SYSTEMS LAB
(LEAVE IN LAB)

Programming
Windows NT 4

UNLEASHED

Mickey Williams

David Hamilton

SAMS
PUBLISHING

03rd Street
dianapolis, IN 46290

D1377562

As always, for René, Alexandria, and Mackenzie—Mickey Williams

Copyright © 1996 by Sams Publishing

Trademarks

President and Publisher	*Richard K. Swadley*
Team Leader	*Greg Wiegand*
Managing Editor	*Cindy Morrow*
Director of Marketing	*John Pierce*
Assistant Marketing Managers	*Kristina Perry*
	Rachel Wolfe

Acquisitions Editors
Christopher Denny
Brad Jones

Development Editor
Anthony Amico

Software Development Specialist
Steve Straiger

Production Editor
Johnna L. VanHoose

Copy Editors
Fran Blauw, Howard Jones

Technical Reviewers
Robert Bogue
Donald Doherty

Editorial Coordinator
Bill Whitmer

Technical Edit Coordinator
Lynette Quinn

Resource Coordinator
Deborah Frisby

Formatter
Frank Sinclair

Editorial Assistants
Carol Ackerman, Andi Richter, Rhonda Tinch-Mize

Cover Designer
Tim Amrhein

Book Designer
Gary Adair

Copy Writer
Peter Fuller

Production Team Supervisor
Brad Chinn

Production
Carol Bowers, Paula Lowell, Dana Rhodes, Laura A. Smith, Susan Van Ness, Mark Walchle

Indexer
Johnna VanHoose

What's on the Disc

The companion CD-ROM contains all the source code and project files developed by the authors.

Windows NT Installation Instructions

1. Insert the CD-ROM disc into your CD-ROM drive.
2. From File Manager or Program Manager, choose Run from the File menu.
3. Type *<drive>*\install and press Enter, where *<drive>* corresponds to the drive letter of your CD-ROM. For example, if your CD-ROM is drive D:, type D:\INSTALL and press Enter.
4. Follow the on-screen instructions in the installation program. Source code files will be installed to the \PROGNT4 directory unless you choose a different directory. Installation also creates a program manager group named "Programming WinNT 4 Unleashed."

Overview

Contents

Part II   Programming the WinNT Desktop

Part III Application-Level Program Communication

Part IV Low-Level Process Communications

Part V   WinNT Network Programming

Part VII Extending Windows NT

Acknowledgements

As with my other books, I had a great deal of help during the writing process. I am grateful for the help these people have provided—I couldn't have done this without their help.

First of all, thanks to all the people at Sams Publishing. My acquisitions editors, Bradley Jones and Chris Denny, convinced me to do this book, then helped keep me on track during the writing process. My development editor, Tony Amico, helped out with advice on the book's contents, as well as tips on DLLs and figure cropping. Also, thanks to Fran Blauw and Howard Jones, who did a great job editing my original manuscript, and Donald Doherty and Robert Bogue, who did a great technical review. Thanks to Johnna VanHoose, the production editor, who managed the project.

Thanks to Bob O'Brien and all the folks at Nu-Mega Technologies for their help. Thanks also to my friends at Ericsson, who were a great source of help and inspiration. Thanks to Cherif Gad, Cuyler Buckwalter, Bo Stenlund, and Lars Karlsson.

I should also thank Paul Stephenson, once of Ericsson, and now working at ObjectSpace, who was a great source of information about STL, exception handling, and other programming topics.

And last but not least, thanks to my wife, René, my best friend, favorite reviewer, and ski instructor. In addition to her usual job of running her own consulting business, she managed the household single-handedly while I was busy writing this book.

—Mickey Williams

About the Authors

Mickey Williams

Mickey Williams is the author of *Essential Visual C++ 4* and *Develop a Professional Visual C++ Application in 21 Days*, both from Sams Publishing. Mickey is a software engineer at PairGain Technologies, where he develops network management software. He is a member of the Association for Computing Machinery and the IEEE Computer Society. Mickey lives in Laguna Hills, California, with his wife, René, and daughters Alexandria and Mackenzie. He can be reached at mickeyw@deltanet.com, or on CompuServe at 75460,2102.

David Hamilton

David Hamilton is the president of SOAP Notes, Inc., a small medical software company in Lincoln, Nebraska. He has been using NT and writing C/C++ software on NT since the earliest betas. Dave is also a private pilot, amateur astronomer, and weekend farmer.

Tell Us What You Think

As a reader, you are the most important critic and commentator of our books. We value your opinion and want to know what we're doing right, what we could do better, what areas you'd like to see us publish in, and any other words of wisdom you're willing to pass our way. You can help us make strong books that meet your needs and give you the computer guidance you require.

Do you have access to CompuServe or the World Wide Web? Then check out our CompuServe forum by typing **GO SAMS** at any prompt. If you prefer the World Wide Web, check out our site at http://www.mcp.com.

> **NOTE**
>
> If you have a technical question about this book, call the technical support line at (800) 571-5840, ext. 3668.

As the team leader of the group that created this book, I welcome your comments. You can fax, e-mail, or write me directly to let me know what you did or didn't like about this book—as well as what we can do to make our books stronger. Here's the information:

Fax: 317/581-4669

E-mail: programming_mgr@sams.mcp.com

Mail: Greg Wiegand
          Comments Department
          Sams Publishing
          201 W. 103rd Street
          Indianapolis, IN 46290

Introduction

The information in this book is based on beta software. Because this information was made public before the final release of the product, there may be some changes to the product by the time it is finally released. After the final product has begun shipping, we encourage you to visit our Web site, `http://www.mcp.com/sams`, for an electronic update beginning 09/01/96.

Additionally, if you have access to the Internet, you can always get up-to-the-minute information about Windows NT Server and Windows NT Workstation directly from Microsoft at the following locations:

```
http://www.microsoft.com/ntserver
http://www.microsoft.com/ntworkstation
```

Windows NT has been Microsoft's quietest success. After its 1992 introduction, there has been little fanfare, but slowly momentum has built. As companies outgrew their Windows for Workgroups networks they introduced dedicated NT servers. Programmers and power users slowly shifted to NT Workstation. It seemed that as the media was reporting it dead, everyone else was deploying it.

In 1995, Windows 95 got all the fanfare—it seemed that it was destined to be Microsoft's operating system. In reality, Windows 95 just took some of the parts of NT to merge with its Windows roots. While Windows 95 got the press, International Data Corporation estimated sales of NT grew 163% over the prior year.

NT was designed from the ground up by Microsoft. They had MS-DOS, Zenix, Windows, and OS/2 experience as their microcomputer background. They hired from Digital Equipment Company people who knew operating systems for minicomputers. NT was designed with these criteria:

> Portability between platforms
>
> Extensibility as market requirements changed
>
> Multiprocessing and scalability
>
> Reliability and robustness; the system should protect itself
>
> Distributed computing
>
> POSIX compliance
>
> Government certifiable security
>
> Compatibility with prior Microsoft software
>
> Performance, as fast as possible given the above criteria

In 1996, Windows NT 4.0 was released with a new user interface. Microsoft has stated its direction is to build an object-oriented file system with NT, code-named Cairo, by 1997. OLE and database access are marrying to become Nile. These may be out by the time you are reading this. All of Microsoft's new technologies for the future are being introduced on NT.

Companies that have had minicomputers in the past have found more and more users that attach PCs to the network. The minicomputer has become a file/printer server. When it gets replaced, a PC network gets its job. An NT network! Many of you have picked this book up for that very reason—you are "rightsizing" at work from a mainframe or minicomputer to a network of computers. You are considering Microsoft NT as the network operating system.

The Developer

This book is written for an intermediate-to-advanced level C/C++ programmer, someone who is developing commercial applications and needs to know the new features of NT 4.0 and Visual C++ 4.0. It is also written for corporate developers whose users are asking for new features and want full access to the power of Windows NT. It is a developer-based book.

For you the developer, Visual C++ 4.0 and MFC 4.0 allow you to build 32-bit applications for Windows NT. Many of the concepts and function calls will be familiar to Windows programmers.

Visual C++ allows for rapid prototyping using Wizards. It also allows code to be reused via the Component Gallery and OCX controls. A full interactive debugger is built in. The integrated development environment is extendible to include such products as Crystal Reports, SourceSave, and various resource editors.

The Code

In the examples in this book, you will see code snippets developed with Visual C++. We tried to give you examples, not large code dumps to fill pages. The accompanying CD-ROM has the full demonstration applications containing the code snippets. We have tried to build applications to demonstrate and test each snippet, but in some cases you will need to use the Visual C++ online help to get all of a function's parameters or usage.

At the end of many chapters, you will see an application built to demonstrate that chapter's ideas. These applications are included on the CD-ROM.

The Layout

The first step of writing this book was to develop the table of contents. We enumerated areas we as developers use and weighed the page allocation to areas that we found were used most in our day-to-day development. I think that this led to a mix quite different from most programming texts. We have included topics almost never addressed, such as printing, low-level communication, OpenGL, Microsoft BackOffice, and the Cross Development edition.

However, we placed the emphasis on where we spend a larger portion of our time, database access, program communications, and the user interface.

Some areas such as the DAO SDK, multimedia SDK, and BackOffice SDK are only documented in their online help and don't appear in much, if any, text.

Part I: The WinNT Platform

Part I is an introduction to the concepts of the NT environment, with little actual code but lots of definitions. In many instances, this lays the groundwork for future topics. In Part I we look at NT itself, how multitasking and multiprocessor support are implemented, and the architecture.

Part II: Programming the WinNT Desktop

Part II introduces you to programming the NT Desktop, the user interface. Each of the major components of Visual C++ 4.0 is reviewed as well as general NT programming techniques such as structured exception handling and memory management. This part is to introduce you to developing a Windows NT application. We examine the basics such as the graphical user interface, structured exception handling, memory management, and templates. There is one chapter dedicated to printing and another to building DLLs, two subjects often given only the lightest treatments in other texts.

Part III: Application-Level Program Communication

Part III dives deeper into application development and the application-level communication of one program to another. This is given considerable emphasis because modern programs need to intercommunicate data with other unknown programs. All five chapters have OLE as their basis because this technology is becoming a much larger part of Windows NT.

Part IV: Low-Level Process Communications

Part IV goes one step deeper into the lower-level communications between threads, named pipes, and remote procedure calls. This is intra-application communication. Multithreading makes your NT application much more robust. We look at how NT uses a local form of remote procedure calls to handle its internal messaging. Remote procedure calls enable you to use other processors on your network to speed up your application.

Part V: WinNT Network Programming

Part V comes back to the surface to introduce several APIs that are coming more to the forefront with the emergence of the Internet. WinSockets allow your network to easily access the Internet and develop internal applications for mail and telephone routing.

Part VI: Windows NT Database Interfaces

Part VI looks at four ways databases are accessed and the Microsoft API's supporting database access. Every application manages data. ODBC allows your application access to data in many different databases. A new technology, DAO, is emerging that combines OLE and database access in a way that is easy to implement.

Part VII: Extending Windows NT

Part VII is a mix of additional APIs included in Windows NT programming, including the multimedia extensions and OpenGL graphics development. We will also look at how you develop the help system you ship with your application and how to write your installation software.

The WinNT Platform

PART

I

Modes of Operation

1

by David Hamilton

Early MS-DOS programs were simple. You ran one program, and when it finished, you ran another. A program was a static sequence of instructions that you, the programmer, controlled. Life was simple back then: one user, one application, one thing happening at a time.

Learning to write Windows software and specifically writing software for Windows NT is a life-long endeavor. There are no real experts, and it's a rapidly moving target. Windows NT is constantly evolving at the forefront of the computer industry, making it easier for the user, adding support for the advances in the industry, and adding to what you, the programmer, need to implement those changes in your organization.

Each project exposes you to a new API (Application Programming Interface) with an entire new set of functions. An API is a related grouping of function calls, one API may provide database access, another graphics, and yet another controls how you distribute e-mail. Fortunately, Windows NT programming can be broken down into pieces based on which set of APIs provides the functionality you need in your current project. Fortunately, it's a building process where what you have learned makes learning a new API easier.

In developing the layout for Programming Windows NT 4.0 Unleashed I tried to look back on past Windows projects and assign weight in book pages based on the areas of Windows programming, such as database access, where you will spend your time. I also tried to give emphasis to areas where Windows NT is evolving the fastest such as OLE.

In order to begin you need to understand a little bit about Windows NT itself, where it came from and where it's headed. The first two chapters look at the structure of NT workstation and NT server. This first chapter looks at the architecture of Windows NT. With the new user interface of NT 4.0, it looks like Windows 95, but it is so much more. We begin with the evolution of Windows.

A Brief History of Operating Modes

Several early task-switching programs enabled you to freeze your program, work in another, and then return to the first program. These programs developed at about the same time of some early network operating systems (NOSs). The first NOSs were layered on top of MS-DOS to provide printer- and file-sharing capabilities between computers. The NOS managed a queue of packets that the CPU processed one at a time. Early code was called *non-reentrant code* because you entered the code segment once and executed it in its entirety. If two packets tried to use a single system resource one after another, your system often crashed because slower devices had not finished the first packet's request when the CPU was working on the second packet's request. This led to the development *of reentrant code* (code that you or multiple processes can reenter and execute).

Microsoft developed MSNET and 3COM developed 3Slave, which together became LAN Manager, a concurrent I/O system with pieces of reentrant code that tracked resources. Similar work was being done by IBM with its PCLP NOS and by Banyan VINES with its Vines product for UNIX System V. UNIX had a big advantage back then because the operating system was both multitasking and reentrant.

Microsoft developed Windows, in which multiple programs seem to be running concurrently. Actually, each application is doing its individual thing. In earlier versions of Windows, the application is in control. When an application is done with the CPU, it enters a loop to wait for a message telling Windows that another person can use the CPU. You actually can see this as software-performance spurts during disk access when Windows appears to freeze while the CPU gets new instructions from the drive. In this case, neither the user nor Windows is in control: the software application is. This is like running an entire auto race under a "yellow caution flag" where each car has to slow down and maintain its relative position in the race.

Windows (prior to Windows 95 and Windows NT) relies on the application to tell it when to multitask—usually, when the application is waiting for a user message. To write a CPU-friendly application, the programmer must call the SetTimer() and pass WM_TIMER messages, which are difficult to develop. The program must track the progress of itself. WM_TIMER also is set in milliseconds, which doesn't give you a speed advantage with all the emerging, faster hardware. Another CPU-friendly technique is using PeekMessage(), but the application must be asynchronous. This leads to many system hangs during which the PeekMessage() never gets a return. It is impossible to check all the potential actions that could occur while you wait for the function's return. If any application using the CPU goes into an infinite loop, the system hangs because Windows has no way of interrupting. Microsoft realized that a preemptive operating system would be a better design. The operating system had to be "in charge."

Microsoft and IBM realized that the operating system had to support the multitasking and reentrant code, so they developed OS/2, released in 1987. This is a true multitasking operating system with several reentrant packets of code processed seemingly at once. With this new operating system came the concept that the multitasking environment and the networking can't just run on top of an operating system; it must *be* the operating system. OS/2 relied on another layer: the NOS. Microsoft therefore started over and NT was designed from the ground up to be reentrant, to use preemptive multitasking, and to be the NOS.

Understanding NT Design

NT was designed along two paths. NT workstation is a peer-to-peer environment sharing files, printers, and applications with other NT workstations, Windows 95 clients, and also with Windows for Workgroups (Windows 3.11) clients. NT server is a centralized file/print/applications server whose clients can be NT workstation, OS/2, Windows 95, Windows 3.11 or Macintosh users. NT server brought along the concept of *domains*, in which several servers and workstations form a logical group. A user can log in just once to gain access to the group's resources.

Users no longer speak of programs; they speak of *processes*—the dynamic allocation of system resources. A process is the loaded and called instance of your program along with the system resources it requires. What is important here is the tying of an instruction sequence with system resources. A process combines an executable program's code and data, a private address space, system resources, and at least one thread of execution.

One of NT's major design criteria was that one process could not exercise unlimited control over other processes. This was done via virtual memory. With virtual memory, a programmer or his process has a logical view of memory that does not correspond to the physical memory layout. Each process sees only its 4 GB virtual address space. It is prevented from accessing another process's 4 GB address space. NT can access operating system memory only by switching to Kernel mode. (You sometimes may see kernel mode referred to as restricted mode and user mode referred to as unrestricted mode. In *kernel mode*, your thread surrenders itself to the operating system for the execution and then is switched back to you.) Kernel mode is discussed in Chapter 2, but most of your time as a programmer will be spent in User mode making API function calls that Windows NT executes in Kernel mode.

Processes and Threads

NT manages the creation and deletion of processes. The NT Process Manager also manages the interprocess communication. The Process Manager provides low-level services that each of the environmental subsystems uses to emulate their unique process structures.

NT makes some processes more important than others. No process is excluded from CPU time. Each process is served in a round-robin fashion but given an amount of CPU time according to its importance. When its slice of time is up, the process is interrupted and the next process starts. NT enables the process to finish the instruction it is executing and then preempts the process, saving the process state until it is its turn again. Making something *preemptive* also means that no single process can control all the system resources.

NT also manages multiple operating subsystems within User mode. User mode is discussed in greater detail in the next chapter; for now, just remember that *User mode* is the way in which NT restricts a process from having unlimited resources. An NT process has its own address space in which it manages its multiple threads.

In a *single-threaded process*, the CPU follows a linear path from function to function. When its CPU time slice is up, NT stores the registers and state of the resources in use. It restores another process's state and gives the second its due time slice.

> **NOTE**
>
> Before you continue reading this section, you should understand four terms. A *module* is a block of your EXE loaded into memory. A *task* is the module (now a memory resource) plus the other system resources required by the loaded module. NT breaks the task into *processes*, which are the instances of a running program, and *threads*, which are the paths of execution through the processes.

You double-click your application's icon to evoke your EXE. At this point, NT creates a single process and a single thread. NT tells the CPU to begin executing at the CRuntime code, which calls the function WINMAIN. A return from WINMAIN tells NT to destroy the process and thread it created.

Each process has at least one thread. Chapter 3, "Execution Models," dives deeper into the concept of threads, and Chapter 22, "Threads," discusses programming multithreaded applications. For now, you just need to look at a few basics to understand processes.

The CPU

NT schedules CPU time slices among threads rather than processes. When a thread is executing, NT can steal the CPU (preempt it) between instructions. The life of a process is the lifetime of its threads. One thread can create another thread. Remember that a *thread* is the path of execution through the process. During a process, new threads are created, some are paused and then restarted, and some are terminated. After all threads are terminated, the process is terminated.

Objects allocated by a thread are owned by the process rather than the thread. Memory belongs to the process. Any variables you create therefore belong to your process.

You need to understand who owns what in order to understand who can share what. A thread owns its user objects like the window, the menu, and the accelerator table. It can share these with other threads. Everything else is owned by the process. When a thread allocates objects or memory, these belong to the process, not the thread requesting the allocation. An important point is that when your thread creates a variable (allocates memory) that variable belongs to the process not the thread. The thread cannot share that variable with another thread, but the process could share the variable with another process. All threads have equal access to their process's resources.

Each thread has its own set of registers, kernel stacks, and environmental blocks. Together, these form the thread's context. When a thread is preempted, the context is stored. This preemption actually is performed by a system-called context switching within the kernel component of the NT Executive. This enables a thread to run until the thread pauses to wait on a resource or until the time slice is over. At this point, the context is saved and the next thread's context is loaded. It is the context switcher's job to ensure that the CPU isn't wasted and to put the time limitations on the threads (time allotment or slices).

The NT Executive

The NT Executive manages low-level objects. Every object your application creates is built from objects that were built from these low-level objects. Suppose that you create an object based on the class `CFile`. If you go into the MFC source code, you will find that `CFile` is derived from `CObject`. You also will find somewhere in the code that it wraps function calls to the Win32 API function `CreateFile()`. You don't have the source code for `CreateFile()` available, but if you did, you would find that the Microsoft system programmer who wrote that API function built it out of lower level Executive file objects.

This is not to say that NT is an object-oriented operating system in the strictest sense. It is not. The NT Executive was written in straight C and some assembler language. The C language does not have the dynamic binding of data types, polymorphic functions, or class inheritance that you use in MFC C++ programming. This difference in binding is always the basis of arguments as to what is an object-oriented operating system. Without getting into the religion, just think of it as similar to the difference between a C structure and a C++ object class. On the surface, they are the same, but in their use the class has internal data that is hidden from the outside world. The NT Executive provides services, object services, that work just like your public functions: it gets data out and puts data into objects.

The NT Executive isn't really just one piece of software but is instead a management team of software, as shown in Figure 1.1. The *NT Executive* is the software that creates and manages system objects. The team includes the Process Manager, Memory Manager, I/O Manager, Local Procedure Call facility, security system, Object Manager, kernel, Configuration Manager, and executive support services. Any management team is assembled to make the best use of limited resources. So too, the NT Executive's mission is making user-friendly names for resources, sharing resources between processes, and protecting resources from unauthorized use.

FIGURE 1.1.

The NT Executive team.

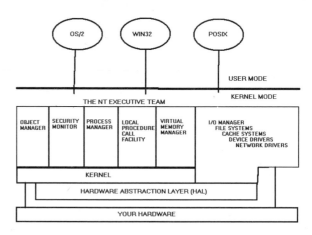

Processes and threads are system objects. Because many processes may use the same resources, one program must control the creation of system objects and the deletion of them when no process is using them. It does this by passing out handles. A handle is a pointer to an object that holds private data in a structure and in most cases that data is only important to the operating system. Each window for your application has a handle in which NT has stored the data necessary to draw that window. If you wish to modify some element of that window, you must first get a handle to the window. There are handles for devices and nearly every object your application will manipulate. If two processes need the same object and have the security permissions to it, they are given the same handle. In the Win32 subsystem, these handles have the same value so that processes can intercommunicate. On the system level, the handles have different values as part of the NT security system. One thread can pass a handle to another thread in the same process. A thread cannot pass a handle to a thread in another process. That is up to the NT Executive.

You're in Control

Chapters 3 and 22 show you that the programmer has great control over the priority of threads. In the function CreateProcess, you can set the priority of a process you create via the flags in fdwCreate. The NT user also has control of priorities, as shown in Figure 1.2. From the command prompt, you can use the new NT command START which has switches for LOW, NORMAL, HIGH, and REALTIME priorities. Also, from the Control Panel, the user can set up the relative responsiveness of foreground versus background processes as in Figure 1.2. In PVIEW.EXE, users can adjust any current process's priority, but it's often not wise to do so!

FIGURE 1.2.

Setting the process priority via the Control Panel settings.

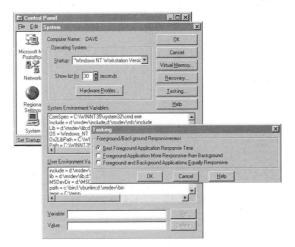

Your power users may have found the Process Viewer (PVIEW.EXE) shown in Figure 1.3, with its three settings for process priority and five settings for thread priority. When you use the Process Viewer with the NT Performance Monitor software, you can fine-tune NT to give the highest performance in your particular setting. The NT Resource Kit also has guidelines and samples for tuning your system's performance. To tune your application's performance under NT, you also might want to use NTPERF—a sample application on the MSDN disks. The NT Resource Kit has an entire volume on performance tuning of NT. It's also a prime learning tool to use in getting to know Windows NT.

You can use the Performance Monitor software to examine many characteristics of processes and threads running on your system, as shown in Figure 1.4.

FIGURE 1.3.

The NT PVIEW.EXE software.

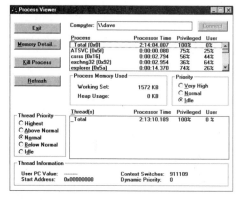

FIGURE 1.4.

The NT Performance Monitor software.

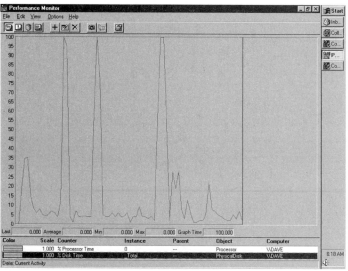

The processors in today's computers are so fast that it appears as though several things are happening simultaneously. After reading this far in the chapter, however, you know that they are not. Most threads really don't execute continuously for their entire time slice. They stop to wait on resources from other threads or to wait on input and output. In these cases, the threads preempt themselves. The processor still performs one thing at a time in round-robin fashion.

Threads are created at the priority of the process that creates them. After you create them, you can raise or lower their relative priority via a call to SetThreadPriority(), as you will see in Chapters 3 and 22.

One process can spawn another and then use interprocess communication. Device driver programmers also can actually change the value of the time slices by changing their *granularity* (the duration of each time slice).

NT also can support systems with multiple processors. This involves the use of a *shared memory pipe*, which is a buffer the processors share to jointly work on your executable, each processing a thread simultaneously. When you design software, you don't need to do anything special to use the multiprocessing of Windows NT. If your application uses multiple threads, NT parses them out to the processors. You do need to be aware of the synchronization problems that any multi-threaded application must address, however. Chapter 22 discusses this topic in more detail.

Using the File/Print Sharing Server

If you have used NT 4.0 or Windows 95 you have become familiar with the NT Explorer, My Computer, and Network Neighborhood, all of which enable you to access other drives and access files across the network in the same fashion the NT Print Manager lets the NT user attach to the remote printers available across the network.

Almost every office, and even some homes, have networks set up to share files and printers between several computers. With the current explosive growth of the Internet, users have found it's just as easy to access files on thousands of remote networks. In writing software for Windows NT, the programmer must plan for this distribution and sharing of files. This section examines how NT shares file and printer resources. Chapter 2 looks at some of the security issues and in Chapter 5 you examine the different file systems available with NT.

Using NT as an Application Server

Working with and sharing files is something every application must do. Windows NT enables you to allocate an address space for a disk file and access it as if the entire file was resident in the local machines memory. Memory-mapped files are discussed in Chapter 13, "Windows NT Virtual Memory and Memory Management." NT provides memory-mapped files to enable you to share blocks of memory between processes. When you create a file via `CreateFile()`, for example, you set a parameter, `dwShareMode`, that allows sharing of this file with other processes. If `dwShareMode` is 0, no sharing is allowed; or, you can set it to `FILE_SHARE_READ` and/or `FILE_SHARE_WRITE`. You then can create a memory-mapped file by using `MapViewOfFile()`.

Your *entire* file or database isn't getting moved into memory; only portions are kept in memory. Earlier, you learned that each application has a 4 GB address space; 2 GB is used for the application and its data, and you probably don't have 2 GB of free physical memory. Each portion of your file or database kept in memory is called a *view*. Memory-mapped files are used on a single machine to share writeable files between processes. You should not use these types of files on writeable data across the network.

Memory-mapped files are discussed here because that is how NT handles creating a new process for an application that already is running. NT recognizes that an instance is running and opens another memory-mapped view of the executable file's image. Using memory-mapped files enables multiple instances of the same application to share code and data. This is how DLLs are used as well.

Suppose that you are typing in your Microsoft Word application. Several other people may be using Microsoft Word off your NT server. Each of you has accessed the same executable, which is loaded into the individual machines' address spaces. As you and the other users move between the many functions, DLLs are loaded and freed. Each machine behaves as if Word is a local application. This work is done by the Redirector part of NT. The Redirector's job is to ensure that your application sees its files as if they are in a local directory. If your network connection fails, the Redirector recovers the connection if possible, and you don't even realize that the failure has occurred. A second process called the *server* is responsible for actually reading and writing the data from the NT application server to your workstation. In NT, the server is actually a driver rather than a process.

Using NT as a Network File Server

A file server makes excellent use of a multi-threaded approach to an application. On your file server, the same operations are happening over and over. A file is open, read, written to, and closed. Each process is the same; only the file name is changed. NT Server then has just one process for these operations always loaded into memory. Each request simply creates another thread of execution, sharing the server functions in the process's address space.

Earlier in this chapter, you learned that NT is a peer-to-peer networking environment and NT server is a dedicated file/application/printer environment. Certainly how you set up a network affects the performance as viewed by the clients. NT server is optimized for file/print services and is most efficient when applications are not running. This topic is the focus of this section. The next section examines NT server as a gateway, in which its use is optimized as a database server.

Using Peer-to-Peer Networks

Peer-to-peer networks definitely are less expensive than dedicated servers. Peer-to-peer networks usually are adequate for the needs of 25 or fewer users. By now, you have seen how easily you can use Windows for Workgroups and Windows 95 as peer-to-peer clients with NT. Any machine on the network can become a server simply by offering one of its resources to the network. If you asked most network users what they need in a network, the bottom line probably would first be that they share a printer, and then that they can share access to a few data files. This would be the response regardless of the complexity of their networks.

Peer-to-peer networks are easy to install and administrate. You can restrict access to files on your computer simply by not offering them to the network or by offering them only to certain groups of users.

Using a Dedicated Server

Peer-to-peer networks have drawbacks. The biggest disadvantage as a developer probably is that several users are accessing a database that resides on one workstation. That workstation may be shut off or rebooted before other users are done working. Also, as more and more users access files and printers on your computer, your workstation grows increasingly less responsive. As you get more users, it becomes more difficult to administrate who has access to what. Leaving the administration to many users can cause problems and defeats any idea of having some security for sensitive data. As your network grows, you reach a point with so many users that you must have central network administration.

NT has two forms: NT Workstation and NT Server. In the largest sense, NT is NT: they are the same. Microsoft has tweaked the software of one to optimize it as a print/file server, however, and the other as a workstation.

Files Are Objects, Too

NT treats all system resources, including files, as objects. The NT Object Manager is an executive component of the kernel that names, creates, and deletes objects. When your application issues a call to NT to create a file, NT transfers that call to the I/O Manager. The I/O Manager's job is to maintain the hierarchy of files on your drive and your network. The I/O Manager calls the Object Manager to create an object. It is during this call that the Security Reference Monitor (SRM) gets involved. For now, you should just know that if the SRM finds the proper security token matches for your process and the file, it allows the call to pass to the Object Manager. The Object Manager creates the file and sends back a status code to tell the I/O Manager that everything is OK.

Why a file object? Objects are the central focus of the design of NT. The parts of NT like SRM and the I/O Manager work on a variety of objects by always treating them the same. SRM doesn't need to know whether an object is round, flat, or correctly formatted; it only needs to know that it has a consistent interface to its security tokens. The I/O Manager doesn't care whether the object is a word processing file or a printer—only that its interface is correct for I/O Manager operations.

The Object Manager gives all objects a name for internal use and sets up a hierarchical tree to track them. If you call your file C:\DOCS\MyWord.DOC, for example, the Object Manager maps it to \Device\HardDisk0\DOCS\MyWord.DOC. You often will hear the word *namespace*.

To the file system, namespace is the \DOC\MyWord.DOC. To the Object Manager, its namespace is the \Device\HardDisk0 part. The *namespace* is the area that controls the naming of the directory. Somewhere, an alias was set up that mapped drive C to \Device\HardDisk0. An *alias* is a symbolic link to a physical device. In the File Manager, you can assign this when you set up a sharename. You can assign the name DOCS to those files on a server in the F:\NTS\WORDDOCS directory. This then would be a shared directory that other users can access by the alias as "DOCS." This solves the problem that allows various users the capability to assign different shared drive letters to the server path. In NT Workstation, 10 users can access this directory simultaneously. In NT Server, no user limit exists.

Printer Sharing

NT recognizes two types of printers: physical or printing devices and logical devices (the software interface to NT's Print Manager). If you are in Print Manager, you see both listed. One logical printer may have a device driver for an HP IIP and another for an Epson label printer, for example. In another setup, one logical printer can be set up to print jobs on demand to the HP while another can be set up to print jobs at night to the same HP. You even might have logical printers such as LETTER_HEAD or OLD_GREEN_STRIPE. In a large network, you might have one logical printer, HP, which is assigned to a pool of physical printers. The important point is the distinction between physical and logical.

NT doesn't have print queues; it has lists of print jobs in a logical printer. A print queue has the concept of an order, whereas a list of jobs, although usually printed in the order in which they arrive, can be processed in any order or by priority.

When your application sends a print job to a logical printer, this sequence of events is depicted in Figure 1.5 and described as follows:

FIGURE 1.5.

NT Printing sequence of events.

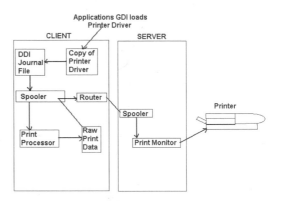

1. The printer driver is loaded.
2. The DDI generates an output file (journal file) with device driver interface calls to the print driver you loaded.

3. The spooler (WINSPOOL.DRV) passes the journal file to a print processor. The spooler performs a certain amount of rendering on the print job.

4. The print processor (WINPRINT.DLL) creates raw print data consistent with the physical printing device. Rendering is finished and returned to the appropriate machine's spooler.

5. The client computer NT router sends the raw data to the appropriate client computer's NT print server spooler and returns any error messages.

6. The print server spooler passes the document to the Print Monitor (LOCALMON.DLL or HPMON.DLL), which redirects data to ports such as LPT1, COM2, or MACINTOSH. Spooler examines the Registry key value in DefaultSpoolDirectory located in HKEY_LOCAL_MACHINE\SYSTEM\CurrentControlSet\Control\Print\Printers to determine where to make the spool file.

7. Printing occurs or error messages are passed back.

Why all the steps? NT has some very powerful and broad features. Data from a Macintosh, for example, can be printed by NT Server as if the attached printer were PostScript. A PC can share a Macintosh printer, however, without knowing anything about PostScript. Chapter 34, "Cross-Platform Development," discusses this topic in more detail. This is just one of the behind-the-scenes actions of this operating system.

A printer driver consists of a DLL (more specifically, a set of DLLs), the Print Graphics DLL, the Printer Interface DLL, and a configuration file. Your application's GDI API calls are sent to the Print Graphics DLL. The Print Manager uses the configuration file and the Printer Interface DLL to administrate using the printer. In the past, each printer supplied all three elements. Now NT has a universal raster driver. NT loads the printer driver DLLs, RASDD.DLL, RASDDUI.DLL, PSCRIPT.DLL, and PSCRPTUI.DLL as defaults. The manufacturer only supplies the configuration files that tell NT about paper trays, memory, and resolution.

When using the printer driver within your application, Windows NT does most of the work for you. You probably are familiar with the common dialog boxes shown in Figure 1.6, which most applications use to set and get printer information.

FIGURE 1.6.

Common dialog box printer settings.

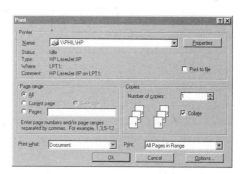

In general, access to printer-specific information is not necessary; Windows NT handles it for you. The Win32 API does provide methods for you to poll NT for the device-specific information in its calls to EnumPrinterDrivers and EnumPrinters, however. If your application needs to get this information directly and cannot use the common dialog boxes, you can use the sample program Microsoft provides on the Win32 SDK CD. It's in the MSTOOLS/SAMPLE/ PRINTER directory. Figure 1.7 uses the EnumPrinterDrivers and EnumPrinters calls with their various parameters to poll for printer-specific information. Also notice that Windows NT and Windows 95 handle many things differently in this area.

FIGURE 1.7.

The Printer.C sample program and the EnumPrinter *options.*

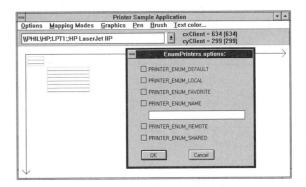

You can control many aspects of the print server from the NT Registry. Usually, you set these via the Print Manager, but you might need to manage in the Registry under the \HKEY_LOCAL_MACHINE\SYSTEM\CurrentControlSet\Control\Print\Printers directory, including the following:

```
BeepEnabled
DisableServerThread
EventLog
FastPrintSlowDownThreshold
FastPrintThrottleTimeout
FastPrintWaitTimeout
NetPopup
NetPrinterDecayPeriod
PortthreadPriority
PriorityClass
SchedulerThreadPriority
ServerThreadTimeout
```

Examining the Gateway Mode of Operation

In a large network, one NT server may serve as the gateway to a mainframe computer or to computers that use dissimilar languages and file formats. In this section you examine ways NT can act as a gateway to translate data and then as a bridge to dissimilar network protocols. An example of such a gateway is in Figure 1.8 where the NT box reformats the requests from ODBC database users to poll a large mainframe database. You examine this closer in Chapter 29, "ODBC Concepts," and discuss a two-tiered ODBC setup in which client requests for information are passed to a gateway that reformats the information and then passes it to a large ODBC server.

FIGURE 1.8.

NT as an ODBC database gateway.

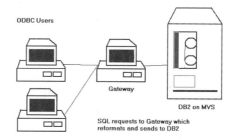

A second example is that you can use the Macintosh services of NT server to store Mac files and provide Mac printing. This server also allows PC users to access common files. Files created by programs such as Microsoft Word or Excel certainly can be used by Macintosh or PC users. The Macs using AppleTalk can print to network printers on other NT machines.

An NT server also can act as the bridge between networks running IPX/SPX and your WFW and Windows 95 clients. The NT machine may have multiple network cards to provide this bridge as in Figure 1.9 where the NT machine has both an Ethernet card and a Token Ring card to form the bridge. In this configuration, as one machine sends a packet to another, NT realized that the second machine is on another type of network and replaces the Ethernet header with a Token Ring header.

My organization does something similar; it uses one machine that has an IP address and polls the Internet for mail and newsgroups. That machine then reposts the mail into our Microsoft Exchange Mail on the network. It stores newsgroup information in a file structure that our off-line readers use. In fact, without probably realizing it, you set up a similar situation when you access the Internet via a SLIP or PPP connection with a modem.

In all of these cases, an NT machine is acting as a gateway between networks. NT is not tied to the NetBIOS protocol; it also can have NetBEUI, TCP/IP, AppleTalk, IPX/SPX, SLIP, PPP, SNA, DLC, and several others all loaded. You can set these up by using the Control Panel's Network applet under the Protocol tab.

FIGURE 1.9.

NT with two network cards acting as a bridge.

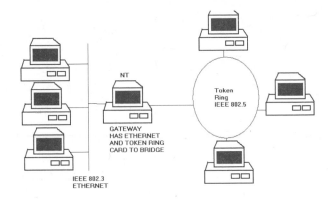

A machine that contains two network cards is referred to as a *bridge*. If NT is relied on to switch protocols, it is referred to as a *router*.

When NT acts as a router, it examines the network layer source and destination of a packet. Packets don't know what route they will take—only where they need to go. NT Redirector figures out the best path.

More and more, Visual C++ is used to develop front-end applications that access data on mainframes and minicomputers. Typically, this data is stored in an RDBMS such as DB2 from IBM or Rdb from Digital Equipment Corporation. Companies such as Oracle, Sybase, and IBM have recognized this and built gateway products called MiddleWare. These pieces of *in-between software* can access that mainframe data as well as talk to ODBC applications. Several other tools translate ODBC's SQL language into queries required by these large databases.

Gateways provide connectivity between PC LANS and their larger computer relatives. An example is the IBM Token-Ring gateway for the AS/400 minicomputer and its larger mainframe computers. Gateways are software that run on both the mainframe and the NT machine. Another example of this is Information Builder, Inc.'s EDA/SQL combined with EDA/Link for Windows. This combination allows a Windows front-end application to access data stored in a DB2 database on an MVS mainframe from IBM.

With the advent of personal digit assistants (PDAs), you can even expand the concept of a gateway in one more dimension. You can use a PDA to attach to your MSExchange or MSSchedule+ and move the day's messages and schedule to a device you carry in your pocket. This requires two pieces of software. First, an NT application gets the Exchangemail or Schedule+ data file, reformats it, and sends it out a serial or IR port. The second software residing on the PDA reads the serial stream and stores and displays the information appropriately. I don't think the original concept of a gateway embodied using NT and a PDA, but it is just as viable and probably becoming as important in this mobile world. With the new shell for Windows NT and with Windows 95, the concept of a desktop briefcase builds on this with information you plan to take from the workplace, use, and then return.

Earlier, this chapter mentioned the NT Resource Kit. The Resource Kit is available in printed form and is included on the MSDN CDs by subscription. If you are going to set up an NT machine as a gateway or any specific task, look into the area of performance monitoring and tuning. NT allows your application to feed the Performance Monitor software and to make adjustments. One whole book of the Resource Kit is dedicated to tuning your NT system. With a database gateway, this is required reading! In one NT training exercise, a large file was copied back and forth. It was simply amazing the differences that settings made on the time to copy this large file. These settings will make your application shine, too.

Probably the most common gateway other than your Internet connection is the Gateway Service for NetWare (see Figure 1.10). Microsoft network clients can use the Gateway Service for accessing file and print services on the NetWare server.

FIGURE 1.10.

Using Gateway Service for NetWare.

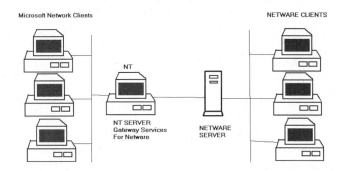

The NT machine running Gateway Service for NetWare receives the Server Message Blocks requests and translates these into Network Control Protocol requests that the NetWare server can use. This is adequate for a small network setup. If you have a larger Novell network, NT workstations probably also would run Client Services for NetWare, in which each workstation is configured to run as an actual NetWare client. This product is available from Novell.

Contrasting NT Workstation with Windows 95

Windows 95 was released with many of the features NT users have grown to know. It uses preemptive multitasking, long file names, threads, virtual memory, structured exception handling, and a long list of other features thought to belong to the NT operating system. Microsoft had such a large introduction, most programmers thought all their clients would have Windows 95 by the end of 1995. Although many did, you know that you still have many Windows 3.11 users. With your users on both Windows 95 and Windows 3.11, why would you develop on Windows NT? Stability. It's a major design emphasis of NT and it is a design criterion that NT meets fully.

NT is also where your clients are going. International Data Corporation reports that in 1995 sales of NT grew by 370 percent and both they and Forrester Research, Inc., predicted NT sales would double in 1996 and 1997.

As a programmer you are a power user, and NT is your only real serious choice. You need to get everything possible out of your machine to build tomorrow's software.

The Microsoft NT team is building the operating systems of the future. The Windows 95 team is implementing NT-developed concepts. It takes you a long time to write software. You need to develop for where your users will be next year.

Win32 is an API that Microsoft claims will run on all the systems. Differences exist in how Windows 95 and Windows NT uses the Win32 API, however. NT is optimized for larger machines with more memory. NT 4.0 requires at least a 486 with 16 MB of memory. Windows 95 is optimized to run with less requirements.

A Brief History

Windows 95 provides only a subset of the full Win32 APIs as defined for Windows NT. Originally, this subset was called Win32c (Chicago) but since has dropped this distinction. Win32s allowed Windows 3.11 to use a subset of the full Win32 API. But Win32s has gotten a bad reputation as "buggy," so there was an effort not to introduce another Win32c API. The problem wasn't so much that Win32s was buggy as that it lies in the difficult task of running a true 32-bit application in a 16-bit environment (Windows 3.1). The problem is compounded since Windows 3.1 runs on top of MS-DOS. Win32c inherited all of Win32s API functions (the bridge for 32-bit programs to run on Windows 3.11) and it also got most of the NT Win32 API calls. As Win32s, Win32c, and Win32 became confusing to programmers, Microsoft dropped the name designations. They still matter to you, the programmer. If you explore the APIs you see a lot of differences between function calls for the two APIs. For example, use the books-on-line to examine the `EnumPrinters` and `EnumPrinterDrivers` API functions.

Examining the Differences

Actually Windows 95 is closer to Windows 3.11 than it is to Windows NT. A large part of the Windows 95 code is in 16-bit system DLLs, which are thunked to 32-bit programs. This includes the messaging and window code in USER.EXE, which had to stay to provide compatibility to Windows 3.1 applications. Windows 95 uses combinations of the 16-bit GDI.DLL and the GDI32.DLL. And Windows 95's KERNEL32 calls down to the KRNL386.EXE. Windows 95 is only truly preemptive if you run strictly 32-bit code. This is almost never done because there is a lot of 16-bit code in the OS itself.

Although Windows 95 implements preemptive multitasking, it had to be done in such a way as to be backward compatible. So 16-bit DLLs still are nonreentrant and don't expect control to be yanked away. Microsoft got around the mix of 16-bit code with the *Win16Mutex*, which is a semaphore acquired upon entry into a 16-bit DLL. Thus, only one 16-bit code segment can operate at a time—the one that is holding the semaphore. If that program doesn't break to wait for a message or grant another process to run (the friendly CPU coding stuff), the application can take and hold the CPU.

The Windows 95 team did not intend their operating system to run on platforms other than Intel, so that code is missing and the Windows 95 code is optimized for the 80386 class of CPU. Windows NT's primary design goal was to be robust and portable to other platforms.

Stability and portability cost NT. It is a larger code base, requires more memory, and at least a 486 processor. Many users have pointed out places where OS/2 or Windows 95 is faster running X's software than Windows NT. They forget all the other things NT is doing at the time, such as implementing security. While one programmer may scoff at the last sentence, another demands it. One reason for the slowdown is the client/server model in NT. When your application makes a simple call, it doesn't directly go to the base code for that function. Instead, it is routed to GDI32.DLL where the parameters are copied into a region of memory accessible by both your process and the Win32 system subprocess. A message is sent to the Win32 subprocess that something is waiting to be executed. The subprocess processes the function call and notifies your thread that it is done. This client calling to server and then server sending results to client causes the slowdown. It also provides multiprocessor support, however—support for other operating system interfaces such as OS/2 and POSIX.

The client/server model provides stability by protecting subsystems against memory overwrites and bugs. Windows 95 doesn't have the subsystem, so is faster but far less stable. In NT, the overhead is that every call to an operating system function requires a process switch and memory context change. NT also runs 16-bit processes in their own memory space known as *Windows on Windows* (WOW). This allows these applications a walled-off area where they can do what they want but need to send messages in an organized manner to get resources outside the box. Building this box and using the message structure also takes time and gives NT the rap that 16-bit programs run slower.

This all may be somewhat fuzzy to you as a programmer trying to decide on a development platform. What really matters is that with Windows 95, you need to reboot your machine much more often than with Windows NT. Development somewhat implies that somewhere you will meet failures that put your computer in an unstable state. With NT, you kill the process; with Windows 95, you reboot.

Windows 95 does not have near the same level of object security. It does not support Unicode (although it may by the time you read this). When you call a Unicode version of a function, you get a stub reply. Because OLE programming is becoming more and more Unicode-centric and OLE is at the heart of NT and Microsoft's future software development, this is a big missing feature.

Windows 95 didn't ship with the OpenGL 3D graphics library (it also may be coming later on the MSDN CDs) and more importantly, Windows 95 reused the old FAT file system. Although

Windows 95 gave FAT new support for long file names, FAT is still inefficient for today's larger media sizes. Windows 95 also doesn't support multiple processors.

Some subtle differences still exist. Windows 95 still has some 16-bit code that can cause some Win32 API functions to fail, but very few. Where Win32 API calls are not supported, Windows 95 has provided stub functions that allow the software to simply report that the function isn't there. This keeps NT-specific software from crashing and allows it to exit gracefully. In general, the 16-bit implementation within Windows 95 doesn't cause the programmer difficulty. These limits are fairly obscure. In Windows 95, for example, you still can have only 64 KB of text in an edit box, you can have only 16,000 plus window handles and menu handles, a listbox can have only 32,767 items, and so on. You won't run into these often and if you do, maybe your user interface could use some refinement anyway. At other times these differences can be quite significant as in graphics programming where NT's 32-bit integer values allow for much richer looking output.

Other minor differences include differences in the Registry and that Windows 95 still has some 16-bit implementations. This shows up in that Windows 95 can do large integer math and some differences in functions that actually use the upper 16 bits of `lParam` and `wParam`. With Windows 95, kernel call programming and remote procedure calls are not provided. Named pipes can be used but not created under Windows 95. Remote Access Services (RAS) is part of NT's networking. This allows clients to dial into the NT network as well as access remote computers. An RAS server is available for Windows 95 with the MS Plus! Software.

Choosing NT as Your Development Platform

If you ask programmers why they choose to work on NT workstations, you will get one response over and over. It's rock stable. This is what is important to a programmer; the development platform must be stable. With NT, when your debug program version is hung, you can perform a postmortem. Another NT machine can be used to examine why the program hung and where.

Security is important to some programmers, and NT 4.0's new cryptography API is such a feature.

Other programmers would point out the POSIX element for porting existing UNIX applications. The capability to cross-develop Macintosh applications is important to some developers. The NT interface on RISC, PowerPC, and DEC Alpha is the same.

In spite of the fact that NT 4.0 got the new shell after Windows 95, NT is the platform that new technology is deployed on by Microsoft. With the release of NT 4.0, several things came from Windows 95: Telephony API, the Internet Explorer, Exchange, and the Unimodem drivers.

When Windows 95 gets a Win32 function that it hasn't implemented, it provides a *stub function*. Stub functions do nothing but return an error code. This allows most programs to continue to load and function but notifies the user that a certain action is not supported on her platform.

But in another sense, Windows 95 isn't NT; it just inherited a lot from it. It doesn't provide the level of security a large network requires. It doesn't offer the network management functionality. The choices of network protocols aren't included. No Windows 95 server product exists to handle domains with the flexibility to be nearly as fine tuned.

Because you already have chosen to use NT as your development platform, how do you target a user with Windows 95? Follow these steps:

■ **Test under Windows 95.** This might seem like an obvious statement. Your development environment probably includes programmers using NT but users on Windows 3.1, Windows 95, and DOS. Within these larger groups are users with every possible network, all types of machines, and every memory configuration available. If you implement a feature on your NT machine without a defined testing process, it goes out having never been tested on your user's platform. I recently found this out with the new "common" controls for CPropertySheet while making an AppWizard. My buttons moved when I built under Windows 95 from where I placed them under NT!

■ **Review the code for features not available under Windows 95.** These features include Unicode support and the security features, for example. You can use GetVersionEx() from winbase.h to write a common executable and switch on its return value. With both NT 4.0 and Windows 95 having the same GUI, this is your probable route. If you get and set values in the Registry, remember that differences exist between the NT Registry and the Windows 95 Registry index values and test for this.

■ **Test with memory constraints.** Develop a simple "EatMem" application that restricts your Windows 95 test machine's base and extended memory. At least knowing at what level your application will fail enables you to notify the users going in that they are a little short.

■ **Use structure exception handling.** Don't just let your application hang under Windows 95 if something unusual happens. By writing termination routines, you can exit gracefully.

■ **Use the common dialog boxes and new GDI common features.** Even though the underlying implementation is different, they give you consistency.

The bottom line to most programmers is that NT is rock stable.

Operating System Architecture

2

by David Hamilton

IN THIS CHAPTER

NT is an operating system designed to run programs from different environments. You can have DOS programs, 16-bit Windows 3.11 programs, 32-bit NT programs, POSIX (UNIX) applications, and OS/2 programs all running at the same time and sharing the same data. Windows NT accomplishes this by having subsystems for each of these respective operating systems.

The above lists the set of subsystems available today; NT is designed so that others can be added in the future. Each of these subsystems has its own set of function calls to use system resources; they ask for I/O in different ways, they access the network via different protocols, and they get data in different formats. They also need to be able to share data and send messages to each other.

To implement this seemingly impossible task, NT uses a client server model. Each of the applications (Win32, POSIX, and OS/2) runs in User mode as a client. The application sends API calls to its own environmental subsystem, which repackages these into local procedure calls (LPCs). The LPC is the interface between User mode and Kernel mode. It's the method that allows each subsystem to use its own functions with its own parameter lists but submit system calls in a uniform way.

Applications still link to DLLs using their function calls as on their native operating systems. Each DLL provides entry points to its functions called *stubs*. Stubs package the caller's parameters into messages and send the messages to the correct server. The server implements the function call and returns results back to the DLL via an LPC. All this is invisible to the application programmer, who writes code-calling functions in the DLL as before by their familiar parameter lists. After the stub packages the call into a message, it sends those messages across the User mode/Kernel mode barrier to the system services of the NT Executive.

In Chapter 1, you looked at what NT can do as well as the basics of the NT operating system. In this chapter, you examine the NT architecture that allows it to accomplish so much. This has been broken down into four sections, The Kernel, Security, The Registry, and Memory Management.

The NT Executive

The NT Executive is a team of objects. Various Win32 API functions create these objects by building on smaller objects—the Kernel objects. In object-oriented programming you derive one object based on a previously created object that has some functionality you wish to use. If you want to create a data file you first create an object based on a CFile object and use its CreateFile member function. Microsoft derived this base CFile object from a more basic class, CObject. CObject itself was derived from Executive objects by a Microsoft systems programmer. These Executive objects were built from even more primitive Kernel objects. Table 2.1 lists these Executive objects.

Table 2.1. The `Executive` objects.

Executive object	*Represents*
Process	A program invocation
Thread	An executable entity within a process
Section	A region of shared memory
File	An instance of an opened file or I/O device
Port	A destination for messages passed between processes
Access token	A ID containing security information about a user
Event	An announcement that a system event has occurred
Event pair	A notification that a client has copied a message
Semaphore	A counter that regulates the number of threads that can use a resource
Mutant	A mechanism to provide mutual exclusion capabilities
Timer	A counter that records the passage of time
Object directory	A memory-based repository for object names
Symbolic link	A mechanism for indirectly referring to an object name
Profile	A mechanism for measuring the distribution of execution time within a block of code
Key	An index for refer to records in the NT registry

Figure 2.1 shows the NT Executive. The kernel is part of the Executive, but there is a definite division of labor. The other `Executive` objects are in charge of setting policy, whereas the kernel is in charge of implementation—it is the mechanic that makes sure the tasks are performed. The kernel is in direct communication with the hardware abstraction layer (HAL), and HAL talks to the CPU or CPUs directly.

NT 4.0 added the GDI32 and USER32 elements to the Executive, thereby making the system more responsive to the user. It also moves these two areas out of User mode into Kernel mode.

The various subsystems such as Win32, POSIX, and OS/2 all have their individual policies or rules. The Executive is the area where these rules are brought together into the operating system policies. Again, it is important to understand who owns what. The simplest way to decide whether an object is owned by a subsystem or by the Executive is to ask, "What does my object mean to the POSIX subsystem?" If your object is a file that both the WIN32 and POSIX or OS/2 subsystems can use, it is an `Executive` object. If your object is a menu or window, it means nothing to the character-based OS/2 system, so it must be a WIN32 subsystem object.

FIGURE 2.1.
The NT Executive team.

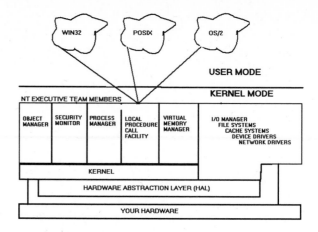

It becomes somewhat hard to discuss the kernel without discussing threads. If these objects are foreign to you, you might find it easier to read the next chapter on threads and then return to this point.

The Kernel

Microsoft calls the kernel the bottom of the food chain. NT is built by layers upon layers of code. Each layer is made up of lower, more primitive objects. When you get to the kernel, you have only the most fundamental functions and objects. The VMS OS kernel for the DEC VAX series was written before the NT kernel. This is the final layer that everything had to pass through between the operating system and the CPU. The kernel performs these actions:

- Scheduling threads
- Transferring control on interrupts and exceptions
- Synchronizing multiprocessor operations
- Initiating system recovery after a power failure

Some unique features of the kernel are that it is never paged out of memory and that it is never preempted. In fact, when a kernel thread is run, multitasking itself is preempted. Although the kernel can't be preempted, it can be interrupted by a high-level interrupt, as you will see later in this chapter.

The Kernel objects can be divided into two classes:

- **Dispatcher objects:** These include the `Kernel Thread` objects, `Kernel Mutant` objects, `Kernel Event` objects, `Kernel Event Pair` objects, `Kernel Mutext` object, and `Kernel Semaphore` objects.
- **Control objects:** These include `I/O` objects, `Kernel Process` objects, `Asynchronous Procedure Call` objects, and `Deferred Procedure Call` objects. The `I/O` objects include the `Interrupt` object, the `Power Notify` object, and the `Power Status` object.

Each of these `Kernel` objects is a more primitive set of objects implemented by the NT Kernel. An example is the `Kernel Thread` object, shown in Figure 2.2, which has a subset of the attributes available in the `User Thread` object.

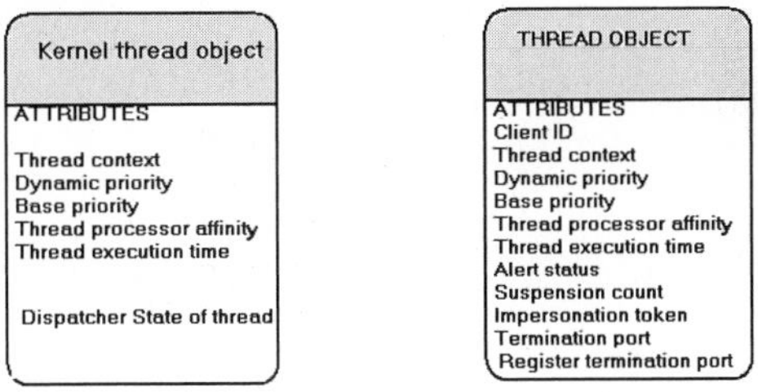

FIGURE 2.2.

Attributes of `Kernel` `Thread` *objects and a* `Process Thread` *object.*

```
Kernel thread object

ATTRIBUTES

Thread context
Dynamic priority
Base priority
Thread processor affinity
Thread execution time

Dispatcher State of thread
```

```
THREAD OBJECT

ATTRIBUTES
Client ID
Thread context
Dynamic priority
Base priority
Thread processor affinity
Thread execution time
Alert status
Suspension count
Impersonation token
Termination port
Register termination port
```

Figure 2.2 makes it easy to see that your process's `Thread` object was built on a more primitive object—the `Kernel Thread` object.

When an event occurs that changes the status of a thread, the Kernel suspends the thread that is running and changes its dispatcher state from running to waiting. This process is called a context switch. The kernel's dispatcher software (The Dispatcher) uses a priority scheme to determine the order of thread execution, scheduling higher priority threads before those with lower priority.

Context switches are discussed in a minute but, basically, the current state of the thread is its *context*. If the context is preempted, it must be saved in order to restore the thread to its current state until it again gets access to the CPU.

Thread Scheduling

The Dispatcher maintains a Dispatcher Ready Queue, a table as shown in Figure 2.3, in which all threads in a ready state are ordered by priority. Each thread receives a slice of time from the CPU and is served in its order of priority.

A thread is assigned a priority from 1 to 31. All threads at the same priority level get equal access to the CPU. Using Figure 2.3 as an example, the CPU must handle the first priority 25 thread (Thread E) and then the next priority 25 thread (Thread F). It then returns to the first 25 thread (Thread E) and finishes all priority 25s before any priority 24 threads (Threads C and D). Threads usually don't have real-mode priorities this high, and not even something important like the Flight Simulator can get priority 31 threads (Thread G). A thread at this level would suspend all processing until it was finished. Your joystick won't work, the video won't update, this is system starvation.

Most threads are variable priority (priority 0 to 15). The only priority 0 thread is the idle thread created by the `Kernel Thread` object to watch for `Deferred Process` objects to become available.

FIGURE 2.3.

The Dispatcher Ready Queue.

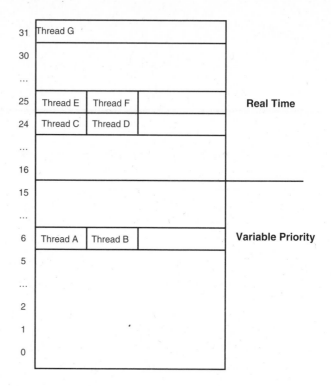

Scheduling Priority

To prevent starvation, the variable priority threads are boosted, such as when your foreground task gets a +2 priority boost for performance, or they decay in priority if they begin to hog resources. A process that has a high priority and is CPU-intensive decays −1 priority each time it is active. It decays back to its base priority. This changing of priorities keeps NT robust.

In the next chapter, you will learn more about priorities and scheduling.

Context Switching

After a thread has executed for its time slice, if it is preempted, or if it needs to wait for a resource, the Kernel Dispatch object saves its context, restores the next-up thread's context, and executes that next thread.

A thread may be preempted if it no longer is the highest priority thread. It also may enter a wait state if it needs some resource that is not available.

A thread's context includes a program counter, the processor status register, the other register contents, the user and kernel stack pointers, and a pointer to the address space in which the thread runs. The kernel saves all this data by pushing it onto the current thread's Kernel mode stack and updating the stack pointer.

In the next chapter, you will look closer at context switching. For now, just remember that if you are going to execute a small segment of one process, then another, and then return to the first, you need some method of storing and restoring your current work on that first processes.

Interrupt and Exception Handling

Interrupts and *exceptions* are operating system events that change the current flow of execution. They are detected by the software or the hardware. When an interrupt or exception occurs, the processor must stop and transfer control to the code that handles the condition that threw the exception or issued the interrupt. This code is called the *trap handler*. If the interrupt is from a device driver, the processor executes its trap handler, which is called the *interrupt service routine* (ISR), in this case.

All devices supply their own ISRs; when you press a mouse button, press a key, access the disk drive, or use your network, you are interrupting the processor to run the ISR of that device.

Jumping to the code at the trap handler requires a context switch. When this type of context switch is entered, NT creates a trap frame. The *trap frame* is just a subset of the entire thread's context.

If an interrupt can happen at any time, it is said to be an *asynchronous* event. An exception happens at a certain instruction and can be reproduced by running the same program under identical conditions. It therefore is *synchronous*. In Chapter 12, "Structured Exception Handling," you look at structured exception handling—a way that your software can use exceptions to gracefully handle unusual conditions sometimes referred to as *bugs* or *features*.

Just as threads have priority levels, interrupts have priority levels called *interrupt request levels* (IRQLs), as shown in Figure 2.4. This is kind of intuitive; a power off interrupt is more important to the CPU than a mouse click.

FIGURE 2.4.

Interrupt request levels.

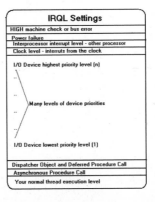

The kernel treats IRQL settings just like thread priorities. If a higher level interrupt occurs, it preempts a lower level interrupt. If the Dispatcher hides or ignores all lower IRQLs, this is called *masking an interrupt*. NT is secure, and such things as a drop in voltage to the CPU trigger events such as recording critical information. The amount of recording is up to you in a way; if you don't use a battery backup system, NT naturally can't restart with all the data intact as it was designed.

If your system does have a battery, backup data can be restored from memory when the system returns. Two Kernel objects are in charge of this: the Power Notify object and the Power Status object. These are used in device driver development to implement a power-recovery routine. If a device has such a routine, it is registered with the Kernel Interrupt object. You will see in Chapter 5, "File Systems," that the NTFS file system also has ways in which to recover itself.

More important to you, the developer, are software interrupts. On the basic level, by issuing a software interrupt, the Kernel Dispatcher preempts a thread during its normal course of work. Using *deferred procedure calls* (DPCs) is another way to process a less critical task. The task may be one you want to run just when the CPU is idle or it may be one that needs to run at the specific time or on a specific event's occurrence. DPCs usually also are performed in device driver development. *Asynchronous procedure calls* (APCs) are performed in both User mode and Kernel mode. These calls are threads that are in the waiting state. A software sets a timer that tells the kernel when to move the thread to the ready state.

Finally, there are exceptions. An exception occurs in a synchronous fashion whenever your application reaches a certain instruction. The following conditions throw an exception:

> Data-Type Mismatch
> Debugger Breakpoint
> Debugger Single Step
> Floating-Point Divide by Zero
> Floating-Point Overflow/Underflow
> Floating-Point Reserved Operand
> Guard Page Violation
> Illegal Instruction
> Integer Divide by Zero
> Integer Overflow
> Memory Access Violation
> Page Read Error
> Paging File Quota Exceeded
> Privileged Instruction

The kernel handles some of these conditions by sending back an Unsuccessful message to the user. Some exceptions are not handled by the operating system, such as a memory-access violation; instead, these are handled by the WIN32 subsystem. When an exception occurs, the kernel searches for an exception handler in the current stack frame. If it doesn't find it, the kernel continues searching back to previous stack frames until it exhausts its search. At that point, it calls its own default handler. When it calls its default, it sends a message out the exception port of the subsystem responsible for the thread. A WIN32 user therefore gets a WIN32 exception and a POSIX user gets a POSIX exception.

These other `Kernel` objects are used in thread synchronization:

- **Mutex object (mutual exclusion):** Ensures that only one thread can access a particular resource at a time. `Mutant` objects ensure that only one thread at a time holds a `Mutex` object.
- **Semaphore objects:** Keep count of how many threads can access a certain resource.
- **Event objects:** Announce that a certain event has occurred.
- **Event Pair objects:** Allow the kernel to link two events in an `if`, `then` fashion.

The kernel is a busy place: it does the mechanical work of scheduling tasks, interrupts, and exceptions.

The I/O Manager

The Executive's I/O system is all the code that gets and sets data to and from devices such as disk drives, mice, video, CD-ROM, and so on. Before you look at the other elements of NT, you should have a general understanding of I/O. NT uses packets of information; every I/O request is represented by an *I/O request packet* (IRP). The I/O Manager is a Kernel mode system charged with the task of attaining the necessary resources that a process needs. It treats everything like a device driver—even the file system. When it gets called, it sends an IRP out to the appropriate device. NT followed in UNIX's footsteps by treating all data as just a stream of bytes, or a file. All sources and destinations of data are treated as if they are files. You need to get a handle to open and access them just as you do a disk file.

NT also uses a uniform structure for drivers; a device and the file system have the same design. Named pipes and network Redirectors are viewed as file systems and are used as a file system driver. IRPs are reused as they pass through the system, and the I/O Manager synchronizes their access to global data.

The I/O Manager performs its tasks asynchronously. The processor preempts a thread that needs data and performs another task while the I/O Manager is getting the data. A call from User mode to read data is passed via an IRP to the I/O Manager, which then checks the parameters and security. It then queues the request at the particular device and notifies the User mode program that I/O is pending. When the data is available, the device driver sends an interrupt that the I/O Manager translates by setting the file handle's signal state. This tells the User mode program to context switch to the waiting thread. Turning a signal bit on means that an object is available. If you see that a resource is *signaled*, it is available.

NT device drivers use DPCs to tell NT that they have data ready. This is a two-step process. The device sends an interrupt that is intercepted by the ISR for the device. The ISR saves any information it receives, sends a DPC, and then quits. NT then resumes what it was doing before the interrupt occurred and processes the DPC whenever the system drops to that DPC priority level. Therefore, most other threads run before a device, such as a printer that usually has a very low-level DPC. Some devices have a much higher level of interrupt, such as the mouse or keyboard. These devices are serviced before most other threads.

After the DPC finishes, a process called *I/O completion* occurs, during which the I/O services record the outcome in an I/O status block. This status block may be the actual data transferred, so it may need to be written to the calling process's virtual address space. The I/O Manager must wait until the thread actually is running before it can get a handle on the process's memory space. It does this by creating a Kernel mode APC, which triggers a software interrupt the next time the thread runs. When the trigger goes off, the thread again is preempted so that the data actually can be copied into the address space. Finally, it can use the data!

This is the easy, one-layered example. In a typical disk drive/file system configuration, you add another layer as the IRP comes from the I/O Manager, to the file system device driver, to the disk drive's driver, and then to the drive itself. Then it goes all the way back up the chain.

Each NT driver has a standard set of components:

- An initialization routine that creates the System objects that the I/O Manager uses to access the driver
- A set of dispatch routines that are the functions the driver can perform
- A start I/O routine that initiates data transfer
- An ISR
- An interrupt-servicing DPC routine
- A completion routine
- A Cancel I/O routine
- An unload routine
- Error-handling routines

Throughout this chapter and the next, you will look at priorities and interrupt levels in much greater detail.

NT's I/O Manager has a Cache Manager component that places frequently accessed file data in memory to provide better response for I/O bound programs. This is a dynamic process in which the size of the cache grows and shrinks, depending on the memory available. NT uses virtual memory pages to bring 4 KB pages into memory. The paging mechanism always is balancing how may pages are read into memory and adjusting the cache size to optimize its work.

Security

As unlikely as it may seem, the Department of Defense (DoD) set the design specifications for the NT security system by requiring an operating system at Class C2 level security. The DoD had defined security requirements that had to be met for an operating system to be used in defense-related government agencies and industries. Microsoft built NT with an eye to these requirements. Level C2 security consists of the following requirements:

■ **A secure login facility with both a user name and password.** NT implements this by trapping the Ctrl+Alt+Del combination; this is one interrupt no other process can see. This prevents programs from intercepting the user name and password.

■ **Discriminating access control.** The owner of a resource says who can access the resource and what they can do with it. The owner must grant access rights to users or groups of users.

■ **An auditing system.** This detects and records security events whenever someone tries to create, access, or delete a resource.

■ **Protecting memory from a second process reading what a first had written into memory.** You will see later in this chapter how NT initializes a block of memory by filling it with zeroes to blank it out.

In NT's future releases there will be even more security as the system moves to DoD level B2 with security-clearance levels and compartments that separate groups of users from one another. NT Server calls these compartments *domains.* Security-clearance levels prevent a user from giving resource access to any second user with a lower clearance level than the first. In DoD spy terms, top-secret clearance level users can't share their resources with someone who is just cleared at the secret-user level.

NT names resources and shares user accounts across the network in a uniform way. Although the system Administrator may choose not to use all the levels of security, he can't bypass the process. Every object NT creates must pass through a gate in the Object Manager and have its access token compared to its proposed user's access token. (See Figure 2.5.) This gate is called the *Security Resource Monitor* (SRM).

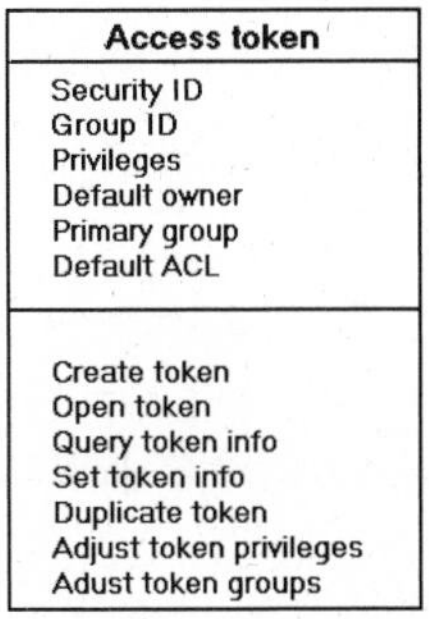

FIGURE 2.5.

An NT security access token.

Access token
Security ID
Group ID
Privileges
Default owner
Primary group
Default ACL
Create token
Open token
Query token info
Set token info
Duplicate token
Adjust token privileges
Adust token groups

When you logon to NT, it attaches an access token to your user process, which passes to all other processes you create. The SRM always is comparing your token with that of the resources your process requests. Within the token is an *access control list* (ACL), which just lists rights called *access control entries* (ACEs), such as "Dave can read," "The Accounting group can read/write," or "The world can execute." This actually happens when you open a handle to an object, not every time you reuse the handle. The SRM processes the ACL list item by item and stops whenever it gets the first level where you have access.

The SAM Database

Pressing Ctrl+Alt+Del from within NT starts its *local security authority* (LSA), which authenticates your user ID and password against that in the Security Access Monitor database. This also happens when a logon comes from another computer on your network. If the logon is successful, you are assigned a *security access token* (SAT). The Win32 API has a number of functions to manipulate SAT tokens.

```
AdjustTokenGroups
AdjustTokenPrivileges
GetTokenInformation
OpenProcessToken
OpenThreadToken
SetTokenInformation
```

Each user has a unique security ID value in the form S-1-5-21-81-0. The S is for SID, 1 is the revision level, 5 identifies who created the SID, and 21, 81, and subsequent values are subauthority values. If you are doing security programming, you can use a number of functions to authenticate your users based on this SID and look up accounts in the SAM database.

```
EqualPrefixSid
EqualSid
GetLengthSid
GetSidIdentifierAuthority
GetSidLengthRequired
GetSidSubAuthority
GetSidSubAuthorityCount
IsValidSid
LookupAccountName
LookupAccountSid
AllocateAndInitializeSid
CopySid
FreeSid
InitializeSid
```

You use these functions to retrieve the account name of a current thread on your machine and determine access rights. To do this in your software security system, you need to have corresponding functions to retrieve and set security on objects that your application creates. These functions are

```
GetFileSecurity
GetKernelObjectSecurity
GetUserObjectSecurity
QueryServiceObjectSecurity
RegGetKeySecurity
RegSetKeySecurity
SetFileSecurity
SetKernelObjectSecurity
SetServiceObjectSecurity
SetUserObjectSecurity
```

Another part of NT's security is the *system logon* where the user is authenticated no matter where in the domain they log on. A domain controller maintains the SAM database of users. When a trusted second domain controller is added to the network, the first domain controller synchronizes the SAM databases on the two. This allows a user with domain privileges to log on anywhere with the same user ID and password.

Security Access Control

When a new object is created, it gets its security descriptor from a variety of sources. If you pass a SECURITY_ATTRIBUTES parameter in the Create function, you define the attributes. Usually, you will pass NULL for this parameter and let NT assign default values. NT gets these default values from the creator's access token, so the object is available to the same group to which you belong.

When a child process inherits from its parent, the new handle has the same security attributes as the parent. Using DuplicateHandle(), you can create a mask to change the child's security. You actually can create a handle with even a higher security than you have; you won't be able to use it, but a higher security level process will.

Whenever a resource's security token is examined, the Object Manager also must know how you intend to use the object. You define this when you flag objects as GENERIC_READ or GENERIC_WRITE. This further gives you the ability to control how your objects are used.

Network operations become interesting when two processes are working on one project. One process without the access may attempt to gain access to resources through the other process with which it is sharing. In these cases, the server security comes into play. The server does a double check; it doesn't rely on the security system to validate use. With Dynamic Data

Exchange (DDE), named pipes, and remote procedure call programming, it becomes necessary sometimes for one process to impersonate the other's security. In keeping with discriminating access control, though, the thread controls who can impersonate it with `ImpersonateSelf()` and `DuplicateToken()`. After a thread allows itself to be impersonated, the other thread can use `DdeImpersonateClient()`, `ImpersonateDDEClientWindow()`, `ImpersonateNamedPipeClient`, and `RpcImpersonateClient` to get the job done. It resets with `RpcRevertToSelf()` or `RevertToSelf()`.

Security Auditing

When you log on to your domain server as an Administrator, you can enable auditing via the Policies Audit option in the User Manager. This enables you to audit the success or failure of the following actions:

- Login or logoff
- File and object access
- Use of user rights
- User and group management
- Security policy changes
- Restart, shutdown, and system configuration changes
- Process tracking

After auditing is enabled, you can use the Explorer to further define what types of files and which directories you are watching. You also can assign read, write, execute, delete, change password, and take ownership attributes to your files.

With auditing enabled, all changes you define are written to a security log. To view these security logs use the Event Viewer program and open the security log you are watching. This program details the source, category, event, user, and computer, as well as the date and time, of each event.

Shared Memory Security

In the last section of this chapter, you look at memory management in detail, how NT manages memory and where you the programmer can make choices. In order to have a secure system, one process should not be allowed to overwrite memory needed by another process or control all available memory. This is the cause of many of the general protection faults you've seen in Windows. Security also requires that a user cannot write a process that can read another process memory in an unrestricted manner. Restricting memory access not only impacts system security but also how responsive and robust the system is to the user.

With NT, memory protection is provided in four forms:

■ A separate address space for each process in which hardware disallows any thread from accessing the virtual address of another process.

■ Two modes of operation. User mode cannot access system code or data; instead, you must use Kernel mode.

■ A page-based protection mechanism in which each virtual page has a set of security flags that determine who can use it and how. Pages are marked as private, read-only, read/write, execute only, guarded, no-access, and copy-on-write.

■ Every object must be used via a handle. The Security Reference Monitor's handle is checked for user access privileges before any handle is opened.

Each process sees its own 4 GB memory space, but that virtual memory is mapped into physical memory. When two instances of an executable are run, NT doesn't load the executable image twice; it just maps the first image into the second process's virtual memory. Before it makes this mapping, memory, like every other resource, is checked by the Security Resource Monitor. That is the first level of security. When a process wants to have an area of memory to write data into, it initializes a block for its use. During this initialization, NT blanks out every byte in the memory with a 0 to prevent the process from viewing what was in left over in the block from a past use.

The application also may have various security measures, such as a database's access rights, which are checked. If both processes have the access, they can share memory for writing. Now it becomes somewhat tricky: Should each process see its own data or should they share the changed data? This is a policy set up by the process that created the data. Without a policy, NT uses copy-on-write. In this situation, as one process needs to write data, NT makes a copy of the original that the second process still sees. The first process writes to the copy.

The Registry

The *Registry* is an internal database that contains information not only on NT configuration, but on the configuration of many of your applications (see Figure 2.6). Programs should use the Registry instead of the outdated INI files for their configuration storage.

When you installed NT, your SYSTEM.INI file was copied to this directory:

`HKEY_LOCAL_MACHINE\Software\Microsoft\Windows NT\CurrentVersion\WOW`

Your WIN.INI files are in this directory:

`HKEY_CURRENT_USER and HKEY_CURRENT_USER\SOFTWARE\MicrosoftWindows NT`

FIGURE 2.6.

The Registry database.

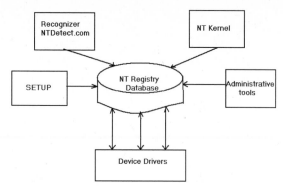

The network settings, however, are copied to this directory:

```
HKEY_LOCAL_MACHINE\SOFTWARE\MicrosoftWindows NT\CurrentVersion
```

The setup component of the Registry database is used when your application's setup writes configuration information to the database. When your application starts, it reads and uses that information.

NTDETECT.COM runs when NT starts to get the configuration options you have set up. It probes the system hardware and checks against your prior configuration. It detects changes to the configuration and adjusts NT for you in some situations. It uses this information to load device drivers.

After NTDETECT runs, NT loads the kernel, which actually loads the device drivers and passes information to the subsystem. Device drivers send and get information from the Registry, such as hardware available, DMA channels to use, I/O port addresses, and base memory. NTDETECT checks for the following:

> Bus/adapter type
> Video adapter
> Keyboard
> Floating-point coprocessor
> SCSI adapter
> Mouse
> Communications ports
> Floppy drives
> Machine ID
> Parallel ports

The administrative tools are like the User Manager, which writes the security IDs to the Registry. Programs register their own settings in the Registry, such as when ODBC drivers register the ODBC database names you use and the ODBC drivers that each database requires.

REGEDIT.EXE enables you to view and edit Registry information, as shown in Figure 2.7. Each computer has five subtrees in the Registry:

- `HKEY_LOCAL_MACHINE`
- `HKEY_CLASSES_ROOT`
- `HKEY_CURRENT_USERS`
- `HKEY_USERS`
- `KEY_CURRENT_CONFIG`

These subtrees form a tree of information. Each entry is flagged as `REG_MULTI_SZ` if it is a string, `REG_EXPAND_SZ` if it is a variable representing a string, `REG_BINARY` for binary data, and `REG_FULL_RESOURCE_DESCRIPTOR` to contain device driver parameters. The three parts of every entry are the name, the data type, and the value represented in the form `Name:DATAType:Value`, as in `CurrentUser:REG_SZ:USERNAME`.

FIGURE 2.7.

Using REGEDIT.EXE.

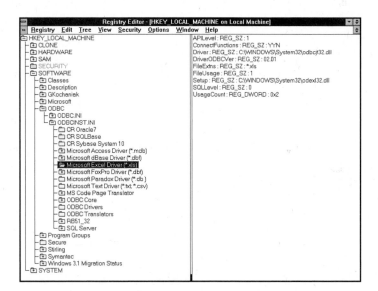

`HKEY_LOCAL_MACHINE` has subbranches for `HARDWARE`, `SAM SECURITY` (policy settings), `SOFTWARE`, and `SYSTEM`. Expanding each of these displays a seemingly endless list of key entry values. You often will see these subbranches referred to as *hives*.

Your application can use the Registry to store configuration settings with the following API functions:

RegCloseKey	RegOpenKey
RegConnectRegistry	RegOpenKeyEx
RegCreateKey	RegQueryInfoKey
RegCreateKeyEx	RegQueryMultipleValues

RegDeleteKey	RegQueryValue
RegDeleteValue	RegQueryValueEx
RegEnumKey	RegReplaceKey
RegEnumKeyEx	RegRestoreKey
RegEnumValue	RegSaveKey
RegFlushKey	RegSetKeySecurity
RegGetKeySecurity	RegSetValue
RegLoadKey	RegSetValueEx
RegNotifyChangeKeyValue	RegUnLoadKey

In addition to REGEDIT.EXE, the NT Resource Kit provides these files:

■ **REGBACK.EXE:** Creates backups of Registry files (Backup does not back up a remote Registry)

■ **REGENTRY.HLP:** Documents Registry entries

■ **REGINI.EXE:** Makes Registry changes by script

■ **REGREST.EXE:** Restores Registry hives using the ReplaceKey function

When you installed NT, the default hive values were written to the Emergency Repair disk. It's a good idea to periodically create a new Emergency Repair disk so that you have a copy of your hive values. Going back to the originals won't help much if you have been using NT for quite some time!

The REGENTRY.HLP file is almost a necessity to decipher the sometimes cryptic Registry key names. You will find many services listed in your control set, but often it isn't apparent that Cdfs is the SCSI CD-ROM or that spock and sparrow are your SCSI adapters.

Before you modify many of the basic Registry values, you can use several of the performance-monitoring tools included with the NT Resource Kit to find the best values for critical items, such as page sizes, pages to swap, and a host of other NT settings. If you haven't worked with the NT Resource Kit, it's an excellent learning tool as well.

CAUTION

Changing Registry values can cause extreme difficulties, so be sure to know what the value you are changing will do!

Memory Management

Virtual memory isn't new. I first worked on a VAX system in which each user had his own 512 KB address space on a computer with only 16 MB of memory. That doesn't seem like a big deal by today's PC standards until you realize that there were dozens of user processes going on at any one time. In Windows NT, each process has its own 4 GB: 2 GB contain the User mode space and 2 GB contain the process's Kernel mode and system space.

NT's Virtual Memory Manager was designed with these requirements in mind:

- ■ It must be portable.
- ■ It should be reliable without system Administrator or user tuning.
- ■ It should contain memory-mapped files with copy-on-write capabilities for multi-user access.
- ■ It should allow the process to manage its private memory.
- ■ It should allow for various subsystems such as POSIX and OS/2.
- ■ It should balance the needs of multiprocessing and memory access.

Virtual Memory

Virtual memory has three parts: the physical memory layout, the logical memory layout, and the process that maps the two. The *logical memory layout* (virtual memory) is the memory as the process views it: one contiguous, flat, 4 GB block of memory. Being able to treat the memory as one large linear space is much easier on the programmer than working with 64 KB segments of memory.

Mapping this large virtual memory space in the actual computer's physical memory requires swapping unused areas out to the disk drive when your process extends beyond the physical memory space. The large paging file, pagefile.sys, is used for this.

Take a break and watch this happen. Fire up the Performance Monitor software and then use the Visual C++ compiler to begin building a larger project. In Figure 2.8, my computer is building the CIRC3 sample included with Visual C++ 4.0. By watching the number of page faults per second and the copy on writes per second, you can get a good idea whether your computer would benefit from added memory. When you run into performance problems you can decide what area of your computer is causing the bottleneck. The NT Resource Kit book on performance testing does a good job of illustrating what each type of bottleneck looks like with the performance monitor and what parameter you need to measure to demonstrate the bottleneck.

As you can see, my 486/66 with only 24 MB of memory does quite a bit of paging while building the sample CIRC3 software. This takes time. The guy down the hall has a 486/33 with 32 MB and builds software in almost one-third the time. Processor speed isn't everything, so I won't even tell you big Pentium users out there the amount of time this build takes: a P133 with 32 MB takes less than one-tenth of my own speed. (OK, it takes Visual C++ 4.1 160 seconds to rebuild the entire application, go out and buy a second copy of this book!)

FIGURE 2.8.

Performance Monitor while VC++ is building the CIRC3 sample.

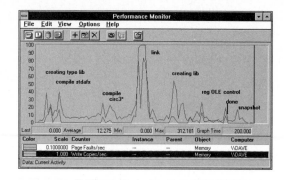

Paging

Moving this data back and forth between memory and the hard drive takes a lot of processor power. To make this process more efficient, NT moves the memory in 4 KB blocks called *pages*. The 4 GB space is divided into a million pages, each 4 KB. The 4 GB space is used by your process in sections as in Table 2.2.

Table 2.2. NT use of your 4 GB address space.

Virtual Address	Contents
0 KB to 64 KB	Reserved
64 KB and above	Executables file images
above the file image	Heaps and thread stacks
above the heap & stack	Application DLLs
above the app DLLs	System DLLs you use, such as Kernel32, User32, GDI32, and NT
2 GB to 4 GB	Reserved for operating system

When a page is in physical memory, it is said to be *valid*. When it is not in physical memory, it is *invalid*. Each time you need to access a page that has been swapped to disk (an invalid page), the processor issues a system trap called a *page fault*.

Deciding which pages to swap out is a complex process. Two processes may be sharing memory, private memory must be protected from access, some memory is locked, and multiprocessor systems really inundate the Virtual Memory Manager.

To the user, process memory is an object that is named, protected, and manipulated like any other Executive object. Your process can allocate memory, read and write to virtual memory, lock pages in virtual memory, get information on virtual pages, protect pages, and flush virtual pages to disk.

Allocating memory is a two-step process. First, you reserve the memory that tells the Virtual Memory Manager to set aside a block for your use. When you then commit memory, the Virtual Memory Manager actually sets aside a piece of its paging file for your use. Reserving virtual memory is a cheap operation in Windows NT programming, but actually committing it is expensive because NT deducts committed memory from your paging file quota. By not committing memory, you free paging file space for processes that actually need to use it at the moment. For time-critical operations, you can lock pages in memory to save the overhead of having to retrieve them from the paging file. You can pick a memory address to reserve or let NT assign one for you. The following code would allocate memory at a specific memory address:

```
LPVOID VirtualAllocate(LPVOID lpAddress, DWORD dwSize, DWORD flAllocationType,
DWORD flProtect);
LPVOID VirtualFree(LPVOID lpAddress, DWORD dwSize, DWORD dwFreeType);
```

NT allocates memory in 64 KB blocks, beginning on 64 KB boundaries, so make sure that lpAddress and dwSize are multiples of 64×1024. Actually, NT rounds down if you can't do the math. The parameter flAllocationType is MEM_COMMIT or MEM_RESERVE. The flProtect is PAGE-NOACCESS, PAGE_READONLY, or PAGE_READWRITE. The dwFreeType is MEM_RELEASE or MEM_DECOMMIT.

Three other useful functions enable you to change the protection of the memory, as this code shows:

```
BOOL VirtualProtect(LPVOID lpAddress, DWORD dwSize, DWORD dwNewProtect, DWORD
dwOldProtect);
BOOL VirtualLock(LPVOID lpvMem, DWORD cbMem);
BOOL VirutalUnlock(LPVOIC lpvMem, DWORD cbMem);
```

You also can query the state of the memory by using this code:

```
DWORD VirutalQuery(LPVOID lpAddress, PMEMORY_BASIC_INFORMATION, DWORD lpBuffer,
DWORD dwLength);

typedef struct _MEMORY_BASIC_INFORMATION {
  PVOID baseaddress;
  PVOID allocationbase;
  DWORD allocationProtect;
  DWORD regionsize;
  DWORD state;  //MEM_FREE, MEM-RESERVE, MEM_COMMIT
  DWORD protect;
  DWORD type;//MEM_MAPPED, MEM_PRIVATE, MEM_IMAGE
} MEMORY_BASIC_INFORMATION, *PMEMORY_BASIC_INFORMATION;
```

You already have learned how executables and DLLs share memory. Each process sees the shared code or data in its process address space, but the shared code is really just in memory once. Figure 2.9 shows a section of identical memory in the address spaces of two processes while it only resides once in actual physical memory.

Mapping of the memory from its physical location to the virtual address space is a simple concept, as long as you are just reading from the memory and not writing to it.

FIGURE 2.9.

Two virtual process's views
of physical memory.

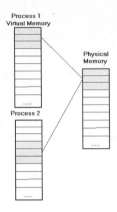

Memory Access

WIN32 applications have access to virtual memory through the WIN32 API. Your process actually can manipulate the memory of another process by knowing that process's handle and using `ReadProcessMemory()` and `WriteProcessMemory()`, assuming that you have the security level. These two functions are intended to be used only in User mode debuggers. Normally, processes share memory by granting each other access.

Shared memory is classified further as a `Section` object or a `File-Mapping` object. To share memory, a thread creates a `Section` object and gives it a name so that other processes can get a handle to it. Because an executable or file may be much larger than can fit even in virtual memory, NT creates a view of a section of the memory. The best analogy is a large database that is being displayed. The Virtual Memory Manager moves sections of the database table into memory, and multiple users may have different views of that database. It would make no sense to copy the entire database to a paging file and then display it. Instead, the Virtual Memory Manager uses a second type of object called a `Mapped-File` object. In a sense, with the database, the Virtual Memory Manager is using the database itself as the paging file. A `Section` object has attributes of maximum size, page protection, paging file/mapped file, and based/not based. The based attribute specifies that the `Section` object should appear at the same base address in each virtual address space that shares it.

The synchronization of the data in the `Section` object can come from many sources outside the Virtual Memory Manager. In the database example, the DBMS is doing record locking. Win32 applications can use events, mutexes, semaphores, and critical sections to provide the synchronization between a process's view of a `Section` object and another process's view.

NT provides protection of the virtual memory by assigning a separate address space to each process, using two modes of operation, allowing only Kernel mode processes to access system code, flagging pages as protected, and using the Security Reference Monitor. Each page is designated as a User mode page or a Kernel mode page and as read only or read/write. Pages also are flagged as execute only, guard, no access, and copy-on-write. NT further marks some areas where memory is never paged out, this includes most of its 2 GB system memory area as in Figure 2.10.

FIGURE 2.10.

Your process's 4 GB address space.

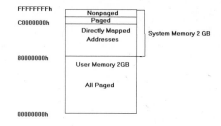

Copy-on-Write

Copy-on-write specifies that as long as two processes are reading shared memory, they each have a view of the same section of physical memory. As soon as one process wants to write to that memory, the Virtual Memory Manager makes a copy of the page to be written to and maps that copy to the process that wants to perform the write. This is illustrated in Figure 2.11 where just the page that is written to needs to be copied. Actually, NT uses an optimization technique called *lazy evaluation* so that even though you designate the memory as read/write, it doesn't do the actual copying until you actually write something and then only after ensuring that you have the proper security to do so.

FIGURE 2.11.

Using the copy-on-write attribute.

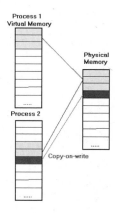

The paging mechanism is quite involved in giving NT the robustness it needs. First, a table is set up with the most recently used pages; this is *the translation lookaside buffer* (TLB). It tries to maximize the mapping of virtual memory to physical memory. NT looks here first for that mapping. If it doesn't find it, it moves on to the paging tables. These tables contain all the information the Virtual Memory Manager needs to find any page a thread might need. Mor than 1 million pages may exist, however, and NT sets up a directory for each process to fin that process's pages faster

Further optimization is performed by clustering the pages into memory. When a page fault occurs, NT loads a number of pages surrounding the needed page in the event that your next request will be for data or code near the current request.

When physical memory is full, NT uses a FIFO (first-in-first-out) algorithm to decide which pages are swapped out to the paging file (or mapped file). This simply means that the pages that have been in physical memory the longest are swapped out first. Pages that your application has most recently loaded into memory are assumed to be those that it will need access to more immediately and are left in physical memory. One process is restricted from starving other process's access to physical memory by NT's automatic working set trimming techniques.

Each process is assigned a maximum and minimum working set size (the minimum number of pages it will have in physical memory). When plenty of physical memory exists, the process can load pages up to its maximum working set size. As memory fills, the Virtual Memory Manager swaps pages out back to the process's minimum working set. The Virtual Memory Manager keeps track of the number of page faults each process causes. If there is plenty of physical memory and the process is causing many page faults, the Virtual Memory Manager increases the process's working set. If a process is not causing page faults, its working set is decreased. The Virtual Memory Manager therefore always is minimizing the number of page faults for you, and it often is counterproductive to take over management by your application.

To keep track of all the possibilities, the Virtual Memory Manager uses its own database: the page frame database. Each page frame is marked as one of the following:

State	Indicates
Bad	A parity error or hardware error occurred while the page was in use
Free	Available but not yet initialized
Modified	Contents have changed but have not been written to disk
Standby	Recently removed from the working set
Valid	In use
Zeroed	Empty and initialized with all zeros

You can see that the Virtual Memory Manager is also a very busy place in NT. When you look at things on this level, it is quite amazing that your lowly software gets any resources at all. Only the many optimization techniques used in NT enable it to have the robustness it does and yet be a rock-solid development platform.

Summary

Chapter 2 looked at the NT architecture as the basis for your understanding of how to write software for Windows NT. Each area of this chapter is built on in a future chapter. In the next chapter, "Execution Models," you look more closely at processes and threads, and in Chapter 22, "Threads," learn to write multithreaded NT applications. Chapter 3 also looks at the executable you will build and how it's loaded by NT. You examine dynamic link libraries (DLLs), which are the building blocks of nearly all your Window NT applications. You also look at new powerful features NT has added to batch file programming.

There are many examples throughout the book in which applications write or read from the Registry. In Chapter 36, "Smart Install and Uninstall Programming," you develop methods your application will use to register itself on installation and politely unregister when it's uninstalled.

Using memory and virtual memory management also show up in many areas of the book but are covered in detail in Chapter 13, "Windows NT Virtual Memory and Memory Management," where you learn how your application can use the virtual memory manager to create memory-mapped files and to program link lists for rapid data access.

In Chapter 14, "Files," you learn how to use the NT security features to access files throughout the network and implement security features in your application.

Execution Models

3

by David Hamilton

In this chapter you take a closer look at processes and threads in order to learn about NT's execution models. You will see how the executable you build is loaded into memory and how multiple users can be accessing the same executable simultaneously. You will look at how your application can share code with other applications through the use of dynamic link libraries (DLLs). NT's own DLLs allow you to integrate common controls and dialog boxes into your application, making it look like an application written for Windows NT.

In the chapter's last section you look at the NT command language and writing batch files to automate daily tasks. In this chapter and in Chapter 26, "Using the Remote Access Server," you develop a batch command that gathers your company's Internet mail and Usenet news. In Chapter 27, "Using the Messaging API," you see how that mail can be redistributed to each individual mail account.

A FEW DEFINITIONS

Processes, threads, executables, dynamic link libraries (DLLs), and batches. The definitions all seem to blend, so here's a short list to help you out:

Executable: A static sequence of instructions. It is the file your compiler builds, which it loads into memory when you run a program.

Process: A unit of resource ownership. It is the address space where the sequence of instructions (the executable) is loaded.

Thread: Executes sequences in the process's memory space resource.

DLL: A sequence of instructions, dynamically linked at runtime and meant to be shared by several processes. *Dynamically linked* means that it is loaded into memory when it is needed.

Batch: A list of NT operating system command instructions. Windows NT has an enhanced set of batch commands, including network management commands, which you can use in a .CMD file, just like the .BAT files you build under MS-DOS.

Processes

A *process* is the running instance of an application. It consists of blocks of code in memory loaded from executables and DLLs. Each process has its own 4 GB address space and owns resources such as threads, files, and dynamically allocated memory. Processes don't execute code; they are the address space resources in which code resides. Code in a process's address space is executed by a thread. Every NT process has at least one thread of execution.

NT processes have several characteristics:

- They are implemented as objects and accessed using object services.
- They can have multiple threads executing in their address space.

- Both process objects and thread objects have built-in synchronization.
- NT does not use a parent/child relationship with the processes it creates.

The process consists of multiple threads, each executing for a slice of time (a *quantum*) allocated by the NT kernel in a cyclic fashion. If your machine has multiple CPUs, each thread is assigned transparently to a CPU. On each CPU, the threads execute seemingly simultaneously. When the last thread finishes its task, the process terminates.

To prevent any one process from gaining unlimited control over another, each process has its own 4 GB address space in which its threads run. This memory space is split into 2 GB for the system's processes and 2 GB for the user's processes. Each time a process uses its address space, the virtual memory system maps the virtual address to a physical address. One process cannot directly access the virtual memory of another without the second process giving the first process access. To execute operating system code or to access operating system memory, a process must have a thread running in the unrestricted processor mode called *Kernel mode*.

Your application, as well as NT's own subsystems, almost always run in User mode. When a thread calls a system service, the processor traps the thread, actually takes ownership of the thread, and validates its arguments. The operating system then executes the thread in Kernel mode, switches it back to User mode, and then returns control to your process.

Processes are simply objects created by the Object Manager. Like any object, they have a header to store attributes and a body that provides the interface or services available to other objects. Table 3.1 lists these attributes.

Table 3.1. A process object's attributes.

Attribute	Description
Process ID	A unique value to identify the process
Access Token	Security information about the user of a process
Base Priority	Execution priority of a process's threads
Default Processor Affinity	Default set of processors that will run in a multiprocessor environment
Quota Limits	Maximum amount of memory space, file size, and processor time a user process can have
Execution Time	Cumulative time all threads have used
I/O Counter	Counters for number and type of I/O operations
VM Counters	Counters for number and type of virtual memory (VM) operations
Exception and Debugging Port	Interprocess communication ports to which the Process Manager should send exception messages
Exit Status	Indicates why the process terminated

A process can contain several threads The first thread, or primary thread, is created by NT. This primary thread then can create other threads. In a large symmetric multiprocessor (SMP) machine like a Sequent, many CPUs (up to 30) can exist. NT handles all the scheduling of the threads. When you design multi-threaded software, you don't need to make special programming changes in order for your application to run in a multiprocessor environment. When writing multi-threaded code, however, you need to synchronize the actions of the threads. Because of a multiprocessor system's speed and complexity, any synchronization you missed most likely will show up.

Creating a Process

When your program or NT's Program Manager needs to create a process, it calls the CreateProcess function. Don't faint if you have been spoiled by Windows' 3.11 simple WinExec function. Most parameters are passed NULL for the default. This section of the chapter focuses on concepts, not source code functions. However, you first need to examine this function so that you can look at the parameter, fdwCreate, for your process priority. Also, you'll look at wShowWindow, which is where all the SW_* flags you set in MFC's nCmdShow are passed. Listing 3.1 presents the code for CreateProcess.

Listing 3.1. Using CreateProcess.

```
BOOL CreateProcess(
  LPCTSTR LpszImageName, //process name usually exe name
  LPCTSTR lpszCommandLine, //command line parameters
  LPSECURITY_ATTRIBUTES lpsaProcess,
  LPSECURITY_ATTRIBUTES lpsaThread,
  BOOL fInheritHandles,
  DWORD fdwCreate,  //flags for if debug, console app and priority
  LPVOID lpEnvironment, //pointer to environmental strings, NULL if default
  LPTSTR lpszCurDir, //working and directory for new process
  LPSTARTUPINFO lpsiStartInfo, // see start up struct
  LPPROCESS_INFORMATION lppiProcInfo); //see process info struct

  typedef struct _SECURITY_ATTRIBUTES{
  DWORD nLength;   //size of this struct
  LPWORD lpSecurityDescriptor;  //if NULL then default
  BOOL bInheritHandle; //set TRUE if NT Executive handle
} SECURITY_ATTRIBUTES

 typedef struct _STARTUPINFO {    //for setting GUI, Console or both
  DWORD cb;
  LPSTR lpReserved;
  LPSTR lpDesktop;
  LPSTR lpTitle;
  DWORD dwX;
  DWORD dwY;
  DWORD dwXSize;   //size of your first window
  DWORD dwYSize;
  DWORD dwXCountChars;
```

```
    DWORD dwYCountChars;
    DWORD dwFillAttribute;  //background color
    DWORD dwFlags;  //where you set wait cursor
    DWORD wShowWindow;
    DWORD cbReserved2;
    LPBYTE lpReserved2;
    HANDLE hStdInput;
    HANDLE hStdOutput;
    HANDLE hStdError;
}  STARTUPINFO, *LPSTARTUPINFO;

typedef struct _PROCESS_INFORMATION; {
    HANDLE hProcess;
    HANDLE hThread;
    DWORD dwProcessID;
    DWORD dwThreadID;
} PROCESS_INFORMATION
```

In the SECURITY_ATTRIBUTES structure, you can set whether you want to be able to pass handles from your base process to any subprocesses it creates. The real point you should make on process priorities is via the fdwCreate parameter. This is the creation flag, which you can set to IDLE_PRIORITY_CLASS, NORMAL_PRIORITY_CLASS, HIGH_PRIORITY_CLASS, or REALTIME_PRIORITY_CLASS.

Because most of this book focuses on building MFC Windows applications, the function CreateProcess is not discussed further here. NT calls CreateProcess for you; the purpose of this section was just to point out where you can influence the call NT makes.

Getting to Know Your Process

After you start a process, you might want to know more about it. Processes are identified by a handle and an ID number.

Referring to any object by its handle is faster than using its name, because the Object Manager doesn't have to do a name lookup to find the object. In Windows NT, a handle is an index to a process-specific object table. This table contains pointers to all the objects for which the process has opened a handle. It gets a new entry in the table each time it creates a new object, opens a handle to an existing object, inherits a handle from a process, or is given a duplicate by another process. Each entry has the handle's access rights and its inheritance designation. An *inheritance designation* specifies whether processes created by this process get a copy of the handle in their object tables. Technically, a handle refers only to the index; however, when you see the word *handle* in a programming manual, it usually refers to the entire table entry.

In the Win32 and POSIX subsystems, resources can be inherited. The creator of an object decides whether the handle to the object can be inherited by another process. This is the discretionary access control security discussed in Chapter 2.

When a parent starts a process via CreateProcess, it receives both a handle and an ID. A child can get its name via GetCurrentProcess and GetCurrentProcessID calls. This returns a pseudohandle. *Pseudohandles* are valid only in the current process. If you need to use a pseudohandle outside that process, it must be converted using DuplicateHandle to get the address of the real handle. The syntax follows:

```
HANDLE GetCurrentProcess(void);
DWORD GetCurrentProcessID(void);
```

Remember, these functions return a pseudohandle. You can get at the real handle by using a trick with the DuplicateHandle function, where you pass it the pseudohandle as both the handle to copy and as the copy address, as shown in Listing 3.2.

Listing 3.2. The DuplicateHandle function.

```
DuplicateHandle(GetCurrentProcess(),
                GetCurrentProcess(),
                GetCurrentProcess(),
                &hProcess,  //this is the result you can use, the real handle
                0,
                False,
                DUPLICATE_SAME_ACCESS);
```

All User mode processes that access objects must first get a handle to the object. The Object Manager then can track which processes and how many processes need a certain object. It uses this information to decide how long an object should be retained before it is destroyed and the memory it is using is freed.

Object retention is performed in two phases:

■ **Name retention:** Every object belongs to the namespace of the Object Manager. When a handle is opened to an object, the Object Manager increments the object's usage count. When the handle is closed, it decrements the counter. When a usage counter goes to 0, the object is deleted.

■ **Reference counting:** This method is very similar to name retention. NT itself uses objects by pointers instead of handles. After the Object Manager gives the operating system a pointer, it increments the reference count. Likewise, the operating system frees a pointer and decrements the reference count. The Object Manager therefore can have a namespace counter that is 0 but doesn't delete the object because its reference count is not 0.

Object retention ensures that when two of your processes share any object, even if the first process dies, the second process still has the resources it was sharing.

Management is optimizing the allocation of limited resources. In order to optimize resources, you need to have an accounting of what is available. In NT's management, that is called *resource accounting*. Each user has a *resource quota*—a limit on the amount of the system's memory that his processes can use. Each object's header has an attribute called a *quota charge* that is the charge for getting a handle to that object. When your process's thread opens a handle to an object, the process is charged the amount of the quota charge. Threads open many handles during their execution, and each involves a charge. At some point, threads must close some objects before they can open any more. So just as NT is allocating the amount of CPU time, it is allocating the number of resources by imposing a quota on the number of handles available to a process and thus to the user.

Earlier in you saw how to set the priority of a process when it was created. To alter an existing processes priority you use the following code:

```
DWORD GetPriorityClass(HANDLE hProcess);
BOOL SetPriorityClass(HANDLE hProcess, DWORD fdwPriority);
```

CAUTION

You can change the priority of a process. You should do this only for short periods, however. For example, you might need to raise the priority if you are working with something that is really time critical. Then be sure to set it back. Failure to raise priorities only for time-critical tasks and then immediately resetting can impair the performance of other processes on your machine.

The four possible values of fdwPriority follow:

- IDLE_PRIORITY_CLASS
- NORMAL_PRIORITY_CLASS
- HIGH_PRIORITY_CLASS
- REAL_TIME_PRIORITY_CLASS

Remember this warning: Using REAL_TIME_PRIORITY_CLASS can slow down NT to the point where you can't even start PView to kill your favorite infinite-loop application.

Before you try to change a priority, read the section "Threads," later in this chapter. Although it's best to think of all processes as getting CPU time in a round-robin fashion, there is more to the story!

Pipes enable processes to communicate; Chapter 23, "Pipes," explores that topic. For now, you should just know that a *pipe* is a memory buffer where the system holds data between the time a process writes it and another process reads it. A *one-way* pipe has two ends: one for writing and one for reading. A *two-way* pipe allows both ends to read and write. You can create a name for your pipe or leave it as anonymous.

Terminating a Process

You can terminate a process by using the `ExitProcess` or `TerminateProcess` function.

```
VOID ExitProcess(UINT fuExitcode)
```

This doesn't return a value, but it does set the exit code.

```
BOOL TerminateProcess(HANDLE hProcess, UINT fuExitCode)
```

This code enables you to specify which process to terminate. This second function is used only to force termination and not as a usual call to end your application.

Again, these are functions you don't usually see in a one-process Windows application. You send `WM_CLOSE` or simply return from `WinMain`, and the `CRuntime` codes the function `ExitProcess`. If your application is going to create multiple processes, however, you need to terminate them. If your program terminates the process, NT terminates any threads running in the process. This is different than the usual behavior in which, after all threads are terminated, NT terminates the process.

When a process ends, NT first terminates all threads. It then closes all object handles and sends a signal to all other operating threads. The reason for the signal is that you still can have child processes executing after that parent terminates.

One last function that might be useful to check whether a process has terminated and its exit code follows:

```
BOOL GetExitCodeProcess(HANDLE hProcess, LPDWORD lpdwExitcode);
```

Threads

You learned a little about threads in Chapters 1 and 2 during discussions of multi-tasking and Kernel mode. If a process is a job that your application needs to perform, the thread is a task within that job. A *thread* is a unit of execution in a process. Each thread is just a sequence of CPU instructions with its own set of registers, two stacks (one for when it is in User mode and the other for when it is in Kernel mode), and a private storage area. The thread uses this private storage area to pass information to subsystems, DLLs, and runtime libraries.

A thread is an object with a header of attributes and a body of services it provides. Table 3.2 lists these attributes.

Table 3.2. Thread attributes.

Attribute	Description
Alert Status	A flag indicating whether a thread should execute an asynchronous procedure call (APC)

Attribute	Description
Base Priority	The lower limit of a thread's priority
ClientID	Unique value to identify the thread
Dynamic Priority	Priority at any given moment
Impersonation Token	A token to allow a thread to perform on behalf of another process (Win32 subsystem only)
Suspension Count	Number of times a thread has been suspended and not resumed
Termination Port	The channel that Process Manager should use to send a message when a thread dies
Thread Context	Register values and data to define state
Thread Exit Status	Indicates why a thread died
Thread Processor Affinity	The set of processors on which a thread can run in a multiprocessor environment

In OS/2, the primary thread was designed with a special attribute: When this primary thread dies, its process dies. NT has a different design: The process doesn't die until the last of its threads dies. The primary thread may have died long before. NT actually creates the primary thread when you run your executable. NT calls the C Runtime function, which then calls WinMain. The process is created on the call to WinMain, and this primary thread dies when WinMain returns.

The NT SDK and Visual C++ 4.0 have three libraries you can use in thread management:

- **LIBC.LIB:** A static link library for single-threaded applications
- **LIBCMT.LIB:** A static link library for multi-threaded applications
- **CRTDLL.LIB:** A dynamic link library for both single and multi-threaded applications

To Thread or Not to Thread

Your application can create other threads to help the process do its job. The idea is to use the CPU as much as possible to get a smooth-flowing application. When NT was first released, many programmers went overboard in creating threads and found that sometimes the overhead did not give better performance. And threads have to be synchronized in their actions.

Every time you create a thread, the Win32 subsystem creates a matching thread for its use, causing more overhead. A thread resides in the process's virtual address space. If you create multiple threads, they all share the address space and all the process's resources. Creating multiple threads is far more efficient than creating multiple processes. By sharing the same address space, one thread can write some data that a later thread can read.

Suppose that you are typing a large document in Microsoft Word. As you type, one thread ensures that the text appears as quickly you type. Another thread is assigned to repaginate the document. If the document is long and you are inserting a large block of text at the beginning of the document, the repagination may take some time, so it's done in the background. But what if you immediately press Undo (wiping out the large insertion) before the first repaginate thread finishes but when another repaginate thread needs to work? Now, as you print the document, you expect that you can return immediately and start typing. Should the thread to print this document print it as it was when you pressed Print or as it exists when it is ready to print the page on which you are working? These are the complexities of multi-threaded applications. (Actually, in printing, a temporary copy is stored and printed.)

Before you create a thread, you need to think through the process's flow. Is there an operation that can be performed asynchronously? In other words, can this second thread perform some task without regard to the main flow of the process? Another example you can consider is when Microsoft Word auto-saves the file on which you are working. These additional threads also may monitor devices such as the mouse for input.

The Life of a Thread

As with processes, threads have defined points of creation, actions, and deaths. Microsoft's documentation on NT says threads die of natural causes, commit suicide, or are murdered. This section builds on this image because it is one that will stick with you.

Creating a Thread

You learned earlier in this chapter that the primary thread for a process is created by NT when you run your application. That thread can create other threads in the same process. Listing 3.3 shows how you can do this with `CreateThread`.

Listing 3.3. Using `CreateThread`.

```
HANDLE CreateThread(
  LPSECURITY_ATTRIBUTES lpsa,
  DWORD cbstack, //normally the size you set in linker with the /STACK
  LPTHREAD_START_RUNTIME lpStartAddr,  // you can define address where thread is to
➥start
  LPVOID lpvThreadParam, //pointer to thread's data you wish to pass to another
➥thread
  DWORD fdwCreate,  //either 0 if active or CREATE_SUSPENDED
  LPDWORD lpIDThread); //valid address of thread ID
```

It's a Thread's Life

Now that your thread is alive, you have the usual functions to get at the thread:

```
HANDLE GetCurrentThread(VOID)
DWORD GetCurrentThreadID(VOID)
```

All active threads get time slices from the NT kernel. A *time slice* is a portion of the CPU's time, and often is referred to as a *quantum*. This chapter uses the term *time slice*. Threads spend most of their lives sleeping or suspended. When a thread stops at `GetMessage` and no messages are waiting, it is suspended and doesn't get CPU time until something sends it a message. If you create the thread with `CREATE_SUSPENDED`, it is born sleeping.

After a thread is created, it passes through the following states:

- **Ready:** These threads are ready to execute and are the only threads that will be considered by the Scheduler.
- **Standby:** This is the next "at bat" thread. Unless the system changes another thread's priority or an interrupt occurs, this thread runs next.
- **Running:** This thread executes until its time slice runs out, it voluntarily goes into the wait state, it is interrupted, or it terminates.
- **Waiting:** Usually, the thread enters a wait state for I/O information it needs in order to proceed. When that resource becomes available, the thread enters the ready state.
- **Transition:** A thread that is ready, but its resources are not available.
- **Terminated:** When a thread is terminated, a thread's object sometimes is not deleted; it may be kept around to be reinitialized and used again.

You may see graphs that give the impression all threads get CPU time in a round-robin fashion. This really isn't true, as you have seen in Chapter 2. If it weren't for the fact that a thread spends most of its time sleeping, the system would slow to an extreme crawl (starvation). Use caution when playing with these settings, or you will see starvation. Several times, I have managed to starve my system to the point at which the mouse barely crawls, and pressing a button doesn't create an action.

In the last chapter we showed how all threads at the same priority level get equal access to the CPU. The CPU won't even address the priority 24 threads if a 25 priority thread is waiting. If you have several threads at this high a priority that don't ever go to sleep, then no lower priority threads ever get executed. This is referred to as *starvation*. This means that some threads get run more often than others. All threads normally run briefly, go to sleep, wake up, and run briefly.

In a more normal example, a priority 5 thread is executing and a priority 6 thread comes along. The priority 5 thread is preempted after it finishes its current instruction. The priority 6 thread is given its time slice and then the priority 5 thread is resumed.

You cannot really assign a number to a thread's priority. The process you create has a base priority in its creation or is modified by this code:

```
BOOL SetPriorityClass(HANDLE hProcess, DWORD fdwPriority);
```

The fdwPriority settings follow:

IDLE_PRIORITY_CLASS	4
NORMAL_PRIORITY_CLASS	7 or 9
HIGH_PRIORITY_CLASS	13
REALTIME_PRIORITY_CLASS	24

When you change a thread's priority with SetThreadPriority, it is always in relation to its base priority that you assigned with SetPriorityClass.

```
BOOL SetThreadPriority(HANDLE hThread, int nPriority);
```

The values of nPriority follow:

THREAD_PRIORITY_LOWEST	-2
THREAD_PRIORITY_BELOW NORMAL	-1
THREAD_PRIORITY_NORMAL	0
THREAD_PRIORITY_ABOVE_NORMAL	+1
THREAD_PRIORITY_HIGHEST	+2

This relative system ensures that no thread in a process can totally dominate. Threads have a priority relative to the others in their process. You also can see that you can't get to 31. As in life, some things are reserved for the executives!

NT boosts and decays priorities for you as well. Notice that when you make an application come to the foreground, after a second it gets a performance boost by NT that gives its thread a +2 priority increase. NT also notices whether a thread is CPU bound and lowers its dynamic priority back to its base priority.

You also can suspend threads and resume threads to do synchronization by using this code:

```
DWORD ResumeThread(HANDLE hThread);
DWORD SuspendThread(HANDLE hThread);
```

Chapter 22, "Threads," examines this topic in more detail.

The Death of a Thread

I like the image of death by natural causes, suicide, or murder. To a thread, natural causes is the usual state; the thread returns from its function and dies. All threads are owned by the process that created them. When a thread dies, its objects die (the window, accelerators, and hooks it owns).

A thread commits suicide when it calls

```
VOID ExitThread(DWORD fdwExitCode)
```

In other words, it stops itself instead of returning. A thread would behave in this fashion if you used structured exception handling and determined that you could not go on, for example.

When a thread dies naturally or by suicide, the normal clean-up process occurs: The thread's stack is destroyed and NT notifies all DLLs that the thread has died so that the DLLs can do their own clean up.

A thread is murdered by another thread that calls

```
BOOL TerminateThread(HANDLE hThread, DWORD fdwExitCode)
```

When a thread is murdered, the murderer must do the clean up. NT doesn't destroy the thread's stack because the murderer may want something from its victim. NT doesn't notify DLLs either. If you're going to commit murder, you need to clean up.

Threads often need to know whether another is alive and can do so by calling this code:

```
BOOL GetExitCodeThread(HANDLE hThread, LPDWORD lpdwExitCode).
```

The return value if the other thread is still alive is STILL_ACTIVE (TRUE).

After any death, NT does perform these actions:

- Closes all related Win32 object handles
- States whether the thread is signaled
- Changes all STILL_ACTIVE code to the exit code
- Allows the process to die if the thread was the last in its process

Synchronizing Threads

In Chapter 22, you will learn several methods used to synchronize threads in a multi-threaded application. Synchronization becomes very important on multiprocessor machines because one thread has to perform its functions and have the results ready before the next thread can perform its functions.

Threads need to communicate with one another and to coordinate their activities. You learned that threads can send information via a pipe to another thread. Synchronization is even simpler; it is the process by which one thread knows to stop and wait for the other thread to execute. If one thread needs to read a buffer for the data it is going to process, it cannot run until the thread that writes the data in the buffer has run. NT supplies the method the threads use to notify each other when they are done with their part. This method is implemented in the operating system by the synchronization objects mentioned in Chapter 2: the Executive object, Event object, Event Pair object, Semaphore object, Timer object, and Mutant object. Each of these has a state: signaled or unsignaled. When an Executive object is signaled, it is available. The Executive's other objects—Process objects, Thread objects, and File objects—also have the same state attribute.

The concept of signaled/unsignaled is a little confusing. When an object is *signaled*, it is available for someone else to use. This is a straightforward process with a thread that during its lifetime is unsignaled as it executes. After a thread terminates, it becomes signaled, which means that the thread hasn't yet been deleted, just in case you want to reactivate it. When a timer is waiting to go off, it is counting down the seconds and is in an *unsignaled* state. When it is done counting, it goes off; instead of making a ringing bell sound, however, it just becomes signaled, which tells any threads waiting on the timer that they are free to execute themselves (this fits into the death analogy but is really just when they change from the waiting state to the ready state). Table 3.3 shows the effects on objects when various events occur.

Table 3.3. Signal states.

Object	Set to Signaled When	Effect on Threads Waiting
Process	Last thread terminates	All released
Thread	Thread terminates	All released
File	I/O completes	All released
Event	Thread sets an event	All released
Event Pair	Client server dedicated and thread sets dedicated	Other thread released
Semaphore	Semaphore count drops to 0	All released
Timer	Set time arrives or interval expires	All released
Mutant	Thread releases mutant	One thread released

A mutant is created by a Win32 Mutext object. *Mutext* is mutually exclusive, meaning that a resource is used by one and only one thread—the one with a handle to the Mutant object. When a Mutant object is signaled, the kernel assigns it to one thread. That one thread has all access to the resource associated with the Mutant object.

Threads also can synchronize by notifying another thread to stop what it is doing. This is called an *alert operation*. Because the executing thread might get this alert at any time, this is an *asynchronous* event. NT uses alert operations in asynchronous procedure calls (APCs). These are used by the operating system extensively but are available to your application in User mode as well. APCs are discussed under general and network I/O in the next chapter, "NT Is the Network." When the user makes an I/O request, the executing process must wait for the results of the request to proceed. NT lets another thread do its thing until the I/O request finishes. NT then interrupts the thread to copy the data to its address space. This interrupt is via an APC. A Kernel mode APC can interrupt any thread at any time. A User mode APC can be delivered only when the thread says it is ready to execute it. This happens by the thread testing to see whether an APC has arrived or by waiting on an object handle that becomes available when the APC is ready.

Executables

When you build your 32-bit application, all the data and code are assembled into one large file—your executable. The executable is a mixture of the data and code, broken into sections. Each section starts on a page boundary. If you build on an Intel-based machine, each page is 4 KB; if you build on a MIPs machine, it is 4 KB; and if you build on a DEC Alpha, it is 8 KB and maybe even 16 KB on other platforms. Code is in one section, followed by global variables in another section.

When you run the application, these pages are loaded into your 4 GB virtual address space and then are mapped by NT to an application address space, as shown in Figure 3.1.

FIGURE 3.1.

Two instances of an executable share the same virtual memory space.

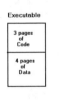 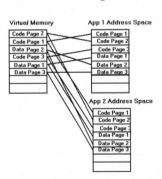

When you run a second instance of the application, NT recognizes what code is loaded and creates a memory-mapped view of the first file's image. NT allows this second process and thread to share the same code and data in memory. If either instance alters the data, NT does a copy-on-write operation with the memory-mapped file and creates a new block of memory that the process that wants to write sees. Now the other process still sees the original data it is relying on, whereas the process that is modifying memory sees its changed data as in Figure 3.2. The majority of the code is being shared. You also can write the application so that when a change is made, both processes see the changed data. This is done with the #pragma data_seg compiler directive (Chapter 13, "Windows NT Virtual Memory and Memory Management," discusses memory-mapped files in more detail).

FIGURE 3.2.

A second executable shares the memory-mapped file but not its changes.

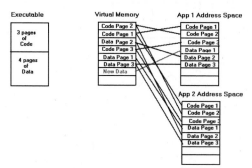

As you can see, this method allows the memory in your application's view to be much larger than physical memory and also expands the available virtual memory by copying only what is necessary.

You usually build applications without really caring what goes into the executable, unless, of course, the Linker gives you the message that it can't find a library. You rely on Visual C++'s Linker to put in what you need to run the application. The Linker also can tell you what it has done with a DLL or an EXE. As an example, build the programmer's basic application as shown in Listing 3.4 and look at the EXE. No, not hello.c—you can create something just as stupid for this illustration.

Listing 3.4. A very basic Windows application.

```
//on CD as pkill.exe
#include <windows.h>
#include <winbase.h>

int WINAPI WinMain(HANDLE hInstance, HANDLE hPrevInstance, LPSTR lpszCmdLine, int
➥nCmdShow)
{
char str[256];
wsprintf(str, "          Die Process no. 0x%x \n",GetCurrentProcessId());
MessageBox(NULL, str, "Press OK to kill this Process", MB_OK);
return (TRUE);
}
```

This is built as a release to keep the next output short. To look at this EXE file, type the following:

```
LINK -dump -headers pkill.exe
```

The results should yield a listing similar to Listing 3.5.

Listing 3.5. An example of EXE dump.

```
Microsoft (R) COFF Binary File Dumper Version 3.00.5270
Copyright  Microsoft Corp 1992-1995. All rights reserved.


Dump of file pkill.exe

NT signature found

File Type: EXECUTABLE IMAGE

FILE HEADER VALUES
         14C machine (i386)
           5 number of sections
    312773E5 time date stamp Sun Feb 18 12:45:57 1996
           0 file pointer to symbol table
           0 number of symbols
          E0 size of optional header
         10E characteristics
                 Executable
                 Line numbers stripped
                 Symbols stripped
                 32 bit word machine

OPTIONAL HEADER VALUES
         10B magic #
        3.00 linker version
        2000 size of code
        2E00 size of initialized data
           0 size of uninitialized data
        1050 address of entry point
        1000 base of code
        3000 base of data
             ----- new -----
      400000 image base
        1000 section alignment
         200 file alignment
           2 subsystem (Windows GUI)
        4.00 operating system version
        0.00 image version
        4.00 subsystem version
        9000 size of image
         400 size of headers
           0 checksum
      100000 size of stack reserve
        1000 size of stack commit
```

continues

Listing 3.5. continued

```
 100000 size of heap reserve
   1000 size of heap commit
      0 [       0] address [size] of Export Directory
   7000 [      3C] address [size] of Import Directory
      0 [       0] address [size] of Resource Directory
      0 [       0] address [size] of Exception Directory
      0 [       0] address [size] of Security Directory
   8000 [     290] address [size] of Base Relocation Directory
      0 [       0] address [size] of Debug Directory
      0 [       0] address [size] of Description Directory
      0 [       0] address [size] of Special Directory
      0 [       0] address [size] of Thread Storage Directory
      0 [       0] address [size] of Load Configuration Directory
      0 [       0] address [size] of Bound Import Directory
   70C8 [      8C] address [size] of Import Address Table Directory
      0 [       0] address [size] of Reserved Directory
      0 [       0] address [size] of Reserved Directory
      0 [       0] address [size] of Reserved Directory


SECTION HEADER #1
   .text name
   1F02 virtual size
   1000 virtual address
   2000 size of raw data
    400 file pointer to raw data
      0 file pointer to relocation table
      0 file pointer to line numbers
      0 number of relocations
      0 number of line numbers
60000020 flags
         Code
         (no align specified)
         Execute Read

… much more follows
```

There are four more section heads just for this one little four-line program! If you type the following code, you will see a summary as shown in Listing 3.6:

```
LINK -dump -summary pkill.exe
```

Listing 3.6. Link's summary output.

```
Microsoft (R) COFF Binary File Dumper Version 3.00.5270
Copyright  Microsoft Corp 1992-1995. All rights reserved.


Dump of file pkill.exe
```

```
File Type: EXECUTABLE IMAGE

    Summary

        3000 .data
        1000 .idata
        1000 .rdata
        1000 .reloc
        2000 .text
```

The code is in the section marked `.text`, all uninitialized data is in `.bss`, and initialized data is in `.data`. Table 3.4 lists the executable file sections.

Table 3.4. Executable file sections.

Section Name	Contains
.bss	Uninitialized data
.CRT	Read-only CRuntime data
.data	Initialized data
.debug	Debugging information
.edata	Exported names table
.idata	Image-activation table
.rdata	Read-only data
.reloc	Fix-up table data
.rsrc	Resources
.sdata	Shared data
.text	EXE or DLL code
.tls	Thread local storage
.xdata	Exception-handling data

This is getting a little deep, and a picture is worth a thousand more words—in this case, two pictures.

For more information on these file formats, you can look in the books on line in Win32 Binary Resource Formats. The sample program with PVIEW.EXE is a good, simple way to play. Using LINK -dump with its various switches is a good way to examine what the Linker is up to. Try LINK -dump /? to see your many other choices.

FIGURE 3.3.

*Microsoft executable file
format.*

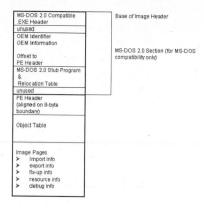

FIGURE 3.4.

*NT's new Common Object
File Format (COFF) file
format.*

DLLs

DLLs enable you to break your software into modules. These modules can be reused in other software projects. When two applications need to use the same DLL, it can be shared in memory. DLLs are basically a set of functions that are exported to the client software. The DLL *exports* the function and the client application *imports* the function. With Windows NT, a DLL can export global data as well.

When the DLL software calls the code

```
__declspec(dllexport) int MyFunc(int);
```

and the client application calls

```
__declaspec(dllimport) int MyFunc(int);
```

NT matches the import to the export calls and maps the DLL's function address into the .EXE file's image-activation table. A twist on this arrangement is that DLLs are also usually clients because they call other DLLs. This is just another layer of matching imports to exports, in which, to fill the application's order, the first DLL needs to import something from another DLL before it can export the entire function back to the application.

You can examine DLLs in the same fashion as you just did with executables using with the Linker's "dump" switch. DLLs load into virtual memory and are shared as memory-mapped files.

All Win32 API functions are contained in a DLL; that's what makes Windows NT function so efficiently.

A Brief History

To understand current DLLs, it might help to look at how DLLs were used under 16-bit Windows and OS/2. With Windows 3.11, the DLL became part of the operating system and was available to every application that was running. The application directly called functions in the DLL and each application could modify data in the DLL's common memory locations. To load a DLL, you first checked to see whether it was loaded by calling this function:

```
HMODULE GetModuleHandle(LPCSTR lpszModule);
```

If the DLL was loaded, you got a handle. If it was not loaded, you had to load the DLL by using this code:

```
HINSTANCE LoadLibrary(LPCSTR lpszLibFileName);
```

Then you could get the memory address of your function by using this code:

```
FARPROC GetProcAddress(HINSTANCE hinst, LPCSTR lpszProcName);
```

Lastly, you freed the DLL by calling this code:

```
void FreeLibrary(HINSTANCE hinst);
```

This decremented the usage count, and if the count became 0, it freed the memory it used by unloading the DLL. It was a pretty efficient and simple method to share code at runtime. It violated NT design goals for security, however, because you were in fact making the DLL's functions part of the operating system.

NT architects used a client/server model to overcome this security breach and to make NT much more stable, as shown in Figure 3.5. In this new model, each Win32 DLL had entry points called *stubs*. A *stub* packages the caller's parameters into a message.

The client DLL sends this message to the Local Procedure Call Facility (LPCF). The LPCF is modeled after remote procedure calls (RPCs), which you will explore in Chapter 24, "Local and Remote Procedure Calls." One machine can send a message to another machine by using RPCs. The second machine executes the instructions and sends a message back with the results. This allows machines that may be very different to communicate and work together to perform a process faster. LPCs work similarly but on the same machine to coordinate the activities of processes that may use very different function calls, such as the Win32 and POSIX subsystems. Both machines use the same system services by sending the same messages. The messages all go to the LPCF that validates the parameters and executes and sends results to the appropriate subsystem. Remember that Win32 is only one of the possible subsystems; your user also may be an OS/2, POSIX, or future subsystem client. A programmer writing for each subsystem can use that subsystem's features and API calls to the DLLs, but the stubs in the DLLs send a common message to the system services.

FIGURE 3.5.

NT client/server model for DLL use.

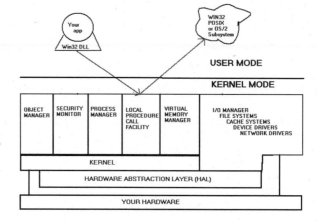

Notice that the entire subsystem is in User mode and therefore cannot modify any of the Executive's data. This is much more secure but somewhat less efficient. Your thread must be suspended, a context switch must occur, a thread must be started for Win32 to use, another context switch must occur, and then your thread must be restarted with the results. There is always a thread created that mirrors the one you have running.

Using DLLs the NT Way

As you see in Figure 3.5, the DLL is now part of the process that is using it. But the overhead of this calling is much more. To make this more efficient, Microsoft developers first made DLLs that held the most common API calls and didn't modify global data. These DLLs were secure without the LPCFs checking their parameters. A system was developed to cache API calls. You see this when you create an object and it is held in the cache for each screen redraw. Lastly, they developed a way to batch API calls and submit them to Win32 as a set. An example of this is when you change your pen color; that call isn't submitted until the next screen redraw call.

Just as you saw with executables and running multiple instances of an application, NT treats the DLL code as a memory-mapped file. It makes a mapping of the DLL to the address space of the process. When a second process wants the same DLL, NT makes a view in that second process's address space. Note, however, that the address of a function in one process and the same function in another process may be different. You still need to get the address of the procedure call via `GetProcAddress` for each process.

Each 16-bit Windows DLL has its own data segment. This allows sharing of data between processes using `SetData` and `GetData` calls. NT DLLs don't have their own data segment; instead, they use the space of the calling process. When two processes both modify DLL data, each is done via a copy-on-write, as you saw with executable files and memory mapping.

When you built a 16-bit Windows DLL, you had to link in a bit of Microsoft assembler code that made the DLL work and call your `LibMain` function. This is similar to how your executable causes `CRuntime` to call your `WinMain` function. But NT was designed to be processor independent. If you're using Visual C++, the DLL Wizard does a lot of the work for you, as you will see in Chapter 16, "Dynamic Link Libraries." One thing the Wizard does is create a function `DllMain` or a function `DllEntryPoint`, which is both your `LibMain` and Windows Exit procedure (WEP) combined. If you're building a regular DLL using AppWizard, functions like `WinMain` are hidden from you (the Linker also actually adds a function if you don't with the Win32 API). The code you use follows:

```
BOOL    WINAPI   DllMain (HANDLE hInst, ULONG ul_reason_for_call, LPVOID lpReserved);
```

The `reason_for__call` parameters can be any of the following:

- **DLL_PROCESS_ATTACH:** A new process is attempting to access the DLL; one thread is assumed.
- **DLL_PROCESS_DETACH:** A process is detaching from the DLL.
- **DLL_THREAD_ATTACH:** A new thread of an existing process is attempting to access the DLL; this call is made beginning with the second thread of a process attaching to the DLL.
- **DLL_THREAD_DETACH:** One of the additional threads (not the first thread) of a process is detaching from the DLL.

When your application makes a function call to a DLL, the DLL is loaded into the process address space with `DLL_PROCESS_ATTACH`. Actually, when a thread is started or terminated, the `DllMain` function is always called.

Each DLL is identified to the system by a unique 32-bit `HINSTANCE` value, just like each .EXE had a unique value. You saw this earlier in the following function:

```
GetProcAddress(hinst, lpcszFuncName)
```

When you build a DLL in the .DEF file, you can define which functions are exported. You must have the same string in the `EXPORTS` section as you use in the `GetProcAddress` function. With 16-bit Windows, many function names also are assigned an ordinal value, as in this code:

```
EXPORTS
  MyFunc @2
```

You also can use this code to call the same function:

```
GetProcAddress(hinst, MAKEINTRESOURCE(2))
```

This is faster than using the names and saved memory space. If you examine a .MAP file, you will see that the names actually are based on 32-bit values using this function, which is quite long:

```
Class@Function@ParameterList
```

NT has optimized this process so that it is not nearly as lengthy. In fact, 16-bit Windows loads all the functions of the DLL into the image-activation file, where NT loads only what is needed. You still may want to use ordinal values for security reasons, however, to hide function name methods from users. You do this by using the switch NONAME after the ordinal value, which does not export the name, class, or parameter list.

One more switch is important: CONSTANT. Windows NT also can export global variables via the DLL. In the .DEF file, this is done as the following:

```
EXPORTS
  g_hGlobal  @3 NONAME CONSTANT
```

You can use the global variable in the client application as in the following function code:

```
lpghVal = g_hGlobal
extern HVAL *lpg_hVal
```

When your application needs to load a DLL, NT has a specific search list it uses to find the DLL:

1. Directory of .EXE file
2. Current directory of process
3. Windows System32 directory
4. Windows directory
5. PATH environmental variable

Almost every application calls functions in a DLL—certainly, any Windows NT application. When the Compiler and Linker created your application, it created an image-activation table. This table exists inside the .EXE file. Every DLL also has an image-activation table. When you make a function call, the loader determines the virtual address of your function and maps a "jump" instruction from this table to the function's address. This makes the system much more responsive. Only the functions your application uses are mapped, and the system only needs to look in one place for the address.

Long before you build a DLL, you need to learn to use those DLLs that already exist. If you have been using MFC, many things are being done for you, and you may think that you have never written a call to a function in a DLL. Take a look at your .MAK file: a bunch of DLLs are getting linked.

Using Visual C++ to Build DLLs

Visual C++ 4.0 helps you build three types of DLLs: a Win32 DLL without MFC, an extension DLL that has links to the MFC40D.DLL, and a regular DLL that has MFC linked in to create a standalone module. Regular DLLs are larger, but you can export C-type functions that other products, such as Visual Basic, can use. Regular DLLs also can export classes that your application will use. You can statically link in a copy of the MFC Library or dynamically link in the MFC at runtime. Dynamic linking implies that your users always will have the MFC DLLs on their computers. The MFC DLLs follow:

- **MFC40D.DLL:** Core MFC classes
- **MFCO40D.DLL:** OLE classes
- **MFCD40D.DLL:** Database classes DAO and ODBC
- **MFCN40D.DLL:** Winsock classes

To tell MFC which type of DLL and linking you will use, you use #define statements, as shown in Table 3.5 which lists common DLLs you will include in MFC programming.

Table 3.5. MFC's DLLs and their link type usage.

DLL Type	Dynamic Link	Static Link
Regular	_AFXDLL, _USRDLL	_USRDLL
Extension	_AFXEXT, _AFXDLL	Not applicable
Client .EXE	_AFXDLL	

Chapter 16, "Dynamic Link Libraries," goes into much more detail on using Visual C++ to create DLLs, but there is one more concept topic that can be very interesting: using hooks.

Using Hooks

Hooks are used to notify a process when an event occurs in another process. To set up a hook, use this code:

```
HHOOK SetWindowsHookEx(int idHook, HOOKPROC hkProc, HINSTANCE hinst, DWORD
dwThreadID);
```

Table 3.6 lists the possible integer values for the first parameter, idHook. The second parameter, hkProc, is the address of the function you want to run if notified, hinst is your instance, and dwThreadID is the thread you are going to watch (NULL means to watch all threads).

Table 3.6. Hook identification parameters.

Hook	Indicates
WH_CALLWNDPROC	The Call Window procedure
WH_CBT	Window created, destroyed, sized, or moved
WH_DEBUG	Hook function is being called
WH_GETMESSAGE	Get message
WH_JOURNALPLAYBACK	Journal playback hardware event from input queue
WH_JOURNALRECORD	Journal record hardware event from input queue
WH_KEYBOARD	Keyboard message
WH_MOUSE	Mouse message
WH_MSGFILTER	Dialog box, menu, or scroll bar message
WH_SHELL	Overlapped window created, destroyed, sized, or moved
WH_SYSMSGFILTER	Dialog box, menu, or scroll bar system message

What is interesting about hooks is that the function maps the DLL with your hook function into the address space of another process. You can use hooks to put code into another process. To learn more about hooks, look at the source code for the SPY.EXE program on the MSDN sample disk. Microsoft has begun to supply the source code for many of NT's tools and they are a valuable learning resource.

Batches—Using NT's New Command Language

The command prompt is the character-based interface to Windows NT or one of the other subsystems. Although it is clearly derived from MS-DOS's batch commands, NT has added many command prompts specific to its environment, as shown in Table 3.7. You can run an application from a command prompt; this includes applications written for Windows NT, Windows 3.1, MS-DOS, MS OS/2 1.x, or POSIX. The command prompt also supports batch programs; redirection between subsystems; cutting and pasting information between subsystems; and file management for both the NTFS and the FAT file systems.

Table 3.7. New NT commands.

Command	Function
&&	The command following this symbol runs only if the command preceding the symbol succeeds.
¦ ¦	The command following this symbol runs only if the command preceding the symbol fails.
&	Separates multiple commands on the command line.
( )	Groups commands.
^	Works as an Escape character. Allows input of command symbols as text.
; or ,	Separates parameters.
aclconv	Restores OS/2 HPFS386 ACLs to NTFS volumes.
at	Schedules commands and programs to run on a computer at a specified time and date.
cacls	Displays or modifies access control lists (ACLs) of files.
convert	Converts file systems from FAT or HPFS to NTFS.
diskperf	Starts, stops, and displays system disk performance counter use.
dosonly	Prevents starting applications other than MS-DOS-based applications from the COMMAND.COM prompt.
echoconfig	Displays messages when reading the MS-DOS subsystem CONFIG.NT file.
endlocal	Ends localization of environment variables.
findstr	Searches for text in files using regular expressions.
ntcmdprompt	Runs the Windows NT command interpreter, CMD.EXE, rather than COMMAND.COM after running a TSR or after starting the command prompt from within an MS-DOS application.
popd	Changes to the directory last set with the pushd command.
pushd	Saves the current directory for use by the popd command, and then changes to the specified directory.
setlocal	Begins localization of environmental variables.
start	Runs a specified program or command in a secondary window and in its own memory space.
title	Sets the title of the command prompt window.

Many common MS-DOS commands received added functionality or were changed to fit into the NT multi-subsystem world, as Table 3.8 shows.

Table 3.8. MS-DOS commands that changed under NT.

Command	Description
chcp	Changes code pages for full-screen mode only.
cmd	CMD.EXE replaces COMMAND.COM.
del	New switches provide many more functions for deleting files with attributes previously set.
dir	New switches provide many more functions for directories by date, time, attributes and greater long file name support.
diskcomp	Switches /1 and /8 are not supported.
diskcopy	Switch /1 is not supported.
doskey	Available for all character-based programs that accept buffered input. Several other enhancements improve doskey.
format	20.8 MB floptical drive supported. Switches /b, /s, and /u are not supported.
keyb	KEYBOARD.SYS no longer is used.
label	The symbols ^ and & can be used in a volume label.
mode	Extensive changes.
more	New switches provide many more functions.
path	The %PATH% environment variable appends the current path to a new setting at the command prompt.
print	Switches /b, /c, /m, /p, /q, /s, /t, and /u are not supported.
prompt	New character combinations allow you to add ampersands ($a), parentheses ($c and $f), and spaces ($s) to your prompt.
recover	Recovers files only.
rmdir	New /s switch deletes directories containing files and subdirectories.
sort	Does not require TEMP environment variable. File size is unlimited.
xcopy	New switches provide many more functions.

Lastly, some commands were made obsolete by Windows NT or could no longer be supported due to NT's security. Table 3.9 lists these commands.

Table 3.9. MS-DOS commands no longer available under NT.

Command	Description
assign	Not supported in Windows NT.
choice	Not supported in Windows NT.
ctty	Not supported in Windows NT.
dblspace	The Dblspace program is not supported.
defrag	Windows NT automatically optimizes disk use.
deltree	NT uses the command rmdir /s to delete directories containing files and subdirectories.
dosshell	Unnecessary with Windows NT.
drvspace	The Drvspace program is not currently supported.
emm386	Unnecessary with Windows NT.
fasthelp	This MS-DOS 6.0 command is the same as the Windows NT Help command. Windows NT also provides an online command reference from the Windows NT Help icon in the Main program group.
fdisk	The Disk Administrator prepares hard disks for use with Windows NT.
include	Multi-configurations of the MS-DOS subsystem are not supported.
interlnk	The Interlnk program is not supported, functionality now built in to RAS.
intersrv	The Intersrv program is not supported, functionality now built in to RAS.
join	Increased partition size and an improved file system eliminate the need to join drives.
memmaker	Windows NT automatically optimizes the MS-DOS subsystems that memory use.
menucolor	Multi-configurations of the MS-DOS subsystem are not supported.
menudefault	Multi-configurations of the MS-DOS subsystem are not supported.
menuitem	Multi-configurations of the MS-DOS subsystem are not supported.
mirror	Not supported in Windows NT.
msav	The Msav program is not supported.
msbackup	Windows NT provides the Backup utility (in the Administrative Tool group) for computers with tape drives, or the backup and xcopy commands for computers without tape drives.

continues

Table 3.9. continued

Command	Description
mscdex	It is unnecessary to configure the MS-DOS subsystem to use CD-ROM drives. Windows NT provides access to CD-ROM drives for the MS-DOS subsystem.
msd	Use the Windows NT Diagnostics program in the Administrative Tools group.
numlock	The numlock command is not currently supported.
power	The Power utility is not supported.
scandisk	The Scandisk utility is not supported.
smartdrv	Windows NT automatically provides caching for the MS-DOS subsystem.
submenu	Multi-configurations of the MS-DOS subsystem are not supported.
sys	Windows NT will not fit on a standard 1.2 MB or 1.44 MB floppy disk.
undelete	Not supported in Windows NT.
unformat	Not supported in Windows NT.
vsafe	The Vsafe program is not supported.

Most of the network management can be done from the command line instead of using File Manager. Table 3.10 lists the NT implementation of the Lan Manager commands.

Table 3.10. NT Lan Manager commands.

Command	Description
at	In addition to local scheduling, you can remotely schedule events on a computer.
ipxroute	This new command supports routing for the NWLink protocol on a token-ring network.
net accounts	Server roles cannot be set. Windows NT security controls lockout.
net computer	This new command enables you to add or delete computers from a domain database. This command is available only on computers running Windows NT Server.
net config	Peer functionality is inherent to Windows NT. Separate commands, such as net config peer, no longer are required.

Command	Description
net config server	Most network services are self-configuring. The switches /autodisconnect, /srvcomment, and /hidden can be configured. The switch /srvhidden now is /hidden.
net config workstation	Most network services are self-configuring. The switches /charcount, /chartime, and /charwait can be configured.
net continue	Use Print Manager to control printing. *See net pause for the list of pausable services that can be continued.*
net group	Manages global groups and is only for computers that are members of a domain.
net localgroup	This new command manages local groups.
net pause	You can pause these network services: File Server for Macintosh and Remoteboot. (Windows NT Server only) ftp server lpdsvc net logon network dde network dde dsdm nt 1m Security Support Provider Remote Access Server scheduler server simple TCP/IP services workstation
net print	Use Print Manager to manage printers.
net send	Sending files is not supported. The /broadcast switch is not supported.
net share	Remote administration is automatic. Use Print Manager to share printers. Com queues are not supported in this release.

continues

Table 3.10. continued

Command	Description
`net start`	You can start these network services:
	Alerter
	Client Service for NetWare
	Clipbook Server
	Computer Browser
	DHCP client
	Directory Replicator
	Event log
	ftp server
	`lpdsvc`
	Messenger
	`net logon`
	`network dde`
	`network dde dsdm`
	Network Monitoring Agent
	`nt lm` Security Support Provider
	OLE
	Remote Access Connection Manager
	Remote Access `isnsap` Service
	Remote Access Server (RAS)
	remote procedure call (RPC) locator
	remote procedure call (RPC) service
	scheduler
	server
	simple TCP/IP services
	SNMP
	spooler
	TCP/IP NETBIOS helper
	UPS
	workstation
	These services are available only on Windows NT Server:
	File Server for Macintosh
	Gateway Service for NetWare

Command	*Description*
	Microsoft DHCP Server
	Print Server for Macintosh
	Remoteboot
	Windows Internet Name Service
	Note that services can be configured to start automatically.
`net start alerter`	Self-configuring
`net start directory replicator`	Use Server Manager to configure the Replicator service.
`net start eventlog`	This new service logs any significant system, security, and application occurrences that require users to be notified.
`net start messenger`	Self-configuring
`net start net logon`	Self-configuring
`net start server`	Use Server Manager to configure the Server service.
`net start snmp`	New options permit logging.
`net start workstation`	Workstation is configured at setup and in various applications.
`net statistics`	Peer functionality is an inherent part of Windows NT and no longer requires separate commands. The statistics log cannot be cleared.
`net stop`	You can stop all network services except eventlog. *See* `net start` *for a list of services that can be started and stopped.*
`net use`	The `/persistent` switch has only yes and no values. Comm queues are not supported in this release. You can use NetWare volumes.
`net user`	Switches `/logonserver`, `/maxstorage`, `/operator`, and `/privilege` are not supported.
`net view`	New switch `/domain` permits viewing of domains and viewing of computers in a specified domain. You can view servers on NetWare networks.
`Route`	An NT 4.0 new parameter, `-p`, has been added to the TCP/IP route command that enables you to specify persistent IP routes. The `-p` parameter, when used with the `add` command, indicates that you want the IP route to be preserved when the computer is restarted. Using this parameter with the `print` command displays all routes that are marked as persistent.

Examining Update Information for NT 4.0

NT 4.0 added the capability to format diskettes as NTFS.

The biggest change is in the ability to use the right mouse button to modify the look, font size, and other characteristics of the window you see in Command mode (see Figure 3.6).

FIGURE 3.6.

NT 4.0 Console settings.

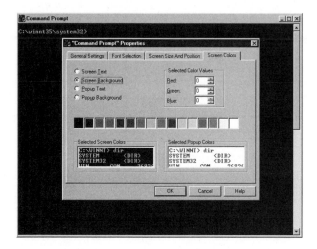

The command interpreter, cmd, no longer is loaded by default when running the Scheduler service. Certain commands, however, do not work without cmd—for example, dir, copy, and > or >> (for redirection). This solves problems you might have had doing your backup via a scheduled service. When you use the AT command, you also should specify the cmd command with it unless you are scheduling an executable file (a file with the .EXE extension) to run. You need to put a /c after cmd to get commands after the one executing to finish. If you do not include the /c parameter with the cmd command, the command interpreter terminates when the operation is complete. An example of this follows:

```
cmd /c dir > com1
cmd /c f: & cd directory name > batch.out
```

When using the AT command from the command line with redirection or conditional processing symbols, you must include the command in quotation marks, as in this example:

```
at 16:30 "cmd.exe /c type backup.log > prn"
```

Using .CMD Files

You can use *multitasking* so that NT can run processes for you unseen. You can schedule a backup to run every night at midnight, for example. You also can set up certain tasks to be done periodically, such as the .CMD file shown in Listing 3.7. This program runs every hour, dials into your Internet provider, and downloads the mail for each person from the POP server to MSMAIL. It then places each person's subscribed newsgroups into a structure for offline reading. The NT Resource Kit WinAT.EXE software easily manages your multiple scheduled .CMD files, running each at different hours of the day or in different day patterns. Operations such as backup and virus scanning therefore are performed each night, and their results are written to log files, which are printed for morning review during the tape change.

In Chapter 27, "Using the Messaging API," you will develop the NNTP32.EXE file under MAPI as an example of getting information from a POP mail server, sorting as to user, and sending back out via Microsoft Mail's SMTPGATE.

Listing 3.7. NT batch command file to gather and redistribute Usenet news and POP3 mail.

```
echo off

set _NEWSDRIVE=O
set _NEWSARCHIVE=%_NEWSDRIVE%:\news
set _NEWSBIN=%_NEWSDRIVE%:\x\news\bin\
set _NEWSFILE=%_NEWSDRIVE%:\x\news\spool\newsbat

rasdial INTERNET soapnotes password

c:\netware\nntp32 all  //this is a winsocket that gets all users mail and newsgroups

%_NEWSDRIVE%:

cd \

copy %_NEWSFILE% %_NEWSARCHIVE%

%_NEWSBIN%unbatch

del %_NEWSFILE%

c:

set _NEWSDRIVE=
set _NEWSARCHIVE=
set _NEWSBIN=
set _NEWSFILE=

rasdial INTERNET /d
```

Figure 3.7 shows how the application should look.

The batch file shown in Listing 3.8 is driven by an .INI file that is a combination of each person's individual subscriptions and mail accounts. The executable you will build in Chapter 26, "Using the Remote Access Server," uses this to identify which newsgroups each person uses and to identify the POP mail accounts.

FIGURE 3.7.

*The NNTP32.EXE
application.*

Listing 3.8. NNTP32's .INI file.

```
[groups]
1=comp.os.ms-windows.networking.tcp-ip,0,26055,26055
2=comp.os.ms-windows.nt.misc,5,115398,115403
3=comp.os.ms-windows.programmer.networks,507,107505,108012
4=comp.os.ms-windows.programmer.win32,3,34264,34267
5=comp.sys.newton.programmer,248,30300,30548
6=comp.os.ms-windows.programmer.tools.mfc,2,8941,8943
7=rec.games.programmer,5,69470,69475

[Mail]
hostname=MyInternetProvider
postoffice=SOAPNOTES

[MailBoxes]
hamilton="password1,Dave Hamilton"
sampson="password2,Bill Sampson"
```

Because this book is about Programming Windows NT, I won't go into MS-DOS's batch file programming. If you don't have one, a good batch file programming book can be quite useful in setting up little command sets that you want to execute on a repeated basis or at given times using NT's Scheduler.

Summary

Chapter 3 studied what makes NT 4.0 the operating system for your future. NT's multiprocessing and virtual memory capabilities make it the most robust environment in which to develop and deploy your software. The ability to control processes makes it the only operating system choice for the serious Windows developer. Throughout the remainder of the book you will build on what you have learned about processes and threads.

In nearly every chapter of this book you build executables and DLLs. This chapter gave you the insight into what NT does with your executable. You also examined the many enhancements NT brought to the command line language.

NT is not just the operating system, it is also the network. In the next chapter, "NT Is the Network," you see that networking is no longer something added to an operating system. With Windows NT, the operating system was designed for networking. NT workstations can be integrated into existing network protocols or computers running dissimilar operating systems can be attached to an NT network. NT server introduces the concept of breaking the enterprise into globally manageable groups called *domains.* Domains allow for the efficient rapid growth of networks in today's businesses.

NT Is the Network

4

by David Hamilton

You can't look at NT's architecture without seeing all its network components. Networking is an integral part of NT all the way down to its roots. In the past three chapters you have looked deep into the NT operating system and Chapter 1 touched on NT as a file and printer server. The architects of NT designed it as the network. Networking is no longer layered on the operating system.

In this chapter you focus on NT, the network. You first examine NT's family tree to see how networking has been done in the past. NT was designed to co-exist within many networking environments and you next look at the various protocols in which NT performs. Lastly, you study how domains and workgroups make administration of a growing network easier.

To start, you examine the evolution of networks and how NT took the best of what was out there and put it into its new model.

Networking Models

NT is the network, and networking is what NT does. Windows NT inherited many features from MS-NET, which was released in 1984. MS-NET was the forerunner of LAN Manager and was a means by which an MS-DOS computer could share files and printers.

Three elements of NT are direct descendants of MS-NET:

■ **Redirector:** Redirects I/O requests from a computer's local disk drive to the network, steering requests in the right direction.

■ **Server Message Block (SMB) Protocol:** A protocol for packaging messages to be sent across a network. NetBIOS was the API released to pass I/O requests structured in the SMB format.

■ **Server:** The software on the other computer that receives the SMBs and transfers the messages into file or print I/O requests.

The SMB Protocol was developed by IBM, Microsoft, and Intel as a series of commands used to pass information between computers. The Redirector packages network control blocks into SMBs, which it sends across the network. The server listens for SMBs directed toward itself and removes the data from those it gets. The SMBs can be one of four types of messages:

■ **Session control messages:** Start and stop the Redirector connection.

■ **File messages:** Tell the Redirector to get access to a file on a server.

■ **Printer messages:** Tell the Redirector to send data to a print queue on a server and return status information.

■ **Simple messages:** Send messages to and from another workstation.

In a peer-to-peer network, both computers have the Redirector and the server software running. The second computer repackages the results and redirects them back to the server on the first computer. Networks today are layers upon layers of software that enable a wide variety of computers to recognize and service each others' requests.

In Windows NT, a network operation starts out when your application issues a remote I/O request. The operating system forwards that request to a Redirector, which to NT is just a remote file system. After the remote file system fills your request and returns results, your network card issues an interrupt. The kernel handles the interrupt, and the original I/O operation completes. In the process, the messages have to be repackaged in a format the remote computer can understand. Network protocols are these layers of translations.

Protocols

The *Open Systems Interconnection* (OSI) model defines seven layers of the network, as Figure 4.1 shows. On any level, the message is formatted and sent through all the lower layers, across the wire, up the corresponding layers, and to the layer at the same level on the other machine. The packets must be coded and decoded, broken into smaller bits, and then reassembled. Both computers only need to speak the same language (use the same protocol) on the same level.

FIGURE 4.1.

The OSI protocol stack.

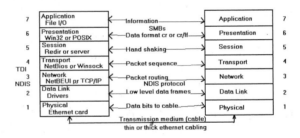

The OSI model defines the layers as the following:

7. The *application layer* handles security and the correspondence between two network applications: the sender and receiver of the messages. This is the layer for file I/O, named pipes, and mailslots.

6. The *presentation layer* is where the data is reformatted in a form usable by the applications. This layer performs such operations as deciding whether to use carriage returns or CR/LF pairs. This is where the data is coded and encoded for transfer. You also see this referred to as the environmental layer. It is where NT's I/O system services exists for User mode programming.

5. The *session layer* manages the communications: who is talking and who is listening. It also is known as the *handshaking layer*. This is the Redirector/server layer all within I/O Kernel mode.

4. The *transport layer* divides the messages into packets and numbers the packets to ensure that all are delivered in the right order. This is the first layer that knows anything about the hardware that is the physical network. This is the layer of NetBIOS and Winsockets.

3. The *network layer* handles the routing of the packets. This layer knows which machines are talking to which machines and the type of cabling, bandwidth, and transfer speed. This is the familiar layer of NetBEUI, IPX/SPX, and TCP/IP.

2. The *data link layer* transfers the low-level data frames and waits for an acknowledgment that they were received. If they were not, they are retransmitted. This is the *Network Driver Interface Specification* (NDIS) layer, which is standardized to allow all kinds of hardware to connect.

1. The *physical layer* puts bits of data on the wire and reads bits of data off the wire. This is the Ethernet or token-ring layer.

It all seems a little complex until you step back and see that NT treats the whole process like file I/O. Your Win32 API function issues an I/O request to NT's I/O system services. The I/O Manager creates an *I/O request packet* (IRP) and passes it to the Redirector. The Redirector uses the *Transport Driver Interface* (TDI) to decide which transport driver should receive the IRP. These network transport drivers put the request on the network.

When the data comes back, the network transport drivers copy the information into a buffer and pass it to the server file system. The server is part of the I/O Manager and uses normal file I/O and the local file system driver to store the data on the hard drive.

As a programmer, you use the Win32 I/O API, the WNet API, named pipes, mailslots, the NetBIOS API, the Winsockets API, or *remote procedure calls* (RPCs) to build the User mode access to the network. Each of these is a different route to the network resources. The WNet API is for broadcasting information to multiple places. Mailslots are also messages to multiple sites. Winsockets and NetBIOS are both DLLs that talk directly to lower-level drivers within the I/O Manager. The rest use the NT Redirector.

To better understand this process, look at some of these terms:

■ **NetBIOS:** The *Network Basic Input/Output System.* In Windows peer-to-peer networks, this is the session layer. NetBIOS is a session-level interface and a standard set of API function calls. The Redirector is implemented as a NetBIOS application within the NT I/O Manager. *NetBEUI* is an extended API version of NetBIOS.

■ **Windows Sockets (Winsockets):** A Windows implementation of the UNIX socket protocol. These are DLLs that provide APIs to write network applications used in TCP/IP communications. A socket provides an endpoint to a connection; two sockets form a path. Winsockets function as bidirectional pipes for the incoming and outgoing communications between two computers. Many of the Internet applications you use, such as FTP or Telnet, are built using the Winsockets API. In Part 5 of this book, "Windows NT Network Programming," you will build a Winsocket application.

- **Named pipes and mailslots:** These are NT file systems. You can find a list of these named pipes and mailslots in your Registry. A pipe enables computers to communicate without going through all the network components. A pipe goes from one place to another, whereas a mailslot goes from one place to many others. Mailslots are used to broadcast messages to several computers.

- **Remote procedure call (RPC):** A standard way for dissimilar computers to pass messages. Using RPCs, one computer can parse work out to others on the network. RPCs communicate with the other computer via Winsockets, named pipes, or NetBIOS. The client application is built with a special stub library. When the application makes a function call to a stub, it sees the stub as part of its DLL's subroutines. The stub actually transfers data to a module called the *RPC runtime*, which searches the network for a server with an RPC runtime that has the capability of performing the stub's task. When it locates this second server computer, the stub's function is executed by the server computer and the return values are sent back to the client computer's RPC runtime module. The client sees the function return from the stub as if it had been executed locally.

- **Remote Access Service (RAS):** Part of NT that can connect to another computer and run applications using the other computer's CPU. You probably have your NT machine set up to run RAS to provide PPP service to an Internet provider.

- **Point-to-Point Protocol (PPP):** Defines a standard set of frames that are transferred to remote computers via modem. PPP can use NetBEUI, IPX, or TCP/IP to interface to the remote computer. PPP largely has replaced *Serial Line Internet Protocol* (SLIP) as the standard for modems to access UNIX computers. NT can be configured as a SLIP client as well, or a PPP client, but NT cannot be configured as a SLIP server.

All these terms are NT services or drivers. NT's service controller loads and unloads drivers as required. Some drivers are loaded upon boot up, whereas others are started as needed. The NT Redirector is unique because it can coexist with Redirectors from other vendors and also can handle requests from NT's multiprocessor support.

The Redirector and Server

The Redirector and server are implemented as file system drivers in the Executive. This makes use of the cache and can work with as many transport drivers as necessary. Your NT workstation probably uses NetBEUI to talk to other Windows 3.11 or Windows 95-based computers and TCP/IP for your Internet connection. It also might, at the same time, be using IPX/SPX to talk to NetWare clients and AppleTalk to share files or printers with your Macintosh. To support this group and more, NT provides each Redirector with an open single common interface. NT also has an open common interface to NDIS, so the network card drivers also can be as varied.

The Redirector is a file system driver. When it is initialized, it creates a device object, \Device\Redirector, and provides a file system that behaves like the local file system. The NT

Redirector also monitors the connection; if it is dropped, the Redirector tries to reestablish the link and reopen files that were open when the drop occurred. It needs to work asynchronously, taking the User mode request and steering its IRP in the right direction. It then must return immediately for more I/O, regardless of whether the first remote I/O operation is finished.

The interface over which the Redirector sends the SMP packets is called the *transport driver interface* (TDI). To use the TDI functions, the Redirector creates virtual circuits to each machine to which you are connected. Using virtual circuits allows the Redirector to multiplex the SMB packets. NT's SMB packets are enhanced, but they are similar to SMB packets from MSNet and LAN Manager. This allows the use of primitive SMBs from Windows 3.11. The enhanced NT SMBs have security ACLs and pass text strings as unicode to allow for international data sets.

The NT server also is implemented as a driver and uses the I/O Manager cache. Transferring data from the cache directly to the network often avoids a costly write to the disk drive. The Virtual Memory (VM) manager controls the cache writing as necessary. The server even may copy data into and out of the cache directly without forming IRPs. Because the cache is part of the I/O Manager, it uses the I/O completion routine to initiate context switching.

With everything being treated like normal file I/O, there has to be a way to get handles and to track namespaces. Namespaces are simply directory trees, as shown in Figure 4.2.

FIGURE 4.2.

A namespace.

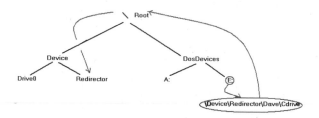

You use the Explorer to assign logical drive E to the network path \\dave\cdrive. To access this network drive, simply use drive E:. NT has actually mapped the drive to \Device \Redirector\dave\cdrive as illustrated by the arrow in Figure 4.2. Later, to parse a file name on drive E:, NT uses this mapped path following it down the namespace.

Deciding which Redirector to use is based on the calling API. The Win32 I/O API uses the *multiple UNC provider* (MUP) to make its decisions based on the uniform naming conventions (names that begin with \\, as in \\dave\cdrive) in the namespace of Figure 4.2 to decide which network to access. If the request doesn't have a UNC name, like a request to several providers, the *multiple provider router* (MRP) is used to determine which network to access.

When the request reaches the Redirector, it is up to the Redirector to steer it along a path to its destination. Many transport protocols may be available, each needing data in a different format. NT provides a common interface, the TDI, so that any Redirector can use any transport mechanism.

The Networking Process

Before you look at how various protocols handle the network transfer, look at networking in general. You first see the process from the client application's viewpoint, then from the server application's viewpoint. It's really just one process, but the two computers see it from their different vantage points.

The process for networking viewed from the client side follows:

1. The application requests a file that resides on NT Server.
2. The I/O Manager on the workstation creates an I/O request packet (IRP) and passes it to the file system driver, which, in this case, is the Redirector.
3. The Redirector steers the request to a network transport driver.
4. The network transport driver adds the network and transport headers, and then sends the request on through the NDIS interface.
5. The NDIS drivers format the packet, add data-link headers, and place the packet onto the physical network.

Networking viewed from the server side follows:

6. The NDIS drivers on the server side take the packet from the network card and strip off the data-link header.
7. The packet is forwarded to the network transport driver, where it strips off its headers.
8. The packet is sent to the server module.
9. The server module decides what is needed to fulfill the request by the local file system. If it can handle it, it makes a local file system I/O request or sends the packet on to a gateway.
10. The local file system gets the requests from its hard drive and sends results back the way they came.

Drivers

The protocol drivers don't actually place the bits of data onto the network. In Figure 4.3 you see that all protocols pass the data to the NDIS Wrapper DLL. In the past, network card providers had one standard driver that their card used. NT allows many different protocols and many different drivers to share a network card, however. By using a common interface (the NDIS Interface in Figure 4.3), vendors can write using a one-to-one interface. The user can communicate using TCP/IP, NetBEUI, AppleTalk, NetWare, and so on, using a single network card and a single network driver.

NT also can be extended as other transport protocols become available. In this chapter, you will closely examine these four protocols most common in an NT network.

FIGURE 4.3.

NT's TDI and NDIS common interfaces.

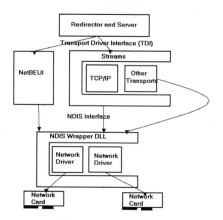

NetBEUI

The original NetBIOS API consisted of 17 commands that enabled you to connect, use, and disconnect with a remote computer. NetBEUI originally was an extension on those commands by IBM to work within Microsoft's NetBIOS network interface. NetBIOS now is defined as the API and NetBEUI as the protocol. Because the API now is separated from the transport protocol, other protocols can function with the same API. Protocols such as IPX/SPX and TCP/IP therefore could be extended to also support the NetBIOS API.

NetBEUI is adequate for a single network without routers. In this setup, you have several work-stations and possibly a dedicated server. This is a typical Windows for Workgroups network and was the original NT default network protocol. With NT 3.5, NetBEUI and IPX/SPX were given equal billing. Currently, when you set up an NT 4.0 workstation, IPX/SPX is the default. On NT server, both IPX/SPX and NetBEUI are the default settings.

The Windows NT implementation of NetBEUI is extended over that provided by LAN Manager and now is referred to as an *NBF* (*NetBIOS frame*). NBF provides for traffic that is either connection-oriented or connectionless. NBF also handles the unreliable nature of a network connection. Both connection-oriented and connectionless networks must handle equipment failures such as someone tripping over a network cable. In the past this would lock up the entire network and requiring on many occasions shutting down the entire network and rebooting all the machines. With Windows NT when the connection is again available it is restored, usually without the other network users having been aware of a problem.

NBF uses the values set up in the following directory of the NT Registry:

```
HKEY_LOCAL_MACHINE\SYSTEM\CurrentControlSet\Services\Nbf
```

NBF sends out a certain number of frames, depending on the command. It gets from the Registry the number of times to retry, to send, and how long to wait before a TimeOut. When you type **NET USE**, NBF sends out *Unnumbered Information* (UI) frames to look for the remote server.

If it gets a reply (an unnumbered acknowledgment UA frame), it initializes a link; if not, you see the TimeOut message.

The initial frame sent is always a NameQuery frame. All listening computers read the frame and check to see whether the name is in their namespace. The sending computer also has a *local session number* (LSN values are 0 to 255) in the frame. The receiving computer generates a new LSN for itself and reads the network SourceAddress from the frame. Using the SourceAddress, NBF can send subsequent frames directly. Originally, the LSN values in NetBIOS limited the number of sessions to 254 (0 is a special network test value). NBF extended this, however, by using a matrix of LSN values and network addresses.

If connected, NBF sends a Session Initialize frame and the server responds with a Session Confirm frame. At this point, the session is ready to handle application-level frames, the Server Message Blocks (SMBs).

If NBF had to send and wait on every frame, it would be too slow. Instead, it can send a number of frames (MaximumIncomingFrames) while waiting for the acknowledgment to return. The frames are numbered before they are sent, and the receiver can ask to have a frame resent.

In the Registry, you will see three timer values:

- **DefaultT1Timeout:** Specifies how long to wait before you assume that the frame is lost.
- **DefaultT2Timeout:** Specifies how often to send acknowledgments.
- **DefaultTiTimeout:** Indicates the inactivity timeout value used to determine when to assume that the link has been lost.

T2 is always less than T1, which is always less than Ti. These values can be adjusted if you have an unusually slow network medium, but the defaults are best for most modern network links.

TCP/IP

The *Transmission Control Protocol/Internet Protocol* (TCP/IP) was developed by the Department of Defense specifically to connect a wide variety of computers running UNIX. The TCP/IP transport operates within a STREAMS environment. *STREAMS* is a driver development environment designed to provide a high degree of portability from one operating system to another. Other STREAMS drivers can be plugged into Windows NT with little or no modification, allowing your computer to use many other transports.

TCP is the transport layer, and IP is the network layer in the OSI model.

IP is a suite of protocols that form a best-effort connectionless system: IP packets are not guaranteed to arrive at their destinations and they may arrive in a varied sequence. IP only does checksums on the IP header; the data is the responsibility of TCP. TCP, in contrast to IP, assumes a reliable connection-based system. TCP guarantees delivery and ordering of packets and provides a checksum on both the packet header and the data. TCP requires an acknowledgment on everything it sends. The *User Datagram Protocol* (UDP) is the connectionless TCP complement that does not provide flow control but does provide for one-to-many broadcast/multicast capabilities. Many other protocols, such as FTP, SMTP, SNTP, and Telnet, are part of the TCP/IP suite.

FTP, SMTP, and Telnet

File Transfer Protocol (FTP) uses the fact that TCP guarantees delivery to transfer files between computers. It allows for the uploading, downloading, listing, renaming, and deleting of files (the last two actions assume that you have permission). *Trivial FTP* (tFTP) uses UDP in situations in which the network is more unreliable. Someday, you may be using tFTP built into a CD-ROM to transfer files by a wireless network.

The *Simple Mail Transfer Protocol* (SMTP) is probably the Internet's most-used protocol. With SMTP, a user interacts with his local mail system through a *User Agent* (UA) and his mail is deposited in a local mailbox. SMTP periodically polls the outgoing mailbox. If it finds mail, it sets up a TCP connection with the host, sending the mail onto your Internet provider and picking up any incoming mail. On your provider, the process is the same: Periodically, SMTP moves the mail along to the next part of its path—your destination's Internet provider's computer. You can see these steps in the header of any mail you get. Usually, your workstation is not available on the network around the clock. SMTP assumes that it can make a connection or it returns the mail. To handle computers that dial into the network periodically to collect mail, another protocol is available: *Post Office Protocol version 3* (POP3). The SMTP host holds the mail until the POP3 client comes and gets it.

Telnet is terminal emulation; it makes your NT workstation behave as a terminal on a remote computer. Telnet uses TCP to send keystrokes from your keyboard and to place letters on your monitor. Your NT workstation is running Telnet client software and your Internet host is running Telnet server software. To log on, you need an account on the remote machine.

IP Addresses

Within IP are also the *Address Resolution Protocol* (ARP) and the *Internet Control Message Protocol* (ICMP). IP packets contain the source address, the destination IP addresses, and the destination hardware address. IP acquires the hardware address by broadcasting a special inquiry packet (an ARP request packet) with the destination's IP address, and the system replies by sending its hardware address in an ARP reply packet. ICMP allows nodes to share IP status and error information. The Internet Ping protocol uses ICMP echo request and echo reply packets to show you its information.

A *host* is any device attached to the network that provides an IP address, subnet mask, and default gateway. IP addresses are unique 32-bit values, but they are displayed in the familiar *dotted-decimal* notation. You attain an IP address from hostmaster@internic.net.

An address, that to the computer is a 32-bit value, is usually written as `123.456.789.123`. As Table 4.1 shows, IP address classes refer to whether you were given in class A all the 123.* addresses, with the first decimal in the 1–126 range; in class B, all the 128.456.* addresses, with the first decimal in the 128–191 range; or in class C, all the 192.456.789.* addresses, with the first decimal in the 192–223 range. There is also a class D for multicasting and a future class E. Obviously, you have to be a major player to get a Class A or B IP address. Most companies have a class C address. To determine which computer in the company you are addressing, you apply a mask to hide the upper values. A class C subnet mask would be 255.255.255.0, which, when masked with the IP address, gives you the value in the last decimal notation. This use of class and IP address provides the routing of the packet through the huge web that is the Internet.

Table 4.1. IP address classes.

Class	Values	NetID	HostID	Available	Possible Hosts
A	1–126	a	b.c.d	126	16,777,214
B	128–191	a.b	c.d	16,384	65,534
C	192–223	a.b.c	d	2,097,151	254

As the Internet growth has exploded, just assigning IP addresses throughout large companies has become burdensome. In addition, network providers have many dial-in clients that may not be able to configure their IP addresses and subnet masks. NT has a Dynamic Host Configuration Protocol (DHCP) that allows the system Administrator to lease out addresses on a login-term basis (assigned addresses being valid only for that particular login session), thus sharing addresses between many users. This is the BOOTP protocol many providers supply instead of a permanent IP address.

Computers use IP addresses to talk to each other, but people find it easier to use names. Just as Windows NT setup gives your computer a name when it is set up on the Internet, it gets a name composed of that computer plus the DNS domain name. The *Domain Name System* (DNS) provides a way to look at names based on IP addresses and is a database distributed throughout the Internet. If you are the NT Network Administrator, you use the Windows Internet Names Service (WINS) server to manage your local names database. A WINS server is able to keep track of who has your local BOOTP addresses, IP addresses, and the distant DNS databases. The DNS database is a simple listing of IP addresses and aliases. On Windows NT, this file is kept in the \WINNT\System32\drivers\etc\hosts file. Windows NT workstation uses a similar LMHOSTS file for NetBIOS over TCP/IP applications. Windows NT server uses a NetBIOS name server called WINS for resolving NetBIOS names. You can find DNS software on the resource kit CD to set up your own internal DNS.

Datagrams

IP packets are called *datagrams* and can vary in size from 576 bytes to 65,535 bytes. The header is 64 bytes and contains data that indicates both its military and Internet origins. The precedence field is normally a 0 for civilians, but the DoD uses values for ASAP, within four hours, within the same day, and within one day. The TOS field also is interesting because it can designate its queuing algorithm. Also, the Time to Live field indicates how long the datagram will stay alive on the network. Each time the datagram passes through a router, it is decremented, so it is discarded by all routers except the destination host. The Protocol field designates which upper layer protocol is to receive the IP data. There also are options for security, strict routing, record route, and timestamps. Take a look at the IP packet in Figure 4.4 and think of the Internet, banks sharing data, military, and us common nonsense e-mail people.

FIGURE 4.4.

IP packet structure.

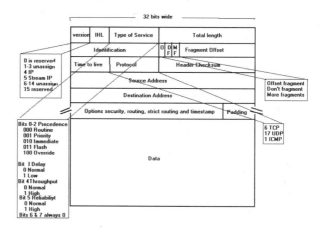

IPX/SPX

Internet Packet Exchange (IPX) is a set of protocols within a STREAMS environment and is used in Novell NetWare. IPX is also a connectionless datagram service that uses data-link protocols such as Ethernet, token ring, ARCnet, and PPP. *Connectionless* means that prior to the data transmission, no control packets are sent to establish a connection. The data packets have both the source and destination address, and no guarantees are made about the success of the packet. To provide guarantees, upper layers such as SPX are used to perform error checking. IPX addresses are composed of a 32-bit network number installed by Novell for each physical network and a 48-bit address pair. The IPX packet also has a socket number that identifies which process is doing the communicating.

Sequenced Packet Exchange (SPX) is a transport layer protocol that provides connection-oriented services. It uses a reliable virtual circuit and performs the flow control and sequencing of packets. SPX sends control packets to establish the virtual connection and assign connection IDs. SPX uses a time-out algorithm in which it sends a packet. Then, if an acknowledgment is not received by the time-out value, it increases the time-out value 50 percent and resends the packet. SPX also sends probes to verify the connection. Many SPX connections can use the same IPX socket by multiplexing the connection IDs.

Packet Exchange Protocol (PXP) is a less reliable service than SPX. It uses a request/response sequence called a *transaction*. PXP is used by NetWare in its NetBIOS emulation.

The *NetWare Core Protocol* (NCP) implements NetWare's file services, print services, name management, and file locking. It also maintains a database of NetWare objects called the *bindary*. Windows NT Server provides a binary-emulation mode to implement NCP for NetWare 3.*x* and 4.*x*. NT workstation must make requests for service to an NCP server. NCP directly uses IPX to be more efficient and handles its own error detection, session controls, and retransmissions.

AppleTalk

AppleTalk is the protocol Apple Macintoshes use to communicate between each other and with Windows NT. Macintosh clients on an NT network communicate with the AppleTalk protocols built into every Macintosh computer. This provides file sharing, printer sharing, administration, and routing support. AppleTalk is implemented as part of the Macintosh operating system. Macintosh users have a familiar graphical user interface to access network services.

To the Macintosh user, the NT file server looks like an AppleShare server. The server manages file names, icons, and access permissions. NT Server provides multistream file access, both resource and data forks, and 31-character long file names.

The *AppleTalk Address Resolution Protocol* (AARP) is modeled on TCP/IP's ARP protocol, with binding between OSI's upper layer network addresses and the data-link layer addresses. AARP uses simple addresses, 1 to 254, which are much easier to handle than the common 123.456.789.123 IP address format you saw earlier. AARP makes it possible to use different data-link technologies that Apple calls EtherTalk, TokenTalk, FDDITalk, as well as the Macintosh standard AppleTalk. A data-link address is required in order to send a frame over the physical link.

The network layer uses sockets similar to IPX and TCP/IP sockets. AppleTalk calls this the *Datagram Delivery Protocol* (DDP). The network layer also defines the *Name Binding Protocol* (NBP), which is similar to the DNS name on TCP/IP networks. This is a binding between the addresses, and uses the easier-to-use symbolic name of the *Network Visible Entries* (NVEs).

AppleTalk sets up zones as a collection of nodes. This is similar to NT Server workgroups but without the associated security issues. When the Macintosh boots, it polls its Zone Information Table (ZIT) to determine which zone it belongs in. This table is maintained on the router.

The transport layer is broken into a transaction protocol (ATP) and a data-stream protocol (ADSP). An *ATP transaction* is a request and response between the client and the server machine. In ATP, each transaction is numbered, which enables the client to determine whether it gets the correct response to its request. The *ADSP protocol* is full-duplex flow between two sockets, similar to TCP, with a maximum stream size of 64 KB. ADSP uses two types of packets: control and data.

This session layer provides session protocols and printer-access protocols. The *AppleTalk Session Protocol* (ASP) uses the concept of transactions, in which a series of commands are sent from the client to the server and executed. The *Printer Access Protocol* (PAP) creates, maintains, and disconnects connections to remote printers. PAP polls the *Name Binding Protocol* (NBP) from the network layer to map addresses from the server to printer settings on the client.

AppleTalk does not have the OSI presentation layer. In the application layer, the *AppleTalk Filing Protocol* (AFP) is defined to locate files across the network or locally on the client. AFP defines the write-, read-, and search-access controls as well as user names, passwords, and directory-access controls. *AppleTalk Print Services* (APS) communicate with the PAP layer to give the application printer access.

Workgroups

Workgroups are networks of Windows-based computers running Windows 95, Windows 3.11, or Windows NT. These usually are small networks with a peer-to-peer setup. There may or may not be a central file server that the entire workgroup uses. In the most common setup, illustrated in Figure 4.5, each workstation acts as a server, sharing its files and printers with every other workstation. Each workstation is also a client using resources shared by other workstations.

FIGURE 4.5.

Windows NT Workgroup in a peer-to-peer network.

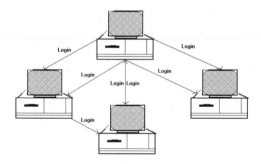

At first, workgroups may seem ideal because every user has access to all the workgroups' resources. Workgroups have their limitations, however; as the network grows, it is harder to administer because each workstation has to give access to each new workstation. Each computer maintains its own security database (SAM) with its own group definitions, passwords, and access rights. The Administrator must coordinate the SAM databases on each computer. The Administrator has to create user accounts on each workstation in the workgroup. There is no password synchronization within the workgroup, so each user's password has to be changed on each workstation. A larger problem occurs when users begin to share files, such as databases. Several users may be accessing a database on one worker's computer. If that one worker shuts down, all connections to the database are lost. If that shutdown occurs during a file write, damage to the database may occur.

Notice that when you log onto your workstation, you have only one choice in the listbox: your workgroup. If you are a part of a domain, you may have several choices in this listbox. You supply your user name and password, and the computer checks the SAM database and assigns you a security token. This token is attached to any processes you start.

The security access token contains a *SID identifier*, which is a unique identifier based on user name, group name, computer name, and computer clock time. This SID value is checked against the resource's access control lists that grant your permissions.

If you start File Manager, you can see the computers in your workgroup and in other workgroups. File Manager sends a query packet out to all computers and lists which ones respond that they are part of that workgroup. You may have workgroups for certain departments in your organization or certain projects in your development group.

There is really no security that limits you to just your workgroup. You just as easily can log onto a computer that is part of another workgroup, if you have the permissions to do so as in Figure 4.6. Up to 10 simultaneous users can be connected to any workstation at one time.

FIGURE 4.6.

Logons across workgroups.

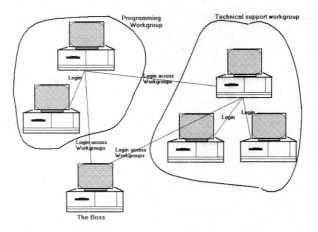

At some point in your company's growth, you will begin to use one workstation as a central point from which to share files and printers. This becomes a server in the client/server model. The advantage of a dedicated server is that now your shared databases have a point where a user is not going to shut down at any time. You also can perform backups on the central server and know that all critical data is being backed up. Also, you can administer access to those shared files at one point.

Further on in the company growth, you need to have central administration of the network. NT Server is a version of NT that has had certain areas of the software fine-tuned to perform better as a file/printer server. The software has many additional utilities for administrating the network. NT Server has one additional function: to provide a domain model for networking.

NT Server has the following features not found in NT Workstation:

- NT server implements the Domain network model for centralized account administration
- Disk fault tolerance is available by implementing RAID, which you look closer at in Chapter 5, "File Systems."
- NT Server provides remote access of up to 256 dial-up modem links
- NetWare account migration allows for preservation of existing netware privileges
- NetWare gateway service in which NT Server provides a bridge between an existing Netware network and an NT network
- Macintosh File/Printer services are provided to NT Server based networks.
- NT Server can be a remoteboot server
- WINS Internet Name Service translates name addresses to IP addresses locally
- Dynamic Host Configuration Protocol (DHCP)
- Directory replication. NT workstation allows for import of directories; NT Server allows replication by both import and export.

Domains

A domain has at least one NT Server. The primary feature is a centralized SAM database from which you can administrate user accounts and passwords that propagate to workstations in the domain. One of the NT Servers in the domain is designated as the primary domain controller (PDC), whereas another NT server may be designated as the backup domain controller (BDC). The PDC has the master copy of the SAM database, and a copy of the SAM database is placed on the BDC. If the PDC fails, you can promote the BDC to be the PDC without losing the SAM database.

Domain clients can be Windows NT workstations, Windows 95, Windows 3.11, OS/2 workstations, MS-DOS LAN Manager clients, or NetWare clients. Each computer still controls access to its own resources by offering to share a certain resource. The NT Server in Figure 4.7 is the primary domain controller. The domain controller's SAM database is used to hold user names, passwords, and group definitions. When a workstation joins a domain, it can choose to take logons using its own NT workstation SAM or the domain's SAM.

FIGURE 4.7.
The NT Server domain.

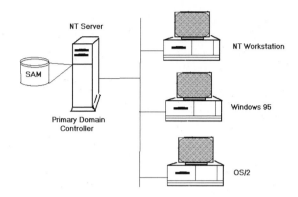

To access a domain server, you must be a member of the domain or be given a trust relationship to the domain. A company will have multiple domains—for example, accounting, manufacturing, administration, and so on. All Windows NT machines are members of one domain. In order to access resources on another domain, one domain sets up a trust relationship with the other domain.

Trust Relationships

You can have two types of trust relationships: one-way trusts or bidirectional trusts. A *trust relationship* allows a user account in one domain to access another domain. In Figure 4.8, a user in the Accounting domain with privileges can access data in the Manufacturing domain and the Administration domain. You can administrate several domains from one central location and use trust relationships to fine tune the user access rights. You also can access a resource in a domain—even those domains in which you don't have a user account due to your domain's trust relationship.

FIGURE 4.8.
The domain model.

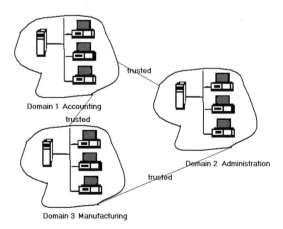

In a *one-way* trust relationship, users in one domain (the *trusted* domain) can access resources in another domain (the *trusting* domain). This may be the situation when the administration domain can access the accounting domain's files, but accounting cannot access administration's files, for example.

A *bidirectional* trust allows both domains to access resources from each other. When a trust relationship exists, the trusting server passes logon requests for validation by the trusted server. This means that Jane, who is a user in the trusted server, Administration, does not need an account on the trusting server, Accounting, in order to log onto Accounting if she has privileges in her domain. The trusting domain passes through the validation to the trusted domain and receives authorization for Jane. (See Figure 4.9.)

FIGURE 4.9.

Pass-through validation.

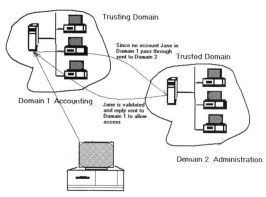

In keeping with the NT design of discretionary access, a domain that trusts another doesn't automatically become trusted by any others in other words, no trust relationships are transitive. This is illustrated in Figure 4.10 where just because Domain 1 trusts Domain 2, and Domain 2 trusts Domain 3, does not imply that Domain 1 trusts Domain 3.

FIGURE 4.10.

Domain trust relationships are defined, never assumed.

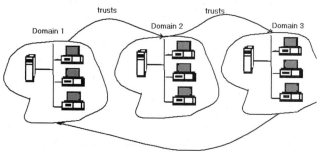

Two types of groups in Windows NT exist: the global group (called a domain group) and the local groups defined on the individual machines. The scope of a global group is the entire domain; the scope of a local group is the individual machine. Each local machine controls its own resources. Users typically are defined on the domain server and are assigned to various domain groups. This allows for central administration of policies but individual administration of one's own computer. A global group contains users in the domain. A local group contains local users, global groups from this domain, global groups from trusted domains, and user accounts from other domains.

Domain Models

Microsoft suggests four domain models under which you can define trust relationships. Without a general design plan, your network can get complex as each domain decides who it trusts and is trusted by. Remember that, inside the domain security arrangements, you have domain groups of users with group rights, local groups of users, and individuals within groups with their access rights. The four types of domain models follow:

- **A single domain model for a small network:** In a single domain, you use a common SAM database and central administration. A disadvantage is that, as the number of users increases, performance can suffer. Also, no grouping of resources occurs around the business model. Figure 4.11 shows an example of a single domain model.

FIGURE 4.11.

A single domain model.

- **The master domain model:** This allows for multiple domains with centralized administration as in Figure 4.12. All domains trust the central domain in a one-way fashion. All logons therefore are passed through to the central domain server. Users in the master domain can access resources in any domain, but users within the other domains are confined to the resources within their domains.

  An MIS department is a typical example of this type of domain. Here, MIS is the master domain and each business unit is a separate domain that trusts the master. A local computer shares its resources with local groups. Each local group contains global groups rather than users. The users are all grouped into global groups on the master domain server rather than the local machine. When a user is added to a global group, she automatically gets access to the local resources. This model is a good choice for companies with fewer than 10,000 users, but performance suffers as the number of users grows because all validations come from a central point.

FIGURE 4.12.

A master domain model.

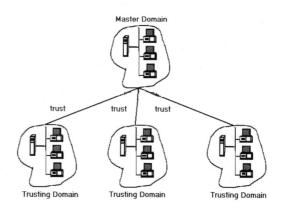

■ **The multiple master domain model:** This model has two or more master domains as in Figure 4.13. The domains has a two-way trust relationships between them. All the other domains trust these two master domains. The number of master domains times the number of resource domains is the total number of one-way trust relationships you need to define. This model allows for a larger-sized network because it is scaleable. As the number of master domains grows, however, there is increased network traffic. MIS doesn't have its own domain and now must manage multiple trust relationships.

FIGURE 4.13.

A multiple master domain model.

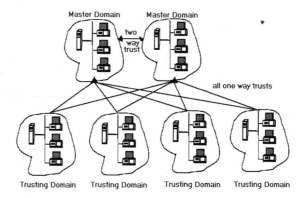

■ **The complete trust model:** In this model, every domain has a two-way trust relationship with every other domain, as shown in Figure 4.14. There will be *(n–1)×(n/2)* two-way trust relationships to maintain and *(n–1)×n* trust relationships to maintain. This leads to a much higher level of complexity but assumes that each domain is administered to protect its resources. This model is for companies without a central MIS department and can be scaleable to very large organizations. The disadvantage is that everyone relies on the domain Administrators to not put inappropriate users and global groups into their local groups.

FIGURE 4.14.

A complete trust domain model.

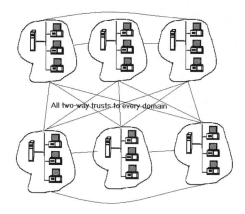

All two-way trusts to every domain

Administrating a Domain

NT Server has Server Manager software that enables you to join domains, change domain names, delete computers from the domain, synchronize the DNC and BNC databases, and set up properties of the domain. These properties can include the number of users connected to the domain, the number of files open, the number of file locks, and the number of named pipes (See Figure 4.15).

FIGURE 4.15.

The NT Server Manager.

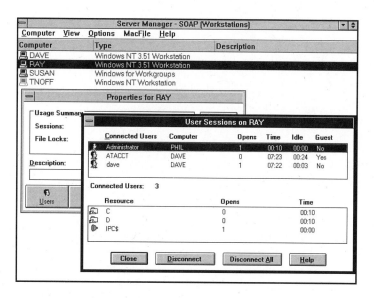

From the Server Manager, the Administrator can disconnect users. This may be necessary to stop a runaway service, to shut down the NT server, or to balance the load on the NT server. You can broadcast to all users in the case of an impending shutdown. Also from the Server Manager, you can examine resources in use and user connection properties to further fine tune your network security and resource allocation.

The User Manager will be the primary tool you use to manage accounts and groups. It allows each NT Server to define trusted domains and which domains are permitted to trust this domain. You can see from the definition process that you must designate one at a time who you trust and who can trust you. The discriminating security in the relationship therefore isn't defined; it isn't assumed to exist by prior relationship definitions. To set up a two-way trust relationship, you need to define the relationship twice.

FIGURE 4.16.

Setting up trust relationships with the User Manager.

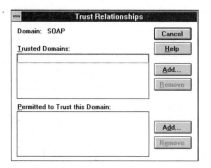

The NT Server domain user policy setup allows for much sharper definition of users than is available under workgroups. In the Policy screen, you can define various characteristics of the passwords and logon (see Figure 4.17). When managing accounts, you might want to force the user to change passwords after a certain number of days. This practice keeps passwords from becoming commonly known and abused. You also can set up accounts so that the new password must be one your users haven't used recently. You can set uniqueness from 1 to 24, indicating how infrequently users can use the same password. You also can specify a minimum number of days the user must use that password before he can change it, as well as the minimum length of a password. Accounts can be locked out automatically after a certain number of unsuccessful password attempts. Accounts also can be forced to log out at a certain time of day. You can lock accounts that the user hasn't accessed for a certain number of days by using Password Change options and the Must Logon option.

Each user account has a set of properties, commonly thought of as read access, write access, execute capabilities, or delete capabilities. Windows NT enables you to specify in much greater detail who can access resources and in what way. The user rights policy is broken up into the rights for normal users and rights typically restricted for programmers on Windows NT. Table 4.2 lists the first basic set of rights and properties that all users have.

FIGURE 4.17.

User Manager for Domain policy settings.

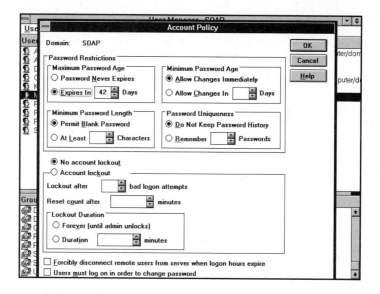

Table 4.2. Basic user settings.

Property	Description
Account disabled	Specifies that the account still exists; it is just disabled.
Account locked out	Specifies that if too many unsuccessful password attempts occur, the account becomes locked until the Administrator clears it.
Account type	Specifies global or local accounts.
Change password next login	Forces user to change password on new accounts.
Expiration date	Specifies the date on which the account will be disabled.
Full name	Specifies the user's full name.
Groups	Specifies a list of groups of which the user is a member.
Home directory	Specifies a private directory for the users.
Logon script	Specifies a batch file, command file, or executable to run when a user logs on.
Logon hours	Sets hours during which users can access an account on NT Server.

continues

Table 4.2. continued

Property	Description
Logon workstations	In NT Server specifies a list of workstations from which a user can log on.
Password	Consists of 14 characters and is case sensitive. Allows only one-way encryption so that the Administrator can change but not view the password.
Password never expires	Ensures that Replicator accounts are set to Yes, or you'll never be able to login after password expires.
Profile	A descriptive file of the user's desktop.
User can't change guest pswd	Changing the password for guest accounts is an adminstrative function
Username	Specifies a unique user name that is not case sensitive.

User rights administration is set up into predefined groups by Microsoft. It's best to try to use these groups, if possible. User rights can be fine tuned. The more advanced possibilities follow:

User rights as an administrator:

> Access from network
> Add workstations to domain
> Back up files
> Change system time
> Force shutdown from a remote computer
> Load or change drivers
> Log on locally
> Manage auditing and security logs
> Restore files
> Shut down
> Take ownership of files

User rights as a programmer:

> Act as part of operating system
> Bypass transverse checking
> Create a pagefile
> Create a token
> Create permanent shared object
> Debug programs
> Generate security audits

Increase quotas
Increase priorities
Load and unload drivers
Lock pages into memory
Log on as a batch job
Log on as a service
Modify firmware variables
Profile a process
Profile system performance
Replace a process level token

Drawbacks of the Domain Model

Although the Domain Model has greatly enhanced network administration, it's not yet perfect. Businesses are becoming more global as are their networks. Some of the drawbacks to the Domain Model are:

■ It isn't hierarchical like a business chart and is hard to match business models that are geographically or market based.

■ As the network grows, the maintenance of trust relationships increases.

■ It is easy with two-way trust relationships to get a user in a group with access rights that he shouldn't have.

■ If you are not careful about trust relationships, all models can become the complete trust model.

■ Businesses need to plan ahead when using the network trust model. The use of business computers sometimes outpaces the planning and trust relationships defined on-the-fly.

■ The BDC database is read-only and must be replicated from the PDC often or it can become stale. The Administrator needs to keep the BDC fresh, or it can be authenticating users based on old data. Typically, the BDC database is refreshed every five minutes with NT Server, but at times, it can get out of synchronization and the Administrator may need to use the Server Manager tool to resynchronize it.

Summary

NT is the network. You saw in this chapter that the NT operating system was designed for the network from the ground up. NT's designers recognized the many existing network protocols and the dissimilar computers sharing resources on the network, and they developed NT to cooperate with them. The designers also build NT for the future and designed NT to accept new advances in network technology.

This chapter just scratched the surface of networking with Windows NT. To learn more in-depth details about this topic, use the NT Resource Kit manuals. Chapters 25 through 27 deal with programming NT using Winsockets, MAPI, and RAS to get more from your NT network.

In Chapter 5, "File Systems," you build on what you learned about networking, as NT was also designed to work with dissimilar file systems existing on the network. You look closely at how NT's new file system was developed out of the best of the past file systems such as FAT and HPFS. This new file system is much more capable given the rapid changes in storage technology the computer industry will bring into your environment.

File Systems

5

by David Hamilton

IN THIS CHAPTER

Just as quickly as the computer on which you program advanced from your old PC XT or Apple II to your new NT workstation, so have the computer's storage requirements grown. In 10 years we have gone from the 10MB PC hard drive as standard, to where a several gigabyte drive is now the desktop standard, and recent commercials for the 1996 Olympics talk of managing a 4 terrabyte database. Amazingly, somehow MS-DOS's File Allocation Table (FAT) file system survived the entire time, being extended far past its initial design.

In the last chapter you looked at NT networking and saw that whether local or across the network, NT treated it all as file I/O. With networks and huge databases making increasing I/O demands, NT brought with it a new, more efficient file system: NTFS. NTFS was designed from the best of FAT and what worked well with FAT's earlier replacement, OS/2's High Performance File System (HPFS).

Versions of NT prior to 4.0 still supported HPFS volumes. Both NT and Windows 95 support using FAT volumes and have added long filename support to FAT. In order to see the strength of NTFS, you first look back at both FAT and HPFS. You see how NTFS is superior, how NT handles reading and writing files, and how NTFS protects the file structure. Last, you look at setting up arrays of drives to provide speed or redundancy to file operations.

File Systems in the Past

With MS-DOS, managing files was about all that was asked of the operating system. Even Windows relied on DOS to take care of file details. It wasn't until the introduction of 32-bit disk access that Windows began to bypass DOS and talk directly to the disk controller. Windows NT is responsible for all file I/O. NT was released with the capability to work with four file systems and to be extensible to use future file systems.

Because many users were coming from systems based on FAT, NT had to support that file system and choose to use it for floppy disk access as well. HPFS was supported to provide compatibility with OS/2, because the OS/2 subsystem was part of NT. The *CD-ROM file system* (CDFS) had to be supported because at the time NT was introduced, CD-ROMs were just becoming a more common way to distribute software. Now, at the time of NT 4.0's release, nearly all software is distributed via CD-ROM, and users can hardly imagine loading NT 4.0 from a zillion floppy disks.

One thing all the file systems have in common is that the media is formatted. *Formatting* divides the disk into top and bottom halves. Then each half is divided into rings call *tracks*. Lastly, each track is divided into sectors. A *sector* is the smallest physical unit of storage on a disk— usually 512 bytes. To increase performance with large files, a disk can be formatted with much larger sectors. A *cluster* is defined as 4 sectors.

When you write a file to a disk, the file system allocates the number of clusters needed to store the file. Even if your file is small, it needs one cluster, or 2 KB (512×4). With the FAT system, the number of sectors per cluster varies according to the media in use: a 360 KB floppy has 2 sectors per cluster, a 1.2 MB floppy has 4 sectors per cluster, a 200 MB hard drive has 8 sectors per cluster, and a 400 MB drive has 32 sectors per cluster. The larger the media, the more wasted space in storing small files. If you have a 100 byte file on a 360 KB floppy disk, in this case, it takes 1 cluster (1 KB) of space. The same file on a 200 MB hard drive still takes 1 cluster (4 KB) of space, and on a 400 MB drive, it takes up 1 cluster (16 KB) of space. This was why you often saw larger drives formatted into smaller partitions: You wasted a ton of less space!

As your file grows, more clusters are added. All the file systems try to add clusters in contiguous blocks of space. Often, this is not possible and a cluster is added from another area of the disk, resulting in a fragmented file. The more fragmented a file, the longer it takes to locate all the file pieces and return the file to the user. You can make the sector sizes larger than 512 bytes to reduce the likelihood of fragmentation, but the trade-off is wasted space on small files.

FAT

When IBM introduced the PC in 1981, it ran a new operating system called MS-DOS. MS-DOS's file system is called FAT after its central feature, the *file allocation table*. The FAT's design was more than enough to handle the media sizes of its day and provided a hierarchical directory of the files and directory structures. The biggest testament to its design is that it is still today probably the most-used file system. It initially was designed to handle massive disk sizes of up to 32 MB; who would ever need more? At the time, 5 MB and 10 MB hard drives were the type of power PC users had. The MS-DOS that you use today can handle much larger drives, usually up to 512 MB, but recent extensions are available to allow partitions greater than 1 GB.

You can look at the FAT with many utilities to view a simple listing of cluster numbers and see which clusters form the file. Figure 5.1 shows how you can view the FAT using The Norton Utilities.

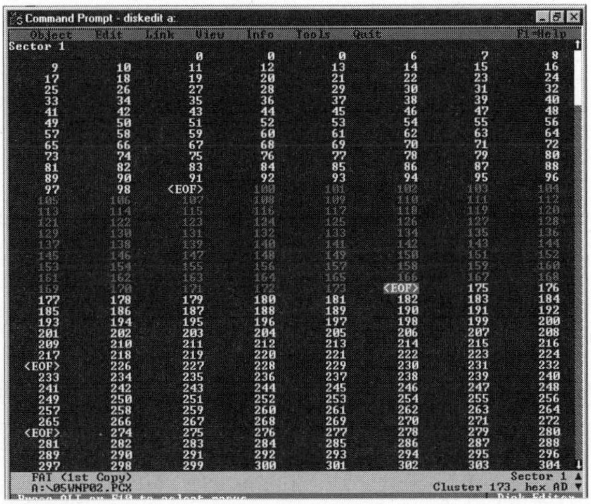

FIGURE 5.1.

Displaying a FAT table with The Norton Utilities.

Figure 5.2 shows a directory listing of three files. The first file uses two clusters, the first at address 0002. Note that the block at address 0002 points to the second block at 0004, which is marked as the end with FFFF. The second file uses just one cluster and is located at address 0001 in the FAT table. The third file uses up four clusters beginning at address 0004. The directory points to the first cluster to be read, and the FAT points you to successive clusters that form the same file. You keep reading until you reach a FFFF, which marks the end of the file.

FIGURE 5.2.

The File Allocation Table (FAT).

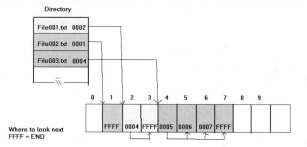

Updating the FAT is very important, as well as time consuming. If the FAT is not updated regularly, it can lead to data loss. It is time consuming because the disk-read heads must be repositioned to the drive's logical track zero each time the FAT is updated. There is no organization to the FAT directory structure, and files are given the first open location on the drive, leading to increased fragmentation as the drive becomes full and multiple small files are deleted.

The FAT is a linked list of the clusters on the hard drive. The clusters are chained together by the FAT—thus, the too common message about lost chains or clusters. FAT marks the *end of file* (EOF) with FFFF, and marks bad clusters with FFF7. Any cluster containing FFF7 is ignored by DOS.

The directory contains first 8 bytes for the file name and then 3 bytes for the file extension. This gives you the 8.3 file name restriction. The directory listing also has a file attribute byte (8 bits), a reserved byte, modification time (16 bits), modification date (16 bits), the starting allocation unit (16 bits, which is the pointer into the FAT you saw in Figure 5.1), and a 32-bit file size.

As files are created, expanded, and deleted, the FAT file system becomes fragmented. It is designed for smaller media; in fact, the FAT system with DOS 1.0 doesn't even know how to handle subdirectories, and the root directory is limited to 64 files (2 KB cluster size/32 bytes per entry). A subdirectory now is a special file that has a 32-byte entry for each of its files. This first FAT system has 12 bits for each entry in the FAT system and, therefore, a 32 MB limit. This was expanded to 16-bit entries, and now larger hard drives can be formatted.

Data recovery is provided by having an entire second copy of the FAT on the drive. The disk is formatted so that the first block is the BIOS area, the next is the primary FAT, and the third is the duplicate FAT. When a disk is damaged in the first cluster, it can't boot or be read. When you try to recover the data, often you will find that the damage extends through the primary FAT into the immediately adjacent FAT duplicate.

The size of every file is stored in the file's directory entry. The *chain size* of any file is the number of clusters on the disk multiplied by the number of bytes in each cluster. CHKDSK compares the two reported sizes to see whether the directory entry and the FAT are comparable. CHKDSK displays the following error message if the sizes are incorrect:

```
Allocation error, size adjusted
```

The error is displayed if the file size located in the directory entry is larger than the chain size, or if the chain size is more than one cluster size larger than the reported file size. To adjust the size of the file, CHKDSK changes the directory entry to match the chain size.

FAT was designed to use 8.3 file names, and there is no structure for security other than the 8 bit attribute byte, which typically is just read-only, archive, hidden, or system.

The basic problem with FAT is not only that it becomes fragmented easily, but, as the media gets larger, it takes longer and longer to search through the FAT.

Windows NT makes a few changes to the implementation of FAT. The POSIX subsystem needs timestamps for file creation and last-accessed files, so NT makes a linked directory entry to save these. To get around the 8.3 file name restriction, both NT and Windows 95 use the attribute bits to signal that there are one or more secondary directory entries each holding the next 13 characters of the file name. By setting the bits for all four attributes (volume, system, read-only, and hidden), NT and Windows 95 can ensure that these special directory entries are not even seen by MS-DOS or OS/2. The directory entries are recombined to form the long file names for use by NT or Windows 95. You can override this process by changing the Registry entry to the following:

```
HKEY_LOCAL_MACHINE\System\CurrentControlSet\Control\FileSystem
```

FAT uses the traditional 8.3 file-naming convention, and all file names must be created with the ASCII character set. The name of a file or directory can contain up to eight characters, followed by a period (.) separator, and then followed by a three-character extension. The name must start with a letter or number and can contain any characters except for the following:

```
. " / \ [ ] : ; ¦ = ,
```

Also, the name cannot contain any spaces. If any of these characters are used, unexpected results may occur. By using the Alt key plus the three-digit ASCII code, however, you can create some fairly "protected" files.

FAT is the most widely used file system for PCs. You can access FAT files via OS/2 and Windows NT. The FAT's other advantage is that you can boot your computer with a DOS disk and undelete files. It is not as robust as HPFS or NTFS, however, and doesn't support long file names or security attributes. The major drawback to FAT is that as drives get larger than 200 MB, performance decreases with size.

HPFS

HPFS was released in 1990 with the OS/2 operating system and was designed to handle increasingly large media and 16-bit processor operations. Almost immediately, HPFS 386 was released to handle the new 80386's 32-bit operations and LAN Manager's needs. It doesn't handle data-corruption problems very well, and it can take hours to perform a CHKDSK to find out whether you have a problem.

HPFS maintains the directory organization of FAT, but adds automatic sorting of the directory based on file names. File names are extended to up to 254 double-byte characters. HPFS also allows a file to be composed of "data" and special attributes to allow for increased flexibility in terms of supporting other naming conventions and security. In addition, the unit of allocation is changed from clusters to physical sectors (512 bytes), which reduces lost disk space by enabling you to allocate a smaller unit for small files.

HPFS introduced some features that eventually became part of NTFS: the new NT file system. HPFS supports file names of up to 254 characters and uses a B-tree to find files much more quickly than the linear list that FAT uses. A linear list is fast up to a point, but you have to search the entire list each time you need a file. Figure 5.3 shows a simple B-tree. If the value you need is less than D, you look left; if it is greater than D but less than H, you look right. The structure is that of a root and nodes. Each node greatly reduces the number of places you need to look.

FIGURE 5.3.

A B-tree makes searching faster.

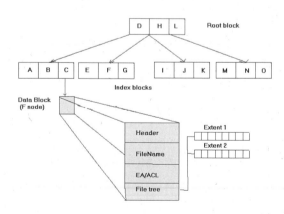

In HPFS, the root block points to index blocks that are the directory entries. Each directory entry points to an Fnode that contains a 512-byte structure that describes the individual file. The Fnode contains a 15-byte file name, the file length, extended attributes (EA), an access control list (ACL), and pointers to the location of file extents. *Extents* are the other clusters in the volume that make up the file. Up to 8 extents can exist, and each extent is a cluster (made up of 2 bands) of up to 16 MB. One Fnode then can describe a file of up to 16×8 MB, or 128 MB. HPFS expanded on this by providing 12 pointers to allocation nodes that give you even more extents.

An HPFS drive is formatted for efficiency with large files and can handle volumes of up to 2 GB. When you format the volume, the first 18 sectors (a sector is still 512 bytes) are used for the boot block, the super block, and the spare block. These three blocks boot the operating system and are used in file maintenance. As you can see in Figure 5.4, each band is 8 MB. The bands are arranged so that two bands are seated together to form a contiguous unit of 16 MB. HPFS leaves room this way for files to grow without fragmentation. By having such large contiguous chunks, files can be retrieved faster. The 2 KB bitmaps are simply a mapping of which parts of the band are in use.

FIGURE 5.4.

HPFS volume format.

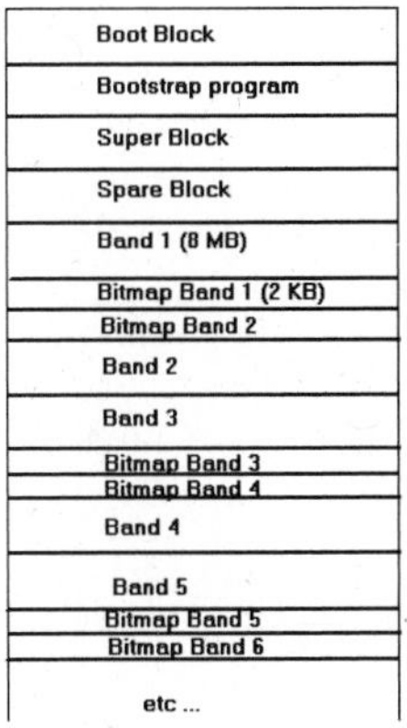

Boot Block
Bootstrap program
Super Block
Spare Block
Band 1 (8 MB)
Bitmap Band 1 (2 KB)
Bitmap Band 2
Band 2
Band 3
Bitmap Band 3
Bitmap Band 4
Band 4
Band 5
Bitmap Band 5
Bitmap Band 6
etc ...

The following listing takes a closer look at these HPFS blocks and includes a couple of other unique special data objects. Although support for HPFS was dropped in NT 4.0, several of its best features went into the design of NTFS, and I have pointed those out.

- ■ **Super block:** Located in logical sector 16 and contains a pointer to the Fnode of the root directory. One of the biggest dangers of using HPFS is that if the super block is lost or corrupted due to a bad sector, so are the contents of the partition, even if the rest of the drive is fine. It is possible to recover the data on the drive by copying everything to another drive with a good sector 16 and rebuilding the super block. This is a very complex task, however.

- **Spare block:** Located in logical sector 17 and contains a table of "hot fixes" and the spare directory block. *Hot fixing* is a technique for handling write errors. Under HPFS, when a bad sector is detected, the "hot fixes" entry is used to logically point to an existing good sector in place of the bad sector. This technique was carried over into the design of NTFS. HPFS introduced this hot fixing to handle write errors. HPFS keeps a section of blocks available, and if it detects a write error, it uses one of these blocks to write the data to and remap the file to use this block instead of the bad block. If this happens too frequently, HPFS warns you to run CHKDSK, which can be a very long operation on HPFS.

- **Hot fixing:** A technique in which, if an error occurs because of a bad sector, the file system moves the information to a different sector and marks the original sector as bad. This is all done transparent to any applications performing disk I/O (that is, the application never knows that there were any problems with the hard drive). Using a file system that supports hot fixing eliminates error messages such as the FAT Abort, Retry, or Fail? error message that occurs when a bad sector is encountered. The version of HPFS included with earlier versions of Windows NT did not support hot fixing, but NTFS does.

- **Disk caching:** A process that increases performance by holding information in memory in case it is needed a second time. The data is written to the drive as a background process.

- **Lazy writes:** Helps increase performance by postponing writes until you have a larger amount to write.

Although HPFS is a major improvement over the FAT file system, it has some problems. All the boot information and root directory still are concentrated at the first part of the volume. If this area is damaged, the whole volume is inaccessible. It still uses 512-byte sectors, which limits it to 2 GB drives. Lastly, CHKDSK runs every time you boot the machine, and if it detected errors, this is a very time-consuming process. When Windows NT uses an HPFS volume, it doesn't support the ACL list or hot-fixing options. Disk caching and lazy writes are part of NT's Cache Manager and are not performed by the file system.

You can access HPFS files by using OS/2 or versions of NT prior to 4.0, which provide faster access than FAT. If your drive is less than 200 MB, the overhead of HPFS can cause slower access than DOS. It also gives OS/2 systems added security and better file-error correction.

NTFS

When designing NFTS, Microsoft learned from its experiences. It borrowed heavily on what it had done right with HPFS but designed out the limitations described earlier. Unlike FAT or HPFS, there are no "special" objects on the disk and there is no dependence on the underlying hardware, such as 512-byte sectors. In addition, there are no special locations on the disk, such as FAT tables or HPFS super blocks.

Microsoft also went back to the FAT concept of clusters in order to avoid the HPFS problem of a fixed sector size. This was done because NT is a portable operating system and different disk technology is likely to be encountered at some point. Therefore, 512 bytes per sector is viewed as having a large possibility of not always being a good fit for the allocation. Microsoft avoided fixed sector size by allowing the cluster to be defined as multiples of the hardware's natural allocation size.

NTFS has the capability to address extremely large media and introduces the NT security features. To NT, files are objects with attributes, and the new NTFS has to treat files as objects and stores the attributes in the object itself—the file. NTFS also knows whether a file is an executable and marks it as execute-only so that no virus can easily attach itself.

Each volume has a *master file table* (MFT), as shown in Figure 5.5. MFTs contain information on each file on the volume; a large volume has multiple MFTs. To provide redundancy, each MFT has a mirror-copy capability. This mirror lies within the volume at its midpoint to provide redundancy. The MFT is a database of records. The first 16 records describe the MFT itself, followed by records for each file or directory. If a file is small (less than 1,500 bytes) it is written right into the MFT data field. This field for larger files contains index pointers to the actual data. These pointers again are called *extents* and point out just the location of external clusters that make up the data. Directories are just a file of indexes to other records (the files in the directory).

FIGURE 5.5.

The master file table (MFT).

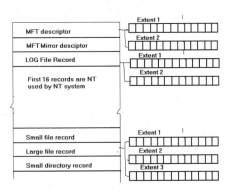

So what you have is the capability to find small files immediately because they exist in the MFT database itself (as resident files). You also can find large files via extents and the B-tree structure (these are nonresident files).

An MFT is a database of records, and each record has fields that allow NTFS to use subsystems, such as POSIX, OS/2, and WIN32. Because files are treated as objects, an object might not have all the possible attributes. A user can design files with new attributes particular to her needs (Table 5.1 lists these attributes). This also allows for variances such as POSIX's use of case-sensitive file names. An object for the POSIX subsystem may have attributes meaningful only to that subsystem. This built-in extendibility enables transaction-based operations to implement their own fault tolerance, version control, multiple data streams, and future higher levels of file security.

Table 5.1. NT attributes.

Attribute	Description
Attribute list	Lists all other attributes in large files only
Bitmap	Map of records in use on the MFT
Data	One unnamed data attribute and as many as needed named data attributes
Extended attribute	Not used by NT for OS/2 consistency
Extended attribute info	Not used by NT for OS/2 consistency
Filename	Up to 255 Unicode characters
Index allocation	Directory files
Index root	Directory files
Security descriptor	Permissions and ownership
Standard information	Timestamps, link count (POSIX), file size
Volume information	Used only in volume system file and includes the version and name of volume

The record in Figure 5.6 shows the basic NT attributes that every file has; OS/2 and POSIX have added attributes that are particular to their subsystem needs. Future subsystems add their own set of attributes. A link count and a hard link occurs when two different file names, which can be located in different directories, point to the same data. These are used by the POSIX subsystem.

FIGURE 5.6.

An MFT record layout.

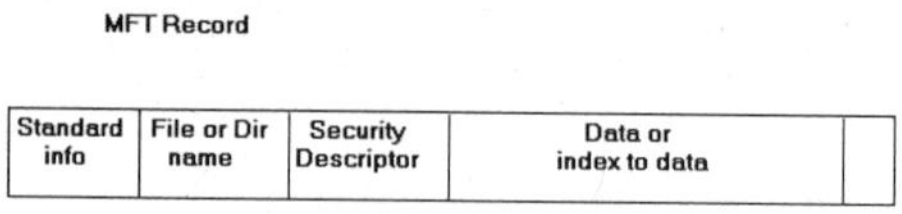

MFT Record

Standard info	File or Dir name	Security Descriptor	Data or index to data	

Streams is a concept that you will hear more about in the future. The easiest example of a stream is in multimedia applications in which you play an .AVI file and the sound comes from one of several streams: the English language stream, the French stream, and so on. When your application reads the .AVI file, it specifies which stream to read. You can think of a stream object as a *smart file* that acts as a source and destination for bytes. A stream's characteristics are determined by its class and by customized insertion and extraction operators. Data can be coming in and going out at the same time. Every database management system uses a logical stream of data in which each user is reading and writing data.

Windows NT also supports *sector sparing*. In this technique, when a drive is formatted, all sectors on the drive are verified. Bad sectors are mapped out and not used. Spare sectors are set aside and used to replace those that are mapped out. When NT writes to the drive, every write is verified when using sector sparing. If NT detects a bad write due to the sector being bad, it maps out the sector and writes to one of the spare sectors instead.

NTFS is a recoverable file system because it keeps track of transactions against the file system. When a CHKDSK is performed on FAT or HPFS, the consistency of pointers within the directory, allocation, and file tables is checked. Under NTFS, a log of transactions against these components is maintained so that CHKDSK only needs to roll back transactions to the last point where transactions were written to the drive as committed (commit point) in order to recover consistency within the file system. NT supports hot fixing.

Each time you boot Windows NT, it performs an autocheck routine on the NTFS volume. If this routine detects an error, it runs the CHKDSK /f command to fix the inconsistency or error.

> **NOTE**
>
> It is normal for CHKDSK to report consistency errors on an NTFS drive containing the page file.

As long as no specific files are listed as damaged and no other errors are detected, the volume is marked as clean. You rarely need to run CHKDSK /f from the command line in this case, and NT has designated that you need Administrator privileges to run CHKDSK. If the CHKDSK command locates files or directories that have lost pointers to their parent directory, they are named FILExxx.CHK and DIRxxx.CHK and are housed in the FOUNDxxx directory of the NTFS volume.

When you format an NTFS volume, the system files are written to the volume and hidden. Table 5.2 lists the system files.

Table 5.2. The NTFS system files.

File	Purpose
$.	Root file name index, the root directory
$AttrDef	Attribute definition file
$BadClus	A table of bad clusters on the volume
$BitMap	A map of allocation units in use
$Boot	The bootstrap program file
$Logfile	Transaction steps used in data recovery
$Mft	Master file table
$MftMirr	Mirror of master file table
$Volume	Volume information, name, and version

NTFS is used only by Windows NT. It supports files and directories with up to 255 extended attributes. It automatically generates 8.3 DOS file names. It is much more reliable with the transaction log file which allows you to return to the last point at which the file system was intact then restore transactions occurring after that point. Security is built into the file system and is extendible as NT grows. DOS, POSIX, and OS/2 subsystems can access the NTFS files.

File and directory names can contain up to 255 characters, including any extensions. Names preserve case but are not case sensitive. NTFS makes no distinction of file names based on case. Names can contain any characters except for the following:

```
?   "   /   \   <   >   *   ¦   :
```

When converting a long file name to 8.3, NT uses the first six characters in the file name, followed by a tilde (~), and then a number 1 through 4 to designate similar named files. If you have more than four similar names, NT switches to a naming convention in which it uses the first two characters, followed by a four-character hash value based on file size, date and time, a tilde, and a number 5 through 9.

Some examples of these file names follow:

NTFS long file name	8.3 file name
ODBCCursor1.cpp	ODBCCU~1.cpp
ODBCCursor2.cpp	ODBCCU~2.cpp
ODBCCursor3.cpp	ODBCCU~3.cpp
ODBCCursor4.cpp	ODBCCU~4.cpp
ODBCCursor5.cpp	ODD942~5.cpp <- notice the switch
ODBCCursor6.cpp	ODDD42~5.cpp <- only uses first two characters

NTFS suffers from overhead space problems on volumes of less than 400 MB. The space overhead for NTFS is 4 MB for each 100 MB of files. In versions of NT prior to 4.0 you could not format a floppy disk as NTFS. As a default, NT still uses FAT formatting for floppy disks. With the introduction of the 144 MB floppy, NT 4.0 actually can format an NTFS floppy disk.

One of the major design goals of Windows NT at every level is to provide a platform that can be added to and built upon, and NTFS is no exception. NTFS provides a rich and flexible platform for other file systems to be able to use.

In addition, NTFS fully supports the Windows NT security model and multiple data streams. Because, in the past, it has been possible to boot under DOS and use low-level tools to examine data on an NTFS volume, NT 4.0 introduced a data-encryption API. No longer is a data file a single stream of data. Finally, under NTFS, a user can add her own user-defined attributes to a file. Table 5.3 shows a comparison of the different file systems.

Table 5.3. A comparison of FAT, HPFS, and NTFS.

Attribute	FAT	HPFS	NTFS
File names	8.3	254 ASCII	255 Unicode
Max path length	64	No limit	No limit
File size in bytes	2E32	2E32	2E64
Partition size in bytes	2E32	2E41	2E64
Fastest drives	<200 MB	200–400 MB	>400 MB
Directories	unsorted	B-tree	B-tree
Operating systems	DOS, OS/2, NT	OS/2, NT versions prior to 4.0	NT, NT's OS/2, or POSIX subsystems
Attributes	Bit flags	Bit flags plus 64 KB extent	All info treated as attribute
NT security	No	No	Yes
Design	Simple	Fast	Fast, secure, recoverable

Performing Disk Operations

NT and Win32's Winbase.h has a good number of functions to access the NTFS file system. In Chapter 14, "Files," you look closely at doing file I/O. This section lists the file functions available and their parameters. In disk operations, you can find out what drives are available, their names, and the amount of available free space.

Listing 5.1. Disk operations.

```
DWORD GetLogicalDrives();

DWORD GetLogicalDriveStrings(DWORD cchBuffer, LPTSTR lpszBuffer);

BOOL GetVolumeInformation(
    LPCTSTR lpRootPathName,              // address of root directory of
                                         //   the file system
    LPTSTR lpVolumeNameBuffer,           // address of name of the volume
    DWORD nVolumeNameSize,               // length of lpVolumeNameBuffer
```

continues

Listing 5.1. continued

```
    LPDWORD lpVolumeSerialNumber,            // address of volume serial
                                             // number
    LPDWORD lpMaximumComponentLength,        // address of system's maximum
                                             // filename length
    LPDWORD lpFileSystemFlags,               // address of file system flags
    LPTSTR lpFileSystemNameBuffer,           // address of name of file system
    DWORD nFileSystemNameSize                // length of
                                             // lpFileSystemNameBuffer
    );

BOOL GetDiskFreeSpace(
    LPCTSTR lpRootPathName,                  // address of root path
    LPDWORD lpSectorsPerCluster,             // address of sectors per cluster
    LPDWORD lpBytesPerSector,                // address of bytes per sector
    LPDWORD lpNumberOfFreeClusters,          // address of number of free
                                             // clusters
    LPDWORD lpTotalNumberOfClusters          // address of total number of
                                             // clusters
    );
```

Performing Directory Operations

Every process has a current directory associated with it. When you create a process, the current directory is inherited from the parent process. In addition, the system files are stored in a directory and NT 4.0 is stored in the Windows directory (C:\WINNT). You can manipulate the directory by using the code shown in Listing 5.2.

Listing 5.2. API directory functions.

```
DWORD GetCurrentDirectory(DWORD cchCurDir, LPTSTR lpszCurDir);

BOOL SetCurrentDirectory(LPTSTR lpszCurDir);

UINT GetSystemDirectory(LPTSTR lpszSysPath, UINT cchSysPath);

UINT GetWindowsDirectory(LPTSTR lpszWinPath, UINT cchWinPath);

BOOL CreateDirectory(LPTSTR lpszPath, LPSECURITY_ATTRIBUTES lpsa);
typedef struct _SECURITY_ATTRIBUTES { // structure for security attributes
    DWORD   nLength;
    LPVOID  lpSecurityDescriptor;
    BOOL    bInheritHandle;
} SECURITY_ATTRIBUTES;

BOOL RemoveDirectory(LPTSTR lpszDir);
```

Performing File Operations

To manipulate files, Win32 has the functions shown in Listing 5.3. To rename a file, move the file from its old name to its new name and location. Unfortunately, none of the following calls supports wild cards (* or ?).

Listing 5.3. API file functions.

```
BOOL CopyFile(LPTSTR lpszExistingFile, LPTSTR lpszNewFile, BOOL fFailIfExists);

BOOL DeleteFile(LPTSTR lpszFileName);

BOOL MoveFile(LPTSTR lpszExisting, LPTSTR lpszNew);

BOOL MoveFileEx(LPTSTR lpszExisting , LPTSTR lpszNew, DWORD fdwFlags);
```

The `fdwFlags` parameter can be:

- `MOVEFILE_REPLACE_EXISTING`   If a file of the name specified by `lpNewFileName` already exists, the function replaces its contents with those specified by `lpExistingFileName`.
- `MOVEFILE_COPY_ALLOWED`   If the file is to be moved to a different volume, the function simulates the move by using the `CopyFile` and `DeleteFile` functions. Cannot be combined with the `MOVEFILE_DELAY_UNTIL_REBOOT` flag.
- `MOVEFILE_DELAY_UNTIL_REBOOT`   Windows NT only: The function does not move the file until the operating system is restarted. The system moves the file immediately after AUTOCHK is executed, but before creating any paging files. Consequently, this parameter enables the function to delete paging files from previous startups.

Creating, Opening, Reading, and Closing Files

In the previous chapter, you learned about the `CreateFile` function and the extended functionality it has over `Openfile`, `_lcreate`, and `_lopen` (its Windows predecessors). The `ReadFileEx` and `WriteFileEx` functions allow for asynchronous I/O, in which you pass the address of the completion routine. Listing 5.4 shows the syntax of these function calls.

Listing 5.4. API file functions.

```
HANDLE CreateFile(
    LPCTSTR lpFileName,                          // pointer to name of
                                                 //   the file

    DWORD dwDesiredAccess,                       // access (read-write)
                                                 //   mode
```

continues

Listing 5.4. continued

```
        DWORD dwShareMode,                                      // share mode
        LPSECURITY_ATTRIBUTES lpSecurityAttributes,            // pointer to security
                                                                  descriptor
        DWORD dwCreationDistribution,                          // how to create
        DWORD dwFlagsAndAttributes,                            // file attributes
        HANDLE hTemplateFile                                   // handle to file with
                                                                  attributes to copy
        );

BOOL ReadFile(
        HANDLE hFile,                       // handle of file to read
        LPVOID lpBuffer,                    // address of buffer that receives data
        DWORD nNumberOfBytesToRead,       // number of bytes to read
        LPDWORD lpNumberOfBytesRead,                    // address of number of
                                                           bytes read
        LPOVERLAPPED lpOverlapped                       // address of structure for
                                                           data
        );

BOOL ReadFileEx(
        HANDLE hFile,                       // handle of file to read
        LPVOID lpBuffer,                    // address of buffer
        DWORD nNumberOfBytesToRead,                    // number of bytes to read
        LPOVERLAPPED lpOverlapped,                     // address of offset
        LPOVERLAPPED_COMPLETION_ROUTINE lpCompletionRoutine
                                                       // address of completion routine
        );

BOOL WriteFile(
        HANDLE hFile,                       // handle to file to write to
        LPCVOID lpBuffer,                   // pointer to data to write to file
        DWORD nNumberOfBytesToWrite,                   // number of bytes to write
        LPDWORD lpNumberOfBytesWritten,                // pointer to number of
                                                          bytes written
        LPOVERLAPPED lpOverlapped                      // addr. of structure needed
                                                          for overlapped I/O
        );

BOOL WriteFileEx(
        HANDLE hFile,                       // handle to output file
        LPCVOID lpBuffer,                   // pointer to input buffer
        DWORD nNumberOfBytesToWrite,                   // number of bytes to write
        LPOVERLAPPED lpOverlapped,                     // pointer to async. i/o data
        LPOVERLAPPED_COMPLETION_ROUTINE lpCompletionRoutine
                                                       // ptr. to completion routine
        };

DWORD SetFilePointer(
        HANDLE hFile,                       // handle of file
        LONG lDistanceToMove,                          // number of bytes to move file
                                                          pointer
        PLONG lpDistanceToMoveHigh,                    // address of high-order word
                                                          of distance to move
        DWORD dwMoveMethod                  // how to move
        );
```

```
BOOL SetEndOfFile(HANDLE hFile);

BOOL FlushFileBuffers(HANDLE hFile);

BOOL LockFile(
    HANDLE hFile,                       // handle of file to lock
        DWORD dwFileOffsetLow,                  // low-order word of lock region
                                                    offset
        DWORD dwFileOffsetHigh,                 // high-order word of lock region
                                                    offset
        DWORD nNumberOfBytesToLockLow,              // low-order word of
                                                        length to lock
        DWORD nNumberOfBytesToLockHigh          // high-order word of
                                                    length to lock
    );

BOOL UnlockFile(
    HANDLE hFile,                       // handle of file to unlock
        DWORD dwFileOffsetLow,                  // low-order word of lock region
                                                    offset
        DWORD dwFileOffsetHigh,                 // high-order word of lock region
                                                    offset
        DWORD nNumberOfBytesToUnlockLow,            // low-order word of
                                                        length to unlock
        DWORD nNumberOfBytesToUnlockHigh        // high-order word of
                                                    length to unlock
    );
```

Chapters 14, "Files," and 15, "Printing," make extensive use of these calls in performing file I/O. This section just lists the file I/O functions in one place and introduces their functionality.

RAID Arrays

NT Server provides for software fault tolerance by using disk mirroring, disk striping with parity, and sector sparing. Fault tolerance generally is done in software in an NT Server or by special RAID arrays of drivers, which can be used on NT Workstation as well. Before you dive into *redundant arrays of inexpensive disks* (RAID), you should examine more basic redundancy methods, such as backup and uninterrupted power supplies (UPSs).

NT backup enables you to perform the following types of backups:

- **Full:** Backs up all files on the drive and is the NT default or normal backup.
- **Incremental:** Backs up only the files that have been changed since the last full or incremental backup session.
- **Differential:** Backs up all the files changed since the last full backup.
- **Custom:** Backs up only the files you select to back up.
- **Daily:** Backs up only files that were modified that day.

■ **Copy:** Backs up the files that do not have their archive bit set. Your paging file, the Registry, and files that are locked by an application's use are not backed up.

As I recently found out the hard way, NT backup does not back up the Registry on remote computers. The Registry always is open, and you need to use REGBACK and REGREST from the NT Resource Kit. You also can use the RDISK.EXE tool, which uses the Emergency Repair disk to fix a broken NT installation.

NT UPS support enables you to define on which serial port the UPS messages are received. The software is set up from a Control Panel applet, and you configure it with the characteristics of the UPS, such as battery life, recharge time, time between power failure and warning, and the delay between warning messages. You also can designate a .CMD file to execute when the UPS service initiates power shutdown. You can start and stop the UPS service by using the Services option of the Control Panel. Or, you can use the NET START UP, NET STOP UPS, NET PAUSE UPS, and NET CONTINUE UPS commands from the command line.

This section is really about RAID, but it is important that you have in place the basics, such as a good backup scheme and a UPS prior to other data-redundancy techniques. RAID is not intended to replace backups.

NT supports hardware RAID devices from Conner, Micropolis, Professional Concept, and Storage Solutions. As RAID becomes increasingly more important, more companies will release clusters of drives to be used as RAID Arrays. SCSI devices are available that have RAID built into the controller's ROM. They can be used with NT Workstation or NT Server.

NT Server also can implement RAID in software, supporting RAID levels 0, 1, and 5. You will look at each of the levels; in order to understand level 5, you have to understand the concepts of the prior levels.

RAID first was proposed in 1987 as a way an array of disks could improve reliability of data and increase disk performance. Disk drives always have been a bottleneck to computers. Table 5.4 lists the six levels of RAID.

Table 5.4. RAID levels.

RAID Level	Description
0	Disk striping for performance
1	Disk mirroring
2	Bit-level striping with error-correction code (ECC)
3	Byte-level striping with ECC as parity
4	Block-level striping with parity on one drive
5	Block-level striping with distributed parity blocks

The basic concept in RAID is that of striping: writing a part of the data to one drive and another part to another drive. By writing to two or more drives simultaneously, performance is enhanced. Each drive is working independently of the other, so data is transferred in parallel to multiple drives at the same time. At its most basic level, if data is written to three drives simultaneously, it can be written three times as fast.

By combining a check byte, you can improve the reliability of the data written. You can design the check byte so that if one drive fails, data can be restored from the remaining drives, therefore providing redundancy. This section examines each level.

RAID Level 0

Level 0 is for performance only. The data simply is split into stripes and written to two or more drives in a parallel fashion illustrated in Figure 5.7. If there are *n* drives, the data is written in $1/n$ time. There is no check byte or redundancy provided—just speed.

FIGURE 5.7.
RAID level 0.

RAID Level 1

Level 1 is called *disk mirroring*. Here, the same data is written to two drives simultaneously. This does not give the speed improvement of level 0 because all the data is written to both drives. The level 1 advantage is redundancy; if one drive crashes, the data also exists on the other drive. RAID actually defined striping of the drives at level 1, but NT level 1 simply mirrors the data to the second drive.

To implement RAID level 1, you need two drives of the same speed and size. The only performance benefit is when you use a controller that can read and write independently. This design leads to speed improvements because a read request is completed by the first drive that can get the results. Disk mirroring often is referred to as *disk duplexing*. Notice in Figure 5.8 that this only protects your data if a single drive fails and doesn't protect it if the controller fails. It is not a substitute for doing daily backups, but it does provide a high level of redundancy because all data is written in two places.

NT also supports hot fixing with mirror sets. When the NT mirror support code encounters a sector-read error on one drive of the mirror set, it corrects the error if the underlying hardware supports this (SCSI drives support). After correcting the error on one of the drives, the mirror set code returns an informational status to the file system, indicating that the data was recovered by reading from the secondary drive. This informational status causes NTFS to scan both drives of the mirror set for faulty sectors (including the secondary drive, which the mirror set code did not scan for faulty sectors). If faulty sectors are located on the secondary drive, NTFS maps this sector for use at the file system level instead of having the mirror set code map it for use at the hardware level.

FIGURE 5.8.

RAID level 1 disk mirroring.

RAID Level 2

Level 2 seldom is used in microcomputers, but I will use level 2 to illustrate the concept of RAID's data redundancy. A bit is written to drive 1, the second bit is written to drive 2, and the XOR value of the bits is written to drive 3. XOR stands for an *exclusive OR* operation which works like this: if bit 1 is a 1 and bit 2 is a 0, then on drive 3, the ECC bit (XOR value) is a 1. Figure 5.9 graphically displays level 2 RAID. If drive 2 would fail, you still recover the data from bit 1 on drive 1 and the ECC bit on drive 3 by applying another XOR operation. ECC is error-correcting code and the most basic is the XOR method.

FIGURE 5.9.

Raid level 2 bit with ECC.

RAID Level 3

Level 3 is the same thing by using bytes of data instead of bits of data. Again the values are combined with XOR to give the value written to drive 3.

```
Data drive 1          11110011
Data drive 2          11101100
XOR drive 3           00011111
```

If drive 2 fails, you still can read its data by using drive 1's data and the XOR drive's data—again, doing a second XOR to get back to 11101100 as in this illustration.

```
Data drive 1          11110011
Data drive 3          00011111
XOR recovery          11101100 voila the original data on drive 2
```

Level 3 is not actually used by NT Server; it is just used here as an example upon which to build on how RAID provides redundancy.

RAID Level 4

Level 4 uses blocks of data as the stripes. A *block* is the amount of data in a single read/write operation. Drive 3, in this case, holds a parity check on that block. The parity check is just the XOR values of all the bytes in the block. The layout is the same as in level 3, with the last drive containing all the parity information. In Figure 5.10 you can see the parity data is still all written to one drive. Level 4 is not used by NT Server, but NT uses blocks as the stripes in RAID level 5.

FIGURE 5.10.

RAID level 4.

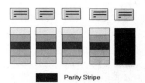

Parity Stripe

RAID Level 5

Level 5 normally is referred to simply as *RAID*. When you hear of RAID arrays, they usually are hardware. NT Server implements RAID level 5 in software. The error-correcting parity stripe is distributed across all the drives as in Figure 5.11. You can use a set of similar IDE (integrated device electronics) drives to implement this type of RAID, but SCSI (Small Computer Systems Interface) drives are more reliable, provide hot fixing, are more flexible, and are recommended by Microsoft. Notice that this approach gives both speed improvements and data redundancy.

FIGURE 5.11.

RAID level 5.

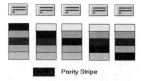

Parity Stripe

In RAID level 5, each stripe is a block (the amount of data in one read/write operation). The parity stripes are interwoven across all the drives. Any one drive can fail and the data still is available from the other drives. Five drives normally are used as a RAID array.

Disk mirroring and RAID are set up on NT Server using the Disk Administrator. You select the first partition, press and hold down the Ctrl key to select the next partition, and then use the options on the Fault Tolerance menu. If you have an error in a mirrored set, you need to go into Disk Administrator and choose Break Mirror. To regenerate a RAID level 5 set, you use Regenerate. Again, these methods provide a higher level of data redundancy and data speed in transfer, but are no substitute for daily backups.

RAID level 0, disk striping, is optimized for performance only, whereas RAID level 5, disk striping with parity, offers a configuration that provides both high performance and fault tolerance using data redundancy. If you require optimum performance as well as data redundancy, you should configure your stripe set for RAID level 5. Microsoft recommends that you low-level format your disk(s) before you begin. You can implement RAID level 0 from both a Windows NT Workstation computer and Windows NT Server computer. You can run RAID level 5 from the Windows NT Server operating system only, because it implements fault tolerance.

Summary

This has been a general review of NT's file system options. You looked at the format in which data is actually stored on the media and the advances in NTFS that make it the file system for your future.

The past five chapters (Part 1) have described the architecture of Windows NT 4.0 as a basis for learning to write NT software. Although a few API function calls were listed, it was done to illustrate what is available, not as documenting the functions usage. In the remainder of the entire book you will be actually developing software that takes advantage of the new features in NT 4.0.

We begin immediately in Part II, "Programming the WinNT Desktop," with an introduction to Visual C++ 4.0 and MFC 4.0. This is the programming environment for the remainder of this book. In Part II you learn to write software with the new look of NT 4.0.

PART

II

Programming the WinNT Desktop

Visual C++ 4.0 and the Microsoft Foundation Classes

6

by Mickey Williams

IN THIS CHAPTER

In this chapter I discuss Developer Studio, the Visual C++ development environment, and how it can be used to create great Windows NT Workstation and Server applications. In addition to the actual development environment, I discuss the basic architecture of the MFC class library and how it can be used to simplify creating Windows NT applications. I also discuss how Developer Studio can easily be integrated with other tools you may already own, including tools made by third parties.

I include a discussion on creating custom AppWizards. Using a custom AppWizard is a great way to tailor Visual C++ so that it meets your exact needs. A custom AppWizard that you can add to your Developer Studio environment is created and is included on the CD that accompanies this book.

The Visual C++ Developer Studio

The central part of the Visual C++ package is the Developer Studio. Developer Studio is an Integrated Development Environment (IDE) where you can edit, compile, and debug your application without needing to launch several different tools.

Tools Included with Developer Studio

Developer Studio includes a number of tools you can use to create applications for Windows NT. Until recently, you would have purchased many of these tools separately; integrating them into your development environment would have been up to you. Today, all the tools you need to create great Windows NT workstation and server applications come in one package:

- An advanced C++ compiler includes many of the latest ANSI C++ enhancements, including support for Runtime Type Identification, templates, and namespaces.

- An integrated editor mimics several different popular editors, including Brief. If you're a long time Brief or Epsilon user, you'll be able to remap the Developer Studio editor to follow the keyboard commands you're accustomed to.

- With Component Gallery you can store, organize, and reuse software in your projects. One of the primary uses of Component Gallery is to store OLE Custom Controls.

- An integrated debugger enables you to step through your source code and check for errors. Because the debugger is part of Developer Studio, it's easy to correct an error in the source code, recompile, and resume testing. As will be discussed later, you can also attach the debugger to a process that is already running or use Just In Time (JIT) debugging to launch the debugger after a program crashes.

Integration with Other Tools

Beginning with Visual C++ 4.0, the IDE can be integrated with other Microsoft tools, including Microsoft Test and the *Microsoft Developer's Network* (MSDN). MSDN is a subscription service that keeps you updated with information about developing applications for Windows 95 and Windows NT. The integration with MSDN is especially helpful because you can search for help using either the MSDN contents or the Developer Studio online help.

Integrating Visual Source Safe with Developer Studio

If you write software as part of a team, you probably use some sort of source code control tool. With source code control you can track changes to your source code modules and ensure that only one person is modifying a source file at any given time.

Microsoft's source code management tool, Visual Source Safe, can be integrated into Developer Studio. This integration makes it easy to check out and update files without leaving the Developer Studio environment. For example, you can check out files directly from the File View display in the project workspace; files that are already checked out are displayed with a checkmark, as shown in Figure 6.1.

FIGURE 6.1.

Visual Source Safe integrates with Developer Studio.

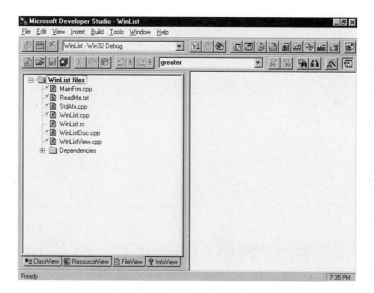

Figure 6.1 also includes the file properties dialog box. At the bottom edge of the dialog box, notice that it displays the current source code control status for the file; the `MainFrame.cpp` file is checked out for exclusive use.

Many other source code control tool vendors are expected to make use of the same interfaces used by Visual Source Safe in their new versions now that Visual C++ 4 has been released. If you have written a custom-made, in-house source code management system, you're out of luck; these API's have only been exposed to commercial tool vendors.

Integrating BoundsChecker with Developer Studio

In addition to Microsoft, other companies offer development tools that can be integrated with Developer Studio. BoundsChecker from NuMega Technologies is one such tool. It is a tool that checks your program for memory leaks, misuse of pointers, and verifies API calls.

When BoundsChecker and Visual C++ are installed on the same machine, BoundsChecker adds items to the tools menu that make it possible to launch and configure BoundsChecker without leaving Developer Studio. BoundsChecker also adds a new BoundsChecker toolbar, as shown in Figure 6.2.

FIGURE 6.2.

The BoundsChecker toolbar in Developer Studio.

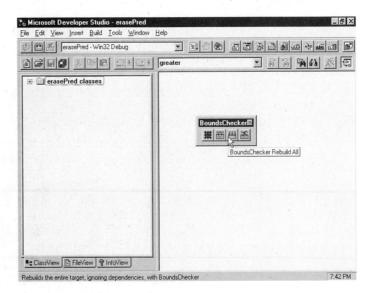

The Microsoft Foundation Classes

The Microsoft Foundation Classes help to simplify the task of writing programs in two ways.

First, the MFC class library provides a simplified wrapper around the Windows NT API. Many of the objects and function calls are much easier to use, primarily due to the use of C++ features such as inheritance and default parameters. Of course, you could write your own classes, but MFC 4 includes more than 150 fully documented classes.

Second, the MFC class library supplies a number of high-level abstractions that you can take advantage of by using just a few lines of code. For example, the OLE source code alone approaches 100,000 lines of C++ code.

Classes Included in MFC 4.0

Visual C++ 4 includes version 4.0 of the Microsoft Foundation Classes (MFC), a class library that makes programming for Windows NT much easier. Most of the MFC classes fall into these major categories:

- Application Architecture, which includes classes that help provide the basic plumbing for applications written using MFC.
- Dialog boxes, which are derived from CDialog, a basic dialog box class. This category includes classes that handle the common dialog boxes included in Windows NT.
- Views, which are used in the Document/View architecture to represent the program's output. Classes that support scrolling, editing, and windows based on dialog boxes are included in this category.
- Controls, which are used to provide easy access to all the controls offered by Windows 95 and Windows NT. Included in this category are classes that manage tree controls, list views, and combo boxes.
- Graphics Objects, used for creating the output in a Windows program. This category includes classes for pens, brushes, icons, and bitmaps.
- Exceptions, which are used to indicate that an unexpected event has occurred during a program's execution.
- Collections, a special type of class that is used to contain objects from another class. Some of the collection classes offered in the MFC class library are template based, which allows them to be used with almost any object.
- OLE classes, which are used to provide support for creating OLE-aware applications.
- Miscellaneous classes, which include classes for strings, rectangles, and WOSA services such as socket-based communication and MAPI.

By using the MFC classes when you write programs for Windows NT, you are able to take advantage of a large amount of source code that has been written for you. You can concentrate on writing the important parts of your code instead of worrying about the details of Windows programming.

Installing Visual C++

The first step toward using Visual C++ is to install it on your computer. Like all well-behaved programs written for Windows NT, Visual C++ is installed using a Windows-based setup program. When the Visual C++ CD is initially inserted into a local CD drive, an autorun startup dialog box is displayed. One option offered by this dialog box is to install Visual C++. Alternatively, you can begin setup from the Start menu. To launch the setup program, follow these steps:

1. Press the Start button on the task bar and select Run.
2. When the Run dialog box is displayed, press the button labeled Browse.
3. When the Browse dialog box is displayed, go to the root directory for the CD drive, usually D: or E:.
4. Go to the \Msdev directory and select the Setup program icon.
5. Close the Browse dialog box and close the Run dialog box by pressing the button labeled OK. This will start the Visual C++ setup wizard.

Using the Setup Wizard

Most setup programs for applications written for Windows NT use a setup wizard. A setup wizard is an easy-to-use tool that guides the user through the installation process. With a setup wizard a user can navigate forward and backward through the setup process. The user can also ask for help or cancel the setup process at any time.

The opening screen for the Visual C++ setup wizard displays a welcome message and explains the setup process in general terms. This screen has no user options as it's only used to introduce the setup program.

Pressing the button labeled Next> displays the next screen, which is a software licensing agreement for the Visual C++ compiler. This screen must be dismissed by pressing either the button labeled Yes or the button labeled No. Pressing the No button stops the installation process; the Yes button allows the installation to continue.

The next screen collects user information. On this screen, you should enter your name, your company or organization's name, and the CD key that is located on the CD package or liner notes. This information will be displayed in the Developer Studio startup screen and also in the About box.

The next screen presents a list of installation options. The option you select depends on the amount of free space on your hard disk, as well as the types of programs that will be developed using Visual C++. The installation options for Visual C++ are

- Typical, which installs the most commonly used Developer Studio and Visual C++ components and leaves the remaining components on the CD. This option requires slightly more than 107M of disk space.
- Minimum, which installs only components that are absolutely required. This option requires approximately 70M of disk space.

■ CD, which installs only Developer Studio to the hard disk and assumes that the Visual C++ CD is always available. The compiler and all libraries remain on the CD, so that this installation uses only about 10M of disk storage.

■ Custom, with which you can pick the options to be installed on your hard disk. If you use this option, you can specify which components are immediately available on the hard disk and which items must be fetched from the CD. The best response time for Developer Studio and its tools is obtained by installing all components to the hard disk, which will take up about 250M of disk space.

If you don't remember exactly how much space is available on your hard drive, don't worry; this setup wizard displays the amount of space required for each option and the amount of free space available on the hard drive. If you select an option and find later that you need more components installed on the hard drive, you can add Visual C++ components at any time by running the setup program again or by running the Control Panel Add/Remove Programs applet.

After selecting the installation option, the next page is used to tell you how the installation will proceed. To begin the installation, press the button labeled Next. The setup wizard copies files needed for Visual C++, as indicated by the installation options you selected earlier.

When all files have been copied to your hard disk, the setup wizard adds the Microsoft Visual C++ 4.0 group to your Program menu and adds several icons for Developer Studio and other programs to it. This completes the installation process.

What's Not Installed

The Visual C++ CD includes a special version of InstallShield, a program used to create setup programs similar to the one used to setup Visual C++. To set up InstallShield, run its setup program, located in the `\Ishield\Disk1` directory.

The Visual C++ CD includes the Standard Template Library, or STL, a set of algorithms and classes that are part of the ANSI C++ Draft Standard. The STL is located in the `\Stl` directory on the Visual C++ CD. There is no setup program, but installing and using the STL is discussed in Chapter 9, "Standard Template Library Programming."

The Visual C++ CD also includes the following tools:

■ Crystal Reports, a report generator library that includes MFC-compatible classes. This is a "light" version of the full product.

■ The MFC Migration Kit, which helps move your applications written in C to MFC and C++.

■ The Data Access Objects (DAO) SDK.

■ WinCIM, the Windows-based interface used to access CompuServe.

■ A demo of BoundsChecker Pro from NuMega.

With the exception of the MFC Migration Kit, none of these optional applications are installed by default. Use the Visual C++ main setup screen to install each of these applications, as needed.

Building Applications Using Visual C++ and MFC

In addition to tools that are used for debugging, editing, and creating resources, Developer Studio includes five "wizards" that are used to simplify developing your windows programs:

- AppWizard, used to create the basic outline of a Windows program. Three types of programs are supported by AppWizard: Single Document and Multiple Document applications based on the Document/View architecture and dialog box-based programs, where a dialog box serves as the applications' main window.

- MFC DLL AppWizard, used to create DLLs that use the MFC class library. Three types of DLL projects are supported: regular DLLs that use static linking to MFC, regular DLLs dynamically linked to MFC, and extension DLLs, that are always dynamically linked to MFC.

- Custom AppWizard, which allows you to create your own customized AppWizards. A custom AppWizard can be created from scratch based on an existing AppWizard type or based on an existing project. Later in this chapter, I create a custom AppWizard.

- ClassWizard, used to define the classes used in a program created with AppWizard. Using ClassWizard, you can add classes to your project. You can also add functions that control how messages received by each class are handled. ClassWizard also helps to manage controls that are contained in dialog boxes, by allowing you to associate an MFC object or class member variable with each control.

- OLE ControlWizard, used to create the basic framework of an OLE control. An OLE control is a customized control that supports a defined set of interfaces and is used as a reusable component. OLE controls replace Visual Basic Controls or VBXs that were used in 16-bit versions of Windows.

AppWizard Builds Skeleton Applications

As discussed previously, Developer Studio includes a tool, AppWizard, that is used for creating a skeleton application. AppWizard asks you a series of questions about your program and then generates a project and much of the source code for you, allowing you to concentrate on the code that makes your program unique.

Even if you use the MFC class library, there is still a learning curve before you can write a moderately sized Windows NT program with it. In addition, much of the code that is used as a starting point for many Windows programs is generic, "skeleton" code similar for all Windows applications.

The MFC class library is built around the Document/View programming model. Using AppWizard to create the skeleton code for your program is the quickest way to get started writing Document/View programs.

A Quick Overview of the Document/View Architecture

The AppWizard uses MFC classes to create applications that are based on the MFC Document/View architecture. The basic idea behind Document/View is to separate the data handling classes from the classes that handle the user interface.

Separating the data from the user interface allows each of the classes to concentrate on performing one job, with a set of interfaces defined for interaction with the other classes involved in the program. A view class is responsible for providing a "viewport" through which you can see and manage the document. A document class is responsible for controlling all the data, including storing it when necessary. Figure 6.3 shows how the document and view classes interact with each other.

FIGURE 6.3.

The Document/View architecture.

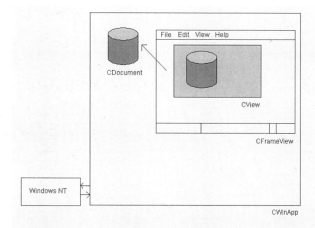

I discuss the Document/View architecture in detail in Chapter 7, "Document/View Architecture." For now, just be aware that there are four main "super classes" used in a Document/View application:

- The document class, which controls the data used by an application. The data doesn't have to be an actual page of text; for example, a spreadsheet or project plan can easily be represented as a document.
- The view class, used to display information about the document to the user and to handle any interaction that is required between the user and the document.
- The frame class, used to physically contain the view, menu, toolbar, and other physical elements of the program.
- The application class, which controls the application-level interaction with Windows.

In addition to these four classes, we discuss in Chapter 7 some specialized classes that are used in Document/View programs.

How to Use AppWizard

The first step in using AppWizard is to create a new project workspace. Begin by selecting New from the File menu and select Project Workspace from the New dialog box. When the New Project Workspace dialog box appears, select MFC AppWizard (exe) as the type. You must also specify a name and a location for your project, such as \MSDEV\Projects\Hello. Click the Create button to start AppWizard.

The opening screen for AppWizard is shown in Figure 6.4.

FIGURE 6.4.

The opening screen for AppWizard.

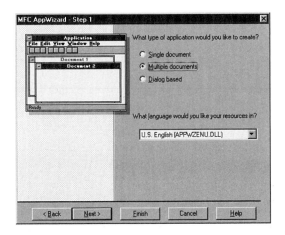

AppWizard sets up the following types of generic programs for you:

- Single document, or SDI; a program that controls a single document at a time
- Multiple document, or MDI; a program that can control several different documents at once
- Dialog box-based; a program that has a dialog box as its main display window

After you select one of these application types, you are asked for more information about the new program.

An SDI Application Created with AppWizard

To create a simple SDI program, select Single document on the opening AppWizard screen. AppWizard displays six Wizard pages filled with default information for a typical SDI program. For now, just accept the default information—later in the book I discuss some of the options available for programs developed with AppWizard. You can move to the next page by pressing the button labeled Next and to the previous page by pressing the button labeled Back. At any time you can tell AppWizard to create the project for you by pressing the button labeled Finish.

AppWizard creates several classes and files for you and creates a project that you can use to manage the process of compiling the program. AppWizard creates these classes for a program named Hello:

- `CHelloApp`, derived from `CWinApp`, the application class for the program
- `CHelloDoc`, the program's document class, derived from `CDocument`
- `CHelloView`, the program's view class derived from `CView`
- `CMainFrame`, the main frame class for the program

The class declaration for each of these classes is stored in a .h file with the filename based on the name of the class. For example, the `CHelloView` class declaration can be found in the file HelloView.h. The implementation of each class is found in a .cpp file that follows the same naming convention. For example, the implementation of `CHelloView` can be found in HelloView.cpp. In addition, there are a number of files created by AppWizard that aren't used for C++ classes. AppWizard creates these files:

- `ReadMe.txt`, a file that has information about all the files created by AppWizard.
- `Hello.rc`, a resource file that contains information about dialog boxes, menus, and other resources used by the program.
- `Hello.mak`, the project file used by Developer's Studio to build the program.
- Hello.ncb, the Developer Studio parser file. This contains class information and is used by the Developer Studio Class View and by Component Gallery.

- Hello.clw, the ClassWizard database file. ClassWizard uses this file to track the status of classes, message handling functions, and member variables added to your project.
- StdAfx.cpp, a file included in all AppWizard programs and which includes all the standard *include* files.
- StdAfx.h, a standard header file included in all AppWizard programs, and which is used to include other files that are included in the precompiled headers.

Creating a Windows program using AppWizard is easy. In fact, you can compile and run the program as it is now, although it doesn't really do anything.

Customization of a Skeleton Program Built Using AppWizard

To add a Hello World! message to this simple SDI program, open the file HelloView.cpp by selecting the FileView tab at the bottom of the project tree, then clicking on the HelloView.cpp icon, or by using the Open file icon on the toolbar.

There are several ways to find a particular function using Developer Studio. The most obvious way is to open the file and find the function by searching for it. Another method is to click on the ClassView tab and locate the function in the class tree. Double-clicking on a member function name takes you directly to the member function. Use one of these methods to locate the CHelloView::OnDraw function and edit the function so it looks like the code provided in Listing 6.1.

Listing 6.1. The `CHelloView::OnDraw` function for an SDI version of `Hello World!`.

```
void CHelloView::OnDraw(CDC* pDC)
{
    CHelloDoc* pDoc = GetDocument();
    ASSERT_VALID(pDoc);

    // TODO: add draw code for native data here
    CRect    rcClient;
    GetClientRect( rcClient );
    pDC->DrawText( "Hello World!", -1, rcClient,
                DT_SINGLELINE | DT_CENTER | DT_VCENTER );
}
```

The CHelloView::OnDraw function is called whenever the view must be drawn. If you're familiar with Windows programming, you're probably familiar with the WM_PAINT message. OnDraw is called whenever a view window receives a WM_PAINT message from the operating system. In a

Document/View application, WM PAINT also is called when the view is printed or during a print preview. I discuss these topics later, in Chapter 15, "Printing."

Creation of Custom AppWizards

One of the new features offered by Developer Studio is the open AppWizard interface. Now you can easily add extensions to the AppWizard, ranging from simple extensions to entirely new project types. In this section, we create a custom AppWizard project that extends the built-in MFC project AppWizard.

Creating a custom AppWizard is an advanced topic. If you aren't comfortable discussing dialog boxes, DLLs, and the MFC classes, you may want to return to this section after reading the remaining chapters in Part II.

The Custom AppWizard Architecture

Developer Studio includes a number of different options for new projects. When you select New from the File menu and then select Project Workspace, a list of different project types is displayed, as shown in Figure 6.5.

FIGURE 6.5.

Developer Studio's default project types.

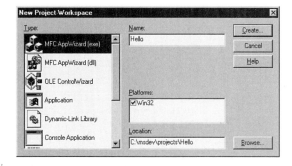

In addition to the built-in types shown in Figure 6.5, Developer Studio also displays any available custom AppWizards. The interface between Developer Studio and AppWizard has been exposed through a set of classes and components that you can use to create custom AppWizards. Custom AppWizards are physically located in DLLs placed in the \MSDEV\Template directory. The basic architecture is shown in Figure 6.6.

When you add a custom AppWizard to Developer Studio, you don't replace any of the existing AppWizard options. Rather, you are extending the number of project types, not replacing any.

FIGURE 6.6.

*The AppWizard
architecture.*

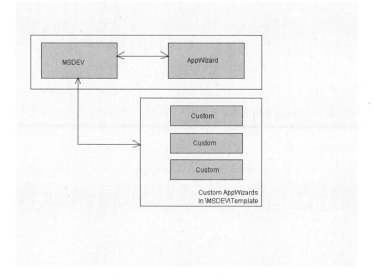

There are three basic methods that you can use to create a custom AppWizard. Each of these methods uses a different starting point for creating the new AppWizard project. The three options are

- Use an existing project to create a custom AppWizard. In order to use this method, the project must be completely created using AppWizard. A project with small modifications may continue to work, but a project with large changes won't be successfully translated.

- Use the standard AppWizard steps, adding custom steps if needed. This is a flexible approach to creating a custom AppWizard. Your AppWizard follows the default AppWizard logic and enables you to add one or more custom dialog boxes to the wizard sequence. This is the method I use for the Unleashed AppWizard example discussed later in this chapter.

- Use a completely new sequence of dialog boxes and steps. This is the most flexible approach to building a custom AppWizard, and it's also the most difficult. You must create all the dialog boxes used by the AppWizard, and you must manage all the information collected by the user.

Depending on the type of custom AppWizard that is created, you will need to modify some of the custom AppWizard components. Each of these components is used for a different purpose; your custom AppWizard may not need to modify or interact with all the different parts of the AppWizard architecture. However, if you're creating a new AppWizard based on the default AppWizard or a completely custom AppWizard project, you will need to understand the different components that are used to create an AppWizard. These components are shown in Figure 6.7.

FIGURE 6.7.

The components used to create a custom AppWizard.

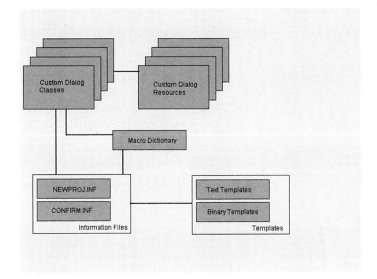

Each of these components is described in the following sections.

Custom Dialog Boxes

Custom dialog boxes are used to interact with the user of your custom AppWizard. As the AppWizard uses nested dialog boxes, you are only responsible for the interior dialog box. The exterior dialog box is maintained by the AppWizard framework. The relationship between your dialog box and the one provided by the AppWizard framework is shown in Figure 6.8.

FIGURE 6.8.

A custom AppWizard dialog box is nested inside the framework's wizard page.

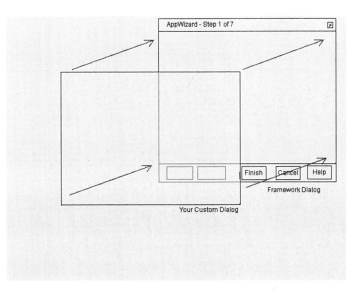

The number of steps used by a custom AppWizard is defined when the project is created. AppWizard creates the required dialog box templates and classes automatically. Unlike normal dialog box classes, all dialog box classes used in a custom AppWizard are derived from CAppWizStepDlg.

As in other MFC dialog boxes, every control in your dialog box can be associated with a member variable using ClassWizard. You must manually add the controls required for your dialog box, as well as any logic required for your dialog box class.

The dialog box class OnDismiss function is called when a user clicks the Next, Back, or Finish buttons. If this function returns FALSE, the AppWizard page won't be dismissed. If the data entered by the user is acceptable, you should return TRUE. A simple version of this function is included for every AppWizard dialog box class. To validate data that has been entered on one of your custom AppWizard pages, you must edit the OnDismiss member function, like this:

```
BOOL CCustom1Dlg::OnDismiss()
{
    if (!UpdateData(TRUE))
        return FALSE;
    if( m_szAuthor.IsEmpty() == FALSE )
        // Store a default value
    else
        // Store the data from m_szAuthor
    return TRUE;
}
```

The OnDismiss function begins by calling OnUpdate(TRUE), an MFC function that verifies the contents of controls and transfers the data into member variables. If the transfer is unsuccessful, OnUpdate returns FALSE, and the user is not allowed to move to a new page. If the transfer is successful, member variables such as m_szAuthor are updated with new values from the controls they are associated with. After using the value of m_szAuthor, TRUE is returned, allowing the user to move to a new page.

Macros

Macros are stored in a map collection named m_Dictionary that associates each macro name with a value. Information collected in your custom AppWizard is stored in the macro dictionary for use later. There are two types of macros.

- Standard AppWizard macros are used to track information entered by the user as the project is created, and the user follows the basic AppWizard steps.
- Custom macros are defined and used by your custom AppWizard.

The m_Dictionary map is a CMapStringToString object that is a member of the CCustomAppWiz-derived class for your custom AppWizard. Macro names are used as keys into the map collection. For example, to create a new macro named PROJ_DATE that contains the current date, you can use a code fragment like this:

```
CTime date = CTime::GetCurrentTime();
CString szDate = date.Format( "%A, %B %d, %Y" );
Demoaw.m_Dictionary["PROJ_DATE"] = szDate;
```

The name of the AppWizard object is always the project name, plus aw. In the previous example, the name of the custom AppWizard is Demo. The macro dictionary is accessed as Demoaw.m_Dictionary. To retrieve a value from the dictionary, just use the macro name as an index.

```
szDate = Demoaw.m_Dictionary["PROJ_DATE"];
```

After a macro has been defined, the macro value can also be used in text templates and project information files.

A number of standard AppWizard macros are defined for every AppWizard project. For example, a standard naming convention is used for class- and filenames. First, there is a set of prefixes that are used for macro names:

- DOC refers to the application's document class.
- APP refers to the application's CWinApp-derived class.
- FRAME refers to the application's main frame class.
- CHILD_FRAME refers to the application's MDI child frame class, if any.
- VIEW refers to the application's view class.
- DLG refers to the application's main dialog box class in dialog box-based applications.
- RECSET refers to the application's main recordset class, if any.
- SRVRITEM refers to the application's main server-item class, if any.
- CNTRITEM refers to the application's main container-item class, if any.
- IPFRAME refers to the application's in-place frame class, if any.

Next, there are a set of component names that can be combined with the previous prefixes list.

- CLASS, refers to the class name.
- BASE_CLASS, refers to the base class name.
- IFILE, refers to the class implementation filename (without the extension).
- HFILE, refers to the class header filename (without the extension).

Uppercase and lowercase versions of the _IFILE and _HFILE macros are defined. If the macro name is uppercase, its value is uppercase. If the macro name is lowercase, its value is lowercase, as shown in Table 6.1.

Table 6.1. Standard macro translations for a project named Foo.

Macro	*Translation*
APP_CLASS	CFooApp
VIEW_IFILE	FOOVIEW
DOC_HFILE	FOODOC
doc_hfile	foodoc
view_hfile	fooview

There is also a ROOT macro, which refers to the project name. Three versions of ROOT are provided. The macro ROOT is translated into the project name using all uppercase letters, root is translated using all lowercase, and Root is translated according to the capitalization used when the project was created.

Text Templates

A text template is used by a custom AppWizard to create source files that will be included in a project. A text template is a mixture of macros, directives, and plain source code. Directives are covered in the section *Directives*.

Macros are always surrounded by pairs of dollar signs, like this:

```
$$MY_MACRO$$
```

When the parser reaches a pair of dollar signs, the macro is evaluated. If the symbol is a macro, a text substitution is made. For example, the following code fragment is a simplified version of the template used to create the OnNewDocument function for AppWizard applications:

```
BOOL $$DOC_CLASS$$::OnNewDocument()
{
    if (!$$DOC_BASE_CLASS$$::OnNewDocument())
        return FALSE;
    // TODO: add reinitialization code here
    // (SDI documents will reuse this document)
    return TRUE;
}
```

As you can see, this example is a mixture of macros and plain source code. As the parser scans this function, it makes the following substitutions:

- $$DOC_CLASS$$ is replaced by the document class name. For example, if your project name is Foo, $$DOC_CLASS$$ is replaced by CFooDoc.

- $$DOC_BASE_CLASS$$ is replaced by the immediate base class of the document. For example, if this isn't an OLE document, it becomes CDocument.

All other text in this example is copied directly into the source file.

Binary Templates

Binary templates are resources that are copied into a project's directory. Every bitmap, icon, and cursor that can be included in a project has a binary template. By modifying these templates you can change the appearance of projects created with your custom AppWizard.

Information Files

Information files are used by the custom AppWizard to create the actual project. An information file is very much like a "make" file; it's used to create projects and output based on user input stored in various macros.

There are two information files created as part of a custom AppWizard project:

- NEWPROJ.INF contains directives and information used by your custom AppWizard to create a project.
- CONFIRM.INF contains the directives used to create the information displayed in the project confirmation dialog box.

Like the text template files, information files make heavy use of directives and macros.

In most cases, you don't edit information files. The information file needs editing only if the rules for creating a particular file are to be changed or if a new source file is added to a project.

Directives

A directive always begins with $$ and is used to control the flow of the text template or information file, just like simple C or C++ statements. A directive must always appear in the first column of a text template file. A directive can have one of the following values:

- $$IF
- $$ELIF
- $$ELSE
- $$ENDIF
- $$BEGINLOOP
- $$ENDLOOP
- $$SET_DEFAULT_LANG
- $$//
- $$INCLUDE

The $$IF, $$ELIF, $$ELSE, and $$ENDIF directives are commonly used to control which lines of code are inserted in a source code module. For example, this code fragment is from the StdAfx.h text template:

```
$$IF(CRecordView)
#include <afxdb.h>          // MFC ODBC database classes
$$ELIF(CDaoRecordView)
#include <afxdao.h>         // MFC DAO database classes
$$ELIF(DB ¦¦ PROJTYPE_DLL)
$$// Here, minimal DB support is requested, or we're a DLL.
#ifndef _AFX_NO_DB_SUPPORT
#include <afxdb.h>          // MFC ODBC database classes
#endif // _AFX_NO_DB_SUPPORT
#ifndef _AFX_NO_DAO_SUPPORT
#include <afxdao.h>         // MFC DAO database classes
#endif // _AFX_NO_DAO_SUPPORT
$$ENDIF // database/DLL options
```

The $$IF and $$ELIF directives test a macro to see whether it's defined in the directory. If so, the directive evaluates as TRUE. The $$IF and $$ELIF and $$ELSE directives are similar to the if, else if, and else statements used in C and C++, except that no braces are required. As shown in the previous example, macros tested by the $$IF and $$ELIF directives can be combined using the logical or symbol, ¦¦. For example, the line

```
$$ELIF(DB ¦¦ PROJTYPE_DLL)
```

evaluates as TRUE if DB or PROJTYPE_DLL is defined in the macro dictionary. Macro names also can be preceded by the not symbol, !. Using ! changes a TRUE value to FALSE and vice versa. For example,

```
$$IF(!PROJTYPE_DLL)
```

evaluates as TRUE if PROJTYPE_DLL is *not* defined in the macro dictionary.

Execution continues until the next directive. Every $$IF is terminated by a single $$ENDIF. After an $$IF directive, there may be one or more $$ELIF directives and a maximum of one $$ELSE directive that is executed only if none of the $$IF or $$ELIF directives were TRUE.

The $$BEGINLOOP and $$ENDLOOP directives are used to create loops inside a text template or information file. Every $$BEGINLOOP must be matched with a $$ENDLOOP. These directives cannot be nested. The macro that is tested must be a string that contains a numeric value. For example,

```
$$BEGINLOOP(NUM_LANGS)
// Do some work here...
$$ENDLOOP
```

executes NUM_LANG loops. If NUM_LANG contains the string "25", 25 loops are executed.

The $$INCLUDE directive is used to include other templates. This can be useful if you need to perform the same processing in multiple locations. The macro used as a parameter must specify a template filename.

The `$$//` directive is used to indicate a comment in the template or information file. To embed a comment into a source file, just use comments.

```
$$//This is a template comment, it is not written into the source.
//This is a source file comment.
```

In the next section, the Unleashed custom AppWizard uses directives in its modified text templates.

The Unleashed AppWizard

I have created an example custom AppWizard named Unleashed, which can be found on the CD that accompanies this book. The Unleashed AppWizard has two features that aren't found in the standard AppWizard.

First, all `include` files have protection against multiple inclusion, using `#ifndef`/`#endif` preprocessor directives:

```
#ifndef WNT_H
#define WNT_H
// Header information.
#endif //WNT_H
```

There are also expanded comments at the beginning of every file, including the author's name, the date the project was created, the purpose of the file, and a comment that is embedded in all project source files.

```
/*

    This project was created using the "Windows NT Programming
    Unleashed" custom AppWizard.

    This is the first Unleashed AppWizard project.

    Author : Mickey Williams
    File   : ChildFrm.cpp
    Project: Foo
    Date   : Tuesday, December 26, 1995

    This file provides the interface for the
    CChildFrame class.

*/
```

Planning the Custom AppWizard

Like any software project, it's a good idea to have a plan before you start coding. Like most custom AppWizards, the Unleashed AppWizard has two main parts.

- A wizard page that collects information from the user.
- Modifications to the text templates that control how the source code is generated.

The new wizard page collects the project author's name and a project-wide comment that will be added to every source file. This information, along with the current date, is stored in the macro dictionary. Every source code text template is modified to use the new macros when generating source code files.

Creating the Custom AppWizard Project

Creating a custom AppWizard is much like creating any other MFC project. Developer Studio includes a wizard that automates the process, so most of the hard work is done automatically.

The first step in creating the Unleashed AppWizard is to create a custom AppWizard project. Begin by selecting New from the File menu and select Project Workspace from the New dialog box. When the New Project Workspace dialog box appears as shown in Figure 6.9, select Custom AppWizard as the type. You must also specify a name and a location for your project. In Figure 6.9, the name is `Unleashed`, and the location is `C:\WNP\Unleashed`.

FIGURE 6.9.

The New Project Workspace dialog box.

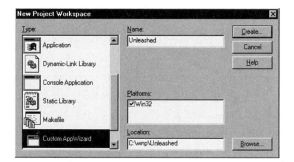

After you have filled in the New Project dialog box, click the Create button. A wizard is displayed to help guide you through the process of creating a custom AppWizard. The first wizard page is used to collect basic information about the new AppWizard.

- The project starting point, either an existing project, the standard AppWizard steps, or completely custom steps. For the Unleashed AppWizard, I wanted to add to the existing AppWizard functions, so I chose Standard AppWizard Steps.

- The name of the AppWizard as it will be displayed in the list of project types. For the Unleashed AppWizard, I kept the default name `Unleashed AppWizard`.

- The number of custom steps in the custom AppWizard. The Unleashed AppWizard has one additional wizard page to collect information; enter a `1` here.

When you're satisfied with the contents of the first wizard page, click the Next button. The contents of the second wizard page presented to you depend on the project starting point that you selected on the first wizard page:

- If the custom AppWizard is based on an existing project, the second wizard page asks for the path to this project.

- If the custom AppWizard is based on the standard AppWizard steps, the second wizard page collects two key pieces of information: the type of application built with the new AppWizard—either executable or dynamic link library—and the languages that will be supported by the custom AppWizard. For the Unleashed AppWizard, select the AppWizard Executable radio button and select US English as a supported language.

- If the custom AppWizard is based on completely new steps, there is no second page; the only available buttons are Cancel and Finish.

After you have completed the second wizard page, click the Finish button. The New Project Information dialog box is presented. Click OK to dismiss the dialog box, and the wizard creates the custom AppWizard skeleton project.

The skeleton project will compile and run; however, it will have an extra, blank wizard page and the same functionality as the standard AppWizard. To complete the Unleashed AppWizard, the following steps are required:

1. Edit the dialog box resource for the seventh page and add class member variables for the new controls that collect the author's name and a project comment.

2. Edit the `CCustom1Dlg::OnDismiss` function to collect user input from the seventh wizard page.

3. Edit the text templates for all the AppWizard source files to make use of the new information collected on the new wizard page.

These steps are covered in the next three sections.

Editing the Dialog Box Resource

The Unleashed AppWizard has one dialog box resource, `IDD_CUSTOM1`, which was created as part of the default project. Open the `IDD_CUSTOM1` dialog box resource by double-clicking on the `IDD_CUSTOM1` icon in the Dialog resource, which can be found in the Resource View. Add two edit controls as shown in Figure 6.10.

FIGURE 6.10.

The IDD_CUSTOM1 *dialog box resource from the Unleashed AppWizard project.*

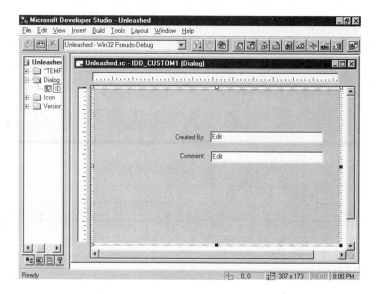

Name the two edit controls and using the values from Table 6.2, associate them with member variables in the CCustom1Dlg class.

Table 6.2. Member variables added to the CCustom1Dlg class.

Control ID	Name	Category	Variable Type
IDC_EDIT_AUTHOR	m_szAuthor	Value	CString
IDC_EDIT_COMMENT	m_szComment	Value	CString

Providing an OnDismiss Function

As discussed earlier, the OnDismiss function is called when a user is moving from a new wizard page. This function should validate data contained in the dialog box and store user input in the macro dictionary. The CCustom1Dlg::OnDismiss function used in the Unleashed AppWizard project is shown in Listing 6.2.

Listing 6.2. The CCustom1Dlg::OnDismiss function.

```
BOOL CCustom1Dlg::OnDismiss()
{
    if (!UpdateData(TRUE))
        return FALSE;
    if( m_szAuthor.IsEmpty() == FALSE )
        Unleashedaw.m_Dictionary["PROJ_AUTHOR"] = m_szAuthor;
    else
        Unleashedaw.m_Dictionary["PROJ_AUTHOR"] = "";
```

```
    if( m_szComment.IsEmpty() == FALSE )
        Unleashedaw.m_Dictionary["PROJ_COMMENT"] = m_szComment;
    else
        Unleashedaw.m_Dictionary["PROJ_COMMENT"] = "";

    CTime date = CTime::GetCurrentTime();
    CString szDate = date.Format( "%A, %B %d, %Y" );
    Unleashedaw.m_Dictionary["PROJ_DATE"] = szDate;

    szDate = Unleashedaw.m_Dictionary["PROJ_DATE"];
    return TRUE;
}
```

In addition to storing user input in the macro dictionary, OnDismiss also calculates and stores the current time. The PROJ_DATE macro will be used to print the date that the project was created.

Editing the Text Templates

Every custom AppWizard project includes a Template directory, which contains the information and template files used by the custom AppWizard. For the Unleashed AppWizard, every source file is modified to use the information that has been stored in the OnDismiss function. In addition, every header file will have #include protection added.

For this custom AppWizard, you only modify the .h and .cpp template files. These files will be used by the custom AppWizard to create the source files used by projects it creates. The first few lines of all .cpp and .h source files are modified as shown in Listing 6.3, which contains the changes made to the ChildFrm.cpp text template. Most of the modifications shown in Listing 6.3 are used in all .cpp and .h source files, except for the parts that refer specifically to the child frame class.

Listing 6.3. Modifications made to the beginning of the `ChildFrm.cpp` text template.

```
/*

    This project was created using the "Windows NT Programming
    Unleashed" custom AppWizard.

    $$PROJ_COMMENT$$

    Author : $$PROJ_AUTHOR$$
    File   : $$child_frame_ifile$$.cpp
    Project: $$Root$$
    Date   : $$PROJ_DATE$$

    This file provides the implementation for the
    $$CHILD_FRAME_CLASS$$ class.

*/
```

The line:

```
File   : $$child_frame_ifile$$.cpp
```

will be translated into:

```
File   : CChildFrm.cpp
```

Every text template will have a different macro used on this line, depending on the filename. In addition, the comment

```
This file provides the implementation for the
    $$CHILD_FRAME_CLASS$$ class.
```

is slightly different for every text template file.

Listing 6.4. contains the modifications made to the ChildFrm.h text template. In addition to modifications similar to the ones shown in Listing 6.3, a set of #include guards have been added. Note that the #include guards use the name of the header class to make each guard unique, and the #ifndef is paired with one #endif at the end of the file.

Listing 6.4. Modifications made to the ChildFrm.h text template.

```
/*

        This project was created using the "Windows NT Programming
        Unleashed" custom AppWizard.

        $$PROJ_COMMENT$$

        Author : $$PROJ_AUTHOR$$
        File   : $$child_frame_hfile$$.cpp
        Project: $$Root$$
        Date   : $$PROJ_DATE$$

        This file provides the interface for the
        $$CHILD_FRAME_CLASS$$ class.

*/

#ifndef NTPRG_UNLEASHED_$$CHILD_FRAME_CLASS$$_H
#define NTPRG_UNLEASHED_$$CHILD_FRAME_CLASS$$_H

class $$CHILD_FRAME_CLASS$$ : public $$CHILD_FRAME_BASE_CLASS$$
{
    DECLARE_DYNCREATE($$CHILD_FRAME_CLASS$$)
public:
    $$CHILD_FRAME_CLASS$$();

// ....
// Remaining text template remains unchanged.
// ....

};
#endif //NTPRG_UNLEASHED_$$CHILD_FRAME_CLASS$$_H
```

Using the Custom AppWizard

To use the Unleashed AppWizard, compile the Unleashed AppWizard project. After the project is built, the `Unleashed.awx` DLL will be automatically copied into the `\MSDEV\Template` directory. Optionally, the CD includes a compiled version of Unleashed that you can manually copy into the `\MSDEV\Template` directory.

When a new project is opened, a new selection named Unleashed AppWizard should be displayed in the New Project Workspace Menu, as shown in Figure 6.11.

FIGURE 6.11.

The New Project Workspace dialog box containing the custom Unleashed AppWizard.

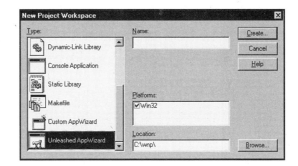

Summary

In this chapter, I discussed the Microsoft Visual C++ Developer Studio and how it can be used to create great Windows NT Workstation and Server applications. The tools included with Developer Studio were covered, as was its integration with tools supplied by third parties.

This chapter also included a custom AppWizard that adds `#include` guards to every header file. It also adds extra information to every project source file, including a project comment, such as a copyright message.

Document/View Architecture

7

by Mickey Williams

IN THIS CHAPTER

This chapter discusses the Document/View architecture and how it is used with the MFC class library to create applications for Windows NT. After reading this chapter, you will understand how the MFC class library uses the Document/View model to divide an application into well-defined parts. This chapter also covers two sample programs that can be found on the CD: ViewCount, which demonstrates how document and view classes update each other, and Split, which shows how to implement a dynamic split view.

Document/View Overview

Writing applications for Windows can be difficult. The MFC class library uses the Document/View model to divide the work performed by a Windows program into easily manageable pieces. The Document/View defines four major class categories:

- The document class contains the data managed by the application. Although the name seems to suggest that the application must be a word processor, the class can actually handle any sort of data.

- The view class manages most of the application's user interface. View classes are windows that display information and collect user input.

- The frame class controls the placement of views, and it owns the menus, toolbars, and status bars displayed by the application.

- The application class is the starting point for program execution and handles any general purpose interaction with Windows NT.

The Document/View architecture provides for two basic types of applications:

- Single Document Interface (SDI) programs work with a single document and view at any given time.

- Multiple Document Interface (MDI) programs can work with multiple documents of different types at the same time. Each document can have one or more views open at once.

The Document Class

The document class is responsible for maintaining the document or data used by the MFC-based application. In simple applications, maintaining the data is simple and straightforward, and usually includes support for serializing the document's data to and from storage.

As shown in Figure 7.1, most document classes provide an interface to their data in addition to the standard document interfaces. The document class in Figure 7.1 is taken from the ViewCount example covered later in this chapter.

FIGURE 7.1.

*Document class interfaces
for the ViewCount
application.*

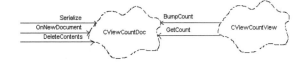

In simple applications, the document class may work with data directly, although in more complicated applications it is a good idea to separate the actual data model from the document class.

The View Class

The view class is responsible for managing the user interface for the document. The view class is not responsible for storing any information that is contained in the document class; rather, the view object should ask its document for any data as it is needed.

Every view is connected to exactly one document. A view object gains access to its attached document by using the GetDocument member function. The CView base class provides an implementation of GetDocument that returns a pointer to CDocument. If the base class function is used directly it must be cast to the proper document type, like this:

```
CViewCountDoc* pDoc = dynamic_cast<CViewCountDoc*>(GetDocument());
```

If a view was created with AppWizard, a new version of GetDocument is included that performs the necessary cast to the proper CDocument class. It's a good idea to implement a specialized GetDocument function for any view classes that you write, because it helps reduce the number of casts in your program.

```
CViewCountDoc* CViewCountView::GetDocument()
{
    CViewCountDoc* pDoc = dynamic_cast<CViewCountDoc*>(GetDocument());
    ASSERT_VALID( pDoc );
    return pDoc;
}
```

To enable RTTI support, select Settings from the Build menu, and select the C/C++ tab. Select C++ Language from the Category drop down list. A number of C++ language options are presented, including RTTI. Select the check box labeled Enable Run-Time Type Information (RTTI).

The two previous examples use the improved casting operators that are available if you enable Run Time Type Information (RTTI) for your project. If you like to live dangerously, and don't enable RTTI, you can still use the older style cast.

```
CViewCountDoc* CViewCountView::GetDocument()
{
    CViewCountDoc* pDoc = (CViewCountDoc*)GetDocument();
    ASSERT_VALID( pDoc );
    return pDoc;
}
```

The Frame Classes

The frame classes used in the Document/View architecture create frame windows that contain the views. There are two types of frames: the main frame that contains the main application window, and a child frame used to contain MDI child views.

Main Frame Windows

In an SDI application, the CMainFrame class is derived from CFrameWnd, while in an MDI application, the CMainFrame class is derived from CMDIFrameWnd. This class is responsible for the menu, toolbar, status bar, and the frame around the main window.

In an SDI application, the view completely fills the main frame window, while an MDI frame can contain multiple views. The relationship between main frame windows and a view in an SDI application is shown in Figure 7.2.

FIGURE 7.2.

The relationship between frame and view windows in an SDI application.

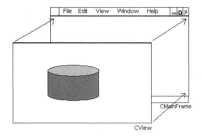

Child Window Frames

In an MDI application, each view is associated with its own frame window. This frame window is responsible for controlling the frame edges of the view, including the sizing controls, caption, and other frame attributes. Figure 7.3 shows how the view and frame windows are related in an MDI application.

FIGURE 7.3.

The relationship between view and frame windows in an MDI application.

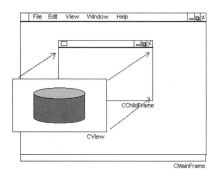

The MDI child views are actually child windows of their associated frame window. MDI child frames are derived from CMDIChildWnd. Projects built with AppWizard include the CChildFrame class, which is derived from CMDIChildWnd.

To override the current behavior of your project's MDI child frame, you must modify the CChildFrame class. For example, most MDI child windows allow themselves to be resized by using the mouse to drag the frame. To prevent an MDI child view from being resized, the frame window style bits are changed by overriding the OnPreCreateWindow function.

```
BOOL CChildFrame::PreCreateWindow(CREATESTRUCT& cs)
{
    cs.style &= ~WS_THICKFRAME;
    return CMDIChildWnd::PreCreateWindow(cs);
}
```

The OnPreCreateWindow function is often used to change the behavior of a frame class. As you can probably tell by its name, the function is called just before a window is created. The CREATESTRUCT structure gives you access to all the member variables listed in Table 7.1.

Table 7.1. CREATESTRUCT member variables.

Variable	Type	Description
lpCreateParams	LPVOID	Data used to create the window
hInstance	HANDLE	Instance handle of the window's owner
hMenu	HMENU	Menu used for a new window
hwndParent	HWND	Handle of parent window
cy	int	Window height
cx	int	Window width
y	int	Y coordinate of the upper-left window corner
x	int	X coordinate of the upper-left window corner
style	LONG	Window style flags
lpszName	LPCSTR	Window name
lpszClass	LPCSTR	Window class name
dwExStyle	DWORD	Extended style flags

The Application Class

The application class in an MFC-based program is derived from CWinApp. The application class is responsible for initializing and running your application, as well defining and storing general information about it, such as the document templates and icons. There is only one application class per Document/View program.

Document Templates

The document, view, and frame classes are connected to each other using a document template. As discussed later in this chapter, CSingleDocTemplate is used for SDI applications, and CMultiDocTemplate is used for MDI applications.

Each document template contains information about one document class, one view class, and one frame class. The document template also stores the *shared resource identifier*. This value is used to identify several different resources that are used by the document template.

■ A resource string specifying the file type, file extension, and document name used by the document

■ An icon for the view

■ A menu used when the view is active

The resource string has this format:

```
\nSplit\nSplit\n\n\nSplit.Document\nSplit Document
```

There are seven sections to a resource string, each separated by \n. If a section is not used, it's left empty. Table 7.2 lists the purpose of each section, with example values from the Split example, which is presented later in this chapter.

Table 7.2. Resource string sections with example values.

Section	IDR_SPLITTYPE
Title	
Document Name	Split
New File Name	Split
Filter Name	
Filter Extension	
Type ID	Split Document
Type Name	Split Document

When an MDI application supports more than one view or document class, it creates additional document templates as needed. The document templates for an application are stored by the application class in a list, as shown in Figure 7.4.

FIGURE 7.4.

An MDI application may contain several document templates.

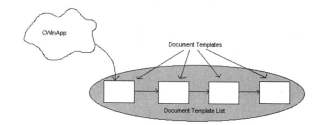

If you're interested in how the CWinApp class keeps track of its document templates, you can always browse through the MFC source code. In MFC 4.0, the CWinApp class uses an undocumented class called CDocManager to handle a collection of document templates. The CDocManager class stores document templates in a list and handles most of the interaction with the document list collection. In fact, many of the document and view interfaces exposed by the CWinApp class are actually delegated directly to CDocManager.

Document and View Life Cycles

In your MFC application, you will derive your own classes from CDocument, CView, and the other Document and View classes. In most cases, you will probably have AppWizard create the initial application and class structure for you.

Because a great deal of work in a default application seems to be done magically by the base classes, the next few sections discuss important milestones in the life of an MFC application.

Creating a New Document

As shown in Figure 7.5, SDI and MDI documents are treated differently. SDI applications create one document object and reuse it when new documents are loaded. MDI applications create new document objects whenever a new document is needed. The document object is not destroyed until the associated document is closed.

FIGURE 7.5.

The life cycle of SDI and MDI documents.

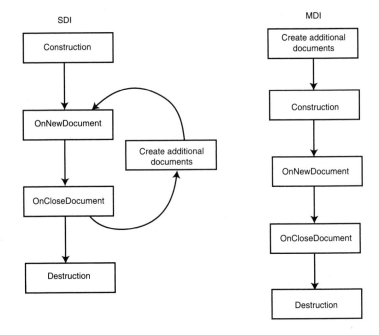

When creating a new, empty document using the standard MFC implementation, the user selects New from the File menu. The CWinApp::OnFileNew creates the new document in one of two ways.

- If there is only one document template defined for the application, that document is created.
- If there is more than one document template defined for the application, the user is prompted to select one of the available document types. The CWinApp\:OnFileNew function uses the selected document template to create the new document.

After a document type has been selected, the MFC framework calls the document's OnNewDocument function. OnNewDocument is called in both SDI and MDI applications and is the proper place for you to perform any special initialization required for new documents. The default version of OnNewDocument calls the DeleteContents member function and clears the modification flag. This is good enough for most document classes.

Almost all document classes must provide a version of DeleteContents. The DeleteContents function is used to release any resources that have been allocated for the document, and it should reset the document to its initial state.

Opening an Existing Document

Opening an existing document is similar to creating a new document. The CWinApp::OnFileOpen function handles prompting the user for a file name by using the FileOpen common dialog.

The MFC framework calls the document class's OnOpenDocument, which by default calls DeleteContents, then calls serialization functions to create the document's data from the stored document. In most cases, the default implementation of OnOpenDocument is used, with any special needs being handled by specialized versions of DeleteContents and the serialization functions.

Destroying a Document

As discussed previously, when a document is destroyed in an SDI application, the actual document object is not destroyed. For this reason, it's a good idea to develop document classes that release their resources when they receive DeleteContents, rather than during destruction.

Updating Documents and Views

The Document/View architecture is designed to separate the application's data from its user interface. The document classes handle the data, and the view classes handle the user interface. In general, the only time that document and view classes need to interact directly is when one of these classes must update the other.

When the view or document classes need to be updated, they communicate using four well-defined interfaces, as shown in Figure 7.6.

FIGURE 7.6.

Interfaces used for Document/View interaction.

The commonly used interfaces used for updating document and view objects are:

- GetDocument is a CView member function used to fetch a pointer to the document attached to a view. The document pointer is then used to access document class member functions. This is the only way for the view class to update the document.

- UpdateAllViews is a CDocument function used to update all views attached to a document. Calling this function results in an OnUpdate function call from the MFC framework to all a document's views. As discussed in the next section, it's possible for the document class to pass *hint* information using this function in order to optimize the updating process.

- OnInitialUpdate is a CView member function that is called when a view is initially displayed. In most cases a view class initializes itself during this function.

- OnUpdate is called when the document attached to a view has called UpdateAllViews. A simple version of OnUpdate causes the view to be completely redrawn using new information from the document. More advanced versions use information passed by the document class to optimize the updating process.

Optimizing the Update Process

The view that updates a document often has enough information to update its own view immediately. MFC allows a document to skip updating a particular view by passing a `CView` pointer in the call to `UpdateAllViews`.

```
UpdateAllViews( pView );
```

As a further optimization, a document can pass parameters in the call to `UpdateAllViews`, which are then passed to every view as parameters in the call to `CView::OnUpdate`. There are two different hint parameters.

- An `LPARAM` suitable for storing an index or other scalar value.
- A pointer to a `CObject` that can be used to store information about the update. This can be used to pass a pointer to anything derived from `CObject` that can help speed up the update process.

For example, a document that stores objects in an array or a list can pass the index of the object that has been updated, and a pointer to that object to all views during updates. When documents and views store large amounts of data, this can really speed up the update process.

An Example of Document/View Interaction

I've created a small example demonstrating how documents and views interact with each other. The ViewCount application is an MDI program that tracks the number of currently open views for each open document. Figure 7.7 shows ViewCount running with several views open for a single document.

FIGURE 7.7.

The ViewCount example with four views displayed.

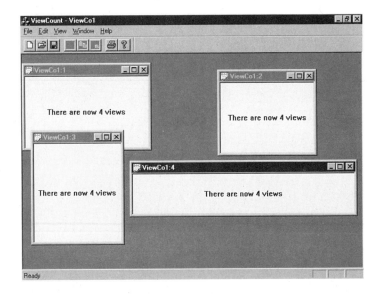

As new views for a document are opened, all view windows attached to that document are updated. The document class for ViewCount has one data member that tracks the number of open views. When a view is created or destroyed, the following steps take place:

1. The view gets a pointer to its document by calling GetDocument.

2. The view calls a function in the document class to increment or decrement the view counter, depending on whether it is being created or destroyed. The view passes a pointer to itself, which is used to optimize the updating process in the next step.

3. The document class updates the view counter and calls UpdateAllViews, passing the pointer to the changed view as a parameter. The framework updates all the other views, but it does not update the view whose pointer was passed to it. This allows the update process to be optimized if a view is capable of keeping itself updated.

4. The MFC framework calls the OnUpdate member function for each view. The OnUpdate member function invalidates the view client area.

5. Windows sends a WM_PAINT message to every visible view, resulting in OnDraw being called for every view object. The view classes collect the current view count from the document and display their text message.

The ViewCount project is on the CD. After launching the application, a single view is displayed. To open additional views, select New from the Window menu. As each new view is opened, the message displayed in each of the views is updated.

Most of the ViewCount application is a standard MDI skeleton created by AppWizard except for the modifications to the document and view classes discussed in the next two sections.

Modifying the CViewCountDoc Class

The CViewCountDoc class contains one new data member that is used to track the number of views connected to the document. The m_nViews variable is accessed through two new member functions, GetCount and BumpCount. In addition, ClassWizard was used to add a DeleteContents member function. The changes to the CViewCountDoc header are shown below.

```
class CViewCountDoc : public CDocument
{

//...

// Operations
public:
    int GetCount() const;
    void BumpCount( CView* pView, int nBump = 1 );
// ...
// Implementation
protected:
    int m_nViews;
};
```

As discussed earlier, the DeleteContents member function is used to initialize the contents of the document. For CViewCountDoc, that means that the m_nViews member variable should be set to zero. The new member functions for the CViewCountDoc class are provided in Listing 7.1.

Listing 7.1. New member functions for the CViewCountDoc class.

```
void CViewCountDoc::DeleteContents()
{
    m_nViews = 0;
    CDocument::DeleteContents();
}
int CViewCountDoc::GetCount() const
{
    return m_nViews;
}

void CViewCountDoc::BumpCount( CView *pView, int nMoveBy )
{
    // nMoveBy may be positive or negative.
    m_nViews += nMoveBy;
    UpdateAllViews( pView );
}
```

The CViewCountDoc::BumpCount function increments the m_nViews variable and calls UpdateAllViews. Any view that calls BumpCount is expected to pass its pointer as the first argument to BumpCount. In turn, this pointer is passed to UpdateAllViews, resulting in OnUpdate calls being made to all views attached to this document except for the view that originally called BumpCount.

Modifying the CViewCountView Class

The CViewCountView class is responsible for notifying the document class when it is created or destroyed. It also invalidates its client area when notified that the document has been updated and collects new information when its client area is redrawn. Four member functions are used to perform this work:

- OnInitialUpdate is called when the view is initially created.
- OnUpdate is called when the document attached to this view calls UpdateAllViews.
- OnDraw is called when the client area of the view needs to be redrawn.
- PostNcDestroy is called after the view client and non-client areas have been destroyed.

When creating an MDI project using AppWizard, the OnDraw member function is created for you automatically. For the ViewCount example, the OnInitialUpdate, OnUpdate and PostNcDestroy member functions were added using ClassWizard.

The implementation of these functions is shown in Listing 7.2. The unchanged parts of the CViewCountView class are not shown here, but they can be found on the CD-ROM.

Listing 7.2. Modified member functions in the `CViewCountView` class.

```
void CViewCountView::OnInitialUpdate()
{
    CView::OnInitialUpdate();

    CViewCountDoc* pDoc = GetDocument();
    ASSERT_VALID( pDoc );
    pDoc->BumpCount( this );
}

void CViewCountView::OnUpdate(CView* pSender,
                             LPARAM lHint,
                             CObject* pHint)
{
    InvalidateRect( NULL );
}

void CViewCountView::PostNcDestroy()
{
    CViewCountDoc* pDoc = GetDocument();
    ASSERT_VALID( pDoc );

    pDoc->BumpCount( this, -1 );
    CView::PostNcDestroy();
}

void CViewCountView::OnDraw(CDC* pDC)
{
    CViewCountDoc* pDoc = GetDocument();
    ASSERT_VALID(pDoc);
    // Get the document pointer and format the display message.
    int nViews = pDoc->GetCount();
    CString szMsg;
    szMsg.Format( _T("There are now %d views"), nViews );
    // Calculate the view client area and display the message.
    CRect rcView;
    GetClientRect( rcView );
    pDC->DrawText( szMsg, rcView,
                DT_VCENTER | DT_SINGLELINE | DT_CENTER );
}
```

In Listing 7.2, the `OnInitialUpdate` and `PostNcDestroy` functions notify the document that the number of views is changing by calling the document's `BumpCount` member function. The `this` pointer is passed to the document because neither view needs to be updated by the document. In fact, after the `PostNcDestroy` function is completed, the view will no longer exist, and any attempts to update it will result in an exception error.

The `OnUpdate` function is called by the MFC framework when the attached document has called `UpdateAllViews`. In this application, that happens when *another* view has been opened or closed. The only action required is to invalidate the client area, which eventually results in the view's `OnDraw` function being called.

The `OnDraw` function fetches the current view count from the document and displays the number of open views in the center of the view's client area using `DrawText`.

View Classes Provided in MFC 4.0

The ViewCount example uses `CView` as the `CViewCountView` base class. The MFC class library provides nine view classes that can be used as base classes in your application.

- `CView` provides a standard child window for your view.
- `CScrollView` adds automatic scrolling to your view.
- `CFormView` uses a dialog template to embed controls in a view.
- `CRecordView` is a special form view used to work with ODBC databases.
- `CDaoRecordView` is similar to `CRecordView`, but is used with DAO database classes.
- `CEditView` contains an edit control that fills the view client area.
- `CTreeView` contains a tree view control that fills the view client area.
- `CRichEditView` contains a rich edit control that fills the view client area.
- `CListView` contains a list view control that fills the view client area.

The relationships between these view classes is shown in the class diagram in Figure 7.8. If you aren't familiar with Booch notation, each "cloud" represents a class, and arrows are drawn between classes to indicate inheritance, with the arrow pointing toward the base class.

FIGURE 7.8.

*The Inheritance relation-
ships for view classes in
MFC 4.0.*

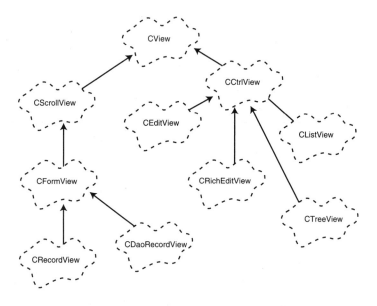

Form views and the view classes that have embedded controls are discussed in detail in Chapter 10, "Menus and Dialog Boxes." All these classes are used throughout the remainder of this book.

Multiple Documents

When MFC is used to create MDI applications, it is very easy to add support for new document types. Using ClassWizard, a new document can be added to your application with a few mouse clicks.

There are five steps involved in adding a new document to an existing MDI application.

1. Create a new resource string and give it an identifier beginning with IDR_. The easiest way to add a new resource string is to copy and paste the existing resource string.

2. Create new menu and icon resources that share the same IDR_ resource ID as the resource string.

3. Use ClassWizard to create new classes based on CDocument and CView.

4. If necessary, use ClassWizard to create a new child frame window class. In most cases, you should be able to use the standard CChildFrameWnd class.

5. Modify the application class to create a new document template for the new document and view, and add it to the application's document template list. This step is described in the next section.

These steps add the basic skeleton for a new pair of document and view classes for your application.

Using Document Templates

The document template accepts four parameters.

- The resource ID shared by the resource string, icon, and menu.
- A pointer to the CRuntime class that refers to the class derived from CDocument.
- A pointer to the CRuntime class that refers to a class derived from CFrameWnd.
- A pointer to the CRuntime class that refers to a class derived from CView.

When AppWizard creates the InitInstance function for an application class, it generates this code for the document template:

```
CMultiDocTemplate* pDocTemplate;
pDocTemplate = new CMultiDocTemplate(
    IDR_TWOVIETYPE,
    RUNTIME_CLASS(CTwoViewsDoc),
    RUNTIME_CLASS(CChildFrame), // custom MDI child frame
    RUNTIME_CLASS(CTwoViewsView));
AddDocTemplate(pDocTemplate);
```

To take advantage of built-in support for multiple documents, just cut and paste the code created by AppWizard and add a new document template to the application class. In most cases, you only need to change the names of the resource ID and the document and view classes. The following source code creates a new document template for CNewDoc, a new document class, and CNewView, a new view class:

```
pDocTemplate = new CMultiDocTemplate(
    IDR_NEWVIETYPE,
    RUNTIME_CLASS(CNewDoc),
    RUNTIME_CLASS(CChildFrame), // custom MDI child frame
    RUNTIME_CLASS(CNewView));
AddDocTemplate(pDocTemplate);
```

Using Split Views

A *split view* allows a child window to display two or more views at the same time. Split views are very useful when two related views must be displayed simultaneously. Split views come in two different types:

■ *Dynamic split views* are initially displayed as a single view. The user can create another view of the same type by dragging a special button located near the view's scroll bar.

■ *Static split views* are split into two or more panes when they are initially displayed. Unlike dynamic split views, a static split view can contain different types of views in each of its *panes*, or subwindows.

A split view is managed by the CSplitterWnd class, which is owned by the child frame window. The CSplitterWnd class creates panes that are used to contain the individual views. The relationship between the various windows involved with a split view is shown in Figure 7.9.

FIGURE 7.9.

The relationship between the elements involved in a split view.

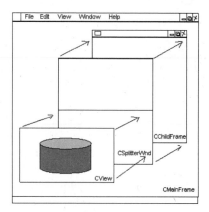

An Example of a Dynamic Split View

The CD contains a sample MDI program named Split that demonstrates how a dynamic split view is implemented. Like the ViewCount example presented earlier in this chapter, most of the application's source code is generated by AppWizard. The CSplitterWnd implements most of the functionality required for a dynamic split view; the entire split view implementation requires only a few lines of code.

When the Split program is run, the view displays an ellipse drawn inside of its initial view. By dragging the splitter button located above the scroll bar, the view can be split into two views.

Modifying the Child Frame Class

The first modification that was done to Split was to add a CSplitterWnd variable to the child frame class. The following code was added to the CChildFrame class declaration:

```
// Implementation
private:
    CSplitterWnd      m_wndSplitter;
```

In a larger application that provides more than one view, a new child frame class specifically for the split view must be created. Because Split only offers split views, the AppWizard-provided CChildFrame class is used.

The next step is to add a message-handling function for OnCreateClient to the CChildFrame class using ClassWizard. The source code for the new version of OnCreateClient is shown in Listing 7.3.

Listing 7.3. Creating a dynamic split view.

```
BOOL CChildFrame::OnCreateClient(LPCREATESTRUCT lpcs,
                                  CCreateContext* pContext)
{
    CSize    size( 10, 10 );
    return m_wndSplitter.Create( this, 2, 2, size, pContext);
}
```

Believe it or not, that's all that is required to implement a dynamic split view. Of course, the actual view doesn't do anything yet, but that's covered in the next section.

Modifying the CSplitView Class

In order to show that the split views are actually being displayed, the CSplitView::OnDraw function was modified to display an ellipse inside the view window. The following source code listing is a simple function that draws an ellipse around the entire client area of the view.

```
void CSplitView::OnDraw(CDC* pDC)
{
    CRect    rcClient;
    GetClientRect( rcClient );
    pDC->DPtoLP( rcClient );

    pDC->SelectStockObject( BLACK_PEN );
    pDC->Ellipse( rcClient );
}
```

Using Static Split Views

Implementing a static splitter requires just slightly more code than the previous example. For a static split view, you must create the views inside the OnCreateClient member function. To give the Split program static split views, replace the CChildFrame::OnCreateClient member function provided earlier with the source code in Listing 7.4.

Listing 7.4. Creating a static split view.

```
BOOL CChildFrame::OnCreateClient(LPCREATESTRUCT lpcs,
                                 CCreateContext* pContext)
{
    if( m_wndSplitter.CreateStatic(this, 2, 1) == FALSE )
    {
        TRACE0("Failed to CreateStaticSplitter\n");
        return FALSE;
    }
    BOOL bCreated = m_wndSplitter.CreateView( 0,
                                              0,
                                              pContext->m_pNewViewClass,
                                              CSize(100, 115),
                                              pContext );
    if( bCreated == FALSE )
    {
        TRACE0("Failed to create first pane\n");
        return FALSE;
    }
    // add the second splitter pane
    bCreated = m_wndSplitter.CreateView( 1,
                                         0,
                                         RUNTIME_CLASS(CSplitView),
                                         CSize(0, 0),
                                         pContext);
    if( bCreated == FALSE )
    {
        TRACE0("Failed to create second pane\n");
        return FALSE;
    }
    // activate the input view
    SetActiveView((CView*)m_wndSplitter.GetPane(0,0));
    return TRUE;
}
```

There are two function calls that do most of the work in the OnCreateClient member function:

- CreateStatic is used to create a static split view. A pointer to the child frame that owns the split view is passed as a parameter. The number of panes displayed by the splitter is also passed; in this case, the split view has two rows and one column.

- The first call to CreateView uses the runtime class stored in pContext to create the first view. The first two parameters to CreateView specify which pane will be used to display the view. The pane at position 0,0 is the upper-left pane. The second call to CreateView uses the pane at 1,0, which is the lower pane.

Before compiling the modified class, add these two include statements to the ChildFrame.cpp file, just after the other #include statements:

```
#include "SplitDoc.h"
#include "SplitView.h"
```

Summary

In this chapter I have discussed the document view architecture and how it is used with the MFC class library. I have also discussed two sample programs that demonstrate how documents and views interact with each other.

Windows and the Graphical Device Interface

IN THIS CHAPTER

In this chapter, I discuss the Graphical Device Interface (GDI) provided by Windows NT. The basic differences between the GDI offered by Windows 95 and Windows NT are covered, as well as the various types of GDI objects offered by Windows NT. Example programs that demonstrate how GDI objects are used are provided also.

This chapter also discusses 256-color bitmaps and the steps required to modify the system color palette to display 256-color bitmaps properly. An example program that loads and displays 256-color bitmaps is provided; this application includes two reusable classes that you can include in your own programs.

This chapter also covers using enhanced metafiles, which are used to store GDI functions for playback at a later time, and GDI paths, which can be used to draw irregular or unusual shapes. Example programs for each of these topics are provided also.

GDI Basics

The Windows NT GDI is similar to the GDI offered in Windows 95 and earlier versions of 16-bit Windows. However, it also includes some enhancements that make Windows NT a preferred choice for some types of graphics applications.

> **NOTE**
>
> Many of the differences between the GDI offered by Windows NT and that offered by Windows 95 are a result of Windows 95's need to offer backward compatibility to applications that ran on Windows 3.1. Too many Windows 3.1 applications rely on implementation details with regard to GDI objects, and these applications tend to break when these structures change. In addition, Microsoft made certain trade-offs to reduce the memory footprint required by Windows 95. These trade-offs include some Win32 functions that aren't implemented in Windows 95.
>
> In fact, much of the Windows 95 GDI is 16-bit code. Many parameters and values are truncated at 16 bits. Most of these issues are only minor problems for most people. Still, it's nice to know where possible problems are. Of course, this is only an issue if you write code that must run on Windows 95 and Windows NT. A list of differences between Windows 95 and Windows NT GDI is provided in the following sections.
>
> There are two major problems when moving GDI code between Windows NT and Windows 95:
>
> - ■ In Windows 95, all coordinates are 16-bit values. If you use a 32-bit value, the least significant 16 bits are truncated.
>
> - ■ In Windows 95, if you delete a GDI object that is selected into a device context (DC), the operation succeeds. The deleted object is still selected into the DC,

but the DC destroys the object when the DC is deleted. However, in Windows NT, the call to `DeleteObject` will fail, and you will have a memory leak unless you unselect the GDI object and delete it again.

In addition to these issues, some GDI calls and options aren't supported between the two platforms. All these differences are documented, and there is always a way around the limitation. These differences will probably not cause you any trouble, in most cases.

Device Contexts

A DC is an important part of the Windows NT GDI. A DC is a structure maintained by Windows, which stores information needed when a Windows NT application must display output to a device. The DC stores information about the drawing surface and its capabilities. Before using any of the GDI output functions, you must create a DC for that device.

Windows NT and the MFC class library provide the following four different basic types of DCs. Although you use these DCs in different situations, the basic rules for their use are consistent.

- Display DCs are used to display information to a standard video terminal. These are the most commonly used DCs in a Windows program.
- Printer DCs are used to display output on a printer or plotter.
- Memory DCs, sometimes called *compatible DCs*, are used to perform drawing operations on a bitmap.
- Information DCs are used to collect information on a device. These DCs cannot be used for actual output. However, they're extremely fast and have little overhead and therefore are ideal for use when information is being collected.

With the exception of the information DCs, each of the different DC types is used for creating a different sort of output. That's why the MFC class library offers five classes that help encapsulate Windows NT DCs. These five classes are shown in Figure 8.1.

The DC classes provided by MFC are

- `CDC` is the base class for all the DC classes.
- `CPaintDC` performs some useful housekeeping functions that are needed when a window responds to `WM_PAINT`.
- `CMetaFileDC` is used when creating metafiles, which are records of GDI commands that can be used in place of bitmaps.

■ CClientDC is used when a DC will be used only for output to a window's client area.

■ CWindowDC is used when the entire window may be drawn on.

FIGURE 8.1.

The relationships between MFC DC classes.

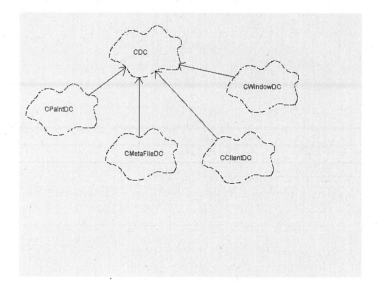

The GDI Map Modes

In Windows, you use *mapping modes* to define the size and direction of units used in drawing functions. As a Windows programmer, there are several different coordinate systems available to you. Mapping modes can use physical or logical dimensions, and they can start at the top, at the bottom, or at an arbitrary point on the screen.

There are a total of eight different mapping modes available in Windows. You can retrieve the current mapping mode used by a DC using the GetMapMode function and set a new mapping mode using SetMapMode. The available mapping modes are

■ MM_ANISOTROPIC uses a viewport to scale the logical units to an application-defined value. The SetWindowExt and SetViewportExt member functions are used to change the units, orientation, and scaling.

■ MM_HIENGLISH, where each logical unit is converted to a physical value of 0.001 inch. Positive x is to the right; positive y is up.

■ MM_HIMETRIC, where each logical unit is converted to a physical value of 0.01 millimeter. Positive x is to the right; positive y is up.

■ MM_ISOTROPIC, similar to MM_ANISOTROPIC, where logical units are converted to arbitrary units with equally scaled axes. This means that 1 unit on the x-axis is always equal to 1 unit on the y-axis. Use the SetWindowExt and SetViewportExt member functions to specify the desired units and orientation of the axes.

- ■ MM_LOENGLISH, where each logical unit is converted to a physical value of 0.01 inch. Positive x is to the right; positive y is up.

- ■ MM_LOMETRIC, where each logical unit is converted to a physical value of 0.1 millimeter. Positive x is to the right; positive y is up.

- ■ MM_TEXT, where each logical unit is converted to 1 device pixel. Positive x is to the right; positive y is down.

- ■ MM_TWIPS, where each logical unit is converted to 1/20 of a point. Because a point is 1/72 inch, a *twip* is 1/1440 inch. This mapping mode is useful when sending output to a printer. Positive x is to the right; positive y is up.

GDI Objects and Their Use

When a DC is created, it has a number of default GDI objects assigned to it, as shown in Figure 8.2. Each of the GDI objects shown in Figure 8.2 has a default value. For example, the bitmap is always a one-pixel, monochrome bitmap. The pen is always a solid black pen. Before a DC can be used, it almost always needs to be massaged in some way.

FIGURE 8.2.

A DC is created with a set of default GDI objects.

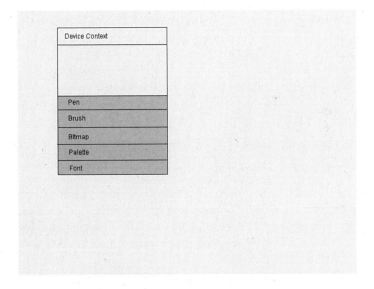

Each of these default objects can be replaced by calling SelectObject to replace the current GDI object with a new one. When a new GDI object is selected, the current object is passed back to the caller as a return value. Failure to return a DC to its original state is a common source of memory leaks. Code that selects a new object should always look something like this:

```
CBitmap* pbmpOld = dcMem.SelectObject( &bmpHello );
if( pbmpOld != NULL )
{
```

```
    // Use the bitmap...
    //
    // Return the old bitmap to the DC.
    dcMem.SelectObject( pbmpOld );
}
```

Notice that the pbmpOld value is checked to make sure that it isn't NULL. If the call to SelectObject fails, the original bitmap isn't returned. In that case, there's no need to return the original bitmap to the DC, because a new one was never selected.

One last point about DCs and GDI objects: In 16-bit versions of Windows, it was possible to exchange DCs and GDI objects between processes. This was due to the fact that the old Windows 3.1 GDI had no protection model, and all the applications shared a common GDI segment. In Windows NT, this is a definite no-go, and you will find that any GDI handles or pointers you attempt to pass between processes yield unpredictable results.

Pens

A pen is a Windows GDI object used to draw lines and figures. A pen is perfect in situations where you must draw a geometric shape or line. Although you might use a bitmap for complicated images, you easily can draw squares, rectangles, circles, and other basic shapes using pens. Think of a Windows pen as being like an ink pen at your desk.

A Windows pen object has three attributes.

■ Width, usually one pixel wide, although a pen can be as wide as you like.

■ Style, which can be any of the pen styles discussed later.

■ Color, which can be any Windows color packed into a COLORREF structure and which is discussed in the section *Using Color with Pens*.

Programs written for Windows use two types of pens.

■ Cosmetic pens, which are always drawn in device units, regardless of the current mapping mode. Cosmetic pens are extremely quick, and are mapped directly into device units. This makes them useful for drawing things like frames, borders, grid lines, and other screen objects that should not be affected by the current DC mapping mode.

■ Geometric pens, which are drawn in logical units and are affected by the current mapping mode. Geometric pens have more style and drawing options than cosmetic pens. Geometric pens require more CPU power, but offer more styles. You can manipulate geometric pens using any of the available mapping modes.

Understanding Cosmetic Pens

Cosmetic pens aren't affected by the current mapping mode's scaling factor, because they are always drawn in device units. This makes them useful for work in which a line must overlay another view that may be scaled. These basic styles are available for cosmetic pens:

- ■ PS_SOLID, which creates a solid pen.
- ■ PS_DASH, used to create a dashed pen. If the pen width is greater than 1, the pen is drawn as PS_SOLID.
- ■ PS_DOT, which creates a dotted pen. This style is also only valid for pens with a width of 1. Wider pens are drawn as PS_SOLID.
- ■ PS_DASHDOT, which creates a pen with alternating dashes and dots. If the pen width is greater than 1, a solid pen is drawn instead.
- ■ PS_DASHDOTDOT, which creates a pen with alternating dashes and double dots. If the pen width is greater than 1, a solid pen is drawn instead.
- ■ PS_NULL, which creates a null pen; this pen doesn't draw at all.
- ■ PS_INSIDEFRAME, which creates a pen that draws a line inside the frame of closed shapes produced by GDI functions, such as the Ellipse and Rectangle functions.
- ■ PS_ALTERNATE, which can be applied only to cosmetic pens and which creates a pen that sets every other pixel.

Figure 8.3 shows examples of each of these pen styles.

FIGURE 8.3.

Examples of the styles available for pens.

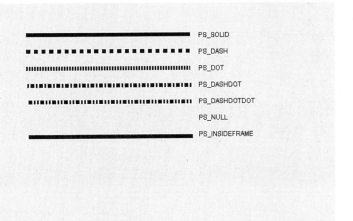

Using Geometric Pens

Geometric pens can use all of the styles available for cosmetic pens except for the PS_ALTERNATE style, and they also have access to three additional attributes:

- A pattern used to draw the pen
- End cap styles used for terminating a line
- A joining style, used when two lines intersect

Defining Pattern Styles for Pens

In addition to other styles shared with cosmetic pens, a geometric pen can be associated with a brush style by passing a LOGBRUSH, or *logical brush structure,* as a parameter when the pen is created. Using a LOGBRUSH structure enables you to specify patterns and hatching styles for a pen, just like a brush.

Defining End-Cap Styles

When a line drawn with a pen terminates, an *end cap* is drawn. If the line is drawn with a geometric pen, you can specify the style of the end cap. The following end cap styles are available:

- PS_ENDCAP_ROUND, which draws rounded end caps after the line's end point
- PS_ENDCAP_SQUARE, which draws a square box extending slightly past the line's end point as an end cap
- PS_ENDCAP_FLAT, which draws a line that ends exactly on the end point, with a flat end cap

These three styles are shown in Figure 8.4. The square and round end caps actually extend past the end of the line drawn by the pen. The flat end cap style extends only to the end of the line.

Defining Joining Styles

A *joining style* is used to determine how the intersection of two lines should be drawn. This attribute is only used for geometric pens; cosmetic pens are simply joined at right angles to each other. The join can be one of the following styles:

- PS_JOIN_BEVEL, which specifies a beveled join
- PS_JOIN_MITER, which specifies a miter join, but only if the join is within limits set by ::SetMiterLimit. If the join exceeds this limit, it is drawn as a beveled join.
- PS_JOIN_ROUND, which specifies a rounded joint

Examples of each join type are shown in Figure 8.5.

FIGURE 8.4.

End-cap styles available for geometric pens.

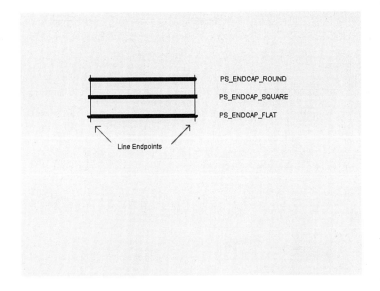

FIGURE 8.5.

Join styles available for geometric pens.

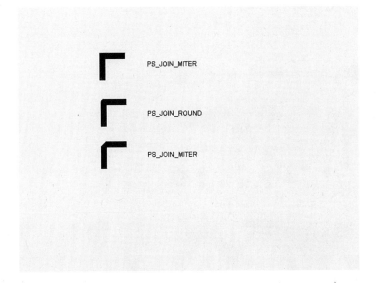

Using Color with Pens

All pens are given a color by passing a COLORREF structure as a parameter when they are created. A COLORREF structure is used commonly to pass color information as a parameter in Windows programs. A COLORREF is a 32-bit value, made up of four bytes (where each byte contains eight bits). Three of the bytes specify the relative intensities of red, green, and blue for a particular color, and the fourth byte is left unused.

A COLORREF is created using the RGB macro, which takes three parameters, each ranging from 0 to 255, with 255 signifying that the maximum amount of that color should be included in the COLORREF. For example, to create a COLORREF with a white value, the definition would look like this:

```
COLORREF clrWhite = RGB(255,255,255);
```

For black, the definition would look like this:

```
COLORREF clrBlack = RGB(0,0,0);
```

Using the CPen Class

The CPen class is simple, as there are only a few things that can be done to a pen object; most of the fun occurs when the pen object is selected into a DC. The CPen class provides three constructors: two simple constructors primarily for cosmetic pens and another extremely flexible constructor primarily for geometric pens.

The first constructor has no arguments.

```
CPen     aGreenPen;
aGreenPen.Create( PS_SOLID, 1, RGB(0,255,0);
```

If you use this constructor, use the Create member function to actually create the pen and make it ready for use.

The second constructor provided for CPen also is used for cosmetic pens:

```
CPen     penDottedAndRed( PS_DOT, 1, RGB(255,0,0) );
```

This version of the constructor accepts three parameters: the pen style, width, and pen color.

The third constructor used for CPen objects allows any sort of pen to be created. It also uses more parameters.

```
LOGBRUSH     lbrGrnHatch;

lbrGrnHatch.lbStyle = BS_HATCHED;
lbrGrnHatch.lbColor = RGB(0,255,0);
lbrGrnHatch.lbHatch = HS_DIAGCROSS;

CPen     penGeometric( PS_DOT ¦ PS_GEOMETRIC ¦ PS_ENDCAPROUND,
                       50,
                       &lbrGrnHatch,
                       0,
                       NULL );
```

The constructor's first parameter is the pen's style, with the or operator used to combine all styles that are applied to the pen. The second parameter for the constructor is the width; if the pen is cosmetic, it must be set to 1. The third parameter is a pointer to a LOGBRUSH structure. In this example, lbrGrnHatch is defined as a diagonally cross-hatched green brush.

The last two parameters are rarely used; they define a user-supplied pattern for the pen. These two parameters are used only if the pen is created with the PS_USERSTYLE attribute. The fourth parameter is the number of elements in the style array, and the fifth parameter is an array of DWORD values, each used to define the length of a dash or space in the pen's pattern.

Using Stock Pens

The simplest pens to use are known as *stock objects*. Each type of GDI object has a certain number of stock objects that belong to the operating systems and are easy to use because they don't have to be constructed or deleted. There are three stock pens provided by Windows.

- BLACK_PEN, which, oddly enough, provides a black pen
- WHITE_PEN, which provides a white pen
- NULL_PEN, which provides a NULL pen and is exactly the same as creating a pen with the PS_NULL style

Each of these pens is exactly one unit wide. If you need a wider pen, you must create one using the CPen class. These pens are used through a CDC object by calling the SelectStockObject function, passing the stock object as a parameter, as follows:

```
CPen* pOldPen = pDC->SelectStockObject( BLACK_PEN );
```

As with other GDI objects, it's a good idea to maintain the pattern of storing the first GDI object returned from a SelectObject function so that it can be returned to the operating system.

Drawing with Pens

Pens are just one of the GDI objects that you can use with a DC. After a pen has been selected into a DC, there are several different drawing functions that can be performed with the DC. The CDC class used to represent DCs includes these drawing functions often used with pens:

- Ellipse, used to draw an ellipse. This function is also used to draw circles, because a circle is just a special type of ellipse.
- Arc, used to draw a portion of an ellipse.
- LineTo and MoveTo, used to draw lines. Together they're often used to draw highlighting, squares, rectangles, and other types of figures.

Brushes

A brush is a GDI object used to fill a control, window, or other area with a color or bitmap pattern. A brush is much like a pen; you select them the same way, some of the attributes are similar, and there are a series of stock objects that you can use without much overhead. However, you use a brush to fill an area rather than draw a line or a figure. A common use for brushes is to color windows, controls, or dialog boxes.

A brush has three attributes:

■ Color, used to specify the brush color. You use a COLORREF value, just as when you specify a pen color.

■ Pattern, used to define the pattern used by the brush.

■ Hatching Style, used when a hatch pattern is specified.

Later in this chapter, the Meta example project uses a brush to fill a circle with color. Removing the metafile-specific code, a simplified version of the code used to draw a red circle looks like this:

```
CBrush brRed( RGB(255,0,0) );
CBrush* pOldBrush = pDC->SelectObject( &brBlue );
ASSERT( pOldBrush );
CRect rcCircle(0,0,50,50);
pDC->Ellipse( rcCircle );
pDC->SelectObject( pOldBrush );
```

After creating a brush using an RGB value, the brush is selected into a DC. As with the previous pen example, if the return value from SelectObject is NULL, the GDI object was not selected. The circle is drawn using the Ellipse function, and the original brush is reselected into the DC.

Fonts

Fonts are GDI objects, much like the pens and brushes discussed earlier, and are used to define the characters used for output in a Windows program. A collection of characters and other symbols that share the same attributes is called a *font*.

Strictly speaking, fonts aren't necessary for most programs written for Windows. A default font is selected into every DC automatically, and it may work just fine for most applications. However, almost every program can benefit from using fonts that have been selected to suit its specific needs.

Before going on, I'll define some terms that are unique to programming with fonts:

■ A *glyph* is an individual character.

■ *Font pitch* refers to the width of individual characters; *fixed pitch* means that each character has the same width, *variable pitch* means that some characters will be wider than others.

■ A *serif* is the small cross at the ends of some characters. A font with a serif has short crosses at the ends of lines making up the font; Times New Roman is such a *serif* font. A font without serifs is often called a *sans serif* font. Figure 8.6 shows examples of a serif and a sans serif font.

Fonts are maintained by Windows. Information about each currently installed font is stored in a system table known as the *font table*.

FIGURE 8.6.

Serif and sans serif fonts.

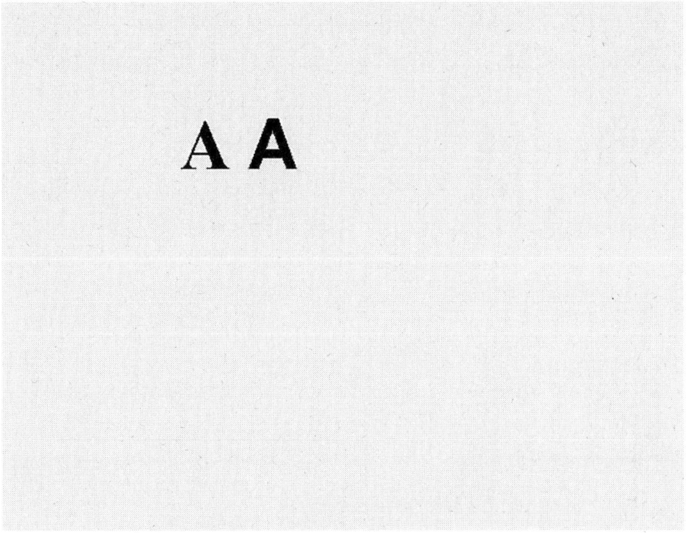

There are three different types of fonts; each type has different capabilities.

■ Raster fonts are created from bitmaps and are stored in resource files with a .FON extension. Each bitmap is created for a specific screen resolution and is used by Windows to map out exactly how the glyph looks when it is displayed.

■ Vector fonts consist of a series of endpoints that are connected together to create each glyph and also are found in files with a .FON extension. Unlike raster fonts, vector fonts are device-independent but are the slowest of the three font types.

■ TrueType fonts are the most flexible of all Windows fonts. First introduced in Windows 3.1, TrueType fonts consist of line and curve information, as well as hints about each glyph. Each TrueType font is stored in two files: one with an .FOT extension, the other with a .TTF extension.

Fonts are also arranged into six families that define the general attributes of the font. Fonts in the same family share similar strokes, serifs, or pitch.

The six font families are

■ Decorative, which specifies novelty fonts such as Old English.

■ Dontcare, which specifies a generic group of fonts; either the information doesn't exist or is unimportant.

■ Modern, which specifies fonts that have fixed pitch and may or may not have serifs. Courier New is an example of a modern font.

■ Roman, which specifies fonts that have variable pitch and have serifs, such as Times New Roman.

- Script, which specifies fonts that are similar to handwriting.
- Swiss, which specifies a font that is fixed pitch and does not have serifs, such as Arial.

Using the MFC `CFont` Class

Like other GDI objects, the easiest way to use a font is to use the MFC class library. Like other GDI objects, fonts must be used with a DC and are influenced by the current state of the DC, such as mapping mode and color definitions. When you're working with text output, the `CFont` class helps make using a font easy.

There are two basic ways to use a font in your program:

- You can specify exactly what sort of font should be used.
- You can specify font general attributes and let Windows select a font for you.

Using Font Attributes

In addition to the font families I discussed earlier, there are other general attributes you can use to specify a font. There are a lot of font attributes, mainly because there are so many different ways to display characters in a program written for Windows. Don't worry; after you've used fonts a few times, you'll be able to create fonts with no trouble at all.

The Font Height and Width

You can specify the height of the font using one of the methods:

- If a height greater than zero is specified, Windows tries to match the requested height with one of the available fonts, and the font is mapped using logical units.
- If a font height of zero is specified, a reasonable default font is used. In this case, "reasonable" is defined by Windows.
- If the specified height is a negative number, the font is mapped using hardware units. Windows searches for a font that matches the absolute value of the size provided.

Logical units usually are used for screen display, and physical units are usually used for printing. In Chapter 15, "Printing," you use `MM_TWIPS` to create fonts based on device units.

The width of a font usually is set to zero, which tells Windows to select an appropriate default width. However, in some cases you may want to specify your own font width to display compressed or elongated text.

The Font Character Set

Every font is made up of a large number of characters and other symbols that can be displayed. The actual symbols contained in a font depend on the character set supported by that font. These three-character sets are available:

- ANSI_CHARSET, used for most output when programming in Windows. This is the character set you're most likely to use. The symbol ANSI_CHARSET is defined as equal to zero, which makes it easy to use as a default parameter.

- OEM_CHARSET, used mainly for console mode programs, is almost identical to the ANSI character set. This character set is system-dependent and can't be used reliably for every machine capable of running Windows. Some of the low- and high-numbered characters are different, but these are rarely used in Windows.

- SYMBOL_CHARSET, used to display symbols, such as the ones used in math formulas.

Attributes That Affect Font Output

Three parameters specify output attributes of the selected font: *output precision, clipping precision,* and *output quality.*

Output precision is used to specify how closely the font returned by Windows must match the requested font. A range of options is available, from allowing Windows to select a reasonable match to requiring an exact match:

- OUT_DEFAULT_PRECIS, used when Windows can choose a "reasonable" font. This is the option selected most often and is equivalent to using zero as a parameter.

- OUT_STRING_PRECIS, used to specify that the font chosen by Windows must match the requested font's size.

- OUT_CHARACTER_PRECIS, used to specify that the font must match all requested attributes except orientation and escapement.

- OUT_STROKE_PRECIS, used to specify that the font chosen must exactly match the requested font.

Clipping precision is used to specify how characters are treated when they cross a clipping boundary. There are three options.

- CLIP_DEFAULT_PRECIS, which allows Windows to select a "reasonable" font. This is the option selected most often and is equal to zero.

- CLIP_CHARACTER_PRECIS, which requires Windows to select a font that allows individual characters to be clipped if any part of the character lies outside the clipping region.

- CLIP_STROKE_PRECIS, which requires Windows to choose a font that allows portions of an individual character to be clipped if a character falls on the clipping boundary.

The output quality of the font refers to the degree to which GDI routines must match logical font attributes to the physical representation of the font. Here, again, there are three options.

- DEFAULT_QUALITY, where appearance doesn't matter; Windows is free to provide a "reasonable" font. This is a commonly selected option and is equivalent to using 0 as a parameter.

- DRAFT_QUALITY, where fast output is given higher priority than print quality. Some effects, such as strikethrough, bold, italics, and underlined characters are synthesized by GDI routines if necessary.

- PROOF_QUALITY, where the output quality is given higher priority than output speed. The quality of the font is more important than exact matching of the logical font attributes. Some effects, such as strikethrough, bold, italics, and underlined characters are synthesized by GDI routines if necessary.

Font Pitch and Family Attributes

As discussed earlier, all fonts have a certain pitch. When you request a font from Windows, there are three different choices for the pitch.

- DEFAULT_PITCH, where Windows selects a reasonable font based on other specified attributes.

- FIXED_PITCH, where the font created by Windows must have a fixed pitch.

- VARIABLE_PITCH, where the font is specified to have a variable pitch.

As discussed earlier, the font family describes general characteristics for a type of font and can be used when a specific font may not be available on all machines. Here are the values for font families:

- FF_DECORATIVE
- FF_DONTCARE
- FF_MODERN
- FF_ROMAN
- FF_SCRIPT
- FF_SWISS

The pitch attribute can be combined with a font family attribute using the bitwise OR operator, like this:

```
lfHeading.lfPitchAndFamily = DEFAULT_PITCH | FF_SWISS;
```

It isn't always necessary to combine the pitch and family attributes. For example, in the preceding example it's possible to specify just FF_SWISS.

Font Weights

You can specify the relative weight of a font, based on a scale from 0 to 1,000. A weight of 400 describes a "normal" font, and 700 is used for a "bold" font. If you use 0, Windows uses a reasonable default weight for the font. Each of the weight options between 0 and 900 have symbolic names, as shown in Table 8.1.

Table 8.1. Symbolic names for font weights.

Symbol	Weight
FW_DONTCARE	0
FW_THIN	100
FW_EXTRALIGHT	200
FW_ULTRALIGHT	200
FW_LIGHT	300
FW_NORMAL	400
FW_REGULAR	400
FW_MEDIUM	500
FW_SEMIBOLD	600
FW_DEMIBOLD	600
FW_BOLD	700
FW_EXTRABOLD	800
FW_ULTRABOLD	800
FW_BLACK	900
FW_HEAVY	900

Although not every weight is available for every font, Windows tries to select a font weight close to the requested value.

Other Font Attributes

It's possible to define the escapement and orientation of a font. The *escapement* is the angle, in tenths of a degree, formed by a line of text in relation to the bottom of the page. For example, an escapement of 900 describes a font where each line of text is rotated 90 degrees counter-clockwise. The *orientation* of a font is similar to the escapement, but applies to each character rather than to an entire line of text.

Italic, underline, or strikethrough effects are assigned by specifying TRUE or FALSE for each of these attributes.

Finally, you can specify the typeface name. This is the name of a font that should be a good match for the parameters specified in other parts of the font description. If this parameter is set to NULL, Windows uses the other parameters when searching for a font. If you specify a name, that name is used to search for a font. If a font with that name is found, it's used.

Creating a Font Using CFont

The first time you consider creating a CFont object, you may be intimidated by the large number of parameters it takes. Don't worry; most of the parameters can actually be set to default values, or zero, and the Windows NT font mapper will select a font for you.

The following source code creates two fonts. One font, fntArial, uses zero for all the parameters and specifies a font name. The other font, fntBoldSwiss, specifies many of the characteristics of a desired font, and the font mapper determines a reasonable font.

```
void CDCTestView::OnDraw(CDC* pDC)
{
    CRect rcClient;
    GetClientRect( rcClient );
    pDC->DPtoLP( rcClient );
    COLORREF clrOld = pDC->SetTextColor( RGB(0,255,0) );
    int nOldMode = pDC->SetBkMode( TRANSPARENT );
    CFont   fntArial, fntBoldSwiss;
    fntArial.CreateFont( 0, 0, 0, 0, 0, 0, 0, 0,
                         0, 0, 0, 0, 0, "Arial" );
    fntBoldSwiss.CreateFont( rcClient.Height()/20, 0, 0, 0,
                      FW_BOLD, TRUE, FALSE, 0, ANSI_CHARSET,
                      OUT_TT_PRECIS, CLIP_DEFAULT_PRECIS,
                      DEFAULT_QUALITY, DEFAULT_PITCH | FF_SWISS,
                      NULL );
    CString szMsg = "Hello! Change the color and mapping mode";
    CFont* pOldFont = pDC->SelectObject( &fntArial );
    pDC->TextOut( 0, rcClient.Height()/4, szMsg );
    pDC->SelectObject( &fntBoldSwiss );
    pDC->TextOut( 0, rcClient.Height()/2, szMsg );
    // Restore the old GDI objects
    pDC->SelectObject( pOldFont );
    pDC->SetTextColor( clrOld );
    pDC->SetBkMode( nOldMode );
}
```

Creating a Font Using a LOGFONT Structure

The LOGFONT structure is often used to describe a font. Just as the LOGBRUSH structure discussed earlier was used to describe a particular brush, the LOGFONT structure is used to describe a particular font. A LOGFONT isn't a font; it's just a description, so it contains members for all the attributes available for a font.

Using a LOGFONT simplifies creating fonts, because many of the attributes for a series of fonts can be shared. This code uses a LOGFONT structure to create several different fonts:

```
void CMyView::OnDraw(CDC* pDC)
{
    COLORREF clrOld = pDC->SetTextColor( RGB(255,0,0) );
    int nOldMode = pDC->SetBkMode( TRANSPARENT );

    TEXTMETRIC tm;
    pDC->GetTextMetrics( &tm );
    int cy = tm.tmExternalLeading + tm.tmHeight;
    int yPos = cy;

    LOGFONT lf;
    memset( &lf, 0, sizeof(LOGFONT) );

    CString szMsg = "Hello! I'm an Arial font";
    CFont    fntArial;
    lstrcpy( lf.lfFaceName, "Arial" );
    fntArial.CreateFontIndirect( &lf );
    CFont* pOldFont = pDC->SelectObject( &fntArial );
    pDC->TextOut( 0, yPos, szMsg );

    yPos += cy;
    szMsg = "Hello! I'm a Courier font";
    CFont fntCourier;
    lstrcpy( lf.lfFaceName, "Courier New" );
    fntCourier.CreateFontIndirect( &lf );
    pDC->SelectObject( &fntCourier );
    pDC->TextOut( 0, yPos, szMsg );

    yPos += cy;
    szMsg = "Hello! I'm a Times font";
    CFont fntTimes;
    lstrcpy( lf.lfFaceName, "Times New Roman" );
    fntTimes.CreateFontIndirect( &lf );
    pDC->SelectObject( &fntTimes );
    pDC->TextOut( 0, yPos, szMsg );

    pDC->SelectObject( pOldFont );
    pDC->SetTextColor( clrOld );
    pDC->SetBkMode( nOldMode );
}
```

Bitmaps

Every DC stores a handle to a bitmap as one of its attributes. As discussed earlier, this is a one-pixel monochrome bitmap that isn't useful for much; you will almost always select a new bitmap rather than using the default bitmap.

DDBs Versus DIBs

Bitmaps come in two basic flavors: Device-Independent Bitmaps (DIB) and Device Dependent Bitmaps (DDB). In early versions of 16-bit Windows, only DDBs were supported. Beginning with Windows 3.0, and on all versions of Windows NT, DIBs are also supported.

A DDB is tightly coupled to the device that it's intended to be displayed on. The memory that is used to store the bitmap is actually allocated by the device driver, and an application that needs to change the contents of the bitmap must do so indirectly, a slow and inefficient process. Figure 8.7 shows how a DDB is controlled by a device driver, and the application has only indirect access to the bitmap.

FIGURE 8.7.

A device-dependent bitmap is controlled by the device driver.

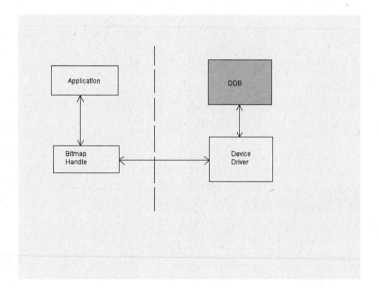

One of the problems with DDBs is that an application must supply bitmaps in a format supported by the device driver. The application must either store bitmaps in multiple formats, or it must be capable of converting a bitmap from one format into another. Either way, dealing with a DDB can be difficult and time consuming.

The DIB Format

To get around these problems, all versions of Windows since the Jurassic era (Windows 3.0) support DIBs. A DIB has a known structure that can be converted easily into a DDB whenever necessary.

A DIB can exist in two formats, the Windows format and the OS/2 format. Because the OS/2 format is rarely used, my examples assume the DIB is in the Windows format. A DIB bitmap stored in a file consists of four sections, as shown in Figure 8.8.

FIGURE 8.8.

DIBs contain four data structures.

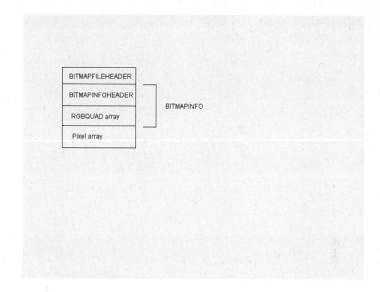

The **BITMAPFILEINFO** Structure

The BITMAPFILEINFO structure has the following members:

```
WORD     bfType;
DWORD    bfSize;
WORD     bfReserved1;
WORD     bfReserved2;
DWORD    bfOffBits;
```

The value of bfType is always 0x4D42, the ASCII value for the characters B and M. The value of bfSize is supposed to be the size of the bitmap file; however, in many bitmaps this value is incorrect due to an early SDK documentation error. The value of bfOffBits is the distance to actual bitmap data, and is rarely used. The remaining structure members are reserved and should always be set to zero.

The BITMAPFILEINFO structure is used only when the bitmap is read or stored to disk. When a DIB is manipulated in memory, the BITMAPFILEINFO structure is often discarded. The remaining parts of the DIB structure follow the same format whether they're located in RAM or in a disk file.

The **BITMAPINFO** Structure

The actual bitmap header consists of a BITMAPINFO structure that has the following members:

```
BITMAPINFOHEADER bmiHeader;
RGBQUAD          bmiColors[]; // contains zero or more palette values
```

The BITMAPINFO structure contains a BITMAPINFOHEADER and zero or more palette values for pixels stored in the bitmap. BITMAPINFOHEADER contains information about the dimensions, color format, and compression information for the bitmap. The BITMAPINFOHEADER structure contains the following members:

```
DWORD    DbiSize
LONG     biWidth
LONG     biHeight
WORD     biPlanes
WORD     biBitCount
DWORD    biCompression
DWORD    biSizeImage
LONG     biXPelsPerMeter
LONG     biYPelsPerMeter
DWORD    biClrUsed
DWORD    biClrImportant
```

DbiSize is intended to be the size of the bitmap structure. However, due to documentation errors in the early versions of the Windows SDK, this value cannot be trusted as accurate.

biWidth and biHeight are the bitmap dimensions in pixels. If the height is a negative number, the bitmap is a "top-down" bitmap (see the following note). The value of biPlanes is the number of planes supported by the bitmap. This value is always 1 in Windows NT.

> **NOTE**
>
> Until recently, all bitmaps were "bottom-up," meaning that the first pixel stored in the bitmap was the lower-left pixel in the displayed image. The pixels stored in a bottom-up bitmap are stored in order, with the last pixel representing the upper-right pixel in the displayed image.
>
> Top-down bitmaps reverse the order of the stored pixels. The first pixel in the bitmap refers to the top-left pixel in the displayed image, and the last pixel in the bitmap refers to the bottom-right pixel in the displayed image.

The value of biBitCount is the number of bits used to represent each pixel in the bitmap. This value must be either 1, 4, 8, 16, 24, or 32.

The type of compression, if any, is determined by the value of biCompression. Top-down bitmaps are never compressed. biCompression has one of the following values.

- BI_RGB indicates that the bitmap is not compressed.
- BI_RLE8 is a run-length encoded (RLE) format for bitmaps with 8 bits per pixel.
- BI_RLE4 is an RLE format for bitmaps with 4 bits per pixel.

- BI_BITFIELDS is used to specify that the bitmap isn't compressed, and the color table is made up of three RGB doubleword values for each pixel in the bitmap. This value is used when biBitCount is 16 or 32.

The size of the bitmap image in bytes is given in the biSizeImage member. If the value of biCompression is BI_RGB, this value may be zero.

The values of biXPelsPerMeter and biYPelsPerMeter can be used to help an application select the most appropriate bitmap for a particular resolution, if multiple resources are available.

The value of biClrUsed specifies the number of valid entries in the bitmap's color table. If this value is zero, the maximum number of entries should be assumed, based on the value of biBitCount.

The number of colors considered "important" is stored in biClrImportant. If this value is zero, all colors are considered important. This information is never used by any of the GDI functions; rather it's meant for use by applications. If an application is unable to create a palette that contains all the bitmap's colors, this value can be used to determine whether the result is acceptable.

After the BITMAPINFOHEADER structure, the bmiColors variable marks the beginning of the color table. This table is used if the bitmap is not a 16, 24, or 32 bit-per-pixel bitmap. The color table is an array of RGBQUAD structures, with each entry storing one of the colors used by the bitmap. The members of the RGBQUAD structure are

```
BYTE      rgbBlue;
BYTE      rgbGreen;
BYTE      rgbRed;
BYTE      rgbReserved; // Always set to zero
```

The members of the RGBQUAD structure represent the red, green, and blue color intensity for a color stored in the color table. Each structure member has a range of 0–255. If all members have a value of zero, the color is black; if all members have a value of 255, the color is white.

The DIB Image Array

An array of pixel information follows the color table. Every pixel in the bitmap is represented by one element of this array. Each of the elements contains a value that represents one of the color map entries. For example, if the first element in the array has a value of 32, the first pixel in the bitmap will use the color found in color table entry number 32, as shown in Figure 8.9.

If this is a 16-, 24-, or 32 bit-per-pixel bitmap, there was no color table, and each element of the array contains the RGB color for a single pixel. In effect, the palette has been moved out to the pixel array for these types of bitmaps.

FIGURE 8.9.

Every entry in the image array refers to a pixel in the displayed image.

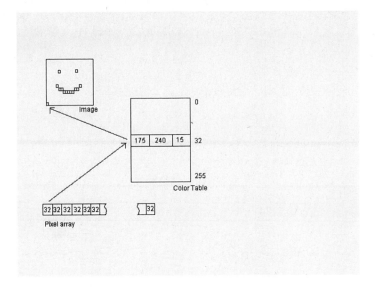

16-Color DIBs

The CBitmap class is often used to manipulate monochrome and 16-color bitmaps. Loading and displaying a bitmap with the CBitmap class is easy, requiring only a few lines of code. To display a bitmap with a resource ID of IDB_HELLO in a view, edit the view's OnDraw function like this:

```
void CBitmapView::OnDraw(CDC* pDC)
{
    CBitmap        bmp;
    bmp.LoadBitmap( IDB_HELLO );
    // Calculate bitmap size using a BITMAP structure.
    BITMAP         bm;
    bmp.GetObject( sizeof(BITMAP), &bm );
    // Create a memory DC, select the bitmap into the
    // memory DC, and BitBlt it into the view.
    CDC            dcMem;
    dcMem.CreateCompatibleDC( pDC );
    CBitmap* pbmpOld = dcMem.SelectObject( &bmp );
    pDC->BitBlt( 10,10, bm.bmWidth, bm.bmHeight,
                 &dcMem, 0,0, SRCCOPY );
    // Reselect the original bitmap into the memory DC.
    dcMem.SelectObject( pbmpOld );
}
```

256-Color DIBs

You might think that manipulating a 256-color bitmap is just as easy as loading a 16-color bitmap. Unfortunately, that's not the case. When a 256-color DIB is displayed on a 256-color device, the colors are almost never correct because of how Windows NT (as well as other Windows flavors) handles the color palette.

Before I present the code used to display 256-color bitmaps, I need to review how Windows NT determines the colors available to your application. Unfortunately, when a bitmap is loaded, Windows NT doesn't make any special effort to make sure that color entries in the bitmap's color table are added to the system's color palette. The result is an ugly-looking bitmap. To display a 256-color bitmap, you must always create and manage a logical palette for your application.

An Overview of the Windows NT Palette

The Windows NT GDI uses palettes to manage color selection for 256-color devices. There are actually several different types of palettes, as shown in Figure 8.10.

FIGURE 8.10.

The different types of color palettes used in Windows NT.

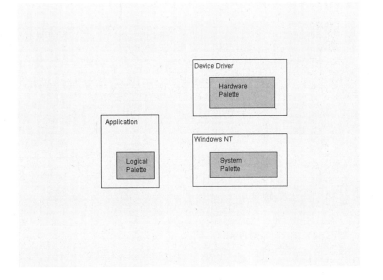

Device drivers that use palettes have an internal palette that stores the current set of colors available for display. This means that 256-color devices have 256 entries in the hardware palette.

The Windows NT palette manager maintains a system palette that (we hope) matches the hardware palette.

Every application can have one or more logical palettes. An application interacts with the system palette in order to control the colors that are currently available for display.

To maintain some level of consistency, Windows NT reserves the first and last 10 palette entries, leaving 236 palette entries for application use, as shown in Figure 8.11.

At first glance, it might seem unfair for 20 entries to be removed from the system palette. The reason that these entries are removed is to keep the basic window display predictable. The 20 reserved palette entries include the colors used by 16-color VGA devices. As long as these palette entries are available, Windows applications that don't use the palette are displayed as expected.

FIGURE 8.11.

Windows NT makes 236 palette entries available to applications.

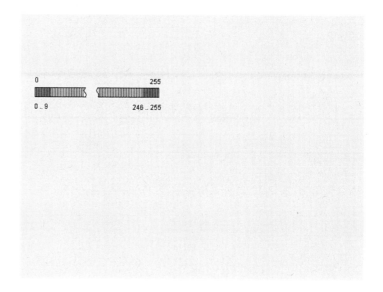

The System Palette

A palette is one of the attributes that belongs to a DC. Once you have decided to use a palette in your application, you must follow these basic steps:

■ Create a logical palette. This is the process of allocating space for the palette entries and describing the colors that will be included in the palette. As we'll demonstrate, this process is much easier than it sounds. In most cases, when you need to create a palette you copy the colors from a bitmap or other object into the new palette. This step is usually performed once, and the logical palette is stored by the application so that it can be used whenever needed.

■ Select the palette into a DC. Unlike other GDI objects, `SelectObject` doesn't work for logical palettes. You must use the `SelectPalette` function.

■ Realize the palette. Basically, realizing the palette asks the Windows NT palette manager to add your palette to the system palette or map your palette to a reasonably close substitute. Selecting and realizing the palette always happen at the same time; there's no point in selecting a palette unless you intend to realize it immediately.

■ Use the palette. If the system palette was updated, the application should redraw itself. This is usually done by invalidating any windows that depend on palette entries.

■ Unselect the palette by selecting the previous palette back into the DC.

■ Delete the palette object. This step is usually performed only when you're sure the palette is no longer needed.

There are two messages related to palettes that are sent to your application.

■ When a window moves into the foreground, Windows NT sends it a WM_QUERYNEWPALETTE message. In response to this message your application should realize its palette.

■ If the system palette is changed, all windows in the background receive a WM_PALETTECHANGED message. An application in the background should rerealize its palette to attempt to reassert colors in the system palette. If no free positions in the system palette are available, the Palette Manager maps the requested color to the closest palette entry.

In any case, you should invalidate any parts of your application that depend on your logical palette if the system palette is updated.

The DIB Example

As an example of how 256-color bitmaps are displayed, I have created an MFC example, Dib. The complete Dib example project can be found on the CD. The design of the Dib project uses a basic AppWizard SDI skeleton with these modifications:

■ A class that handles the display of DIBs, CDIBitmap

■ A class that handles creating a new 256-color palette, CBmpPalette

■ Additional palette message-handling functions

The CDIBitmap class

The CDIBitmap class does most of the work in the Dib project. The CDIBitmap class provides an easy to use interface for handling 256-color DIBs. The class interface for CDIBitmap is shown in Listing 8.1. It is also included in the Dib project as dib256.h.

Listing 8.1. The CDIBitmap class interface.

```
#ifndef DIBMP_UNLEASHED
#define DIBMP_UNLEASHED
class CDIBitmap
{
    friend class CBmpPalette;
//constructors
public:
    CDIBitmap();
    virtual ~CDIBitmap();
private:
    CDIBitmap( const CDIBitmap& dbmp ){};
```

continues

Listing 8.1. continued

```
//operations
public:
    inline BITMAPINFO* GetHeaderPtr();
    inline BYTE* GetPixelPtr();
    virtual void DrawDIB( CDC* pDC, int x, int y );
    virtual BOOL Load( CFile* pFile );
    RGBQUAD* GetColorTablePtr();

protected:
    int GetPalEntries() const;
    int GetPalEntries( BITMAPINFOHEADER& infoHeader ) const;
protected:
    int GetWidth() const;
    int GetHeight() const;

//implementation
private:
    BITMAPINFO* m_pInfo;
    BYTE*       m_pPixels;
};
#endif
```

Note that `CDIBitmap` isn't derived from `CBitmap`, or `CObject` for that matter. The class itself consumes only a few bytes, requiring space for two pointers and a virtual function table.

`CDIBitmap` has five public functions.

- ▪ `GetHeaderPtr` returns a pointer to the `BITMAPINFO` structure.
- ▪ `GetPixelPtr` returns a pointer to the beginning of the pixel image array.
- ▪ `DrawDIB` draws the DIB at a specified location.
- ▪ `Load` reads a DIB from a .BMP file, and initializes the `CDIBitmap` object.
- ▪ `GetColorTablePtr` returns a pointer to the color table.

The source code for the implementation of `CDIBitmap` is provided in Listing 8.2. Remember, you don't actually have to type all this source code yourself, because it's located on the CD in the Dib project as `dib256.cpp`.

Listing 8.2. The implementation of the `CDIBitmap` class.

```
#include "stdafx.h"
#include "dib256.h"

CDIBitmap::CDIBitmap()
{
    m_pInfo = 0;
    m_pPixels = 0;
}

CDIBitmap::~CDIBitmap()
{
```

```
        delete [] (BYTE*)m_pInfo;
        delete [] m_pPixels;
}

BOOL CDIBitmap::Load( CFile* pFile )
{
    ASSERT( pFile );
    BOOL fReturn = TRUE;
    try
    {
        delete [] (BYTE*)m_pInfo;
        delete [] m_pPixels;
        m_pInfo = 0;
        m_pPixels = 0;
        DWORD       dwStart = pFile->GetPosition();
        //
        // Check to make sure we have a bitmap. The first two bytes must
        // be 'B' and 'M'.
        BITMAPFILEHEADER fileHeader;
        pFile->Read(&fileHeader, sizeof(fileHeader));
        if( fileHeader.bfType != 0x4D42 )
            throw TEXT("Error:Unexpected file type, not a DIB\n");

        BITMAPINFOHEADER infoHeader;
        pFile->Read( &infoHeader, sizeof(infoHeader) );
        if( infoHeader.biSize != sizeof(infoHeader) )
            throw TEXT("Error:OS2 PM BMP Format not supported\n");

        // Store the sizes of the DIB structures
        int cPaletteEntries = GetPalEntries( infoHeader );
        int cColorTable = 256 * sizeof(RGBQUAD);
        int cInfo = sizeof(BITMAPINFOHEADER) + cColorTable;
        int cPixels = fileHeader.bfSize - fileHeader.bfOffBits;
        //
        // Allocate space for a new bitmap info header, and copy
        // the info header that was loaded from the file. Read
        // the file and store the results in the color table.
        m_pInfo = (BITMAPINFO*)new BYTE[cInfo];
        memcpy( m_pInfo, &infoHeader, sizeof(BITMAPINFOHEADER) );
        pFile->Read( ((BYTE*)m_pInfo) + sizeof(BITMAPINFOHEADER),
                    cColorTable );
        //
        // Allocate space for the pixel area, and load the pixel
        // info from the file.
        m_pPixels = new BYTE[cPixels];
        pFile->Seek(dwStart + fileHeader.bfOffBits, CFile::begin);
        pFile->Read( m_pPixels, cPixels );
    }
    catch( TCHAR* psz )
    {
        TRACE( psz );
        fReturn = FALSE;
    }
    return fReturn;
}

//
```

continues

Listing 8.2. continued

```
// DrawDib uses StretchDIBits to display the bitmap.
void CDIBitmap::DrawDIB( CDC* pDC, int x, int y )
{
    ASSERT( pDC );
    HDC     hdc = pDC->GetSafeHdc();
    if( m_pInfo )
        StretchDIBits( hdc,
                       x,
                       y,
                       GetWidth(),
                       GetHeight(),
                       0,
                       0,
                       GetWidth(),
                       GetHeight(),
                       GetPixelPtr(),
                       GetHeaderPtr(),
                       DIB_RGB_COLORS,
                       SRCCOPY );
}

BITMAPINFO* CDIBitmap::GetHeaderPtr()
{
    ASSERT( m_pInfo );
    ASSERT( m_pPixels );
    return m_pInfo;
}

RGBQUAD* CDIBitmap::GetColorTablePtr()
{
    ASSERT( m_pInfo );
    ASSERT( m_pPixels );
    RGBQUAD* pColorTable = 0;
    if( m_pInfo != 0 )
    {
        int cOffset = sizeof(BITMAPINFOHEADER);
        pColorTable = (RGBQUAD*)(((BYTE*)(m_pInfo)) + cOffset);
    }
    return pColorTable;
}

BYTE* CDIBitmap::GetPixelPtr()
{
    ASSERT( m_pInfo );
    ASSERT( m_pPixels );
    return m_pPixels;
}

int CDIBitmap::GetWidth() const
{
    ASSERT( m_pInfo );
    return m_pInfo->bmiHeader.biWidth;
}

int CDIBitmap::GetHeight() const
{
```

```
    ASSERT( m_pInfo );
    return m_pInfo->bmiHeader.biHeight;
}

int CDIBitmap::GetPalEntries() const
{
    ASSERT( m_pInfo );
    return GetPalEntries( *(BITMAPINFOHEADER*)m_pInfo );
}

int CDIBitmap::GetPalEntries( BITMAPINFOHEADER& infoHeader ) const
{
    int nReturn;
    if( infoHeader.biClrUsed == 0 )
    {
        nReturn = ( 1 << infoHeader.biBitCount );
    }
    else
        nReturn = infoHeader.biClrUsed;

    return nReturn;
}
```

Most of the work in the `CDIBitmap` class is done by the `CDIBitmap::Load` member function. This member function takes a pointer to a `CFile` object as its only parameter. Depending on your application, you could modify this routine to accept a filename. However, in an MFC application, a `CFile` pointer is easy to get from the MFC framework during serialization.

After verifying that the `CFile` object refers to a Windows bitmap, the `Load` function reads each part of the bitmap data structure and creates a DIB dynamically. Note that there are actually two calls to the `new` operator; there is no requirement that the DIB exist in one solid chunk of memory. The `BITMAPINFOHEADER` is stored in one location, and the pixel image array is stored in another location.

The `CDIBitmap::DrawDIB` member function calls `StretchDIBits` to display the DIB. Very little work is actually done in this function. For example, the width and height of the DIB are calculated using `CDIBitmap` member functions.

The remaining member functions are used to calculate various bits of information about the DIB. Only a pointer to the beginning of the `BITMAPINFO` structure and a pointer to the beginning of the pixel image array are stored; all other information is calculated as it's needed.

The `CBmpPalette` Class

The `CBmpPalette` class is used to create a logical palette that contains the colors used by a `CDIBitmap` object. Although the MFC class library includes a `CPalette` class, you must derive your own class from it in order to do any meaningful work. Listing 8.3 contains the class declaration for `CBmpPalette`. This class is included in the Dib project as `dibpal.h`.

Listing 8.3. The `CBmpPalette` class interface.

```
#ifndef BMP_PAL_UNLEASHED
#define BMP_PAL_UNLEASHED
class CBmpPalette : public CPalette
{
public:
    CBmpPalette( CDIBitmap* pBmp );
};
#endif
```

All the work done by `CBmpPalette` is done in the constructor; there are no member functions other than the functions inherited from `CPalette`. The `CPalette` class is always used together with `CDIBitmap`. A pointer to a `CDIBitmap` object is passed to `CBmpPalette` as a constructor parameter.

`CBmpPalette` allocates a logical palette with enough entries to store the palette required by the `CDIBitmap` object. After storing some basic palette information, the palette entries are filled in, using the values collected from the `CDIBitmap` object. After the palette is created, the logical palette is deleted. The implementation for `CBmpPalette` is provided in Listing 8.4 and is included in the Dib project as `dibpal.cpp`.

Listing 8.4. The implementation of the `CBmpPalette` class.

```
#include "stdafx.h"
#include "dib256.h"
#include "dibpal.h"

CBmpPalette::CBmpPalette( CDIBitmap* pBmp )
{
    ASSERT( pBmp );
    int cPaletteEntries = pBmp->GetPalEntries();
    int cPalette = sizeof(LOGPALETTE) +
                   sizeof(PALETTEENTRY) * cPaletteEntries;
    // Since the LOGPALETTE structure is open-ended, you
    // must dynamically allocate it, rather than using one
    // off the stack.
    LOGPALETTE* pPal = (LOGPALETTE*)new BYTE[cPalette];
    RGBQUAD*    pColorTab = pBmp->GetColorTablePtr();
    pPal->palVersion = 0x300;
    pPal->palNumEntries = cPaletteEntries;
    // Roll through the color table, and add each color to
    // the logical palette.
    for( int ndx = 0; ndx < cPaletteEntries; ndx++ )
    {
        pPal->palPalEntry[ndx].peRed   = pColorTab[ndx].rgbRed;
        pPal->palPalEntry[ndx].peGreen = pColorTab[ndx].rgbGreen;
        pPal->palPalEntry[ndx].peBlue  = pColorTab[ndx].rgbBlue;
        pPal->palPalEntry[ndx].peFlags = NULL;
    }
    VERIFY( CreatePalette( pPal ) );
    delete [] (BYTE*)pPal;
}
```

CDibDoc **Class Changes**

In the Dib example, the CDibDoc class will be responsible for the bitmap objects and will have two new member functions:

■ GetBitmap will return a pointer to a CDIBitmap object.

■ GetPalette will return a pointer to a CBmpPalette object.

The CDibDoc class will contain a CDIBitmap object and a pointer to a CBmpPalette object. The CDibDoc class header is shown in Listing 8.5, with changes in bold type.

Listing 8.5. The CDibDoc **class header, with changes in bold type.**

```
#include "dib256.h"
#include "dibpal.h"

class CDibDoc : public CDocument
{
protected: // create from serialization only
    CDibDoc();
    DECLARE_DYNCREATE(CDibDoc)

// Attributes
public:

// Operations
public:
    CDIBitmap* GetBitmap();
    CPalette*  GetPalette();
// Overrides
    // ClassWizard generated virtual function overrides
    //{{AFX_VIRTUAL(CDibDoc)
    public:
    virtual BOOL OnNewDocument();
    virtual void Serialize(CArchive& ar);
    //}}AFX_VIRTUAL

// Implementation
protected:
    CDIBitmap     m_dib;
    CBmpPalette* m_pPal;
public:
    virtual ~CDibDoc();
#ifdef _DEBUG
    virtual void AssertValid() const;
    virtual void Dump(CDumpContext& dc) const;
#endif

// Generated message map functions
protected:
    //{{AFX_MSG(CDibDoc)
        // NOTE - the ClassWizard will add and remove member functions here.
        //    DO NOT EDIT what you see in these blocks of generated code !
    //}}AFX_MSG
    DECLARE_MESSAGE_MAP()
};
```

The CDIBitmap object will be loaded during serialization. After it has been loaded, the CBmpPalette object will be created dynamically. m_pPal, the pointer to CBmpPalette, will be initialized in the constructor and deleted in the distracter. The changes for the constructor, destructor, OnNewDocument, and Serialize member functions for the CDibDoc class are shown in Listing 8.6. All changed lines are marked in bold.

Listing 8.6. Changes to CDibDoc member functions, with changes in bold type.

```
CDibDoc::CDibDoc()
{
    m_pPal = 0;
}

CDibDoc::~CDibDoc()
{
    delete m_pPal;
}

BOOL CDibDoc::OnNewDocument()
{
    if (!CDocument::OnNewDocument())
        return FALSE;
    delete m_pPal;
    m_pPal = 0;
    return TRUE;
}

void CDibDoc::Serialize(CArchive& ar)
{
    if (ar.IsStoring())
    {
        TRACE( TEXT("Storing a bitmap is not supported") );
        ASSERT(FALSE);
    }
    else
    {
        CFile* pFile = ar.GetFile();
        ASSERT( pFile );
        ar.Flush();
        BOOL fLoaded = m_dib.Load( pFile );
        if( fLoaded != FALSE )
        {
            delete m_pPal;
            m_pPal = new CBmpPalette( &m_dib );
            UpdateAllViews( NULL );
        }
        else
            AfxMessageBox( TEXT("Error Loading Bitmap") );
    }
}
```

As discussed earlier, the CDibDoc class has two new member functions to return pointers to the bitmap and palette data members. Add the source code provided in Listing 8.7 to the CDibDoc class.

Listing 8.7. New `CDibDoc` member functions to return the bitmap and palette pointers.

```
CDIBitmap* CDibDoc::GetBitmap()
{
    return &m_dib;
}

CPalette* CDibDoc::GetPalette()
{
    return m_pPal;
}
```

Main Frame Class Changes

When the Dib application receives a palette message, Windows NT actually sends the message to the application, where it will be routed to the `CMainFrame` class. Because the `CMainFrame` class has no knowledge about how the bitmap or palette is organized, it must forward these messages to the view class. When `CMainFrame` receives a palette message from Windows, it must determine the active view and send it the message.

Using ClassWizard, add message handling functions for `WM_PALETTECHANGED` and `WM_QUERYNEWPALETTE`. Accept the default names, and edit the functions using the source code provided in Listing 8.8.

Listing 8.8. The new `CMainFrame` message handling functions.

```
void CMainFrame::OnPaletteChanged(CWnd* pFocusWnd)
{
    CView* pView = GetActiveView();
    if( pView )
    {
        HWND hWndFocus = pView->GetSafeHwnd();
        pView->SendMessage( WM_PALETTECHANGED,
                            (WPARAM)hWndFocus,
                            (LPARAM)0 );
    }
}

BOOL CMainFrame::OnQueryNewPalette()
{
    CView* pView = GetActiveView();
    if( pView )
    {
        HWND hWndFocus = pView->GetSafeHwnd();
        pView->SendMessage( WM_QUERYNEWPALETTE,
                            (WPARAM)hWndFocus,
                            (LPARAM)0 );
    }
    return TRUE;
}
```

CDibView **Class Changes**

The CDibView class has two main functions: drawing the 256-color bitmap and responding to palette messages. The CDibView::OnDraw function must be modified to draw the bitmap, as shown in Listing 8.9.

Listing 8.9. A new version of CDibView::OnDraw.

```
void CDibView::OnDraw(CDC* pDC)
{
    CDibDoc* pDoc = GetDocument();
    ASSERT_VALID(pDoc);

    CPalette* pPal = pDoc->GetPalette();
    CPalette* pOldPal = pDC->SelectPalette( pPal, FALSE );
    pDC->RealizePalette();

    CDIBitmap* pBmp = pDoc->GetBitmap();
    pBmp->DrawDIB( pDC, 0, 0 );

    pDC->SelectPalette( pOldPal, FALSE );
}
```

OnDraw fetches pointers to the bitmap and palette from CDibDoc, using the new member functions added to the document class earlier. The palette is selected and realized and then the bitmap is drawn. After drawing the bitmap, the previous palette is selected back into the DC.

The CMainFrame class forwards WM_PALETTECHANGED and WM_QUERYNEWPALETTE messages to the view class. However, there is one small problem: ClassWizard does not offer direct support for palette messages sent to child window classes such as CDibView. Therefore, some trickery is required. To add the palette handling functions, follow these steps:

1. Open ClassWizard.
2. Select the CDibView class.
3. Select the Class Info tab.
4. In the Advanced Options group, click the Message filter combo box, and select Topmost Frame instead of Child Window.
5. Select the Message Map tab, and add the message handling functions for WM_PALETTECHANGED, and add WM_QUERYNEWPALETTE to the CDibView class.
6. Select the Class Info tab.
7. In the Advanced Options group, click the Message filter combo box and select Child Window, instead of Topmost Frame.
8. Close ClassWizard.

The source code for the palette message handling functions is provided in Listing 8.10.

Listing 8.10. New functions added to the `CDibView` class.

```
// OnPaletteChanged - Handles WM_PALETTECHANGED, which is a
// notification that a window has changed the current palette. If
// this view did not change the palette, forward this message to
// OnQueryNewPalette so the palette can be updated, and redrawn
// if possible.
void CDibView::OnPaletteChanged(CWnd* pFocusWnd)
{
    if( pFocusWnd != this )
        OnQueryNewPalette();
}
// Notification that the view is about to become active,
// and the view should realize its palette.
BOOL CDibView::OnQueryNewPalette()
{
    CDibDoc* pDoc = GetDocument();
    ASSERT_VALID(pDoc);

    CBmpPalette* pPal = (CBmpPalette*)pDoc->GetPalette();
    if( pPal )
    {
        CDC*     pDC = GetDC();
        CPalette* pOldPal = pDC->SelectPalette( pPal, FALSE );
        UINT uChanges = pDC->RealizePalette();
        pDC->SelectPalette( pOldPal, FALSE );
        ReleaseDC( pDC );
        if( uChanges != 0 )
            InvalidateRect( NULL );
    }
    return TRUE;
}
```

In most cases, `OnPaletteChanged` calls the `OnQueryNewPalette` function directly. The only exception is when the `WM_PALETTECHANGED` message was sent because this view had updated the system palette. If this view is the foreground window, the Windows NT palette manager gives you first crack at setting the system's palette. If you are in the background, you have access to the unused entries only. If there's no more room in the palette, your palette is mapped to the closest possible match.

Remember to include the declarations for the `CDIBitmap` class at the top of the `dibView.cpp` source file:

```
#include "dib256.h"
```

Compile and run the Dib example. If you have a 256-color display, load a 256-color bitmap and notice that you get all of the colors. If you run several instances of the program using different 256-color bitmaps, you may notice the palette change if you switch between windows. Figure 8.12 shows the Dib example displaying the 256-color Windows NT logo.

FIGURE 8.12.

The Dib example program displaying a 256-color bitmap.

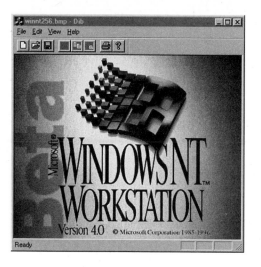

Paths

A path is a GDI object that was first introduced in Windows NT 3.1. A path is a collection of figures or shapes that can be combined to draw shapes or figures or to create irregular clipping regions. When you use a path to describe a shape, Windows NT GDI can display the path in one operation instead of a series of small building blocks. Although Windows 95 now supports GDI paths, it only supports a subset of the functions available to you as a Windows NT programmer.

A path is created by calling BeginPath, describing the path endpoints, and calling EndPath. This series of function calls is known as *a path bracket*. An example path bracket is shown in Figure 8.13.

As shown in Figure 8.13, there are 21 functions that can be called in a path bracket. By combining these functions in a path, you can create a wide range of complicated shapes.

Once you have created a path, you can draw its outline, fill its interior, or use it as a clipping region. To demonstrate using paths to create clipping regions, I have created an example named Path that can be found on the CD.

The Path example is a standard AppWizard SDI application. All the interesting work in this example is done in the CPathView::OnDraw function, shown in Listing 8.11.

FIGURE 8.13.

An example of a path bracket.

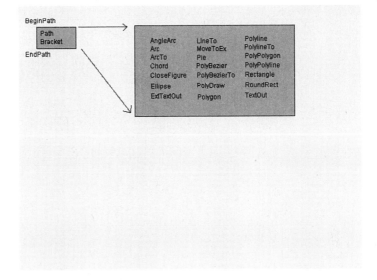

Listing 8.11. Using a path to create a clipping region.

```
void CPathView::OnDraw(CDC* pDC)
{
    // Calculate the size of the clipping area
    CRect rcClient;
    GetClientRect( rcClient );
    int xBorder = rcClient.Width()/4;
    int yBorder = rcClient.Height()/4;
    int cxRect  = rcClient.Width()/2;
    int cyRect  = rcClient.Height()/2;

    //
    // Create a large Arial font, and select it into
    // the device context. This font will be part of
    // the clipping path.
    CFont   fntClip;
    LOGFONT lf;
    memset( &lf, 0, sizeof(LOGFONT) );
    lstrcpy( lf.lfFaceName, "Arial" );
    lf.lfWeight = FW_BOLD;
    lf.lfHeight = yBorder;
    fntClip.CreateFontIndirect( &lf );
    CFont* pOldFont = pDC->SelectObject( &fntClip );

    // Create a path, and use it as a clipping area
```

continues

Listing 8.11. continued

```
HDC hdcPath = pDC->GetSafeHdc();
pDC->BeginPath();
    MoveToEx( hdcPath, xBorder, yBorder, NULL );
    LineTo( hdcPath, xBorder + cxRect, yBorder );
    LineTo( hdcPath, xBorder + cxRect, yBorder + cyRect );
    LineTo( hdcPath, xBorder, yBorder + cyRect );
    LineTo( hdcPath, xBorder, yBorder );
    DrawText( hdcPath, TEXT("SUN"), 3, &rcClient,
                DT_CENTER | DT_SINGLELINE| DT_VCENTER );
pDC->EndPath();
pDC->SelectClipPath( RGN_COPY );
//
// Create red brushes and pens for the sun burst, and
// select them into the device context.
CBrush  brRed( RGB(255,0,0) );
CPen    penRed( PS_SOLID, 1, RGB(255,0,0) );
CBrush* pOldBrush = pDC->SelectObject( &brRed );
CPen*   pOldPen = pDC->SelectObject( &penRed );

CSize   sizeOfSun( cxRect/2, cxRect/2 );
CPoint  ptSun( cxRect + (xBorder/2), yBorder/2 );
CRect   rcSun( ptSun, sizeOfSun );
//
// Calculate the sin and cosine of one 90 degree
// quadrant.
double rgSin[90], rgCos[90];
const  double pi = 3.14159;
CPoint ptCenter( xBorder + cxRect, yBorder );
for( int nAngle = 0; nAngle < 90; nAngle++ )
{
    rgSin[nAngle] = sin( (((double)nAngle)/180.0) * pi );
    rgCos[nAngle] = cos( (((double)nAngle)/180.0) * pi );
}
//
// Starting from the upper-right corner of the rectangle,
// draw rays across the clipping path, then draw an ellipse
// centered in the upper-right corner.
double flSegment = (double)(rcClient.Width());
for( nAngle = 0; nAngle < 90; nAngle++ )
{
    pDC->MoveTo( ptCenter.x, ptCenter.y );
    int x = (int)(rgCos[nAngle] * flSegment);
    int y = (int)(rgSin[nAngle] * flSegment);
    pDC->LineTo( ptCenter.x - (int)(rgCos[nAngle]*flSegment),
                ptCenter.y + (int)(rgSin[nAngle]*flSegment));

}
pDC->Ellipse( rcSun );

pDC->SelectObject( pOldBrush );
pDC->SelectObject( pOldPen );
pDC->SelectObject( pOldFont );
}
```

In Listing 8.11, a path is created containing a rectangle, along with a text string. After the path is selected as a clipping region, all drawing functions are affected by it, as shown in Figure 8.14.

FIGURE 8.14.

The Path example uses a path as a clipping region.

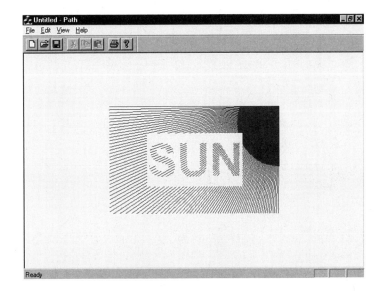

Metafiles

A metafile is a collection of GDI function calls that have been stored in a binary format. Windows NT uses Enhanced Metafiles, which have more capabilities than the ordinary metafiles used in 16-bit versions of Windows.

A metafile is often used to exchange drawing information via the Clipboard. In fact, a metafile is useful in any case where a bitmap image would take up too much storage. Although a metafile requires much less storage than a bitmap, it takes more time to display a metafile than to `BitBlt` a bitmap.

A metafile is created by creating a metafile DC and then drawing it just like any other DC. After the GDI calls have been drawn into the metafile DC, the metafile is "played" in order to display its contents.

The MFC class library includes a `CMetaFileDC` class that can be used to simplify creating and playing both plain metafiles and enhanced metafiles. To create an enhanced metafile, the `CreateEnhanced` member function is used.

```
CMetaFileDC dcMetaFile;
dcMetaFile.CreateEnhanced( pDC ,
                           TEXT("C:\\FOO"),
                           NULL,
                           TEXT("Unleashed MetaFile Example") );
```

228

The `CreateEnhanced` function has four parameters.

- A reference DC, which indicates the resolution and device units used by the current device.

- A filename, if any, that stores the metafile after it is closed. If a metafile is created by an application for temporary purposes, this parameter will be NULL, and the metafile will be destroyed when its handle is deleted.

- A bounding rectangle for the image stored in the metafile. If this value is NULL, an appropriate size will be selected, based on the size of the image drawn into the metafile.

- A description of the metafile image, if any. Otherwise, NULL is entered for this parameter.

After the metafile is created, it can be used just like any other DC, except that instead of drawing an image, the function calls are stored in the metafile.

```
dcMetaFile.MoveTo( rcDot.TopLeft() );
dcMetaFile.LineTo( rcDot.BottomRight() );
```

After all the required GDI function calls have been recorded in the metafile, the metafile is closed, using the `CloseEnhanced` function.

```
HENHMETAFILE          m_hmf;
m_hmf = dcMetaFile.CloseEnhanced();
```

The handle to the metafile is returned when closing an enhanced metafile. This handle can be played on any DC, using the `CDC::PlayMetaFile` function.

```
pDC->PlayMetaFile( m_hmf, rc );
```

A Metafile Example

We have created an example named `Meta`, which can be found on the CD. Meta is a standard AppWizard SDI application with a few simple modifications.

When the Meta application starts, a metafile is created, and the handle is stored by the view class. When a left-button mouse click is detected in the Meta client area, a metafile is played in the location of the mouse click. In addition, the location of the mouse click is stored so that the client area is updated correctly when it is repainted.

`CMetaView` Class Declaration Changes

The `CMetaView` class handles creating and playing the enhanced metafile, as well as storing the collection of points that have received mouse clicks. The `CMetaView` class needs two new member variables:

- m_rgPoints is a CArray object that stores an array of CPoint objects. The location of left-button mouse clicks is stored in this array.
- m_hmfTarget is a handle to an enhanced metafile.

Listing 8.12 shows the changes to the CMetaView class in boldface type. Because this class is created by AppWizard, most of the unchanged parts of the declaration are omitted from the listing.

Listing 8.12. Changes to the CMetaView class declaration.

```
class CMetaView : public CView
{
...
// Implementation
protected:
    CArray<CPoint,CPoint> m_rgPoints;
    HENHMETAFILE          m_hmfTarget;
...
}
```

CMetaView Destructor Changes

The only cleanup required for the CMetaView class is to delete the metafile handle when the view is destroyed. Listing 8.13 contains the source code for the CMetaView destructor.

Listing 8.13. The CMetaView destructor.

```
CMetaView::~CMetaView()
{
    DeleteEnhMetaFile( m_hmfTarget );
}
```

CMetaView::OnInitialUpdate Changes

When a view is initially displayed, the OnInitialUpdate function is called. The CMetaView class creates an enhanced metafile during OnInitialUpdate and stores the metafile handle for later use. The OnInitialUpdate function must be added to CMetaView using ClassWizard. Listing 8.14 contains the source code for CMetaView::OnInitialUpdate.

Listing 8.14. Creating an enhanced metafile during `OnInitialUpdate`.

```
void CMetaView::OnInitialUpdate()
{
    CMetaFileDC dcMetaFile;

    CDC* pDC = GetDC();
    dcMetaFile.CreateEnhanced( pDC , NULL, NULL, NULL );

    CRect rcCircle(0,0,50,50);
    CRect rcDot(20,20,30,30);

    CBrush brRed( RGB(255,0,0) );
    CBrush brBlue( RGB(0,0,255) );

    CBrush* pOldBrush = dcMetaFile.SelectObject( &brBlue );
    ASSERT( pOldBrush );
    CPen*   pOldPen = (CPen*)(dcMetaFile.SelectStockObject( BLACK_PEN ));

    dcMetaFile.Ellipse( rcCircle );
    dcMetaFile.SelectObject( &brRed );
    dcMetaFile.Ellipse( rcDot );

    dcMetaFile.MoveTo( rcDot.TopLeft() );
    dcMetaFile.LineTo( rcDot.BottomRight() );
    dcMetaFile.MoveTo( rcDot.left, rcDot.bottom );
    dcMetaFile.LineTo( rcDot.right, rcDot.top );

    dcMetaFile.SelectObject( pOldBrush );
    dcMetaFile.SelectObject( pOldPen );

    m_hmfTarget = dcMetaFile.CloseEnhanced();
}
```

The source code in Listing 8.14 creates an enhanced metafile that contains two circles arranged like a target, with a smaller red circle located inside a larger blue circle. An x is drawn to mark the center of the circles.

Note that the source code used to draw the metafile is almost exactly like the source code used to draw on a normal DC. In fact, it's easy to use a generic routine that draws to either a metafile DC, or a normal DC, like this:

```
DrawImage( CDC* pDC )
{
    CRect rcCircle(0,0,50,50);
    CBrush brBlue( RGB(0,0,255) );
    CBrush* pOldBrush = pDC->SelectObject( &brBlue );
    pDC->Ellipse( rcCircle );
    // Remaining drawing functions...
}
```

Left-Button Mouse Clicks

When a user clicks the Meta client area using the left mouse button, the metafile is played using the CDC::PlayMetaFile function. Windows NT sends a WM_LBUTTONDOWN message to a window when a user clicks the left mouse button. To handle the left mouse button, use ClassWizard to add a message handling function for WM_LBUTTONDOWN to the CMetaView class. The source code that the Meta application uses for OnLButtonDown is provided in Listing 8.15.

Listing 8.15. Playing a metafile at the point of a mouse click.

```
void CMetaView::OnLButtonDown(UINT nFlags, CPoint point)
{
    CDC* pDC = GetDC();
    ASSERT( pDC );
    if( pDC )
    {
        CRect rcTarget( point.x-25,
                        point.y-25,
                        point.x+25,
                        point.y+25 );
        pDC->PlayMetaFile( m_hmfTarget, rcTarget );
    }
    m_rgPoints.Add( point );
}
```

The source code in Listing 8.15 creates a rectangle, rcTarget, 50 units square around the point that was clicked. The metafile is then played in that rectangle. To make larger or smaller images, you can vary the size of rcTarget.

In addition, the location of the mouse click is added to the m_rgPoints collection. In the next section, the OnDraw function will use m_rgPoints to redraw the client area.

CMetaView::OnDraw Changes

The OnDraw function must be provided in case the client area is redrawn. For example, if the client area is hidden by another window or if the Meta application is minimized and restored, the client area must be redrawn. The source code for CMetaView::OnDraw is provided in Listing 8.16.

Listing 8.16. Redrawing the Meta client area using metafiles.

```
void CMetaView::OnDraw(CDC* pDC)
{
    int limPoints = m_rgPoints.GetSize();
    if( limPoints > 0 )
```

continues

Listing 8.16. continued

```
    {
        CPoint pt = m_rgPoints[0];
        for( int n = 1; n < limPoints; n++ )
        {
            pt = m_rgPoints[n];
            CRect rc( pt.x-25,
                      pt.y-25,
                      pt.x+25,
                      pt.y+25 );
            pDC->PlayMetaFile( m_hmfTarget, rc );
        }
    }
}
```

The source code in Listing 8.16 is similar to the source code provided in Listing 8.15 for the OnLButtonDown function. However, instead of playing a single metafile at one point, OnDraw plays the metafile for every point stored in m_rgPoints.

Compile and run the Meta application. Figure 8.15 shows the Meta application after several mouse clicks have been registered.

FIGURE 8.15.

The Meta example program after the metafile has been played several times.

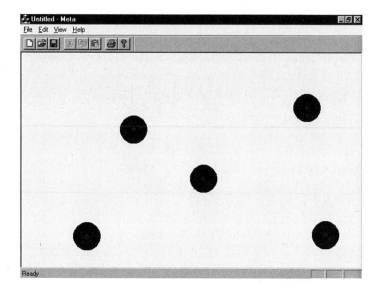

Summary

In this chapter, I have discussed the Windows NT GDI. The GDI objects used when programming for Windows NT have also been discussed, and several example programs have been presented.

Standard Template Library Programming

9

by Mickey Williams

In this chapter, you learn about the Standard Template Library (STL) and how you can use it to create Windows NT applications. You learn about the various components that make up the STL, and several short example programs are provided. Later in this chapter, you see how you can modify the generic STL distribution so that you can use it with the MFC Class Library.

Understanding the STL

The C++ language is currently undergoing official standardization by two bodies: the American National Standards Institute (ANSI), and the International Organization for Standardization (ISO). Committees working on the standardization process are developing a standards document that will serve as the official definition of the C++ language. At the time of this writing, a draft standard has been released for public review.

The *Standard Template Library* is a set of collections, algorithms, and functions recently added to the C++ Draft Standard. As part of the C++ standardization process, some of the members of the C++ community thought there was a need for a basic C++ library that would take advantage of the C++ language and be available on all compilers. The STL was selected by the C++ standardization committees to be this standard library.

As its name suggests, the STL makes heavy use of templates in its library classes and functions. The STL classes grew out of research on generic programming performed at Hewlett-Packard; the STL uses templates extensively to provide a set of collections and algorithms that truly are generic.

The examples in this chapter are different from most of the C and C++ programs you have encountered. Functions and algorithms are treated as objects that can be created and used just like other objects; collections often are created using two or more templates at a time (if you aren't familiar with the details involved with using templates, you will be soon). Functions and objects in the STL are classified by what they do, not by the way in which they are implemented.

The Advantages of the STL

The STL offers generic containers and algorithms that you can apply to a wide variety of objects. The containers and algorithms included in the STL also, to a large extent, are interchangeable. This is the major strength of the STL because it enables the containers and algorithms in an application to be separated completely from the application's data.

All STL containers and algorithms use templates that easily can be used for almost any data type. The containers, functions, and algorithms used by the STL can be adapted to any data type and, in many cases, can be used interchangeably with C++ arrays. The functions and helper objects you use with STL vectors also can be used with built-in arrays.

Installing the STL

The STL is not installed by the default Visual C++ Setup program. To use the STL, you must add the STL files to the #include file search path. You also might consider copying the \STL directory to your hard drive to speed up access time, especially if your other #include files are located on the hard disk.

To add the STL directory to the include file search path, follow these steps:

1. Choose Options from the Tools menu. The Options dialog box appears.
2. Select the Directories tab.
3. Select Include files from the Show directories for: combo box.
4. Add the STL directory to the Directories listbox. The STL directory on the CD is \Stl. If you copied the STL files to your hard disk, enter that location.
5. Click the OK button.

The STL was not created by Microsoft; the version on the distribution CD-ROM is the public domain version available to everyone. A reference manual for the STL is included in the STL directory. Although the Visual C++ compiler offers excellent support for the STL, be aware that some of the template constructions used by the library push the envelope as far as template support is concerned. It's not uncommon to receive warning messages when using the STL.

If you plan to use the STL to create MFC programs or programs that use Windows NT API functions, you must modify the STL sources; this procedure is described later in this chapter, in the section *Modifying the STL Sources.*

STL Components

The STL includes five types of components:

- **Containers:** Also known as *collections.* These are used to store other objects. Containers are classified according to the methods used to access items stored in the container.
- **Iterators:** Used to move through items stored in a container. An iterator is similar to a cursor in a word processor. In the STL, there are several types of iterators.
- **Function objects:** Used to wrap a commonly performed function in a generic object. Function object classes use templates that make them flexible, as well as typesafe. Typesafety helps the compiler guarantee that the proper parameter and return values are used in your code.
- **Adapters:** Used to map a new interface for an existing class. In the STL, for example, stack is an adapter class applied on top of another class, such as list or vector.
- **Algorithms:** Used to perform specified operations on objects. You use the sort algorithm, for example, to sort a container.

Understanding the STL Basics

Before you look at the different STL components in detail, you should know a few basic STL components and concepts. This section introduces you to some of these elements.

Using the `pair` Class

A key STL component is the `pair` class. The STL makes heavy use of `pair` objects as parameters and return values. The `pair` template allows two objects to be combined into a single object, as shown in Figure 9.1.

FIGURE 9.1.

A pair *object contains two sub-objects:* first *and* second.

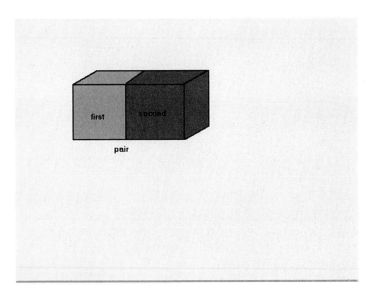

The library includes a `make_pair` function used to initialize a pair object. To create a pair of integer values, you can use this syntax:

```
pair<int,int>  agePair = make_pair(35,33);
```

One of the most common uses of `pair` objects is as function return values. How many times have you wanted to return two values from a function call? The `pair` class makes this easy:

```
typedef pair<int,int> return_type;
//...
return_type GetAges()
{
    return make_pair(35,33);
}
```

The `pair` class also is used in other ways. Later in this chapter, in the section *Using the* map *and* multimap *Classes*, you'll see how the map class uses `pair` objects to associate a particular key with its stored value.

Using the `basic_string` Class

The version of the STL distributed on the Visual C++ CD-ROM also includes an implementation of `basic_string` from Modena Software. `basic_string` is a template-based string class that will be part of the ANSI C++ standard. The `basic_string` class will work with any underlying data type for its strings. You must specify a type when declaring the object:

```
basic_string<int>    strInt;
basic_string<char>   strChar;
basic_string<TCHAR>  strTchar;
```

Of course, with Windows NT, you can use `TCHAR` to help make internationalization easier.

TIPS FOR WORKING WITH THE STL

- Separate nested template declarations so that your declaration is understood by the compiler. All C++ compilers have difficulty understanding nested template declarations if the trailing angle brackets are not separated, as in this example:

  ```
  list<int,less<int>> listOfInts; // syntax error
  ```

  In this line of code, the compiler mistakes the last two angle brackets as the right-shift operator and generates a syntax error. All the nested template declarations in this book separate nested templates with an extra space between the angle brackets, as shown in this code:

  ```
  list<int,less<int> > listOfInts;
  ```

- Use `typedef` to simplify your template declarations. It can be difficult to read STL template declarations without `typedef`. A declaration for a map collection, for example, follows:

  ```
  map<int, basic_string<TCHAR>, less<int> > theMap;
  ```

  Writing out the same declaration dozens or hundreds of times in your source can quickly get tiring. In this chapter's STL examples, a `typedef` is used to simplify the source code. A `typedef` for the preceding line of code, for example, follows:

  ```
  typedef map<int, basic_string<TCHAR>, less<int> >  CMapIntToString;
  ```

  By using a `typedef`, you can use `CMapIntToString` to simplify declarations and make your source code much more readable.

- Use an stl.h include file to isolate all your STL modifications in one place. For more information on the stl.h file included on the CD-ROM included with this book, see *Modifying the STL Sources*, later in this chapter.

- Finally, use `#pragma warning` to disable common warnings generated by the STL source. The stl.h header on the CD-ROM included with this book disables warning numbers `4018`, `4114`, `4146`, and `4786`, which are generated for practically all programs that use the STL with Visual C++ 4.0.

Using Containers

The STL provides a set of generic containers. This means that the library is generally not concerned with what types of objects are stored in the containers. The containers with the STL also are generic with respect to each other; a common set of interfaces are shared by all STL container classes, as shown in Table 9.1.

Table 9.1. Common interfaces supported by STL containers.

Interface	Returns
begin()	An iterator that points to the start of the container
end()	An iterator that points past the end of the container
max_size()	The maximum size of the container
empty()	Non-zero if the container is not empty
operator==()	Tests equivalence with another container
operator!=()	Negates the value of operator==()
operator<()	Depends on the container's comparison function
operator>()	Depends on the container's comparison function
operator<=()	Negates operator>()
operator>=()	Negates operator<()

Many class libraries include a great deal of functionality into container classes, such as ordering or sequence information. In contrast, STL containers are concerned with managing memory locations and nothing else. A container class is concerned only with containing objects, as well as the boundaries for the beginning and end of the collection. To traverse or iterate a collection, you use an STL object known as an iterator, as in this code:

```
vector<int>::iterator    iter;
for( iter = vect.begin(); iter != vect.end(); iter++ )
    cout << *iter << endl;
```

Iterators are special objects that override the asterisk (*) operator and behave like pointers. Iterators are covered in "Using STL Iterators," later in this chapter.

The vector class is the simplest of the STL collection classes. An STL *vector* is similar to an array except that it automatically expands as needed when additional items are added. To declare a vector of integers named v, for example, you use this syntax:

```
vector<int> v;
```

To add an item to a vector, you use the `push_back` function:

```
v.push_back(42);
```

The `vector` class is only one of several containers provided by the STL. The STL containers are separated into two types: sequential and associative containers, as shown in Figure 9.2.

FIGURE 9.2.

Containers provided by the STL.

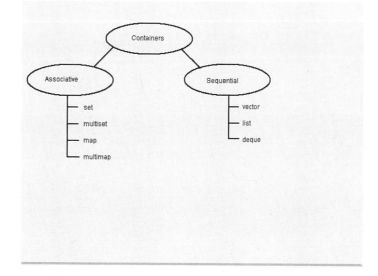

Sequences are collections implying that items are stored based on the order in which they were inserted into the collection. *Associative* containers are sorted or retrieved on the basis of a key or other mapping.

Using Sequence-Based Containers

Sequence-based containers order their contents in a linear fashion. The STL offers three types of sequence-based containers (see Figure 9.3):

- **list**   This class is optimized to allow easy insertions and removals from any known point in the container. This class offers the best possible performance if you need to insert or remove items from the middle of a sequence.

- **deque**   This class is well suited for situations in which insertions and deletions are made from each end of the sequence.

- **vector**   This class is a basic container that you should use in general-purpose situations, when you don't need a container that is tuned for a particular purpose.

FIGURE 9.3.

Sequential containers included in the STL.

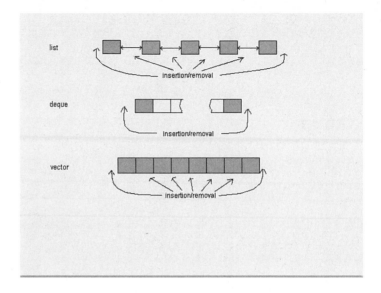

Each of these classes supports a different set of interfaces, as Table 9.2 shows.

Table 9.2. Common interfaces for sequential containers.

Interface	Vector	List	Deque	Action
front()	X	X	X	Returns first element
back()	X	X	X	Returns last element
push_front()		X	X	Adds to front of sequence
push_back()	X	X	X	Adds to back of sequence
pop_front()		X	X	Removes from front of sequence
pop_back()	X	X	X	Removes from back of sequence
operator[int]()	X		X	Returns specified element

Listing 9.1 uses a vector to store an array of integer values.

Listing 9.1. Using a vector to store integers.

```
#include <iostream.h>
#include <vector.h>
#include <algo.h>

int main()
{
```

```
    vector<int> v;
    v.push_back( 434 );
    v.push_back( 356 );
    v.push_back( 267 );
    v.push_back( 987 );
    for( unsigned n = 0; n < v.size(); n++ )
    {
        cout << v[n] << endl;
    }
    return 0;
}
```

You learn about a more flexible way to access vector contents using iterators in *Using Iterators*, later in this chapter.

Using Associative Containers

Associative containers use a key to identify values stored in the container. Every associative container has a key; this key is used when searching for values stored in the container. A container that stores employee data, for example, may use an employee number as the key. Associative containers are constructed so that it is very efficient to look up a known key value in the container; however, associative containers are less efficient when iterating over an entire collection.

The STL offers four types of associative containers:

- **set**   Stores unique keys.
- **multiset**   Supports duplicate key values.
- **map**   Associates a unique key with a particular value.
- **multimap**   Similar to a map, but duplicate keys are allowed.

These containers are described in this section.

Using the `set` and `multiset` Containers

The `set` class stores keys. Unlike in the `map` class, discussed in the next section, the only data stored in a `set` is the key. The `set` class supports unique keys; each key inserted into the set is expected to be unique. This type of data is useful when a key value does not need to be associated with any other data, such as a list of valid window handles.

The `multiset` class is similar to the `set` class, but multiple key values are supported. Allowing multiple keys is useful if you need to store the number of times a particular key is represented in a set. You can use a `multiset` to track user connections to a server application, for example.

Using the `map` and `multimap` Classes

The map class enables you to associate a key with a particular value. Like set containers, a map cannot contain multiple keys. If you attempt to store a second value for a particular key, the first value is overwritten.

The map class associates a key with a particular value using the `pair` class. Every container supports a value_type expression that can be used to create the `pair` stored in a container. You can use the value_type expression or the make_pair function to create elements for a map container:

```
map<int,char,less<int> > theMap;
pair<int,char> foo = make_pair(42,'A');
pair<int,char> bar = map<int,char,less<int> >::value_type(42,'A');
```

Of course, this code looks a little cleaner with a couple of typedefs added:

```
typedef map<int,char,less<int> > CMapType;
typedef pair<int,char> CPairType;
CMapType theMap;
CPairType foo = make_pair(42,'A');
CPairType bar = CMapType::value_type(42,'A');
```

The console mode program provided in Listing 9.2 uses the STL map class as a simple employee database. This listing is included on the CD-ROM as part of the Employee project, in the file Employee.cpp.

Listing 9.2. Using the `map` class for a simple employee database.

```
#include <iostream.h>
#include "stl.h"

// These two typedefs help make the map and pairs easier to
// use. Instead of the template syntax, you can just use a
// new type name. Remember, typedef is your friend.
typedef map< int, basic_string<char> , less<int> >  CIntToString;
typedef pair<int,basic_string<char> > CMapPair;

// Define three pairs that will be used as map values. The
// other five employees are left to the reader as extra credit.
// Note that all of the pairs are constructed as map value_types.
CMapPair grumpy = CIntToString::value_type(123,"Grumpy");
CMapPair sleepy = CIntToString::value_type(202,"Sleepy");
CMapPair sneezy = CIntToString::value_type(716,"Sneezy");

int main()
{
    // Create map and insert three employees.
    CIntToString    empMap;
    empMap.insert(grumpy);
    empMap.insert(sleepy);
    empMap.insert(sneezy);

    // Calculate the size of the map.
```

```
cout << "The map contains " << empMap.size()
    << " elements." << endl;

// Find a particular map item using a specific key.
CMapPair employee = *(empMap.find(123));
cout << "Employee 123 is:" << employee.second << endl;

cout << "ID\tName" << endl;
// Create an iterator, and display the map contents. Since
// the map stores a pair, the contents are referred to as
// first and second. The key is (*iter).first, and the value
// is (*iter).second.
CIntToString::iterator iter;
for( iter = empMap.begin(); iter != empMap.end(); iter++ )
{
    cout << (*iter).first << '\t' << (*iter).second << endl;
}
return 0;
}
```

The Employee project uses the unmodified STL sources. It does use a header file, stl.h, however, that includes all the STL source files. Listing 9.3 shows a version of stl.h for the unmodified STL source. Store this copy of stl.h in the Employee project directory.

Listing 9.3. A version of stl.h for use with the unmodified STL source.

```
#ifndef STL_H
#define STL_H
// Disable common warnings from the compiler.
#pragma warning(disable: 4018)
#pragma warning(disable: 4114)
#pragma warning(disable: 4146)
#pragma warning(disable: 4786)
#include <algo.h>
#include <algobase.h>
#include <bstring.h>
#include <bool.h>
#include <defalloc.h>
#include <deque.h>
#include <function.h>
#include <heap.h>
#include <iterator.h>
#include <list.h>
#include <map.h>
#include <multimap.h>
#include <multiset.h>
#include <pair.h>
#include <projectn.h>
#include <set.h>
#include <stack.h>
#include <tree.h>
#include <vector.h>
#endif
```

Later in this chapter, in *Modifying the STL Sources*, a new version of stl.h is provided for use with STL sources that have been modified to work in MFC and Windows NT applications.

Using Iterators

As discussed earlier, an STL iterator works very much like a pointer. An iterator is used to move forward or backward through a container or other structure, and it is declared in the following way:

```
vector<int>::interator   nIterator;
```

This line declares nIterator to be an iterator for a vector of integers. Before an iterator is used, it must be given a position, much like a pointer must be initialized, as shown in this code:

```
nIterator = v.begin();
```

The begin function returns an iterator position that points to the first element in a container. There is also a function named end that returns a position *past* the end of the container, as shown in this example:

```
for( nIter = v.begin(); nIter != n.end(); nIter++ )
    cout << *nIter << endl;
```

This code looks almost exactly like a for loop that would be used to display the contents of a built-in array. In fact, you can use STL iterators with built-in arrays.

```
int     arAges[] = { 5, 27, 38, 45 };
vector<int>::iterator nIter = arAges;
for(nIter = arAges; nIter != arAges + 4; nIter++)
    cout << *nIter << endl;
```

You can use and declare iterators for all types of STL containers. This helps make the STL very flexible; not only are the containers generic, but your algorithms also can be generic.

You also can use a set of iterators to iterate a container in reverse. A *reverse* iterator works very much like the forward iterators discussed previously, except that when incremented, it moves to the previous item in a container. A reverse iterator must be explicitly declared.

```
vector<int>::reverse_iterator  revIter;
```

A different set of positioning functions is used with reverse iterators. The rbegin function returns the iterator position to the last collection item, and the rend function returns an iterator position *before* the first container item, as shown in this code:

```
for( revIter = v.rbegin(); revIter != v.rend(); revIter++ )
```

When a container is altered, any iterators that point at altered elements are invalidated. A common mistake in STL programming is the use of an invalid iterator, as demonstrated in the following code:

```
// Faulty code, do not use!
// This code shows how iterators should not be used.
vector<int>::iterator   start_iter; // iterator defined
vector<int>::iterator   end_iter;   // iterator defined
end_iter = v.end();                 // iterator valid
for( start_iterator = v.begin();
     start_iterator != end_iterator;
     start_iterator++ )
{
     v.erase( start_iterator );  // start_iterator invalidated
}
```

Using the STL Algorithms

The STL also offers generic algorithms that can be applied to any type of object or container. This is the major strength of the STL. All STL algorithms are template functions that can be used for almost any data type. This enables the STL to be truly generic; the STL source code is a good role model for designing extendible libraries.

As an example of the algorithms provided in the STL, look at the sorting algorithms. Each of the sorting algorithms comes in two flavors: one version that automatically uses the < operator to compare items and another version that uses a function object to compare items. The sorting algorithms in the STL follow:

- ▪ **sort:** Orders a container with fairly good performance on average, although its worst-case time can be very poor. On average, the sort is *logarithmic*, meaning that the time required to sort the collection approaches *NlogN*, where *N* is the number of items in the collection. This is good performance for a general-purpose sort algorithm.
- ▪ **stable_sort:** Guarantees that the relative order of objects that compare equally is preserved. If enough resources are available, the sort time is *NlogN*.
- ▪ **partial_sort:** Orders only a part of a container.
- ▪ **partial_sort_copy:** Copies the results of a partial sort into a new container.

Using an STL algorithm is just like calling any other function. To sort a vector of integers named v using the greater function object, for example, the function call looks like the following:

```
sort( v.begin(), v.end(), greater<int> );
```

Using Function Objects

One of the unusual features of STL is its use of function objects. In C libraries, it's common to pass a pointer to a function that will be used to perform some work. In the standard C library, for example, the qsort function uses a pointer to a comparison function supplied by you in order to sort a set of values.

An STL function object provides a generic function that can be applied to any object type. Containers and algorithms in the STL often use function objects to perform a task (such as comparing two objects) or to test whether a certain condition has been met. A greater function object, for example, often is used when sorting a container. An instance of greater used to compare integers looks like this:

```
greater<int>   IsGreater;
```

The reason for using function objects is the same as the rest of the STL: Components should be general enough to be completely interchangeable. To sort a vector, v, in ascending order, you can use the sort function and the greater function object, as in this code:

```
sort( v.begin(), v.end(), greater<int> );
```

If you decide to sort in descending order, you can just use the less function object, like this:

```
sort( v.begin(), v.end(), less<int> );
```

A function object overloads the () operator to provide a result based on its arguments. A simple example of a function object is the greater class mentioned earlier:

```
template <class T>
struct greater : binary_function<T, T, bool> {
    bool operator()(const T& x, const T& y) const { return x > y; }
};
```

As you can see from this code, greater is derived from the binary_function class, which defines how function objects with two parameters behave. There is also a unary_function base class for functions that work with a single argument.

Function Objects Used for Comparison

The greater and less function objects are examples of comparison function object classes. A *comparison* function determines how two other objects are related to each other, and operator() always is defined as returning a Boolean value. Although the most common use for function objects is as arguments to STL algorithms, you also can use function objects by themselves, like this:

```
greater<int> isGreater;
if( isGreater(a,b) )
    cout << "a is greater than b" << endl;
else
    cout << "a is not greater than b" << endl;
```

Table 9.3 lists more STL comparison functions.

Table 9.3. Comparison functions in the STL.

Function	Returns True If
equal_to(x,y)	x == y
not_equal_to(x,y)	x != y

Function	*Returns* True *If*
greater(x,y)	x > y
greater_equal(x,y)	x >= y
less(x,y)	x < y
less_equal(x,y)	x <= y

All the function objects listed in Table 9.3 are *binary*—they accept two parameters. In addition to comparison function objects, the STL also includes predicate and general-purpose function objects.

Predicate Function Objects

You use a predicate function object to determine whether an event or action should take place. All predicate function objects return Boolean `true` or `false` values. A commonly used predicate is the `logical_not` function, for example, which returns `true` if its parameter is `false`. `logical_not` is an example of a *unary* function (a function object that accepts only one parameter) as shown in this code:

```
logical_not<int> isnt;
isnt(0); // returns true
isnt(1); // returns false
```

Predicate functions often are used with STL algorithms that end with `_if`, such as `count_if` and `replace_if`. The `replace_if` algorithm, for example, uses a predicate function object to determine whether a value in a container should be replaced:

```
vector<int> v;
// Add items to vector
replace_if( v.begin(), v.end(), logical_not<int>, 80 );
```

This code tests all the values stored by the `vector`, `v`, and replaces any zeros with 80.

Table 9.4 lists the STL predicate functions.

Table 9.4. Predicate functions included in the STL.

Function	*Returns* True *If*
logical_not(x)	x==0
logical_and(x,y)	x&&y
logical_or(x,y)	x||y

You are not limited to using the predicate functions included in the STL. It's easy to create your own predicate functions. The source code provided in Listing 9.4, for example, uses the count_if algorithm and the logical_not function object to determine the number of vector elements equal to zero, and then uses count_if with a user-defined BiggerThanTen function to count the number of elements with values larger than 10. Listing 9.4 uses the stl.h file provided earlier in Listing 9.3. You must copy that version of stl.h into the project's source code directory.

Listing 9.4. Using predicate functions to count array elements.

```
#include <iostream.h>
#include "stl.h"

int LessThanTen( int n )
{
    return n < 10;
}

int main()
{
    vector<int> v;
    v.push_back(0);
    v.push_back(20);
    v.push_back(10);
    v.push_back(0);
    v.push_back(8);

    int nZero = 0;
    count_if( v.begin(), v.end(), logical_not<int>(), nZero );
    cout << "There are " << nZero << " elements containing zero."
        << endl;

    int nBigger = 0;
    count_if( v.begin(), v.end(), LessThanTen, nBigger );
    cout << "There are " << nBigger << " elements less than ten."

        << endl;

    return 0;
}
```

Both binary and unary predicate function objects exist. Algorithms that use predicate functions specify a particular type of function. The count_if and remove_if algorithms use unary predicate function objects, for example, because the algorithms test a single element at a time. One version of the adjacent_find algorithm uses a binary predicate function object to determine whether two adjacent items in a container are equivalent, however, as in the following code:

```
#include <iostream.h>
#include "stl.h"
```

```
int main()
{
    vector<bool> v;
    v.push_back( true );
    v.push_back( false );
    v.push_back( true );
    vector<bool>::iterator matchPoint;
    matchPoint = adjacent_find( v.begin(), v.end(),
                                logical_and<bool>() );
    if( matchPoint == v.end() )
        cout << "No adjacent values are true." << endl;
    else
    {
        cout << "Adjacent values are true." << endl;
    }
    return 0;
}
```

In this example, the `logical_and` function compares adjacent values in the `vector`, `v`. If any two compared values are both `true`, the `logical_and` predicate function returns `true`, and the `adjacent_find` algorithm returns an iterator that points to the first of two container elements. If no adjacent `true` elements are discovered in `v`, an iterator equal to `v.end()` is returned.

General Function Objects

The STL also includes a set of general function objects. General function objects often are used with STL algorithms to apply functions to every element in a container. Table 9.5 lists the general function objects included in the STL.

Table 9.5. General functions included in the STL.

Function	Returns
`divides(x,y)`	x/y
`modulus(x,y)`	x%y
`minus(x,y)`	x−y
`plus(x,y)`	x+y
`negate(x)`	−x
`times(x,y)`	x*y

The source code in Listing 9.5 uses the `times` function object and the `accumulate` algorithm to calculate the factorial of eight, or the product of every number from one to eight multiplied together.

Listing 9.5. Using the `times` function object to calculate a factorial.

```
#include "stl.h"
#include <iostream.h>

const int nArraySize = 8;
int main()
{
    vector<int> v(nArraySize);
    for( int n = 0; n < nArraySize; n++ )
        v[n] = n+1;

    int nTotal = accumulate( v.begin(), v.end(), 1, times<int>() );
    cout << "Total = " << nTotal << endl;

    return 0;
}
```

The accumulate algorithm runs through a container and applies a function to a start value and the first element in the container. The function then is applied, along with the previous result, to each element in the container. If the plus function object is used, the total of all elements in the container is returned. If the times object is used, the product of all container elements is returned.

Using STL for Windows NT Applications

The STL examples presented so far in this chapter have been straightforward, very portable programs that run with any compiler that supports the STL, and on any operating system. In this section, you'll learn some of the steps required to make STL work with Windows NT.

Modifying the STL Sources

Unfortunately, the STL conflicts with both MFC and definitions found in the Windows #include file, windows.h. When writing MFC-based applications using the STL, remember to do the following:

- Wrap the STL in the std namespace and use namespaces to refer to STL components.
- Modify the STL sources so that namespaces are used correctly.
- Ensure that the min and max macros from windows.h are not used.

The STL distribution included on the Visual C++ CD-ROM includes a readme.wri file that specifies how the STL source must be modified in order to work with MFC. In order to wrap the stl source in the std namespace, the stl.h header file must be modified, as shown in Listing 9.6. All remaining examples in this chapter assume that you are using a modified version of the STL and the modified #include file from Listing 9.6. The modified STL source and stl.h #include file used to build the remaining examples in this chapter are provided on the accompanying CD-ROM.

NOTE

In addition to the modifications listed by Microsoft in the Readme.wri file in the STL directory, there are two more changes that must be made. In the bstring.h file, change line 1093 so it looks like this:

```
if (cap == std::reserve)
```

In the same file, change line 1099 to look like this:

```
else if ((cap == std::default_size) && (size != NPOS))
```

Listing 9.6. The modified stl.h `#include` file used for MFC and Windows NT examples.

```
#ifndef STL_H
#define STL_H
//
// Handle the collision between STL and the normal Windows
// include definition for min and max. If this file is included
// before windows.h, defining the NOMINMAX macro prevents the
// Windows header from defining min and max. If min and max are
// already defined, the definition is removed.
#define NOMINMAX
#ifdef min
#undef min
#endif
#ifdef max
#undef max
#endif
//
// Disable common warnings from the compiler.
#pragma warning(disable: 4018)
#pragma warning(disable: 4114)
#pragma warning(disable: 4146)
#pragma warning(disable: 4786)
//
// Include headers that are needed before the namespace is
// created. This list has evolved over time, so it's possible
// that more headers should be included here.
#include <new.h>
#include <typeinfo.h>
#include <stddef.h>
#include <stdlib.h>
#include <limits.h>
#include <iostream.h>
//
// Namespace std is used for the STL library header files.
namespace std {
#include <algo.h>
#include <algobase.h>
#include <bstring.h>
#include <bool.h>
#include <defalloc.h>
```

continues

Listing 9.6. continued

```
#include <deque.h>
#include <function.h>
#include <heap.h>
#include <iterator.h>
#include <list.h>
#include <map.h>
#include <multimap.h>
#include <multiset.h>
#include <pair.h>
#include <projectn.h>
#include <set.h>
#include <stack.h>
#include <tree.h>
#include <vector.h>
}
#endif
```

After using the new version of the stl.h header provided in Listing 9.6, you must use a namespace qualifier in front of every STL component or a using directive. When using fully qualified names, code that uses the STL looks like this:

```
std::vector<int>  v;
std::vector<int>::iterator  iter = v.begin();
```

When a using directive is used, you add the following code before any of your code using any of the STL components:

```
using namespace std;
```

The examples in the remaining chapters of this book contain using directives because this approach leads to clearer source code.

Looking at the List Example

I have created a small program named List as an example of a practical application that uses STL. The List project is included on the CD-ROM with this book and is a simple Windows NT console-mode application that lists all the top-level windows currently on the desktop.

As discussed in the previous section, the List application uses a modified version of the STL located on the accompanying CD-ROM, along with the stl.h header file. You can run the List application off the CD-ROM, or you can create it from scratch by creating a console-mode application and adding the source code from Listing 9.7 to the project as source file List.cpp.

Listing 9.7. A console-mode program that lists all top-level windows.

```
#include <iostream.h>
#include "windows.h"
#include "stl.h"
```

```
using namespace std;

//
// Define a typedef that simplifies the template syntax. I
// don't want to type map<HWND,basic_string<TCHAR>,less<HWND> >
// everywhere.
//
typedef map<HWND,basic_string<TCHAR>,less<HWND> >  CHwndToString;

int  CALLBACK CollectWindowHandles( HWND, LPARAM );
void DisplayWindowHandles( CHwndToString& hwndToSzWnd );

int main()
{
    CHwndToString hwndToSzWnd;
    EnumWindows( (WNDENUMPROC)CollectWindowHandles,
                 (LPARAM)&hwndToSzWnd );
    DisplayWindowHandles( hwndToSzWnd );
    return 0;
}

int CALLBACK CollectWindowHandles( HWND hWnd, LPARAM lpMap )
{
    CHwndToString* pMap = (CHwndToString*)lpMap;
    TCHAR    tchTitle[40];
    GetWindowText( hWnd, tchTitle, 40 );
    pMap->insert( CHwndToString::value_type(hWnd, tchTitle) );
    return TRUE;
}

void DisplayWindowHandles( CHwndToString& theMap )
{
    CHwndToString::iterator  mapIter;

    for( mapIter = theMap.begin();
         mapIter != theMap.end();
         mapIter++ )
    {
        if( (*mapIter).second.length() != 0 )
            cout << (*mapIter).first << '\t' << (*mapIter).second
                 << endl;
        else
            cout << (*mapIter).first << '\t' << TEXT("<No Title")
                 << endl;
    }
}
```

When the main function in Listing 9.7 begins executing, it creates an instance of an STL map, hwndToSzWnd, that associates a window handle (HWND) with a basic_string object that will contain the window caption.

The hwndToSzWnd map is filled inside the CollectWindowHandles function, which is an example of an enumeration procedure. *Enumeration procedures* are callback functions that are called one or more times by Windows NT in response to a function call you have made—in this case,

EnumWindows. As shown in Figure 9.4, when EnumWindows is called, the address of an enumeration procedure and an LPARAM containing user data are passed as parameters. Windows NT uses these values to call the enumeration procedure once for every top-level window.

FIGURE 9.4.

Using the Windows NT
EnumWindows *function.*

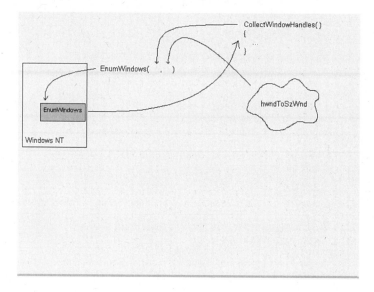

In the List example, the address of the hwndToSzWnd map is passed as an LPARAM to the CollectWindowHandles procedure, which adds the window handle and window caption to the map for each top-level window.

Compile and run the List example. Notice that there are a number of top-level windows that have no captions.

Using STL in an MFC Application

I also have created a program that illustrates how you can use the STL in an AppWizard MFC application. The WinList example is an SDI program similar to the List example in the previous section. WinList displays a list of all top-level windows in an SDI scroll view and enables you to update the list by pressing a toolbar button. Figure 9.5. shows the WinList example running.

You can find the WinList project on the accompanying CD, or you can create the WinList project using AppWizard and the steps in the following sections. If you create the project from scratch, change the base class for CWinListView to CScrollView in AppWizard step 6.

The WinList document class, CWinListDoc, has a map object that stores the HWND and caption for every top-level window. The document class also has member functions for updating and retrieving the map's contents. The view class, CWinListView, is derived from CScrollView and displays all the HWND and caption information in a scrolling view.

FIGURE 9.5.

Displaying top-level windows with the WinList application.

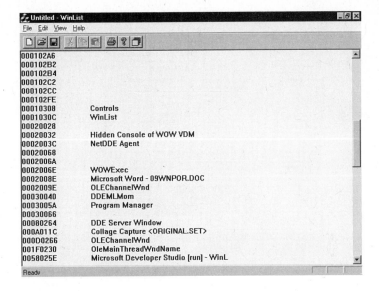

Creating a New Toolbar Button

WinList provides a toolbar button to update the window list. To add a button to the toolbar, first open the toolbar resource for editing by following these steps:

1. Click on the Resource View tab in the project workspace.
2. Expand the resource tree and open the Toolbar folder.
3. Click on the toolbar resource.

The toolbar is displayed in an Image Editor. Edit the empty button on the toolbar so that it looks like the button shown in Figure 9.6.

After editing the toolbar button, set the button's properties as in the following example. Use ClassWizard to add a message-handling function to the CWinListDoc:

ID: ID_UPDATE_LIST

Caption: Update List\nUpdate

Class: CWinListDoc

Function: OnUpdateList

Making Changes to the Document Class

As in the preceding example, the CWinListDoc class uses a map to store the HWND and a caption for every top-level window. After a new document is created, or after the Update button on the toolbar is clicked, CWinListDoc enumerates all the top-level windows, updates the window map, and updates the view associated with the document.

FIGURE 9.6.

Adding a new toolbar button using the Developer Studio Image Editor.

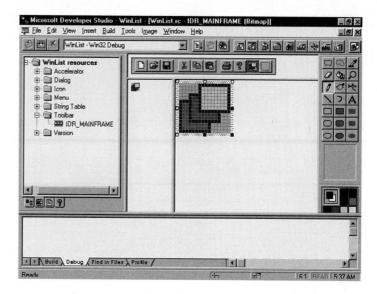

In addition to the map data member, there are two new member functions for the CWinListDoc class: CollectWindowHandles is a static callback function used as a window enumeration procedure, and GetHwndMap returns a reference to the map object.

Listing 9.8 shows the modifications to the CWinListDoc class in boldface type. Most of the CWinListDoc class declaration created by AppWizard has been removed for clarity; you can find the entire file on the accompanying CD-ROM.

Listing 9.8. Changes to the CWinListDoc class declaration.

```
using namespace std;
typedef map<HWND, CString, less<HWND> >  CHwndToString;

class CWinListDoc : public CDocument
{

// ...

// Operations
public:
    CHwndToString& GetHwndMap();

// ...

// Implementation
private:
    CHwndToString m_hwndToSzWnd;
    static int CALLBACK CollectWindowHandles( HWND, LPARAM );

};
```

The `CWinListDoc::CollectWindowHandles` function in Listing 9.9 is almost exactly like the window enumeration function used in the List project presented earlier in this chapter.

Listing 9.9. The static `CollectWindowHandles` function.

```
int CALLBACK CWinListDoc::CollectWindowHandles( HWND hWnd, LPARAM lpMap )
{
    CHwndToString* pMap = (CHwndToString*)lpMap;
    TCHAR   tchTitle[40];

    GetWindowText( hWnd, tchTitle, 40 );
    pMap->insert( CHwndToString::value_type(hWnd, tchTitle) );
    return TRUE;
}
```

Listing 9.10 shows the `CWinListDoc::OnUpdateList` function. This function is called after a new document is created, or after a user clicks the toolbar's Update button. As in the List project discussed earlier, a pointer to the window enumeration function and a pointer to the map object are passed as parameters to `EnumWindows`. The `CollectWindowHandles` function is called once for each top-level window and updates the map with the window handle and caption for each window.

Listing 9.10. The message-handling function for the Update button.

```
void CWinListDoc::OnUpdateList()
{
    ::EnumWindows( (WNDENUMPROC)CollectWindowHandles,
                   (LPARAM)&m_hwndToSzWnd );
    UpdateAllViews( NULL );
}
```

Listing 9.11 shows the changes to the `CWinListDoc::OnNewDocument` class. After initializing the window map, `OnUpdateList` is called to collect the top-level windows.

Listing 9.11. Changes made to the `OnNewDocument` function.

```
BOOL CWinListDoc::OnNewDocument()
{
    if (!CDocument::OnNewDocument())
        return FALSE;

    m_hwndToSzWnd.erase( m_hwndToSzWnd.begin(),
                         m_hwndToSzWnd.end() );
    OnUpdateList();
    return TRUE;
}
```

Listing 9.12 shows the final change to the CWinListDoc class. The GetHwndMap function returns a reference to the window map.

Listing 9.12. The GetHwndMap function.

```
CHwndToString& CWinListDoc::GetHwndMap()
{
    return m_hwndToSzWnd;
}
```

Making Changes to the View Class

There are two changes to the CWinListView class: the OnDraw function must be modified to display the window map contents, and the OnInitialUpdate function must initialize the scroll sizes for the view.

Listing 9.13. contains the source code for CWinListView::OnDraw. First, the height required for each line is displayed in the view using the GetTextMetrics function. Next, a reference to the window map object is retrieved from the document class, and the map contents are displayed using TabbedTextOut.

Listing 9.13. Using the OnDraw function to display map information.

```
void CWinListView::OnDraw(CDC* pDC)
{
    CWinListDoc* pDoc = GetDocument();
    ASSERT_VALID(pDoc);
    CHwndToString& theMap = pDoc->GetHwndMap();

    TEXTMETRIC tm;
    pDC->GetTextMetrics(&tm);
    int cy = tm.tmHeight + tm.tmExternalLeading;
    int x= 0, y = 0;

    CHwndToString::iterator iter = theMap.begin();
    while( iter != theMap.end() )
    {
        y += cy;
        CString szWindow;
        szWindow.Format( "%p\t%s",
                         (*iter).first,
                         (*iter).second );
        pDC->TabbedTextOut( x, y, szWindow, 0, NULL, 0 );
        iter++;
    }
}
```

Listing 9.14 shows the final modification to the `CWinListView` class. The scroll sizes for the view must be set in order for the scroll bars to work correctly; in this case, a default value of 100 lines is used.

Listing 9.14. Setting scroll sizes during `OnInitialUpdate`.

```
void CWinListView::OnInitialUpdate()
{
    CScrollView::OnInitialUpdate();

    CDC* pDC = GetDC();
    TEXTMETRIC tm;
    pDC->GetTextMetrics(&tm);
    int cy = tm.tmHeight + tm.tmExternalLeading;

    CSize sizeTotal;
    sizeTotal.cx = 100;
    sizeTotal.cy = 100 * cy;
    SetScrollSizes(MM_TEXT, sizeTotal);
    InvalidateRect(NULL);
}
```

The `document` and `view` classes in the WinList project must have access to the STL header files. Before compiling the WinList project, add an `#include` directive to the StdAfx.h header file in the project directory:

```
#include "stl.h"
```

This adds the STL source to the project's precompiled header and speeds up compilation. Remember to copy the stl.h file into the project directory. Alternatively, you can add the stl.h file to the STL directory.

Summary

This chapter introduced you to the Standard Template Library. You learned how to use the STL to create Windows NT applications, as well as the steps required to modify the STL so that it can be integrated with the MFC Class Library.

In the next chapter, "Menus and Dialog Boxes," I discuss using menus and dialog boxes in a Windows NT application.

Menus and Dialog Boxes

10

by Mickey
Williams

IN THIS CHAPTER

Menus and dialog boxes are essential parts of most Windows NT applications. With the exception of some simple dialog box–based applications, all Windows programs offer several dialog boxes and some sort of menu. Menus and dialog boxes are used for much of the interaction between the user and a Windows program.

In this chapter, you'll see how menu and dialog resources are used in Windows NT programs. You'll modify a menu created by AppWizard and also create a floating pop-up menu as examples. You'll also learn about the different types of dialog boxes and the steps required to add them to a project using Developer Studio.

Using Menus

A *menu* is a list of command messages that can be selected and sent to a window. To the user, a menu item is a string that indicates a task that can be performed by the application. Each menu item also has an ID that identifies the item when routing window messages. This ID also is used when modifying attributes for the menu item.

Menus usually are attached to a window, although many applications support floating pop-up menus that can appear anywhere on the desktop. Later in this chapter, you will create a floating pop-up menu that is displayed after the right mouse button is pressed. These menus often are used to provide context-sensitive help and offer different menu choices, depending on the window that creates the menu.

You can create menus dynamically or as static resources that are added to your program. If you use Visual C++, the MFC class library provides a CMenu class that simplifies menu handling and is used for most of the examples in this chapter.

The Visual C++ AppWizard generates a menu resource for programs that it creates. You can edit this menu resource to add extra menu items for your application, or you can create new menu resources for your application.

Message Routing

Before you look at creating and modifying menus, look at how menu messages are handled by Windows programs in general and MFC programs in particular.

A menu always is associated with a particular window. When a menu item is selected, a WM_COMMAND message is sent to the window that owns the menu. In most MFC programs, the menu is associated with the main frame window, which also contains the application's toolbar and status bar. When a menu item is selected, a WM_COMMAND message is sent to the main frame window; this message includes the ID of the menu item. The MFC framework and your application convert this message into a function call that can be handled by other classes in your MFC program, such as your document or view classes.

In an MFC application, many windows can receive a menu-selection message. In general, any window derived from `CCmdTarget` is plugged into the MFC framework's message loop. When a menu item is selected, the message is offered to all the command target objects in your application in the following order:

- The `CMainFrame` object
- The main MDI frame window
- The active child frame of an MDI frame window
- The view associated with the MDI child frame
- The document object associated with the active view
- The document template associated with the document object
- The `CWinApp` object

This list might seem like a large number of steps to take, but it's actually not very complicated in practice. Usually, a menu item is handled by one type of object: a view or main frame. Menu messages rarely are handled directly by the document template or child frame objects. Figure 10.1 shows a simplified map of how commands are routed in an MFC application.

FIGURE 10.1.

Menu command routing in an MFC application.

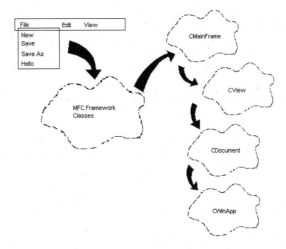

In most cases, you can use ClassWizard to configure the message maps required to route menu-selection messages to their proper destinations.

Adding New Menu Items

One of the easiest tasks to perform with a menu is adding a new menu item. In order to use a new menu item, you must do two things:

■ Modify the menu resource to include the new menu item.

■ Add message-handling routines to your application. If you are using Visual C++ and MFC, you will add a message-handling function using ClassWizard.

Adding a menu item using Visual C++ is explained in the following sections.

Opening the Menu Resource

To display the current menu resources for an MFC project, select the Resource View tab in the project workspace window. Expand the resource tree to show the different resource types defined for the current project; one of the folders is labeled Menu.

Open the menu folder to display the resources defined for the project's menus. Every multiple-document application created by AppWizard has two menu resources. MDI applications use an IDR_MAINFRAME menu when no views are active. They also have an additional menu item used when a view is active. The name of this menu resource is based on the application name, as IDR_*xxx*TYPE, where *xxx* is replaced by the program's name. For example, IDR_FOOTYPE is the second menu resource created for a program named Foo.

SDI applications have a single menu created by AppWizard named IDR_MAINFRAME. This is the menu displayed by default for single-document applications. Every AppWizard program begins with the exact same menu; it's up to you to supply any modifications required for your application.

Editing the Menu Resource

Open the menu resource by double-clicking the Menu Resource icon. The menu is displayed in the Resource Editor ready for editing. When the menu initially is loaded into the Editor, only the top-level menu bar is displayed. Clicking any top-level menu item displays the pop-up menu associated with that item, as shown in Figure 10.2.

The last item of every menu is an empty box. You can use this box to add new menu items to the menu resource. All menu items initially are added to the end of a menu resource and then moved to their proper positions.

To add a new menu item to the File menu, follow these steps:

1. Double-click the empty box on the File menu to display the Menu Properties dialog box. Alternatively, you can type a caption directly into a blank menu item box; as you enter the caption, the properties dialog box is displayed.

2. To add a menu item, provide a menu ID and caption for the new menu item. By convention, menu IDs begin with ID_, followed by the name of the top-level menu. For this example, enter ID_FILE_HELLO as the menu ID and &Hello as the menu caption.

3. Optionally, you can provide a prompt that is displayed in the status bar when the new menu item is highlighted.

4. Click anywhere outside the Menu Properties dialog box to return to the Editor.

After you've added the new menu item, you can move it to a new position by dragging it with the mouse. Changing the menu position does not change any of its attributes. Alternatively, you can move the empty menu item rectangle to a new position, and then follow the above steps to add the menu item.

FIGURE 10.2.

Using the Developer Studio Resource Editor to edit a menu resource.

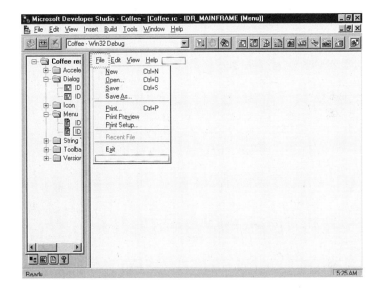

Adding a Message-Handling Function

After adding a menu item to the application's menu, the next step is to add a message-handling function to handle the new menu item. As discussed in Chapter 7, "Document/View Architecture," when using Visual C++, ClassWizard is used to create message-handling functions for MFC-based Windows programs.

To add a message-handling function for a new menu item ID_FILE_HELLO, in the File menu, follow these steps:

1. Open ClassWizard by pressing Ctrl+W or by right-clicking in a source code window and selecting ClassWizard from the menu.

2. Select the Message Maps tab and select the class that will handle the message from the Class Name combo box—in this case, CMainFrame.

3. Select the object that is generating the message from the Object ID listbox—in this case, ID_FILE_HELLO. Two message-handling functions are displayed in the Messages listbox.

4. Select the COMMAND message from the Messages listbox and click the Add Function button. Accept the default name suggested by ClassWizard for the function name—OnFileHello.

5. Click the Edit Code button to close ClassWizard, and open the editor at the OnFileHello function.

Edit the CMainFrame::OnFileHello function so that it looks like the function that follows:

```
void CMainFrame::OnFileHello()
{
    AfxMessageBox( "Hello from the File menu" );
}
```

The AfxMessageBox function displays a simple message dialog box and is discussed in detail later in this chapter.

Creating Menu Resources by Hand

In addition to the visual editing tools offered by Visual C++ and other compilers, you can create menu resources by hand. A menu resource is defined in the project's .rc file and looks something like Listing 10.1.

Listing 10.1. An example of a menu resource created by hand.

```
IDR_MAINFRAME MENU DISCARDABLE
BEGIN
    POPUP "&File"
    BEGIN
        MENUITEM "&New\tCtrl+N",             ID_FILE_NEW
        MENUITEM "&Open...\tCtrl+O",         ID_FILE_OPEN
        MENUITEM "&Save\tCtrl+S",            ID_FILE_SAVE
        MENUITEM "Save &As...",              ID_FILE_SAVE_AS
        MENUITEM SEPARATOR
        MENUITEM "E&xit",                    ID_APP_EXIT
    END
END
```

Creating menus like this is tedious, and it is difficult to see exactly what the finished menu will look like, especially for large menus. You always have the option of creating or modifying your menu resources by hand, however.

Creating a Pop-Up Menu

Creating a floating pop-up menu is similar to modifying an existing menu, except that a new menu resource must be created as the first step. Most floating pop-up menus are displayed in response to the WM_XBUTTONDOWN message, where *X* is replaced by *R* for a right-button click or *L* for a left-button click.

If you are supplying a context-sensitive pop-up menu, you should display the menu in response to the WM_CONTEXTMENU message. This message is sent after the user right-clicks in a window, as well as after a user presses the Menu key on a Microsoft natural keyboard. The source code for a typical CMyView::OnContextMenu message-handling function is provided in Listing 10.2.

Listing 10.2. Popping up a context-sensitive menu in response to WM_CONTEXTMENU.

```
void CMyView::OnContextMenu(CWnd* pWnd, CPoint point)
{
    CMenu   menu;
    menu.LoadMenu( ID_POPUP );
    CMenu* pPopup = menu.GetSubMenu( 0 );
    ASSERT( pPopup );
    pPopup->TrackPopupMenu( TPM_LEFTALIGN¦TPM_RIGHTBUTTON,
                            point.x,
                            point.y,
                            this );
}
```

When a right mouse click is detected, the WM_CONTEXTMENU message is sent to the application, and the MFC framework calls the OnContextMenu message. The OnContextMenu function creates a CMenu object and loads the ID_POPUP menu resource. The floating menu is displayed by calling GetSubMenu and TrackPopupMenu.

The GetSubMenu function is used to skip past the dummy menu item at the top of the ID_POPUP menu resource. The GetSubMenu function returns a temporary pointer to the pop-up menu. Calling TrackPopupMenu causes the pop-up menu to be displayed and the menu item selection automatically to follow the mouse cursor.

Using Dialog Boxes

Dialog boxes, often just called *dialogs*, are used to present information and collect input from the user. Dialog boxes come in all shapes and sizes, ranging from simple message boxes that display a single line of text to large dialog boxes that contain sophisticated controls.

Dialog boxes usually are used to collect information and to provide feedback to a program's user. The most commonly used type of dialog box is a *modal dialog box*, which usually contains several controls used to interact with a program.

Dialog boxes also are used for one-way communication with a user, such as *splash screens* used to display copyright and startup information as a program is launched. The opening screens displayed by the Visual C++ Developer Studio and Microsoft Word are two examples of dialog boxes used for one-way communication. Dialog boxes sometimes are used to notify the user about the progress of a lengthy operation.

Several types of dialog boxes exist, each with a specific purpose. In this chapter, I discuss these three main types of dialog boxes:

- **Message box:** Displays information to the user.
- **Modal dialog box:** Must be closed before a user can perform another task.
- **Modeless dialog box:** Enables you to perform other activities while the dialog box still is open.

Understanding Message Boxes

The simplest type of dialog box is the *message box*, which is used to display information to the user. This type of dialog box is so simple you can call it with just one line of code, using the MFC Class Library. To display a message box using default parameters supplied by MFC, for example, just use this line:

```
AfxMessageBox( "Hello World" );
```

This line of code creates a message box with an exclamation mark inside a yellow triangle. Several additional options for the icon are available, as discussed later in the section *Adding Message Boxes*.

Using Dialog Boxes for Input

When most people think of dialog boxes, they think of the dialog boxes that collect input from a user. Dialog boxes often are used to contain controls used to handle user input. There are a wide range of controls that you can include in a dialog box.

Some dialog boxes are needed so often in Windows programs that they have been included as part of the operating system. These dialog boxes, known as *common dialog boxes*, are available by calling a function and don't require you to create a dialog resource. Common dialog boxes can be used for opening and selecting files, choosing fonts and colors, and performing find-and-replace operations.

Most dialog boxes are *modal*, which means that they must be closed before a user can perform another task. A dialog box that is *modeless* allows other activities to be carried out while the dialog box still is open.

An example of a modeless dialog box is the Find and Replace dialog box used by Developer Studio. When the dialog box is open, you still can make selections from the main menu and even open other dialog boxes. In contrast, all other Developer Studio dialog boxes are modal. As long as they are open, the user cannot interact with the other parts of Developer Studio.

Adding Message Boxes

As I discussed earlier, you can add message boxes to your program using a single line of code. You must supply at least a single parameter: the text that is displayed inside the dialog box. Optionally, you can specify an icon style and a button arrangement pattern. Each of the icons has a specific meaning. When most Windows programs display a message box, they use a standard icon for each message. When programs use the same icons consistently, users find it much easier to understand the meanings of information provided with message boxes.

In addition, you can specify a button arrangement to be used in the message box. By default, a single button labeled OK is included in the message box. Sometimes it's convenient to ask a user a simple question and to collect an answer, however. One use for these button arrangements is to ask the user what action to take during an error. This code displays a message box that contains a question mark icon, for example, and asks the user whether the current file should be deleted:

```
int nChoice = AfxMessageBox( "Overwrite existing file?",
                        MB_YESNOCANCEL | MB_ICONQUESTION );
if( nChoice == IDYES )
{
    // Overwrite file
}
```

The user can choose the Yes, No, or Cancel button. Table 10.1 lists the different button arrangements possible for a message box.

Table 10.1. Message-box button arrangements.

Message Box Style	Buttons Included in Dialog Box
MB_ABORTRETRYIGNORE	Abort, Retry, and Ignore
MB_OK	OK
MB_OKCANCEL	OK and Cancel
MB_RETRYCANCEL	Retry and Cancel
MB_YESNO	Yes and No
MB_YESNOCANCEL	Yes, No, and Cancel

The message-box return value indicates the button selected by the user. Table 10.2 lists the possible return values and the choice made by the user.

Table 10.2. Message-box return values.

Return Value	Button Pressed
IDABORT	Abort
IDCANCEL	Cancel
IDIGNORE	Ignore
IDNO	No
IDOK	OK
IDRETRY	Retry
IDYES	Yes

Adding a Dialog Box

Adding a dialog box to a program using Visual C++ usually takes four steps:

1. Design and create a dialog resource.
2. Use ClassWizard to create a C++ class derived from CDialog that will manage the dialog box.
3. Add functions to handle messages sent to the dialog box, if needed.
4. If the dialog box is selected from the main menu, modify the menu resource and message-handling functions created using ClassWizard.

Each of these steps is discussed in the following sections.

Understanding Resources

Dialog boxes are just a specialized type of window. Because they commonly are used for short periods of time, however, they are usually stored as program resources and loaded only when needed. Program resources are stored in a program's EXE file but are loaded only when they actually are needed. You can see this behavior when running a Windows program on a machine that has little free memory. Every time a dialog box is opened, the hard disk is accessed to load the dialog box resources from the EXE.

Menus, which I covered earlier in this chapter, are one type of resource. Here are some of the other resource types used by Windows programs:

- **Accelerators**: Key combinations used to simulate selecting menu items.
- **Bitmaps:** Store images such as the logo from the Visual C++ opening, or "splash" screen.

- **Cursors:** Indicate the current mouse position. A program can modify the cursor to indicate that a specific action can be taken with the mouse at its current position or for other user-feedback purposes.
- **Dialog boxes:** Windows used for interaction with a program's user.
- **Icons:** Small bitmaps in a special format that can be used to represent another object in a Windows program.
- **String tables:** Contain text strings that can be changed without recompiling the application.
- **Version information:** Tags an executable file with version data.

Creating the Dialog Resource by Hand

There are two ways to create a dialog resource. The first way, which is tedious and error-prone, is to code the resource statements by hand and then add them to your resource file. Listing 10.3 shows a dialog box resource definition.

Listing 10.3. A typical dialog box resource coded by hand.

```
IDD_ABOUTBOX DIALOG DISCARDABLE  34, 22, 217, 55
STYLE DS_MODALFRAME ¦ WS_POPUP ¦ WS_CAPTION ¦ WS_SYSMENU
CAPTION "About Hello World"
FONT 8, "MS Sans Serif"
BEGIN
    ICON            IDR_MAINFRAME,IDC_STATIC,11,17,20,20
    LTEXT           "Hello World 1.0",IDC_STATIC,40,10,119,8
    LTEXT           "Copyright \251 1994",IDC_STATIC,40,25,119,8
    DEFPUSHBUTTON   "OK",IDOK,176,6,32,14,WS_GROUP
END
```

The first five lines of Listing 10.3 describe the dialog box, and the remaining lines define the controls contained by the dialog box. Each element of the definition, including the dialog box and all the controls, is given a name and position. Creating a dialog resource this way is almost impossible without a lot of time and effort. You almost always will want to use the easier method described in the next section, which takes advantage of the tools included in Developer Studio.

Working with a Menu and Dialog Box Example

As an example of using menus and dialog boxes, I have created a simple SDI application named Coffee, which is included on the accompanying CD-ROM. Coffee displays a welcome greeting and pretends to place coffee orders for you.

The Coffee application has two menus: the IDR_MAINFRAME menu that every AppWizard SDI application has, and ID_COFFEE, a pop-up menu displayed after a user right-clicks in the View window, as shown in Figure 10.3.

FIGURE 10.3.

The pop-up coffee order menu from the Coffee application.

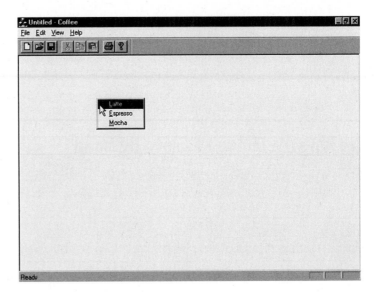

The Coffee application also has a new menu item on the Edit menu's Name submenu, which asks for your name and displays it back to you. This isn't extremely exciting, but it shows the basic method for exchanging data with dialog box controls.

To create your own version of the Coffee application by hand, start with a default AppWizard SDI application named Coffee. The following sections guide you through the following steps:

1. Create the IDD_NAME dialog box resource, which will be used to collect the user's name.
2. Add a class derived from CDialog, CNameDlg, to handle interactions with the dialog box resource.
3. Add a new menu item, Name, to the IDR_MAINFRAME menu resource.
4. Add a new coffee-ordering pop-up menu, ID_COFFEE.
5. Add message-handling functions for the ID_COFFEE menu items.

Creating a Dialog Resource Using Developer Studio

The Visual C++ Developer Studio enables you to create a dialog box and configure it visually. You can add and size controls by using a mouse. You can set attributes for the dialog box and its controls with a click of a mouse button.

To create a new dialog resource for the Coffee project, use either of the following methods:

- Select Resource from the Insert menu, and then select Dialog as the resource type.
- Right-click the Dialog folder in the Resource tree, and then choose Insert Dialog from the pop-up menu.

After using either of these methods, the Dialog Editor is displayed, as shown in Figure 10.4.

FIGURE 10.4.

The Developer Studio Dialog Editor.

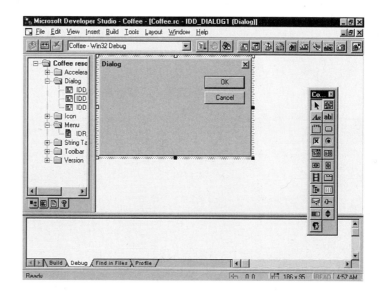

The dialog box displayed for editing initially contains two button controls: OK and Cancel. As I discuss in Chapter 11, "Common Controls," these are two standard dialog box controls.

Bring up the new dialog box's Properties dialog box by double-clicking on the dialog box, by choosing Properties from the Edit menu, or by pressing Alt+Enter. Change the dialog box's resource ID to IDD_NAME and the caption to User Name. All other properties can remain set to their default values.

Adding Controls to a Dialog Box Resource

The IDD_NAME dialog box uses an Edit control to collect a user's name, as well as a Static Text control used as a prompt. The Static Text control requires no interaction with the dialog box; it often is used as a plain text label for other controls contained by the dialog box. To add the Static Text control, follow these steps:

1. Select the Static Text control icon on the Control toolbar. The cursor changes shape to a plus sign (+) when moved over the dialog box.
2. Center the cursor over the dialog box and click the left mouse button. A Static Text control is created with the label Static.

3. Change the label of the Static Text control by double-clicking the control, and then changing the caption to Your Name:. As with other resources, another way to edit the caption is by selecting the resource item and typing the caption. As you type, the caption is replaced, and the Properties dialog box is displayed.

The Static Text control is visible whenever the dialog box is displayed. Text controls are an excellent choice for labeling controls or messages that are not likely to change. Experiment with changing the size and position of the Static Text control by dragging its edges with the mouse.

Adding the Edit control is almost exactly like adding the Static Text control:

1. Select the Edit Control icon.
2. Place the control on the dialog box.

Arrange the Edit control so that the dialog box resembles the one shown in Figure 10.5.

FIGURE 10.5.

The dialog box used in the Coffee application.

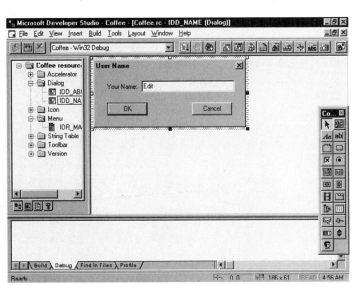

The resource ID for the new Edit control is set by default to IDC_EDIT1 or a similar name. Change the ID to IDC_NAME, leaving the other properties set to their default values, by clicking the Edit control. A Properties dialog box is displayed which gives you easy access to the resource ID and other properties for the control.

Creating a Class for the Dialog Box

You can use the CDialog class to manage most of the interaction with a dialog box in your program. The CDialog class provides member functions that make a dialog box easy to use. You should derive a class from CDialog that is specifically tailored for your dialog box using ClassWizard.

To start ClassWizard, use any of these methods:

- Press Ctrl+W almost anytime in Developer Studio.
- Click on the ClassWizard toolbar icon.
- Select ClassWizard from the View menu.
- Right-click anywhere in the Dialog Editor and select ClassWizard from the pop-up menu.

If ClassWizard knows that a new resource has been added, a dialog box appears, asking you to choose between three options for the new dialog box resource:

- Create a new class.
- Import an existing class.
- Select an existing class.

You almost always should choose to create a new dialog box class, unless you are reusing some existing code. An example of the Adding a Class dialog box is shown in Figure 10.6.

FIGURE 10.6.

The ClassWizard and Adding a Class dialog boxes.

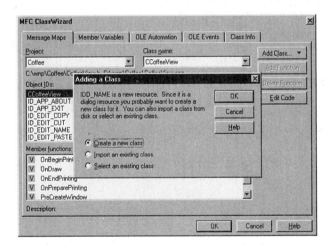

Select the Create a new class radio button, and click OK. The Create New Class dialog box is displayed. Values provided to the Create New Class dialog box are used by ClassWizard to create a class that will manage the new dialog box resource. Use the values from Table 10.3 to fill in the values for the IDD_NAME dialog box.

Table 10.3. Example values for the Create New Class dialog box.

Control	Value
Name	CNameDlg
Base Class	CDialog

continues

Table 10.3. continued

Control	Value
File	NameDlg.cpp
Dialog ID	IDD_NAME
OLE Automation	None
Add to Component Gallery	Cleared

Press the Create button. The CNameDlg class is generated, and two files are added to your project:

- The NameDlg.h file contains the class declaration.
- The NameDlg.cpp file contains the class definitions.

The IDC_NAME Edit control must be associated with a CNameDlg member variable in order to use its value outside the CNameDlg class. Using ClassWizard, add a CString member variable to the CNameDlg class by following these steps:

1. Open ClassWizard if you closed it after creating the CNameDlg class.
2. Select the CNameDlg class.
3. Select the Member Variables tab.
4. Select the control ID representing the control associated with the new member variable—in this case, IDC_NAME.
5. Click the Add Variable button. An Add Member Variable dialog box appears. Enter the control's name, category, and variable type, and then click OK. For this example, use the following values:

   Control ID: IDC_NAME

   Variable name: m_szName

   Category: Value

   Type: CString

After making these changes, the MFC framework uses the m_szName variable to pass values to and from the IDC_NAME Edit control.

Adding a Menu Choice for the New Dialog Box

Add a menu choice to the Edit menu called Name using the procedure I discussed earlier in this chapter, in *Adding New Menu Items*. Use these values for the menu item:

   Menu ID: ID_EDIT_NAME

   Caption: &Name...

Adding a Message-Handling Function for the New Menu Item

The `CCoffeeView` class creates the dialog box when the new menu item is selected. Use the following steps to add a message-handling function for the new menu item and display the `IDD_NAME` dialog box:

1. Using ClassWizard, add a message-handling function to `CCoffeeView` for the menu ID named `OnEditName`. This function creates a `CNameDlg` object and executes the dialog box.

2. Add an `#include` statement in `CoffeeView.cpp` that includes the class definition for `CNameDlg`, found in NameDlg.h. Add the following line just above the `include` statement for CoffeeView.h:

   ```
   #include "NameDlg.h"
   ```

Listing 10.4 provides the source for `CCoffeeView::OnEditName`.

Listing 10.4. The message-handling function for the Name menu item.

```
void CCoffeeView::OnEditName()
{
    CNameDlg    dlgName;

    if( dlgName.DoModal() == IDOK )
    {
        CString szReply;
        szReply.Format( TEXT("Hello, %s, right-click for a menu"),
                        dlgName.m_szName );
        AfxMessageBox( szReply );
    }
}
```

Adding a Pop-up Menu

Use the Developer Studio Resource Editor to create the floating pop-up menu. To create the new menu resource, use one of the following techniques:

- Choose Resource from the Insert menu and then select Menu from the Insert Resource dialog box.
- Right-click on the Menu folder in the Resource View and then choose Insert Menu from the pop-up menu.

Both these methods open a new menu resource for editing. Add a dummy caption for the first top-level item on the menu bar. This caption is not displayed by the pop-up menu; it is used only as a placeholder.

Open the Properties dialog box for the menu resource by double-clicking on the edge of the menu resource, and change the resource ID to ID_COFFEE. Use the values from Table 10.5 to add three menu items under the dummy label.

Table 10.5. Menu items for the ID_COFFEE pop-up menu.

Menu ID	Caption
ID_LATTE	&Latte
ID_ESPRESSO	&Espresso
ID_MOCHA	&Mocha

When you open ClassWizard for the first time after adding a menu resource, the Add Class dialog box appears. Because a dynamic menu is being added, there is no need for a new class, and you can just click Cancel.

The CCoffeeView class handles displaying the pop-up menu and any menu selections made from it. Using the steps discussed earlier in *Adding New Menu Items*, add the message-handling functions listed in Table 10.6 to the CCoffeeView class with ClassWizard.

Table 10.6. Values for new member functions in CCoffeeView.

Object ID	Class Name	Message	Function
CCoffeeView	CCoffeeView	WM_CONTEXTMENU	OnContextMenu
ID_LATTE	CCoffeeView	COMMAND	OnLatte
ID_ESPRESSO	CCoffeeView	COMMAND	OnEspresso
ID_MOCHA	CCoffeeView	COMMAND	OnMocha

The source code for the CCoffeeView::OnContextMenu function looks very much like the source code from Listing 10.1. The other message-handling functions display a message dialog box indicating that the selected coffee is temporarily out of stock. Listing 10.5 shows the source code for all the message-handling functions.

Listing 10.5. Message-handling functions for the CCoffeeView class.

```
void CCoffeeView::OnContextMenu(CWnd* pWnd, CPoint point)
{
    CMenu   menu;
    menu.LoadMenu( ID_COFFEE );
    CMenu* pPopup = menu.GetSubMenu( 0 );
    ASSERT( pPopup );
```

```
        pPopup->TrackPopupMenu( TPM_LEFTALIGN¦TPM_RIGHTBUTTON,
                                point.x,
                                point.y,
                                this );
}

void CCoffeeView::OnEspresso()
{
    AfxMessageBox( TEXT("Sorry, we're out of Espresso") );
}

void CCoffeeView::OnLatte()
{
    AfxMessageBox( TEXT("Sorry, we're out of Latte") );
}

void CCoffeeView::OnMocha()
{
    AfxMessageBox( TEXT("Sorry, we're out of Mocha") );
}
```

Summary

This chapter showed you how to use menus in Windows NT applications built using Visual C++ and MFC. You learned about the routing of menu-command messages, as well as methods for modifying and creating menu resources. As an example, you created an application that displays a floating pop-up menu when the right mouse button is clicked.

You also learned about dialog box basics and how they are used in programs written for Windows. You also were introduced to the support provided by Developer Studio, including ClassWizard, the MFC Class Library, and the Dialog Editor.

The next chapter discusses many of the new common controls used in Windows NT, such as the Tree View, List View, and rich edit controls.

Common Controls

This chapter discusses the new common controls first introduced with Windows 95, and introduced for Windows NT beginning with version 3.51. It begins with a section on image lists, which provide bitmaps for many of the new common controls.

Each section includes an example program that demonstrates how you can use the control in a Windows NT application. The complete project for each example is included on the CD-ROM that accompanies this book, and interesting parts of the project are discussed in the text here.

Image Lists

An *image list* is similar to an array of bitmaps, just like a roll of film is an array of images. Unlike rolls of film, an image list can grow, if needed, as extra images are added to the list. Each bitmap stored in an image list is associated with an index, which can be used to retrieve a particular image.

Image lists are used by four of the new common controls used in Windows NT: Tree Views, List Views, Tab controls, and toolbars. All these controls use image lists to store their bitmaps. Image lists also can be used outside of these new controls, and they provide an easy way to store a series of bitmaps, because you only need to handle a single image list object instead of separate objects for each bitmap.

Even if you aren't using common controls, there still are reasons to use image lists in your Windows NT applications. If your program needs to manage several different bitmapped images, a single image list is easier to use than a series of bitmaps. Accessing and displaying multiple images from an image list is easier than handling multiple CBitmap objects. In addition, two features are offered by image lists that are difficult to duplicate with regular bitmaps:

- **Transparent images:** A transparent image is difficult to achieve using a normal bitmap. In the simplest cases, about twice as many lines of code are required to draw a bitmap transparently as are required to draw it as an opaque image against a drawing surface. Using an image list, drawing a transparent bitmap is almost effortless, requiring little more than parameters that are set correctly.

- **Overlaid images:** An overlaid image is created by combining two images to form a single, combined image. This is useful when showing special attributes for items represented by images stored in an image list. When a shared directory is shown in the Explorer, for example, a server "hand" is superimposed over the directory's folder. This is an overlaid image.

Using an Image List

As for almost everything else in Windows, there is an MFC class for image lists, too. The CImageList class is used to create, display, and otherwise manage image lists in an MFC-based Windows program.

The first step in creating an image list is to create a series of bitmaps, each of which is the same size. Adding a bitmap resource to an image list consists of three steps:

1. Loading the bitmap.
2. Adding the bitmap to the image list.
3. Deleting the bitmap object.

The bitmap object is deleted because the image list makes a copy of the bitmap and stores the image internally. As discussed in Chapter 8, "Windows and the Graphical Device Interface," any time a Windows NT GDI object is loaded, it should be deleted to prevent memory leaks. The steps just outlined usually are handled by a helper function, such as AddBitmapToImageList, as shown in Listing 11.1.

Listing 11.1. Adding a bitmap resource to an image list.

```
BOOL AddBitmapToImageList( CImageList& imageList, UINT nResourceID )
{
    BOOL bReturn;
    CBitmap bmp;

    bReturn = bmp.LoadBitmap( nResourceID );
    if( bReturn != FALSE )
    {
        // Add bitmap to image list, set white as the background
        // transparent color.
        bReturn = imageList.Add( &bmp, RGB(255,255,255) );
        bmp.DeleteObject();
    }
    return bReturn;
}
```

Adding the bitmaps using a helper function reduces the amount of code you must write and helps reduce the chance of errors, because every bitmap is loaded using the same function. In an MFC application, the helper function is often a member function of the View or Dialog Box class.

If an image list is owned by a View or Dialog Box class, the actual work of creating the image list is done when the view or dialog box is constructed. The image list can be built at any time; however, it is costly to create an image list in terms of computing power. Creating the image list in the constructor enables you build it once, rather than each time it is used. Listing 11.2 shows a typical view constructor.

Listing 11.2. Using the `AddBitmapToImageList` function to initialize an image list.

```
CMyView::CImageListView()
{
    m_imageList.Create( 32, 32, TRUE, 4, 1 );

    AddBitmapToImageList( IDB_CROSS );
    AddBitmapToImageList( IDB_CHECK );
    AddBitmapToImageList( IDB_BANG );
    AddBitmapToImageList( IDB_BALL );
}
```

The image list is created using one of the `CImageList::Create` functions. This version of `Create` is useful when an image list is used as a bitmap collection; I use other versions of `Create` in the following sections. This version of `Create` has five parameters:

- The height of each bitmap (in this case, 32 pixels)
- The width of each bitmap (in this case, 32 pixels)
- Whether the image list can be masked for transparency (in this case, `TRUE`)
- The number of bitmaps stored initially in the image list (in this case, 4)
- The *grow-by*, or the number of bitmaps added when the image list is expanded (in this case, 1)

If the image list will be expanded, the grow-by parameter should be a larger number, because expanding a bitmap consumes a lot of computing power.

Displaying an Image List Element

Individual items stored in an image list can be drawn using the `CImageList::Draw` member function, as Listing 11.3 shows.

Listing 11.3. Drawing items stored in an image list.

```
void CMyView::OnDraw(CDC* pDC)
{
    CPoint ptImage( 0, 0 );
    for( int nImage = 0; nImage < 3; nImage++ )
    {
        m_imageList.Draw( pDC, nImage, ptImage, ILD_NORMAL );
        ptImage.x += 50;
    }
}
```

The individual image bitmaps stored in an image list also can be extracted as icons using the `ExtractIcon` member function:

```
HICON hicon = m_imageList.ExtractIcon( nImage );
```

The only parameter needed for ExtractIcon is the image index. You then can use the icon extracted just like any icon handle.

Displaying a Transparent Image

You can use one of two methods to display a bitmap transparently. The easiest way is to define a background color mask for the bitmap, as done earlier in AddBitmapToImageList. You then can adjust the background color of the image list to allow the background color of the drawing surface to "shine through," giving the image a transparent effect, as Listing 11.4 shows.

Listing 11.4. Drawing image list items with transparent backgrounds.

```
void CMyView::OnDraw(CDC* pDC)
{
    m_imageList.SetBkColor( CLR_NONE );
    CPoint ptImage( 0, 0 );
    for( int nImage = 0; nImage < 3; nImage++ )
    {
        m_imageList.Draw( pDC, nImage, ptImage, ILD_TRANSPARENT );
        ptImage.x += 50;
    }
}
```

Two image list features are used in this version of OnDraw making it possible to draw the image list transparently. First, the background color is set to CLR_NONE using the CImageList::SetBkColor function. The CLR_NONE parameter tells a masked image list to prepare to use the color mask when drawing any images. If you use non-transparent bitmaps, you can set the image background to any color by using the SetBkColor function.

Second, the ILD_TRANSPARENT flag is used when CImageList::Draw is called. This tells the image list to combine the image mask with the bitmap, if a mask exists. In this case, the bitmap uses a color mask, so the background color is made transparent.

Displaying an Overlapped Image

An overlapped image consists of two images from the same image list, with one image superimposed over the other. Before using an image as an overlay, you must define it as an overlay image. You can define up to four bitmaps per image list as overlays by using the CImageList::SetOverlayImage function:

```
m_imageList.SetOverlayImage( 0, 1 );
```

The SetOverlayImage function takes two parameters: the image index used as the overlay, and the overlay index used to identify the overlay. Just to make things even easier, unlike every other index used in Windows, the overlay index starts at 1 instead of 0.

To use an overlaid image, you use the `CImageList::Draw` function as in previous examples, except that you use the `ILD_OVERLAYMASK` flag. The `INDEXTOOVERLAYMASK` macro is combined with `ILD_OVERLAYMASK` flag to specify the overlay image index to be combined with the base image. Listing 11.5 is a new version of `OnDraw` that displays an overlaid image using an image list.

Listing 11.5. Using the `CImageList::Draw` function to display an overlapped image.

```
void CImageListView::OnDraw(CDC* pDC)
{
    m_imageList.SetBkColor( CLR_NONE );
    CPoint ptOverlay( 50, 80 );
    m_imageList.SetOverlayImage( 0, 1 );
    m_imageList.Draw( pDC,
                      3,
                      ptOverlay,
                      ILD_OVERLAYMASK | INDEXTOOVERLAYMASK(1) );
}
```

List View Controls

List View controls are one of the new common controls first released with Windows 95. You can use a List View control to display information and an associated icon in one of four formats:

- **Icon view:** Displays a 32×32 pixel icon next to a list item label.
- **Small Icon view:** Displays a smaller, 16×16 pixel icon next to a list item label.
- **List View:** Displays small icons and list items arranged in a row.
- **Report view:** Displays items and their associated icons, along with subitems that are arranged in columns.

When you use a List View control, you can provide a menu or other method to enable the user to switch between the different viewing modes.

The Windows NT Explorer uses a list view control and offers all four view styles. The Explorer is shown in Figure 11.1 with the contents of the `c:\` directory contained in a report view.

List views are very popular with users because they offer several ways to display information. When you allow the user to switch between view styles, the List View control puts the user in charge of how information is displayed.

You can use List View controls to associate icons with information, as the Explorer does for file names. The user is free to select between different-sized icons, or even the Report view, which can display extra information about each item. List View controls also support drag-and-drop operations, label editing, and sorting on different columns when using the Report view.

FIGURE 11.1.

The Windows NT Explorer uses a List View control.

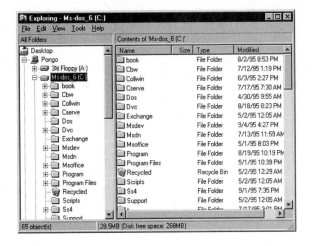

As with the Tree View controls discussed later in this chapter, there are two ways to use List View controls in your MFC-based programs. The most common way to use a List View control is to embed it into a dialog box resource, as with any other control. You use the MFC class `CListCtrl` to interact with List View controls and you can associate it with a List View control by using ClassWizard.

You also can use List View controls in a view. The `CListView` class is a specialized view that consists of a single List View control.

Using the List View Control Properties

You set the properties for the List View control by using the Properties dialog box, just as you set other controls. Some of the properties available for List View controls also are available for listboxes. Table 11.1 shows the List View control property options.

Table 11.1. The List View control property options.

Option	Function
Align	Specifies whether the items are aligned to the top or left sides of the control. This property only applies in the Icon or Small Icon view.
Auto arrange	Specifies that items should be kept arranged when viewed in the Icon or Small Icon view.
Border	Indicates that a border should be drawn around the control.
Disabled	Indicates that the list initially should be disabled. This checkbox usually is cleared.

continues

Table 11.1. continued

Option	Function
Edit labels	Enables the user to edit labels. If this property is enabled, you must handle edit-notification messages sent by the control. This is discussed later in "Editing Labels In-Place."
Group	Marks the first control in a group. This checkbox usually is cleared.
Help ID	Indicates that a context-sensitive Help ID should be created for this control. This checkbox usually is cleared.
ID	Used for the List View control resource ID. A default resource ID, such as IDC_LIST1, is supplied by Developer Studio.
No column header	Removes the header control that usually is included in the Report view.
No label wrap	Specifies that each item label must be displayed on a single line, instead of wrapping the label, as is the standard behavior.
No scroll	Disables scrolling.
No sort header	Disables the sorting function that is available through the Header control.
Owner draw fixed	Indicates that the owner of the control has responsibility for drawing the control, instead of Windows NT.
Share image list	Indicates that image lists used by the List View control can be used by other controls and should not be destroyed automatically by the control.
Single selection	Enables a single List View item to be selected.
Sort	Enables items to be sorted based on their labels as they are entered into the List View control. This item usually is set to None.
Tabstop	Indicates that this control can be reached by pressing Tab on the keyboard. This checkbox usually is checked.
View	Specifies the initial view used by the List View control. Possible values are Icon, Small Icon, List, or Report view.
Visible	Indicates that the control initially is visible. This checkbox usually is checked.

Associating Image Lists with a List Control

The images displayed in the List view next to each item are stored in image lists that are associated with the List View control. You can add an image list to a List View control by using the SetImageList function:

```
m_listCtrl.SetImageList( &m_imageSmall, LVSIL_SMALL );
```

Two parameters are passed to the List View control: a pointer to the image list and a style parameter that indicates the type of images stored in the image list. There are three types of image lists:

- **LVSIL_NORMAL:** Used for the image list used in the Icon view.
- **LVSIL_SMALL:** Used for the image list used in the Small Icon view.
- **LVSIL_STATE:** Used for state images, if there are any.

After the Image List control is added to the List View control, the List View control takes responsibility for destroying the image list.

Adding Items to a List View Control

You use the LV_ITEM structure to represent an item in a List View control. You use this structure when adding, modifying, or fetching List View items. The data members for the LV_ITEM structure follow:

- **mask:** Indicates which members are being used for the current function call. Possible values for this member are given later in this section.
- **item:** Contains the index of the item referred to by this structure.
- **iSubItem:** Contains the index of the current subitem. A *subitem* is a string displayed in a column to the right of an item's icon and label in the Report view. All items in a List view have the same number of subitems. If there is no current subitem, this field should be set to 0.
- **state** and **stateMask:** Contain the current state of the item and the valid states of the item.
- **pszText:** Contains the address of a string used as the item's label. This member must be assigned the LPSTR_TEXTCALLBACK value if a callback function is used to set the item's text. Using text callbacks is discussed later in this chapter, in the section, "Inserting an Item Using LVN_GETDISPINFO."
- **cchTextMax:** Specifies the size of the buffer provided in the pszText member if the structure is receiving item attributes. Otherwise, this member is not used.
- **iImage:** Contains the image list index for this item.
- **lParam:** An application-specific, 32-bit value associated with this item.

You use the LV_ITEM structure's mask member to indicate which parts of the structure are valid or should be filled in. This member can be one or more of the following values:

- **LVIF_TEXT:** Indicates that the pszText member is valid.
- **LVIF_IMAGE:** Indicates that the iImage member is valid.
- **LVIF_PARAM:** Indicates that the lParam member is valid.
- **LVIF_STATE:** Indicates that the state member is valid.

Inserting a List View Item

You use the `InsertItem` function to add an item to a List View control. When using MFC, four versions of `InsertItem` are available. The simplest version of `InsertItem` requires only a text label and a position for the new item:

```
m_listItem.InsertItem( 0, TEXT("Foo") );
```

Another version of `InsertItem` enables you to specify an image list index for the item:

```
m_listItem.InsertItem( 0, TEXT("Bar"), 3 );
```

The most complex version of `InsertItem` has seven parameters:

```
m_listItem.InsertItem( LVIF_TEXT¦LVIF_IMAGE,
                       0,
                       TEXT("Rama"),
                       0,
                       0,
                       3,
                       (LPARAM)0 );
```

The seven parameters in this version of `InsertItem` correspond to members found in the `LV_ITEM` structure.

The most flexible version of `InsertItem`, and the one that is used for the List view samples in this section, has one parameter: a pointer to an `LV_ITEM` structure, as shown in this code:

```
m_listItem.InsertItem( &listItem );
```

When using this version of `InsertItem`, `LV_ITEM` data members are filled with data for the new item before it is inserted, as shown in this code:

```
listItem.mask = LVIF_TEXT;
listItem.iItem = 0;
listItem.pszText = szText;
m_listCtrl.InsertItem( &listItem );
```

Inserting an Item Using `LVN_GETDISPINFO`

Image, text, and state information can be supplied when the item is inserted into the List control, or it can be supplied in response to a notification message. Providing the text information for the contents of a List control on demand is often more efficient than providing the information when the item is created. Because most applications store this information internally, it often is very easy to supply it when needed, as shown in Figure 11.2.

Each item and subitem in the List View control receives one `LVN_GETDISPINFO` message when the item or subitem is displayed. If image and state information change often, they also can be supplied through the `LVN_GETDISPINFO` notification message.

FIGURE 11.2.

The List View control uses an LVN_GETDISPINFO *message to collect display information.*

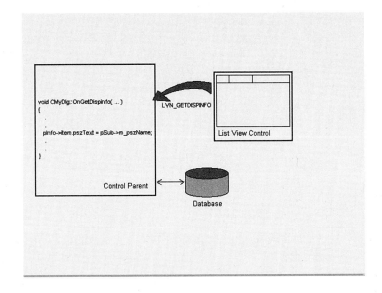

The LVN_GETDISPINFO message includes a pointer to a notification message structure:

```
typedef struct tagLV_DISPINFO {
    NMHDR   hdr;
    LV_ITEM item;
} LV_DISPINFO;
```

Like all notification messages, the first part of the LV_DISPINFO structure is a NMHDR, or notification message header. The second part of the structure is an LV_ITEM structure that represents the item or subitem being displayed. You must fill in the LV_ITEM structure with the information requested.

Listing 11.6 shows an example of adding an item that uses callback notification messages. Typically, an item is created on the heap, and a pointer to it is stored in the LV_ITEM lParam structure member.

Listing 11.6. Using text callbacks to add items to a List View control.

```
LV_ITEM        listItem;
CSubscriber* pSub = new CSubscriber( szName, szTelNumber );

listItem.mask = LVIF_TEXT¦LVIF_IMAGE¦LVIF_PARAM;
listItem.iSubItem = 0;
listItem.iItem = 0;    //First item in list view
listItem.pszText = LPSTR_TEXTCALLBACK;
listItem.cchTextMax = 40;
listItem.iImage = I_IMAGECALLBACK;
listItem.lParam = (LPARAM)pSub;  //Store subscriber info in lParam
VERIFY( listCtrl.InsertItem(&listItem) != -1 );
listCtrl.SetItemText( 0, 1, LPSTR_TEXTCALLBACK );
```

The LVN_GETDISPINFO message is sent to the List view control owner with the iItem, iSubItem, and lParam values filled. The message handler must determine how to fill in the remaining parts of the structure. The mask structure member is set to the fields that must be filled in. You must test the mask structure member to determine whether the List View control is requesting text, image, or state information, as shown in Listing 11.7.

Listing 11.7. Handling the LVN_GETDISPINFO message.

```
void CMyDlg::OnGetdispinfoList(NMHDR* pNMHDR, LRESULT* pResult)
{
    LV_DISPINFO* pInfo = (LV_DISPINFO*)pNMHDR;

    CSubscriber* pSub = (CSubscriber*)pInfo->item.lParam;
    if( pInfo->item.mask & LVIF_TEXT )
    {
        switch( pInfo->item.iSubItem )
        {
        case 0:
            pInfo->item.pszText = (char*)(LPCTSTR)pSub->m_szName;
            break;
        case 1:
            pInfo->item.pszText = (char*)(LPCTSTR)pSub->m_szNum;
            break;
        default:
            ASSERT(0);
        }
    }
    if( pInfo->item.mask & LVIF_IMAGE )
    {
        pInfo->item.iImage = pSub->GetLineType();
    }
    *pResult = 0;
}
```

If your List View control only handles one type of callback, it is not necessary to test the value of the mask variable.

When assigning text strings to a List View item, you can copy the string to pszText using lstrcpy, as in Listing 11.7, or change pszText to point at a static char buffer. The LV_ITEM cchText contains the size of the pszText label.

Adding Column Information for the Report View

Unlike the other three List View styles, the Report View displays additional information for each item contained in the list. The extra items are subitems arranged in columns. Each List View item must have the same number of subitems. Later in the section *Sorting Items in Report View*, you will see how you can sort the List View contents using the column headers.

You can add subitems to a List View control in two steps: First, you initialize the header control and then you add the subitems. You insert List View columns using LV_COLUMN structures and the InsertColumn function. The LV_COLUMN structure has the following members:

- **mask:** Specifies the member variables used for the current function call. Values for the mask member variable are discussed at the end of this section.
- **fmt:** Specifies the alignment used for the column. There are three possible values: LVCFMT_LEFT, LVCFMT_RIGHT, and LVCFMT_CENTER. The first column must use the LVCFMT_LEFT value.
- **cx:** Specifies the width of the column in pixels.
- **pszText:** Points to a string containing the column text. If the structure is used to fetch information, this member holds the address of the buffer that contains the column heading text.
- **cchTextMax:** Stores the size of the buffer pointed to by pszText. This member is used only when receiving data.
- **iSubItem:** Specifies the column number.

You use the mask member variable to specify which member values are valid, in the same way you use the LV_ITEM structure's mask member variable. Possible values follow:

- **LVCF_FMT:** Indicates that the fmt member is valid.
- **LVCF_SUBITEM:** Indicates that the iSubItem member is valid.
- **LVCF_TEXT:** Indicates that the pszText member is valid.
- **LVCF_WIDTH:** Indicates that the cx member is valid.

After you fill in the values for an LV_COLUMN structure, you add the column to the List View control using the InsertColumn function:

```
m_listCtrl.InsertColumn( nColumn, &listColumn );
```

Changing the Current View for a List View Control

Switching views in a List View control requires just a few lines of code. The current view style is stored in a structure maintained by Windows. You can retrieve this information by using the GetWindowLong function:

```
DWORD dwOldStyle = GetWindowLong( hWndList, GWL_STYLE );
```

The GetWindowLong function has two parameters:

- A window handle to the Image List control
- A GWL constant that specifies the type of information requested (in this case, GWL_STYLE)

The return value from GetWindowLong contains all the Windows style information for the image list. If you are interested in the current view, you should mask off the unnecessary information by using LVS_TYPEMASK:

```
dwOldStyle &= ~LVS_TYPEMASK; // Mask off extra style info
```

After the mask has been applied, the style information is one of the following values:

- ■ `LVS_ICON`
- ■ `LVS_SMALLICON`
- ■ `LVS_LIST`
- ■ `LVS_REPORT`

To change to another view, you use the `SetWindowLong` function. When applying a new List View style, you must make sure that the style bits not associated with the List View style are left undisturbed. You usually can do this in four steps:

1. Get the existing window style bit information using `GetWindowLong`.
2. Strip off the List View style information, leaving the other style information intact.
3. Combine a new List View style with the old style information.
4. Apply the new style information using `SetWindowLong`.

These steps often are combined into a few lines of code in the following way:

```
DWORD dwNewStyle = LVS_ICON;
DWORD dwOldStyle = GetWindowLong( hWndList, GWL_STYLE );
dwNewStyle |= ( dwOldStyle &= ~LVS_TYPEMASK );
SetWindowLong( hWndList, GWL_STYLE, dwNewStyle );
```

Editing Item Labels In Place

The List View control offers a built-in Edit control that you can use to edit items contained in the control. In order to take advantage of this capability, the List View control must have the `LVS_EDITLABELS` style. If you are using the Visual C++ Developer Studio, you can just click the `Edit labels` checkbox.

In addition to setting the List View control style, you must handle two notification messages that relate to label editing:

- ■ **`LVN_BEGINLABELEDIT`:** Sent just before label editing begins.
- ■ **`LVN_ENDLABELEDIT`:** Sent after editing is completed.

You can prevent a label from being changed by setting `*pResult` to `TRUE`. You should set `*pResult` to `FALSE` if you want to allow the edit to begin. Occasionally, you may respond to the `LVN_BEGINLABELEDIT` message in order to take control of the List View control's Edit control. Listing 11.8 shows how you can change the behavior of the Edit control.

Listing 11.8. Limiting the number of characters entered into a List View edit control.

```
void CMyDlg::OnBeginlabeleditList(NMHDR* pNMHDR, LRESULT* pResult)
{
    LV_DISPINFO* pDispInfo = (LV_DISPINFO*)pNMHDR;
    // Get pointer to the list view's edit control
```

```
CEdit* pEdit = m_listCtrl.GetEditControl();
// Set maximum text length to 15 characters
pEdit->LimitText( 15 );
*pResult = 0;
}
```

In most cases, you respond to the LVN_ENDLABELEDIT message and update the application's data. If you allow the user to change a label, you probably need to update the underlying data. There are two cases in which you should not update your data: if the LV_ITEM pszText member is NULL, and if the LV_ITEM iItem is set to –1. In these cases, the user has canceled the label-editing operation. Listing 11.9 shows an example of a message-notification handler for LVN_ENDLABELEDIT.

Listing 11.9. Handling the LVN_ENDLABELEDIT message.

```
void CMyDlg::OnEndlabeleditList(NMHDR* pNMHDR, LRESULT* pResult)
{
    LV_DISPINFO* pDispInfo = (LV_DISPINFO*)pNMHDR;
    if( (pDispInfo->item.pszText != NULL) &&
        (pDispInfo->item.iItem != -1) )
    {
        CSubscriber* pSub = (CSubscriber*)pDispInfo->item.lParam;
        ASSERT( pSub );
        pSub->m_szName = pDispInfo->item.pszText;
    }
    *pResult = 0;
}
```

Remember that the Edit control only updates what is displayed in the List View control; you must update your document or other database in response to LVN_ENDLABELEDIT.

Performing Drag-and-Drop Operations

Performing a drag-and-drop operation within a List View control is fairly easy. You must handle three messages and track a few variables, but it actually is surprisingly painless. You must handle three messages:

- **LVN_BEGINDRAG:** Sent when the drag operation is detected by the control.
- **WM_MOUSEMOVE:** Sent as the cursor moves across the control.
- **LVN_ENDDRAG:** Sent after the user releases the left mouse button and completes the drag operation.

You must begin the drag-and-drop operation in response to LVN_BEGINDRAG. In response to this message, you must create a dithered drag image, capture the cursor, and store the dragging item ID, as Listing 11.10 shows.

Listing 11.10. Handling the LVN_BEGINDRAG message.

```
void CMyDlg::OnBegindragList(NMHDR* pNMHDR, LRESULT* pResult)
{
    NM_LISTVIEW* pNMListView = (NM_LISTVIEW*)pNMHDR;
    m_nDragItem = pNMListView->iItem;
    CImageList* pDragImage;
    pDragImage = m_listCtrl.CreateDragImage( m_nDragItem,
                                             &pNMListView->ptAction );
    pDragImage->BeginDrag( 0, CPoint(0,0) );
    pDragImage->DragEnter( &m_listCtrl, pNMListView->ptAction );
    SetCapture();
    m_fIsDragging = TRUE;
    *pResult = 0;
}
```

Inside the message handler for LVN_BEGINDRAG, a temporary drag image list is created by calling the CreateDragImage function. The image list returned by this function is used to update the cursor position. The BeginDrag function associates an image index with the drag operation, and the DragEnter function "locks" the window so that it can't be updated and enables the drag image to be displayed.

As the mouse is moved across the screen during the drag-and-drop operation, WM_MOUSEMOVE messages are sent to the dialog box. The OnMouseMove function checks to see whether a drag-and-drop operation is in progress. If so, the drag image is moved to the new mouse position using the DragMove function. Because this is a static function, you can call it without specifying a CImageList object. A *hit test* also is performed to determine whether the mouse cursor is over a list item; if so, a handle to the item is stored for future use as a possible drop target. If the hit test fails, the m_nDragTarget member variable is set to –1, indicating that a drop is not possible.

Note that the drag item ID is stored as an integer, representing the item's position in the control. This complicates the drag-and-drop process, because the relative positions of the items are changed during a drag-and-drop operation.

As the item is moved to a new position, WM_MOUSEMOVE messages are sent to the owner of the List View control. If dragging is in progress, you must update the position of the drag image and determine whether the cursor is over any List View items, as shown in Listing 11.11.

Listing 11.11. Handling the WM_MOUSEMOVE message.

```
void CMyDlg::OnMouseMove(UINT nFlags, CPoint point)
{
    if( m_fIsDragging == TRUE )
    {
        // Convert point to client coordinates, and
        // update the drag image position.
        CPoint ptList(point);
        MapWindowPoints( &listCtrl, &ptList, 1 );
        CImageList::DragMove( ptList );
        // Make a hit-test to determine if the cursor is over
        // any list view items.
        UINT    uHitTest = LVHT_ONITEM;
```

```
        m_nDragTarget = m_listCtrl.HitTest( ptList, &uHitTest );
    }
    CDialog::OnMouseMove(nFlags, point);
}
```

In Listing 11.11, the `CListView::HitTest` function is used to determine whether the cursor is over a List View item. `HitTest` returns the index of the list item under the cursor, or −1 if the cursor is not over any of the List View's items.

When the user releases the left mouse button to complete the drag-and-drop operation, Windows NT sends a `WM_LBUTTONUP` message to the List View's parent window. If this message is received while a drag operation is in progress, the drag image must be released. If the cursor is over a valid drop target, you must take the appropriate action. The code in Listing 11.12, for example, moves the drag item to a new position as a result of a successful drag-and-drop operation.

Listing 11.12. Handling the WM_LBUTTONDOWN message.

```
void CTravelDlg::OnLButtonUp(UINT nFlags, CPoint point)
{
    if( m_fIsDragging == TRUE )
    {
        CImageList::DragLeave( &m_listCtrl );
        CImageList::EndDrag();
        ReleaseCapture();
        m_fIsDragging = FALSE;
        // Test for valid drop target.
        if((m_nDragTarget != -1)&&(m_nDragTarget != m_nDragItem))
        {
            // Create a copy of the drag item.
            LV_ITEM theItem;
            theItem.iItem = m_nDragItem;
            theItem.iSubItem = 0;
            theItem.mask = LVIF_PARAM;
            m_listCtrl.GetItem( &theItem );
            CSubscriber* pSub;
            pSub = new CSubscriber((CSubscriber*)theItem.lParam);
            // Change the new item number to the drop target's
            // item number.
            theItem.iItem = m_nDragTarget;
            theItem.iImage = I_IMAGECALLBACK;
            theItem.pszText = LPSTR_TEXTCALLBACK;
            theItem.mask = (LVIF_TEXT | LVIF_IMAGE);
            theItem.lParam = (LPARAM)pNew;
            // Delete the old drag item, but first adjust the
            // item number to account for the new item.
            m_listCtrl.InsertItem(&theItem);
            if( m_nDragTarget < m_nDragItem )
                m_nDragItem++;
            m_listCtrl.DeleteItem( m_nDragItem );
        }
    }
    else
        CDialog::OnLButtonUp(nFlags, point);
}
```

Determining Which Items Are Selected

Unlike a listbox control, no single message or function exists to determine which list items are selected. Instead, you must use the CListCtrl::GetNextItem function, as in this example:

```
int nSel = m_listCtrl.GetNextItem( -1, LVNI_SELECTED );
```

This code returns the index of the first selected item in the List View control. GetNextItem has two parameters: the start item and a search flag. If the start item is –1, the search starts with the first item. The flag variable can include one geometric value and one state value. The geometric values follow:

- **LVNI_ABOVE:** Searches for an item above the start item.
- **LVNI_ALL:** Searches for the next indexed item. This is the default value.
- **LVNI_BELOW:** Searches for an item below the start item.
- **LVNI_TOLEFT:** Searches for an item to the left of the start item.
- **LVNI_TORIGHT:** Searches for an item to the right of the start item.

The possible state values follow:

- **LVNI_DROPHILITED:** Searches for an item that has the LVIS_DROPHILITED state flag set.
- **LVNI_FOCUSED:** Searches for an item that has the LVIS_FOCUSED state flag set.
- **LVNI_HIDDEN:** Searches for an item that has the LVIS_HIDDEN state flag set.
- **LVNI_MARKED:** Searches for an item that has the LVIS_MARKED state flag set.
- **LVNI_SELECTED:** Searches for an item that has the LVIS_SELECTED state flag set.

If no item can be found that matches the search parameters, –1 is returned. Otherwise, the index of the first list item that satisfies the criteria is returned.

Sorting Items in Report View

One of the best features of the Report view is its capability to sort items after a user clicks on a column header. By implementing a simple notification message handler, you can provide this sorting capability.

The listbox sends an LVN_COLUMNCLICK message to its parent window. To provide column sorting for your List View control, you must supply a pointer to a comparison function to the control by calling CListCtrl::SortItems. The message-handling function shown in Listing 11.13 passes the address of SortList, a sort function.

Listing 11.13. Sorting list view columns in response to a `LVN_COLUMNCLICK` message.

```
void CMyDlg::OnColumnclickList(NMHDR* pNMHDR, LRESULT* pResult)
{
    NM_LISTVIEW* pNMListView = (NM_LISTVIEW*)pNMHDR;
    m_listCtrl.SortItems(SortList, (LPARAM)pNMListView->iSubItem);
    *pResult = 0;
}
```

In Listing 11.13, the `iSubItem` value is provided as an extra parameter that is passed to the comparison function. This allows the comparison function to determine which column should be used as a basis for the sort. The comparison function prototype follows:

```
int CALLBACK SortList( LPARAM lp1, LPARAM lp2, LPARAM lpArg );
```

The List View control calls the comparison function repeatedly with pairs of list items. The comparison function must return the following:

- ▪ `-1` if the first item sorts before the second item.
- ▪ `0` if both items sort equal.
- ▪ `1` if the first item sorts after the second item.

A comparison function looks similar to the function provided in Listing 11.14.

Listing 11.14. A comparison function used to sort List View items.

```
int CALLBACK SortList( LPARAM lpOne, LPARAM lpTwo, LPARAM lpArg )
{
    int       nResult;
    CSubscriber* pFirst = (CSubscriber *)lpOne;
    CSubscriber* pSecond = (CSubscriber *)lpTwo;
    switch( lpArg )
    {
    case 0:
        // Sort based on the main item column
        break;
    case 1:
        // Sort based on the first subitem column
        break;
    case 2:
        // Sort based on the second subitem column
        break;
    default:
        nResult = 0;
    }
    return nResult;
}
```

A full example of a comparison function is provided in the List View control example in the next section.

Looking at a List View Control Example

As an example of how List View controls are used, I have created a dialog box-based application named Travel using AppWizard. You can find Travel on the accompanying CD-ROM. This program initially displays a List View control containing three items.

Travel is a dialog-based application that displays information about hotels, along with simple ranking information. Travel supports in-place label editing, drag-and-drop operations, adding and deleting items dynamically, text and image callback message notifications, and column sorting in Report view.

Adding Controls to the Travel Dialog Box

Start by customizing the standard dialog box provided by AppWizard. You must add a total of three controls to the Travel main dialog box: two additional pushbuttons and one List View control. Add the controls to the dialog box, as shown in Figure 11.3.

FIGURE 11.3.

The Travel main dialog box in the Dialog Editor.

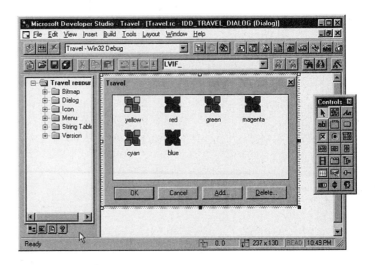

Table 11.2 lists the properties for the List View and pushbutton controls. Properties not listed should be set to the default values.

Table 11.2. Property values for controls in the Travel main dialog box.

Control	Resource ID	Caption
Add button	IDC_ADD	&Add...
Delete button	IDC_DELETE	&Delete...
List View control	IDC_LIST	none

Use ClassWizard to associate a `CListCtrl` member variable with `IDC_LIST`, using the values shown in Table 11.3.

Table 11.3. Values for a new `CListCtrl` member variable in `CTravelDlg`.

Control ID	Variable Name	Category Type
IDC_LIST	m_listCtrl	Control CListCtrl

Next, use ClassWizard to create message-handling functions called when the pushbuttons are clicked. Add two member functions to the `CTravelDlg` class, using the values listed in Table 11.4.

Table 11.4. Values for new member functions in `CTravelDlg`.

Object ID	Class Name	Message	Function
IDC_ADD	CTravelDlg	BN_CLICKED	OnAdd
IDC_DELETE	CTravelDlg	BN_CLICKED	OnDelete

Creating the Image Lists

You must create two bitmaps for the Travel application. One bitmap is used for the large icon bitmap and one for the small icon bitmap. Figure 11.4 shows the two bitmaps. Each of the bitmaps contains six hotel icons of the same size.

FIGURE 11.4.

Bitmaps used for the Travel image lists.

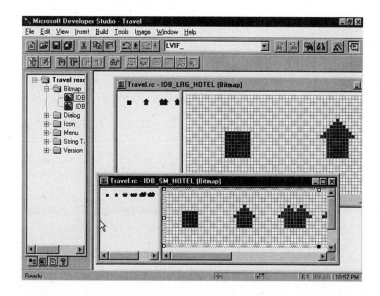

Table 11.5 lists the properties for the two bitmaps.

Table 11.5. Properties for the Travel image list bitmaps.

Resource ID	Width	Height	Background
IDB_LRG_HOTEL	192	32	White
IDB_SM_HOTEL	96	16	White

Modifying the CTravelDlg Class

You must make two small manual modifications to the CTravelDlg class declaration:

- You must add two CImageList member variables for the List View control.
- You must add three variables to support drag-and-drop operations. One BOOL variable is used to indicate that a drag operation is in progress, and two int variables are used to identify List View items involved in a drag-and-drop operation.

Add the source code shown in bold in Listing 11.15 to the implementation section of the CTravelDlg class declaration. Most of the code that is not changed is not shown for clarity.

Listing 11.15. Changes to the CTravelDlg class declaration.

```
class CTravelDlg : public CDialog
{
// Construction
public:
    CTravelDlg(CWnd* pParent = NULL);
...
// Implementation
protected:
    HICON       m_hIcon;
    CImageList  m_imageLarge;
    CImageList  m_imageSmall;
    int         m_nDragItem;
    int         m_nDragTarget;
    BOOL        m_fIsDragging;
    // Generated message map functions
    //{{AFX_MSG(CTravelDlg)
...
    DECLARE_MESSAGE_MAP()
};
```

Some of the new member variables for CTravelDlg must be initialized when a new instance is constructed. Add the source code shown in bold in Listing 11.16 to the CTravelDlg class constructor.

Listing 11.16. The `CTravelDlg` constructor.

```
CTravelDlg::CTravelDlg(CWnd* pParent /*=NULL*/)
    : CDialog(CTravelDlg::IDD, pParent)
{
    //{{AFX_DATA_INIT(CTravelDlg)
        // NOTE: the ClassWizard will add member initialization here
    //}}AFX_DATA_INIT
    m_hIcon = AfxGetApp()->LoadIcon(IDR_MAINFRAME);
    m_nDragItem = -1;
    m_nDragTarget = -1;
    m_fIsDragging = FALSE;
}
```

The CHotel structure is used to model each Hotel object stored in the List View control. CHotel objects are created dynamically as needed, and their pointers are stored in the List View control. Listing 11.17 contains the definition of the CHotel structure, which should be added to the TravelDlg.cpp file just before any of the CTravelDlg member functions.

Listing 11.17. The `CHotel` structure used in the Travel application.

```
struct CHotel
{
    CString m_szName;
    CString m_szCity;
    CString m_szCost;
    int     m_nRank;
    CHotel() : m_nRank(0) {};
    CHotel( const CString& szName, const CString& szCity,
            const CString& szCost, int nRank ) :
            m_szName(szName), m_szCity(szCity),
            m_szCost(szCost), m_nRank(nRank) {};
};
```

The CTravelDlg::OnInitDialog member function is called when the main dialog box is initialized. Add the source code shown in bold in Listing 11.18 to the OnInitDialog function.

Listing 11.18. Changes to the `CTravelDlg::OnInitDialog` member function.

```
BOOL CTravelDlg::OnInitDialog()
{
    CDialog::OnInitDialog();

    // AddWizard code omitted

    // TODO: Add extra initialization here
    // Create image lists for the list view icons
    m_imageLarge.Create( IDB_LRG_HOTEL, 32, 1, RGB(255,255,255) );
    m_imageSmall.Create( IDB_SM_HOTEL, 16, 1, RGB(255,255,255) );
    m_listCtrl.SetImageList( &m_imageLarge, LVSIL_NORMAL );
    m_listCtrl.SetImageList( &m_imageSmall, LVSIL_SMALL );
```

continues

Listing 11.18. continued

```
    //
    // Create a header control for three columns, and add
    // it to the list control.
    LV_COLUMN    listColumn;
    TCHAR*       rgszColumns[] = { TEXT("Name"),
                                   TEXT("City"),
                                   TEXT("Cost") };
    listColumn.mask = LVCF_FMT¦LVCF_WIDTH¦LVCF_TEXT¦LVCF_SUBITEM;
    listColumn.fmt = LVCFMT_LEFT;
    listColumn.cx = 60;
    for( int nColumn = 0; nColumn < 3; nColumn++ )
    {
        listColumn.iSubItem = nColumn;
        listColumn.pszText = rgszColumns[nColumn];
        m_listCtrl.InsertColumn( nColumn, &listColumn );
    }
    //
    // Add three initial hotel values.
    //
    CHotel* rgpHotels[3];
    rgpHotels[0] = new CHotel( TEXT("Ritz"),
                               TEXT("London"),
                               TEXT("High"),
                               5);
    rgpHotels[1] = new CHotel( TEXT("Flora"),
                               TEXT("Venice"),
                               TEXT("Medium"),
                               4);
    rgpHotels[2] = new CHotel( TEXT("George V"),
                               TEXT("Paris"),
                               TEXT("High"),
                               5);
    LV_ITEM      listItem;
    listItem.mask = LVIF_TEXT¦LVIF_IMAGE¦LVIF_PARAM;
    listItem.iSubItem = 0;
    for( int nItem = 0; nItem < 3; nItem++ )
    {
        listItem.iItem = nItem;
        listItem.pszText = LPSTR_TEXTCALLBACK;
        listItem.cchTextMax = 40;
        listItem.iImage = I_IMAGECALLBACK;
        listItem.lParam = (LPARAM)(rgpHotels[nItem]);
        VERIFY( m_listCtrl.InsertItem(&listItem) != -1 );
        for( int nSub = 1; nSub < 3; nSub++ )
            m_listCtrl.SetItemText(nItem, nSub, LPSTR_TEXTCALLBACK);
    }
    return TRUE;
}
```

The source code provided in Listing 11.18 creates two image lists for the List View control and then creates the control's column headers. After the columns are created, the three list items are inserted into the List View. The SetItemText function is used to add subitem text strings to each list item—in this case, `LPSTR_TEXTCALLBACK` is inserted, which causes the List View control to ask for each item as it is displayed.

Using ClassWizard, select `IDC_LIST` from the Object IDs list, and add a message-handling function for `LVN_GETDISPINFO`, which is sent by the control to request text and image information. Listing 11.19 shows the source code used to handle the `LVN_GETDISPINFO` notification message.

Listing 11.19. A message-handling function for `LVN_GETDISPINFO`.

```
void CTravelDlg::OnGetdispinfoList(NMHDR* pNMHDR, LRESULT* pResult)
{
    LV_DISPINFO* pDispInfo = (LV_DISPINFO*)pNMHDR;

    CHotel* pHotel = (CHotel*)pDispInfo->item.lParam;
    if( pDispInfo->item.mask & LVIF_TEXT )
    {
        switch( pDispInfo->item.iSubItem )
        {
        case 0:
            pDispInfo->item.pszText = (char*)(LPCTSTR)pHotel->m_szName;
            break;
        case 1:
            pDispInfo->item.pszText = (char*)(LPCTSTR)pHotel->m_szCity;
            break;
        case 2:
            pDispInfo->item.pszText = (char*)(LPCTSTR)pHotel->m_szCost;
            break;
        default:
            ASSERT(0);
        }
    }
    if( pDispInfo->item.mask & LVIF_IMAGE )
    {
        pDispInfo->item.iImage = pHotel->m_nRank;
    }
    *pResult = 0;
}
```

Freeing Dynamically Created List Items

The items added to the List View control have been allocated dynamically on the heap. If they are not explicitly deleted when the List View control is destroyed, a memory leak occurs. Fortunately, when an item in a List View control is destroyed, the control sends a notification message, `LVN_DELETEITEM`, to the parent of the List View control.

Using ClassWizard, select `IDC_LIST` from the Object IDs list, and add a message-handling function for the `LVN_DELETEITEM` message to the `CTravelDlg` class. Listing 11.20 shows the source code for `CTravelDlg::OnDeleteitemList`.

Listing 11.20. A message-handling function for `LVN_DELETEITEM`.

```
void CTravelDlg::OnDeleteitemList()
{
    int nSel = m_listCtrl.GetNextItem( -1, LVNI_SELECTED );
    if( nSel == -1 )
        AfxMessageBox( TEXT("Please select an item first") );
    else
        m_listCtrl.DeleteItem( nSel );
}
```

Sorting Columns in the List View

To add sorting capability to the List View control, use ClassWizard to create a message-handling function for `LVN_COLUMNCLICK`. Listing 11.21 shows the source code for the message-handling function and an associated comparison function.

Listing 11.21. A message-handling function for `LVN_COLUMNCLICK`.

```
void CTravelDlg::OnColumnclickList(NMHDR* pNMHDR, LRESULT* pResult)
{
    NM_LISTVIEW* pNMListView = (NM_LISTVIEW*)pNMHDR;
    m_listCtrl.SortItems(SortList, (LPARAM)pNMListView->iSubItem);
    *pResult = 0;
}

int CALLBACK SortList( LPARAM lpOne, LPARAM lpTwo, LPARAM lpArg )
{
    int     nResult;
    CHotel* pFirst = (CHotel*)lpOne;
    CHotel* pSecond = (CHotel*)lpTwo;
    ASSERT( pFirst && pSecond );
    switch( lpArg )
    {
    case 0:
        nResult = pFirst->m_szName.Compare( pSecond->m_szName );
        break;
    case 1:
        nResult = pFirst->m_szCity.Compare( pSecond->m_szCity );
        break;
    case 2:
        nResult = pFirst->m_szCost.Compare( pSecond->m_szCost );
        break;
    default:
        nResult = 0;
    }
    return nResult;
}
```

Adding Items to the List View Control

When an item is added to the List View control, a dialog box is used to collect information from the user. A new CHotel object then is created on the heap and inserted into the List View control.

Using Figure 11.5 as a guide, create a dialog box resource to collect new hotel information from a user. Give the dialog box a resource ID of IDD_ADD_HOTEL.

FIGURE 11.5.

The Add Hotel dialog box used by the Travel example.

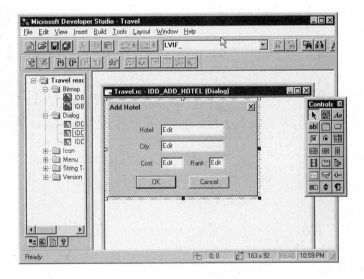

Table 11.6 shows the resource IDs used by the new dialog box's Edit controls.

Table 11.6. Edit controls used by the Add Hotel dialog box.

Edit Control	Resource ID	Category	Type	Member Variable
Hotel	IDC_HOTEL_NAME	Value	CString	m_szName
City	IDC_HOTEL_CITY	Value	CString	m_szCity
Cost	IDC_HOTEL_COST	Value	CString	m_szCost
Rank	IDC_RANK	Value	int	m_nRank

Using ClassWizard, associate a CDialog-derived class named CAddHotelDlg with the new dialog box resource. With ClassWizard, associate each Edit control with a member variable, using the values provided in Table 11.6.

Add an #include statement in TravelDlg.cpp that includes the class definition for CAddHotelDlg, found in AddHotelDlg.h. Add the following line after the other #include statements at the top of TravelDlg.cpp:

```
#include "AddHotelDlg.h"
```

Listing 11.22 provides the source code for the CTravelDlg::OnAdd member function.

Listing 11.22. Adding a new hotel to the List View control.

```
void CTravelDlg::OnAdd()
{
    CAddHotelDlg     dlg;

    if( dlg.DoModal() )
    {
        CHotel* pHotel = new CHotel( dlg.m_szName,
                                     dlg.m_szCity,
                                     dlg.m_szCost,
                                     dlg.m_nRank );
        int nItem = m_listCtrl.GetItemCount();
        LV_ITEM     listItem;
        listItem.mask = LVIF_TEXT¦LVIF_IMAGE¦LVIF_PARAM;
        listItem.iSubItem = 0;

        listItem.iItem = nItem;
        listItem.pszText = LPSTR_TEXTCALLBACK;
        listItem.cchTextMax = 40;
        listItem.iImage = pHotel->m_nRank;
        listItem.lParam = (LPARAM)pHotel;
        VERIFY( m_listCtrl.InsertItem(&listItem) != -1 );
        m_listCtrl.SetItemText( nItem, 1, LPSTR_TEXTCALLBACK );
        m_listCtrl.SetItemText( nItem, 2, LPSTR_TEXTCALLBACK );
    }
}
```

Deleting Items from the List

The Travel application deletes an item from the List View control in two steps:

- The selected item in the List View control is identified.
- The selected item is deleted.

These steps occur after a user clicks the Delete button. Listing 11.23 shows the source code for CTravelDlg::OnDelete.

Listing 11.23. Deleting an item from the List View control.

```
void CTravelDlg::OnDelete()
{
    int nSel = m_listCtrl.GetNextItem( -1, LVNI_SELECTED );
    if( nSel == -1 )
```

```
            AfxMessageBox( TEXT("Please select an item first") );
        else
            m_listCtrl.DeleteItem( nSel );
}
```

Note that the OnDelete function does not call delete to free the memory allocated for the CHotel object; instead, it calls the CListCtrl::DeleteItem member function. In turn, the List View control generates an LVN_DELETEITEM notification message—the message handler for LVN_DELETEITEM frees the memory allocated for this object.

Handling Drag-and-Drop Operations

As discussed earlier, handling drag-and-drop operations requires you to handle three messages. With ClassWizard, add message handlers to the CTravelDlg class, using the values in Table 11.7.

Table 11.7. Message-handling functions used for drag-and-drop operations.

Object ID	Message	Function
IDC_LIST	LVN_BEGINDRAG	OnBegindragList
CTravelDlg	WM_MOUSEMOVE	OnMouseMove
CTravelDlg	WM_LBUTTONUP	OnLButtonUp

Listing 11.24 shows the source code for these three functions.

Listing 11.24. CTravelDlg functions used to implement drag-and-drop operations.

```
void CTravelDlg::OnBegindragList(NMHDR* pNMHDR, LRESULT* pResult)
{
    NM_LISTVIEW* pNMListView = (NM_LISTVIEW*)pNMHDR;

    m_nDragItem = pNMListView->iItem;
    CImageList* pDragImage;
    pDragImage = m_listCtrl.CreateDragImage( m_nDragItem, &pNMListView->ptAction );
    ASSERT( pDragImage );

    pDragImage->BeginDrag( 0, CPoint(0,0) );
    pDragImage->DragEnter( &m_listCtrl, pNMListView->ptAction );
    SetCapture();
    m_fIsDragging = TRUE;

    *pResult = 0;
}
```

continues

Listing 11.24. continued

```cpp
void CTravelDlg::OnMouseMove(UINT nFlags, CPoint point)
{
    if( m_fIsDragging == TRUE )
    {
        CPoint ptList(point);
        MapWindowPoints( &m_listCtrl, &ptList, 1 );
        CImageList::DragMove( ptList );
        UINT    uHitTest = LVHT_ONITEM;
        m_nDragTarget = m_listCtrl.HitTest( ptList, &uHitTest );
    }
    CDialog::OnMouseMove(nFlags, point);
}

void CTravelDlg::OnLButtonUp(UINT nFlags, CPoint point)
{
    if( m_fIsDragging == TRUE )
    {
        CImageList::DragLeave( &m_listCtrl );
        CImageList::EndDrag();
        ReleaseCapture();
        m_fIsDragging = FALSE;
        if((m_nDragTarget != -1)&&(m_nDragTarget != m_nDragItem))
        {
            LV_ITEM theItem;
            theItem.iItem = m_nDragItem;
            theItem.iSubItem = 0;
            theItem.mask = LVIF_PARAM;
            VERIFY( m_listCtrl.GetItem( &theItem ) );


            CHotel* pOldHotel = (CHotel*)theItem.lParam;
            ASSERT(pOldHotel);

            CHotel* pNewHotel = new CHotel(*pOldHotel);
            ASSERT(pNewHotel);

            theItem.iItem = m_nDragTarget;
            theItem.iImage = pNewHotel->m_nRank;
            theItem.mask |= (LVIF_TEXT | LVIF_IMAGE);
            theItem.pszText = LPSTR_TEXTCALLBACK;
            theItem.cchTextMax = 40;
            theItem.lParam = (LPARAM)pNewHotel;
            VERIFY( m_listCtrl.InsertItem(&theItem) != -1 );
            m_listCtrl.SetItemText( m_nDragTarget, 1, LPSTR_TEXTCALLBACK );
            m_listCtrl.SetItemText( m_nDragTarget, 2, LPSTR_TEXTCALLBACK );

            if( m_nDragTarget < m_nDragItem )
                m_nDragItem++;

            VERIFY( m_listCtrl.DeleteItem( m_nDragItem ));
        }
    }
    else
        CDialog::OnLButtonUp(nFlags, point);
}
```

Performing In-Place Label Editing

As discussed earlier in this chapter, support for in-place label editing is managed through two messages: LVN_BEGINLABELEDIT and LVN_ENDLABELEDIT. Add handling functions for these two messages, using the values shown in Table 11.8.

Table 11.8. Message-handling functions used for label editing.

Object ID	*Message*	*Function*
IDC_LIST	LVN_BEGINLABELEDIT	OnBeginlabeleditList
IDC_LIST	LVN_ENDLABELEDIT	OnEndlabeleditList

Listing 11.25 shows the source code for these two functions.

Listing 11.25. `CTravelDlg` functions used to implement label editing.

```
void CTravelDlg::OnBeginlabeleditList(NMHDR* pNMHDR, LRESULT* pResult)
{
    LV_DISPINFO* pDispInfo = (LV_DISPINFO*)pNMHDR;
    CEdit* pEdit = m_listCtrl.GetEditControl();
    pEdit->LimitText( 15 );
    *pResult = 0;
}

void CTravelDlg::OnEndlabeleditList(NMHDR* pNMHDR, LRESULT* pResult)
{
    LV_DISPINFO* pDispInfo = (LV_DISPINFO*)pNMHDR;

    if((pDispInfo->item.pszText != NULL)&&
       (pDispInfo->item.iItem != -1))
    {
        CHotel* pHotel = (CHotel*)pDispInfo->item.lParam;
        ASSERT( pHotel );
        pHotel->m_szName = pDispInfo->item.pszText;
    }
    *pResult = 0;
}
```

Switching Between View Styles

In the Travel application, you can switch between different List View styles by selecting a new view style from a pop-up menu displayed after the user right-clicks over the List View control.

To create this pop-up menu, begin by adding a new menu resource to the Travel project. This menu will be used as a pop-up menu, so create a dummy caption for the first item on the top level of the menu.

Open the Properties dialog box for the menu resource by double-clicking on the edge of the menu resource, and change the resource ID to IDM_LISTVIEW. Using the values shown in Table 11.9, add four menu items under the dummy label.

Table 11.9. Menu items added to the IDM_LISTVIEW menu resource.

Menu ID	Caption
IDM_LARGE_ICON	&Large Icon
IDM_SMALL_ICON	&Small Icon
IDM_REPORT	&Report
IDM_LIST	&LIST

Figure 11.6 shows the pop-up menu in the Developer Studio Resource Editor.

FIGURE 11.6.

The IDM_LISTVIEW menu.

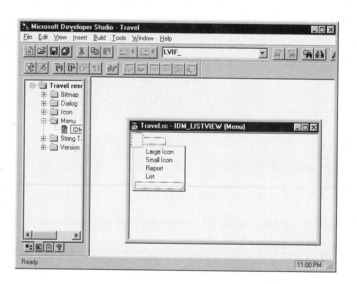

To pop up the menu after the right mouse button is clicked, you must add a message-handling function to the CTravelDlg class. With ClassWizard, add a message-handling function for NM_RCLICK, using the values shown in Table 11.10.

Table 11.10. Handling a notification message for a right-mouse click.

Class Name	Object ID	Message	Function
CTravelDlg	IDC_LIST	NM_RCLICK	OnRclickList

Listing 11.26 provides the source code for `CTravelDlg::OnRclickList`.

Listing 11.26. Displaying a pop-up menu in response to a right-mouse click.

```
void CTravelDlg::OnRclickList(NMHDR* pNMHDR, LRESULT* pResult)
{
    POINT   pt;
    GetCursorPos( &pt );

    CMenu   theMenu;
    theMenu.LoadMenu( IDM_LISTVIEW );
    CMenu* pPopup = theMenu.GetSubMenu(0);
    ASSERT( pPopup );
    pPopup->TrackPopupMenu( TPM_LEFTALIGN¦TPM_RIGHTBUTTON,
                            pt.x,
                            pt.y,
                            this );
    *pResult = 0;
}
```

The four menu selection messages from the pop-up menu are handled by the `CTravelApp` class. Use ClassWizard to add the message-handling functions listed in Table 11.11.

Table 11.11. Message-handling functions used for changing List View styles.

Object ID	Message	Function
IDM_LARGE_ICON	COMMAND	OnLargeIcon
IDM_SMALL_ICON	COMMAND	OnSmallIcon
IDM_LIST	COMMAND	OnList
IDM_REPORT	COMMAND	OnReport

In addition to the member functions listed in Table 11.11, you must add manually another member function to the `CTravelApp` class. Add a declaration for `SetListView` in the `Implementation` section of the `CTravelApp` class declaration:

```
// Implementation
private:
    void SetListView( DWORD dwNewStyle );
```

Listing 11.27 provides the source code for the List view selection messages.

Listing 11.27. Functions used to change the List View control's view style.

```
void CTravelApp::OnLargeIcon()
{
    SetListView( LVS_ICON );
}

void CTravelApp::OnList()
{
    SetListView( LVS_LIST );
}

void CTravelApp::OnReport()
{
    SetListView( LVS_REPORT );
}

void CTravelApp::OnSmallIcon()
{
    SetListView( LVS_SMALLICON );
}

void CTravelApp::SetListView( DWORD dwNewStyle )
{
    ASSERT( m_pMainWnd );
    CWnd* pList = m_pMainWnd->GetDlgItem( IDC_LIST );
    ASSERT( pList );
    HWND    hWndList = pList->GetSafeHwnd();
    ASSERT( hWndList );
    DWORD   dwOldStyle = GetWindowLong( hWndList, GWL_STYLE );
    if( (dwOldStyle & LVS_TYPEMASK) != dwNewStyle )
    {
        dwOldStyle &= ~LVS_TYPEMASK;
        dwNewStyle |= dwOldStyle;
        SetWindowLong( hWndList, GWL_STYLE, dwNewStyle );
    }
}
```

Compile and run the Travel example project. The List View initially displays its contents in the Icon view. Try using the right mouse-click menu to switch between views. When the Report view is displayed, use the header control to change the spacing between columns and sort the items. You also can experiment with adding and deleting hotel items from the List View control.

Tree View Controls

Tree controls are similar to the List View controls discussed in the preceding section, except that they display information in a tree, or hierarchy. Tree View controls often are used to display disk directories or the contents of books or other documents.

Items in a Tree View control are arranged into groups, with child items located under parent items. Child items are indented, or nested, under a parent. The Visual C++ Developer Studio is one of the applications that uses the new tree control, shown in Figure 11.7.

FIGURE 11.7.

The Tree View control used by Developer Studio.

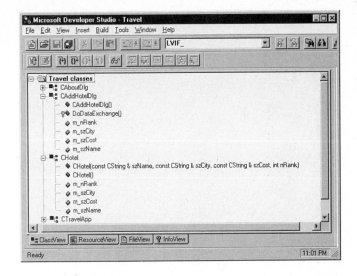

You can create Tree View controls with several different styles. Many Tree View controls display a bitmap next to each item, for example. Many also display a Tree Control button next to each item. This button contains a plus sign if an item can be expanded. If the button is clicked, the Tree View expands to display the item's children. Once expanded, the item displays a button with a minus sign.

Tree controls often are used to contain a large amount of information. The user can control the amount of information displayed by expanding or collapsing tree items. When more horizontal or vertical room is needed, the tree control automatically displays scroll bars.

The Tree control is a popular control because it enables you to display a great deal of information in a hierarchy. Unlike with a listbox, a small amount of high-level information can be presented initially, enabling the user to decide which parts of the tree should be expanded. The Tree control also enables information to be displayed so that you can view relationships between different items in the control. In the Explorer, subdirectories are nested in order to show their positions in the directory, for example. Tree views are popular because they offer a wide range of options. As with List View controls, Tree View controls put the user in charge.

When a Tree control is used in a dialog box, the control is added just as buttons, listboxes, and other controls are added—by using a Resource Editor. The MFC class `CTreeCtrl` is used to interact with Tree controls and is associated with a Tree View control using ClassWizard.

Setting Tree View Control Properties

When creating a Tree View control in a dialog box resource, you can set the Tree View control's properties by using the Properties dialog box. Some of the properties available for Tree View controls also are available for List View controls. Table 11.12 lists the Tree Control property options.

Table 11.12. Tree Control property options.

Option	Function
Border	Indicates that a border should be drawn around the Tree control. This checkbox usually is checked.
Disable drag drop	Prevents drag-and-drop operations for items contained in the Tree View control. This item usually is cleared.
Disabled	Indicates that the list initially should be disabled. This checkbox usually is cleared.
Edit labels	Enables a user to change the values of labels in the control. This checkbox usually is cleared.
Group	Marks the first control in a group. This checkbox usually is cleared.
Has buttons	Indicates that the control should be drawn with buttons. For each Tree Control item that can be expanded, a button appears to the left of the item. This checkbox usually is cleared.
Has lines	Indicates that lines should be drawn connecting items in the control. This checkbox usually is cleared.
Help ID	Indicates that a context-sensitive Help ID should be generated for this control.
ID	Used for the Tree View control resource ID. A default resource ID, such as IDC_TREE1, is supplied by Developer Studio.
Lines at root	Indicates that lines should be drawn at the first, or root, level of the control. This option is ignored if the Has Lines checkbox is not selected.
Show selection always	Uses the system highlight colors for selected items. This item usually is cleared.
Tabstop	Indicates that this control can be reached by pressing Tab. This checkbox usually is checked.
Visible	Indicates that the control initially is visible. This checkbox usually is checked.

Using Image Lists with a Tree View Control

The Tree View control uses image lists as the source of bitmap information displayed in a Tree View control. Like the List View control discussed in the preceding section, an image list first is created, and then is associated with a Tree View control using the SetImageList function:

```
m_imageList.Create( IDB_TREE, 14, 1, RGB(255,0,0) );
m_tree.SetImageList( &m_imageList, TVSIL_NORMAL );
```

> **NOTE**
>
> At first glance, you might think that the List View and Tree View controls almost are identical as far as the API goes. The key word, unfortunately, is *almost.*
>
> The biggest difference between List View and Tree View controls is in how individual items are referenced. In List View controls, an item index is used when communicating with the control. Because Tree View controls allow the tree to be expanded and collapsed, however, the concept of an index doesn't work. An item handle, or HTREEITEM, therefore is used when referring to an item contained in a Tree View control.
>
> In addition, there are a number of smaller differences that can tend to be a bit aggravating. For example, CListView::CreateDragImage takes two parameters, whereas CTreeView::CreateDragImage accepts only one.

Examining Tree View Data Structures

The primary Tree View data structure is TV_ITEM, which is used when inserting or retrieving an item from the Tree View control. Table 11.13 lists the members of the TV_ITEM structure.

Table 11.13. Members of the TV_ITEM structure.

Member	Description
cChildren	A flag that indicates whether the item has any children. If this member is set to 0, the item has no children. If it is set to 1, the item has one or more children. If it has the value I_CHILDRENCALLBACK, a callback is used to determine whether the item has any children.
cchTextMax	Specifies the size of the buffer provided in the pszText member if this structure is receiving attributes. Otherwise, this structure is not used.
hItem	A handle to the Tree View item to which this structure refers.
iImage	Contains the normal image list index for this item, or I_IMAGECALLBACK when a callback is used to set the item's image data.
iSelectedImage	Contains the image list index for the item displayed when the item is selected, or I_IMAGECALLBACK when a callback is used to set the item's image data.
lParam	An application-specific, 32-bit value associated with the item.

continues

Table 11.13. continued

Member	Description
mask	Indicates which structure members are valid for the current function call. Possible values are provided later in this section.
pszText	Contains the address of a string used as the item's label. This item is assigned a value of LPSTR_CALLBACK when a callback function is used to set the item's text.
state	Contains the current state of the item and stateMask and the valid states contained in the state variable.

You use TV_ITEM structures much like LV_ITEM structures were used earlier in this chapter. Specific explanations are provided in the following sections.

Adding an Item to a Tree View Control

As with the List View controls discussed earlier, you can add items to the Tree View control in several ways. In fact, no matter what parameters you have available, you probably can find some way to insert an item into a Tree View control.

When using MFC, the InsertItem function is overloaded to provide four methods to insert Tree Control items. In addition, most of these methods have default parameters, simplifying their use.

Inserting Items Directly into the Tree View Control

When adding simple items to a Tree control, you can use the text-label version of CTreeCtrl::InsertItem:

```
HTREEITEM InsertItem( LPCTSTR lpszItem,
                      HTREEITEM hParent = TVI_ROOT,
                      HTREEITEM hInsertAfter = TVI_LAST );
```

In this prototype, hParent is a handle to the new item's parent. Because the last two parameters have default values, only the label for the item must be provided:

```
HTREEITEM hItem = tree.InsertItem( "Foo" );
```

This line adds an item to the Tree control at the first, or root, level. The return value from InsertItem is a handle to the new item if it was inserted successfully, or NULL if the item could not be inserted. To add an item as a child, pass the parent's handle as a parameter when inserting the item:

```
tree.InsertItem( "Bar", hItem );
```

This item is inserted as the last child because the default value of TVI_LAST is used for the hInsertAfter parameter. There are three predefined values for this parameter:

- **TVI_FIRST:** Inserts the item as the first child, as used in this example.
- **TVI_LAST:** Inserts the item as the last child.
- **TVI_SORT:** Sorts the item alphabetically.

To specify a particular location for the new item, pass that item's handle as a parameter for InsertItem:

```
tree.InsertItem( "Bar", hItem, hPrevious );
```

The source code in Listing 11.28 uses the functions discussed previously to add items in a dialog box's OnInitDialog function.

Listing 11.28. Adding items to a Tree View control.

```
void CMyDlg::OnInitDialog()
{
    // m_tree is a CTreeCtrl object
    HTREEITEM hAuthor = m_tree.InsertItem(TEXT("Shakespeare"));
    HTREEITEM hType   = m_tree.InsertItem(TEXT("Tragedy"),hAuthor);
    m_tree.InsertItem( TEXT("Hamlet"), hType );
    m_tree.InsertItem( TEXT("Richard III"), hChapter );
    m_tree.InsertItem( TEXT("Othello"), hChapter );
    hType = m_tree.InsertItem( TEXT("Comedy"), hAuthor );
    m_tree.InsertItem( TEXT("A Midsummer Night's Dream"), hType );
}
```

In order to add image information for a Tree View item, you must use a different version of InsertItem:

```
HTREEITEM InsertItem( LPCTSTR lpszItem,
                      int nImage,
                      int nSelectedImage,
                      HTREEITEM hParent = TVI_ROOT,
                      HTREEITEM hInsertAfter = TVI_LAST);
```

Typically, a Tree View control displays several images next to items stored in the control, with each image representing a specific nesting level or item type. You must specify two image indexes—one for the normal image and another for the selected image. If the image doesn't change, just pass the same value for both parameters:

```
m_tree.InsertItem( TEXT("Foo"), 3, 3, hParent );
```

The most flexible insertion method uses the TV_INSERTSTRUCT. The actual call to InsertItem is simple enough:

```
TV_INSERTSTRUCT    tvis;
// Initialize tvis
m_tree.InsertItem( &tvis );
```

The definition of TV_INSERTSTRUCT looks like this:

```
typedef struct _TV_INSERTSTRUCT {
    HTREEITEM hParent;
    HTREEITEM hInsertAfter;
    TV_ITEM   item;
} TV_INSERTSTRUCT;
```

Using this version of the InsertItem function enables you to fill a TV_ITEM structure and insert it at a specific location in the Tree View control using the hParent and hInsertAfter parameters. The source code in Listing 11.29 shows an example of using TV_INSERTSTRUCT.

Listing 11.29. Using TV_INSERTSTRUCT to add items to a Tree View control.

```
TV_INSERTSTRUCT      tviAuthor;
TV_INSERTSTRUCT      tviCategory;

tviAuthor.hParent = TVI_ROOT;
tviAuthor.hInsertAfter = TVI_FIRST;
tviAuthor.item.mask = TVIF_TEXT;
tviAuthor.item.pszText = TEXT("Shakespeare");
tviAuthor.item.cchTextMax = 40;
HTREEITEM hAuthor = m_tree.InsertItem( &tviAuthor );

tviCategory.hParent = hAuthor;
tviCategory.hInsertAfter = TVI_FIRST;
tviCategory.item.mask = TVIF_TEXT;
tviCategory.item.pszText = TEXT("Tragedy");
tviCategory.item.cchTextMax = 40;
HTREEITEM hCategory = m_tree.InsertItem( &tviCategory );

tviCategory.hInsertAfter = hCategory;
tviCategory.item.pszText = TEXT("Comedy");
hCategory = m_tree.InsertItem( &tviCategory );
```

Using the TVN_GETDISPINFO Callback Message

Like the List View control, the Tree View control uses callback notification messages to retrieve display information about an item. The TVN_GETDISPINFO message is sent to the Tree View control's parent window when the control needs to collect display information.

In order to use the TVN_GETDISPINFO message, you must use the version of CTreeCtrl::InsertItem that takes TV_INSERTSTRUCT as a parameter. In place of the pszText, iImage, iSelectedImage, or cChildren members of TV_ITEM, you can use special values to specify that the information is provided in response to TVN_GETDISPINFO, as shown in Table 11.14.

Table 11.14. Callback message symbols for Tree View control items.

TV_ITEM *member*	*Symbol*
pszText	LPSTR_TEXTCALLBACK
iImage	I_IMAGECALLBACK
iSubImage	I_IMAGECALLBACK
cChildren	I_CHILDRENCALLBACK

After defining the TV_ITEM members that use the TVN_GETDISPINFO callback message, ClassWizard creates a message handler. Listing 11.30 shows a typical message handler.

Listing 11.30. A typical TVN_GETDISPINFO message handler.

```
void CTreeDispDlg::OnGetdispinfoTree(NMHDR* pNMHDR, LRESULT* pResult)
{
    TV_DISPINFO* pTVDispInfo = (TV_DISPINFO*)pNMHDR;

    CItem* pItem = (CItem*)pTVDispInfo->item.lParam;
    if( pTVDispInfo->item.mask & TVIF_TEXT )
    {
        lstrcpy( pTVDispInfo->item.pszText, pItem->m_szLabel );
    }
    *pResult = 0;
}
```

Performing In-Place Label Editing

Like the List View control, the Tree View control offers a built-in Edit control that you can use to edit items contained in the control. In order to take advantage of this capability, the List View control must have the TVS_EDITLABELS style. If you are using the Visual C++ Developer Studio, you can just click the Edit labels checkbox.

In addition to setting the List View control style, there are two notification messages that relate to label editing:

- **TVN_BEGINLABELEDIT:** Sent just before label editing begins.
- **TVN_ENDLABELEDIT:** Sent after editing is completed.

These messages are handled exactly as they are for a List View control. You can prevent a label from being changed by setting *pResult to TRUE, and you should set *pResult to FALSE if you want to allow the edit to begin. In addition, you can use the LVN_BEGINLABELEDIT message to take control of the Tree View control's Edit control.

The TVN_ENDLABELEDIT message is used exactly as with a List View control. If you update underlying data when you receive TVN_ENDLABELEDIT, make sure to look out for cases in which pszText is NULL or iItem is set to –1. Either of these conditions indicate that the user has canceled the label-editing process. Listing 11.31 shows an example of a message notification handler for TVN_ENDLABELEDIT.

Listing 11.31. Handling the TVN_ENDLABELEDIT message.

```
void CMyDlg::OnEndlabeleditTree(NMHDR* pNMHDR, LRESULT* pResult)
{
    LV_DISPINFO* pDispInfo = (LV_DISPINFO*)pNMHDR;
    if( (pDispInfo->item.pszText != NULL) &&
        (pDispInfo->item.iItem != -1) )
    {
        CSubscriber* pSub = (CSubscriber*)pDispInfo->item.lParam;
        ASSERT( pSub );
        pSub->m_szName = pDispInfo->item.pszText;
    }
    *pResult = 0;
}
```

Using Drag-and-Drop Support

The steps required to support drag-and-drop operation in a Tree View control are very similar to the steps required for List View controls discussed earlier in this chapter. In order to handle drag-and-drop operations inside a Tree View control, you must handle the following three messages:

- **TVN_BEGINDRAG:** Notifies the Tree View control's parent that a drag operation has been started.

- **WM_MOUSEMOVE:** Sent as the mouse is moved. If a drag operation is in progress, the drag image is moved to the new cursor position.

- **WM_LBUTTONUP:** Sent as the left mouse button is released. If a drag operation is in progress, the drag is completed by moving the drag item into the new position.

The drag sequence starts with the Tree View control sending the TVN_DRAGBEGIN to the control's parent. If you are using MFC, the MFC framework translates this message into an OnBegindrag function call. Inside this function, you should store a reference to the drag item, just as for List View controls earlier in this chapter. Because the Tree View controls use handles instead of indexes, however, the drag item is stored as a handle instead of an int.

Inside the message handler for TVN_BEGINDRAG, a temporary drag image list is created by calling the CreateDragImage function. The image list returned by this function is used to update the cursor position. The BeginDrag and DragEnter functions start the drag process and lock the window so that it can't be updated during the drag-and-drop operation, as shown in Listing 11.32.

Listing 11.32. Handling the `TVN_BEGINDRAG` message.

```
CImageList* pDragImage;
pDragImage = m_tree.CreateDragImage( m_hDragItem );

... calculate cursor position ...

pDragImage->BeginDrag( 0, ptDrag );
pDragImage->DragEnter( &m_tree, pNMTreeView->ptDrag );
```

As with the List View control discussed earlier in the chapter, `WM_MOUSEMOVE` messages are sent to the control's owner during the drag process. The message handler updates the drag image using the `DragMove` function, if a drag is in progress. A hit test is performed to determine whether the mouse cursor is over a tree item; if so, a handle to the tree item is stored for future use as a possible drop target. If the hit test fails, the `m_dragTarget` member variable is set to `NULL`, indicating that a drop is not possible.

At some point, the user releases the left mouse button, resulting in a `WM_LBUTTONUP` message. If a drag-and-drop operation is in progress, the operation is completed by calling the `DragLeave` and `EndDrag` functions. The mouse capture is released, and the dragging flag is set to `FALSE`.

If the drop target is valid, the drag item is inserted by calling `CTreeCtrl::InsertItem`. For drag-and-drop operations, calls to the `InsertItem` function often use a fourth parameter, which is a handle for the item just before the new item.

After the drag item is inserted in a new position, you can remove the old position by using the `DeleteItem` function:

```
m_tree.DeleteItem( m_hDragItem );
```

Looking at a Tree View Control Example

As an example of using a Tree View control that supports drag-and-drop operations, I have created an example program named TreeDisp included on the accompanying CD-ROM. TreeDisp is a dialog-based application that displays a tree containing a list of teams at the root level. Expanding a team displays the players assigned to that particular team. Players can be moved between teams by dragging them to a new team. You also can add teams and players. Figure 11.8 shows the TreeDisp application running with its team nodes expanded.

To begin the TreeDisp project, use ClassWizard to create a skeleton dialog-based application named TreeDisp. Add a Tree View control and three pushbutton controls, as shown in Figure 11.9.

FIGURE 11.8.

The main dialog box for the TreeDisp application.

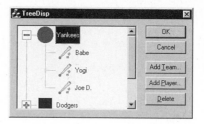

FIGURE 11.9.

Adding controls to the main dialog box for the TreeDisp application.

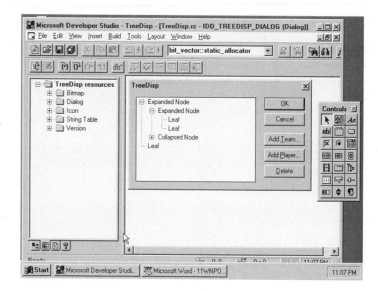

Open the Properties dialog box for the Tree View control and change the resource ID to IDC_TREE. All other properties should be set to their default values except for the following items, which should be checked:

- Has lines
- Lines at root
- Edit labels
- Has buttons

Using ClassWizard, associate a CTreeCtrl member variable with the new Tree View control, using the values shown in Table 11.15.

Table 11.15. Values used to add a CTreeCtrl member variable for CTreeDispDlg.

Control ID	Variable Name	Category	Type
IDC_TREE	m_tree	Control	CTreeCtrl

Using ClassWizard, create three message-handling functions for the pushbutton controls added to the dialog box. Table 11.16 contains the resource IDs for the new controls, as well as information about the message-handling functions.

Table 11.16. Values for new member functions in `CTreeDispDlg`.

Object ID	Class Name	Message	Function
IDC_ADD_TEAM	CTreeDispDlg	BN_CLICKED	OnAddTeam
IDC_ADD_PLAYER	CTreeDispDlg	BN_CLICKED	OnAddPlayer
IDC_DELETE	CTreeDispDlg	BN_CLICKED	OnDelete

Creating an Image List Control

The version of the Tree View control used in the TreeDisp project displays two types of bitmaps next to Tree View items:

- A circle, square, or diamond for root-level items representing teams
- A baseball and bat icon for second-level items representing players

As discussed earlier in this chapter, an image list consists of a single bitmap that has one or more segments. The bitmap shown in Figure 11.10 contains all the images used by the Tree View control.

FIGURE 11.10.

Bitmaps displayed in the Tree View control.

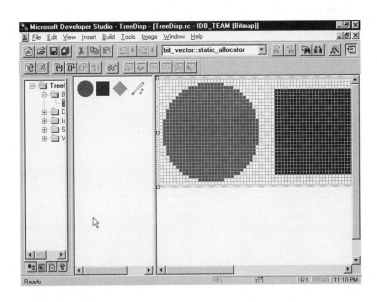

Use the Image Editor to create the bitmap in Figure 11.10. Use white as a background color for the bitmap to make it easier to draw the bitmap transparently. Use the values shown in Table 11.17 for the bitmap.

Table 11.17. Attributes for the image list bitmap used in TreeDisp.

Resource ID	Height	Item Width	Total Width
IDB_TEAM	32	32	192

Modifying the Dialog Box Class

The CTreeDispDlg class must be modified in order to handle the Tree View control. You must add a total of four new member variables to the CTreeDispDlg class:

- A CImageList variable supplies the images displayed next to each item in the Tree control.
- A BOOL flag indicates that a drag-and-drop operation is in progress.
- An HTREEITEM variable refers to an item being dragged.
- Another HTREEITEM variable refers to the current drop target.

Add the source code shown in bold type in Listing 11.33 to the Implementation section of the CTreeDispDlg class declaration.

Listing 11.33. Additions to the CTreeDispDlg class declaration.

```
class CTreeDispDlg : public CDialog
{
    ...
// Implementation
private:
    CImageList   m_imageList;
    HTREEITEM    m_hDragItem;
    HTREEITEM    m_hDragTarget;
    BOOL         m_fIsDragging;
protected:
    HICON m_hIcon;
    ...
};
```

The Tree control is initialized when the CTreeDispDlg class receives the WM_INITDIALOG message. Add the source code in Listing 11.34 to the OnInitDialog member function.

Listing 11.34. The `CTreeDispDlg::OnInitDialog` member function.

```
BOOL CTreeDispDlg::OnInitDialog()
{
    CDialog::OnInitDialog();

    // Existing code omitted

    // TODO: Add extra initialization here
    m_imageList.Create( IDB_TEAM, 32, 1, RGB(255,255,255) );
    m_tree.SetImageList( &m_imageList, TVSIL_NORMAL );

    HTREEITEM    hTeamItem;

    hTeamItem = m_tree.InsertItem( TEXT("Yankees"), 0, 0 );
    m_tree.InsertItem( TEXT("Babe"), 3, 3, hTeamItem );
    m_tree.InsertItem( TEXT("Yogi"), 3, 3, hTeamItem );
    m_tree.InsertItem( TEXT("Joe D."), 3, 3, hTeamItem );

    hTeamItem = m_tree.InsertItem( TEXT("Dodgers"), 1, 1 );
    m_tree.InsertItem( TEXT("Garvey"), 3, 3, hTeamItem );
    m_tree.InsertItem( TEXT("Sutton"), 3, 3, hTeamItem );
    m_tree.InsertItem( TEXT("Drysdale"), 3, 3, hTeamItem );

    hTeamItem = m_tree.InsertItem( TEXT("Cubs"), 2, 2 );
    m_tree.InsertItem( TEXT("Tinker"), 3, 3, hTeamItem );
    m_tree.InsertItem( TEXT("Evers"), 3, 3, hTeamItem );
    m_tree.InsertItem( TEXT("Chance"), 3, 3, hTeamItem );
    return TRUE;
}
```

Adding Drag-and-Drop Support

Using ClassWizard, add message-handling functions for the messages sent during a drag-and-drop operation, using the values shown in Table 11.18.

Table 11.18. Message-handling functions used for drag-and-drop procedures.

Object ID	Message	Function
IDC_TREE	TVN_BEGINDRAG	OnBegindragTree
CTreeDispDlg	WM_MOUSEMOVE	OnMouseMove
CTreeDispDlg	WM_LBUTTONUP	OnLButtonUp

Listing 11.35 shows the source code for the three drag-and-drop functions.

Listing 11.35. Functions used to implement simple drag-and-drop operations.

```cpp
void CTreeDispDlg::OnBegindragTree(NMHDR* pNMHDR, LRESULT* pResult)
{
    NM_TREEVIEW* pNMTreeView = (NM_TREEVIEW*)pNMHDR;
    // In this tree, root nodes aren't allowed to move.
    if(m_tree.GetParentItem(pNMTreeView->itemNew.hItem) != NULL)
    {
        m_hDragItem = pNMTreeView->itemNew.hItem;
        CImageList* pDragImage;
        pDragImage = m_tree.CreateDragImage( m_hDragItem );
        ASSERT( pDragImage );
        CRect    rcDrag;
        CPoint   ptCursor;
        m_tree.GetItemRect( m_hDragItem, rcDrag, TRUE );
        rcDrag.left -= 32;   // Adjust by width of image
        GetCursorPos( &ptCursor );
        m_tree.ScreenToClient( &ptCursor );
        CPoint ptDrag( ptCursor - rcDrag.TopLeft() );
        pDragImage->BeginDrag( 0, ptDrag );
        pDragImage->DragEnter( &m_tree, pNMTreeView->ptDrag );
        SetCapture();
        m_fIsDragging = TRUE;
    }
    *pResult = 0;
}


void CTreeDispDlg::OnMouseMove(UINT nFlags, CPoint point)
{
    if( m_fIsDragging == TRUE )
    {
        CPoint ptTree(point);
        MapWindowPoints( &m_tree, &ptTree, 1 );
        CImageList::DragMove( ptTree );

        UINT    uHitTest = TVHT_ONITEM;
        m_hDragTarget = m_tree.HitTest( ptTree, &uHitTest );
    }
    CDialog::OnMouseMove(nFlags, point);
}


void CTreeDispDlg::OnLButtonUp(UINT nFlags, CPoint point)
{
    if( m_fIsDragging == TRUE )
    {
        CImageList::DragLeave( &m_tree );
        CImageList::EndDrag();
        ReleaseCapture();
        m_fIsDragging = FALSE;
        // Test for valid drop target.
        if((m_hDragTarget != NULL)&&(m_hDragTarget != m_hDragItem))
        {
            // Create a copy of the drag item.
            HTREEITEM    hParent;
            hParent = m_tree.GetParentItem( m_hDragTarget );
            CString szLabel = m_tree.GetItemText( m_hDragItem );
```

```
        if( hParent != NULL )
            m_tree.InsertItem( szLabel, 3, 3, hParent,
                                    m_hDragTarget );
        else
            m_tree.InsertItem( szLabel, 3, 3, m_hDragTarget,
                                    TVI_FIRST );
        // Remove the existing copy of the drag item.
        m_tree.DeleteItem( m_hDragItem );
    }
}
else
    CDialog::OnLButtonUp(nFlags, point);
}
```

Adding a New Team to the Tree View Control

You can add two types of items to the Tree View control used by TreeDisp. Team items are added at the root level and display one of three team icons. Player icons are inserted as child items to a team and always use the same icon.

Add a dialog box to the TreeDisp project that will be used to add team items to the Tree View control. Figure 11.11 shows the dialog box.

FIGURE 11.11.

The Add Team dialog box used by TreeDisp.

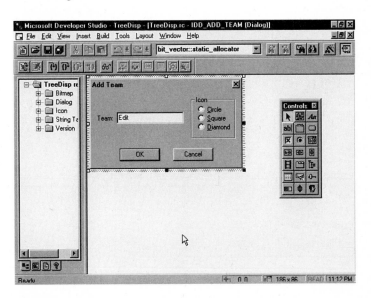

Give the new dialog box a resource ID of IDD_ADD_TEAM. Properties for the radio button and Edit controls are listed in Table 11.19. All properties that aren't listed should be set to the default values.

Table 11.19. Property values for controls in the Add Team dialog box.

Control	Resource ID	Caption	Properties
Circle radio button	IDC_CIRCLE	&Circle	Group
Square radio button	IDC_SQUARE	&Square	
Diamond radio button	IDC_DIAMOND	&Diamond	
Team Edit control	IDC_TEAM	none	Group

Using ClassWizard, add a new class derived from CDialog named CAddTeamDlg to the TreeDisp project. Table 11.20 lists the properties for the new dialog class.

Table 11.20. Values used for the CAddTeamDlg class.

Control	Value
Name	CAddTeamDlg
Base Class	CDialog
File	AddTeamDlg.cpp
Dialog ID	IDD_ADD_TEAM
OLE Automation	None
Component Gallery	Cleared

Click the Create button. The CAddTeam class is generated and added to your project. Change to the Member Variables tab and add member variables to the CAddTeam class using the values in Table 11.21.

Table 11.21. Values for new member variables in CAddTeamDlg.

Control ID	Variable Name	Category	Type
IDC_CIRCLE	m_nImage	Value	int
IDC_TEAM	m_szTeam	Value	CString

Next, edit the CTreeDispDlg::OnAddTeam function as shown in Listing 11.36, adding the source lines shown in bold type. These changes create a CAddTeamDlg object and insert a new team item into the Tree View control after the user clicks the OK button.

Listing 11.36. Inserting a new team into the Tree View control.

```
void CTreeDispDlg::OnAddTeam()
{
    CAddTeamDlg      dlg;
    if( dlg.DoModal() == IDOK )
    {
        int nImage = dlg.m_nImage;
        m_tree.InsertItem( dlg.m_szTeam, nImage, nImage );
    }
}
```

Remember to add an #include directive at the top of the TreeDispDlg.cpp source file, just after the existing #include directives:

```
#include "AddTeamDlg.h"
```

Adding a New Player to the Tree View Control

Add a new dialog box to the TreeDisp project that will be used to add player items to the Tree View control. Figure 11.12 shows the dialog box.

FIGURE 11.12.

The Add Player dialog box used by TreeDisp.

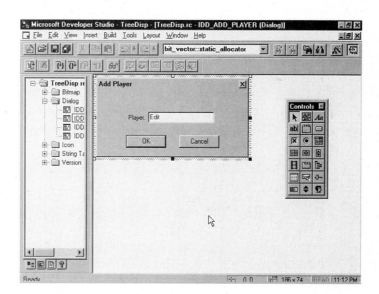

Give the new dialog box a resource ID of IDD_ADD_PLAYER. Table 11.22 lists the properties for the Edit control. All other properties should be set to the default values.

Table 11.22. Property values for the Edit control in the Add Player dialog box.

Control	Resource ID
Player edit control	IDC_Player

Using ClassWizard, add a new class derived from CDialog named CAddPlayerDlg to the TreeDisp project. Table 11.23 lists the properties for the new dialog class.

Table 11.23. Values used for the CAddTeamDlg class.

Control	Value
Name	CAddPlayerDlg
Base Class	CDialog
File	AddPlayerDlg.cpp
Dialog ID	IDD_ADD_PLAYER
OLE Automation	None
Component Gallery	Cleared

Click the Create button. The CAddPlayer class is generated and added to your project. Change to the Member Variables tab and add an Edit control member variable to the CAddPlayer class, using the values from Table 11.24.

Table 11.24. Values for a new member variable in CAddTeamDlg.

Control ID	Variable Name	Category	Type
IDC_PLAYER	m_szPlayer	Value	CString

Next, edit the CTreeDispDlg::OnAddPlayer function as shown in Listing 11.37, adding the source lines shown in bold. These changes create a CAddPlayerDlg object and insert a new player item into the Tree View control after the user clicks the OK button.

Listing 11.37. Adding a player to the Tree View control.

```
void CTreeDispDlg::OnAddPlayer()
{
    CAddPlayerDlg   dlg;
    if( dlg.DoModal() == IDOK )
    {
        HTREEITEM hItem = m_tree.GetSelectedItem();
```

```
            if( hItem != NULL )
            {
                HTREEITEM hParent = m_tree.GetParentItem( hItem );
                if( hParent == NULL )
                    m_tree.InsertItem(dlg.m_szPlayer, 3, 3, hItem);
                else
                    m_tree.InsertItem(dlg.m_szPlayer, 3, 3, hParent);
            }
            else
            {
                AfxMessageBox( TEXT("Please select a team first") );
            }
        }
    }
}
```

Remember to add an #include directive at the top of the TreeDispDlg.cpp source file, just after the existing #include directives:

```
#include "AddPlayerDlg.h"
```

Deleting Items from the Tree View Control

Edit the CTreeDispDlg::OnDelete function as shown in Listing 11.38, adding the source lines shown in bold. These changes remove the currently selected item from the Tree View control.

Listing 11.38. Deleting items from the Tree View control.

```
void CTreeDispDlg::OnDelete()
{
    HTREEITEM hItem = m_tree.GetSelectedItem();
    if( hItem != NULL )
    {
        VERIFY( m_tree.DeleteItem( hItem ) );
    }
    else
    {
        AfxMessageBox( TEXT("Please select an item first") );
    }
}
```

Running the TreeDisp Example

After you make the changes in the previous sections, compile and run the TreeDisp project. The dialog box contains three teams when it is displayed initially. Experiment with adding and deleting items using the Add Team, Add Item, and Delete pushbuttons. You also can move players by dragging them from their current team to a new team.

Property Pages, Property Sheets, and Tab Controls

Property pages, property sheets, and Tab controls are some of the hottest new user interface elements in Windows NT programs. A *property sheet* looks like a normal modal dialog box but instead contains one or more views, called *property pages*, with a *Tab control* you can use to select one page at a time.

Property sheets often are called tabbed dialog boxes, due to the tabs used to switch between the property sheet pages. A property sheet consists of three parts:

- A Tab control is used to switch between the property sheet pages.

- One or more property sheet pages are associated with one tab each in the Tab control. Only one of the property pages is visible. Property sheet pages contain controls in the same way as dialog boxes.

- A property sheet object is similar to a dialog box. It contains the Tab control and one or more property sheet pages. You never see an empty property sheet; at least one property sheet page must always exist.

Using property sheets is an easy way to group a large number of controls into a single dialog box. Instead of requiring a user to navigate through a series of cascading dialog boxes, you can use several pages, each with a specific purpose.

You also can combine several dialog boxes into a single property sheet and its associated property sheet pages. Figure 11.13 shows how you can combine several related dialog boxes into a single property sheet.

FIGURE 11.13.

Combining several related dialog boxes into a single property sheet.

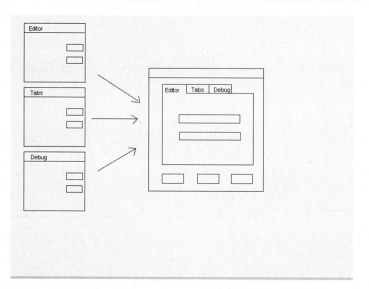

The Windows NT property sheet and property pages provide an easy-to-use method for implementing tabbed windows. If property pages and property sheets don't meet your needs, however, you can use the Tab control as a stand-alone control. This results in more work, because you must manage the interaction between each window and the Tab control, but it provides the maximum flexibility when working with tabs.

Using Property Pages and Property Sheets

Property pages and property sheets are used almost exactly in the same way as dialog boxes. The MFC `CPropertySheet` and `CPropertyPage` classes are used as base classes instead of the `CDialog` class. In general, you use the following steps to create a property sheet:

1. Create a `CPropertySheet` object.
2. Create one or more property page objects and add them to the property sheet.
3. Call the property sheet's `DoModal` member function.
4. Update property sheet data exactly as you would for modal dialog boxes.

Each of these four steps is discussed in the next few sections. The steps involved are fairly simple and very much like the steps used to add dialog boxes to an application using ClassWizard and the `CDialog` class.

Creating a `CPropertySheet` Object

The `CPropertySheet` class serves as a container for property sheet pages. In most cases, such as the example presented here, the default behavior offered by `CPropertySheet` is sufficient, and you can create a `CPropertySheet` object directly—usually with a single parameter specifying the caption for the property sheet.

```
CPropertySheet    nameSheet( "Names" );
```

Creating a Property Page

In contrast to the `CPropertySheet` class, each page class must be a new class derived from `CPropertyPage`. At least one property page must be contained by the property sheet; if the last page is removed, the property sheet is closed automatically.

Before adding a `Property Page` class to your project, you must create the dialog resource for the property page. Use ClassWizard to add a class derived from `CPropertyPage` to the project for each property page.

Creating a Dialog Resource for a Property Page

Every property page must have a dialog resource created for it. The property page uses this dialog resource to lay out controls in the property page, much in the same way a form view uses a dialog resource to determine how to lay out controls.

Every dialog resource used as a property page must follow these guidelines:

- It must have a caption because the dialog box caption labels the tab associated with the property page.
- The window style must be set to Child.
- The frame style must be set to Thin. Developer Studio refers to the frame style as the border style.
- The Disabled and Titlebar options must be selected.

In addition, the first property page added to the property sheet is used to determine the size for the sheet and all pages added to the dialog box. For this reason, you should add your largest property page first or coordinate the sizes of the property pages.

Deriving a Class from CPropertyPage Using ClassWizard

After you create the dialog resource, you must add a class derived from CPropertyPage to the project. This step is exactly the same as adding a class based on CDialog except that the base class is CPropertyPage. Three classes derived from CPropertyPage are created in the example later, in the section *Looking at a Property Sheet Example*.

Adding Message-Handling Functions to CPropertyPage

Two message-handling functions are used often by property pages:

- **OnApply:** Called for each property page after a user clicks the Apply Now button. The default version of OnApply calls the OnOk member function and validates any input made so far. You can use ClassWizard to add your own version of the OnApply function if you want to perform additional work when the user clicks the Apply Now button.
- **OnKillActive:** Called as a user changes to a new property page. This is a good place to verify input. If the page is not changed, you can keep the current tab active by returning FALSE from this function.

Other message-handling functions have default implementations that you don't usually need to override in simple property sheets. These additional member functions follow:

- **OnCancel:** Called by the MFC framework after the property sheet's Cancel button is clicked and after all property pages acknowledge the OnQueryCancel function.
- **OnOK:** Called by the MFC framework after the property sheet's OK, Apply Now, or Close button is clicked.
- **OnQueryCancel:** Called by the MFC framework after the property sheet's Cancel button is clicked but before the cancel operation takes place. This gives each page a chance to veto the cancellation.

■ **OnReset:** Called by the MFC framework after the property sheet's Reset button is clicked.

■ **OnSetActive:** Called by the MFC framework as the property page becomes the active page.

Calling the Property Sheet's `DoModal` Function

You can use the `DoModal` and `Create` member functions to create modal and modeless property sheets. To display a modal property sheet, call the `DoModal` member function, but to display a modeless property sheet, use the `Create` member function. You can test the return value from `DoModal` to determine whether the dialog box was closed or canceled:

```
if( nameSheet.DoModal() != IDCANCEL )
{
    // Update data
}
```

Exchanging Data with Property Sheets and Property Sheet Pages

Data is exchanged with a property sheet much as it is with a dialog box. The data contained in a property sheet, however, is actually member data that belongs to the individual property sheet pages. Therefore, the simplest way to exchange data with a property sheet is to interact with each page individually.

Each `CPropertyPage` object handling a property sheet page can have class member variables associated with dialog box controls using ClassWizard. After the property sheet is dismissed, you can update the property sheet page member variables, as with `CDialog` member variables.

Looking at a Property Sheet Example

As a property sheet example, I have included a project on the accompanying CD-ROM named TabExample that contains a property sheet with two pages: The first page contains a name and address, and the second page stores hobby information. Each page contains controls and includes an icon with the tab caption.

To get started on this example, use AppWizard to create an SDI project named TabExample. Alternatively, you also can use an existing project as a starting point, because this example focuses on the property sheet rather than the application around it.

Creating the Dialog Box Resources

As discussed earlier in this section, every property sheet page needs a dialog box resource. When creating dialog box resources for the property pages, remember to apply the styles provided in the section *Creating a Dialog Box Resource for a Property Page*, earlier in this chapter. Also, the first property sheet page is used to determine the size for the entire property sheet and subsequent pages. Make sure that the dialog box resource used for the first page is the largest page or that all the pages are the same size.

Creating the Name Page

You use the first dialog box to store name and address information, as shown in Figure 11.14.

FIGURE 11.14.

The dialog box resource used for the name and address property sheet page.

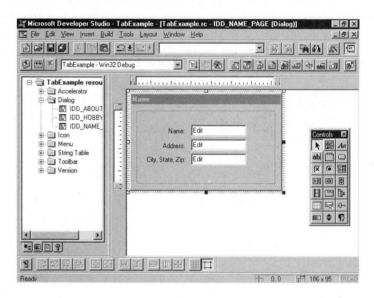

Use the resource ID `IDD_NAME_PAGE` for the dialog box. Use the values from Table 11.25 for the dialog box's attributes. Use the values from Table 11.26 for Edit controls added to the dialog box.

Table 11.25. Attributes for the `IDD_NAME_PAGE` dialog box.

Name	Value
Style	Child
Border	Thin
Disabled	Checked
System Menu	Unchecked
Titlebar	Checked
Caption	Name

Table 11.26. Values used for the `IDD_NAME_PAGE` dialog box resource.

Edit Control	Resource ID	Category	Type	Member Variable
Name	IDC_EDIT_NAME	Value	CString	m_szName
Address	IDC_EDIT_ADDRESS	Value	CString	m_szAddress
City, State, ZIP	IDC_EDIT_CITY	Value	CString	m_szCity

Use ClassWizard to create a new class to handle the `IDD_NAME_PAGE` property page. Use the values from Table 11.27 for the Add Class dialog box. Note that the base class for the `CNamePage` class is `CPropertyPage` rather than `CDialog`.

Table 11.27. Values used for the Add Class dialog box.

Control	Value
Name	CNamePage
Base Class	CPropertyPage
File	NamePage.cpp
Dialog ID	IDD_NAME_PAGE
OLE Automation	None
Component Gallery	Cleared

Click the Create button. The `CNamePage` class is generated and added to your project. Change to the Member Variables tab and add control member variables to the `CNamePage` class, using the values from Table 11.27.

Creating the Hobby Page

You use the second dialog box resource to collect information about hobbies, as shown in Figure 11.15. Create this dialog box resource using the same attributes used for the preceding dialog box, but instead make the dialog box caption "Hobbies" and its resource ID `IDD_HOBBY_PAGE`.

Use the values from Table 11.28 for the checkboxes added to the `IDD_HOBBY_PAGE` dialog box resource.

FIGURE 11.15.

The hobby page resource ID in the Developer Studio Dialog Editor.

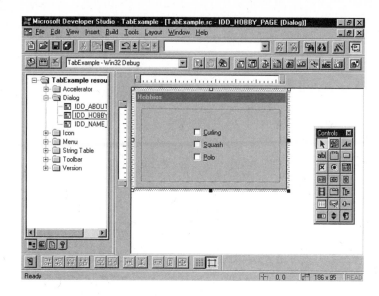

Table 11.28. Values used for the IDD_HOBBY_PAGE dialog box resource.

Checkbox	Resource ID
Curling	IDC_CHECK_CURLING
Squash	IDC_CHECK_SQUASH
Polo	IDC_CHECK_POLO

Use ClassWizard to create a new class to handle the IDD_HOBBY_PAGE property page, using the values from Table 11.29.

Table 11.29. Values used for the Add Class dialog box.

Control	Value
Name	CHobbyPage
Base Class	CPropertyPage
File	HobbyPage.cpp
Dialog ID	IDD_HOBBY_PAGE
OLE Automation	None
Component Gallery	Cleared

Click the Create button to add the CHobbyPage class to your project. Unlike the Name page, the Hobby page has no member variables.

Creating the Property Sheet

In this example, the CMainFrame class handles a menu item that creates the property sheet. Create a new menu item under the View menu, using the values from Table 11.30 for the menu item and its message-handling function. Use ClassWizard to add a message-handling function for the new menu item.

Table 11.30. New member functions for the CMainFrame class.

Menu ID	Caption	Event	Function Name
ID_VIEW_NAMES	&Names...	COMMAND	OnViewNames

Listing 11.39 contains the source code for the OnViewNames function, which handles the message sent when the Names menu item is selected.

Listing 11.39. Creating a property sheet in the CMainFrame::OnViewNames function.

```
void CMainFrame::OnViewNames()
{
    CPropertySheet   nameSheet( "Hobby List" );

    CNamePage        pgName;
    CHobbyPage       pgHobby;

    nameSheet.AddPage( &pgName );
    nameSheet.AddPage( &pgHobby );

    nameSheet.DoModal();
}
```

The CNamePage and CHobbyPage class declarations must be included in the source file. Add the #include statements that follow to the MainFrm.cpp source file after the other #include statements:

```
#include "NamePage.h"
#include "HobbyPage.h"
```

Compile and run the project. The property sheet is displayed after you choose Names from the View menu.

Handling the Apply Button

The current property page example works fine, but the Apply button is disabled. The button remains disabled unless a property page explicitly enables it by calling the SetModified function.

Enabling the Apply Now Button

The best place to call `SetModifed` is after a control has been changed. The `CNamePage` class, for example, can call `SetModified` after an Edit control is updated. Using ClassWizard, add a message-handling function for the `EN_CHANGE` message sent from the `IDC_EDIT_NAME` Edit control. Listing 11.40 provides the source code for the `CNamePage::OnChangeEditName` function.

Listing 11.40. Handling Edit control updates in the `CNamePage` class.

```
void CNamePage::OnChangeEditName()
{
    SetModified();
}
```

In Listing 11.40, after the user updates the Edit control used to collect the name, the Apply button is enabled. You also can have more complicated requirements for enabling the button, such as verifying input or requiring that more than one control has valid input.

For the Hobby property page, the Apply button should be enabled after the user changes any of the checkboxes. Using ClassWizard, add message-handling functions for `BN_CLICKED` for every checkbox, accepting the default names suggested by ClassWizard. Listing 11.41 shows the source code for these functions.

Listing 11.41. Handling checkbox updates in the `CHobbyPage` class.

```
void CHobbyPage::OnCheckCurling()
{
    SetModified();
}

void CHobbyPage::OnCheckPolo()
{
    SetModified();
}

void CHobbyPage::OnCheckSquash()
{
    SetModified();
}
```

Receiving Messages from the Apply Button

Clicking the Apply button calls the `OnApply` function for every loaded property page. Property pages that have not been loaded are not called because they haven't had any data changed yet. Listing 11.42 provides an example of an `OnApply` function that was added with ClassWizard. This function displays a message box after the Apply button is clicked.

Listing 11.42. The `CHobbyPage::OnApply` member function.

```
BOOL CHobbyPage::OnApply()
{
    AfxMessageBox( "Hobby Page Applied" );
    return CPropertyPage::OnApply();
}
```

Toolbars and Status Bars

Toolbars and status bars are two examples of *control bars*, which are user interface elements used to contain other controls or windows. Three types of control bars exist:

- **Status bars:** The simplest type of control bar. Status bars are attached permanently to the bottom of a frame window.
- **Toolbars:** Contain buttons that are used as menu shortcuts.
- **Dialog box bars:** Contain buttons and other types of controls, such as combo boxes, listboxes, or progress controls.

In an MFC-based application, control bars usually are owned by the main frame window. Dialog box bars and control bars can be *docked* on the frame window or *free floating*. Docked toolbars and control bars can be *torn off*, or *undocked*. When a control bar is floating, it has a small title bar that displays the window caption.

The CtrlBar Sample Program

To illustrate how control bars are used, I have created an example program named CtrlBar, which is included on the CD-ROM with this book. If you want to follow the steps used to create the project, read the next few sections. To get started creating the CtrlBar project, begin with these steps:

1. Open a new project workspace named CtrlBar.
2. After AppWizard appears, select the Single document option and click the Finish button.
3. After the New Project Information dialog box appears, click the OK button. AppWizard creates the files needed to generate the CtrlBar sample program.

If you compile and run the skeleton CtrlBar program generated by AppWizard, you see that there is already a large amount of control bar functionality in the program, even without any programming on your part. You get this basic functionality for free; later, you will see how to extend the basic toolbar and status bar provided by AppWizard.

Defining Status Bars

A *status bar* is a control bar attached to the bottom edge of an application's frame window. Most status bars provide a method to hide the status bar if more screen real estate is needed. This is considered good style from a user-interface perspective, and all applications created by AppWizard enable you to hide the status bar.

Status bars usually are split into several panes, also known as *indicators*. The CtrlBar program has panes dedicated to displaying the status of the Caps Lock and Num Lock keys, for example.

Using Status Bars

In an MFC-based program, all control bars are owned and controlled by the main frame window. The main frame class, CMainFrame, includes a CStatusBar object named m_wndStatusBar. The m_wndStatusBar object is constructed with the CMainFrame object and is created and initialized during the CMainFrame::OnCreate function, as Listing 11.43 shows.

Listing 11.43. Creating an instance of `CStatusBar`.

```
if (!m_wndStatusBar.Create(this) ||
    !m_wndStatusBar.SetIndicators(indicators,
    sizeof(indicators)/sizeof(UINT)))
{
    TRACE0("Failed to create status bar\n");
    return -1;      // fail to create
}
```

Before you create a status bar, you must create an array of resource IDs used for each pane of the status bar. This array of resource IDs is passed as a parameter to the SetIndicators function. The IDs are used to identify each status pane and the default text string for each pane. A default string resource must be assigned for each pane added to the status bar.

You set the properties for a status bar pane by calling the SetPaneInfo function:

```
m_wndStatusBar.SetPaneInfo(4, ID_INDICATOR_TIME, SBPS_POPOUT, 80);
```

The SetPaneInfo function takes four parameters: the pane index, the pane ID, the pane style, and the pane width. The available pane styles follow:

- **SBPS_DISABLED:** Indicates that no text should be drawn.
- **SBPS_NOBORDERS:** Indicates that no 3D border should be drawn around the pane.
- **SBPS_NORMAL:** Creates a status bar without stretch, borders, or pop-out effects.
- **SBPS_POPOUT:** Specifies that a reverse border should be drawn so that the pane "pops out."
- **SBPS_STRETCH:** Indicates that this pane can stretch to fill unused space. Only one pane per status bar can have this attribute. AppWizard gives this attribute to the first pane.

Looking at a Status Bar Example

For a status bar example, add an extra status bar pane that displays the current time. To add an extra status bar pane, follow these steps:

1. Add a new ID to the indicator array.

2. Add a new default text item to the string table.

3. Add an update command handler for the status bar pane.

In addition, you must add a function to handle a timer message used to update the time.

Adding a New Status Bar Indicator ID

To define a new resource symbol, open the Resource Symbols dialog box by choosing Resource Symbols from the View menu. You see a list of resource symbols defined for the CtrlBar application. To add a new resource, click the New button and enter `ID_INDICATOR_TIME` as the new symbol name.

In the MainFrame.cpp source file, an array of `UINT` is used to define the layout of the status bar. Edit the `indicators` array so that it resembles the source code provided in Listing 11.44. You have to add the last item in the array.

Listing 11.44. Changes to the `indicators` array in MainFrame.cpp.

```
static UINT indicators[] =
{
    ID_SEPARATOR,           // status line indicator
    ID_INDICATOR_CAPS,
    ID_INDICATOR_NUM,
    ID_INDICATOR_SCRL,
    ID_INDICATOR_TIME
};
```

Follow these steps to add a string table resource using the `ID_INDICATOR_TIME` symbol:

1. Click the ResourceView tab in the project workspace window.

2. Display the resource types used in the project by opening the top-level resource folder.

3. Open the String Table resource folder.

4. Open the String table for editing by double-clicking the String Table icon.

5. Insert a new item into the String table by pressing the Ins key. Enter a value of `ID_INDICATOR_TIME` as the ID and `Time not set` as the caption.

Defining the Timer and Pane Styles

Define a style for the new status bar item and begin a timer that expires every second in the CMainFrame::OnCreate function. Add the source code from Listing 11.45 at the end of the OnCreate function. The return statement already is included in the function by AppWizard.

Listing 11.45. Changes to the CMainFrame::OnCreate member function.

```
// Start timer for the status bar clock
m_wndStatusBar.SetPaneInfo(4, ID_INDICATOR_TIME, SBPS_POPOUT, 80);
SetTimer( 1, 1000, NULL );
return 0;
```

Handling the Timer

Using ClassWizard, add a message-handling function for WM_TIMER to the CMainFrame class. This function is called every time the timer set in Listing 11.45 expires—once per second. When the timer expires, the main frame should invalidate the status bar rectangle, causing it to be repainted. Add the source code in Listing 11.46 to the CMainFrame::OnTimer function.

Listing 11.46. Invalidating the status bar in the OnTimer function.

```
void CMainFrame::OnTimer(UINT nIDEvent)
{
    m_wndStatusBar.InvalidateRect( NULL );
}
```

When the status bar is invalidated, the MFC framework updates each pane using a CCmdUI handler. Although you can use ClassWizard to create CCmdUI handlers for most user-interface objects, you must create status bar pane handlers by hand. When adding message handlers manually, you must be very careful not to modify any source code located between // AFX comments because this code is reserved for ClassWizard.

Add a declaration for a CCmdUI update function to the CMainFrame class declaration, as shown in bold in Listing 11.47.

Listing 11.47. Changes to the CMainFrame class declaration.

```
// Generated message map functions
protected:
    //{{AFX_MSG(CMainFrame)
    afx_msg int OnCreate(LPCREATESTRUCT lpCreateStruct);
    afx_msg void OnTimer(UINT nIDEvent);
    //}}AFX_MSG
    afx_msg void OnUpdateTimer(CCmdUI* pCmdUI);
    DECLARE_MESSAGE_MAP()
```

Next, add the entry in the message map found in MainFrame.cpp, as shown in bold in Listing 11.48. Again, only the `OnUpdateTimer` line must be added.

Listing 11.48. The `CMainFrame` message map after adding `OnUpdateTimer`.

```
BEGIN_MESSAGE_MAP(CMainFrame, CFrameWnd)
    //{{AFX_MSG_MAP(CMainFrame)
    ON_WM_CREATE()
    ON_WM_TIMER()
    //}}AFX_MSG_MAP
    ON_UPDATE_COMMAND_UI(ID_INDICATOR_TIME,OnUpdateTimer)
END_MESSAGE_MAP()
```

Add the `OnUpdateTimer` function, as shown in Listing 11.49.

Listing 11.49. The `OnUpdateTimer` member function.

```
void CMainFrame::OnUpdateTimer(CCmdUI* pCmdUI)
{
    pCmdUI->Enable();
    CTime   theTime = CTime::GetCurrentTime();
    CString szTime = theTime.Format( "%I:%M:%S %p" );
    pCmdUI->SetText( szTime );
}
```

Compile and run the CtrlBar example. The status bar has a new pane at its far right side that contains the current time.

Dialog Bars

Dialog bars are similar to modeless dialog boxes except that they can be embedded in or docked against the main frame or free floating on the Windows workspace. This property makes dialog bars similar to toolbars, except that they can contain any type of control, just like a dialog box.

Dialog bars often contain combo boxes, listboxes, and Edit controls. Users can press Tab to move from control to control and can dock or float the dialog bar if that capability is enabled by the dialog bar's properties.

Understanding How Dialog Box Bars Are Used

The first step in using a dialog box bar is defining a dialog box resource using the Developer Studio Dialog Box Editor. If the dialog box bar is docked against the top or bottom edge of the main frame, the dialog box resource usually is "stretched."

Unlike with the CDialog class, you usually don't need to derive your own class from CDialogBar. Messages from controls in the dialog box bar are routed to the dialog box bar's owner—usually, CMainFrame. Unfortunately, ClassWizard does not manage these message maps for you; they must be edited by hand.

Creating a Dockable Dialog Box Bar

To prepare a dialog box bar for docking, you must call the CControlBar::EnableDocking member function:

```
m_dlgBar.EnableDocking( CBRS_ALIGN_ANY );
```

The single parameter passed to the EnableDocking function specifies the docking alignment for the control bar. Table 11.31 lists the values you can specify for this parameter.

Table 11.31. Specifying parameters for the EnableDocking function.

Parameter	Function
CBRS_ALIGN_TOP	Enables docking along the top edge of the client area.
CBRS_ALIGN_BOTTOM	Enables docking along the bottom edge of the client area.
CBRS_ALIGN_LEFT	Enables docking along the left edge of the client area.
CBRS_ALIGN_RIGHT	Enables docking along the right edge of the client area.
CBRS_ALIGN_ANY	Enables docking along any edge of the client area.
CBRS_NOALIGN	Specifies that the control bar is not repositioned when the parent is resized.
CBRS_SIZE_DYNAMIC	Indicates that the control bar is dynamic.
CBRS_FLOATING	Indicates that the control bar is floating.
CBRS_SIZE_FIXED	Indicates that the control bar is fixed.
CBRS_HIDE_INPLACE	Specifies that the control bar is not displayed to the user.
CBRS_FLOAT_MULTI	Enables several toolbars to be docked in the same row of the frame window.

When you create a dockable dialog box bar, you should set the caption for the window by using SetWindowText. This gives the dialog box bar a title when it is floated off the frame window.

Adding a Dialog Box Bar Example to the CtrlBar Project

To see an example of a dialog box bar, add a dialog box bar to the CtrlBar sample project. The new dialog box bar initially is docked in the main frame window, just below the existing toolbar.

Creating the Dialog Box Resource

Using the Developer Studio Dialog Box Editor, create a new dialog box resource, using IDD_BAR as the resource ID. Make sure that the dialog box resource has the following properties:

- Child Style
- No Border
- Visible checkbox not checked

Add two child controls to the dialog box: a button and a combo box, as shown in Figure 11.16.

FIGURE 11.16.

The IDD_BAR *resource in the Developer Studio Dialog Box Editor.*

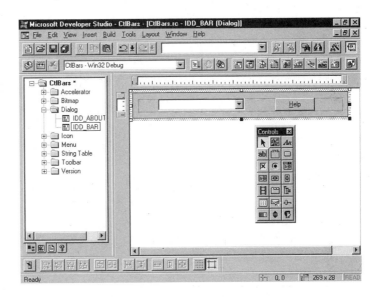

Use the values shown in Table 11.32 for the controls added to the dialog box resource.

Table 11.32. Controls added to the IDD_BAR dialog box.

Control	*Caption*	*Resource ID*
Button	&Help	IDC_BAR_HELP
Combo box	—	IDC_COMBO

Modifying the CMainFrame Class

The new CDialogBar object is a member variable in the CMainFrame class. Add the following source code to the Implementation section of the CMainFrame class declaration:

```
protected:  // control bar embedded members
    CDialogBar  m_dlgBar;
```

The dialog box bar is created and initialized in the `CMainFrame:OnCreate` function. Add the source code in Listing 11.50 to the `OnCreate` function, after the changes made earlier in Listing 11.45.

Listing 11.50. Additions to the `CMainFrame::OnCreate` function.

```
// Create a dialog bar
m_dlgBar.Create( this, IDD_BAR, CBRS_TOP, IDD_BAR );
m_dlgBar.SetWindowText( "Dialog Bar" );
m_dlgBar.EnableDocking( CBRS_ALIGN_ANY );
// Dock the control bar on the main frame window.
DockControlBar( &m_dlgBar );
```

As discussed earlier, messages from controls located in a dialog box bar are routed to the parent of the dialog box bar, and the message maps are not managed by ClassWizard. Edit the message map function declaration in MainFrame.h so that it resembles the source code provided in Listing 11.51. You need to add only one line of code: the line in bold that declares the `OnBarHelp` function.

Listing 11.51. Updates to the `CMainFrame` message map declarations.

```
// Generated message map functions
protected:
    //{{AFX_MSG(CMainFrame)
    afx_msg int OnCreate(LPCREATESTRUCT lpCreateStruct);
    afx_msg void OnTimer(UINT nIDEvent);
    //}}AFX_MSG
    afx_msg void OnUpdateTimer(CCmdUI* pCmdUI);
    afx_msg void OnBarHelp();
    DECLARE_MESSAGE_MAP()
```

Next, add the entry in the message map found in MainFrame.cpp, as shown in Listing 11.52. Again, only the `OnBarHelp` line must be added.

Listing 11.52. Updates to the `CMainFrame` message map.

```
BEGIN_MESSAGE_MAP(CMainFrame, CFrameWnd)
    //{{AFX_MSG_MAP(CMainFrame)
    ON_WM_CREATE()
    //}}AFX_MSG_MAP
    ON_UPDATE_COMMAND_UI(ID_INDICATOR_TIME,OnUpdateTimer)
    ON_BN_CLICKED(IDC_BAR_HELP, OnBarHelp)
END_MESSAGE_MAP()
```

Add the `OnBarHelp` function provided in Listing 11.53 to the MainFrame.cpp source file. This function is called when the `IDC_BAR_HELP` button is clicked on the dialog box bar.

Listing 11.53. The `CMainFrame::OnBarHelp` function.

```
void CMainFrame::OnBarHelp()
{
    AfxMessageBox( "Dialog bar help has been selected" );
}
```

Compile and run the new version of the CtrlBar sample program. Notice that the dialog box bar can be undocked and moved around the desktop. Clicking the dialog box bar's Help button pops up a message box. When the dialog box bar is undocked, the title is displayed.

Toolbars

Toolbars contain buttons used to send commands to an application. They generally are used to provide quick and easy access to commands that also are available as menu items. The properties for toolbar items are similar to the properties for menu items. Instead of checking a menu item, however, a toolbar button is "pressed down" to indicate that it is selected.

Toolbars are similar to dialog box bars except that they contain only buttons. As with dialog box bars, they can be docked against a main frame or free floating.

Understanding How Toolbars Are Used

You use the MFC `CToolbar` class to manage the toolbar control. The `CToolbar` object is declared as a member variable of the `CMainFrame` class, just as are `CDialogBar` objects.

When toolbar control items use the same resource IDs as the menu items they represent, it is very easy to add a toolbar to an MFC-based application. The menu and toolbar generate the same commands for the application and use the same message-handling functions. When the status for a menu item is updated, the status of the toolbar also is updated.

Creating the Bitmap Resource

The first step in creating a toolbar is creating a bitmap to be used for the toolbar's button faces. Each button face must be the same size; the default is 16 pixels wide and 15 pixels high.

Creating a Toolbar Control

You use the `LoadToolbar` function to load the toolbar bitmap. After you load the toolbar bitmap, you set the position of each button in the toolbar by calling the `SetButtons` member function:

```
m_toolBar.LoadBitmap( IDB_TOOLS );
m_toolBar.SetButtons( arToolButtons,
                 sizeof(arToolButtons)/sizeof(UINT) );
```

The SetButtons function has two parameters: an array of UINT containing the resource ID for each toolbar item and the number of items in the toolbar. The array is exactly like the status bar indicator array used earlier in the section *Adding a New Status Bar Indicator ID*.

You can give a toolbar floating and dockable properties just as you can give a dialog box bar these properties:

```
m_toolBar.EnableDocking( CBRS_ALIGN_ANY );
```

All the alignment options used for dialog box bars also apply for toolbars. In addition, the following control bar options generally are used only for toolbars:

- **CBRS_FLYBY:** Indicates that the status bar displays information about a button when it is selected.
- **CBRS_TOOLTIPS:** Indicates that the control bar displays tool tips when the cursor passes over a toolbar button.

Adding a Toolbar Example to the CtrlBar Project

To better understand how toolbars are used, add a second toolbar to the CtrlBar project. The new toolbar is dockable and handles the following three menu functions:

- Displaying the About dialog box
- Toggling the original toolbar on or off
- Toggling the status bar on or off

Creating a Toolbar Bitmap

Using the Developer Studio Image Editor, create the bitmap shown in Figure 11.17. The bitmap is 48 pixels wide and 15 pixels high. Use IDB_TOOLS as the bitmap's resource ID.

Modifying the CMainFrame Class

The new CToolbar object is a member variable in the CMainFrame class. Add the declaration of m_toolBar to the CMainFrame class declaration, as shown in Listing 11.54, just after the existing declaration of m_dlgBar.

Listing 11.54. Additions to the CMainFrame class declaration.

```
protected:  // control bar embedded members
    CDialogBar  m_dlgBar;
    CToolBar    m_toolBar;
```

FIGURE 11.17.

The IDB_TOOLS *bitmap in Developer Studio's Image Editor.*

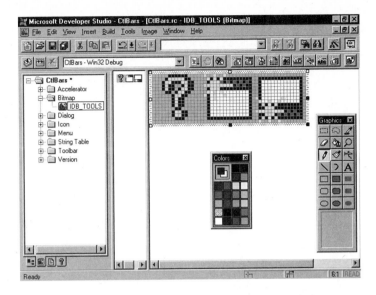

Every toolbar is created using an array of UINT that represents the menu ID of every toolbar item. Add the arToolButtons array shown in Listing 11.55 to the MainFrame.cpp source file, just below the other control bar arrays. Note that each array member is a menu ID. The ID_SEPARATOR value is used to create a space between adjacent toolbar items.

Listing 11.55. The resource ID array used by the new toolbar.

```
static UINT BASED_CODE arToolButtons[] =
{
    ID_APP_ABOUT,
        ID_SEPARATOR,
    ID_VIEW_TOOLBAR,
    ID_VIEW_STATUS_BAR,
};
```

Add the source code in Listing 11.56 to the CMainFrame::OnCreate member function. This source code creates a new toolbar using the IDB_TOOLS bitmap and floats the toolbar instead of docking it.

Listing 11.56. Additions to the CMainFrame::OnCreate function.

```
// Create a floating toolbar
m_toolBar.Create( this );
m_toolBar.SetWindowText( "Tools" );
m_toolBar.LoadBitmap( IDB_TOOLS );
m_toolBar.SetButtons( arToolButtons,
                    sizeof(arToolButtons)/sizeof(UINT) );
// Enable docking, even though the toolbar will float initially.
```

continues

Listing 11.56. continued

```
m_toolBar.EnableDocking( CBRS_ALIGN_ANY );
// Calculate the location to float the toolbar.
CRect   rc;
GetClientRect( &rc );
ClientToScreen( &rc );
FloatControlBar( &m_toolBar, rc.TopLeft() );
UINT nOldStyle = m_toolBar.GetBarStyle();
m_toolBar.SetBarStyle(nOldStyle | CBRS_TOOLTIPS | CBRS_FLYBY);
```

Compile and run the CtrlBar sample program. You can use the new toolbar to display or hide the status bar and original toolbar and also to display the CtrlBar About box.

Up-Down Controls

Up-down controls, often called *spin controls*, are a pair of small arrows that resemble the ends of a scroll bar but are smaller. Up-down controls often are used to adjust the value of another control associated with the up-down control. Known as a *buddy* control, this usually is an Edit control.

An up-down control also can be aligned horizontally. A horizontal up-down control is not called a left-right control; it keeps its original name.

By default, clicking the up arrow decreases the value of the buddy control, and clicking the down arrow increases the value contained in the buddy control. This behavior is confusing to most people; fortunately, it's easy to change, as you will see in the section *Using an Up-Down Control.*

Up-down controls often are used with an Edit control as the buddy control. The up-down control easily can run through a range of available values for the Edit control. By setting a range for the up-down control, you can ensure that the user selects a value within the acceptable range for the Edit control.

Up-down controls are ideal for situations in which a set of values can be scrolled by a user. If the values are adjusted up or down by a few units, an up-down control is perfect because it enables the user to select a new value with a few key presses,.

Using an Up-Down Control

An up-down control is very easy to use. To use the default functionality of the up-down control, you need to write exactly zero lines of source code! Even the most advanced uses for up-down controls require just a few lines of source code; most of the code is written by ClassWizard.

To illustrate how the up-down, progress, and slider controls are used, I have created an example program named Controls, which is included on the CD-ROM with this book. If you want to follow the steps used to create the project, read the next few sections. This project starts in this section by adding an up-down control to a dialog-based project.

To get started creating the Controls project, use AppWizard to create a new project workspace. Select a dialog-based project and click the Finish button.

Adding an Up-Down Control to a Dialog Box

Adding an up-down control to the Controls dialog box is just like adding other controls. Open the main dialog box in the Dialog Box Editor by selecting the ResourceView tab in the project workspace and opening the Dialog folder. Open the IDD_CONTROLS_DIALOG by double-clicking the Dialog Box icon or by right-clicking the icon and choosing Open from the pop-up menu.

You can drag and drop an up-down control from the Control palette to the main dialog box. Or, you can select the up-down control on the Tool palette using the mouse and then click the desired position in the main dialog box. Remember, Developer Studio calls this control a Spin control.

Open the Properties dialog box for the up-down control by double-clicking the control and change the resource ID to IDC_SPIN. All other properties should be set to their default values.

Using Up-Down Control Properties

As with other controls, up-down controls have properties that you can change using the Developer Studio Resource Editor. Table 11.33 lists the properties available for an up-down control.

Table 11.33. Up-down control properties.

Property	Function
Alignment	Specifies how the buddy control and up-down control are associated with each other. Possible values are Right, Left, and Unattached. The default value is Unattached, but in most cases, you should select Left or Right.
Arrow key	Indicates that the keyboard's arrow keys can be used to change the value of the up-down control. This checkbox usually is cleared.
Auto buddy	Indicates whether the up-down control should use the preceding control in the Tab order as its buddy control. This checkbox is cleared by default but should be checked in most cases.
Disabled	Indicates that the control should be disabled initially. This checkbox usually is cleared.

continues

Table 11.33. continued

Property	Function
Group	Marks the first control in a group. This checkbox usually is cleared.
Help ID	Indicates that a context-sensitive Help ID should be generated for this control.
ID	Used for the up-down control's resource ID. A default resource ID, such as IDC_SPIN1, is supplied by Developer Studio.
No thousands	Indicates that no comma should be provided for a value greater than 1,000 in the up-down control. This checkbox usually is cleared.
Orientation	Indicates whether the up-down control should be vertical or horizontal. The default selection is vertical.
Set buddy integer	Indicates that the up-down control should set the value of the attached buddy control. This checkbox is cleared by default but should be checked in most cases.
Tabstop	Indicates that this control can be reached by pressing Tab on the keyboard. This checkbox usually is checked.
Visible	Indicates that the control initially is visible. This checkbox usually is checked.
Wrap	Indicates that the up-down control should "wrap around" after reaching its maximum value. If this option is not selected, the up-down control stops after reaching its maximum limit. This checkbox usually is cleared.

Adding a Buddy Control

The easiest way to add a buddy control to an up-down control requires no source code; instead, you use the Dialog Box Editor. Follow these steps to associate an Edit control with an up-down control:

1. Add an Edit control to the dialog box. Most users expect the up-down control to be placed against the buddy control; it helps emphasize the connection between the two controls.

2. Open the Properties dialog box for the Edit control and change the resource ID to IDC_EDIT. All other properties should be set to their default values.

3. Set the tab order for the Edit control so that it is the control immediately before the up-down control. You can select the tab order by choosing Tab Order from the Layout menu or by pressing Ctrl+D. Each control is displayed with a small label that

represents the control tab order. To change the tab order, use the mouse to click each control in the new tab order sequence.

4. Open the Properties dialog box for the up-down control and set the alignment value to Right. This aligns the up-down control on the right side of the buddy control.

5. Keep the Properties dialog box open and check the Auto Buddy and Set Buddy Integer checkboxes.

Figure 11.18 shows the IDD_CONTROLS_DIALOG with an up-down control and the buddy Edit control.

FIGURE 11.18.

The main dialog box used in the Controls sample program.

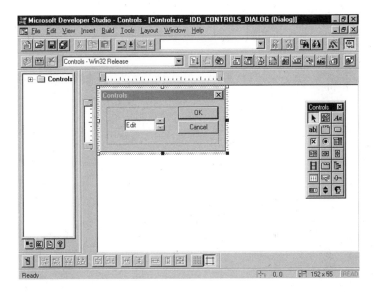

Believe it or not, that's all there is to using an up-down control. If you compile and execute the Controls project, you can use the up-down control to change the value contained in the Edit control.

To set, validate, or retrieve the value of the Edit control, use ClassWizard to associate a member variable with the Edit control.

Changing the Range of the Up-Down Control

As discussed earlier, the default behavior for an up-down control is to increment the control if the down arrow is clicked and decrement the control if the up arrow is clicked. You can change this behavior by reversing the range of the up-down control.

You can use the MFC class CSpinButtonCtrl to manage an up-down control. To change the range of an up-down control, use the CSpinButtonCtrl's SetRange function:

```
m_spin.SetRange( 100, 0 );
```

Use ClassWizard to associate the IDC_SPIN control with a CSpinButtonCtrl object, using the values in Table 11.34.

Table 11.34. Values used to add a CSpinButtonCtrl member variable for CControlsDlg.

Control ID	Variable Name	Category	Type
IDC_SPIN	m_spin	Control	CSpinButtonCtrl

To set a new range for the up-down control, add the following source code to the CControlsDlg::OnInitDialog member function. You should add this source code just after the // TODO comment:

```
// TODO: Add extra initialization here
   m_spin.SetRange( 0, 100 );
```

Compile and execute the Controls project. The up-down control increments the Edit control when its up arrow is clicked and decrements the Edit control when its down arrow is clicked.

Slider Controls

A slider control, also known as a trackbar control, is a control that contains a slide bar that you can move between two points. A slider is used in the Display applet that is part of the Windows Control Panel. The Settings property page uses a slider to set the screen resolution.

The user moves the slide bar by dragging it with the mouse or by setting the keyboard focus to the slider and using the arrow keys on the keyboard. You can create sliders with optional tick marks that help the user to judge the position of the slide bar.

Sliders are useful when a user is asked to select a value within a certain range. A slider gives the user immediate feedback about the control's current value, as well as the value's relationship to the high and low ranges.

Using a Slider Control

You use sliders in the same way as most other controls. Although you can create a slider from scratch, it's much easier to add one in the Developer Studio Dialog Box Editor.

Open the IDD_CONTROLS_DIALOG resource and add a slider control by dragging a slider control from the Control palette and dropping it on the dialog box. Figure 11.19 shows the Controls dialog box after you add the slider control.

FIGURE 11.19.

The main dialog box from the Controls project after you add a slider.

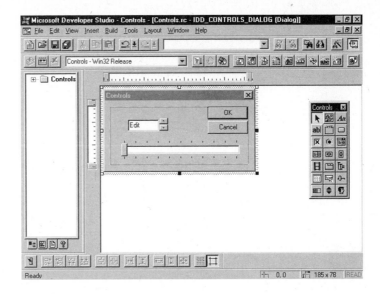

Open the Properties dialog box for the slider control and change the resource ID to IDC_SLIDER. All other properties can remain set to their default values for now. In the next section, you'll learn about the properties offered for slider controls.

Examining Slider Control Properties

The Properties dialog box for a slider control contains many of the same options offered for up-down controls, as well as a few exclusive to slider controls. Table 11.35 lists the available options.

Table 11.35. Slider control properties.

Property	Function
Autoticks	Indicates that tick marks should be drawn at intervals along the slider control. This option checkbox usually is cleared.
Border	Specifies that a border should be drawn around the control. This checkbox usually is checked.
Disabled	Indicates that the control should be disabled initially. This checkbox usually is cleared.
Enable selection	Enables the slider to be used to select a range of values. This checkbox usually is cleared.
Group	Marks the first control in a group. This checkbox usually is cleared.

continues

Table 11.35. continued

Property	Function
Help ID	Indicates that a context-sensitive Help ID should be generated for this control.
ID	Used for the slider's resource ID. A default resource ID, such as IDC_SLIDER1, is supplied by Developer Studio.
Orientation	Specifies whether the slider is vertical or horizontal. The default value is vertical.
Point	Indicates the position of optional tick marks. There are three options: Top/Left, Bottom/Right, or Both. The default value is Bottom/Right.
Tabstop	Indicates that this control can be reached by pressing Tab. This checkbox usually is checked.
Tick marks	Indicates that tick marks should be drawn for the slider. This checkbox usually is cleared.
Visible	Indicates that the control initially is visible. This checkbox usually is checked.

In the next section, you use a slider to control a slider. To prepare for that example, open the Properties dialog box and make sure that the following slider properties are selected:

- Tick marks
- Autoticks
- Enable selection

Progress Controls

A *progress control,* also known as a *progress bar,* is commonly used to indicate the progress of an operation and usually is filled from left to right as the operation is completed. You also can use progress controls for indicating temperature, water level, or similar measurements. In fact, an early term for this type of control was *gas gauge,* back in the old days when programmers had mules and most Windows programs were written in C.

Progress controls are used in Developer Studio to indicate the progress of saving or loading a project workspace. Progress controls also are used by the Windows Explorer when copying or moving files.

Using Progress Controls

You add a progress control to a dialog box in the same way that you added the up-down and slider controls discussed earlier. Using the Developer Studio Dialog Box Editor, add a progress control to the Controls project main dialog box. Figure 11.20 shows the main dialog box from the Controls project after the progress control is added.

FIGURE 11.20.

The Controls dialog box after adding the progress control.

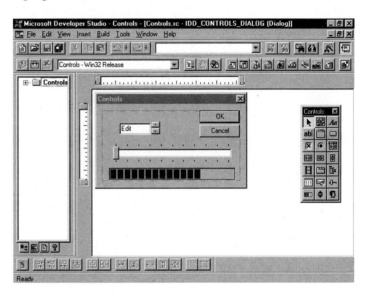

After you add the control, open the Properties dialog box and change the resource ID to IDC_PROGRESS. A progress control doesn't have optional properties, other than those available on all controls. Table 11.36 lists these properties.

Table 11.36. Progress control properties.

Property	Function
Border	Specifies that a border should be drawn around the control. This checkbox usually is checked.
Disabled	Indicates that the control should be disabled initially. This checkbox usually is cleared.
Group	Marks the first control in a group. This checkbox usually is cleared.
Help ID	Indicates that a context-sensitive Help ID should be generated for this control.

continues

Table 11.36. continued

Property	Function
ID	Used for the progress control's resource ID. A default resource ID, such as IDC_PROGRESS1, is supplied by Developer Studio.
Tabstop	Indicates that this control can be reached by pressing Tab. This checkbox usually is checked.
Visible	Indicates that the control initially is visible. This checkbox usually is checked.

For this example, you can set the progress control properties to their default values.

Using a Slider to Update a Progress Control

In this section, you use the IDC_SLIDER slider control to change the value displayed by the progress control. Using ClassWizard, add two new member variables associated with the slider and progress controls to the CControlsDlg class. Use the values from Table 11.37 for the new controls.

Table 11.37. Values for slider and progress control member variables.

Control ID	Variable Name	Category	Type
IDC_SLIDER	m_slider	Control	CSliderCtrl
IDC_PROGRESS	m_progress	Control	CProgressCtrl

Initializing the Slider and Progress Controls

The slider and progress controls must be initialized before you can use them. The CProgressCtrl and CSliderCtrl classes each provide a SetRange function used to set minimum and maximum values for their respective controls:

```
m_slider.SetRange( 0, 100 );
```

The slider also enables you to place tick marks along the slider control, if the Autoticks checkbox is selected. Use the SetTicFreq function to specify the distance between each tick mark. To add tick marks every 10 positions, pass a value of 10 to SetTicFreq:

```
m_slider.SetTicFreq( 10 );
```

Listing 11.57 contains new source code for the initialization section of OnInitDialog. Add this source code just after the // TODO comment.

Listing 11.57. Initializing the controls in `CControlsDlg::OnInitDialog`.

```
// TODO: Add extra initialization here
m_spin.SetRange( 0, 100 );
m_slider.SetRange( 0, 100 );
m_slider.SetTicFreq( 10 );
m_progress.SetRange( 0, 100 );
```

Handling Messages from the Slider

When a slider is moved, it notifies its parent using WM_SCROLL and WM_HSCROLL messages. Because the slider in this example is a horizontal slider, it sends WM_HSCROLL messages to the main dialog box. Using ClassWizard, add a message-handling function to the CControlsDlg class for the WM_HSCROLL message. Listing 11.58 shows the source code for the OnHScroll function.

Listing 11.58. Using slider scroll messages to update the progress control.

```
void CControlsDlg::OnHScroll(UINT nSBCode, UINT nPos,
                             CScrollBar* pScrollBar )
{
    int nSliderPos = m_slider.GetPos();
    m_progress.SetPos( nSliderPos );
}
```

The code in Listing 11.58 is called whenever the slider position is changed. The `CSliderCtrl::GetPos` function is used to collect the current slider position, which then is used to update the progress control using the `CProgressCtrl::SetPos` function.

The Rich Edit Control

The Rich Edit control is an Edit control that uses a subset of the rich text format (RTF) to store text contained in the control. The Rich Edit control is almost like having a complete word processor in a single control.

The Edit control uses the RTF format to store its text while keeping the low-level details about RTF hidden from the user of the control. Although the Rich Edit control does not support the entire RTF specification, it supports the most commonly used parts, and it simply ignores any input that it can't handle.

Understanding the Rich Text Format

The *rich text format* is a specification that defines how applications can embed formatting information inside a document. Unlike a proprietary formatting scheme supported by a single application, the RTF specification is used by many applications to store data. This is important for situations in which a document must be shared on different types of computers or by different applications. An RTF document created by FrameMaker on a UNIX machine, for example, can be used by Word for Windows without losing formatting information.

If you are interested in the details about RTF, the specification is available from Microsoft and can be downloaded from the CompuServe MSWORD forum. You can also download this information directly from Microsoft. The current version of the RTF specification (1.4) is available directly from Microsoft in application note GC0165 .

To download the Application Note directly from Microsoft's web page, use this URL:

```
http://www.microsoft.com/KB/SoftLib/MSLFiles/Gc0165.EXE
```

If you're not concerned with the details of RTF, don't worry; the Rich Edit control handles all the difficult work for you.

Deciding When to Use the Rich Edit Control

The Rich Edit control enables you to have Edit controls capable of displaying multiple formats in a single control window. When you use a standard Edit control, the font, color, and other formatting options must be consistent for all text contained in the control. Using the Rich Edit control enables you to be flexible; every character can have its own formatting style.

The Rich Edit control also enables you to specify paragraph styles—something that is not possible using a standard Edit control. You can independently specify tab positions, indentations, and paragraph alignment styles for each paragraph.

Even with all the extra functionality offered by a Rich Edit control, it still is compatible with the original Edit control. All messages and functions you use for standard Edit controls can be used with Rich Edit controls.

Using the MFC Rich Edit Control Classes

You can use the Rich Edit control in two ways. First, you can use it to replace a standard Edit control in a dialog box to collect and display user input. The MFC CRichEditCtrl class is used to wrap the Edit control and to provide access to its advanced functions, much in the same way that the CEdit class provides easy access to the standard Edit control. You also can integrate the Rich Edit control into the MFC Document/View architecture, using the CRichEditView and CRichEditDoc classes.

Using the Rich Edit Document/View Classes

The Rich Edit Document/View classes help simplify the creation of simple word processing applications. The three Rich Edit classes that work together for document/view integration follow:

- **CRichEditView:** Actually contains the Rich Edit control and is responsible for all the interaction with the control for user input and formatting.
- **CRichEditDoc:** Serializes the data in the control to and from storage.
- **CRichEditCntrItem:** Handles the OLE interface for items embedded in the Rich Edit control.

The CRichEditView class contains a CRichEditCtrl object. This MFC class is discussed in the next section and provides access to the actual Rich Edit control. To retrieve a reference to the CRichEditCtrl object, use the GetRichEditCtrl function:

```
CRichEditCtrl&  rtfEdit = GetRichEditCtrl();
```

Using the CRichEditCtrl Class

You use the MFC CRichEditCtrl class to interact with a Rich Edit control. This class is similar to the CEdit class, but there are many more options available for formatting text.

Controlling Character Formatting

The CRichEditCtrl class offers two functions for controlling character formatting: GetSelectionCharFormat and SetSelectionCharFormat. These functions work for individual characters or with the currently selected text area. You use the GetSelectionCharFormat function to collect information about a character's format:

```
CHARFORMAT     chFormat;
DWORD dwSel = rtfEdit.GetSelectionCharFormat( chFormat );
```

You use the SetSelectionCharFormat function to set the format attributes for a character:

```
rtfEdit.SetSelectionCharFormat( chFormat );
```

The CHARFORMAT structure contains information about the character selection and is used for retrieving or setting character format information. The return value from GetSelectionCharFormat is a mask that represents which CHARFORMAT structure members are valid for the entire selection. Table 11.38 lists the members of the CHARFORMAT structure.

Table 11.38. Members of the CHARFORMAT structure.

Parameter	Function
bCharSet	Can be any of the values allowed by the LOGFONT structure's lfCharSet member variable. Using the LOGFONT structure is discussed in Chapter 32, "Fonts."
bPitchAndFamily	Specifies the font family and pitch. This member supports the same values as the LOGFONT structure's lfPitchAndFamily member variable.

continues

Table 11.38. continued

Parameter	Function
cbSize	Specifies the size of this CHARFORMAT structure. You must fill in this value if you create the structure. If the structure is returned as a result from Windows, this value should not be changed, even if you pass it as a parameter in a later function call.
crTextColor	Specifies the character text color. This value is used only if the CFE_AUTOCOLOR flag is not set in the dwEffects member.
dwEffects	Specifies the effects applied to the selection. The possible values for this member are discussed after this table.
dwMask	Determines the valid members of the structure. This member is discussed in detail at the end of this table.
szFaceName	A null-terminated string that specifies the font face used by the character.
yHeight	Specifies the character height in twips. *Twips* are one-twentieth of a point. Because there are approximately 72 points in an inch, each twip is about 1/1440 of an inch.
yOffset	Specifies the character's offset relative to the baseline. If this value is positive, the character is a superscript; if negative, it is a subscript.

Using the dwMask and dwEffects Flags

You use the dwMask member to specify which structure members contain valid data. More than one of the values for dwMask can be combined by using ¦, the bitwise OR operator. Table 11.39 lists the values for dwMask.

Table 11.39. Values for dwMask.

Value	Function
CFM_BOLD	Indicates that the state of the dwEffects CFE_BOLD flag is valid.
CFM_COLOR	Indicates the crTextColor value, as well as the dwEffects CFE_AUTOCOLOR flag, is valid.
CFM_FACE	Indicates that the szFaceName value is valid.
CFM_ITALIC	Indicates that the dwEffects CFE_ITALIC flag is valid.
CFM_OFFSET	Indicates that the yOffset value is valid.
CFM_PROTECTED	Indicates that the dwEffects CFE_PROTECTED flag is valid.
CFM_SIZE	Indicates that the yHeight value is valid.

Value	Function
CFM_STRIKEOUT	Indicates that the dwEffects CFE_STRIKEOUT flag is valid.
CFM_UNDERLINE	Indicates that the dwEffects CFE_UNDERLINE flag is valid.

The dwEffects member contains the formatting flags for the character selection. Before using any information from dwEffects, test dwMask to make sure the data is valid. Table 11.40 lists the dwEffects members.

Table 11.40. Formatting flags in the CHARFORMAT dwEffects member.

Flag	Indicates the Character Is
CFE_AUTOCOLOR	Default Color
CFE_BOLD	Bold
CFE_ITALIC	Italic
CFE_PROTECTED	Protected
CFE_STRIKEOUT	Struck Out
CFE_UNDERLINE	Underlined

When the CFE_AUTOCOLOR flag is set, the default color can be obtained by calling the GetSysColor function:

```
GetSysColor( COLOR_WINDOWTEXT );
```

As with the flags and attributes from other Windows structures that use combined values, the dwMask and dwEffects member variables are used with the ¦ (bitwise OR) and & (bitwise AND) operators. To determine whether a flag is set, use the bitwise AND operator:

```
if( chFormat.dwMask & CFM_BOLD > 0 )
```

To set a flag, use the bitwise OR operator; you can use the form that combines the OR and assignment operators:

```
chFormat.dwEffects ¦= CFE_BOLD;
```

To clear a flag, use the bitwise AND operator with the negation operator:

```
chFormat.dwEffects &= ~CFE_BOLD;
```

Controlling Paragraph Formatting

In addition to offering character formatting, the CRichEditCtrl class offers two functions for controlling paragraph formatting: GetParaFormat and SetParaFormat. These functions work for individual paragraphs or for multiple paragraphs in a text-selection area. Use the `GetParaFormat` function to retrieve paragraph information:

```
PARAFORMAT    parFormat;
DWORD dwSel = rtfEdit.GetParaFormat( parFormat );
```

Use the `SetParaFormat` function to set the format attributes for a paragraph:

```
rtfEdit.SetParaFormat( parFormat );
```

Like the `CHARFORMAT` structure, the `PARAFORMAT` structure contains information about the paragraph and is used for retrieving or setting paragraph format information. Table 11.41 lists the members of the `PARAFORMAT` structure.

Table 11.41. Members of the PARAFORMAT structure.

Member	Function
cbSize	Specifies the size of the `PARAFORMAT` structure. You must fill in this value if you create the structure. If the structure is returned as a result from Windows, this value should not be changed, even if you pass it as a parameter in a later function call.
cTabCount	Contains the number of tab positions stored in the `rgxTabs` array.
dwMask	Determines the valid members of the structure. This member is discussed in detail at the end of this table.
dxOffset	Specifies the indentation for lines after the first line. This value is relative to the first line's starting indentation. If `dxOffset` is negative, the first line of the paragraph is indented. If `dxOffset` is positive, the first line is outdented.
dxRightIndent	Specifies the right indentation, relative to the right margin.
dxStartIndent	Specifies the first line indentation for the paragraph. If `dwMask` includes the `PFM_OFFSETINDENT` style bit, this member refers to the relative offset added to the starting indentation of the paragraph.
rgxTabs	An array that contains tab stop positions for the paragraph. The maximum number of tab positions is defined as `MAX_TAB_STOPS`.
wAlignment	Specifies how the paragraph text is aligned. For left alignment, use `PFA_LEFT`; for right alignment, use `PFA_RIGHT`; for paragraphs that are centered, use `PFA_CENTER`.
wNumbering	Specifies the paragraph's numbering and bulleting options. This member can be 0 or `PFN_BULLET`.

You use the PARAFORMAT structure's dwMask member variable in the same way that you use the dwMask member variable found in the CHARFORMAT structure. In both cases, dwMask specifies which member variables can be used. Of course, the PARAFORMAT's dwMask member variable has different flags, as Table 11.42.

Table 11.42. Flags used for the PARAFORMAT dwMask member variable.

Flag	Function
PFM_ALIGNMENT	Indicates that the wAlignment value is valid.
PFM_NUMBERING	Indicates that the wNumbering value is valid.
PFM_OFFSET	Indicates that the dxOffset value is valid.
PFM_OFFSETINDENT	Indicates that the dxStartIndent is valid and specifies a relative offset.
PFM_RIGHTINDENT	Indicates that the dxRightIndent value is valid.
PFM_STARTINDENT	Indicates that the dxStartIndent value is valid and contains an absolute indentation value.
PFM_TABSTOPS	Indicates that the cTabStops and rgxTabStops values are valid.

It's possible to specify both PFM_STARTINDENT and PFM_OFFSETINDENT. If that happens, PFM_STARTINDENT takes precedence.

Looking at a Rich Edit Control Example

As an example of how the Rich Edit controls are used, I have created an example application named RichText, which you can find on the CD-ROM that accompanies this book. If you want to create the application yourself, follow the steps in the next few sections.

To get started creating the RichText application, create an SDI project named RichText using AppWizard. For AppWizard step 3, select the OLE Container option, which is required when using the Rich Edit control. In the final AppWizard page, a checkered flag is displayed along with a listbox containing classes generated for the application. Follow these steps to use the Rich Edit Document/View classes:

1. Select the view class in the Class listbox—in this case, CRichTextView.
2. Select CRichEditView from the Base combo box.
3. Click the Finish button to complete the AppWizard process.

AppWizard might display a message box notifying you of new options that will be added to your project. Accept any suggested changes. You can compile and run the RichText application; however, no character formatting options have been added to the project. In the next section, you will see how to perform character formatting.

Creating a Format Dialog Box

Using Figure 11.21 as a guide, create a Character Format dialog box. You use this dialog box to display or change character formatting for text in the RichText application. Give the dialog box a resource ID of IDD_FORMAT.

FIGURE 11.21.

The Character Formatting dialog box from the RichText example.

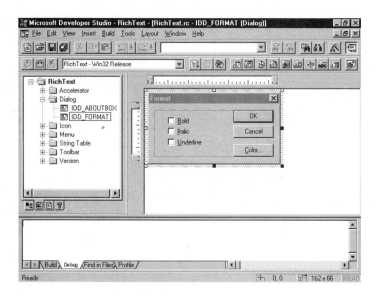

The dialog box contains four new controls: three checkboxes and one pushbutton. You use the checkboxes to set or clear character formatting flags and the pushbutton to display a common Color dialog box so that the user can select the text color. Table 11.43 provides the resource IDs for each of these controls.

Table 11.43. Control properties from the Format dialog box.

Control	Resource ID
Bold checkbox	IDC_BOLD
Italic checkbox	IDC_ITALIC
Underline checkbox	IDC_UNDERLINE
Color pushbutton	IDC_COLOR

Creating the `CFormatDlg` Class

Use ClassWizard to create a new class to handle the Format dialog box, using the values from Table 11.44 for ClassWizard's Add Class dialog box.

Table 11.44. Values for the Add Class dialog box.

Control	Value
Name	CFormatDlg
Base Class	CDialog
File	FormatDlg.cpp
Dialog ID	IDD_FORMAT
OLE Automation	None
Add to Component Gallery	Cleared

Next, associate `CFormatDlg` member variables with the controls included in the Format dialog box, using ClassWizard and the values listed in Table 11.45. You use these variables to report and set formatting flags in the Rich Edit control.

Table 11.45. Values used to add member variables for `CFormatDlg`.

Control ID	Variable Name	Category	Type
IDC_BOLD	m_bBold	Value	BOOL
IDC_ITALIC	m_bItalic	Value	BOOL
IDC_UNDERLINE	m_bUnderline	Value	BOOL

Add a message-handling function for the `IDC_COLOR` button using ClassWizard and the values listed in Table 11.46. You use this function to display the common Color dialog box in order to select the current text color.

Table 11.46. Adding a message-handling function for the Format dialog box.

Object ID	Message	Class	Function
IDC_COLOR	BN_CLICKED	CFormatDlg	OnColor

Listing 11.59 provides the source code for the `OnColor` function.

Listing 11.59. The `CFormatDlg::OnColor` member function.

```
void CFormatDlg::OnColor()
{
    CColorDialog    dlg;
    dlg.m_cc.rgbResult = m_clrText;
    if( dlg.DoModal() )
```

continues

Listing 11.59. continued

```
        {
            m_clrText = dlg.GetColor();
        }
}
```

When the OnColor function is called, the common Color dialog box is displayed. If the Color dialog box is dismissed with the OK button, the selected color is stored in the m_clrText member variable.

Add a declaration for the m_clrText member variable to the CFormatDlg class declaration. Add the declaration of m_clrText in the Implementation section under a public label, as shown in Listing 11.60.

Listing 11.60. Changes to the CFormatDlg class declaration.

```
// Implementation
public:
    BOOL    m_clrText;
```

Making Changes to the CRichTextView Class

The Format dialog box is displayed after a user right-clicks inside the view window. Using ClassWizard, add a message-handling function for WM_RBUTTONUP to the CRichTextView class, using the values from Table 11.47.

Table 11.47. Values for the new CRichTextView message-handling function.

Object ID	Message	Class	Function
CRichTextView	WM_RBUTTONUP	CRichTextView	OnRButtonUp

Listing 11.61 provides the source code for the OnRButtonUp function.

Listing 11.61. The CRichTextView::OnRButtonUp member function.

```
void CRichTextView::OnRButtonUp(UINT nFlags, CPoint point)
{
    CRichEditView::OnRButtonUp(nFlags, point);
    CRichEditCtrl&  rtfEdit = GetRichEditCtrl();
    WORD wSelType = rtfEdit.GetSelectionType();
    if( wSelType & SEL_TEXT )
    {
        CFormatDlg  dlg;
        CHARFORMAT  chFormat;
        DWORD dwSel = rtfEdit.GetSelectionCharFormat( chFormat );
```

```
        if( dwSel & CFM_BOLD )
            dlg.m_bBold = chFormat.dwEffects & CFE_BOLD;
        if( dwSel & CFM_ITALIC )
            dlg.m_bItalic = chFormat.dwEffects & CFE_ITALIC;
        if( dwSel & CFM_UNDERLINE )
            dlg.m_bUnderline = chFormat.dwEffects & CFE_UNDERLINE;
        if( dwSel & CFM_COLOR )
            dlg.m_clrText = chFormat.crTextColor;

        if( dlg.DoModal() == IDOK )
        {
            if( dlg.m_bBold == TRUE )
                chFormat.dwEffects |= CFE_BOLD;
            else
                chFormat.dwEffects &= ~CFE_BOLD;
            if( dlg.m_bItalic )
                chFormat.dwEffects |= CFE_ITALIC;
            else
                chFormat.dwEffects &= ~CFE_ITALIC;
            if( dlg.m_bUnderline )
                chFormat.dwEffects |= CFE_UNDERLINE;
            else
                chFormat.dwEffects &= ~CFE_UNDERLINE;
            chFormat.crTextColor = dlg.m_clrText;
            rtfEdit.SetSelectionCharFormat( chFormat );
        }
    }
    else
    {
        AfxMessageBox( "Please select some text" );
    }
}
```

Add an `#include` statement in RichTextView.cpp that includes the class definition for `CFormatDlg`, found in FormatDlg.h. Add the following line just above the `#include` statement for RichTextView.h:

```
#include "FormatDlg.h"
```

Compile and run the RichText example. You can select a block of text using the mouse and change the format of the characters by right-clicking anywhere in the view window.

The Animation Control

You use the Animation control to "play" bitmaps stored in an AVI file as an animation sequence. The Animation control is used in several places in Windows NT and Windows 95. The flying paper displayed when a file is copied or deleted, for example, is displayed in an Animation control.

The source AVI file consists of a sequence of bitmaps that are organized as shown in Figure 11.22. As the AVI file is played, the control seems to be animated.

FIGURE 11.22.

An AVI clip is made up of a series of bitmaps.

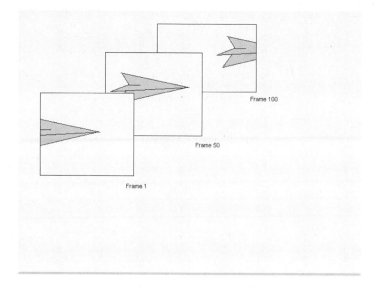

Frame 100

Frame 50

Frame 1

The Animation control is useful in situations in which you need to convey that an action is taking place—such as moving files, printing documents, or waiting for a connection to be established. Using an Animation control does not affect your application performance significantly, because Windows NT runs the animation as a separate thread.

Only simple AVI files can be used by the Animation control. In order to be used by an Animation control, an AVI file must meet these requirements:

- It must have RLE compression or no compression at all.
- It must have only one video stream and a maximum of one additional stream (usually audio), which is ignored.
- It must use only one palette.

These requirements make it difficult to use AVI video clips in a control because they usually are compressed and use multiple palettes.

Using an Animation Control

An Animation control is extremely simple to use. In fact, the most difficult part of using an Animation control is creating its AVI source file. In this section, you'll create a dialog-based project that plays an Animation control on demand.

Creating an AVI File

The Win32 SDK includes the AVIEDIT sample application, a tool for editing AVI files. Unfortunately, this tool is rather primitive, and there is no documentation. Even worse, it isn't included with Visual C++, only with the full Win32 SDK. If you have the Win32 SDK installed, the AVIEDIT sample is found in the MSTOOLS\SAMPLES\MM\AVIEDIT directory.

Basically, AVIEDIT works like this:

1. Create individual bitmaps using Paint or some other image editor.

2. Copy the images to AVIEDIT using the Windows NT clipboard.

3. Save the images into an AVI stream.

I use Digital Video Producer from Asymetrix to create all my AVI clips. DVP provides storyboarding, drag-and-drop editing, and an intuitive user interface.

Creating an AVI clip for an Animation control consists of creating the individual bitmaps that represent each frame of the animation sequence. Figure 11.23 shows an example of one bitmap.

FIGURE 11.23.

Editing an animation bitmap.

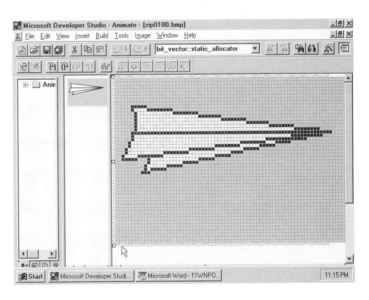

After a series of bitmaps has been edited, you can use Digital Video Producer or a similar tool to create an AVI clip. Figure 11.24 shows an AVI clip being created inside Digital Video Producer.

FIGURE 11.24.

Using Digital Video Producer to create an AVI clip.

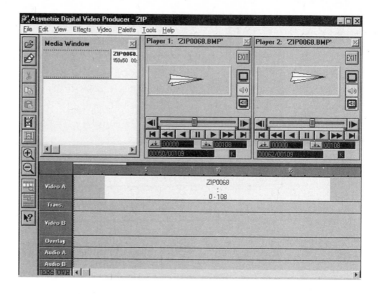

Examining Animation Control Properties

Three optional properties exist for Animation controls. If you create an Animation control using Visual C++, these properties are exposed in a Properties dialog box that is displayed by double-clicking the Animation control:

- **Center:** Causes the control to be centered in the Animation control's window. Selecting this option applies the ACS_CENTER style to the control.

- **Transparent:** Specifies that the animation should be drawn using a transparent background instead of the background used in the AVI clip. Selecting this option applies the ACS_TRANSPARENT style to the control.

- **Autoplay:** Starts playing the AVI clip as soon as the file is opened. After the clip ends, it is restarted from the beginning. Selecting this option applies the ACS_AUTOPLAY style to the control.

Using the CAnimateCtrl Class

The MFC CAnimateCtrl class provides an easy-to-use wrapper for the Animation control. Actually, the wrapper is very thin because there are only a few things you can do with an Animation control.

To open an Animation control, use the CAnimateCtrl::Open function. This function takes as a parameter a resource ID or the name of the file containing the AVI clip:

```
m_aniCtrl.Open( TEXT("foo.avi") );
m_aniCtrl.Open( IDR_AVI_CLIP );
```

If the control has the automatic play style, the clip immediately starts playing after it is opened. Otherwise, the first frame of the AVI clip is displayed.

To start the animation, use the `CAnimateCtrl::Play` member function:

```
BOOL CAnimateCtrl::Play( UINT nFrom, UINT nTo, UINT nRep );
```

This function has three parameters:

- ■ **nFrom:** The frame that will start the animation, with 0 as the first frame.
- ■ **nTo:** The last frame in the animation sequence. Use –1 to indicate that the entire clip must be played. Because the parameter is (for some reason) typed as UINT, you must cast –1 if you want to avoid compiler warnings.
- ■ **nRep:** The number of times the AVI clip is repeated. Use –1 to indicate that the clip is repeated indefinitely. Because the parameter is (for some reason) typed as UINT, you must cast –1 if you want to avoid compiler warnings.

The source code that follows, for example, is used to play an Animation control repeatedly from beginning to end:

```
m_aniCtrl.Play( 0, (UINT)-1, (UINT)-1 );
```

To stop an Animation control, you use the cleverly named function `CAnimateCtrl::Stop`:

```
m_aniCtrl.Stop();
```

The `Open`, `Play`, and `Stop` functions all return `FALSE` if they fail and non-zero if they are successful.

Adding an Animation Control to a Dialog Box

As an example of using an Animation control in a dialog box, I have created an example program named Animate that is located on the CD-ROM that comes with this book. Animate is a dialog-based application that displays an Animation control in the center of its main dialog box. Figure 11.25 shows the Animate program running, with an Animation control displayed inside the dialog box. As the Animation control plays, the paper airplane flies across the dialog box.

Start the Animate project by using AppWizard to create a dialog-based application. Feel free to accept or change any of the default parameters.

FIGURE 11.25.

The Animate example program.

Creating the AVI File

On the CD, I have included the bitmaps used to create the AVI file used by the Animation control. In the project's BMP subdirectory, you will find 119 bitmaps, named Zip0068.bmp through Zip0176.bmp. These bitmaps will be merged together to create the Zip.AVI file that also is included in the BMP subdirectory.

As discussed earlier, I used Asymetrix Digital Video Producer to create the AVI clip, using the bitmap images as source files. Whatever method you use, be sure to create a single, uncompressed or RLE-encoded video stream. Compressed AVI clips are not supported by the current version of the Animation control.

Adding the AVI File to the Project

As discussed earlier, you can open the Animation control with an AVI file name or with a resource ID. In order to use a resource ID, you must add the AVI file to your project as a resource. Trouble is, there isn't a predefined resource type for AVI files.

To add the AVI file to your project as a custom resource, follow these steps:

1. Copy the AVI file into your project's RES subdirectory. For this project, you can find the file Zip.avi on the CD-ROM in the project's BMP subdirectory.
2. Open the Resource view in the project workspace window and right-click on the root folder.
3. Choose Import from the pop-up menu.
4. Select the AVI from the Open File dialog box and click the Import button. A Custom Resource Type dialog box is displayed.
5. Enter AVI as the Resource type and click OK.
6. The new resource is given a default name, such as IDR_AVI1. For this project, change the name to IDR_AVI_ZIP.

Adding an AVI Control to the Animate Project

Using the Dialog Box Editor, add an Animation control to the IDD_ANIMATE_DIALOG dialog box, as shown in Figure 11.26. You add the Animation control just like any other control: Just drag and drop the control or select the control and click on the new location.

FIGURE 11.26.

The main dialog box used in the Animate example.

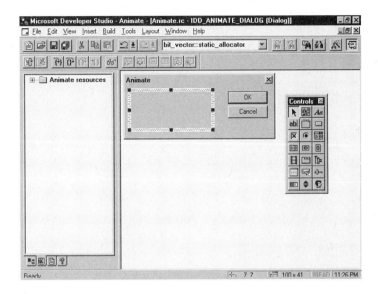

Open the Properties dialog box for the Animation control and change the resource ID to IDC_ANIMATE. All other properties should be set to their default values.

Using ClassWizard, associate a CAnimateCtrl member variable with the new Animation control, using the values shown in Table 11.48.

Table 11.48. Values used to add a CAnimationCtrl member variable for CAnimateDlg.

Control ID	Variable Name	Category Type
IDC_ANIMATE	m_animate	Control CAnimateCtrl

The Animation control is opened when the dialog receives WM_INITDIALOG. Listing 11.62 shows the modifications to CAnimateDlg::OnInitDialog in bold type. Because there are only two new lines, most of the existing function is not shown.

Listing 11.62. Starting an AVI control in OnInitDialog.

```
BOOL CAnimateDlg::OnInitDialog()
{
    CDialog::OnInitDialog();
    ...
    // TODO: Add extra initialization here
    m_animate.Open( IDR_AVI_ZIP );
    m_animate.Play( 0, -1, -1 );
    return TRUE;
}
```

Compile and run the Animate project. When the dialog box initially is displayed, the paper airplane flies across the dialog box. The AVI clip continues to repeat until the dialog box is closed.

Summary

In this chapter, you examined the most popular common controls that first were introduced in Windows 95 and Windows NT 3.51. The MFC classes that interact with the new controls were covered, and example programs were used to demonstrate how the controls are used in Windows NT applications.

In the next chapter, "Structured Exception Handling," you learn about how Windows NT offers advanced error-handling features. You also learn how Windows NT structured exception handling can be integrated with C++ exception handling.

Structured Exception Handling

12

by Mickey Williams

IN THIS CHAPTER

This chapter explains how you can use exception handling to make your Windows NT applications more robust. You'll learn about structured exception handling (SEH) offered by Windows NT and the ANSI C++ standard exception handling. You'll also see how ANSI C++ exception handling and Windows NT SEH can be integrated with each other.

Looking at the Exception-Handling Basics

Handling errors and special cases is a major cause of frustration for many programmers. Much of the code presented in examples in programming books or in sample programs deals with the *normal case*—code executed when a program is executed as expected. Adding source code that checks for errors often clutters a listing and makes it less clear. Listing 12.1 tests the return value of all function calls and handles errors by displaying a message to the user.

Listing 12.1. Handling errors by testing return values.

```
int ConcatStrings( TCHAR* pszDest, TCHAR* pszSrc, int cDest )
{
    TCHAR* pResult = NULL;
    if( pszDest && pszSrc )
    {
        int nDest = lstrlen( pszDest );
        int nSrc = lstrlen( pszSrc );
        if( (nDest + nSrc) < cDest )
            pResult = lstrcat( pszDest, pszSrc );
    }
    if( pResult )
        return lstrlen( pResult );
    else
        return 0;
}
```

The general term *exception handling* refers to using mechanisms that separate error-handling code from source code executed in the normal case. These mechanisms help separate source code used for normal processing from the source code executed to recover from errors. Listing 12.2 shows an example of exception handling using Windows NT structured exception handling to handle error conditions.

Listing 12.2. Dealing with errors using structured exception handling.

```
int ConcatStrings( TCHAR* pszDest, TCHAR* pszSrc, int cDest )
{
    __try
    {
        TCHAR* pResult = lstrcat( pszDest, pszSrc );
        return lstrlen( pResult );
    }
```

```
    __except( EXCEPTION_EXECUTE_HANDLER )
    {
        return 0;
    }
}
```

As you can see, exception handling is useful because it helps preserve the flow of the essential source code by moving the error-handling code into a separate block. The second version of ConcatStrings catches every error that was caught by the first version, using less code and simpler construction.

When programming for Windows NT, you have three exception-handling options:

- Use structured exception handling offered by the Windows NT operating system.
- Use ANSI C++ exception handling offered by your C++ compiler.
- Integrate the exception handling between Windows NT and your C++ compiler.

All three approaches are discussed in this chapter.

Understanding How SEH Works

When an exception is detected by Windows NT, the executing thread is suspended immediately, and processing shifts from User mode to Kernel mode. Control is transferred to the *exception dispatcher*, which is responsible for finding a way to handle the new exception.

If there is no exception handler available for the exception, the exception dispatcher transfers control to a system-wide exception handler, which displays a dialog box similar to the one shown in Figure 12.1.

FIGURE 12.1.

The standard dialog box displayed for unhandled exceptions.

On the other hand, if an exception handler can be found, control is passed to it, and the application can, if it is coded to take advantage of exception handling, handle the error gracefully. Even if you choose to terminate your application, catching exceptions enables you to do the following:

- Clean up data in external databases.
- Restore allocated resources.

■ Send detailed information to the event log.

■ Provide detailed failure information to the user to help debug the problem.

Any of these options is much better than displaying an Application Error dialog box to the user.

Using Termination Handlers

The most basic form of structured exception handling offered by Windows NT is the termination handler. A *termination handler* is a block of code that always is guaranteed to be executed. Termination handlers often are used in situations in which memory or other resources must be freed before a function returns. Listing 12.3 shows how a termination handler is used to ensure that heap memory is released inside a function.

Listing 12.3. Using a termination handler to guarantee memory is released.

```
BOOL SomeFunc()
{
    int*    p = 0;
    __try
    {
        // Use p in here
    }
    __finally
    {
        delete [] p;
    }
    return fReturn;
}
```

The SEH keywords in the code fragment follow:

■ **__try:** Marks the beginning of an exception try block.

■ **__finally:** Marks the beginning of a termination handler block.

Note that in Listing 12.3, the return statement is outside the try and finally blocks. This is good coding practice, which encourages an easy-to-follow structure for your code. You can include return and goto statements inside a try block, but the path of execution can become difficult to trace, and your code will suffer performance-wise.

Listing 12.4 shows an example of source code that exits prematurely from a try block.

Listing 12.4. An example of the wrong way to exit from a __try block.

```
long CalcAndLogFactorial( int n )
{
    long  lResult;
    __try
    {
        if( n > 2 )
        {
            for( lResult = 1; n > 1; n-- )
                lResult *= n;
        }
        else
            return (long)n;
    }
    __finally
    {
        // Store result in log file.
    }
    return lResult;
}
```

If CalcAndLogFactorial is called with a parameter of 2 or less, the parameter value is returned from the function. For a larger value of n, the factorial is calculated as the sum of the product of all integers from 1 to n.

If the value of n is greater than 2, the factorial is calculated, and execution flows through to the body of the __finally block. After the __finally block is executed, the factorial is returned by the return lResult statement. The flow of execution is more complicated for cases in which the value of n is 2 or less. First, the return value is stored, and then the code inside the termination handler is executed. After the termination handler executes, control returns to the return statement, and the value of n is returned to the caller.

Whenever a premature exit from a __try block is detected, the termination block must be called. If the premature exit occurs due to a return, the return value is stored until after the termination handler executes.

This can lead to even more complex cases. Listing 12.5 shows a case in which the last return statement is inside the termination handler.

Listing 12.5. Using return inside a termination handler.

```
long CalcAndLogFactorial( int n )
{
    long  lResult;
    __try
```

continues

Listing 12.5. continued

```
    {
        if( n > 2 )
        {
            for( lResult = 1; n > 1; n-- )
                lResult *= n;
        }
        else
            return (long)n;
    }
    __finally
    {
        return lResult;
    }
}
```

In Listing 12.5, the return statement inside the __try block causes the termination handler to be called. The termination handler also contains a return, however. In this case, the return value from the __finally block is returned to the caller.

Obviously, all these twists and turns, caching and retrieving, come at a performance penalty. If possible, you always should avoid premature exits from __try - __finally blocks.

Using __leave to Exit a __try Block

If you must exit a __try block, Windows NT offers a controlled way to exit the __try block that is more efficient than using return. The __leave keyword enables you to make a controlled jump to the termination handler without incurring the extra overhead that results in a goto or return. The syntax is very simple:

```
__try
{
    ...
    __leave;
    ...
}
```

After a __leave is encountered, execution continues at the exception handler.

Using Normal and Abnormal Termination

When executing the code in a termination handler, you may need to know whether the termination handler was called due to an error or as a result of normal processing. There are basically two ways to reach a termination handler:

■ The __try block was executed normally, and execution continued into the __finally block.

■ An abnormal exit occurred due to a premature exit from the __try block, such as an exception or a goto or return statement.

The AbnormalTermination function returns FALSE if the termination handler was reached via normal execution. If an abnormal exit from the __try block was detected, AbnormalTermination returns a non-zero value. If the __try block was exited due to a __leave statement, AbnormalTermination returns FALSE, as shown in the console mode program provided in Listing 12.6.

Listing 12.6. A console-mode program that tests for abnormal exit using AbnormalTermination.

```
#include <iostream.h>
#include <windows.h>

int main()
{
    __try
    {
        __leave;
        cout << "never" << endl;
    }
    __finally
    {
        if( AbnormalTermination() != FALSE )
            cout << "Abnormal termination" << endl;
        else
            cout << "Normal termination" << endl;
    }
    return 0;
}
```

The program in Listing 12.6 displays Normal termination. If the __leave statement is replaced by return or goto, the program displays Abnormal termination.

The only way for you to avoid a termination handler is if you kill the currently executing thread. If abort is called inside a __try block, for example, the process is killed, and the termination handler is never called.

Using Exception Handlers

Of course, the real highlight of structured exception handling is handling errors encountered while executing your program. SEH uses exception filters to determine how errors detected in your application should be handled. Two keywords are used when building an exception handler:

■ **__try:** Marks the beginning of a guarded block, much as it is used in termination handlers discussed earlier in this chapter.

■ **__except:** Marks the beginning of an exception filter that may be capable of handling an exception.

The syntax for an exception handler is similar to that used by termination handlers. In Listing 12.7, using *p generates an access violation, and control immediately is passed to the __except block. The string "Never got here" is not sent to cout.

Listing 12.7. Handling an access violation with an exception handler.

```
__try
{
    char *p = NULL;
    *p = 'A';
    cout << "Never got here" << endl;
}
__except( EXCEPTION_EXECUTE_HANDLER )
{
    cout << "Caught exception" << endl;
}
```

The value used with __except is an *exception filter* and is discussed in the next section.

Using Exception Filters

An *exception filter* indicates how your application will handle an exception; it can have one of three values:

■ **EXCEPTION_EXECUTE_HANDLER:** Indicates that the exception handler should pass control to the __except block, which takes responsibility for handling the exception. This symbol is equivalent to using the value 1.

■ **EXCEPTION_CONTINUE_SEARCH:** Indicates that the exception handler is not interested in handling the exception. The exception dispatcher should look further for an exception handler. This symbol is equivalent to using a value of 0.

■ **EXCEPTION_CONTINUE_EXECUTION:** Indicates that the exception handler will handle the exception, and execution should resume at the instruction following the instruction that generated the exception. This symbol is equivalent to using a value of –1.

> **CAUTION**
>
> Take extreme care with EXCEPTION_CONTINUE_EXECUTION as an exception filter. In practice, it often is impossible to predict exactly what is "next" after the instruction that generates an exception.
>
> Remember that Windows NT determines the next instruction, not the programming language you currently are using. Many assembly instructions may be generated for a single statement, particularly if you are using languages such as C++ or Visual Basic.

Handling Specific Exception Codes

One way to use exception handling is to just catch every possible exception raised in a particular function or even the entire application. It is much more likely, however, that you are interested in catching a few specific exceptions. If you are interested in specific exception code, you can use the GetExceptionCode function to retrieve the value of the current exception being handled, as shown in Listing 12.8.

Listing 12.8. Using GetExceptionCode to determine the current exception value.

```
__except( GetExceptionCode() == EXCEPTION_ACCESS_VIOLATION )
{
    cout << "Caught exception" << endl;
}
```

This example exception filter expression is TRUE for access violations. The exception filter expression evaluates TRUE as equal to EXCEPTION_EXECUTE_HANDLER.

The GetExceptionCode function can be called only from the exception filter expression, as shown in Listing 12.8, or from within the body of an exception handler. If you are interested in a set of exceptions, you can use a filter function, as shown in Listing 12.9.

Listing 12.9. An exception filter function that tests for access violations and divide-by-zero exceptions.

```
int ExceptionFilter( int nException )
{
    int nReturn;
    switch( nException )
    {
    case EXCEPTION_ACCESS_VIOLATION:
```

continues

Listing 12.9. continued

```
        nReturn = EXCEPTION_EXECUTE_HANDLER;
        break;

    case EXCEPTION_INT_DIVIDE_BY_ZERO:
        nReturn = EXCEPTION_EXECUTE_HANDLER;
        break;

    default:
        nReturn = EXCEPTION_CONTINUE_SEARCH;
    }
    return nReturn;
}
```

The exception filter function must be called from inside the exception filter, as shown in this code:

```
__except( ExceptionFilter(GetExceptionCode()) )
```

Understanding the Exception Record Information

In addition to the exception code, it is possible to determine a wide range of information about the exception currently being handled. You can use the GetExceptionInformation function to return all the information you could ever need about an exception.

You can call the GetExceptionInformation function only from within the exception filter expression. The return value from GetExceptionInformation is a pointer to an EXCEPTION_POINTERS structure. This value usually is passed to a filter function that returns a value to be used by the exception filter expression.

The EXCEPTION_POINTERS structure contains two pointers:

■ **ExceptionRecord:** A pointer to an EXCEPTION_RECORD structure. This structure contains information about the exception currently being handled.

■ **ContextRecord:** A pointer to a CONTEXT structure, which contains information about the CPU state. This structure is dependent on the CPU. Intel and PowerPC CPUs, for example, generate CONTEXT structures with different semantics.

In practice, the CONTEXT structure rarely is used. It is so processor-dependent that using it requires an in-depth knowledge of the CPU on which your application actually is running. If you need to know the contents of a particular register or flag during an exception, for example, this information is available to you.

The EXCEPTION_RECORD structure has the following members:

■ **ExceptionCode:** Indicates the reason the exception occurred. Possible values for the exception code are discussed in the next section.

- **ExceptionFlags:** Indicates whether the exception is continuable. If this flag is 0, the exception is continuable. If this flag is `EXCEPTION_NONCONTINUABLE`, the exception cannot be continued. If you attempt to resume after a non-continuable exception, an `EXCEPTION_NONCONTINUABLE_EXCEPTION` is raised.

- **ExceptionRecord:** Points to another `EXCEPTION_RECORD` structure that is chained to this record. This typically is done in case of nested exceptions.

- **ExceptionAddress:** Indicates the address where the exception occurred.

- **NumberParameters:** Contains the number of elements in the `ExceptionInformation` array.

- **ExceptionInformation:** An array of 32-bit values that describe the exception. Only one exception from Windows NT uses this array. If the exception code is `EXCEPTION_ACCESS_VIOLATION`, the first element of the array indicates whether a read or write operation caused the exception. A value of 0 indicates a read, and a value of 1 indicates a write.

Using Exception Codes

The following list of exception codes can be raised by Windows NT while your application is executing:

- **`EXCEPTION_ACCESS_VIOLATION`:** Indicates that the thread attempted to read from or write to a virtual address without the appropriate access.

- **`EXCEPTION_BREAKPOINT`:** Indicates that a debugging breakpoint was encountered while executing the program. This exception is only useful to debuggers.

- **`EXCEPTION_DATATYPE_MISALIGNMENT`:** Raised when a thread attempts to read or write misaligned data. On some non-Intel processors, data must be properly aligned. For example, a long integer may be required to be aligned on an even address boundary. Because Windows NT automatically fixes alignment errors for you (at a large performance cost), you won't see this exception.

- **`EXCEPTION_SINGLE_STEP`:** Indicates that a trace trap or other single-instruction mechanism signaled that one instruction was executed.

- **`EXCEPTION_ARRAY_BOUNDS_EXCEEDED`:** Thrown when a thread attempts to access an array element that is out of bounds when using hardware that supports bounds checking.

- **`EXCEPTION_FLT_DENORMAL_OPERAND`:** Indicates that one of the operands in a floating-point operation is too small to represent as a standard floating-point value.

- **`EXCEPTION_FLT_DIVIDE_BY_ZERO`:** Indicates that the thread attempted to divide a floating-point value by a floating-point divisor of zero.

■ **EXCEPTION_FLT_INEXACT_RESULT:** Indicates that the result of a floating-point operation cannot be represented exactly as a decimal fraction.

■ **EXCEPTION_FLT_INVALID_OPERATION:** Indicates that a floating-point exception (other than the types listed here) has occurred.

■ **EXCEPTION_FLT_OVERFLOW:** Indicates that the exponent of a floating-point operation is greater than the magnitude allowed by the corresponding type.

■ **EXCEPTION_FLT_STACK_CHECK:** Indicates that the stack overflowed or underflowed due to a floating-point operation.

■ **EXCEPTION_FLT_UNDERFLOW:** Indicates that the exponent of a floating-point operation is less than the magnitude allowed by the corresponding type.

■ **EXCEPTION_INT_DIVIDE_BY_ZERO:** Indicates that the thread attempted to divide an integer value by 0.

■ **EXCEPTION_INT_OVERFLOW:** Indicates that the result of an integer operation caused an overflow in the result register. The processor's "carry flag" will contain the most significant bit of the result.

■ **EXCEPTION_PRIV_INSTRUCTION:** Indicates that the thread attempted to execute an instruction for which the operation is not allowed in the current machine mode.

■ **EXCEPTION_NONCONTINUABLE_EXCEPTION:** Indicates that the thread attempted to continue execution after a non-continuable exception occurred.

Handling Floating-Point Exceptions

By default, floating-point exceptions are not raised. Instead, predefined error values such as NAN and INFINITY are returned when error cases are detected. To enable floating-point exceptions, you must use the _controlfp function. The following code, for example, enables EXCEPTION_FLT_DIVIDE_BY_ZERO exceptions:

```
int n = _controlfp(0,0);
n &= ~EM_ZERODIVIDE;
_controlfp( n, MCW_EM );
```

Table 12.1 lists the five flags for enabling floating-point exceptions.

Table 12.1. Flags used to enable floating-point exceptions.

Flag	Enables
EM_OVERFLOW	EXCEPTION_FLT_OVERFLOW
EM_UNDERFLOW	EXCEPTION_FLT_UNDERFLOW
EM_INEXACT	EXCEPTION_FLT_INEXACT_RESULT
EM_ZERODIVIDE	EXCEPTION_FLT_DIVIDE_BY_ZERO
EM_DENORMAL	EXCEPTION_FLT_DENORMAL_OPERAND

To use more than one of these flags, you can combine them using the | operator.

When a floating-point exception is caught, you must use the _clearfp function to clear the floating-point exception flag. You must clear this flag before you perform any additional floating-point calculations. Listing 12.10 shows an example of enabling and handling floating-point exceptions.

Listing 12.10. Enabling and handling floating-point exceptions.

```
double CalcAverageRate( double* pdTotal, double* pdTime )
{
    double dResult;

    int n = _controlfp(0,0);
    n &= ~EM_ZERODIVIDE;
    _controlfp( n, MCW_EM );

    __try
    {
        dResult = *pdTotal / *pdTime;
    }
    __except( EXCEPTION_EXECUTE_HANDLER )
    {
        dResult = 0.0;
        _clearfp();
    }
    return dResult;
}
```

C++ Exception Handling

So far, this chapter has focused on the structured exception handling offered in Windows NT. If you are using C++ to write your applications, you also can take advantage of the exception-handling capabilities that are part of the C++ language specification.

In this section, you'll learn about using C++ exception handling, as well as how you can integrate C++ exception handling with the Windows NT SEH.

Using Exceptions to Detect Errors

The general idea behind C++ exception handling is similar to that of structured exception handling: A section of code that fails can throw, or raise, an exception that can be caught by an exception handler. The simplest example is when an exception is handled within a single function, as Listing 12.11 shows.

Listing 12.11. Throwing and catching a C++ exception inside a single function.

```cpp
int Divide( int n1, int n2 )
{
    int nReturn = 0;
    try
    {
        if( !n2 ) throw range_error();
        nReturn = n1/n2;
    }
    catch( range_error& e )
    {
        cout << "Caught divide by zero attempt" << endl;
    }
    return nReturn;
}
```

The try keyword marks the beginning of a try block. Inside a try block, any exceptions that are thrown are handled by exception handlers that follow the try block. An exception handler specifies the exceptions that it handles by using the catch keyword. A single try block may throw several types of exceptions, as Listing 12.12 shows.

Listing 12.12. Throwing multiple exceptions from a single try block.

```cpp
try
{
    if( nIndex < 0 )
        throw range_error();
    else if( nIndex >= m_cbText )
        throw range_error();
    else if( check_lock( nIndex ) == CL_LOCKED )
        throw "Element is locked";

    .
    . Normal processing
    .
}
catch( const char* psz )
{
    cout << *pszErr << endl;
}
catch( logic_error& e )
{
    cout << e.what() << endl;
}
```

In Listing 12.12, a pointer to char is thrown to the exception handler. The result of the throw expression is used to evaluate which catch clause should be used to resume processing.

> **NOTE**
>
> The ANSI C++ Draft Standard specifies a standard exception-handling library. This library is not included with Visual C++. I have included an exception library on the CD-ROM included with this book, however, that conforms to the latest draft.

Usually, a function throws exceptions intended to be caught by the calling function. If no suitable `catch` expression can be found in the calling function, the next higher-level function is checked for a `try` block and a suitable exception handler. If no exception handler can be found, a special, high-level function named `terminate` is called. This function usually terminates the program.

A `catch` expression matches the thrown exception if it is an exact match for the thrown object. The standard conversions also are allowed; for example, a pointer to a base class catches a pointer to a derived class. A `catch` expression that contains an ellipse (...) catches all exceptions. The block of code following a `catch` expression is called a `catch` block and must be enclosed in curly braces.

Using Exceptions to Clean Up After Errors Are Detected

When an exception is thrown, any objects that have been constructed are guaranteed to be destroyed properly. This is one of the big benefits of using exception handling, because it ensures that your program cleans up properly, even in error conditions.

Using the Standard Exception Library

The *Standard Exception Library* is part of the ANSI C++ Draft Standard. It defines a hierarchy of exception types that can be thrown to indicate an exception condition. The only mandatory exception is `bad_alloc`, which is thrown to indicate a failed request for memory allocation. The ANSI draft requires a conforming implementation to throw `bad_alloc` instead of returning 0 for the allocation request. Unfortunately, at the time of this writing, the current version of the Microsoft C++ compiler (4.1) does not properly implement this behavior.

Other than `bad_alloc`, there is no requirement that these exception types be used; as shown in earlier examples, any type of object can be thrown as an exception. A standard set of exceptions helps to provide an easy way to handle exceptions thrown by code written by others, however. Figure 12.2 shows the ANSI C++ exception hierarchy.

FIGURE 12.2.
*The ANSI C++ Standard
Exception Library.*

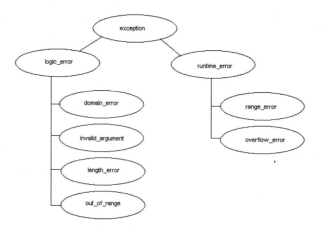

The standard exception hierarchy is divided into two sections:

- **Runtime errors:** Indicate problems that are not possible to predict—for example, lack of memory or hardware failure.

- **Logic errors:** Indicate a problem with function processing, such as illegal function parameter values or other preconditions.

Using Runtime Exceptions

Runtime exceptions usually are used to indicate problems that have occurred outside of the program's control. Problems with hardware, lack of memory, or other resources are examples of runtime errors. These problems generally are difficult, if not impossible, to predict when the program is compiled.

When a runtime error is encountered, it often is possible to take some sort of alternative action without terminating the current process. If memory cannot be allocated, it may be possible to process an operation differently. Likewise, if a disk is full, you might want to ask the user to take some action and then try the operation again.

All runtime exception classes included in the Standard Exception Library are derived from `runtime_error`. Any runtime exception can be caught by specifying `runtime_error` in the catch expression, as shown in Listing 12.13.

Listing 12.13. Throwing and catching a `runtime_error` exception.

```
void SomeFunc()
{
    try
    {
        TCHAR szDest[] = TEXT("Hello");
        TCHAR szSrc[] = TEXT("World");
```

```
        Concatenate( szDest, sizeof(szDest), szSrc );
    }
    catch( runtime_error e )
    {
        cout << e.what() << endl;
    }
}

void Concatenate( TCHAR szDest[], int nSize, TCHAR szSrc[] )
{
    int nStrlen = lstrlen( szSrc ) + lstrlen( szDest );
    if( nStrlen < nSize )
        lstrcat( szDest, szSrc );
    else
        throw range_error( "Concatenate:Destination too small" );
}
```

Using Logic Exceptions

Logic exceptions normally are used to indicate a problem in the coding or logic used in the program. A parameter that is out of range is a logic error, for example. Logic errors are difficult to recover from because they often result from a misunderstanding about how a particular object or function is meant to be used.

All logic error exception classes included in the Standard Exception Library are derived from the `logic_error` class. Four classes are used to throw logic error exceptions:

- **domain_error:** Indicates an internal processing error.
- **invalid_argument:** Indicates that a faulty parameter argument has been detected.
- **length_error:** Indicates an attempt to create or use an object of illegal size.
- **out_of_range:** Indicates that a parameter is out of range.

Any logic error exception can be handled by specifying `logic_error` in the `catch` expression, as Listing 12.14 shows.

Listing 12.14. Throwing and catching `logic_error` exceptions.

```
void SomeFunc()
{
    try
    {
        CMySafeArray    ar;
        int nVal = ar[5];
    }
    catch( logic_error e )
    {
```

continues

Listing 12.14. continued

```
        cout << e.what() << endl;
    }
}

int CMySafeArray::operator[](int nIndex)
{
    if( nIndex < 0 )
        throw domain_error( "Negative index" );
    else
        return m_nData[nIndex];
}
```

Detecting Errors During Construction

As discussed earlier, one of the reasons exceptions were added to the C++ language was to handle errors that occur inside constructors. Because a constructor does not have a return value, there are only two ways to handle errors during construction if exceptions are not used:

- Using *two-stage construction*, in which only "safe" operations that cannot fail are performed during construction. A separate Create or Init function then is used to complete construction of the object.

- Using a *test function* that returns an error code if construction failed.

Each of these methods has drawbacks. Two-stage construction results in code that is difficult to read and write. One of the advantages of using constructors is that initialization is done automatically inside the constructor. When two-stage construction is used, this benefit is reduced. Also, two-stage construction cannot be used for copy constructors and doesn't work well with assignment operators, so those operations must be handled in other ways.

The primary difficulty with using a function to determine whether construction was successful is that a great deal of extra source code must be added. There is also a problem using copy constructors and assignment operators, because it might not always be obvious when a test function should be called.

Exception handling is easier to use than either of these methods. As shown in the Console Mode program in Listing 12.15, the try block should enclose all objects that might throw exceptions when they are constructed.

Listing 12.15. Throwing and catching errors during construction.

```
CSafeArray::CSafeArray( int nArraySize )
{
    try
    {
        m_nData = new int[nArraySize];
```

```
        m_pLogger = new CLog;
    }
    catch(...)
    {
        cout << "Error constructing CSafeArray" << endl;
        throw;
    }
}
```

Using `throw` with no argument inside a `catch` block re-throws the currently executing exception, just as if it had not been handled. This allows the expression to be caught and handled by an enclosing set of `try` and `catch` blocks.

Integrating Win32 SEH with C++ Exception Handling

Using C++ exceptions and structured exception handling together requires a small amount of planning on your part. The basic problems with mixing these two exception-handling mechanisms follow:

- Using SEH can cause an object's destructor to be bypassed.
- Failing to handle SEH exceptions makes your application less robust.
- Many ANSI standard library functions throw C++ exceptions when they fail. If your compiler doesn't support this yet, it will—it's part of the standard.

Fortunately, there is a way to integrate SEH with C++ exceptions. Windows NT provides the `_set_se_translator` function, which enables you to define a function that translates SEH exceptions into C++ exceptions. The new translation function must use an unsigned `int` and a pointer to an `EXCEPTION_POINTERS` structure as parameters:

```
void new_xlation_func( unsigned int nCode,
                       EXCEPTION_POINTERS* pEx );
```

These values are used exactly as if they were returned from `GetExceptionCode` and `GetExceptionInformation`.

The `_set_se_translator` function takes one parameter: the address of the new translation function:

```
_se_translator_function  fnOld;
fnOld = _set_se_translator( nex_xlation_func );
```

The return value from `_set_se_translator` is the address of the current translation function, if any. You should restore the previous value when exiting your exception-handling code.

Inside the translation function, you can throw a C++ exception, using information about the structured exception that has been raised. You simply can throw a char string or any of the Standard Exception Library exception objects.

Listing 12.16 contains the source code for the CWin32Except class, which I use when translating a structured exception into a C++ exception.

Listing 12.16. The CWin32Except class.

```
#include <eh.h>
class CWin32Except
{
    unsigned int m_nCode;
public:
    CWin32Except( unsigned int nCode ) : m_nCode(nCode) {};
    unsigned int Code() const { return m_nCode; };
};
```

Listing 12.17 shows an example of using this code in a console-mode program. First, a translation function is defined that throws a CWin32Except object. When an SEH exception is sent to this function, the exception code is stored in the CWin32Except object and is caught by a catch expression that specifies a CWin32Except object.

Listing 12.17. Using the CWin32Except class to handle structured exceptions.

```
#include <iostream.h>
#include <windows.h>
#include "w32ex.h"

void SEH_TransFunc( unsigned int nCode, EXCEPTION_POINTERS* pExp )
{
    throw CWin32Except( nCode );
}

void DoAccessViolation()
{
    int* p = 0;
    *p = 42;
}

void main( void )
{
    // Set the translation function, and save
    // the previous function address as fnOld.
    _se_translator_function  fnOld;
    fnOld = _set_se_translator( SEH_TransFunc );
    try
    {
        DoAccessViolation();
    }
    catch( CWin32Except& e )
    {
```

```
        cout.flags( ios::hex );
        cout << "Caught a __try exception with CWin32Except." << endl;
        cout << "Exception number " << e.Code() << endl;
    }
    // Restore the previous translation function
    _set_se_translator( fnOld );
}
```

Before any code in the main function starts executing, the translation function is enabled using the _set_se_translation function. When the access violation occurs, it is translated into a C++ exception and is caught and handled in the program.

Summary

In this chapter, you learned how you can use exception handling to improve the readability and robustness of programs written for Windows NT. This chapter also discussed using Windows NT structured exception handling to create termination and exception handlers, as well as the exception handling built into the C++ language. The Standard Exception Library included in the ANSI Draft C++ Standard also was discussed.

In the next chapter, "Windows NT Virtual Memory and Memory Management," you learn how Windows NT manages the virtual memory space. You also learn about Win32 heap management and how you can write C++ classes that take advantage of advanced memory-handling techniques.

Windows NT Virtual Memory and Memory Management

13

by Mickey Williams

IN THIS CHAPTER

This chapter discusses memory management functions offered by Windows NT. You learn about the virtual memory management functions, which enable you to directly manage virtual memory addresses. You also see an example program that illustrates how virtual memory is used; this is provided on the accompanying CD-ROM.

You also learn about the Windows NT *heap memory API*, a set of functions that provide higher-level management of virtual memory in Windows NT. You see an example of using the heap API to manage memory privately in C++ classes as well.

Using Virtual Memory

Virtual memory enables you to allocate and use a much larger range of memory addresses than you have available on your computer. Windows NT makes extensive use of virtual memory; every application behaves as though it is running in a 4GB address space, regardless of how much RAM actually is installed on the computer.

The 4GB address space is divided into two sections: The upper 2GB are used by the operating system, and the lower 2GB are available to the application, as shown in Figure 13.1.

FIGURE 13.1.

The Windows NT address space.

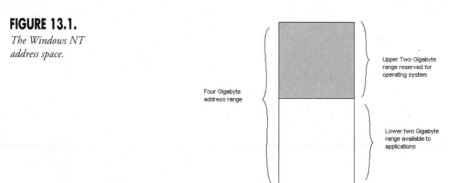

Four Gigabyte address range

Upper Two Gigabyte range reserved for operating system

Lower two Gigabyte range available to applications

Obviously, the 4GB range of virtual memory address is not directly mapped to actual memory hardware. Instead, a Windows NT application works with virtual addresses, which can be moved to different physical locations in memory or out to page file storage on the hard disk.

Windows NT deals with virtual memory in pages. Each page is a fixed size, which can be determined by calling the `GetSystemInfo` function. The `GetSystemInfo` function fills a `SYSTEM_INFO` structure; the `dwPageSize` member will contain the virtual memory page size, as shown in this code:

```
SYSTEM_INFO inf;
GetSystemInfo( &inf );
cout << "Page size = " << inf.dwPageSize << endl;
```

Deciding When to Use Virtual Memory

Virtual memory is ideal in situations in which you're not sure how much memory will be used. If you implement a private heap, as discussed earlier in this chapter, you actually allocate memory from Windows NT. With virtual memory, you can reserve a large range of addresses and only allocate, or commit, the pages you actually use.

Virtual memory also is useful when implementing a sparse memory data structure. A sparse memory scheme reserves a large range of virtual memory and uses only a few pages at a time. This is an easy way to implement grid- or spreadsheet-based applications because you can reserve a large virtual address range that represents the entire grid and commit only the pages that represent cells that actually are used, as shown in Figure 13.2.

FIGURE 13.2.

Sparse memory allocation in a spreadsheet.

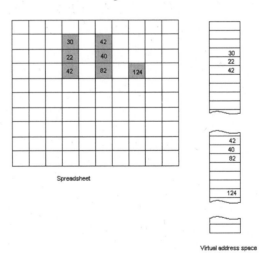

Figure 13.2 shows a typical sparse memory data structure used to implement a spreadsheet. When a grid initially is used, the page used by that grid is committed. Until a page is committed, no memory actually is allocated by Windows NT.

If you have programmed for 16-bit Windows, you might be familiar with the older heap-management functions. These functions still are supported in 32-bit versions of Windows, but their use is discouraged. When programming under Windows NT, you use Win32 heap API functions to manage the heap. These functions are discussed in the next few sections.

Reserving a Range of Virtual Memory

The first step in using virtual memory in your Windows NT application is to allocate a range of addresses. The VirtualAlloc function returns a pointer to the base of a range of virtual memory that has been reserved for your application:

```
pMem = VirtualAlloc(NULL, cAllocSize, MEM_RESERVE, PAGE_NOACCESS);
```

The first parameter passed to VirtualAlloc is the base address of the virtual memory range. That's right—in Windows NT, you actually can specify the virtual memory address that the system should return to you. If Windows NT cannot allocate memory at that address, NULL is returned. In most cases, you pass NULL as the base address, which enables Windows NT to select an address for you.

The second parameter passed to VirtualAlloc is the size of the requested memory reservation. In most cases, you should ask for as much memory as you are likely to use. The time required for reserving a large number of pages doesn't vary in relation to the amount of memory requested; there's no advantage to being thrifty here.

The MEM_RESERVE flag is passed as the third parameter to VirtualAlloc. MEM_RESERVE is one of three memory-allocation flags you can use with VirtualAlloc, and is used to reserve memory using VirtualAlloc. The other two flags follow:

- **MEM_COMMIT:** Commits a range of virtual memory. If combined with MEM_RESERVE, the virtual memory range is reserved and then committed during the same function call.
- **MEM_TOP_DOWN:** Specifies that the virtual memory should be allocated from the top of the virtual memory address range. You can combine this flag with the MEM_TOP_DOWN and MEM_RESERVE flags.

The fourth parameter is the page-access flag, which enables you to set the access permission for virtual memory pages. There are seven page-access flags:

- **PAGE_READONLY:** Allows read access to the committed region of pages. An attempt to write to the committed region results in an access violation.
- **PAGE_READWRITE:** Allows both read and write access to the committed region of pages.
- **PAGE_EXECUTE:** Allows execute access to the committed region of pages for systems that differentiate between read and execute access. An attempt to read or write to the committed region results in an access violation.

- **PAGE_EXECUTE_READ:** Allows both execute and read access to the committed region of pages. An attempt to write to the committed region results in an access violation.

- **PAGE_EXECUTE_READWRITE:** Allows execute, read, and write access to the committed region of pages.

- **PAGE_GUARD:** Specifies that pages in the region are guard pages. A guard page can be used as a boundary page when using virtual memory. An exception is raised when a page with this attribute is initially accessed. Using guard pages is discussed later in this chapter, in the section *Using Guard Pages.*

- **PAGE_NOCACHE:** Specifies that no caching of the committed regions of virtual memory is allowed. This generally is used only when writing device drivers.

The page-access flags only apply after a page is committed. If a page is free or reserved, any attempt at access causes an access violation exception to be raised.

Committing a Page of Virtual Memory

After you reserve a range of the virtual memory address space, you must commit it before you actually can use it. You must commit virtual memory in one-page chunks; if you need only part of a page, the entire page is committed. To commit a page of virtual memory, use the `VirtualAlloc` function with the `MEM_COMMIT` flag:

```
pv = VirtualAlloc( pMem, cPageSize, MEM_COMMIT, PAGE_READWRITE );
```

In this code, the `PAGE_READWRITE` flag indicates that the page is now both readable and write-enabled. It also is possible to use the `PAGE_NOACCESS` flag to prevent the page from being written to or used. If you use this flag, you must change the access rights for the page before using it.

The idea behind reserving a range of virtual memory addresses and committing them as needed is simple enough, but deciding on a mechanism for committing new pages is difficult. You can commit new pages in one of three ways:

- Keep track of the number of allocated pages manually and increase the allocation when needed. This involves a lot of bookkeeping because you need to remember how you have committed objects into the committed virtual memory space. This approach adds processing costs to every virtual memory access.

- Use guard pages as boundary markers in your virtual memory, and commit more pages when a guard page is touched and a structured exception is raised. This approach works well for some types of applications and is discussed later in *Using Guard Pages.*

- Use Windows NT structured exception handling to help determine which pages should be committed. Write your code so that all your pages are assumed to be committed, and catch access exceptions. Inside the access exception handler, commit the page and repeat whatever access was made on the page.

The fastest methods I have found for committing pages involve using structured exception handling; these are discussed in the next two sections.

Using Exceptions

A simple approach to using structured exceptions is very useful when using sparse memory schemes. The basic idea is to attempt to write to a page, and if an access violation exception is thrown, to commit the page and write to the page again. Listing 13.1 shows an example of this.

Listing 13.1. Allocating virtual memory as needed using structured exceptions.

```
__try
{
    g_ptrGridArray[nGridIndex] = pGrid;
}
__except( GetExceptionCode() == EXCEPTION_ACCESS_VIOLATION )
{
    VirtualAlloc( g_rgGridArray + nGridIndex * sizeof(CGridItem*),
                  sizeof(CGridItem),
                  MEM_COMMIT,
                  PAGE_READWRITE );
    g_ptrGridArray[nGridIndex] = pGrid;
}
```

In Listing 13.1, a pointer to a CGridItem object is stored in the g_ptrGridArray array. If the requested page has not been committed, Windows NT generates an EXCEPTION_ACCESS_VIOLATION exception. The exception handler commits the page and stores a pointer to the object on the new page. This approach is very fast because it doesn't require you to track the currently committed pages.

Using Guard Pages

Another approach to committing pages in virtual memory is useful when the memory is used from the "bottom up." This type of allocation model can take advantage of virtual memory *guard pages*, which generate exceptions when they are used. Figure 13.3 shows an example of virtual memory using guard pages.

FIGURE 13.3.

Virtual memory using guard pages.

In Figure 13.3, (a) shows a new virtual memory area with two pages committed, one of which is a guard page. Storage is used from the bottom of the committed address space as shown in (b), and when the first access is made on the guard page in (c), an EXCEPTION_GUARD_PAGE exception is raised by Windows NT. At this point, your application has two choices:

■ Allocate additional pages.

■ Stop using virtual memory before the storage on the guard page is exhausted.

The EXCEPTION_GUARD_PAGE exception is raised only for the first access made to a guard page. After the exception is raised, no more exceptions are raised for that page, no matter how many times it is accessed. Listing 13.2 shows an example of using guard pages.

Listing 13.2. Using guard pages to efficiently commit virtual memory.

```
#include <iostream.h>
#include <windows.h>
#include <limits.h>

char* g_rgChar = NULL;
const int nAllocLimit = 0x100000;
int main()
{
    cout.flags(ios::hex);
    SYSTEM_INFO  inf;
    GetSystemInfo( &inf );

    g_rgChar = (char*)VirtualAlloc( NULL,
                                    nAllocLimit,
                                    MEM_RESERVE,
                                    PAGE_READWRITE );
    cout << "Reserved range based at " << (void*)g_rgChar << endl;
    // Commit the first page in the virtual address space,
    // and mark it as a guard page.
    VirtualAlloc( g_rgChar,
                  inf.dwPageSize*1,
                  MEM_COMMIT,
                  PAGE_READWRITE ¦ PAGE_GUARD);
    int nPagesCommitted = 1;
    for( int nIndex = 0; nIndex < nAllocLimit; nIndex++ )
```

continues

Listing 13.2. continued

```
    {
        __try
        {
            g_rgChar[nIndex] = (nIndex%26)+'A';
        }
        __except( GetExceptionCode() == EXCEPTION_GUARD_PAGE )
        {
            // A guard page has been touched, commit a new one.
            g_rgChar[nIndex] = (nIndex%26)+'A';
            void* pvNewPage;
            pvNewPage = g_rgChar+nPagesCommitted*inf.dwPageSize;
            if( pvNewPage < g_rgChar + nAllocLimit )
            {
                void* pv = VirtualAlloc(pvNewPage,
                                        inf.dwPageSize,
                                        MEM_COMMIT,
                                        PAGE_READWRITE|PAGE_GUARD);
                cout << "Committed a new page at " << pv << endl;
                nPagesCommitted++;
            }
        }
    }
    VirtualFree( g_rgChar, nAllocLimit, MEM_RELEASE );
    return 0;
}
```

The Console Mode program in Listing 13.2 reserves 100KB of virtual address space and then commits one page at a time. Each page is committed as a guard page. The first time the guard page is accessed, an EXCEPTION_GUARD_PAGE exception is raised, and an additional guard page is committed.

Locking a Page of Virtual Memory

Normally, you should let the virtual memory management functions built into Windows NT determine which pages are loaded into RAM or swapped out to a page file. Sometimes it is necessary to guarantee that a page always is loaded in RAM for performance reasons, however. You can lock a page of virtual memory by using the VirtualLock function:

```
VirtualLock( pvPageAddr, inf.dwPageSize );
```

The VirtualLock function takes two parameters:

- The address that marks the beginning of the locked region of virtual memory.
- The number of bytes that should be locked.

The VirtualLock function affects your virtual memory in one-page chunks, but the values passed to VirtualLock can specify any address—not necessarily a page boundary.

Now that I've shown you how to shoot yourself in the foot, here are some things to remember:

- If you lock a range of virtual memory, you increase the chance that code will be swapped out. This causes total system performance to decrease in many cases.

- If you lock a large range of virtual memory, other applications are more likely to be swapped out, and total system performance decreases in many cases.

In the overwhelming majority of cases, the Virtual Memory Manager makes intelligent choices about which pages currently should be loaded. Unless you are writing device drivers or other time-critical software, the pain is probably not worth the gain.

Freeing a Page of Virtual Memory

Freeing sparse pages of virtual memory is quite a bit more difficult than efficiently committing memory. Fortunately, the virtual memory swapping algorithm used by Windows NT swaps out unused pages to the hard disk. Once swapped out, these pages are made active only when they are accessed. In almost all cases, this is sufficient for most applications. Typically, you can defer free virtual memory until the entire range no longer is needed and then use the VirtualFree function:

```
VirtualFree( pvAddr, dwSize, MEM_RELEASE );
```

The VirtualFree function is called with three parameters: the base address of the memory to be released, the size of the range to be released, and a release flag (in this case, MEM_RELEASE).

If you need to uncommit virtual memory, you can explicitly uncommit pages of virtual memory by using the VirtualFree function with the MEM_DECOMMIT flag:

```
VirtualFree( pvAddr, dwSize, MEM_DECOMMIT );
```

Virtual memory that has been uncommitted still is marked as reserved and is available to be committed.

Looking at an Example That Uses Virtual Memory

As an example of how the virtual memory functions can be used, I have created a sample project named VMGrid, which is located on the accompanying CD-ROM. You can compile and use the VMGrid project on the CD-ROM, or you can follow the steps outlined here. VMGrid uses an OLE custom grid control to display the status of a range of virtual memory.

To begin the VMGrid project, use AppWizard to create a dialog-based project named VMGrid. When asked by AppWizard, select the optional support for OLE controls.

Using Figure 13.4 as a guide, modify the main dialog box, IDD_VMGRID_DIALOG.

FIGURE 13.4.

The main dialog box from the VMGrid example.

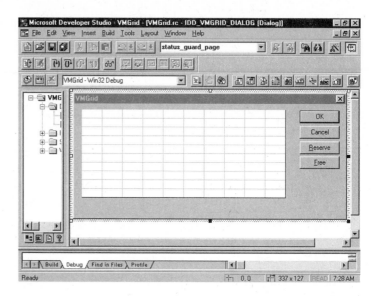

The dialog box has two additional pushbutton controls and one grid control from the Component Gallery. Use the values from Table 13.1 to assign resource IDs to the new controls.

Table 13.1. Control properties for VMGrid's main dialog box.

Control	Resource ID
Free pushbutton	IDC_FREE
Reserve pushbutton	IDC_RESERVE
Grid control	IDC_GRID

To add the OLE grid control to your project, follow these steps:

1. Select Component from the Insert menu. The Component Gallery dialog box is displayed.
2. Select the OLE Controls tab in Component Gallery. The Active controls registered on your computer are displayed.

3. Select the Grid Control icon, and click the Insert button. A Confirm Classes dialog box is displayed.

4. Click the OK button on the Confirm Classes dialog box. The OLE grid control is added to your project and inserted into the control palette displayed when editing a dialog box resource.

5. Close Component Gallery by clicking the Close button.

To add a grid control to the dialog box resource, just drag it from the control palette and drop it on the dialog box just like any other control. Use the values from Table 13.2 to set the properties for the Grid control. All properties not listed should be set to their default values.

Table 13.2. Properties for the Grid control used in VMGrid.

Property	Value
Rows	10
Cols	10
FixedRows	0
FixedCols	0
BorderStyle	0
ScrollBars	0
Highlight	Cleared

Next, associate CVMGridDlg member variables with the controls added to the main dialog box using ClassWizard and the values listed in Table 13.3.

Table 13.3. Values used to add member variables for CVMGridDlg.

Control ID	Variable Name	Category	Type
IDC_FREE	m_btnFree	Control	CButton
IDC_RESERVE	m_btnReserve	Control	CButton
IDC_GRID	m_grid	Control	CGridCtrl

Add message-handling functions for the IDC_GRID, IDC_FREE, and IDC_RESERVE controls using ClassWizard and the values listed in Table 13.4.

Table 13.4. Adding message-handling functions for the main dialog box.

Object ID	Message	Class	Function
IDC_GRID	MouseDown	CVMGridDlg	OnMouseDownGrid
IDC_FREE	BN_CLICKED	CVMGridDlg	OnFree
IDC_RESERVE	BM_CLICKED	CVMGridDlg	OnReserve

A CGridItem structure is used to represent 1KB chunks of virtual memory used by VMGrid. Add the class definition provided in Listing 13.3 to the VMGridDlg.cpp file before any CVMGridDlg class member functions.

Listing 13.3 The CGridItem structure used by VMGrid.

```
struct CGridItem
{
    char m_chData[1024];
};
```

The VMGrid application uses VirtualAlloc to reserve a 100KB range of addresses when it is initialized. Add the source code shown in bold in Listing 13.4 to the CVMGrid::OnInitDialog function.

Listing 13.4. Changes made to the CVMGridDlg::OnInitDialog function.

```
BOOL CVMGridDlg::OnInitDialog()
{
    CDialog::OnInitDialog();

...

    // TODO: Add extra initialization here
    m_pVirtualAlloc = (char*)VirtualAlloc( NULL,
                                   100 * sizeof(CGridItem),
                                   MEM_RESERVE,
                                   PAGE_NOACCESS );
    ASSERT( m_pVirtualAlloc );
    m_btnReserve.EnableWindow(FALSE);
    UpdateGrid();
    return TRUE;
}
```

After the Free button is clicked, all the virtual memory is released by the VMGrid application through the VirtualFree function. After the Reserve button is clicked, the 100KB range of virtual memory addresses is reserved, just as in OnInitDialog. Listing 13.5 shows the source code for the OnFree and OnReserve functions.

Listing 13.5. Reserving and freeing virtual memory in VMGrid.

```
void CVMGridDlg::OnReserve()
{
    ASSERT( m_pVirtualAlloc == NULL );
    if( m_pVirtualAlloc == NULL )
    {
        m_pVirtualAlloc = (char*)VirtualAlloc(NULL,
                                    100 * sizeof(CGridItem),
                                    MEM_RESERVE,
                                    PAGE_NOACCESS);
        ASSERT( m_pVirtualAlloc );
        m_btnFree.EnableWindow();
        m_btnReserve.EnableWindow(FALSE);
        UpdateGrid();
    }
}

void CVMGridDlg::OnFree()
{
    ASSERT( m_pVirtualAlloc != NULL );
    if( m_pVirtualAlloc != NULL )
    {
        VirtualFree( m_pVirtualAlloc, 0, MEM_RELEASE );
        m_pVirtualAlloc = NULL;
        m_btnFree.EnableWindow(FALSE);
        m_btnReserve.EnableWindow();
        UpdateGrid();
    }
}
```

After a range of virtual memory is reserved, the user can commit a page of virtual memory by clicking on a grid cell. Each cell represents a 1KB chunk of virtual memory. Because virtual memory is managed in pages, clicking on an uncommitted cell results in several cells being committed. Listing 13.6 shows the source code that handles mouse clicks reported from the Grid control.

Listing 13.6. Handling mouse clicks in the Grid control.

```
void CVMGridDlg::OnMouseDownGrid(short Button, short Shift, long X, long Y)
{
    if( m_pVirtualAlloc != NULL )
    {
        int nIndex = m_grid.GetRow() * 10 + m_grid.GetCol();
        CommitAt( nIndex );
        UpdateGrid();
    }
}
```

Two new member functions for the `CVMGridDlg` class must be added manually:

- **CommitAt:** Copies a string to a section of virtual memory, committing the page if needed.
- **UpdateGrid:** Runs through the virtual address space reserved by VMGrid and displays the status of the memory addresses represented by the grid.

Listing 13.7 contains the source code for these functions.

Listing 13.7. Memory-handling and reporting functions for the `CVMGridDlg` class.

```
void CVMGridDlg::CommitAt( int index )
{
    __try
    {
        // Try a simple access to test if the page is committed.
        char chTest = *(m_pVirtualAlloc + index*sizeof(CGridItem));
        // The page is committed, just do a string copy.
        lstrcpy( m_pVirtualAlloc + index*sizeof(CGridItem),
                 TEXT("Committed") );
    }
    __except( GetExceptionCode() == EXCEPTION_ACCESS_VIOLATION )
    {
        VirtualAlloc( m_pVirtualAlloc + index*sizeof(CGridItem),
                      sizeof(CGridItem),
                      MEM_COMMIT,
                      PAGE_READWRITE );
        lstrcpy( m_pVirtualAlloc + index*sizeof(CGridItem),
                 TEXT("Committed") );
    }

}

void CVMGridDlg::UpdateGrid()
{
    MEMORY_BASIC_INFORMATION    mbi;
    char* pAddr = m_pVirtualAlloc;

    do{
        int cQuery = VirtualQuery( pAddr, &mbi, sizeof(mbi) );
        if( cQuery != sizeof( MEMORY_BASIC_INFORMATION ) )
            break;
        // Change the status of the grid control.
        TCHAR    chMsg[10];
        switch( mbi.State )
        {
        case MEM_RESERVE:
            lstrcpy( chMsg, TEXT("Res") );
            break;
        case MEM_COMMIT:
            lstrcpy( chMsg, TEXT("Com") );
            break;
        case MEM_FREE:
            lstrcpy( chMsg, TEXT("Free") );
            break;
        default:
            lstrcpy( chMsg, TEXT("Unk") );
```

```
            break;
        }
        int nGridStart =
            ((char*)mbi.BaseAddress - m_pVirtualAlloc)/1024;
        int cGrids = mbi.RegionSize/sizeof(CGridItem);

        while( cGrids != 0 && nGridStart < 100 )
        {
            int nCol = nGridStart%10;
            int nRow = nGridStart/10;
            m_grid.SetRow( nRow );
            m_grid.SetCol( nCol );
            m_grid.SetText( chMsg );
            nGridStart++;
            cGrids--;
        }
        // Get the next Chunk O' RAM.
        pAddr = (char*)mbi.BaseAddress + mbi.RegionSize;
    } while( pAddr );
}
```

The `CommitAt` function provided in Listing 13.7 tries to access an address represented by a grid location clicked by a user. It first tries to access the first address represented by the cell; if the cell is not committed, an `EXCEPTION_ACCESS_VIOLATION` exception is raised. The exception handler first commits the page and then copies a string at the address.

The `UpdateGrid` function uses `VirtualQuery` to walk through the virtual address range used by VMGrid. Each call to `VirtualQuery` returns the status of a single block of virtual memory. This block may be as small as a page or as large as the entire range. `UpdateGrid` calculates the grid cell that represents each 1KB chunk of memory and labels the grid with the virtual memory status.

As the final step, add the `UpdateGrid` and `CommitAt` member functions to the `CVMGridDlg` class declaration. At the same time, declare a new member variable, `m_pVirtualAlloc`, which will serve as a pointer to the block of virtual memory used by VMGrid. These changes are shown in bold in Listing 13.8.

Listing 13.8. Modifications (in bold) to the `CVMGridDlg` class declaration.

```
class CVMGridDlg : public CDialog
{
        .
        .
        .
// Implementation
protected:
    HICON m_hIcon;
    void UpdateGrid();
    void CommitAt( int index );
    char* m_pVirtualAlloc;
        .
        .
        .
};
```

Compile and run the VMGrid application, and experiment by clicking on different cells in the Grid control. Each click commits one page's worth of cells in the grid. For Intel platforms, each click changes four cells. Figure 13.5 shows the VMGrid main dialog box after several cells have been clicked.

FIGURE 13.5.

The VMGrid application after several pages of virtual memory have been committed.

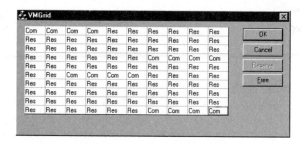

Using Windows NT Heap Functions

Unlike 16-bit versions of Windows, under Windows NT, there is no difference between the local and global heap. When accessing the heap, you always get access to the 2GB virtual address space maintained by Windows NT for your application. Although many of the heap-management functions available under 16-bit Windows also are available in Windows NT, you should use the newer heap API functions introduced specifically for Win32.

If your application allocates and frees small amounts of data, runs for a relatively short lifetime, or has only moderate demands on its performance, you will be very happy using the default memory allocation offered by your C or C++ compiler. The runtime libraries included with your compiler include memory suballocation schemes that effectively manage the heap in most cases.

These built-in memory-allocation schemes are created for general-purpose computing, however; you might have needs that aren't addressed by the default compiler libraries. You might constantly allocate and free small objects of different sizes, for example. This often causes heap fragmentation and poor performance using most default suballocation schemes. Using the heap-management API functions offered by Windows NT can help you solve this and many other memory-management problems.

Performing Heap Management Under Windows NT

Windows NT offers a set of memory functions that allow for a higher level of memory management than the virtual memory APIs, while still allowing for a great deal of control over heap-allocated memory. The Windows NT heap-management APIs include functions that create, manage, and destroy private heaps.

Every process has a default heap provided by the operating system. The handle to this heap can be retrieved via the GetProcessHeap function:

```
HANDLE hDefaultHeap = GetProcessHeap();
```

The only difference between this heap and a heap created dynamically is that this one is created for you based on link information embedded in your executable file. The default heap is used for C++ runtime library malloc and new allocations. You can use this default heap or create one or more dynamic heaps.

Creating a Heap

To create a dynamic heap, you use the HeapCreate function:

```
HANDLE hHeap = HeapCreate( HEAP_GENERATE_EXCEPTIONS,
                           0x01000,
                           0 );
```

The HeapCreate function has three parameters:

- Options for the dynamic heap. In this case, HEAP_GENERATE_EXCEPTIONS is used.
- The initial size for the heap, which is rounded up to the next page boundary. In this case, 4KB is allocated for the heap.
- The maximum size for the heap. In this case, 0 is used, which indicates that the heap is limited only by the amount of virtual memory that can be committed by Windows NT.

You can use two option flags when a dynamic heap is created:

- **HEAP_GENERATE_EXCEPTIONS:** Specifies that the heap should generate structured exceptions instead of returning NULL in error conditions.
- **HEAP_NO_SERIALIZE:** Specifies that the heap should not synchronize access. This flag should be used with care because unsynchronized access to a heap by multiple threads corrupts the heap. Use this flag only if you are sure that two threads will not attempt to manipulate the heap at the same time.

Allocating from a Heap

The HeapAlloc function is used to allocate memory from a heap. You can use this function with default or dynamic heaps because the first parameter is a heap handle that specifies the heap used to allocate the memory. HeapAlloc returns a pointer to the memory allocated from the heap, as shown in this code:

```
TCHAR pszName = HeapAlloc( hHeap,
                           HEAP_GENERATE_EXCEPTIONS,
                           cName );
```

The `HeapAlloc` function has three parameters:

- A handle to the heap that is servicing the allocation request.
- Optional flags used to specify how the memory is allocated. In this example, `HEAP_GENERATE_EXCEPTIONS` is used. Other values for this parameter follow.
- The size of the requested memory allocation.

Three heap-allocation flags are used for `HeapAlloc`:

- **HEAP_GENERATE_EXCEPTIONS:** Specifies that Windows NT should use exceptions to indicate error conditions instead of returning `NULL`.
- **HEAP_NO_SERIALIZE:** Indicates that the heap does not need to synchronize this call to the heap with other heap-management functions. This flag should be avoided unless you can guarantee that multiple threads will not access the heap at the same time.
- **HEAP_ZERO_MEMORY:** Tells the heap to initialize the contents of the allocated memory to 0.

As with `HeapCreate`, you can pass a value of 0 to indicate that no flags are used, or you can combine two or more flags if more than one option is needed.

Freeing Heap Memory

To release a block of memory allocated with `HeapAlloc`, use the `HeapFree` function. `HeapFree` takes only three parameters: the heap handle, an optional flag, and a pointer to the memory to be freed:

```
BOOL bFreed = HeapFree( hHeap, 0, pszName );
```

The second parameter passed to `HeapFree` can be 0, as in this example, or `HEAP_NO_SERIALIZE`. As in the previously discussed heap functions, you should use this flag only if you are certain that only one thread will attempt to manage the heap at any given time.

Using Private Heaps in C++ Classes

As an example of how you can use dynamic heaps to manage private memory heaps in C++ programs, I have created a Console Mode project named PrivHeap, which you can find on the CD-ROM included with this book. The PrivHeap application creates a simple linked list using C++ classes that manage their own private heaps so that the main application doesn't need to perform any memory management.

As shown in Figure 13.6, two classes are used to implement the linked list used by PrivHeap. The `CVMListNode` class is a *payload* class that is stored in the linked list. The `CVMList` class maintains a link to one `CVMListNode` object and a link to the next `CVMList` object in the list.

The `CVMList` and `CVMListNode` objects are different sizes. If you create a database that allocates and frees these objects at random for a long period of time, the heap becomes fragmented, as shown in Figure 13.7.

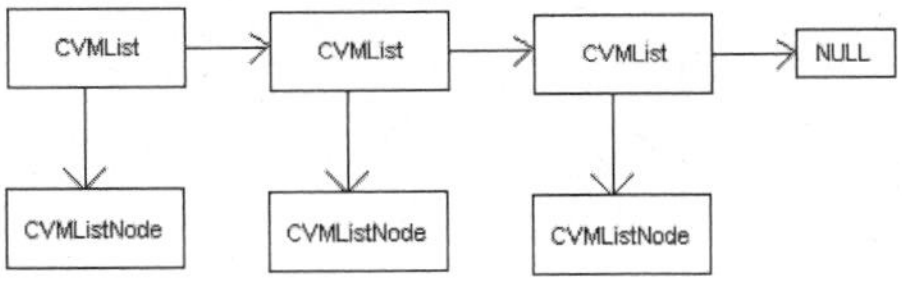

FIGURE 13.6.

The relationship between `CVMList` *and* `CVMListNode` *objects.*

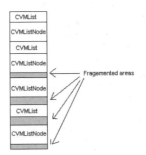

FIGURE 13.7.

Fragmentation of heap memory.

By allowing each class to manage a private dynamic heap in which the allocations are always the same size, fragmentation is avoided.

The C++ language allows a class to provide an implementation of the `new` operator, which allows a class to control how memory is allocated before the constructor is called. The classes used in PrivHeap include specialized versions of the `new` operator and follow this basic scheme:

- If a private heap is not created, create one and initialize a reference counter.
- Allocate the number of requested bytes from the heap.
- Increment the reference counter.

In addition, the C++ language allows a class to define how memory is released by implementing an `operator delete` function. The classes used in PrivHeap use the following method for `operator delete`:

- Release the requested memory block to the heap.
- Decrement the reference counter.
- If the reference counter is 0, destroy the heap.

Using the `CVMListNode` Class

The `CVMListNode` class is very simple and only stores one integer as its data; most of the work done by the class is concerned with memory management. Listing 13.9 shows the `CVMListNode` class declaration. You can find this class on the CD-ROM as listnode.h in the PrivHeap project directory.

Listing 13.9. The CVMListNode class declaration.

```
class CVMListNode
{
    int          m_n;
    static HANDLE  m_hHeap;
    static int     m_nRef;
public:
    CVMListNode() {};
    CVMListNode( int n ) : m_n(n) {};
    virtual ~CVMListNode() {};
    void* operator new( size_t s );
    void  operator delete( void* p );

    virtual int Get() const { return m_n; };
    virtual void Set( int n ){ m_n = n; };
};
```

Listing 13.10 provides the implementation of the CVMListNode class. This file is located on the accompanying CD-ROM as listnode.cpp in the project directory.

Listing 13.10. The implementation of the CVMListNode class.

```
#include <iostream.h>
#include <windows.h>
#include "listnode.h"

HANDLE CVMListNode::m_hHeap = NULL;
int    CVMListNode::m_nRef = 0;

void* CVMListNode::operator new( size_t size )
{
    void* p;
    if( m_hHeap == NULL )
    {
        SYSTEM_INFO inf;
        GetSystemInfo( &inf );
        m_hHeap = HeapCreate( 0, inf.dwAllocationGranularity ,0 );
        cout << "List Node: Private heap Allocated" << endl;
    }
    if( (p = HeapAlloc( m_hHeap, 0, size )) != NULL )
    {
        m_nRef++;
        cout << "List Node: Allocated "<< size <<" bytes" << endl;
    }
    return p;
}

void CVMListNode::operator delete( void* p )
{
```

```
    if( HeapFree( m_hHeap, 0, p ) != FALSE )
    {
        m_nRef--;
        cout << "List Node: Released one chunk" << endl;
    }
    if( m_nRef == 0 )
    {
        HeapDestroy( m_hHeap );
        m_hHeap = NULL;
        cout << "List Node: Heap destroyed" << endl;
    }
}
```

Listing 13.11 shows the implementation of the CVMList class. This file is located on the accompanying CD-ROM as list.cpp in the project directory.

Listing 13.11. The implementation of the CVMList class.

```
#include <iostream.h>
#include <windows.h>
#include "listnode.h"
#include "list.h"


HANDLE CVMList::m_hHeap = NULL;
int    CVMList::m_nRef = 0;

CVMList::CVMList():m_pNext(0)
{
    m_pNode = new CVMListNode(0);
}
CVMList::CVMList( int n ) : m_pNext(0)
{
    m_pNode = new CVMListNode(n);
}
CVMList::~CVMList()
{
    delete m_pNext;
    delete m_pNode;
}
CVMList* CVMList::Insert( int n )
{
    CVMList* pTemp = NULL;
    pTemp = new CVMList(n);
    if( m_pNext != NULL )
    {
        pTemp->m_pNext = m_pNext->m_pNext;
    }
    pTemp->m_pNext = m_pNext;
    m_pNext = pTemp;
    return pTemp;
}
void* CVMList::operator new( size_t size )
{
```

continues

Listing 13.11. continued

```
    void* p;
    if( m_hHeap == NULL )
    {
        SYSTEM_INFO inf;
        GetSystemInfo( &inf );
        m_hHeap = HeapCreate( 0, inf.dwAllocationGranularity ,0 );
        cout << "List: Private heap Allocated" << endl;
    }
    if( (p = HeapAlloc( m_hHeap, 0, size )) != NULL )
    {
        m_nRef++;
        cout << "List: Allocated "<< size << " bytes" << endl;
    }
    return p;
}

void CVMList::operator delete( void* p )
{
    if( HeapFree( m_hHeap, 0, p ) != FALSE )
    {
        m_nRef--;
        cout << "List: Released one chunk" << endl;
    }
    if( m_nRef == 0 )
    {
        HeapDestroy( m_hHeap );
        m_hHeap = NULL;
        cout << "List: Heap destroyed" << endl;
    }
}
```

Listing 13.12 shows the `main` function for the PrivHeap program; you can find this on the accompanying CD-ROM as main.cpp in the project directory.

Listing 13.12. The `main` function for PrivHeap.

```
#include <iostream.h>
#include <windows.h>
#include "listnode.h"
#include "list.h"

int main()
{
    CVMList    listHead;

    listHead.Insert(5);
    listHead.Insert(3);
    listHead.Insert(2);

    return 0;
}
```

In the main function, a CVMList object is created, and several items are added to the list. The first CVMList object is created on the stack frame, and all other CVMList and CVMListNode objects are created using private dynamic heaps.

Using the CVMList Class

The CVMList class is a simple linked list; again, most of the work done by the class is concerned with memory management. Listing 13.13 shows the CVMList class declaration. This class is included on the accompanying CD-ROM as list.h in the PrivHeap project directory.

Listing 13.13. The CVMList class declaration.

```
class CVMList
{
    CVMListNode*    m_pNode;
    CVMList*        m_pNext;
    static HANDLE   m_hHeap;
    static int      m_nRef;
public:
    int Get() { return m_pNode->Get(); }
    CVMList* Next() {return m_pNext;}
    void Set(int n) {m_pNode->Set(n);}

    CVMList();
    CVMList( int n );
    virtual ~CVMList();

    void* operator new( size_t s );
    void  operator delete( void* p );

    CVMList* Insert( int n );
};
```

Summary

In this chapter, you looked at the virtual memory management functions used when programming for Windows NT. You also examined an example showing how virtual memory is used to implement a sparse memory array in an application. You learned about the Windows NT heap-management API and how you can use it to create dynamic heaps in your applications. An example of using heaps to implement private memory management in C++ classes was presented in a small example.

In the next chapter, "Files," you learn about file-based input and output in Windows NT, including asynchronous I/O and file completion routines.

Files

14

by Mickey Williams

This chapter discusses how files are used in applications written for Windows NT. You will learn about the basics of file input and output, and then move on to more advanced topics, such as asynchronous file I/O and using file I/O completion routines. Along the way, I present two sample programs included on the CD-ROM with this book.

Using Windows NT File Systems

Windows NT 4 supports several types of file systems. Unlike some operating systems, each of these systems can be used on the same Windows NT installation. Unlike previous versions of Windows NT, the OS/2 High Performance File System (HPFS) no longer is supported. The file systems included with Windows NT 4 follow:

- **The File Allocation Table file system (FAT):** Included for backward compatibility with MS-DOS and Windows 95 files. It offers no security, has poor performance with large volumes, and minor errors can wipe out your entire volume.
- **The New Technology File System (NTFS):** Developed for Windows NT. It has excellent performance for large volumes. It also has excellent security and recovery functions.
- **The Compact Disk File System (CDFS):** Included to support CDs, which are used in most Windows NT installations. In fact, most development tools, including Visual C++, are delivered on CD-ROM.

Performing General File Operations

Windows NT has a rich set of functions used to interact with files. The most basic of these functions create, open, read, write, and delete files. The next few sections cover these functions and how they are used.

Opening, Closing, and Deleting Files

You open files by using the `CreateFile` function. You can use `CreateFile` to open existing files as well as new files. To open an existing file, you use the `OPEN_EXISTING` flag, as Listing 14.1 shows.

Listing 14.1. Using `CreateFile` to open an existing file.

```
TCHAR  szFile[255] = ("TestFile.txt");
HANDLE   hReadFile = CreateFile( szFile,
                                 GENERIC_READ,
                                 0,
                                 (LPSECURITY_ATTRIBUTES)NULL,
                                 OPEN_EXISTING,
                                 FILE_ATTRIBUTE_NORMAL,
                                 (HANDLE)NULL );
```

The return value from `CreateFile` is a file handle that identifies the created file.

> **NOTE**
>
> It is possible for a valid handle to have a value of 0, so you must test the returned handle against `INVALID_FILE_HANDLE`, rather than zero or `NULL`.

The parameters used by `CreateFile` specify the following:

- The name of the file—`TestFile.txt`, in the example in Listing 14.1.
- The read and write attributes for the file; in this case, the file is opened as read-only. Other values for this parameter are discussed later.
- The share-mode attributes for this file; in this case, 0 prevents any file sharing. Other values for this parameter are discussed later.
- The security descriptor for this access of the file. This parameter has no effect when used on file systems that don't support security, such as FAT or CDFS.
- A flag that states how the file should be opened—in this case, the call to `CreateFile` opens only existing files. Other values for this parameter are discussed later.
- A flag that specifies the file-level attributes for the file—in this case, `FILE_ATTRIBUTE_NORMAL`. Other values for this parameter are discussed later.
- An optional handle to a template file that specifies extended attributes for the file.

The parameter used to specify read and write permission can be one or more of these values:

- **`GENERIC_READ`:** Opens the file with read access
- **`GENERIC_WRITE`:** Opens the file with write access

If a value of 0 is used, the file is created or opened without read or write permission, and the file handle can be used to collect information about the file. Note that `GENERIC_WRITE` does not imply automatic read access. If you want both read and write access, you must specify `GENERIC_READ|GENERIC_WRITE`.

The share attributes for the file can be 0, indicating that file sharing is not allowed, or one or both of the following flags:

- **`FILE_SHARE_READ`:** Indicates that other read operations can be performed on the file.
- **`FILE_SHARE_WRITE`:** Indicates that other write operations can be performed on the file.

The most flexible of the `CreateFile` parameters are the flags that specify how the file will be created. Table 14.1 lists the possible values for this parameter.

Table 14.1. Parameters for `CreateFile`.

Parameter	Function
CREATE_ALWAYS	Creates a new file and overwrites the specified file if it exists.
CREATE_NEW	Creates a new file and fails if the specified file already exists.
OPEN_ALWAYS	Opens the file, creating it first if necessary.
OPEN_EXISTING	Opens the specified file and fails if it does not exist.
TRUNCATE_EXISTING	Opens the file and truncates its size to 0 bytes. The file must have been opened with write access.

The file attribute parameter can be a combination of one or more of the values shown in Table 14.2.

Table 14.2. File attribute parameters.

Parameter	Function
FILE_ATTRIBUTE_ARCHIVE	Indicates that the file is an archive file.
FILE_ATTRIBUTE_COMPRESSED	Indicates that the file or directory is compressed. If a file is created, the file will be compressed. If a directory is created, all files stored in it will be compressed by default.
FILE_ATTRIBUTE_HIDDEN	Creates a hidden file or directory.
FILE_ATTRIBUTE_NORMAL	Used when no other flags apply. This flag is ignored if it is combined with any other flags.
FILE_ATTRIBUTE_READONLY	Creates a read-only file.
FILE_ATTRIBUTE_SYSTEM	Marks a file as used by the operating system.
FILE_FLAG_BACKUP_SEMANTICS	Used during backups or restore operations. An application also can set this flag to obtain a handle to a directory, which can be passed to some Win32 functions in place of a file handle.
FILE_FLAG_DELETE_ON_CLOSE	Notifies the operating system that it must delete the file immediately after all its handles have been closed.

Parameter	Function
FILE_FLAG_NO_BUFFERING	Specifies that the file must be opened with no intermediate buffering or caching, which can improve performance. If this flag is used, you must access the file in multiples of the file's sector size. You can get the sector size used by a volume with the GetDiskFreeSpace function.
FILE_FLAG_OVERLAPPED	Indicates that ReadFile and WriteFile operations will use an OVERLAPPED structure, and asynchronous file I/O will be performed using this file. This topic is covered in detail later in this chapter.
FILE_FLAG_POSIX_SEMANTICS	Indicates that the file will be accessed according to POSIX rules, which include case-sensitivity on file systems that support case-sensitive naming. Files created with this flag may not be accessible by applications written for Windows NT.
FILE_FLAG_RANDOM_ACCESS	Indicates that the file will be accessed randomly. This flag gives Windows NT a chance to optimize file caching.
FILE_FLAG_SEQUENTIAL_SCAN	Indicates that the file is to be accessed sequentially from beginning to end. This flag gives Windows NT a chance to optimize file caching.
FILE_FLAG_WRITE_THROUGH	Indicates that the operating system must write through any intermediate cache and write directly to the file.

To close a file, use the CloseHandle function:

```
CloseHandle( hReadFile );
```

After all open handles for a file have been closed, you can delete the file using the DeleteFile function:

```
DeleteFile( "Foo.txt" );
```

Writing to Files

You use the WriteFile function to write to files. An example of using the WriteFile function follows:

```
WriteFile( hWriteFile, szBuff, dwRead, &dwWritten, NULL );
```

WriteFile has five parameters:

- The file handle to be written to
- The address of a buffer containing the data to be written
- The number of bytes to be written
- A pointer to a DWORD that will contain the number of bytes actually written after WriteFile returns
- An optional OVERLAPPED structure used for asynchronous write requests (this parameter is discussed later in this chapter)

In addition to WriteFile, Windows NT also offers the WriteFileEx function, which is used exclusively for asynchronous file output. The WriteFileEx function is discussed later in this chapter, in the section *Using File-Completion Routines*.

Reading From Files

You use the ReadFile function to read data from files. Listing 14.2 shows how to use the read file function.

Listing 14.2. Using ReadFile to read data from a file.

```
const int cBufferSize = 0x1000;
char szBuff[cBufferSize];
DWORD dwRead;
do{
    ReadFile( hReadFile, szBuff, cBufferSize, &dwRead, NULL );
    ...
    // use data from file here
    ...
}while( dwRead == cBufferSize );
```

ReadFile has five parameters:

- The file handle to be read from
- The address of a buffer that will receive the transferred data
- The maximum number of bytes to be read

- A pointer to a DWORD that will contain the number of bytes actually read after WriteFile returns

- An optional OVERLAPPED structure used for asynchronous read requests (this parameter is discussed later in this chapter)

In addition to ReadFile, Windows NT also offers the ReadFileEx function, which is used exclusively for asynchronous file output. The ReadFileEx function is discussed later in this chapter, in the section *Using File-Completion Routines.*

The Console Mode program in Listing 14.3 is an example of opening a file and reading its contents. After promoting a user for a path name, the file is opened, and its contents are displayed in the Console window.

Listing 14.3. Reading a file using ReadFile under Windows NT.

```c
#include <windows.h>
#include <iostream.h>
int main()
{
    // Get path name to file from user, and open
    // file as read-only.
    TCHAR szFile[MAX_PATH];
    cout << "File name:";
    cin.getline( szFile, sizeof(szFile) );
    HANDLE   hReadFile = CreateFile( szFile,
                                     GENERIC_READ,
                                     0,
                                     (LPSECURITY_ATTRIBUTES)NULL,
                                     OPEN_EXISTING,
                                     FILE_ATTRIBUTE_NORMAL,
                                     (HANDLE)NULL );
    if( hReadFile == INVALID_HANDLE_VALUE )
    {
        MessageBox( NULL,
                    TEXT("Can't Open File"),
                    TEXT("Console File"),
                    MB_ICONHAND );
        return 1;
    }
    // Read the file, one 4K chunk at a time, and display it
    // on the console.
    const int cBufferSize = 0x1000;
    char szBuff[cBufferSize+1];
    DWORD dwRead;
    do{
        ReadFile( hReadFile, szBuff, cBufferSize, &dwRead, NULL );
        szBuff[dwRead] = '\0';
        cout << szBuff;
    }while( dwRead == cBufferSize );
    ClseHandle( hReadFile );
    return 1;
}
```

Performing Other File Operations

Windows NT offers other file operations; the most commonly used are covered in this section. These include functions that copy files, set the current position of the file pointer, and get file size information.

Using `CopyFile`

You use the `CopyFile` function to copy the contents of a file from one location to another:

```
CopyFile( szSourcePath, szDestPath, TRUE );
```

`CopyFile` has three parameters:

- The path name of the existing file.
- The path name of the new file.
- A flag that indicates whether the function should fail if the destination already exists. If this flag is `FALSE`, the destination is overwritten. If this flag is `TRUE`, the function fails.

Using `MoveFile`

You use the `MoveFile` function to move a file from one location to another. You can rename a file using this function by specifying a new filename while keeping the same directory path:

```
MoveFile( szOldPath, szNewPath );
```

`MoveFile` takes two parameters:

- The current path name for the file to be moved
- The path name to the location the file is to be moved to

The `MoveFile` function fails if you attempt to move a file to a different volume.

Using `SetFilePointer`

In situations in which you use random file access, such as a disk-based database, you must change the position of the file pointer. To move the file pointer to a new position, you use the `SetFilePointer` function, as shown in Listing 14.4.

Listing 14.4. Using the `SetFilePointer` function.

```
DWORD dwPos = SetFilePointer( hFile, dwOffset, NULL, FILE_BEGIN );
if( dwPos != 0xffffffff )
{
    // seek succeeded
}
```

In Listing 14.4, SetFilePointer is used to move to a known offset from the beginning of the file. SetFilePointer has four parameters:

- The handle to the file.
- The number of bytes to move the file pointer. If the value is positive, the pointer moves forward, negative moves it backward. Internally, Windows NT uses 64-bit values to move the file pointer. If the file pointer is moved more than 2^{31} bytes in one direction, you must use the next parameter for the higher 32-bit portion of the total 64-bit distance value.
- A pointer to an optional higher order word to move the file pointer. If this value is NULL, the previous 32-bit value is used to move the file pointer. If this value is not NULL, it is used as the higher 32-bit part of a 64-bit quantity used to move the file pointer. This is useful in cases in which your file sizes exceed 2^{32} bytes.
- A move method for the seek request—in this case, FILE_BEGIN, which moves the file pointer to a position measured from the beginning of the file.

Three values are possible for the move method:

- **FILE_BEGIN:** Specifies that the file pointer should be moved to a new position measured from the beginning of the file.
- **FILE_CURRENT:** Specifies that the file pointer is moved to a new position measured from its current location.
- **FILE_END:** Specifies that the file pointer is moved to a new location measured from the end of the file.

SetFilePointer returns 0xffffffff on failure. You can determine the cause of the error by calling GetLastError. When SetFilePointer is successful, the return value is the new file position. If the upper 32-bit parameter is not NULL, the DWORD variable pointed to by this parameter is filled with the higher order word for the new file position.

A special case can occur when dealing with file sizes greater than 2^{32}—sometimes 0xffffffff really is a valid value. When the 32-bit higher order word is used, GetLastError returns NO_ERROR if the return value is 0xffffffff and there is no error. Listing 14.5 demonstrates how to handle this case.

Listing 14.5. Proper handling of return values from SetFilePointer.

```
DWORD dwLow = SetFilePointer( hFile, dwOffset, &dwHigh, FILE_BEGIN );
if( dwPos == 0xffffffff )
{
    if( GetLastError() != NO_ERROR )
    {
        // Handle error
        return;
    }
}
__int64 cFilePos = dwHigh;
cFilePos << 32;
cFilePos += dwLow;
```

If you use this function in a multithreaded application or with asynchronous I/O, you must be careful not to change the pointer while it is being used. Protect your calls to `SetFilePointer` using a `CriticalSection` or `Mutex` if necessary.

Using `GetFileSize`

You use the `GetFileSize` function to retrieve the size of a file:

```
DWORD cFile = GetFileSize( hFile, NULL );
```

`GetFileSize` has two parameters:

- A file handle.
- An optional pointer to a `DWORD`, which stores the upper 32 bits of the file size if the file size can't be stored in a 32-bit value.

`GetFileSize` returns the size of the file unless the file size cannot be stored in a 32-bit variable. If you are working with very large files that require 64-bit file sizes, you must pass a pointer to a `DWORD` that stores the higher order 32-bit value of the file size if needed, and then convert the two `DWORD`s to a 64-bit quantity, as Listing 14.6 shows.

Listing 14.6. Handling large file sizes with `GetFileSize`.

```
DWORD dwHigh;
DWORD dwLow = GetFileSize( hFile, &dwHigh );
if( dwLow == 0xffffffff )
{
    if( GetLastError() != NO_ERROR )
    {
        // Handle error here
        return;
    }
}
__int64 cFileSize = dwHigh;
cFileSize << 32;
cFileSize += dwLow;
```

Using Asynchronous Input and Output

The one bottleneck that most Windows NT applications have in common is input and output. Unless you have a very simple application that never needs to read or write to a file, your application probably spends at least some of its time waiting for file I/O to be completed.

With Windows NT, you can take advantage of asynchronous file routines that enable your application to continue working while the operating system handles your input and output. Under 16-bit Windows and MS-DOS, a call to an input or output function was blocked or waited until the request was satisfied. Because disk I/O is much slower than memory access, this means that your program has to wait, as shown in Figure 14.1. This is known as *synchronous I/O.*

FIGURE 14.1.

Synchronous file input and output.

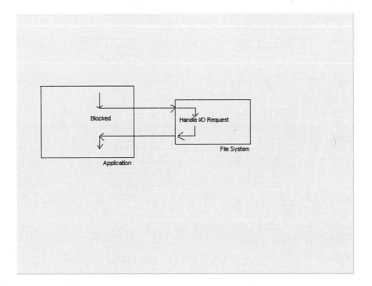

If you use the Windows NT asynchronous file routines, your application can continue to do other work while the operating system satisfies your I/O request, as shown in Figure 14.2.

FIGURE 14.2.

Asynchronous file input and output.

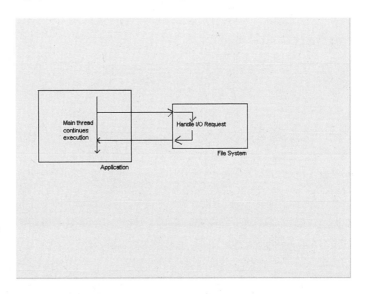

You will achieve better overall performance by using asynchronous I/O because you will use your processing power more efficiently.

Using Overlapped Input and Output

Windows NT offers an easy way for you to spin off asynchronous file input and output, and perform other work while waiting for the I/O work to be completed. This sort of file I/O is called *overlapped I/O* because other work can be performed while the operating system handles your I/O request.

Using overlapped I/O is useful in situations in which you know that data must be read to or written from a file, and you can structure your code so that other work can be done while waiting for the I/O to be completed.

Using the OVERLAPPED Structure

You use the OVERLAPPED structure to manage overlapped I/O. Because multiple reads and writes can be requested and can remain pending for relatively long periods of time, it can be difficult to keep track of the file location and other information related to the I/O request. You use the OVERLAPPED structure to track this information. The OVERLAPPED structure has five members:

- **Offset:** The lower 32-bit value specifying the read or write location.
- **OffsetHigh:** The upper 32-bit value specifying the read or write location.
- **hEvent:** An event handle that is alerted when the I/O request is satisfied. This enables you to create an event that is associated with this OVERLAPPED structure, instead of waiting on the file handle associated with the file. This approach allows multiple overlapped reads or writes to be performed at the same time.
- **Internal:** Reserved for operating system use.
- **InternalHigh:** Reserved for operating system use.

Two common mistakes are made when using overlapped I/O:

- Allowing the OVERLAPPED variable to go out of scope before the I/O request is satisfied.
- Failing to set OffsetHigh to a value. If this member is not used, it must be set to 0.

Looking at an Overlapped I/O Example

You need to follow five steps to use overlapped I/O:

1. Create a file handle using the FILE_FLAG_OVERLAPPED attribute.
2. Initialize an OVERLAPPED structure.
3. Perform a ReadFile or WriteFile function.

4. Sleep or wait for the file handle to be alerted.

5. Get the result of the I/O operation.

These steps are demonstrated in the Console Mode application provided in Listing 14.7. This application is similar to the program provided in Listing 14.3, except that it now makes use of overlapped input and output.

Listing 14.7. Using overlapped I/O in a Console Mode program.

```
#include <windows.h>
#include <iostream.h>

int main()
{
    // Get path name to file from user, and open
    // file as read-only.
    TCHAR szFile[MAX_PATH];
    cout << "File name:";
    cin.getline( szFile, sizeof(szFile) );

    HANDLE    hReadFile = CreateFile( szFile,
                                      GENERIC_READ,
                                      0,
                                      (LPSECURITY_ATTRIBUTES)NULL,
                                      OPEN_EXISTING,
                                      FILE_FLAG_OVERLAPPED,
                                      (HANDLE)NULL );
    if( hReadFile == INVALID_HANDLE_VALUE )
    {
        MessageBox( NULL,
                    TEXT("Can't Open File"),
                    TEXT("Console File"),
                    MB_ICONHAND );
        return 1;
    }
    // Read the file, one 4K chunk at a time, and display it
    // on the console.
    OVERLAPPED ov;
    ov.Offset = 0;
    ov.OffsetHigh = 0;
    ov.hEvent = NULL;

    const int cBufferSize = 0x1000;
    char szBuff[cBufferSize+1];
    DWORD dwRead;
    do{
        BOOL fReadStarted = ReadFile( hReadFile,
                                      szBuff,
                                      cBufferSize,
                                      NULL,
                                      &ov );
        if( fReadStarted )
        {
```

continues

Listing 14.7. continued

```
        // Simulate useful work
        for( int n = 0; n < 10; n++ )
            cout << "Lah te dah" << endl;
        // Wait for handle to be signaled
        WaitForSingleObject( hReadFile, INFINITE );
        GetOverlappedResult( hReadFile,
                             &ov,
                             &dwRead,
                             TRUE );
        szBuff[dwRead] = '\0';
        cout << szBuff;
    }
    ov.Offset += dwRead;
}while( dwRead == cBufferSize );

CloseHandle( hReadFile );
return 1;
}
```

The Console Mode program provided in Listing 14.7 opens an existing file using a name supplied by a user. Unlike the previous file I/O example in Listing 14.3, the FILE_FLAG_OVERLAPPED attribute is used to open the file with an overlapped file handle.

Next, an OVERLAPPED structure is created and initialized. In this case, the file is read from the beginning—that is, stating offset 0. The OVERLAPPED structure and its offset information are updated after every iteration of the do/while loop.

The do/while loop has four parts:

■ A call to ReadFile, in which the overlapped structure is passed to Windows NT and the file read is started.

■ Work that is done while the operating system handles the file request—in this case, a few calls to cout.

■ A call to WaitForSingleObject, in which the thread waits for the file handle to become signaled. A file handle becomes signaled when a pending I/O request is satisfied.

■ A call to GetOverlappedResult that returns the result of the file read.

Note that the call to ReadFile passes NULL instead of a pointer to a variable to hold the number of bytes read. This is because an overlapped call to ReadFile returns almost immediately, and the number of bytes read hasn't been determined. The call to GetOverlappedResult includes a parameter that determines the number of bytes actually read.

Using File-Completion Routines

A more sophisticated form of asynchronous I/O involves completion routines. A *completion routine* is a function that you specify to be called when your asynchronous I/O request is satisfied. When the thread that made the I/O request sleeps or waits in an alertable state, the completion routine is called to handle the completion of the I/O request. Figure 14.3 shows how this works in a typical Windows NT application.

FIGURE 14.3.

Alertable file input and output using completion routines.

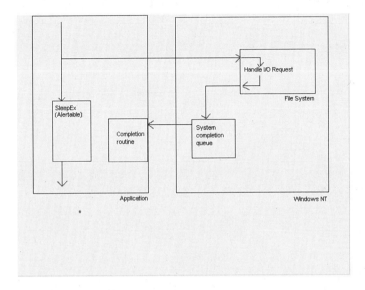

The completion routine is a callback function that follows the general form shown in Listing 14.8.

Listing 14.8. Typical format for file completion routines.

```
void WINAPI ReadComp( DWORD dwErr, DWORD dwBytes, OVERLAPPED* pOv )
{
    if( dwErr == 0 )
        // Handle completed I/O
    else if( dwErr == ERROR_HANDLE_EOF )
        // Handle end-of-file
    else
        // Handle error
}
```

Three parameters are required for a completion routine:

- An error code for the I/O request, if any. This variable is 0 if no error exists.
- The number of bytes written or read during the I/O request.
- A pointer to the OVERLAPPED structure passed to ReadFileEx or WriteFileEx.

To take advantage of completion routines, you must use `ReadFileEx` and `WriteFileEx` in place of the `ReadFile` and `WriteFile` functions. These functions accept an extra parameter that is used for the address of the completion routine:

```
BOOL fWrite = ReadFileEx( hWriteFile,
                          szBuffer,
                          dwWrite,
                          pOverlapped,
                          ReadCompletion );
```

Except for the extra parameter, the behavior of `ReadFileEx` and `WriteFileEx` is exactly like that overlapped I/O using `ReadFile` and `WriteFile`.

Looking at an Example Using File-Completion Routines

As an example of using file-completion routines, I have created a sample program named AsynchCopy that copies a file using `ReadFileEx` and `WriteFileEx`. This program works exactly like the `CopyFile` function, but it shows how you can use file-completion routines and asynchronous I/O in a Windows NT application.

You can open this project and follow along as I describe the various parts of the project, or you can create the project yourself using the steps presented in the next few sections. To begin, create a dialog-based project named AsynchCopy using ClassWizard.

Modifying the Main Dialog Box

Using Developer Studio, add a progress control and three pushbutton controls to the main dialog box, as shown in Figure 14.4.

FIGURE 14.4.

Adding controls to the main dialog box for the AsynchCopy application.

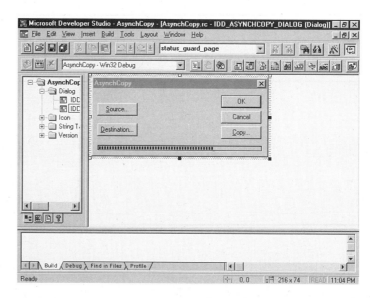

Table 14.3 lists the resource IDs used by the main dialog box controls. Clear the `Visible` property for the progress control; leave all other control attributes set to their default values.

Table 14.3. Controls used by the main dialog box.

Control	Resource ID
Source button	IDC_SOURCE
Destination button	IDC_DEST
Copy button	IDC_COPY
Progress control	IDC_PROGRESS

Using ClassWizard, associate a `CAsynchCopyDlg` member variable with the progress control, using Table 14.4 as a guide.

Table 14.4. Values for the `CAsynchCopyDlg` member variable.

Resource ID	Category	Type	Name
IDC_PROGRESS	Control	CProgressCtrl	m_progressCtrl

Adding Message-Handling Functions

Using ClassWizard, add three message-handling functions for the `CAsynchCopyDlg` class—one for each of the three button controls added to the dialog box. Use the values from Table 14.5 when adding these message-handling functions.

Table 14.5. Values for new member functions in `CAsynchCopyDlg`.

Object ID	Class Name	Message	Function
IDC_SOURCE	CAsynchCopyDlg	BN_CLICKED	OnSource
IDC_DEST	CAsynchCopyDlg	BN_CLICKED	OnDest
IDC_COPY	CAsynchCopyDlg	BN_CLICKED	OnCopy

Modifying the `CAsynchCopyDlg` Class

Add new member variables and member functions to the implementation section of the `CAsynchCopyDlg` class, as shown in bold in Listing 14.9. Unchanged parts of the class declaration have been removed to save space.

Listing 14.9. New `CAsynchCopyDlg` member variables.

```
class CAsynchCopyDlg : public CDialog
{
    .
    .
    .
// Implementation
private:
    CString       m_szSourcePath;
    CString       m_szDestPath;
    HANDLE        m_hReadFile;
    HANDLE        m_hWriteFile;
    BOOL          m_fDone;
    DWORD         m_dwReadChunk;
    TCHAR         m_szBuffer[4096];
    MY_OVERLAPPED m_overlapped;
void WriteBuffer( DWORD dwWrite, OVERLAPPED* pOverlapped );
    void ReadBuffer( OVERLAPPED* pOverlapped );
    static void WINAPI ReadCompletion( DWORD dwErr,
                                       DWORD dwBytes,
                                       OVERLAPPED* pOv );
    static void WINAPI WriteCompletion( DWORD dwErr,
                                        DWORD dwBytes,
                                        OVERLAPPED* pOv );
protected:
    .
    .
    .
};
```

One of the variables in Listing 14.9, m_overlapped, is a MY_OVERLAPPED variable. MY_OVERLAPPED is a structure that has an OVERLAPPED structure as its first member. The second member of MY_OVERLAPPED is a pointer to the CAsynchCopyDlg object that "owns" the structure. This is necessary because you will use static member functions as file-completion routines. By passing a pointer to MY_OVERLAPPED instead of OVERLAPPED to Windows NT, you will be able to find your way back to the instance of CAsynchCopyDlg performing the I/O.

Listing 14.10 provides the definition of MY_OVERLAPPED. You must add this declaration to the AsynchCopyDlg.h file just before the class declaration.

Listing 14.10. The `MY_OVERLAPPED` structure definition.

```
struct MY_OVERLAPPED
{
    OVERLAPPED ov;
    CWnd* pWnd;
};
```

Three pushbuttons must handle user clicks in the main dialog box, and each of these buttons has a member function associated with it:

- **OnSource:** Creates a File Open common dialog box and collects a filename to be used as a source file for the copy operation.

- **OnDest:** Creates a File Open common dialog box and collects a filename to be used as a destination file in the copy operation.

- **OnCopy:** Opens the source and destination files and starts the copy process.

Listing 14.11 provides the source code for these three functions.

Listing 14.11. Message-handling functions for the `CAsynchCopyDlg` class.

```
void CAsynchCopyDlg::OnDest()
{
    CFileDialog     fileDlg( FALSE );
    if( fileDlg.DoModal() == IDOK )
    {
        m_szDestPath = fileDlg.GetPathName();
        CWnd* pWnd = GetDlgItem( IDC_LABEL_DEST );
        ASSERT( pWnd );
        CString szTitle = fileDlg.GetFileTitle();
        szTitle += "." + fileDlg.GetFileExt();
        pWnd->SetWindowText( szTitle );
    }
}

void CAsynchCopyDlg::OnSource()
{
    CFileDialog     fileDlg( TRUE );
    if( fileDlg.DoModal() == IDOK )
    {
        m_szSourcePath = fileDlg.GetPathName();
        CWnd* pWnd = GetDlgItem( IDC_LABEL_SRC );
        ASSERT( pWnd );
        CString szTitle = fileDlg.GetFileTitle();
        szTitle += "." + fileDlg.GetFileExt();
        pWnd->SetWindowText( szTitle );
    }
}

void CAsynchCopyDlg::OnCopy()
{
    m_hReadFile = CreateFile( m_szSourcePath,
                              GENERIC_READ,
                              0,
                              (LPSECURITY_ATTRIBUTES)NULL,
                              OPEN_EXISTING,
```

continues

Listing 14.11. continued

```
                                FILE_FLAG_OVERLAPPED,
                                (HANDLE)NULL );
    m_hWriteFile = CreateFile( m_szDestPath,
                                GENERIC_WRITE,
                                0,
                                (LPSECURITY_ATTRIBUTES)NULL,
                                CREATE_ALWAYS,
                                FILE_FLAG_OVERLAPPED,
                                (HANDLE)NULL );

    if( m_hReadFile == INVALID_HANDLE_VALUE )
    {
        AfxMessageBox( TEXT("Can't Open Source File") );
        return;
    }
    if( m_hWriteFile == INVALID_HANDLE_VALUE )
    {
        AfxMessageBox( TEXT("Can't Open Destination File") );
        CloseHandle( m_hReadFile );
        return;
    }

    m_progressCtrl.SetRange( 0, 100 );
    m_progressCtrl.ShowWindow( SW_SHOW );

    m_fDone = FALSE;
    m_overlapped.ov.hEvent = NULL;
    m_overlapped.pWnd = this;
    m_dwReadChunk = 4096;
    m_overlapped.ov.OffsetHigh = 0;
    m_overlapped.ov.Offset = 0;

    ReadBuffer( (OVERLAPPED*)&m_overlapped );
    while( m_fDone == FALSE )
        SleepEx( INFINITE, TRUE );

    m_progressCtrl.ShowWindow( SW_HIDE );
    CloseHandle( m_hReadFile );
    CloseHandle( m_hWriteFile );
}
```

The OnSource and OnDest functions are straightforward; they use the Open File common dialog box to get source and destination filenames from the user, and store the filenames in member variables.

The OnCopy member function is slightly more complicated. It attempts to open the source and destination files with the overlapped file flag. If the files are opened successfully, OnCopy initializes the progress control and makes it visible.

Next, m_overlapped is initialized, and the copy process is kicked off by a call to the ReadBuffer member function, followed by a call to SleepEx. The main thread sleeps until alerted by a completed I/O function. If the m_fDone flag is still FALSE, SleepEx is called again. This process continues until m_fDone is set to TRUE.

Several member functions are involved in the I/O processing in the AsynchCopy project, as shown in Figure 14.5.

FIGURE 14.5.

Adding controls to the main dialog box for the AsynchCopy application.

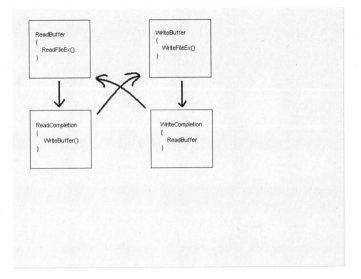

The ReadBuffer function calls ReadFileEx to read a buffer from the source file and specifies ReadCompletion as its completion routine. If the read is successful, ReadCompletion calls WriteBuffer to write the buffer contents. WriteBuffer calls WriteFileEx and uses WriteCompletion as its completion routine. WriteCompletion calls ReadBuffer, and the entire process starts again. If, at any time, an end-of-file marker is detected, the m_fDone flag is raised and I/O stops.

Listing 14.12 provides the source code for the remaining I/O functions.

Listing 14.12. Alertable file I/O functions from the `CAsynchCopyDlg` class.

```
void CAsynchCopyDlg::ReadBuffer( OVERLAPPED* pOverlapped )
{
    int nPos = pOverlapped->Offset * 100;
    nPos /= GetFileSize( m_hReadFile, NULL );
    m_progressCtrl.SetPos( nPos );
    BOOL fRead = ReadFileEx( m_hReadFile,
                             m_szBuffer,
                             sizeof(m_szBuffer),
                             pOverlapped,
                             ReadCompletion );
    if( fRead == FALSE )
    {
        if( GetLastError() == ERROR_HANDLE_EOF )
        {
            // End of file
            m_fDone = TRUE;
```

continues

Listing 14.12. continued

```
        }
        else
        {
            TRACE( "ReadBuffer error = %l\n", GetLastError() );
            // Some other error
        }
    }
}

void CAsynchCopyDlg::WriteBuffer( DWORD dwWrite, OVERLAPPED* pOverlapped )
{
    BOOL fWrite = WriteFileEx( m_hWriteFile,
                               m_szBuffer,
                               dwWrite,
                               pOverlapped,
                               WriteCompletion );
    if( fWrite == FALSE )
    {
        if( GetLastError() == ERROR_HANDLE_EOF )
        {
            // End of file
            m_fDone = TRUE;
        }
        else
        {
            // Some other error
            TRACE( "WriteBuffer error = %l\n", GetLastError() );
        }
    }
}

void WINAPI CAsynchCopyDlg::ReadCompletion( DWORD dwErr,
                                            DWORD dwBytes,
                                            OVERLAPPED* pOv )
{
    MY_OVERLAPPED* pOverlapped = (MY_OVERLAPPED*)pOv;
    CAsynchCopyDlg* pDlg = (CAsynchCopyDlg*)pOverlapped->pWnd;

    ASSERT( pDlg );

    if( dwErr == 0 )
        pDlg->WriteBuffer( dwBytes, pOv );
    else if( dwErr == ERROR_HANDLE_EOF )
        pDlg->m_fDone == TRUE;
    else
        AfxMessageBox( "Error in Read Completion" );
}

void WINAPI CAsynchCopyDlg::WriteCompletion( DWORD dwErr,
                                             DWORD dwBytes,
                                             OVERLAPPED* pOv )
{
    MY_OVERLAPPED* pOverlapped = (MY_OVERLAPPED*)pOv;
    CAsynchCopyDlg* pDlg = (CAsynchCopyDlg*)pOverlapped->pWnd;

    ASSERT( pDlg );
```

```
    if( dwErr == 0 )
    {
        pOverlapped->ov.Offset += pDlg->m_dwReadChunk;
        pDlg->ReadBuffer( (OVERLAPPED*)pOverlapped );
    }
    else if( dwErr == ERROR_HANDLE_EOF )
        pDlg->m_fDone == TRUE;
    else
        AfxMessageBox( "Error in Write Completion" );
}
```

Compile and run the AsynchCopy project. Select the source and destination file and copy a file to a new location. You might need to choose very large files; on my machine, anything smaller than 1MB barely shows the progress control. Figure 14.6 shows the AsynchCopy dialog box copying a file.

FIGURE 14.6.

Copying a file with AsynchCopy.

Summary

In this chapter, you learned how files are manipulated in Windows NT applications. Asynchronous file input and output was presented as a method to improve program performance, and an example of using file I/O completion routines was presented.

In the next chapter, "Printing," I discuss printing under Windows NT using the MFC class library.

Printing

15

by Mickey Williams

This chapter discusses printing using the MFC Class Library and Windows NT. Printing using the MFC Class Library is much simpler than printing in a straight SDK and C environment. At the end of this chapter, you will create a small sample program to demonstrate how you can print for a Document/View application.

Collecting Printer Information

Every printer installed on a Windows NT Workstation or Server has specific information associated with it. This information includes its name, capabilities, security attributes, and optional information, such as its location.

You can use this information to decide which printers should be offered to a user as print options, or you can change your print output based on the capabilities of the selected printer. You also can provide feedback to the user during the print job, such as scheduling information or printer location.

Windows NT provides functions that enable you as an application programmer to collect this information. The next two sections discuss commonly used functions for collecting print-related information under Windows NT.

You use the `EnumPrinters` function to create a list of installed printers available for a Windows NT application. The `EnumPrinters` function returns an array of printer information structures. Listing 15.1 shows a sample call to `EnumPrinters`.

Listing 15.1. A sample call to `EnumPrinters`.

```
pInfo = (PRINTER_INFO_4*)HeapAlloc(GetProcessHeap(),
        HEAP_ZERO_MEMORY,
        sizeof(PRINTER_INFO_4);
EnumPrinters( PRINTER_ENUM_LOCAL,
            NULL,
            4,
            (LPBYTE)pInfo,
            sizeof(PRINTER_INFO_4),
            &cBytes,
            &cPrinters );
```

Listing 15.1 collects information about a single printer and assumes that only one printer is installed. In most cases, you must call `EnumPrinters` twice: the first time to determine the size of the printer information array and the second time to actually fill the array with useful information. An example of using `EnumPrinters` in this way is provided in an example later in this section.

The EnumPrinters function has seven parameters:

- A flag that indicates what sort of printers are to be enumerated—in this case, PRINTER_ENUM_LOCAL, which enumerates only locally attached printers.

- An optional name of a printer object—in this case, NULL. If a name is specified, only that printer object is enumerated.

- The type of printer information structure. Because this example uses a PRINT_INFO_4 structure, a value of 4 is used.

- A pointer to an array of printer information structures. If NULL is passed as this parameter, the size required for an array of appropriate print information structures is calculated.

- The number of bytes in the array of printer information structures. If the previous parameter is NULL, this value must be 0.

- A pointer to a DWORD that contains the number of bytes copied to the array of printer information structures. If the array is too small, this value contains the number of bytes required for the array.

- A pointer to a DWORD that contains the number of printer information structures copied into the array.

The flag variable used to specify the types of printers included in the enumeration must be one or a combination of the following flags:

- PRINTER_ENUM_CONNECTIONS: Enumerates a list of printers with which the user has been connected.

- PRINTER_ENUM_LOCAL: Ignores the optional printer object name parameter and enumerates the locally installed printers.

- PRINTER_ENUM_NAME: Enumerates only the printer identified by the optional printer object name parameter. If this parameter is NULL, the function enumerates available print providers.

- PRINTER_ENUM_NETWORK: Enumerates network printers in the computer's domain. This value is valid only if the PRINTER_INFO_1 structure is used.

- PRINTER_ENUM_REMOTE: Enumerates network printers and print servers in the computer's domain. This value is valid only if the PRINTER_INFO_1 structure is used.

- PRINTER_ENUM_SHARED: Enumerates printers that have the shared attribute. This flag must be used with at least one other flag.

Four print information structures are possible when programming on Windows NT:

- PRINTER_INFO_1: Contains general information about the printer, such as its name and description.

■ PRINTER_INFO_2: Contains detailed information about the printer, such as its location (if available), its status, and its sharepoint, if any.

■ PRINTER_INFO_3: Contains a pointer to a SECURITY_DESCRIPTOR structure that describes the printer's security information.

■ PRINTER_INFO_4: Contains information found in the Registry, such as the printer name, the machine it is connected to, and whether it is a local or remote printer. This is the fastest structure for Windows NT to fill because the information is available immediately.

There is a fifth structure, PRINTER_INFO_5, that is available only on Windows 95.

Listing 15.2 is a Console Mode sample program that demonstrates how the EnumPrinters function is used.

Listing 15.2. Collecting printer information using EnumPrinters.

```
#include <windows.h>
#include <iostream.h>

int main()
{
    PRINTER_INFO_4*    pInfo = 0;
    DWORD              cBytes;
    DWORD              cPrinters;
    DWORD              dwFlags = PRINTER_ENUM_LOCAL;

    EnumPrinters( dwFlags,
                  NULL,
                  4,
                  NULL,
                  0,
                  &cBytes,
                  &cPrinters );
    //
    // Alloc enough memory from the default heap for the printer
    // info structure. Use cBytes - not cPrinters, which will be
    // zero. (The return value of zero indicates that no structures
    // were filled.)
    pInfo = (PRINTER_INFO_4*)HeapAlloc(GetProcessHeap(),
            HEAP_ZERO_MEMORY,
            cBytes);
    //
    // Now that the printer info structure is allocated, fetch
    // the printer data.
    EnumPrinters( dwFlags,
                  NULL,
                  4,
                  (LPBYTE)pInfo,
                  cBytes,
                  &cBytes,
```

```
            &cPrinters );
    cout << "Fetched " << cPrinters << " printers." << endl;
    //
    // Spin through the printer info structures, and display
    // information to the console window.
    for( UINT ndxPrn = 0; ndxPrn < cPrinters; ndxPrn++ )
    {
        cout << pInfo[ndxPrn].pPrinterName;
        if( pInfo[ndxPrn].Attributes == PRINTER_ATTRIBUTE_LOCAL )
            cout << " is a local printer" << endl;
        else
            cout << " connected to " << pInfo[ndxPrn].pServerName
                << endl;
    }
    //
    // Avoid the noid - free the printer info structure.
    HeapFree( GetProcessHeap(), 0, pInfo );
    return 0;
}
```

When the Console Mode program in Listing 15.2 is executed on my computer, the following information is displayed:

```
Fetched 3 printers.
Jennifer is a local printer
Gwendolyn is a local printer
Perditta is a local printer
```

Printing in a Windows NT Application

Programs written for Windows should display their information in a hardware-independent manner. This extends to the printer, where all output is performed through device contexts, much as displays to the screen are performed.

The Document/View architecture and the MFC Class Library help make it easy to create hard-copy printouts in a Windows program. You can use the common Print dialog box and reuse view functions that are used for displaying information to the screen.

Using the Printer in an MFC Program

Printing in an MFC program is almost effortless. If your program uses the Document/View architecture and does all its drawing in the OnDraw function, you might not need to do anything to get basic printing to work. The source code shown in Listing 15.3 is an example of a simple OnDraw function that you can use for screen and printer output.

Listing 15.3. A minimal `OnDraw` function used for screen and printer output.

```
void CMyView::OnDraw(CDC* pDC)
{
    CString szMsg = "Hello printer and view example.";

    pDC->TextOut( 0, 50, szMsg );
}
```

Using the view's `OnDraw` member function is an easy way to take advantage of the hardware independence offered by Windows. If your code is portable enough to run on a variety of screen displays, you probably will get an acceptable printout using most printers available for Windows.

On the other hand, there might be times when you will want to get more involved in the printing. If your view is not WYSIWYG, for example, the printed output might not be suitable. If your view is a Form view, for example, you might want to print your document's data in another form, such as a list of items in the entire document or detailed information about an item in the current form.

When you customize the view functions responsible for printing, you also can offer nice user-interface elements, such as headers, footers, page numbers, or special fonts.

Examining the MFC Printing Routines

If you want to get involved in printing, here are the `CView` routines you can use to print a view:

- **`OnBeginPrinting`:** Specifies where GDI resources specific to using the printer should be allocated.

- **`OnEndPrinting`:** Called once after all pages have been printed or after the job is canceled. This is where GDI resources specific to using the printer are released.

- **`OnPrepareDC`:** Called once per page just before the printout begins.

- **`OnPreparePrinting`:** Called before the common Print dialog box is displayed.

- **`OnPrint`:** Called to actually draw to the printer's Device Context.

These member functions are called by the MFC framework as the print routine progresses. Figure 15.1 shows the relationship between these routines.

As shown in Figure 15.1, only the `OnPrepareDC` and `OnPrint` member functions are called for every page sent to the printer. The other functions are used to initiate variables in preparation for the printout or to clean up and free resources after the printout is completed.

When AppWizard creates a `View` class for your program, the `OnPreparePrinting`, `OnBeginPrinting`, and `OnEndPrinting` functions are provided automatically for you. You can add the other member functions with ClassWizard if you need to override the basic functionality.

FIGURE 15.1.
CView *member functions called while printing a document.*

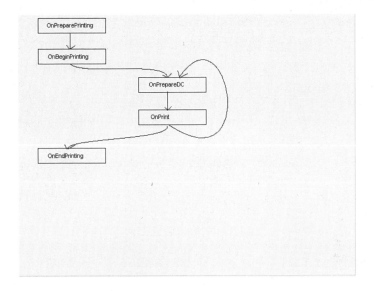

Exploring the CPrintInfo Class

You use the CPrintInfo class to store information about the current state of a printout. A pointer to a CPrintInfo object is passed as a parameter to functions involved in the printout. You can access attributes of the CPrintInfo object for information about the printout. Or, in some cases, you can change the attributes to customize the printout. Table 15.1 lists the most commonly used CPrintInfo members.

Table 15.1. Commonly used CPrintInfo members.

Value	Function
GetFromPage	Returns the number of the first page being printed
GetMaxPage	Returns the value previously set as the document's last page number
GetMinPage	Returns the value previously set as the document's first page number
GetToPage	Returns the number of the first page being printed
m_bContinuePrinting	A flag set to FALSE to stop the print loop
m_bPreview	A flag set to TRUE if the document is being previewed
m_nCurPage	Contains the currently printing page number
m_rectDraw	Contains the current printout rectangle
SetMaxPage	Sets the document's last page number
SetMinPage	Sets the document's first page number

Some of these members are used in a particular function. As each function is discussed in the next few sections, the commonly used CPrintInfo members also are covered.

Using the OnPreparePrinting Function

The OnPreparePrinting function is generated by AppWizard for a project's initial View class. This function is called before the common Print dialog box is displayed, and it gives you an opportunity to change the values displayed in the Print dialog box.

If your document has more than one page, you should calculate the number of pages, if possible. This allows the maximum number of pages to be displayed in the Print dialog box. You can set the number of pages by calling the CPrintInfo::SetMaxPages function:

```
pInfo->SetMaxPages( 2 );
```

You should not allocate any resources in this function, because you are not notified if the user cancels the print dialog box. The next section discusses allocating resources for printing.

Using the OnBeginPrinting Function

The OnBeginPrinting function is called after the user clicks OK in the Print dialog box in order to start the printout. This function is the proper place to allocate resources such as fonts, brushes, and pens that might be needed for the printout. In the example presented later in the section *Looking at a Printing Example*, this function is used to create CFont objects.

The OnBeginPrinting function is called only once for each printout. If this function is called by the framework, you can rely on the OnEndPrinting function to be called after the printout is finished in order to give you a chance to free resources allocated here.

Using the OnPrepareDC Function

The OnPrepareDC function is called just prior to a page being printed or displayed in the view. If OnPrepareDC is called with the CPrintInfo pointer set to NULL, the document is not being printed.

This function often is overridden for multiple-page documents in order to continue the printout over multiple pages. To print another page, set the CPrintInfo::m_bContinue member variable to TRUE:

```
pInfo->m_bContinuePrinting = TRUE;
```

By default, only one page is printed, unless you override this function and set this flag to TRUE.

Using the `OnPrint` Function

The `OnPrint` function is the printing counterpart to `OnDraw`. In fact, some programs can just use the default version of `OnPrint`, which calls `OnDraw`. Most printouts can benefit from providing page numbers, headers, footers, or special fonts that aren't displayed in the view, however.

When printing, the `MM_TWIPS` Mapping mode is used. A *twip* is one-twentieth of a point, which is, in turn, almost exactly 1/72 of an inch. If you need help on the math, that's about 1,440 twips per inch. The really odd thing about `MM_TWIPS` is that the Mapping mode begins with the upper-left corner at (0,0) and runs in a negative direction down the page, making the point one inch below the origin (0,–1440). Like other modes, the Mapping mode extends in a positive direction to the right side of the page.

The `OnPrint` function is called once for every page. If you're printing data arranged so that the page number can easily be determined, it's a good idea to use the `CPrintInfo` parameter to determine the current page number. Remember that the user may ask for just a range of pages to be printed instead of the entire document.

Using the `OnEndPrinting` Function

The `OnEndPrinting` function is called after the printout is finished. This function may be called because the job was completed successfully or because it has failed; you don't really know. The purpose of this function is to release any resources allocated in the `OnBeginPrinting` function.

Querying the Printing Device Context

Unlike video displays, printing devices offer a large variation in their capabilities. It is a good idea to determine the capabilities of a printout device before attempting graphics functions.

You use the `CDC::GetDeviceCaps` function to retrieve information about a selected output device, as Listing 15.4 shows.

Listing 15.4. Using `GetDeviceCaps` to determine if `BitBlt` is allowed.

```
int nRasterFlags = pDC->GetDeviceCaps( RASTERCAPS );
if( nRasterFlags & RC_BITBLT )
{
    // BitBlt is allowed
}
```

`GetDeviceCaps` accepts an index as a parameter. This index specifies the sort of information returned from the function. In Listing 15.4, the `RASTERCAPS` index results in a return value that contains flags that indicate the raster capabilities of the device. If the `RC_BITBLT` flag is set, the `BitBlt` function can be applied to the output device.

You can use this function for any type of device—not just printers. Dozens of possible indexes and return flags are available. Check the online documentation for details.

Looking at a Printing Example

As an example of the MFC print functions, I have created an MFC project named MFCPrint, which is located on the accompanying CD. You can open this project and follow along as I describe the various printing functions, or you can create the project yourself using the steps presented in the next few sections. To begin, create an SDI project named MFCPrint using ClassWizard.

Using ClassWizard, add two message-handling functions for the `CMFCPrintView` class: `OnPrepareDC` and `OnPrint`. The other printing functions already have been included in the `CMFCPrintView` class by AppWizard.

Add five new member variables, and two new member functions to the `Implementation` section of the `CMFCPrintView` class, as shown in bold in Listing 15.5. Unchanged parts of the class declaration have been removed to save space.

Listing 15.5. New `CMFCPrintView` member variables and functions.

```
class CMFCPrintView : public CView
{
    .
    .
    .
// Implementation
private:
    int     m_nCurrentPrintedPage;
    CFont* m_pFntBold;
    CFont* m_pFntBanner;
    CFont* m_pFntHighlight;
    CPen    m_penBlack;
    void PrintHeader( CDC* pDC );
    void PrintFooter( CDC* pDC );
    .
    .
    .
};
```

These new member variables and functions are used during the printout.

The `CMFCPrintView` Constructor and Destructor

The member variables added in the preceding section must be initialized in the `CMFCPrintView` constructor and freed in the destructor. Listing 15.6 shows the source code for the `CMFCPrintView` constructor and destructor.

Listing 15.6. The constructor and destructor for CMFCPrintView.

```
CMFCPrintView::CMFCPrintView()
{
    COLORREF clrBlack = GetSysColor( COLOR_WINDOWFRAME );
    m_penBlack.CreatePen( PS_SOLID, 0, clrBlack );
    m_pFntBold = 0;
    m_pFntBanner = 0;
    m_pFntHighlight = 0;
}

CMFCPrintView::~CMFCPrintView()
{
    // These fonts must be released explicitly
    // since they were created with new.
    delete m_pFntBold;
    delete m_pFntBanner;
    delete m_pFntHighlight;
}
```

The usual practice with GDI objects is to defer actually creating the object until it is needed. The constructor for CMFCPrintView sets the CFont pointer variables to 0; these objects are created on the heap when the print job begins.

The destructor for CMFCPrintView deletes the dynamically allocated CFont objects. Under normal execution, these pointers do not need to be freed because the resources are released at the end of the print job. It is guaranteed safe to invoke delete on a 0 or NULL pointer, however, so this code protects you in the case of abnormal termination.

The OnBeginPrinting Function

As you learned earlier, the OnBeginPrinting function is called just before printing begins. Add the source code provided in Listing 15.7 to the OnBeginPrinting function. This version of OnBeginPrinting creates three new fonts used in the printout. To avoid compiler warnings about unused variables, AppWizard comments out the pDC and pInfo parameters. If you use these parameters, you must remove the comments manually, as shown in Listing 15.7.

Listing 15.7. Allocating new fonts in the OnBeginPrinting function.

```
void CMFCPrintView::OnBeginPrinting(CDC* pDC, CPrintInfo* pInfo)
{
    ASSERT( m_pFntBold == 0 );
    ASSERT( m_pFntBanner == 0 );
    ASSERT( m_pFntHighlight == 0 );

    m_nCurrentPrintedPage = 0;
    pDC->SetMapMode( MM_TWIPS );
```

continues

Listing 15.7. continued

```
// Create the bold font used for the fields. TimesRoman,
// 12 point semi-bold is used.
m_pFntBold = new CFont;
ASSERT( m_pFntBold );
m_pFntBold->CreateFont( -240,
                        0,
                        0,
                        0,
                        FW_SEMIBOLD,
                        FALSE,
                        FALSE,
                        0,
                        ANSI_CHARSET,
                        OUT_TT_PRECIS,
                        CLIP_DEFAULT_PRECIS,
                        DEFAULT_QUALITY,
                        DEFAULT_PITCH | FF_ROMAN,
                        "Times Roman" );
// Create the normal font used for the Headline banner.
// TimesRoman, 18 point italic is used.
m_pFntBanner = new CFont;
ASSERT( m_pFntBanner );
m_pFntBanner->CreateFont( -360,
                          0,
                          0,
                          0,
                          FW_NORMAL,
                          TRUE,
                          FALSE,
                          0,
                          ANSI_CHARSET,
                          OUT_TT_PRECIS,
                          CLIP_DEFAULT_PRECIS,
                          DEFAULT_QUALITY,
                          DEFAULT_PITCH | FF_ROMAN,
                          "Times Roman" );
// Create the normal font used for the Headline highlight.
// This is the text used under the headline banner, and in
// the footer. TimesRoman, 8 point is used.
m_pFntHighlight = new CFont;
ASSERT( m_pFntHighlight );
m_pFntHighlight->CreateFont( -160,
                             0,
                             0,
                             0,
                             FW_NORMAL,
                             TRUE,
                             FALSE,
                             0,
                             ANSI_CHARSET,
                             OUT_TT_PRECIS,
                             CLIP_DEFAULT_PRECIS,
                             DEFAULT_QUALITY,
                             DEFAULT_PITCH | FF_ROMAN,
                             "Times Roman" );
CView::OnBeginPrinting(pDC, pInfo);
}
```

The `OnEndPrinting` Function

The `OnEndPrinting` function is called once per print job, but only if the `OnBeginPrinting` function has been called. Use this function to release the resources allocated in `OnBeginPrinting`. You must match all your allocations in `OnBeginPrinting` with deallocations in `OnEndPrinting`.

Listing 15.8 provides the source code for the `OnEndPrinting` function used in `CMFCPrintView`. As in the `OnBeginPrinting` function presented in Listing 15.7, AppWizard comments out the `pDc` and `pInfo` parameters. If you use these parameters, you must remove these comments, as shown in Listing 15.8.

Listing 15.8. Releasing resources in the `OnEndPrinting` function.

```
void CMFCPrintView::OnEndPrinting(CDC* pDC, CPrintInfo* pInfo)
{
    delete m_pFntBold;
    delete m_pFntBanner;
    delete m_pFntHighlight;
    // Since the destructor also deletes these fonts, we have
    // to set pointers to 0 to avoid dangling pointers and exceptions
    // generated by invoking delete on a non-valid pointer.
    m_pFntBold = 0;
    m_pFntBanner = 0;
    m_pFntHighlight = 0;
    CView::OnEndPrinting(pDC, pInfo);
}
```

The `OnPrint` Function

The default implementation of `OnPrint` calls the `OnDraw` member function. For this example, add the source code from Listing 15.9 to `OnPrint`, which sends a header, two rows of text, and a footer to the printer.

Listing 15.9. Printing a page using the `OnPrint` function.

```
void CMFCPrintView::OnPrint(CDC* pDC, CPrintInfo* pInfo)
{
    CPoint      pt( 5000, -7000 );
    TEXTMETRIC  tm;

    //Since the DC has been modified, it's always a good idea to reset
    //the mapping mode, no matter which one you use. In our case, since
    //we use MM_TWIPS, we have to reset the mapping mode for each page.
    pDC->SetMapMode( MM_TWIPS );
    PrintHeader( pDC );
    CFont* pOldFont = pDC->SelectObject( m_pFntBold );
    pDC->GetTextMetrics( &tm );
    int cyText = tm.tmHeight + tm.tmExternalLeading;
```

continues

Listing 15.9. continued

```
    m_nCurrentPrintedPage++;
    pDC->TextOut( pt.x, pt.y, "Hello Printer!!!" );

    pt.y += cyText;
    CString  szPageInfo;
    szPageInfo.Format( TEXT("Page number %d"),
                        m_nCurrentPrintedPage );
    pDC->TextOut( pt.x, pt.y, szPageInfo );

    pDC->SelectObject( pOldFont );
    PrintFooter( pDC );
}
```

Listing 15.10 provides the source code used to print the header and footer. Add these two functions to the MFCPrintView.cpp source file, and add declarations for these functions to the CMFCPrintView class declaration.

Listing 15.10. Printing the header and footer.

```
void CMFCPrintView::PrintFooter( CDC* pDC )
{
    ASSERT( pDC );
    TEXTMETRIC  tm;
    CPoint  pt( 0, -14400 );

    //Select the smaller font used for the file name.
    ASSERT( m_pFntHighlight );
    CFont* pOldFont = pDC->SelectObject( m_pFntHighlight );
    ASSERT( pOldFont );
    pDC->GetTextMetrics( &tm );
    int cyText = tm.tmHeight + tm.tmExternalLeading;

    // Print the underline bar. This is the same pen used to draw
    // black lines in the control. 10000 twips is about 7 inches or so.
    CPen* pOldPen = pDC->SelectObject( &m_penBlack );
    ASSERT( pOldPen );
    pt.y -= (cyText / 2);
    pDC->MoveTo( pt );
    pDC->LineTo( 10000, pt.y );

    pt.y -= cyText;
    pDC->TextOut( pt.x, pt.y, TEXT("Every page needs a footer") );
    // Restore GDI objects.
    pDC->SelectObject( pOldFont );
    pDC->SelectObject( pOldPen );
}
void CMFCPrintView::PrintHeader( CDC* pDC )
{
    ASSERT( pDC );
    TEXTMETRIC  tm;
```

```
CPoint      pt( 0, 0 );

// Select the banner font, and print the headline.
CFont* pOldFont = pDC->SelectObject( m_pFntBanner );
ASSERT( pOldFont );
pDC->GetTextMetrics( &tm );
int cyText = tm.tmHeight + tm.tmExternalLeading;
pt.y -= cyText;
pDC->TextOut( pt.x, pt.y, "Windows NT 4.0 Programming Unleashed" );
// Move down one line, and print an underline bar. This is the same
// pen used to draw black lines in the control. 10000 twips is about
// 7 inches or so.
CPen* pOldPen = pDC->SelectObject( &m_penBlack );
ASSERT( pOldPen );
pt.y -= cyText;
pDC->MoveTo( pt );
pDC->LineTo( 10000, pt.y );
// We move down about 1/2 line, and print the report type using the
// smaller font.
VERIFY( pDC->SelectObject( m_pFntHighlight ) );
pDC->GetTextMetrics( &tm );
cyText = tm.tmHeight + tm.tmExternalLeading;
pt.y -= (cyText / 2);
pDC->TextOut( pt.x, pt.y, "Printing Demonstration" );
// Restore GDI objects.
pDC->SelectObject( pOldFont );
pDC->SelectObject( pOldPen );
}
```

The OnPrepareDC Function

The OnPrepareDC function is called just before each page is printed. The default version of this function allows one page to be printed. By modifying the bContinuePrinting flag, you can use this function to cause the printout to continue.

Add the source code provided in Listing 15.11 to the OnPrepareDC function.

Listing 15.11. The OnPrepareDC function.

```
void CMFCPrintView::OnPrepareDC(CDC* pDC, CPrintInfo* pInfo)
{
    CView::OnPrepareDC(pDC, pInfo);
    if( pInfo )
    {
        if( m_nCurrentPrintedPage < 3 )
            pInfo->m_bContinuePrinting = TRUE;
        else
            pInfo->m_bContinuePrinting = FALSE;
    }
}
```

In the MFCPrint example, the print job is hard-coded to stop after three pages. In your applications, you can determine the number of pages to be printed in advance or test some other condition in `OnPrepareDC`.

Compile and run the Print project, and send the output to the printer using the File menu.

Summary

This chapter discussed the print functions and support offered by both Windows NT and MFC and the Document/View architecture. You looked at two example programs provided on the CD-ROM: a Console Mode program that demonstrates how to enumerate the printers installed under Windows NT, and a small MFC program that sends three pages of text to the printer.

In the next chapter, "Dynamic Link Libraries," I discuss how dynamic link libraries are created and used in Windows NT applications.

Dynamic Link Libraries

16

by Mickey Williams

In this chapter, you learn about dynamic link libraries (DLLs) and how you can use them to write programs for Windows NT. Different approaches for writing and using DLLs are presented, and several examples are provided, including examples that demonstrate how to use DLLs when programming with MFC.

Understanding Libraries

Simply put, a *library* is a file that contains functions or other resources available for use in applications. These resources usually are general purpose, allowing many different applications to share the same code or resources easily.

Libraries used in Windows applications come in two basic flavors: *static libraries* and *dynamic libraries*. Figure 16.1 illustrates the difference between these two types.

FIGURE 16.1.

Calling a function in static library versus calling a function in a Dynamic Link Library.

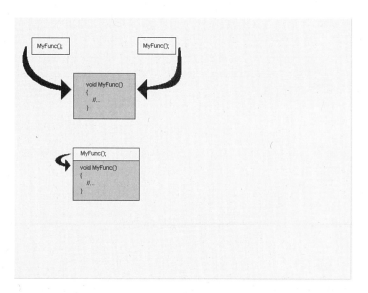

Static libraries are groups of reusable functions that are linked with a Windows NT application. The static library is part of the application's executable file and is not shared with other applications that may be using the same functions. Static linking is very easy to implement; however, updating the library requires that the program be re-linked.

DLLs are often used for common functions that are used by several applications simultaneously. For example, the MFC runtime code is contained in a DLL. The first MFC-based application started by Windows NT loads the DLL. Once the MFC library DLL is loaded by Windows NT, launching another application that uses the DLL proceeds much more quickly.

Only one instance of a DLL is actually loaded at any particular time. If a DLL is already loaded and in use by another process, the DLL is simply mapped into the address space of the new process that depends on it. A DLL can be easily updated without modifying the programs that depend on it, as long as the interfaces supported by the DLL are not changed.

Examining Static Libraries

Static linked libraries normally are reserved for relatively small, stable function libraries such as the standard C library, which provides functions such as `strlen` or `memcpy`. Static libraries are often used for small libraries due to the cost of creating and maintaining a DLL. A static library is very easy to create and maintain, and the behavior of a static library is very similar to that of a DLL, for most small libraries.

Examining Dynamically Linked Libraries

Dynamic link libraries are executable files containing functions, data, or resources available to other applications. As the name suggests, a DLL is loaded when needed—at load time or while an application is running. This is in contrast to static linking, in which a library is added to an executable when it is compiled and linked.

Dynamically linked libraries are useful when functions or other resources may be used by multiple processes on a single machine. The contents of each DLL loaded by an application are mapped into the calling application process address space and linked as the DLL is loaded. A good example of a DLL used in Windows NT is MFC40.DLL, which is used by programs built using MFC 4.0. Most of the MFC code in a typical MFC-based application actually is located in the DLL. Because MFC40.DLL is a shared DLL, many MFC applications can use it simultaneously.

If an application needs a DLL that is already loaded, two things happen:

- It maps the DLL into the address space of the new process.
- It increases a reference counter kept by Windows NT for this DLL. If this counter drops to 0, Windows NT unloads the DLL.

Unlike 16-bit versions of Windows, under Windows NT, a DLL is loaded in the address space of the calling process instead of a global address space. This protects the DLL from faulty applications, because only the calling process has access to the DLL. It also changes the way in which DLLs are used, however. If you're accustomed to using DLLs in 16-bit versions of Windows, you will need to make some changes in the way you use DLLs in your applications.

The biggest change in how DLLs are used is that, by default, all data in a DLL is mapped into the address space of the calling process, as shown in Figure 16.2.

FIGURE 16.2.

DLLs use data in the context of the process that loaded the DLL.

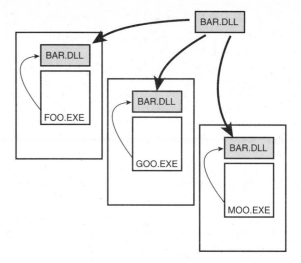

This means that the process that loaded the DLL gets its own copy of global data. Any heap memory allocation made by the DLL is made in the context of the process that loaded the DLL, and is "owned" by that process. In addition, the DLL uses the process's stack, unlike 16-bit Windows, in which each DLL allocates a private stack.

Later in this chapter, you will learn some methods for sharing variables in a DLL.

Looking at the Advantages of Using DLLs

Most non-trivial Windows NT applications use one or more DLLs. There are four main advantages to using DLLs in a Windows NT application:

- Executable code size can be reduced, because several applications can use the same library.
- A central code base isolated in a library is more economical to develop than similar functions used in multiple projects. Reusing code contained in DLLs can look very attractive when several projects need similar functionality.
- Large projects can be broken up into smaller, easier-to-manage subprojects.
- DLLs make it easy to implement new functions: just release a new version of the DLL. As long as the existing interface doesn't change, you can add new functions without recompiling existing clients.

Looking at the Disadvantages of Using DLLs

The advantages of using DLLs don't come without a price. You should consider a few issues before you break your project into hundreds of tiny DLLs:

- Using DLLs results in more deliverables. Your main EXE may be smaller, but now you need to track more than one binary file.

- DLLs increase project complexity. DLLs must be released and maintained through the development and testing process. These intraproject dependencies grow exponentially with the number of DLLs if you don't plan your project carefully.

- You must deal with version issues with a DLL. Because a DLL is a compiled product, you should use version resources discussed later, in the section *Using Version Control with DLLs*, to mark your DLLs.

If any of the above issues apply to your project, consider using static libraries.

Creating and Using Dynamic Link Libraries

Dynamic link libraries usually are created using your C or C++ compiler, although you can use other development tools—for example, Delphi from Borland can create DLLs. In this section, you learn the steps required to create a DLL using Visual C++. Tools from other vendors are similar; see your documentation for the exact details.

The next few sections cover several issues involved in creating and using DLLs:

- Initializing a DLL
- Exporting functions and data from a DLL
- Loading a DLL when an application starts
- Loading a DLL during runtime
- Using version control with a DLL
- Shared memory in a DLL

Following these general topics, example projects are developed that demonstrate each of these subjects.

Understanding DLL Initialization

In 16-bit Windows, separate entry and exit points exist for a DLL. `LibMain` is called when the DLL is loaded, and `WEP` is called when the DLL is freed. The performance of `LibMain` and `WEP` were never spectacular, and they are horrendous when handling runtime error conditions.

Under Windows NT, you can define the name of the DLL's main entry point. By convention, the name of this function is `DllMain`. This entry point is a function called by the operating system at the following times:

- When a process calls the DLL for the first time
- When a new thread is created by a process attached to a DLL

■ When a thread owned by a process attached to a DLL is destroyed

■ When a process releases a DLL

If you are using Visual C++, you can change the entry point for the DLL by following these steps:

1. Choose Settings from the Build menu.
2. Click on the Link tab.
3. Select Output from the Category drop-down list.
4. Enter a new name as the entry-point symbol. This will be the function name called when the DLL is loaded.

Listing 16.1 shows a typical example of a DLL entry-point function.

Listing 16.1. A generic DLL entry-point function.

```
BOOL DllMain( HINSTANCE hLibInstance,
              DWORD     dwReason,
              LPVOID    lpvReserved )
{
    BOOL fResult = FALSE;
    switch( dwReason )
    {
        case DLL_PROCESS_ATTACH:
        // A process has loaded the library
        // Set fResult to TRUE if initialization
        // is successful.
        break;

        case DLL_PROCESS_DETACH:
        // A process has unloaded the library
        break;

        case DLL_THREAD_ATTACH:
        // A new thread has loaded the library
        break;

        case DLL_THREAD_DETACH:
        // A thread has unloaded the library
        break;

        default:
        break;
    }
    return fResult;
}
```

If your DLL has no global data or initialization or cleanup functions that must be performed when it is loaded or unloaded, you can safely omit the DllMain function from your DLL. If you don't create an entry point, the compiler and linker generate a default version that returns TRUE for every case.

Exporting and Importing DLL Functions

By default, no functions or data located in a DLL are visible to the process that loads the DLL. All functions, data, and resources must be explicitly exported from the DLL using one of these methods:

- Placing the names of the exported items in the EXPORTS section of the library's .DEF file

- Using a tool-specific method, such as the __declspec(dllexport) keyword used by Visual C++

Once upon a time, when wheels were made of stone and real programmers used C but preferred assembler, all the symbols exported from a library were entered into a library's definition (DEF) file. You still can use this method. In fact, the MFC Library explicitly lists every exported symbol in the DLL version of the MFC Library. If you are using a newer compiler, however, you don't even need a DEF file in many cases—you can just use the __declspec method to export symbols.

Examining the Module Definition File

In 16-bit Windows development, the DEF file has a much more central role than it does in 32-bit Windows. For a 32-bit DLL, there are at least two entries in a DEF file, if it exists:

- **LIBRARY:** Specifies the name of the DLL
- **EXPORTS:** Marks the beginning of a list of exported symbols

A minimal DEF file that exports no symbols looks like this:

```
LIBRARY     "FOO"
EXPORTS
            ; No exports
```

Exporting Symbols in a DEF File

Every symbol that is exported from the DLL must appear after an EXPORTS label in the DEF file. The following DEF file exports two functions, for example:

```
LIBRARY     "FOO"
EXPORTS
            GetData
            SetData
```

Beware of C++ name mangling. If the DLL is compiled with a C++ compiler, you have two options if you want to use the EXPORTS section of the DEF file:

- Compile the DLL as a C project in order to turn off name-mangling.
- Determine the mangled names for each of your exported functions and enter the mangled names in the EXPORTS portion of the DEF file.

In order to determine the mangled names for C++ symbols included in your DLL, build the DLL with no exports and have the linker generate a MAP file. To create a MAP file using Visual C++, follow these steps:

1. Choose Settings from the Tools menu.
2. Click on the Link tab.
3. Select General from the Category drop-down list.
4. Click the Generate Mapfile checkbox.

A map file is fairly large, even for small C++ programs. The section you are interested in looks something like this:

```
Address         Publics by Value         Rva+Base   Lib:Object

0001:00000000   ??2CVMListNode@@SAPAXI@Z   00401000 f listnode.obj
0001:000000b2   ??3CVMListNode@@SAXPAX@Z   004010b2 f listnode.obj
0001:000001f0   ??0CVMList@@QAE@XZ         004011f0 f list.obj
```

The symbol names in the Publics by Value column are the mangled C++ names used by this C++ application.

If you are exporting a large number of symbols from your DLL, you should export your symbols *by ordinal*, meaning that they are referenced by number instead of name. This speeds up the search for individual symbols in a library; this approach is used in the MFC DLLs.

To export by ordinal, add an ampersand (&) followed by an ordinal number after every symbol in the EXPORTS portion of the DEF file:

```
LIBRARY      "FOO"
EXPORTS
             GetData  @1
             SetData  @2
```

The Linker generates export and import libraries that use the associated ordinal instead of the name to reference each symbol. The numbers used as ordinals must begin with 1, and they must be consecutive.

Using __declspec, dllimport, and dllexport

As you can see, managing the DEF file can be a big headache. If you are using a current C++ compiler, you probably can avoid dealing with the EXPORTS section of the DEF file altogether. Visual C++ uses the __declspec keyword, for example, to add extra attributes when declaring a function or variable name:

```
int __declspec(dllexport) foo();
```

The `__declspec` keyword first was introduced in Visual C++ 2.0 and has four possible parameters:

- **dllexport:** Declares a function or variable as exported from a DLL.
- **dllimport:** Declares a function or variable as imported from a DLL.
- **naked:** Declares a function that should not have prologue or epilogue code generated for it.
- **thread:** Declares a variable as a thread local storage variable.

In some cases, using `dllexport` and `dllimport` enables the compiler to generate more efficient code because it can identify which symbols are exported and imported from the DLL.

A slight amount of complexity is added to your declarations when using `__declspec`. Consider a DLL that exports a function named `foo`:

```
int foo( int )
{
    // Does something useful...
    return 1216;
}
```

When building the DLL, `foo` is declared using `dllexport`:

```
int __declspec(dllexport) foo( int );
```

When importing the DLL, `foo` is declared using `dllimport`:

```
int __declspec(dllexport) foo( int );
```

Instead of using two header files, the examples in this chapter use conditional compilation to ensure that the proper declaration is used, as Listing 16.2 demonstrates.

Listing 16.2. Using `__declspec` with conditional compilation.

```
#ifdef FOO_DLL
// export function from library
#define FUNC_DECL   __declspec(dllexport)
#else
// import function from library
#define FUNC_DECL   __declspec(dllimport)
#endif

int  FUNC_DECL GetFoo( void );
void FUNC_DECL SeFoo( int nFoo );
```

In the DLL implementing these functions, `FOO_DLL` is defined, resulting in `__declspec(dllexport)` being used for the declarations. When this header is used without defining `FOO_DLL`, the `__declspec(dllimport)` declaration is used.

Loading a DLL at Load Time

An executable can contain information about the DLLs it needs to have loaded. This information is placed into the EXE file by the Linker and is used by Windows NT when an application is launched.

Windows NT searches for these DLLs in the following order:

1. The directory containing the EXE file that owns the process
2. The current directory
3. The Windows NT system directory
4. The Windows NT directory
5. The directories listed in the PATH environment variable

If any of the DLLs associated with an application cannot be found or fail to load for any other reason, the application terminates.

Every DLL that is found is treated like a memory-mapped file, and its contents are mapped into the process of the starting application. Because it is treated like a memory-mapped file, only the parts of the DLL that actually are used are loaded into physical memory.

As discussed earlier in the chapter, if a DLL used by an application is already in use by another process, Windows NT creates another mapping for the new process and increments a reference count stored internally by the operating system. This counter is incremented when processes attach to a DLL and decremented when processes detach or are terminated. When this counter reaches 0, the DLL is released.

To notify the Linker that your application depends on a DLL, you must link your application with an import library created for the DLL. Visual C++ creates an import library automatically when building DLL projects created by AppWizard.

Loading a DLL at Runtime

The second method you can use to load a DLL is *runtime* or *dynamic loading*. With this method, you can attempt to explicitly load a DLL using LoadLibrary, as Listing 16.3 shows.

Listing 16.3. Using LoadLibrary to load a DLL at runtime.

```
typedef int(*PFUNC)(void);
.
.
.
HINSTANCE   hLibInstance;
hLibInstance = LoadLibrary( "FuncDll" );
if( hLibInstance != NULL )
{
    PFUNC pFunc = (PFUNC)GetProcAddress( hLibInstance,
```

```
                                  "GetUltimateAnswer" );
    if( pFunc != NULL )
    {
        int n = pFunc();
        cout << "The answer is " << n << endl;
    }
    FreeLibrary( hLibInstance );
}
else
{
    cout << "Couldn't load library" << endl;
}
```

The `LoadLibrary` function returns an instance handle that refers to the DLL. If `LoadLibrary` is not successful, `NULL` is returned. In order to use any functions exported by the DLL, you must call `GetProcAddress` with the library's instance handle and the name of the function:

```
pFunc = (PFUNC)GetProcAddress( hLibInstance, "GetUltimateAnswer" );
```

The function name must be spelled exactly as it is exported. Alternatively, you can use the ordinal export value, if one exists, like this:

```
pFunc = (PFUNC)GetProcAddress( hLibInstance, MAKEINTRESOURCE(1) );
```

The return value from `GetProcAddress` is typed as a `FARPROC`. In most cases, you must cast it to the proper type, as shown in the preceding example.

After you get the address, you use it like any other function pointer:

```
int n = pFunc();
```

After you finish using the library, you should release it by calling `FreeLibrary`:

```
FreeLibrary( hLibInstance );
```

When using `LoadLibrary`, you don't need to link your application with an import library for the DLL. Because you don't explicitly call any of the DLL functions, the Linker doesn't complain about missing references.

This method is extremely useful in situations in which a DLL may not exist on a particular installation. You can use `LoadLibrary` to load a DLL containing optional resources or functions; if it's not found, you can take some alternative action.

Using Version Control with DLLs

One of the types of resources that can be bound to executable files is the version resource. The *version resource* tags the executable files and font resources with the company name, file name, and other version information. Other programs can use this information to compare files to determine the revision level of the file. Windows NT offers version control functions that can be used to query standard version resources.

Adding version information to a DLL project is easy and takes only a few minutes. To take advantage of the standard version control functions, you must define a version resource for your project. Figure 16.3 shows a version resource being edited.

FIGURE 16.3.

Using Developer Studio to edit a version resource.

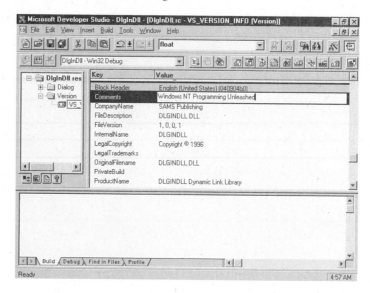

If you use Developer Studio to edit your version resource, the individual fields are conveniently displayed for editing. Just fill in the relevant information and rebuild the DLL project.

That's all there is to marking your files with version information. You can see this information easily by using the Windows NT Explorer and displaying the file properties. Figure 16.4 shows an example of version information for a DLL.

FIGURE 16.4.

Displaying version information for a DLL.

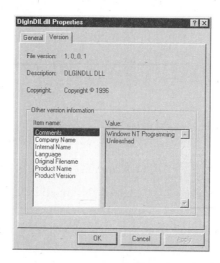

Creating Shared Memory for a DLL

It sometimes is necessary for processes that use a DLL to share information. In 16-bit versions of Windows, this usually is done through shared memory owned by the DLL. Because the DLL in 16-bit Windows is mapped into the global address space, all applications have access to data owned by the DLL, so this scheme is easy to implement.

When running on Windows NT, where each DLL is mapped into the address space of the process that loaded the DLL, any memory used by the DLL is actually in the address space of the calling process. You still can share memory—it just takes a little more work.

A section of memory used by a DLL is defined as sharable by using the SECTIONS keyword in a module definition file. Listing 16.4 defines a section named .shared as a readable, writable, and shared section of memory. Windows NT memory sections always begin with a ., but you can give them any name you want.

Listing 16.4. A DEF file defining a shared data section.

```
LIBRARY       "FOODLL"
DESCRIPTION   'FOODLL Windows Dynamic Link Library'

SECTIONS
    .shared   READ WRITE SHARED

EXPORTS
    ; Explicit exports can go here
```

After you define a memory section, you must place your shared memory into that section and initialize it. Only initialized data can be shared using this method; uninitialized data is not placed into the shared memory section. If you are using Visual C++, the data_seg pragma is used to mark the beginning and end of a data segment, as Listing 16.5 shows.

Listing 16.5. Using the data_seg pragma to mark a data segment.

```
#pragma data_seg(".shared")
int nFoo = 0;
#pragma data_seg()

int GetFoo( void )
{
    return ++nFoo;
}
```

The code fragment in Listing 16.5 creates a data segment named .shared that contains one variable: nFoo. When this code is used in a DLL, every process will share the nFoo variable. When GetFoo is called, nFoo is incremented and the new value is returned.

When this code is run on a Windows NT installation with one processor, it works as expected. On my machine with two processors, however, it has a fatal flaw. It is possible for more than one CPU to attempt to change the value of nFoo, resulting in undefined results.

To demonstrate this problem, I wrote a simple driver program that called GetFoo 5,000 times and ran 10 instances of the test program. The last instance of the program should have finished with a count of 50,000. As you can see in Figure 16.5, this was not the case.

FIGURE 16.5.

Lost iterations after calling
GetFoo *50,000 times.*

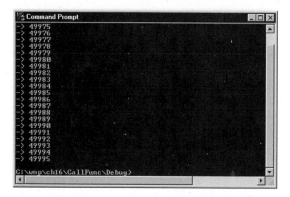

At some point, both CPUs on my machine tried to increment nFoo at the same time. This situation is known as a *race condition*—two or more processes each contend for a single variable or function, without synchronization. The basic problem is that a C++ language statement such as the following is not atomic—that is, it's translated into several CPU instructions:

```
return ++nFoo;
```

If you are using shared memory in a DLL, beware of using non-atomic operations on data or functions that may be used by multiple threads simultaneously.

Fortunately, Windows NT offers an API function you can use to increment and store a variable in an atomic operation. This guarantee is extended to all platforms, including RISC processors. The InterlockedIncrement function increments a variable stored at an address passed to it as a parameter:

```
InterlockedIncrement( &nFoo );
```

Listing 16.6 shows an improved version of GetFoo. Using a test driver, this version of GetFoo compiled into a DLL, which ran without losing any transactions.

Listing 16.6. A multiprocessor safe version of GetFoo.

```
#pragma data_seg(".shared")
int nFoo = 0;
#pragma data_seg()
```

```
int GetFoo( void )
{
    InterlockedIncrement( &nFoo );
    return nFoo;
}
```

The `InterlockedIncrement` function is used as the foundation for many synchronization primitives. In Chapter 22, "Threads," you learn other ways to synchronize threads and processes in a Windows NT application.

Using AppWizard to Create a DLL

If you are using Visual C++ to develop DLLs, you should use AppWizard to start your DLL projects. AppWizard sets up the build environment, including Linker and compiler settings needed to properly create DLLs.

Looking at a Simple DLL Example

As an example of how DLLs are used in Windows NT applications, I have created several example programs that are located on the CD-ROM included with this book. These examples range from simple examples involving Console Mode applications to MFC-based DLLs.

The first example program demonstrates how different applications can use a DLL as a "function warehouse." The FuncDll project creates a DLL that exports a single function; later, shared memory is added. I also create a Console Mode program and a dialog-based MFC application that use the DLL.

The final version of the DLL and its clients are included on the CD-ROM. You can use those projects or create them from scratch by following the steps presented here.

Creating the FuncDll DLL Project

The first version of the FuncDll project exports a single function: `GetCounter`. I used AppWizard to create `FuncDll` as a dynamic link library project.

Two files are added to the first version of the project:

- **FuncDll.c:** Contains the DLL source code
- **FuncDll.h:** Contains the declarations for FuncDll.c

Listing 16.7 provides the source code for the FuncDll.h source file. Enter the source code as shown here, and save it in the project directory.

Listing 16.7. The FuncDll.h header file used by FuncDll.

```
#ifdef __cplusplus
extern "C" {
#endif
// Define FUNC_DECL to be either an imported or exported
// library symbol, depending on whether we are building the
// DLL or using it in a client.
#ifdef FUNCDLL_DLL
// export function from library
#define FUNC_DECL   __declspec(dllexport)
#else
// import function from library
#define FUNC_DECL   __declspec(dllimport)
#endif
int FUNC_DECL GetCounter( void );
#ifdef __cplusplus
}
#endif
```

The FuncDll.h header file is used by the FuncDll.c source file, as well as by any applications that use load-time or implicit linking to the DLL. When used in FuncDll.c, the symbol FUNCDLL_DLL is defined, causing GetCounter to be exported. All other users of the header file do not define this symbol, so GetCounter is imported.

Listing 16.8 contains the FuncDll.c source file. This is the main source file used by the FuncDll project. Enter the source code as shown here, and save it in the project directory. After saving the file, add it to the project.

Listing 16.8. The FuncDll.c source file used by FuncDll.

```
#define   FUNCDLL_DLL
#include "funcdll.h"

int GetCounter( void )
{
    return 42;
}
```

FuncDll.c defines no DLL entry point because no initialization is performed. All FuncDll does is export a simple function from a DLL.

Compile the FuncDll project. Visual C++ creates a DLL and LIB file and stores them in the project's Debug subdirectory.

Using FuncDll in a Console Mode Application

The simplest type of Windows NT program that can use a DLL is a Console Mode application. Use AppWizard to create a Console Mode project named CallFunc, which demonstrates how to use a DLL in a Console Mode application.

After creating the CallFunc project using AppWizard, copy the FuncDll.h header file into the CallFunc project directory, where it is used by the Linker to generate a list of DLLs on which CallFunc depends.

Only one file exists in the CallFunc project. Listing 16.9 provides the source code for CallFunc.cpp. Enter the source code as shown here, and save it in the project directory. Remember to add the CallFunc.cpp file to the CallFunc project.

Listing 16.9. The CallFunc.cpp source file used by CallFunc.

```
#include <iostream.h>
#include "FuncDll.h"

int main()
{
    cout << "The counter is " << GetCounter() << endl;
    return 0;
}
```

In order to specify that Windows NT must load FuncDll.dll as the CallFunc application is loaded, you must link CallFunc with FuncDll.lib, the FuncDll import library. Copy FuncDll.lib into the CallFunc project directory, and change the project's Linker options by following these steps:

1. Choose Build and then Settings from the main menu.
2. Click on the Link tab.
3. Select Input from the Category drop-down list control.
4. Enter **FuncDll.lib** in the Object/Library module's Edit control.
5. Close the Settings dialog box.

Build the CallFunc project. If there are no errors, you can start the CallFunc application. You first must copy the FuncDll into the CallFunc project's Debug directory, however. This ensures that FuncDll is found when the application is started.

Open an MS-DOS console and change to the CallFunc project's Debug subdirectory. Start the application by typing **CallFunc** at the DOS prompt. If everything goes as planned, the following output appears:

```
The counter is 43
```

Using FuncDll in an MFC Application

Using a DLL such as FuncDll in an MFC application is very simple. In fact, you follow exactly the same steps used in the Console Mode example. If your DLL does not use any of the MFC Class Library, just use exactly the same steps outlined in the earlier sections. Situations in which you need access to the MFC Class Library in your DLL are covered later in this chapter, in the section *Using MFC and DLLs.*

Adding Shared Memory Functions to FuncDll

To add shared memory to FuncDll, I have edited the FuncDll library to include a shared memory section named .shared, as discussed earlier in this chapter. The new version of FuncDll stores a global counter that is incremented every time the GetCounter function is called.

Listing 16.10 contains a module definition file for FuncDll. Enter the source code as shown, and save it as FuncDll.def in the project directory.

Listing 16.10. The module definition file for FuncDll.

```
LIBRARY      "FUNCDLL"
DESCRIPTION  'FUNCDLL Windows Dynamic Link Library'

SECTIONS
   .shared  READ WRITE SHARED

EXPORTS
   ; Explicit exports can go here
```

In addition, the FuncDll.c source file must be edited. Listing 16.11 shows the new version of FuncDll.c.

Listing 16.11. The new version of FuncDll.c.

```
#include <windows.h>
#define   FUNCDLL_DLL
#include "funcdll.h"

#pragma data_seg(".shared")
int nCounter = 0;
#pragma data_seg()

int GetCounter( void )
{
    InterlockedIncrement( &nCounter );
    return nCounter;
}
```

After making these changes, rebuild the FuncDll project. To test the new version of FuncDll, start several instances of the CallFunc project created earlier. Every time GetCounter is called, it returns a higher value. You also can modify the CallFunc project to call GetCounter repeatedly, like this:

```
for()
```

Several versions of CallFunc modified in this way are running in Figure 16.6.

FIGURE 16.6.

Several instances of CallFunc using shared memory in FuncDll.

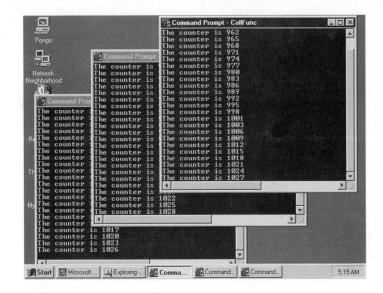

Using C++ and DLLs

The previous DLL examples export C functions because they are the simplest functions to export. You also can export C++ classes and member functions from a DLL, however. If you use a C++ interface in your DLL, be warned: A DLL that exports classes created with Visual C++ cannot be used by applications created with a compiler that uses different object-management or name-mangling schemes.

When exporting class or member function symbols, __declspec is used much as it is for standard C functions. To export a class, __declspec follows the class keyword:

```
class __declspec(dllexport) CFoo {
// class info here
};
```

To export an individual function from a class, __declspec is included in the function declaration:

```
class CFoo{
public:
    int __declspec(dllexport) GetCount() const;
};
```

Examining a Payroll Record Class Stored in a DLL

As an example of exporting a C++ class from a DLL, I have created a DLL project named ClassDll. The ClassDll project builds a DLL that exports CPayrollRec—a C++ class that represents a payroll record.

To get started with the ClassDll project, use AppWizard to create the project. Listing 16.12 shows the CPayrollRec class declaration. Enter the source code as shown, and save it as payrec.h in the project directory.

Listing 16.12. The class declaration for CPayrollRec.

```
#ifdef PAYREC_DLL
#define CLASS_DECL __declspec(dllexport)
#else
#define CLASS_DECL __declspec(dllimport)
#endif

class CLASS_DECL CPayrollRec
{
public:
    CPayrollRec();
    CPayrollRec( double dRate, double dHours = 0.0 );
    double GrossPay() const;
private:
    double m_dRate;
    double m_dHours;
};
```

Listing 16.13 contains the source code for the CPayrollRec function definitions. Enter the source code as shown, and save it as payrec.cpp in the project directory. Remember to add the source file to the ClassDll project.

Listing 16.13. The class definition for CPayrollRec.

```
#define PAYREC_DLL
#include "payrec.h"

CPayrollRec::CPayrollRec(): m_dRate(0.0), m_dHours(0.0)
{
}

CPayrollRec::CPayrollRec( double dRate, double dHours )
           :m_dRate(dRate), m_dHours(dHours)
{
}

double CPayrollRec::GrossPay() const
{
    return m_dRate * m_dHours;
}
```

Compile the ClassDll project. Visual C++ creates a DLL and an import LIB file for ClassDll.

Using the ClassDll Example in an Application

I also have created a project that demonstrates how you can use ClassDll in a Windows NT application. The Payroll project is a Console Mode application that creates and uses a CPayrollRec object defined in ClassDll.

After creating the Payroll project using AppWizard, copy the payrec.h header file and the ClassDll.lib import library into the Payroll project directory, where they will be used by the Linker to generate a list of DLLs on which Payroll depends.

Only one file exists in the Payroll project. Listing 16.14 provides the source code for Payroll.cpp. Enter the source code as shown here, and save it in the project directory as Payroll.cpp. Insert this file into the Payroll project.

Listing 16.14. The source code for Payroll.cpp.

```
#include <iostream.h>
#include "payrec.h"

int main()
{
    CPayrollRec    theRec( 2.5, 42.00 );
    cout << "Current gross pay is $" << theRec.GrossPay() << endl;
    return 0;
}
```

Before building the Payroll project, change the build settings to include ClassDll.lib as a library used by the linker. Follow these steps:

1. Choose Build and then Settings from the main menu.
2. Click on the Link tab.
3. Select Input from the Category drop-down list control.
4. Enter **ClassDll.lib** in the Object/Library module's Edit control.
5. Close the Settings dialog box.

Build the Payroll project. As with the earlier examples, you first must copy the ClassDll into the Payroll project's Debug directory. This ensures that ClassDll is found when the application is started.

Open an MS-DOS console and change to the Payroll project's Debug subdirectory. Start the application by typing **Payroll** at the DOS prompt. If everything goes as planned, the following output appears:

```
Current gross pay is $105
```

As you can see, using a C++ class exported by a DLL is almost exactly like using a standard C function exported from a DLL.

Using MFC and DLLs

Three basic ways exist to mix MFC and DLLs with your Windows NT application:

- Use MFC in a shared DLL.
- Use MFC in a DLL and load the DLL from a non-MFC application.
- Use MFC in a DLL and load the DLL from an MFC application.

When using MFC as a Windows application, the default behavior is to use MFC in a shared DLL, as shown in Figure 16.7. This helps reduce the size of your application and helps your application load faster if another MFC application is already running.

FIGURE 16.7.

MFC application using the MFC core code from the shared MFC DLL.

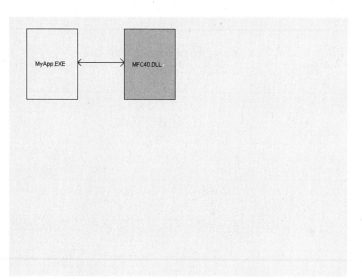

Another way to use the shared MFC DLL is by creating a DLL that uses the MFC DLL. The main application does not have to be MFC-based. In fact, it is possible to use a C interface between the main application and the DLL. Figure 16.8 illustrates this sort of interface.

The most common way to use MFC in a DLL is with an extension DLL, as shown in Figure 16.9. An *extension DLL* uses the shared MFC library and is called by an MFC-based application.

The next few sections discuss the steps required to create and use MFC-extension DLLs.

FIGURE 16.8.

Non-MFC applications using MFC code via a DLL.

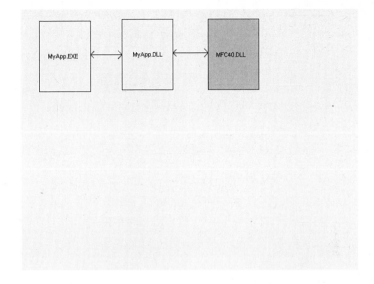

FIGURE 16.9.

Using an extension DLL in an MFC application.

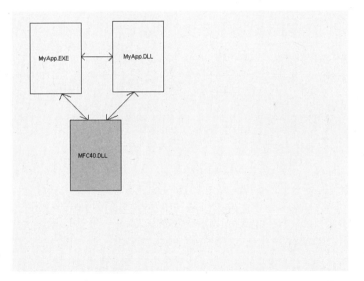

Initializing an MFC Extension DLL

Every MFC-extension DLL must perform some initialization in its DLL entry-point function. Listing 16.15 provides an example of a typical DLL entry point for an extension DLL. Actually, this function was created by AppWizard as part of an extension DLL project. I usually try to avoid showing AppWizard-generated code, but in this case, it's short and relevant.

Listing 16.15. Source code created by AppWizard for MFC-extension DLLs.

```
static AFX_EXTENSION_MODULE fooDLL = { NULL, NULL };
extern "C" int APIENTRY
DllMain(HINSTANCE hInstance, DWORD dwReason, LPVOID lpReserved)
{
    if (dwReason == DLL_PROCESS_ATTACH)
    {
        TRACE0("DLGINDLL.DLL Initializing!\n");
        // Extension DLL one-time initialization
        AfxInitExtensionModule(fooDLL, hInstance);
        // Insert this DLL into the resource chain
        new CDynLinkLibrary(DlgInDllDLL);
    }
    else if (dwReason == DLL_PROCESS_DETACH)
    {
        TRACE0("DLGINDLL.DLL Terminating!\n");
    }
    return 1;
}
```

Even if you do not use AppWizard to create your extension DLL project, you should copy this function because it shows exactly how an extension DLL must be started and registered with the MFC framework.

When a process is attached to an extension DLL, the global AFX_EXTENSION_MODULE variable is used to track classes and other objects used in the DLL. A CDynLinkLibrary object is created on the heap; this object is inserted into a list that is searched when resources are required by the process that loaded the DLL.

Creating an Extension DLL

In this section, I create an MFC-extension DLL project named DlgInDll that exports a dialog box resource and an associated CDialog-based class used to manage it. Like the earlier projects in this chapter, the complete project can be found on the accompanying CD-ROM. You can use that project, or you can follow along with the steps presented here to create the project from scratch.

To get started on the DlgInDll project, use AppWizard to create an MFC-extension DLL. First, select MFC AppWizard(dll) as the project type, as shown in Figure 16.10.

After clicking Create, a Wizard page appears, as shown in Figure 16.11. Select MFC Extension DLL (using shared MFC DLL).

Using Developer Studio, add a dialog resource type to the project. Give this dialog box a resource ID of IDD_EXT_NAME. Add an Edit control to the dialog, as shown in Figure 16.12.

FIGURE 16.10.

Using AppWizard to create a DLL that uses MFC.

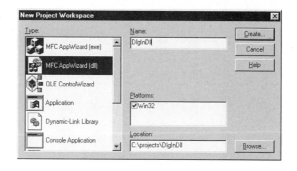

FIGURE 16.11.

Selecting MFC Extension DLL as the project type.

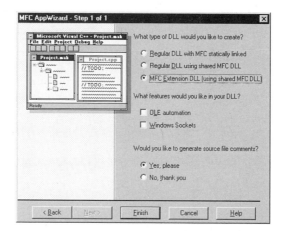

FIGURE 16.12.

Adding an Edit control to the DlgInDll dialog box.

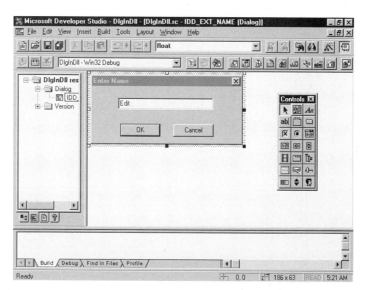

Table 16.1 provides the resource ID used by the Edit control. Use ClassWizard to associate a member variable with the Edit control, using the values from the same table.

Table 16.1. Edit control resource information.

Control Name	Resource ID	Category	Type	Variable
Name edit	IDC_NAME	Value	CString	m_szName

Using ClassWizard, create a class derived from CDialog named CNameDlg to manage the new dialog resource. Use the values in Table 16.2 to create the new class.

Table 16.2. Values used for the dialog box.

Control	Value
Name	CNameDlg
Base Class	CDialog
File	NameDlg.cpp
Dialog ID	IDD_EXT_NAME
OLE Automation	None
Component Gallery	Cleared

In order to export the CNameDlg class from the library, the CNameDlg class declaration must be edited. Listing 16.16 shows changes made to the NameDlg.h header file in bold.

Listing 16.16. The CNameDlg class declaration.

```
#ifndef _AFXEXT
#define IDD_EXT_NAME 129
#else
#include "resource.h"
#endif

class AFX_EXT_CLASS CNameDlg : public CDialog
{
// Construction
public:
    CNameDlg(CWnd* pParent = NULL);

// Dialog Data
    //{{AFX_DATA(CNameDlg)
    enum { IDD = IDD_EXT_NAME };
```

```
    .
    .
    .
};
```

Two changes are made in the NameDlg.h header file:

- ■ The symbol used to define the dialog box is hard-coded in the header. This resource symbol is hard-coded because there is a dependency between the class declaration and the IDD_EXT_NAME symbol. If you use Visual C++ 4.0 or 4.1, and follow the steps described, this value is correct. You can always determine the actual value by selecting Resource Symbols from the Developer Studio View menu.

- ■ The AFX_EXT_CLASS symbol is used in the CNameDlg class declaration. This symbol is used exactly as other placeholders used in previous examples. When an MFC-extension DLL is built, the AFX_EXT_CLASS symbol expands to __declspec(dllexport). For all other builds, it expands to __declspec(dllimport).

Compile the DlgInDll project. Visual C++ creates a DLL and an import LIB file for DlgInDll.

Looking at an Example Using an Extension DLL

As an example of using an MFC-extension DLL, I have created a program that uses the DlgInDll DLL project created in the preceding section.

Once again, you can open this project and follow along as I describe the various parts of the project, or you can create the project yourself using the steps presented in the next few sections. To begin, create a dialog-based project named Hello using ClassWizard.

Modifying the Main Dialog Box

Using Developer Studio, add a new pushbutton control to the main dialog box, as shown in Figure 16.13.

Table 16.3 shows the resource IDs used by the main dialog box controls. Note that the static control has a new resource ID and caption.

Table 16.3. Controls used by the main dialog box.

Control	Resource ID	Caption
Name button	IDC_NAME	&Name...
Static control	IDC_NAME_LABEL	Hello! Click Name...

FIGURE 16.13.

Adding controls to the main dialog box for the Hello application.

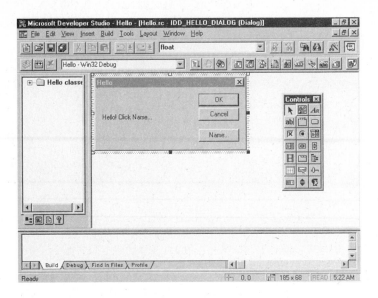

Using ClassWizard, add a message-handling function for the CHelloDlg class. Use the values from Table 16.4 when adding this message-handling function.

Table 16.4. Values for new member functions in CHelloDlg.

Object ID	Class Name	Message	Function
IDC_NAME	CHelloDlg	BN_CLICKED	OnBtnName

Using ClassWizard, associate a CStatic member variable named m_wndNameLabel with the IDC_NAME_LABEL static control.

Listing 16.17 provides the source code for the CHelloDlg::OnBtnName function.

Listing 16.17. Calling a dialog box class located in an extension DLL.

```
void CHelloDlg::OnBtnName()
{
    CNameDlg    dlg;
    if( dlg.DoModal() == IDOK )
    {
        CString szHello = "Hello ";
        m_wndNameLabel.SetWindowText( szHello + dlg.m_szName );
    }
}
```

Remember to add the following code to the top of the HelloDlg.cpp source file, just after the standard #include files:

```
#include "NameDlg.h"
```

Before compiling the Hello project, copy DlgInDll.lib, the import library from the DlgInDll project into the Hello project directory. Also copy the NameDlg.h header file into the Hello project directory.

Add the import library from the DlgInDll DLL to the Hello project by following these steps:

1. Choose Build and then Settings from the main menu.
2. Click on the Link tab.
3. Select Input from the Category drop-down list control.
4. Enter **DlgInDll.lib** in the Object/Library module's Edit control.
5. Close the Settings dialog box.

Build the Hello project. As with the earlier examples, you must copy the DlgInDll DLL into the Hello project's Debug directory before running the application. This ensures that the DLL is found when the application is started.

Start the Hello application. If you click the Name button, the dialog box from the DlgInDll DLL is displayed, as shown in Figure 16.14. After entering a name in the dialog box, the static label in the main dialog is updated.

FIGURE 16.14.

The Hello application after creating the Name dialog box.

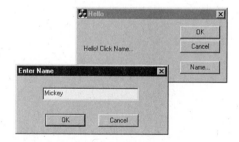

Summary

This chapter discussed many of the issues involved with building and using DLLs when programming for Windows NT. The differences between DLLs written for 16-bit versions of Windows and Windows NT were also discussed.

Several projects were provided to illustrate how to export standard C functions, C++ classes, and MFC objects. An example illustrating how to avoid synchronization problems in shared DLL memory was also presented.

The next chapter, "OLE and DDE Concepts," discusses how OLE and DDE are used for interprocess communication. The chapter includes examples using DDE and OLE for integration with the Windows NT Shell.

PART

Application-Level Program Communication

OLE and DDE Concepts

17

by Mickey Williams

OLE 2.0 and Dynamic Data Exchange (DDE) are two methods commonly used for interprocess communication in Windows NT. This chapter focuses on the concepts behind these two communications methods and presents sample programs that demonstrate how they are used.

Looking at an Overview of OLE and DDE

DDE is an interprocess communication protocol originally introduced for 16-bit Windows. DDE is an attractive mechanism for interprocess communication because it allows applications to communicate over defined, open interfaces. In order to communicate, applications only need to know the DDE services exposed by another application; it isn't necessary for applications to share DLLs or other binary components.

OLE 2.0 is based on the *component object model*—a specification for communications between software components. COM is discussed in more detail later in this chapter, beginning with the section *Looking at the Component Object Model*. OLE 1.0 was a much simpler method of interprocess communication. In fact, back then, OLE actually stood for *object linking and embedding*. Nowadays, OLE 2.0 has so much more functionality that the marketing department in Redmond has decided that OLE is just plain OLE—it isn't limited to linking and embedding.

Using DDE for Interprocess Communication

DDE is used for interprocess communication in three ways:

- For a DDE client to transmit information to or from a DDE server
- For a DDE client to request status updates from a DDE server
- For a DDE server to expose commands that can be executed by DDE client applications

The Microsoft Office applications are examples of programs that can be used as DDE servers or DDE clients. It's fairly simple to create a DDE client application that establishes a DDE conversation with an Excel spreadsheet and uses DDE to extract or update information contained in the spreadsheet. You also can use MS-Word as a DDE server to create word processing documents.

Examining the Roles of Clients and Servers

Two applications exchange information using DDE by establishing a DDE conversation. A conversation always consists of a client that initializes the conversation and a server that serves the needs of the client. The client requests or transmits information to the server, and the server provides or accepts information from the client, as shown in Figure 17.1.

FIGURE 17.1.

Client and server roles in a DDE conversation.

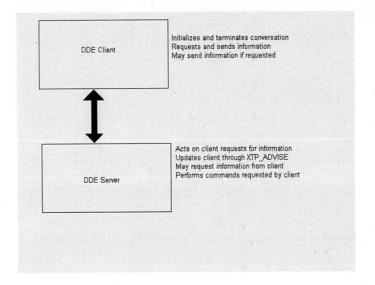

Examining DDE Basics

The original version of DDE was based on the Windows message protocol. Client and server DDE applications communicate by sending formatted messages, much like sending any other message between two applications. In Windows 3.0, the DDE Management Library (DDEML) was introduced to simplify the use of DDE. Instead of explicitly sending messages between applications, Windows API functions can be used for DDE programming.

When a client establishes a conversation with a DDE server, the client must specify an application and a topic name. A conversation can refer to a single topic only; to change topics, a new conversation must be started. Table 17.1 lists examples of application names for common Windows applications.

Table 17.1. DDE application names for common Windows applications.

Application	DDE Application Name
Microsoft Access	MSAccess
Microsoft Excel	Excel
Microsoft FoxPro	FoxPro
Microsoft Project	WinProj
Microsoft Word	WinWord
Windows shell	ProgMan

In addition to the application and topic, an item name is specified for any information exchanged between client and server. You can think of an item name as a subtopic, and you can change it during a conversation.

Initializing DDE

Before calling any of the DDEML functions, an application must call DDEInitialize in order to register with the DDE management library. Listing 17.1 shows how the DDEInitialize function is called.

Listing 17.1. Registering an application with the DDE management library.

```
DWORD dwID = 0;
UINT uErr = DdeInitialize( &dwID,
                           (PFNCALLBACK)&DdeCallback,
                           APPCMD_CLIENTONLY,
                           0 );
if( uErr != DMLERR_NO_ERROR )
{
    // Handle error
}
```

DDEInitialize takes four parameters:

- The address of a DWORD variable that will contain the instance identifier for this DDE session. This variable must be set to 0 when calling DDEInitialize and contains the instance ID if the function call succeeds. This value must be retained because it is required for some DDEML functions.
- A pointer to a callback function used for DDE messages.
- One or more flags that specify characteristics about the DDE services required by this application. In this case, APPCMD_CLIENTONLY indicates that this application will never be a server. Any server requests directed at this application will fail immediately. This helps reduce the resources committed by the DDE management library.
- A reserved parameter that must be set to 0.

The DDE callback function passed as the second pointer to DDEInitialize is called by the operating system to handle messages sent by the server. Listing 17.2 shows a minimal version of a DDE callback function.

Listing 17.2. A minimal version of a DDE callback function.

```
HDDEDATA EXPENTRY DdeCallback( UINT  uType,
                               UINT  uFmt,
                               HCONV hconv,
                               HSZ   hsz1,
                               HSZ   hsz2,
```

```
                  HDDEDATA hdata,
                  DWORD dwData1,
                  DWORD dwData2 )

{
    return (HDDEDATA)NULL;
}
```

If the call to DDEInitialize succeeds, the DDE management library must be released by calling DDEUninitialize, passing the instance identifier as a parameter:

```
DdeUninitialize( dwID );
```

Looking at a DDE Client Example

As an example of using DDE, I have created an MFC project named DdePm on the accompanying CD-ROM. This project uses DDE to communicate with the Windows NT Shell. I chose a Shell DDE interface example because every Windows NT installation is likely to have it. The DdePm application enables you to create, modify, and delete program groups from the Program menu. You can use DdePm directly from the CD, or you can follow along as I create the project from scratch.

To get started with the DdePm project, use AppWizard to create a dialog-based project named DdePm. Feel free to accept or change any of the project options offered by AppWizard.

Open the main dialog box resource and modify it, as shown in Figure 17.2. Note that a new edit control and three new pushbutton controls are included.

FIGURE 17.2.

The main dialog box for DdePm.

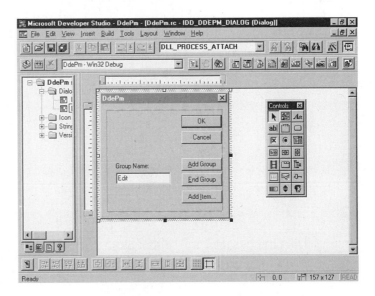

Use the values from Table 17.2 for the new controls added to the main dialog box resource.

Table 17.2. Resource and control information for the main dialog box.

Control	Resource ID	Caption
Static text control	IDC_STATIC	Group Name:
Edit control	IDC_EDIT_GROUP	
Add group button	IDC_ADD_GROUP	&Add Group
End group button	IDC_END_GROUP	&End Group
Add item button	IDC_ADD_ITEM	Add &Item

Use ClassWizard to associate a new member variable with the IDC_EDIT_GROUP edit control, using the values from Table 17.3.

Table 17.3. Values for new member variables in CDdePmDlg.

Control ID	Variable Name	Category	Type
IDC_EDIT_GROUP	m_szEditGroup	Value	CString

Using ClassWizard, add message-handling functions to the CDdePmDlg class to handle messages from the new controls, using the values provided in Table 17.4.

Table 17.4. Message-handling information for CDdePmDlg.

Class Name	Object ID	Message	Member Function
CDdePmDlg	IDC_ADD_GROUP	BN_CLICKED	OnAddGroup
CDdePmDlg	IDC_END_GROUP	BN_CLICKED	OnEndGroup
CDdePmDlg	IDC_ADD_ITEM	BN_CLICKED	OnAddItem

The CDdePmDlg class is modified by adding a new member function that handles the display of common DDE errors. Make the changes shown in bold in Listing 17.3 to the CDdePmDlg class declaration.

Listing 17.3. Changes (in bold) to the CDdePmDlg class declaration.

```
class CDdePmDlg : public CDialog
{
.
.
```

```
.
.
.
// Implementation
protected:
    HICON    m_hIcon;
    void     HandleError( UINT u );
.
.
.
};
```

Add declarations for two functions used by the `CDdePmDlg` class to the top of the DdePmDlg.cpp source file, just below the #include directives, as shown in Listing 17.4.

Listing 17.4. Declarations for functions used by the `CDdePmDlg` class.

```
BOOL ProgManDde( DWORD dwInst, LPCTSTR lpszCommand );
HDDEDATA EXPENTRY DdeCallback( UINT  uType,
                              UINT  uFmt,
                              HCONV hconv,
                              HSZ   hsz1,
                              HSZ   hsz2,
                              HDDEDATA hdata,
                              DWORD dwData1,
                              DWORD dwData2 );
```

Listing 17.5 contains the source code for the new member functions added to the `CDdePmDlg` class, as well as the `ProgManDde` and `DdeCallback` functions.

Listing 17.5. `CDdePmDlg` member functions.

```
void CDdePmDlg::OnAddGroup()
{
    UpdateData();
    if( m_szGroup.IsEmpty() == FALSE )
    {
        DWORD dwID = 0;
        UINT u = DdeInitialize( &dwID,
                                (PFNCALLBACK)&DdeCallback,
                                APPCMD_CLIENTONLY,
                                0 );
        if( u != DMLERR_NO_ERROR )
        {
            HandleError( u );
            return;
        }
        CString szCommand;
        szCommand.Format( "[CreateGroup(\"%s\")]", m_szGroup );
        BOOL fResult = ProgManDde( dwID, szCommand );
        if( fResult == FALSE )
        {
```

continues

Listing 17.5. continued

```
                AfxMessageBox( "Command Failed", MB_ICONHAND );
        }
        DdeUninitialize( dwID );
    }
    else
    {
        AfxMessageBox( "Please enter a group name" );
    }
}

void CDdePmDlg::OnAddItem()
{
    UpdateData();
    if( m_szGroup.IsEmpty() == FALSE )
    {
        CFileDialog     dlg(TRUE);
        if( dlg.DoModal() == IDOK )
        {
            DWORD dwID = 0;
            UINT u = DdeInitialize( &dwID,
                            (PFNCALLBACK)&DdeCallback,
                            APPCMD_CLIENTONLY,
                            0 );
            if( u != DMLERR_NO_ERROR )
            {
                HandleError( u );
                return;
            }
            CString szCommand;
            szCommand.Format( "[CreateGroup(\"%s\")]", m_szGroup );
            BOOL fResult = ProgManDde( dwID, szCommand );
            if( fResult == FALSE )
            {
                AfxMessageBox( "Command Failed", MB_ICONHAND );
            }
            szCommand.Format( "[AddItem(\"%s\")]",
                            (LPCTSTR)dlg.GetPathName() );
            ProgManDde( dwID, szCommand );
            DdeUninitialize( dwID );
        }
    }
    else
    {
        AfxMessageBox( "Please enter a group name" );
    }
}

void CDdePmDlg::OnEndGroup()
{
    UpdateData();
    if( m_szGroup.IsEmpty() == FALSE )
    {
        DWORD   dwID = 0;
        UINT u = DdeInitialize( &dwID,
                            (PFNCALLBACK)&DdeCallback,
                            APPCMD_CLIENTONLY,
```

```
                                   0 );
        if( u != DMLERR_NO_ERROR )
        {
            HandleError( u );
            return;
        }
        CString szCommand;
        szCommand.Format( "[DeleteGroup(\"%s\")]", m_szGroup );
        BOOL fResult = ProgManDde( dwID, szCommand );
        if( fResult == FALSE )
        {
            AfxMessageBox( "Command Failed", MB_ICONHAND );
        }
        DdeUninitialize( dwID );
    }
    else
    {
        AfxMessageBox( "Please enter a group name" );
    }
}

void CDdePmDlg::HandleError( UINT u )
{
    CString szMsg;
    switch(u)
    {
    case DMLERR_DLL_USAGE:
        szMsg = "DMLERR_DLL_USAGE";
        break;
    case DMLERR_INVALIDPARAMETER:
        szMsg = "DMLERR_INVALIDPARAMETER";
        break;
    case DMLERR_NO_CONV_ESTABLISHED:
        szMsg = "DMLERR_NO_CONV_ESTABLISHED";
        break;
    case DMLERR_SYS_ERROR:
        szMsg = "DMLERR_SYS_ERR";
        break;
    default:
        szMsg = "Unknown DDE Initialization Error";
        break;
    }
    AfxMessageBox( szMsg );
}
//
// ProgManDde - A basic function that sends a command string
//              to the program manager.
//
BOOL ProgManDde( DWORD dwInst, LPCTSTR lpszCommand )
{
    BOOL fResult = FALSE;
    HSZ hszTopic = DdeCreateStringHandle( dwInst,
                                          "PROGMAN",
                                          CP_WINANSI );

    ASSERT( hszTopic );
    HCONV hConversation = DdeConnect( dwInst,
                                      hszTopic,
                                      hszTopic,
```

continues

Listing 17.5. continued

```
                                        NULL );
        if( hConversation != NULL )
        {
            int   cString = lstrlen( lpszCommand );
            DWORD    dwResult;
            HDDEDATA hResult;
            hResult = DdeClientTransaction( (LPBYTE)lpszCommand,
                                            cString + 1,
                                            hConversation,
                                            0L,
                                            CF_TEXT,
                                            XTYP_EXECUTE,
                                            10000,
                                            &dwResult );

            if( hResult != NULL )
                fResult = TRUE;

            DdeDisconnect( hConversation );
        }
        DdeFreeStringHandle( dwInst, hszTopic );
        return fResult;
}

HDDEDATA EXPENTRY DdeCallback( UINT   uType,
                              UINT   uFmt,
                              HCONV  hconv,
                              HSZ    hsz1,
                              HSZ    hsz2,
                              HDDEDATA hdata,
                              DWORD dwData1,
                              DWORD dwData2 )
{
    return (HDDEDATA)NULL;
}
```

Three of the CDdePmDlg member functions are called in response to the user clicking a button in the main dialog box:

- OnAddGroup
- OnAddItem
- OnEndGroup

Each of these functions initializes the DDE library, creates a command string to be sent to the Windows NT shell, and passes the command string to the ProgManDde function. The syntax for each command string is documented in the Win32 SDK, below the topic "Shell Dynamic Data Exchange Interface." After ProgManDde sends the command to the Windows NT shell, the DDE library is freed using DDEUninitialize.

The ProgManDde function handles the actual conversation with the shell. ProgManDde creates a DDE string handle for the ProgMan topic and initiates a conversation with the shell. If the conversation is established, the command string is sent to the shell.

In order to use DDE management library functions, you must include the ddeml.h header file. Add the following line after the other include statements in stdafx.h:

```
#include <ddeml.h>
```

Compile and run the DdePm project. Figure 17.3 shows DdePm running with a new Program Group window displayed in the background. Experiment by adding, modifying, and deleting program groups, but be careful not to delete groups you really need.

FIGURE 17.3.
*Using the DdePm
application to modify
Program groups.*

To add a new group to the Programs menu, enter a group name and click the Add Group button. If the group already exists, it is opened; otherwise, a new group is added. To add an item to the group, click the Add Item button and select an item from the File Open dialog box.

Looking at the Component Object Model

As discussed earlier, the component object model (COM) is the foundation on which OLE rests. COM is a specification for a number of technologies that define how objects and systems can interact with each other in an open and scaleable manner.

Examining Commonly Used COM and OLE Technologies

OLE and COM define several technologies that can be used to create component-based software. The most commonly used COM and OLE technologies follow:

- OLE Clipboard
- Drag and drop
- Compound documents
- Visual editing
- OLE Automation
- Integration with other applications

Each of these technologies is discussed in the following sections.

Compound Documents

One of the original big-ticket items that came with OLE 2.0 were compound documents. A compound document can be used to integrate content from multiple OLE servers—including text, graphics, audio, or any other data that might be generated. Each document stores the *CLSIDs* of the servers used to create and manage individual portions of the document. A CLSID is a unique 128-bit identifier used to identify different types of COM components.

Storing information in a compound document enables a user to focus on the document rather than on each application used to create the content stored in the document. Because a component object in the compound document requires editing, that object's server can be activated automatically, using the CLSID for the object's server. Of course, this happens without the user needing to understand the underlying mechanism involved.

A component object can be stored in a compound document in two ways: by linking and by embedding.

A *linked* component resides outside the compound document, and the compound document keeps a moniker that points to the linked component's location. This reduces the size of the compound document and is very useful when a single item is "owned" by another user, or when a single item is shared among multiple documents, as shown in Figure 17.4.

FIGURE 17.4.

A linked object is physically located outside the compound document.

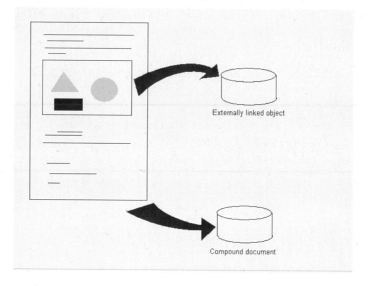

Externally linked object

Compound document

An *embedded* component object actually is stored inside the compound document, as shown in Figure 17.5. Using embedding is useful when a document must be transferred or relocated, because all the information is stored inside the compound document. In addition, embedded objects can take advantage of visual editing, which is discussed in the next section.

FIGURE 17.5.

An embedded object is physically stored inside the compound document.

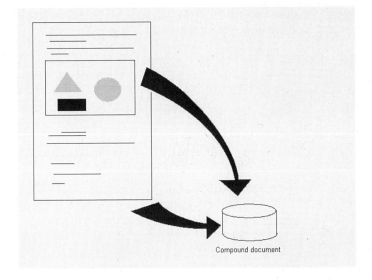

Compound document

Visual Editing

Visual editing allows an OLE container to activate a server for an embedded component object *in-place*. The container and the server share the user interface, enabling a user to interact with a component object without switching applications. This greatly simplifies the user's view of how a document is managed. From the user's perspective, the entire document seems to be edited within a single application.

As an example, consider a spreadsheet object embedded in a word processing compound document, as shown in Figure 17.6.

FIGURE 17.6.

An Excel spreadsheet embedded in a Word document.

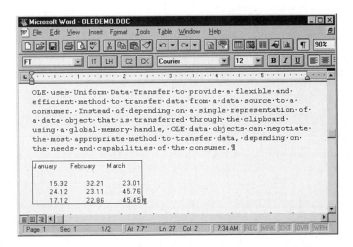

If the spreadsheet object is edited, the server for the spreadsheet object, Microsoft Excel, activates in-place, as shown in Figure 17.7.

FIGURE 17.7.

Microsoft Excel activated inside the Word container.

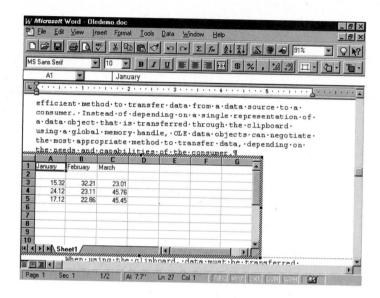

As you can see in Figure 17.7, the container and server have merged various elements of their user interface. Although the container has not changed, it now hosts many of the menus and toolbar items that belong to the Excel spreadsheet.

After editing is complete, the container resumes control of the user interface, as shown in Figure 17.6.

OLE Automation

OLE Automation involves the exposure of programmable interfaces by an application. Automation always involves an automation controller—usually a programming environment such as Visual Basic—and an automation server that exposes a set of programmable interfaces.

Automation allows an application to be controlled by a script or another program, in much the same way that DDE controls applications. In fact, many DDE servers also are OLE Automation servers, such as Microsoft Word and Excel.

Automation is a large topic—in fact, Chapter 19, "OLE Automation," is devoted entirely to this topic.

Uniform Data Transfer

OLE uses uniform data transfer to provide a flexible and efficient method to transfer data from a data source to a consumer. Instead of depending on a single representation of a data object transferred through the Clipboard using a global memory handle, OLE data objects can negotiate the most appropriate method to transfer data, depending on the needs and capabilities of the consumer.

When using the Clipboard, data must be transferred via a global memory handle, which is extremely inefficient for large items such as bitmaps or multimedia clips. Uniform data transfer allows data to be transferred as a reference to a file or other storage object, speeding up the transfer operation.

Uniform data transfer also supports the idea of notifications when a data source changes its representation of a data object. These notifications are similar to the XTP_ADVISE messages used with DDE, although they occur through OLE interfaces.

Drag and Drop

OLE drag and drop is built on top of the uniform data transfer mechanism discussed in the preceding section. OLE provides a large set of functions and interfaces that can be used to manage the transfer of data from one object to another visually, instead of through the Clipboard. Chapter 18 discusses OLE drag and drop in detail.

Integration with Other Applications

In addition to the OLE capabilities discussed earlier, the component object model implies even greater possibilities yet to come. COM defines a model that can extend the services offered by Windows in a general, flexible way. In fact, many of the new technologies released for Windows NT and Windows 95, such as MAPI, use COM-style interfaces.

Programming with COM and OLE

Before you look at an OLE example, you should know some of the basics involved with programming using COM and OLE. These basic topics follow:

- Understanding and using COM interfaces
- Identifying COM objects and interfaces
- The IUnknown and the QueryInterface functions
- Creating COM objects

After looking at these basic topics, you'll learn about using OLE and COM to create shell extensions for the Windows NT shell.

Using COM Interfaces

Under COM, direct access to an object is never permitted. Communication with an object takes place through well-defined interfaces. Restricting access to objects allows COM to be an environment and language-neutral model—nothing in the COM specification restricts you to using C++. In fact, Visual Basic, Delphi, and C all are used to program OLE and COM applications.

All interfaces in the component object model begin with *I* as a standard naming convention (*I* stands for *interface*). A COM interface usually is drawn as shown in Figure 17.8.

FIGURE 17.8.

Diagramming the interfaces supported by an object.

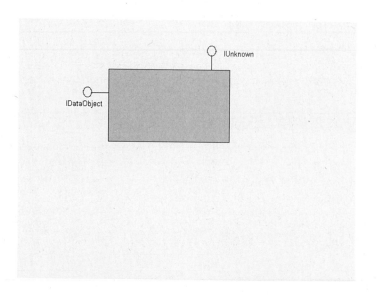

The object is shown as a square box, with one or more open circles, representing jacks, extended from it. These jacks symbolize interfaces supported by the object. Because every object implements the IUnknown interface, it usually is shown alone at the top of the box. When dealing with well-known interfaces, such as those defined by COM or a Windows NT subsystem such as MAPI, the names of individual functions on an interface are not shown.

Identifying COM Interfaces and Objects

The component object model specifies that interfaces and objects are identified by 128-bit numbers known as *globally unique identifiers* (GUIDs). A GUID can be used to identify two types of items:

■ A GUID used to identify an interface is known as an *interface identifier* (IID).

■ A GUID used to identify a type of object is known as a *class identifier* (ClassID, or CLSID).

Due to the sheer size of a GUID, it is very unlikely that two randomly chosen GUIDs will ever be identical. Even given large numbers of randomly chosen GUIDs, the possibility of a name collision is extremely small.

> **NOTE**
>
> *Never* attempt to reuse GUIDs published in books, magazines, or elsewhere. This is much worse than sharing a toothbrush with someone and has the potential of causing you (and others) endless and difficult-to-resolve pain and suffering. The Windows NT Registry and COM are not built to handle the possibility of GUID collisions, which never happen as long as everyone plays by the rules.

To generate your own set of GUIDs, run the UUIDGEN from a console window. If you have a network interface card installed on your machine, you will receive a unique GUID of your very own similar to the following:

```
d3d834c1-9a3b-11cf-82a0-00608cca2a2a
```

You can display a complete list of UUIDGEN options by using the -? switch. You also can ask for a GUID preformatted into an interface structure as used in the DEFINE_GUID macro by using the -s switch, as shown in Listing 17.6.

Listing 17.6. A preformatted GUID generated by UUIDGEN.

```
INTERFACENAME = { /* d3d834c1-9a3b-11cf-82a0-00608cca2a2a */
    0xd3d834c1,
    0x9a3b,
    0x11cf,
    {0x82, 0xa0, 0x00, 0x60, 0x8c, 0xca, 0x2a, 0x2a}
};
```

The DEFINE_GUID macro is used to initialize a class ID or interface ID to be equal to a particular GUID. To define a GUID representing an OLE class named Foo, a CLSID_Foo symbol is initialized using the DEFINE_GUID macro:

```
DEFINE_GUID( CLSID_Foo, 0xd3d834c0, 0x9a3b, 0x11cf, 0x82,
             0xa0, 0x00, 0x60, 0x8c, 0xca, 0x2a, 0x2a );
```

If your machine does not have a network interface card, a pseudo-random GUID is synthesized for you. There is a slight chance that this GUID may collide with other GUIDs assigned at random to other COM and OLE programmers. If you are writing an OLE application for distribution, you must install a network interface card for maximum safety. If installing a network card for a few GUIDs is too painful for some reason, drop me an e-mail message at:

```
mickeyw@deltanet.com
```

and I'll be happy to create some safe GUIDs for you.

Handling GUIDs

Due to the length of a GUID, handling GUIDs tends to be more difficult than passing around 32-bit handles. Listing 17.7 shows the structure of a GUID.

Listing 17.7. The GUID `struct` declaration.

```
typedef struct _GUID
{
    unsigned long  Data1;
    unsigned short Data2;
    unsigned short Data3;
    unsigned char  Data4[8];
}GUID;
```

In the Win32 Registry, a GUID is stored with curly braces at each end, like this:

```
{d3d834c0-9a3b-11cf-82a0-00608cca2a2a}    // Another one of *My* GUIDs!
```

The Win32 SDK also provides several functions used to handle GUIDs, which are listed in Table 17.5.

Table 17.5. Win32 GUID handling functions.

Function	Description
CLSIDFromString	Converts a string into a CLSID
CoCreateGuid	Generates a new GUID
IIDFromString	Converts a string into an IID
IsEqualCLSID	Compares two class IDs
IsEqualGUID	Compares two GUIDs
IsEqualIID	Compares two interface IDs
StringFromCLSID	Converts a CLSID into a string
StringFromGUID2	Formats a GUID into a supplied buffer
StringFromIID	Converts an IID into a string

Handling the Versioning Problem

The notion of interfaces in COM is meant to solve two common problems that occur when trying to develop component-based software: tracking versions and maintaining backward compatibility.

After a traditional software component is released, its interfaces must be frozen. Any changes to the component's interface risks breaking existing programs that depend on the current interface. Any change to an existing interface may make the new interface unusable to existing clients of the component. Additionally, any new interfaces remain undiscovered until the client program is rebuilt.

COM removes these issues by defining *interfaces* as groups of one or more related functions that can be applied to an object. Once defined, an interface is never changed. Modifying an interface does not create a new version of an existing interface; instead, it creates a brand new interface, with a new identity and responsibilities.

Using the `IUnknown` Interface

Every COM object supports the `IUnknown` interface. Every COM interface also includes the `IUnknown` interface, which is used as a starting point for all communication in COM. The `IUnknown` interface has three simple but very important functions:

- **`AddRef`:** Increments an internal reference counter and is called once for every pointer created to a COM interface. Reference counting is discussed in the next section.

- **`Release`:** Decrements an internal reference counter and is called when pointers to COM interfaces are released. When the counter reaches 0, the object destroys itself.

- **`QueryInterface`:** Returns a pointer to other COM interfaces supported by the same object. This is the mechanism used to move on past the `IUnknown` interface and is discussed later, in the section *Querying for Another Interface*.

Reference Counting

The lifetime of an OLE object is strictly controlled by an internal reference count maintained by the object, representing the number of pointers that clients have created to its interfaces. Several rules apply to reference counting:

- When an object is created, its constructor sets the reference count to 0.

- Whenever a pointer to an interface is provided to a client of the object, the reference count is incremented by the function that creates the pointer—usually, by calling the `AddRef` function.

- When a pointer no longer is used, the internal reference count is decremented by calling `Release`. This enables each object to know how many external clients currently are connected to it. When the internal counter transitions to 0, the object destroys itself.

As an example, look at the OLE interfaces involved in ringing a simulated telephone. In Figure 17.9, a `TelephoneCall` object is created by calling the `CoCreateInstance` function (this function is discussed later, in the section *Creating an Object*). Because this function returns a pointer to the `IUnknown` interface for the `TelephoneCall` object, the reference count for the object already is incremented when the pointer is returned. At this point, the reference count is 1, because there is one pointer to the `TelephoneCall` object.

FIGURE 17.9.

A `TelephoneCall` *object is created with one interface pointer, and the reference count is set to 1.*

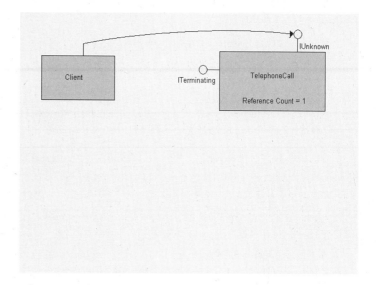

You now have a pointer to an interface for the `TelephoneCall` object, but it's a pointer to its `IUnknown` interface. In order to get a pointer to the `ITerminating` interface, you must ask your current interface for a pointer to `ITerminating`. When this pointer is passed back to you, the interface count on the `TelephoneCall` object is incremented, as shown in Figure 17.10.

FIGURE 17.10.

A new pointer to a `TelephoneCall` *interface is created, and the reference count is incremented.*

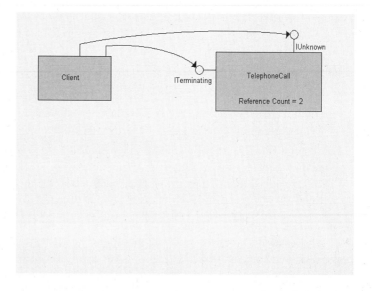

After you have the pointer to the ITerminating interface, you can start performing useful work like ringing the telephone. You don't need the original IUnknown interface pointer, however. Before discarding or overwriting this pointer, you must call the IUnknown::Release function, which decrements the TelephoneCall object's reference count back to 1, as shown in Figure 17.11.

FIGURE 17.11.

A TelephoneCall *interface pointer is destroyed, and the reference count is decremented.*

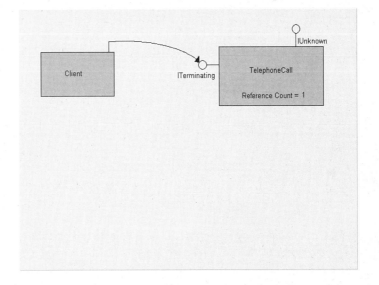

For the purposes of this simple example, assume that the telephone remains unanswered. After you decide to stop ringing the telephone, you call Release through the ITerminating interface pointer, decrementing the TelephoneCall object's reference count to 0 and destroying the object, as shown in Figure 17.12.

In practice, there is no way to reliably determine whether you have the last interface pointer to an object. Although Release returns the current reference count, in a multithreaded environment, this information is useful only if you are looking for the last call to Release, which always returns 0. For that reason, it is considered "A Very Bad Thing" to use an interface pointer after calling Release.

FIGURE 17.12.

The last interface pointer to a TelephoneCall *object is released, and the object is destroyed.*

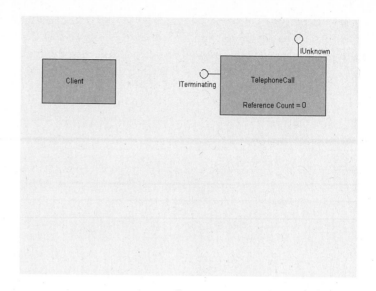

Querying for Another Interface

A pointer to any interface supported by an object can be retrieved by calling QueryInterface. Along with AddRef and Release, QueryInterface is part of the IUnknown interface, so it is safe to call QueryInterface through any interface pointer. QueryInterface accepts two parameters and returns a handle to a result code, as Listing 17.8 shows.

Listing 17.8. Using QueryInterface **to get a pointer to** IFoo**.**

```
IFoo    *pFoo;
HRESULT hr;
hr=pIUnknown->QueryInterface( IID_IFoo, &pFoo );
if( FAILED(hr) )
{
    // Interface not obtainable, report error or work
    // with other interfaces.
}
else
{
    // Use the IFoo interface, and release it when finished.
    pFoo->Release();
}
```

Several rules define how an object must behave with respect to its implementation of QueryInterface:

- For successful calls, the interface reference count must be incremented before the new interface pointer is returned to the caller.

- For one instance of an object, the same pointer value must be consistently returned for a given interface. If you ask for the IFoo interface and get a certain pointer value, any future QueryInterface calls for IFoo on the same object's interface must return the same value.

- Objects are not allowed to grow new interfaces. If QueryObject fails once, it is expected to fail consistently. Likewise, if QueryInterface is successful, it must consistently return a pointer to the requested interface.

- There must not be a "maze" in the interface hierarchy. If a QueryInterface call returns a pointer to a new interface, it must be possible to call QueryInterface to return to the previous interface. Similarly, it must be possible to traverse interfaces by obtaining a pointer to interface A, interface B, interface C, and then back to interface A.

Handling Return Values

The return value from QueryInterface, like most OLE interfaces and functions, returns an HRESULT or handle to a result code. This is a structured 32-bit value that includes more than just the usual pass/fail information returned from a return code. An HRESULT is structured very much like a Win32 error code, as shown in Figure 17.13.

FIGURE 17.13.

The format for an HRESULT *return code.*

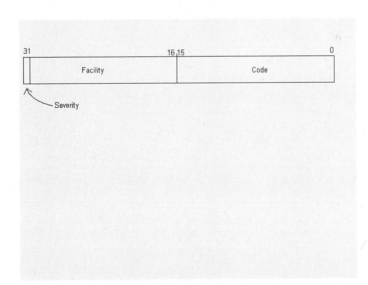

It is possible for a function to return several different flavors of success and failure. In order to determine whether a function has succeeded, you must use the SUCCEEDED and FAILED macros, as Listing 17.9 shows.

Listing 17.9. Using the SUCCEEDED and FAILED macros.

```
HRESULT hr = pObj->GetData( &fetc, &stg );
if( FAILED(hr) )
{
    // Handle failed condition
}
hr = pObj->DoSomethingElse();
if( SUCCEEDED(hr) )
{
    // Handle successful return
}
```

Creating an Object

A client creates an OLE object by calling CoCreateInstance and passing a CLSID for the object to be created, as shown in Listing 17.10.

Listing 17.10. Creating an object using CoCreateInstance.

```
IFoo* pFoo = 0;
HRESULT hr = CoCreateInstance( CLSID_FooBar,
                               NULL,
                               CLSCTX_INPROC_SERVER,
                               IID_IFoo,
                               &pFoo );
if( FAILED(hr) )
{
    // Handle error
}
// Use pFoo
.
.
.
pFoo->Release();
```

In Listing 17.10, a FooBar object is created (identified by CLSID_FooBar) by calling CoCreateInstance. If the object is created successfully, a pointer to the IFoo interface is returned.

Several steps are involved in creating a COM object. All COM objects are created by one of three types of servers:

- In-process servers are implemented in a DLL and run in the client's address space.
- Local servers are EXEs, and like all EXEs, run in their own address space on the same machine as the client.
- Remote servers are EXEs that run on a machine out on the network.

Working with Class Factories

A COM object server must implement a *class factory*—a special interface responsible for creating instances of the requested object. The class factory implements the `IClassFactory` interface, as shown in Figure 17.14.

FIGURE 17.14.

An object that implements the `IClassFactory` *interface.*

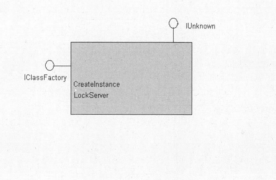

A class factory creates an instance of a COM object through the `IClassFactory::CreateInstance` function, as Listing 17.11 shows.

Listing 17.11. An example of a class factory `CreateInstance` function.

```
STDMETHODIMP CClassFactory::CreateInstance( LPUNKNOWN punk,
                                            REFIID riid,
                                            LPVOID* ppv )
{
    *ppv = NULL;
    if( punk != NULL )
        return ResultFromScode( CLASS_E_NOAGGREGATION );
```

continues

Listing 17.11. continued

```
    CCFoo* pFoo = new CFoo;
    if( pFoo == NULL )
        return ResultFromScode( E_OUTOFMEMORY );

    return pFoo->QueryInterface( riid, ppv );
}
```

In Listing 17.11, the CreateInstance function for this particular class factory creates a CFoo object and performs an initial QueryInterface on the new object. Most class factories are like this one—tightly coupled to one particular CLSID.

Finding the Custom Component Server

The module containing the COM component's server is found through the system Registry. If this CLSID is an in-process server, the path to the server's DLL is stored in the InProcServer32 key:

```
HKEY_CLASSES_ROOT\CLSID\<GUID>\InProcServer32 = Foo.dll
```

In this example, <GUID> is replaced by the full CLSID identifying the object. The name of the requested COM object's server is Foo.dll. You can speed loading by specifying a complete path to the server, or you can just place all your server modules in the Windows NT System directory.

Looking at In-Process Server Requirements

An in-process server must implement three functions, in addition to the functions required by the class factory:

- **DllMain:** The module's entry point. The only work done in this function is to stash the instance handle in case it's needed later.
- **DllGetClassObject:** Must be exported from the module and is called by Windows NT when a new COM object is created.
- **DllCanUnloadNow:** Called by Windows NT to test whether the DLL can be unloaded. Every object created in the module must increment a global reference counter during construction and decrement this counter when destroyed.

Figure 17.15 shows the typical layout for an in-process server. An in-process server contains DLL-specific functions, at least one IClassFactory interface, and interfaces supporting at least one OLE custom component.

FIGURE 17.15.

Contents of a typical COM custom component server.

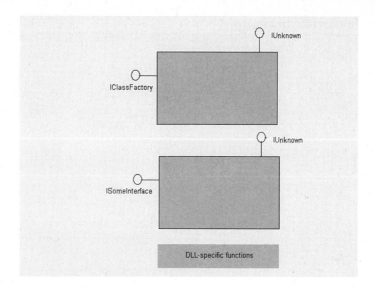

Looking at an OLE Example

As an example of how a simple custom component server is implemented, I have created a sample project on the accompanying CD-ROM. The CppExt project is a Windows NT shell extension that creates a custom context menu after you right-click a C++ file in the shell.

Using the Shell Extension Mechanism

The new shell user interface released with Windows NT 4.0 uses COM to support user extensions to the shell. By creating and registering in-process servers supporting the shell extension interfaces, you can create several types of shell extensions, as shown in Table 17.6.

Table 17.6. Windows NT shell extension types.

Shell Extension	Function
Icon handlers	Change the appearance of a file's icon on a per-file object basis. By implementing this interface, for example, you can change the icon displayed for a file object based on its internal state, its age, or any other criteria.
Copy hook handlers	Invoked when a file object is copied, moved, or deleted. By implementing this interface, you can supplement or prevent the operation.

continues

Table 17.6. continued

Shell Extension	Function
Context menu extensions	Add items to the context menu displayed after a file object is right-clicked.
Property sheet extensions	Add pages to the property sheet displayed by the shell for a particular type of file object.
Drag-and-drop handlers	Called after a drag-and-drop operation. They are almost identical to context menu extensions.
Drop target handlers	Control the activity that occurs when a file object is dropped after a drag-and-drop operation.
Data object handlers	Supply the file object during drag-and-drop operations.

All shell extensions implement the `IShellExtInit` or the `IPersistFile` interfaces. They also support additional interfaces used to implement their particular service.

Understanding Context Menu Extensions

A context menu extension supports two interfaces:

- **`IShellExtInit`:** An interface implemented by several types of shell extensions. `IShellExtInit` defines one function, `Initialize`, that provides information a shell extension can use to initialize itself.

- **`IContextMenu`:** Implemented exclusively by context menu extensions. `IContextMenu` defines three functions. `QueryContextMenu` requests that the shell extension add items to the context menu. `GetCommandString` is used by the shell to collect string descriptions of the added menu items. `InvokeCommand` signals the shell extension that a new menu item has been selected. Each of these interfaces is discussed later in this chapter.

When a user right-clicks on a file object that is handled by a context menu extension, the Windows NT shell creates an instance of the shell extension, using the mechanism discussed earlier for in-process servers.

Next, the shell uses `QueryInterface` for the `IShellExtInit` interface and calls the `Initialize` function, allowing the context menu to store initialization information. A context menu extension must collect information about the file object in this function.

The shell then queries for the `IContextMenu` interface and calls the `QueryContextMenu` function. The shell extension must add all its menu items to the context menu during this function call. The extension is not allowed to remove items or to make any assumptions about the final configuration of the menu. It is possible for several shell extensions to be registered for a single file type, and there is no way to ensure that your extension is called last (or first, for that matter). The shell also calls the `GetCommandString` function in order to collect strings used as canonical verbs and status bar text.

If a menu item added by a context menu extension is selected by the user, `IContextMenu::InvokeCommand` is called by the shell. This is the function that carries out whatever activity is represented by the menu item.

That's all there is to context menu extensions. In addition to the general-purpose code that must be written for all in-process servers, you really need to implement only four functions for your server.

Creating the Example

As with other examples in this book, you can use the project directly from the accompanying CD-ROM, or you can follow the steps described here to create the project from scratch.

> **WARNING**
>
> If you modify this project, you must not reuse my GUID—use UUIDGEN to create your own CLSID.

Get started with the example by using Developer Studio to create a new dynamic link library project workspace named CppExt. Unlike most AppWizard projects, absolutely no code is written for you; you must enter it yourself (or copy from the CD-ROM).

Exporting the Required DLL Functions

The first file to create for the CppExt project is the module definition file, provided in Listing 17.12. Enter the source code as it is presented here, save it as CppExt.def, and add it to the CppExt project.

Listing 17.12. The module definition file for CppExt.

```
LIBRARY      CppExt
DESCRIPTION "Shell extension for CPP files"

EXPORTS
    DllCanUnloadNow
    DllGetClassObject
```

Notice that only two functions are exported: `DllCanUnloadNow` and `DllGetClassObject`.

Creating the Class Declarations

Two classes are declared in the CppExt.h header file. The CCppShellExt class is the actual context menu extension class. The CClassFactory class is used to create instances of CCppShellExt. My normal practice is to put each C++ class in its own header file, but because class factories are coupled tightly to the classes they create, I make an exception for them.

Save the contents of Listing 17.13 as CppExt.h. There's no need to add it to the CppExt project, because it is included in the main .CPP file.

Listing 17.13. The CppExt.h header file.

```
// The class ID for the CPP file extension
/* d3d834c0-9a3b-11cf-82a0-00608cca2a2a */
DEFINE_GUID( CLSID_CppExtension, 0xd3d834c0, 0x9a3b, 0x11cf, 0x82,
             0xa0, 0x00, 0x60, 0x8c, 0xca, 0x2a, 0x2a );

#define     OFFSET_COUNTLINES   0
//
// A typical class factory, nothing out of the ordinary. Includes
// the IClassFactory and IUnknown interfaces
class CClassFactory : public IClassFactory
{
public:
    CClassFactory();
    ~CClassFactory();

    // IUnknown
    STDMETHODIMP QueryInterface( REFIID riid, LPVOID* ppv );
    STDMETHODIMP_(ULONG) AddRef();
    STDMETHODIMP_(ULONG) Release();

    // IClassFactory
    STDMETHODIMP CreateInstance( LPUNKNOWN punk,
                                 REFIID riid,
                                 LPVOID* ppv );
    STDMETHODIMP LockServer( BOOL f );

protected:
    ULONG    m_cRef;
};
//
// The CCppShellExt class
// As a context menu handler, the CCppShellExt class implements the
// IContextMenu and IShellExtInit interfaces.
class CCppShellExt: public IContextMenu, IShellExtInit
{
    ULONG    m_cRef;
    char     m_szFile[MAX_PATH];
public:
    CCppShellExt();
    ~CCppShellExt();
    //
    // IUnknown
    STDMETHODIMP QueryInterface( REFIID riid, LPVOID* ppv );
```

```
        STDMETHODIMP_(ULONG) AddRef();
        STDMETHODIMP_(ULONG) Release();
        //
        // IContextMenu
        STDMETHODIMP QueryContextMenu( HMENU  hMenu,
                                       UINT   nMenuIndex,
                                       UINT   nFirstID,
                                       UINT   nLastID,
                                       UINT   nFlags );
        STDMETHODIMP InvokeCommand( LPCMINVOKECOMMANDINFO pInfo );
        STDMETHODIMP GetCommandString( UINT   nItemID,
                                       UINT   nFlags,
                                       UINT*  pReserved,
                                       LPSTR  pszName,
                                       UINT   cchMax );
        //
        // IShellExtInit
        STDMETHODIMP Initialize( LPCITEMIDLIST pidl,
                                 LPDATAOBJECT  pObj,
                                 HKEY          hKeyProgID );
private:
        //
        // Operations
        void DoCountCppFile( LPCMINVOKECOMMANDINFO pInfo );
};
```

There are two sections to the CppExt.h file. The first half of the file is almost identical to any header file that declares a class that implements the `IClassFactory` interface. The `CClassFactory` class implements the `IClassFactory` and `IUnknown` interfaces; this declaration can be copied and pasted into any server module you implement.

The second half of the file declares the `CCppShellExt` class. This class implements three interfaces: `IUnknown`, `IShellExt`, and `IShellExtInit`. With the exception of the `DoCountCppFile` function, this code can be reused for any server that implements a context menu extension.

Implementing the In-Process Server Module

The actual implementation of the in-process server is spread out over the next few pages. All this code is physically located in the CppExt.cpp source file. Separating it into three separate listings, however, helps simplify my explanations.

Listing 17.14 presents the first part of the CppExt.cpp source file and deals with the basic DLL functions performed by all in-process servers.

Listing 17.14. Basic in-process server functions in CppExt.cpp.

```
#define STRICT
#define INC_OLE2            // WIN32, get ole2 from windows.h

#include <windows.h>
#include <windowsx.h>
```

continues

Listing 17.14. continued

```cpp
#include <shlobj.h>
#pragma data_seg(".text")
#define INITGUID
#include <initguid.h>
#include <shlguid.h>
#pragma data_seg()

#include "CppExt.h"

LONG    g_cRef = 0;
HANDLE  g_hInst = NULL;

// ------------------------------------------------------------
// General DLL functions
// ------------------------------------------------------------
// Main DLL entry point - stash the module instance handle for use
// later, return TRUE in all cases.
extern "C" int APIENTRY
DllMain( HANDLE hInst, ULONG uReason, LPVOID pRes )
{
    if( uReason == DLL_PROCESS_ATTACH )
        g_hInst = hInst;
    return TRUE;
}
//
// Every InProc server must support DllGetClassObject. The only
// object supported by this server is CLSID_CppExtension, all
// other requests are rejected. For our extension, a ClassFactory
// object is created, and a QIF is performed for the requested
// interface through the ClassFactory.
STDAPI DllGetClassObject(REFCLSID rcid, REFIID riid, LPVOID *ppv)
{
    HRESULT hr;
    *ppv = NULL; // Always clear the "out" parameter
    if( IsEqualCLSID( rcid, CLSID_CppExtension ) == FALSE )
        hr = ResultFromScode( CLASS_E_CLASSNOTAVAILABLE );
    else
    {
        CClassFactory* pFactory = new CClassFactory;
        if( pFactory == NULL )
            hr = ResultFromScode( E_OUTOFMEMORY );
        else
        {
            hr = pFactory->QueryInterface( riid, ppv );
        }
    }
    return hr;
}
//
// DllCanUnloadNow is called by the OS to determine if the inproc
// server can be unloaded. If the global reference count is greater
// than zero, S_FALSE is returned to prevent unloading.
STDAPI DllCanUnloadNow()
{
    HRESULT hr = S_FALSE;
    if( g_cRef == 0 )
```

```
        hr = S_OK;
    return hr;
}
```

The `DllGetClassObject` function is very similar to a class factory. This function checks that the requesting CLSID matches `CLSID_CppExtension` and creates an instance of the class factory. The class factory then is queried for the requested interface, and the result is returned to the shell.

Listing 17.15 contains the next set of functions implemented in CppExt.cpp. This listing contains the `CClassFactory`, which implements the `IClassFactory` interface.

Listing 17.15. The class factory implementation from CppExt.cpp.

```
// ------------------------------------------------------------
// IClassFactory implementation
// ------------------------------------------------------------
// The IClassFactory interface is responsible for creating an
// instance of the shell extension. The ctor and dtor increment
// and decrement the DLL's global reference count.
CClassFactory::CClassFactory()
{
    m_cRef = 0L;
    InterlockedIncrement( &g_cRef );
}
CClassFactory::~CClassFactory()
{
    InterlockedDecrement( &g_cRef );
}
// IUnknown interfaces for CClassFactory
STDMETHODIMP CClassFactory::QueryInterface( REFIID riid, LPVOID* ppv )
{
    *ppv = NULL;
    if( IsEqualIID( riid, IID_IUnknown ) == TRUE )
    {
        *ppv = (LPUNKNOWN)this;
        m_cRef++;
        return NOERROR;
    }
    else if( IsEqualIID( riid, IID_IClassFactory ) == TRUE )
    {
        *ppv = (LPCLASSFACTORY)this;
        m_cRef++;
        return NOERROR;
    }
    else
    {
        return ResultFromScode( E_NOINTERFACE );
    }
}
STDMETHODIMP_(ULONG) CClassFactory::AddRef()
{
    return ++m_cRef;
```

continues

Listing 17.15. continued

```
}
STDMETHODIMP_(ULONG) CClassFactory::Release()
{
    if( --m_cRef )
        return m_cRef;
    delete this;
    return 0L;
}
// IClassFactory interfaces - CreateInstance and LockServer.
//
// CreateInstance creates a CCppShellExt object, and returns
// the result of QIF on the requested interface.
STDMETHODIMP CClassFactory::CreateInstance( LPUNKNOWN punk,
                                            REFIID riid,
                                            LPVOID* ppv )
{
    *ppv = NULL;
    if( punk != NULL )
        return ResultFromScode( CLASS_E_NOAGGREGATION );

    CCppShellExt* pShellExt = new CCppShellExt;
    if( pShellExt == NULL )
        return ResultFromScode( E_OUTOFMEMORY );

    return pShellExt->QueryInterface( riid, ppv );
}
// Simple implementation of LockServer, this just increments and
// decrements the global reference count.
STDMETHODIMP CClassFactory::LockServer( BOOL f )
{
    if( f )
        InterlockedIncrement( &g_cRef );
    else
        InterlockedDecrement( &g_cRef );
    return NOERROR;
}
```

The constructor for CClassFactory sets its internal reference count to and increments the module's global reference count, which represents the number of objects created in the entire module. The destructor decrements this same value. Note that the Win32 InterlockedIncrement and InterlockedDecrement functions are used to change these values. With Windows NT, it is possible for a single process to run with more than one thread at any given time. You must use these functions to ensure that they are properly incremented and decremented.

In addition to the IUnknown interfaces, CClassFactory implements the two IClassFactory functions: CreateInstance and LockServer. CreateInstance uses the new operator to create a new instance of CppShellExt and returns the result of QueryInterface to the client—in this case, the Windows NT shell.

LockServer is used by the shell to ensure that the DLL stays loaded, even if all of its objects are destroyed. For an in-process server, a simple solution is to increment and decrement the global object reference count, depending on the value of the flag passed to LockServer. There is a great deal of sample code in other books, and even sample programs available from Microsoft imply that this function need not be implemented. This is not correct; all class factories must implement LockServer.

Listing 17.16 contains the last group of functions contained in CppExt.cpp. These are the CCppShellExt functions, which implement the IShellExtInit and IContextMenu interfaces.

Listing 17.16. The shell extension implementation from CppExt.cpp.

```
// --------------------------------------------------------------
// Shell extension implementation
// --------------------------------------------------------------
// There are three interfaces supported by a context menu extension
// - IccontextMenu, IShellExtInit, and IUnknown. Additionally,there
// is one private member function, DoCppCount.
//
// The ctor and dtor for the CppShellExt class increment and decre-
// ment the global reference count for the DLL. The ctor also
// handles initialization of member variables.
CCppShellExt::CCppShellExt()
{
    m_cRef = 0L;
    m_szFile[0] = '\0';
    InterlockedIncrement( &g_cRef );
}
CCppShellExt::~CCppShellExt()
{
    InterlockedDecrement( &g_cRef );
}
// IUnknown interfaces for the Shell Interfaces
STDMETHODIMP CCppShellExt::QueryInterface( REFIID riid, LPVOID* ppv )
{
    if( IsEqualIID( riid, IID_IUnknown ) == TRUE )
    {
        *ppv = (LPUNKNOWN)(LPCONTEXTMENU)this;
        m_cRef++;
        return NOERROR;
    }
    else if( IsEqualIID( riid, IID_IContextMenu ) == TRUE )
    {
        *ppv = (LPCONTEXTMENU)this;
        m_cRef++;
        return NOERROR;
    }
    else if( IsEqualIID( riid, IID_IShellExtInit ) == TRUE )
    {
        *ppv = (LPSHELLEXTINIT)this;
        m_cRef++;
        return NOERROR;
    }
    else
    {
        *ppv = NULL;
        return ResultFromScode( E_NOINTERFACE );
```

continues

Listing 17.16. continued

```
    }
}
STDMETHODIMP_(ULONG) CCppShellExt::AddRef()
{
    return ++m_cRef;
}
STDMETHODIMP_(ULONG) CCppShellExt::Release()
{
    if (--m_cRef)
        return m_cRef;
    delete this;
    return 0L;
}
// ------------------------------------------------------------
// IShellExtInit interface
// ------------------------------------------------------------
// IShellExtInit only has one function - Initialize is called to
// prepare your shell extension for calls that will be made on
// other interfaces - in this case, through IContextMenu. The main
// point of interest for a context menu is the name of the file
// object receiving the mouse-click, which is collected using
// DragQueryFile.
STDMETHODIMP CCppShellExt::Initialize( LPCITEMIDLIST pidl,
                                       LPDATAOBJECT  pObj,
                                       HKEY          hKeyProgID )
{
    STGMEDIUM   stg;
    FORMATETC   fetc = { CF_HDROP,
                         NULL,
                         DVASPECT_CONTENT,
                         -1,
                         TYMED_HGLOBAL };
    if( pObj == NULL )
        return ResultFromScode( E_FAIL );
    HRESULT hr = pObj->GetData( &fetc, &stg );
    if( FAILED(hr) )
        return ResultFromScode( E_FAIL );

    UINT cFiles = DragQueryFile( (HDROP)stg.hGlobal,
                                 0xFFFFFFFF,
                                 NULL,
                                 0 );
    if( cFiles == 1 )
    {
        DragQueryFile( (HDROP)stg.hGlobal,
                       0,
                       m_szFile,
                       sizeof(m_szFile) );
        hr = NOERROR;
    }
    else
        hr = ResultFromScode( E_FAIL );

    ReleaseStgMedium( &stg );
    return hr;
}
```

```
// -----------------------------------------------------------
// IContextMenu interfaces
// -----------------------------------------------------------
//
// QueryContextMenu is called when the shell requests the extension
// to add its menu items to the context menu. It's possible to get
// a NULL menu handle here. Also note that the current (As of this
// writing) Win32 SDK documentation is wrong regarding the nFlags
// parameter. This function should always return the number of new
// items added to the menu.
STDMETHODIMP CCppShellExt::QueryContextMenu( HMENU hMenu,
                                             UINT  nMenuIndex,
                                             UINT  nFirstID,
                                             UINT  nLastID,
                                             UINT  nFlags )
{
    char szMenu[] = "Count Lines and Statements";
    BOOL fAppend = FALSE;
    if( (nFlags & 0x000F) == CMF_NORMAL )
    {
        fAppend = TRUE;
    }
    else if( nFlags & CMF_VERBSONLY )
    {
        fAppend = TRUE;
    }
    else if( nFlags & CMF_EXPLORE )
    {
        fAppend = TRUE;
    }
    if( fAppend && hMenu )
    {
        BOOL f = ::InsertMenu( hMenu,
                    nMenuIndex,
                    MF_STRING | MF_BYPOSITION,
                    nFirstID,
                    szMenu );
        return ResultFromScode( MAKE_SCODE(SEVERITY_SUCCESS,
                                    0,
                                    USHORT(1)) );

    }
    return NOERROR;

}
//
// InvokeCommand is the "Money Shot". This is a notification that
// the user has clicked on one of the selected items in the context
// menu. The name of the file is not passed to you in this function
// since it was passed in the IShellExtInit::Initialize  function.
STDMETHODIMP
CCppShellExt::InvokeCommand( LPCMINVOKECOMMANDINFO pInfo )
{
    if( HIWORD(pInfo->lpVerb) != 0 )
        return ResultFromScode( E_FAIL );

    if( LOWORD(pInfo->lpVerb) > OFFSET_COUNTLINES )
        return ResultFromScode( E_INVALIDARG );
```

continues

Listing 17.16. continued

```
    if( LOWORD(pInfo->lpVerb) == OFFSET_COUNTLINES )
        DoCountCppFile( pInfo );
    return NOERROR;
}
//
// GetCommandString is called by the shell to retrieve a string
// associated with a new menu item.
STDMETHODIMP CCppShellExt::GetCommandString( UINT   nItemID,
                                             UINT   nFlags,
                                             UINT*  pReserved,
                                             LPSTR  pszName,
                                             UINT   cchMax )
{
    if( nItemID == OFFSET_COUNTLINES )
    {
        switch( nFlags )
        {
        case GCS_HELPTEXT:
            lstrcpy( pszName,
                        "Counts lines and semicolons in a file");
            return NOERROR;
            break;
        case GCS_VALIDATE:
            return NOERROR;
            break;
        case GCS_VERB:
            lstrcpy( pszName, "Count" );
            break;
        }
    }
    return ResultFromScode(E_INVALIDARG);
}
//
// DoCountCppFile opens the file which is located under the mouse
// click. The name of this file was passed to us in the Initialize
// member function that is part of the IShellExtInit interface. The
// file name was stored in m_szFile. This function opens the file
// and counts the number of newlines and semicolons in the file.
void CCppShellExt::DoCountCppFile( LPCMINVOKECOMMANDINFO pInfo )
{
    HANDLE  hFile = CreateFile( m_szFile,
                                GENERIC_READ,
                                FILE_SHARE_READ,
                                NULL,
                                OPEN_EXISTING,
                                FILE_ATTRIBUTE_COMPRESSED,
                                NULL );
    if( hFile == INVALID_HANDLE_VALUE )
    {
        ::MessageBox( pInfo->hwnd,
                        m_szFile,
                        "Can't open file",
                        MB_ICONHAND );
        return;
    }
    BOOL  fRead;
```

```
    DWORD dwRead;
    DWORD cSemi = 0L;
    DWORD cLines = 0L;
    while(1)
    {
        char rgBuffer[1024];
        fRead = ReadFile( hFile,
                          rgBuffer,
                          sizeof(rgBuffer),
                          &dwRead,
                          NULL );
        if( fRead == FALSE || dwRead == 0 )
            break;
        for( DWORD dw = 0; dw < dwRead; dw++ )
        {
            if( rgBuffer[dw] == ';' )
                cSemi++;
            else if( rgBuffer[dw] == '\n' )
                cLines++;
        }
    }
    TCHAR szMsg[80];
    TCHAR szSemi[] = "Total Semicolons = ";
    TCHAR szLines[] = "Total Lines = ";
    wsprintf( szMsg,"%s%ld\n%s%ld",
              (LPCTSTR)szSemi,
              (DWORD)cSemi,
              (LPCTSTR)szLines,
              (DWORD)cLines );
    ::MessageBox( pInfo->hwnd, szMsg, "C++ File", MB_ICONINFORMATION );
    CloseHandle( hFile );
}
```

Save the contents from Listings 17.14, 17.15, and 17.16 as CppExt.cpp and add this file to the CppExt project. After compiling the CppExt project, you are ready to register the extension and copy the DLL into the Windows NT system directory, which is covered in the next section.

Registering the Shell Extension

Like all in-process servers, a shell extension must be registered before it is used. All in-process servers must be registered in the HKEY_CLASSES_ROOT\CLSID key. The simplest way to implement these changes is to create a Registry file, which will be merged into the system Registry.

Create a new key for the CLSID used by the shell extension and give it a string value with an easy-to-read name—in this case, C++ Line Counter. Under this key, add an InProcServer32 key that marks this class as an in-process server. The value associated with this key is the name of the DLL that implements the server—in this case, CppExt.dll. You also must add a ThreadingModel key, which always is set to Apartment, as shown in Listing 17.17.

Listing 17.17. Registry file entries required for a thread-safe in-process server.

```
[HKEY_CLASSES_ROOT\CLSID\<GUID>]
    @="C++ Line Counter"
[HKEY_CLASSES_ROOT\CLSID\<GUID>\InProcServer32]
    @="CppExt.dll"
        "ThreadingModel"="Apartment"
```

As in earlier examples, substitute the proper GUID for <GUID> in the above registry file fragment.

It is possible to register a context menu handler for all files or for a single file extension. For CppExt, the .cpp file extension was used, as Listing 17.18 shows.

Listing 17.18. Registry file entries required for a context-menu handler.

```
[HKEY_CLASSES_ROOT\.cpp]
    @="cpp_auto_file"
[HKEY_CLASSES_ROOT\cpp_auto_file]
    @="C++ File"
[HKEY_CLASSES_ROOT\cpp_auto_file\shellex\ContextMenuHandlers]
    @="CppLC"
[HKEY_CLASSES_ROOT\cpp_auto_file\shellex\ContextMenuHandlers\CppLC]
    @="{d3d834c0-9a3b-11cf-82a0-00608cca2a2a}"
```

In addition, when registering a shell extension for Windows NT, you must add the CLSID for the shell extension under the following key:

```
HKEY_LOCAL_MACHINE\SOFTWARE\Microsoft\Windows\CurrentVersion\Shell
Extensions\Approved
```

The CppExt.reg Registry file provided on the accompanying CD-ROM contains all the entries required to register a context menu shell extension on Windows NT. To merge this file with your current Registry, right-click on the file in the Explorer and choose Merge from the context menu.

Debugging a Shell Extension

Debugging an extension to the Windows NT shell requires a few steps you might not be accustomed to using. You restart your machine, close the shell, and reload the shell into the Developer Studio debugger. The steps involved are similar to the steps used to debug any DLL:

1. Close all running applications and folders.
2. Restart Windows NT.
3. Open Visual C++ and ensure that it is the only open application.
4. Close the shell by following the usual steps to shut down Windows NT. This time, however, click the No button in the confirmation dialog box while pressing Ctrl+Alt+Shift.

5. After the shell shuts down, choose Setting from the Build menu. A dialog box appears.

6. Click on the Debug tab, and enter the path to the Windows NT Explorer in the Executable for Debug Session edit control. The path usually is something like `WINNT\EXPLORER.EXE`.

7. Close the dialog box.

After completing these steps, start a debug session. The shell restarts and runs inside the Developer Studio debugger. You will be able to set breakpoints and step through the code in your shell extension.

Summary

This chapter presented an overview of OLE and DDE concepts, and provided examples showing how you can use OLE and DDE to interact with the Windows NT shell. OLE is definitely the wave of the future—you should use DDE only for existing applications or to provide backward compatibility. Use OLE whenever possible for all your new projects.

The next chapter, "OLE Drag and Drop," discusses uniform data transfer, the OLE Clipboard, and moving data between applications using drag and drop.

OLE Drag and Drop

18

by Mickey Williams

IN THIS CHAPTER

OLE applications use a mechanism known as uniform data transfer to exchange information. *Uniform data transfer* is a much more extendible way of exchanging data than using the traditional Windows NT Clipboard operations. Although the basic Windows NT Clipboard works fine for transferring small amounts of text, it is not very useful when transferring large objects.

This chapter discusses uniform data transfer, the OLE Clipboard, and OLE drag and drop. You'll also add OLE drag and drop to an MFC application as an example.

Understanding the OLE Clipboard

As you may know, the Clipboard functions offered by Windows NT—`OpenClipboard`, `SetClipboardData`, `GetClipboardData`, and so on—work with a handle to global data. When transferring large objects, such as bitmaps or multimedia clips, these objects must be loaded from disk, created in global memory, and transferred to another program. All this work consumes a large amount of your system's resources and slows down performance. A mechanism that works fine for small text strings really bogs down when transferring 20MB AVI clips.

The OLE Clipboard uses uniform data transfer as its underlying transport. The OLE Clipboard enables you to describe the data to be transferred, as well as its current storage medium. This enables you to avoid transferring megabytes of data unnecessarily instead of consuming all the global memory available on your machine just to paste a large bitmap.

OLE objects that are the source of a data-transfer operation expose the `IDataObject` interface, and are known as *data objects*. The `IDataObject` interface works primarily with two structures:

- **FORMATETC:** Describes the data to be transferred
- **STGMEDIUM:** Describes the current location of the data

Using the FORMATETC and STGMEDIUM Structures

The `FORMATETC` structure describes the contents involved in an OLE data transfer. When using the Windows NT Clipboard, you are limited to describing the data to be transferred as a `DWORD` variable. When using OLE uniform data transfer, an entire structure is used to describe the data, as Listing 18.1 shows.

Listing 18.1. The FORMATETC structure.

```
typedef struct tagFORMATETC
{
    CLIPFORMAT      cfFormat;
    DVTARGETDEVICE  *ptd;
    DWORD           dwAspect;
    LONG            lindex;
    DWORD           tymed;
}FORMATETC;
typedef FORMATETC* LPFORMATETC;
```

The five member variables of the FORMATETC structure specify much more than the format of the data to be transferred. As shown in the list below, descriptions of the target device, the storage medium, and the amount of detail in the data are also supplied:

- **cfFormat:** Specifies the format of the data represented by this structure. This value can be any of the traditional Windows Clipboard formats, such as CF_TEXT or CF_BITMAP. This value also can refer to formats registered privately by applications using RegisterClipboardFormat. Although Clipboard formats can be used as values, remember that this structure is used for OLE data transfer and has nothing to do with the traditional Windows NT Clipboard.

- **ptd:** Points to a DVTARGETDEVICE structure containing information about the target device for which the data is being composed. This value can be NULL, as when the data is created independently of any particular device, such as a metafile. If a target device is required, an appropriate default device must be selected. The DVTARGETDEVICE structure is discussed immediately after this list.

- **dwAspect:** Specifies the amount of detail present in the format. This allows multiple views to be supported for a single object on the Clipboard. A bitmap may be present as a metafile, as a thumbnail, as an icon, and in a native 20MB BITMAP structure, for example. Possible aspect values are presented after this list.

- **lindex:** Identifies a portion of the aspect when data is split across page boundaries. If data is not split across a page boundary, this value is set to -1, which refers to the entire data.

- **tymed:** Specifies how the data is stored and is taken from one of the TYMED constants, which is discussed later in the *Using the STGMEDIUM Structure* section.

Handling FORMATETC Structures

Filling in a FORMATETC structure every time you transfer or query the OLE Clipboard can be a real pain. So much so that I use a C++ wrapper class to make using the structure less painful. Listing 18.2 provides the source code for the CFormatEtc class. This class is used in the sample program presented later in this chapter, and can be found on the CD-ROM in the OleTree project directory as fmtetc.h.

Listing 18.2. A C++ wrapper for the FORMATETC structure.

```
// CFormatEtc - a C++ class that wraps the FORMATETC structure.
// All ctor arguments have default values - no arguments are
// required for transferring text.
struct CFormatEtc : public FORMATETC
{
    CFormatEtc( CLIPFORMAT cf = CF_TEXT,
                DWORD dwTymed = TYMED_HGLOBAL,
```

continues

Listing 18.2. continued

```
                DWORD aspect = DVASPECT_CONTENT,
                DVTARGETDEVICE* ptd = NULL,
                LONG lindex = -1 );
};
CFormatEtc::CFormatEtc( CLIPFORMAT cf,
                        DWORD dwTymed,
                        DWORD aspect,
                        DVTARGETDEVICE* pTargDevice,
                        LONG lDataIndex )
{
    cfFormat = cf;
    tymed = dwTymed;
    dwAspect = aspect;
    ptd = pTargDevice;
    lindex = lDataIndex;
}
```

The CFormatEtc class initializes itself according to default arguments declared for its constructor. To construct a CFormatEtc object suitable for text data transfer, you can just declare an object, like this:

```
CFormatEtc fe; // Text format transfer
```

To create more elaborate format descriptions, pass parameters to the constructor when initializing the object, like this:

```
CFormatEtc  fe( CF_HBITMAP, TYMED_HGLOBAL, DVASPECT_CONTENT );
```

Any function that accepts a pointer to a FORMATETC structure will accept a pointer to CFormatEtc.

Using the DVTARGETDEVICE Structure

The DVTARGETDEVICE structure looks a great deal like the DEVNAMES structure, as Listing 18.3 shows.

Listing 18.3. The DVTARGETDEVICE structure.

```
typedef struct tagDVTARGETDEVICE
{
    DWORD tdSize;
    WORD  tdDriverNameOffset;
    WORD  tdDeviceNameOffset;
    WORD  tdPortNameOffset;
    WORD  tdExtDevmodeOffset;
    BYTE  tdData[1];
}DVTARGETDEVICE;
```

Think of the DVTARGETDEVICE structure as a header for a block of data. Immediately following the structure is a series of Unicode strings that contain information that can be used to create a device context. Each entry in the DVTARGETDEVICE structure contains an offset into the block of data. For example, tdDriverNameOffset contains the number of bytes from the beginning of the structure to the beginning of the string that holds the driver name string, as shown in Figure 18.1.

FIGURE 18.1.

The offsets stored in DVTARGETDEVICE *are offsets into a Unicode data block.*

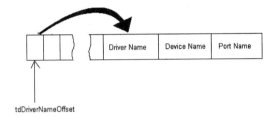

tdDriverNameOffset

The DVASPECT enumerated type specifies the amount of detail present in a particular rendering of the data. If you are dealing with text, this value almost certainly will be DVASPECT_CONTENT, meaning that the rendering should represent the full content of the data. When dealing with graphical data or more complex items, however, other values often are used. The possible values for this type follow:

- **DVASPECT_CONTENT:** Specifies full content. This value requests a representation of an object so that it can be displayed as an embedded object inside a container.
- **DVASPECT_DOCPRINT:** Specifies a representation of the data content as though it were printed to a printer using the Print command from the File menu. The described data may represent a sequence of pages.
- **DVASPECT_ICON:** Specifies an iconic representation of an object.
- **DVASPECT_THUMBNAIL:** Specifies a small thumbnail sketch of the data content. A typical thumbnail is approximately a 120×120 pixel, 16-color (recommended), device-independent bitmap potentially wrapped in a metafile.

Only one of the listed values can be used at any given time—no bitwise ORing is allowed.

Using the STGMEDIUM Structure

The STGMEDIUM structure represents a general-purpose storage object. It basically replaces the global memory handle used to transfer data with the Windows NT Clipboard. Listing 18.4 shows the declaration of STGMEDIUM.

Listing 18.4. The STGMEDIUM structure.

```
typedef struct tagSTGMEDIUM
{
    DWORD tymed;
    union
    {
        HBITMAP hBitmap;
        HMETAFILEPICT hMetafilePict;
        HENHMETAFILE hEnhMetaFile;
        HGLOBAL hGlobal;
        LPWSTR lpszFileName;
        IStream *pstm;
        IStorage *pstg;
    } u;
    IUnknown *pUnkForRelease;
}STGMEDIUM;
typedef STGMEDIUM *LPSTGMEDIUM;
```

The members of the STGMEDIUM structure follow:

- tymed specifies the type of storage used to represent the data object. A list of possible values is provided later in this section.

- A union of several variables used to refer to the data object's storage. The variable in use can be determined by examining the tymed variable.

- pUnkForRelease is a pointer to an IUnknown method that can be called to release storage for IStorage and IStream objects. This value may be NULL.

The possible values for tymed and the corresponding union variable used to refer to the data object are provided in Table 18.1.

Table 18.1. Possible values for tymed and relevant union members.

Value of tymed	Corresponding Union Member
TYMED_NULL	No data
TYMED_HGLOBAL	hGlobal
TYMED_FILE	lpszFileName
TYMED_ISTREAM	pstm
TYMED_ISTORAGE	pstg
TYMED_GDI	hBitmap
TYMED_MFPICT	hMetaFilePict
TYMED_ENHMF	hEnhMetaFile

As you'll see later in this chapter, during a drag-and-drop operation, you often need to free storage. If you find yourself in a position where you must release the storage contained in a STGMEDIUM structure, call ReleaseStgMedium, passing the address of the STGMEDIUM structure as a parameter:

```
ReleaseStgMedium( &stg );
```

ReleaseStgMedium takes care of determining the proper release method for a STGMEDIUM object.

Using the `IDataObject` Interface

All data objects must expose the IDataObject interface. Through IDataObject, a data object provides access to all the information required for implementing all sorts of data transfer. The OLE Clipboard, OLE controls, and OLE drag and drop all make use of this interface.

Listing 18.5 shows how the IDataObject interface is defined.

Listing 18.5. The `IDataObject` interface declaration.

```
interface IDataObject : public IUnknown
{
public:
    HRESULT GetData( FORMATETC* pformatetcIn, STGMEDIUM* pmedium );
    HRESULT GetDataHere(FORMATETC* pformatetc, STGMEDIUM* pmedium);
    HRESULT QueryGetData( FORMATETC* pformatetc );
    HRESULT GetCanonicalFormatEtc( FORMATETC* pformatectIn,
                                   FORMATETC  *pformatetcOut);
    HRESULT SetData( FORMATETC* pformatetc,
                     STGMEDIUM* pmedium,
                     BOOL fRelease);
    HRESULT EnumFormatEtc( DWORD dwDirection,
                           IEnumFORMATETC** ppenumFormatEtc );
    HRESULT DAdvise( FORMATETC* pformatetc,
                     DWORD advf,
                     IAdviseSink* pAdvSink,
                     DWORD* pdwConnection );
    HRESULT DUnadvise( DWORD dwConnection );
    HRESULT EnumDAdvise( IEnumSTATDATA** ppenumAdvise);
};
```

Nine functions are defined as part of the IDataObject interface. Most data objects will provide meaningful implementations of many of these interfaces, although in most cases at least a few of the functions will return not implemented. Table 18.2 lists the purpose of each of these functions.

Table 18.2. Member functions included in the `IDataObject` interface.

Function	Purpose
Dadvise	Used when a client needs to be notified when the contents of a data object are changed. The client passes a pointer to an `IAdviseSink` interface to the data object, which uses the `IAdviseSink` interface to notify the client of changes. This type of interaction is similar to the DDE `XTP_ADVISE` protocol and is used primarily when embedding an object into a container.
Dunadvise	Breaks a connection previously set up with `DAdvise`.
EnumDAdvise	Enumerates the advisory connections established by a data object.
EnumFormatEtc	Enables you to enumerate the formats supported by a data object using the `IEnumFORMATETC` interface.
GetCanonicalFormatEtc	Returns the most general rendering information for a specific data object.
GetData	Returns data in an `STGMEDIUM` structure, depending on the format described in the `FORMATETC` structure. Data returned by this function must be freed by the caller. If the data cannot be rendered as requested, an error `HRESULT` value is returned.
GetDataHere	A rarely used function that enables the caller to specify where to store the contents of data copied by the data object.
QueryGetData	Asks the data object whether data can be transferred in a specific format. This function is one of those rare cases in which you cannot use the `SUCCEEDED` or `FAILED` macro. If the function succeeds, `S_OK` is returned. If the function fails, `S_FALSE` is returned if the requested format is not supported.
SetData	A rarely used function that allows a client (usually a consumer) to change the contents stored by a data object.

When using MFC, the `IDataObject` interface is wrapped by the `COleDataSource` class.

Using OLE Drag and Drop

As discussed earlier, OLE drag and drop uses the OLE Clipboard and uniform data transfer to transfer data from a source and a consumer. Figure 18.2 shows the OLE objects involved in a typical drag-and-drop operation.

FIGURE 18.2.

The various component objects involved in a typical OLE drag-and-drop operation.

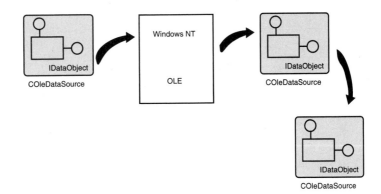

As shown in Figure 18.2, three MFC classes are involved in a drag-and-drop operation:

- **COleDataSource:** Handles collecting the data to be transferred and implements an IDataObject interface. This class handles the source-side interaction with OLE. Unless you need specialized behavior, you can use this class as is, without deriving from it.

- **COleDropTarget:** Handles the consumer or destination side of a drag-and-drop operation. You always will derive a new class from COleDropTarget in order to perform specific behavior required when an object is dropped on a particular window.

- **COleDataObject:** A wrapper for the IDataObject interface, as discussed earlier. A COleDataObject is passed as a parameter in many of the functions called during the drag and drop.

An OLE Drag-and-Drop Source

With a small amount of work, any window can be an OLE drag-and-drop source. If you are using MFC, your CWnd-derived class must implement a COleDataSource member variable.

When a drag is detected, store the data to be transferred in the drag and drop in the COleDataSource member variable. This step is very much like placing an item on the Windows Clipboard. After storing data in COleDataSource, call the COleDataSource::DoDragDrop member function to start the drag-and-drop operation.

DoDragDrop does not return until the drag and drop completes. If DoDragDrop returns DROPEFFECT_MOVE, the drag and drop has been completed successfully, and you should perform whatever tasks are necessary to make the object appear to move. In many cases, this means that the object should be deleted.

An OLE Drag-and-Drop Destination

Implementing a drop target involves a bit more code than implementing a drop source, but it's fairly simple code, especially if you're using MFC. The modifications discussed in this section can be made to any CWnd-derived class, including any control or view.

The key component of an OLE drop target is the IDropTarget interface. MFC wraps the IDropTarget interface in the COleDropTarget class. The first step in implementing a drop target is to derive a class from COleDropTarget and to override three functions:

- ■ **OnDragEnter:** Called during a drag and drop when the cursor initially passes over the window associated with the COleDropTarget object. In almost all cases, this function does nothing except call OnDragOver.

- ■ **OnDragOver:** Called during a drag and drop as the cursor moves over the window associated with the COleDropTarget object. This function sets the current drop effect for the cursor.

- ■ **OnDrop:** Called when the user actually "drops" an object on the window associated with the COleDragTarget object. This function must fetch the data from the OLE Clipboard and paste it into the target window.

The class derived from COleDropTarget must be added to the CWnd-derived class as a member variable. The window class must be registered as a drop target by calling the COleDropTarget::Register function.

Looking at a Drag and Drop Example

As a sample of how you can use OLE drag and drop in any Windows NT application, I have created a sample project located on the accompanying CD-ROM. The OleTree example adds OLE drag-and-drop capability to a pair of tree controls. Items can be exchanged between these controls by dragging them from one tree to the other. Items also can be transferred to or from any other applications that support OLE drag and drop, such as Microsoft Word.

To get started with the OleTree project, use AppWizard to create a dialog-based project named OleTree. Feel free to accept or change any of the project options offered by AppWizard.

Open the main dialog box resource and modify it as shown in Figure 18.3. Note the new edit control, the new pushbutton control, and the two new tree controls.

FIGURE 18.3.

The main dialog box for OleTree.

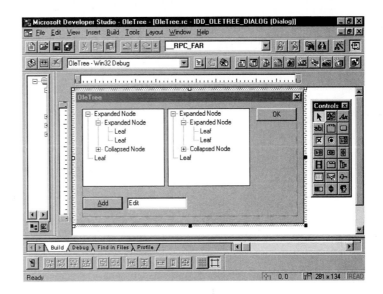

Use the values from Table 18.3 for the new controls added to the main dialog box resource.

Table 18.3. Resource and control information for the main dialog box.

Control	Resource ID	Caption
Edit control	IDC_EDIT	
Add pushbutton	IDC_ADD	&Add
Left tree control	IDC_LEFT	
Right tree control	IDC_RIGHT	

Using the control property sheets, enable the following properties for the two tree controls:

- Has buttons
- Has lines
- Border
- Lines at root

Using ClassWizard, add a new class derived from `CTreeCtrl` to manage the tree controls to the OleTree project. The new class, `CDragTree`, will include OLE drag-and-drop functionality. Click the Add Class button and choose New from the pop-up menu. Use the values from Table 18.4 for the new class.

Table 18.4. Attributes for the `CDragTree` class.

Attribute	Value
Name	CDragTree
Base Class	CTreeCtrl
File	DragTree.cpp
OLE Automation	None
Component Gallery	Cleared

The next step is to use ClassWizard to associate member variables with controls located in the main dialog box. Click on the Member Variables tab and add the member variables listed in Table 18.5 to the OleTree project.

Table 18.5. Control member variables added to the `OleTreeDlg` class.

Control ID	Category	Variable Type	Variable Name
IDC_EDIT	Value	CString	m_szEdit
IDC_LEFT	Control	CDragTree	m_treeLeft
IDC_RIGHT	Control	CDragTree	m_treeRight

Using ClassWizard, add message-handling functions to the OleTree project to handle messages from the new controls, using the values provided in Table 18.6. Note that messages reflected from the tree view control are prefixed by "=" inside the ClassWizard Message list box.

Table 18.6. Message-handling information for the OleTree project.

Class Name	Object ID	Message	Member Function
COleTreeDlg	IDC_ADD	BN_CLICKED	OnAdd
CDragTree	CDragTree	=TVN_BEGINDRAG	OnBegindrag

Create a class derived from `COleDropTarget` that will handle drag-and-drop operations to the tree controls. The declaration for the `CTreeDropTarget` class is provided in Listing 18.6. Save this listing as DropTarg.h in the project directory.

Listing 18.6. The `CTreeDropTarget` class declaration.

```
#ifndef TREEDROPTARGET_INC
#define TREEDROPTARGET_INC
class CTreeDropTarget : public COleDropTarget
{
// Constructor
public:
    CTreeDropTarget();

// Interfaces
public:
    virtual DROPEFFECT OnDragEnter( CWnd*            pWnd,
                                    COleDataObject* pObj,
                                    DWORD           dwKeyState,
                                    CPoint          pt );
    virtual DROPEFFECT OnDragOver( CWnd*            pWnd,
                                   COleDataObject* pObj,
                                   DWORD           dwKeyState,
                                   CPoint          pt );
    virtual BOOL OnDrop( CWnd*           pWnd,
                         COleDataObject* pObj,
                         DROPEFFECT      de,
                         CPoint          pt );
// Operations
public:
    void SetDragItem( HTREEITEM hItem );
    void SetParent( CTreeCtrl* pTree );

// Implementation
private:
    CTreeCtrl* m_pTree;
    BOOL       m_fIsDragging;
    HTREEITEM  m_hDragItem;
};
#endif
```

Listing 18.7 provides the implementation of the `CTreeDropTarget` class. Save this file as DropTarg.cpp and insert it into the OleTree project.

Listing 18.7. The implementation of the `CTreeDropTarget` class.

```
#include "stdafx.h"
#include "DropTarg.h"
#include "fmtetc.h"
//
// CTreeDropTarget constructor
CTreeDropTarget::CTreeDropTarget()
{
    m_pTree = NULL;
    m_fIsDragging = FALSE;
    m_hDragItem = NULL;
```

continues

Listing 18.7. continued

```
}
//
// OnDragEnter - called when a drag item initially passes over
// the window associated with this object. In most cases, this call
// is delegated to OnDragOver.
DROPEFFECT CTreeDropTarget::OnDragEnter(CWnd*          pWnd,
                                        COleDataObject* pObj,
                                        DWORD          dwKeyState,
                                        CPoint         pt )
{
    return OnDragOver( pWnd, pObj, dwKeyState, pt );
}
//
// OnDragOver - called as a drag item passes over the window
// associated with this object. Two things happen in this
// function. First, the tree control item under the mouse is
// highlighted to provide feedback to the user. Second, the
// mouse cursor is set to the move cursor if the OLE Clipboard
// has text data avilable, or the copy cursor if the text is
// available and the Control key is pressed.
DROPEFFECT CTreeDropTarget::OnDragOver(CWnd*          pWnd,
                                       COleDataObject* pObj,
                                       DWORD          dwKeyState,
                                       CPoint         pt )
{
    UINT uHitTest = TVHT_ONITEM;
    HTREEITEM hTarget = m_pTree->HitTest( pt, &uHitTest );
    m_pTree->SelectDropTarget( hTarget );

    DROPEFFECT deResult = DROPEFFECT_NONE;
    if( pObj->IsDataAvailable(CF_TEXT) )
    {
        if( dwKeyState & MK_CONTROL )
            deResult = DROPEFFECT_COPY;
        else
            deResult = DROPEFFECT_MOVE;
    }
    return deResult;
}
//
// OnDrop - called when the user drops the drag item on our window
// The text string is collected from the OLE Clipboard, and a new
// item is created for the tree control.
BOOL CTreeDropTarget::OnDrop(CWnd*          pWnd,
                             COleDataObject* pObj,
                             DROPEFFECT     de,
                             CPoint         pt )
{
    CFormatEtc  fe;
    STGMEDIUM   stg;
    // Test to see if the dropper can give us text
    BOOL fHasText = pObj->GetData( CF_TEXT, &stg, &fe );
    if( fHasText == FALSE )
        return FALSE;
    LPCSTR pszObj = (LPCSTR)GlobalLock( stg.hGlobal );
    if( pszObj )
    {
```

```
        HTREEITEM hNewItem;
        UINT uHitTest = TVHT_ONITEM;
        HTREEITEM hTarget = m_pTree->HitTest( pt, &uHitTest );
        // Drop to self is not allowed.
        if( m_fIsDragging && (hTarget == m_hDragItem) )
            return FALSE;

        if( hTarget != NULL )
        {
            hNewItem = m_pTree->InsertItem( pszObj,
                                            hTarget,
                                            TVI_FIRST );
        }
        else // Add at root
        {
            hNewItem = m_pTree->InsertItem( pszObj,
                                            TVI_ROOT,
                                            TVI_LAST );
        }
        m_pTree->SelectDropTarget( NULL );
        m_pTree->SelectItem( hNewItem );
        GlobalUnlock( stg.hGlobal );
        GlobalFree( stg.hGlobal );
        return TRUE;
    }
    return FALSE;
}
//
// SetParent - called by the CTreeCtrl object associated with this
// drop target. The pointer to the CTreeCtrl object is used to add
// items to the tree, and highlight the drop target.
void CTreeDropTarget::SetParent( CTreeCtrl* pCtrl )
{
    m_pTree = pCtrl;
}
//
// SetDragItem - called by the CTreeCtrl object when a drag begins
// or ends. The drag item is used to prevent dropping an object on
// itself, which is a meaningless operation.
void CTreeDropTarget::SetDragItem( HTREEITEM hItem )
{
    m_hDragItem = hItem;
    if( hItem )
        m_fIsDragging = TRUE;
    else
        m_fIsDragging = FALSE;
}
```

DropTarg.cpp includes the fmtetc.h file, which is the CFormatEtc class, provided earlier in Listing 18.2. DropTarg.cpp defines six functions:

- ■ **CTreeDropTarget:** The constructor for the CTreeDropTarget class.

- ■ **SetParent:** Sets a pointer to the CTreeCtrl object that owns this particular instance of CTreeDropTarget. This pointer is used to add items to the tree control after a successful drop.

- ■ **SetDragItem:** Caches the current item involved in a drag and drop. Unless steps are taken to prevent it, it is possible for a user to drag an item and drop it on itself. This operation has no purpose and is usually the result of an error. This function is called by the CTreeCtrl object associated with this drop target when a drag is started. If a drop is attempted over the item that started a drag and drop, it is ignored.

- ■ **OnDragEnter:** Calls the OnDragOver function.

- ■ **OnDragOver:** Determines the type of feedback returned to the user. In this case, DROPEFFECT_MOVE is returned when the cursor is over a valid target, unless the Control key is pressed, in which case DROPEFFECT_COPY is returned.

- ■ **OnDrop:** Manages the actual drop event. If a "drop to self" is attempted, the drop attempt is ignored. If a valid drop is attempted, the data is fetched from the OLE Clipboard and inserted into the tree control associated with this drop target.

The CDragTree class needs a few minor modifications, as shown in bold type in Listing 18.8. First, the DropTarg.h header file must be included. Next, two member variables must be added: a CTreeDropTarget member variable and a COleDataSource member variable. In addition, a new member function named Register is added to the class.

Listing 18.8. Modifications (in bold) to the CDragTree class declaration.

```
#include "DropTarg.h"
#ifndef DRAGTREECTRL_INC
#define DRAGTREECTRL_INC
class CDragTree : public CTreeCtrl
{
.
.
.
// Operations
public:
    void Register();

// Implementation
protected:
    CTreeDropTarget m_dropTarget;
    COleDataSource  m_dragSource;
.
.
.
};
#endif
```

Listing 18.9 provides the implementation of the CDragTree class. This listing includes only new functions or functions that require modifications. The constructor provided by ClassWizard is not included, for example, because it is not changed.

Listing 18.9. Member functions added to the `CDragTree` class.

```
// Handle the start of a drag. Since the tree control detects that
// the drag has actually begun, it isn't necessary to detect the
// mouse drag. The text of the drag item is placed onto the OLE
// Clipboard, and DoDragDrop is called. The handle of the item that
// is dragged is passed to m_dropTarget to prevent tree items being
// dropped on themselves.
void CDragTree::OnBegindrag(NMHDR* pNMHDR, LRESULT* pResult)
{
    NM_TREEVIEW* pNMTreeView = (NM_TREEVIEW*)pNMHDR;
    // Only nodes without children are eligible for dragging
    HTREEITEM hDragItem = pNMTreeView->itemNew.hItem;
    if( ItemHasChildren(hDragItem) == FALSE )
    {
        CString szItem = GetItemText( hDragItem );
        if( szItem.IsEmpty() == FALSE )
        {
            HGLOBAL hGlobal = GlobalAlloc( GMEM_SHARE,
                                           szItem.GetLength() + 1 );
            LPSTR   pszGlobal = (LPSTR)GlobalLock( hGlobal );
            ASSERT( pszGlobal );
            lstrcpy( pszGlobal, szItem );
            GlobalUnlock( hGlobal );
            m_dragSource.CacheGlobalData( CF_TEXT, hGlobal );

            m_dropTarget.SetDragItem( hDragItem );
            DROPEFFECT  de;
            de = m_dragSource.DoDragDrop( DROPEFFECT_COPY|
                                          DROPEFFECT_MOVE );
            // The drop is over - delete the drag item if
            // neccessary, and reset the drop target.
            if( de == DROPEFFECT_MOVE )
                DeleteItem( hDragItem );
            m_dropTarget.SetDragItem( NULL );
            SelectDropTarget( NULL );
        }
    }
    *pResult = 0;
}
//
// Register the tree control window as a drop target, and
// pass a pointer to this window, so that the drop target
// can pass messages back to us.
void CDragTree::Register()
{
    m_dropTarget.Register(this);
    m_dropTarget.SetParent(this);
}
```

Two functions are added to DragTree.cpp:

- **OnBegindrag:** Handles the notification message sent after a user begins a drag in the tree control. If the drag item has no children, the text label associated with that item is placed on the OLE Clipboard through m_dragSource and the COleSource object, and a drag and drop is started.
- **Register:** Called by the window that contains the CDragTree object—for example, a dialog box or view. Calling this function registers the tree control as an OLE drop target.

Listing 18.10 contains modifications to the COleTreeDlg class, with the changed lines shown in bold. Two lines must be added to the COleTreeDlg::OnInitDialog function. The Register function is called for each tree view control. In addition, the function body must be supplied for the OnAdd function. This function is called after the user clicks the Add button in the main dialog box. The function checks to make sure that a string has been entered by the user and then inserts the item at the root level.

Listing 18.10. Message-handling functions added to the COleTreeDlg class.

```
BOOL COleTreeDlg::OnInitDialog()
{
    CDialog::OnInitDialog();
    // Add "About..." menu item to system menu.
    // IDM_ABOUTBOX must be in the system command range.
    ASSERT((IDM_ABOUTBOX & 0xFFF0) == IDM_ABOUTBOX);
    ASSERT(IDM_ABOUTBOX < 0xF000);

    CMenu* pSysMenu = GetSystemMenu(FALSE);
    CString strAboutMenu;
    strAboutMenu.LoadString(IDS_ABOUTBOX);
    if (!strAboutMenu.IsEmpty())
    {
        pSysMenu->AppendMenu(MF_SEPARATOR);
        pSysMenu->AppendMenu(MF_STRING, IDM_ABOUTBOX, strAboutMenu);
    }

    // Set the icon for this dialog.  The framework does this
    //  automatically when the application's main window is not
    //  a dialog
    SetIcon(m_hIcon, TRUE);      // Set big icon
    SetIcon(m_hIcon, FALSE);     // Set small icon
    // TODO: Add extra initialization here
    m_treeLeft.Register();
    m_treeRight.Register();
    return TRUE;
}


void COleTreeDlg::OnAdd()
{
    UpdateData();
    if( m_szEdit.IsEmpty() == FALSE )
```

```
    {
        HTREEITEM hItem = m_treeRight.InsertItem( m_szEdit );
        ASSERT( hItem );
        m_treeRight.SelectItem( hItem );
    }
}
```

Add an #include directive at the top of the OleTreeDlg.h file, just before the declaration of the COleTreeDlg class:

```
#include "DragTree.h"
```

Before compiling the OleTree project, include MFC OLE support by including afxole.h to the stdafx.h header file, just after the existing #include directives:

```
#include <stdafx.h>
```

Compile and run the OleTree project. Add a few items to the tree control, and experiment by dragging items between the tree controls. Note that only leaf nodes can be moved. Figure 18.4 shows the OleTree main dialog box after adding several items to the tree controls.

FIGURE 18.4.

The OleTree main dialog box after several drag-and-drop operations.

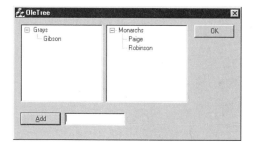

You also can experiment with drag and drops to and from other applications that support OLE drag and drop, such as Microsoft Word.

Summary

This chapter discusses data transfer using OLE uniform data transfer, the OLE Clipboard, and OLE drag and drop. You learned about the MFC classes used to implement OLE drag and drop, and you also looked at a sample project that adds drag-and-drop capability to a pair of tree controls.

The next chapter, "OLE Automation," discusses using OLE Automation and the IDispatch interface. OLE Automation is used by many applications to expose functions and properties to external programs.

OLE Automation

19

by Mickey Williams

IN THIS CHAPTER

OLE Automation is probably the most commonly used OLE technology. By exposing portions of their applications that use OLE Automation interfaces, the developers of programs such as Visio and Microsoft Word have made their programs much more flexible and open to extension by end users.

In this chapter, I discuss OLE Automation and the IDispatch interface. I also cover the steps required to add OLE Automation to your MFC-based applications, and I create an OLE Automation controller using Visual Basic.

Creating Programmable Applications Using OLE Automation

OLE Automation allows applications to expose to the outside world selected parts of their functionality. An OLE Automation server exposes properties and methods through the IDispatch interface. Tools such as Visual Basic, Visual Basic for Applications (VBA), and other programs that are clients of an OLE Automation server are known as OLE Automation controllers. The relationship between OLE Automation servers and controllers is shown in Figure 19.1.

FIGURE 19.1.

OLE Automation controllers and servers communicate through IDispatch.

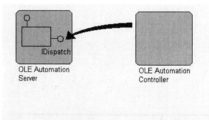

OLE Automation methods are functions exposed to the outside world. For example, Microsoft Word allows you to create and print documents through its OLE Automation methods. A property corresponds to an attribute of an object exposed through OLE Automation. Examples of properties include the size of a document or the font and color used by a particular object.

The `IDispatch` Interface

The primary interface used for OLE Automation is `IDispatch`. The `IDispatch` interface is implemented by any object that supports OLE Automation as a server. To determine if a particular COM object supports OLE Automation, an OLE controller can simply call `QueryInterface` for `IDispatch`. If an interface pointer is returned, the COM object is an OLE Automation server, and the controller can access the server's properties and methods.

Data Types Used with `IDispatch`

OLE Automation is a language-independent interface primarily used by scripting languages such as Visual Basic and VBA. Data passed through this interface must be represented so that a majority of languages can understand it. OLE defines language-neutral strings, characters, arrays, and other data types that can be exchanged by OLE Automation controllers and servers.

There are two data types associated with OLE Automation.

- `BSTR` is a basic string type that is language independent.
- `VARIANT` is a tagged union type used to portably transfer various types across a single interface.

Each of these types is discussed in the following sections.

The Basic String Type

The C and C++ languages define a simple string type as an array of characters terminated by a zero. Unfortunately, most other languages use different representations for their string types. For this reason, OLE defines its own "Basic String" type, or `BSTR`.

A `BSTR` consists of a C-style string, prefixed by a 4-byte value containing the length of the string, as shown in Figure 19.2. When using a `BSTR` in a C or C++ program, you can treat the `BSTR` much like an ordinary string.

FIGURE 19.2.

A BSTR *includes the length of the string.*

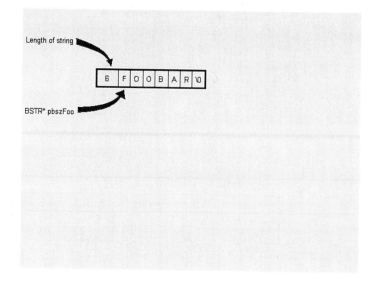

Although a BSTR may look very much like a C-style string while reading it, take care when modifying a BSTR. In particular, never free a BSTR using `free` or `delete`. Also, you should never change the length of a BSTR using the C string library because these routines will not change the prefixed length of the BSTR.

Windows NT provides alternate functions that must be used to manipulate BSTRs. The most commonly used functions include the following:

- `SysAllocString` creates a BSTR containing the contents of a string passed as a parameter.
- `SysFreeString` frees a previously allocated BSTR.
- `SysReAllocString` changes the contents of a BSTR to contain the contents of a string passed as a parameter.
- `SysAllocStringLen` creates a BSTR and copies a string to it.
- `SysReAllocStringLen` changes the contents of a BSTR to contain a substring of a string passed as a parameter.
- `SysStringLen` returns the length of a BSTR.

The VARIANT Type

The OLE VARIANT is a tagged union that contains practically any type of object. The IDispatch interface uses VARIANT objects to pass data to and from OLE Automation servers. The VARIANTARG structure is a typedef of the VARIANT structure—it can be used in place of a VARIANT. The VARIANT structure is defined like this:

```
typedef struct tagVARIANT  {
    VARTYPE vt;
    unsigned short wReserved1;
    unsigned short wReserved2;
    unsigned short wReserved3;
    union {
        unsigned char      bVal;
        short              iVal;
        long               lVal;
        float              fltVal;
        double             dblVal;
        VARIANT_BOOL       bool;
        SCODE              scode;
        CY                 cyVal;
        DATE               date;
        BSTR               bstrVal;
        Iunknown       FAR* punkVal;
        Idispatch      FAR* pdispVal;
        SAFEARRAY      FAR* parray;
        unsigned char  FAR *pbVal;
        short          FAR* piVal;
        long           FAR* plVal;
        float          FAR* pfltVal;
        double         FAR* pdblVal;
        VARIANT_BOOL   FAR* pbool;
        SCODE          FAR* pscode;
        CY             FAR* pcyVal;
        DATE           FAR* pdate;
        BSTR           FAR* pbstrVal;
        IUnknown FAR*  FAR* ppunkVal;
        IDispatch FAR* FAR* ppdispVal;
        SAFEARRAY FAR* FAR* parray;
        VARIANT        FAR* pvarVal;
        void           FAR* byref;
    };
};
```

The actual data type contained in the union is contained in the vt member. Possible values for vt are listed in Table 19.1.

Table 19.1. Possible values for the vt member of the VARIANT structure.

Value	*Meaning*
VT_EMPTY	No value was specified.
VT_EMPTY ¦ VT_BYREF	Invalid value.
VT_UI1	Unsigned 1-byte character stored in bVal.
VT_UI1 ¦ VT_BYREF	A pointer to an unsigned 1-byte character is stored in pbVal.
VT_I2	A 2-byte integer value is stored in iVal.

continues

Table 19.1. continued

Value	*Meaning*
VT_I2 ¦ VT_BYREF	A pointer to a 2-byte integer is stored in piVal.
VT_I4	A 4-byte integer value is stored in lVal.
VT_I4 ¦ VT_BYREF	A pointer to a 4-byte integer is stored in plVal.
VT_R4	An IEEE 4-byte real value is stored in fltVal.
VT_R4 ¦ VT_BYREF	A pointer to an IEEE 4-byte real value is stored in pfltVal.
VT_R8	An 8-byte IEEE real value is stored in dblVal.
VT_R8 ¦ VT_BYREF	A pointer to an 8-byte IEEE real value is stored in pdblVal.
VT_CY	A currency value is stored in cyVal.
VT_CY ¦ VT_BYREF	A pointer to a currency value is stored in pcyVal.
VT_BSTR	A BSTR is stored in bstrVal.
VT_BSTR ¦ VT_BYREF	A pointer to a BSTR is stored in pbstrVal.
VT_NULL	A SQL NULL value was specified.
VT_NULL ¦ VT_BYREF	Invalid value.
VT_ERROR	An SCODE is stored in scode.
VT_ERROR ¦ VT_BYREF	A pointer to an SCODE is stored in pscode.
VT_BOOL	A Boolean (True/False) value is stored in bool.
VT_BOOL ¦ VT_BYREF	A pointer to a Boolean value is stored in pbool.
VT_DATE	A value representing a date and time is stored in date.
VT_DATE ¦ VT_BYREF	A pointer to a date is stored in pdate.
VT_DISPATCH	A pointer to an object supporting IDispatch is stored in pdispVal.
VT_DISPATCH ¦ VT_BYREF	A pointer to a pointer to an object supporting IDispatch is stored in the location referred to by ppdispVal.
VT_VARIANT	Invalid value.
VT_VARIANT ¦ VT_BYREF	A pointer to another VARIANTARG is stored in pvarVal.
VT_UNKNOWN	A pointer to an object that implements IUnknown is stored in punkVal.
VT_UNKNOWN ¦ VT_BYREF	A pointer to a pointer to IUnknown is stored in ppunkVal.
VT_ARRAY ¦ <anything>	An array of data type <anything> is passed, with information stored in an array descriptor pointed to by pByrefVal.

When handling a VARIANT object, it's a good idea to use the Variant*xxx* API functions. These functions automatically handle the type contained inside the VARIANT properly. For example, if you are clearing a VARIANT, you must call IUnknown::Release if the stored element is a pointer to IUnknown or IDispatch. The most commonly used VARIANT handling functions are as follows:

■ VariantClear properly frees the contents of a VARIANT; BSTR and OLE interface types are freed properly, and the vt member is set to VT_EMPTY.

■ VariantCopy copies one VARIANT to another, adjusting reference counts if needed.

■ VariantInit initializes a VARIANT structure.

■ VariantChangeType safely converts a VARIANT from one type to another, performing initialization and release operations as required.

Functions Included in `IDispatch`

The IDispatch interface includes four functions and is implemented by any COM object that supports OLE automation. A somewhat simplified version of the IDispatch interface looks like this:

```
interface IDispatch : public IUnknown
{
public:
    HRESULT GetTypeInfoCount( UINT *pctinfo );
    HRESULT GetTypeInfo( UINT itinfo,
                         LCID lcid,
                         ITypeInfo **pptinfo );
    HRESULT GetIDsOfNames( REFIID riid,
                           LPOLESTR *rgszNames,
                           UINT cNames,
                           LCID lcid,
                           DISPID *rgdispid );
    HRESULT Invoke( DISPID dispidMember,
                    REFIID riid,
                    LCID lcid,
                    WORD wFlags,
                    DISPPARAMS *pdispparams,
                    VARIANT *pvarResult,
                    EXCEPINFO *pexcepinfo,
                    UINT *puArgErr );
};
```

Depending on how you use the IDispatch interface, you may implement some or all of these functions.

■ GetTypeInfo is used to get a pointer to an ITypeInfo interface, which is used to determine the automation support provided by an OLE Automation server.

■ GetTypeInfoCount is used to get the number of ITypeInfo interfaces (either 0 or 1) supported by an OLE Automation server.

- ▆ GetIDsOfNames converts method, property, and parameter names into dispatch IDs, or DISPIDs. A DISPID is an index to a name that is used in calls to IDispatch.

- ▆ Invoke is used to gain access to the properties and methods exposed by the OLE Automation server.

The heart of the IDispatch interface is the Invoke function. Invoke is called by an OLE Automation controller in order to call the programmable interfaces exposed by the automation server. As I'll demonstrate later, the MFC library hides much of the complexity of IDispatch from you.

Creating an OLE Automation Server Using MFC

As an example of an OLE Automation server, I have created an MFC-based project named AutoBub that can be found on the CD. AutoBub can be run as a stand-alone application or driven by an OLE Automation controller. AutoBub is an SDI application that displays bubbles in its main view, as shown in Figure 19.3.

FIGURE 19.3.

Autobub running as a stand-alone application.

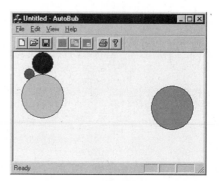

The AutoBub project is created in two steps. First the AutoBub project is created as a stand-alone application, then OLE Automation is added.

You can compile and run the project "as-is" from the CD, or you can follow along as I create the project in the following chapters. To get started, use AppWizard to create an SDI application named AutoBub. As you step through the AppWizard pages, select the OLE Automation support checkbox in step 3, as shown in Figure 19.4.

FIGURE 19.4.

Selecting OLE Automation support using AppWizard.

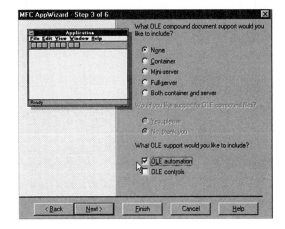

Modifying the OLE Automation Options

In the AppWizard step 4 dialog box, click the Advanced button. This displays the Advanced Options dialog shown in Figure 19.5. Notice that some of the fields have been truncated— instead of `AutoBub`, `AutoBu` is displayed. Change the File new name value to `AutoBub`, and the File type name value to `AutoBub.Document`, as shown in Figure 19.5.

FIGURE 19.5.

Changing the Advanced Options for AutoBub.

Modifications to the Document Class

A CBubble structure is used to model each bubble displayed by the AutoBub application. In addition to this structure, the CAutoBubDoc class must be modified to provide functions to add, count, and retrieve bubble objects. Modifications to the AutoBubDoc.h file are shown in Listing 19.1. Changed lines are shown in bold type, and most lines created by AppWizard are not shown.

Listing 19.1. Modifications to the CAutoBubDoc class declaration.

```
struct CBubble
{
    COLORREF    m_clr;
    int         m_nRadius;
    CPoint      m_ptCenter;
};

class CAutoBubDoc : public CDocument
{
.
.
.
// Operations
public:
    void AddBubble( const CBubble& bub );
    BOOL GetBubble( int nBubble, CBubble* pBub );
    int  GetCount() const;
.
.
.
// Implementation
protected:
    CArray<CBubble,CBubble> m_rgBubble;
.
.
.
};
```

Because the CArray class is used, you must add a line to the stfafx.h header file:

```
#include <afxtempl.h>
```

This includes the declarations for the MFC template-based collection classes.

Listing 19.2 contains the implementations of three new member functions for the CAutoBubDoc class. These functions handle adding and retrieving CBubble objects into the CArray structure maintained by the document.

Listing 19.2. New and modified functions for the `CAutoBubDoc` class.

```
void CAutoBubDoc::AddBubble( const CBubble& bub )
{
    m_rgBubble.Add( bub );
}

BOOL CAutoBubDoc::GetBubble( int nIndex, CBubble* pBub )
{
    BOOL fReturn = FALSE;
    if( nIndex < GetCount() )
    {
        *pBub = m_rgBubble.GetAt( nIndex );
        fReturn = TRUE;
    }
    return fReturn;
}

int CAutoBubDoc::GetCount() const
{
    return m_rgBubble.GetSize();
}
```

Creating a Dialog Box for AutoBub

Add a dialog box to the AutoBub project that will be used to add bubbles to the document. Figure 19.6 shows the dialog box.

FIGURE 19.6.

The Add Bubble dialog box used by AutoBub.

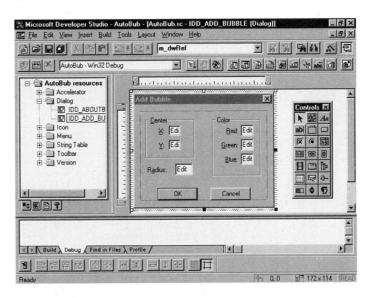

Give the new dialog box a resource ID of IDD_ADD_BUBBLE. Properties for the controls added to the dialog box are listed in Table 19.2 in tab order. All properties that aren't listed should be set to the default values.

Table 19.2. Property values for controls in the Add Bubble dialog box.

Control	Resource ID	Properties
Center Group	IDC_STATIC	Group
X Edit control	IDC_EDIT_X	
Y Edit control	IDC_EDIT_Y	
Color Group	IDC_STATIC	Group
Red Edit control	IDC_EDIT_RED	
Green Edit control	IDC_EDIT_GREEN	
Blue Edit control	IDC_EDIT_BLUE	
Radius Edit control	IDC_EDIT_RADIUS	Group

Using ClassWizard, add a new class derived from CDialog named CAddBubDlg to the TreeDisp project. Table 19.3 lists the properties for the new dialog class.

Table 19.3. Values used for the CAddBubDlg class.

Control	Value
Name	CAddBubDlg
Base Class	CDialog
File	AddBubDlg.cpp
Dialog ID	IDD_ADD_BUBBLE
OLE Automation	None
Component Gallery	Cleared

Click the Create button. The CAddBubDlg class is generated and added to your project. Change to the Member Variables tab, and add member variables to the CAddBubDlg class using the values in Table 19.4.

Table 19.4. Values for new member variables in `CAddBubDlg`.

Control ID	Variable Name	Category	Type	Min	Max
IDC_EDIT_X	m_nX	Value	int		
IDC_EDIT_Y	m_nY	Value	int		
IDC_EDIT_RED	m_nRed	Value	int	0	255
IDC_EDIT_GREEN	m_nGreen	Value	int	0	255
IDC_EDIT_BLUE	m_nBlue	Value	int	0	255
IDC_EDIT_RADIUS	m_nRadius	Value	int	0	32000

Add a menu item to the IDR_MAINFRAME menu resource, as shown in Figure 19.7. Add the new menu item as the last item on the Edit menu, using a resource ID of ID_EDIT_ADD_BUBBLE and a caption of "&Add Bubble...".

With ClassWizard, add a message-handling function to handle the new menu item using the values shown in Table 19.5.

FIGURE 19.7.

The new Add Bubble menu selection added to IDR_MAINFRAME.

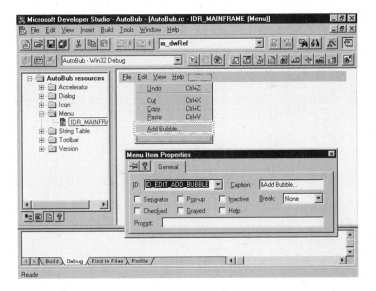

Table 19.5. Handling the Add Bubble menu item.

Class Name	Object ID	Message	Function
CAutoBubView	ID_EDIT_ADD_BUBBLE	COMMAND	OnEditAddBubble

The source code for CAutoBubView::OnEditAddBubble is provided in Listing 19.3.

Listing 19.3. Handling the Add Bubble menu item.

```
void CAutoBubView::OnEditAddBubble()
{
    CAddBubDlg    dlg;
    if( dlg.DoModal() == IDOK )
    {
        CBubble bub;
        bub.m_clr = RGB(dlg.m_nRed, dlg.m_nGreen, dlg.m_nBlue);
        bub.m_ptCenter = CPoint( dlg.m_nX, dlg.m_nY );
        bub.m_nRadius = dlg.m_nRadius;

        CAutoBubDoc* pDoc = GetDocument();
        ASSERT_VALID(pDoc);

        pDoc->AddBubble( bub );
        Invalidate();
    }
}
```

Remember to add an #include directive at the top of the AutoBubView.cpp source file, just after the existing #include directives:

```
#include "AddBubDlg.h"
```

Drawing Bubble Objects for AutoBub

Bubbles are drawn in the CAutoBubView::OnDraw member function, which is called when the view is redrawn. The source code for OnDraw is provided in Listing 19.4.

Listing 19.4. Drawing a collection of bubbles.

```
void CAutoBubView::OnDraw(CDC* pDC)
{
    CAutoBubDoc* pDoc = GetDocument();
    ASSERT_VALID(pDoc);

    for( int n = 0; n < pDoc->GetCount(); n++ )
    {
        CBubble aBubble;
        BOOL fResult = pDoc->GetBubble( n, &aBubble );
        if( fResult == FALSE )
```

```
        break;

    CBrush  br( aBubble.m_clr );
    CBrush* pbrOld = pDC->SelectObject( &br );
    ASSERT( pbrOld );

    CSize   offset( aBubble.m_nRadius, aBubble.m_nRadius );
    CRect   rcBoundary( aBubble.m_ptCenter - offset,
                        aBubble.m_ptCenter + offset );
    pDC->Ellipse( rcBoundary );
    pDC->SelectObject( pbrOld );
    }
}
```

At this point, the AutoBub project can be compiled and run as a stand-alone application. Try it out now, before adding the OLE Automation support, so that you can get a feel for adding bubbles using the Add Bubble dialog box.

Adding OLE Automation Support to AutoBub

Of course the point of this chapter is OLE Automation, so let's expose some of the AutoBub properties and methods using ClassWizard. Open ClassWizard, and click on the OLE Automation tab. Add a Count property to the CAutoBubDoc class by clicking the Add Property button and using the values from Table 19.6.

Table 19.6. AutoBub Count OLE automation properties.

Implementation	Type	External Name	Get Function	Set Function
Get/Set	long	Count	CountIs	(none)

Add two methods for the CAutoBubDoc class using the values from Tables 19.7 and 19.8.

Table 19.7. Values used to add the Clear method to the CAutoBubDoc class.

Control	Value
External name	Clear
Internal name	Clear
Return type	void
Parameter list	(none)

Table 19.8. Values used to add the Add method to the CAutoBubDoc class.

Control	Value	Type
External name	Add	
Internal name	Add	
Return type	void	
Parameter list	clr	short
	nYPos	short
	nXPos	short
	nRadius	short

After making these changes, close ClassWizard by clicking the OK button. ClassWizard adds the necessary OLE Automation skeleton functions to your project. ClassWizard also adds dispatch maps to the CAutoBubDoc class and modifies the AutoBub.odl file.

The complete implementation for the new OLE Automation functions is provided in Listing 19.5.

Listing 19.5. Automation methods added to the CAutoBubDoc class.

```
void CAutoBubDoc::Clear()
{
    m_rgBubble.RemoveAll();
    UpdateAllViews( NULL );
}

void CAutoBubDoc::Add(long clr, short nYPos, short nXPos, short nRadius)
{
    CBubble    bub;

    bub.m_nRadius = nRadius;
    bub.m_ptCenter.x = nXPos;
    bub.m_ptCenter.y = nYPos;
    bub.m_clr = clr;

    AddBubble( bub );

    UpdateAllViews( NULL );
}

long CAutoBubDoc::CountIs()
{
    return GetCount();
}
```

Note that the OLE Automation functions make use of the existing functions whenever possible.

The ODL file created by ClassWizard is provided in Listing 19.6. I have removed some of the comments for clarity. You don't have to enter this code yourself—I just inserted it here so that you can see how the OLE Automation methods and properties are declared using the Microsoft ODL syntax.

Listing 19.6. The AutoBub .ODL file.

```
[ uuid(06A6EDEB-A2FD-11CF-9C7D-000000000000), version(1.0) ]
library AutoBub
{
    importlib("stdole32.tlb");

    //  Primary dispatch interface for CAutoBubDoc

    [ uuid(06A6EDEC-A2FD-11CF-9C7D-000000000000) ]
    dispinterface IAutoBu
    {
        properties:
            //{{AFX_ODL_PROP(CAutoBubDoc)
            [id(1)] long Count;
            //}}AFX_ODL_PROP

        methods:
            //{{AFX_ODL_METHOD(CAutoBubDoc)
            [id(2)] void Clear();
            [id(3)] void Add(long clr, short x, short y, short r);
            //}}AFX_ODL_METHOD
    };

    //  Class information for CAutoBubDoc
    [ uuid(06A6EDEA-A2FD-11CF-9C7D-000000000000) ]
    coclass CAutoBubDoc
    {
        [default] dispinterface IAutoBu;
    };
    //{{AFX_APPEND_ODL}}
};
```

One final change must be done for the AutoBub project. By default, OLE Automation servers are not displayed when launched by an OLE Automation controller. This behavior is useful for many OLE Automation servers, however, it defeats the purpose of the AutoBub application. The CAutoBubApp::InitInstance function must be modified as shown in Listing 19.7. InitInstance is a fairly large function, so I've highlighted the changed lines and omitted most of the unchanged lines.

Listing 19.7. Modifications (in bold) to the `CAutoBubApp::InitInstance` **function.**

```
BOOL CAutoBubApp::InitInstance()
{
    .
    .
    .

    // Parse command line for standard shell commands, DDE, file
    // open
    CCommandLineInfo cmdInfo;
    ParseCommandLine(cmdInfo);

    // Check to see if launched as OLE server
    if(cmdInfo.m_bRunEmbedded ¦¦ cmdInfo.m_bRunAutomated)
    {
        // Register all OLE server (factories) as running.  This
        // enables the OLE libraries to create objects from other
        // applications.
        COleTemplateServer::RegisterAll();

        // Application was run with /Automation.  Okay to show the
        // main window in this case.
        if (!ProcessShellCommand(cmdInfo))
            return FALSE;
        return TRUE;
    }
    .
    .
    .
    .
}
```

After making the changes shown above, compile and run the AutoBub project. AutoBub is now ready to be used as a OLE Automation server. In the next section I cover creating OLE Automation controllers using Visual Basic.

Using Visual Basic to Create an Automation Controller

The classic automation controller is Visual Basic. In this section, I'll create a 32-bit application that drives AutoBub through its OLE Automation interface. This application, named Auto, displays a dialog box that can be used to add bubbles to an instance of AutoBub. The main form used in the Auto project is shown in Figure 19.8.

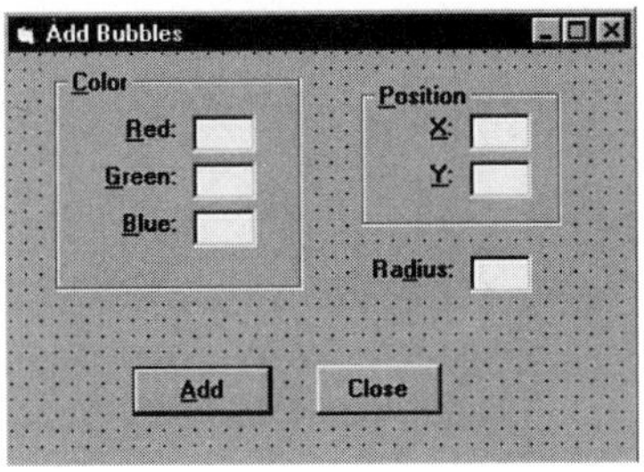

FIGURE 19.8.

The main form used by the Auto project.

The control name properties are listed in Table 19.9. Properties not listed should be set to their default values.

Table 19.9. Name properties for controls in the Auto form.

Control	Resource ID
X Edit control	IDC_POS_X
Y Edit control	IDC_POS_Y
Add pushbutton	IDC_ADD
Close pushbutton	IDC_CLOSE
Red Edit control	IDC_RED
Green Edit control	IDC_GREEN
Blue Edit control	IDC_BLUE
Radius Edit control	IDC_RADIUS

Code in a Visual Basic project is placed into procedures, depending on the object and event affected by the code. Declarations that are used for the entire project belong in the (General) object section. Add a declaration under (General) for the OLE Automation object. It should look like this:

```
Dim BubbleMachine As Object
```

Before the automation object can be used, it must be initialized by calling the `CreateObject` function. `CreateObject` locates the AutoBub server, creates an instance of it, and initializes the `BubbleMachine` object. Add the code provided in Listing 19.8 as the `Load` procedure for the `Form` object.

Listing 19.8. Initializing the OLE Automation object.

```
Private Sub Form_Load()
    Set BubbleMachine = CreateObject("AutoBub.Document")
End Sub
```

After the OLE Automation object has been used, it must be released by assigning the `BubbleMachine` object the special value of `Nothing`. Add the code provided in Listing 19.10. as the `Unload` procedure for the `Form` object.

Listing 19.9. Releasing an OLE Automation object.

```
Private Sub Form_Unload(Cancel As Integer)
    Set BubbleMachine = Nothing
End Sub
```

In order to close the Auto application, `End` must be called. In the Auto project, the `Click` procedure for the `IDC_CLOSE` pushbutton object closes the application. Add the code provided in Listing 19.10 as the `Click` procedure for the `IDC_CLOSE` object.

Listing 19.10. Closing the Auto application.

```
Private Sub IDC_CLOSE_Click()
    End
End Sub
```

And finally, the `Click` procedure for the `IDC_ADD` object is used to add a new bubble. Add the code provided in Listing 19.11. as the `Click` procedure for the `IDC_ADD` object.

Listing 19.11. Creating a new bubble via OLE Automation.

```
Private Sub IDC_ADD_Click()
  Static ColorRef As Long, R As Integer, G As Integer, B As Integer
  Static nX As Integer, nY As Integer, nRadius As Integer
  ' Make the COLORREF from the RGB components
  R = Val(IDC_RED.Text) And &HFF&
  G = Val(IDC_GREEN.Text) And &HFF&
  B = Val(IDC_BLUE.Text) And &HFF&
  ColorRef = RGB(R, G, B)
  ' Save the position coords as ints
```

```
nX = Val(IDC_POS_X.Text)
nY = Val(IDC_POS_Y.Text)
nRadius = Val(IDC_RADIUS.Text)
 ' Create a new bubble
 BubbleMachine.Add ColorRef, nX, nY, nRadius
End Sub
```

An instance of the AutoBub application is displayed when you run the Auto project. Remember, this isn't the default behavior; usually an MFC-based automation server remains hidden. Use the Auto dialog box to add bubbles to AutoBub. Figure 19.9 shows both applications running after adding a few bubbles.

FIGURE 19.9.

The Auto and AutoBub applications after adding a few bubbles.

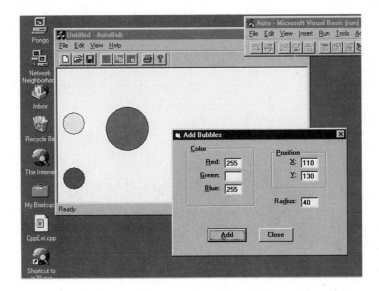

Summary

This chapter discussed OLE Automation and the IDispatch interface. OLE Automation is one of the hottest OLE technologies right now, primarily because it enables you to easily expose parts of your applications to the outside world. OLE Automation servers such as Excel, Word, and Visio can easily be controlled by OLE Automation controllers, such as Visual Basic. In this chapter, examples of an OLE Automation server and OLE Automation controllers were created.

The next chapter, "Developing ActiveX Controls," covers creating and using ActiveX and OLE controls. An example of an ActiveX control, OleEdit, is created and tested.

Developing ActiveX Controls

20

by Mickey Williams

ActiveX Controls are the new name for what were previously known as OLE custom controls. An ActiveX Control is a functional piece of code that is packaged into a reusable component, and offers some guarantees about how it interacts with its clients. Although many ActiveX Controls are user interface components, just like the built-in Windows NT controls, it is not required that an ActiveX Control must be visible.

In this chapter, I discuss ActiveX Controls and how they are implemented using Developer Studio and MFC. I also create an ActiveX Control and test it inside the OLE control test container that is shipped with Developer Studio and the Win32 SDK.

What Is an ActiveX Control?

At a minimum, an ActiveX Control must be a COM object. This means that an ActiveX Control must support the IUnknown interface. This allows for a great deal of latitude when deciding how a control is to be implemented—previously, the OLE custom control architecture required support of at least fourteen interfaces, as will be discussed later.

Reducing the number of interfaces required for ActiveX Controls makes it possible to create much smaller controls, and makes it feasible to use ActiveX Controls to implement functionality where the size of the control is an important factor. Web pages can be more intelligent when a control is downloaded and activated to your browser. For example, Microsoft's Internet Explorer 3.0 has support for downloading ActiveX Controls from a web page. Although this opens a lot of exciting functionality, the size of the control to be downloaded must be kept as small as possible.

ActiveX Controls are almost always in-process servers. This is due to several factors.

- Although it isn't required, many controls present a user interface through the IViewObject2, and this interface is not marshaled across a process boundary.

- A control loaded in-process has much faster response time than a local EXE server.

- Historical reasons. OLE controls could only be in-process, and the version of the Control Development Kit shipped with Visual C++ 4 supports only in-process servers. If you want an out-of-process server, you must create it from scratch.

ActiveX Control Interfaces

An ActiveX Control typically implements a large number of interfaces. Although the number of mandatory interfaces has been greatly reduced from the number required by the original OLE Controls specification, there is still a great deal of work required to implement a control or container from scratch. In the original OLE Control specification, an OLE control was expected to support the interfaces listed in Table 20.1. For comparison, the requirements for ActiveX Controls are also listed.

Table 20.1. Interfaces required for ActiveX and OLE custom controls.

Interface	OLE Control	ActiveX Control
IUnknown	Yes	Yes
IClassFactory or IClassFactory2	Yes	Optional
IConnectionPointContainer	Yes	Optional
IDataObject	Yes	Optional
IDispatch	Yes	Optional
IOleCache2	Optional	Optional
IOleControl	Yes	Optional
IOleInPlaceActiveObject	Yes	Optional
IOleInPlaceObject	Yes	Optional
IOleObject	Yes	Optional
IPersistStorage	See note	Optional
IPersistStream	See note	Optional
IPersistStreamInit	See note	Optional
IProvideClassInfo	Yes	Optional
IRunnableObject	Yes	Optional
ISpecifyPropertyPages	Yes	Optional
IViewObject2	Yes	Optional

An OLE control is required to implement one of the IPersistXxx interfaces—IPersistStorage, IPersistStream, or IPersistStreamInit. An ActiveX Control is not required to support any of these interfaces, unless the control is persistent. Because a control usually saves only its internal properties, the control usually implements the simplest of these interfaces—IPersistStream.

Although an ActiveX Control need not support all the interfaces supported by an OLE Control, most ActiveX Controls will continue to be very "control-like." That is, they will still appear to be connectable objects, will be embeddable, and will draw themselves through IViewObject2.

Understanding Connectable Objects

Connectable objects communicate with their containers through connection point interfaces. These are *back-channel* interfaces that allow the embedded control to notify the container of events. There are two interfaces implemented by a connectable object:

- IConnectionPoint is implemented by a control or other COM object and allows a container or client of the COM object to request event notifications.

- IConnectionPointContainer is used to query the object about IConnectionPoint interfaces supported by the object. This interface includes functions that return a pointer to a known IConnectionPoint interface, or enumerate IConnectionPoint interfaces supported by a control.

Most ActiveX Controls are connectable objects. However, other types of COM objects can implement the IConnectionPointContainer and IConnectionPoint interfaces, and thus become connectable objects. The coupling between a connectable client and server is shown in Figure 20.1.

FIGURE 20.1.

The interfaces used to implement connectable objects.

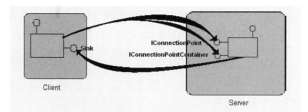

A client interested in a specific IConnectionPoint interface first invokes QueryInterface, requesting the IConnectionPointContainer interface. If an interface pointer is returned, the particular IConnectionPoint interface is requested through IConnectionPointContainer. If the request is successful, the client passes a pointer to its notification sink to the server, through the IConnectionPoint interface. The server transmits event notifications to the client using the pointer to the notification sink.

ActiveX Control Properties, Events, and Methods

Interaction with an ActiveX component takes place via properties, events, and methods.

- A property is an attribute associated with the control.
- An event is a notification message passed to the container by the control.
- A method is an exposed function that can be applied to the control via IDispatch.

I'll discuss each of these interaction methods in the next few sections.

Properties

Properties are exposed by ActiveX Controls as well as by the client site where the control is located. There are four basic types of properties.

- *Ambient properties* are provided to the control by the container. The control uses these properties in order to "fit in" properly. Commonly used ambient properties include the container's background color, default font, and foreground color.
- *Extended properties* are implemented by the container, but appear to be generated by the control. For example, the tab order of various controls in a container are extended properties.
- *Stock properties* are control properties implemented by the ActiveX Control development kit. Examples of stock properties are the control font, the caption text, and the foreground and background colors.
- *Custom properties* are control properties that you implement.

Methods

Methods implemented by ActiveX Controls are exactly like the methods implemented for OLE Automation discussed in Chapter 19. In fact, methods are implemented through OLE Automation using the IDispatch interface.

Events

An *event* is used to send a notification message to the control's container. Typically, events are used to notify the container when mouse clicks or other events take place. There are two basic types of events.

- *Stock events* are implemented by the ActiveX Control development kit, and are invoked just like a function call, such as `FireError`.

- *Custom events* are implemented by you, although the MFC class library and ClassWizard handle much of the work for you.

An ActiveX Control Example

As an example of creating an ActiveX Control, I have created an ActiveX Control that subclasses the existing Windows NT Edit control. The OleEdit project can be found on the CD. You can either use the completed project from the CD, or follow along as I create the control from scratch.

The OleEdit control is similar to the basic Windows NT edit control, except that it exposes properties that allow it to accept only numbers, letters, or a combination of both. When WM_CHAR is received by the control, it is processed as shown in Figure 20.2.

FIGURE 20.2.

Handling WM_CHAR *in OleEdit.*

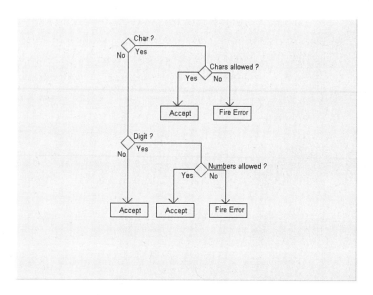

The property flags `m_fTextAllowed` and `m_fNumbersAllowed` are exposed as properties that can be changed by the OleEdit control's container.

Creating the Project

To get started creating the OleEdit control, use ControlWizard to create an OLE custom control project. The initial page from the ControlWizard is shown in Figure 20.3. This page allows you to specify the basic characteristics of the project, such as the number of controls handled by this server, if help files should be generated, and so on. Accept all the default options presented on this page by clicking the Next button.

FIGURE 20.3.

The first page of the OLE ControlWizard.

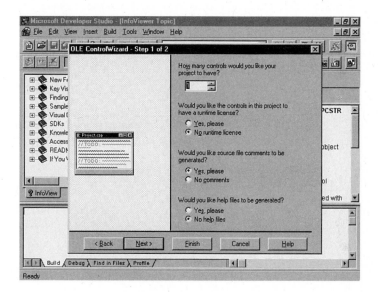

The second ControlWizard page is shown in Figure 20.4. This page allows you to change the names associated with the control and its OLE interfaces, as well as defining properties for the control. There is also a drop-down list that allows a base class to be specified for the control. Select EDIT from the drop-down list to make the OleEdit control a subclass of the standard edit control.

FIGURE 20.4.

The second page of the OLE ControlWizard.

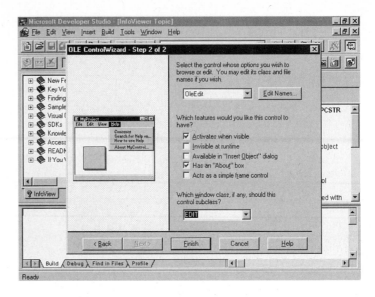

Click the button labeled Finish. As with other ControlWizard projects, a list of the files to be created is displayed. Click the OK button, and the skeleton project is created.

Drawing the Control

All visible OLE controls must be capable of drawing themselves. Even controls that aren't visible when active should draw something as an aid during program development. The OleEdit control is visible at runtime, and it should appear to be a standard edit control.

You might think that because OleEdit is subclassed from the standard edit control, it can draw itself. Unfortunately, the only control I've found that can draw itself correctly is the pushbutton control. For most controls, you must be prepared to handle the drawing yourself.

When an OLE control project is initially created, the control's OnDraw function draws an ellipse inside the bounding rectangle. The changes to OnDraw required for the OleEdit control are provided in Listing 20.1.

Listing 20.1. OnDraw.

```
void COleEditCtrl::OnDraw(
          CDC* pdc, const CRect& rcBounds, const CRect& rcInvalid)
{
    COLORREF    clrBackground = TranslateColor( GetBackColor() );
    CBrush*     pOldBrush;
    CBrush      brBackground( clrBackground );
```

```
    pdc->FillRect( rcBounds, &brBackground );
    pOldBrush = pdc->SelectObject( &brBackground );
    pdc->SelectObject( pOldBrush );
    DoSuperclassPaint(pdc, rcBounds);
    CRect rc(rcBounds);
    pdc->DrawEdge( rc, EDGE_SUNKEN, BF_RECT );
}
```

The code provided in Listing 20.1 does three things. First, it fills the control's bounding rectangle with the ambient background color. Next, it calls `DoSuperclassPaint` to allow the edit control a chance to not draw itself properly. Finally, it draws a three-dimensional edge along the control's bounding rectangle.

Defining Properties for OleEdit

There are four properties used by OleEdit: The `Font` and `Text` stock properties, and the `fTextAllowed` and `fNumbersAllowed` custom properties.

Using ClassWizard, add the stock properties for the OleEdit control. Select the OLE Automation tab, and click the Add Property button. Fill in the dialog box using the values provided in Table 20.2.

Table 20.2. Stock properties for the OleEdit control.

External name	Implementation
Font	Stock
Text	Stock

Use ClassWizard to add a custom property named `fNumbersAllowed` to the OleEdit project. Click the Add Property button, and use the values provided in Table 20.3.

Table 20.3. The `fNumbersAllowed` custom property for the OleEdit control.

Control	Value
External name	fNumbersAllowed
Type	BOOL
Variable name	m_fNumbersAllowed
Notification function	OnFNumbersAllowedChanged
Implementation	Member variable

Use ClassWizard to add the `fTextAllowed` property, following the steps used to add the previous properties. Use the values provided in Table 20.4.

Table 20.4. The `fTextAllowed` custom property for the OleEdit control.

Control	Value
External name	`fTextAllowed`
Type	`BOOL`
Variable name	`m_fTextAllowed`
Notification function	`OnFTextAllowedChanged`
Implementation	Member variable

Modify the `COleEditCtrl` class constructor to contain code that initializes the custom properties added in the previous steps. The modified constructor is shown in Listing 20.2 with changed lines shown in bold type.

Listing 20.2. Modifications (in bold) to the `COleEditCtrl` constructor.

```
COleEditCtrl::COleEditCtrl()
{
    InitializeIIDs(&IID_DOleEdit, &IID_DOleEditEvents);
    m_fTextAllowed = TRUE;
    m_fNumbersAllowed = TRUE;
}
```

Every control created using AppWizard includes a default property page. The OleEdit property page is modified by adding two checkboxes that control the states of the `m_fTextAllowed` and `m_fNumbersAllowed` flags. Open the `IDD_PROPAGE_OLEEDIT` dialog box resource, and add two checkbox controls as shown in Figure 20.5.

FIGURE 20.5.

The property page used by OleEdit.

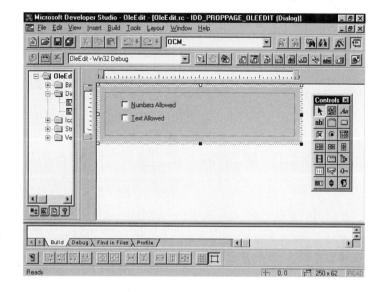

Table 20.5 lists the properties for the checkbox controls. All properties that aren't listed should be set to the default values.

Table 20.5. Property values for checkbox controls in the OleEdit property page.

Control	Resource ID	Caption
Numbers checkbox	IDC_CHECK_NUMBERS	&Numbers Allowed
Text checkbox	IDC_CHECK_TEXT	&Text Allowed

Use ClassWizard to associate COleEditPropPage member variables with the controls, using the values shown in Table 20.6.

Table 20.6. Values for new member variables in COleEditPropPage.

Control ID	Variable Name	Category	Type	Property Name
IDC_CHECK_NUMBERS	m_fNumbersAllowed	Value	BOOL	fNumbersAllowed
IDC_CHECK_TEXT	m_fTextAllowed	Value	BOOL	fTextAllowed

The optional OLE property name field is used by ClassWizard to generate source code that exchanges the values from the property sheet to the control class. The DDP_ and DDX_ macros are used to transfer and validate property page data. The code used to transfer the value of the IDC_CHECK_TEXT control looks like this:

```
//{{AFX_DATA_MAP(COleEditPropPage)
DDP_Check(pDX,IDC_CHECK_TEXT, m_fTextAllowed, _T("fTextAllowed"));
DDX_Check(pDX, IDC_CHECK_TEXT, m_fTextAllowed);
//}}AFX_DATA_MAP
DDP_PostProcessing(pDX);
```

Inside the control class, you must collect the values from the property page during DoPropExchange, as shown in Listing 20.3.

Listing 20.3. The Property Exchange control.

```
void COleEditCtrl::DoPropExchange(CPropExchange* pPX)
{
    ExchangeVersion(pPX, MAKELONG(_wVerMinor, _wVerMajor));
    COleControl::DoPropExchange(pPX);

    PX_Bool(pPX, _T("fNumbersAllowed"), m_fNumbersAllowed );
    PX_Bool(pPX, _T("fTextAllowed"), m_fTextAllowed );
}
```

The OleEdit control supports the stock font property. An easy way to give the control access to all the available fonts is to add the standard font property page to the control. The property pages associated with an ActiveX Control are grouped together between the BEGIN_PROPPAGEIDS and END_PROPPAGEIDS macros. Listing 20.4 shows how the standard font property page is added to the control, using the PROPPAGEID macro. Remember to change the second parameter passed to the BEGIN_PROPPAGEIDS macro, which is the number of property pages used by the control object.

Listing 20.4. Adding the standard font property page to OleEdit.

```
BEGIN_PROPPAGEIDS(COleEditCtrl, 2)
    PROPPAGEID(COleEditPropPage::guid)
    PROPPAGEID(CLSID_CFontPropPage)
END_PROPPAGEIDS(COleEditCtrl)
```

As I'll demonstrate when I discuss testing the control later in this chapter, adding the font property page, along with exposing the stock font property, allows a user to easily change the control font. The only code that is written is shown in Listing 20.4.

Handling Character Input

As discussed earlier, OleEdit uses exposed properties to determine if characters entered on the keyboard are stored in the edit control. If an invalid character is input, an Error event is fired to the control's container.

The message sent to the control as characters are input to the control is WM_CHAR. Using ClassWizard, add a message-handling function to the COleEditCtrl class, using the values from Table 20.7.

Table 20.7. Handling the WM_CHAR message in COleEditCtrl.

Class Name	Object ID	Message	Function
COleEditCtrl	COleEditCtrl	WM_CHAR	OnChar

The source code for the COleEditCtrl::OnChar function is provided in Listing 20.5.

Listing 20.5. Handling the WM_CHAR message in COleEditCtrl::OnChar.

```
void COleEditCtrl::OnChar(UINT nChar, UINT nRepCnt, UINT nFlags)
{
    if( _istdigit(nChar) )
    {
        if( m_fNumbersAllowed == FALSE )
        {
            FireError( CTL_E_INVALIDPROPERTYVALUE,
                        _T("Numbers not allowed") );
        }
        else
        {
            COleControl::OnChar(nChar, nRepCnt, nFlags);
        }
    }
    else if( _istalpha(nChar) )
    {
        if( m_fTextAllowed == FALSE )
        {
            FireError( CTL_E_INVALIDPROPERTYVALUE,
                        _T("Characters not allowed") );
        }
        else
        {
            COleControl::OnChar(nChar, nRepCnt, nFlags);
        }
    }
    else
        COleControl::OnChar(nChar, nRepCnt, nFlags);
}
```

The OnChar handler tests for valid characters based on the property flags m_fTextAllowed and m_fNumbersAllowed. Valid characters are passed to COleControl::OnChar, the base class handler for WM_CHAR. If an invalid character is detected, an Error event is fired to the control's container.

Modifying the Control's Bitmap

When an ActiveX Control is used in a tool such as Developer Studio, Visual Basic, or the OLE control test container, a bitmap associated with the control is displayed to the user. In Developer Studio, the bitmap is added to the control palette used to design dialog box resources. In the test container, a toolbar button displaying the bitmap is added to the container's toolbar.

Open the IDB_OLEEDIT bitmap resource and edit the bitmap image as shown in Figure 20.6. Save the bitmap and compile the OleEdit project.

FIGURE 20.6.

The IDB_OLEEDIT *bitmap resource.*

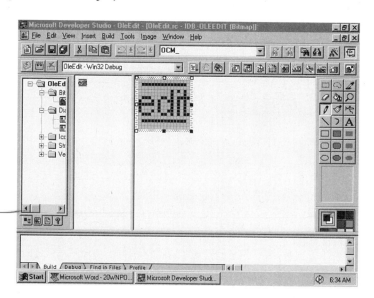

Testing an ActiveX Control

After following the steps in the previous sections, you are in possession of an OleEdit ActiveX Control. However, because the control is an in-process server located in a DLL, it can't be run as an EXE. Testing an ActiveX Control requires a few extra steps, which are discussed in this section.

Choosing a Test Container for Your Control

Every ActiveX Control requires a control container. The simplest control container is the OLE control test container included with Developer Studio and the Win32 SDK. Other OLE control containers include Microsoft Access and Visual Basic 4.0. At the time of this writing, the only container specifically for ActiveX Controls is Internet Explorer 3.0. However, if your control follows the OLE control specification, there's no problem testing it with OLE control containers.

You should test an ActiveX Control using as many test containers as possible. In this chapter, I test OleEdit in two containers. First, I use TSTCON32.EXE, the test container included with Developer Studio.

Using the TSTCON32 Test Container

In order to launch the OleEdit control in the Developer Studio debugger, you must specify the application to be used to load the control. You can do this by following these steps:

1. Select Settings from the Build menu in Developer Studio. The Build Setting dialog box is displayed.
2. Click on the tab labeled Debug.
3. In the edit control labeled "Executable for debug session," enter the path to the test container, which is usually something like `C:\MSDEV\BIN\TSTCON32.EXE`. If you have installed Visual C++ in a directory other than `C:\MSDEV`, you must change the path accordingly.
4. Click the OK button to dismiss the dialog box and save your changes.

After you have made these changes, the Developer Studio debugger can be used to launch the test container. Clicking on the Go icon in the toolbar or otherwise starting a debug session causes the test container to be displayed as shown in Figure 20.7.

FIGURE 20.7.

The OLE control test container.

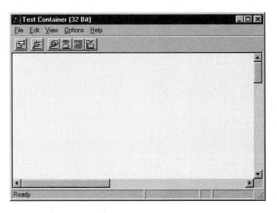

When an ActiveX Control created by ControlWizard is compiled, the control is automatically registered. To display a list of all registered controls, select "Insert OLE Control..." from the Edit menu. A dialog box containing all available OLE controls is displayed. Select the OleEdit edit control, and click the OK button. The OleEdit control is inserted into the test container, as shown in Figure 20.8. Note that an OleEdit icon is also added to the test container toolbar.

FIGURE 20.8.

The OLE control test container and OleEdit control.

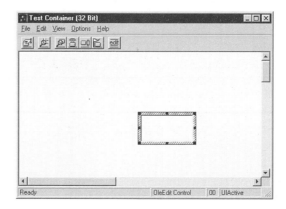

Testing Properties

The test container can be used to test your control's properties in two ways:

- Through an OLE Automation interface that lists all exposed properties.
- Through your control's property sheet.

To access all the properties implemented by an OLE control, select Properties from the View menu. A properties dialog box is displayed as shown in Figure 20.9.

FIGURE 20.9.

Accessing the properties exposed by OleEdit.

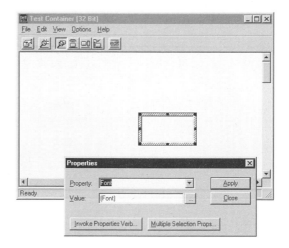

Using Component Gallery

21

by Mickey
Williams

IN THIS CHAPTER

Component Gallery is a tool included with Developer Studio. Component Gallery serves as a database that stores information about components that can be inserted into your Visual C++ projects. In this chapter I discuss Component Gallery and how it is used to manage components—both those supplied with Developer Studio and those components created by you.

What Is Component Gallery?

Component Gallery is a new feature of Visual C++ introduced with Developer Studio 4.0. Component Gallery is a database used for storing Active Controls, reusable classes, and other code fragments used for creating Windows NT applications.

When Visual C++ is initially installed, Component Gallery contains a variety of OLE controls and reusable classes provided by Microsoft. Using Visual C++, you can automatically add Active Controls and other components to the Component Gallery as you create them. This makes it easy to reuse your code.

Adding Components to the Component Gallery

Because Component Gallery is part of Developer Studio, it is not necessary to create a project in order to add an existing component. There are several ways to add components to the Component Gallery.

- By using ClassWizard to create a new class as a component.
- By importing an existing component into the Component Gallery.
- By installing a component acquired elsewhere using the component's setup program. Typically, only commercial components will have setup programs.
- By registering an Active Control, which automatically adds the control to the Component Gallery database.

Using ClassWizard to Create Components

To create a reusable class component, you must use ClassWizard. In addition, if the class uses a dialog box resource, it's a very good idea to create the dialog box resource before creating the class. When adding a new class to a project, make sure the checkbox labeled "Add to Component Gallery" is checked.

After creating the reusable component, it is added to the Component Gallery under its project's tab. For example, if you create a class named CFoo, as part of a project named Bar, information about the CFoo component is stored under the Component Gallery Bar tab.

A component is not stored in two places—Component Gallery is just a database that stores the location of your components. If a component is moved or erased, the component is not available, even though information about it is stored in Component Gallery.

Before a reusable class component can be used, it must be exported into a single file from Component Gallery. This file contains all the component's class information as well as any resources used by the component.

An Example of a Reusable Dialog Box Component

As an example of a reusable component, I have created an About box that displays available memory and CPU information. By packaging the dialog box and its associated class as a component named XAbout, it can easily be reused in other projects.

The first step in creating a reusable component is to create a project to contain the original class and dialog box. The HostAbout project will contain the original implementation of the CXAbout class and its associated resources. The HostAbout project included on the CD is a dialog-based project. However, feel free to start with an existing MDI or SDI project; it doesn't matter for the purposes of this example.

Creating the Dialog Resource

Add a dialog box to the HostAbout project to be used to replace the existing About box. Figure 21.1 shows the dialog box in the Developer Studio resource editor.

FIGURE 21.1.

The About dialog box used by HostAbout.

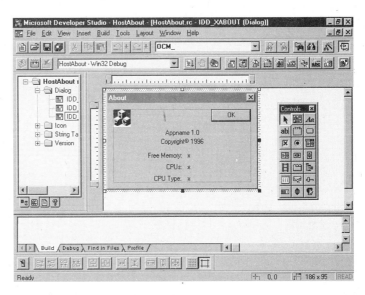

Give the new dialog box a resource ID of IDD_XABOUT. Remove the Cancel button supplied by the resource editor. Properties for the controls added to the dialog box are listed in tab order in Table 21.1. All properties that aren't listed should be set to their default values.

Table 21.1. Property values for controls in the IDD_XABOUT dialog box.

Control	Resource ID	Caption	Image
Icon	IDC_STATIC	N/A	IDR_MAINFRAME
Copyright label	IDC_COPYRIGHT	Copyright© 1996	
Application label	IDC_APPNAME	Appname 1.0	
Free Memory label	IDC_STATIC	Free Memory:	
CPU label	IDC_STATIC	CPUs:	
CPU Type label	IDC_STATIC	CPU Type:	
Free Memory value	IDC_MEM_FREE	X	
CPU label	IDC_CPU_COUNT	X	
CPU Type label	IDC_CPU_TYPE	X	

Note that there are three static text controls inserted in the dialog with a caption of X. The caption is changed at runtime to contain system information.

Creating the CXAbout Class

Using ClassWizard, to the HostAbout project add a new class named CXAbout derived from CDialog. Table 21.2 lists the properties for the new dialog class.

Table 21.2. Values used for the CAddBubDlg class.

Control	Value
Name	CXAbout
Base Class	CDialog
File	XAbout.cpp
Dialog ID	IDD_XABOUT
OLE Automation	None
Component Gallery	Checked

Click the Create button. The CXAbout class is generated and added to the HostAbout project. With ClassWizard, add a message-handling function to handle the WM_INITDIALOG message, using the values shown in Table 21.3.

Table 21.3. Handling the WM_INITDIALOG message.

Class Name	Object ID	Message	Function
CXAbout	CXAbout	WM_INITDIALOG	OnInitDialog

The source code for CXAbout::OnInitDialog is provided in Listing 21.1.

Listing 21.1. Handling the WM_INITDIALOG message.

```
BOOL CXAbout::OnInitDialog()
{
    TCHAR   szBuff[64];
    CDialog::OnInitDialog();

    // Collect free memory size
    MEMORYSTATUS ms;
    ms.dwLength = sizeof( MEMORYSTATUS );
    GlobalMemoryStatus( &ms );
    wsprintf(szBuff, _T("%ld K"), (DWORD)(ms.dwTotalPhys / 1024L));
    SetDlgItemText( IDC_MEM_FREE, szBuff );

    // Determine the number of CPUs installed
    SYSTEM_INFO si;
    GetSystemInfo( &si );
    wsprintf(szBuff, _T("%ld"), (DWORD)si.dwNumberOfProcessors);

    // Determine the CPU type
    SetDlgItemText( IDC_CPU_COUNT, szBuff );
    switch( si.wProcessorArchitecture )
    {
    case PROCESSOR_ARCHITECTURE_INTEL:
        wsprintf(szBuff, _T("Intel"));
        break;

    case PROCESSOR_ARCHITECTURE_MIPS:
        wsprintf(szBuff, _T("MIPS"));
        break;

    case PROCESSOR_ARCHITECTURE_ALPHA:
        wsprintf(szBuff, _T("DEC Alpha"));
        break;

    case PROCESSOR_ARCHITECTURE_PPC:
        wsprintf(szBuff, _T("PowerPC"));
        break;
```

continues

Listing 21.1. continued

```
case PROCESSOR_ARCHITECTURE_UNKNOWN:
default:
    wsprintf(szBuff, _T("Unknown CPU Type"));
    break;
}
SetDlgItemText( IDC_CPU_TYPE, szBuff );

return TRUE;
}
```

To substitute the CXAbout class for the CAboutDlg class, make the changes shown in Listing 21.2 to the CHostAboutDlg::OnSysCommand function. The changed lines are shown in bold type, and they create an instance of the CXAbout class and display the dialog box by calling DoModal.

Listing 21.2. Modifications (in bold) to the OnSysCommand function.

```
void CHostAboutDlg::OnSysCommand(UINT nID, LPARAM lParam)
{
    if ((nID & 0xFFF0) == IDM_ABOUTBOX)
    {
        CXAbout dlg;
        dlg.DoModal();
    }
    else
    {
        CDialog::OnSysCommand(nID, lParam);
    }
}
```

After making the changes in Listing 21.2, add the following line near the top of the HostAboutDlg.cpp file, just after the other include directives:

```
#include "XAbout.h"
```

Compiling and Testing the Project

Test the changes made in the previous sections by compiling the HostAbout project. After compiling the project successfully, test the CXAbout class by selecting About from the system menu. The About dialog box displayed by the CXAbout class is shown in Figure 21.2.

FIGURE 21.2.

The CXAbout dialog box used by the HostAbout project.

Creating an XAbout Category in Component Gallery

Component Gallery components are arranged in categories, with each category containing one or more components. Each category has its own tab, as shown in Figure 21.3.

FIGURE 21.3.

Each component category is stored under a unique tab.

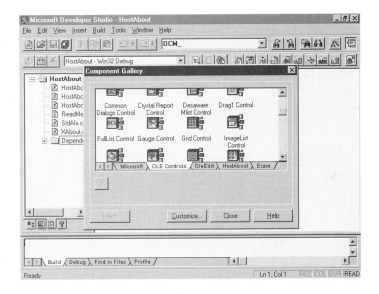

When Developer Studio is initially installed, there are two Component categories.

- OLE Controls contains all the registered Active Controls on your system, not just the controls installed as part of the Visual C++ installation. For example, I have Visual Basic 4.0 installed, and all the OLE controls I use with Visual Basic are also available through the Component Gallery OLE Controls tab.

- Microsoft contains a number of reusable components that you can use to add extra functionality to your application. There are components for adding MAPI and WinSock support, dialog bars, and improved status bar handling.

As you create new projects, Component Gallery automatically adds a new tab containing project components. For the HostAbout project, the only component that will be reused is the XAbout component. Figure 21.4. shows all the components created by Component Gallery including the XAbout component created earlier in this chapter.

To create a new category for a component, click the button labeled Customize. A dialog box that allows you to customize Component Gallery is displayed. The Categories list box has an entry for every category contained by Component Gallery. To change a component's name, click on the component's name, and an edit control is displayed that can be used to enter the new name for the component.

FIGURE 21.4.

Components created as part of the HostAbout project.

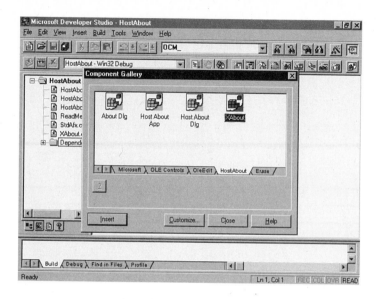

After the last component entry, there is an extra "empty" entry that is just a focus rectangle. Click on the focus rectangle and an edit control pops up, allowing you to enter the new category directly into the list box, as shown in Figure 21.5.

FIGURE 21.5.

Creating a new category inside Component Gallery.

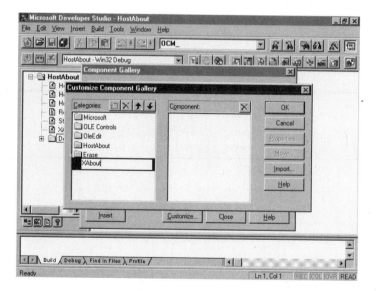

To move a component to the new category, highlight the component in the right list box, and click the Move button. A dialog containing a list box filled with the available categories is displayed. Select the target category, and click OK.

Exporting Components

In order to use components you created in other projects on your computer, you can simply double-click on the component. Component Gallery adds the necessary source files and resources to the current project automatically. However, if you want to share components with others, you must first export the component into an OGX file. This file contains all the information necessary to create the component on another machine.

To export a component, follow these steps:

1. Open Component Gallery.
2. Click on the Customize button to display the Customize Component Gallery dialog box.
3. Display the property sheet for the selected component by selecting the component to be exported then clicking the Properties button.
4. Select the Custom tab on the property sheet, then click the Export button.
5. A Save File common dialog box is presented—use this dialog box to select a destination for the OGX file, then click OK. Component Gallery then creates the OGX file.

The resulting OGX file can be used on other machines, and imported into Developer Studio using the procedure outlined in the next section, *Importing Existing Components*.

Importing Existing Components

To import an existing Active Control or a component stored as an OGX file, click the Import button in the Customize Component Gallery dialog box. A modified Open File common dialog box is displayed; use this dialog to select the component to be imported. This dialog box is shown in Figure 21.6.

The dialog box used to import components has a checkbox that is used to copy the component into the Component Gallery subdirectory. If this checkbox is cleared, the component is not copied; rather, a reference is kept to its current location. If you are importing from a floppy or other temporary location, you should check this option.

FIGURE 21.6.

The Insert Component dialog box.

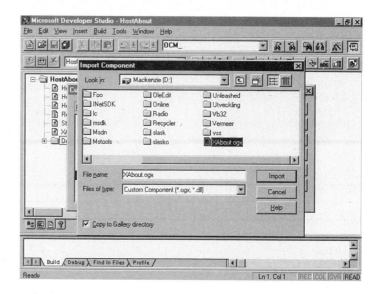

Removing Items From the Component Gallery

Components and categories are removed from Component Gallery by using the Customize Component Gallery dialog box. To remove a category or component, select the item to be removed and click the red "X" above the list box. Alternatively, you can select the item to be deleted, and then press the Delete key on your keyboard.

> **NOTE**
>
> **Preventing AppWizard From Adding Projects to the Component Gallery**
>
> By default, AppWizard adds every project to the Component Gallery. I'm sure someone finds this useful, but everyone I know thinks that this is a major hassle. After creating a project using AppWizard, you may want to immediately open the Component Gallery, and remove the current project.
>
> At the time of this writing, the current versions of Visual C++ versions 4.0 and 4.1 do not provide a checkbox or similar method to request that a particular project not be added to the Component Gallery. However, by making a small modification to the registry you can prevent AppWizard from automatically adding your new projects as components.
>
> Follow these steps to modify the registry:
>
> 1. Open regedt32.exe, the Windows NT registry editor.
> 2. Open the HKEY_CURRENT_USER\Software\Microsoft\Developer key.

3. Add a new key named Gallery by selecting New, then Key from the Edit menu.

4. Select the new Gallery key, and add a new DWORD value named ScanProjects. To add this value, select New, then DWORD from the Edit menu.

5. Double-click on the ScanProjects label, and set its value to 0 to prevent AppWizard from adding projects to the Component Gallery.

The steps listed above prevent AppWizard from adding new projects to the Component Gallery. To change this behavior, change the value of the ScanProjects key to 1 instead of 0, or delete the key.

Using an Active Control

To insert an Active Control into an AppWizard project, follow these steps:

1. Open Component Gallery.

2. Select the component category that contains the Active Control, and highlight the control to be inserted.

3. Click the Insert button.

4. A dialog box is displayed, asking you to confirm that the control is to be inserted into the project; confirm the operation.

5. Close Component Gallery.

After following the above steps, the component is inserted into your project. Classes used to manage the control are added automatically to your project.

To insert a class component such as the XAbout component created earlier in this chapter, the same steps are followed as with Active Controls.

Summary

This chapter has discussed Component Gallery, a Developer Studio tool that helps you create and reuse your components. Component Gallery automatically stores information about new projects created in Developer Studio. New classes can be added to Component Gallery by simply marking a checkbox when creating the class.

Reusable classes, as well as ActiveX Controls, can be stored and reused through Component Gallery. The steps required to create a reusable class was covered in this chapter, as well as the steps required to share the class with other developers.

The next chapter, "Threads," discusses how process and threads are managed in Windows NT. Several examples are provided, including examples of multithreaded applications using MFC.

PART

IV

IN THIS PART

Low-Level Process Communications

Threads

by Mickey
Williams

22

This chapter continues the discussion of processes and threads begun in Chapter 3, "Execution Models." It will cover how processes and threads are created and managed, as well as how they are used in developing multithreaded applications in Windows NT.

A major portion of this chapter is used to discuss synchronization between threads and processes. Windows NT provides a number of ways to efficiently synchronize your multithreaded applications, and this chapter discusses them all.

As always, this chapter also includes a number of sample projects that can be found on the CD. These projects illustrate the concepts of multithreading and synchronization.

Processes and Threads

As discussed in Chapter 3, a process is started by Windows NT when an application is launched. The process owns the memory, resources, and threads of execution associated with that particular instance of running an executable program. When a process is started, a primary thread is started as well. As long as at least one thread is associated with a process, the process will be alive.

A thread, sometimes called a *thread of execution,* is the smallest unit of execution in Windows NT. A thread is always associated with a process, and always lives within a particular process. Although many processes have only a single thread that lasts for the life of the process, it is not unusual for a process to have many threads over its lifetime, as shown in Figure 22.1.

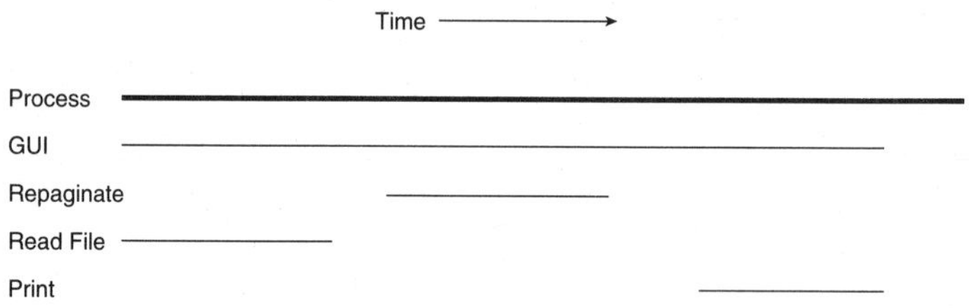

FIGURE 22.1.

A typical Windows NT process has many threads over its lifetime.

Thread Scheduling

Threads are scheduled according to their priority, and within a certain priority, in a circular, or "round-robin" fashion. There are 31 different priority levels, as shown in Figure 22.2.

As discussed in Chapter 3, a thread can be in one of six states:

- Waiting
- Ready
- Running
- Standby
- Terminated
- Transition

FIGURE 22.2.

There are 31 different priority levels available in Windows NT.

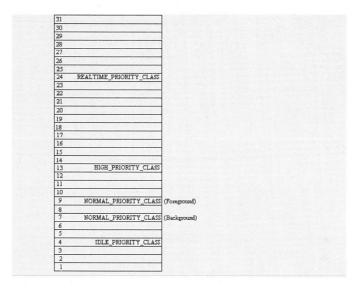

The last three states in the preceding list are really "substates." That is, the thread is either waiting, as in the case of thread in the standby state, or running, in the case of the transition state.

At any given time, there is only one thread per system processor in running state. All other threads are either waiting, or ready. A running thread is allowed to run until one of the following things occurs:

- It exceeds its maximum allotted execution time, known as a quantum.
- A higher priority thread marked as waiting becomes waiting.
- The running thread decides to wait for an event or object.

When a thread exceeds its time quantum, Windows NT marks the thread as ready and looks for the highest priority ready thread in the system. If there are other ready threads with the same priority level as the previously running thread, the next thread is marked as running, and starts executing. In this way, threads at the same priority level are serviced in a circular, or "round-robin" sort of queue. If a thread is waiting for an I/O event or waiting for some other object to be signaled, another thread is selected to run using the same scheduling process.

In order to make Window-based applications appear more responsive, the thread that owns the foreground window is usually boosted by two priority levels. This boost only applies if the thread is running at the usual priority class. If a thread has an idle, high, or real-time priority class, switching to the foreground does not effect its priority level.

When a thread is prevented from running due to a large number of higher-priority work, it is said to be *starved*. Threads that have an extremely low priority are occasionally given a "boost" in their priority that enables them to be scheduled for one execution cycle. This is enough in most cases to guarantee that all threads get at least some chance to compete for CPU cycles.

Managing Processes

One of the most common ways to start a process is to launch it from the Windows NT Explorer, by launching it from the Start menu, or by typing the name of the program at the console command line. Windows NT also includes a number of functions that can be used to create and manage processes.

Using the `CreateProcess` Function

A process can be begun in many ways, such as by launching from the Windows NT Start menu, or clicking on an icon. To start a process from within another Windows NT application, you must call the `CreateProcess` function:

```
STARTUPINFO si;
memset( &si, 0, sizeof(STARTUPINFO) );
si.cb = sizeof(STARTUPINFO);
PROCESS_INFORMATION pi;
BOOL fCreated = CreateProcess( TEXT("C:\\foo.exe"),
                               NULL,
                               NULL,
                               NULL,
                               FALSE,
                               CREATE_NEW_CONSOLE,
                               NULL,
                               TEXT("C:\\"),
                               &si,
                               &pi );
HANDLE hProcess = pi.hProcess;  // Process handle
```

The `CreateProcess` function has ten parameters:

- The path to the executable file that is to be started. If this parameter is NULL, the next parameter is used to determine the filename.

- The command line used to start the process. This parameter can be NULL if no command line arguments are passed to the new process.

- A pointer to a SECURITY_ATTRIBUTES structure that specifies the security attributes for the new process. Using NULL for this parameter causes the operating system to give the new process a default security descriptor.

- A pointer to a SECURITY_ATTRIBUTES structure that specifies the security attributes for the primary thread created by the new process. A NULL value causes a default security descriptor to be used.

- A flag that specifies if the new process will inherit the handles owned by the current process, in this case FALSE.

- A flag that specifies how the process will be created and its priority level, in this case, the flag is CREATE_NEW_CONSOLE. Other possible values for this flag are discussed later.

- A pointer to an environment block used by the new process, or NULL if the new process will use the environment block of the parent process.

- The current drive and directory for the new process, or NULL if the new process will use the same drive and current directory as the parent process.

- A pointer to a STARTUPINFO structure, which can be used to set various attributes for the new process, such as its title and window position. The STARTUPINFO structure should be initialized as shown in the example, particularly the cb member, which must be initialized with the size of the STARTUPINFO structure.

- A pointer to a PROCESS_INFORMATION structure, which will be filled in by Windows NT while creating the new process.

The CREATE flag parameter has one or more of the following values:

- CREATE_DEFAULT_ERROR_MODE prevents the new process from inheriting the error mode set by the parent process.

- CREATE_NEW_CONSOLE gives the new process its own console, instead of inheriting the one owned by the parent process. This flag cannot be used with the DETACHED_PROCESS flag.

- CREATE_NEW_PROCESS_GROUP specifies that the new process is the root member of a new process group.

- CREATE_SEPARATE_WOW_VDM is used when creating a 16-bit process. This flag specifies that the new process is given its own Windows On Windows (WOW) Virtual DOS Machine.

- CREATE_SHARED_WOW_VDM is used when creating a 16-bit process. This flag specifies that the new process will share a Windows On Windows (WOW) Virtual DOS Machine.

- CREATE_SUSPENDED specifies that the primary thread of the new process is created in a suspended state.

- CREATE_UNICODE_ENVIRONMENT specifies that the environment block uses Unicode instead of ANSI characters.

- DEBUG_PROCESS specifies that the parent process is interested in receiving debug events generated from the new process.

- DEBUG_ONLY_THIS_PROCESS is used to specify that the new process should not be debugged using the same debugger used for the parent process.

- DETACHED_PROCESS prevents the new process from accessing the console window of the parent process. This flag cannot be used with the CREATE_NEW_CONSOLE flag.

- NORMAL_PRIORITY_CLASS is used to specify a process without special scheduling requirements. This thread priority value should be used for almost all cases.

- IDLE_PRIORITY_CLASS specifies that the threads owned by the process only run when the system is idle. This value is the default if the parent process has this attribute.

- HIGH_PRIORITY_CLASS specifies that the threads in the process need to perform delay-sensitive tasks that must be executed with a minimum amount of delay. This flag should be used with care, because it causes the thread to preempt most other threads in the system.

■ REALTIME_PRIORITY_CLASS specifies that the threads owned by the process must be given the highest possible priority. Threads running at this level literally outrun the operating system. Because threads with this attribute execute faster than the virtual memory management system and other internal processes, they may become dead-locked and cause the system to behave erratically.

The CreateProcess function returns TRUE if it was able to begin launching the new process. If the process cannot be started, it is usually considered a fault in the new process; as far as CreateProcess is concerned, its work is finished.

The PROCESS_INFORMATION structure contains information about the new process and its primary thread. The PROCESS_INFORMATION structure has four members:

■ hProcess is a handle for the new process.

■ hThread is a handle to the primary thread of the new process.

■ dwProcessId is an ID number for the new process. Take care when using this value—it's only valid as long as the process is running, and Windows NT may reassign it to a new process immediately after this process is finished.

■ dwThreadId is an ID number for the primary thread of the new process.

Ending a Process

There are two ways to end a process. The preferred way is to call the ExitProcess function from within one of the threads executing the process:

```
ExitProcess( NO_ERROR );
```

Calling ExitProcess enables a process to perform an orderly exit—such as calling the DLL entry point functions for any DLLs that the process has loaded, signaling threads that may be waiting for it to finish, and closing all of the object handles owned by the process.

After the process has ended, the GetExitCodeProcess function returns the value passed as a parameter to ExitProcess. If the GetExitCodeProcess function is called before the process ends, the return value is STILL_ACTIVE.

Another way to end a process is to call TerminateProcess, passing the handle of the process to be ended:

```
TerminateProcess( hProcess, NO_ERROR );
```

This method should be avoided when possible, because it does not unload DLLs and perform other types of system cleanup that are normally performed when a process terminates.

The third way to kill a process is to terminate all of the threads owned by the process. Killing a thread is discussed in the next section.

Managing Threads

Unlike many popular multithreaded operating systems, Windows NT offers true threads. Most multithreaded operating systems require you to create a new process when creating a new path of execution. However, a Windows NT thread is much less expensive to create than a typical UNIX process in terms of computing resources, and offers a wide range of management options. The next few sections discuss how threads are created and managed in a Windows NT application.

Creating Threads

A thread is created by calling the `CreateThread` function:

```
long WINAPI ThreadEntry( LPARAM lparam )
{
    // ...
}
unsigned long nThreadID;
HANDLE hThread = CreateThread( NULL,
                               0,
                               (LPTHREAD_START_ROUTINE)ThreadEntry,
                               (void*)szHello,
                               0,
                               &nThreadID );
```

The `CreateThread` function takes six parameters:

■ A pointer to a `SECURITY_ATTRIBUTES` structure that specifies the security attributes for the new thread. Using `NULL` for this parameter causes the operating system to give the new thread a default security descriptor.

■ The initial stack size for the new thread. If zero is passed as this parameter, the new thread is given a stack the same size as the primary thread. This is usually a good value to use as a default, because Windows NT will increase the size of the stack, if necessary.

■ The address of a start function where the thread begins executing.

■ A 32-bit parameter passed to the new thread's start function. The new thread begins executing in this function, and when the thread exits this function, it is terminated.

■ A flag that specifies how the thread is created. This flag can either be `CREATE_SUSPENDED`, which creates the flag in a suspended state, or zero, which enables the thread to begin executing. A thread that is suspended does not execute until the `ResumeThread` function has been called for it.

■ The address of a 32-bit variable that is filled with the thread ID when `CreateThread` returns.

Ending a Thread

There are three ways to end a thread. The "normal" way to end a thread is to call the `ExitThread` function from within the thread that is ending. When `ExitThread` is called, a thread exit code is passed as a parameter:

```
ExitThread( NO_ERROR );
```

The `ExitThread` function is called implicitly when you exit from the thread's start function. For example, the following thread start function executes a `for` loop five times, then returns `NO_ERROR` as the thread's exit code:

```
long WINAPI ThreadFunc( long lParam )
{
    for( int n = 0; n < 5; n++ )
    {
        // Work with thread
    }
    return NO_ERROR;
}
```

The least preferred method to end a thread is to use `TerminateThread`. Calling `TerminateThread` does not give a thread a chance to clean up any partially completed work; the thread may own critical sections that are not released, or it may have partially completed work that cannot be concluded. The call to `TerminateThread` looks like this:

```
HANDLE hThread = CreateThread( .... );
.
.
TerminateThread( hThread, NO_ERROR );
```

The `TerminateThread` function has two parameters: the thread handle, and an exit code for the thread.

If any of these methods is used to kill the last remaining thread owned by a process, the process terminates.

The exit code for a thread can be retrieved by calling `GetExitCodeThread`:

```
DWORD dwResult;
GetExitCodeThread( hThread, &dwResult );
if( dwResult != NO_ERROR )
{
    // Handle error case
}
```

The `GetExitCodeThread` function has two parameters: the thread handle, and the address of a 32-bit variable that will be filled with the thread's exit code. If `GetExitCode` thread is called for a thread that has not yet exited, the return value is `STILL_ACTIVE`.

Fetching and Changing a Thread's Priority

Windows NT enables you to dynamically change the priority of a thread. You should take extreme care when changing the priority of a thread—it's easy to severely impact the performance of your entire system by raising a thread's priority too high.

As discussed in Chapter 3, there are four process priority classes:

- `IDLE_PRIORITY_CLASS`
- `NORMAL_PRIORITY_CLASS`
- `HIGH_PRIORITY_CLASS`
- `REALTIME_PRIORITY_CLASS`

Within a single process, every thread has the same process priority class. You can't have one thread running at `HIGH_PRIORITY_CLASS`, and several other threads running at `NORMAL_PRIORITY_CLASS`. You can, however, change the relative priority of threads within a process using the `SetThreadPriority` function:

```
SetThreadPriority( hThread, THREAD_PRIORITY_LOWEST );
```

Every thread can be set to run within a range of five priority levels, no matter what its priority class:

- `THREAD_PRIORITY_LOWEST` is two steps below the priority class assigned to the process.
- `THREAD_PRIORITY_BELOW_NORMAL` is one step below the priority class assigned to the process.
- `THREAD_PRIORITY_NORMAL` is the same as the priority class assigned to the process.
- `THREAD_PRIORITY_ABOVE_NORMAL` is one step above the priority class assigned to the process.
- `THREAD_PRIORITY_HIGHEST` is two steps above the priority class assigned to the process.

In addition, there are two special priority levels that can be passed to `SetThreadPriority`:

- `THREAD_PRIORITY_IDLE` always sets the thread's priority level to one, unless the process priority class is `REALTIME_PRIORITY_CLASS`, in which case it is set to 16.
- `THREAD_PRIORITY_TIME_CRITICAL` always sets the thread's priority to 15, unless the process priority class is `REALTIME_PRIORITY_CLASS`, in which case it is set to 31. This is the only way a thread can run at priority level 31.

Thread-Local Storage

Automatic variables, such as the variables declared inside a function body, are created in the context of the currently running thread. This means that every thread has its own copy of every automatic variable. This is usually a good thing, because it means that you don't need to synchronize access to variables created on the stack.

When it is necessary to use global variables, threads tend to complicate your life quite a bit. First, access to the variable must be synchronized so that multiple threads don't attempt to modify the variable at the same time. Second, a normal global variable is shared between all threads—unless you use an array, there's no way to store data on a per-thread basis.

Windows NT has a specific way of dealing with this problem. Thread-local storage enables you to create variables that are maintained on a per-thread basis, with very little bookkeeping or maintenance required by the programmer. There are two types of thread-local storage:

- Static thread-local storage
- Dynamic thread-local storage

The advantages of both methods are discussed in the next two sections.

Using Static Thread-Local Storage

Static thread-local storage is very easy to use. There are no functions to call, no special precautions to take, and no weird compiler switches to set.

Static thread-local storage lives in a special memory section named `.tls` created in the address space of your process. When a new thread is created, Windows NT makes a new copy of the thread-local storage for the new thread, and destroys the block of memory when the thread is killed. A thread can only access the thread-local variables used for its thread.

To declare a thread-local storage variable, use `__declspec(thread)` as part of the variable's declaration:

```
__declspec(thread) int nMeals = 0;
```

To make your code more readable, you can also use a `typedef`:

```
typedef __declspec(thread) TLS;
TLS int nMeals = 0;
```

A thread-local storage variable is used just like any other variable. You can read to it, write to it, or take its address, just as you can with other global variables. You don't need to synchronize access to it, because only one thread can touch it.

A thread-local storage variable can be declared in global scope, or as a static variable in a function. It can never be declared as a plain automatic variable.

Using Dynamic Thread-local Storage

Dynamic thread-local storage is created and used at runtime by your application. Although it is slightly more complex than static thread-local storage, dynamic thread-local storage is much more flexible, because it can be allocated and freed as needed.

Windows NT maintains the dynamic thread-local storage, and each process accesses the thread-local storage using indexes, as shown in Figure 22.3.

FIGURE 22.3.

Thread-local storage uses indexes maintained by Windows NT.

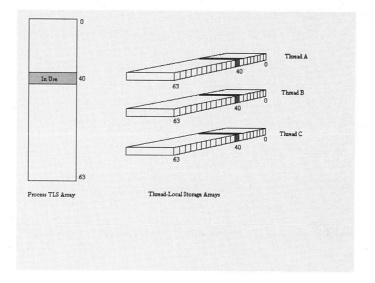

Each thread in a process has its own copy of the thread-local storage. Windows NT maintains a status flag for each thread-local storage index, and allocates a new one for any process requesting a new storage index. There are four functions used to manage the thread-local storage:

- TlsAlloc is used to request a new thread-local storage index from Windows NT.
- TlsSetValue is used by a thread to store a 32-bit value in its copy of the thread-local storage.
- TlsGetValue is used by a thread to retrieve a 32-bit value previously stored in thread-local storage.
- TlsFree is used to notify Windows NT that a process no longer needs a particular thread-local storage index.

Each thread in the process has access to its own copy of the thread-local storage. It cannot change the values used by any other threads.

Getting Multiple Threads to Cooperate

The need to manage threads and processes in an application is not something unique to Windows NT. Once you break an application into more than one thread, you may need to handle problems you never knew existed under single-threaded programming.

For example, cout, the standard iostream console output object, is often used to display text information to the console. You may not believe it, but plain old cout can be a problem for multithreaded applications. Consider a simple function like this:

```
void bugMsg( TCHAR* psz )
{
    cout << TEXT("A bug lives here ") << *psz << end;
}
```

This function fails if called by more than a single thread. If the cout object is manipulated by two threads simultaneously, the result is undefined. On a Windows NT installation with a single CPU, the likelihood of two threads interfering with each other is remote. However, the console-mode program provided in Listing 22.1 fails after a short period of time when run on a machine with multiple processors.

Listing 22.1. Unsynchronized access to the global cout object.

```
#include "windows.h"
#include "iostream.h"
long g_nCounter = 0;
long WINAPI Print( long lParam )
{
    while (1)
    {
        cout << TEXT("Thread # ") << lParam
            << TEXT(" Count = ")  << g_nCounter << endl;
        InterlockedIncrement( &g_nCounter );
    }
    return NO_ERROR;
}
int main()
{
    unsigned long nThreadID;
    for( int cThread = 0; cThread < 2; cThread++ )
    {
        CreateThread( NULL,
                      0,
                      (LPTHREAD_START_ROUTINE)Print,
                      (void*)cThread,
                      0,
                      &nThreadID );
    }
    Sleep( 5000 );
    return 0;
}
```

Listing 22.1 demonstrates what is known as a synchronization problem. Another example of a synchronization problem was discussed in Chapter 16, "Dynamic Link Libraries," specifically, how multiple processes could access a variable in shared memory at the same time.

Any operating system that supports multiple threads of execution must provide some way for you to handle these synchronization issues. What makes Windows NT unique is its large number of management options. Windows NT is chock-full of methods to help you manage threads and processes. These methods are discussed in detail in the section *Synchronization* later in this chapter.

When to Create a Thread

There are several problems that are easily solved by splitting an application into two or more threads. Your application is probably a good candidate for multithreading if it:

- Spends a lot of time testing to check for completed I/O
- Has a number of "background" tasks to perform asynchronously
- Has other tasks that can be performed independently without much synchronization

Using multiple threads tends to make applications with these properties easier to program. However, it's easy to go overboard when using threads for the first time. Consider the next section.

When Not to Create a Thread

There are some types of applications that are not good candidates for becoming multithreaded. Your application may not be a great candidate for multithreading if it:

- Is basically monolithic
- Does not consume existing computing resources
- Has complex synchronization issues
- Has many dependencies between tasks

Remember, adding multiple threads to your application may solve some of your problems, but it will create new issues—synchronization, thread, and object lifetime—as well as increased complexity during testing. And remember this: Your program will not, in most cases, run any faster on a single CPU machine.

Synchronization

As discussed earlier, when two or more threads use a common variable, problems can result. If multiple threads attempt to read a variable, there's no problem; however, if one thread attempts to modify a common variable, access to that variable must be synchronized.

A synchronization primitive is an object that helps you manage a multithreaded application. There are five basic types of synchronization primitives available in Windows NT:

- *Events* are objects created by you and used to signal that a variable or routine is available for access.
- *Critical sections* are areas of code that can be accessed by a single thread at any given time.
- *Mutexes* are Windows NT objects used to ensure that only a single thread has access to a protected variable or code.

- *Semaphores* are similar to mutexes, but behave like counters, allowing a specified number of threads access to a protected variable or code.

- API-level *atomic* operations are provided by Windows NT to enable you to increment, decrement, or exchange the contents of a variable in a single operation.

Each of these synchronization primitives is useful in certain situations. Each is discussed in turn in the next few sections.

Critical Sections

A critical section is a section of code that must be used by only one thread at any given time. If two or more threads attempt to access a critical section at the same time, only one thread must be allowed control of the critical section, and all other threads are *blocked*, or kept waiting, until the critical section is free, as shown in Figure 22.4.

FIGURE 22.4.

A critical section only enables one thread to execute.

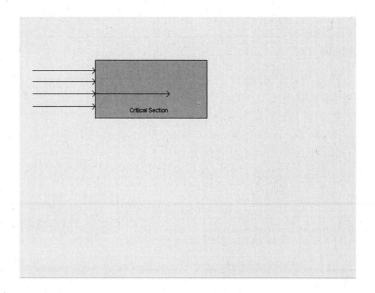

Compared with other synchronization methods discussed later, creating a critical section is very inexpensive in terms of computing resources. However, unlike other Windows NT synchronization primitives, a critical section can only be used within a single process.

A critical section is guarded by a CRITICAL_SECTION variable. This variable must be initialized before it is used, and must be in-scope for every thread that uses it. It must not be allowed to go out of scope while in use, and for this reason critical section variables are often given global scope.

The InitializeCriticalSection function is used to initialize the CRITICAL_SECTION variable:

```
CRITICAL_SECTION cs;
InitializeCriticalSection(&cs);
```

To take possession of a critical section, a thread must call the EnterCriticalSection function:

```
EnterCriticalSection(&cs);
```

If the critical section is not in use, the critical section is marked as busy, and the thread immediately continues execution. If the critical section is already in use, the thread blocks it until it becomes free.

When a thread has finished working with the protected variable or function, the critical section is released by calling LeaveCriticalSection:

```
LeaveCriticalSection(&cs);
```

One thread blocked on this CRITICAL_SECTION variable is able to take control of the variable.

A single CRITICAL_SECTION variable can protect many related variables or functions. The console mode examples in this chapter use critical sections to ensure that only one thread attempts to use cout for console output at a time.

Later in this chapter, a single CRITICAL_SECTION variable is used to ensure that only one of eight threads is working with the controls in a dialog box.

Once a thread takes control of a critical section, it is blocking other threads waiting to gain control of the critical section. For best results, it is important for threads to hold a critical section as little as possible.

Every call to EnterCriticalSection must be balanced with a call to LeaveCriticalSection. If you forget to call LeaveCriticalSection, threads waiting to enter the critical section are blocked forever, or until the process ends, whichever comes first. Unless the work performed inside a critical section is very simple, it's a good idea to use __try and __finally blocks to make sure that your calls to EnterCriticalSection and LeaveCriticalSection are balanced, as shown below:

```
void DoSomething()
{
    __try
    {
        EnterCriticalSection( &csOutput );
        .
        .
        // Do some interesting work here
        .
    }
    __finally
    {
        LeaveCriticalSection( &csOutput );
    }
}
```

In the code fragment above, the LeaveCriticalSection function is always called, even if an exception is thrown while executing inside the critical section.

A single thread is permitted to call EnterCriticalSection multiple times using the same CRITICAL_SECTION variable. This is because it can be difficult to determine all of the possible nested critical sections in a large application. For example, the following code calls the EnterCriticalSection function twice with the same CRITICAL_SECTION variable:

```
void CIsdnTerminal::HandleKeyPress()
{
    EnterCriticalSection( &m_csAction );
    if( ReceivedRelease() == FALSE )
        TranslateKey();
    LeaveCriticalSection( &m_csAction );
}
BOOL CIsdnTerminal::ReceivedRelease()
{
    BOOL fResult;
    EnterCriticalSection( &m_csAction );
    if( m_state == CLEARING )
        fResult = TRUE;
    else
        fResult = m_fReleaseStored;
    LeaveCriticalSection( &m_csAction );
    return fResult;
}
```

In the example above, each call to EnterCriticalSection is balanced with a call to LeaveCriticalSection. When a thread that owns a CRITICAL_SECTION variable calls EnterCriticalSection with the same variable, an internal counter is incremented, and the thread is allowed to continue without blocking. When the internal counter decrements to zero, other threads are allowed to take control of the critical section.

Managing Events

Critical sections are useful when protecting data or functions from multiple threads. However, in a multithreaded application, sometimes you need to notify another thread that an event has occurred. With Windows NT, this is done by creating events.

An event is a Windows NT synchronization object that is managed by the operating system. Each event can have an associated name; this allows multiple processes to share the same event handle.

Events are used when one thread must wait for another thread to complete a task, or when a thread must sleep and wait for another thread to indicate that an event has occurred.

Once created, an event can be in one of two states:

■ Signaled means that a wait request on this event will be satisfied.

■ Not signaled means that wait requests on this thread will not be satisfied, and the waiting thread will be blocked.

Typically, an event is used to indicate a particular task is completed. A thread waiting for this task to be completed waits until the event is signaled, then continues processing, as shown in Figure 22.5.

FIGURE 22.5.

Multiple threads using events for synchronization.

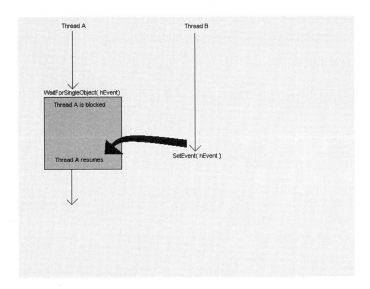

Usually, an event that is signaled is immediately reset to the not-signaled state in an atomic operation. This prevents another thread from reusing the event. Manual-reset events that stay signaled, even after a wait request has been satisfied, are discussed later in this chapter.

Creating and Closing Event Handles

The CreateEvent function is used to create an event:

```
HANDLE hEvent = CreateEvent( NULL, FALSE, FALSE, "EventName" );
```

The CreateEvent function takes four parameters:

- A pointer to a SECURITY_ATTRIBUTES structure. If you aren't concerned about security issues, you can use a NULL for this parameter.
- A flag that indicates whether or not this is to be a manual-reset event. Manual-reset events are described in detail later; this parameter is usually FALSE.
- A flag that indicates the initial state of the event. If this parameter is TRUE, the event is signaled; a value of FALSE indicates this event should be placed into a not-signaled state.
- An optional name for the event. Keep in mind that all event, mutex, and file-mapping objects use the same namespace, so you must take care not to reuse names accidentally. In most cases, this value is NULL, especially when not sharing events across process boundaries.

If the event is successfully created, a handle to the event is returned. If an error occurs, NULL is returned.

Event handles are Windows NT objects, much like file, thread, and process handles. When you are finished using an event handle, the `CloseHandle` function is used:

```
CloseHandle( hEvent );
```

Signaling and Resetting Event Handles

To change the state of an event handle to signaled, the `SetEvent` function is used:

```
SetEvent( hEvent );
```

The `SetEvent` function takes a handle as its only parameter.

Once signaled, an auto-reset event handle is reset after it is used to satisfy a wait request. Manual-reset events must be explicitly reset, using the `ResetEvent` function:

```
ResetEvent( hEvent );
```

Auto-reset events are often used when performing initializations or other events that must be broadcast to a number of threads. In this case, it makes sense to leave a thread signaled, even though it has been used to satisfy a wait request. This enables all waiting threads to be satisfied by setting a single event.

When using manual-reset events to signal a group of threads, it can be difficult to determine when all waiting threads have been released. Windows NT includes a `PulseEvent` function for this very purpose:

```
PulseEvent( hEvent );
```

The `PulseEvent` function signals the event handle, and resets it after all of the waiting threads have been released.

Waiting on a Handle

When a thread needs to wait for a handle to be signaled, there are several different ways to do so. There are two functions that are used to put a thread into a wait state while waiting for a handle to be signaled:

■ `WaitForSingleObject` is used when waiting for one handle to be signaled.

■ `WaitForMultipleObjects` is used when testing an array of handles.

`WaitForSingleObject` tests a handle passed to it as a parameter, and returns immediately if the handle is signaled:

```
DWORD dwResult = WaitForSingleObject( hEvent, INFINITE );
```

The `WaitForSingleObject` function takes two parameters:

■ The handle to be tested

■ A time-out value in milliseconds, or `INFINITE` for no time-out limit

The event remains signaled for a manual-reset event handle even after the first thread's wait request has been satisfied. All other events are set to their non-signaled state by `WaitForSingleObject` after satisfying a wait request.

There are three possible return values for `WaitForSingleObject`:

- ■ `WAIT_OBJECT_0` is returned when the handle is signaled. Note that the last character of this symbol is a zero, not the letter "O."

- ■ `WAIT_TIMEOUT` is returned when the handle is not signaled, and the time-out limit has expired.

- ■ `WAIT_ABANDONED` is returned only when waiting on a mutex handle.

Beware of nested calls to `WaitForSingleObject`. At times, a thread may need to wait for several handles to become signaled. Using nested calls to `WaitForSingleObject` can be risky in cases where multiple threads are contending for multiple objects, as shown in Figure 22.6.

FIGURE 22.6.

An example of deadlock.

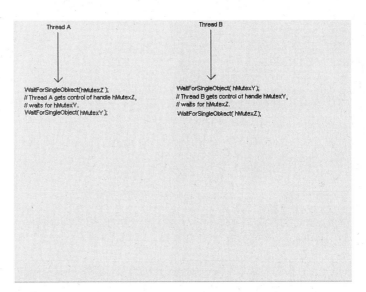

In Figure 22.6, both Thread A and Thread B have one of the resources needed to continue. Unfortunately, neither can continue unless the other thread relinquishes the resource of which it has already taken possession. Fortunately, Windows NT enables you to wait for several synchronization objects at the same time, as discussed in the next section.

Waiting on Multiple Handles

The `WaitForMultipleObjects` function is similar to `WaitForSingleObject`, except that it works with an array of handles. All handles are supervised at the same time, and none are favored with respect to the others. The call to `WaitForMultipleObjects` looks like this:

```
HANDLE hEvents[2];
  .
  .
  .
DWORD dw = WaitForMultipleObjects( 2, hEvents, TRUE, INFINITE );
```

`WaitForMultipleObjects` has four parameters:

- The number of object handles to be tested.
- The base address of the handle array.
- A flag that specifies if all handles must be signaled, or just one. In this case, TRUE indicates that all event handles must be signaled.
- A time-out value in milliseconds, or INFINITE for no time-out limit.

If TRUE is specified as the third parameter to `WaitForMultipleObjects`, no event handle has its state altered unless all handles are available. This is necessary to prevent deadlock conditions that might occur if threads were allowed to take control of a subset of the threads needed to continue.

The return values for `WaitForMutipleObjects` are slightly more complex that `WaitForSingleObject`:

- WAIT_OBJECT_0 through WAIT_OBJECT_0 + (number of handles -1) is returned when the handle is signaled. The return value indicates the index of the lowest numbered handle that has become signaled.
- WAIT_TIMEOUT is returned when the handle is not signaled, and the time-out limit has expired.
- WAIT_ABANDONED_0 through WAIT_ABANDONED_0 + (number of handles -1) is returned only when waiting on a mutex handle.

If you are interested in exactly which handle has been signaled, use a code fragment like this:

```
HANDLE rghEvents[63];
  .
  .
  .
DWORD dw = WaitForMultipleObjects( 63, rghEvents, FALSE, 0x10000 );

if( (dw >= WAIT_OBJECT_0)&&(dw <= WAIT_OBJECT_0 + 63) )
{
    int ndx = dw - WAIT_OBJECT_0;
    HANDLE hSignaled = rghEvents[ndx];
      .
    // Use hSignaled
      .
}
```

Using Event Handles Across a Process Boundary

As discussed earlier, you can use event handles between processes. An event handle can be inherited, passed to a new process during `CreateProcess`, or duplicated using `DuplicateHandle`.

In addition, if an event object was created with an optional name, you can use `CreateEvent` or `OpenEvent` to get a handle to that event object from another process. For example, assume that an event object was created with a name of `"Shared"`:

```
HANDLE hEvent = CreateEvent( NULL, FALSE, FALSE, "Shared" );
```

Another process can get a handle to the same event by calling `CreateEvent` with the same parameters. The `OpenEvent` function also can be used by another process:

```
HANDLE hEvent = OpenEvent( EVENT_ALL_ACCESS, FALSE, "Shared" );
```

Two small console-mode applications on the CD provide examples of using an event handle across process boundaries. The WaitEvent project creates an event handle and waits for it to be signaled. The SigEvent project opens a copy of this event handle, and signals it, allowing WaitEvent to complete its execution.

The complete source code for WaitEvent is provided in Listing 22.2.

Listing 22.2. The WaitEvent program.

```
#include <iostream.h>
#include <windows.h>

int main()
{
    HANDLE hEvent = CreateEvent( NULL, FALSE, FALSE, "WaitEvent" );

    cout << "Waiting for SigEvent" << endl;
    WaitForSingleObject( hEvent, INFINITE );
    cout << "Caught event handle, all done." << endl;
    CloseHandle( hEvent );
    return 0;
}
```

The complete source code for SigEvent is provided in Listing 22.3.

Listing 22.3. The SigEvent program.

```
#include <iostream.h>
#include <windows.h>

int main()
{
    HANDLE hEvent = OpenEvent(EVENT_ALL_ACCESS, FALSE,"WaitEvent");
    cout << "Signaling WaitEvent handle" << endl;
    SetEvent( hEvent );
    return 0;
}
```

Compile both programs. Run the WaitEvent program first. The console displays the following:

```
Waiting for SigEvent
```

Launching the SigEvent program in a different console window displays the following:

```
Signaling WaitEvent handle
```

The SigEvent program signals the event handle, and enables the WaitEvent program to finish. The WaitEvent console window displays the following:

```
Caught event handle, all done
```

Figure 22.7 shows two console mode windows used to run these two programs at the same time.

FIGURE 22.7.

Running the WaitEvent and SigEvent programs.

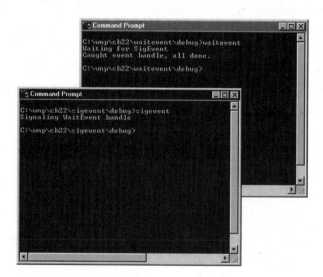

Mutexes and Mutual Exclusion

A mutex is a Windows NT object used as a mutual exclusion primitive. Like critical sections, only one thread can have possession of a mutex object. However, unlike critical sections, mutexes are Windows NT objects and are managed by the operating system. They can also be named and shared between processes.

To take possession of a mutex, a thread must perform a wait on the mutex handle. A mutex is considered signaled when available, and not signaled when in use.

A common synchronization example that illustrates mutual exclusion is the "Dining Philosophers" problem. Several philosophers are sitting at a table, with one chopstick between each philosopher. A philosopher must have possession of both chopsticks before eating, and must put down both chopsticks before thinking. Each philosopher will spend an arbitrary amount of time thinking and eating.

The problem is to design the program such that:

- No philosopher goes hungry, or literally, is starved for both CPU cycles and food.
- No philosopher is forced to eat continuously, and is prevented from thinking.
- Most importantly, no deadlock condition is created.

The mutual exclusion part of the dining philosophers problem occurs when two philosophers attempt to gain control of the same chopstick. Mutual exclusion can be used to ensure that only one of the philosophers can grab a free chopstick.

When designing an algorithm for selecting a chopstick, care must be taken to avoid deadlocks. If the philosophers are able to grab one chopstick and wait for the other chopstick to become free, every philosopher could have one chopstick and a deadlock situation could occur.

One solution to the dining philosophers problem has been included on the CD. The Philo project is a console mode program that uses mutex objects to represent the chopsticks used by the dining philosophers. When a philosopher wants to eat, WaitForMultipleObjects is used to wait for both mutex handles at the same time. Because neither mutex is acquired until both are ready, deadlock conditions are avoided.

The source code for the solution on CD is provided in Listing 22.4. This version of the source code models three philosophers. You can increase the number of philosophers by changing the value of nMaxPhil.

Listing 22.4. The "Dining Philosophers" problem using Windows NT synchronization primitives.

```cpp
#include <iostream.h>
#include <windows.h>
#include <time.h>

long  g_fDone = FALSE;

struct CPhilosopher
{
    int     m_nID;
    HANDLE  m_hForks[2];
    int     m_nMeals;
};

CRITICAL_SECTION csOutput;

void SayEat( CPhilosopher* pPhilo )
{
    __try
    {
        EnterCriticalSection( &csOutput );
        cout << "Philosopher " << pPhilo->m_nID << " eats a while"
            << endl;
    }
    __finally
```

continues

Listing 22.4. continued

```cpp
        {
            LeaveCriticalSection( &csOutput );
        }
        pPhilo->m_nMeals++;
}

void SayThink( int nPhilo )
{
    __try
    {
        EnterCriticalSection( &csOutput );
        cout << "Philosopher " << nPhilo << " thinks a while"
            << endl;
    }
    __finally
    {
        LeaveCriticalSection( &csOutput );
    }
}

void SayDone( CPhilosopher* pPhilo )
{
    __try
    {
        EnterCriticalSection( &csOutput );
        cout << "Philosopher " << pPhilo->m_nID << " had "
            << pPhilo->m_nMeals << " meals.(burp)" << endl;
    }
    __finally
    {
        LeaveCriticalSection( &csOutput );
    }
}

long WINAPI WaitToEat( long lParam )
{
    CPhilosopher* pPhilo = (CPhilosopher*)lParam;

    while( g_fDone == FALSE )
    {
        WaitForMultipleObjects( 2,
                                pPhilo->m_hForks,
                                TRUE,
                                INFINITE );
        //
        // Wait satisfied - I have both forks
        SayEat( pPhilo );
        Sleep( (rand() % 1000) + 1000 );
        SayThink( pPhilo->m_nID );
        // Release the "right" fork, give up my time slice,
        // then release the "left" fork.
        ReleaseMutex(pPhilo->m_hForks[1]);
        Sleep(0);
        ReleaseMutex(pPhilo->m_hForks[0]);
        Sleep( (rand() % 1000) + 1000 );
```

```
    }
    SayDone( pPhilo );
    return 0;
}

int main()
{
    const int nMaxPhil = 63;
    srand((unsigned)time(NULL));

    HANDLE          rghFork[nMaxPhil];
    CPhilosopher    rgPhilosophers[nMaxPhil];
    unsigned long   nThread;

    InitializeCriticalSection( &csOutput );

    for( int nFork = 0; nFork < nMaxPhil; nFork++ )
        rghFork[nFork] = CreateMutex(NULL,FALSE,NULL);

    // Kick off the philosopher threads, using WaitToEat
    // as the thread function.
    for( int nPhilo = 0; nPhilo < nMaxPhil; nPhilo++ )
    {
        rgPhilosophers[nPhilo].m_nID = nPhilo;
        rgPhilosophers[nPhilo].m_nMeals = 0;
        rgPhilosophers[nPhilo].m_hForks[0] = rghFork[nPhilo];
        if( nPhilo < nMaxPhil-1 )
            rgPhilosophers[nPhilo].m_hForks[1] = rghFork[nPhilo+1];
        else
            rgPhilosophers[nPhilo].m_hForks[1] = rghFork[0];
        HANDLE hThread = CreateThread( NULL,
                                        0,
                                        (LPTHREAD_START_ROUTINE)WaitToEat,
                                        (void*)&rgPhilosophers[nPhilo],
                                        0,
                                        &nThread );
        CloseHandle( hThread );
    }
    Sleep( 100000 );  // Run for ~ 100 seconds
    g_fDone = TRUE;
    Sleep( 8000 );    // Wait ~ 8 seconds for thread completion.
    DeleteCriticalSection( &csOutput );
    return 0;
}
```

Semaphores

The semaphore was one of the first synchronization primitives described in computer science literature. Semaphores were invented by Edsger Dijkstra (pronounced Dike-stra) as a tool to be used in multithreaded computing, which was a new field in the mid-1960s. A semaphore is like a counter that acts as a guardian over a section of code or a resource. In fact, semaphores are sometimes referred to as *Dijkstra Counters*.

The semaphore maintains an internal counter that is decremented or incremented as operations are performed on the semaphore. If the semaphore's internal counter reaches zero, any new thread attempting to decrement the counter must wait until another thread increments it. Two operations can be performed on a semaphore:

- P, sometimes called DOWN, is used to indicate that a resource is not available. P is short for "proberen te verlagen," a Dutch phrase which roughly translates to "attempt to decrease."

- V, sometimes called UP, is used to indicate that a resource has become available. V is short for "verhogen," a Dutch word that translates to "increase."

Semaphores and Wait Functions

Before using a resource guarded by a semaphore, a thread must always perform a wait on the semaphore's handle. This enables the thread to be blocked, if the semaphore is not signaled. It also enables the semaphore's internal counter to be decremented after the thread's wait is completed. This is the "P" or "attempt to decrease" function described in the previous section.

When a thread is finished using a controlled resource, the semaphore is released by calling the ReleaseSemaphore function. This function increases the semaphore's internal counter, and enables another waiting thread to take control of the semaphore. This is the "V" or "increase" function described in the preceding section.

Figure 22.8 illustrates how a semaphore is initialized, used, and released.

FIGURE 22.8.

Using a semaphore to control resources.

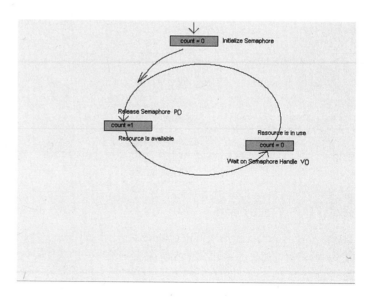

A semaphore can be used with either of the wait functions discussed earlier in this chapter. A semaphore is considered to be signaled when its counter is greater than zero; it is not signaled as long as the count equals zero.

The semaphore's internal counter should always reflect the number of resources available for consumption. Any threads that take possession of a resource controlled by a semaphore must perform a wait function on the semaphore object. If the semaphore counter is zero, no resources are available, and the thread is blocked until it either times out or until a resource becomes available.

Applications for Semaphores

A semaphore is more flexible than a critical section because it enables a quantity of resources to be guarded, rather than enabling a single thread's access to a certain part of the code. For example, a typical exercise in multithreaded computing deals with allocating scarce resources to a group of consumers, as shown in Figure 22.9.

FIGURE 22.9.

Three available barbers controlled by a semaphore.

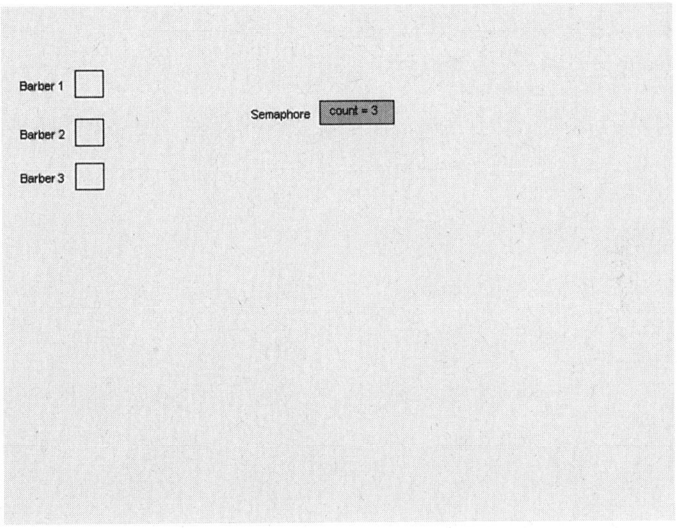

In Figure 22.9, a group of barbers is controlled using a semaphore. Initially this semaphore is set with a maximum value of three, to indicate that three barber resources are available. As customers enter the barber shop, the semaphore is decremented, as shown in Figure 22.10.

As the semaphore is decremented for each new customer, eventually the semaphore's internal counter reaches zero, indicating that no barbers are available, as shown in Figure 22.11.

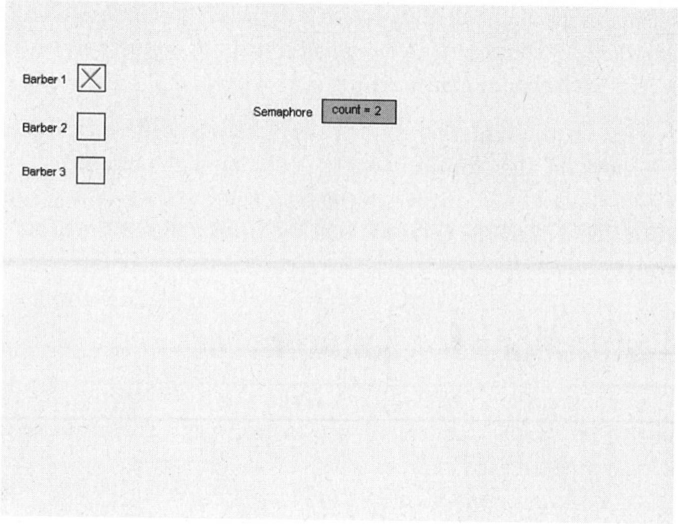

FIGURE 22.10.

Consuming a barber resource decrements the semaphore counter.

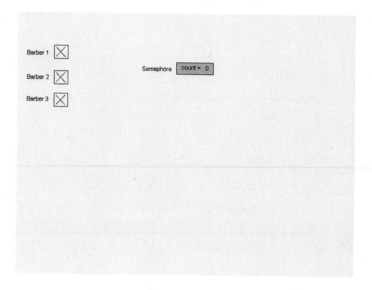

FIGURE 22.11.

Blocking access to the barbers using a semaphore.

As a barber finishes with a customer, that customer releases the semaphore, allowing the internal counter to increase, and allowing one more customer to be served, as shown in Figure 22.12.

These are the basic steps in the life cycle of producer/consumer application. The barbers are "producing" haircuts, and the customers in line are "consuming" them. Later in this chapter a dialog-based application that uses semaphores in a similar manner is introduced.

FIGURE 22.12.
Releasing a semaphore enables a new customer to be served.

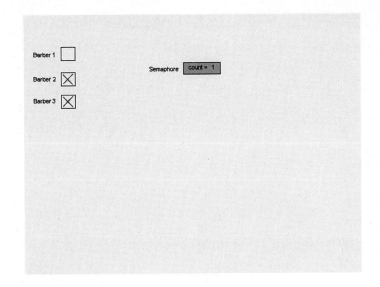

Creating Semaphores

A semaphore is created by calling `CreateSemaphore`:

```
HANDLE hsemBarbers = CreateSemaphore( NULL,
                                      0,
                                      5,
                                      NULL );
if( hsemBarbers == NULL )
{
    // Handle Error
}
```

The call to `CreateSemaphore` has four parameters:

- A pointer to a `SECURITY_ATTRIBUTES` structure: Using this structure is discussed later in this chapter.

- An initial value for the semaphore's counter: This value must be greater than, or equal to, zero.

- A maximum value for the semaphore's counter: This value must be at least one; it must also be at least as large as the initial value for the counter.

- An optional name for the semaphore. Keep in mind that all event, mutex, and file-mapping objects use the same namespace, so you must take care not to reuse names. In most cases, this value is NULL.

Returning Semaphore-Controlled Resources

When a semaphore-controlled resource becomes available, the resource counter must be incremented by calling `ReleaseSemaphore`:

```
BOOL fReleased = ReleaseSemaphore( hSemBarbers,
                                   1,
                                   NULL );

if( fReleased == FALSE )
{
    // Handle Error
}
```

The call to `ReleaseSemaphore` has three parameters:

- A handle to the semaphore to be released
- The number of steps the semaphore counter is to be incremented by
- An optional pointer to a long variable to hold the previous counter value, otherwise, `NULL`

Using Semaphores and Critical Sections in an Application

An example of using semaphores in an MFC-based Windows NT application, a program named SkiLift, can be found on the CD. SkiLift is a dialog-based application that displays the status of a group of skiers using a ski lift.

A semaphore controls access to the ski lift, enabling a maximum of four skiers at a time to use the lift. After reaching the top of the mountain, each skier takes a semi-random amount of time to enter the lift line at the base of the mountain. Figure 22.13. shows the SkiLift application in use.

FIGURE 22.13.

The SkiLift application uses semaphores to control lift access.

To begin the SkiLift project, use ClassWizard to create a skeleton dialog-based application named SkiLift. Add a new pushbutton control, and 20 checkbox controls, as shown in Figure 22.14.

FIGURE 22.14.

Adding controls to the main dialog box for the SkiLift project.

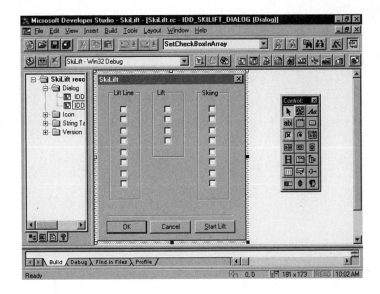

Properties for the checkbox and pushbutton controls are listed in Table 22.1. All properties that aren't listed should be set to the default values. The checkbox controls must be assigned sequentially, with IDC_CHECK1 through IDC_CHECK8 in the first column, IDC_CHECK9 through IDC_CHECK12 in the middle column, and IDC_CHECK13 through IDC_CHECK20 in the last column.

Table 22.1. Property values for controls in the SkiLift main dialog box.

Control	Resource ID	Caption
Start button	IDC_START	&Start Lift
Status static control	IDC_STATUS	
Checkbox buttons	IDC_CHECK1 through IDC_CHECK20	empty

Next, use ClassWizard to create a message-handling function that is called when the Start pushbutton is clicked. Add a member function to the CSkiLiftDlg class, using the values from Table 22.2.

Table 22.2. Values for message handling functions in CSkiLiftDlg.

Object ID	Class Name	Message	Function
IDC_START	CSkiLiftDlg	BN_CLICKED	OnStart

Modify the class declaration for the `CSkiLiftDlg` class, found in SkiLiftDlg.h, as shown in Listing 22.5. Most of the unchanged lines have been removed for clarity.

Listing 22.5. Changes to the `CSkiLiftDlg` class.

```cpp
// Forward declaration required for CSkiLiftDlg
class CSkiLiftDlg;
struct CSkier
{
    int             m_nID;
    CSkiLiftDlg*    m_wnd;
};

class CSkiLiftDlg : public CDialog
{
.
.

.
// Implementation
protected:
    HICON               m_hIcon;

    HANDLE              m_hChairLift;
    CRITICAL_SECTION    m_cs;
    CSkier              m_rgSkier[8];
    BOOL                m_fLiftStopped;

    // Static members used as thread functions
    static void Ski( LPARAM lparam );
    static void Clean( LPARAM lparam );

    // Implementation member functions
    void WaitForLift( CSkier* pSkier );
    void GetOnLift( CSkier* pSkier );
    void SkiAWhile( CSkier* pSkier );
    void SetCheckBoxArray( UINT nLow, UINT nHigh, BOOL fSet );
    .
    .

    .
};
```

Listing 22.5 adds a structure named `CSkier`, which represents each skier in the SkiLift project. An array of eight `CSkier` structures are used in the `CSkiLiftDlg` class. In addition, a `CRITICAL_SECTION` variable is used to synchronize control of dialog items. A semaphore handle is used to control access to the chair lift, so that only four skiers are permitted to use the ski lift at any given time. Finally, a flag is used to indicate when the ski lift is running. When the ski lift is stopped, `m_fLiftStopped` is set to `TRUE`, and all running threads stop using the ski lift.

There are a total of six new member functions added to the `CSkiLiftDlg` class. The `Ski` function is static, and is used as a thread start function. This function is called by threads that represent skiers in the SkiLift project. These threads cycle through calling the `WaitForLift`, `GetOnLift`, and `SkiAWhile` member functions. The `SetCheckBoxArray` member function is used to check or clear checkboxes that indicate the current status of the application.

The clean function is a static member function used to clean up the application before exiting.

Modify the constructor for the CSkiLiftDlg class as shown in Listing 22.6. There is one line of new code, shown in bold type, that sets the m_fLiftStopped variable to TRUE.

Listing 22.6. Modifications to the CSkiLiftDlg class.

```
CSkiLiftDlg::CSkiLiftDlg(CWnd* pParent /*=NULL*/)
    : CDialog(CSkiLiftDlg::IDD, pParent)
{
    //{{AFX_DATA_INIT(CSkiLiftDlg)
        //NOTE: the ClassWizard will add member initialization here
    //}}AFX_DATA_INIT
    m_fLiftStopped = TRUE;
    m_hIcon = AfxGetApp()->LoadIcon(IDR_MAINFRAME);
}
```

Listing 22.7. contains the source code for the remaining member functions. ClassWizard provides a skeleton of the OnStart function for you; all the other source code listed must be added. As always, the source code for these functions is also located on the CD.

Listing 22.7. New member functions for the CSkiLiftDlg class.

```
void CSkiLiftDlg::OnStart()
{
    CWnd* pWnd = GetDlgItem( IDC_START );
    if( m_fLiftStopped != FALSE )
    {   // It's time to open the lift - perform some
        // initializations
        m_fLiftStopped = FALSE;
        const int      nMaxOnLift = 4;
        const int      nMaxSkiers = 8;
        srand( (unsigned)time( NULL ) );
        pWnd->SetWindowText( "&Stop Lift" );
        // Initialize the critical section used for the GUI,
        // and create a semaphore with four slots used for
        // the ski lift.
        InitializeCriticalSection( &m_cs );
        m_hChairLift = CreateSemaphore( NULL,
                                        0,
                                        nMaxOnLift,
                                        "ChairLift" );
        ASSERT( m_hChairLift );
        // Create eight skiers, each with their own thread.
        // Each of the skiers knows it's skier number and
        // window handle.
        for( int n = 0; n < nMaxSkiers; n++ )
        {
            m_rgSkier[n].m_nID = n;
            m_rgSkier[n].m_wnd = this;
            unsigned long nThread;
            HANDLE hThread;
```

continues

Listing 22.7. continued

```
                    hThread = CreateThread( NULL,
                                            0,
                                            (LPTHREAD_START_ROUTINE)Ski,
                                            (void*)&m_rgSkier[n],
                                            0,
                                            &nThread );
                CloseHandle( hThread );
            }
            // After all of the skiers have been created, release
            // all of the semaphore resources.
            ReleaseSemaphore( m_hChairLift, nMaxOnLift, NULL );
        }
        else
        {   // We are stopping the lift. Create a "cleaner" thread
            // which will clean up all of the synchronization
            // resources. The start/stop button is disabled until
            // the cleanup process is completed.
            unsigned long nThread;
            m_fLiftStopped = TRUE;
            pWnd->EnableWindow( FALSE );
            pWnd->SetWindowText( "&Start Lift" );
            HANDLE hCleanThread;
            hCleanThread = CreateThread(NULL,
                                        0,
                                        (LPTHREAD_START_ROUTINE)Clean,
                                        (void*)this,
                                        0,
                                        &nThread );
            CloseHandle( hCleanThread );
        }
}
// Static thread-procedure member function used
// to run the skier threads. The skiers run around
// like little, er, skiers until the m_fLiftStopped
// flag is set to TRUE.
void CSkiLiftDlg::Ski( LPARAM lparam )
{
    CSkier* pSkier = (CSkier*)lparam;
    CSkiLiftDlg*    pWnd = pSkier->m_wnd;
    while( pWnd->m_fLiftStopped == FALSE )
    {
        pWnd->WaitForLift( pSkier );
        pWnd->GetOnLift( pSkier );
        pWnd->SkiAWhile( pSkier );
    }
}
// Static thread-procedure member function used
// to clean up the synchronization resources used
// by the dialog. The thread immediately sleeps
// for six seconds to give the threads enough time
// to finish, then cleans up its resources.
void CSkiLiftDlg::Clean( LPARAM lparam )
{
    Sleep( 6000 );
    CSkiLiftDlg* pDlg = (CSkiLiftDlg*)lparam;
    CloseHandle( pDlg->m_hChairLift );
    DeleteCriticalSection( &pDlg->m_cs );
    // Restore the start button, and cleanup the
```

```
    // status window.
    CWnd* pWnd = pDlg->GetDlgItem( IDC_START );
    pWnd->EnableWindow();
    pWnd = pDlg->GetDlgItem( IDC_STATUS );
    pWnd->SetWindowText( "" );
}

void CSkiLiftDlg::WaitForLift( CSkier* pSkier )
{
    CString szMsg;
    szMsg.Format( TEXT("Skier %d starts waiting in line"),
                  pSkier->m_nID );
    // Update status window with information about this skier, and
    // put a check mark in the lift line column.
    EnterCriticalSection( &m_cs );
    SetCheckBoxArray( IDC_CHECK1, IDC_CHECK8, TRUE );
    SetDlgItemText( IDC_STATUS, szMsg );
    Sleep( 100 );
    LeaveCriticalSection( &m_cs );
    // Wait on the chair lift semaphore. If a resource is not yet
    // available, the thread will block here until one is ready.
    // If a chair is ready, it will be allocated to this thread,
    // and execution continues in the GetOnLift function.
    WaitForSingleObject( m_hChairLift, INFINITE );
}

void CSkiLiftDlg::GetOnLift( CSkier* pSkier )
{
    CString szMsg;
    szMsg.Format( TEXT("Skier %d gets on lift"), pSkier->m_nID );
    // Update status window with information about this skier,
    // remove a check from the lift line column, and put a check
    // mark in the lift column.
    EnterCriticalSection( &m_cs );
    SetCheckBoxArray( IDC_CHECK1, IDC_CHECK8,  FALSE );
    SetCheckBoxArray( IDC_CHECK9, IDC_CHECK12, TRUE );
    SetDlgItemText( IDC_STATUS, szMsg );
    Sleep( 100 );
    LeaveCriticalSection( &m_cs );
    // Spend a short (fixed) amount of time on the chair lift, then
    // return one chair lift resource. Execution continues in the
    // SkiAWhile function.
    Sleep( 2000 );
    ReleaseSemaphore( m_hChairLift, 1, NULL );
}

void CSkiLiftDlg::SkiAWhile( CSkier* pSkier )
{
    CString szMsg;
    szMsg.Format( TEXT("Skier %d starts downhill"), pSkier->m_nID );
    // Move a skier from the lift line check boxes to the
    // skiing checkboxes. After updating the status display, hold
    // the status window for 100 milliseconds so it can be read.
    EnterCriticalSection( &m_cs );
    SetCheckBoxArray( IDC_CHECK9, IDC_CHECK12,  FALSE );
    SetCheckBoxArray( IDC_CHECK13, IDC_CHECK20, TRUE );
    SetDlgItemText( IDC_STATUS, szMsg );
    Sleep( 100 );
    LeaveCriticalSection( &m_cs );
```

continues

Listing 22.7. continued

```
    // Simulate skiing by sleeping a random amount of time
    // between 0 and 1999 milliseconds.
    Sleep( rand() % 2000 );
    // Finished skiing, clear one of the skiing checkboxes.
    EnterCriticalSection( &m_cs );
    SetCheckBoxArray( IDC_CHECK13, IDC_CHECK20, FALSE );
    LeaveCriticalSection( &m_cs );
}


//
// This function is used to set or clear one checkbox from
// an array of checkboxes. The checkboxes are always set
// from the "top", and cleared from the "bottom". This function
// assumes the checkboxes are assigned in sequential order.
void CSkiLiftDlg::SetCheckBoxArray(UINT nLow,UINT nHigh,BOOL fSet)
{
    UINT nResIndex;
    if( fSet == TRUE )
    {   // We are setting a check mark, find a clear checkbox.
        for( nResIndex = nLow; nResIndex <= nHigh; nResIndex++ )
            if( IsDlgButtonChecked(nResIndex) == FALSE )
                break;
    }
    else
    {   // Clearing a check mark
        for( nResIndex = nHigh; nResIndex >= nLow; nResIndex— )
            if( IsDlgButtonChecked(nResIndex) == TRUE )
                break;
    }
    CheckDlgButton( nResIndex, fSet );
}
```

Compile and run the SkiLift application. Press the Start Lift button. Eight checkmarks appear in the left column, representing eight skiers waiting in line for a ski lift. Four of the checkmarks immediately move to the center column, representing four skiers that enter the ski lift. When these skiers reach the top of the mountain, four more skiers enter the ski lift.

Each skier thread takes a random amount of time to re-enter the ski lift line. After a few cycles of the lift line, the load balances out; however, the ski lift will always tend to be a bottleneck, just as in real life.

Summary

This section discussed thread, synchronization, and security primitives. It also covered the methods used to create and manage threads and processes, as well as the pros and cons of creating multithreaded applications.

Finally, a few sample projects that demonstrate how threads and synchronization primitives are used together to write Windows NT applications were introduced.

Pipes

23

by Mickey Williams

IN THIS CHAPTER

This chapter focuses on the interprocess communication using pipes. A *pipe* is a point-to-point protocol used to exchange data between two Windows processes. In this chapter, you'll learn about anonymous and named pipes and create several sample applications that demonstrate how pipes are used in Windows NT applications.

Examining Pipe Types

A *pipe* is a communications channel that Windows applications can use for interprocess communications. Two basic types of pipes exist:

- **Anonymous pipes:** Used primarily for communication between related processes, such as a parent and a child process. Anonymous pipes cannot be used over a network.
- **Named pipes:** Used for communication between any two processes that know the name of the pipe. Unlike anonymous pipes, named pipes can be accessed over a network.

When opening, reading, and writing to pipes, the standard Windows NT file-handling functions are used: `ReadFile`, `ReadFileEx`, `WriteFile`, `WriteFileEx`, and `CreateFile`. In addition, named pipes support overlapped, asynchronous I/O, as discussed in Chapter 14, "Files." Using named pipes for asynchronous I/O is discussed later in this chapter, in the section, *Using Named Pipes*.

Using Anonymous Pipes

An anonymous pipe is used only for communication on the same machine, and almost always between a parent and a child process. An anonymous pipe is always asymmetrical: One end of the pipe always is used for writing, and one end always is used for reading. For bidirectional communication, you must use two pipes.

When a parent process needs to communicate with a child process, anonymous pipes are used, as shown in Figure 23.1. The parent process substitutes the standard input and output handles of the child process with anonymous pipe handles. From the point of view of the child process, it is communicating with the standard input and output.

Communication using anonymous pipes always involves blocking or polling. *Blocking*, which was discussed in Chapter 22, "Threads," occurs when a thread is kept waiting for an operation to complete. *Polling*, as it relates to pipes, requires the calling process to continuously check to see if an operation has completed.

Overlapped communication is supported only for named pipes. Overlapped I/O was discussed in Chapter 14, and is discussed later in this chapter, in the section *Using Named Pipes*.

FIGURE 23.1.

Substituting pipe handles for standard input and output.

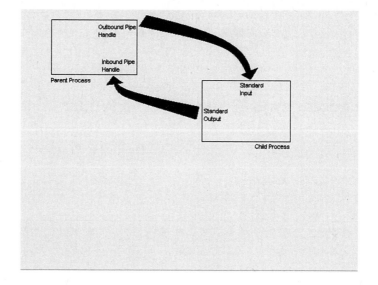

Creating and Closing an Anonymous Pipe

You create an anonymous pipe by calling the CreatePipe function. CreatePipe returns a TRUE or FALSE value, indicating whether the pipe was created:

```
BOOL fCreated = CreatePipe ( &hRead, &hWrite, &sec, 0 );
```

CreatePipe uses four parameters:

- The address of the variable that will store the pipe's read handle
- The address of the variable that will store the pipe's write handle
- The address of a SECURITY_ATTRIBUTES structure or NULL to use a default security descriptor
- The buffer size for the pipe, or 0 to use system default sizes

Anonymous pipe handles usually are inherited by a child process, which means that a valid SECURITY_ATTRIBUTES structure almost always is used with anonymous pipes because the default security descriptor will not allow a pipe handle to be inherited. The following code initializes a SECURITY_ATTRIBUTES structure and uses it to create an anonymous pipe with inheritable handles:

```
SECURITY ATTRIBUTES sec;
sec.nLength = sizeof(SECURITY ATTRIBUTES);
sec.lpSecurityDescriptor = NULL;
sec.bInheritHandle = TRUE;
CreatePipe(&hRead, &hWrite, &sec, 0 );
```

To close an anonymous pipe handle, you use the general-purpose `CloseHandle` function:

```
CloseHandle ( hRead );
```

A pipe is not destroyed until all open handles, including inherited handles, are closed.

Reading and Writing to Anonymous Pipes

You use the `ReadFile` and `WriteFile` functions to read and write to anonymous pipes. These functions always are blocking; they return only when the specified number of bytes are transferred or an I/O error occurs.

To read from a pipe, the pipe's read handle is passed to the `ReadFile`, as in this example:

```
BOOL fRead = ReadFile ( hRead,
                        szBuffer,
                        sizeof(szBuffer),
                        &dwRead,
                        NULL );
if( fRead == FALSE ¦¦ dwRead == 0 )
{
    // Handle error
}
```

The fifth parameter to `ReadFile` normally is an `OVERLAPPED` structure. This parameter always should be `NULL` for anonymous pipes because asynchronous communication is not performed. Feel free to create an `OVERLAPPED` structure; Windows NT will just ignore it.

To write to a pipe, the pipe's write handle is passed to the `WriteFile` function, as shown in this code:

```
BOOL fWrite = WriteFile ( hWrite,
                          szBuffer,
                          sizeof(szBuffer),
                          &dwWritten,
                          NULL );
if( fWritten == FALSE ¦¦ dwWritten == 0 )
{
    // Handle error
}
```

As with `ReadFile`, the fifth parameter passed to `WriteFile` is ignored by Windows NT when writing to anonymous pipes.

Communicating with Another Process Using Anonymous Pipes

The parent process typically creates two anonymous pipes and allows the child process to inherit the pipe handles. As Figure 23.1 shows, the child process must have access to at least two of the four pipe handles—the other two handles do not need to be inherited.

In many cases, the child process may not be aware that it is communicating over a pipe. As discussed earlier, a common method for communicating with a child process is to change the standard input and output handles for the child process to use the pipe handles. The child process then can read and write to its standard input and output handles. When started from the command line, the child process acts like any other console mode application; when launched as a child process, it communicates exclusively with the parent process.

To enable a parent process to communicate with a child process using anonymous pipes, follow these steps:

1. Save the standard input and output handles used by the parent process for later use.

2. Create the anonymous pipes used for communication with the child process. This results in the creation of four pipe handles: two pipes, each with two ends.

3. Arbitrarily define how each pipe handle will be used. The parent process uses the write handle for one pipe and the read handle for the other pipe, whereas the child process uses the remaining handles.

4. Create a non-inheritable copy of the parent pipes write handle. This handle must not be inherited by the child process because the parent will close the pipe to signal that all data has been written to the pipe.

5. Close the parent pipe's original write handle.

6. Set the standard input and write handles to use the child process's read and write handles.

7. Create the child process.

8. Close the child pipe's write handle from within the parent process.

9. Change the standard input and output handles for the parent process back to the original values stored in step 1.

The parent and child processes now can communicate over the anonymous pipes. Each of the pipes can be read from and written to until the pipe is destroyed. In practice, you must create a protocol based on the message length, or read and write from the pipe until the pipe is destroyed, as demonstrated in the following section.

Looking at an Example Using Anonymous Pipes

As an example of how anonymous pipes are used, I have created two example programs that are located on the accompanying CD. The first program, Hex, reads characters from standard input, converts them into hexadecimal format, and sends the result to standard output.

The Hex application believes that it is reading and writing to its standard input and output devices. In fact, when run as a console application, Hex accepts characters from the keyboard and echoes their ASCII hexadecimal equivalents to the display.

Create a console mode project named Hex, and add the source code from Listing 23.1 to the project as Hex.cpp.

Listing 23.1. The Hex.cpp source used to filter input into hexadecimal output.

```cpp
#include <windows.h>
#include <iostream.h>

#define IN_BUF_SIZE  256
#define OUT_BUF_SIZE 3*IN_BUF_SIZE

int main()
{
    char    szInputBuff[IN_BUF_SIZE];
    char    szOutputBuff[OUT_BUF_SIZE];
    HANDLE  hStdInput  = GetStdHandle( STD_INPUT_HANDLE );
    HANDLE  hStdOutput = GetStdHandle( STD_OUTPUT_HANDLE );
    DWORD   dwRead;
    DWORD   dwWritten;
    BOOL    fResult = TRUE;

    do{
        fResult = ReadFile( hStdInput,
                            szInputBuff,
                            IN_BUF_SIZE - 1,
                            &dwRead,
                            NULL );
        if( fResult == FALSE || dwRead == 0 ) break;

        for( DWORD dw = 0; dw < dwRead; dw++ )
        {
            int ch = szInputBuff[dw];
            wsprintf( &szOutputBuff[dw*3], " %02X", ch );
        }

        fResult = WriteFile( hStdOutput,
                             szOutputBuff,
                             dwRead*3,
                             &dwWritten,
                             NULL );
    }while ( fResult == TRUE && dwWritten > 0 );

    return 0;
}
```

Compile and run the project. Any input provided to the program is returned in hexadecimal format. Pressing A and then Enter, for example, displays the following:

`41 0D 0A`

The ASCII value for A is 41, and the ASCII values for the line-feed and carriage-return characters are 0D and 0A, respectively.

The second program used in this example is AnonPipe. The AnonPipe project creates a child process using Hex.exe and uses a pair of anonymous pipes to communicate with the child process. Create a console mode project named AnonPipe, and add the source code provided in Listing 23.2 to the project as AnonPipe.cpp.

Listing 23.2. The AnonPipe.cpp source used to create two anonymous pipes.

```cpp
#include <windows.h>
#include <iostream.h>

int ErrorHandling( LPTSTR lpszMsg );

int main()
{
    // These handles are used to cache the standard input and
    // output handles.
    HANDLE hStdIn   = GetStdHandle( STD_INPUT_HANDLE );
    HANDLE hStdOut  = GetStdHandle( STD_OUTPUT_HANDLE );
    // Create two anonymous pipes, defining child and
    // parent ends for each pipe:
    // hChildRead   <------  hParentWrite
    // hChildWrite  ------>  hParentRead
    HANDLE hChildRead;
    HANDLE hChildWrite;
    HANDLE hParentRead;
    HANDLE hParentWrite;
    SECURITY_ATTRIBUTES sec;
    sec.nLength = sizeof(SECURITY_ATTRIBUTES);
    sec.lpSecurityDescriptor = NULL;
    sec.bInheritHandle = TRUE;
    CreatePipe( &hChildRead, &hParentWrite, &sec, 0 );
    CreatePipe( &hParentRead, &hChildWrite, &sec, 0 );
    // Change the standard input and output handles to
    // use the "child" ends of the anonymous pipes.
    SetStdHandle( STD_INPUT_HANDLE, hChildRead );
    SetStdHandle( STD_OUTPUT_HANDLE, hChildWrite );
    // Make a non-inheritable duplicate of the pipe handle
    // used to communicate between parent and child — this way
    // the child won't increment the usage count on this handle.
    HANDLE hProcess = GetCurrentProcess();
    HANDLE hDuplicateWrite;
    DuplicateHandle ( hProcess,
                      hParentWrite,
                      hProcess,
                      &hDuplicateWrite,
                      0,
                      FALSE,
                      DUPLICATE_SAME_ACCESS );
    CloseHandle( hParentWrite );
    // Start the child process
    STARTUPINFO si;
    memset( &si, 0, sizeof (STARTUPINFO) );
    si.cb = sizeof(STARTUPINFO);
    PROCESS_INFORMATION pi;
    BOOL fCreated = CreateProcess( TEXT("hex.exe"),
                                   NULL,
                                   NULL,
                                   NULL,
                                   TRUE,
                                   0,
                                   NULL,
                                   NULL,
                                   &si,
                                   &pi );
```

continues

Listing 23.2. continued

```c
    if( fCreated == FALSE )
    return ErrorHandling( TEXT("Creating Child Process") );
    // Restore the original standard input and output handles.
    SetStdHandle( STD_INPUT_HANDLE, hStdIn );
    SetStdHandle( STD_OUTPUT_HANDLE, hStdOut );
    // Send a message to the child process, then close the
    // pipe handle, in order to notify the child that the message
    // is finished.
    TCHAR szBuff[] = TEXT( "Fuzzy Wuzzy was a bear" );
    TCHAR szTrans [255];
    DWORD dwRead, dwWritten;
    WriteFile( hDuplicateWrite,
               szBuff,
               sizeof( szBuff ),
               &dwWritten,
               NULL );
    CloseHandle( hDuplicateWrite );
    //Read the result from the child process, and display it
    //to the standard output.
    ReadFile(hParentRead, szTrans, sizeof(szTrans), &dwRead, NULL);
    WriteFile(hStdOut, szTrans, dwRead, &dwWritten, NULL);

    return 0;
}

//
//Display an error message based on the operating system's
//latest error.
int ErrorHandling( LPTSTR lpszTitle )
{
    TCHAR szBuffer[256];
    FormatMessage( FORMAT_MESSAGE_FROM_SYSTEM,
                   NULL,
                   GetLastError(),
                   MAKELANGID(LANG_ENGLISH, SUBLANG_ENGLISH_US),
                   szBuffer,
                   256,
                   NULL ),
    MessageBox( NULL, szBuffer, lpszTitle, MB_ICONSTOP );
    return 1;
}
```

Compile the AnonPipe project. Before executing AnonPipe, make sure that the Hex.exe executable created by the previous project is found somewhere in the path. When AnonPipe is launched, it creates a Hex child process and sends the string "Fuzzy Wuzzy was a bear" to the child process for translation. The Hex child process converts the string to hexadecimal and returns it to the AnonPipe process, which appears in hexadecimal format, like this:

```
46 75 7A 7A 79 20 57 75 7A 7A 79 20 77 61 73 20 61 20 62 65 61 72 00
```

You can extend this example to use any sort of child process that expects to read and write from its standard input and output handles.

Using Named Pipes

Named pipes are similar to anonymous pipes, except that they have several features that make them well suited for communication between unrelated processes:

- Named pipes can be referenced by name, instead of just by a handle.
- Named pipes have more flexible connection options than anonymous pipes.
- Unlike anonymous pipes, named pipes can be used over a network.
- Named pipes can use asynchronous, overlapped I/O.

The name of a named pipe always follows this format:

```
\\machine_name\pipe\pipe_name
```

A pipe named "Foo" on a machine named "Pongo," for example, looks like this:

```
\\pongo\pipe\foo
```

When a pipe is referred to on its own machine, a dot is substituted for the machine name:

```
\\.\pipe\foo
```

Note that pipe names are not case-sensitive.

A named pipe instance connects one server with one client. If multiple clients connect to a server using the same named pipe, multiple instances of the named pipe are created; there is no communication directly between the clients.

Examining the Types of Named Pipes

You can create named pipes as blocking or non-blocking. The *non-blocking* type of pipe is not really asynchronous; after you issue a read or write request to the pipe, you must continue to call the read or write request until the pipe finishes the operation. These pipes often are called *polling pipes*. In almost all cases, pipes should be opened in *blocking* mode, with asynchronous read and write operations implemented using overlapped structures or completion routines, if needed.

You can create pipes as byte-type or message-type pipes. A *byte-type* pipe sends and receives data as a stream of bytes, with no implied division of data sent in separate writes to the pipe. A *message-type* pipe separates the data written to the pipe into a separate packet that can be read from the pipe as a single chunk of data.

After a byte-type pipe is created, it can be opened and read from only as a byte-type pipe. After creating a message-type pipe, however, you can read it as a message-type pipe or a byte-type pipe.

As an option, a pipe can wait to return a result of a write operation until the data is delivered to the other end of the named pipe; this option is called *write-through*. A message-type pipe always has write-through enabled, whereas this option must be requested for byte-type pipes.

Creating and Closing a Named Pipe

You can create a named pipe by calling the `CreateNamedPipe` function. `CreateNamedPipe` returns a handle to a created pipe instance if successful, or `INVALID_HANDLE_VALUE` if the pipe can't be created:

```
HANDLE hPipe = CreateNamedPipe( TEXT("\\\\.\\pipe\\Foo"),
                                PIPE_ACCESS_DUPLEX,
                                PIPE_TYPE_MESSAGE¦
                                PIPE_READMODE_MESSAGE¦
                                PIPE_WAIT,
                                PIPE_UNLIMITED_INSTANCES,
                                4096,
                                4096,
                                INFINITE,
                                &sa );
if( hPipe == INVALID_HANDLE_VALUE )
{
    // Handle error
}
```

The parameters used by `CreateNamedPipe` follow:

- The name of the pipe. The pipe always is created initially on the local machine, using a dot in place of the machine name, as shown in the preceding code.

- The read, write, and security attributes for the pipe. In this case, the pipe is opened in *duplex* mode, meaning that the pipe is bidirectional.

- The pipe mode and blocking characteristics of the pipe. In this case, the pipe is created in message mode for both reading and writing and is created as a blocking pipe.

- The number of instances allowed for the pipe, or `UNLIMITED_PIPE_INSTANCES`, to indicate that an unlimited number of instances is permitted.

- The number of bytes reserved for the pipe's output buffer.

- The number of bytes reserved for the pipe's input buffer.

- The time-out period for a pipe operation in milliseconds, or `INFINITE` for no timeout.

- A pointer to a `SECURITY_ATTRIBUTES` structure. If `NULL` is passed as this parameter, the pipe receives the security descriptor of the current access token.

Table 23.1 lists the read, write, and security attributes for the pipe.

Table 23.1. Read, write, and security attributes for named pipes.

Attributes	Function
ACCESS_SYSTEM_SECURITY	Specifies that the client side of the pipe will have write access to the named pipe's system ACL
FILE_FLAG_OVERLAPPED	Specifies that read, write, and connect operations can be performed asynchronously using an OVERLAPPED structure
FILE_FLAG_WRITE_THROUGH	Indicates that write-through mode is enabled
PIPE_ACCESS_DUPLEX	Specifies a bidirectional pipe
PIPE_ACCESS_INBOUND	Specifies a pipe used for incoming traffic to the server side of the pipe
PIPE_ACCESS_OUTBOUND	Specifies a pipe used for outgoing traffic from the server side of the pipe
WRITE_DAC	Indicates that the client side of the pipe will have write access to the named pipe's discretionary access control list
WRITE_OWNER	Indicates that the client side of the pipe will have write access to the named pipe's owner

Table 23.2 lists the pipe mode and blocking characteristics of the pipe.

Table 23.2. Mode and blocking attributes for named pipes.

Attribute	Function
PIPE_NOWAIT	Indicates that nonblocking mode is enabled. As discussed earlier, this mode should be avoided in most cases.
PIPE_READMODE_BYTE	Indicates that data is read from the pipe as a stream of bytes.
PIPE_READMODE_MESSAGE	Indicates that data is read from the pipe as a stream of messages.
PIPE_TYPE_BYTE	Indicates that data is written to the pipe as a stream of bytes.
PIPE_TYPE_MESSAGE	Indicates that data is written to the pipe as a stream of messages.

You close a named pipe handle by calling the ever popular CloseHandle function:

```
CloseHandle( hPipe );
```

Connecting and Using a Named Pipe

A pipe must be placed into listening mode by the pipe's server process before a client can use it. A server process places a pipe into listening mode by calling the `ConnectNamedPipe` function. If the pipe is not using overlapped I/O, the call to `ConnectNamedPipe` blocks, or waits, until it times out or a client is connected to the pipe. Listing 23.3 shows a typical call to `ConnectNamedPipe`.

Listing 23.3. Placing a named pipe into listening mode using `ConnectNamedPipe`.

```
BOOL fConnected = ConnectNamedPipe( hPipe, NULL );
if( fConnected ¦¦ GetLastError() == ERROR_PIPE_CONNECTED )
{
    // Connected to a client
}
else
{
    // Handle error condition
}
```

The `ConnectNamedPipe` function has two parameters:

- The pipe handle
- The address of an `OVERLAPPED` structure, which is used for overlapped I/O

The `ConnectNamedPipe` function returns `TRUE` if a client connects to the pipe successfully or `FALSE` if an error occurs. If a client connects to a pipe after the pipe is created but before the server process calls `ConnectNamedPipe`, the return value is `FALSE`, and `GetLastError` returns `ERROR_PIPE_CONNECTED`.

In most cases, it's perfectly okay to continue processing, as shown in Listing 23.3. Be aware that if you attempt to call `ConnectNamedPipe` on a pipe handle that already is open, however, you receive the same error message. It's up to you to structure your code so that you can separate these cases.

A client process opens a handle to a named pipe by using the `CreateFile` function and passing the full name of the pipe as the filename. If a handle to the pipe cannot be opened using the parameters passed to `CreateFile`, `INVALID_HANDLE_VALUE` is returned, as Listing 23.4 shows.

Listing 23.4. Opening the client side of a named pipe.

```
HANDLE  hPipe = CreateFile( TEXT("\\\\pongo\\pipe\\lucky"),
                            GENERIC_READ ¦ GENERIC_WRITE,
                            0,
                            NULL,
```

```
                        OPEN_EXISTING,
                        0,
                        NULL );
if( m_hPipe == INVALID_HANDLE_VALUE )
{
}
DWORD dwPipeState = PIPE_READMODE_MESSAGE;
BOOL fChangedState = SetNamedPipeHandleState( hPipe,
                        &dwPipeState,
                        NULL,
                        NULL );
```

By default, `CreateFile` opens a pipe handle as a byte-type pipe. In Listing 23.4, `Set-NamedPipeHandleState` specifies a message-type pipe.

When opening named pipe handles, the parameters for `CreateFile` are very similar as when opening existing disk files:

- The full pipe name
- The read and write access for the pipe handle
- The share mode, which always is set to 0 for named pipes
- A pointer to a `SECURITY_ATTRIBUTES` structure, or `NULL` if the pipe handle will use the security descriptor of the current access token
- The handle-creation information, which always is set to `OPEN_EXISTING` for named pipes
- The file attribute flags, set to 0 for named pipes
- The address of an `OVERLAPPED` structure if the pipe is opened in `OVERLAPPED` mode, or `NULL` if the pipe will block until the `CreateFile` function is completed

Looking at a Named Pipe Example

As an example of using named pipes to communicate between two unrelated processes, I have created two projects that are included on the accompanying CD. BardServ provides a series of quotations from Shakespeare via a named pipe named "Quote." NPClient is a dialog-based MFC program that connects to the named pipe supplied by BardServ and displays a quotation in its main dialog box. Although the source code assumes that both programs are located on the same machine, it's easy to modify NPClient to work across a network.

As with the other example projects, you can use the project as is or follow the steps provided in the next few sections.

A Named Pipe Server Application

The BardServ application is a fairly simple server application. It spins in a `while` loop, creating and connecting named pipes for client processes, as Figure 23.2 shows.

FIGURE 23.2.

The basic architecture of BardServ.

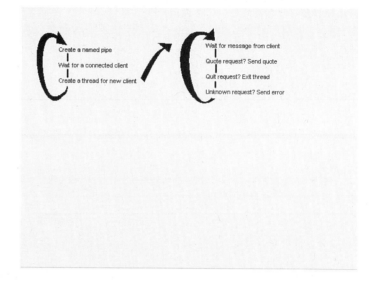

Most of the time, BardServ is blocked on a call to `ConnectNamedPipe`, waiting for a client process to connect to the other side of a pipe. When a client connects to the named pipe, BardServ creates a thread to service that client, creates a new pipe, and blocks again on a call to `ConnectNamedPipe`.

Listing 23.5 shows the complete source code for the BardServ project. Create a console mode project named BardServ, and add the source code in Listing 23.5 to the project as BardServ.cpp.

Listing 23.5. The BardServ source code.

```cpp
#include <windows.h>

// BardServ —
// A server that supplies quotations from Shakespeare via named
// pipes. This version supplies three quotations, and others easily are
// added.
const int cBuffer = 256;
const int cTimeout = INFINITE;

const TCHAR g_szPipe[] = TEXT("\\\\.\\pipe\\Quote");
const TCHAR g_szUnknown[] = TEXT("Unknown request");
const TCHAR g_rgszQuotes[][350] = {
    //Henry V
    {TEXT("We few, we happy few, we band of brothers;\n"
        "For he today that sheds his blood with me\n"
        "Shall be my brother; be he ne'er so vile,\n"
        "This day shall gentle his condition.\n"
        "And gentlemen in England, now abed,\n"
        "Shall think themselves accursed they were not here;\n"
        "And hold their manhoods cheap whiles any speaks\n"
        "That fought with us upon Saint Chrispin's day.\n") },
```

```
    //Hamlet
    {TEXT("There are more things in heaven and earth, Horatio,\n"
          "Than are dreamt of in your philosophy.\n") },
    //Richard III
    {TEXT("Now is the winter of our discontent\n"
          "Made glorious summer by this sun of York;\n") }
};

int   ErrorHandling( LPCTSTR lpszTitle );
DWORD PipeFunc( LPARAM lparam );
void  MessageWrite( LPCTSTR lpszMsg );

int main()
{
    // Create a security descriptor that has a NULL ACL
    // that allows unlimited access.
    SECURITY_ATTRIBUTES      sa;
    SECURITY_DESCRIPTOR*     psd;
    psd = (SECURITY_DESCRIPTOR*)LocalAlloc( LPTR,
                                 SECURITY_DESCRIPTOR_MIN_LENGTH);
    InitializeSecurityDescriptor(psd,SECURITY_DESCRIPTOR_REVISION);
    SetSecurityDescriptorDacl( psd, TRUE, NULL, FALSE );
    sa.nLength = sizeof(sa);
    sa.lpSecurityDescriptor = psd;
    sa.bInheritHandle = TRUE;

    // Hang in a loop, creating named pipe instances and
    // waiting for a client to connect.  There is a teeny,
    // tiny hole where two clients might try to connect
    // at the same time; however this is an extremely small
    // time gap.
    while(1)
    {
        HANDLE hPipe = CreateNamedPipe( g_szPipe,
                                        PIPE_ACCESS_DUPLEX,
                                        PIPE_TYPE_MESSAGE ¦
                                        PIPE_READMODE_MESSAGE ¦
                                        PIPE_WAIT,
                                        PIPE_UNLIMITED_INSTANCES,
                                        cBuffer,
                                        cBuffer,
                                        cTimeout,
                                        &sa );
        if( hPipe == INVALID_HANDLE_VALUE )
            return ErrorHandling( TEXT("CreatePipe Failed") );

        MessageWrite( TEXT("Main thread waiting for a client\n") );
        BOOL fConnected = ConnectNamedPipe( hPipe, NULL );
        if( fConnected ¦¦ GetLastError() == ERROR_PIPE_CONNECTED )
        {
            // Connected -- now spin off a thread to manage this
            // pipe. Execution continues in PipeFunc.
            HANDLE hThread;
            DWORD  dwThreadID;
            hThread = CreateThread(NULL,
                                   0,
                                   (LPTHREAD_START_ROUTINE)PipeFunc,
                                   (LPVOID)hPipe,
```

continues

Listing 23.5. continued

```c
                                      0,
                                      &dwThreadID );
            TCHAR szMsg[80];
            wsprintf( szMsg,
                     TEXT("Thread 0x%02X connected to a client\n"),
                     dwThreadID );
            MessageWrite( szMsg );
            if( hThread == INVALID_HANDLE_VALUE )
                ErrorHandling( TEXT("CreateThread Failed") );
        }
        else
        {
            CloseHandle( hPipe );
                return ErrorHandling(TEXT("Connect Failed") );
        }
    }
    LocalFree( psd );
    return 0;
}
//
// Display an error message based on the operating system's
// latest error.
int ErrorHandling( LPCTSTR lpszTitle )
{
    TCHAR szBuffer[256];
    FormatMessage( FORMAT_MESSAGE_FROM_SYSTEM,
                   NULL,
                   GetLastError(),
                   MAKELANGID (LANG_ENGLISH, SUBLANG_ENGLISH_US),
                   szBuffer,
                   256,
                   NULL );
    MessageBox( NULL, szBuffer, lpszTitle, MB_ICONSTOP );
    return 1;
}

// PipeFunc —
// Manages a thread containing one pipe instance. If the client
// sends "Quit", the thread exits; otherwise, a new quotation is sent
// to the client.
DWORD PipeFunc( LPARAM lparam )
{
    HANDLE hPipe = (HANDLE)lparam;
    static int ndx = 0;
    TCHAR szBuffer[cBuffer];
    DWORD dwRead, dwWritten;
    while (1)
    {
        LPCTSTR pszWrite;
        BOOL fRead = ReadFile( hPipe,
                               szBuffer,
                               cBuffer,
                               &dwRead,
                               NULL );
        if( fRead == FALSE || dwRead == 0 ) break;
        if( lstrcmpi( TEXT("Quit"), szBuffer ) == 0 )
        {
```

```
            TCHAR szMsg[80];
            DWORD dwThreadID = GetCurrentThreadId();
            wsprintf( szMsg,
                     TEXT("Thread 0x%02X closing connection\n"),
                     dwThreadID );
            MessageWrite( szMsg );
            break;
        }
        else if( lstrcmpi( TEXT("Quote"), szBuffer ) == 0 )
        {
            pszWrite = g_rgszQuotes[ndx];
            if( ++ndx == 3 )
            ndx = 0;
        }
        else
            pszWrite = g_szUnknown;

        BOOL fWrite = WriteFile( hPipe,
                                 pszWrite,
                                 lstrlen(pszWrite) +1,
                                 &dwWritten,
                                 NULL );
        if( fWrite == FALSE || dwWritten == 0 ) break;
    }
    FlushFileBuffers( hPipe );
    DisconnectNamedPipe( hPipe );
    CloseHandle( hPipe );

    return NO_ERROR;
}

void MessageWrite( LPCTSTR lpszMsg )
{
    DWORD dwWritten;
    WriteFile( GetStdHandle(STD_OUTPUT_HANDLE),
              lpszMsg,
              lstrlen(lpszMsg),
              &dwWritten,
              NULL );
}
```

Inside main, BardServ creates a SECURITY_ATTRIBUTES structure that allows any client to connect to the pipe. BardServ then enters a loop, creating and connecting pipes for clients. When a client is connected to a pipe, BardServ spins up a thread for that client and passes the pipe handle to the thread function for handling.

In addition to main, BardServ has three functions:

- **ErrorHandling:** Displays a system-supplied text string when an error is detected.
- **MessageWrite:** Displays a status message to the standard output.
- **ThreadFunc:** Handles the threads that are spun up for every connected pipe. A client can request a quotation by sending the string "Quote" to BardServ. If the client sends "Quit," the thread closes the pipe and exits. If the client sends anything else, an error message is returned.

A Named Pipe Client Application

The NPClient project is an example of a dialog-based MFC application that uses named pipes to exchange information with another process. In this case, NPClient connects to BardServ via a named pipe and displays a quotation from Shakespeare in its main dialog box.

To get started with the NPClient project, use AppWizard to create a dialog-based project named NPClient. Feel free to accept or change any of the project options offered by AppWizard.

Open the main dialog box resource and modify it as shown in Figure 23.3. Notice that a new static text control is included that covers most of the dialog box area, as well as a new pushbutton control.

FIGURE 23.3.

The main dialog box for NPClient.

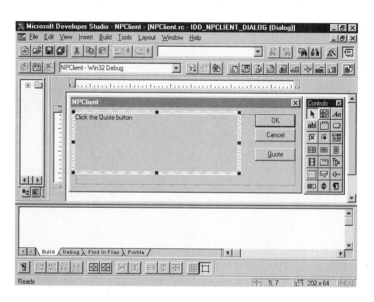

Use the values from Table 23.3 for the new controls added to the main dialog box resource.

Table 23.3. Resource and control information for the main dialog box.

Control	Resource ID	Caption
Static text control	IDC_MSG	Click the Quote button
Quote button	IDC_QUOTE	&Quote

Using ClassWizard, add a message-handling function to the CNPClientDlg class to handle BN_CLICKED messages from the Quote button, using the values provided in Table 23.4.

Table 23.4. Message-handling information for `CNPClientDlg`.

Class Name	Object ID	Message	Member Function
CNPClientDlg	IDC_QUOTE	BN_CLICKED	OnQuote

The `CNPClientDlg` class is modified by adding a named pipe handle and extra member functions to handle the communications through the named pipe. Make the changes shown in bold in Listing 23.6 to the `CNPClientDlg` class declaration.

Listing 23.6. Changes (in bold) to the `CNPClientDlg` class declaration.

```
class CNPClientDlg : public CDialog
{
.
.
.
// Implementation
protected:
    HICON  m_hIcon;
    HANDLE m_hPipe;

    void SendQuitMsg();
    int  ErrorHandling( LPCTSTR lpszTitle );
    void GetQuote();
.
.
.
};
```

Listing 23.7 contains the source code for the `CNPClientDlg::OnQuote` member function, which is called when the user clicks the Quote button. The `OnQuote` function attempts to open the client side of the named pipe, fetches a quotation, and releases the named pipe.

Listing 23.7. The `CNPClientDlg::OnQuote` member function.

```
void CNPClientDlg::OnQuote()
{
    m_hPipe = CreateFile( TEXT("\\\\.\\pipe\\Quote"),
                          GENERIC_READ | GENERIC_WRITE,
                          0,
                          NULL,
                          OPEN_EXISTING,
                          0,
                          NULL );
    if( m_hPipe == INVALID_HANDLE_VALUE )
    {
        ErrorHandling( TEXT("CreateFile Failed") );
        return;
    }
```

continues

Listing 23.7. continued

```
DWORD dwPipeState = PIPE_READMODE_MESSAGE;
BOOL fChangedState = SetNamedPipeHandleState( m_hPipe,
                                              &dwPipeState,
                                              NULL,
                                              NULL );
if( fChangedState == FALSE )
{
    ErrorHandling( TEXT("SetNamedPipeHandleState Failed") );
    return;
}
//Get a quotation from the BardServer, and quit the connection
GetQuote();
SendQuitMsg();
CloseHandle( m_hPipe );
}
```

Three additional functions exist for `CNPClientDlg`:

- **ErrorHandling:** Handles system error messages, just as in BardServ.
- **GetQuote:** Sends the string "Quote" to BardServ and waits for the quotation to be returned. After reading the quotation from the pipe, `GetQuote` displays the message in the dialog box.
- **SendQuitMessage:** Sends the string "Quit" to BardServ in order to shut down the pipe.

Listing 23.8 shows the source code for the remaining `CNPClientDlg` member functions.

Listing 23.8. Additional member functions for `CNPClientDlg`.

```
void CNPClientDlg::GetQuote()
{
    const int cBuffer = 512;
    TCHAR szBuffer[cBuffer];
    ASSERT( m_hPipe != INVALID_HANDLE_VALUE );

    TCHAR szMsg[] = TEXT("Quote");
    DWORD dwWritten, dwRead;

    BOOL fWritten = WriteFile( m_hPipe,
                               szMsg,
                               lstrlen(szMsg) + 1,
                               &dwWritten,
                               NULL );
    if( fWritten == FALSE ¦¦ dwWritten == 0 )
    {
        ErrorHandling( TEXT("WriteFile failed") );
        return;
```

```
    }
    BOOL fRead = ReadFile( m_hPipe,
                           szBuffer,
                           cBuffer,
                           &dwRead,
                           NULL );
    if( fRead == FALSE || dwRead == 0 )
    {
        ErrorHandling( TEXT("ReadFile failed") );
        return;
    }
    szBuffer[dwRead] = '\0';
    SetDlgItemText( IDC_MSG, szBuffer );
}

void CNPClientDlg::SendQuitMsg()
{
    ASSERT( m_hPipe != INVALID_HANDLE_VALUE );
    DWORD dwWritten;
    TCHAR szQuit[] = TEXT("Quit");
    BOOL fWritten = WriteFile( m_hPipe,
                               szQuit,
                               strlen(szQuit)+1,
                               &dwWritten,
                               NULL );
}

int CNPClientDlg::ErrorHandling( LPCTSTR lpszTitle )
{
    TCHAR szBuffer[256];
    FormatMessage( FORMAT_MESSAGE_FROM_SYSTEM,
                   NULL,
                   GetLastError(),
                   MAKELANGID(LANG_ENGLISH, SUBLANG_ENGLISH_US),
                   szBuffer,
                   256,
                   NULL );
    MessageBox( szBuffer, lpszTitle, MB_ICONSTOP );
    return 1;
}
```

Compile and run the BardServ and NPClient projects. While debugging or testing named pipes, I find it helpful to run two instances of the Visual C++ Developer Studio at the same time—one for each end of the pipe.

Figure 23.4 shows three copies of NPClient running with one copy of BardServ. Note the status messages displayed in the BardServ console window.

FIGURE 23.4.

Three instances of NPClient running with BardServ.

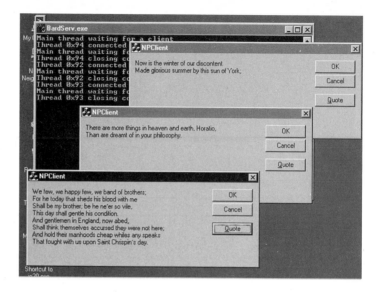

Summary

This chapter explained how you can use pipes for interprocess communications in Windows NT applications. You learned about using named and anonymous pipes. You also created two sets of sample applications—two programs that demonstrate how anonymous pipes are used, and two programs that demonstrate named pipes.

The next chapter, "Local and Remote Procedure Calls," explains how Windows NT applications can use LRPC and RPC for interprocess communication.

Local and Remote Procedure Calls

24

by David Hamilton

Remote Procedure Calls (RPCs)

Throughout this book we have seen many procedure calls; C and C++ are procedure-call based. The basic structure is one function (a procedure that returns a value), `main`, which calls other procedures. In Chapter 16, "Dynamic Link Libraries," we saw that these procedures can be shared and in a separate file, the DLL. Related procedures are grouped into DLLs.

The Remote Procedure Call is a low-level interprocess communication method where the procedure you call may be on another network computer. The RPC model was defined in the Open Software Foundation's (OSF) Distributed Computing Environment (DCE). A remote computer acts as the "compute server" sharing its CPU cycles with other computers on the network. Microsoft's RPC is an implementation of the RPC standard.

The DCE standard for RPC allows for use of the client server model with an RPC seen by the client as a function call. The client sees the call as a local procedure call but RPC translates the function across the network. A Windows NT application can be either a client or a server, while DOS and Windows 95 applications must be clients.

Like any function call, the remote server performs the procedure and returns results. Remember a return can also be `VOID`.

Benefits of RPC

The primary benefit is to enhance performance by using the network's available CPU power. Using RPC, processing can be directed from client machines to more powerful, or specialized, computing resources that exist out on the network. For example, one multiprocessor Windows NT machine may be able to serve database queries for a large number of smaller client machines. When using Windows NT, both client and server can execute an RPC call asynchronously, in its own thread, optimizing computing resources. This allows CPU power to be distributed throughout the network and used by clients when needed, rather than providing clients with extra CPU power that may never be needed.

RPC follows closely the function call model or local procedure calls (LPCs) so that when the first procedure calls the second, it gets a return and doesn't know or care how the second procedure got the answer. From a client's point of view, the function call looks exactly like a local procedure call, it just gets executed on another machine. The RPC standard allows for calls between dissimilar computers on the network, allowing UNIX machines to be servers to Windows clients, for example. RPC is independent of the network transport or protocol in use.

The benefit to you, the programmer, is that RPC hides the complexity of the network. RPC calls look like local procedure calls. RPC handles the differences in the hardware, such as different endian schemes and different network protocols.

All Windows NT hardware uses the "little-endian" convention, where the least significant bit is located first in memory. Motorola 68x00 machines, as well as many flavors of UNIX, use the "big-endian" convention, where the bit order is reversed. As you can imagine, this can cause big headaches when communicating between machines with different architectures. RPC smoothes out this problem by encoding the type of bit-ordering scheme used by a machine when transporting the RPC call across the network. This allows the RPC implementation on each machine to be responsible for translating the incoming data into the proper endian format.

The process is simple, as illustrated in Figure 24.1. The client program makes a function call into a local stub procedure. Stubs are code compiled and linked into the application, and instead of executing the function, they perform the RPC. The stub takes the parameters and translates them into the standard network representation format (NDR). It then calls the RPC client runtime library to send the request. The runtime translates the information into a network message and places the call on the network. The server side runtime translates the network message back into NDR and calls the server stub procedure. The stub on the server unpacks the NDR into parameters in the format the server application can use, then calls the remote procedure on the server. The remote procedure is executed. The server stub repackages the procedure results in an NDR and places them back on the network and the sequence is repeated in reverse. The last step is that the client stub gives the return value to the client application.

FIGURE 24.1.

The RPC sequence.

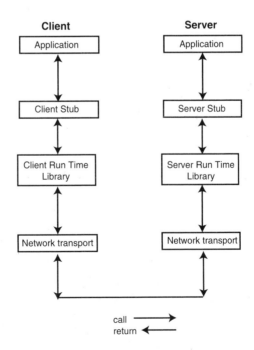

Open Software Foundation's DCE Model

The goal of the Open Software Foundation in creating the DCE standard was to allow interoperability between dissimilar platforms. In a large company, computers can range from mainframes to PCs, all of which need to share data.

DCE supports three models of distributed computing.

- The client/server model, which uses RPC in applications such as Microsoft SQL Server.
- The RPC model, where the client makes a local procedure call which is translated into a network message.
- The data sharing model, where data is distributed as in the Lotus Notes software.

We usually think of a server as providing file sharing, printer sharing, centralized communications, and acting as a data warehouse. In the RPC model, the server has evolved to also share its CPU power.

OSF sets the following list of goals for the RPC model:

- RPC should be simple, transparent, and provide high performance.
- RPC should adhere to the local procedure call format to minimize complexity to the developer.
- RPC should provide interoperability between platforms.
- RPC should allow applications to remain independent of network transports and protocols.
- RPC should work with the other components of DCE such as the Security Service, DCE Time, the Directory Service, and DCE threads.

DCE threads are important in programming RPC applications on Windows NT. Threads allow for concurrent programming in which the application can perform several tasks simultaneously. In RPC programming this allows the user to continue working in the application while a separate thread performs the RPC. Because the NT operating system supports multithreading, it does not require special DCE threads.

Windows NT's RPC Components

Microsoft's RPC includes the following components:

- MIDL Compiler
- Runtime library and header files

- ■ Transport interface modules
- ■ Name Service provider
- ■ Endpoint supply service

OSF has defined the Network Interface Definition Language (IDL) which Microsoft has implemented as MIDL. This language defines the interface between the client and server. All communication between the client and the server pass through the MIDL interface. By using a common interface, one team of developers can work on the client application while another works on the server application. Server applications can also be built to work with a variety of client applications.

MIDL is really a translator, not a compiler. It translates IDL code into C. The MIDL compiler builds the stubs used by both the client and the server. IDL is not a separate language by itself; it is the interface. To the programmer, the only feature of IDL you need to be aware of is that it is strongly typed and you cannot cast variables into different types. MIDL must interface not only between different applications, but also possibly different computer architectures. As such, it uses an exact definition of variable types as listed in Table 24.1.

Table 24.1. MIDL base types and properties.

Base Type	Description
boolean	A data item with values of TRUE or FALSE
byte	An 8-bit data item transmitted without modification
char	An 8-bit unsigned character
double	A 64-bit floating point data item
float	A 32-bit floating point data item
handle_t	A primitive handle used in RPC binding
hyper	A 64-bit integer, signed or unsigned
long	A 32-bit integer declared as either signed or unsigned
short	A 16-bit integer declared as either signed or unsigned
small	An 8-bit integer declared as either signed or unsigned
wchar_t	Wide character type used by Microsoft's MIDL. To use wchar_t the MIDL compiler needs the -ms_ext switch

IDL, the Glue That Binds the Client and the Server

In order to build the client and server stubs, MIDL needs an interface definition file. This file has an .IDL extension that contains the name, version, UUID or Universally Unique Identifier of the interface, and a list of procedures forming the interface. The most basic IDL file is shown in Listing 24.1.

Listing 24.1. A sample.idl file.

```
[uuid (ea981110-af4f-11cf-9aa4-d4b43b630000),
version(1.0)
]
interface sample
{
void SampleProc([out, string] unsigned char * pszString);
}
```

The IDL file has two parts: the header and the body. The header contains the UUID, the version number, the keyword `interface` and the name of the interface. The version number ensures that only compatible versions (with the same major version number) get connected. As an example, version pairs 1.3 and 1.7 would connect but versions 1.3 and 2.0 would not. The UUID ensures that your application is calling the appropriate server application on the network. The body contains the function prototype. Notice the bracketed `[out, string]`, this signifies that the function sends a string from the server back to the client. Conversely, `[in, string]` would signal that a string was being sent from the client to the server and `[in, out, string]` would mean the string was sent both ways.

> **TIP**
>
> You can save yourself some typing by using the NT utility program, UUIDGEN.EXE, as
>
> ```
> C:\UUIDGEN > Sample.H
> ```
>
> UUIDs are five groups of hexadecimal digits separated by hyphens. The first group is based on the date/time and will change, while the remainder is based on the network card and a random number. You will also see these referred to in NT as GUID.

When the IDL file is compiled, MIDL generates the C language client and server stubs along with their header files. The above listing would generate

```
/*file: sample.h */
#include <rpc.h>
void SampleProc(unsigned char * pszString);
```

Your application would include sample.h and would call the function in the usual fashion, like

```
SampleProc(pszString);
```

The Application Configuration File (ACF)

In the DCE standard the developer needs to also include one other definition file, the application configuration file, ACF, which contains RPC data that is not transmitted to the server. The main feature of this file is the binding handle. This handle represents the connection between the client and the server. In RPC, *binding* is a term used in a similar manner to the more familiar term *linking*. However, in RPC you can't actually perform linking because you don't know the exact memory address of the procedure; it's on the server. The client calls runtime functions to establish a valid binding handle that is used whenever the client calls a remote procedure. The binding handle is not a parameter in the function prototype and is not transmitted over the network. It is defined in the ACF file as in this listing:

```
/* file sample.acf */
[implicit_handle(handle_t sample_IfHandle)
] interface sample
{
}
```

Notice the similarity to the IDL file, attributes are in brackets, and again you see the keyword `interface`. The interface name in the IDL file and in the ACF file must match. The attribute, `implicit_handle`, indicates that the handle is a global variable and precedes the handle type and its name. Before you dive deeper into binding, the process of building an RPC application is diagrammed in Figure 24.2.

FIGURE 24.2.

Building an RPC application.

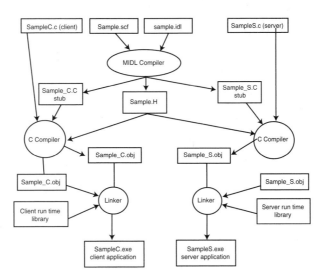

In Figure 24.2 you see that MIDL compiler takes the ACF and IDL files and builds the two stub files (labeled Sample_C.c and Sample_S.c). It also builds a common header file to include the RPC header file. These are passed to the C compiler with the client and server code files. The compiler builds the object code files for both the stubs and the source files. The linker then puts all this together with the appropriate RPC runtime libraries and builds both the client application and the server application.

The server application is run and informs the system what procedures are available, then it sits and waits for a client request.

Differences Between LPC and RPC Function Calls

Although RPC is designed to be transparent to the developer, it cannot be completely transparent. There are differences in operating systems, address spaces, exception handling, and binding requirements that the programmer must be aware of.

> **TIP**
>
> When writing an RPC application, it is best to start with a single application written so that the procedures you will call remotely are in separate files. You build a standalone program calling these procedures in the usual fashion and debug the code before converting to a distributed application. Once this is working, the same procedure source files can be used to build the server application.

The primary difference is global variables. Because the client and the server applications are two executables, each running on a separate computer, they cannot share global variables. The global variable, in order to be shared, must be passed to the remote procedure as a function parameter. If the client relies on a global variable that the server or another thread may change, the programmer has to be careful to synchronize global variable access

You saw in Chapter 22, "Threads," how NT supports multithreading. Combining RPC and multithreading makes NT a powerful development platform. A server application can handle several client applications and still the server can be used locally. Conversely, an application could be written with one client calling server applications on several other network computers. By using threads, the client application doesn't have to stop and wait for the RPC return value. Other functions can execute in the meantime to enhance your application's performance. However, this all comes at a price to the developer. Every thread must be re-entrant because NT can interrupt a thread at any time. While local variables are saved on the stack when a thread is interrupted and thus are thread save, this is not true with global variables. As I said above, the programmer must insure that global variables stay synchronized.

Binding

A *binding* is a logical connection between the client and the server. The concept of binding is similar to dynamic linking in that external references are unresolved until runtime. RPC never, in fact, links to a function in the usual sense. In a distributed application, the client application doesn't know the memory address of the remote procedure even at runtime. The client actually doesn't call the remote procedure, it sends a request to the server application to call it. Instead of actually linking, the application creates a dynamic binding that is used to call the function.

Each binding is uniquely identified by the UUID, the protocol sequence, the network address, the endpoint, and some network specific options. You saw the UUID earlier. The protocol sequence specifies the network protocol in use on your network; the most common is named pipes (ncacn_np), but you can also use Internet address (ncacn_ip_tcp), NetBios (ncacn_nb), local rpc (ncalrpc), or several others. The network address is usually in the form of \\Servername. The endpoint specifies the network endpoint at which the server application is listening, or the pipe on which the server is listening, and is specified as \pipe\pipename. The network options for named pipes are set to security=NULL, or TRUE, the only options at this time. These are set up in the server application as in Listing 24.2.

Listing 24.2. Registering a protocol sequence and endpoint with the RPC runtime library.

```
RPC_STATUS status;
unsigned char *pszEndpoint = "\\pipe\\auto";
unsigned char *pszProtocolSequence = "ncacn_np";
unsigned char *pszSecurity = NULL;
unsigned int *cMaxCalls = 20;  //maximul concurrent calls
status = RpcServerUseProtseqEp(pszProtocolSequence, cMaxCalls, pszEndpoint,
pszSecurity);
```

After the server calls RpcServeruseProtseqEp, it then calls RpcServerRegsiterIf to make the binding information available to the client. Lastly, the server calls RpcServerListen to indicate that it's ready and listening for RPC calls. This last function call turns execution over to the RPC runtime module. You will see these at the end of the chapter in your sample server application.

Binding handles can be created either automatically or manually. With automatic binding, the stubs create and maintain the binding handle. With manual, your client application calls the RPC runtime to create and manage the binding handle.

Although all handles eventually get mapped to primitive binding handles of type handle_t, you can also create a user-defined binding handle that has data associated with the handle. If you create an RPC application with a user-defined binding handle the RPC runtime will no longer know the structure of your defined binding handle. Therefore, you must write the marshalling and unmarshalling routines the stub will use to package and unpackage the data with each function call.

Passing Pointers, Arrays, and Strings

MIDL was designed to solve the problem of passing data between different computer architectures and different operating systems. As listed in Table 24.1 there are well-defined base types, because in a distributed application even the size of an integer can be variable. That is why small, short, long, and hyper exists to MIDL, and int doesn't.

Because a remote procedure is running in the address space of a remote machine, if you pass a pointer it would be a pointer to the variable's address on the client. This would mean nothing to the server and you would be told that you tried to access memory the server application didn't own. To solve this, RPC treats pointers differently. When a client passes a pointer, the stub recognizes the potential problem and transmits the pointer and the data to which it points. This is called *pointer emulation.* Passing a pointer in this way involves as much data copying as passing the data directly. In pointer emulation, when the server stub unpackages the data, it allocates memory, copies the data to that memory, and adjusts the pointer value accordingly. After the data is manipulated, the process is reversed to return the data to the client. While in LPC, passing pointers is very efficient, in RPC it is very inefficient. To use pointer emulation you need to supply a custom memory allocation routine and clean up after yourself. These functions can be implemented as user functions in the IDL file using malloc and free as in Listing 24.3.

Listing 24.3. A custom memory allocation routine.

```
void __RPC_FAR * __RPC_USER midl_user_allocate(size_t len)
{
  return (malloc(len));
}
void __RPC_USER midl_user_free(void __RPC_FAR * ptr)
{
  free(ptr);
}
```

To get around this inefficiency in passing pointers, RPC has its own methods using reference pointers, unique pointers, and full pointers. Reference pointers are the most efficient but also the most restrictive. A *reference pointer* must always point to valid memory, it must never change its value. No other pointers can point to the same data object, and a reference pointer can never contain the value NULL. A *unique pointer* can have the value NULL and the value of the pointer can change during the procedure call. When a data object is returned from the remote procedure, it is written over the original object so no other pointer can point to the same object. Full pointers are not supported by Microsoft's RPC 2.0 but in the DCE standard, full pointers let the stubs do all the worrying about what goes where and who accesses what. Full pointers are the least efficient because the stubs can't make any assumptions about the data, its size, and whether it's been changed.

Because the RPC runtime transmits the data across the network, it needs to know exactly the size of the data object. You, the programmer, can control the amount of data sent, like in the case of an array; you may not need to send the entire array. The size of an array and the number of elements to send can be either a constant or a variable amount. If the size will be variable, the IDL file must contain a special attribute for this variable size. These attributes are

first_is	Index of first array element to send
last_is	Index of last array element to send
length_is	Total number of array elements to send
min_is	Lowest valid array element (always set to 0 in Microsoft's RPC)
max_is	Highest valid array element
size_is	Total number of elements to allocate for array

An attribute in the IDL file is defined as in Listing 24.4.

Listing 24.4. Defining an attribute.

```
size_is          //attribute name
interface RPC_Array
{
  extern short Size;
  void MyArray([in, size_is(Size) char Array[*]_;  //the * is a place holder for
➡the variable
                                           //array size
}
```

The variable `Size` must be defined in the client application.

Strings are treated like variable length arrays. RPC uses the keyword `string` to signal the compiler of this special case. This tells the compiler to use `strlen()` or `_wstrlen()` to determine the size of the null-terminated string and send an array of that size with the `NULL`. You declare this in the IDL file as

```
RPC_Array
{
  Void MyString([in,out,string] char Array[*]);
}
```

Exception Handling

With RPC, structure exception handling is not an option: it's required. In Chapter 12, "Structured Exception Handling," you saw that NT had powerful ways to gracefully handle exceptions. In an RPC application the possible exceptions are multiplied by the complexity of two applications on two or more computers, connected by a possibly unreliable network.

Microsoft's RPC has its own set of functions and macros to handle exceptions. These get included with the rpc.h header file and include

- RpcAbnormalTermination
- RpcendExcept
- RpcEndFinally
- RpcExcept
- RpcExceptionCode
- RpcFinally
- RpcTryExcept
- RpcTryFinally

Probably the most common type of exception handing routine you will write will be simply to affirm that the server is online and listening. This provides a good example as in Listing 24.5 where you sit in a while loop calling the function ServerStatus until you get a return of TRUE.

Listing 24.5. Using exception-handling to affirm that the server is online and listening.

```
RpcTryExcept
{
  if(RemoteIsPrime(PrimerServerHandle, temp -1, !=0)
  {
      //do your RPC procedure
  }
RpcExcept(1)
{
  while(ServerStatus())
  {
    //if exception sit and wait
  }
}
RpcEndExcept
char ServerStatus(void)
{
  char value = FALSE;
  RpcTryExcept
  {
    PrimerServerHandle = InitializePrimerServer(server_name);
  }
  RpcExcept(1)
  {
   value = TRUE;
  }
  RpcEndExcept
  return value;
}
```

A Basic Sample Application

If a picture is worth a thousand words, to a programmer working sample code is worth hours of trial and error. Microsoft provides many RPC samples on the VC++ 4 CD-ROM but even their "Hello World" sample gets pretty involved. What I have is a variation using the snippets from the previous code listings that tells your co-worker you want to order a pizza.

The first step is the client application, Listing 24.6, which opens the RPC connection, passes a string via the function pizzaRPC, and closes the connection.

Listing 24.6. Using RPC in a client application.

```
#include <STDIO.H>
#include <RPC.H>
#include "pizza.h"

void _CRTAPI1 main(void)
   {
   RpcTryExcept
      pizzaRPC("Do You want to order a pizza via RPC?");
      Shutdown();
   RpcExcept(1)
      printf("The RPC runtime module reported an exception.\n");
   RpcEndExcept
   }
```

The two functions are in a separate file, Listing, 24.7. Remember it's best first to build a standalone application, debug it, then move it to RPC.

Listing 24.7. The RPC procedures.

```
// listing 24.6 the RPC procedures
#include <STDLIB.H>
#include <STDIO.H>
#include <TIME.H>
#include <RPC.H>
#include "pizza.h"

void pizzaRPC(unsigned char *string)
   {
   printf(string);
   }

void Shutdown(void)
{
   RPC_STATUS status;

   status = RpcMgmtStopServerListening(NULL);
   if (status) {
      exit(status);
   }
```

continues

Listing 24.7. continued

```
    status = RpcServerUnregisterIf(NULL, NULL, FALSE);
    if (status) {
        exit(status);
    }
}
```

The pizza.h file is created by the MIDL compiler for you, but you need to provide the `#in-clude` statement. The file it created is in Listing 24.8, and you need to also include it in the server application.

Listing 24.8. The pizza.h file.

```
/* this ALWAYS GENERATED file contains the definitions for the interfaces */


/* File created by MIDL compiler version 2.00.0102 */
/* at Mon May 20 15:42:52 1996
 */
//@@MIDL_FILE_HEADING(  )
#include "rpc.h"
#include "rpcndr.h"

#ifndef __pizza_h__
#define __pizza_h__

#ifdef __cplusplus
extern "C"{
#endif

/* Forward Declarations */

void __RPC_FAR * __RPC_USER MIDL_user_allocate(size_t);
void __RPC_USER MIDL_user_free( void __RPC_FAR * );

#ifndef __pizza_INTERFACE_DEFINED__
#define __pizza_INTERFACE_DEFINED__

/*****************************************
 * Generated header for interface: pizza
 * at Mon May 20 15:42:52 1996
 * using MIDL 2.00.0102
 *****************************************/
/* [auto_handle][unique][version][uuid] */
/* size is 0 */

void pizzaRPC(
/* [string][in] */
unsigned char __RPC_FAR *string);
/* size is 0 */

void Shutdown( void);
```

```
extern RPC_IF_HANDLE pizza_ClientIfHandle;
extern RPC_IF_HANDLE pizza_ServerIfHandle;
#endif /* __pizza_INTERFACE_DEFINED__ */

/* Additional Prototypes for ALL interfaces */

/* end of Additional Prototypes */

#ifdef __cplusplus
}
#endif

#endif
```

The server application is where all the work gets done. You set up the binding vector and the procedure sequence to be used. The handle is registered then used to export the binding information. Lastly, the server begins to sit and wait for an RPC call. The server application is Listing 24.9.

Listing 24.9. Pizza server application.

```
#include <STDLIB.H>
#include <STRING.H>
#include <STDIO.H>
#include <RPC.H>
#include "pizza.h"

void _CRTAPI1 main(int argc, char *argv[])
    {
    RPC_STATUS status;
    RPC_BINDING_VECTOR *pBindingVector;

    unsigned char *pszAutoEntryName   = "/.:/Autohandle_sample";
    unsigned char *pszEndpoint        = "\\pipe\\auto";
    unsigned char *pszProtocolSequence = "ncacn_np";
    unsigned char *pszSecurity        = NULL;
    unsigned int   cMinCalls          = 1;
    unsigned int   cMaxCalls          = 20;
    unsigned int   fDontWait          = FALSE;
    unsigned int   fNameSyntaxType    = RPC_C_NS_SYNTAX_DEFAULT;

    status = RpcServerUseProtseqEp(pszProtocolSequence,
                                   cMaxCalls,      /* max concurrent calls */
                                   pszEndpoint,
                                   pszSecurity);   /* Security descriptor  */

    if(status)
        exit(status);

    status = RpcServerRegisterIf(
        pizza_ServerIfHandle, /* interface to register    */
        NULL,                 /* MgrTypeUuid               */
```

continues

Listing 24.9. continued

```
        NULL);                  /* MgrEpv; null means use default */

    if(status)
        exit(status);

    status = RpcServerInqBindings(&pBindingVector);

    if(status)
        exit(status);

    status = RpcNsBindingExport(
        fNameSyntaxType,   /* name syntax type    */
        pszAutoEntryName,  /* nsi entry name      */
        pizza_ServerIfHandle,
        pBindingVector,    /* set in previous call */
        NULL);             /* UUID vector         */

    if(status)
        exit(status);

    status = RpcServerListen(cMinCalls, cMaxCalls, fDontWait); /* wait flag */

    if(status)
        exit(status);

    if(fDontWait)
        {

        status = RpcMgmtWaitServerListen(); /* wait operation */

        if(status)
            exit(status);
        }
    }

/* MIDL allocate and free */
void __RPC_FAR *__RPC_API midl_user_allocate(size_t len)
    {
    return(malloc(len));
    }

void __RPC_API midl_user_free(void __RPC_FAR *ptr)
    {
    free(ptr);
    }
```

The last two things you need to write are the IDL and the ACF files. Both of these are short as in Listing 24.10 and 24.11.

Listing 24.10. pizza.idl.

```
[ uuid (e3aa0c40-b281-11cf-9aa4-d4b43b630000),
  version(1.0),
  pointer_default(unique)]
```

```
interface pizza
{
void pizzaRPC([in, string] unsigned char *string);

void Shutdown(void);

}
```

Listing 24.11. pizza.acf.

```
//listing 24.1 the pizza.acf
[auto_handle]
interface pizza
{
}
```

One more file is always needed to build an application: the makefile. In RPC this saves you a lot of work as it calls the MIDL compiler with the proper switch settings, compiles the source, and links both the client and the server application into the two EXE files. The pizza makefile is shown in Listing 24.12, the last.

Listing 24.12. The pizza makefile.

```
!include <ntwin32.mak>

all : pizzac pizzas

# Make the client side application pizzac
pizzac : pizzac.exe
pizzac.exe : pizzac.obj pizza_c.obj
    $(link) $(linkdebug) $(conflags) -out:pizzac.exe \
        pizzac.obj pizza_c.obj \
        rpcrt4.lib rpcns4.lib $(conlibs)

# pizzac main program
pizzac.obj : pizzac.c pizza.h
    $(cc) $(cdebug) $(cflags) $(cvars) $*.c

# pizzac stub
pizza_c.obj : pizza_c.c pizza.h
    $(cc) $(cdebug) $(cflags) $(cvars) $*.c

# Make the server side application
pizzas : pizzas.exe
pizzas.exe : pizzas.obj pizzap.obj pizza_s.obj
    $(link) $(linkdebug) $(conflags) -out:pizzas.exe \
        pizzas.obj pizza_s.obj pizzap.obj \
        rpcrt4.lib rpcndr.lib rpcns4.lib $(conlibsmt)

# pizza server main program
pizzas.obj : pizzas.c pizza.h
```

continues

Listing 24.12. continued

```
    $(cc) $(cdebug) $(cflags) $(cvarsmt) $*.c

# remote procedures
pizzap.obj : pizzap.c pizza.h
    $(cc) $(cdebug) $(cflags) $(cvarsmt) $*.c

# pizzas stub file
pizza_s.obj : pizza_s.c pizza.h
    $(cc) $(cdebug) $(cflags) $(cvarsmt) $*.c


# Stubs and header file from the IDL file
pizza.h pizza_c.c pizza_s.c : pizza.idl pizza.acf
    midl -oldnames -cpp_cmd $(cc) -cpp_opt "-E" pizza.idl

# Clean up everything
cleanall : clean
    -del *.exe

# Clean up everything but the .EXEs
clean :
    -del *.obj
    -del *.map
    -del pizza_c.c
    -del pizza_s.c
    -del pizza.h
```

Summary

This chapter has just scratched the surface of a new and exciting technology, RPC. You will see and learn much more about it as more applications begin to use the CPU power of a network of computers. Unfortunately, outside of the manuals-on-line, there isn't much documentation yet for doing RPC in the Windows NT world. There are, however, many samples programs on the CD-ROM.

In this Part IV, "Low-Level Process Communications," you have looked at the possibilities Windows NT brings to the developer. Development options like RPC have been reserved in the past for mini- and mainframe developers mainly using UNIX.

In the next part, "WinNT Network Programming," you will look at four more APIs the NT developers have available to access the Internet, share mail, and bring telephony to the small business.

IN THIS PART

PART

WinNT Network Programming

Windows Sockets

25

by David Hamilton

In network programming you will see the client/server model over and over again. A client application makes a request, then is recognized by another computer on the network. This second computer is running a server application that fulfills the client's request and returns the information.

As networks grew to include computers outside the immediate location, the need grew to have a standardized way for clients and servers to talk.

With the advent of the Internet, many client and server applications were developed that were freely distributed to allow for the sharing of information. Most of these were distributed as small programs that could be compiled on the local machine and give that machine new network functionality or the ability to access data in a new standardized way. These small applications were called sockets.

As Microsoft Windows became a common user interface, many of these sockets were ported to give the user a "Windows-like" interface. These became known as Winsockets. Before we go into developing Winsockets, let's step back and take a closer look at their background.

The Internet, a Little History

By now, you've heard that the Internet is big news. Vice President Al Gore really didn't invent it—it has been around for more than 30 years. The U.S. Department of Defense started the project as ARPANET to share research among its computers. Its design, implemented in 1968, was to use leased phone lines to send messages in packets of 1,024 bits and to perform cyclic redundancy checking (CRC) with a 24-bit check value. Bolt, Beranek, and Newman from Cambridge, Massachusetts, won the contract from the military to actually build the network to link Stanford Research, University of Utah, UC Santa Barbara, and UCLA in 1969. In 1970, five more research centers were added. By 1983, the network had grown to 320; by 1987, it had grown to 20,000; and by 1990, it had grown to 200,000 computers. Since then, nearly everyone else seemingly has been given an address. Today, there are millions of computers all over the globe connected to the Internet, and many use some of the initial ARPANET protocols, such as telnet, finger, ping, and FTP on a daily basis.

Many of the ideas in the initial Network Control Protocol (NCP) became part of today's Transmission Control Protocol (TCP). As more computers came online with different maximum packet sizes, TCP had to be redefined into two layers: one for the software protocols and one for lower level protocols called Internet Protocol (IP). The OSI model discussed in Chapter 4, "NT Is the Network," was the final result of ARPANET research. Along with the spread of the network, a new operating system, Berkeley Software Distribution UNIX, was becoming the choice of the university computer departments. BSD UNIX used the TCP/IP protocol and had an application programming interface known as Berkeley Sockets. Instead of each research center writing all its own software, centers could get source code for standard utilities from each other and then plug them into their existing network software.

In the OSI model, IP is the networking layer protocol, TCP or UDP are the transport layer protocols, and utilities such as FTP and SMTP are at the top application layer. In Chapter 4, you learned that IP doesn't guarantee that a packet will arrive or that a packet will arrive in any specific order; it just delivers packets the best that it can, and it's up to TCP to check that they are not corrupt and are in the correct order. You learned in Chapter 4 that each packet has the IP address of the sender and the receiver. TCP sets up a connection between two computers and breaks the data into chunks, adds a check sum value to each chunk, and packages the chunks into IP packets.

Just as TCP uses IP addresses to route packets, applications use the concept of ports to direct their data. Suppose that your SMTP mail server waits for connections on port 25. If I mail something to you, my computer sends the mail through port 25 to your computer's port 25 for mail. If it's network news (NNTP), it is port 119, telnet port 23, and FTP for 21. After these ports are open on both computers, all data in a certain stream is directed by TCP to that port. Your mail therefore doesn't include part of the FTP download going on at the same time.

One last element of routing is the *domain name service* (DNS). Computers like IP addresses that tell the computer all it needs to know to route a packet anywhere. Computers find IP addresses easy to remember, whereas humans seem to relate more to names. Each computer used to have a HOST file with all the names and IP addresses it knew. Your NT machine still has an internal similar file, HOSTS, which your internal network may be using via LMHOSTS. Every so often, the computers would share this file so that others knew the routes. Eventually, the HOSTS file became too large to store on each computer and it was just stored on central computers using DNS. A DNS has a hierarchical tree to look up IP addresses that are given names. Figure 25.1 shows that structure.

FIGURE 25.1.

The DNS hierarchical name tree.

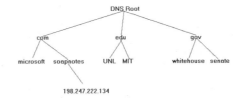

Windows Sockets Implementation

BSN Unix and its sockets API became the standard in network programming because one installation could port the C source code easily, recompile it, and plug it into its existing TCP/IP utilities. The installation knew whether the other installation had the same socket; the two used a common language. As more users started to access the Internet, they were running computers with Windows rather than UNIX. Windows TCP/IP developers came up with their own standard API called WinSock, which has most of the standard BSD API functions and some extensions to support Windows-style messages. The WinSock API is a DLL named WINSOCK.DLL on 16-bit Windows or WSOCK32.DLL on your NT machine. You implement it by using the WINSOCK.H include file. You write an application that talks to WSOCK32.DLL, and it knows how to communicate with TCP/IP. This chapter focuses on connecting to TCP/IP, but connecting to IPX/SPX, AppleTalk, and other protocols also is possible.

A *socket* describes a file handle; it's a positive integer value that identifies the endpoint for communication. The data is buffered both by the server application sending the data and the client application receiving the data. A socket is not the same as a TCP port value. Instead, it is a handle to the data that includes the IP addresses as well as the port doing the communicating. This data may be a stream or a datagram. When you create a socket with the Socket() function, you state whether the data is a stream or datagram. Datagrams use User Datagram Protocol (UDP) and streams use TCP. Streams are bidirectional TCP connections.

To better understand this scenario, suppose that the Federal Express delivery person comes into my office with a package of data for me, but he says that he needs to call his home office first. I direct him to a phone that he can use to make the call and answer if the Federal Express office needs to call him back. At his office, an operator is listening for driver support calls, accepts calls from valid Federal Express drivers, and passes those calls onto the support staff. The support staff and the driver solve the problem, hang up, and I get my package of data. The part of the client socket is played by the Federal Express guy. The bind is when I tell him he can use only that particular phone. His port is the special driver service phone number only he can use. His operator (server socket) accepts the call and creates another socket played by the support person who sends and receives information with the client socket (driver) while the server socket (operator) is free to listen for other calls. I'm the application that got the data from Federal Express (played by TCP/IP) and couldn't care less about the rest of the story.

Socket programming can be broken down into two parts: what the client does and what the server does. The client creates a socket, binds the socket to the local address and port, connects to a server, sends/receives, and then closes the socket. The server creates the socket, binds to its address and port, and sits and listens for the client to connect and start something. After the client connects, the server accepts by creating a new socket for the client's use. The original socket waits for a second client to connect. The new socket performs the receive/send operation with the client and then closes. Figure 25.2 provides a view of this process.

Earlier in this book, you learned that objects have states and Windows NT implements WinSock objects very similar to the way in which it implements file I/O objects. A thread object is in a *signaled* state when it is available, a *waiting* state when it is paused for a resource, or an *executing* state when it has the CPU. Sockets are the same; the socket can be in an open state, a bound state, a connected state, or a listening state.

FIGURE 25.2.

Client server socket interaction.

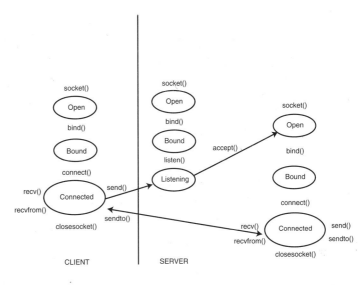

Circled items = State

The WinSock API

In order to understand the MFC WinSock classes and C++ programming, you need some background of the functions they wrap. This will enable you to understand what is going on inside the classes. This section lists the basic API functions and briefly describes what each does. This section doesn't include all the flags and options for the functions; it is just a basic listing. The next section looks at the classes and develops a sample application.

The Windows socket API consists of 44 functions grouped into four classes: conversion functions, database functions, socket functions, and extensions. They are named to be consistent with the BSD socket functions, so you will see that if BSD has a function sockaddr_in for the Internet address, the WinSock API has the function SOCKADDR_IN. The extension functions behave in a similar manner; for example, for the network down error, BSN uses ENETDOWN, whereas WinSock uses WSAENETDOWN.

The basic concept is that two sockets are communicating and need to know the socket number of each other. Each sends messages with this socket number. Windows NT has another API for network programming called the WNet API that is focused on the network resources. The WinSock API focuses on the connection.

The conversion functions are necessary to handle the big-endian versus little-endian issues. On Intel x86 machines, the least significant byte is first in a multiple-byte integer. On Macintosh and most UNIX-based machines, the most significant byte is first, however (big-endian). To ensure that dissimilar machines can talk together, the Internet defines *big-endian* as the *network byte order* (NBO). Table 25.1 lists the six functions for this conversion that you will need to use in your WinSock API programming.

Table 25.1. WinSock API conversion functions.

Function	Converts
htonl	32-bit long to NBO
htos	16-bit short to NBO
inet_addr	IP address string to 32-bit IP address
inet_ntoa	32-bit IP address to IP address string
ntohl	NBO to 32-bit long
ntohs	NBO to 16-bit short

Table 25.2 lists the database functions, which retrieve information about the hosts, the services available, and the protocols in use. These functions enable you to access information by IP address or by name.

Table 25.2. WinSock API database functions.

Function	Retrieves
gethostbyaddr	Host by its IP address
gethostbyname	Host by its host name
gethostname	Name of the local host
getprotobyname	Protocol by familiar protocol name
getprotobynumber	Protocol by protocol number
getservbyname	Service by familiar service name
getservbyport	Service information by port number

These function calls return pointers to structures with the information. Listing 25.1 shows these structures.

Listing 25.1. The `hostent`, `protoent`, and `servent` data structures.

```
struct hostent {
 char FAR * h_name;
 char FAR * FAR * h_alias;
 short h_addrtype;
 short h_length;
 char FAR * FAR * h_addr_list;
};

struct protoent {
 char FAR * p_name;
 char FAR * FAR * p_aliases;
 short p_proto;
};

struct servant {
 char FAR * s_name;
 char FAR * FAR * s_aliases;
 short s_port;
 char FAR * s_proto;
};
```

Given these three data structures, you can get each data element you need in order to establish the communication. The function to get the local host's address isn't included. The host name provides this information. The following function in Listing 25.2 does just that.

Listing 25.2. Function to get local host's address from `gethostname`.

```
char FAR * FAR * gethostaddr(void)
{
 char szhostname[40];
 int iAddofName = gethostname(szHostName, sizeof(szHostName);
   if (iAddofName !=0) ¦¦ (lstrcmp(szHostName,"") == 0)
     return NULL;
 HOSTENT FAR * lphostent = gethostbyname(szHostName);
   if (lphostent == NULL)
     return NULL;
   else
     return lphostent->h_addr_list;
}
```

You already saw some of the socket functions in Figure 25.2. Each of these uses one of three structures to store and get information on the socket. Table 25.3 lists more of the available socket data structures in the Windows API.

Listing 25.3. Data structures to get Internet address, TCP/IP address, and IP address.

```
struct sockaddr {                    //Internet address and port
 u_short sa_family;
 char sa_data[14];
};

stuct sockaddr_in {            //TCP/IP addresses
 short sin_family;
 u_short sin_port;
 struct in_addr sin_addr;
 char sin_zero[8];
};

struct in_addr {                     //access portions of an IP address
 union {
  struct {uchar s_b1,s_b2,s_b3,s_b4;} s_un_b;
  struct {ushort s_w1,s_w2;} S_un_w;
  ulong S_addr;
 } S_un;
};
```

Table 25.3. WinSock API socket functions.

Function	Action
accept	Accepts a connection on a listening socket and returns a newly created connected socket
bind	Binds a local address and port to a socket
closesocket	Closes the socket and releases a descriptor
connect	Establishes a connection to a remote host
getpeername	Gets address and port of a remote host
getsockname	Gets address and port of a socket
getsockopt	Gets the value of a socket option
ioclsocket	Gets or sets the parameters of a socket
listen	Tells socket to listen for incoming connections
recv	Receives data from socket
recvfrom	Receives data from socket and returns host address
select	Determines write and readability error status of socket
send	Sends data to a connected socket
sendto	Sends data to a specific remote host address and port
setsockopt	Sets a local socket's options
shutdown	Disables sending and receiving of data on a socket
socket	Creates a socket

Table 25.4 lists the last class of functions, which handle the conversion from BSD sockets to Windows (a message-based environment). These functions provide control of asynchronous operations, manage the blocking hook loop for 16-bit Windows, and start and stop WinSock usage. Blocking and non-blocking functions allow Windows 3.11 to function even though it is not a preemptive multitasking system. Windows NT takes a blocking call and simply suspends the current thread until the data is available, which enables the user interface to continue to be responsive.

Table 25.4. WinSock API extension functions.

Function	*Action*
WEAStartup	Starts WinSock
WESUnlockBlockingHook	Restores blocking hook to the default
WSAAsyncGetHostByAddr	Asynchronously retrieves host by address
WSAAsyncGetHostByName	Asynchronously retrieves host by name
WSAAsyncGetProtoByName	Asynchronously gets protocol by name
WSAAsyncGetProtoByNumber	Asynchronously gets protocol by number
WSAAsyncGetServByName	Asynchronously gets service by name
WSAAsyncGetServByPort	Asynchronously gets service by port
WSAAsyncSelect	Asynchronously gets events of a socket
WSACancelAsyncRequest	Cancels an in-progress database operation
WSACancelBlockingCall	Cancels an in-progress function that is blocked
WSACleanup	Terminates use of WinSock
WSAGetLastError	Gets the last error code of this thread
WSAIsBlocking	Returns TRUE if blocking is in progress
WSASetBlockingHook	Installs a blocking hook
WSASetLastError	Sets an error code

The MFC WinSock Classes

MFC supplies two models for writing WinSock applications. CAsyncSocket encapsulates the WinSock API and enables you to use callback functions to get notification of network events. The main class is CSocket, which is derived from CAsyncSocket and enables you to work with sockets with MFC CArchive objects.

A socket is a communications endpoint—an object through which you send and receive packets of data. Each socket has a type and is associated with a running process. Sockets still can be a *stream* socket, which is a bidirectional stream of bytes delivered in the correct sequence, and you get each packet once. Sockets also can be *datagram* sockets, which are record oriented, may be duplicated, and are not guaranteed to be delivered in any specific sequence. A socket is a handle to an object of type SOCKET. The class CSocket handles packing and unpacking of data into stream packets. Class CSocket does not enable you to use socket type SOCK_DGRAM. By using CSocket with a CArchive object, you can serialize the data to and from the socket object. CSocket also provides the blocking needed so that your Windows NT user messages get through to you.

The CSocket programming model follows:

1. Construct an object of type CSocket:

   ```
   CSocket sockSrve or CSocket sockClient
   ```

2. Use the object to create a SOCKET handle. If it is a server, specify the port:

   ```
   sockSrve.Create(nPort) or sockClient.Create()
   ```

3. If the socket is a client, call CAsyncSocket::Connect. If the socket is the server, call CAsyncSocket::Listen. After receiving a request, the server accepts by calling CAsyncSocket::Accept. The Accept member function takes a parameter to a second empty CSocket object used in the actual communication:

   ```
   sockSrvr.Listen() or sockClient.Connect(strAddr, nPort)
   CSocket sockRecv;
   sockSrvr.Accept(sockRecv);
   ```

4. Create a CSocketFile object and associate the CSocket object to it:

   ```
   CSocketFile file(&sockRecv);
   ```

5. Create a CArchive object and associate the CSocketFile object to it:

   ```
   CArchive arIn(&file, CArchive::load);
   CArchive arOut(&file, CArchive::store);
   ```

6. Use one CArchive object to send and another to receive data. Any given CArchive object can pass data in only one direction. You use the IsBufferEmpty member function to loop until all the data is read and the buffer is cleared:

   ```
   arIn >> dwValue            or            arIn >> dwValue
   arOut << dwValue                         arOut << dwValue
   ```

7. When finished, destroy the CArchive, CSocket, and CSocketFile objects.

By using CArchive, you can treat the packet using the Serialize function. The only difference is that the archive is attached to a CSocketFile instead of a CFile object. CArchive manages the buffer for you. CSocket is a two-state object. In its asynchronous state, it receives notification that data is coming. Once the data is being received or sent, it switches to its synchronous state, which forces it to handle that communications session before taking on data from another. When the communication is finished, it switches back to an asynchronous state. (See Figure 25.3.)

FIGURE 25.3.

Using CArchive, CSocket, *and* CSocketFile.

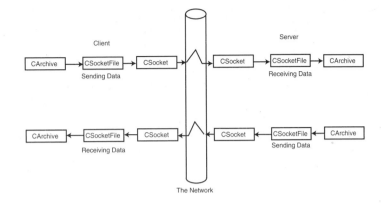

CAsyncSocket

A CAsyncSocket object is a Windows socket—the endpoint of network communication. An endpoint exists usually on two machines: the client and the server. This class wraps the WinSock API for MFC programming. With a CAsyncSocket, you handle the blocking and byte ordering; with CSocket, however, the class handles these for you. To use CAsyncSocket, you call its constructor and then the Create function to create a handle of type SOCKET. From that point on, the member functions mirror what you saw earlier with Listen, Connect, Accept, and Close sequences. To create an instance of the CAsyncSocket class use:

```
CAsyncSocket mysock;
mysock.Create(); // the default parameters
```

or

```
CAsyncSocket* pmysock = new CAsyncSocket;
int nPort = 27;
pmysock->Create(nPort, SOCK_DGRAM);
```

The CAsyncSocket class has one data member: m_hSocket, the handle to the socket. You gain access by using the <afxsock.h> header file. Table 25.5 lists the member functions.

Table 25.5. The CAsyncSocket class member functions.

Constructor	Function
CAsyncSocket	Constructs an object
Create	Creates a socket

continues

Table 25.5. continued

Attribute	Function
Attach	Attaches a socket handle to a CAsyncSocket object
Detach	Detaches a socket handle from a CAsyncSocket object
FromHandle	Returns a pointer to a CAsyncSocket object, given a socket handle
GetLastError	Gets the error status for the last operation that failed
GetPeerName	Gets the address of the peer socket to which the socket is connected
GetSockName	Gets the local name for a socket
GetSockOpt	Retrieves a socket option
SetSockOpt	Sets a socket option

Operation	Function
Accept	Accepts a connection on the socket
AsyncSelect	Requests event notification for the socket
Bind	Associates a local address with the socket
Close	Closes the socket
Connect	Establishes a connection to a peer socket
IOCtl	Controls the mode of the socket
Listen	Establishes a socket to listen for incoming connection requests
Receive	Receives data from the socket
ReceiveFrom	Receives a datagram and stores the source address
Send	Sends data to a connected socket
SendTo	Sends data to a specific destination
ShutDown	Disables send and/or receive calls on the socket

Overridable	Function
OnAccept	Notifies a listening socket that it can accept pending connection requests by calling Accept
OnClose	Notifies a socket that the socket connected to it has closed
OnConnect	Notifies a connecting socket that the connection attempt is complete, whether successfully or in error

Overridable	Function
OnOutOfBandData	Notifies a receiving socket that there is out-of-band data to be read on the socket—usually, an urgent message
OnReceive	Notifies a listening socket that there is data to be retrieved by calling Receive
OnSend	Notifies a socket that it can send data by calling Send

As you can see, most of these member functions closely mirror what you use with the WinSock API.

CSocket

The CSocket class is derived from CAsyncSocket and provides a higher level template for you to use to derive your classes. The CSocket class takes care of blocking and byte ordering for you by calling the CArchive class to read and write synchronously. Table 25.6 shows the member functions in the CSocket class.

Table 25.6. The CSocket class member functions.

Construction	Function
Create	Creates a socket
CSocket	Constructs a CSocket object

Attribute	Function
Attach	Attaches a SOCKET handle to a CSocket object
FromHandle	Returns a pointer to a CSocket object, given a SOCKET handle
IsBlocking	Determines whether a blocking call is in progress

Operation	Function
CancelBlockingCall	Cancels a blocking call that is in progress

Overridable	Function
OnMessagePending	Called to process pending messages while waiting for a blocking call to complete

The use of class CSocket is much the same as calling the constructor and then Create to create a handle of type SOCKET. The default is to create a stream socket, as shown in this example:

```
BOOL Create( UINT nSocketPort = 0, int nSocketType = SOCK_STREAM, LPCTSTR
lpszSocketAddress = NULL )
```

The nSocketType also can be SOCK_DGRAM. The default nSocketPort = 0 allows MFC to select the appropriate port. The last parameter is the address of the SOCKADDR structure.

CSocketFile

The CSocketFile class is derived from CFile and is specialized to send and receive data via sockets. You normally attach a CSocketFile to a CArchive and use serialization. This handles the buffering of data using the insert (<<) and extract (>>) Serialize functions. Because you are looking at a stream of data, you don't have all the CFile member functions, such as Seek(). The constructor for CSocketFile is:

```
CSocketFile( CSocket* pSocket, BOOL bArchiveCompatible = TRUE );
```

The CSocketFile class assumes that data is message-based. The buffer can contain multiple messages, so you can continue reading or writing until the buffer is empty.

Listing 25.4 shows a typical Serialize function to read or write a stream of data.

Listing 25.4. Calling the Serialize function with CArchive.

```
void CMyMsg::Serialize(CArchive& ar)
{
  if (ar.IsStoring())
  {
    ar << m_strText;
  }
  else
  {
ar >> m_strText;
  }
m_msgList.Serialize(ar);
}
```

A Simple Application to Check Whether You Have Any POP Mail

If you haven't done so, look at CHATTER and CHATSRVR, the MFC sample programs included with Visual C++ 4.0 that use MFC's CSocket class. This interesting sample enables you to have a chat server on your local network that multiple chat sessions go through. Several clients therefore can be chatting together.

This application is quite a bit simpler. POPCHK is a dialog-based application that does no more than display an iconized mailbox when minimized, as shown in Figures 25.4 and 25.5.

To create POPCHK use Visual C++ AppWizard to create a dialog-based application, POPCHK. The only option you need to add is the checkbox for Winsocket support.

If you have POP mail, the icon changes so that the flag of the mail box is in the up position. The source code is on the CD-ROM included with this book. In Chapters 26 and 27, you will build on this concept to create a program called NNTPBAT that periodically checks the mail and newsgroups, gets the data, and distributes it throughout your local network. This allows multiple users to have MSMAIL and an offline reader for newsgroups.

FIGURE 25.4.

The POPCHK dialog box.

FIGURE 25.5.

The POPCHK minimized icons. The icon on the left indicates you have mail.

POPCHK has three classes: the application, a dialog box, and `CPopSocket`, which you derive from `CSocket`, as shown in Listing 25.5.

Listing 25.5. The Popsock.H header file.

```
//POPSOCK.H
class CPopSocket : public CSocket
{
DECLARE_DYNAMIC(CPopSocket);

// Construction
public:
CPopSocket();

// Operations
public:
UINT m_messages;
int  m_bSent;
BOOL m_bWait;

enum{
  POP_HELO,
  POP_USER,
  POP_PASS,
  POP_STAT,
  POP_QUIT
};
```

continues

Listing 25.5. continued

```
BOOL GetPopMsg(int nSentFlag);

// Implementation

protected:
virtual void OnReceive(int nErrorCode);
};
```

POP3 is a simple protocol that you probably have seen working if you use Eudora or another common mail reader. You send simple messages like USER dave for the user name and PASS *mypassword* for the password. You probably have seen STAT, RETR 1, DELE 1, and QUIT flip by as your mail was retrieved. The CPopSocket class only has two member functions: one to get these POP3 messages and the other to handle error codes. Listing 25.6 shows the CPopSocket class.

Listing 25.6. POPSOCK.CPP file.

```
#include "stdafx.h"
#include "popchk.h"
#include "popsock.h"
#include <stddef.h>

#ifdef _DEBUG
#undef THIS_FILE
static char BASED_CODE THIS_FILE[] = __FILE__;
#endif

IMPLEMENT_DYNAMIC(CPopSocket, CAsyncSocket)

CPopSocket::CPopSocket()
{
  m_messages = 0;
}

void CPopSocket::OnReceive(int nErrorCode)
{
  CSocket::OnReceive(nErrorCode);
}

BOOL CPopSocket::GetPopMsg(int nSentFlag)
{
char buf [512];

if (Receive(buf, sizeof(buf)) > 0)
 {
  switch (nSentFlag)
   {
     case CPopSocket::POP_HELO:
     case CPopSocket::POP_QUIT:
     case CPopSocket::POP_USER:
     case CPopSocket::POP_PASS:
        if (strnicmp(buf,"-ERR", 4) == 0)
          {
          AfxMessageBox(IDS_BADPASSWD);
```

```
          return FALSE;
        }
        break;
    case CPopSocket::POP_STAT:
        if (strnicmp(buf,"-ERR", 4) == 0)
        {
        AfxMessageBox(IDS_BADSTATMSG);
        return FALSE;
        }

        for (char *p = buf; *p != '\0'; p++)
          {
           if (*p == '\t' || *p == ' ')
             {
             m_messages = atoi(p);
             return TRUE;
             }
          }
        break;
    }
 }
 return TRUE;
}
```

The only code here that you may not be familiar with is the call to the atoi function. This allows you to take a number passed to you as a string and transform it back to its integer values.

All the work in this application is done in the dialog class CPOPCHKDLG. The dialog-based application in Figure 25.4, allows the user to enter the four text fields m_mailbox, m_passwd, m_server, and m_minutes. When you start the program, InitDialog starts a timer with the member variable m_TimerID. Your OnPaint() checks whether you are IsIconic() and whether you received mail, and switches the icon to IDI_GOTMAIL.

When the timer goes off, it calls OnTimer(), which checks the mail via OnCheckMail(), as shown in Listing 25.7. This is the guts of the sample.

Listing 25.7. The Winsock is actually used in the OnCheckMail function.

```
BOOL CPopChkDlg::OnCheckMail()
{

  CPopSocket sock;
  char buf [40];

  sock.Create();
  if (!sock.Connect(m_server, 110)) // 110 Pop3 Port
    {
    AfxMessageBox(IDS_BADCONNECT);
    return FALSE;
    }
  sock.GetPopMsg(CPopSocket::POP_HELO);
```

continues

Listing 25.7. continued

```
wsprintf (buf, "USER %s\r\n", (LPCSTR) m_mailbox);
sock.Send(buf, strlen (buf));
sock.GetPopMsg(CPopSocket::POP_HELO);

wsprintf (buf, "PASS %s\r\n", (LPCSTR) m_passwd);
sock.Send(buf, strlen (buf));
sock.GetPopMsg(CPopSocket::POP_PASS);

strcpy (buf, "STAT\r\n");
sock.Send(buf, strlen (buf));
sock.GetPopMsg(CPopSocket::POP_STAT);

strcpy (buf, "QUIT\r\n");
sock.Send(buf, strlen(buf));
sock.GetPopMsg(CPopSocket::POP_QUIT);
sock.Close();

return sock.m_messages;
}
```

POP3 uses a well-known port, 110, with TCP, so you create a socket and then connect to the user's mail server, m_server, and port 110. To begin the conversation, you say hello as POP_HELO, send the user name and the password, get the status of the mail, and then quit.

You can use another function to reuse and hide passwords in other similar edit boxes, as shown in Listing 25.8.

Listing 25.8. Reusing and hiding passwords.

```
void CPopChkDlg::Crypt(CString &szPasswd, BOOL bEncode)
{
 int k = 0xAF;
 int c = 0;

 if (szPasswd.IsEmpty())
   return;

 for (int i = 0; i < szPasswd.GetLength(); i++)
 {
   c = szPasswd.GetAt(i); // get charcter at position i
   c = c ^ k;        //encrypt by OR with dec 175
   k = (bEncode) ? c : c ^ k;  //if bEncode true then return encrypt else decrypt
   szPasswd.SetAt(i, c);  //set character at position i
 }
}
```

This might be old hat to you, but if you are just starting out, it would take several minutes to decipher. This method steps through the password character by character in the for() loop. You assign the character at each position to c and then use the bitwise OR operator to mask with

0xAF (decimal 175) that you show the user. To get back, you just repeat this process, depending on whether you passed TRUE or FALSE to Crypt(). This function is called when you click the Apply button or change anything in the dialog's edit boxes. UpdateProfile() uses MFC's capability to save data in the POPCHK.INI file, so you write the actual OR value to this string as well.

The simplicity of this example should show you how easy it is to use these three classes to write a WinSock. You will find most of the common Winsocket source code on the Internet. These include such things as finger, MIME encoding, UUENCODE, and NNTP.

By collecting and building your own versions of these, you can enhance them to work in your environment. One simple step I took recently was to add a button bar item to my newsreader. All this button does is open an Access database, parse the news message I am reading, and store it. This way, I have a database of messages I read that I can sort and recall for a future book or when I get stuck but know I have read the answer before somewhere.

Summary

This chapter reviewed the history of the Internet and the development of small applications called sockets that work together across the many dissimilar computers making up the Internet. You have learned that by using standard protocols you can develop Winsockets to access data from the Internet.

You built a basic Winsocket that periodically alerts you if POP3 mail is available.

In the next chapter, "Using the Remote Access Server," you will see how your Windows NT computer can connect to remote computers or the Internet. You also see the host of NT features that allow it to work with a variety of network protocols.

Using the Remote Access Server

26

by David Hamilton

Prior to 1995, when we spoke of a network we usually meant our in-house connection between computers. Various software applications allowed you to use a modem to dial into a remote bulletin board or to allow your laptop to access files on the company's network. Then came the Internet explosion.

We now view our in-house network as a piece of a global network, the Internet. Many large companies have permanent Internet connections, but for most of us access to the Internet is still via modem. We dial-in to an Internet service provider. To make the Internet connection available to a host of NT applications, we make the connection through an application called the Remote Access Server (RAS).

Configuring RAS for NT 4.0

Before you can use RAS, you must set it up in NT 4.0. Follow these steps:

1. From the Control Panel, double-click the Network applet. The Network dialog box appears, as shown in Figure 26.1. Select the Services property page.

FIGURE 26.1.

The Network dialog box.

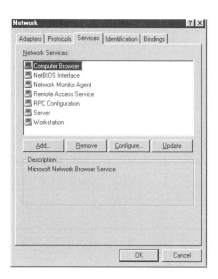

2. Choose Add, and select Remote Access Service (RAS) from the Select Network Service list box. If you haven't added RAS, you need to supply the path of the NT 4.0 CD-ROM with the "Have Disk" option.

3. When RAS is added, you are given the opportunity to configure it. The Remote Access Setup dialog box appears to confirm that your modem is your only network device, as shown in Figure 26.2. If you have installed an ISDN card, X.25 card or other multiport adapter you will also see these listed. NT will try to detect the modem on a serial port and list that for you. If its choice is wrong, you can choose configure and select the appropriate one from the list.

FIGURE 26.2.

The Remote Access Setup dialog box.

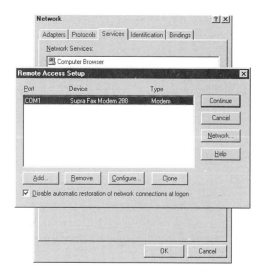

4. Click the Network button to display the Network Configuration dialog box (see Figure 26.3). You see three buttons under the heading Dial Out Protocols. NetBEUI and TCP/IP are selected. Leave only TCP/IP selected for now. Later if you have NetBEUI clients that wish to dial into your computer you can change this. Click OK, and then press OK in the Remote Access Setup dialog box. You then return to the Network dialog box.

FIGURE 26.3.

The Network Configuration dialog box.

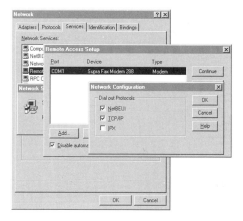

5. Confirm that both Remote Access Service and TCP/IP Protocol are installed, then click OK to exit the Network dialog box.

6. NT reconfigures your network bindings and then NT will ask if it's OK to restart your computer in order for your changes to take effect.

7. Start the Remote Access software and choose Add to set up a new phone book entry as in Figure 26.4.

FIGURE 26.4.

Adding a Phone Book entry to Remote Access Service.

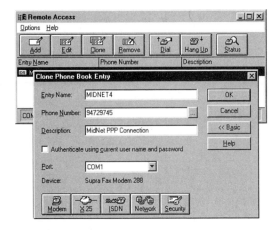

8. Confirm that your appropriate port and modem are shown. From the line of buttons at the bottom of the dialog box, click Modem. Set the initial speed and enable hardware flow control and modem error control. Then click OK.

9. Click the Network button in the bottom row and select PPP and TCP/IP as the protocol. Enable the Request LCP Connections checkbox. Then press the TCP/IP Settings button to access the PPP TCP/IP Settings dialog box (see Figure 26.5).

10. Your provider may not be PPP, but a SLIP connection. In this case, skip the next step.

11. Select Server Assigned IP Address, then select Use Specific Name Server Addresses, and fill in the primary and backup DNS addresses. Leave the WINS and WINS backup addresses at 0. Enable the Use VJ Header Compression checkbox, and enable the Use Default Gateway on Remote Network checkbox.

FIGURE 26.5.

Configuring RAS using a PPP connection.

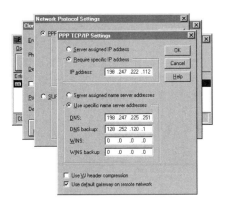

12. Click the Security button to access the Security Settings dialog box, as shown in Figure 26.6. Enable the Use Clear Text Terminal Logon Only checkbox. For Terminal or Script, set Before and After to None. Then click OK to exit this dialog box.

FIGURE 26.6.

The Security Settings dialog box.

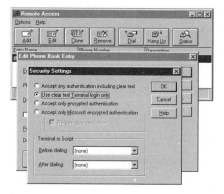

13. Highlight the phone book entry you just set up and click the Dial button. After the connect, the RAS Terminal window opens, and you are prompted by your ISP to log on.

14. When prompted, enter your Username followed by your password in the Password field. Next, you see a series of characters, just random ASCII characters coming across the phone line. When they start to appear, click the Done button. A `Verifying Username and Password` message appears. Then a message appears telling you that it is logging your computer onto the network. When the dialog box disappears, you are successfully logged on, and you can switch to your third-party network application.

15. Now you have confirmed that RAS works. The Remote Access application is minimized on NT 4.0's bottom service bar; maximize it and click the Hang Up button within Remote Access.

16. You can set up RAS so that you don't need to enter the username and password each time you connect. To do this you create a RAS script by editing the Switch.Inf file, which is located in WINNT\System32\RAS directory. You can edit the generic script by substituting your username and password; this is usually the only change needed.

17. Go back to the Remote Access software and choose the button to edit your current phone book entry. Check the Authenticate Using Current Username and Password. Click the Security button and the Security Settings dialog box appears, as shown in Figure 26.6. Select Accept Any Authentication Including Clear Text. In the Terminal or Script group, select the entry that corresponds to the script you added for your ISP in the After Dialing drop-down listbox. Then click OK to save the phone book entry. Choose the Dial button to confirm your script is working.

Remote Access Administrator Software to Allow Dial-in to Your NT Computer

Remote Access also enables remote users to connect to your Windows NT computer via dial-up lines using SLIP or PPP connections. We saw that your NT Workstation can dial-in to your Internet provider using RAS and then uses the host of WinSockets available as shareware to perform the usually Internet socket function. You also can use direct connections to an NT machine using RAS via ISDN, X.25, or a null modem.

NT can also be configured to accept remote access by using Remote Access Administrator software. This software starts the Remote Access Service and allows you to set up permissions for the users dialing in to your machine.

An NT Workstation can support two remote RAS clients dialing in to it. NT Advanced Server can support 256 clients. The Remote Access Administrator uses the same authentication and security features you are familiar with when logging onto any NT machine. Remote Access Server uses TCP/IP as its default, but clients can use either TCP/IP or NetBEUI to connect.

The NT software you will use is *Remote Access Administrator* (RASADMIN.EXE), shown in Figure 26.7, which enables you to grant access rights to dial-in users and restrict what they have access to on your machine and network.

FIGURE 26.7.

Remote Access Administrator defines the Permissions for remote users.

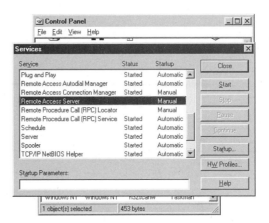

Writing Scripts to Control RASPHONE

In many applications you will have NT make the remote connection in the background using a RASPHONE script. A common use of a script would be a command file that on an hourly basis called your Internet provider and checked for mail and new postings to your subscribed Usenet groups.

RASPHONE.EXE has several switches to make its use easier in a command file. The syntax for RASPHONE follows:

```
rasphone [[[-e¦c¦r¦d¦h¦s¦q] entry]¦-a] [-f file]
```

Explanations of the syntax follow:

-a	Add Phone Book Entry mode
-c	Clone Phone Book Entry mode
-d	Dial Entry mode
-e	Edit Phone Book Entry mode
-f *file*	Full path for the phone book
-h	Hang Up Entry mode
-q	Prompt user before entering Dial Entry mode
-r	Remove Phone Book Entry mode
-s	Status Entry mode
entry	Entry name

Batch Programming

The mail application you started building in Chapter 25, "Windows Sockets," needs a simple command file that runs on a scheduled basis to get the company Internet mail and Usenet groups. This first command file sets up the Windows NT scheduler, or you can use WINAT.EXE from the resource kit:

```
//SceduleAt.cmd with new NT 4.0 batch cmd /c
for %%a in (5:00 9:00 10:00 11:00 12:00 13:00 14:00 15:00 16:00 17:00) do at %%a
/every:M,T,W,Th,F,S,Su "cmd.exe /c c:\netware\batch.cmd"
at
```

This causes your batch.cmd to run each hour, to get the POP3 mail, to convert it to MSMail, and also to get the newsgroups listed in the NNTPBAT.INI file you developed at the end of Chapter 3, "Execution Models." In the batch file, the only lines addressing RAS follow:

```
rasdial MIDNET Username Password
rasdial MIDNET /d
```

RasDial takes several other parameters, as shown in this example:

```
rasdial entryname [username [password¦*]] [/DOMAIN:domain]
                  [/PHONE:phonenumber] [/CALLBACK:callbacknumber]
                  [/PHONEBOOK:phonebookfile] [/PREFIXSUFFIX]
rasdial [entryname] /DISCONNECT
rasdial
```

The *entryname* is an entry in the phone book, rasphone.pbk, which looks much like an INI file. *domain* is the domain name of the NT Server that authenticates the logon. The documentation for manually editing the phone book files can be found in the Rasread.txt file in your WINNT\SYSTEM32\RAS directory. Windows 95 writes the same entries to the Registry, and you edit with the Dial-Up Networking folder. The PHONE and CALLBACK parameters enable you to designate an alternative number to call and to set up a system in which the called system calls you back to establish the connection.

An example of a RASPHONE command file is to automate Netscape to dial in, connect, and disconnect when you finish, as in the following code.

```
RASPHONE -d Entry-Name
RASMON
cd c:\netscape
c:\netscape\program\netscape.exe
RASDIAL Entry-Name /DISCONNECT
exit
```

Or, you might want to access CompuServe via PPP, as this code shows:

```
rasdial  -d CIS-PPP
RASMON
cd C:\CSERVE\WinCim
c:\cserve\wincim\wincim.exe
rasdial CIS-PPP /DISCONNECT
exit
```

To use CompuServe via a PPP connection instead of a direct dial-in, see the notes located at http:\\www.compuserve.com.

Here is my security setting, which points to a sequence of commands to execute. The after-dialing script is stored in the SWITCH.INF file under the [CIS-Internet] heading.

```
Security settings
   check Accept any authentication ....
   Terminal Scripts
     Before dialing    [none]
     After  dialing    [CIS-Internet]
```

In addition to the phone book entries, you can create logon scripts that are held together in a single file: SWITCH.INF. Because RAS reads this file only when it starts, if you modify a script in this file, you must restart RAS. The documentation for SWITCH.INF scripts is included in the file itself. The scripts are quite simple, as Listing 26.1 shows.

Listing 26.1. A sample SWITCH.INF file listing.

```
Switch.inf entry
[CIS-Internet]
COMMAND=<cr>
OK=<match>"e:"
ERROR_NO_CARRIER=<match>"NO CARRIER"
LOOP=<ignore>
COMMAND=+<cr>
OK=<match>"e:"
ERROR_NO_CARRIER=<match>"NO CARRIER"
LOOP=<ignore>
COMMAND=CIS<cr>
OK=<match>"D:"
ERROR_NO_CARRIER=<match>"NO CARRIER"
```

```
LOOP=<ignore>
COMMAND=YourCompuServeId/GO:PPPCONNECT<cr>
OK=<match>":"
ERROR_NO_CARRIER=<match>"NO CARRIER"
LOOP=<ignore>
COMMAND=YourPassword<cr>
CONNECT=<ignore>

[Dave's Login]  //script delimiter
COMMAND=     //set up the conversation
OK=<match>"ogin:" //wait for remote to ask login:
LOOP=<ignore>   //wait and ignore anything else sent
COMMAND=DaveHamilton<cr>  //send my username
OK=<match>"password:" //watch for remote to ask for password:
LOOP=<ignore>    //wait and ignore anything else sent
COMMAND=DaveH<cr>   //send my password
OK=<ignore>  //ignore rest of login info from remote
```

In this sample application, you set up a schedule that dials into the Internet provider on an hourly basis. It gets POP3 mail and converts that to SMTP mail. All the mail for all the users is put into the POSTMASTER account and then is re-sent out over your MSMAIL to each user. The application also gets the most recent postings from the subscribed Usenet newsgroups and puts them into the appropriate directories on the news spooler. The news is deleted on a periodic basis to keep the spoolers small. This application runs mainly in the background. It does have a simple dialog-based user interface that you can run manually (see Figure 26.8). In the next chapter, you develop the actual MAPI application and the mail spooler.

FIGURE 26.8.

Our sample dialog-based application, NNTP32.EXE.

Using the RASDial API

Microsoft has a sample program, RASberry, available in the books online, that uses the RasDial API. This sample dials into a service and also shows you how to access the rasphone.pbk file to get your existing connection information.

The DLL for this is RASAPI32.DLL, with the functions in the RASAPI32.LIB file. To access these functions, include RAS.H and RASERROR.H header files.

The function RasDial() establishes the connection by calling the Remote Access Connection Manager Service on your NT machine. When starting the connection, RasDial() specifies whether it is asynchronous or synchronous, and any RAS extensions that it will use. If this is a synchronous connection, RasDail() doesn't return until the connection is established or until it returns with an error code. An asynchronous connection returns immediately and you receive further connection information from a notification handler. This notification handler can be a window you specify for messages or the callback function RasDialFunc() or RasDialFunc1().

A callback function enables your application to go on doing its thing but to be notified if something happens to the RAS connection. This may be something like a line drop; if it is, you need to be told so that you can reestablish the connection.

Listing 26.2 shows the RasDial function.

Listing 26.2. The `RasDial` function syntax.

```
DWORD RasDial(
  LPRASDIALEXTENSIONS lpRasDialExtensions, // pointer to function extensions data
  LPTSTR lpszPhonebook,    // pointer to full path and filename of phonebook file
  LPRASDIALPARAMS lpRasDialParams,    // pointer to calling parameter's data
  DWORD dwNotifierType,    // specifies type of RasDial event handler
  LPVOID lpvNotifier,    // specifies a handler for RasDial events
  LPHRASCONN lphRasConn    // pointer to variable to receive connection handle
  );
```

The parameter is lpRasDialExtensions, which is NULL, or the RASDIALEXTENSIONS structure shown in Listing 26.3. The second parameter is a pointer to a string with the path of the phone book file, or NULL if you want to use rasphone. The third parameter, lpRasDialParams, points to the RASDIALPARAMS structure in Listing 26.3. The fourth and fifth parameters are dwNotifierType and lpvNotifier, which say where to notify if there is an error or change in connection state in asynchronous connections.

If dwNotifierType is 0, then lpvNotifier points to the function to call with RasDialFunc(). If dwNotifierType is 1, then lpvNotifier points to the function to call with RasDialFunc1(). Because 16-bit Window applications don't use callback functions, dwNotifierType can also be set to 0xFFFFFFFF. In this last case lpvNotifier is a handle to the window that should receive the error message. The value of NULL for lpvNotifier, indicates synchronous communication where there is no interruption.

Listing 26.3 shows the two structures.

Listing 26.3. The RASDIALEXTENSIONS and RASDIALPARAMS structures.

```
typedef  struct  _RASDIALEXTENSIONS {
    DWORD    dwSize; //size of this structure usually sizeof(RASDIALEXTENSIONS)
    DWORD    dwfOptions;
    HWND     hwndParent; //security login window handle or NULL
    DWORD    reserved;
} RASDIALEXTENSIONS;
```

```
typedef struct _RASDIALPARAMS {
  DWORD   dwSize;
  TCHAR   szEntryName[RAS_MaxEntryName + 1];
  TCHAR   szPhoneNumber[RAS_MaxPhoneNumber + 1]; //override phone book entry
  TCHAR   szCallbackNumber[RAS_MaxCallbackNumber + 1];
  TCHAR   szUserName[UNLEN + 1];
  TCHAR   szPassword[PWLEN + 1];
  TCHAR   szDomain[DNLEN + 1] ; //remote domain name that will authenticate
} RASDIALPARAMS;
```

Table 26.1 lists the parameters for dwfOptions.

Table 26.1. Possible settings for dwfOptions in the RASDIALEXTENSIONS structure.

Parameter	Function
RDEOPT_IgnoreModemSpeaker	Uses the setting in the phone book.
RDEOPT_SetModemSpeaker	Sets the modem speaker.
RDEOPT_IgnoreSoftwareCompression	Uses phone book settings.
RDEOPT_PausedStates	Specifies that you want RasDial to accept a paused state (like waiting for a callback connection).
RDEOPT_SetSoftwareCompression	Enables you to set the compression manually.
RDEOPT_UsePrefixSuffix	Uses the prefix and suffix from the phone book.

An asynchronous RasDial call must specify a notification handler. If the connection state changes or an error occurs, the Remote Access Connection Manager uses this handler to inform you, the RAS client, of the change.

In Win32, you are notified of the connection state change or error via a callback function; in 16-bit Windows, you use a window that receives the messages. If the callback indicates an error, you usually call RasHangUp to end the connection.

RasDialFunc() and RasDialFunc1() are for asynchronous connections, and your RasDial connection operation is suspended during a call to a RasDialFunc callback function. For that reason, your RasDialFunc implementation should generally return as soon as possible. The RasDailFunc function syntax is as follows:

```
VOID RasDialFunc(
  UINT unMsg,  // must by WM_RASDIALEVENT
  RASCONNSTATE rasconnstate,  // connection state from enum RASCONNSTATE
  DWORD dwError  // error that may have occurred or zero
  );
```

`RasDialFunc1()` is the same, but with extended error information provided by having a handle to the RAS connection. The syntax for `RasDainFunc1` is as follows.

```
VOID RasDialFunc1(

   HRASCONN hrasconn,  // handle to RAS connection
   UINT unMsg, // type of event that has occurred will be WM_RASDIALEVENT
   RASCONNSTATE rascs,  // connection state about to be entered
   DWORD dwError, // error that may have occurred
   DWORD dwExtendedError  // extended error information for some errors
   );
```

Both these functions take the connection state you are entering, which can be one of the values in the RASCONNSTATE enumeration, as Listing 26.4 shows.

Listing 26.4. The definition of the RASCONNSTATE enumeration.

```
typedef enum _RASCONNSTATE {
    RASCS_OpenPort = 0,  //port about to be opened
    RASCS_PortOpened, //port opened
    RASCS_ConnectDevice, //device is about to be connected
    RASCS_DeviceConnected, //device is successfully connected
    RASCS_AllDevicesConnected, //all devices successfully connected
    RASCS_Authenticate, //authenticate process starting
    RASCS_AuthNotify, //authenticate has occurred
    RASCS_AuthRetry, //client is retry on authenticate
    RASCS_AuthCallback, //remote is requesting a callback
    RASCS_AuthChangePassword, //client wants to change password
    RASCS_AuthProject, //projection phase is starting
    RASCS_AuthLinkSpeed, //link speed calculation is starting
    RASCS_AuthAck, //authentication is acknowledged
    RASCS_ReAuthenticate, //reauthentication is starting
    RASCS_Authenticated, //client is authenticated
    RASCS_PrepareForCallback, //line is about to disconnect to wait for callback
    RASCS_WaitForModemReset, //client is delayed to give modem time to reset
    RASCS_WaitForCallback,//client is waiting for callback
    RASCS_Projected, //projection results are available
 #if (WINVER >= 0x400) //for Windows 95
    RASCS_StartAuthentication,    // Windows 95 only
    RASCS_CallbackComplete,       // Windows 95 only
    RASCS_LogonNetwork,           // Windows 95 only
#endif
      RASCS_Interactive = RASCS_PAUSED, //terminal state of RASPHONE.EXE
    RASCS_RetryAuthentication, //RASPHONE.EXE is retry on authentication
    RASCS_CallbackSetByCaller, //RASPHONE.EXE is callback state
    RASCS_PasswordExpired, //RASPHONE.EXE reports password expired
      RASCS_Connected = RASCS_DONE,
    RASCS_Disconnected
} RASCONNSTATE ;
```

A RAS connection is in one of three states: running, paused, or done. Using Listing 26.4, you can determine which state your connection is in and write your application to respond by using this code:

```
fDoneState = (state & RASCS_DONE);
fPausedState = (state & RASC_PAUSED);
fRunState = !(fDoneState ¦¦ fPausedState);
```

`RasEnumConnections` and `RasEnumEntries` give you information about the connection and the entry. They both return this information via buffers, as Listing 26.5 shows.

Listing 26.5. The syntax for the `RasEnumConnections` and `RasEnumEntries` functions.

```
DWORD RasEnumConnections(
    LPRASCONN lprasconn,  // buffer to receive connections data
    LPDWORD lpcb,  // size in bytes of buffer
    LPDWORD lpcConnections  // number of connections written to buffer
  )

DWORD RasEnumEntries (
    LPTSTR reserved,  // reserved, must be NULL
    LPTSTR lpszPhonebook,  // pointer to full path and filename of phonebook file
    LPRASENTRYNAME lprasentryname,  // buffer to receive phonebook entries
    LPDWORD lpcb,  // size in bytes of buffer
    LPDWORD lpcEntries  // number of entries written to buffer
  );
typedef struct _RASCONN {
    DWORD      dwSize; //size of this struct usually sizeof(RASCONN)
    HRASCONN   hrasconn; //your connection handle
    TCHAR      szEntryName[RAS_MaxEntryName + 1]; //phone book entry
} RASCONN ;

typedef struct _RASENTRYNAME {
    DWORD  dwSize; //usually sizeof(RASENTRYNAME)
    TCHAR  szEntryName[RAS_MaxEntryName + 1]; //remote phonebook entry
}RASENTRYNAME;
```

The other last status functions are `RasGetConnectStatus`, `RasGetErrorString`, and `RasGetProjectionInfo`. `RasGetConnectStatus` tells you whether you are connected or disconnected, to what device, and the device name. `RasGetErrorString` returns a string with the RAS error that you pass in the error code. `RasGetProjectionInfo` tells you whether the connection is IPX, IP, AMB (NetBIOS), or Nbf (NetBEUI).

Listing 26.6. The `RasGetConnectStatus`, `RasGetErrorString`, and `RasGetProjectionInfo` functions and their syntax.

```
DWORD RasGetConnectStatus(
    HRASCONN hrasconn,  // handle to RAS connection of interest
    LPRASCONNSTATUS lprasconnstatus  // buffer to receive status data
  );

typedef struct _RASCONNSTATUS {
    DWORD          dwSize; //size of this struct usually sizeof(RASCONNSTATUS)
    RASCONNSTATE   rasconnstate; //either RASCS_Connected or RASCS_Disconnected
```

continues

Listing 26.6. continued

```
    DWORD        dwError; //if non zero error code
    TCHAR        szDeviceType[RAS_MaxDeviceType + 1]; //
"modem","pad","sitch","isdn"or "null"
    TCHAR        szDeviceName[RAS_MaxDeviceName + 1]; //"Supra288"
} RASCONNSTATUS;


DWORD RasGetErrorString (
    UINT uErrorValue,  // error to get string for
    LPTSTR lpszErrorString,  // buffer to hold error string
    DWORD cBufSize  // size, in characters, of buffer
    );

DWORD RasGetProjectionInfo(
    HRASCONN hrasconn,    // handle that specifies remote access connection of
➥interest
    RASPROJECTION rasprojection,      // specifies type of projection information
➥to obtain
    LPVOID lpprojection,    // points to buffer that receives projection
➥information
    LPDWORD lpcb    // points to variable that specifies buffer size
    );
typedef enum _RASPROJECTION {

    RASP_Amb = 0x10000,
    RASP_PppNbf = 0x803F,
    RASP_PppIpx = 0x802B,
    RASP_PppIp = 0x8021
} RASPROJECTION ;
```

The RasHangUp function hangs up the connection and cleans up after RAS. RasHangUp takes just the handle to the connection, as shown in this code:

```
DWORD RasHangUp( HRASCONN hrasconn );
```

Your connection is terminated even if the RasDial call has not yet been completed. An application should not call RasHangUp and then immediately exit. The connection state machine needs time to properly terminate. If the system prematurely terminates the state machine, the state machine may fail to properly close a port, leaving the port in an inconsistent state. A simple way to avoid this problem is to call Sleep(3000) after returning from RasHangUp; after that pause, the application can exit. This is the method you usually will see, but the recommended way is to call RasGetConnectStatus(hrasconn) and Sleep(0) in a loop until RasGetConnectStatus returns ERROR_INVALID_HANDLE.

Four functions use the Windows 95 Registry to get and set phone book entries: RasCreatePhonebookEntry, RasEditPhonebookEntry, RasGetEntryDialParams, and RasSetEntryDialParams.

There are four possible structures depending on the network protocol you're using.

The RAS-AMB structure is defined as follows.

```
RASAMB
typedef  struct  _RASAMB {
    DWORD     dwSize; //sizeof(RASAMB)
    DWORD     dwError; //if non zero this is error code
    TCHAR     szNetBiosError[ NETBIOS_NAME_LEN + 1 ];
    BYTE      bLana; //NetBIOS addapter LANA or 0xFF is not connected
} RASAMB;
```

If the function returns the value `ERROR_NAME_EXISTS_ON_NET` then `szNetBiosError` contains a string with the NetBIOS name that caused the error. In addition to AMB, there are structures for PPP via IP, NBF, and IPX.

The RAS-PPP-IP structure is defined as follows.

```
typedef  struct  _RASPPPIP {
    DWORD     dwSize; //usually sizeof(RASPPPIP)
    DWORD     dwError; //if not zero then error code
    TCHAR     szIpAddress[ RAS_MaxIpAddress + 1 ]; //clients IP address
} RASPPPIP;
```

The RAS-PPP-IPX structure is defined as follows.

```
typedef  struct  _RASPPPIPX {
    DWORD     dwSize; //usually sizeof(RASPPPIPX)
    DWORD     dwError; //if not zero then error code
    TCHAR     szIpxAddress[ RAS_MaxIpxAddress + 1 ]; //clients IPX address
} RASPPPIPX;
```

The RAS-PPP-NBF structure is defined as follows.

```
typedef  struct  _RASPPPNBF {
    DWORD     dwSize; // usually sizeof(RASPPPNBF)
    DWORD     dwError; //if not zero then error code
    DWORD     dwNetBiosError;
    TCHAR     szNetBiosError[ NETBIOS_NAME_LEN + 1 ];
    TCHAR     szWorkstationName[ NETBIOS_NAME_LEN + 1 ]; //local computer name
    BYTE      bLana; //NetBios adapter LANA or 0xFF if no connection
} RASPPPNBF;
```

If `dwError` has the value `ERROR_SERVER_NOT_RESPONDING` or `ERROR_NETBIOS_ERROR`, the `dwNetBiosError` field contains the NetBIOS error that occurred. If `dwError` has the value `ERROR_NAME_EXISTS_ON_NET`, the `szNetBiosError` field contains a zero-terminated string that is the NetBIOS name that caused the conflict.

Dialing in to RAS

With NT 4.0 and RAS, you can dial-in to your NT workstation or server using the RASADMIN software. This functions like Symantec's PCANYWHERE software and enables the computer dialing in to see the entire network if it has permissions. Figure 26.9 shows a sample dialog box for RASADMIN.

FIGURE 26.9.

Setting up RASADMIN to enable the dial-in capability.

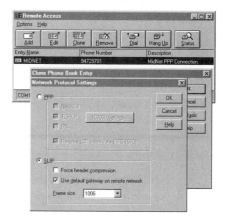

NT maintains security with the dial-in clients, and you can enforce callback connections for even greater security. The dial-in machine needs to have privileges set up like any other NT user.

After it is connected, the NT client sees the network just as a local machine would. Drives can be mapped and the NT Explorer software can be used to copy files. I use this type of setup with a null-modem cable when I bring my laptop to the office. The laptop calls into my NT Workstation and transfers files. Remote users can do the same and retrieve their mail.

Because the modem connection is slow compared to 10mbps or 100mbps Ethernet cards, you shouldn't expect to see blazing speed. With Windows NT and RAS you can also run applications remotely. They actually seem much faster than you would expect over a modem. This is because Windows sends messages rather than an entire screen. Still, don't expect to run Visual C++ 4.1 over a phone line and set any records building your application.

Summary

In this chapter you learned how to install Remote Access Services. You saw how to create phone book entries and use RAS scripts to automate on-line connections. You also learned how NT 4.0's WinSocket applications can perform common activities on the Internet. You developed sample scripts for RAS then wrote command files to automate the gathering of Internet mail to be read later offline.

In the next chapter you learn how to program the messaging API, MAPI. This small API is used to coordinate e-mail within an NT environment. Your Windows NT application can forward mail, reformat the mail, and finally store mail in the NT Exchange database. You will develop a sample application that transfers Internet mail from POP3 to NT's local SMTP mail environment.

Using the Messaging API

27

by David Hamilton

Nearly all organizations during the past five years have found that e-mail has grown from a convenience to a central function. When it first was introduced, most companies thought it was a waste of time; hundreds of messages did no more than document the latest Elvis sightings or gossip, and the sheer volume took up tons of hard drive space. But its usefulness grew: It was a way to contact others in the same office or across the world without both parties having to stop work to answer the phone. You could now contact people whose exact location you didn't know. E-mail became the method to send and receive documents in a form that both parties could edit. It also was a way to distribute organizational materials in a rapid, timely manner and receive notification that the materials were received.

I remember working at Comdex in a booth next to a vendor selling uninterruptible power supplies. I really had an awakening as I watched their staff from the show floor entering marketing reports on the competition, which were sent back immediately to the home office using Lotus Notes. Applications such as Lotus Notes allowed businesses to organize around a centralized information application. People from all around the company filed marketing reports into a central area where people in marketing could actually see them. Policy manuals were stored in another area, and users could check that they actually had been read. Administration could quickly supply employees with the information they needed to do their jobs. E-mail had become the centralized information backbone of the enterprise. If only all that mail was now organized.

A second revelation came at a developers' conference, where an acquaintance from another small medical company had a Motorola version of the Apple Newton, which silently sat and blinked red and green lights. As we sat through the sessions, he was quietly sending and receiving customer support e-mail. If only all mail came across the ARDIS network. ARDIS is a two-way packet radio network available in approximately 90% of the U.S. Initially it was developed as IBM's internal field service network but has been expanded to many commercial uses and now allows for individual customers. It provides communication at 19200 bps from inside buildings and also includes a gateway to the Internet.

One problem I found while developing our company's e-mail solution was that hundreds of messaging programs and solutions existed, and each used their own format and interface. The mail programs used internally didn't talk to the Internet mail. Microsoft and other mail software vendors recognized this and formed a common way to share information called the *Messaging API* (MAPI).

MAPI is a common application interface that enables developers to shield users from the differences in the various mail systems they use. In this chapter, you develop a sample application that retrieves mail from a POP3 server for a group of people and redistributes that mail to each user's desk via MSMail. It collects their outbound mail and sends it to the POP3 server. This application runs hourly.

Using the MAPI

MAPI is a DLL, MAPI32.DLL (16 bit is MAPI.DLL), and a series of header files—the most often used is MAPI.H for the MAPI32.LIB. These provide an open programming interface that is integrated with the NT operating system. Your messages can come from a wide variety of sources, such as a fax, the Internet, voice mail, or documents. These messages are stored in a central inbox. Microsoft describes this as a concept similar to Windows printing. The software doesn't care what printer is installed; it prints to Windows in a consistent fashion and lets Windows handle the print driver. MAPI is the same: Your application doesn't need to know which application generated the messages or to which it is being sent, and messages are handled in a similar fashion.

MAPI-compliant objects conform to the OLE Component Object Model (COM), which is becoming part of nearly every API you as a programmer will use. Again, you don't need to be able to write an OLE application to use MAPI—the complexity is hidden within the API.

Adding MAPI support to your application could not be easier. There really is no reason why you shouldn't enable most applications when you create a new AppWizard application. In the AppWizard's step 4, you simply check the MAPI (Messaging API) support box, as Figure 27.1 shows.

FIGURE 27.1.

Adding basic MAPI support.

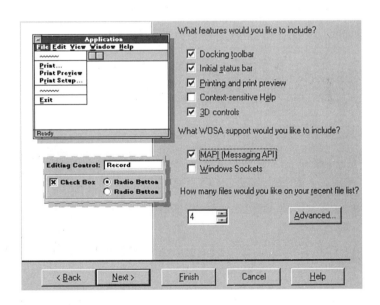

When you enable this checkbox, the AppWizard adds a Send option that is added to the File menu. This menu item has the ID assigned to it ID_FILE_SEND_MAIL. In the AppWizard's document file for the application you will see AppWizard added these two lines:

```
ON_COMMAND(ID_FILE_SEND_MAIL, OnFileSendMail)
ON_UPDATE_COMMAND_UI(ID_FILE_SEND_MAIL, OnUpdateFileSendMail);
```

You can just as quickly add MAPI send support to any existing application by adding the Send menu item and calling the `CDocument:OnFileSendMail` function, which works like saving files using the `Serialize` function. The `Serialize` function call is equivalent to a File Save command that saves (serializes) the document's contents to the mail message instead of a file. This implementation calls on the MSMail client on the user's machine to give the user the opportunity to address the mail and to add subject and message text to the mail message. You can see it takes very little effort to add the most basic MAPI support to your application.

The functions `OnFileSendMail` and `OnUpdateFileSendMail` are in the MFC source file DOCMAPI.CPP. This is a good place to begin to understand MAPI and would be worth your time to print the file and study it. The `OnFileSendMail` first ensures that MSMail is available. It takes the current frontmost document and makes up a title calling `MAPIFileDesc` and then uses `MAPIMessage` to hold the document's data. Lastly, it uses the function `MAPISendMail`.

Microsoft divides applications into three types: messaging-aware, messaging-enabled, and messaging-based. The first two types are applications that have another primary function but can benefit from using a MAPI interface, especially like the sample application, which robs existing code and uses a familiar existing MAPI interface: MSMail. MSMail is a messaging-enabled application, whereas the simple example used here is messaging-aware. The third type is an application that is based primarily on messaging. It exchanges information from one format to another. Scheduling and work-flow applications are messaging-based.

Although you usually will build client applications, MAPI is a dual interface with separate APIs for the client and the messaging systems.

The sample application just uses the MAPI spooler and the MSMail interface. MAPI supplies the common dialog boxes used with MSMail, but your application can use its own interface. Client applications also can use three other interfaces to MAPI:

- **Simple MAPI:** The C++ or Visual Basic API interface using the MAPI32.DLL.
- **Common messaging calls (CMC):** Another API function-based interface for C/C++ clients for the cross-platform XAPIA development. Similar CMC function calls exist that correspond to each of the MAPI API function calls.

NOTE

You use full MAPI to design a work group application in which you provide services such as the phone book, a transport, or a full messaging system to the user. Lotus Notes is an example of a full MAPI-enabled application.

- **OLE messaging:** The developer uses direct OLE Automation programming and the OLE Messaging Library functions. MAPI inherits from OLE's `IUknown` and enables you to use OLE objects to write an application that deals with messaging on a much lower level.

Table 27.1 compares the four routes your application might use in providing MAPI services. You would choose the route based on the level of support you want to provide, your programming experience, the platform for which you are developing, and whether you want to control the MAPI process by using your own forms presented to your user to gather the necessary message and routing information.

Table 27.1. OLE Messaging Library allows C/C++, VB, and VBA developers to use OLE objects to support messaging when each form of MAPI is used.

Issues	CMC	Simple MAPI	MAPI	OLE Messaging
Messaging support	Low	Low	High	Medium
Prerequisite knowledge	None	None	OLE COM	OLE Automation
Forms support	None	None	Full	Some
Platforms	Cross	Windows	Windows	Windows

Figure 27.2 shows the basic MAPI architecture.

FIGURE 27.2.

MAPI architecture.

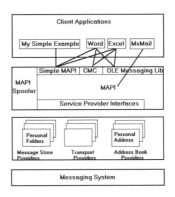

MAPI is a set of components: the client, the messaging service, the spooler, and the transport service. All these components work together, as shown in Figure 27.3.

A client application with the simple Send option is messaging-aware. MAPI provides a powerful set of object-oriented functions to the client that enable you to share structure and behavior between objects—in other words, to use a common interface. By using the COM model and OLE, developers create objects in a common way, access messages, assign recipient properties, customize views of messages, and use the address book.

FIGURE 27.3.

MAPI components.

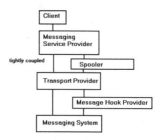

Three types of service providers exist: the message store, the address book, and the message transport. A vendor may provide all of these in one application or just a single service, such as a new address book. The providers each have profiles in the MAPISVC.INF file. One user can have several profiles—one might be internal messages, whereas another might be messages to be posted on the Internet.

The Messaging Service Provider usually sets up a hierarchy of folders that hold messages. This may be a simple structure, such as an inbox and outbox, or it may be as complex as the CompuServe forums. The folders organize the messages. The service provider's job is to be the message store. The message store provider checks the recipient address and puts the message in the outbound queue. This can be directly routed to the transport provider in a tightly coupled application or to the spooler when the transport is not available.

The spooler sends and receives messages from the message system. It also stores the messages and delivers them when the transport or message service becomes available. Remember that messages are bidirectional. The spooler tracks the recipients, informs clients when new messages are available, may do some pre- or post-transport processing of the message, generates delivery reports, and maintains the status of recipients.

Messages are created in a form appropriate for the type of message. You usually have a note and one or more recipients. This can become much more complex when you think of an OLE compound document, however. A form has three components. The *Form Registry Provider* is a library of all the forms available to the user. The *form server* displays the form. The *Form view* is the container for the display.

A recipient can be in an address book or a custom recipient for one-time delivery.

The transport provider performs pre- and post-transport processing. The spooler decides which transport can handle the message and forwards the message.

Service providers translate requests from MAPI-compliant applications into specific messages that the provider can understand. MAPI has strong ties to database and data-handling APIs. Remember that a message doesn't need to be just text e-mail. Messages can be OLE objects, video, sound, or graphics.

Using the MAPI SDK

MAPI was installed with VC++ 4.x, or you can install the MAPI SDK from the Win32 SDK provided on the MSDN Level 2 CD-ROMs. Both VC++ 4.x and the SDK consists of a setup program, several header files, the libraries and DLLs, the MAPI executables, the samples and service provider DLLs, the spooler, and the Help files. The only added benefit with the Win32 SDK is that you have access to the 16-bit development tools that are not included with VC++ 1.52c.

Table 27.2 lists the sample code included in the SDK.

Table 27.2. SDK sample code.

Code	Function
ABVIEW.DLL	Tool for displaying and changing address book objects
MDBVIEW.DLL	Tool for displaying and changing message store objects
PROPVU.DLL	Tool for displaying and changing properties
SAMPLE.AB	Sample address book provider written in C
SAMPLE.ABS	Sample address book provider written in C++
SAMPLE.CLI	Sample Simple MAPI client application
SAMPLE.EXT	Sample client extensions
SAMPLE.MS	Sample message store provider written in C
SAMPLE.MXP	Sample transport provider written in C
SAMPLE.PR	Sample profile provider written in C
SAMPLE.RAD	Sample server-based messaging host
SAMPLE.SH	Sample hook service provider written in C
SAMPLE.TNF	Sample transport provider written in C++
SAMPLE.XCL	Sample MAPI client application
SAMPLE.XP	Sample transport provider written in C
SAMPLE1.FRM	Sample form
SMH	Sample message-handling hook written in C
SMPCLI	Sample Simple MAPI client application
SMPCMC.CLI	Sample CMC client application
SMPLROUT.CLI	Sample MAPI client application for routing

The MAPI functions are broken into two sets: the core set for the Simple MAPI features and an auxiliary set. This chapter focuses on the core functions you will use in your sample application. As you develop more complex applications, you can use a combination of several of the MAPI forms, and Microsoft provides a set of functions that enable you to combine the forms and move messages between formats.

Table 27.3 lists the 12 high-level Simple MAPI functions that enable a client application to send, address, receive, and reply to messages. Messages sent using Simple MAPI even can include file attachments and OLE objects.

Table 27.3. Simple MAPI function calls.

MAPI Call	*Function*
MAPIAddress MAPIDetails MAPIResolveName	Handle addressing chores, such as creating addresses, looking up addresses, and resolving friendly names with e-mail names.
MAPIDeleteMail	Saves or deletes a specified mail message.
MAPIFindNext	Lists information about messages meeting specific criteria.
MAPIFree	Frees the memory allocated by the messaging service.
MAPILogoff	Terminates a session with the messaging service.
MAPILogon	Establishes a session with the messaging service.
MAPIReadMail	Read a specified mail message.
MAPISaveMail	Saves a specified mail message.
MAPISendDocuments	Sends a standard mail message. This call always prompts with a dialog box for the recipient's name and other sending options. It is intended primarily for use with a scripting language, such as a spreadsheet macro.
MAPISendMail	Sends a standard mail message. Messages can be sent without any user interaction, or users can be prompted via a common user interface (dialog box).

MAPI provides a set of common dialog boxes that enable you to present a familiar interface to the user. The MAPI user interface includes many different dialog boxes—some for session startup, some for addressing, and some for message composition. You use the message composition dialog boxes to create interpersonal messages, to create messages of other types, and to implement special dialog boxes or forms that can be provided by the originator of the message type.

It's a good idea to review the sample application you are developing before beginning to build it. You started out with a CMD file that runs on an hourly basis. It uses RASDIAL to call your local Internet provider and to download the POP3 mail for a group of users, as well as the Usenet newsgroups to which the users have subscribed. After you gather this information, you send the POP3 mail to the Postmaster account in MSMail, where it is redistributed internally to the users. The main application is nntpbat32.exe, which you will develop here and is included on the accompanying CD-ROM.

Getting Started with MAPI Development, the Session

Before your application can call the available messaging system, you need to log on (or *establish a session*, as it's referred to in MAPI). Simple MAPI clients call the MAPILogon function. This is a four-step process:

1. Determine that Simple MAPI is available by checking the Registry [MAIL] Windows Messaging Subsystem key for the MAPI entry. This entry has a value of 1 if Simple MAPI is installed or 0 if it is uninstalled.

2. Load the correct DLL for your operating system by calling the Windows LoadLibrary function:

   ```
   hlibMAPI = LoadLibrary("MAPI32.DLL");
   ```

3. Set the pointer variable to the actual address of the MAPILogon function:

   ```
   lpfnMAPILogon = (LPFNMAPILOGON) GetProcAddress (hlibMAPI, "MAPILogon")
   ```

4. Call the function, as in this line from the example POP3.C:

   ```
   (*lpfnMAPILogon)(hDlg, (LPSTR) "Postmaster",(LPSTR) "password",
   MAPI_NEW_SESSION,0L,  (LPLHANDLE) &hMAPISession );
   ```

Listing 27.1 provides the format of the function.

Listing 27.1. The MAPILogon function syntax.

```
ULONG FAR PASCAL MAPILogon {ULONG ulUIParam, //parent window
  LPTSTR lpszProfileName, //username
   LPTSTR lpszPassword, //password
  FLAGS flFlags,
  ULONG ulReserved,  //always OL
  LPLHANDLE lplhSession //handle to session
   )
```

The `flFlags` parameter can be one of the parameters listed in Table 27.4.

Table 27.4. `flFlags` parameters.

Parameter	Function
MAPI_FORCE_DOWNLOAD	Indicates that an attempt should be made to download all the user's messages before returning. If the MAPI_FORCE_DOWNLOAD flag is not set, messages can be downloaded in the background after the function call returns.
MAPI_LOGON_UI	Indicates that a logon dialog box should be displayed to prompt the user for logon information. If the user needs to provide a password and profile name to enable a successful logon, MAPI_LOGON_UI must be set.
MAPI_NEW_SESSION	Indicates that an attempt should be made to create a new session rather than acquire the environment's shared session. If the MAPI_NEW_SESSION flag is not set, MAPILogon uses an existing shared session.
MAPI_PASSWORD_UI	Indicates that MAPILogon should prompt only for a password and not allow the user to change the profile name. MAPI_PASSWORD_UI and MAPI_LOGON_UI should not be set, because the intent is to select between two dialog boxes for logon.

Table 27.5 lists the values returned from the `MAPILogon` function.

Table 27.5. The `MAPILogon` function's possible return values.

Value	Indicates That
MAPI_E_FAILURE	One or more unspecified errors occurred during logon. No session handle was returned.
MAPI_E_INSUFFICIENT_MEMORY	There was insufficient memory to proceed. No session handle was returned.
MAPI_E_LOGIN_FAILURE	There was no default logon, and the user failed to log on successfully when the logon dialog box was displayed. No session handle was returned.

Value	Indicates That
MAPI_E_TOO_MANY_SESSIONS	The user had too many sessions open simultaneously. No session handle was returned.
MAPI_E_USER_ABORT	The user canceled the logon dialog box. No session handle was returned.
SUCCESS_SUCCESS	The call succeeded and a Simple MAPI session was established.

Everything in Simple MAPI is centered on this session, and the handle you received with the call to MAPILogon. Two types of sessions exist: temporary and persistent. A *temporary* session exists only for the lifetime of a single Simple MAPI call. A *persistent* session exists until the session is explicitly closed. Establishing a temporary session is referred to as *implicit* logon; establishing a persistent session is called *explicit* logon. Clients can use a persistent session for all calls that require the same set of providers and a temporary session for single calls that do not require the same context.

To end a session, you log off by calling the MAPILogoff function to close the session. You then call the MAPIFreeBuffer function to release any buffers allocated by Simple MAPI calls and returned to your client for its use. Calling MAPILogoff does not cause buffers allocated by Simple MAPI calls to be released. Your client has that responsibility.

In this chapters sample application, POP3, this is done with the following code:

```
(*lpfnMAPILogoff)(hMAPISession, hDlg, 0L, 0L);
GlobalUnlock (hMailUsers);
GlobalFree (hMailUsers);
```

The parameters are the session handle, the dialog handle, and two reserved parameters that are always 0. Table 27.6 lists the values returned by the MAPILogoff function.

Table 27.6. The MAPILogoff function's possible return values.

Value	Indicates That
MAPI_E_FAILURE	The flFlags parameter is invalid, or one or more unspecified errors occurred.
MAPI_E_INSUFFICIENT_MEMORY	There was insufficient memory to proceed. The session was not terminated.
MAPI_E_INVALID_SESSION	An invalid session handle was used for the lhSession parameter. The session was not terminated.
SUCCESS_SUCCESS	The call succeeded and the session was terminated.

Moving Messages and Using the Session

To create a new message, your application first allocates a MAPIMessage structure, fills the structure members, and submits the structure to the messaging system by calling MAPISendMail. In the POP3.C sample code, this converts the POP3.C message, reformats it, and sends it, as shown in Listing 27.2.

Listing 27.2. The POP3 sample's code to format POP3 mail to MSMail.

```
int Pop3ToMSMail (LPSTR lpszName)
{
MAPIMessage mmMessage;
MAPIRecipDesc mmRecip;

DWORD ulResult;
char subject [256];

memset (&mmMessage, '\0', sizeof (MAPIMessage));
memset (&mmRecip, '\0', sizeof (MAPIRecipDesc));

GetSubjectLine ((LPSTR) &subject [0], sizeof (subject));

mmRecip.ulReserved = 0L;
mmRecip.ulRecipClass = MAPI_TO;
mmRecip.lpszName = lpszName;

mmMessage.nRecipCount = 1L;
mmMessage.lpRecips = &mmRecip;
mmMessage.lpszNoteText = FixText ();
mmMessage.lpszSubject = (LPSTR) &subject [0];


mmMessage.lpOriginator = NULL;
mmMessage.nFileCount = 0L;
mmMessage.lpFiles = NULL;
mmMessage.flFlags = MAPI_UNREAD;

// send the message to MSMail
// check the return value here

ulResult = (*lpfnMAPISendMail)(
    hMAPISession,
    0L,
    (lpMAPIMessage) &mmMessage,
    0L,
    0L);

return (SUCCESS_SUCCESS == ulResult);
}
```

A MAPIMessage structure contains information about a message, as shown in Listing 27.3.

Listing 27.3. The MAPIMessage structure.

```
typedef struct {
     ULONG ulReserved;  //must be zero
     LPTSTR lpszSubject; //subject line 256 bytes
     LPTSTR lpszNoteText; //message text
     LPTSTR lpszMessageType; //message type
     LPTSTR lpszDateReceived; //Date received
     LPTSTR lpszConversationID; //thread to which message belongs
     FLAGS flFlags;       //MAPI_SENT. MAPI_UNREAD or MAPI_RECEIPT_REQUESTED
     lpMAPIRecipDesc lpOriginator; // sender
     ULONG nRecipCount;      //number of recipient structures
     lpMAPIRecipDesc lpRecips;       //recipient structure
     ULONG nFileCount;      //attached file number
     lpMAPIFileDesc lpFiles; //attached files
} MAPIMessage, FAR *lpMAPIMessage;
```

Listing 27.4 shows the MAPISendMail function syntax.

Listing 27.4. The MAPISendMail function's syntax.

```
ULONG FAR PASCAL MAPISendMail (
   LHANDLE lhSession,  //session handle
   ULONG ulUIParam, //dialog handle
   lpMAPIMessage lpMessage, //our MAPI message structure
   FLAGS flFlags, //MAPI_DIALOG, MAPI_LOGIN_UI or MAPI_NEW_SESSION
   ULONG ulReserved  //always zero
   )
```

To forward an existing message, you use the same process as in sending a message. You first retrieve the message by calling the MAPIReadMail function. Modify the message structure as you want and add the new recipients' addresses in the message's lpRecips member. Modify the subject line to indicate that the message has been forwarded. Allow the user to edit the message body. Submit it to the messaging system by calling the MAPISendMail function.

Listing 27.5 shows the syntax of MAPIReadMail.

Listing 27.5. The MAPIReadMail function's syntax.

```
ULONG FAR PASCAL MAPIReadMail (
   LHANDLE lhSession,   //session handle
   ULONG ulUIParam, //dialog handle
   LPTSTR lpszMessageID, //message stucture
   FLAGS flFlags, //MAPI_BODY_AS_FILE, MAPI_ENVELOPE_ONLY,
MAPI_PEEK,MAPI_SUPPRESS_ATTACH
   ULONG ulReserved, //always zero
   lpMAPIMessage FAR * lppMessage
   )
```

You reply to a message in much the same way that you retrieve the message—by calling the MAPIReadMail function. Modify the message as appropriate. Put the original sender's address into the lpRecips member. Change the subject line to indicate that the message is a reply to an earlier message. Allow the user to edit the message body then submit the message to the MAPISendMail function.

To send a message, create a MAPIMessage structure. Then create one or more MAPIRecipDesc structures describing the recipients of the message and place them in the lpRecips member of the MAPIMessage structure. Then create a text string containing the subject, and place it in the lpszSubject member of the MAPIMessage structure. Create a text string containing the message text, if any, and place it in the lpszNoteText member of the MAPIMessage structure. Create an array of MAPIFileDesc structures, if necessary, to contain any attachments and place it in the lpFiles member of the MAPIMessage structure. Submit the message by calling the MAPISendMail function.

Listing 27.6 shows the MAPIRecipDesc function.

Listing 27.6. The MAPIRecipDesc function's syntax.

```
typedef struct {
    ULONG ulReserved; //must be zero
    ULONG ulRecipClass;  //MAPI_ORIG, MAPI_CC, MAPI_BCC or MAPI_TO
    LPTSTR lpszName; //name of recipient
    LPTSTR lpszAddress; //address of recipient
    ULONG ulEIDSize; //size in bytes
    LPVOID lpEntryID; //phone book entry id
} MAPIRecipDesc, FAR *lpMAPIRecipDesc;
```

Listing 27.7 shows the MAPIFileDesc structure.

Listing 27.7. The MAPIFileDesc structure.

```
typedef struct {
    ULONG ulReserved;   //must be zero
    ULONG flFlags;       //MAPI_OLE or MAPI_OLE_STATIC
    ULONG nPosition;     //where in file to place attachment
    LPTSTR lpszPathName; //path to attachment
    LPTSTR lpszFileName; //name of attachment file
    LPVOID lpFileType;   //file type
} MAPIFileDesc, FAR *lpMAPIFileDesc;
```

Using Auxiliary MAPI Functions

Nearly everything you will need to do with MAPI can be done with the basic functions if you are writing a messaging-aware or messaging-enabled application. If you are designing the next greatest Internet mail client, however, you need access at a lower level and more control over the services. Table 27.7 lists the MAPI auxiliary functions.

Table 27.7. MAPI auxiliary functions.

Function	Action
ChangeIdleRoutine	Changes some or all of the characteristics of an idle function.
CloseIMsgSession	Closes a message session.
DeinitMAPIUtil	Releases utility functions that the ScInitMAPIUtil function called explicitly or the MAPIInitialize function called implicitly.
EnableIdleRoutine	Enables or disables an idle function (that is, a function based on the FNIDLE function prototype).
FBadColumnSeT	Tests the validity of one or more table column sets for use by a service provider in a subsequent call to the IMAPITable::SetColumns method.
FBadEntryList	Validates a list of MAPI entry identifiers.
FBadProp	Validates a specified property.
FBadPropTag	Validates a specified property tag.
FBadRestriction	Validates a restriction used to limit a table.
FBadRglpNameID	Validates an array of pointers that specify name identifier structures and verify their allocation.
FBadRglpszW	Validates all strings in an array of Unicode strings.
FBadRow	Validates a row in a table.
FBadRowSet	Validates all table rows included in a set of table rows.
FBadSortOrderSet	Validates a sort order set by verifying its memory allocation.
FBinFromHex	Converts a string representation of a hexadecimal number to binary data.
FEqualNames	Determines whether two MAPI name identifiers are equal.
FPropCompareProp	Compares two properties using a binary relational operator.
FPropContainsProp	Compares two property values—generally, strings or binary arrays—to see whether one value contains the other.
FPropExists	Searches for a given property tag in an IMAPIProp interface or an interface derived from IMAPIProp, such as IMessage or IMAPIFolder.

continues

Table 27.7. continued

Function	Action
FtAddFt	Adds one unsigned, 64-bit integer to another.
FtgRegisterIdleRoutine	Adds a client application or service provider function based on the FNIDLE function prototype to the idle table.
FtgRegisterIdleRoutine FNIDLE	The FNIDLE function prototype represents a client application or service provider idle function that the MAPI idle engine calls periodically according to priority. The specific functionality of the idle function is defined by the client or provider.
FtMulDw	Multiplies an unsigned, 64-bit integer indicating a time value by an unsigned, 32-bit integer in DWORD format.
FtMulDwDw	Multiplies one unsigned, 32-bit integer in DWORD format by another.
FtNegFt	Computes the two's complement (arithmetic negative operation) of an unsigned, 64-bit integer indicating a time value.
FtSubFt	Subtracts one unsigned, 64-bit integer indicating a time value from another.
GetInstance	Copies one value within a multi-valued property to a single-valued property of the same type.
HexFromBin	Converts a binary number into a string representation of a hexadecimal number.
HrAllocAdviseSink	Creates an advise sink object, given a context specified by the calling implementation and a callback function to be triggered by an event notification.
HrAllocAdviseSink NOTIFCALLBACK	The NOTIFCALLBACK function prototype defines a client application or service provider callback function that MAPI calls to send an event notification. This callback function can be used only when wrapped in an advise sink object created by calling the HrAllocAdviseSink function.
HrComposeEID	Creates a compound entry identifier for an object—usually, a message in a message store.
HrComposeMsgID	Creates an ASCII entry-identifier string for an object—usually, a message in a message store.

Function	Action
HrDecomposeEID	Breaks apart the compound entry identifier of an object—usually, a message in a message store—into the entry identifier of that object and the entry identifier of its store.
HrDecomposeMsgID	Breaks apart the compound entry identifier of an object—usually, a message in a message store—into the entry identifier of that object within a particular store and the entry identifier for that store.
HrEntryIDFromSz	Creates an entry identifier from an ASCII-encoded string and allocates memory for the entry identifier.
HrGetOneProp	Retrieves the value of a single property from an IMAPIProp interface or an interface derived from IMAPIProp.
HrSetOneProp	Changes one property of an object.
HrSzFromEntryID	Creates an entry identifier from an ASCII-encoded string and allocates memory for the entry identifier.
HrValidateIPMSubtree	Adds one or more standard interpersonal message (IPM) folders to a message store.
LPropCompareProp	Compares two property values to determine whether they are equal.
MAPIDeInitIdle	Shuts down the DLL for the idle engine.
MAPIInitIdle	Initializes the DLL for the idle engine.
MapStorageSCode	Maps an HRESULT return value from an OLE storage object to a MAPI return value of the SCODE type.
OpenIMsgSession	Groups the creation of messages within a session, so that closing the session also closes all messages created within that session.
PpropFindProp	Searches for a specified property in a property set.
PreprocessMessage	The PreprocessMessage function prototype, implemented by transport providers, preprocess message contents, or the format of a message.
PropCopyMore	Copies a single property value from a source location to a destination location.

continues

Table 27.7. continued

Function	Action
RemovePreprocessInfo	Removes from a message preprocessed information written by a function based on the PreprocessMessage function prototype.
ScBinFromHexBounded	Converts the specified portion of a string representation of a hexadecimal number into a binary number.
ScCopyNotifications	Copies a group of event notifications to a single block of memory.
ScCopyProps	Copies the properties defined by an array of SPropValue structures to a new destination.
ScCountNotifications	Copies a group of event notifications to a single block of memory.
ScCountProps	Copies the properties defined by an array of SPropValue structures to a new destination.
ScLocalPathFromUNC	Locates a local path counterpart to the given UNC path.
ScRelocNotifications	Adjusts a pointer within a specified event notification array.
ScRelocProps	Adjusts the pointers in an SPropValue array after the array and its data have been copied or moved to a new location.
ScUNCFromLocalPath	Locates a UNC path counterpart to the given local path.
UIAddRef	Provides an alternative way to invoke the OLE method IUnknown::AddRef.
UIPropSize	Obtains the size of a single property value.
UIReleasex	Provides an alternative way to invoke the OLE method IUnknown::Release.

Using the Extended MAPI

Using the Extended MAPI, you have much greater control over messaging services like message stores, address books, and message transports. It is more complex and intended for applications that make heavy use of the mail system. The examples in this book concentrate on the Basic MAPI functions, but you should know that many more are available if you are designing a new workgroup application or business mail-reliant system.

Summary

In this chapter you learned how MAPI has standardized the access and routing of mail. You learned how simple it is to make your application messaging aware. You also built a small, simple application that moves your Internet POP3 mail to your in-house MSMail. Lastly, you saw a large group of functions the Messaging API provides to develop more complex mail applications.

In the next chapter you see a new API for telephony, TAPI. Telephony is the combination of your computer and phone system. You have experienced telephony many times when you call a system with call forwarding menus or the new automated fax back systems. TAPI is now part of Windows NT 4.0.

TAPI

28

by David Hamilton

Telephony is the integration of computers and telephones. The *Telephony API* (TAPI) enables you to dial phone numbers automatically, send documents as faxes, manage voice mail, use caller ID, control a remote computer, and access data from news retrieval services. The TAPI interface gives your application access to the telephone network.

Most people have experienced telephony; they have just called it something else—usually, something not too complimentary. You call an organization and are given a list of numbered options from which to choose. These systems have become inexpensive, existing on a single PC board or built into some modems, with the software included with them.

When Intel began to write specifications for PC telephone boards, it found that the PBXs (Private Branch Exchanges) many businesses were using supported a host of advanced features, but there was no standardization of the way in which these features could be implemented. In 1993, Intel and Microsoft released a preliminary specification called TAPI that standardized telephony services.

Microsoft's Telephone API, TAPI

TAPI14 was released for Windows 95 and TAPI20 is built into NT 4.0. You configure TAPI from the Control Panel's Telephony applet, the General "My Locations" property sheet, as shown in Figure 28.1.

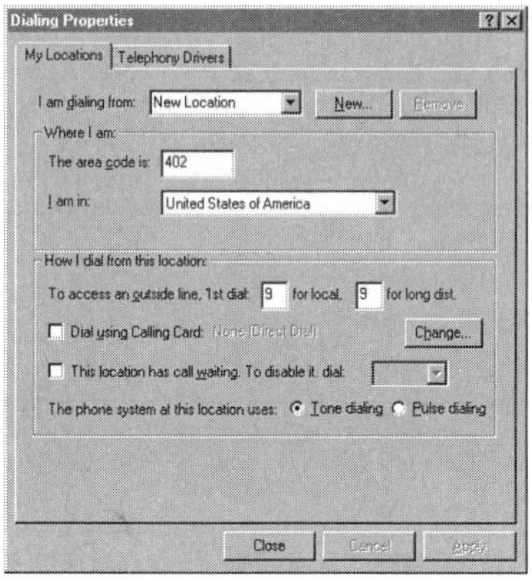

FIGURE 28.1.

TAPI configuration in NT 4.0.

Making a phone call involves first taking the phone off the hook, dialing a number or answering an incoming call, exchanging data, and then hanging up the connection. These steps don't vary much according to whether the call is voice, fax, modem, or video conferencing.

Telephone service can be analog or digital. Your modem takes digital data from your computer and converts it to an analog signal. The modem on the other end reverses the process. Most telephone connections are called *plain old telephone service* (POTS); here, you communicate locally via analog. When you go outside your local loop, the signal is converted to digital at the central switching office of your phone company. *Integrated Services Digital Network* (ISDN) connections are becoming more common; here, the entire communication is digital. As the price of ISDN service continues to come down, you eventually will replace your modem with an ISDN card.

ISDN has the advantages that it is all digital and can achieve much faster data-transmission rates at a lower error rate. ISDN can transfer up to 128 Kbps and can carry both voice and data simultaneously. *Primary Rate Interface* (PRI-ISDN) lines are available, which can offer even faster rates. These ISDN lines are broken into at least three and as many as 32 channels of simultaneous transmissions of data and voice. The *Basic Rate Interface* ISDN (BRI-ISDN) is usually two B channels at 64 Kbps of voice or data and one D channel of data only at 16 Kbps. The two B channels are combined when you need to establish a 128 Kbps connection.

Other types of digital networks exist, such as T1, Centrex, PBX, and Switched56. TAPI is independent of the underlying telephone network, so an application designed now to use your existing POTS environment can be moved to ISDN, PBX, or Centrex as your company grows.

Looking at the TAPI Programming Model

In the other APIs discussed in this book, you controlled the data stream. TAPI is different because you control the line and phone device but not the data stream. The Telephony API is actually three parts: TAPI.H, TAPI.DLL, and a support service application, TAPISRV.EXE. TAPISRV.EXE is loaded by the DLL and is used by the system to allocate memory and to enable data structures to be swapped out to disk.

The API simplifies development by hiding the low-level communications programming. Regardless of the telephone network or type of computer connection, the API calls are handled in a consistent manner. Microsoft has divided the API into four levels:

- **Assisted telephony:** Supplies the basic capability to establish a connection, as in a phone-dialing application
- **Basic telephony:** Minimum functionality of the POTS environment
- **Supplementary telephony:** Adds advanced switching features, such as hold and call transfer
- **Extended telephony:** An API extension mechanism that enables developers to access service provider specific functions not defined in TAPI

Using Assisted Telephony

Assisted telephony is a small set of the function calls that enable you to implement telephony in your Windows application (see Table 28.1). Assisted telephony is just four function calls, but two no longer are used in Windows 32-bit programming. The most common use is to add the Dial menu option as provided by many common desktop applications, such as Symantec's ACT for Windows. Your database application would store client phone numbers and give your user the option to dial the number when that client's record was accessed.

Table 28.1. Assisted TAPI functions.

Function	Action
tapiGetLocationInfo	Get default country code and city (area) code from the Control Panel
tapiRequestDrop	Function no longer in use for Win32
tapiRequestMakeCall	Requests establishment of voice call
tapiRequestMediaCall	Function no longer in use for Win32

The syntax for tapiGetLocationInfo and tapiRequestMakeCall follows:

```
LONG tapiRequestMakeCall(LPCSTR lpszDestAddress, LPCSTR lpszAppName, LPCSTR
➥lpszCalledParty, LPCSTR lpszComment);

LONG tapiGetLocationInfo(LPCSTR lpszCountryCode, LPCSTR lpszCityCode);
```

To TAPI, an address is a phone number. This call returns 0 if successful or these negative values:

```
TAPIERR_INVALDADDRESS
TAPIERR_INVALPOINTER
TAPIERR_NOREQUESTRECIPIENT
TAPIERR_REQUESTFAILED
TAPIERR_REQUESTQUEUEFULL
```

You can add the OnDial function to any Windows application, as Listing 28.1 shows.

Listing 28.1. OnDial, a basic TAPI function to dial a phone number.

```
#include "tapi.h" //put up top

int OnDial()
{
    long tapiRetCode;

    /* Get number from some dialog box in szDialNumber */
tapiRetCode = tapiRequestMakeCall(szDialNumber,NULL, NULL,NULL);

    switch (tapiRetCode)
    {
        case 0:  AfxMessageBox(_T("Call placed successfully"));
                 break;
```

```
        case TAPIERR_NOREQUESTRECIPIENT:
                AfxMessageBox(_T("Call manager app is not running")); //dll not
➡loaded
                break;
        case TAPIERR_REQUESTQUEUEFULL:
                AfxMessageBox(_T("Request Queue full; try again later"));
                break;
        case TAPIERR_INVALDESTADDRESS:
                AfxMessageBox(_T("Invalid phone number"));
                break;
        default: AfxMessageBox(_T("Unrecognized error"));
    }
    return (int)tapiRetCode;
}
```

On the accompanying CD-ROM, you will find a simple dialer application that dials numbers from an Access database. It was built with all the default settings and uses the simple function in Listing 28.1 to OnDial(). In the books online, you can find sample demos to write a macro to dial a number from your spreadsheet. You also can find a complete application, TAM, which is a telephone answering machine, to develop a complete answering machine in software using a SoundBlaster card to provide the storage and retrieval of wave files. The main sample is Dialer, which implements a full TAPI dialer.

Using Basic Telephony

At the end of this chapter, Tables 28.2 through 28.10 list all the TAPI.DLL functions. The best way to learn these functions is via the TB14.EXE (TAPI32 Browser) application, which is available from the WINEXT forum on CompuServe. This online source is also mirrored by Digital Equipment Corporation at

`http://dec2000.faf.cuni.cz/mirrors/gowinnt/developr/TAPI/README.TXT.`

These sites have the most recent releases of the TAPI files available. Figure 28.2 shows the TAPI32 browser.

This application enables you to exercise each TAPI function and to check your parameters. A second useful piece of shareware and a good sample application is ENUMTAPI.C, which also is located on the CD-ROM included with this book. Its output is simple, as shown in Figure 28.3, but it is very useful in tracking down your problems.

The next three chapters focus on the concepts of each area of telephony. The topic easily could fill this book; this is a just a short chapter to warm you up and let you know where else to look if you're going to develop telephony applications.

The TAPI functions can be grouped into three classes as shown in the following section. The most basic functions are the Fundamental API, which allow you to initialize TAPI, open a line device, close the line device, and shut down TAPI. The second set of functions allows you to determine the capabilities of a line device and determine the status of the current connection. Lastly, there are the operations functions that do the actual dialing and answering of calls and let you control a phone call with features like call forwarding.

FIGURE 28.2.

TB14.EXE: the best learning tool.

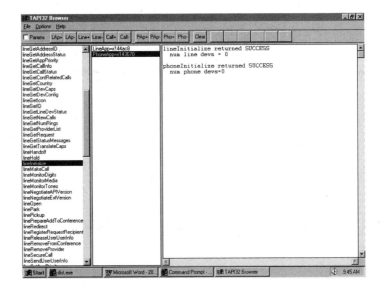

FIGURE 28.3.

ENUMTAPI.C output.

```
<- dwDeviceID
 |  <- Max dwAPIVersion
 |  |  <- Number of addresses
 |  |  |  <- Capable of making voice comm/datamodem calls?
 |  |  |  |  <- Capable of making automated voice calls?
 |  |  |  |  |  <- Call in progress?
 |  |  |  |  |  |  <- Any application waiting for calls?
 |  |  |  |  |  |  |  <- Service Povider - Line Device Name
V  V  V V V V V
0, 1.4,1,Y,N,N,N, UNIMDM.TSP - Sportster 28800 Internal
1, lineNegotiateAPIVersion error: LINEERR_INCOMPATIBLEAPIVERSOIN
```

Fundamental API interactions

- Initialization and shutdown of the Telephony API
- Negotiation of API version
- Filtering of status messages to be received
- Opening and closing line devices

Capabilities and status

- Querying line device and address capabilities, associated media stream devices, icons, and so on
- Querying line device, address, and call status
- Querying and setting media device configurations

Operations

- Translating addresses and setting associated parameters
- Dialing and answering calls
- Dropping calls
- Controlling call privileges and handing off call control

If you read the section *Looking at the TAPI Function List* at the end of this chapter, you will notice a large number of line functions. *Lines* are physical devices in TAPI. They are the modem, ISDN card, fax board, and so on. They are connected physically to a telephone line. TAPI is desktop focused because you have a single PC and telephone. The line functions refer to the connection, whereas the phone functions usually are features associated with a handset.

Basic telephony provides the minimum set of functions needed to write applications using POTS. All TAPI-compatible devices support this minimum set of functions.

Devices are placed into classes so that those with similar capabilities can be treated the same by your software application. You therefore have line devices and phone devices. If you are writing an application that uses a single-channel modem line, you easily can extend this with a second identical channel for an ISDN line. The phone classes are an abstraction of a telephone set. These classes are treated separately; you can have a phone without a line or a line without a phone. A phone handset therefore can record your greeting message as a wave file, which stays locally and doesn't go out over a line.

An address is a telephone number. You can have multiple addresses per phone. On my Centrex system, for example, I have a phone number that an outside caller uses to ring my phone and also a second, two-digit number that another employee uses to ring my phone. A *call* is defined as the connection of two addresses. This seems simple enough until you remember that calls can be interrupted, as in call-waiting, or can be multiple, as in a conference call.

Each of the basic function begins with line. These functions are like lineDial, lineMakeCall, lineDrop, lineAnswer, and lineSetNumRings, and allow for both synchronous and asynchronous use of the line. The example TAM application uses most of these functions. It answers the phone on a specific number of rings, plays a wave file greeting, or—if the phone call is a fax—routes the data. It then captures a wave file that is the voice message.

Examining a Basic Telephony Application Flow

No matter how complex your application becomes, the TAPI component follows a very simple sequence. You will always initialize TAPI, determine what API functionality your application and the device have in common, open a line, dial or answer a call, monitor the line, close the line, free up the device, then shut down TAPI. The following checklist goes into greater detail.

1. **Initialize TAPI.** Before you can place a call, you need to establish a means of communication between your application and TAPI. You tell TAPI the address of your chosen callback function. TAPI notifies this function when relevant events occur.

2. **Negotiate the API version.** In order to communicate, your application and the device must be using the same API version. The versions are built on each other so that you will find the highest level you have in common. Invoking the function `lineGetDevCaps` returns information in a data structure, `LINEDEVCAPS`. This also gives the application the address of the line device.

3. **Open a line.** Applications need to get the ownership and privilege to a line and the calls it creates. The option `LINECALLPRIVILEGE_NONE` enables your application to place outbound calls but protects it from inbound calls.

4. **Translate the address string to one the device recognizes.** Your application will have phone numbers in authorized form (human readable). Your line might be (555) 434-2929, for example. The device might need more information, however, such as a prefix to dial to get an outside line, whether dialing needs pauses, and whether it is tone or pulse.

5. **Place the call.** After you open a line device, you place a call via `lineMakeCall` with the phone address and the media mode (data modem, voice, fax, and so on). Calls represent the connection between two or more addresses. TAPI represents a call via a handle.

6. **Monitor the status of the device.** TAPI uses a callback mechanism to notify your application of events. This callback function carries a request ID and an error indication. By switching on the error indication, the application processes the information flowing via the call. TAPI doesn't actually send data over the line; it establishes the connection and then gives control back to the user. TAPI manages the open line, but your COMM API does the actual data transfer.

7. **Drop the line.** To finish the conversation, the process is reversed. You "go on hook" by calling the `lineDrop` function. This places the call in the idle state. The call still exists and your application still has a handle to the call to use in writing phone logs. The function `lineDeallocateCall` actually frees the handle.

8. **Close the device.** If you are finished using the line, `lineClose` closes the line and frees the handle.

9. **Shut down TAPI.** The application invokes `lineShutdown` to end the TAPI session.

Go through this checklist using the actual functions your application would use.

Before your application can use the TAPI functions, you need to initialize the environment and enable callback functions. You can do this via the `lineInitialize` function, as this code shows:

```
LONG lineInitialize(LPHLINEAPP lphLineApp, HINSTANCE hInstance, LINECALLBACK
➡lpfnCallback, LPCSTR lpszAppName, LPDWORD lpdwNumDevs)
```

This code initializes and returns the number of line devices available, which are addressed using the values 0 through `lpdwNumDevs` −1.

After success, your application can receive information in two ways: solicited and unsolicited. You request *solicited* by making function calls, and *unsolicited* by receiving messages. The pointer to the callback function is used by all lines opened with the same instance handle.

In order to communicate, you need to ensure that both your application and the line device are using the same language by using this code:

```
LONG lineNegotiateAPIVersion(HLINEAPP hLineApp, DWORD dwDeviceID,
    DWORD dwAPILowVersion, DWORD dwAPIHighVersion,
    LPDWORD lpdwAPIVersion, LPLINEEXTENSIONID lpExtensionID)
```

This gives you the pointer to the API version needed in subsequent calls.

After your application and line device are initialized and both are speaking the same language, you can open a line via `lineOpen`, as this code shows:

```
LONG lineOpen(HLINEAPP hLineApp, DWORD dwDeviceID, LPHLINE lphLine,
    DWORD dwAPIVersion, DWORD dwExtVersion, DWORD dwCallbackInstance,
    DWORD dwPrivileges, DWORD dwMediaModes,
    LPLINECALLPARAMS const lpCallParams)
```

This code opens the line device specified by its device ID and returns a line handle for the corresponding opened line device. This line handle is used in subsequent operations on the line device.

After the line is open, you need to translate the phone number from the authorized format (+1(555)434-2929) to a dialable string (t9w15554342929). This says to dial using tones, dial a 9, and wait for the dialing tone before sending the rest of the string. This translation is done by the function `lineTranslateAddress`, as this code shows:

```
LONG lineTranslateAddress(HLINEAPP hLineApp, DWORD dwDeviceID,
    DWORD dwAPIVersion, LPCSTR lpszAddressIn, DWORD dwCard,
    DWORD dwTranslateOptions, LPLINETRANSLATEOUTPUT lpTranslateOutput
```

The dialable address is returned in `lpTranslateOutput` which you use to place the call. LineMakeCall and `lineDial` usually are used together. If the dialable address needs to pause for a dial tone, `lineMakeCall` begins the sequence. If it needs to pause, it sets `fCallMade`; then, after the pause, `lineDial` finishes, as shown in this sequence from the Dialer sample:

```
if (!fCallMade)
  lresult = lineMakeCall(lpdcr->hLine,&(lpdcr->hCall),lpchdialStart,0,lpParams);
else
  lresult = lineDial(lpdcr->hCall, lpchDialStart,0);
```

The function syntax for `lineMakeCall` is as follows:

```
LONG lineMakeCall(HLINE hLine, LPHCALL lphCall, LPCSTR lpszDestAddress,
    DWORD dwCountryCode, LPLINECALLPARAMS const lpCallParams)
```

and

```
LONG lineDial(HCALL hCall, LPCSTR lpszDestAddress, DWORD dwCountryCode)
```

The `lineDial` function returns 0 for success after you dial the number. After a call is placed using `lineMakeCall`, `LINE_CALLSTATE` messages are sent to your application through the callback function from the `lineInitialize` function you started with. Depending on the messages, you might want to do some processing, such as checking whether the state is `LINECALLSTATE_DISCONNECTED`, at which point you call the `lineDrop` function. `LINECALLSTATE_BUSY` notifies users that one session already was using the line.

To finish the call, or after your user selects your Hang up button, you call `lineDrop`, as in this code:

```
lresult = lineDrop(lpdcr->hCall, NULL,0);
```

Then you close the line via this code:

```
lineClose(hpdcr->hLine);
```

You still are not done. You need to shut down TAPI and free the handles by using this code:

```
lineShutdown(hApp);
```

Your application probably will have a large middle step during which the information is processed via another API, but TAPI doesn't handle the message itself—just the connection to the phone network.

Using Supplemental Telephony

These functions take TAPI one step further into typical PBX areas, such as call hold, call transfer, conference calls, call park (a special type of call hold where you can pick up from another phone), and others that you find on a modern phone system. Your application first queries the line to see what supplemental functionality is provided and then implements it.

In addition to the above basic functions that provide telephony services, TAPI provides a set of supplementary functions your application can use to give it features usually found in today's phone systems. The functionality provided by this set of functions is listed below.

- Holding and unholding calls
- Transferring calls—both blind and with consultation

- Conferencing
- Forwarding calls
- Parking and unparking calls. A parked call is like a call put on hold but you can pick it up from any other handset
- Picking up calls that are ringing elsewhere
- Camp-on and other automatic call completion. A camp-on call would be one that is set to ring the phone you are calling as soon as the call in progress on that phone ends
- Accepting, rejecting, and redirecting incoming calls
- Securing calls from interruptions
- Generating in-band dial digits and tones like the beeps you hear when your phone call is being recorded
- Monitoring media mode, received DTMF digits, and tones
- Controlling the routing of media-stream information
- Sending data simultaneously from one user to another with a phone call using ISDN
- Changing call parameters on-the-fly
- Controlling the physical phone terminal (speakers, microphones, ringers, display, lamps, buttons, and so on)

To query the line capabilities, you can use functions such as `lineGetDevCaps` and `lineGetAddressCaps`. The corresponding functions get the capabilities of the phone, as in `phoneGetDevCaps`.

Using Extended Telephony

Microsoft provides a way to extend TAPI as new capabilities are made available by hardware vendors. Vendors can define new values for some enumeration types and add fields to data structures. Two functions, `lineDevSpecific` and `phoneDevSpecific`, enable the application to communicate with these vendor-provided structures and the new capabilities.

Looking at the TAPI Function List

TAPI has more than 60 functions for working with logical phone lines. Although discussing each is beyond the scope of this chapter, I briefly list each and its use in Tables 28.2 through 28.10. They include the basic telephony functions as well as the supplementary functions.

Table 28.2. Line call setup and takedown.

Function	Action
Information Functions	Return information about the features or status of a line, address, or call
lineAccept	Closes an open line device
lineAnswer	Answers the offering call
lineClose	Closes an open line device
lineDeallocateCall	Deallocates a call handle
lineDial	Dials a number on a call
lineDrop	Drops or disconnects a call
lineGetAddressCaps	Queries an address on a line to determine its telephony capabilities
lineGetAddressID	Returns the ID associated with an address
lineGetAddressStatus	Queries an address for its current status
lineGetCallInfo	Obtains static information about a call
lineGetCallStatus	Returns the current status of a call
lineGetConfRelatedCalls	Returns a list of calls that are part of a conference
lineGetDevCaps	Queries a line to determine its telephony capabilities
lineGetID	Returns a device ID for a device class associated with the specified line, address, or call
lineGetLineDevStatus	Queries an open line for its current status
lineGetNewCalls	Returns handles to calls on a line or address for which the application currently does not have handles
lineGetNumRings	Determines the number of times an inbound call on an address should ring prior to answering the call
lineGetRequest	Retrieves the next by-proxy request for the specified request mode
lineGetStatusMessages	Queries for which notification messages it is set to receive
lineInitialize	Initializes the application's use of the Telephony API DLL

Function	Action
lineMakeCall	Places a call on a line to the specified destination address
lineOpen	Opens a line specified by a device ID and returns a line handle for the opened line
lineShutdown	Shuts down the application's usage of the line interface

Table 28.3. Line setup functions.

Function	Action
lineMonitorDigits	Sets the unbuffered detection of digits on the call
lineMonitorMedia	Sets the detection of media modes on a call
lineMonitorTone	Sets and disables the detection of inband tones on a call
lineSetAppSpecific	Sets the application-specific field of a call's call information record
lineSetCallParams	Sets the bearer mode and/or the rate parameters of an existing call
lineSetCallPrivilege	Sets the application's privileges to a call
lineSetMediaControl	Sets control actions on the media stream associated with the specified line, address, or call
lineSetNumRings	Sets the number of rings for an incoming call prior to answering the call
lineSetStatusMessages	Sets which status changes are reported on a line
lineSetTerminal	Sets the terminal to which information is to be routed

Table 28.4. Line-control functions.

Function	Action
lineBlindTransfer	Performs a blind or single-step transfer of the call to the specified destination address
lineCompleteCall	Specifies how a call that could not be connected normally should be completed

continues

Table 28.4. continued

Function	Action
lineCompleteTransfer	Completes the transfer of a call to the consultation call
lineForward	Forwards calls destined for an address on the line
lineGatherDigits	Initiates the buffered gathering of digits on a call
lineGenerateDigits	Initiates the generation of digits on a call as inband tones using the specified signaling mode
lineGenerateTone	Generates tones inband over a call
lineHold	Places a call on hold
linePark	Parks a call
linePickup	Picks up a call
lineRedirect	Redirects an offering call to the specified destination address
lineSecureCall	Secures a call from any interruptions or interference that might affect its media stream
lineSendUserUserInfo	Sends user-to-user information to the remote party on a call
lineSetupTransfer	Initiates the transfer of a call
lineSwapHold	Swaps an active call with a call on consultation hold
lineUncompleteCall	Cancels a call-completion request on a line
lineUnhold	Retrieves a held call
lineUnpark	Retrieves a parked call

Table 28.5. Line-conferencing functions.

Function	Action
lineAddToConference	Adds a call to a conference call
linePrepareAddToConference	Prepares a conference call for the addition of another party
lineRemoveFromConference	Removes a call from a conference
lineSetupConference	Sets up a conference call for the addition of the third party

Table 28.6. Line miscellaneous functions.

Function	Action
lineDevSpecific	An extension mechanism to enable service providers to provide access to features not described in other lineDevSpecificFeature operations
lineHandoff	Used to give ownership of a call to another application
lineNegotiateAPIVersion	Negotiates an API version to use
lineNegotiateExtVersion	Negotiates an extension version to use with a line device
lineRegisterRequestRecipient	Registers the invoking application as a recipient of requests for the specified request mode
lineTranslateAddress	Translates between an address in authorized format and its dialable address

Table 28.7. Phone-related functions.

Function	Action
phoneClose	Closes an open phone device
phoneInitialize	Initializes the application's use of the Telephony API DLL for use of the phone abstraction
phoneOpen	Opens a phone device
phoneShutdown	Shuts down the application's use of TAPI's phone abstraction

Table 28.8. Phone information functions.

Function	Action
phoneGetButtonInfo	Returns information about a button
phoneGetData	Uploads the information from a data buffer in the open phone device
phoneGetDevCaps	Queries a phone to determine its telephony capabilities

continues

Table 28.8. continued

Function	Action
phoneGetDisplay	Returns the current contents of the phone display
phoneGetGain	Returns the gain setting of a phone's hookswitch microphone
phoneGetHookSwitch	Returns the current hookswitch mode of an open phone device
phoneGetID	Returns a device ID for the device class associated with a phone
phoneGetLamp	Returns the current lamp mode of a lamp (a certain button lit on a phone)
phoneGetRing	Queries a phone for its current ring mode
phoneGetStatus	Queries a phone for its overall status
phoneGetStatusMessages	Returns the phone state changes that will generate a message to the application
phoneGetVolume	Returns the volume setting of a phone's hookswitch speaker

Table 28.9. Phone setup functions.

Function	Action
phoneSetButtonInfo	Sets information about a button
phoneSetData	Downloads the information in the buffer to the phone
phoneSetDisplay	Displays the specified string on the phone
phoneSetGain	Sets the gain of the hookswitch microphone
phoneSetHookSwitch	Sets the state of the phone's hookswitch
phoneSetLamp	Causes the lamp to be lit in the specified lamp mode. When you call a certain function like call hold you need to light the hold button.
phoneSetRing	Rings the phone using the specified ring mode and volume
phoneSetStatusMessages	Monitors the phone for selected status events
phoneSetVolume	Sets the volume of the speaker component of the phone hookswitch

Table 28.10. Phone miscellaneous functions.

Function	Action
phoneDevSpecific	A general extension mechanism to the phone API
phoneNegotiateAPIVersion	Negotiates an API version to use for a phone
phoneNegotiateExtVersion	Negotiates an extension version to use with a phone

Summary

This chapter has just briefly introduced what features are available with TAPI 2.0, a new development tool released as part of Windows NT 4.0.

Telephony application development has always been the domain of large companies, large computers, and large budgets. We just recently have seen the release of low-cost products like the PhoneBlaster, which allow a single PC to provide sophisticated telephone services. Another recent development is the ability to use Internet phone utilities to talk via the Internet instead of just typewritten chat.

At the same time, the PC is becoming more dependent on phone-line access. Future applications need to address this marriage of the phone and computer and make it work seamlessly. With the inclusion of TAPI in Windows NT 4.0, Microsoft has given you the tools to write these future applications.

In Part V, "WinNT Network Programming," you have looked at features of Windows NT 4.0 that make it part of a network that extends outside your office. In the next part you spend three chapters looking at how database programming is also expanding to recognize that the data is also widely distributed.

VI

PART

Windows NT Database Interfaces

ODBC Concepts

29

by David Hamilton

In your office, you have large amounts of data, some in text files, some in spreadsheets and some in databases. The concept of the global village and information superhighway embodies the ability for a wide variety of applications to access data in whatever form it currently exists. To write a report you often need to pull data together from many different sources, including computers outside your immediate environment.

Microsoft's *Open Database Connectivity Interface* (ODBC) is a library of functions that enable access to a variety of *Database Management Systems* (DBMSs) using the *Structured Query Language* (SQL). The ODBC interface offers vendor-independent manipulation of a wide variety of DBMS types through this standard set of 57 functions calls. ODBC maximizes the interoperability of the various DBMSs. Your application can access multiple DBMSs and can be built without knowledge of the DBMS's specifications.

DBMS History

In 1969 Dr. E.F. Codd of IBM's San Jose Research Laboratories proposed a relational model with the concept of the tables, indexes, keys, rows, and columns that have become familiar to most database developers. This was a major step forward in DBMS design, and especially in the savings of storage space, in that data was only written in one place in the database. No longer was data duplicated for each similar record. He developed a set of 12 rules that the DBMS had to adhere to in order to be marketed as "relational." In his first model, Relational Model Version 1 (RM/V1), Codd had 50 common functions that must be provided. He expanded on this in RM/V2 with 333 functions. A relational DBMS needed to provide most of the 333, and to be fully relational a DBMS had to provide all 333 functions.

In the 1970s, IBM built on Codd's work and that of mathematical set theory in their Structured English Query Language (SEQUEL). In applying this concept to various computer languages the idea of Embedded SQL was born. With Embedded SQL programmers could access a DBMS using various languages like COBOL, PASCAL, BASIC and C to develop the application. Each language used a common syntax of SQL statements translated by a preprocessor. Embedded SQL was very efficient but recompiling for each new environment was not. The whole concept of using a spreadsheet like Excel to access a wide variety of DBMSs was not possible.

During the 1970s and 1980s, the SQL language itself became well defined, up to the point that it became an ANSI standard language. Each vendor still had its own implementation. "Standards" are basically the definitions of the calls to connect and log on, and the SQL language grammar is a standard set of error codes and data types, and the definition of how to disconnect and log off.

Other standards based on ANSI SQL also developed, such as the International Standards Organization (ISO SQL). The UNIX world united the ANSI and ISO standards in their X/Open SQL. The SQL Access Group (SAG) defined their own standards of the language. Both the SAG and X/Open groups have now come to an understanding called a Common Application

Environment (CAE). The current working standard is the CAE 1992 specifications. In 1995 SAG and X/Open formally merged and are working closely with ISO to keep SQL one standard. Microsoft helped define the Call Language Interface (CLI) specifications and was the first to commercialize it with their Open Database Connectivity software (ODBC) version 1.0 in 1992. This set of C function calls enabled a developer to write an application that could open and query data from a variety of DBMS structures. In 1994 ODBC 2.0 was released and Microsoft has announced ODBC 3.0 will be released in 1996, fully aligned with both ISO and SAG's CLI specifications. A brief review of ODBC 3.0 can be found at the end of Chapter 30, "ODBC Implementation."

The concept of a preprocessor had to be eliminated in order for the dreams of interactive DBMS access to be realized. ODBC allows applications to use the SQL language to access DBMSs without prior knowledge of the structure or data.

An example of embedded SQL (it almost made C a 4GL!) follows:

```
main()
{
EXEC SQL BEGIN DECLARE SECTION;
char NAME[30], PNUM[15];
EXEC SQL END DECLARE SECTION;

EXEC SQL INCLUDE SQLCA;

EXEC SQL DECLARE C1 CURSOR FOR SELECT LASTNAME, PHONE FROM   EMPLOYEE;

EXEC SQL OPEN C1

while (SQLCODE == 0)
   {
     EXEC SQL FETCH C1 INTO :NAME :PNUM
   }

EXEC SQL CLOSE C1
}
```

Although the preceding example seems simple, its precompiler made the source look like spaghetti. More problematically, each DBMS's precompiler generated a vastly different flavor of spaghetti. Even though embedded SQL was efficient and simple, the SQL statements had to always be static (known at compile time). In modern applications, SQL statements were built at runtime by the user (dynamic). Eventually dynamic SQL was developed, and was still DBMS dependent.

An Introduction to ODBC

In ODBC the SQL statement is a string, usually constructed at runtime. It is flexible enough that the same object is used against different DBMSs. The application can ignore the communication with the DBMS and know that data is being returned to it in the application's own formats.

The idea is very much the same as printer drivers in Windows NT. You are able to format text and send it out to the device context for the printer without knowing what printer is attached. ODBC embodies a similar set of database drivers, each a DLL. ODBC was a division of labor. The application, the ODBC Driver Manager, and the ODBC driver DLLs all had separate chores.

FIGURE 29.1.

The relationship of the application to the Driver Manager, the drivers, and the DBMS data.

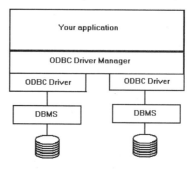

ODBC has three components: your application, the Driver Manager, and the DBMS's ODBC driver. Each has specific tasks; the power of ODBC is that you have to provide only the tasks for the application. Two thirds of the work is done for you.

The application requests the connection to the DBMS and defines the data storage formats. Once connected, the application sends SQL statements. The SQL statements are the requests for results from the DBMS and the method the application uses to process errors. The application also reports the query results to the user. In transaction processing the application requests the commit and rollbacks. Lastly, it is the application's job to terminate the connection to the DBMS.

Before your application can use ODBC to connect to a database, you have to link the database with the appropriate Driver Manager. This is done through ODBCAD32.EXE, the ODBC Administrator, shown in Figure 29.2. This manages entries in the NT Registry's ODBC key values.

FIGURE 29.2.

The Data Sources dialog box.

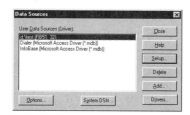

The ODBC Driver Manager loads the appropriate driver when it receives the calls of either SQLBrowseConnect, SQLConnect, or SQLDriverConnect. It uses the Registry key values to get the mappings from the DBMS to the appropriate driver. The Driver Manager then processes the ODBC initialization and provides ODBC entry point addresses for the function calls available. The Device Manager also has the job of validating the parameters passed by the ODBC function calls.

ODBCAD32.EXE provides a list of the drivers available (as seen listed in Figure 29.3). You may have many databases, all of which use the same driver. When a DBMS system is installed, if it provides ODBC support, it will install a new driver in this list.

FIGURE 29.3.
Installed ODBC drivers.

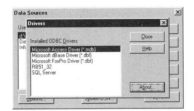

The ODBC Driver Manager's jobs include establishing the connection to the database. The requests from the application are submitted to the DBMS in the form it recognizes. The driver translates data into the format the DBMS requires as well as returns results in the format the application requires. Different DBMSs use different error code values and these are translated into those standard to ODBC. The driver manages the position of the cursors you have set, pointing to the row of data your manipulating. Lastly the Driver Manager handles transaction processing, storing changes until your application calls for them to be committed to the database.

What this all means to you, the programmer, is that two-thirds of the work is being done for you by the Driver Manager and the ODBC driver. You are responsible for one-third, the application.

ODBC and SQL Programming

From the developer's standpoint, it would be ideal if all DBMSs supported the same set of ODBC function calls and SQL statements. This is not the case. Each DBMS has its own set of features, strengths, and weaknesses. To address this, ODBC has conformance levels for its drivers. These conformance levels address two areas, the ODBC API, and the SQL grammar. To claim that it supports a conformance level, the driver must support all the functionality at that level. It may provide more, but it can not provide less. Three calls can be used to determine what conformance level is supported: SQLGetInfo, SQLGetFunctions, and SQLGetTypeInfo. These are discussed in Chapter 30, "ODBC Implementation."

The X/Open and SAG groups have defined three levels of ODBC compliance—Core level, Level 1, and Level 2.

Core API

1. To be Core-level compliant, the ODBC application interface must be able to allocate and free the ODBC environment handle, establish a connection handle, and process statement handles.

2. With a Core-level ODBC API, you must be able to connect to a data source and use multiple SQL statements on a single connection.

3. Core-level ODBC APIs should prepare and immediately execute SQL statements.

4. Core-level ODBC APIs should be able to assign storage space for SQL function parameters and the results of the SQL statements.

5. The Core-level APIs should retrieve data from a result set and retrieve basic information about the result set.

6. Core-level APIs should support commit and roll back transaction processing.

7. Lastly, the Core level APIs must be able to retrieve error information.

CORE SQL Grammar

At the Core level the API should support the following SQL language features:

1. Data Definition Language (DDL) commands: `CREATE TABLE`, `DROP TABLE`, `ALTER TABLE`, `CREATE INDEX`, `DROP INDEX`, `CREATE VIEW`, `DROP VIEW`, `GRANT`, and `REVOKE`

2. Data Manipulation Language (DML): full `SELECT`, `INSERT`, `UPDATE`, `SEARCHED`, and `DELETE SEARCHED`

3. Simple expressions and functions, `MAX` and `MIN`

4. Data types: `CHAR`, `VARCHAR`, or `LONG VARCHAR`, `DECIMAL`, `NUMERIC`, `SMALLINT`, `INTEGER`, `REAL`, `FLOAT`, `DOUBLE PRECISION`

Level 1 API

For a DBMS vendor to label their API product as Level 1 compliant, the API must provide added functionality.

1. All Core level API functionality listed previously must be supported.

2. The Level 1 API must supply the ability to connect to a data source with driver-specific dialog boxes.

3. The Level 1 API must be able to set and get values of SQL statement options and connection options.

4. Level 1 APIs should be able to set part or all of the SQL statement parameter values.

5. Level 1 APIs should be able to retrieve all or part of result column's values.

6. Level 1 APIs must have the ability to provide a description of the database to the application by retrieving catalog information.

7. Level 1 APIs must be able to retrieve information about the ODBC driver's and DBMS's capabilities, available data types, and supported functions.

Extended SQL Grammar

With Level 1 compliance comes extended SQL functionality. To claim that the vendor's product has Extended SQL Grammar capabilities, the product must support the following:

1. All the previously listed Core SQL grammar and data types must be supported.

2. Data Manipulation Language extended functions include: outer joins, positioned UPDATEs, positioned DELETE, SELECT FOR UPDATE, unions.

3. Extended SQL Grammar has the added expressions of: SUBSTRING, ABS, date functions, time functions, and timestamps.

4. Data types are extended to include: BIT, TINYINT, BIGINT, BINARY, VARBINARY, LONG VARBINARY, DATE, TIME, and TIMESTAMP.

5. With Extended SQL the API should support batching of SQL statements.

6. Extended SQL Grammar also provides for procedure calls enabling the development of client/server applications.

Level 2 API

The highest level of API compliance is level 2, which many DBMS vendors are just now beginning to fully support.

1. A Level 2 compliant API would support all Core level and Level 1 API capabilities.

2. A Level 2 compliant API should provide for the ability to browse connection information and provide a list of available data sources.

3. In Level 2 the API should support sending arrays of parameter values and retrieve arrays of results.

4. In Level 2 APIs you can retrieve the number of parameters an SQL statement requires and also a description of individual parameters.

5. Level 2 compliant APIs support scrollable cursors.

6. When a DBMS has its own SQL dialect, the Level 2 API should be able to process this native form of SQL statements as well as standard SQL statements.

7. Level 2 compliant APIs are able to retrieve security privilege information, list the database keys, and list what stored procedures are available.

8. Lastly, a Level 2 compliant API can call functions provided in a transaction Dynamic Linked Library.

ODBC Basics

When you installed NT 4.0, the ODBC DLLs were installed in your WINNT\SYSTEM32 directory and the ODBC 32-bit administrator was installed as an applet in the Control Panel. As you install a DBMS, it installs its own ODBC drivers. When you define a database using the DBMS, you need to go into the ODBC administrator applet and link the appropriate driver to your database.

The first step in using an ODBC database is to tell NT where to find the driver for that database using the NT Control Panel's applet, ODBCAD32.EXE, the Driver Manager. With Windows NT and ODBC the information is written into the registry. With versions of ODBC prior to 2.1, information is written to the ODBCINST.INI file. The file's first section is simply a listing of installed drivers, followed by each driver's path to its particular DLL, and lastly the conformance level the driver can provide.

Figure 29.4 shows the registry listing for my SQL Server database. The same information would have been written to the ODBCINST.INI file on an earlier version of ODBC.

FIGURE 29.4.

The registry has values under the key ODBCINST.INI.

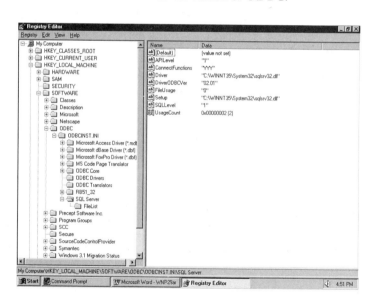

This provides NT with the same information that both the older files ODBCINST.INI and ODBC.INI did.

This following is an older ODBCINST.INI file listing for Microsoft's SQL Server.

```
[ODBC Drivers]
SQL Server=Installed
```

```
[ODBC 32 bit Drivers]
SQL Server (32 bit)=Installed

[SQL Server]
Driver=C:\WINDOWS\SYSTEM\sqlsrvr.dll
Setup=C:\WINDOWS\SYSTEM\sqlsrvr.dll
APILevel=1
ConnectFunctions=YYY
DriverODBCVer=02.01
FileUsage=0
SQLLevel=1


[ODBC Translators]
MS Code Page Translator=Installed

[MS Code Page Translator]
Translator=C:\WINDOWS\SYSTEM\MSCPXLT.DLL
Setup=C:\WINDOWS\SYSTEM\MSCPXLT.DLL
```

The format for the driver section is:

```
[Driver description]
```

The setting options for both the Registry or the older ODBCINST.INI file are as follows. The `APILevel` can be 1, 2, or 0. The value `CreateDSN` is just the data source name. The `ConnectFunctions` values are either Y or N for each of `SQLConnect`, `SQLDriverConnect`, and `SQLBrowseConnect`. The DriverODBCVer is the major version number that can be 1.00, 2.00, or 3.00. The value `FileUsage` which can be 0, 1, or 2 where 0 is not single-tier (usually a client/server DBMS in which a client passes SQL statements that it processes to server software), 1 is single-tier with data files as tables (as in XBase), and 2, which is a driver, treats files in data files as a qualifier like Microsoft's Access where one file contains many tables. The `FileExtensions` value is simply that, the file extension like *.mdb for Access or *.dbf for Xbase. Lastly, the `SQLLevel` is the level of grammar supported where a 0 is for minimal grammar, 1 is core grammar, and 2 is extended grammar.

The translators key of the Registry is what ODBC uses in processing the SQL statements between your application and the driver when a different character format is used.

Once the driver for a DBMS is set up under NT, you can use the ODBC Administrator from the Control Panel to register your application's data source. This information is written to the ODBC.INI file in the Windows directory for ODBC 2.0 or to the ODBC.INI area of the Registry for current versions. The system is very important because it enables the application to change data sources without being recompiled. It is common to build an application using a data source file called MYSOURCE, typically a Microsoft Access database. When the application is finished and is to be deployed in the work environment, you define an SQL Server database with the same tables and columns. The SQL Server database is named MYSOURCE. Go into the ODBC Administrator and change MYSOURCE to point to the SQL Server database instead of the Access database. This last ability is what makes ODBC a powerful tool for you to use in writing applications.

A sample ODBC.INI file listing shows mappings:

```
[ODBC Data Sources]
MS Access Databases=Access Data (*.mdb)

[ODBC 32 bit Data Sources]
testsql=SQL Server (32 bit)
MagicODBC=Microsoft Excel Driver (*.xls) (32 bit)
MS Access 7.0 Database=Microsoft Access Driver (*.mdb) (32 bit)

[testsql]
Driver32=C:\WINDOWS\System32\sqlsrv32.dll
[MS Access Databases]
Driver32=C:\WINDOWS\System32\odbcjt32.dll
FileType=RedISAM
SingleUser=False
UseSystemDB=False
[MagicODBC]
Driver32=C:\WINDOWS\System32\odbcjt32.dll
[ODBC]
TraceAutoStop=1
Trace=0
TraceFile=\SQL.LOG
```

The first section is the [ODBC Data Sources] and is a simple list of the data files and their respective drivers. The second section is the data source specifications. The format for this section is:

```
[data source name]
Driver32= the path to the DLL driver
Description = user defined description of database
TranslationDLL = the path to the translation DLL
TranlationName = the name of the translation DLL
TranslationOptions = options available with the translation DLL
```

This is followed by a list of keywords specific to that database:

```
Server=Accounting
UserID=Dave
UserPassword=evad
```

The last section, [ODBC] includes the options you set in the ODBC Administrator.

Trace is set to 1 when tracing is enabled. In Windows 3.1 tracing was always enabled for all ODBC applications, but in NT it is enabled by individual applications, beginning when an application calls SQLAllocEnv.

TraceFile is the output filename. The default, SQL.LOG, is in the preceding list.

TraceAutoStop is like Trace. In NT, the individual application disables tracing when you call SQLFreeEnv.

Developing an Application

An ODBC application follows the flow of Table 29.1. You initialize the connection, process a set of SQL statements, and then terminate the connection. Throughout this and the following two chapters, you will find the process keeps following these same steps.

Table 29.1. Always the same steps!

Connect	Allocate environment handle, SQLAllocEnv
	Allocate connection handle, SQLAllocConnect
	Connect to server, SQLConnect
	Allocate statement handle, SQLAllocStmt
SQL Processing	Submit statements
	Retrieve results
	Process results
Disconnect	Free statement handle, SQLFreeStmt
	Disconnect from server, SQLDisconnect
	Free connection handle, SQLFreeConnect
	Free environment handle, SQLFreeEnv

The environment handle is of type HENV, the connection handle of type HDBC and the statement handle of type HSTMT. Each of these is a memory storage location holding the specifics of the DBMS to which you are connecting. An environment handle can contain multiple connection handles but each connection handle is associated with only one environment handle. Likewise, each connection handle can have many statement handles, but each statement handle is associated with only one connection handle.

Your application passes data to the driver as the address and length of an input buffer. Afterwards you receive data back as an address, length, and possibly the address of the maximum amount of data available in the output buffer. The application needs to allocate memory for these buffers. When the driver returns data that may be in its own SQL format, it is responsible for converting it into the format ODBC SQL requires. This usually applies to providing NULL-terminated strings.

Whenever you call an ODBC function, the driver returns a predefined code. The following are the return codes:

```
SQL_SUCCESS              SQL_INVALID_HANDLE
SQL_SUCCESS_WITH_INFO    SQL_STILL_EXECUTING
SQL_NO_DATA_FOUND        SQL_NEED_DATA
SQL_ERROR
```

Both SQL_ERROR and SQL_SUCCESS_WITH_INFO return additional information that is accessed through a call to SQLError. One of the important functions of the driver is to return a pre-defined set of error codes.

The syntax for SQLError is:

```
RETCODE SQLError(henv, hdbc, hstmt, szSQLState, pfNativeError, szErrorMsg,
cbErrorMsgMax, pcbErrorMsg)
```

szSQLState is a pointer to the null-terminated 5-byte string, the output of the call. Every error has an associated SQLSTATE return code. These state strings are checked by the application in structure error handling. The SQLSTATE code is a two character class value followed by a three character subclass value. The class values of "01" indicate warnings and are accompanied by SQL_SUCCESS_WITH_INFO. Class "IM" indicates an ODBC implementation warning or error. SQL_SUCCESS has an SQLSTATE return value of 00000. These values were standardized in the ANSI SQL-92 document.

pfNativeError is the database's native error code, output.

szErrorMsg is a pointer to the error message string, output.

cbErrorMsgMax is the maximum length of the szErrorMsg.

pcbErrorMsg is a pointer to the maximum number of bytes in szErrorMsg.

These error codes tell you if the error came from the database or in one of the components of the ODBC connection, such as the driver. The format changes to indicate the source of the error.

A component error would have the text form of the following:

```
[vendor][component identifier]error text
```

Here is an example of the error message string:

```
"[Microsoft][ODBC dBase Driver]Unable to allocate sufficient memory."
```

An error from the database itself would also identify the data source as:

```
[vendor][component identifier][data source]error text
```

The following is an example of the error message string:

```
"[Microsoft][ODBC dBase Driver][dBase]Invalid file name: file TEST.DBF not found."
```

Throughout the following two chapters, error handling is usually omitted for clarity, but you should use it. The following is an example of using an error string in try/catch error handling:

```
try{
  m_pSet->ReQuery();
  }
catch (CDBException* e) {
```

```
    AfxMessageBox(e->m_strError);
    }
```

or

```
try{
  m_pSet->ReQuery();
    }
catch (CDBException* e) {
    AfxMessageBox(e->m_strStateNativeOrigin);
    }
```

The second form gives you the complete error string, including the native error code, which is useful if you are familiar with the DBMS and its error codes. The results of m_strStateNativeOrigin follow:

`"State:S0022,Native:207,Origin:[Microsoft][ODBC SQL Server Driver][SQL Server]"`

m_strError would just be: `"Invalid column name, MyColumn"`.

Summing Up

The first portion of this chapter examined the history of SQL and ODBC. It defined the basic components of ODBC: the driver and the Driver Manager. It listed the basic process of writing an ODBC application, first getting the environment handle, the connection handle, and the statement handle—you must process multiple SQL statements and then reverse the process, freeing the handles. Lastly, an outline of the error-handling process was provided. Microsoft has wrapped the database API into several classes, which will be examined before SQL statements and ODBC are again discussed, in Chapter 30.

MFC Database Class Programming

In MFC 3.2 Microsoft introduced four new classes to wrap the most frequent ODBC functions. Using the Application Wizard in Visual C++, it became trivial to build a simple ODBC application. All the connection and data exchange was handled for one table in the initial frame through a CRecordView. Visual C++ even provided a set of VCR type controls to step through the database. It used CDatabase and CRecordSet to open a connection, retrieve a table's data, and close the connection. This chapter assumes that you are familiar with this process and have looked at the sample ODBC tutorial included with Visual C++ 4.0.

In the VC++ 4.0 ODBC tutorials, you had to get a connection to a database before you could use a CRecordSet object. You constructed a CDatabase object and called its Open member function. When you constructed the CRecordSet object you passed a pointer to the CDatabase object. You finished by calling the CDatabase Close member and destroyed the CDatabase object. This is the basic design of the MFC Database classes. You may not know, however, you did all of this, because the AppWizard handled all of the work!

Class `CDatabase`

`CDatabase` provides member functions to open a database, close a database, begin, end, and reverse transactions, and query the database via SQL statements. `CDatabase` is derived from `CObject` and has one data member, `m_hdbc`, the connection handle of type `HDBC`. You construct the object, then call `Open` to initialize or establish a connection to the database.

The following example shows a typical code snippet to declare an instance of a C database and open that database.

```
class CMyDocument : public Cdocument
{
public:
  CDatabase m_myDB;
}

CDatabase* CMyDocument::GetDatabase()
{
  if(!m_myDB.IsOpen() && !m_myDB.Open(NULL))
    return NULL;
  return &m_myDB;
}
```

Creating the class doesn't open the data source—you must call `CDataBase`'s member function `Open` to make the connection.

`CDataBase::Open`

```
virtual BOOL Open(LPCSTR lpszDSN = NULL, BOOL bExclusive = FALSE, bReadOnly =
➥FALSE, LPCSTR lpszConnect = "ODBC;", BOOLbUseCursorLib = TRUE)
```

Parameters:

`lpszDSN` is a string of the data source name. If you pass `NULL`, the Data Source dialog box asks you to which data source it should connect. If you specify the `lpszConnect` string as previously, it will just be ignored for now, but in future versions of ODBC this may change. Normally, just set this value to `NULL`.

`BExclusive` is always `FALSE` in current versions of MFC because a data source must be shared (non-exclusive).

`BReadOnly` is usually `FALSE`. You want to be able to read and write to the database. You would set this to `TRUE` for a data source from which you read data but don't want the user to change.

`LpszConnect` is a connect string. It always begins with the characters `ODBC`, but future versions of `CDatabase` may support other types of connections. The data source name, the user ID, the user password (if required), and the other information required by your particular database follows. If you don't supply the required information, the Data Source dialog is presented to the user.

BUserCursorLib is TRUE when you use the ODBC Cursor library DLL. Set to FALSE if you wish to use dynasets. The default is TRUE using static snapshots and forward-only cursors.

If Open fails, the function evaluates to zero and throws a CDBException. The function returns nonzero if a successful connection is made.

The following shows an example of Open where every part of the connection information is hard coded into the application:

```
CDatabase m_myDB;

try {
  CString odbc="ODBC;";
  CString dsn="MyDataBase";
  CString uid="Dave";
  CString password="evad";
  CString connect = odbc+"DSN=";

  connect +=dsn;
  connect +="; UID=";
  connect +=uid;
  connect +="; PWD=";
  connect +=password;

pD0c->m_myDB.Open(NULL,FALSE,FALSE,connect,FALSE);
}
```

The following shows another example of Open where the application hard codes the database name and connection information:

```
CDatabase m_myDB();
m_myDB.Open("MYDATABASE",FALSE,FALSE,"ODBC;");
```

You also can query the user for connection information by using just the Open(NULL).

```
m_myDB.Open(NULL);
```

It is important to note that opening the database can take several seconds. Most applications open the database once globally and then use that connection throughout the application. Open is usually stored in either the CDocument class or the main application's InitInstance. In this example we open the database in the application's call to InitInstance:

In the application's header file:

```
CDatabase myDB;
```

In the application's InitInstance:

```
try
{
  myDB.Open("MYDATABASE",FALSE,FALSE,"ODBC;");
}
catch (CDBException *e)
```

```
{
  AfxMessageBox(CString("Didn't open database.\n") + e->m_strError);
  throw;
}
```

Wherever you need to open a CRecordset to get a pointer to the application, open the record-set as

```
CMyApp *app=(CMyApp *)AfxGetApp();
CMyRecordSet myset(&(app->myDB));
myset.Open(CRecordset::dynaset);
...
```

If you open the database in the document, you need a pointer to the database. The pointer is gotten from the document as the following example shows:

```
CDatabase *pDoc = GetDocument()->m_pDatabase;
CDatabase::Close();
virtual void Close();
```

The only thing to remember about CDatabase::Close is that you need to close the recordsets before you close the database connection. If you don't, the record set is left in an undefined state and transaction processing rolls back. This close does not destroy the CDatabase object, you may need it to connect to a different data source.

The preceding example uses the attribute IsOpen, which returns nonzero if the CDatabase object is connected. Also available are GetConnect(), the ODBC connect string; GetDatabaseName(), a string of the database in use; CanUpdate(), which returns nonzero if you didn't make the connection read only; CanTransact(), which returns nonzero if the database supports transaction processing; InWaitForDataSouce(), which returns nonzero when the CDatabase object is waiting for a server response; SetLoginTimeout() and SetQueryTimeout(), which enable you to specify how many seconds to wait; and, SetSynchronousMode(), which enables synchronous processing for recordsets and SQL statements. Asynchronous processing is the default. CDatabase::Cancel is used to cancel an asynchronous operation in progress.

CDatabase supports transaction processing, which is a set of reversible SQL calls—the AddNew(), Edit(), Delete(), and Update() member functions of CRecordSet. If the data source supports transaction processing, all the statements are held in a state in which they can each be reversed. To begin, the statement BeginTrans() is called, followed by a set of statements. When the user specifies that all is okay, CommitTrans() is called and the set of statements is executed. In addition to the above, CDatabase has the operation RollBack() to reverse changes since BeginTrans().

One of the most used database operations is CDatabase::ExecuteSQL. The member function takes a pointer to the SQL statement. The next chapter looks at two ODBC functions, SQLExecDirect and SQLExecute, which enable you to pass every SQL statement to your DBMS driver and get back recordsets of data. However, CDatabase::ExecuteSQL is not used to retrieve datasets—it's used in row operations such as UPDATE and DELETE. In MFC programming you should try to limit direct SQL calls via ::ExecuteSQL so that functionality is not supported by the MFC class. This function doesn't return an MFC dataset.

```
Void ExecuteSQL(LPCSTR lpszSQL);
```

An example code snipped using ExecuteSQL to execute an SQL statement:

```
CString myName = "Update CLIENTS Set LASTNAME = "Hamilton"   where CLIENTNO eq
➥1345";
if(!m_myDB.ExecuteSQL(myName);
{
//handle error
}
```

CRecordset

The CRecordset class encapsulates a collection of database records called a recordset. CRecordset supports scrolling through records, adding, editing, and deleting records, specifying filters to the records, sorting, and parameterization of the recordset. You need a separate CRecordset class for every database table and every join you use. The ClassWizard creates this for you and sets up member variables to handle the data exchange between the class and the dialog or the view where you manage the data. Don't modify the code generated by ClassWizard in this class. If you redefine the database table, ClassWizard regenerates over your changes. The class specific code to manipulate the data can be either in the Dialog class or a separate class you inherit from your CRecordset class.

The CRecordset class should be created and deleted as needed. Each instance takes up RAM, but creating and deleting is fast and efficient. Don't open the classes globally, as you did with the database connection. Open recordsets as you need them, then close them after you use them. You can also let them go out of scope by opening in your dialog class functions. In the OnOK() function listed below for a dialog box you see the recordset object will be deleted after the OnOK() function is complete, because the function's local variables go out of scope and die. As the following example shows:

```
void CMyDialog::OnOK()
{
  UpdateData(TRUE);
  try
  {
    CMyApp *app=(CMyApp *)AfxGetApp();
    CMyRecordSet myset(&(app->myDB));
    myset.Open(CRecordset::dynaset);
    myset.AddNew();
    myset.m_name = m_NameID;
    myset.Update();
  }
catch(CDBException *e)
```

```
{
  AfxMessageBox(e->m_strError);
  e->Delete();
  return;
}
Cdialog::OnOK();
}  //after this function exits the above CRecordset goes out of scope and is
➥deleted
```

Deleting the recordset frees up the RAM.

CRecordset is a large class. Recordsets come in two types: dynasets and snapshots. A dynaset stays synchronized with updates the user makes while a snapshot is a set of the data from the database at the time you created the CRecordset. A snapshot is a copy of the data at that point in time. There is also an open type, Forward Only, which sets up a read-only forward scrolling recordset. This enables the MFC classes to work with older drivers that only support this type scrolling.

The functions of CRecordset enable you to scroll through the data, update the data, sort the data, further filter the data, and parameterize the recordset. Parameterizing enables you to change the filter without parsing the entire SQL phrase again. The Open member function has already been discussed. There is also a Close member function.

The data members of CRecordset are simple:

m_hstmt is the statement handle.

m_pDatabase is a pointer to the database's CDatabase class.

m_nFields is a UINT to the number of data fields in the recordset.

m_nParams is the number of parameter data members.

m_strFilter is a CString with the SQL WHERE clause.

m_sort is a CString with the SQL ORDER BY clause.

CRecordset operations edit the data set and move through the data set.

AddNew prepares the recordset for a new row, UPDATE actually adds it.

Delete deletes the current record from the recordset.

Edit prepares the recordset for changes, while UPDATE actually changes it.

Update completes the AddNew and Edit member functions.

Move positions the recordset at one record.

MoveFirst positions to the first record in the recordset.

MoveLast positions to the last record in the recordset.

MoveNext and *MovePrev* positions the record in the recordset.

DoFieldExchange implements RFX between field member data of the recordset and the database.

GetDefaultConnect gets the default connect string.

GetDefaultSQL gets the default SQL string.

OnSetOptions sets options for the ODBC statement.

OnWaitForDataSource is called to yield processing time to other applications during asynchronous operations.

When moving through the recordset you need to check if you are at the end or beginning of the recordset with the following:

```
if (!myRecset.IsBOF() && !myRecset.IsEOF())
    myRecset.MoveNext();
```

CRecordset has a large set of attributes (see Table 29.2) to give you information on the recordset and changes to the field. All attributes that are "check whether" return nonzero if TRUE.

Table 29.2. CRecordset attributes.

Attribute	Purpose
CanAppend	Checks whether new records can be added
CanRestart	Checks whether requery can be called
CanScroll	Checks whether you can scroll through the records
CanTransact	Checks whether transactions are supported
CanUpdate	Checks whether the recordset can be updated
GetRecordCount	Gets the number of records in the recordset
GetStatus	Gets the status of the recordset: the index of the current record and whether a final count of the records has been obtained
GetTableName	Gets name of the table of the recordset
GetSQL	Gets the SQL string used to select the recordset
IsOpen	Checks whether Open has been called previously
IsBOF	Checks whether the recordset has been positioned before the first record. There is no current record.
IsEOF	Checks whether the recordset has been positioned after the last record. There is no current record.
IsDeleted	Checks whether the recordset is positioned on a deleted record

CRecordView

CRecordView enables your application to display fields in a dialog box. Dialog Data Exchange (DDX) and Record Field Exchange (RFX) enable you to automatically exchange data between your view and the dialog box. CRecordView supports movement between records, updating records, and automatically closing the recordset when the view closes.

In MFC programming the standard approach to developing a database application is via document/view as you saw in Chapter 7, "Document/View Architecture." You open a file and have multiple "views" on the data in that file. If this still confuses you, think about Microsoft's Word. When you type a .DOC file, you can change how you view the text in four ways: Normal, Outline, Page Layout, and Master Document. When creating a document, you use Normal to view spacing. When reviewing a document, you probably switch to Master, a more convenient reading mode.

The concept of multiple views becomes nebulous with databases. The document is actually a collection of files or tables. You often want to look at a union of several tables. Multiple views are even harder to define in client/server applications when you are passing messages to another application. In database applications the recordset is the document. It is often easier to embed the recordset in the frame window, but this precludes having multiple views on the data. CRecordView is a class developed as a view directly connected to a recordset.

CRecordView is a view created from a dialog template that displays the fields in a CRecordset. This class uses both DDX and RFX to automate the movement of data between controls and fields in the recordset. When you did your first ODBC tutorial you saw the power of CRecordView when the AppWizard created a view and recordset. AppWizard even created a toolbar to navigate through the recordset. However, in most cases you will use CRecordset and a CView and not CRecordView. CRecordset has many more features to manipulate data from your database dialog box.

CFieldExchange (RFX) and Special Handling of CLongBinary

CFieldExchange is a helper class for the RFX mechanism. It facilitates the movement between the recordset to the database. It exchanges data between the recordset class and the actual database. CFieldExchange supports a number of operations, including binding parameters, binding data members, and setting flags on the current record. It has two class members: IsFieldType returns the number of the field (if the operation is appropriate for the type) and SetFieldType specifies the type of the recordset data member. The ClassWizard, you saw, generates a field map and handles the typing for you as the following example shows:

```
//enroll tutorial
void CSectionSet::DoFieldExchange(CFieldExchange* pFX)
{
//{{AFX_FIELD_MAP(CSectionSet)
```

```
pFX->SetFieldType(CFieldExchange::outputColumn);
RFX_Text(pFX, _T("[CourseID]"), m_CourseID);
RFX_Text(pFX, _T("[SectionNo]"), m_SectionNo);
RFX_Text(pFX, _T("[InstructorID]"), m_InstructorID);
RFX_Text(pFX, _T("[RoomNo]"), m_RoomNo);
RFX_Text(pFX, _T("[Schedule]"), m_Schedule);
RFX_Int(pFX, _T("[Capacity]"), m_Capacity);
//}}AFX_FIELD_MAP
pFX->SetFieldType(CFieldExchange::param);
RFX_Text(pFX,"CourseIDParam",m_strCourseIDParam);
}
```

The pFX is the context for doing the data exchange and is similar to CArchive::Serialize. It gets and sets data to an external data source, in our case, a CDatabase class member variable. RFX supports the following operations shown in Table 29.3.

Table 29.3. Operations supported by RFX.

Name	Operation
BindParam	Indicates where ODBC should retrieve parameter data
BindFieldToColumn	Indicates where ODBC must retrieve/deposit outputColumn data
Fixup	Sets CString/CByteArray lengths, sets NULL status bit
MarkForAddNew	Marks dirty if value has changed since AddNew call
MarkForUpdate	Marks dirty if value has changed since Edit call
Name	Appends field names for fields marked dirty
NameValue	Appends <column name>=? for fields marked dirty
Value	Appends "?" followed by separator, like ',' or ' '
SetFieldDirty	Sets status bit dirty (that is, changed) field
SetFieldNull	Sets status bit indicating NULL value for field
IsFieldDirty	Returns value of dirty status bit
IsFieldNull	Returns value of NULL status bit
IsFieldNullable	Returns TRUE if field can hold NULL values
StoreField	Archives field value
LoadField	Reloads archived field value
GetFieldInfoValue	Returns general information on a field
GetFieldInfoOrdinal	Returns general information on a field

If your binary data is long, you will need to retrieve it into a CLongBinary, which can be as large as the available memory. One additional step is needed to do the field exchange—calling SetFieldDirty to ensure the field is included in UPDATE operations.

Class CLongBinary simplifies working with BLOBs (binary large objects) in a database. A BLOB is an object, such as a bitmap, in the database but it may be larger than available memory. In this case you would need to process in a piecemeal fashion using ODBC's function SQLGetData. When you create a CRecordset the CLongBinary object is an embedded member of that class. RFX handles loading the data and storing it back in the database. CLongBinary has two class members, m_hData, an HGLOBAL handle to the actual data, and m_dwDataLength, the object's size in bytes. If the BLOB is too large you get an AFX_SQL_ERROR_SQL_NO_TOTAL or a standard memory exception. You can check this by calling ::GlobalSize on the m_hData member. The next chapter discusses the ODBC function SQLGetData.

CDBException

The class CDBException provides exception handling for runtime errors during ODBC processing. It provides member functions to enable your application to access both the error return codes and the string associated with them. Its format is as follows:

```
try
  {

    CMyApp *app=(CMyApp *)AfxGetApp();
    CMyRecordSet myset(&(app->myDB));
    myset.Open(CRecordset::dynaset);
    myset.AddNew();
    myset.m_name = m_NameID;
    myset.Update();
  }
catch(CDBException *e)
{
  AfxMessageBox(e->m_strError);
  e->Delete();
  return;
}
```

The next chapter deals extensively with SQL and ODBC errors and their SQLSTATE return codes.

Some Examples

One of the most common questions asked about developing database applications is "How do I create a join?" In the first example I do just that. The second example makes a modified CRecordset base class with added functionality and can be reused, saving you some typing time.

Example 1

A join is a common database activity. To make a join using MFC, you add the second table to the GetDefaultSQL() in your first record class:

```
CString CMyRSet::GetDefualtSQL()
{
```

```
    return _T("Employees', "Payroll");
}
```

This example joins tables `Employees` and `Payroll`. You then assign the new member variables as normal. If you have columns with the same name, you need to remember that column names in `DoFieldExchange` must be unique so you would change a table name to a column name as:

```
void CMyRSet::DoFieldExchange(CFieldExchange* pFX_
{
//{{AFX_FIELD_MAP(CMyRSet)
pFX->SetFieldType(…)
RFX_TEXT(pFX,"Employees.EmpLastName, m_Lastname);
…
//}}AFX_FIELD_MAP
}
```

Also you need to add the table name to the field name in the sort and filter strings. This tells the compiler which table's `EmpLastName` you are referring to. Demarcate the fields with the table name as:

```
m_pSet->m_strFilter = "Employees.EmpLastName = Payroll.EmpLastName";
```

Example 2

Load ComboBox in the `RecordSet` derived class. For every table or view you create, you build a `CRecordSet`. The ClassWizard generates the code for you, but when you change the database schema and regenerate, your custom code changes within the `CRecordset` can be lost. One technique is to create a class derived from your `CRecordSet` and in that class define class functions. This example fills a combo box. The `CRecordSet` used here is `CRSEmployee` and its derived class, `CRSDEmployee`.

```
//RSDemployee.h
#include "rsdemployee.h"
class CRSDEmployee : public CRSEmployee
{
public:
  CRSDEmployee(CDatabase* pDatabase = NULL);
  void LoadCombo(class CComboBox &cb);
  DECLARE_DYNAMIC(CRSDEmployee)
};

//rsdemployee.cpp
#include "stdafx.h"
#include "myCDatabase.h"
#ifdef _DEBUG
#undef THIS_FILE
static char BASED_CODE THIS_FILE[] = _FILE_;
#endif
IMPLEMENT_DYNAMIC(CRDEmployee, CRSEmployee)
CRSDEmployee::CRSDEmployee(CDatabase* pdb)
  :CRSEmployee(pdb)
{
}
```

```
void CRSDEmployee::LoadCombo(CMyApp *)afxGetApp();
int index;
m_strSort = "Lname ASC, Fname ASC";
m_strFilter = "";
try
{
  Requery();
  cb.ResetContext();
  while (!IsEOF())
  {
    index = cb.AddString(m_Lname + ", " + "m_Fname);
    cb.SetItemData(index, m_EmpID);
    MoveNext()
 }
catch(CDBException* e)
{
  AfxMessageBox(e->m_strError);
  e->Delete();
}
#ifdef _DEBUG
… rest of class code
#endif //_DEBUG
```

You would use this class and call this function from your applications `OnInitDialog` as

```
BOOL CMyDialog::OnInitDialog()
{
  CMyApp *app = (CMyApp*)AfxGetApp();
  CRSDEmployee emp(&(app->db));
  emp.Open(CRecordset::dynaset);
  Cdialog::OnInitDialog();
  emp.LoadCombo(m_pSet);  //this is function call
}
```

Summary

The MFC classes enable you to quickly get started using ODBC to access DBMS data. For this ease of use, though, there is a trade-off with flexibility. The MFC classes assume that your application knows the data source schema and that it won't change. In today's world that is not the case—you need to access data from a wide variety of global sources. The next chapter dives deeper into ODBC and looks at 57 ODBC functions which enable you to access and manipulate the data more quickly, and more extensively.

ODBC Implementation

30

by David Hamilton

IN THIS CHAPTER

The Call Level Interface (CLI)

Chapter 29, "ODBC Concepts," skimmed over the basics of ODBC programming by using the MFC Database classes, which wrap the ODBC function calls into easier-to-use classes. This chapter focuses on the specifics of how you implement an ODBC-enabled application using those function calls. In an early Pascal programming class, I remember being assigned a problem where I was given a totally unknown file from which I needed to extract some demographic data. I had to devise a plan to open the file and search for patterns of the data. At the time, it seemed like such an obscure problem. This type of problem, however, exists every day when your company sells software to a new client and you need to convert the existing data to your format. In most cases, you know the file types and data definitions. However, with the new concept of the global village of data, more and more of the time you won't know the data format.

For the sake of example, say you need to write a report that includes sales of widgets by month. You know the sales data is located in the accounting domain's computers. You know that accounting has an SQL Server and you have the correct privileges. In the past you would have called accounting and asked for the data over the "sneakernet," but today you can connect with your spreadsheet or report writer and get the data structure presented to you as a series of list boxes, query the data, and get results in the format your report needs. This chapter discusses writing the report-writing software behind the report.

In the standard CLI (Call Level Interface), there are 57 functions to support database access. At first they seem threatening, but once you know one of the family, they are all similar. They all take input parameters as a pair of string address or NULL, and length or ignore. They all pass back output parameters as string address, length of data you want, and, optionally, the address of the amount of data available to you. This last output parameter can be confusing unless you think of it as having a very long column description available, (like `My_Still_Working_Employees`), though you only need a short report heading (Employees). This chapter uses Hungarian notation as `sz` (a null-terminated string), `cb` (count of bytes), and `pcb` (pointer to a count of bytes). `pcb` is usually the total number of bytes available. If `pcb` is pointing to a string, it is without the NULL terminator. Throughout this chapter NULL-terminated strings are cast as (`UCHAR *`) because .cpp (C++) files and type checking are best generated more tightly than .c (C). Most outside examples you see don't include this cast on the NULL-terminated strings and are thus standard C files.

The Call Level Interface (CLI) specified functions can be broken down into 11 groups. This makes the task of learning all 57 functions somewhat easier. The functions can be broken down as in the following list.

> Allocating and deallocating handles (eight calls)
>
> Getting and setting attributes (ten calls)

Opening and closing database connection (two calls)

Accessing descriptors (six calls)

Executing SQL statements (nine calls)

Retrieving results (eight calls)

Accessing schema metadata (four calls)

Performing introspection (four calls)

Controlling transactions (two calls)

Accessing diagnostic information (three calls)

Canceling functions (one call)

If you're new to ODBC, one of the best resources is included with the ODBC 2.5 SDK, called ODBCTEST (the file is actually ODBCTE32.EXE). The ODBC SDK is available on Level II or Level III MSDN. Each of the SQL functions is listed. ODBCTE32.EXE enables you to execute each statement, one by one, and test your syntax. It's a good idea to add it to your VC++ 4.0 Tools menu so that it's available for debugging your ODBC application. If you have an older version of ODBC, ODBC 2.5 is available on CompuServe's WINEXT forum or through ftp.microsoft.com in the /developer/ODBC/public/subdirectory.

The first portion of the ODBC chapter, between brief explanations of connecting and disconnecting, looks at a large programmer-friendly set of enabling software, the SQL Catalog Functions. Each function is described, its syntax given, its parameters identified, and its possible SQLSTATE return codes listed. To save space, this chapter describes only the SQLSTATEs particular to a function. However, the entire SQLError function is listed at the end of this chapter.

Whether you are writing for a single PC or for a company worldwide application, it is best to envision the client/server model. The application sends messages that the server interprets. The server retrieves data from a DBMS which is sent back to the client with another stream of messages. In ODBC the middleware is the driver.

ODBC defines three types of drivers. Although each type functions differently, the application doesn't have to know about it. In ODBC programming, the application doesn't care if the data is on your local hard drive, across the network, or on a different continent. In ODBC a *one-tier* driver accesses an ISAM or flat file. Usually the database is on your local PC. In this case, the driver is the SQL engine and does all the SQL statement processing.

Figure 30.1 is a one-tier driver typical of what you will use in developing a PC-based database application.

FIGURE 30.1.

ODBC one-tier type driver.

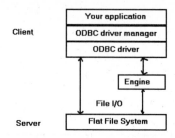

FIGURE 30.2.

SQL Server's two-tier type driver.

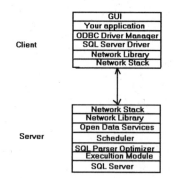

FIGURE 30.3.

A three-tier type driver arrangement.

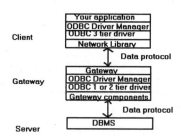

A two-tier driver is the more typical NT office setup. The application is usually placed on an NT workstation and the DBMS on an NT server. This is what is usually referred to as client/ server. ODBC calls the two-tier driver maps to the DBMS's native SQL. Microsoft's SQL Server uses a two-tier ODBC driver. Figure 30.2 shows that the server end of the system is intelligent, parsing and optimizing SQL statements as well as scheduling their execution. The client handles connection to the DBMS and processing of results.

In a three-tier driver, the client connects to a server that acts as a gateway to the network, as shown in Figure 30.3. The DBMS may be on a large mainframe computer. The gateway is responsible for routing and translating requests. In a sense, the application on the client has a one-tier driver to the gateway machine. The gateway machine has either a one-tier or a two-tier driver to the DBMS. The gain is that by off-loading work requirements to a gateway machine, more clients are able to access the DBMS.

Connecting to a Data Source

When connecting to a database, you must evaluate two scenarios—the first where you have a target database in mind and know its schema, and the second where your application must behave like Excel or Crystal Reports and connect to any ODBC data source. In the second case you need to use the ODBC catalog functions to determine what capabilities are available.

SQLAllocEnv

Before you can call any ODBC function, you must initialize ODBC and establish the environment. ODBC uses this environment to keep track of which data sources are in use. Remember that you have one environment per application but can have many connections. The first call is always to SQLAllocEnv, which returns a pointer to the memory location of the environmental handle. The environmental handle privately tracks the number of connections, the connection's state (connected versus disconnected), and the passing of environment errors to SQLError. Within the HENV handle are also the enumerates of the data sources available, the drivers available, and the ability to control the transaction processing on all connections.

This handle is of type HENV. Handles in ODBC are like those you have seen while programming for Windows NT. They are an index into a table entry identifying program data that is private. Windows has all types of handles, memory handles, device contexts, instance handles, and ODBC handles. The privacy is important in that each driver developer can do what they need to get the job done inside a block of code that is used by the application in a consistent way. This is called the interface. Handles have constant interfaces. ODBC drivers provide uniform error handling, tying the error to the function that generated the error condition. In a multithreaded environment like Windows NT, if one process starts a thread to do something, another can control that thread or terminate it. There are actually a pair of handles generated. The application generates a handle passed to the driver manager. The driver manager generates a handle to share with the DBMS's actual ODBC driver.

The return value from SQLAllocEnv is SQL_SUCCESS or SQL_ERROR. Generally the SQL_ERROR means a memory error and handle would be set to SQL_NULL_HENV. The following is a general outline of the process:

```
#include <windows.h>
#include <sql.h>
HENV henv;
HDBC hdbc;
SQLAllocEnv(&henv);
SQLAllocConnect(&hdbc)
SQLConnect(hdbc, MYDATABASE",SQL_NTS,"MYUSERID",SQL_NTS,"MYPASSWORD",SQL_NTS);

//perform application ODBC functions

SQLDisconnect(hdbc);
SQLFreeConnect(hdbc);
SQLFreeEnv(henv);
```

SQLAllocConnect

Just as you got the previous environment handle, you need a handle to the actual connection or connections. For every data source your application uses, you need one connection handle. `SQLAllocConnect` returns a pointer to a memory location, the connection handle, of type `HDBC`. `SQLAllocConnect` can return the same codes as above with the `SQLSTATE` codes of `01000`, `S1000`, `S1001` (memory allocation error), and `S1009` (invalid argument value). `SQLAllocConnect` is a call into the Driver Manager DLL. Inside the private structures of `hdbc` is all the information about one single connection, including the server/directory/file information, the driver to be used. The largest feature of `hdbc` is that all the function calls provided by the driver have pointers stored in a array to provide function call routing. `hdbc` passes connection errors to `SQLError`. Transaction isolation is done within this handle as well as time-out information:

```
HDBC hdbc;
SQLAllocConnect(henv, &hdbc);
```

You also need to allocate a handle to the statements you will use. Again, every connection can have many statements, but each statement applies to only one connection. All SQL statements and catalog functions get the `hdbc` handle from the `hstmt` handle to know what driver to look in for the actual function code. `hstmt` also maintains state information so that the application can call the functions in the correct order. `hstmt` locks results sets together and holds the cursor name and network information. But all of its member variables are private, just for Windows and ODBC to access via an interface. The syntax is

```
rc = SQLAllocStmt(hdbc, phstmt);
```

`phstmt` is a far pointer to the storage area of the statement handle.

`SQLState` return codes are `01000`, `08003` (connection not open), `IM001`, `S1000`, `S1001` (memory allocation failure), and `S1009` (invalid argument).

SQLConnect

At this point you have two handles. The ODBC connection is said to be initialized, but you have not yet said what data source you want and made the actual connection. `SQLConnect` is the only ODBC function available at the core API level to make the connection. Chapter 29 introduced various methods to pass the DSN (data source name) and database specifics like user ID (UID) and password (PWD) via `SQLConnect`. Its parameters are

```
SQLConnect(hdbc, szDSN, cbDSN, szUID, cbUID, szPWD, cbPWD).
```

Throughout this chapter the type definitions are always

```
HDBC hdbc;
char szDSN[SOME_LENGTH];
SDWORD bcDSN;
```

This is a good place to point out a similarity in the parameter values used for all ODBC function calls. First is a handle, then a parameter, then that parameter's size, then another parameter, and then the other parameter's size. This is always the pattern—remember it when you get stuck. This pattern makes internalizing the function calls easier to remember. If the strings are null-terminated, you can pass SQL_NTS for the length of the DSN. In most single-tiered databases, you only need to supply the connection handle and the DSN.

SQLConnect returns general SQLSTATE return codes: 01000, 08001 (unable to connect), 08002 (connection in use), 08004 (data source rejected connection), 08S01 (communication link failure), and 28000 (invalid authorization). It also returns driver codes: IM001 (function not supported), IM002 (no default driver), IM003 (driver not loaded), IM004 (SQLAllocEnv failed), IM005 (SQLAllocConnect failed), and IM006 (SQLSetConnectOption failed). It also returns IM009 and SQL codes: S1000, S1001, S1090 (invalid string length), and S1T00 (time-out). SQL_INVALID_HANDLE sets the hdbc to SQL_NULL_HDBC.

```
RETCODE rc;
rc = SQLConnect(hdbc,
➥"MYDATABASE",SQL_NTS,"MYUSERID",SQL_NTS,"MYPASSWORD",SQL_NTS);
```

In a usual application you might have a dialog box in which the user provides a username and password. In this case you would build a string, the connection string, which could be passed to SQLConnect or its friends, SQLDriverConnect and SQLBrowseConnect. SQLDriverConnect is an extension level 1 function that takes a connection string rather than a set of parameters. SQLDriverConnect uses standard user interface elements. Therefore, if you are writing to Windows, Macintosh OS, or OS/2, this is applicable; if you are writing to MS/DOS, it doesn't help you because you don't have graphical dialog boxes available. You saw SQLDriverConnect wrapped in CDatabase in Chapter 29, with its ability to ask the user for the string information with dialog boxes. In that case, the call was with no supplied parameters:

```
rc = SQLDriverConnect(hdbc, hwnd, NULL, 0, NULL, 0, 0, SQL_DRIVER_COMPLETE);
```

You need to supply the hwnd, a handle to the window in which you want questions asked. The function builds the message boxes and displays them.

```
#define MAXBUF 512
{
HDBC hdbc;
HWND hwnd;
char szConStrIn[MAXBUF+1];  //input string
SWORD cbConStrIn; //length of string
char szConStrOut[MAXBUF+1]; //connection string for later use
SWORD cbConStrOutMax;
SWORD pcbConStrOut; // pointer to total number of bytes in csConStrOut
UWORD fDriverCompletion;
rc = SQLDriverConnect(hdbc, hwnd, szConStrIn, MAXBUF, szConStrOut, MAXBUF,
➥&pcbConStrOut, fDriverCompletion);
```

Using ODBCTEST, you can simulate what your user will see. First choose SQLAllocEnv, SQLAllocConnect, and then SQLDriverConnect, and you are presented with your default dialog boxes as shown in Figure 30.4 and the dialog to input the username and password (in Figure 30.5).

FIGURE 30.4.

SQLDriverConnect *to the data source.*

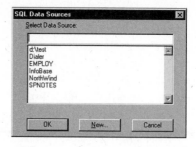

FIGURE 30.5.

SQLDriverConnect *retrieves connection information.*

The magic that brings up these dialog boxes is done in the last parameter which can be either SQL_DRIVER_PROMPT (puts up the SQL Data Sources dialog with all DSNs for the user to pick one), SQL_DRIVER_COMPLETE (checks the szConStrIn for DSN and then connects when enough information is available), SQL_DRIVER_COMPLETE_REQUIRED (same as above but must have full connection string to proceed), or SQL_DRIVER_NOPROMPT (don't ask).

In Windows NT you may be tempted to develop a DLL that encapsulates the application's ODBC functions, sharing them between several applications. ODBC handles are unique to the tasks and cannot be shared because their memory allocation does not use the DDE_SHARE option on the GlobalAlloc() call. A better approach to developing a separate DLL is to develop a DDE server application. By doing so you are not trying to share handles, and the server application would still have all the ODBC calls and would send messages to your other applications.

The return codes for SQLDriverConnect has the same SQLSTATEs as SQLConnect.

SQLBrowseConnect is the third method of connecting to a data source. It enables you to control the user interface. Your application goes step-by-step to first ask the driver what information is needed, and then prompts the user for that information. You repeat the process with the next bit of information until the entire connection string is completed. If you repeatedly called SQLBrowseConnect, the driver gives you the next piece of the connection string and returns SQL_NEED_DATA. Why? You would use SQLBrowseConnect when attempting to connect to a foreign data source, perhaps a source on a mainframe computer where even the format of the data may need to be translated. The database might have many personal attributes, such as HOSTNAME, ALIASes, multiple levels of passwords, and so on. An example follows:

```
HSTMT hstmt
RETCODE rc;
UCHAR szConStrIn[100] = "MYDSN";
UCHAR szConStrOut[100];
SWORD cbConStrOut;
do
{
rc = SQLBrowseConnect(hstmt, szConStrIn, SQL_NTS, szConStrOut,
➥sizeof(szConStrOut),&bcConStrOut);
}
while
{
(rc == SQL_NEED_DATA)
}
```

The input and output strings are always in the following form:

`KEYWORD=VALUE;`

`SQLBrowseConnect` has extensions that enable you to query the user in the form of

`KEYWORD:PROMPT=?;`

`PROMPT` is your string to the user. Another extension uses the form

`KEYWORD:PROMPT={CHOICE1,CHOICE2,CHOICE3}`

This gives the user three choices. The attributes like UID (username) and PWD (password) must be in all capital letters. The prompt can be mixed case. If you precede an attribute with an *, then it is optional.

Now the question of which connection function is best arises. Here are a simple set of rules:

- If the application works with a fixed set of drivers, then use `SQLConnect` or `SQLDriverConnect` and hard-coded connection strings.
- If your data source requires more than the three parameters for `SQLConnect`, you need to use `SQLDriverConnect`.
- If you use dialog boxes to prompt users for information to log in, use `SQLDriverConnect` or `SQLBrowseConnect`.
- If the driver supports only core level functions, then use `SQLConnnect`. If it supports level 1, then use either `SQLConnect` or `SQLDriverConnect`.
- If the application doesn't know what drivers are available, use `SQLDriverConnect`.
- If your application will have multiple users and passwords, it is usually best to prompt the users for data with a dialog box in the application and then call `SQLConnect` or `SQLDriverConnect`.
- If users can decide on a data source, use `SQLDriverConnect` or `SQLBrowseConnect`.
- If the application has no idea what the connection string might look like, use `SQLBrowseConnect`.

You may want to build a quick, simple Visual C++ application to make sure all this really works as described. The following is a fairly basic application. Open a data source and get a piece of data from a table. In Visual C++ you open a new workspace, choose a name, and then choose Application. Add a new file to the project and type it in. This procedure does nothing more than display a list box with the data element you went looking for. All the usual error checking has been removed for simplicity. Your application should function like this, but don't follow this form, because without error handling, ODBC applications become very difficult to debug. You may not even know if the database is open, let alone why you are getting strange characters for the results.

```cpp
//text1.cpp
#include <windows.h>
#include <sql.h>
#include <sqlext.h>
#define MAX_DATA 100

int WINAPI WinMain(HANDLE hInstance, HANDLE hPrevInstance, LPSTR lpszCmdLine, int
➥nCmdShow)
{

HENV henv;
HDBC hdbc;
HSTMT hstmt;
char szData[MAX_DATA];
SDWORD cbData;

SQLAllocEnv(&henv);
SQLAllocConnect(henv, &hdbc);
SQLConnect(hdbc, (UCHAR *)"SPNOTES", SQL_NTS,NULL,0,NULL,0);
SQLAllocStmt(hdbc, &hstmt);

SQLFetch(hstmt);
SQLGetData(hstmt, 2, SQL_C_CHAR, szData, sizeof(szData), &cbData);

MessageBox(NULL, szData, "Chapter 30", MB_OK);

SQLFreeStmt(hstmt, SQL_DROP);
SQLDisconnect(hdbc);
SQLFreeConnect(hdbc);
SQLFreeEnv(henv);
return(TRUE);
}
```

To describe what is happening behind the scenes, back up a bit. When you build your application, Visual C++ links in ODBC32.LIB. When your user runs the application, ODBC.DLL is loaded into memory. The driver manager contains the function entry points for every one of its functions. Windows NT may not load ODBC.DLL if it is already running (the instance count is nonzero). When your application allocates the above handles, two sets are actually allocated, one for the application driver manager connection and the other for the driver manager to driver connection. When you call SQLConnect to the DSN, the driver manager calls LoadLibrary and loads the driver DLL. At this point the driver manager polls the driver DLL, using the Windows function GetProcAddress to build an array of function entry points and associate that array with your HDBC handle. From this point on, the driver DLL is just another data file to Windows NT. The driver manager then uses the second set of HENV and HDBC to make the calls into the driver DLL. It is this two-step process that makes connecting to an ODBC data source time-consuming to the user. After all these steps, the driver sends the user ID and password to the DBMS. Throughout this process your application's call to SQLConnect has been waiting for its return.

Connecting to Unknown ODBC Data Sources

In all of the preceding examples it was assumed that you were writing to a specific data source. But what if you are developing the next GREATER_THAN_EXCEL spreadsheet or a general report writer application, MORE_CLEAR_THAN_CRYSTAL? If you remember, the Driver Manager created a registry entry or an entry in the ODBCINST.INI folder, discussed in Chapter 29. It holds a wealth of information about the data source. To get at that information, you can use the ODBC catalog functions.

SQLDataSources is defined as API level 2, but actually goes through the Driver Manager to poll the registry's ODBCINST.INI folder for the available data sources.

A sample function to load a list box with data source names might be:

```
void CNewtdbView::LoadDataSources ()
{
HENV henv;
SWORD pcbDSN;
SWORD pcbDesc;
UCHAR szDSN [SQL_MAX_DSN_LENGTH + 1];
UCHAR szDesc [255];

    m_lbData = (CListBox *) GetDlgItem (IDC_DATA_SOURCE);
    if (::SQLAllocEnv (&henv) == SQL_ERROR)
    return;

    while (::SQLDataSources (henv, SQL_FETCH_NEXT, szDSN, sizeof (szDSN), &pcbDSN,
    ➥szDesc,sizeof (szDesc),&pcbDesc ) == SQL_SUCCESS)
    {
     m_lbData->AddString ((const char *)szDSN);
    }
    ::SQLFreeEnv (henv);
}
```

SQLDataSources returns SQLSTATEs 01000, 01004 (data truncated), S1000, S1001, S1090, and S1103 (direction out of range).

The preceding sample code can also be used in the common dialog's file open to present your user with a list of data sources in a similar manner as SQLDriverConnect.

The description (szDesc) returned is the setup value from the registry's ODBCINST.INI folder. For example, for an ODBC data source pointing to an Access database, the szDesc value would be "Microsoft Access Driver (*.mdb)," and the szDSN value would be the actual data source name string.

Likewise, you may not know what drivers are available on a system. The function `SQLDrivers` works just like `SQLDataSources`, through the Driver Manager's ODBCINST.INI registry value. It returns the same `SQLSTATE`s, but its parameters are slightly different because it wants drivers returned, not DSNs:

```
rc = SQLDrivers(henv, SQL_FETCH_NEXT, szDriverDesc, sizeof(szDriverDesc),
→&pcbDriverDesc, szDriverAttributes, sizeof(szDriverattributes),
→&pcbDriverAttributes);
```

The attributes are `FileUsage`, `FileExtensions`, and `DirectConnect`. These values are polled by the Driver Manager from the registry values in the ODBCINST.INI folder discussed in Chapter 29.

SQLGetConnectionOption, SQLSetConnectionOption, SQLGetInfo, and SQLGetFunctions

`SQLSetConnectionOptions` enables the application to manipulate the connection parameters. It's a level 1 extended function, so it may not be supported by core ODBC drivers. The format for the function is

```
HDBC hdbc;
UWORD fOption; //option to set
UDWord vParam; //value to set it to
rc = SQLSetConnectionOptions(hdbc, fOption, vParam);
```

The possible values for `fOption` are

Option	Values
SQL_ACCESS_MODE	if read only
SQL_AUTOCOMMIT	SQL_AUTOCOMMIT_OFF or SQL_AUTOCOMMIT_ON
SQL_CURRENT_QUALIFIER	szString with current qualifier or path
SQL_LOGIN_TIMEOUT	32-bit integer in seconds
SQL_ODBC_CURSORS	SQL_CUR_USE_IF_NEEDED, SQL_FETCH_PRIOR, SQL_CUR_USE_ODBC, or SQL_CUR_USE_DRIVER
SQL_OPT_TRACE	SQL_OPT_TRACE_OFF or SQL_OPT_TRACE_ON
SQL_OPT_TRACEFILE	a szFilename of trace file
SQL_PACKET_SIZE	a 32-bit network packet size in bytes
SQL_QUITE_MODE	a 32-bit hwnd as to where dialog boxes are displayed

SQL_TRANSLATE_DLL	the szNameOfDLL of the DLL used in translation
SQL_TRANSLATE_OPTION	a 32-bit translation flag
SQL_TXN_ISOLATION	a 32-bit bitmask for translation level of hdbc

The function SQLGetConnectionOptions uses the same calling syntax and parameter sets.

SQLGetInfo returns information about both the driver and data source. It either returns the information or SQLSTATE 01000 (general error). It's a common function call because you need to know very minute information often. It answers questions like "does this database use double quotes or single quotes?" (SQL_IDENTIFIER_QUOTE_CHAR) or "what ODBC level does it support (SQL_ODBC_SQL_CONFORMACE)?"

SQLGetInfo is used as

```
rc = SQLGetInfo(hdbc, FInfoType,rgbInfoValue, cbInfoValueMax, pcbInfoValue);
```

The following is an example to get the database name:

```
HDBC hdbc;

CHAR szDBMS[100]; //pointer to szString, 16 bit int, 32 bit flag or 32 bit binary
SWORD cbDBMS;
SQLGetInfo(hdbc, SQL_DBMS_NAME, szDBMS, sizeof(szDBMS), &cbDBMS);
```

The volume of information you can query with SQLGetInfo is listed in this table. The returned values can be a null-terminated string, a 16-bit integer, a 32-bit mask, a 32-bit integer, and a 32-bit binary. The descriptions of each are detailed in the books-on-line. Only the fInfoType values are listed because most of the names are pretty self descriptive.

There are over 80 possible values for FInfoType, each giving you a certain piece of information about the DBMS. These range from simple items such as SQL_DATABASE_NAME to values such as SQL_DRIVER_VER. One that is used often is the poll for the escape delimiter to use before you pass in a string with character values, SQL_LIKE_ESCAPE_CLAUSE.

The SQLSTATE return codes are 01000, 01004, 08003, 2203 (number out of range), IM001, S1000, S1009, S1090, S1096 (information type out of range), S1C00, and S1T00.

SQLGetFunctions is similar, but you only use the parameters for the database, the function, and the result (TRUE or FALSE):

```
rc = SQLGetFunctions(hdbc, fFunction, pfExists);
```

You can also use the following:

```
HDBC hdbc;
UWORD fExists;
SQLGetFunctions(hdbc, SQL_API_ALL_FUNCTIONS, &fExists);
if (fExists[SQL_API_SQLBROWSECONNECT])
{
    //do an SQLBrowseConnection
}
```

Like `SQLGetInfo`, `SQLGetFunctions` has an extensive list of possible `fFunction` values that can be polled. All return either `TRUE` or `FALSE` depending on whether the `hdbc` supports that function. The `fFunction` values are all derived from the SQL functions. You are basically asking whether a certain function is supported. For example, for `SQLConnect`, the `fFunction` value would be `SQL_API_SQLCONNECT`, and for `SQLFetch`, the `fFunction` value would be `SQL_API_SQLFETCH`.

SQLGetFunctions' possible fFunction values

`SQLGetFunctions` returns the `SQLSTATE` codes 01000, S1000, S1001, S1010, and S1095 (function type out of range).

Using the Data Source

The data source in ODBC is the combination of the driver and the DBMS. You have already seen the definition of the DBMS in the registry ODBCINST.INI folder, but how did it get there? The obvious way was that the user loaded a new data source with the ODBC applet from the Control Panel. However, most applications install data sources as part of the program installation. This would certainly lower the number of support calls you receive about how to install the data source. You could also manually edit the registry. Telling a user to do so, of course, is guaranteed to get you all the support calls you can handle. The prescribed method is `SQLConfigDataSource`. The prototype is

```
BOOL SQLConfigDataSource(hwnd, UINT fRequest, LPCSTR lpszDriver, LPCSTR
➥lpszAttributes);
```

The following is an example for an Excel spreadsheet you wish to access via ODBC:

```
#include <odbcinst.h>
SQLConfigDataSource(NULL,ODBC_ADD_DSN, "Excel Files (*.xls)",
➥"DSN=MyFancySpreadsheet\0", "Description=Save the Company Spreadsheet\0",
➥"FileType=Excel\0","DataDirectory=C:\\ROOT\0", "MaxScanRows=20\0");
```

The data source in the case of an Excel spreadsheet is the directory of the spreadsheet itself. ODBC 2.5 introduced functions `ConfigDriver`, `SQLConfigDriver`, `SQLInstallTranslator`, `SQLRemoveDriver`, `SQLRemoveDriverManager`, and `SQLRemoveTranslator` These all alter the entries in the NT registry under SOFTWARE/ODBC/ODBCINST.INI.

The following is an example of an Access database:

```
char  szDriverName[] = "Microsoft Access Driver (*.mdb)";
char  szAttributes[] = "DSN=sample\0DefaultDir=\\\0 DriverId=25\0DBQ=sample.mdb\0";
char  szAttributesCreateMDB[] = "CREATE_DB=\\sample.mdb General\0";

SQLConfigDataSource(NULL, ODBC_ADD_DSN, szDriverName,szAttributesCreateMDB);
SQLConfigDataSource(NULL, ODBC_ADD_DSN, szDriverName,szAttributes);
```

The syntax of the new installer functions is:

```
BOOL ConfigDriver(hwnd, fRequest lpszDriver, lpszArgs, lpszMsg cbMsgMax and
➥pcbMsgOut);
BOOL SQLConfigDriver(hwnd, lpszDriver, lpszArgs, lpszMsg cbMsgMax and pcbMsgOut);
```

The difference is that `SQLConfigDriver` calls the driver's `ConfigDriver` routine without knowing the name of the setup DLL. Your setup program would have installed the DLL prior to the call.

The parameters are: `hwnd`, the parent window handle; `fRequest`, either `ODBC_INSTALL_DRIVER` or `ODBC_REMOVE_DRIVER`; `lpszDriver`, the name of the driver to install; `lpszArgs`, a null-terminated string of arguments, `lpszMsg`, a null-terminated string output message, `cbMsgMax`, and `pcbMsgOut`. The function returns `TRUE` or `FALSE`.

```
BOOL SQLRemoveDriver(lpszDriver, FRemoveDSN, lpdwUsageCount)
BOOL SQLRemoveDriverManager(lpdwUsageCount)
```

Both of these return `TRUE` or `FALSE`.

The parameters are: `lpszDriver`, the name of the driver; `fRemoveDSN`, either `TRUE` or `FALSE`, and `lpdwUsageCount`, the usage count of the drive after this function has been called. The last parameter is an output parameter which is decremented with each call until the `UsageCount` goes to 0, at which point the registry entry is removed.

`SQLInstallTranslator` adds information about a translator to the ODBCINST.INI section of the registry and increments the translator's `UsageCount` by one.

```
BOOL SQLInstallTranslator (lpszInfFile, lpszTranslator, lpszPathIn, lpszPathOut,
    cbPathOutMax, pcbPathOut, fRequest, lpdwUsageCount)
BOOL SQLRemoveTranslator(lpszTranslator, lpdwUsageCount);
```

Both functions return `TRUE` if successful.

The parameters are: `lpszInfFile`, the full path of the ODBC.INF file; `lpszTranslator`, the key in ODBC.INF that describes the translator; `lpszPathIn`, where to install it; `lpszPathOut`, path of prior installation; `cbPathOutMax`, length; `pcbPathOut`, pointer to number of bytes available; `fRequest`, either `ODBC_INSTALL_INQUERY` or `ODBC_INSTALL_COMPLETE`; and `lpdwUsageCount`, the usage count after the translator is installed.

In addition to the above functions, ODBC 2.5 introduced eight additional installer functions to support Uninstall software:

- `SQLConfigDataSouce`
- `SQLCreateDataSource`
- `SQLGetPrivateProfileString`
- `SQLInstallDriver`
- `SQLInstallDriverManager`
- `SQLInstallODBC`
- `SQLManageDataSources`
- `SQLWritePrivateProfileString`

The ODBC SDK includes software for installing drivers into the Windows NT registry on your client's machine. While shipping an application, you probably need to check that ODBC itself is installed. The ODBC SDK has samples for writing setup routines to check and install ODBC, your driver, and your application's DSN into the customer machine. You also can use the sample software to install a driver you are missing in your registry. Copy the driver DLLs to the directory where you have the ODBC SDK's SETUP32. Make sure you have the ODBC.INF file, which identifies which DLLs are needed. Once all of these are in the directory, run DRVSTP32.EXE.

Tables, Columns, Indexes, and Stored Procedures

The function of the driver is to let the world know the capabilities of the data source. It does this with a well-defined interface. In SQL-92, DBMSs provided their structure by schema information tables, which are views in the database. These views list the information about tables, columns, sizes, and so on. But these schema tables were not implemented in many DBMSs. Before you access data in an unknown data source, you need to know its schema, and to get that, you query the database.

Querying the database for a list of its tables, columns, indexes, or stored procedures is part of the ODBC catalog functions. All take a similar set of parameter values and include the standard wildcard characters of * for all chars, _ for any one char and % for any combination of zero or more chars. For example, %dave% brings up all fields with *dave* in any position.

The following catalog functions are defined in SQL-92:

- Core Level—none
- Level 1—`SQLTables`, `SQLColumns`, `SQLStatistics`, `SQLSpecialColumns`
- Level 2—`SQLTablePrivileges`, `SQLColumnPrivileges`, `SQLPrimaryKeys`, `SQLForeignKeys`, `SQLProcedures`, `SQLProcedureColumns`

This chapter looks at each of the level 1 functions. Every call has the first seven parameters in common and returns the same first three attributes about their target.

SQLTables

`SQLTables` returns a list of tables in the data source. The syntax is

```
rc = SQLTables(hstmt, szTableQualifier, cbTableQualifier, szTableOwner,
➥cbTableOwner, szTableName, cbTableName, szTableType, cbTableType)
```

In a relational database, each table has a qualifier (usually the database), a table owner, and a name. You can implicitly call any table as in this example. The table type value is either NULL or one or more of the following values: 'TABLE', 'VIEW', 'SYSTEM TABLE', 'GLOBAL TEMPORARY', 'LOCAL TEMPORARY', 'ALIAS', and 'SYNONYM'. The two temporary table types are base tables which hold intermediate results of queries and are flushed at the end of a transaction or session. An example would be Accounting."Dave".AccountsRec, which is the accounts receivable table from the Accounting database owned by Dave. Using wildcards can make this easier:

```
rc = SQLTables(hstmt, "%", SQL_NTS, "%", SQL_NTS, "%", SQL_NTS,
"'TABLE','VIEW','SYSTEM TABLE'", SQL_NTS)
```

The preceding example shows all the tables, views, and system tables. The following example shows all tables:

```
rc = SQLTables(hstmt, "",0,"%",SQL_NTS,"",0,"",0)
```

The following example shows all VIEWS from MYDATABASE owned by DAVE:

```
rc = SQLTables(hstmt, "MYDATABASE", SQL_NTS, "DAVE", SLQ_NTS,"%", SQL_NTS,
"'VIEW'", SQL_NTS)
```

The result set has five items for each table:

TABLE_QUALIFIER	Varchar(128) qualifier name
TABLE_OWNER	Varchar(128) owner of table
TABLE_NAME	Varchar(128) name of table
TABLE_TYPE	Varchar(128) type of table
REMARKS	Varchar(254) remarks

`SQLTables` returns SQLSTATEs 01000, 08S01, 24000 (invalid cursor state), IM001, S1000, S1001, S1008 (operation canceled), S1010, S1090, S1C00 (driver not capable), and S1T00.

It may be, however, that you have a mixed bag of tables when you don't initially know the data source. In that case, extra error checking is required:

```
TRY
{
// set any options, like timeouts, scrolling options
OnSetOptions(m_hstmt);
```

```
// call the ODBC catalog function with data member params

AFX_SQL_ASYNC(this, (::SQLTables)(m_hstmt, (m_strQualifierParam.IsEmpty()?
(UCHAR FAR *)NULL: (UCHAR FAR *)(const char*)m_strQualifierParam), SQL_NTS,
        (m_strOwnerParam.IsEmpty()? (UCHAR FAR *)NULL: (UCHAR FAR *)(const
➥char*)m_strOwnerParam), SQL_NTS,
        (m_strNameParam.IsEmpty()? (UCHAR FAR *)NULL: (UCHAR FAR *)(const
➥char*)m_strNameParam), SQL_NTS,
        (m_strTypeParam.IsEmpty()? (UCHAR FAR *)NULL: (UCHAR FAR *)(const
➥char*)m_strTypeParam), SQL_NTS));

if (!Check(nRetCode))
 {
  AfxThrowDBException(nRetCode, m_pDatabase, m_hstmt);
 }
    // load first record
    MoveFirst();
}
CATCH_ALL(e)
{
  Close();
  THROW_LAST();
}
END_CATCH_ALL
  return TRUE;
}
```

SQLColumns

SQLColumns is just like SQLTables, except that it returns column information. The first seven parameters are the same, and the last two parameters are changed to szColumnName (usually a search string) and cbColumnName. A large database may have hundreds of columns, so you may need to use wildcards to return only a subset with the search string—for example, PAT* for all the "patient"-related columns.

The return set from SQLColumns has 12 items for each column, shown in Table 30.1.

Table 30.1. SQLColumns return set values.

Name	Type	Comments
TABLE_QUALIFIER	Varchar(128)	
TABLE_OWNER	Varchar(128)	
TABLE_NAME	Varchar(128)	
COLUMN_NAME	Varchar(128)	
DATA_TYPE	SMALLINT	ODBC SQL datatype

Name	Type	Comments
TYPE_NAME	Varchar(128)	DBMS data type
PRECISION	int	Maximum digit
LENGTH	int	Length you want
SCALE	SMALLINT	Maximum digits after decimal
RADIX	SMALLINT	*
NULLABLE	SMALLINT	Columns accept NULL as value
REMARKS	Varchar(254)	Remarks

*RADIX is always either 10 or 2. If it is 10, then use precision and scale to get the number of decimal points in the column. If it is 2, then precision and scale define number of bits in column.

The return SQLSTATE values are the same as SQLTables.

SQLStatistics

SQLStatistics is a similar function to SQLTables and SQLColumns, with the same parameters. SQLStatistics returns statistics about a single table and its indexes. The syntax is:

```
rc = SQLStatistics(hstmt, szTableQualifier, cbTableQualifier, szTableOwner,
➥cbTableOwner, szTableName, cbTableName, fUnique, fAccuracy);
```

The first seven parameters are the same as the other catalog functions. The last two parameters are fUnique and fAccuracy. Parameter fUnique is the type of index with values of either SQL_INDEX_UNIQUE (return only unique indexes) or SQL_INDEX_ALL (return all indexes). Parameter fAccuracy tells you whether the CARDINALITY and PAGES parameters in the result set are valid and current. The calculation of these two parameters can take quite some time. If you set fAccuracy to SQL_ENSURE, the driver always retrieves statistics. SQL_QUICK tells the driver to return the statistics which are readily available. The values of CARDINALITY and PAGES may not be current. Many DBMSs do not support these two return values, so for performance reasons, always set SQL_QUICK unless you have a specific need.

Indexes greatly speed access to data in SQL statements using a WHERE clause. An index is an ordered file of the physical disk locations for each value in a column, speeding the database access by directly moving to a location.

The SQLStatistics result set has 13 columns, a row for the table statistics, and a row for each index that satisfies your request. See Table 30.2.

Table 30.2. The `SQLStatistics` result set.

Name	Type	Comment
TABLE_QUALIFIER	Varchar(128)	Same table qualifier you passed
TABLE_OWNER	Varchar(128)	Same table owner you passed
TABLE_NAME	Varchar(128)	Table name of result set
NON_UNIQUE	smallint	TRUE if index enables duplicates
INDEX_QUALIFIER	Varchar(128)	Index qualifier
INDEX_NAME	Varchar(128)	Index name
TYPE	Smallint	SQL_TABLE_STAT, SQL_INDEX_CLUSTERED, SQL_INDEX_HASHED, or SQL_INDEX_OTHER
SEQ_IN_INDEX	Smallint	Column sequence in index; 1 = first
COLUMN_NAME	Varchar(128)	Column identifier
COLLATION	char(1)	Sort sequence; A = Ascending, D = Descending
CARDINALITY	int	Number of unique values in indexes
PAGES	int	Number of pages used to store index
FILTER_CONDITIONS	Varchar(128)	Filter condition

The return SQLSTATE values are the same as SQLTables plus S1100 (invalid FUnique value).

Some DBMSs have special columns. The most common is the column in dBase tables for ROWID or SQLServer's TIMESTAMP. These are not the same as the defined columns in that they don't show up when you SELECT ALL from a table. When they don't show up normally in a SELECT, they are called pseudocolumns. These columns can, however, be very important. ROWID is the quickest method in dBase to get to a particular row.

SQLSpecialColumns

The ODBC function SQLSpecialColumns polls the DBMS for each special column and the description of what these columns do. The syntax for SQLSpecialColumns is

```
rc = SQLSpecialColumns(hstmt, fColType, szTableQualifier, cbTableQualifier,
➥szTableOwner, cbTableOwner, szTableName, cbTableName, fScope, fNullable);
```

FColType is either SQL_BEST_ROWID (rows are uniquely identified by this special column), or SQL_ROWVER (rows are updated automatically by data source). The last two parameters are Fscode, which indicates when special column values go out of scope.

A ROWID may not always point to the same row in the database. In the case of a row counter, it changes when you have deletions. FScode can be SQL_SCOPE_CURROW (the ROWID value is valid only during this position), SQL_SCOPE_TRANSACTION (ROWID scope is guaranteed through this transaction), or SQL_SCOPE_SESSION (ROWID is guaranteed to be valid for this session). Fnullable can be SQL_NO_NULLS or SQL_NULLABLE, depending on whether the special columns you want returned include NULL values.

SQLSpecialColumn returns eight columns of data in the result set, with one row for each special column.

Table 30.3. The SQLSpecialColumns result set.

Name	Type	Comment
SCOPE	Smallint	SQL_SCOPE_CURROW, SQL_SCOPE_TRANSACTION, or SQL_SCODE_SESSION
COLUMN_NAME	Varchar(128)	Name of column
DATA_TYPE	Smallint	SQL data type
TYPE_NAME	Varchar(128)	Data source type
PRECISION	int	Precision
LENGTH	int	Length
SCALE	Smallint	Scale
PSEUDO_COLUMN	Smallint	SQL_PC_UNKNOWN, SQL_PC_PSEUDO, or SQL_PC_NOT-PSEUDO (a pseudo-column) is a value like Oracle's ROWID

The SQLSTATE values are again the same as SQLTables, with the addition of S1097 (invalid FColType value), S1098 (invalid FScope value), and S1099 (invalid FNullable value).

Level 2 Catalog Functions

The level 2 extended functions are SQLTablePrivileges, SQLColumnPrivileges, SQLPrimaryKeys, SQLForeignKeys, SQLProcedures, and SQLProcedureColumns. As you might guess, level 2 catalog functions provide further information about privileges, keys, and procedures. These functions take the same basic set of parameters you have seen in the level 1 functions. However, at this time, most DBMSs don't support these level 2 extended functions. You need to know your data source or poll the driver prior to designing an application around them.

SQLPrimaryKeys does what it claims. From one table it returns the column names of the primary key. This function takes just the seven common parameters. Its syntax is

```
rc = SQLPrimaryKeys(hstmt, szTableQualifier, cbTableQualifier, szTableOwner,
➥cbTableOwner, szTableName, cbTableName);
```

SQLSTATE return codes are 01000, 08S01, 24000, IM001, S1000, S1001, S1008, S1010, S1090, S1C00, and S1T00, the usual set.

SQLPrimaryKeys returns a result set of these columns, one row of data from each primary key column. See Table 30.4.

Table 30.4. SQLPrimaryKeys.

Name	Type	Comment
TABLE_QUALIFIER	Varchar(128)	What you passed
TABLE_OWNER	Varchar(128)	What you passed
TABLE_NAME	Varchar(128)	What you passed
COLUMN_NAME	Varchar(128)	Primary key column
KEY_SEQ	Smallint	Column sequence number
PK_NAME	Varchar(128)	Primary key name

SQLForeignKeys is an extension of SQLPrimaryKeys but works in two ways. You can either get the foreign key columns from your table that are tied to primary keys for another table, or you can get the foreign key columns from other tables that are tied to your table's primary key. Given the options, you have your seven usual parameters, and then the same parameters, except for the foreign key table. If szPTableName is given, you get back the foreign keys from other tables that refer to your table's primary key. If szFTableName is given, you get back the foreign keys in your table that refer to the primary keys of other tables.

```
rc = SQLForeignKeys(hstmt, szPTableQualifier, cbPTableQualifier, szPTableOwner,
➥cbPTableOwner, szPTableName, cbPTableName, szFTableQualifier, cbFTableQualifier,
➥szFTableOwner, cbFTableOwner, szFTableName, cbFTableName);
```

The SQLSTATE return codes are the same as SQLPrimaryKeys.

Table 30.5. The SQLForeignKeys results.

Name	Type	Comment
PTABLE_QUALIFIER	Varchar(128)	Primary key table qualifier
PTABLE_OWNER	Varchar(128)	Primary key table owner
PTABLE_NAME	Varchar(128)	Primary key table name
PCOLUMN_NAME	Varchar(128)	Primary key column name

Name	Type	Comment
FTABLE_QUALIFIER	Varchar(128)	Foreign key table qualifier
FTABLE_OWNER	Varchar(128)	Foreign key table owner
FTABLE_NAME	Varchar(128)	Foreign key table name
FCOLUMN_NAME	Varchar(128)	Foreign key column name
KEY_SEQ	Smallint	Column sequence number
UPDATE_RULE	Smallint	Either SQL_CASCADE, SQL_RESTRICT, or SQL_SET_NULL
FK_NAME	Varchar(128)	Foreign key name
PK_NAME	Varchar(128)	Primary key name

SQLTablePrivileges returns a list of tables and the privileges associated with each table. The function uses the seven common parameters, and the syntax is

```
rc = SQLTablePrivileges(hstmt, szTableQualifier, , cbTableQualifier, szTableOwner,
➥cbTableOwner, szTableName, cbTableName);
```

The SQLSTATE return values are again the same. See Table 30.6.

Table 30.6. SQLTablePrivilege.

Name	Type	Comment
TABLE_QUALIFIER	Varchar(128)	Table qualifier
TABLE_OWNER	Varchar(128)	Table owner
TABLE_NAME	Varchar(128)	Table name
GRANTOR	Varchar(128)	Name of user who granted privilege
GRANTEE	Varchar(128)	Name of user to whom privilege is granted
PRIVILEGE	Varchar(128)	SELECT, INSERT, UPDATE, DELETE, REFERENCE
IS_GRANTABLE	Varchar(3)	YES or NO if grantee can grant privileges to others

SQLColumnPrivileges is a nearly identical catalog function with the additional parameter of the column name and the additional result of the column name:

```
rc = SQLColumnPrivileges(hstmt, szTableQualifier, , cbTableQualifier, szTableOwner,
➥cbTableOwner, szTableName, cbTableName, szColumnName, cbColumnName);
```

The SQLSTATE return values are again the same.

The `SQLColumnPrivileges` results are:

Name	Type	Comment
TABLE_QUALIFIER	Varchar(128)	Table qualifier
TABLE_OWNER	Varchar(128)	Table owner
TABLE_NAME	Varchar(128)	Table name

`SQLProcedures` is like `SQLTables` or `SQLColumns`, except that `SQLProcedures` returns a list of the stored procedure names on a specific data source. A procedure is a generic term used to describe an executable object or a named entity. This is usually an extensive query stored in the data source instead of your application. The usual seven parameters are used again, this time referring to the procedure instead of the table. The syntax is

```
rc = SQLProcedures(hstmt, szProcQualifier, , cbProcQualifier, szProcOwner,
➥cbProcOwner, szProcName, cbTableName);
```

The `SQLSTATE` return values are again the same.

The `SQLProcedures` results are shown in Table 30.7.

Table 30.7. `SQLProcedures` results.

Name	Type	Comment
PROC_QUALIFIER	Varchar(128)	Procedure qualifier
PROC_OWNER	Varchar(128)	Procedure owner
PROC_NAME	Varchar(128)	Procedure name
NUM_INPUT_PARAMS	N/A	Reserved for future use
NUM_OUTPUT_PARAMS	N/A	Reserved for future use
NUM_RESULT_SETS	N/A	Reserved for future use
REMARKS	Varchar(254)	Description of procedures
PROC_TYPE	Smallint	SQL_PT_UNKNOWN, SQL_PT_PROCEDURE, or SQL_PT_FUNCTION

`SQLProcedureColumns` returns a result set with the columns that make up a certain procedure. The function syntax is again the same with the column specified:

```
rc = SQLProcedureColumns(hstmt, szProcQualifier, , cbProcQualifier, szProcOwner,
➥cbProcOwner, szProcName, cbTableName, szColumnName, cbColumnName);
```

The `SQLSTATE` return values are again the same.

The SQLProcedureColumn results are shown in Table 30.8.

Table 30.8. The SQLProcedureColumn results.

Name	Type	Comment
PROC_QUALIFIER	Varchar(128)	Procedure qualifier
PROC_OWNER	Varchar(128)	Procedure owner
PROC_NAME	Varchar(128)	Procedure name
COLUMN_NAME	Varchar(128)	Name of column
COLUMN_TYPE	Smallint	SQL_PARAM_TYPE_UNKNOWN, SQL_PARAM_INPUT, SQL_PARAM_INPUT_OUTPUT, SQL_PARAM_OUTPUT, SQL_RETURN_VALUE, or SQL_RESULT_COL
DATA_TYPE	Smallint	SQL data type
TYPE_NAME	Varchar(128)	Data source type
PRECISION	int	Precision
LENGTH	int	Length
SCALE	Smallint	Scale
RADIX	Smallint	If 10, then precision and scale are used; else if 2 values in precision and scale give number of bits in column
NULLABLE	Smallint	SQL_NO_NULLS, SQL_NULLABLE, or SQL_NULLABLE_UNKNOWN
REMARKS	Varchar(254)	Description of procedure

This discussion of the extended catalog functions may have seemed like a lot of detail, but its implementation is straightforward, as shown in this code snippet using SQLColumns.

```
//wnp chp 30
#include <windows.h>
#include <sql.h>
#include <sqlext.h>
#define MAX_DATA 100
#define MAX_COLNAME 100

int WINAPI WinMain(HANDLE hInstance, HANDLE hPrevInstance, LPSTR lpszCmdLine, int
➥nCmdShow)
{
// setup vars

HENV henv;
HDBC hdbc;
HSTMT hstmt;
RETCODE rc;
```

```
UCHAR   szQualifier[MAX_DATA], szOwner[MAX_DATA];
UCHAR   szTableName[MAX_DATA], szColName[MAX_DATA];
UCHAR   szTypeName[MAX_DATA], szRemarks[MAX_DATA];
SDWORD  Precision, Length;
SWORD   DataType, Scale, Radix, Nullable;
SDWORD  cbQualifier, cbOwner, cbTableName, cbColName;
SDWORD  cbTypeName, cbRemarks, cbDataType, cbPrecision;
SDWORD  cbLength, cbScale, cbRadix, cbNullable;

SQLAllocEnv(&henv);
SQLAllocConnect(henv, &hdbc);
SQLConnect(hdbc, (UCHAR *) "SPNOTES",SQL_NTS,NULL,0,NULL,0);
SQLAllocStmt(hdbc, &hstmt);

rc = SQLColumns(hstmt,
                    NULL, 0,                    /* All qualifiers */
                    NULL, 0,                    /* All owners     */
                    (UCHAR *)"Vdata", SQL_NTS,     /* Vdata table */
                    NULL, 0);                   /* All columns     */

if (rc == SQL_SUCCESS)
 {
    SQLBindCol(hstmt, 1, SQL_C_CHAR, szQualifier, MAX_DATA,&cbQualifier);
    SQLBindCol(hstmt, 2, SQL_C_CHAR, szOwner, MAX_DATA, &cbOwner);
    SQLBindCol(hstmt, 3, SQL_C_CHAR, szTableName, MAX_DATA,&cbTableName);
    SQLBindCol(hstmt, 4, SQL_C_CHAR, szColName, MAX_DATA, &cbColName);
    SQLBindCol(hstmt, 5, SQL_C_SSHORT, &DataType, 0, &cbDataType);
    SQLBindCol(hstmt, 6, SQL_C_CHAR, szTypeName, MAX_DATA, &cbTypeName);
    SQLBindCol(hstmt, 7, SQL_C_SLONG, &Precision, 0, &cbPrecision);
    SQLBindCol(hstmt, 8, SQL_C_SLONG, &Length, 0, &cbLength);
    SQLBindCol(hstmt, 9, SQL_C_SSHORT, &Scale, 0, &cbScale);
    SQLBindCol(hstmt, 10, SQL_C_SSHORT, &Radix, 0, &cbRadix);
    SQLBindCol(hstmt, 11, SQL_C_SSHORT, &Nullable, 0, &cbNullable);
    SQLBindCol(hstmt, 12, SQL_C_CHAR, szRemarks, MAX_DATA, &cbRemarks);

    while(TRUE)
  {
    rc = SQLFetch(hstmt);
    if (MessageBox(NULL, (CHAR *)szColName, "Column Name", MB_OKCANCEL) ==
    ➥IDCANCEL);
     {
     break;
     }
  }
SQLFreeStmt(hstmt, SQL_DROP);
SQLDisconnect(hdbc);
SQLFreeConnect(hdbc);
SQLFreeEnv(henv);
return(TRUE);

}
```

TIP

If you don't like typing SQLBindCol statements and the various type definitions of function variables, take a look at TYPEGEN.EXE from Microsoft's INSIDE ODBC. TYPEGEN.EXE is a 32-bit data type manager that allows you to input an SQL statement. TYPEGEN generates the SQLBindCol statements in a format you can cut and paste into your code.

Disconnecting from the Data Source

The preceding example showed how the process of connecting to the data source was reversed. You will always call SQLDisconnect, SQLFreeConnect, and finally SQLFreeEnv, in that order.

SQLDisconnect

SQLDisconnect was discussed earlier. SQLDisconnect frees allocated statement handles. When your application calls SQLDisconnect, the driver manager calls both SQLFreeConnect and SQLFreeEnv within the driver, and then calls FreeLibrary to unload the ODBC driver DLL and free up memory. If any SQL statements are still executing (you would be in asynchronous mode), then the disconnect fails with SQLSTATE S1010 (function sequence error). Connecting to a data source can take several seconds and slow your application down. In general, you connect to the data source once when you application starts. However, your DBMS might override this decision. An example would be a DBMS such as MicroRim's Rbase, where you purchase connection licenses in groups of five. You might only be able to use five connections at a time and need to disconnect users to enable others' access.

The SQLDisconnect form is

SQLDisconnect(hdbc);

It returns SQLSTATEs 01000, 01002 (disconnect error), 08003 (connection not open), 25000 (invalid transaction state), IM001, S1000, S1001, and S1010. You can reuse the hdbc to connect to another data source after the SQLDisconnect without reallocating the handle.

SQLFreeConnect

SQLFreeConnect releases the resources you allocated for the connection. You cannot reuse the hdbc handle after this call, because it no longer exists—its memory has been freed. The form is simply

```
SQLFreeConnect(hdbc);
```

The SQLSTATE codes returned are 01000, 08S01, S1000, and S1010.

SQLFreeEnv

In closing the application, just before termination you need to free up this memory space with SQLFreeEnv in the same manner. SQLFreeEnv can return SQL_SUCCESS, SQL_SUCCESS_WITH_INFO, SQL_ERROR, or SQL_INVALID_HANDLE. These SQLSTATE return codes are 01000 (general warning), S1000 (general SQL_ERROR), or S1010 (function sequence error). The most common reason for SQL_ERROR is that you haven't freed a connection handle. You would get the S1010 SQLSTATE return code to indicate as such. Always call SQLDisconnect and SQLFreeConnect prior to calling SQLFreeEnv.

SQLExecute

Most SQL statements take a statement handle as their first parameter and return a standard set of SQLSTATE codes and data in a result set of columns and rows. Previously you saw SQL functions that returned information with the output parameters of the function call. From this point on the functions return result sets, which can contain hundreds of rows and columns of data. This becomes somewhat more complicated in that you will always have a two-step process— generate a result set, and then retrieve the results. The next two sections examine both steps. Figure 30.6 is a general outline of the process. This flowchart details the choices after you have initialized the connection and gotten a statement handle. You first ask yourself whether the statement will be executed multiple times and whether you need to know information about the result set prior to execution. If you can answer no to both of these questions, then you proceed using SQLExecDirect; otherwise you need to use the SQLPrepare, SQLExecute combination. This is the first process examined in this section.

Generating Result Sets

Prior to executing a valid SQL Statement, you need to allocate memory for the statement handle. This is done as

```
HSTMT hstmt;
RETCODE rc;
rc = SQLAllocate(hdbc, &hstmt);
```

The SQLSTATE return codes are 01000, 08003, IM001, S1000, S1001, and S1009.

Different DBMSs can support different numbers of open SQL statements. If you are using an unknown data source, this number is obtained with SQLGetInfo's SQL_ACTIVE_STATEMENTS parameter. A value of 0 means that there is no limit. Some DBMSs restrict the number of active statements but enable multiple connections in exchange. This is a poor exchange, for as you have seen, connecting takes time and resources. It is best to allocate a statement handle, use it, free it with SQLFreeStmt, and then reuse it. This minimizes the resources your application needs.

FIGURE 30.6.

General flow of ODBC function processing.

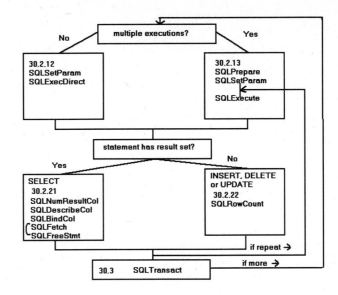

SQLFreeStmt

SQLFreeStmt takes two parameters, the hstmt and an option. The options are: SQL_CLOSE (close cursor and discard results but keep hstmt around and keep bound parameters and results bound), SQL_DROP (close cursor, disregard results, and free hstmt), SQL_UNBIND (release buffers that you bound with SQLBindCol), or SQL_RESET_PARAMS (release all parameter buffers). Binding is the process of associating a data set with the application's variables. You have already seen SQLBinCols. The next section looks at SQLBindParameter, but the basic concept can be summarized by the following: You need to store the results somewhere, or they get discarded.

SQLFreeStmt has the SQLSTATE return codes of 01000, IM001, S1000, S1001, S1010, and S1092 (option type out of range).

ODBC provides several functions to execute SQL statements. Functions are executed either by *direct* or *prepared* execution. Direct execution is fast and the easiest way to execute an SQL statement. Prepared execution is more flexible. Direct execution is used when the SQL statement is to be executed only once and when no information is needed about the result set prior to execution.

SQLExecDirect

SQLExecDirect executes the SQL statement exactly once. Its syntax is

```
rc = SQLExecDirect(hstmt, szSqlStr, cbSqlStr);
```

The szSqlStr is any valid SQL statement; for example "SELECT * FROM ACCOUNTREC". The resulting function example is

```
rc = SQLExecDirect(hstmt, "SELECT * FROM ACCOUNTREC", SQL_NTS);
```

Use `SQLExecDirect` when you want a result set that will not change throughout your application—filling a list box with available products you offer. You generally know the format of the data and the table and type of data being returned.

`SQLExecuteDirect` has the `SQLSTATE` return code:

01000, 01004, 01006, 01S03, 01S04, 07001, 08S01, 21S01, 21S02, 22003, 33005, 22008, 22012, 23000, 24000, 34000, 37000, 40001, 42000, IM001, S0001, S0002, S0011, S0012, S0021, S0022, S1000, S1001, S1008, S1009, S1010, S1090, S1109, S1C00, S1T00

There are six basic steps in executing any SQL statement. Using `SQLExecDirect`, all six steps are executed:

1. The SQL statement is formed by the application or user.
2. The SQL statement is sent to DBMS.
3. The SQL statement is parsed.
4. The parsed SQL statement is optimized to develop the execution plan. The optimizer of each database has rules for using indexes and the ordering of statements to get the result set the quickest way.
5. The execution plan is "executed."
6. Client and server interact to send status information and data to client.

In using `SQLPrepare`, the first four steps are done first and stored. The last two steps are then performed later by the `SQLExecute`. In a stored procedure, these first four steps are stored back into DBMS to be used over and over. By preprocessing the first four steps you can gain more flexibility and speed. The parsing step of a complex SQL statement can be quite time-consuming!

SQLPrepare

Prepared execution is more flexible in that you can break the execution into two steps. The first step is to find information out about the result set, and the second is to execute the statement and get the result set. One example is to know the number of rows returned to format a printed report. A second example is where the user forms the SQL `SELECT` statement at runtime and you need to check its grammar. A final example is to ensure that only one row met your criteria prior to performing a `DELETE`.

The two-step process is

```
rc = SQLPrepare(hstmt, szSqlStr, cbSqlStr);
rc = SQLExecute(hstmt);
```

SQLPrepare returns SQLSTATE codes: 01000, 08S01, 21S01, 21S02, 22005, 24000, 34000, 37000, 42000, IM001, S0001, S0003, S0012, S0021, S0022, S1000, S1001, S1008, S1009, S1010, S1090, S1T00, and ODBC 2.5 added S1C00 (driver not capable).

SQLExecute returns SQLSTATE codes: 01000, 01004, 01006, 01S03, 01S04, 07001, 08S01, 22003, 22005, 22008, 22012, 23000, 24000, 40001, 42000, and IM001.

Always test SQLExecute, SQLExecDirect, and SQLPrepare for return of SQL_SUCCESS or SQL_SUCCESS_WITH_INFO. If you didn't get one of these returned, the statement was not executed. If you don't test, you don't know if you made database changes or not.

SQLPrepare's statement is parsed into its data access path, which makes information about the source available, as you saw with the catalog functions. If you have multiple calls to SQLExecute, the pre-parsed data access path can give you considerable speed as well. This is the same thing you see with parameterized statements.

Let's look again behind the scenes to what is actually happening in a call to SQLExecute. When you called SQLAllocStmt, the driver manager again made a similar call to the driver and allocated a second statement handle for the communication between the driver manager and the driver. It is important to remember that when you are done using an HSTMT handle, reuse it! SQLExecDirect actually sends whatever string you give it to the server. It is the server that parses the string and determines if it can act on the information you provided. It does not return results until you specifically ask for them—it just returns success or failure on your statement.

Parameterization

Parameterized statements are formed by specifying a "?" as a placeholder in an SQL statement. This placeholder gets changed each time the statement is executed, but the entire SQL statement doesn't need to be parsed again—the substitution needs to be made. When you bind a parameter you tie the parameter to a particular storage location of memory, to be retrieved at execution time.

It was mentioned earlier that you need to save the parameters of SQL statements or they get discarded. Binding the results is setting up a pointer to a memory buffer that holds the results. If you had a parameterized statement such as INSERT INTO CLINIC (city, state, zipcode) VALUES (?,?,?), you would need three bindings to retain the three parameter values.

SQLBindParameter binds a buffer to a single parameter. If you want to save multiple parameters, you must call SQLBindParameter multiple times. The syntax is

```
rc = SQLBindParameter(hstmt, ipar, fparType, fCType, fSqlType, cbColDef, ibScale,
rbgValue, cbValueMax, pcbValue);
```

Table 30.9. The `SQLBindParameter` parameters.

Parameter	Description
ipar	Integer for which parameter to save
fparType	Either SQL_PARAM_INPUT, SQL_PARAM_OUTPUT, or SQL_PARAM_INPUT_OUTPUT
fCType	C data type
FSqlType	SQL data type
cbColDef	Precision of column
ibScale	Scale of column
rgbValue	Pointer to buffer for parameter's data
cbValueMax	Maximum length of buffer
pcbValue	Pointer to buffer for parameter length

> **NOTE**
>
> A variation on calling the function `SQLBindParameter` passes the parameter value at execution time. To invoke this form set `pcbValue` to `SQL_DATA_AT_EXEC` and the `rgbValue` to a 32-bit token passed by `SQLParamData` and `SQLPutData`. This is useful when the parameter is a large amount of data such as a binary object.

SQLSTATE return codes for `SQLBindParameter` are 01000, 07006, IM991M, S1000, S1001, S1003 (C type not valid), S1004 (SQL type not valid), S1009, S1010, S1090, S1093 (invalid parameter number), S1094 (invalid scale number), S1104 (invalid precision number), S1105 (invalid parameter type), and S1C00.

The following is an example using `SQLBindParameter`:

```
HSTMT hstmt;
UCHAR szName[NAME_LEN];
SDWORD cbName = SQL_NTS;
//allocate a statement and prepare it
rc = SQLAllocStmt(hdbc, &hstmt);
if (RETCODE_IS_SUCCESSFUL(rc))
  {
    rc = SQLPrepare(hstmt, "INSERT INTO CLINIC (name) VALUES (?)", SQL_NTS);
  }
//bind the parameter
if (RETCODE_IS_SUCCESSFUL(rc))
  {
    rc = SQLBindParameter(hstmt, 1, SQL_PARAM_INPUT, SQL_C_CHAR, SQL_CHAR,
    ➥NAME_LEN, 0, szName, 0, &cbName);
  }
//input the parameter data
strcopy(szName, "Dave's Clinic");
```

```
//execute
if (RETCODE_IS_SUCCESSFUL(rc))
  {
    rc = SQLExecute(hstmt);
  }
```

The preceding example is somewhat contrived. In reality, the whole concept of parameters assumes you will reuse the SQL statement over, and over and the benefit is that you don't need to reparse the entire statement. A collection of parameters is passed with SQLParamOptions as

```
HSTMT hstmt;
UCHAR szNames[][NAME_LEN] = {"Dave's clinic","Bill's clinic","Sam's clinic"};
SDWORD cbName[] = {SQL_NTS, SQL_NTS, SQL_NTS};
UWORD irow;
//allocate a statement and prepare it
rc = SQLAllocStmt(hdbc, &hstmt);
if (RETCODE_IS_SUCCESSFUL(rc))
  {
    rc = SQLPrepare(hstmt, "INSERT INTO CLINIC (name) VALUES (?)", SQL_NTS);
  }
// tell we have 3 parameters, we are going to insert 3 rows, irow is number of
➥current row
if (RETCODE_IS_SUCCESSFUL(rc))
  {
    SQLParamOptions(hstmt, 3, &irow);
  }
//bind the parameter
if (RETCODE_IS_SUCCESSFUL(rc))
  {
    rc = SQLBindParameter(hstmt, 1, SQL_PARAM_INPUT, SQL_C_CHR, SQL_CHAR, NAME_LEN,
    ➥0, szNames, 0, cbName);
  }
//execute
if (RETCODE_IS_SUCCESSFUL(rc))
  {
    rc = SQLExecute(hstmt);
  }
```

The syntax for SQLParamOptions follows:

```
rc = SQLParamOptions (hstmt, crow, pirow);
```

The parameter crow is the number of parameters, and pirow is a pointer to the current row number. If pirow is a null pointer, no row number is returned.

The SQLSTATE return codes are: 01000, IM001, S1000, S1001, S1010, and S1107 (row value out of range).

Getting Results from Result Sets

All the preceding functions address each function's return code, which tells us about success or failure. Where, though, are the actual results? SQL SELECT and the catalog functions each return result sets, rows, and columns of data. SQL DELETE, SQL UPDATE, and SQL INSERT all return a row count, the number of rows affected by the statement.

Once you execute SQLDirect or SQLExecDirect, the results still reside on the server as a subset of the database. Even if you are using a local database, think of it as a server. You still need to fetch the rows from the result set. Why? What if you tried something like SQLExecDirect(hstmt, "SELECT * FROM NY_PHONEBOOK) where NY_PHONEBOOK was immense? Where would the results go? They are still on the server with a *cursor* pointing to the first row of results. A cursor is a pointer to a row. You move the cursor and fetch its contents with SQLFetch and SQLExtendedFetch. Before you gather this information, you still need to know about the result set. You might know a lot about the data, (if you designed the database rows and columns) or you might not even know what data is coming back. The ODBC catalog functions were introduced first because they help you find out what you are going to get back.

Getting to Know the Result Set

Figure 30.7 is an expansion on the lower half of Figure 30.6. The left box shows the process of retrieving results from the result set. You loop through the rows with SQLFetch.

FIGURE 30.7.

ODBC result processing flow chart.

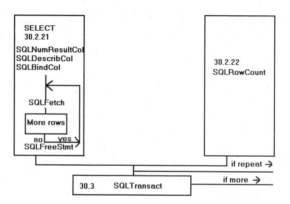

SQLRowCount

If you followed the right half of Figure 30.6, your statement was either INSERT, DELETE, or UPDATE. You could also have used SQLSetPos with SQL_UPDATE, SQL_ADD, or SQL_DELETE. The results are the number of rows you inserted, deleted, or updated. The syntax is

```
rc = SQLRowCount(hstmt, pcrow);
```

pcrow is the output, the number of rows affected by the statement, or -1 if that number is not available.

The SQLSTATE return codes are 01000, IM001, S1000, S1001, and S1010.

SQLNumResultCols

If, on the other hand, your call gives you a result set, the first thing you need to know is the number of columns in that result set. You need this for both allocating memory and displaying the information on your monitor. The simplest way to get this information is with SQLNumResultCols, which has the following syntax:

```
rc = SqlNumResultCols(hstmt, pccol);
```

hstmt is the handle to the statement you just executed, and the pccol is the returned number of columns. If pccol is 0, your executed SQL statement was of the type that returns rows, not a result set, such as INSERT, DELETE, or UPDATE. These statements use SQLRowCount to return number of rows affected by the call.

The SQLSTATE return codes are 01000, IM001, S1000, S1008, S1010 (common error code when your function calls out of sequence), and S1T00.

It has been several pages since you actually typed something into VC++ 4.x to ensure that all this is working. Take the simple console application from earlier in this chapter and modify it as follows. Remember, the "SPNOTES" is the sample data source name and "VDATA" just one of its tables. Change these to test your data source.

```
// chap30

#include <windows.h>
#include <sql.h>
#include <sqlext.h>
#define MAX_DATA 100
#define MAX_COLNAME 100
int WINAPI WinMain(HANDLE hInstance, HANDLE hPrevInstance, LPSTR lpszCmdLine, int
➥nCmdShow)
{
// setup vars
HENV henv;
HDBC hdbc;
HSTMT hstmt;
char szData[MAX_DATA];
SDWORD cbData;
// vars for descriptions
SWORD cCols;
SWORD iCol;
char szColName[MAX_COLNAME +1];
char szTypeName[MAX_COLNAME +1];
SWORD cbColName;
SWORD fSQLType;
UDWORD cbPrec;
SWORD cbTypeName;
SWORD cbScale;
SWORD fNullable;
```

```
SQLAllocEnv(&henv);
SQLAllocConnect(henv, &hdbc);
SQLConnect(hdbc, (UCHAR *)"SPNOTES", SQL_NTS,NULL,0,NULL,0);
SQLAllocStmt(hdbc, &hstmt);

//example of just getting some data
SQLExecDirect(hstmt, (UCHAR *)"SELECT * from VDATA", SQL_NTS);
SQLFetch(hstmt);
SQLGetData(hstmt, 2, SQL_C_CHAR, szData, sizeof(szData), &cbData);
MessageBox(NULL, szData, "Column Data", MB_OK);

//example of getting number of columns
SQLNumResultCols(hstmt, &cCols);
wsprintf(szData, "%d columns returned\n", cCols);
MessageBox(NULL, szData, "Column's received", MB_OK);

//example of column description
for (iCol = 1; iCol <=cCols; iCol++)
{
  SQLDescribeCol(hstmt, iCol, (UCHAR *)szColName, MAX_COLNAME, &cbColName,
&fSQLType,&cbPrec, &cbScale, &fNullable);
  SQLColAttributes(hstmt,iCol, SQL_COLUMN_TYPE_NAME, szTypeName,sizeof(szTypeName),
&cbTypeName,0);
  wsprintf(szData, "Column %d name = '%s'\n type is %02d (%s)\n max length =
%3ld\n", iCol, szColName, fSQLType, szTypeName, cbPrec);
  MessageBox(NULL, szData, "Column description", MB_OK);
}


SQLFreeStmt(hstmt, SQL_DROP);
SQLDisconnect(hdbc);
SQLFreeConnect(hdbc);
SQLFreeEnv(henv);
return(TRUE);
}
```

SQLDescribeCol

Probably the next thing you want to know is the name of the columns and the type of data they hold. The above example shows just how simple it is to get the basic description of a column's data. SQLDescribeCol returns name, type, precision, scale, and nullability of your result set. The syntax is:

```
rc = SQLDescribeCol(hstmt, icol, szColName, cbColName, pcbColName, pfSqltype,
⮕pcbColDef, pibScale, pfNullable);
```

You would call SQLDescribeCol after a call to SQLPrepare and either before or after SQLExecute. You could also call SQLDescribeCol after SQLExecDirect. This function call returns information about one column only, the one you specify in the integer, icol. To get information on all the columns, you need to call SQLDescribeCol once for each result column from 1 to the number you got with `SQLNumResultCols`. The parameter list is: `SzColName` is the column name, `cbColName` is the maximum length of the name you want returned, `pcbColName` is the total maximum length of the column name, `pfSqlType` is the SQL data type, `pcbColDef` is the precision or how large a buffer you need to hold the result set, `pibScale` is the number of digits to the right of the decimal point, and `pfNullable` is either `SQL_NO_NULLS`, `SQL_NULLABLE`, or `SQL_NULLABLE_UNKNOWN`.

SQLSTATE return codes are `01000`, `01004` (data truncated), `24000`, `IM001`, `S1000`, `S1001`, `S1002`, `S1008`, `S1010`, `S1090`, and `S1T00`.

SQLColAttributes

`SQLColAttributes` returns even more detailed information about the columns in the result set. In the sample console application we just built, the `SQLDescribeCol` returned the `SQLType` in the parameter `fSqlType`. If you don't know that type 5 in your data source is a `SHORT`, this doesn't help much. You need to be able to get more detailed information, like the example does, to get the text string representing the various SQL types. The function `SQLColAttributes` is somewhat unusual in that you can get either text returned, as in the preceding example, or a 32-bit signed value. The returned information is in the output parameter `pfDesc` (if `pfDesc` is a signed value, the drive ignores `rbgDesc`, `cbDescMax`, and `pcbDesc`). The syntax is

```
rc = SQLColAttributes(hstmt, icol, fDescType, rgbDesc, cbDescMax, pcbDesc, pfDesc);
```

`SQLColAttributes`' returned information is shown in Table 30.10.

Table 30.10. Returned `SQLColAttributes` information.

fDescType	Output Param	Results
SQL_COLUMN_AUTO_INCREMENT	pfDesc	TRUE or FALSE
SQL_COLUMN_CASE_SENSITIVE	pfDesc	TRUE or FALSE
SQL_COLUMN_COUNT	pfDesc	Number of columns in set
SQL_COLUMN_DISPLAY_SIZE	pfDesc	Number of chars to display columns
SQL_COLUMN_LABEL	rgbDesc	Label or title
SQL_COLUMN_LENGTH	pfDesc	Bytes transferred to each SQLFetch
SQL_COLUMN_MONEY	pfDesc	TRUE or FALSE
SQL_COLUMN_NAME	rgbDesc	Column name
SQL_COLUMN_NULLABLE	pfDesc	SQL_NO_NULLS, SQL_NULLABLE, or SQL_NULLABLE_UNKNOWN
SQL_COLUMN_OWNER_NAME	rgbDesc	Owner of table

continues

Table 30.10. continued

fDescType	Output Param	Results
SQL_COLUMN_PRECISION	pfDesc	Precision
SQL_COLUMN_QUALIFIER_NAME	rbfDesc	Qualifier of table
SQL_COLUMN_SCALE	pfDesc	Scale
SQL_COLUMN_COLUMN_SEARCHABLE	pfDesc	SQL_UNSEARCHABLE, SQL_LIKE_ONLY, SQL_ALL_EXCEPT_LIKE, or SQL_SEARCHABLE
SQL_COLUMN_COLUMN_TABLE_NAME	rgbDesc	Name of table
SQL_COLUMN_COLUMN_TYPE	pfDesc	SQL data type
SQL_COLUMN_TYPE_NAME	rgbDesc	Data source data type
SQL_COLUMN_UNSIGNED	pfDesc	TRUE or FALSE
SQL_COLUMN_UPDATABLE	pfDesc	SQL_ATTR_READONLY, SQL_ATTR_WRITE, SQL_ATTR_READWRITE_UNKNOWN, or SQL_COLUMN_UPDATABLE

The SQLSTATE return codes are: 01000, 01004, 24000, IM001, S1000, S1001, S1002, S1008, S1010, S1090, S1091 (descriptor out of range), S1C00, and S1T00.

The information you choose to retrieve depends on how you use it. If you're going to display to the monitor, you need SQL_COLUMN_DISPLAY_SIZE, and if you're going to do a large UPDATE, you should know beforehand if the column is SQL_COLUMN_UPDATABLE.

Both SQLColAttributes and SQLDescribeCol assume that you don't know about the column. In many of your applications, you will be the person that designed the data source and will execute the SQL statement, bind the columns, and then use the results. A simple example follows:

```
UCHAR szName[30], szAddress[30], szCity[10], szState[3], szZipcode[6];
SDWORD cbName, cbAddress, cbCity, cbState, cbZipcode;
rc = SQLExecDirect(hstmt, "SELECT Name, Address, City, State, Zipcode FROM
➡CUSTOMERS",SQL_NTS);
if (retcode = SQL_SUCCESS)
   {
   SQLBindCol(hstmt, 1, SQL_C_CHAR, szName, 30,&cbName);
   SQLBindCol(hstmt, 2, SQL_C_CHAR, szAddress, 30, &cbAddress);
   SQLBindCol(hstmt, 3, SQL_C_CHAR, szCity, 10, &cbCity);
   SQLBindCol(hstmt, 4, SQL_C_CHAR, szState, 3, &cbState);
   SQLBindCol(hstmt, 1, SQL_C_CHAR, szZipcode, 6, &cbZipcode);
   while (TRUE)
   {
```

```
      retcode = SQLFetch(hstmt);
      if (retcode == SQL_SUCCESS || retcode == SQL_SUCCESS_WITH_INFO)
      {
//print strings 1 less than length for \0
   fprintf(out, "%*s %*s %*s %*s %*s",29,szName,29,szAddress,9,szCity,2,szState,
   ➥5,szZipcode);
      }
      else
      {
      break;
      }
   }
 }
```

ODBC uses either SQLBindCol or SQLGetData to assign a storage location after SQLFetch or SQLExtendedFetch. Use SQLGetData to bind large data objects, which may have to be retrieved in parts due to their size. You can actually mix the two calls as long as you call SQLGetData after you have bound the columns with SQLBindCol. Although you used SQLGetData above, it is discussed in greater detail as it relates to BLOBs near the end of this chapter in our discussion of binary data.

SQLBindCol

SQLBindCol as we have demonstrated is used to pass a pointer to the storage buffer for the column of data. It also specifies how the data is converted from SQL data types to C data types. These default conversions are shown in Table 30.11.

Table 30.11. ODBC 2.0 default data types.

SQL data type	C data type
SQL_CHAR	SQL_C_CHAR
SQL_VARCHAR	SQL_C_CHAR
SQL_LONGVARCHAR	SQL_C_CHAR
SQL_DECIMAL	SQL_C_CHAR
SQL_NUMERIC	SQL_C_CHAR
SQL_BIT	SQL_C_BIT
SQL_TINYINT	SQL_C_STINYINT or SQL_C_UTINYINT
SQL_SMALLINT	SQL_C_SSHORT or SQL_C_USHORT
SQL_INTEGER	SQL_CV_LONG or SQL_C_ULONG
SQL_BIGINT	SQL_C_CHAR
SQL_REAL	SQL_C_FLOAT

continues

Table 30.11. continued

SQL data type	C data type
SQL_FLOAT	SQL_C_DOUBLE
SQL_DOUBLE	SQL_C_DOUBLE
SQL_BINARY	SQL_C_BINARY
SQL_VARBINARY	SQL_C_BINARY
SQL_LONGBINARY	SQL_C_BINARY
SQL_DATE	SQL_C_DATE
SQL_TIME	SQL_C_TIME
SQL_TIMESTAMP	SQL_C_TIMESTAMP

The syntax for SQLBindCol is

```
rc = SQLBindCol(hstmt, icol, fcType, rgbValue, cbValueMax, pcbValue);
```

The columns in the result set are numbered from left to right, with the first column being number 1. fcType is the C data type to which you want the column converted. All SQL types can be converted to SQL_C_CHAR. RgbValue is the pointer to the storage space.

The SQLSTATE return codes are 01000, IM001, S1000, S1001, S1002, S1003, S1009, S1010, S1090, and S1C00.

Once a column is bound it remains bound until you call SQLFreeStmt with either the SQL_UNBIND or SQL_DROP options. You can also unbind any one column by calling SQLBindCol again with that column's number but setting rgbValue to a null pointer.

Columnwise binding is the default. You can also bind rowwise by using the statement SQLSetStmtOption (hstmt, SQL_BIND_TYPE, sizeof(MytableStruc)). In this case "MytableStruc" is a typical C structure, defined as follows:

```
typedef struct {
  UCHAR szLname[30];
  SDWORD cbLname;
  UCHAR szAddress[30];
  SDWORD cbAddress;
} MytableStruc;
```

MytableStruc is declared as

```
MytableStruct rrows[100];
```

and bound as

```
SQLBindCol(hstmt, 1, SQL_C_CHAR. rrow[0].szLname,
➥sizeof(szLname),&rrow[0].cbLname);
```

SQLFetch

As you saw above, SQLFetch simply fetches one row of your result set. You need to call it over once per row to get the entire result set. Its syntax couldn't be simpler:

```
rc = SQLFetch(hstmt);
```

The SQLSTATE return codes are: 01000, 01004, 07006 (could not convert data type), 08S01, 22003 (number out of range), 22012 (division by zero), 24000, 40001 (serialization failed), IM001, S1000, S1001, S1002, S1008, S1008, S1010, S1C00, and S1T00. ODBC 2.5 added 22005 (error in assignment) and 22008 (date/time overflow).

Every call to SQLFetch advances the cursor 1 row until the cursor is positioned after the last row, at which point it returns SQL_NO_DATA_FOUND.

ODBCTEST (ODBCTE32.EXE) has been mentioned before. It is probably the best way to learn the ODBC functions. The next few paragraphs discuss extended ODBC functions. If you find that a section of your application won't work, stepping through the ODBC function calls with ODBCTEST.EXE can ensure that your parameters are correct and also show what results are being returned. This application is part of the ODBC SDK. Nearly every ODBC function is available and in the order you would call the function. Using the SQLError function returns string and SQLSTATE information on each call. Several calls are bundled, such as GetDataAll and FullConnect. You also have the option of building groups of SQL statements into autotest suites. In this manner you can test your application when unusual data is returned. A sample autotest is provided with the ODBC SDK.

FIGURE 30.8.

Microsoft ODBCTE32.EXE input of parameters for SQLTables.

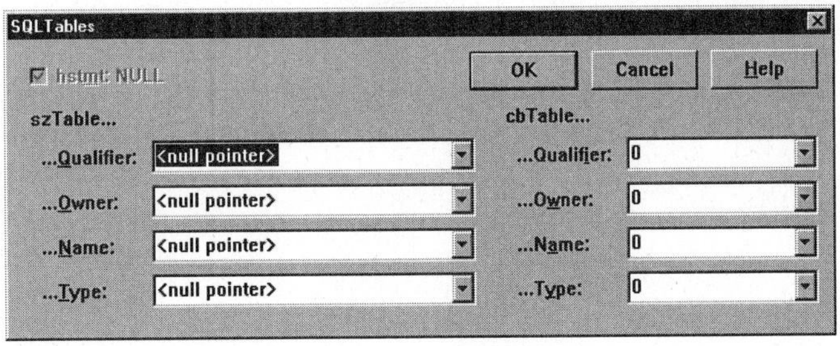

SQLExtendedFetch

ODBC SDK 2.5 provides an extended set of functions that enables you to perform more advanced operations on a result set. These enable block cursors and scrollable cursors, modifying the result set and retrieving multiple result sets. The function returns the result set in the form of an array. SQLExtendedFetch has fFetchType options of SQL_FETCH_NEXT, SQL_FETCH_PRIOR, SQL_FETCH_RELATIVE (use value in irow to move that many rows), SQL_FETCH_FIRST, SQL_FETCH_LAST, SQL_FETCH_ABSOLUTE (use value in irow as starting point), and SQL_FETCH_BOOKMARK. Other options are available by setting parameters in SQLSetStmtOption.

A bookmark is a 32-bit value that uniquely identifies the row. Like the bookmark you're familiar with, it enables you to quickly return to your place (the row) in the result set.

The syntax is

```
rc = SQLExtendedFetch(hstmt, fFetchType, irow, pcrow, rgFRowStatus);
```

The `irow` parameter is the number of rows to return, `pcrow` is the number of rows actually fetched, and `rgfRowStatus` is an array of status values.

The `SQLSTATE` return codes are the same as `SQLFetch`, with the addition of `01S01` (error in row), `S1106` (fetch type out of range), `S1107` (row out of range), and `S1111` (invalid bookmark value).

To use block cursors, you first call `SQLSetStmtOptions` with the `fOption SQL_ROWSET_SIZE` and the `vParam` of the number of rows you want in the block. This can decrease network traffic because you are sending the server that many fewer calls. If your block size was 20, then one call to `SQLExtendedFetch` returns 20 rows, the same as 20 separate calls to `SQLFetch`.

Scrollable cursors enable you to move about the result set. You first call `SQLSetStmtOption` with the `fOption` parameter of `SQL_CURSOR_TYPE` and your choice of `SQL_CURSOR_STATIC` (your result set won't change throughout the calls same as MFC snapshot), `SQL_CURSOR_DYNAMIC` (your result set will change and the cursor should process data as it changes), or `SQL_CURSOR_KEYSET_DRIVEN` (like `SQL_CURSOR_DYNAMIC` with changes and deletions but ignores newly inserted rows).

Just as a cursor marks your position in a word processing document, an ODBC cursor marks your current position in a result set. The simplest type of cursor is forward only where the cursor points to a row in the result set. Each subsequent fetch call moves it forward one row. The forward-only cursor is the most common, but cursors with the ability to scroll backward, page up, and page down, as well as cursors which point to a group of rows, are more flexible in your applications. When a cursor can move back and forth in the result set, it is said to be scrollable. This might seem overly simplistic, but scrollable cursors in result sets are fairly new and may not be supported by your ODBC driver. A cursor that enables you to update the data to which it is pointing is said to be a scrollable, updatable cursor.

In SQL you would say

```
DECLARE MyCursor Cursor for SELECT * FROM client where Lastname like "HAMILTON"
UPDATE client SET Lastname = "Hamilton" WHERE CURRENT of MyCursor
```

This is simple until you examine the effect of more than one user accessing the data at one time. Should user2 or user1 get to update the result set, and after the update who sees what? This is called *sensitivity*, which is the visibility of data after changes are made by a cursor owner. An *insensitive* set of data would be like a *snapshot*, which is a copy of the result set at the point in time the cursor was set. A static cursor is said to give a snapshot view of the data. To change the result set you need to close the cursor and reopen it (a second snapshot). The opposite of this is a dynamic cursor where all changes are immediately visible. In between these two cursor types is keyset. A *keyset* cursor has a unique *keyvalue* for each row in the result set. The keyvalue maintains order, with inserts being put at the end of the result set.

Intertwined in these cursor types are the concept of *row locking*. Once a user gets a result set to work on, should the entire result set be locked for total access by other users by using exclusive locking (X-LOCK), or should it be shown to them in read-only mode with a shared lock (S-LOCK)? Should you just lock the row that is being updated (U-LOCK), or should you lock a page of memory? You might use *optimistic* locking—if no one else is looking at your data when you get it, your application assumes that no other transaction will update your data until you are finished. Suddenly the whole concept of cursors has become quite a bit more complex.

Like so many things in the computer world, row locking is a case of trade-offs. See Table 30.12.

Table 30.12. Cursor models and trade-offs.

Cursor Type	Accuracy	Consistency	Concurrency	Performance
STATIC	Poor	Excellent	Good	Varies
KEYSET_DRIVE	Good	Good	Good	Good
DYNAMIC	Excellent	Poor	Excellent	Varies
MIXED	Varies	Fair	Good	Good

Concurrency is set by the SQLSetStmtOption, SQLSetScrollOptions, or determined with the partner function SQLGetStmtOptions. The choices follow:

SQL_CONCUR_READ_ONLY	No updates will be attempted.
SQL_CONCUR_LOCK	Data is locked as fetched. Some DBMSs use an update lock (U-LOCK).
SQL_CONCUR_ROWVER	Versioning type optimistic locking.
SQL_CONCUR_VALUE	Optimistic locking uses value checking to detect changes.

SQLSetScrollOptions is used as

```
rc = SQLSetScrollOptions(hstmt, fConcurrency, crowKeyset, crowRowset);
```

The fConcurrency values are the SQL_CONCUR_READ_ONLY, SQL_CONCUR_LOCK, SQL_CONCUR_ROWVER, or SQL_CONCUR_VALUES. The crowKeyset is the number of rows to buffer or the scroll method by SQL_SCROLL_FORWARD_ONLY, SQL_SCROLL_STATIC, SQL_SCROLL_KEYSET_DRIVEN, or SQL_SCROLL_DYNAMIC. CrowRowset is the number of rows in the rowset.

The SQLSTATE return codes are 01000, IM001, S1000, S1001, S1010, S1107, S1108 (concurrency option out of range), and S1C00.

Static (snapshot) cursors have the members, order, and values of the result set fixed at the time the cursor is opened. The result set is usually a copy of the data, and it is easiest to think of this result set as a copy. When data is updated in the static cursor result set, it can't be seen by other users because the update was made to the copy. You also cannot see updates made by other cursors because you're working with a local copy of the data. This copy is usually in memory but can be spooled to a file if the data is excessive. In Table 30.12 this data has excellent consistency because you are always looking at the same set of data. The data, however, has poor accuracy because another user may have changed all the data while you were looking at the copy. The database may implement this with a temporary table for the data on the server instead of actually making a copy of the data on the client. Most DBMSs lock all the rows and make other users wait.

Dynamic cursors show you the changes the cursor owner makes as well as changes other cursors make to the data as it is being made. Updates affect the members, order, and values of the result set. The result set is said to be dynamic and have excellent accuracy because it always mirrors the current state of the data. DBMSs usually implement this by assigning an index to the result set. This index is also dynamic, initially set by the ordering you specify in your ORDER BY or GROUP BY clause. As rows are deleted or updated, this index value changes to enable you to move through the result set without holes.

A keyset cursor has a constant set of members and a constant order, but its values can be updated. If another cursor were to delete a row, you would still see that row in your cursor's result set. Inserts by other cursors are not seen, but inserts by your cursor are put at the end of the result set. To develop a keyset cursor you need a unique index column in your result set. The keyset is built from these unique values. When you update a value in a row, using this unique value requerys only the row, not the entire result set. The keyset may also include more rows than just the cursor row. This is to buffer the data, assuming you will be moving through the data by repositioning the cursor, which leads to greater performance. On your network, this larger result set can decrease traffic.

A *mixed* cursor is like the keyset cursor in that it is always larger than the rows specified by the cursor but never larger than the result set itself. It moves through this set like a keyset cursor but can move to rows outside the set and behave like a dynamic cursor. As it moves to the row past the defined keyset, a new keyset is built.

You can set and get the current cursor name with a pair of ODBC functions. Cursor names are used in positioned updates and deletes, like UPDATE variable …WHERE CURRENT of szCursor.

```
rc = SQLGetCursorName(hstmt, szCursor, cbCursorMax, pcbCursor);
rc = SQLSetCursorName(hstmt, szCursor, cbCursorMax);
```

The szCursor name is a pointer to the cursor name, cbCursorMax is the length of szCursor, and pcbCursor is the total bytes available to return in szCursor.

The SQLSTATE return codes are 01000, 01004, IM001, S1000, S1001, S1010, S1015 (no cursor name), and S1090.

```
#include <windows.h>
#include <sql.h>
#include <sqlext.h>
#define MAX_DATA 100
#define MAX_COLNAME 100

int WINAPI WinMain(HANDLE hInstance, HANDLE hPrevInstance, LPSTR lpszCmdLine, int
➡nCmdShow)
{
// setup vars

HENV henv;
HDBC hdbc;
HSTMT hstmt1;
HSTMT hstmt2;
RETCODE rc;

// change lastname of patient via cursors

SQLAllocEnv(&henv);
SQLAllocConnect(henv, &hdbc);
SQLConnect(hdbc, (UCHAR *) "SPNOTES",SQL_NTS,NULL,0,NULL,0);
SQLAllocStmt(hdbc, &hstmt1);
SQLAllocStmt(hdbc, &hstmt2);

UCHAR szLastName[MAX_DATA];
UCHAR szAccount[MAX_DATA];
SDWORD cbLastname;

SQLSetCursorName(hstmt1, (UCHAR *)"MyCursor", SQL_NTS);
SQLExecDirect(hstmt1, (UCHAR *)"SELECT PLastName, PAccount FROM PAT FOR UPDATE of
➡PLastName", SQL_NTS);
SQLBindCol(hstmt1, 1, SQL_C_CHAR, szLastName, MAX_DATA, &cbLastname);
do
SQLFetch(hstmt1);
while ((rc == SQL_SUCCESS ¦¦ rc == SQL_SUCCESS_WITH_INFO) && (strcmp((CHAR
➡*)szLastName, "Boyer")));
if (rc == SQL_SUCCESS ¦¦ rc == SQL_SUCCESS_WITH_INFO)
{
SQLExecDirect(hstmt2,(UCHAR *)"UPDATE PAT SET PLastName = \"Hamilton\" WHERE
CURRENT OF MyCursor", SQL_NTS);
}
SQLFreeStmt(hstmt1, SQL_DROP);
SQLFreeStmt(hstmt2, SQL_DROP);
SQLDisconnect(hdbc);
SQLFreeConnect(hdbc);
SQLFreeEnv(henv);
return(TRUE);
```

As stated previously, there are trade-offs in setting concurrency and setting isolation levels. There is also need of some common sense. If you set the isolation level to SERIALIZABLE, you are saying that no other transactions can affect your result set, nor can you affect theirs. Therefore you need not set further locks. The more you take control over the locking and isolation, the more checking your application needs to do to ensure the data in the result set is correct.

Block cursors and scrollable cursors can be combined to give both traffic savings and flexibility.

Unfortunately, SQLExtendedFetch is a level 2 call and not available to all DBMSs.

The working example can be changed to use SQLExtendedFetch:

```
#define ROWS 100
UCHAR szName[ROWS][30], szAddress[ROWS][30], szCity[ROWS][10];
UCHAR szState[ROWS][3], szZipcode[ROWS][6];
SDWORD cbName, cbAddress, cbCity, cbState, cbZipcode;
UDWORD crow, irow;
UWORD rgfRowStatus[ROWS];
RETCODE rc;
SQLSetStmtOption(hstmt, SQL_CONCURRENCY, SQL_CONCUR_READ_ONLY);
SQLSetStmtOption(hstmt, SQL_CURSOR_TYPE, SQL_CURSOR_KEYSET_DRIVEN);
SQLSetStmtOption(hstmt, SQL_ROWSET_SIZE,ROWS);

rc = SQLExecDirect(hstmt, "SELECT Name, Address, City, State, Zipcode FROM
➥CUSTOMERS",SQL_NTS);

if (rc = SQL_SUCCESS)
    {
    SQLBindCol(hstmt, 1, SQL_C_CHAR, szName, 30,&cbName);
    SQLBindCol(hstmt, 2, SQL_C_CHAR, szAddress, 30, &cbAddress);
    SQLBindCol(hstmt, 3, SQL_C_CHAR, szCity, 10, &cbCity);
    SQLBindCol(hstmt, 4, SQL_C_CHAR, szState, 3, &cbState);
    SQLBindCol(hstmt, 1, SQL_C_CHAR, szZipcode, 6, &cbZipcode);

    while (TRUE)
    {
      rc = SQLExtendedFetch(hstmt, SQL_FETCH_NEXT, 1 &crow, rgfRowStatus);
      if (rc == SQL_SUCCESS ¦¦ retcode == SQL_SUCCESS_WITH_INFO)
      {
//print strings 1 less than length for \0
        for(irow = 0, irow < crow ,irow++)
        {
        if(rgfRowStatus[irow] != SQL_ROW_deleted && rgfRowStatus[irow] !=
        ➥SQL_ROW_ERROR)
        fprintf(out, "%*s %*s %*s %*s
%*s",29,szName[irow],29,szAddress[irow],9,szCity[irow],2,szState[irow],5,szZipcode[irow]);
        }
      }
      else
      {
      break;
      }
    }
  }
```

A good time to remember SQLExtendedFetch is when your application needs to print a long report. You know the page length and the length of the header and footer, so set the block size to the rows of data to print per page. Each page would require only one fetch call to the server.

SQLSetPos

After that long discussion of cursors, most of you want to know how a cursor is actually set. SQLSetPos sets the cursor position in a row set and enables you to refresh, update, delete, or add data to the rowset. The syntax is:

```
rc = SQLSetPos(hsmt, irow, fOption, fLock);
```

The parameter is irow, the number of the row to which the operation is to be performed. If irow is zero, then the operation is on the whole rowset. fOption is either SQL_POSITON, SQL_REFRESH, SQL_UPDATE, SQL_DELETE, or SQL_ADD; fLock is either SQL_LOCK_NO_CHANGE, SQL_LOCK_EXCLUSIVE (row lock), or SQL_LOCK_UNLOCK. Also note that while SQL_ADD can have an irow value of any number, it is logical that the remaining fOption values have irow values less than or equal to the number in the rowset.

The SQLSTATE return codes are 01000, 01004, 01S01, 01S03 (no rows updated or deleted), 21S02, 22003, 22005, 22008, 23000, 24000, 42000, IM001, S0023, S1000, S1001, S1008, S1009, S1010, S1090, S1107 (*row out of range), S1109 (invalid cursor position), S1C00, or S1T00.

Positioned Updates

Another level 2 function is to modify data that is part of the result set. These are called positioned updates, or positioned deletes. The SELECT statement uses the phrase FOR UPDATE which may lock the entire result set on most DBMSs. An example is SELECT * FROM Customers WHERE zipcode eq "68510" FOR UPDATE of zipcode. Although this is a very clean way of updating data in the result set, there are not many DBMSs that support positioned updates. To determine this, you call SQLGetInfo with the fInfoType of SQL_PS_POSITIONED_UPDATE or SQL_PS_SELECT_FOR_UPDATE.

The steps are to first get the name of the cursor for the SELECT FOR UPDATE, then position the cursor with SQLFetch, and then SQLExecute the SELECT using the cursor name. An example is the easiest way to show this.

```
RETCODE rc;
UDWORD fPos
SWORD cbValue;
UCHAR szUpdateSQL{512];
UCHAR szCursor{SQL_MAX_IDENTIFIER+LEN + 1];
HSTMT hstmt;
SWORD cbCursor;
rc = SQLGetInfo(hdbc, SQL_POSITIONED_STATEMENTS, &fPos, sizeof(fPos), &cbValue);
if (RETCODE_IS_SUCCESSFUL(rc)
{
  rc = SQLGetCursorName(hstmt1, szCursor, sizeof(szCursor), &cbCursor);
```

```
}
if (RETCODE_IS_SUCCESSFUL(rc)
{
  rc = SQLAllocStmt(hdbc, &hstmt2);
}
if (RETCODE_IS_SUCCESSFUL(rc)
{
 sprintf(szUpdateSQL, "SELECT * FROM Customers WHERE zipcode eq "68510" FOR UPDATE
➥of zipcode WHERE CURRENT of %s", szCursor);

rc = SQLExecDirect(hstmt2, szUpdateSQL, SQL_NTS);
SQLFreeStmt(hstmt1, SQL_DROP);
}
return rc;
}
```

`SQLGetCursorName` has the following syntax:

```
rc = SQLGetCursorName(hstmt, szCursor, cbCursorMax, pcbCursor);
```

The output parameters are `szCursor` and `pcbCursor`.

The `SQLSTATE` return codes are: `01000`, `01004`, `IM001`, `S1000`, `S1001`, `S1010`, `S1015` (no cursor name), and `S1090`.

Multiple SQL Statements

Some DBMSs enable you to submit more than one SQL statement at once. This would be true in the case of a stored procedure. In this case, you need to be able to retrieve one result set, and then move to the next result set. `SQLMoreResults` simply does that. It moves to the next result set associated with a single `hstmt`. The syntax is

```
rc = SQLMoreResults(hstmt);
```

The `SQLSTATE` return codes are `01000`, `IM001`, `S1000`, `S1001`, `S1008`, `S1010`, and `S1T00`. The following is a simple example:

```
rc = SQLExecDirect(hstmt, "SELECT * FROM Customers"; "SELECT * FROM Friends");
while(rc != SQL_NO_DATA_FOUND)
{
rc = SQLFetch(hstmt);
//nonsense function mail
mail(Christmas cards);
}

SQLMoreResults(hstmt);

while(rc != SQL_NO_DATA_FOUND)
{
rc = SQLFetch(hstmt);
//worked above, use it again
mail(Christmas cards);
}
```

Asynchronous Execution

If your database is huge, some SQL statements can take hours to execute. This is particularly true when you are deleting many rows and the indexes are constantly being rebuilt. Often, a better solution is to remove the indexes and rebuild after the deletes. However, at times you just need to let a long process run its course. In this case, you need to return control back to the application so that the users can get on with their work.

To call asynchronous execution, you first set up the option in the `SQLSetConnectOption` or `SQLSetStatementOption` with the `fOption` parameter of `SQL_ASYNC_ENABLE` with the value of `TRUE`. If you set the connection option, it affects all statements for that connection. If you set the statement option, only that statement is affected. The functions listed in Table 30.13 all can be executed asynchronously. Once a function is executed, it returns `SQL_STILL_EXECUTING` each time you call it. `SQLCANCEL` can cancel the action of an executing statement. Its syntax is:

```
rc = SQLCANCEL(hstmt);
```

`SQLSTATE` has return codes of `01000`, `70100` (operation aborted), `IM001`, `S1000`, and `S1001`. An important point is that when `SQLCANCEL` returns `SQL_SUCCESS`, `SQLCANCEL` was successfully sent, but execution of the statement hasn't actually stopped. You need to call the asynchronous function again until you receive `SQLSTATE` of `S1008` (operation canceled).

Table 30.13. ODBC functions that can be called asynchronously.

SQLColAttributes	SQLForeignKeys	SQLProcedureColumns
SQLColumnPrivileges	SQLGetData	SQLProcudures
SQLColumns	SQLGetTypeInfo	SQLPutData
SQLDescribeCol	SQLMoreResults	SQLSetPos
SQLDescribeParam	SQLNumParams	SQLSpecialColumns
SQLExecDirect	SQLNumResultsCols	SQLStatistics
SQLExecute	SQLParamData	SQLTablePrivileges
SQLExtendedFetch	SQLPrepare	SQLTables
SQLFetch	SQLPrimaryKeys	

`SQLNativeSql` and Extended SQL

ODBC drivers translate SQL statements from the ODBC specification to the DBMS's specific SQL. In order to examine this translation, ODBC provides the function `SQLNativeSql`. When you are tracking down problems with the result set it can be useful to display the SQL statement you sent and the SQL native statement. The syntax is:

```
rc = SQLNativeSql(hdbc, szSqlStrIn, cbSqlStrIn, szSqlStr, cbSqlStrMax, pcbSqlStr);
```

The szSqlStrIn is the string to be translated. It doesn't get executed, just translated. szSqlStr is the translation. The SQLSTATE return codes are 01000, 01004, 08003, 37000 (syntax error), IM001, S1000, S1001, S1009, and S1090.

Date and Time Literals

DBMSs support many different types of date and time formats. The ISO standard represents the date as yyyy-mm-dd. Your application can use a special *escape clause* to pass the ODBC format and the driver interprets. This is done as {d '1996-02-20'}. To Microsoft SQL Server this comes across as '02-20-1996.' There are similar escape clauses for time and timestamps.

Outer Joins

Just as you saw with data escape clauses, ODBC has defined a syntax for an outer join syntax:

```
outer_join ::=table_name[correlation_name] LEFT OUTER JOIN
➥{table_name[correlation_name] ¦ outer_join} ON search_condition
```

Scalar Functions

ODBC supports 60 scalar functions for strings, numerics, system, date/time, and data type conversions. Numeric functions are like "SELECT {fn log10(fMyNumber)} FROM Mytable" or "SELECT {fn rand(iMyint)} FROM Mytable." These take a single parameter and act upon it. String functions extract substrings, determine string length, and concatenate strings as in "SELECT {fn concat(LastName, FirstName)} FROM PAT." Date functions do time-based calculations on a column and work like "SELECT {fn dayofweek(idate)} FROM CALENDAR" or "SELECT * FROM MySchedule WHERE MyTIMESTAMP = {fn now()}." System functions return the name of the database, the user, and if a value is null in the form "SELECT * FROM PATIENTS WHERE PAT = {fn user()}." The data type conversion functions work like "SELECT EMPLOYEENO FROM EMPLOYEES where {fn convert(EMPLOYEENO, SQL_CHAR) LIKE '1%'."

The LIKE predicate is the percent character (%) which matches zero or more of any character. Using the underscore (_) matches any one character. Using these characters in an SQL statement usually requires an escape clause, or the compiler might mix up the number of parameters you are passing. You see this as "SELECT LASTNAME, FIRSTNAME FROM EMPLOYEE WHERE LASTNAME LIKE '\%HAM%' {escape '\'}." This might be messy, but if you have been using C or C++ for a while, you see the problem that it solves. This assumes the escape character is (\). Your DBMS may vary, and you may need to call SQLGetInfo with the SQL_LIKE_ESCAPE_CLAUSE to determine it.

Stored Procedures

In the 1980s, stored procedures were introduced by Sybase as a way to enforce general business rules on its DBMS. An example was that if an order dropped inventory below a certain level, a reorder for a given number of inventory units was automatically created. A stored procedure is a group of SQL statements (get new inventory level, check against rule minimum level if low order level specified) given a procedure name and executed as a unit by calling that name. This procedure would be used by many applications assessing the inventory data. It looks like a function call with a name, parameters, and return values.

DBMSs differ widely in the format of a stored procedure. To overcome this, ODBC has another escape clause:

```
{[?] call procedure)name[(arg1m arg2, …)]}
```

The calling format is

```
{?= CALL monthend (?)}
```

This format calls the monthend procedure. The ?= specifies an output parameter (your results); the second ? specifies the input parameter. Before you call the procedure, you use SQLBindParameter with the fParamType of SQL_PARAM_INPUT_OUTPUT (assuming you have both input and output parameters). The results are returned in a result set in the same fashions as the other SQL statements. To know if your DBMS supports stored procedures you can call SQLGetInfo with fInfoType of SQL_PROCEDURES. The return is either "Y" or "N."

Transaction Processing

Imagine the amount of code you would need to write to track every possible database change and reverse it if necessary. You would need to store the original data so that you could reverse any updates or deletions. You would need to store changes and deletions so that you could reverse. You would need to store the sequence of the changes, and so on. This would be a huge application just to provide the ability to undo. Most true DBMSs provide built-in transaction processing.

A *transaction* is a group of one or more SQL statements, which are to be executed as a unit. Either all or none are executed. *Commit* is the term for executing the unit, and *rollback* is the term to return the database to its state prior to the unit. Transactions are used to maintain data integrity. In accounting, you learned to debit one account and credit another. The two steps are one transaction and must both be performed in order for your accounts to stay in balance. If one cannot be performed, then neither should be, and the transaction is rolled back so that your books are as they were before. That is the basics of transaction processing. If both can be executed, you commit the unit; if not, you reverse the action of the partial steps in a rollback.

The DBMS has to be capable of detecting deadlocks between multiple executing transactions. When a deadlock occurs, the transaction that is initiated must be rolled back and the application informed. The application then restarts the transaction. This is an area were standardization of error codes is essential, as the following example shows:

```
if(!strcmp(SQLSTATE,"40001"))
//restart transaction
```

The first thing your application needs to do is determine if the data source supports transaction processing. You saw this step in SQLGetInfo with the parameter SQL_TXN_CAPABLE. SQLGetInfo returns SQL_TC_NONE if it's not supported, SLQ_TC_DML indicates that data definition language (DDL) statements cannot be used in transactions (like CREATE TABLE or DROP TABLE (to delete a table)). SQL_TC_DDL_COMMIT indicates any DDL statement and fires off a commit. SQL_TC_DDL_IGNORE indicates any DDL statements in the transaction that are ignored. And lastly, SQL_TC_ALL means transaction processing of both DDL and DML statements is supported. You also need to know if multiple transactions can be active at one time on any one connection. SQLGetInfo provides this in the SQL_MULTIPLE_ACTIVE_TXN by returning either "Y" or "N."

Transaction processing involves three steps:

1. Set up transaction processing in SQLSetConnectOptions to manual commit.
2. Execute multiple SQlPrepare, SQLExecute, or SQLExecDirect statements as a unit.
3. Commit or roll back the statements using SQLTransact.

SQLSetConnectOptions

You have two choices in the setup of SQLSetConnectOptions: auto commit and manual commit. Auto commit is the default state, where each SQL statement is committed as it executes. Because auto commit is the default, you must set up manual commit to do the transaction processing yourself.

> **NOTE**
>
> SQLSetConnectOptions (hdbc, SQL_AUTOCOMMIT, SQL_AUTOCOMMIT_OFF) can return SQLSTATE of S1C00 (driver not capable) if the mode is already set to manual. If you hadn't called SQLGetInfo's SQL_TXN_CAPABLE before this call, you wouldn't know why you got this error.

After you set the manual commit mode, every SQL statement is part of a transaction unit. You usually commit if the whole unit succeeds or roll back if any one statement fails. A good example is DELETE, in which you assume that you are only deleting one row. You can save yourself by insuring SQLRowCount is 1 prior to the commit.

In manual commit mode, the driver begins a transaction when an application submits an SQL statement and no transactions are open. It commits or rolls back upon the call to SQLTransact. In auto commit mode, each SQL is a single, complete transaction. The driver commits once per each statement. All statement handles belonging to a single connection handle are in the same transaction space. SQLTransact commits or rolls back all statements in the same transaction space. If you have two statements, you need to be aware that this happens. Each statement is associated with a cursor. If a cursor is open when SQLTransact is called, one of three things can happen:

1. The cursor may be closed and deleted, and any prepared statements will be lost.

2. The cursor may be closed but not deleted. The application needs to re-execute any prepared statements.

3. The cursor is preserved, and the application can continue to use the cursor after the call to SQLTransact.

Your design needs to be aware of possibilities when using multiple statement handles in a transaction mode.

The following is a simple transaction example:

```
RETCODE rc;
SDWORD cRow;
rc = SQLConnectOption(hdbc, SQL_AUTOCOMMIT, SQL_AUTOCOMMIT_OFF);
if (RETCODE_IS_SUCCESSFULL(rc))
  {
    rc = SQLExecute(hstmt);
  }
if (RETCODE_IS_SUCCESSFULL(rc))
  {
    rc = SQLRowCount(hstmt, &cRow);
  }
if (RETCODE_IS_SUCCESSFULL(rc) && cRow <=1L)
  {
    SQLTransact(henv, hdbc, SQL_COMMIT);
  }
else
  {
    SQLTransact(henv, hdbc, SQL_ROLLBACK);
  }
```

SQLTransact

As shown in the preceding example, SQLTransact takes three parameters, the environment handle, the database handle, and either SQL_COMMIT or SQL_ROLLBACK.

The SQLSTATE return codes are: 01000, 08003, 08007 (connect failed during transaction), IM001, S1000, S1001, S1010, S1012 (invalid transaction code), and S1C00.

SQLTransact requests a commit or rollback on all active operations of the statement handles associated with a connnection. This immediately raises questions of multiuser environments and the concept of *transaction isolation levels.* Think of two users: The first edits some data but hasn't committed the changes, and the second user polls the same data. Should they see the edited data or the original? What if they make different changes to the data? What if user 1 is adding a bunch of new data? User 2 polls the same data, and then user 1 decides to roll back so that the data is never in the actual database. Three terms are used to describe the state of the data—*a dirty read* is when user 1 changes data that is read by user 2, and then user 1 rolls back. A *nonrepeatable read* is when both user 1 and user 2 poll the same data, user 2 deletes some data and commits, and user 1 rereads the same data, which has changed. A *phantom read* is when user 1 reads data, user 2 inserts new data, and user 1 requeries and gets the new data.

ODBC provides five sets of locking instructions to prevent the previous situations or combinations of themes as some may be desirable in your situation. The syntax is

```
rc = SQLSetConnectOption(hdbc, SQL_TXN_ISOLATION, SQL_TXN_READ_UNCOMMITTED)
```

There is a trade-off between reading the most current data and reading consistent data. There are also trade-offs when you lock users out of data. This is called *concurrency* locking. The more consistency, the more rows need to be locked, so there is less concurrency. To provide a high level of consistency, like SQL_TXN_SERIALIZABLE, you may need to lock entire tables. Because each DBMS has its own record locking scheme, the best you can do is call SQLGetInfo with fInfoType SQL_TXN_ISOLATION_OPTION and see what levels are available—very few DBMSs support all 5 levels. Often you do the opposite and set up an acceptable level to make the application more robust. This function returns the levels shown in Table 30.14.

Table 30.14. ODBC transaction isolation levels.

Isolation level	Dirty reads	Nonrepeatable reads	Phantom reads
SQL_TXN_READ_UNCOMMITTED	YES	YES	YES
SQL_TXN_READ_COMMITTED	NO	YES	YES
SQL_TXN_REPEATABLE_READ	NO	NO	YES
SQL_TXN_SERIALIZABLE	NO	NO	NO
SQL_TXN_VERSIONING	NO	NO	NO

Read Uncommitted places no restrictions on reads. Data that is inserted, edited, or deleted is immediately available to the next query, therefore you have a high level of concurrency. Because you have no locks, however, you will see all three types of read problems, and thus you have very low consistency.

Read Committed restricts only dirty reads so that transactions do not read uncommitted data. *Read Committed* has slightly better consistency in the data, but the data set is slightly less concurrent.

Repeatable reads is a usual level for multiple user systems. Because reading many rows locks those rows, you should try to have small result sets to enable as many users concurrent access as possible.

Serializable transactions means that if two transactions are executed immediately in order (serial), then you will always get the same result set. However, because this might require an entire table to be locked, your multiuser performance will suffer.

Versioning is when a high performance DBMS keeps separate pages of data for each transaction. Multiple users each have their own page of data, and fewer records need to be locked per transaction. This is a good trade-off for concurrency versus consistency, but this approach can fail if the server goes down while many transactions are pending.

Also note that if you fail to issue `SQLTransact` after a group of statements, the transaction is still open, and further statements are added to that unit. Some DBMSs have limits on the number of transactions in a unit.

Explicit Locking

In most cases you won't have complete control over the preceding transaction options. Instead, the DBMS will have set a default isolation level. Sometimes, though, you cannot let the DBMS manage the locking scheme—the application must control the locks. At this point you need to dig out the API manuals for the DBMS you choose. Some have specific record locking functions; most do not. You need to know about the data source. A `SELECT FOR UPDATE` on some systems does row locking on the rows. You also can use `SQLSetPos` locking functions, discussed earlier. If you're using MFC record sets, you also can use `CRecordset::SetLockingMode` for optimistic or pessimistic locking.

Database Table Creation

Most SQL statements are interchangeable across DBMSs, but `CREATE TABLE` is not, due to the large variety in the naming of data types. Using a database application, you define tables by first assigning a table name, and then, column by column, naming the column and defining what type of data it will hold.

SQLGetTypeInfo

You cannot assume in this area—you need to use `SQLGetTypeInfo` to ensure that the data type exists. This is a simple function:

```
rc = SQLGetTypeInfo(hstmt, fSqlType);
```

The return is a result set containing 15 columns of which you would use TYPE_NAME, DATA_TYPE, PRECISON, CREATE_PARAMS, NULLABLE, UNSIGNED_ATTRIBUTE, MONEY, AUTO_INCREMENT, MINIMUM_SCALE, and MAXIMUM_SCALE in your CREATE TABLE.

The `SQLGetTypeInfo` result set consists of the information shown in Table 30.15.

Table 30.15. The `SQLGetTypeInfo` result set.

Name	Type	Comment
TYPE_NAME	Varchar(128)	Data type name
DATA_TYPE	Smallint	SQL data type
PRECISION	Int	Precision
LITERAL_PREFIX	Varchar(128)	In literals, i.e. "dave," the (")
LITERAL_SUFFIX	Varchar(128)	The second (")
CREATE_PARAMS	Varchar(128)	Parameters, i.e. "max_length"
NULLABLE	Smallint	SQL_NO_NULLS, SQL_NULLABLE, SQL_NULLABLE_UNKNOWN
CASE_SENSITIVE	Smallint	TRUE or FALSE
SEARCHABLE	Smallint	SQL_UNSEARCHABLE, SQL_SEARCHABLE, or SQL_ALL_EXCEPT_LIKE
UNSIGNED_ATTRIBUTE	Smallint	TRUE, FALSE, or NULL
MONEY	Smallint	TRUE or FALSE
AUTO_INCREMENT	Smallint	TRUE, FALSE, or NULL
LOCAL_TYPE_NAME	Varchar(128)	DBMS name for type
MINIMUM_SCALE	Smallint	Minimum scale
MAXIMUM_SCALE	Smallint	Maximum scale

This gives quite a bit more detail than you're likely to need. You typically call `SQLGetTypeInfo` with a type like `SQL_LONGVARCHAR`. If that fails, create the column with type `SQL_VARCHAR` or `SQL_CHAR`.

The `SQLSTATE` return codes are: `01000`, `08S01`, `24000`, `IM001`, `S1000`, `S1001`, `S1004`, `S1008`, `S1010`, `S1C00`, and `S1T00`.

The actual `CREATE TABLE` is part of an `SQLExecDirect`:

```
rc = SQLExecDirect(hstmt, "create table MySales (""Company text(40), ""Contact
➥text(25), ""Order long, ""Today datetime)",SQL_NTS);
rc = SQLExecDirect(hstmt,"create index Coidx on MySales(Company)", SQL_NTS);
```

Your syntax may vary with the most likely use of escape as \" to signify the quote instead of double quotes.

You can see that by using the `SQLConfigDataSource` and `CREATE TABLE` you could build an Access database on-the-fly.

Referential Integrity

SQL defines a set of rules that the database system can use to ensure that its data is valid and conforms to its design schema. There are two types of integrity: referential and entity.

Entity rules apply to records in a table. These rules are those that define the value's limits, prevent fields from being NULL, prevent duplicates, and define default values. Entity rules also define primary key values to ensure that they are unique and not NULL.

Referential integrity rules apply to the relationships between tables. Each customer in a client table might have a CustomerID number that points to the CustomerID field in the sales table. You might have a rule that says you can't update the sales table if the CustomerID doesn't exist in the client table. This is referential integrity. When you delete a customer from the client table, you might have a rule that says all sales table rows for the CustomerID are also deleted.

In general, the database engine is the best place to enforce integrity rules. You build them into the design of the database. In application development, you may need to enforce those rules at entry time. You can either query the database and validate references, or validate against hardcoded values. Most ODBC drivers support some or all of the SQL standard's integrity keywords, such as PRIMARY key and FOREIGN key.

A primary key is a column in a table whose values uniquely identify that row. A foreign key is a column in one table used to reference a unique column in a second table. This designates a one-to-one or one-to-many relationship between the two tables.

In ODBC this is done with SQLExecDirect:

```
rc = SQLExecDirect(hstmt,"create index Coidx on MySales(Company)", SQL_NTS);
```

The "create index" syntax may vary, requiring you to adjust to your particular DBMS vendor. You also may need to use the SQLNativeSql function if your vendor uses a varied syntax.

BLOBs (Binary Large Objects)

You saw SQLGetData in a prior example. It is called once for every column and every row. One thing this enables you to do is retrieve data in a piecemeal type fashion. A BLOB can be a large text block or binary data, like a bitmap or video clip. BLOBs can be large enough that they don't fit into memory at one time. The idea is to use SQLGetData to get a piece of the BLOB, process that piece, and then call SQLGetData again. Each time SQLGetData returns the amount of data left to be retrieved.

ODBC defines three binary types: SQL_BINARY, SQL_VARBINARY, and SQL_LONGVARBINARY. This data type is unique not only in its length but also in that the data usually needs some processing prior to display and use. This data can be BMP, PCX, AVI, PCX, GIF, TIFF, FLI, or of the many other sound, video, or picture types. This data can be larger than can fit into available memory. The process is to use SQLGetData repeatedly with the same set of parameters. Each time you call SQLGetData, it returns the amount of data yet to be retrieved.

SQLPutData

To add binary data to the database, you may need to move it, in pieces, with an AVI file to be stored in a BLOB. The syntax is

```
rc = SQLPutData(hstmt, rgbValue, cbValue);
```

The rgbValue is the pointer to the storage of the data you're going to input and the cbValue, its length. The SQLSTATE return codes are 01000, 01004, 08S01, 22001, 22003, 22005, 22008, IM001, S1000, S1001, S1008, S1009, S1010, S1090, and S1T00.

SQLGetData

SQLGetData was used in several earlier examples. It returns result set data from a single unbound column in the current row. Here it is important because it can retrieve data in parts from a column. Its syntax is

```
rc = SQLGetData(hstmt, icol, fCType, rbgValue cbValueMax, pcbValue);
```

The parameters are icol, the number of the column to retrieve or 0 if a bookmark; fCType, the C data type; rbgValue, a pointer to where you want to store the data; cbValueMax, the maximum length of the buffer; and pcbValue, the total bytes available in the column prior to the call. You can use the pcbValue to get binary fields larger than the buffer or to reduce network traffic by moving larger buffers. For binary data, if this is set to SQL_NO_TYPE, the data is truncated to the length in cbValueMax.

The important item here is the SQLSTATE return codes. If SQLGetData returns SQL_SUCCESS_WITH_INFO and 01004 (data truncated), then you call SQLGetData again with the same column number to retrieve the next amount until SQLGetData returns SQL_NO_DATA_FOUND. The other SQLSTATE return codes are 01000, 01004, 07006, 08S01, 22003, 22005, 22008, 24000, IM001, S1000, S1001, S1002, S1003, S1008, S1009, S1010, S1090, S1109, S1C00, and S1T00. ODBC 2.5 added 22012 (division by zero).

SQLMoreResults

SQLMoreResults really doesn't fit with BLOB data, but it is in the SQLGetData and SQLSetData group, so it is included here. SQLMoreResults simply determines whether there are more results available from the SELECT, UPDATE, INSERT, or DELETE statements. The syntax is

```
rc = SQLMoreResults(hstmt);
```

The function returns more of the result set if it is a SELECT or the number of affected rows. The SQLSTATE return codes are 01000, IM001, S1000, S1001, S1008, S1010, and S1T00.

What's Next?

SAG is working on the next version of the CLI specifications. These extend to interoperability and incorporate new database techniques. These new techniques include XA transaction processing, stored procedures, BLOBs, triggers, and asynchronous calls.

Chapter 29 mentioned that SAG and X/Open have merged and are working with ISO to have one standard. ODBC 2.5 was made available in August of 1995 and included system level data sources, the capability to uninstall components, and new installer functions. Microsoft announced that ODBC 3.0 would ship this year (1996), and you may, in fact, have it as you read this. ODBC 3.0 will take the new ISO functions and map them to existing ODBC functions so that SQL and ISO's CLIs are aligned.

New functions include SQLAllocHandle, which will allocate any of the hdbc, henv, and hstmt handles and the new handle for descriptors. Descriptors are data structures that hold information about columns in a result set or parameters in an SQL statement. Several new functions to get information on the environment are also planned. These include SQLGetStmtAttr, SQLSetStmtAttr, SQLSetEnvAttr, SQLGetEnvAttr, SQLSetConnnectAttr, and SQLGetConnectAttr.

New and extensible error handling will be available with two new functions, SQLGetDiagRec and SQLGetDiagField. These will enable the addition of other types of error data.

Chapter 31, "Database Access Objects (DAO)," gives you a hint of where database programming is headed with the introduction of OLE into database access. In ODBC 3.0, Microsoft will introduce a set of OLE interfaces for manipulating tabular data. This first step will address binding enhancements, positioning enhancements (FETCH Find and enhanced bookmarks), and better support for larger objects. FETCH Find is the ability to find a row in the result set during the FETCH. ODBC 3.0 is also expected to support arrays of parameters with rowwise binding.

Visigenics Corporation has licensed ODBC code from Microsoft and released versions for UNIX and Macintosh. The Macintosh cross compiler edition of VC++ 4.0 ships with the drivers. This ability will be enhanced in ODBC 3.0 to further develop ODBC as the standard CLI. Developers have also requested that ODBC 3.0 include a new, safer installation API with much more extensive error handling.

ODBC and SQL are both dynamic—they will continue to rapidly change. SAG is now defining a set of class library functions (SQL/MM) for multimedia data. This area is rapidly growing as better data engines are available for large amounts of BLOB data. You can monitor the SAG developments at http://www.jcc.com/sql_stnd.html and the ISO work at http://www.iso.ch/welcome.html.

SQLError Return Codes

The entire chapter has referred to SQLError and SQLSTATE return codes. A variable of type RETCODE rc was declared. The possible choices for the return code rc are: -2 SQL_INVALID_HANDLE; -1 SQL_ERROR; 0 SQL_SUCCESS; 1 SQL_SUCCESS_WITH_INFO; 100 SQL_NO_DATA_FOUND; 2 SQL_STILL_EXECUTING; and 99 SQL_NEED_DATA. You will also see Microsoft sample code where macros have been defined. These save space and your typing. Two Microsoft commonly used equivalent macros are

```
#define RC_SUCCESS(rc) (((rc)==SQL_SUCCESS)¦¦((rc)==SQL_SUCCESS_WITH_INFO))
```

and

```
#define RC_SUCCESS(rc) (!((rc)>>1));
```

These are used as

```
rc = SQL…
if (RC_SUCCESS(rc){
…
}
```

This saves you a bunch of typing over the course of your application:

```
if ((rc == SQL_SUCCESS) ¦¦ (rc = SQL_SUCCESS_WITH_INFO))
```

The function SQLError returns error or status information. Its syntax is

```
rc = SQLError(henv, hdbc, hstmt, szSqlState, pfNativeError, szErrorMsg,
➥cbErrorMsgMax, pcbErrorMsg);
```

Your input parameters are henv, hdbc, hstmt, and cbErrorMsgMax (the maximum length of the buffer you're providing for the error message). The return parameters are szSqlState (our SQLSTATE return string), pfNativeError (the data source specific error code), and szErrorMsg (a pointer to the error message text). The only time SQLError returns error information on itself is when none is available. In this case, szSqlState is 00000, and the return code is SQL_NO_DATA_FOUND. This chapter repeatedly listed functions, and then possible SQLSTATEs. The following is a list in the reverse.

Table 30.16. SQLError **codes.**

SQLSTATE	szSqlState	*From functions*
00000	Success	SQLBrowseConnect
		SQLError
01002	Disconnect error	SQLDisconnect

SQLSTATE	szSqlState	*From functions*
01004	Data truncated	SQLBrowseConnect
		SQLColAttributes
		SQLDataSources
		SQLDescribeCol
		SQLDriverConnect
		SQLExtendedFetch
		SQLFetch
		SQLGetCursorName
		SQLGetData
		SQLGetInfo
		SQLNativeSql
01006	Privilege not revoked	SQLExecDirect
		SQLExecute
01S00	Invalid connection string attribute	SQLBrowseConnect
		SQLDriverConnect
07001	Wrong number of parameters	SQLExecDirect
		SQLExecute
07006	Restricted data type attribute violation	SQLExtendedFetch
		SQLFetch
		SQLGetData
		SQLSetParam
08001	Unable to connect to data source	SQLBrowseConnect
		SQLConnect
		SQLDriverConnect
08002	Connection in use	SQLBrowseConnect
		SQLConnect
		SQLDriverConnect
08003	Connection not open	SQLAllocStmt
		SQLDisconnect
		SQLGetConnectOption
		SQLGetInfo
		SQLNativeSql
		SQLSetConnectOption
		SQLTransact
08004	Data source rejected establishment of connection	SQLBrowseConnect
		SQLConnect
		SQLDriverConnect

continues

Table 30.16. continued

SQLSTATE	szSqlState	*From functions*
08007	Connection failure during transaction	SQLTransact
08S01	Communication link during transaction	SQLBrowseConnect
		SQLColumnPrivileges
		SQLColumns
		SQLConnect
		SQLDriverConnect
		SQLExecDirect
		SQLExecute
		SQLExtendedFetch
		SQLFetch
		SQLForeignKeys
		SQLFreeConnect
		SQLGetData
		SQLGetTypeInfo
		SQLParamData
		SQLPrepare
		SQLPrimaryKeys
		SQLProcedureColumns
		SQLProcedures
		SQLPutData
		SQLSetConnectOption
		SQLSetStmtOption
		SQLSpecialColumns
		SQLStatistics
		SQLTablePrivileges
		SQLTables
21S01	Inserted value list does not match column list	SQLExecDirect
		SQLPrepare
21S02	Degree of derived table does not match column list	SQLExecDirect
		SQLPrepare
22001	String data right truncation	SQLExecDirect
		SQLExecute
		SQLPutData

SQLSTATE	szSqlState	*From functions*
22003	Numeric value out of range	SQLExecDirect SQLExecute SQLExtendedFetch SQLFetch SQLGetData SQLGetInfo SQLPutData
22005	Error in assignment	SQLExecDirect SQLExecute SQLPrepare
22008	Date/Time field overflow	SQLExecDirect SQLExecute SQLPutData
22012	Division by zero	SQLExecDirect SQLExecute SQLExtendedFetch SQLFetch
22026	String data, length mismatch	SQLExecDirect SQLPutData
23000	Integrity constraint violation	SQLExecDirect SQLExecute
24000	Invalid cursor state	SQLColAttributes SQLColumnPrivileges SQLColumns SQLDescribeCol SQLExecDirect SQLExecute SQLExtendedFetch SQLFetch SQLForeignKeys SQLGetData SQLGetTypeInfo SQLPrepare SQLPrimaryKeys SQLProcedureColumns

continues

Table 30.16. continued

SQLSTATE	szSqlState	*From functions*
		SQLProcedures
		SQLSetCursorName
		SQLSetPos
		SQLSetScrollOptions
		SQLSpecialColumns
		SQLStatistics
		SQLTablePrivileges
		SQLTables
25000	Invalid transaction state	SQLDisconnect
28000	Invalid authorization specification	SQLBrowseConnect
		SQLConnect
		SQLDriverConnect
34000	Invalid cursor name	SQLExecDirect
		SQLPrepare
		SQLSetCursorName
37000	Syntax error or access violation	SQLExecDirect
		SQLNativeSql
		SQLPrepare
3C000	Duplicate cursor name	SQLSetCursorName
40001	Serialization failure	SQLExecDirect
		SQLExecute
		SQLExtendedFetch
		SQLFetch
42000	Syntax error or access violation	SQLExecDirect
		SQLExecute
		SQLPrepare
70100	Operation aborted	SQLCancel
IM001	Driver does not support this function	All ODBC functions except:
		SQLAllocConnect
		SQLAllocEnv
		SQLDataSources
		SQLError
		SQLFreeConnect
		SQLFreeEnv
		SQLGetFunctions
IM002	Data source name not found and no default driver specified	SQLBrowseConnect
		SQLConnect
		SQLDriverConnect

SQLSTATE	szSqlState	*From functions*
IM003	Driver specified by data source name could not be loaded	SQLBrowseConnect SQLConnect SQLDriverConnect
IM004	Driver's SQLAllocEnv failed	SQLBrowseConnect SQLConnect SQLDriverConnect
IM005	Driver's SQLAllocConnect failed	SQLBrowseConnect SQLConnect SQLDriverConnect
IM006	Driver's SQLSetConnect option failed	SQLBrowseConnect SQLConnect SQLDriverConnect
IM007	No data source specified; dialog prohibited	SQLDriverConnect
IM008	Dialog failed	SQLDriverConnect
IM009	Unable to load translation DLL	SQLBrowseConnect SQLConnect SQLDriverConnect SQLSetConnectOption
S0001	Base table or view already exists	SQLExecDirect SQLPrepare
S0002	Base table not found	SQLExecDirect SQLPrepare
S0011	Index already exists	SQLExecDirect SQLPrepare
S0012	Index not found	SQLExecDirect SQLPrepare
S0021	Column already exists	SQLExecDirect SQLExecute SQLPrepare
S0022	Column not found	SQLExecDirect SQLPrepare
S1000	General error	All ODBC functions except: SQLAllocEnv SQLError

continues

Table 30.16. continued

SQLSTATE	szSqlState	*From functions*
S1001	Memory allocation failure	All functions except: SQLError SQLFreeConnect SQLFreeEnv
S1002	Invalid column number	SQLBindCol SQLColAttributes SQLDescribeCol SQLExtendedFetch SQLFetch SQLGetData
S1003	Program type out of range	SQLBindCol SQLGetData SQLSetParam
S1004	SQL data type out of range	SQLGetTypeInfo SQLSetParam
S1008	Operation canceled	All ODBC functions that can be processed asynchronously: SQLColAttributes SQLColumnPrivileges SQLColumns SQLDescribeCol SQLDescribeParam SQLExecDirect SQLExecute SQLExtendedFetch SQLFetch SQLForeignKeys SQLGetData SQLGetTypeInfo SQLMoreResults SQLNumParams SQLNumResultCols SQLParamData SQLPrepare SQLPrimaryKeys SQLProcedureColumns SQLProcedures SQLPutData

SQLSTATE	szSqlState	*From functions*
		SQLSetPos
		SQLSetScrollOptions
		SQLSpecialColumns
		SQLStatistics
		SQLTablePrivileges
		SQLTables
S1009	Invalid argument value	SQLAllocConnect
		SQLAllocStmt
		SQLBindCol
		SQLExecDirect
		SQLForeignKeys
		SQLGetData
		SQLGetInfo
		SQLNativeSql
		SQLPrepare
		SQLPutData
		SQLSetConnectOption
		SQLSetCursorName
		SQLSetParam
		SQLSetPos
		SQLSetStmtOption
S1010	Function sequence error	SQLBindCol
		SQLColAttributes
		SQLColumnPrivileges
		SQLColumns
		SQLDescribeCol
		SQLDescribeParam
		SQLDisconnect
		SQLExecDirect
		SQLExecute
		SQLExtendedFetch
		SQLFetch
		SQLForeignKeys
		SQLFreeConnect
		SQLFreeEnv
		SQLFreeStmt
		SQLGetConnectOption
		SQLGetCursorName

continues

Table 30.16. continued

SQLSTATE	szSqlState	*From Functions*
		SQLGetData
		SQLGetFunctions
		SQLGetInfo
		SQLGetStmtOption
		SQLGetTypeInfo
		SQLMoreResults
		SQLNumParams
		SQLNumResultCols
		SQLParamData
		SQLParamOptions
		SQLPrepare
		SQLPrimaryKeys
		SQLProcedureColumns
		SQLProcedures
		SQLPutData
		SQLRowCount
		SQLSetConnectOption
		SQLSetCursorName
		SQLSetParam
		SQLSetPos
		SQLSetScrollOptions
		SQLSetStmtOption
		SQLSpecialColumns
		SQLStatistics
		SQLTablePrivileges
		SQLTables
		SQLTransact
S1012	Invalid transaction operation code specified	SQLTransact
S1015	No cursor name available	SQLGetCursorName
S1090	Invalid string or buffer length	SQLBindCol
		SQLBrowseConnect
		SQLColAttributes
		SQLColumnPrivileges
		SQLColumns
		SQLConnect
		SQLDataSources
		SQLDescribeCol

SQLSTATE	szSqlState	*From functions*
		SQLDriverConnect
		SQLExecDirect
		SQLExecute
		SQLForeignKeys
		SQLGetCursorName
		SQLGetData
		SQLGetInfo
		SQLNativeSql
		SQLPrepare
		SQLPrimaryKeys
		SQLProcedureColumns
		SQLProcedures
		SQLPutData
		SQLSetCursorName
		SQLSpecialColumns
		SQLStatistics
		SQLTablePrivileges
		SQLTables
S1091	Descriptor type out of range	SQLColAttributes
S1092	Option type out of range	SQLFreeStmt
		SQLGetConnectOption
		SQLGetStmtOption
		SQLSetConnectOption
		SQLSetStmtOption
S1093	Invalid parameter number	SQLDescribeParam
		SQLSetParam
S1094	Invalid scale value	SQLSetParam
S1095	Function type out of range	SQLGetFunctions
S1096	Information type out of range	SQLGetInfo
S1097	Column type out of range	SQLSpecialColumns
S1098	Scope type out of range	SQLSpecialColumns
S1099	Nullable type out of range	SQLSpecialColumns

continues

Table 30.16. continued

SQLSTATE	szSqlState	*From functions*
S1100	Uniqueness option type out of range	SQLStatistics
S1101	Accuracy option type out of range	SQLStatistics
S1102	Table type out of range	SQLTables
S1103	Direction option out of range	SQLDataSources
S1106	Fetch type out of range	SQLExtendedFetch
S1107	Row value out of range	SQLExtendedFetch SQLParamOptions SQLSetPos SQLSetScrollOptions
S1108	Concurrency option out of range	SQLSetScrollOptions
S1109	Invalid cursor position; no keyset defined	SQLSetPos
S1110	Invalid driver completion	SQLDriverConnect
S1C00	Driver not capable	SQLBindCol SQLColumnPrivileges SQLColumns SQLExtendedFetch SQLFetch SQLForeignKeys SQLGetConnectOption SQLGetData SQLGetInfo SQLGetStmtOption SQLPrimaryKeys SQLProcedureColumns SQLProcedures SQLSetConnectOption SQLSetParam SQLSetPos SQLSetScrollOptions SQLSetStmtOption SQLSpecialColumns

SQLSTATE	szSqlState	*From functions*
		SQLStatistics
		SQLTablePrivileges
		SQLTables
		SQLTransact
S1DE0	No data at execution	SQLParamData
		values pending SQLPutData
S1T00	Time-out expired	SQLBrowseConnect
		SQLColAttributes
		SQLColumnPrivileges
		SQLColumnsSQLConnect
		SQLDescribeCol
		SQLDescribeParam
		SQLDriverConnect
		SQLExecDirect
		SQLExecute
		SQLExtendedFetch
		SQLFetch
		SQLForeignKeys
		SQLGetData
		SQLGetInfo
		SQLGetTypeInfo
		SQLMoreResults
		SQLNumParams
		SQLNumResultCols
		SQLParamData
		SQLPrepare
		SQLProcedures
		SQLPutData
		SQLSetPos
		SQLStatistics
		SQLTablePrivileges
		SQLTables

Data Access Objects (DAO)

31

*by David
Hamilton*

IN THIS CHAPTER

Microsoft Access and the MDB file format have become a standard for PC-based databases, due primarily to Access's ease of use. Chapters 29 and 30 showed ways to build database applications using ODBC in client/server applications.

In 1992, Microsoft released Access and described it as "a significant engine hidden behind an easy user interface." The internal code name for the engine development had been JET, a play on words with engine. It proved to be fast in accessing data in tables and stored queries. More important to Access's success, it couldn't have been much easier to use. Most Windows NT programmers who see Microsoft Access for the first time need only 10 minutes of training because the product is simple to learn. With version 1.1, a DAO interface for Visual Basic 3.0 developers was introduced.

In 1994, after merging technologies with FoxPro, Access 2.0 was released. FoxPro had a technology called Rushmore that enabled data validation, standard SQL syntax, and a full programming interface. DAO version 2.5 added to the ability to access data with ODBC, and the 1995 release (DAO 3.0) enabled more than 10 applications to simultaneously use the engine. Access 7.0 was released updated for Windows 95. With 3.0, DAO became callable as an OLE Automation in-process server. Any program that can call an OLE server can access DAO functionality.

Not only can you rapidly design a database schema with Microsoft Access, you can later use Access to run and optimize your queries and adjust your index designs.

DAO

DAO is built on the concept of collections. Each DBEngine object can contain multiple Workspace objects and error objects. Each Workspace contains multiple database objects, group objects, and user objects. Each database contains multiple TableDef objects, multiple QueryDef objects, and multiple Recordset objects. Each Tabledef contains multiple fields and indexes. This forms a hierarchical tree of branching objects. Each object, as you know, has properties and methods.

DAO, the programming interface to Microsoft Access, was designed to be used by Visual Basic. Visual Basic users and VBA (Visual Basic for Applications) users, however, have been building their applications using classes of a native API, which writes and directly reads the MDB files.

The DAO DLL is an OLE Automation in-process server containing an embedded type library. You saw OLE Automation servers in Chapter 19, "OLE Automation." With Visual C++ 4.0, Microsoft provided header files describing the vtable interfaces for DAO. This eliminated the need to use the Idispatch interface you saw in Chapter 17, "OLE and DDE Concepts." The objects created are OLE Component Object Model (COM) objects.

In Visual C++ 4.0, Microsoft has released DAO to give C/C++ programmers full access to the jet engine used by Access. With the DAO SDK, a set of classes mimics using the Visual Basic classes. With the MFC DAO classes, the classes are wrapped similarly to the MFC ODBC classes. DAO is a set of OLE objects that greatly simplify database programming, together called an OLE Automation Server. The jet engine is a set of DLLs, shown in Figure 31.1. In addition to opening Access databases, you can open ODBC sources directly. You can open ISAM type data sources (dBASE, FoxPro, Paradox, Btrieve, Excel or Text files) either directly or as attached tables to an Access Database.

FIGURE 31.1.

DAO vs. ODBC and their DLLs.

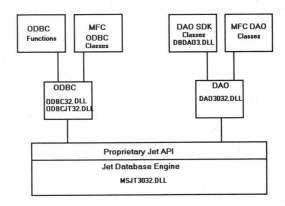

The last two chapters discussed ODBC database development; so a natural question would be why DAO? First of all you need to answer the question of which DBMS you are going to access. Although DAO can read from any ODBC data source, it's usually more efficient to use ODBC directly for many DBMS's not supplied by Microsoft. However, if you will access data in a format the jet engine can read directly, like an Access database, an Excel spreadsheet, or a FoxPro database, DAO is more efficient.

The DAO classes have a richer set of methods. By combining DAO with the fast data-retrieval methods using an Access stored procedure, you can get back complex queries or sorted data searches much quicker. You can also use the jet engine's ability to very quickly do joins with data outside the Access database.

At this time, DAO doesn't support multithreaded applications. For developing true client/server RPC applications, this limits your choice to ODBC. DAO also does not work with Win32's applications. If you expect to have more than 10 simultaneous users accessing the database on a dedicated server, DBMSs such as SQL Server are more efficient than Access.

The last reason may become the most important: the future. DAO is closely linked to OLE, and NT's future is OLE. More and more of the functionality added to Windows NT will rely on data in a format the DAO can read directly. In the future, you will find yourself writing applications that blend functionality from other applications that are themselves OLE automation servers, just like DAO.

Some basic definitions are needed to get started if you do not have experience with OLE. A *method* is still just a function associated with a class of object.

A *property* (or OCX property) is an attribute of an object that does not usually have arguments. Usually a property has a name that is mapped to an integer index value. To set a property value in Visual Basic, you specify an integer index and the value. To get the property, you need only specify the integer index. In C++ the properties are implemented as a pair of methods (Get and Set); and the index value is defined as a name, so properties look and behave just like methods.

A *collection* is a group of like objects accessed together for easier reference. In DAO you are able to do group operations on the entire collection and add or remove objects from collections. Collections contain zero or more objects, all of the same type. You will notice in Table 13.1 that for each Class object, there is a corresponding class collection (except CdbEngine). The collections are named as the plural of their respective classes. In Table 13.1 a collection of CdbDatabase is held in class CdbDatabases. What Microsoft has developed is a hierarchical model of the database structure.

A TableDef object is a table stored in a database. It contains the definitions of the fields but does not contain the data.

A QueryDef object is a saved query in the database. Again, it contains the defintions of the fields but does not contain the data.

Table 31.1. Data access objects and collections.

Object	Collection	Description
CdbContainer	CdbContainers	Storage of information about object type
CdbDatabase	CdbDatabases	An open database
CdbDbEngine		The jet engine
CdbDocument	CdbDocuments	Information on a saved predefined object
CdbError	CdbErrors	Errors associated with object
CdbField	CdbFields	Column in a table, query, index, relation or recordset
CdbGroup	CdbGroups	A group of user accounts
CdbIndex	CdbIndexes	Predefined ordering and uniqueness of values
CdbParameter	CdbParameters	A parameter for a query
CdbProperty	CdbProperties	A built-in or user-defined property
CdbQueryDef	CdbQueryDefs	A saved query definition
CdbRecordset	CdbRecordsets	The records in a table or query
CdbRelation	CdbRelations	The relationships between fields in a table or query

Object	Collection	Description
CdbTableDef	CdbTableDefs	A saved table definition
CdbUser	CdbUsers	A user account
CdbWorkspace	CdbWorkspaces	A session with the jet engine

A *variant* is an OLE automation type which is the union of common C types and several complex types such as date, currency, and BSTR. BSTR is a way to represent character strings. A BSTR variable is a pointer to a zero-terminated character array that has a character count in the front. Variants are a safe way to pass variables between your application and the OLE automation server. They also facilitate the use of Remote Procedure Calls where variables are passed between dissimilar machines. MFC 4.0 introduced the type COleVariant that makes converting from a C++ to a variant easier. To access a variant you need only know the type—if the variant is VT_I2 you read the variant's value from iVal. A string is read from the bstrVal value of the variant. The easiest way to envision this is by examining the Win32 OLE header file definition:

```
struct tagVaRIANT{
  VARTYPE vt; //unsigned short integer type code
  WORD wReserved1;
  WORD wReserved2;
  WORD wReserved3;
  union {
    short      iVal; //VT_I2 short int
    long       iVal; //VT_I4 long int
    float      fltVal; //VT_R4 4 byte float
    double     dblVal; //VT_R8 8 byte IEEE float
    DATE       date; //VT_DATE stored as dbl date.time
    BSTR       bstrVal; //VT_BSTR
    IUnknown   FAR* punkVal; //VT_UNKNOWN
    IDispatch  FAR* pdispVal; //VT_DISPATCH
    short      FAR* piVal;   //VT_BYREF | VT_I2
    long       FAR* plVal;   //VT_BYREF | VT_I4
    float      FAR* pfltVal; // VT_BYREF | VT_R4
    double     FAR* pdblVal; // VT_BYREF | VT_R8
    DATE       FAR* pdate; // VT_BYREF | VT_DATE
    BSTR       FAR* pbstrVal; // VT_BYREF | VT_BSTR
    IUnknown   FAR* FAR* ppunkVal; // VT_BYREF |  VT_UNKNOWN
    IDispatch  FAR* FAR* ppdispVal; // VT_BYREF | VT_DISPATCH
  }
};
typedef struct tagVARIANT VARIANT;
```

The jet engine gives the Visual C++ the power to not only access the data in an MDB file but also to create a JOIN with attached tables from other DBMSs. It also enables the use of stored queries, which can greatly speed up your application. A big advantage of stored queries is that you can change them in Access without changing your application.

DAO3032.DLL is an OLE automation server like you saw in Chapter 17. OLE automation is the process of using code stored in a COM object. In this case, DAO is a new automation interface type called a dual interface, using both OLE programming's interface of objects, `IDispatch` and a `vtable`. Both C++ and Basic programmers are accessing the same code with the COM object.

There are actually three ways to write your application using DAO and C++.

1. Use the OLE automation dual interface directly, which requires knowledge of COM programming but gives you the maximum DAO functionality.

2. Use the DAO SDK classes, which require little COM programming knowledge and also enable you to write a lot less code. These classes handle the reference counting for you (`AddRef` and `Release`), do the allocating and deallocating of objects, give you collection support, and enable direct fetches into data structures. Functions enable you to access security and table definition areas of the jet engine.

3. DAO MFC classes are based on ODBC's `CRecordset` and enable you to use the same programming style and ease you saw in Chapter 29. DAO has MFC classes similar to ODBC, but renamed `CRecordset` becomes `CDAORecordset`. However, some functionality is lost in simplifying the database classes. You also may need to use some function calls from the DAO SDK.

Each of the preceding three ways has advantages and disadvantages. Using the OLE automation interface gives you the most functionality, but programming can be tedious. The DAO MFC classes are the easiest to learn and use if you are familiar with ODBC. If you are coming from Visual Basic, the DAO SDK classes seem familiar to you. You mix the MFC classes with the DAO SDK classes to gain functionality.

Native Jet Engine Access

The DAO SDK is installed separately from the opening screen of the VC++ 4.1 CD. The DAO SDK classes are an application programmer interface based on OLE. The classes are defined in DBDAO.H, and the error classes in DBDAOERR.H and extended functions are defined in DAOGETRW.H. The DAO SDK classes closely model the classes provided to Visual Basic users. By using operator overloading, these classes make programming to the jet engine easy. The DAO SDK classes can be the most efficient way to access MDB files because they map directly to the underlying functions without the translation step MFC may impose.

CdbDBWorkspace, CdbDBEngine, and CdbDBDatabase

While quite a bit has been written about using the MFC DAO classes, there is not much documentation on using the DAO SDK classes. To illustrate how easy using SDK classes is, this chapter concentrates mainly on teaching by example—giving an example then explaining the class members, member functions, collections, and operator overloads. To begin any database project you need to build a basic AppWizard application and open your database. The examples use an Access Database, SPNOTES.MDB, which has four tables, PAT, Groups, Visit, and Doctor. Each patient's demographics are in PAT. Visit is for the daily notes of each patient's visit. Doctor and Groups are simple look-up tables.

To begin, create an AppWizard SDI application with Container support. In this example, its name is Chp31. In the application header, Chp31h, include the dbdao header file in the very first line as

```
#include <dbdao.h>
```

Using the right button popup menus in the class browser document class (CChp31Doc for the following example), add the function ConnectToDatabase as

```
BOOL ConnectToDatabase and check public
```

Also using the right button popup menu add the variables

```
CdbDBEngine m_cDBEngine and check protected
CdbDatabase m_cSNDatabase and check protected
BOOL m_bConnected and check public
```

Call the function ConnectToDatabase in the Document class's OnNewDocument() as

```
BOOL CChp31Doc::OnNewDocument()
{
if (!COleDocument::OnNewDocument())
return FALSE;
if (!ConnectToDatabase())
{
m_bConnected = FALSE;
return FALSE;
}
m_bConnected = TRUE;
return TRUE;
}
```

If you are not already connected, simply call the function ConnectToDatabase(). This function is defined in the Chp31Doc.cpp file as

```
BOOL CChp31Doc::ConnectToDatabase()
{
  CFileDialog cOpenFile(TRUE,_T("MDB"),_T("SPNOTES.MDB"),OFN_HIDEREADONLY |
➥OFN_OVERWRITEPROMPT,
  (_T("Access Files (*.mdb) | *.mdb ||")));
cOpenFile.DoModal();
TCHAR szBuf[256];
try
{
  m_cSNDatabase = m_cDBEngine.OpenDatabase(cOpenFile.m_ofn.lpstrFile);
  wsprintf(szBuf, _T("Database: %s\n"), (LPCTSTR)m_cSNDatabase.GetName());
  AfxMessageBox(szBuf);
}
catch (CdbException e)
```

```
{
  CdbLastOLEError exError;
  wsprintf(szBuf, _T("Error %d : %s\n"), DBERR(e.m_hr),
(LPCTSTR)exError.GetDescription());
  AfxMessageBox(szBuf);
  return FALSE;
}
return TRUE;

}
```

Build and run the very basic application. You need to ensure that dbdao3d.dll is in your path, probably in the WINNT\System32 directory. If it isn't there, you can copy it from the \MSDEV\DAOSDK\LIB\debug folder.

You will have to add this DLL to the project. Open the Project settings dialog box and the Link property sheet. Select General in the Category drop-down listbox and type in dbdao3d.lib into the Object/library modules text box.

The application doesn't appear to do much. It first asks you to find the database, then confirms that the database is open. (See Figures 31.2 and 31.3.)

FIGURE 31.2.

cOpenFile.DoModal() *to find the database.*

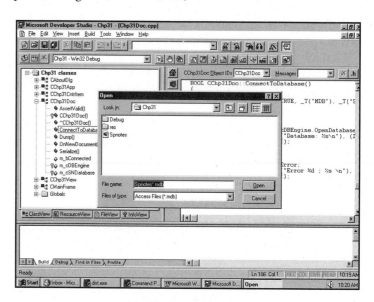

FIGURE 31.3.

Proof that we have the database open!

All you have done so far is initialize the DAO DBEngine object. Using the cOpenFile.DoModal() was just for show. You could have just as easily hard-coded the database name:

```
m_cSNDatabase = m_cDBEngine.OpenDatabase(_T("SPNOTES.MDB"));
```

The `m_cdbEngine.OpenDatabase()` hides quite a bit of behind-the-scenes action. The DAO SDK classes all have default collections defined. (See Table 31.2.) ODBC has the concept of an environment—DAO has a Workspace. Because you didn't specifically declare a Workspace, the default action was to first evoke the default Workspace, Workspace(0). What you typed was

```
m_cSNDatabase = m_cDBEngine.OpenDatabase(…);
```

but what the library saw was:

```
m_cSNDatabase = m_cDBEngine[0L].OpenDatabase(…).
```

The `CdbDBEngine` class has two constructors, the simple form just used, and another constructor that enables you to specify the UserID, password, IniPath, private or shared, and whether to start the engine. The Workspace class enables the application to do transaction processing using the syntax workspace. BeginTrans | CommitTrans | Rollback.

Table 31.2. Class definitions.

Class	*Members/Collections*	*Methods/Properties*
class `CdbWorkspace`	Databases	`OnInterfaceChange(VOID)`
	Users	`GetName(VOID)`
	Groups	`SetName(LPCSTR)`
		`GetUserName(VOID)`
		`GetIsolateODBCTrans(VOID)`
		`SetIsolateODBCTrans(BOOL)`
		`BeginTrans(VOID)`
		`CommitTrans(VOID)`
		`Close(VOID)`
		`Rollback(VOID)`
		`OpenDatabase(LPCTSTR, BOOL)`
		`CreateDatabase(LPCTSTR LPCTSTR)`
		`CreateUser(LPCTSTR, LPCTSTR)`
		`CreateGroup(LPCTSTR, LPCTSTR)`
class `CdbDatabase`	TableDefs	`OnInterfaceChange(VOID)`
	QueryDefs	`GetCollatingOrder(VOID)`
	Relations	`GetConnect(VOID)`

continues

Table 31.2. continued

Class	Members/Collections	Methods/Properties
	Containers	GetName(VOID)
	Recordsets	GetQueryTimeout(VOID)
		SetQueryTimeout(SHORT)
		GetTransactions(VOID)
		GetUpdatable(VOID)
		GetVersion(VOID)
		GetRecordsAffected(VOID)
		Close(VOID)
		Execute(LPCTSTR,LONG)
		OpenRecordset(LPCTSTR, LONG, LONG)
		CreateProperty(LPCTSTR, LONG, LPVARIANT,BOOL)
		CreateRelation(LPCTSTR, LPCTSTR, LPCTSTR, LONG)
		CreateTableDef(LPCTSTR LONG, LPCTSTR, LPCTSTR)
		CreateQueryDef (LPCTSTR LPCTSTR)
class CdbDBEngine	m_bStarted	SetDefaultPassword (LPCTSTR)
	Workspaces	SetDefaultUser(LPCTSTR)
	Errors	SetIniPath(LPCTSTR)
		GetIniPath(LPCTSTR)
		SetLoginTimeout(SHORT)
		GetLoginTimeout(VOID)
		GetVersion(VOID)
		GetSystemDB(VOID)
		SetSystemDB(LPCTSTR)
		CreateWorkspace(LPCTSTR, LPCTSTR)
		OpenDatabase(LPCTSTR, BOOL, BOOL, LPCTSTR)

Class	Members/Collections	Methods/Properties
		CompactDatabase(LPCTSTR, LPCTSTR, LPCTSTR, LONG, LPCTSTR)
		RepairDatabase(LPCTSTR)
		RegisterDatabase(LPCTSTR, LPCTSTR, BOOL, LPCTSTR)
		Idle(LONG)
		Start(VOID)

CdbException, CdbLastOLEError, and cdbError

You also used class CdbException and its HRESULT member, m_hr. Much more error information is available from CdbLastOLEError and CdbError classes. HRESULT members come from OLE programming, a LONG composed of several bit fields. The DBERR macro extracts the information. The error values are listed in DBDAOERR.H. CdbException also has a collection. In a long sequence of statements you can retrieve the error collection as

```
catch (CdbException e)
{
  int iError, cError;
  CString stError = _T("");
  cError = m_cDBEngine.Errors.GetCount();
  for (iError = 0, iError < cError; iError++)
    {
    stError += m_cbDBEngine[iError];
    stError += _T("\n");
    }
}
```

or as:

```
catch (CdbException e)
{
        wsprintf(szBuf, _T("Error %d : %s\n"), m_cDBEngine.Errors[0].GetNumber(),
(LPCTSTR)m_cDBEngine.Errors[0].GetDescription());
  AfxMessageBox(szBuf);
  return FALSE;
}
```

Table 31.3. Class definitions.

Class	Members	Methods
class `CdbException`	`HRESULT m_hr`	
class `CdbError`	`OnInterfaceChange`	`GetNumber(VOID)`
		`GetSource(VOID)`
		`GetDescription(VOID)`
		`GetHelpFile(VOID)`
		`GetHelpContext(VOID)`
class `CdbLastOLEError`		`GetSource(VOID)`
		`GetDesciption(VOID)`
		`GetHelpFile(VOID)`
		`GetHelpContext(VOID)`

`CdbRecordset`, `CdbGetRow`, and `CdbGetRowsEx`

As we saw with ODBC, the DAO SDK uses a class to hold a recordset. The recordset can be opened as either `dbOpenDynaset`, `dbOpenSnapshot`, or the new type, `dbOpenTable`. `dbOpenTable` gives you a spreadsheet-like view of an entire table. It behaves like a dynaset but works only with all the columns in a table. The source of the recordset (either snapshot or dynaset) can be a table name, a query name, or an SQL statement. In addition, the record set has the options of `dbAppendOnly`, `dbForwardOnly`, `dbSQLPassThrough` (pass SQL to ODBC for processing), `dbSeeChanges` (generate an error if another user tries to update your data), `dbDenyWrite`, `dbDenyRead`, `dbReadOnly`, `dbInconsistent`, and `dbConsistent`.

A quick note about dynaset vs. snapshot vs. table-type: If you are looking at the entire table, use table-type, it is fastest. If your data is remote, use snapshot recordsets, they're fastest. If they're memo fields or OLE objects, use dyansets.

The style you see most often in sample applications is to consider the database and recordset as the Document in Document/View architecture. However, in a large database application with many tables, you may want to open the recordset as each dialog box or view is created and move it out of the document class and into your dialog class. An example of opening a recordset follows:

```
BeginWaitCursor();
try
{
  m_database = m_cDBEngine.OpenDatabase(_T("SPNOTES"));
  m_strDatabase = m_database.GetName();
  m_qvrecordset = m_database.OpenRecordset(_T("Visits"));
  if(!m_qvrecordset.GetBOF())
```

```
    {
      m_qvrecordset.MoveLast();
    }
    m_nRowCount = m_qvrecordset.GetAbsolutePosition() +1;
    m_qvrecordset.MoveFirst();
    }
catch (CdbException e)
{
    CdbLastOLEError oe;
    TCHAR szBuf[256];
    wsprintf(szBuf, ("Error: %d : %s\n"), DBERR(e.m_hr),
➡(LPCTSTR)oe.GetDescription());
    AfxMessageBox(szBuf);
    m_bConnected = FALSE;
}
EndWaitCursor();
TRACE(("m_strDatabase: %s m_nRowCount: %d\n"),_T(m_strDatabase), m_nRowCount);
return TRUE;
```

This brief example used several of the member functions of `CdbRecordset`. There are many more listed in Tables 31.1–12. You will notice in the implementation within a recordset that you don't need to bind the variables—however, changing from type `OleVariant` to a string takes just about as much typing. Because dynamic recordsets in ODBC require both the column name and type, Chapter 30 spends a good deal of time just determining those two parameters. DAO makes it much easier because the values are passed as type variant, and the columns can be accessed by numbered index. A DAO recordset only needs a recordset object. To convert from variant to my variable type, I have a short header file, Convert.h, that contains these functions and can be reused. You can also make part of stdafx.h or many of the Microsoft samples add it to the application header file.

```
//Convert.h
inline void VarToCStr(CString *c, COleVariant *v)
{
if(v->vt==VT_BSTR)
  {
  *c = (LPCTSTR)v->bstrVal;
  }
else
{
  *c = _T("");
}
}
#define VTOLONG(v) ((v).vt==VT_I4 ? (LONG)(v).iVal:0L)
#define VTODATE(v) ((v).vt==VT_DATE ? (CTime)(v).iVal:0L)
```

Putting the recordset to work in the `CFormView` is just as simple. A pointer to a `CdbRecordset *` `m_pset` is declared in My29aView.h. First, in the `OnInitialUpdate`, assign this pointer to the recordset as

```
void CMy29aView::OnInitialUpdate()
{
m_pSet = &GetDocument()->m_qvrecordset;
m_pSelection = NULL;    // initialize selection for OLE
CFormView::OnInitialUpdate();
}
```

The preceding code is only called the first time. It then calls `OnUpdate`, which is called every time you redraw the dialog. As such, it's a good place to do the field exchanges as

```
void CMy29aView::OnUpdate(CView* pSender, LPARAM lHint, CObject* pHint)
{
  try
  {
    VarToCStr(&m_pcode,&m_pSet->Fields[0L].GetValue());
    VarToCStr(&m_pfirstname,&m_pSet->Fields[1].GetValue());
    VarToCStr(&m_plastname,&m_pSet->Fields[2].GetValue());
    VarToCStr(&m_doctorname,&m_pSet->Fields[3].GetValue());
    m_visit_date = m_pSet->Fields[4].GetValue();   //defined as OleDateTime
    m_visit_time = m_pSet->Fields[5].GetValue();
  }
  catch (CdbException e)
  {
    CdbLastOLEError eo;
    TCHAR szBuf[256];
    wsprintf(szBuf, _T("Error %d;
➥%s\n"),DBERR(e.m_hr),(LPCTSTR)eo.GetDescription());
    AfxMessageBox(szBuf);
  }
UpdateData(FALSE); //moves member variables to form or dialog variables
}
```

In the first call to `VarToCStr` the `Fields[0L]`, you must use a long, not just a `0`. If the index is not cast as `LONG`, the compiler interprets `0` as `NULL`. It is usually more readable to give your fields either a named or a numbered index like

```
#define PAT_ID 0L
```

To be even more readable, you also can use:

```
VarToCStr(&m_pcode,&m_pSet->Fields[PAT_ID].GetValue());
```

You can continue to access the recordset as

```
void CMy29aView::OnRecordNext()
{
CMy29aDoc* pDoc = GetDocument();
try
  {
    m_pSet->MoveNext();
    if(m_pSet->GetEOF())
    {
      MessageBeep(0);
      m_pSet->MovePrevious();
    }
  else
    {
    pDoc->UpdateAllViews(NULL);
    }
  }
  catch (CdbException e)
  {
    CdbLastOLEError eo;
    TCHAR szBuf[256];
```

```
    wsprintf(szBuf, _T("Error %d;
➡%s\n"),DBERR(e.m_hr),(LPCTSTR)eo.GetDescription());
    AfxMessageBox(szBuf);
  }
}

void CMy29aView::OnRecordFirst()
{
  try
  {
    m_pSet->MoveFirst();
  }
  catch (CdbException e)
  {
    CdbLastOLEError eo;
    TCHAR szBuf[256];
    wsprintf(szBuf, _T("Error %d;
➡%s\n"),DBERR(e.m_hr),(LPCTSTR)eo.GetDescription());
    AfxMessageBox(szBuf);
  }
}
```

The DAO supports the GetRows method for fetching multiple rows of data in one call. This is a holdover from Visual Basic and may not exist much longer in future versions of DAO. It is a fast method of getting large amounts of data, but suffers from problems when an error occurs. If you ask for 20 rows and only 10 are available, you naturally just get the 10. But if you ask for 20 rows and an error occurs, you get the rows prior to the error. This enables you to get error information at the point of the error, but you need to call GetEOF() to determine if you got all the rows (so that you know if an error occurred). GetRows takes only one argument, the number or rows you want. It returns all the fields to a single COleVariant object, a two dimensional array, your table. You need to then parse this array using SafeArrayGetUBound to retrieve the number of records and SafeArrayGetElement to get the field values.

```
void CMy29aDoc::LoadDialogBar()
{
//get pointer to app to get pointer to dialogbar to get pointer to its combobox
CWnd* pWnd = AfxGetApp()->m_pMainWnd;
CDialogBar* pBar = (CDialogBar*)pWnd->GetDlgItem(ID_QUERY_BAR);
CComboBox* pBox = (CComboBox*)pBar->GetDlgItem(IDC_BAR_PATIENT);

COleVariant vRows;
COleVariant vField;
LONG lNumberRows;
CString mrow;
LONG index[2];
TCHAR szBuf[256];

try
    {
  m_qpat = m_database.OpenRecordset(_T("QPats"));
  vRows = m_qpat.GetRows(10);
  SafeArrayGetUBound(vRows.parray,2,&lNumberRows);
  TRACE("Got %ld rows\n"),lNumberRows + 1);
    }
```

```
catch (CdbException e)
  {
  CdbLastOLEError oe;
  wsprintf(szBuf, ("Error: %d : %s\n"), DBERR(e.m_hr),
➥(LPCTSTR)oe.GetDescription());
  AfxMessageBox(szBuf);
  m_bConnected = FALSE;
  }

pBox->ResetContent();

for(index[1] = 0; index[1] <= lNumberRows; index[1]++)
  {
  mrow.Empty();

  index[0] = 0L;
  SafeArrayGetElement(vRows.parray, &index[0], &vField);
  mrow += (LPCTSTR)vField.bstrVal;
  mrow += _T(", ");

  index[0] = 1;
  SafeArrayGetElement(vRows.parray, &index[0], &vField);
  mrow += (LPCTSTR)vField.bstrVal;
  mrow += _T(" ");

  index[0] = 2;
  SafeArrayGetElement(vRows.parray, &index[0], &vField);
  mrow += (LPCTSTR)vField.bstrVal;

  pBox->AddString(mrow);
  }
}
```

The preceding code fills a combo box in the dialog box with the names in the Query. The variant vRows is parsed using SafeArrayGetElement, and a string is built to add to the combo box.

The DAO SDK has a much more powerful method, GetRowsEx, which enables you to forget the conversion of the variant to your C type. GetRowsEx can fetch subsets of the fields in the table and read data into a structure. Although GetRowsEx is slightly more complex, it works just like GetRows but enables you to specify which fields to fetch. To use GetRowsEx you define a standard C structure for your data, and a binding structure that maps your data structure to the fields. To get different subsets of your data you can define multiple structures.

The syntax for GetRowsEx is

```
rc = m_recordset.GetRowsEx(pvBuffer, cbRow, prb, cBinding, pvVarBuffer,
➥cbVarBuffer, lRows);
```

This looks a little daunting until you really use it. Though actually quite simple, the syntax is powerful. The parameters are pvBuffer (buffer to store rows), cbRow (length of row), prb (binding structure), cBinding (number of bindings), pvVarBuffer (pointer to buffer for variable length data), cbVarBuffer (length in bytes of pvVarBuffer), and lRows (number of rows you want). PvVarBuffer is an area of memory used to store variable length data in zero-terminated strings (you don't need to retrieve a VT_BSTR from each that way and it's packed to save memory).

GetRowsEx is easier to use than to explain, so an example follows:

```
typedef struct
  {
  LONG lPatientNo;           // just a long
  TCHAR strFirstName[20];    // zero terminated string
  TCHAR *strLastName;        // pointer into pVarBuffer
  } PATIENT, *LPPAT;
DAORSETBINGING Bindings[] =
// simple list of index type, column, type, offset and offset size
  {
{dbBindIndexINT, PAT_N0, dbBindI4, offsetof(PAT, lPatientNo), sizeof(LONG)},
{dbBindIndexINT, PAT_FNAME, dbBindSTRING, offsetof(PAT,strFirstName),
➥sizeof(TCHAR)* 20)},
{dbBindIndexINT, PAT_LNAME, dbBindLPSTRING, offsetof(PAT,strLastName),sizeof(TCHAR
*)}
};

// Perform dbDAO GetRowsEx against the Patient table

void CPatDlg::DoGetRowsEx()
{
LPPAT pPATRows = new PAT[MAX_PAT_REC];
CListBox *pListBox = (CListBox *)GetDlgItem(IDD_PatList);
CString strLBRow;
TCHAR szId[16];
LONG lNumRecords;
LONG lCount;
TCHAR pBuf[MAX_PAT_REC * 15];

lNumRecords = m_cPatSet.GetRowsEx(
pPatRows,                // Pointer to data buffer.
sizeof(PATIENT),         // Length of row in bytes.
&Bindings[0],            // Pointer to binding structures.
sizeof(Bindings) / sizeof(DAORSETBINDING),  // Number of bindings is size of all /
➥size of one
pBuf,                    // Storage for variable-length data (lastname).
sizeof(pBuf),            // Bytes available for variable-length data.
MAX_PAT_REC);            // Get MAX_EMP_REC rows.

for (lCount = 0; lCount < lNumRecords; lCount++)
{
strLBRow.Empty();
wsprintf(szId, _T("%d,  "), pPatRows[lCount].lPatientNo);
strLBRow += szId;
strLBRow += pPatRows[lCount].strLastName;
strLBRow += _T(", ");
strLBRow += (LPCTSTR) pPatRows[lCount].strFirstName;
pListBox->AddString(strLBRow);
}

delete [] pPatRows;
}
```

The binding structure looks a little complex, but it is just a table of the index type, your column name, binding type, offset, and size of offset. The possible index types (whether field is indicated by name or a string) are dbBindIndexINT for an index and dbBindIndexStr for a name. The possible data types are given in Table 31.4.

Table 31.4. DAORSETBINDING **data types.**

dbBindl2	long
dbBindl4	short
dbBindR4	float
dbBindR8	double
dbBindCY	currency
dbBindDATE	date
dbBindBOOL	VARIENT_BOOL
dbBindUl1	unsigned char
dbBindVARIANT	VARIANT
dbBindWCHAR	wchar_t[]
dbBingSTRING	same as dbBindWHAR for UNICODE or same as dbBindUi1 for ANSI
dbBindLPSTR	char pointer
dbBindLPTSTR	wchar pointer
dbBindLPSTRING	same as dbBindLPTSTR for UNICODE same as dbBindLPSTR for ANSI
dbBindBookmark	CdbBookmark
dbBindBlob	unsigned char pointer

There is a great deal of power in this function call to GetRowsEx. You certainly need to type more than when you use GetRows(). If the typing bothers you, you can use the Microsoft 32-bit ODBC Data Type Mapper program to generate the structures and buffer code. Although you need to set up an ODBC connection for your development work, the ability to cut/paste your structures is worth it.

Table 31.5. Class definitions.

Class	*Members/Collections*	*Methods/Properties*
class CdbRecordset;	GetBOF(VOID)	
	GetBookmark(VOID)	
	SetBookmark(CdbBookmark&)	
	GetBookmarkable(VOID)	GetDateCreated(VOID)
	GetLastUpdated(VOID)	

Class	Members/Collections	Methods/Properties
	GetEOF(VOID)	
	GetFilter(VOID)	
	GetIndex(VOID)	
	SetIndex(LPCTSTR)	
	GetLastModified(VOID)	
	GetLockEdits(VOID)	
	SetLockEdits(BOOL)	
	GetName(VOID)	
	GetNoMatch(VOID)	
	GetSort(VOID)	
	SetSort(LPCTSTR)	
	GetTransactions(VOID)	
	GetType(VOID)	
	GetRecordCount(VOID)	
	GetUpdatable(VOID)	
	GetRestartable(VOID)	
	GetValidationText(VOID)	
	GetValidationRule(VOID)	
	GetCacheStart(VOID)	
	SetCacheStart(CdbBookmark&)	
	GetCacheSize(VOID)	
	SetCacheSize(LONG)	
	GetPercentPosition(VOID)	
	SetPercentPosition(FLOAT)	
	GetAbsolutePosition(VOID)	
	SetAbsolutePostion(LONG)	
	GetEditMode(VOID)	
	CancelUpdate(VOID)	
	AddNew(VOID)	
	Close(VOID)	
	OpenRecordset(LONG, LONG)	

continues

Table 31.5. continued

Class	Members/Collections	Methods/Properties
	`Delete(VOID)`	
	`Edit(VOID)`	
	`FindFirst(LPCTSTR)`	
	`FindLast(LPCTSTR)`	
	`FindNext(LPCTSTR)`	
	`FindPrevious(LPCTSTR)`	
	`MoveFirst(VOID)`	
	`MoveLast(VOID)`	
	`MoveNext(VOID)`	
	`MovePrevious(VOID)`	
	`Seek(LPCTSTR,LONG, COLEVariant)`	
	`Update(VOID)`	
	`Clone(VOID)`	
	`Requery(CdbQuery *)`	
	`Move(LONG, CdbBookmark*)`	
	`FillCache(LONG, CdbBookmark*)`	
	`CopyQueryDef(VOID)`	
	`GetRows(LONG)`	
	`GetRowsEx(LPLONG, LONG LPDAORSETBINDING, LONG LONG, LPVOID, LONG, LONG)`	
	`GetFieldV(COleVariant, COleVariant)`	
	`SetFieldV(COleVariant, LPVariant)`	
	`GetField(LPCTSTR)`	
	`GetField(LONG)`	
	`SetField(LPCTSTR,m_GetRowInt, ➡LPVARIANT)`	
	Fields	`SetField(LONG, LPVARIANT)`
class `CdbGetRowsEx`;	Fields	`OnInterfaceChange(VOID)`

COleVariant **and** CdbBookmark

Microsoft has written a class to wrap the VARIANT structure with constructors for each VARIANT type. Constructors can call VariantInit and destructors can call VariantClear. There are copy constructors using VariantCopy. When a variant object goes out of scope, the destructor is called. There are also comparison operators, assignment operators, conversion operators, and friend insertion/extraction operators for the CArchive and CDumpContext classes. The examples in both code snippets above were

```
mrow += (LPCTSTR)vField.bstrVal;
```

A variant can contain actual data or a pointer to the data. If the variant type (vt) is VT_I2, you read the variant's value from iVal; if it is VT_I8, then dblVal; and if the VT_BYREF bit is set, you access the pointer in piVal or plVal. Strings are a special type. The BSTR type is a pointer to a zero-terminated character array with a character count in front. Perhaps examining the variant definition in the OLE header file (oaidl.h) again makes this most clear.

```
Struct tagVARIANT {
  VARTYPE  vt;
  WORD wReserved1;
  WORD wReserved2;
  WORD wReserved3;
  union {
    short       ival; //VT_I2 short int
    long        lval; //VT_I4 long int
    float       fltVal; //VT_R4 4-byte float
    double      dblVal; //VT_R8 8-byte float
    DATE        date; //VT_DATE dbl date.time
    BSTR        bstrVal; //VT_BSTR
    IUnknown    FAR* punkVal; //VT_UNKNOWN
    IDispatch   FAR* pdispVal; //VT_DISPATCH

    short       FAR* pival; //VT_BYREF|VT_I2
    long        FAR* plval; // VT_BYREF|VT_I4
    float       FAR* pfltVal; // VT_BYREF|VT_R4
    double      FAR* pdblVal; // VT_BYREF|VT_R8
    DATE        FAR* pdate; // VT_BYREF|VT_DATE
    BSTR        FAR* pbstrVal; // VT_BYREF|VT_BSTR
    IUnknown    FAR* FAR* ppunkVal; // VT_BYREF|VT_UNKNOWN
    IDispatch   FAR* FAR* ppdispVal; // VT_BYREF|VT_DISPATCH
  }
};
typedef struct tagVARIANT VARIANT;
```

Strings are special, and they can cause a common problem. To initialize the `COleVariant` properly you use

```
COleVariant varMyStr(_T("MyString"),VT_BSTRT);
```

The `VT_BSTRT` constant specifies that the `BSTR` is a UNICODE `BSTR` with a UNICODE build or an ANSI `BSTR` in a non-UNICODE build. This is an important point with non-UNICODE builds. If you wrongly use

```
COleVariant varMyStr(_T("MyString"));
```

you find that `varMyStr` is set to only the letter M. MFC creates ANSI DAO objects in a non-UNICODE build and UNICODE objects in a UNICODE build.

A bookmark is a variant that uniquely identifies the current record. When you create a recordset, the jet engine assigns a bookmark to each row automatically. You need to assign your bookmark to a variable to use it. You can have any number of bookmarks—just move to the row and assign the value of the bookmark property to any `CString`. When you "Clone" a recordset, the bookmarks move with you.

CdbTableDef **and** CdbQueryDef

If you are working with an Access database, you can store a query back into the database using the `CdbQueryDef` or define a new table with `CdbTableDef`. It's much easier to define the queries and table using Access. However, sometimes you need to define queries at runtime. An example of this would be a report or query that the user can define.

The default collection of a database object is the `TableDefs` collection, and the default collection of a `TableDef` object is the `Fields` collection. To create a new `TableDef` object you use the `CreateTableDef` method. The syntax for this is

```
var = db.CreateTableDef(name, attributes, source, connect);
```

Where `name` is the name of the table you are defining, `source` is the external MDB files table that you are optionally going to use in the definition (like moving a table from one MDB to another); `connect` is the connection string to the current MDB; and `attributes` is a `long` composed of the parts in Table 31.6.

Table 31.6. `CreateTableDef` **attributes from Microsoft DAO reference.**

Attribute	Comments
dbFixedField	The field size is fixed (default for Numeric fields).
dbVariableField	The field size is variable (Text fields only).

Attribute	Comments
dbAutoIncrField	The field value for new records is automatically incremented to a unique long integer that can't be changed (supported only for Microsoft Jet database tables).
dbUpdatableField	The field value can be changed.
dbDescending	The field is sorted in descending (Z to A or 100 to 0) order (applies only to a Field object in a Fields collection of an Index object). If you omit this constant, the field is sorted in ascending (A to Z or 0 to 100) order (default).
dbSystemField	The field is a replication field (on a TableDef object) used on replicable databases and cannot be deleted.
dbRelationUnique	Relationship is one-to-one.
dbRelationDontEnforce	Relationship isn't enforced (no referential integrity).
dbRelationInherited	Relationship exists in a noncurrent database that contains the two attached tables.
dbRelationUpdateCascade	Updates will cascade.
dbRelationDeleteCascade	Deletions will cascade.
dbAttachExclusive	For databases that use the jet database engine, indicates the table is an attached table opened for exclusive use. This constant can be set on an appended TableDef object for a local table, but not for a remote table.
dbAttachSavePWD	For databases that use the jet database engine, indicates that the user ID and password for the remotely attached table are saved with the connection information. This constant can be set on an appended TableDef object for a remote table, but not for a local table.
dbSystemObject	Indicates the table is a system table provided by the jet database engine. This constant can be set on an appended TableDef object.
dbHiddenObject	Indicates the table is a hidden table provided by the jet database engine. This constant can be set on an appended TableDef object.

continues

Table 31.6. continued

Attribute	Comments
dbAttachedTable	Indicates the table is an attached table from a non-ODBC database, such as a Microsoft Jet or Paradox database (read-only).
dbAttachedODBC	Indicates the table is an attached table from an ODBC database, such as Microsoft SQL Server (read-only).

The attribute is defined as a `long`, so you can add the values together such as:

```
var = db.CreateTableDef(name, (dbVariableField+dbUpdatableField), source, connect);
```

To add a field to an existing table, you need to ensure that the table is closed by all other users, then create the new field with the `CreateField` method, and lastly add the new field with the `TableDef` Append method. (See the next example.)

To create a table that is ready for new records in a database, first create a `TableDef` object using `CreateTableDef`, set its properties, and create the fields using the `CreateField` method. Add the field with the `Append` method and `Append` the `TableDef` object to your database's `TableDefs` collection. An example follows:

```
CdbEngine m_cDbEngine;
CdbDatabase m_database;
CdbTableDef m_tabledef;
CdbField m_field;
m_database = m_cDBEngine.OpenDatabase(_T("SPNOTES"));
m_tabledef = m_database.CreateTableDef(_T("MyNewTable"));
m_field = m_tabledef.CreateField(_T("Dave"),dbText,20);
m_tabledef.Fields.Append(m_field);
m_database.TableDefs.Append(m_tabledef);
```

To attach an external table to your database, first create a `TableDef` object by using `CreateTableDef`, set its `Connect` and `SourceTableName` properties, set its `Attributes` property, then add it to the `TableDefs` collection of a database using the `Append` method.

```
CdbEngine m_cDbEngine;
CdbDatabase m_database;
CdbTableDef m_tabledef;
CdbField m_field;
m_database = m_cDBEngine.OpenDatabase(_T("SPNOTES"));
m_tabledef = m_database.CreateTableDef(_T("MyNewTable"));
m_tabledef.Connect = (_T("FoxPro 3.0;DATABASE=c:\book\FPDB"));
m_tabledef.SourceTableName = (_T("Billing"));
m_database.TableDefs.Append(m_tabledef);
```

You can delete a `Field` object from a `TableDefs` collection if it doesn't have any indexes assigned to it, but its underlying data is lost.

Creating queries uses the same methods. However, you also can use SQL statements to create stored queries that later can be accessed like tables in a recordset. A quick example would show this the easiest.

```
CdbDatabase m_database;
CdbQueryDef m_querydef;
CdbRecordset m_recordset;

m_database = m_cDBEngine.OpenDatabase(_T("SPNOTES"));
m_querydef = m_database.CreateQueryDef("QVisits"));
m_querydef.SetSQL = (_T("Select * From Visits"));
m_database.QueryDefs.Append(m_querydef);
m_recordset = m_database.OpenRecordset(_T("Qvisits"));
```

If you don't want to append the QueryDef to the database you also can directly open the recordset from the query as in:

```
m_recordset = m_querydef.OpenRecordset(_T("Qvisits"));
```

As we have seen in ODBC programming, you can define parameterized queries or QueryDefs. The advantage is the parameter can change without the engine having to parse the entire query again. This enables faster lookups. A QueryDef has a collection of Parameters. Each parameter has a name, a value, and a type. You may still have the QueryDef stored in the database, and your programmer will just pass the parameters.

In the preceding example, if the QueryDef stored as Qvisits in the database was

```
SELECT * FROM Patients WHERE (Patients.PATID =[Patient Wanted])
```

It could be accessed as

```
CdbParamter m_parameter;
m_parameter.SetName(_T("Patient Wanted"));
m_paramter.SetValue(382);
m_recordset = m_querydef.OpenRecordset(_T("Qvisits"));
```

Table 31.7. Class definitions.

Class	Members/Collections	Methods/Properties
class CdbQueryDef;	Parameters	OnInterfaceChange(VOID)
		GetDateCreated(VOID)
		GetLastUpdated(VOID)
		GetName(VOID)
		SetName(LPCTSTR)
		GetODBCTimeout(VOID)

continues

Table 31.7. continued

Class	Members/Collections	Methods/Properties
		SetODBCTimeout(SHORT)
		GetType(VOID)
		GetSQL(VOID)
		SetSQL(LPCTSTR)
		GetUpdateable(VOID)
		GetConnect(VOID)
		SetConnect(LPCTSTR)
		GetReturnsRecords(VOID)
		SetReturnsRecords(BOOL)
		GetRecordsAffected(VOID)
		OpenRecordset(LONG, LONG)
		Execute(LONG)
		CreateProperty(LPCTSTR, LONG, LPVARIANT, BOOL)
class CdbTableDef;	Fields	OnInterfaceChange(VOID)
	Indexes	GetAttributes(VOID)
		SetAttributes(LONG)
		GetConnect(VOID)
		SetConnect(LPCTSTR)
		GetDateCreated(VOID)
		GetLastUpdated(VOID)
		GetName(VOID)
		SetName(LPCTSTR)
		GetSourceTableName(VOID)
		SetSourceTableName (LPCTSTR)
		GetUpdatable(VOID)
		GetValidationText(VOID)
		SetValidationText (LPCTSTR)
		GetValidationRule(VOID)
		SetValidationRule

Class	Members/Collections	Methods/Properties
		(LPCTSTR)
		GetRecordCount(VOID)
		OpenRecordset(LONG, LONG)
		RefreshLink(VOID)
		CreateField(LPCTSTR,
		LONG, LONG)
		CreateIndex(LPCTSTR)
		CreateProperty(LPCTSTR
		LONG, LPVARIANT, BOOL)
class CdbParameter;		OnInterfaceChange(VOID)
		GetName(VOID)
		GetValue(VOID)
		SetValue(LPVARIANT)
		GetType(VOID)
class CdbField;		OnInterfaceChange(VOID)
		GetCollatingOrder(VOID)
		GetType(VOID)
		SetType(SHORT0
		GetName(VOID)
		SetName(LPCTSTR)
		GetSize(VOID)
		SetSize(LONG)
		GetSourceField(VOID)
		GetSourceTable(VOID)
		GetValue(VOID)
		SetValue(LPVARIANT)
		GetAttributes(VOID)
		SetAttributes(LONG)
		GetOrdinalPosition(VOID)
		SetOrdinalPosition(LONG)
		GetValidationText(VOID)

continues

Table 31.7. continued

Class	Members/Collections	Methods/Properties
		SetValidationText (LPCTSTR)
		GetValidationOnSet(VOID)
		SetValidationOnSet(LONG)
		GetValidationRule(VOID)
		SetValidationRule (LPCTSTR)
		GetDefaultValue(VOID)
		SetDefaultValue(LPCTSTR)
		GetRequired(VOID)
		SetRequired(BOOL)
		GetAllowZeroLength(VOID)
		SetAllowZeroLength(BOOL)
		GetDataUpdatable(VOID)
		SetForeignName(LPCTSTR)
		AppendChunk(LPVARIANT)
		GetChunk(LONG, LONG)
		FieldSize(VOID)
		CreateProperty(LpCTSTR, LONG, LPVARIANT, BOOL)

CdbIndex, CdbProperty, and CdbRelation

Indexes provide quicker access and ordering of records in a recordset or table. Without indexes you search through every record to find a given value. Unique indexes provide additional data validation. Usually, when you define a table, you define the indexes. However, you can also modify the database definition at runtime and add indexes. Indexes have properties like UNIQUE, REQUIRED, and PRIMARY. These are listed in Table 31.8 and identified by the Set prefix.

```
CdbIndex m_index;
m_index = m_tabledef.CreateIndex(_T("Dave"));
m_field = m_tabledef.CreateField(_T("Dave"),dbText,20);
m_tabledef.Fields.Append(m_field);
```

Every DAO object contains a Properties collection, which has certain built-in Property objects. These Property objects (which are often just called properties) uniquely characterize that instance of the object. You have seen the Name property and Get the Name property of objects set. When you define a new field you specify built-in properties.

An object of class CDbRelation enables you to set or examine the relationships between tables in the database. It enables trappable errors when your application violates those defined relationships.

Classes of type CdbIndex, CdbProperty, or CdbRelation are all created by a method with the similar name, CreateIndex, CreateProperty, and CreateRelation. Usually this is done as part of a TableDef code sequence. You define the table, set its properties, then define the fields with their properties. The following code snippet demonstrates the CreateRelation method.

```
CdbDatabase m_database;
CdbRelation m_relation;
CdbField m_field;

m_relation = m_database.CreateRelation(_T("MyRelation"));
m_relation.SetTable(_T("Patients"));
m_relation.SetForeignTable(_T("Visits"));
m_field = m_relation.CreateField("Visit"));
m_field.SetForeignName(_T("Visit"));
m_relation.Fields.Append(m_field);
m_database.Relations.Append(m_relation);
```

Table 31.8. Class definitions.

Class	Members/Collections	Methods/Properties
class CdbProperty;		GetValue(VOID)
		SetValue(LPVARIANT)
		GetName(VOID)
		SetName(LPCTSTR)
		GetType(VOID)
		SetType(SHORT)
		GetInherited(VOID)
class CdbRelation;	Fields	OnInterfaceChange(VOID)
		GetName(VOID)
		SetName(LPCTSTR)
		GetTable(VOID)
		SetTable(LPCTSTR)
		GetForeignTable(VOID)
		SetForeignTable(LPCTSTR)

continues

Table 31.8. continued

Class	Members/Collections	Methods/Properties
class CdbIndex;	Fields	GetAttributes(VOID)
		SetAttributes(LONG)
		CreateField(LPCTSTR, LONG, LONG)
		OnInterfaceChange(VOID)
		GetName(VOID)
		SetName(LPCTSTR)
		GetForeign(VOID)
		GetUnique(VOID)
		SetUnique(BOOL)
		GetClustered(VOID)
		SetClustered(BOOL)
		GetRequired(VOID)
		SetRequired(BOOL)
		GetIgnoreNulls(VOID)
		SetIgnoreNulls(BOOL)
		GetPrimary(VOID)
		SetPrimary(BOOL)
		GetDistinctCount(VOID)
		CreateField(LPCTSTR LONG, LONG)
		CreateProperty(LPCTSTR LONG, LPVARIANT, BOOL)

CdbUser **and** CdbGroups

Most users of Microsoft Access never see the security system, but it's always enabled. The jet engine checks to ensure that the user has privileges to perform every action the user takes. A local database user normally will have full permissions set for all objects and just never see the security checking system. With users you can set the name, UID, password, group, and change passwords. With CdbGroups, you set the name, the user ID, and create users.

```
CdbDatabase m_database;
CdbUser m_user;
CString m_name;
m_name = (_T("DAVE"));
CString m_oldpassword;
m_oldpassword = (_T("sex"));
CString m_newpassword;
m_newpassword = (_T("work"));

m_user = m_database.Users(m_name);
m_user.NewPassword(m_oldpassword, m_newpassword);
```

Table 31.9. Class definitions.

Class	Members/Collections	Methods/Properties
class CdbUser;	Groups	OnInterfaceChange(VOID)
		GetName(VOID)
		SetName(LPCTSTR)
		SetPID(LPCTSTR)
		SetPassword(LPCTSTR)
		NewPassword(LPCTSTR, LPCTSTR)
		CreateGroup(LPCTSTR,LPCTSTR)
class CdbGroup;	Users	OnInterfaceChange(VOID)
		GetName(VOID)
		SetName(LPCTSTR)
		SetPID(LPCTSTR)
		CreateUser(LPCTSTR,LPCTSTR,LPCTSTR)

These remaining classes are used internally by the DAO SDK classes to start up OLE and track OLE object names. A database has a collection of containers. In each container is a document. The containers are named Databases, Tables, and Relations. The CdbObject and CdbOleObject enable the OLE interface to be started and be queried.

Table 31.10. The collection classes.

Class	Members/Collections	Methods/Properties
class CdbOleObject	m_punkInterface	Exists(VOID)
		SetInterface(LPUNKNOWN, BOOL)

continues

Table 31.10. continued

Class	Members/Collections	Methods/Properties
		GetInterface(BOOL, BOOL)
		OnIterfaceChange(VOID)
		SetRichErrorInfo (LPOLESTR, LPOLESTR, LPOLESTR, ULONG)
		StartOLE(VOID)
class CdbObject		GetName(VOID)
		SetName(LPCTSTR)
class CdbDocument;		OnInterfaceChange(VOID)
		GetName(VOID)
		GetOwner(VOID)
		SetOwner(LPCTSTR)
		GetContainer(VOID)
		GetUserName(VOID)
		SetUserName(LPCTSTR)
		GetPermissions(VOID)
		SetPermissions(LONG)
		GetDateCreated(VOID)
		GetLastUpdate(VOID)
class CdbContainer;	Documents	OnInterfaceChange(VOID)
		GetName(VOID)
		GetOwner(VOID)
		SetOwner(LPCTSTR)
		GetUserName(VOID)
		SetUserName(LPCTSTR)
		GetPermissions(VOID)
		SetPermissions(LONG)
		GetInherit(VOID)
		SetInherit(BOOL)

Class	Members/Collections	Methods/Properties
class `CdbCollection`		`ObItem(LONG)`
		`ObItem(LPCTSTR)`
		`GetCount(VOID)`
		`ObAppend(CdbObject &obj)`
		`Delete(LPCTSTR)`
		`Refresh(VOID)`

MFC Database Classes for DAO

The DAO SDK classes strongly resemble the VisualBasic functions and classes. This enabled Visual Basic programmers to move to Visual C++ 4.0 easier. In order for MFC database programmers to move to DAO classes more easily, Microsoft wrapped the DAO classes in MFC classes. These were given the same names and methods as the MFC ODBC classes. Where you had `CDatabase`, you got `CDAODatabase`; `CRecordset` became `CDAORecordset`; etc. Both the DAO and ODBC setting share the same property page within AppWizard as in Figure 31.4.

FIGURE 31.4.

AppWizard allows you to choose ODBC or the MFC DAO classes.

Creating an application with DAO became as simple as with ODBC. Mostly, you can convert an application from ODBC to DAO by changing the class names. The methods are that similar!

DAO is still a set of OLE interfaces that are pure virtual functions. The classes are

```
CDaoWorkspace
CDaoDatabase
CDaoRecordset
```

```
CDaoRecordView
CDAOTableDef
CDAOQueryDef
CDaoFieldExchange
CDAOException
```

These have names that should be quite familiar after the first half of this chapter. In fact, to gain the full capabilities of the DAO jet engine, you need to blend some DAO SDK functions into your database application, just as you need some Win32 functions in your daily MFC programming.

FIGURE 31.5.

In AppWizard you choose a default database table.

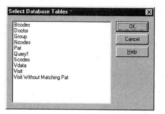

What happened to the other DAO classes? The MFC mapping of the DAO classes is not one-for-one. Classes such as CdbFields, CdbIndexes, CdbParameters, and CdbRelations are not in the list. Their functionality is provided by interfaces (member functions) in the above classes. Fields and indexes are provided with both CDAOTableDef and CDAORecordset, parameters are provided with CDAOQueryDef, and relations provided by CDAODatabase. MFC does supply classes or interfaces to CdbUsers or CdbGroups. CdbEngine is accessed via CDOAWorkspace. MFC has flattened out the DAO classes.

MFC DAO classes make using DAO easier by handling many of the details. This includes the initialization of OLE, the creation and management of the DAO collection objects, error checking, and providing a strongly typed, simpler interface (no VARIANT nor BSTR arguments). Sometimes you still need to make direct DAO calls. The biggest area where MFC does not support all of the DAO SDK is in security, users, and groups. To use a DAO SDK call, all your code has to do is call *Release* for any objects created. If you use the combination, check out the AFXDAO.H for the helper macros: DAO_CHECK, DAO_CHECK_ERROR, DAO_CHECK_MEM, DAO_TRACE, and see AfxDaoCheck and AfxDaoTrace in DAOCORE.CPP. These give you good insights into how Microsoft wrapped the DAO calls into MFC. Also see Microsoft's Technical Note 54 for examples.

You know that you can open Access databases and ISAM databases, and attach to ODBC databases. Opening the databases using DAO is more efficient than using ODBC if they are either Access or ISAM. Attaching a table to a database is fairly efficient. Using DOA to access an ODBC database is less efficient because it adds a second layer of function calls.

Document/View and MFC DAO

When you ran AppWizard as in Figure 31.4, it created a CDAORecordView derived class and connected it to a table you selected in Figure 31.5. This is useful in a simple form-based application where you display one record at a time. You may, however, need more functionality with multiple views or by using CListView or CTreeView.

If you don't need to use MFC serialization, you may not need to use a CDocument derived class. CDocument does enable multiple views on the data and the ability to UpdateAllViews. Many applications make both CDAODatabase and CDAORecordset members of the view derived class. Other options include embedding the data directly in the CFrameWnd class or CDialog class and passing up document/view altogether. AppWizard supports either option in building a dialog based application.

MFC DAO classes can be used in any DLL. That means you can use them in building an OLE control. DOA is not, however, multithread safe. There has been much discussion of this in the Usenet newsgroups, and it seems everyone that has tried to get around this has found that it's best to confine your DAO code to a single thread. Microsoft has its own news source, msnews.microsoft.com, and the group with the most DAO information would be microsoft.public.vc.database. The Usenet group would be comp.os.ms-windows.programmer.tools.mfc.

If you create a basic DAO AppWizard application, you will notice no database code in the document class. The database is opened in your CDaoRecordset class. You've seen the same process before—you create an object, then open it. When you create the object, it can be either on the stack, or, if you use operator new, on the heap. If your object is going to be used throughout the application, create it on the heap. If its use is temporary, for one function, use the stack.

Creating, Opening, and Closing DAO Objects

You will find that MFC relies heavily on the default collection classes without exposing them to you, the developer. When you open a CDaoRecordset object, you can omit opening the CDaoDatabase object, and MFC implicitly creates a CDaoDatabase object. Even though these are implicitly created, you can still access them. If you open a database, dbPatients, its Workspace is found as

```
CDaoWorkspace* pws = dbPatients->m_pWorkspace
```

Sometimes you need to take these two steps, as in the preceding example. You can also open theCDaoRecordset object. The default action would be to open the correspondingCDaoDatabase object.

```
CDaoDatabase* pdb = recsetpatients.m_pDatabase;
CDaoWorkspace* pws = pdb->m_pWorkspace;
```

Before you call Open, the object is constructed, but is uninitialized and unusable. It simply has memory space reserved. It is easy to confuse construction of an object with creation of an object. Create has different meanings in MFC DAO programming. CDaoDatabase::Create actually creates a new MDB file on the disk, a new database. CDaoQueryDef::Create likewise creates a new QueryDef that is not stored until you Append it to the collection. You construct a CDaoRecordset and call its Open member function to actually run the query or open the table. This creates a new CDaoRecordset object, but there is not a Create member function for CDaoREcordset. It can be confusing to use the create word with MFC. I will try to differentiate the construction (calling the constructor operator) and calling the create member function. Only CDaoRecordset and CDaoException do not have Create member functions. Only CDaoException does not have an Open member function.

Open also has different meanings. When you open a CDaoDatabase, you get the usual meaning. When you open a CDaoRecordset, you run a query or open a tabledef in a table-type recordset.

Close is much simpler. Each class has a close member function, and it is considered good programming practice to use it. Close() releases memory associated with an object and releases the object. Closing CDaoQueryDef, CDaoTableDef, and CDaoDatabase leaves the object in its respective collection. CDaoWorkspace and CDaoRecordset objects do not persist between sessions. There is no member function Close() for CDaoException. Calling close does not destroy the MFC object—you must do that by calling its destructor or letting it go out of scope. Good programming practice is to close it yourself.

Collections in MFC

As you have seen, DAO is a hierarchy of collections. MFC DAO tries to hide some of the workings with collections. They aren't gone—MFC provides member functions and data members through which you access the underlying collection. Almost all the functionality is there. However, in the case of recordsets, you only have GetRecordsetCount and GetRecordsetInfo. You need to keep track of remaining recordset information yourself. Every other MFC DAO object has a GetSomeInfo and GetSomeCount member functions, such as GetTableDefInfo, GetDatabaseCount, and so on.

You have seen that collections are zero based. The (0)th element is the default collection. You loop through the collection as

```
CDaoQueryDefInfo qdinfo;
int nQueryDef = pDB->GetQueryDefCount();
for (int i = 0; I < nQueryDef; i++)
{
GetQueryDefInfo( i,qdinfo);
AfxMessageBox(_T("qdinfo.m_strName"));
}
```

To speed up the process, Microsoft has defined three levels of information; the AFX_DAO_PRIMARY_INFO (Name and Type), AFX_DAO_SECONDARY_TYPE (date created, date last updated, returns records, and updatable) and AFX_DAO_ALL_INFO (all primary, secondary, SQL, Connect, and ODBCTimeout). You supply these DWORD options as the third parameter to GetQueryDefInfo:

```
GetQueryDefInfo( i, qdinfo, AFX_DAO_PRIMARY_TYPE);
```

The more information you need to retrieve about the database, the slower it will be to retrieve it; so only use AFX_DAO_ALL_INFO when you actually need all the information.

Class CDaoWorkspace

A CDaoWorkspace object manages the session with the jet database engine. A workspace object contains one or more database objects. Workspace objects also manage transaction processing and security.

In MFC DAO programming, the default Workspace is the first Workspace created. When you open a database, it by default exists in this Workspace. You imply by opening the database that you need to construct a Workspace. You seldom will explicitly create a CDaoWorkspace object; it will be created for you when you open a database. To take this one step farther, you can open a recordset that creates a default database object, which creates a default Workspace. In any case, you seldom construct the CDaoWorkspace object unless you are going to do transaction processing.

You also seldom destruct a CDaoWorkspace object. The workspace exists in memory for the life of the database engine session. When your application quits, the CDaoWorkspace object is destroyed.

CDaoWorkspace provides member functions to GetVersion(), SetDefaultPassword, and SetDefaultUser. There are also two functions to specify an NT registry key to which the current settings can be stored and retrieved, GetInipath and SetIniPath. This enables you to preserve the workspace settings and database settings you had open with a prior session.

The biggest job of class CDaoWorkspace is managing transaction processing.

A transaction is a series of changes made to a database's data or its schema. In order to reverse this series of transactions, CDaoWorkspace provides a way to group the series. You may find that you have a certain action that you only want to perform if all prior actions were completed successfully. If they were not, you want to go back to how the data was before you started the series.

Transactions are global to the workspace in which they are defined. If you have two recordsets that belong to databases in the same workspace, when you roll back a transaction, both recordsets are affected. If this is not what you wanted, you need to define two separate Workspaces. Each call to BeginTrans, CommitTrans, and Rollback applies to all objects in a Workspace.

```
CDaoDatabase m_database;
CDaoRecordset m_recordset(&m_database);
CString strSQL = (_T("SELECT * FROM Patients WHERE PatID eq 12345"));
try
  {
  m_recordset.Open(dbOpenDynaset, strSQL);
  m_database.m_pWorkspace->BeginTrans();
  m_recordset.Delete();
  }
catch (CDaoException* e)
  {
  m_database.m_pWorkspace->Rollback();
  AfxMessageBox("Failed to delete patient");
  e->Delete()
  return FALSE;
  }
m_recordset.CLOSE();
return TRUE;
}
```

The preceding example called the default workspace with the database's data member `m_pWorkspace`.

Table 31.11. `CDaoWorkSpace` **data members and methods.**

`m_pDAOWorkspace`	Member variable that points to the underlying DAO workspace object.
`CDaoWorkspace`	Constructs a workspace object. Afterwards, call `Create` or `Open`.
`GetIsolateODBCTrans`	Returns a value that indicates whether multiple transactions that involve the same ODBC data source are isolated with forced multiple connections to the data source.
`GetName`	Returns the user-defined name for the workspace object.
`GetUserName`	Returns the user name specified when the workspace was created. This is the name of the workspace owner.
`IsOpen`	Returns nonzero if the workspace is open.
`SetIsolateODBCTrans`	Specifies whether multiple transactions that involve the same ODBC data source are isolated by forcing multiple connections to the data source.
`Append`	Appends a newly created workspace to the database engine's Workspaces collection.
`BeginTrans`	Begins a new transaction, which applies to all databases open in the workspace.

Close	Closes the workspace and all of the objects it contains. Pending transactions are rolled back.
CommitTrans	Completes the current transaction and saves the changes.
CompactDatabase	Compacts (or duplicates) a database.
Create	Creates a new DAO workspace object.
GetDatabaseCount	Returns the number of DAO database objects in the workspace's Databases collection.
GetDatabaseInfo	Returns information about a specified DAO database defined in the workspace's Databases collection.
GetWorkspaceCount	Returns the number of DAO workspace objects in the database engine's Workspaces collection.
GetWorkspaceInfo	Returns information about a specified DAO workspace defined in the database engine's Workspaces collection.
Open	Explicitly opens a workspace object associated with DAO's default workspace.
RepairDatabase	Attempts to repair a damaged database.
Rollback	Ends the current transaction and does not save the changes.
Idle	Enables the database engine to perform background tasks.
GetVersion	Returns a string that contains the version of the database engine associated with the workspace.
GetIniPath	Returns the location of the Microsoft Jet database engine's initialization settings in the Windows registry.
GetLoginTimeout	Returns the number of seconds before an error occurs when the user attempts to log in to an ODBC database.
SetDefaultPassword	Sets the password that the database engine uses when a workspace object is created without a specific password.
SetDefaultUser	Sets the username that the database engine uses when a workspace object is created without a specific username.
SetIniPath	Sets the location of the Microsoft Jet database engine's initialization settings in the Windows registry.
SetLoginTimeout	Sets the number of seconds before an error occurs when the user attempts to log in to an ODBC data source.

Class CDaoDatabase

Each CDaoWorkspace contains a collection of open CDaoDatabase objects. Although only one open database has been used as an example, your application will often have more than one. An example would be a database of fixed user records on your local drive and a large database of corporate records on a remote drive. Each CDaoDatabase in this example would be a member of a workspace collection.

Each CDaoDatabase holds collections of tabledefs, querydefs, recordsets and relations. It is these collections your application will manipulate. While your application is running, these database objects exist in memory. The CDaoDatabase object is not the same as the MDB file on the drive. When your application quits, the Workspace object and the Database object cease to exist. The data described by the tabledef or querydef is, however, persistent in the file.

If your application uses a database throughout its existence, construct a CDaoDatabase object that will be used by all recordsets. If your application simply needs some bit of information, then doesn't use the database again, you can construct the recordset and explicitly construct the database. Remember that the most time-consuming step is opening the database. If you are going to reuse it, leave the database open by creating an explicit CDaoDatabase object for the life of the application.

You should also create a CDaoDatabase object if you need to access external data, data in a ISAM database, on a CD-ROM, or in an ODBC database. This is done by either directly opening the external data file or by attaching the file as a table to your Access MDB file.

To attach an external table, you first open your MDB file and either construct a CDaoDatabase object or get a pointer with the open recordsets m_pDatabase member. You then construct and create a new CDaoTableDef object. In the call to Create() you specify the source table and the connection string. Lastly you Append() the CDaoTableDef object.

```
CDaoDatabase m_database;
CDaoTableDef m_tabledef(&m_database);
m_tabledef.Create("New
patients",0,"Patients","ODBC:DSN=aaa,UID=Dave,PWD=password");
m_tabledef.Append();
```

To open the external table directly is just as easy—you use the CDaoRecordset's Open() member function, which is in the next section. Non-ODBC external data sources give better performance when opened directly. ODBC is slower when opened directly than when attached to an MDB file.

You also can create new MDB files via CDaoDatabase's Open() member function as

```
CDaoDatabase::Create(_T("C:\book\MYDB.MDB")),dbLangGeneral, dbVersion30);
```

Table 31.12. `CDaoDatabase` **data members.**

`m_pWorkspace`	A pointer to the `CDaoWorkspace` object that contains the database and defines its transaction space.
`m_pDAODatabase`	A pointer to the underlying DAO database object.
`CDaoDatabase`	Constructs a `CDaoDatabase` object. Call `Open` to connect the object to a database.
`CanTransact`	Returns nonzero if the database supports transactions.
`CanUpdate`	Returns nonzero if the `CDaoDatabase` object is updatable (not read-only).
`GetConnect`	Returns the connect string used to connect the `CDaoDatabase` object to a database. Used for ODBC.
`GetName`	Returns the name of the database currently in use.
`GetQueryTimeout`	Returns the number of seconds after which database query operations will time out. Affects all subsequent open, add new, update, and edit operations and other operations on ODBC data sources (only) such as `Execute` calls.
`GetRecordsAffected`	Returns the number of records affected by the last update, edit, or add operation or by a call to `Execute`.
`GetVersion`	Returns the version of the database engine associated with the database.
`IsOpen`	Returns nonzero if the `CDaoDatabase` object is currently connected to a database.
`SetQueryTimeout`	Sets the number of seconds after which database query operations (on ODBC data sources only) time out. Affects all subsequent open, add new, update, and delete operations.
`Close`	Closes the database connection.
`Create`	Creates the underlying DAO database object and initializes the `CDaoDatabase` object.
`CreateRelation`	Defines a new relation among the tables in the database.
`DeleteQueryDef`	Deletes a `querydef` object saved in the database's QueryDefs collection.
`DeleteRelation`	Deletes an existing relation between tables in the database.
`DeleteTableDef`	Deletes the definition of a table in the database. This deletes the actual table and all of its data.

continues

Table 31.12. continued

Execute	Executes an action query. Calling Execute for a query that returns results throws an exception.
GetQueryDefCount	Returns the number of queries defined for the database.
GetQueryDefInfo	Returns information about a specified query defined in the database.
GetRelationCount	Returns the number of relations defined between tables in the database.
GetRelationInfo	Returns information about a specified relation defined between tables in the database.
GetTableDefCount	Returns the number of tables defined in the database.
GetTableDefInfo	Returns information about a specified table in the database.
Open	Establishes a connection to a database.

Class CDaoRecordset

A *recordset* is the primary method for working with data. It represents a subset of the records in a database table and maintains the current record of that set. Like the DAO SDK, CDaoRecordsets come in three types; snapshot, dynaset, and table-type. Both dynasets and table-type are dynamic and updatable. Table-type must be used with an entire table, not a query. Snapshots are like a report, a view of the data at a particular moment in time.

When ClassWizard in the above examples created a derived CDaoRecordset class for you, it had a data member for each field, a member function to get at the data source name (GetDefaultDBName), and member functions to get the SQL string (GetDefaultSQL), which created the recordset and the DoFieldExchange member function. You saw that creating a CDaoRecordset from a query was the same as creating it from a table.

When ClassWizard constructed your class, it initialized m_nFields data member to the number of field data members. If you manually add to the list, it must be done outside of the //}}AFX_FIELD, and you need to change m_nFields as:

```
m_nFields += 2; //this indicates add 2 to m_nFields above
```

If you use parameterization, you need to initialize m_nParams yourself and manually place the parameter data members outside of //}}AFX_FIELD comment brackets.

The database maintains a collection of recordsets. When you open a recordset, it is automatically appended to the collection.

The recordset maintains a collection of files and indexes. You access those fields and indexes with the member functions GetFieldCount, GetFieldInfo, GetIndexCount, and GetIndexInfo.

You have seen several examples of creating a recordset. The following one is from a temporary QueryDef:

```
CDaoDatabase m_database;
CDaoQueryDef m_querydef(&m_database);
CDaoRecordset m_recordset(;

CString strSQL = (_T("SELECT * FROM Patients WHERE state eq NY"));
m_querydef.Create(_T("MyNewQuery"), strSQL);
m_recordset.Open(&m_querydef);
```

This would really be the same as using open with the strSQL:

```
m_recordset.Open(_T("MyRS"),strSQL);
```

Moving about in a recordset is done by scrolling, Seek, and Find. Scrolling is done with MoveNext, MoveFirst, MoveLast, MovePrev, or Move N, just as in ODBC.

To add a new record, you first call CanUpdate(), then AddNew() member functions. The call to AddNew() prepares the edit buffer by creating a new row with NULL field values. You complete the process with a call to Update(), the member function that actually adds the record. If you are not using double buffering, you need to call SetFieldDirty() and SetFieldNull(FALSE) before you call Update(). The Update() actually moves the data from the edit buffer.

To edit a record, the process is similar. First call CanUpdate(), then call the Edit() member function. To finish, call Update() to flush the buffer.

To delete a record, use the same process. Call CanUpdate(), then the Delete() member function. You do not call Update() after a delete.

To rerun a query you can either close the recordset and then reopen, or call the Requery() member function. This is also the process if you had changed either m_strFilter or m_strSort. You also call Requery() after a change of parameters. Using Open() and Close() when you need to rebuild the SQL string as with a change to m_strFilter is the same as using Requery(). However, if you just change a parameter, the use of Requery() is much faster than Open() and Close().

Because records can be deleted from recordsets, you cannot rely on the absolute position of a record within a recordset. The way to track an individual record is by using a Bookmark. A Bookmark is a unique COleVariant value that points to a record. The member functions are SetBookmark(COleVariant), GetBookmark(COleVariant), and GotoBookMark(COleVariant) used as the following example shows:

```
COleVariant currentrecord;
rs.SetBookmark(currentrecord);
re.GotoBookmark(currentrecord);
```

In addition to Bookmarks, you can move to absolute positions in the recordset or to a percent position in the recordset. The member function GetPercentPosition determines what percentage of the recordset precedes the current record. SetPercentPosition puts you at approximately that point in the recordset. GetAbsolutePosition() gives you the zero-based position of your current record. You can return to that position with SetAbsolutePosition(). Remember that absolute positions change if your recordset is changed by another user deleting a row in the recordset.

Seek() and Find() are powerful ways to navigate a recordset. To find a record where lname equals Hamilton you would use a combination of a Bookmark and a seek:

```
rs.SetCurrentIndex(_T("lnme"));
COleVariant currentrecord = rs.GetBookmark();
if (rs.Seek(_T("="), _T("Hamilton")))
  rs.GotoBookmark(currentrecord);
```

Find is similar, but its relatives, FindNext, FindPrev, FindFirst, and FindLast, give you even more flexibility:

```
CString strFind = (_T("lnme = 'HAMILTON'");
rs.FindFirst(strFind);
```

Table 31.13. CDaoRecordset **data members.**

m_bCheckCacheForDirtyFields	Contains a flag indicating whether fields are automatically marked as changed.
m_pDAORecordset	A pointer to the DAO interface underlying the recordset object.
m_nParams	Contains the number of parameter data members in the recordset class—the number of parameters passed with the recordset's query.
m_pDatabase	Source database for this result set. Contains a pointer to a CDaoDatabase object.
m_strFilter	Contains a string used to construct an SQL WHERE statement.
m_strSort	Contains a string used to construct an SQL ORDER BY statement.
CDaoRecordset	Constructs a CDaoRecordset object.
Close	Closes the recordset.
Open	Creates a new recordset from a table, dynaset, or snapshot.
CanAppend	Returns nonzero if new records can be added to the recordset with the AddNew member function.

CanBookmark	Returns nonzero if the recordset supports bookmarks.
CanRestart	Returns nonzero if `Requery` can be called to run the recordset's query again.
CanScroll	Returns nonzero if you can scroll through the records.
CanTransact	Returns nonzero if the data source supports transactions.
CanUpdate	Returns nonzero if the recordset can be updated (you can add, update, or delete records).
GetCurrentIndex	Returns a `CString` containing the name of the index most recently used on an indexed, table-type `CDaoRecordset`.
GetDateCreated	Returns the date and time the base table underlying a `CDaoRecordset` object was created.
GetDateLastUpdated	Returns the date and time of the most recent change made to the design of a base table underlying a `CDaoRecordset` object.
GetEditMode	Returns a value that indicates the state of editing for the current record.
GetLastModifiedBookmark	Used to determine the most recently added or updated record.
GetName	Returns a `CString` containing the name of the recordset.
GetParamValue	Retrieves the current value of the specified parameter stored in the underlying `DAOParameter` object.
GetRecordCount	Returns the number of records accessed in a recordset object.
GetSQL	Gets the SQL string used to select records for the recordset.
GetType	Called to determine the type of a recordset: table-type, dynaset-type, or snapshot-type.
GetValidationRule	Returns a `CString` containing the value that validates data as it is entered into a field.
GetValidationText	Retrieves the text that is displayed when a validation rule is not satisfied.

continues

Table 31.13. continued

IsBOF	Returns nonzero if the recordset has been positioned before the first record. There is no current record.
IsDeleted	Returns nonzero if the recordset is positioned on a deleted record.
IsEOF	Returns nonzero if the recordset has been positioned after the last record. There is no current record.
IsFieldDirty	Returns nonzero if the specified field in the current record has been changed.
IsFieldNull	Returns nonzero if the specified field in the current record is Null (having no value).
IsFieldNullable	Returns nonzero if the specified field in the current record can be set to Null (having no value).
IsOpen	Returns nonzero if Open has been called previously.
SetCurrentIndex	Called to set an index on a table-type recordset.
SetParamValue	Sets the current value of the specified parameter stored in the underlying DAOParameter object.
SetParamValueNull	Sets the current value of the specified parameter to Null (having no value).
AddNew	Prepares for adding a new record. Call Update to complete the addition.
CancelUpdate	Cancels any pending updates due to an Edit or AddNew operation.
Delete	Deletes the current record from the recordset. You must explicitly scroll to another record after the deletion.
Edit	Prepares for changes to the current record. Call Update to complete the edit.
Update	Completes an AddNew or Edit operation by saving the new or edited data on the data source.
Find	Locates the first, next, previous, or last location of a particular string in a dynaset-type recordset that satisfies the specified criteria and makes that record the current record.

FindFirst	Locates the first record in a dynaset-type or snapshot-type recordset that satisfies the specified criteria and makes that record the current record.
FindLast	Locates the last record in a dynaset-type or snapshot-type recordset that satisfies the specified criteria and makes that record the current record.
FindNext	Locates the next record in a dynaset-type or snapshot-type recordset that satisfies the specified criteria and makes that record the current record.
FindPrev	Locates the previous record in a dynaset-type or snapshot-type recordset that satisfies the specified criteria and makes that record the current record.
GetAbsolutePosition	Returns the record number of a recordset object's current record.
GetBookmark	Returns a value that represents the Bookmark on a record.
GetPercentPosition	Returns the position of the current record as a percentage of the total number of records.
Move	Positions the recordset to a specified number of records from the current record in either direction.
MoveFirst	Positions the current record on the first record in the recordset.
MoveLast	Positions the current record on the last record in the recordset.
MoveNext	Positions the current record on the next record in the recordset.
MovePrev	Positions the current record on the previous record in the recordset.
Seek	Locates the record in an indexed table-type recordset object that satisfies the specified criteria for the current index and makes that record the current record.
SetAbsolutePosition	Sets the record number of a recordset object's current record.
SetBookmark	Positions the recordset on a record containing the specified Bookmark.

continues

Table 31.13. continued

SetPercentPosition	Sets the position of the current record to a location corresponding to a percentage of the total number of records in a recordset.
FillCache	Fills all or a part of a local cache for a recordset object that contains data from an ODBC data source.
GetCacheSize	Returns a value that specifies the number of records in a dynaset-type recordset containing data to be locally cached from an ODBC data source.
GetCacheStart	Returns a value that specifies the bookmark of the first record in the recordset to be cached.
GetFieldCount	Returns a value that represents the number of fields in a recordset.
GetFieldInfo	Returns specific kinds of information about the fields in the recordset.
GetFieldValue	Returns the value of a field in a recordset.
GetIndexCount	Retrieves the number of indexes in a table underlying a recordset.
GetIndexInfo	Returns various kinds of information about an index.
GetLockingMode	Returns a value that indicates the type of locking that is in effect during editing.
Requery	Runs the recordset's query again to refresh the selected records.
SetCacheSize	Sets a value that specifies the number of records in a dynaset-type recordset containing data to be locally cached from an ODBC data source.
SetCacheStart	Sets a value that specifies the Bookmark of the first record in the recordset to be cached.
SetFieldDirty	Marks the specified field in the current record as changed.
SetFieldNull	Sets the value of the specified field in the current record to Null (having no value).
SetFieldValue	Sets the value of a field in a recordset.
SetFieldValueNull	Sets the value of a field in a recordset to Null (having no value).

SetLockingMode	Sets a value that indicates the type of locking to put into effect during editing.
DoFieldExchange	Called to exchange data (in both directions) between the field data members of the recordset and the corresponding record on the data source. Implements DAO record field exchange (DFX).
GetDefaultDBName	Returns the name of the default data source.
GetDefaultSQL	Called to get the default SQL string to execute.

Class CDaoTableDef

As with DAO SDK classes, a TableDef is an object that describes a table (the table's structure, not its data). The table is said to be a base table if it exists in the MDB file or an external table if it's from another database attached to the MDB file. You can modify base tables, but you cannot modify external tables that are attached to the MDB file.

A database has a collection of tabledefs, one for each table in the database. A tabledef has a collection of fields and a collection of indexes.

Again, it's easier to create a table in the MDB file using Microsoft Access, but at runtime that is not possible. To create a tabledef, you first construct a CDaoTableDef object with a pointer to the CDaoDatabase object in which it will belong. Then you set any properties, append the tabledef to the database, and create the fields and indexes.

```
CDaoTableDef m_tabledef(&m_database);
m_tabledef.Create(_T("MyNewTable"));
m_tabledef.Append();
m_tabledef.CreateField(_T("Dave"),dbText,20);
```

Table 31.14. CDaoTableDef data members.

m_pDatabase	Source database for this table.
m_pDAOTableDef	A pointer to the DAO interface underlying the tabledef object.
Append	Adds a new table to the database.
CDaoTableDef	Constructs a CDaoTableDef object.
Close	Closes an open tabledef.
Create	Creates a table that can be added to the database using Append.

continues

Table 31.14. continued

Open	Opens an existing tabledef stored in the database's TableDef's collection.
CanUpdate	Returns nonzero if the table can be updated (you can modify the definition of fields or the table properties).
GetAttributes	Returns a value that indicates one or more characteristics of a CDaoTableDef object.
GetConnect	Returns a value that provides information about the source of a table.
GetDateCreated	Returns the date and time the base table underlying a CDaoTableDef object was created.
GetDateLastUpdated	Returns the date and time of the most recent change made to the design of the base table.
GetFieldCount	Returns a value that represents the number of fields in the table.
GetFieldInfo	Returns specific kinds of information about the fields in the table.
GetIndexCount	Returns the number of indexes for the table.
GetIndexInfo	Returns specific kinds of information about the indexes for the table.
GetName	Returns the user-defined name of the table.
GetRecordCount	Returns the number of records in the table.
GetSourceTableName	Returns a value that specifies the name of the attached table in the source database.
GetValidationRule	Returns a value that validates the data in a field as it is changed or added to a table.
GetValidationText	Returns a value that specifies the text of the message that your application displays, if the value of a Field object does not satisfy the specified validation rule.
IsOpen	Returns nonzero if the table is open.
SetAttributes	Sets a value that indicates one or more characteristics of a CDaoTableDef object.
SetConnect	Sets a value that provides information about the source of a table.
SetName	Sets the name of the table.

SetSourceTableName	Sets a value that specifies the name of an attached table in the source database.
SetValidationRule	Sets a value that validates the data in a field as it is changed or added to a table.
SetValidationText	Sets a value that specifies the text of the message that your application displays if the value of a Field object does not satisfy the specified validation rule.
CreateField	Called to create a field for a table.
CreateIndex	Called to create an index for a table.
DeleteField	Called to delete a field from a table.
DeleteIndex	Called to delete an index from a table.
RefreshLink	Updates the connection information for an attached table.

Class CDaoQueryDef

A query is an instruction to a database to either return a set of records or perform an action on a set of records. Queries are expressed via SQL.

You have seen complex SQL statements that can generate a formatted, complex report with one long obfuscated line of code. There are probably many more of these elegant queries in magazines than in applications. A QueryDef is a query definition that you can choose to store in the database as a persistent object. Once it is stored, you can run it later, pass it parameters, use it to create recordsets, or execute actions against the database.

Filters limit the results of a query. Filters are SQL WHERE clauses such as

WHERE [zipcode] EQ "12345"

In the preceding example, the [] are around a database column name.

Parameters let you design filters that are assigned at runtime. A parameter looks like a filter except for the brackets around the parameter name:

WHERE [zipcode] EQ [zipnumber]

In addition to WHERE clauses, you can use HAVING clauses, and GROUP BY clauses.

To be constant with MFC ODBC you can assign the m_strFilter data member of your CDaoRecordset class. MFC just appends this data member to the recordset's SQL statement for your convenience. You cannot use m_strFilter or m_strSort with CDaoQueryDef or CDaoTableDef, however. If you are not moving to DOA from ODBC, ignore this paragraph because the native DAO method is easier to learn with the default `CDaoRecordset::Open(type, lpszSQL)` syntax.

Using a parameter is easier than in ODBC. A parameter is a value you get from the user at runtime that changes the query. You get better query speed because the query doesn't need to be completely reparsed to execute. You can save large complex queries and change just the WHERE clause with parameters. You also can execute queries that are not known until runtime. First the `QueryDef` is stored into the database, then accessed as

```
CString strParam = "PARAMETERS [Patient Number] TEXT";
CString strSQL = strParam + "Select * form Patients where Patients.PatientID =
➥[Patient Number];
CDaoQueryDef qd(m_dbPatients);
qd.Create("Find Patient", strSQL);
qd.Append();
```

Remember the `Append()` does the actual store—you may not need to store the query to use it. You also can create a temporary `QueryDef` by passing NULL as the name. It is saved as a compiled SQL statement and executes faster because it doesn't need to be parsed and recompiled. The preceding example stores a parameterized query named "Find Patient" in the database object, `m_dbPatients`. The following example executes that query.

```
CString strPatientNo = (_T("P00012334"));
COleVariant varParamValue(strPatientNo);
qd.SetParamValue(_T("[Patient Number]")), varParamValue);
CPatientSet rsPatientset(&m_dbPatients);
rsPatientset.Open(&qd, dbOpenDynaset);
```

You use `QueryDefs` to create recordsets or to execute SQL statements, such as UPDATE or DELETE. `QueryDefs` do not have to return recordsets; they may just affect rows. You also can pass queries through your attached table to ODBC data sources. This uses the DB_SQLPASSTHROUGHT option in Opening a recordset.

Even though this entire book is about programming using C++, it wouldn't be fair not to tell you that building your QueryDefs from inside Access is far easier, or at least much faster.

Table 31.15. `CDaoQueryDef` data members.

m_pDatabase	A pointer to the `CDaoDatabase` object with which the querydef is associated. The querydef might be saved in the database or not.
m_pDAOQueryDef	A pointer to the OLE interface for the underlying DAO querydef object.
CDaoQueryDef	Constructs a `CDaoQueryDef` object. Next, call `Open` or `Create`, depending on your needs.
Create	Creates the underlying DAO querydef object. Use the querydef as a temporary query, or call `Append` to save it in the database.

Append	Appends the `querydef` to the database's QueryDefs collection as a saved query.
Open	Opens an existing `querydef` stored in the database's QueryDefs collection.
Close	Closes the `querydef` object. Destroys the C++ object when you finish with it.
CanUpdate	Returns nonzero if the query can update the database.
GetConnect	Returns the connect string associated with the `querydef`. The connect string identifies the data source. (For SQL pass-through queries only; otherwise an empty string.)
GetDateCreated	Returns the date the saved query was created.
GetDateLastUpdated	Returns the date the saved query was last updated.
GetName	Returns the name of the `querydef`.
GetODBCTimeout	Returns the timeout value used by ODBC (for an ODBC query) when the `querydef` is executed. This determines how long to allow for the query's action to complete.
GetRecordsAffected	Returns the number of records affected by an action query.
GetReturnsRecords	Returns nonzero if the query defined by the querydef returns records.
GetSQL	Returns the SQL string that specifies the query defined by the `querydef`.
GetType	Returns the query type: `delete`, `update`, `append`, `make-table`, and so on.
IsOpen	Returns nonzero if the `querydef` is open and can be executed.
SetConnect	Sets the connect string for an SQL pass-through query on an ODBC data source.
SetName	Sets the name of the saved query, replacing the name in use when the `querydef` was created.
SetODBCTimeout	Sets the timeout value used by ODBC (for an ODBC query) when the `querydef` is executed.
SetReturnsRecords	Specifies whether the `querydef` returns records. Setting this attribute to `TRUE` is only valid for SQL pass-through queries.

continues

Table 31.15. continued

SetSQL	Sets the SQL string that specifies the query defined by the querydef.
Execute	Executes the query defined by the querydef object.
GetFieldCount	Returns the number of fields defined by the querydef.
GetFieldInfo	Returns information about a specified field defined in the query.
GetParameterCount	Returns the number of parameters defined for the query.
GetParameterInfo	Returns information about a specified parameter to the query.
GetParamValue	Returns the value of a specified parameter to the query.
SetParamValue	Sets the value of a specified parameter to the query.

Class CDAOFieldExchange (DFX)

DFX automates moving data between the data source field and the recordset member variables. It is very similar to RFX from ODBC programming. It is type safe and eliminates allocating storage and binding data to it. Like ODBC's RFX, most of the work is hidden from you in MFC programming. When you derive your recordset class from CDaoRecordset, the DFX mechanism is set up. ClassWizard does all of the mapping. You only need to manually add parameter data members, call the SetFieldType for each parameter, and specify the number of parameters in m_nParams. Like ODBC's RFX, you need to specify which table is used for JOIN statements. The rest is handled for you. The ClassWizard even initializes the recordset field data members for you and writes a function to override CDaoRecordset::DoFieldExchange().

DoFieldExchange is called any time you need to move data from a recordset to a data source or vice versa. It also sets up the type of recordset with m_nDefaultType = dbOpenDynaset data member and specifies a "double-buffering" mechanism to check if fields have been edited. This is the m_bCheckCacheForDirtyFields = TRUE data member.

DFX also transfers data between types for you. DFX works by setting up an edit buffer that holds your recordset's field data members. When you open the recordset, DFX binds the address of the field to a field data member. DFX keeps a second buffer (double buffering) or a second copy of the data to use in comparison. This is not true for variable-length data types, such as text or binary data, which may grow quite large. Making a second set of variable-length data types may cause you problems. You can, however, force these types to double buffer or turn off double buffer altogether. If you turn on m_bCheckCacheForDirtyFields = FALSE, you need to provide this function yourself by setting SetFieldDirty each time a field changes. Each time you call AddNew or Update, it restores these buffers. Each time you scroll a record, DFX calls DoFieldExchange. UpdateData(TRUE) moves the data in the direction of the function; FALSE reverses:

```
void CPatientSet::DoFieldExchange(CDaoFieldExhange* pFX)
{
  //{{AFX-FILD_MAP(CPatientSet)
  pfX->SetFieldType(CDaoFieldExchange::outputColumn);
  DFX_Text(pFX, _T("PatientNO"), m_patientNo);
  …
```

When DoFieldExchange is called, the pFX pointer is examined to see what operation to perform and in which direction to transfer data. Then a series of DFX functions calls are run. The first listed here is a call to DFX_Text, which actually transfers text between the field PatientNo and the data member m_patientNo.

Table 31.16. DFX data types.

DFX Function	C++ Data Type	DAO Type
DFX_Binary	CByteArray	DAO_BYTES
DFX_Bool	BOOL	DAO_BOOL
DFX_Byte	BYTE	DAO_BYTES
DFX_Currency	COleCurrency	DAO_CURRENCY
DFX_DateTime	COleDateTime	DAO_DATE
DFX_Double	double	DAO_R8
DFX_Long	long	DAO_I4
DFX_LongBinary	CByteArray	DAO_BYTES
DFX_SHORT	short	DAO_I2
DFX_Single	float	DAO_R4
DFX_Text	CString (ANSI)	DAO_CHAR
DFX_Text	CString (UNICODE)	DAO_WCHAR

Table 31.17. CDaoFieldExchange data members.

m_nOperation	The DFX operation being performed by the current call to the recordset's DoFieldExchange member function.
m_prs	A pointer to the recordset on which DFX operations are being performed.
IsValidOperation	Returns nonzero if the current operation is appropriate for the type of field being updated.
SetFieldType	Specifies the type of recordset data member—column or parameter—represented by all subsequent calls to DFX functions until the next call to SetFieldType.

Class CDAOException

Throughout this chapter and the prior two chapters you have seen exception handling in the form of a try/catch clause. In the catch expression, the CDaoException or CdbException was created, and its data members were used to express the problem. All DAO errors are expressed as exceptions of type CDaoException. The errors are actually in a collection in the CDaoDatabase object. The prior error is available until another occurs. When an error occurs, the collection is cleared out and the new error object is placed in the collection.

Table 31.18. CDaoException class members.

m_scode	The SCODE value associated with the error.
m_nAfxDaoError	Contains an extended error code for any error in the MFC DAO classes.
m_pErrorInfo	A pointer to a CDaoErrorInfo object that contains information about one DAO error object.
CDaoException	Constructs a CDaoException object.
GetErrorCount	Returns the number of errors in the database engine's Errors collection.
GetErrorInfo	Returns error information about a particular error object in the Errors collection.

Class CDaoRecordView

You have seen how easily MFC makes developing a form-based database application. When you built your first DAO AppWizard application, you were given a default CDaoRecordView. This is a CFormView with an attached CDaoRecordset. It set up DFX for you and gave you buttons for MoveFirst, MoveLast, MoveNext, and MovePrev. The recordview tracks the current position in the recordset for you.

One of the quickest ways to get an application going is to define a recordset for each table or query in the database. Then define a recordview for each recordset. Switching between recordview is simple, as shown in the following Mainframe.cpp function:

```
void CMainFrame::OnEditPatients()
{
if(GetActiveView()->IsKindOf(RUNTIME_CLASS(CPatView)))
return;
SwitchToForm(IDW_PAT);
}

void CMainFrame::SwitchToForm(int nForm)
{
```

```
CView* pOldActiveView = GetActiveView();
CView* pNewActiveView = (CDaoRecordView*)GetDlgItem(nForm);
if (pNewActiveView == NULL)
  {
  if (nForm == IDW_DOCTORS)
  pNewActiveView = (CDaoRecordView*)new CDoctorView;
  if (nForm == IDW_GROUPS)
  pNewActiveView = (CDaoRecordView*)new CGroupView;
  if (nForm == IDW_PAT)
  pNewActiveView = (CDaoRecordView*)new CPatView;
  if (nForm == IDW_VISIT)
  pNewActiveView = (CDaoRecordView*)new CVisitView;
  if (nForm == IDW_QVISITS)
  pNewActiveView = (CDaoRecordView*)new CQVisitView;

CCreateContext context;
context.m_pCurrentDoc = pOldActiveView->GetDocument();
pNewActiveView->Create(NULL, NULL, 0L, CFrameWnd::rectDefault, this, nForm,
&context);
pNewActiveView->OnInitialUpdate();
}

SetActiveView(pNewActiveView);
pNewActiveView->ShowWindow(SW_SHOW);
pOldActiveView->ShowWindow(SW_HIDE);
if (pOldActiveView->GetRuntimeClass() == RUNTIME_CLASS(CDoctorView))
  pOldActiveView->SetDlgCtrlID(IDW_DOCTORS);
if (pOldActiveView->GetRuntimeClass() == RUNTIME_CLASS(CGroupView))
  pOldActiveView->SetDlgCtrlID(IDW_GROUPS);
if (pOldActiveView->GetRuntimeClass() == RUNTIME_CLASS(CPatView))
  pOldActiveView->SetDlgCtrlID(IDW_PAT);
if (pOldActiveView->GetRuntimeClass() == RUNTIME_CLASS(CVisitView))
  pOldActiveView->SetDlgCtrlID(IDW_VISIT);
if (pOldActiveView->GetRuntimeClass() == RUNTIME_CLASS(CQVisitView))
pOldActiveView->SetDlgCtrlID(IDW_QVISITS);

pNewActiveView->SetDlgCtrlID(AFX_IDW_PANE_FIRST);
RecalcLayout();
}
```

In the mainfrm.h file, each recordview is given an arbitrary integer value as #define IDW_GROUPS1. This enables you to pass the reference to the view by integer.

Another idea with CDaoRecordView in this type of example is that for each view, you need to define a function for OnMoveLast, OnMoveFirst, OnMovePrev, OnMoveNext, OnAdd, and OnUpdate. It is even simpler to make a new base class derived from CDaoRecordView that includes all of these handler functions, then derive your own recordview class from that base class. ClassWizard sets up a pointer, m_pset for each recordset, and handles tracking the active view. You may even design your base class with standard functions like LoadListBox and LoadComboBox, which you use over and over. The enclosed CD-ROM has a simple forms-based application, My29b, which does just this. Steal class CMyDAORecordset for the CD-ROM for your own reuse.

Table 31.19. Class `CDaoRecordView` members.

CDaoRecordView	Constructs a CDaoRecordView object.
OnGetRecordset	Returns a pointer to an object of a class derived from CDaoRecordset. ClassWizard overrides this function for you and creates the recordset, if necessary.
IsOnLastRecord	Returns nonzero if the current record is the last record in the associated recordset.
IsOnFirstRecord	Returns nonzero if the current record is the first record in the associated recordset.
OnMove	If the current record has changed, updates it on the data source, then moves to the specified record (next, previous, first, or last).

Summary

This chapter has examined the new DAO classes, both the DAO SKD classes and the MFC classes. These were introduced with Visual C++ 4.0. It is significant that the new DAO classes are not only database classes, but also OLE interfaces. Microsoft is using OLE programming more and more in the design of Windows NT. Although the DAO classes are now used primarily to address Microsoft MDB files, rumors have surfaced about DAO being able to access Oracle and Sybase data in the future. Where does this leave ODBC? It is hard to say, but a project called Nile has gotten some press. Supposedly Nile merges ODBC and OLE. It seems that with the DOA classes, a major step is being taken without ODBC! As new multimedia database classes are released and as Windows NT evolves into more OLE-centric, you may be glad you started on the path to DOA programming early in its infancy.

PART

VII

IN THIS PART

Extending Windows NT

Multimedia Programming

32

by Mickey Williams

IN THIS CHAPTER

This chapter discusses the multimedia API provided by Windows NT. It covers functions used to access sound, CD audio, and video devices in your PC; it also provides a sample program that demonstrates how to use these functions.

The term "multimedia" means different things to different people. As it applies to Windows NT, it refers to applications that incorporate sound, video, and three-dimensional graphics. Examples of multimedia devices are CD audio, laser discs, MIDI-compatible devices, and video capture boards.

Using the Multimedia API

Many API functions are available to help you create multimedia applications. When I first began investigating the multimedia API some years ago, I was discouraged by the sheer size of the reference manual. The multimedia architecture actually is exposed in different layers, which leads to a number of API functions that seem to be implemented in more than one way. Figure 32.1 shows the multiple layered API.

FIGURE 32.1.

Exposing the multimedia API in several layers.

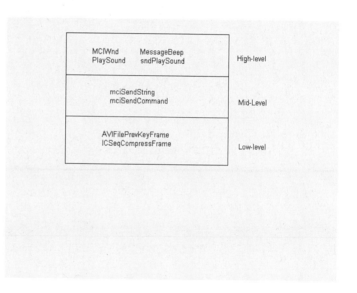

At the top, or highest level, interfaces are built around the MCIWnd window class, which enables easy access to multimedia devices.

The middle range of interfaces uses the *Multimedia Control Interface* (MCI) API to control multimedia devices. These interfaces offer a good balance between flexibility and power, and most of this chapter deals with these interfaces.

The lowest level of the multimedia API provides direct access to multimedia structures and API functions and provides the maximum amount of flexibility when writing an application. It also requires more knowledge and code than the other two approaches, however.

Using High-Level Audio Functions

Because playing a sound or audio message is such a common requirement, Microsoft has made it as easy as possible. Windows NT includes three high-level audio functions to play sounds on your PC:

- `MessageBeep`
- `sndPlaySound`
- `PlaySound`

Each of these functions is covered in this section.

Using `MessageBeep`

Perhaps the simplest way to play a sound is to use the `MessageBeep` function. `MessageBeep` plays a sound much like `MessageBox` displays a message to a user. In fact, it often is used with `MessageBox`:

```
int ErrorMessage( LPCTSTR lpszErrorMsg )
{
    MessageBeep( MB_ICONEXCLAMATION );
    MessageBox( NULL, lpszErrorMsg, "Error", MB_ICONEXCLAMATION );
}
```

The `MessageBeep` function takes one parameter: the type of sound to be played. Table 32.1 lists the values passed to `MessageBox`.

Table 32.1. Parameters passed to the `MessageBeep` function.

Message	Plays
-1	A standard beep using the computer speaker
MB_ICONASTERISK	The Control Panel asterisk sound
MB_ICONEXCLAMATION	The Control Panel exclamation sound
MB_ICONHAND	The Control Panel critical sound
MB_ICONQUESTION	The Control Panel question sound
MB_ICONSTOP	The Control Panel critical sound
MB_OK	The Control Panel default sound

Note that the message values used by `MessageBeep` also are used by `AfxMessageBox` and `MessageBox`. `MB_ICONHAND` and `MB_ICONSTOP` values, for example, are used with the `MessageBox` functions to indicate critical errors in the application. Passing the same value to `MessageBeep` plays the appropriate sound for the event, as defined by the user in the Control Panel Sounds applet.

Using `sndPlaySound`

In addition to `MessageBeep`, Windows NT offers two functions that can play any waveform audio file. The simplest of these functions is `sndPlaySound`:

```
sndPlaySound( lpszFile, nFlags );
```

The `sndPlaySound` function has two parameters:

- A string that contains the path to a waveform audio file or a sound name found in the system Registry or WIN.INI file
- A flag or combination of flags that specify how the sound should be played

Table 32.2 lists the possible values for the second parameter.

Table 32.2. Values used for the second parameter in calls to `sndPlaySound`.

Parameter	Function
SND_ASYNC	Begins playing the sound asynchronously. The function returns immediately, before the sound finishes. To stop an asynchronous sound event, call `sndPlaySound` a second time, with NULL as the first parameter.
SND_LOOP	Plays the sound continuously. This flag must be combined with `SND_ASYNC`.
SND_MEMORY	Plays a waveform located in memory rather than on disk.
SND_NODEFAULT	Quietly returns if the requested file cannot be found. The normal behavior without this flag is to play the system default sound.
SND_NOSTOP	Causes `sndPlaySound` to fail if another sound already is playing, without interrupting the sound currently playing.
SND_SYNC	Plays the sound synchronously—the function does not return until the sound finishes playing.

The requested waveform audio file must fit into available memory. If the sound is played, `sndPlaySound` returns TRUE; otherwise, FALSE is returned. If the request waveform audio file cannot be found, the default sound is played.

Playing Waveform Files Using `PlaySound`

Windows NT also offers a more flexible function for playing waveform audio: `PlaySound`. The `PlaySound` function enables you to specify a file, a sound stored in the Registry, or a waveform audio resource stored in your application. Although `sndPlaySound` is available for Windows NT 4.0, you should try to use the more flexible `PlaySound` for any new applications.

You use the `PlaySound` function very much like you used `sndPlaySound` in the preceding section:

```
PlaySound( lpszFile, hInstance, SND_ASYNC );
```

The `PlaySound` function has three parameters:

- The name of the file, resource, or sound event in the Registry to be played. As with `sndPlaySound`, this parameter is set to `NULL` to interrupt the sound currently playing.

- The instance handle for the module that contains the sound resource. If the first parameter does not specify a resource, this parameter is not used and may be set to `NULL`.

- One or more flags that specify how the sound will be played. `PlaySound` shares many of its flags with `sndPlaySound` and adds several more. The flags used for this parameter are discussed later in this section.

The `PlaySound` function returns `TRUE` if the sound can be stated; otherwise, it returns `FALSE`.

Table 32.3 lists the flags that can be used for the third parameter for PlaySound. Unless otherwise specified, flags can be combined using ¦, the bitwise, or symbol.

Table 32.3. Flags used with `PlaySound`.

Parameter	*Function*
SND_ALIAS	Specifies that the first parameter is a system-event alias in the Registry. This flag cannot be used with SND_FILENAME or SND_RESOURCE.
SND_ALIAS_ID	Indicates that the first parameter is a predefined sound identifier.
SND_APPLICATION	Indicates that the sound is played using an application-specific association.
SND_ASYNC	Starts playing the sound asynchronously. The function returns immediately, before the sound finishes. To stop an asynchronous sound event, call PlaySound a second time, with NULL as the first parameter.

continues

Table 32.3. continued

Parameter	Function
SND_FILENAME	Indicates that the fist parameter is a filename.
SND_LOOP	Plays the sound continuously. This flag must be combined with SND_ASYNC.
SND_MEMORY	Plays a waveform located in memory rather than on disk.
SND_NODEFAULT	Quietly returns if the requested file cannot be found. The normal behavior without this flag is to play the system default sound.
SND_NOSTOP	Causes PlaySound to fail if another sound already is playing, without interrupting the sound currently playing.
SND_NOWAIT	Causes the PlaySound function to return immediately without playing the sound if the sound driver is busy.
SND_PURGE	Causes sounds to be stopped for the calling task. If the first parameter is NULL, all sounds playing on behalf of the calling task are stopped. Otherwise, all currently playing instances of the specified sound are stopped. In the case of resource sound events, you also must specify the instance handle.
SND_RESOURCE	Specifies that the first parameter is a waveform audio resource. The second parameter must be the instance handle that owns the resource.
SND_SYNC	Plays the sound *synchronously*—the function does not return until the sound finishes playing.

Using PlaySound with the Registry

You also can use PlaySound to play a sound event located in the system Registry. The user can select the sound associated with these events or use the default values provided by Windows NT. You can specify sound events associated with your Windows NT application by adding keys to the Registry. Placing these events in the Registry enables users to bind specific sounds to these events.

Six sounds appear on all Win32 systems:

- SystemAsterisk
- SystemExclamation
- SystemExit
- SystemHand

■ SystemQuestion

■ SystemStart

In addition, Windows NT 4.0 adds sounds, such as EmptyRecycleBin, RingIn, and RingOut. You can find a complete list of the sound events available to the current user in the Registry at

```
HKEY_CURRENT_USER\AppEvents\EventLabels
```

To play one of the sound events using PlaySound, pass the name of the sound event as the first parameter and use the SND_ALIAS flag:

```
PlaySound( "RingIn", NULL, SND_ASYNC¦SND_ALIAS );
```

Using PlaySound with Application Resources

You also can use the PlaySound function to play waveform audio resources contained in your application. The resource ID is passed as the first parameter, and the SND_RESOURCE flag must be used:

```
PlaySound( MAKEINTRESOURCE(IDR_ALEX_WAVE),
          hInstance,
          SND_RESOURCE¦SND_ASYNC );
```

Note that the second parameter is not set to NULL; it must be the instance handle of the DLL or application that owns the resource.

Using the MCI Functions

As discussed earlier, Windows NT provides a set of commands known as *Media Control Interface* (MCI) to control multimedia devices. This is a fairly high-level interface that can be used to control multimedia devices. Some of the commands are used for a specific type of device, but most commands can be applied to a wide range of device types. All devices support the MCI_PLAY and MCI_OPEN commands, for example.

Every multimedia device is categorized by MCI as one of the device types shown in Table 32.4. The type of a particular device (as well as its device driver) determines what commands are supported by that device.

Table 32.4. MCI device types.

Device Type	Constant	Description
animation	MCI_DEVTYPE_ANIMATION	Animation device
cdaudio	MCI_DEVTYPE_CD_AUDIO	CD audio player

continues

Table 32.4. continued

Device Type	Constant	Description
dat	MCI_DEVTYPE_DAT	Digital audio tape player
digitalvideo	MCI_DEVTYPE_DIGITAL_VIDEO	Digital video in a window
other	MCI_DEVTYPE_OTHER	Undefined MCI device
overlay	MCI_DEVTYPE_OVERLAY	Overlay (analog video)
scanner	MCI_DEVTYPE_SCANNER	Image scanner
sequencer	MCI_DEVTYPE_SEQUENCER	MIDI sequencer
vcr	MCI_DEVTYPE_VCR	VCR or player
videodisc	MCI_DEVTYPE_VIDEODISC	Videodisc player
waveaudio	MCI_DEVTYPE_WAVEFORM_AUDIO	Audio device

Commands are sent to multimedia devices through a set of Windows NT API functions. Two media control functions are provided by Windows NT:

■ **mciSendCommand:** Uses command messages to control an MCI device, in a manner similar to sending window messages.

■ **mciSendString:** Uses command strings to control an MCI device. Windows NT converts command strings into command messages before passing them to the multimedia driver.

You always will get better performance by using command messages instead of command strings. The command string interface is somewhat easier to use, however, and it's perfectly acceptable to mix both types of MCI commands in your application.

Using mciSendCommand to Control Multimedia Devices

Every MCI command sent to a multimedia device using mciSendCommand follows this basic format:

```
mciSendCommand( nID, MCI_PLAY, MCI_NOTIFY, &playStruct );
```

The mciSendCommand function has four parameters:

■ A device ID that identifies the target of the command message—in this case, nID, which is assumed to have been set to a valid value earlier

■ A constant that specifies the command message to be sent to the device—in this case, MCI_PLAY

■ A set of flags to provide arguments for the command message

■ The address of a structure used to pass arguments to and from the multimedia device

The return value from mciSendCommand is 0 if the function succeeds or an error value if the function fails. This topic is discussed later in *Handling Error Return Values*.

Using mciSendString to Control Multimedia Devices

The mciSendString function gives you easy access to multimedia services and applications written in languages that do not support the C syntax, such as Visual Basic. Although you might pay a small performance penalty when using mciSendString, it is much easier to use than the low-level multimedia API functions. In fact, I often use mciSendString when prototyping.

A command string consists of three basic parts:

■ A command, such as play

■ A device identifier, such as cdaudio

■ A set of arguments or parameters, such as from 1 to 3

The string "play cdaudio from 1 to 3" plays the first two tracks on the computer's cdaudio device. To send this command string, you use the mciSendString function:

```
TCHAR    szReturn[128];
mciSendString( "play cdaudio from 1 to 3",
               szReturn,
               sizeof(szReturn)
               NULL );
```

Four parameters are passed to mciSendString:

■ The actual command string sent to the multimedia device

■ A buffer to hold return information, if any, or NULL if the information is not required

■ The size of the return information buffer

■ A window handle to be used for notification messages if the notify argument is used in the command string, or NULL otherwise

As with the mciSendCommand function, the return value from mciSendString is 0 if the function succeeds or an error value if the function fails. This topic is discussed in more detail in the following section.

Handling Error Return Values

The mciSendString and mciSendCommand functions return 0 if successful, and a non-zero error value if an error is encountered. The Win32 SDK contains a complete list of possible error values. In most cases, all you really need to do is format the error message into a reasonable message and then display it to the user. The mciGetErrorString function returns a formatted text string that describes an error passed to it as a parameter:

```
DWORD dwError;
if( dwError = mciSendString( "play ball", NULL, 0, NULL ) )
{
    TCHAR    szError[129];
    mciGetErrorString( dwError, szError, sizeof(szError) );
    AfxMessageBox( szError );
}
```

This code sends an invalid command string. The error value is passed to `mciGetErrorString`, which returns a formatted string ready for display in a message box, as shown in Figure 32.2.

FIGURE 32.2.

Displaying a multimedia error using `mciGetErrorString`.

Opening a Device

You must open an MCI device before you can use it. If you are using `mciSendString`, the command is fairly simple, even with error handling, as Listing 32.1 shows.

Listing 32.1. Opening the `cdaudio` device using `mciSendString`.

```
DWORD dwError;
TCHAR szMsg[129];
dwError = mciSendString("open cdaudio", szMsg, sizeof(szMsg),NULL);
if( dwError == 0 )
{
    // Device opened
    CString sz = TEXT("Device ID = ");
    AfxMessageBox( sz + szMsg );
}
else
{
    // Handle error
    TCHAR    szError[129];
    mciGetErrorString( dwError, szError, sizeof(szError) );
    AfxMessageBox( szError, MB_ICONHAND );
}
```

The code for using `mciSendCommand` is very similar to the code used for `mciSendString`. In Listing 32.2, note that the device ID is retrieved from the `MCI_OPEN_PARAMS` structure if the device is opened successfully. Any future calls to the MCI device, such as `MCI_PLAY` and `MCI_CLOSE`, rely on the device ID to identify the MCI device.

Listing 32.2. Opening the `cdaudio` device using `mciSendCommand`.

```
DWORD           dwError;
MCIDEVICEID     id;
MCI_OPEN_PARMS  param;
memset( &param, 0, sizeof(param) );
param.lpstrDeviceType = (LPCTSTR)MCI_DEVTYPE_CD_AUDIO;
dwError = mciSendCommand( NULL,
                          MCI_OPEN,
                          MCI_OPEN_TYPE¦MCI_OPEN_TYPE_ID,
                          (DWORD)&param );
if( dwError == 0 )
{
    CString szMsg;
    szMsg.Format( TEXT("Device Id = %d"), param.wDeviceID );
    AfxMessageBox( szMsg );
    id = param.wDeviceID;
}
else
{
    TCHAR   szError[129];
    mciGetErrorString( dwError, szError, sizeof(szError) );
    AfxMessageBox( szError, MB_ICONHAND );
}
```

You use the `MCI_OPEN_PARMS` structure to pass data to and from the device when sending the `MCI_OPEN` command. The `MCI_OPEN_PARMS` structure has five members, as Table 32.5 shows.

Table 32.5. Member variables contained in `MCI_OPEN_PARMS`.

Member Variable	Type
dwCallback	DWORD
lpstrDeviceType	LPCTSTR
lpstrElementName	LPCTSTR
lpstrAlias	LPCTSTR
wDeviceID	MCIDEVICEID

Depending on how the device is opened and the flags that are passed to `MCI_OPEN`, some of the structure variables are optional, and some are passed back to you as outgoing parameters, as Table 32.6 shows.

Table 32.6. `MCI_OPEN_PARMS` **structure member variables.**

Parameter	Function
dwCallback	Stores the window handle used for notification messages. This member variable must be valid if the `MCI_NOTIFY` flag is passed as the third parameter; in all other cases, this flag is ignored.
lpstrAlias	Contains an optional alias name for the device. If this member is valid, the `MCI_OPEN_ALIAS` flag must be passed as the third parameter.
lpstrDeviceType	Contains a device type. If this member is used, the `lpstrElement` name is set to NULL. If this member is valid, the `MCI_OPEN_TYPE` flag must be passed as the third parameter. If this flag is combined with `MCI_OPEN_TYPE_ID`, the low-order part of `lpstrDeviceType` contains a standard device ID and the high-order part contains a device index.
lpstrElementName	Contains an element name—usually, a path to a file. If this parameter is set, the `lpstrDeviceType` member usually is set to NULL.
wDeviceID	Contains the device ID for the opened device if `MCI_OPEN` is successful.

After opening an MCI device, you must use the `MCI_CLOSE` command to close the device. Otherwise, the device may become unavailable.

Playing a Device

After an MCI device has been opened, you can play it by using `mciSendString` or `mciSendCommand`. All MCI devices support the `play` command. Sending a command string is very simple, as shown in Listing 32.3.

Listing 32.3. Using `mciSendString` **to play a** `cdaudio` **device.**

```
DWORD dwError;
TCHAR szMsg[129];
dwError = mciSendString( "play cdaudio from 1 to 3",
                         szMsg,
                         sizeof(szMsg),
                         NULL );
if( dwError == 0 )
{
    // Playing...
}
```

```
else
{
    // Handle error
}
```

The command string sent in Listing 32.3, "play cdaudio from 1 to 3," instructs the cdaudio device to play tracks 1, 2, and 3. The track information is optional—the string "play cdaudio" starts the cdaudio device to play from beginning to end.

Using mciSendCommand is slightly more complicated than sending a command string, but the interface is much more flexible. Listing 32.4 plays a track from a CD that was opened earlier, in Listing 32.2.

Listing 32.4. Using mciSendCommand to play a cdaudio device.

```
DWORD           dwError;
MCIDEVICEID     id;
.
.
.
MCI_PLAY_PARMS  playParam;
memset( &playParam, 0, sizeof(playParam) );
playParam.dwFrom = 1;
playParam.dwTo   = 3;
dwError = mciSendCommand( id,
                          MCI_PLAY,
                          MCI_FROM|MCI_TO,
                          (DWORD)&playParam );
if( dwError == 0 )
{
    // Playing
}
else
{
    TCHAR    szError[129];
    mciGetErrorString( dwError, szError, sizeof(szError) );
    AfxMessageBox( szError, MB_ICONHAND );
}
```

Listing 32.4 assumes that the device ID was stored when the MCI device was opened and that it was stored in the ID variable. When playing an MCI device using MCI_PLAY, an MCI_PLAY_PARMS structure is used to carry parameter information for the command. The following discusses the MCI_PLAY_PARMS member variables. All the structure members are input parameters, but some are optional, depending on the flags passed with the command.

■ **dwCallback:** Stores the window handle used for notification messages. This member variable must be valid if the MCI_NOTIFY flag is passed as the third parameter; in all other cases, this flag is ignored.

- **dwFrom:** Number of the first track or index to play on the MCI device. This member variable is associated with the MCI_FROM flag. If the flag is set, this value must be valid; if the flag is cleared, this member variable is ignored.

- **dwTo:** Number of the track or index to play to. If this member is omitted, the default action is to play until the end of the media. This member variable is associated with the MCI_TO flag. If the flag is set, this value must be valid; if the flag is cleared, this member variable is ignored.

Stopping a Device

You can stop a currently playing MCI device by using the stop command. All MCI devices support the stop command. When using mciSendString, the command string consists of stop and the device name or alias, as shown in Listing 32.5.

Listing 32.5. Using mciSendString to stop a device.

```
dwError = mciSendString( "stop cdaudio", NULL, 0, NULL );
if( dwError == 0 )
{
    // Stopping
}
else
{
    // Handle error
}
```

If you use the stop command string with a digitalvideo device, you can add the hold stop flag to the command to indicate that Windows NT should not release resources needed to redraw the current image.

You can achieve a similar effect using the pause command:

```
dwError = mciSendString( "pause cdaudio", NULL, 0, NULL );
```

The only difference between the stop command and the pause command is that pause keeps a device queued at its present position. A play command resumes play from the location where the device paused. The stop command starts from the beginning. Not all devices support a true pause—those that do not map pause into a stop command.

The mciSendCommand version of stop uses the MCI_STOP symbol and an MCI_GENERIC_PARMS structure, as Listing 32.6 shows.

Listing 32.6. Using `mciSendCommand` to stop a device.

```
DWORD           dwError;
MCIDEVICEID     id;
.
.
.

MCI_GENERIC_PARMS  genericParam;
memset( &genericParam, 0, sizeof(genericParam) );
dwError = mciSendCommand( id,
                          MCI_STOP,
                          MCI_WAIT,
                          (DWORD)&genericParam );
if( dwError == 0 )
{
    // Stopping
}
else
{
    // Handle error
}
```

As you can see, stopping a playing device is a relatively simple operation. Listing 32.6 uses the MCI_WAIT flag to block the current thread until the device actually stops.

Pausing a device using `mciSendCommand` is just as easy—just substitute MCI_PAUSE in place of MCI_STOP:

```
dwError = mciSendCommand( id,
                          MCI_PAUSE,
                          MCI_WAIT,
                          (DWORD)&genericParam );
```

Closing a Device

All open MCI devices must be closed after use. Failure to close open MCI devices can leave them locked up and inaccessible. All MCI devices support the `close` command. When using `mciSendString`, the command string consists of `close` and the device name or alias, as Listing 32.7 shows.

Listing 32.7. Using `mciSendString` to close a device.

```
dwError = mciSendString( "close cdaudio", NULL, 0, NULL );
if( dwError == 0 )
{
    // Closing
}
else
{
    // Handle error
}
```

To close all open devices for your process, use the `"close all"` command string.

The `mciSendCommand` version of `close` uses the `MCI_CLOSE` symbol and an `MCI_GENERIC_PARMS` structure, as Listing 32.8 shows.

Listing 32.8. Using `mciSendCommand` to stop a device.

```
DWORD           dwError;
MCIDEVICEID     id;
.
.
.
MCI_GENERIC_PARMS  genericParam;
memset( &genericParam, 0, sizeof(genericParam) );
dwError = mciSendCommand( id,
                          MCI_CLOSE,
                          MCI_WAIT,
                          (DWORD)&genericParam );
if( dwError == 0 )
{
    // Closed
}
else
{
    // Handle error
}
```

Using the `MCIWnd` Functions

Windows NT 4.0 also offers a high-level, window-oriented set of multimedia functions and macros called `MCIWnd`. The `MCIWnd` family provides an easy-to-use interface ideal for many simple multimedia applications. Later in the section *Handling Digital Video Using MCIWnd*, you will see how you can use `MCIWnd` functions to control a video clip.

Creating a Window with `MCIWnd`

The first step in using the `MCIWnd` functions is to create an MCI window using the `MCIWndCreate` function. This function creates the standard Windows multimedia interface shown in Figure 32.3.

The user interface in Figure 32.3 has several features that you get just by using `MCIWndCreate`:

- A trackbar that shows the relative current position in the multimedia clip. You can use this to change the current position.
- A menu that provides easy access to commonly used functions.
- Pushbuttons to start, pause, and stop the playback.

FIGURE 32.3.

A multimedia window created using the MCIWndCreate *function.*

The MCIWndCreate function is called as shown in this code:

```
HWND hWndVideo = MCIWndCreate( hWndMain,
                               hInstance,
                               MCIWNDF_SHOWALL,
                               szVideoFile );
```

The return value from MCIWndCreate is a handle to the created MCI window. The parameters to MCIWndCreate follow:

■ A handle to the owner of the new MCI window or NULL if the new window will be a top-level window

■ The instance handle that will be associated with the new MCI window

■ One or more MCIWnd flags that specify how the window will be created

■ A name that specifies a multimedia device or a multimedia file that will be opened

Although MCIWndCreate initially was released with Video for Windows 1.1, you can use it to play audio tracks as well as video clips. When used for audio, the video window is not shown. Table 32.7 lists the possible flags for MCIWndCreate.

Table 32.7. MCIWndCreate flags.

Flag	Function
MCIWNDF_NOAUTOSIZEMOVIE	Creates a window that does not change the size of its destination window if the MCIWnd window size changes.
MCIWNDF_NOAUTOSIZEWINDOW	Creates a window that will not change its dimensions if the image size changes.

continues

Table 32.7. continued

Flag	Function
MCIWNDF_NOERRORDLG	Prevents MCI errors from being displayed to users.
MCIWNDF_NOMENU	Hides the menu button on the toolbar.
MCIWNDF_NOOPEN	Hides the open and close commands on the MCIWnd menu.
MCIWNDF_NOPLAYBAR	Hides the entire MCI toolbar.
MCIWNDF_NOTIFYALL	Indicates that Windows NT must send all MCIWNDM_ notification messages.
MCIWNDF_NOTIFYANSI	Indicates that Windows NT must use ANSI strings when generating notification messages to the parent window. This flag must be used with MCIWNDF_NOTIFYMODE.
MCIWNDF_NOTIFYERROR	Indicates that Windows NT must send an MCIWNDM_NOTIFYERROR message if an MCI error occurs.
MCIWNDF_NOTIFYMEDIA	Indicates that Windows NT must send an MCIWNDM_NOTIFYMEDIA message whenever a new device is used or a data file is opened or closed.
MCIWNDF_NOTIFYMODE	Indicates that Windows NT must send an MCIWNDM_NOTIFYMODE message whenever the device changes operating modes.
MCIWNDF_NOTIFYPOS	Indicates that Windows NT must send an MCIWNDM_NOTIFYPOS message whenever a change in the playback or record position within the content occurs.
MCIWNDF_NOTIFYSIZE	Indicates that Windows NT must send an MCIWNDM_NOTIFYSIZE message whenever the MCIWnd window size changes.
MCIWNDF_RECORD	Adds a record button to the toolbar if the MCI device has the recording capability.
MCIWNDF_SHOWALL	Identical to using all the MCIWNDF_SHOW styles.
MCIWNDF_SHOWMODE	Causes the current mode of the MCI device to be displayed in the window title bar.
MCIWNDF_SHOWNAME	Displays the name of the open MCI device or data file in the MCIWnd window title bar.
MCIWNDF_SHOWPOS	Displays the current position within the content of the MCI device in the window title bar.

Opening Files Using `MCIWnd`

The `MCIWnd` family also includes an easy-to-use function that you can use to open a multimedia file and associate it with an MCI window:

```
LONG dwOpen = MCIWndOpenDialog( hWndMci );
```

`MCIWndOpenDialog` is just one of dozens of multimedia macros that simplify use of the multimedia APIs. Although it does a serviceable job of opening a multimedia file, I prefer to use `GetOpenFileNamePreview`. The `GetOpenFileNamePreview` function works just like the common dialog `GetOpenFileName` function, and it also opens a thumbnail preview of the selected file. Listing 32.9 shows a small code fragment that opens a file using this function.

Listing 32.9. Using `GetOpenFileNamePreview` to preview an AVI file before opening it.

```
TCHAR           szFilePath[256] = "*.AVI";
OPENFILENAME    ofn;
memset( &ofn, 0, sizeof(ofn) );
ofn.lStructSize = sizeof(ofn);
ofn.hwndOwner = m_hWnd;
ofn.lpstrFilter = "Video files(*.AVI)\0*.AVI\0";
ofn.Flags = OFN_EXPLORER;
ofn.lpstrFile = szFilePath;
ofn.nMaxFile = 256;

if( GetOpenFileNamePreview( &ofn ) )
{
    m_szVideoFile = ofn.lpstrFile;
    m_hWndVideo = MCIWndCreate( NULL,
                                AfxGetInstanceHandle(),
                                MCIWNDF_SHOWALL,
                                m_szVideoFile );
}
```

Using the `OFN_EXPLORER` flag creates an Explorer-style dialog box that removes the default preview window. Figure 32.4 shows an example of the default dialog box with a preview window. If the multimedia clip has a sound track, it is played with the video.

Looking at a Multimedia Example

As an example of using different multimedia functions in a Windows NT application, I have created an sample program called MM located on the accompanying CD-ROM. The MM application is a property sheet that has several tabs. Each tab contains a different set of multimedia functions, as Figure 32.5 shows.

FIGURE 32.4.

Using the
`GetOpenFileNamePreview`
function to open a
multimedia clip.

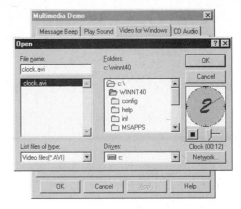

FIGURE 32.5.

The MM application's
main property sheet.

As with the other examples provided on the CD, you can use the complete MM project from the CD, or you can follow the steps described in the next few sections. Begin the project by using AppWizard to create a dialog-based application named MM.

Modifying stdafx.h

Three files must be included in a multimedia project:

- **afxole.h:** Included to prevent duplicate definitions of the BSTR type
- **vfw.h:** Included for MCIWnd functions and macros
- **digitalv.h:** Included for low-level functions

Including these files in stdafx.h, as shown in Listing 32.10, causes them to be included in a precompiled header, speeding your project's compilation time.

Listing 32.10. Modifications to the stdafx.h file (shown in bold).

```
#define VC_EXTRALEAN

#include <afxwin.h>          // MFC core and standard components
#include <afxext.h>          // MFC extensions
#ifndef _AFX_NO_AFXCMN_SUPPORT
#include <afxcmn.h>
#endif                       // _AFX_NO_AFXCMN_SUPPORT

#include <afxole.h>          // Avoid duplicate definition of BSTR
#include <vfw.h>             // For MCIWnd commands
#include <digitalv.h>        // For low-level interfaces
```

In addition, you must link your project with the vfw32.lib and winmm.lib libraries. If you are using Visual C++, follow these steps:

1. Select Build and then Settings from the main menu. The Project Settings dialog box appears.

2. Click on the Link tab. You might need to scroll the tab bar in order to find the proper tab.

3. Enter `vfw32.lib` and `winmm.lib` in the Object/library modules edit control.

4. Close the Project Settings dialog box by clicking the OK button.

Managing High-Level Sound Events

The first property page created for the MM project demonstrates the use of the high-level sound functions provided by Windows NT. Insert a new dialog box resource into the project. Figure 32.6 shows the dialog box resource being edited inside Developer Studio.

FIGURE 32.6.

Creating the Sound *property page using Developer Studio.*

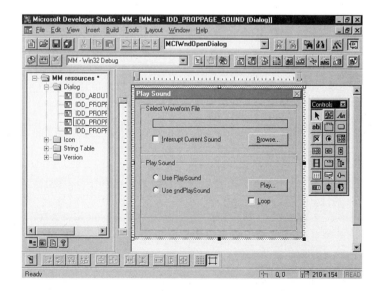

Give the new property page the attributes provided in Table 32.8.

Table 32.8. Attributes for the Sound property page.

Attribute	Value
Resource ID	IDD_PROPPAGE_SOUND
Caption	Play Sound
Style	Child
Border	Thin
Disabled checkbox	Checked
Visible checkbox	Cleared

Use the values from Table 32.9 for the controls added to the Sound property page.

Table 32.9. Controls added to the Sound property page, listed in tab order.

Control	Resource ID	Attributes
Select Waveform group frame	IDC_STATIC	
Static text frame	IDC_WAV_FILE	Border
Interrupt checkbox	IDC_INT_SOUND	
Browse pushbutton	IDC_SND_BROWSE	
PlaySound group frame	IDC_GRP_PLAY	
PlaySound radio button	IDC_PLAYSOUND	Group
sndPlaySound radio button	IDC_SNDPLAYSOUND	
Play pushbutton	IDC_SND_PLAY	Group
Loop checkbox	IDC_LOOP	

Open ClassWizard. Because a new dialog box resource has just been added, ClassWizard automatically prompts you to add a class to handle the new dialog box resource. Use the values provided in Table 32.10 for the new property page class.

Table 32.10. Values used to add a CSoundPage class.

Control	Value
Name	CSoundPage
Base Class	CPropertyPage

Control	Value
File	SoundPage.cpp
Dialog ID	IDD_PROPPAGE_SOUND
OLE Automation	None
Component Gallery	Cleared

The next step is to use ClassWizard to associate CSoundPage member variables with controls located on the property page. Click on the Member Variables tab, and add the member variables listed in Table 32.11 to the CSoundPage class.

Table 32.11. Control member variables added to the CSoundPage class.

Control ID	Category	Variable Type	Variable Name
IDC_INT_SOUND	Value	BOOL	m_fInterrupt
IDC_LOOP	Value	BOOL	m_fLoop
IDC_PLAYSOUND	Value	int	m_nPlayType

Use ClassWizard to add three message-handling functions to the CSoundPage class, using the values in Table 32.12.

Table 32.12. Message-handling events added to the CSoundPage class.

Object ID	Message	Function Name
CSoundPage	WM_INITDIALOG	OnInitDialog
IDC_SND_BROWSE	BN_CLICKED	OnSndBrowse
IDC_SND_PLAY	BN_CLICKED	OnSndPlay

One variable must be added manually to the CSoundPage class. The m_szWavFile member variable is used to track the currently selected waveform audio file. Listing 32.11 shows the CSoundPage class declaration, with the changed lines in bold. Most unchanged lines are omitted for clarity.

Listing 32.11. Modifications made to the `CSoundPage` class (shown in bold).

```
class CSoundPage : public CPropertyPage
{
.
.
.
// Implementation
protected:
    CString m_szWavFile;
.
.
.
};
```

Listing 32.12 contains the source code for the three new member functions added to the CSoundPage class.

Listing 32.12. Functions included in the `CSoundPage` class.

```
void CSoundPage::OnSndBrowse()
{
    TCHAR    szFilePath[256] = "*.WAV";
    OPENFILENAME   ofn;
    memset( &ofn, 0, sizeof(ofn) );
    ofn.lStructSize = sizeof(ofn);
    ofn.hwndOwner = m_hWnd;
    ofn.lpstrFilter = "Sound files(*.WAV)\0*.WAV\0";
    ofn.Flags = OFN_EXPLORER;
    ofn.lpstrFile = szFilePath;
    ofn.nMaxFile = 256;
    if( GetOpenFileNamePreview( &ofn ) )
    {
        m_szWavFile = ofn.lpstrFile;
        SetDlgItemText( IDC_WAV_FILE, m_szWavFile );
    }
}

void CSoundPage::OnSndPlay()
{
    UpdateData();
    UINT nFlags = SND_ASYNC;
    nFlags |= m_fLoop ? SND_LOOP : 0;

    LPCTSTR lpszFile;
    if( m_szWavFile.IsEmpty() || m_fInterrupt )
        lpszFile = NULL;
    else
        lpszFile = m_szWavFile;

    if( m_nPlayType == 0 )
        PlaySound( lpszFile, NULL, nFlags );
    else
        sndPlaySound( lpszFile, nFlags );
}
```

```
BOOL CSoundPage::OnInitDialog()
{
    CPropertyPage::OnInitDialog();

    m_nPlayType = 0;
    UpdateData(FALSE);

    return TRUE;
}
```

The OnInitDialog member function sets the active radio button for the property page.

The OnSndBrowse function initializes an OPENFILENAME structure and uses the GetOpenFileNamePreview function to enable the user to select a WAV file. The name of the selected file is stored in the m_szWavFile member variable.

The OnSndPlay member function plays the file stored in m_szWavFile, using PlaySound or sndPlaySound, depending on the option selected by the user and stored in m_nPlayType.

Handling Digital Video Using MCIWnd

The second property page created for the MM property sheet illustrates using the MCIWnd functions and macros to open an AVI file. Insert a new dialog box resource into the project. Figure 32.7 shows the dialog box resource being edited inside Developer Studio.

FIGURE 32.7.

Creating the Video *property page using Developer Studio.*

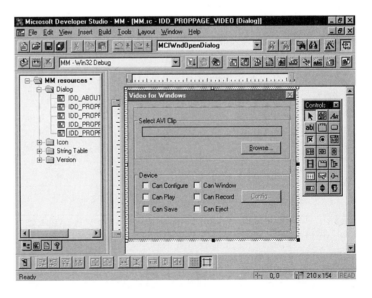

Give the new property page the attributes provided in Table 32.13.

Table 32.13. Attributes for the `Video` property page.

Attribute	Value
Resource ID	`IDD_PROPPAGE_VIDEO`
Caption	`Video for Windows`
Style	Child
Border	Thin
Disabled checkbox	Checked
Visible checkbox	Cleared

Use the values in Table 32.14 for the controls added to the `Video` property page.

Table 32.14. Controls added to the `Video` property page, listed in tab order.

Control	Resource ID	Attributes
Select AVI group frame	`IDC_STATIC`	
Static text frame	`IDC_VIDEO_STAT`	Border
Browse pushbutton	`IDC_VIDEO_BROWSE`	
Device group frame	`IDC_STATIC`	
Can Configure checkbox	`IDC_CAN_CONFIG`	
Can Play checkbox	`IDC_CAN_PLAY`	
Can Save checkbox	`IDC_CAN_SAVE`	
Can Window checkbox	`IDC_CAN_WINDOW`	
Can Record checkbox	`IDC_CAN_RECORD`	
Can Eject checkbox	`IDC_CAN_EJECT`	
Config pushbutton	`IDC_VID_CONFIG`	Disabled

As with the `Sound` property page, use ClassWizard to create a class derived from `CPropertyPage` that will manage the new property page. Use the values provided in Table 32.15 for the new property page class.

Table 32.15. Values used to add a `CVideoPage` class.

Control	Value
Name	CVideoPage
Base Class	CPropertyPage
File	VideoPage.cpp
Dialog ID	IDD_PROPPAGE_VIDEO
OLE Automation	None
Component Gallery	Cleared

The next step is to use ClassWizard to associate `CVideoPage` member variables with controls located on the property page. Click on the Member Variables tab, and add the member variables listed in Table 32.16 to the `CVideoPage` class.

Table 32.16. Control member variables added to the `CVideoPage` class.

Control ID	Category	Variable Type	Variable Name
IDC_CAN_CONFIG	Value	BOOL	m_fCanConfig
IDC_CAN_PLAY	Value	BOOL	m_fCanPlay
IDC_CAN_SAVE	Value	BOOL	m_fCanSave
IDC_CAN_WINDOW	Value	BOOL	m_fCanWnd
IDC_CAN_RECORD	Value	BOOL	m_fCanRecord
IDC_CAN_EJECT	Value	BOOL	m_fCanEject

Use ClassWizard to add two message-handling functions to the `CVideoPage` class, using the values in Table 32.17.

Table 32.17. Message-handling events added to the `CVideoPage` class.

Object ID	Message	Function Name
IDC_VID_CONFIG	BN_CLICKED	OnVidConfig
IDC_VIDEO_BROWSE	BN_CLICKED	OnVideoBrowse

Two variables must be added manually to the `CVideoPage` class:

- The `m_szVideoFile` member variable tracks the currently selected waveform audio file.
- The `m_hWndVideo` member variable contains the window handle returned from `MCIWndCreate`.

Listing 32.13 shows the `CVideoPage` class declaration. Most unchanged lines are omitted for clarity.

Listing 32.13. Modifications made to the `CVideoPage` class.

```
class CVideoPage : public CPropertyPage
{
.
.
.
// Implementation
protected:
    HWND    m_hWndVideo;
    CString m_szVideoFile;
.
.
.
};
```

Listing 32.14 contains the source code for the two new member functions added to the `CVideoPage` class.

Listing 32.14. Functions included in the `CVideoPage` class.

```
void CVideoPage::OnVidConfig()
{
    if( m_hWndVideo == NULL )
        return;
    if( MCIWndCanConfig( m_hWndVideo ) != FALSE )
    {
        UINT nID = MCIWndGetDeviceID( m_hWndVideo );
        mciSendCommand( nID, MCI_CONFIGURE, MCI_WAIT, NULL );
    }
}

void CVideoPage::OnVideoBrowse()
{
    TCHAR    szFilePath[256] = "*.AVI";
    OPENFILENAME    ofn;
    memset( &ofn, 0, sizeof(ofn) );
    ofn.lStructSize = sizeof(ofn);
    ofn.hwndOwner = m_hWnd;
    ofn.lpstrFilter = "Video files(*.AVI)\0*.AVI\0";
    ofn.Flags = OFN_EXPLORER;
    ofn.lpstrFile = szFilePath;
    ofn.nMaxFile = 256;
```

```
    if( GetOpenFileNamePreview( &ofn ) )
    {
        m_szVideoFile = ofn.lpstrFile;
        SetDlgItemText( IDC_VIDEO_STAT, m_szVideoFile );
        m_hWndVideo = MCIWndCreate( NULL,
                                    AfxGetInstanceHandle(),
                                    MCIWNDF_SHOWALL,
                                    m_szVideoFile );
        CWnd* pWnd = GetDlgItem( IDC_VID_CONFIG );
        ASSERT( pWnd );
        pWnd->EnableWindow();

        m_fCanConfig = MCIWndCanConfig( m_hWndVideo );
        m_fCanRecord = MCIWndCanRecord( m_hWndVideo );
        m_fCanEject  = MCIWndCanEject( m_hWndVideo );
        m_fCanSave   = MCIWndCanSave( m_hWndVideo );
        m_fCanWnd    = MCIWndCanWindow( m_hWndVideo );
m_fCanPlay   = MCIWndCanPlay( m_hWndVideo );
        UpdateData( FALSE );
    }
}
```

The `OnVideoBrowse` member function uses `GetOpenFileNamePreview` to enable the user to select an AVI file. After opening the file using `MCIWndCreate`, the property page's checkboxes are set, depending on the attributes of the selected file.

The `OnVidConfig` member function uses `mciSendCommand` to display the standard configuration property page, as described earlier in this chapter.

Handling Audio at a High Level

The third property page created for the MM property sheet illustrates using the `MessageBeep` function to play simple audio events. Figure 32.8 shows the dialog box resource being edited inside Developer Studio.

Give the new property page the attributes provided in Table 32.18.

Table 32.18. Attributes for the `Video` property page.

Attribute	Value
Resource ID	`IDD_PROPPAGE_BEEP`
Caption	`Message Beep`
Style	Child
Border	Thin
Disabled checkbox	Checked
Visible checkbox	Cleared

FIGURE 32.8.

Creating the Message Beep *property page using Developer Studio.*

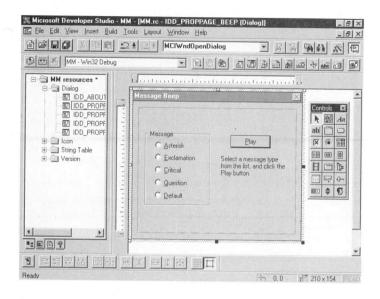

Use the values from Table 32.19 for the controls added to the Message Beep property page. The IDC_BEEP_STAT static text control is not visible in Figure 32.8 because it has no caption. It runs along the bottom of the property page.

Table 32.19. Controls added to the Message Beep property page, listed in tab order.

Control	Resource ID	Attributes
Message group frame	IDC_STATIC	
Asterisk radio button	IDC_ASTERISK	Group
Exclamation radio button	IDC_EXCLAMATION	
Critical radio button	IDC_CRITICAL	
Question radio button	IDC_QUESTION	
Default radio button	IDC_DEFAULT	
Status static control	IDC_BEEP_STAT	
Play pushbutton	IDC_MB_PLAY	Group

As with the previous property pages, use ClassWizard to create a class derived from CPropertyPage that will manage the new property page. Use the values provided in Table 32.20 for the new property page class.

Table 32.20. Values used to add a CBeepPage class.

Control	Value
Name	CBeepPage
Base Class	CPropertyPage
File	BeepPage.cpp
Dialog ID	IDD_PROPPAGE_BEEP
OLE Automation	None
Component Gallery	Cleared

The next step is to use ClassWizard to associate a CBeepPage member variable with the radio button controls located on the property page. Click on the Member Variables tab, and add the member variables listed in Table 32.21 to the CBeepPage class.

Table 32.21. Control member variables added to the CBeepPage class.

Control ID	Category	Variable Type	Variable Name
IDC_ASTERISK	Value	int	m_rbMessage

Use ClassWizard to add message-handling functions to the CBeepPage class, using the values from Table 32.22.

Table 32.22. Message-handling events added to the CBeepPage class.

Object ID	Message	Function Name
IDC_ASTERISK	BN_CLICKED	OnAsterisk
IDC_EXCLAMATION	BN_CLICKED	OnExclamation
IDC_CRITICAL	BN_CLICKED	OnCritical
IDC_QUESTION	BN_CLICKED	OnQuestion
IDC_DEFAULT	BN_CLICKED	OnDefault
IDC_MB_PLAY	BN_CLICKED	OnMbPlay

Listing 32.15 contains the source code for the new member functions added to the CBeepPage class.

Listing 32.15. Functions added to the `CBeepPage` class.

```
UINT g_rgBeepMap[] = { MB_ICONASTERISK, MB_ICONEXCLAMATION,
                       MB_ICONHAND, MB_ICONQUESTION, MB_OK };

void CBeepPage::OnAsterisk()
{
    CString szMsg = TEXT("Plays the system asterisk sound");
    SetDlgItemText( IDC_BEEP_STAT, szMsg );
}

void CBeepPage::OnCritical()
{
    CString szMsg = TEXT("Plays the system critical sound");
    SetDlgItemText( IDC_BEEP_STAT, szMsg );
}

void CBeepPage::OnDefault()
{
    CString szMsg = TEXT("Plays the system default sound");
    SetDlgItemText( IDC_BEEP_STAT, szMsg );
}

void CBeepPage::OnExclamation()
{
    CString szMsg = TEXT("Plays the system exclamation sound");
    SetDlgItemText( IDC_BEEP_STAT, szMsg );
}

void CBeepPage::OnQuestion()
{
    CString szMsg = TEXT("Plays the system question sound");
    SetDlgItemText( IDC_BEEP_STAT, szMsg );
}

void CBeepPage::OnMbPlay()
{
    UpdateData();
    UINT nMessage = g_rgBeepMap[m_rbMessage];
    MessageBeep( nMessage );
}
```

Most of the member functions added to the `CBeepPage` class are called when the user clicks on a radio button. These member functions, such as `OnAsterisk`, display a message to the user indicating the sound event that will be played.

The `OnMbPlay` member function uses the currently selected radio button as an index when selecting the proper sound event from the `g_rgBeepMap` array.

Handling CD Audio Functions

The last property page created for the MM property sheet uses MCI command functions to manage a CD player. Insert a new dialog box resource into the project. Figure 32.9 shows the dialog box resource being edited inside Developer Studio.

FIGURE 32.9.

Creating the CD Audio
*property page using
Developer Studio.*

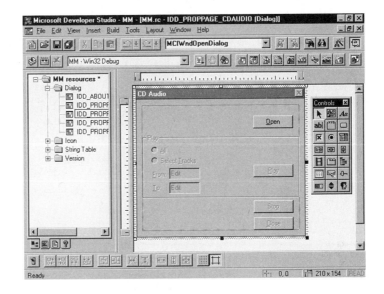

Give the new property page the attributes provided in Table 32.23.

Table 32.23. Attributes for the CD Audio property page.

Attribute	Value
Resource ID	IDD_PROPPAGE_AUDIO
Caption	CD Audio
Style	Child
Border	Thin
Disabled checkbox	Checked
Visible checkbox	Cleared

Use the values from Table 32.24 for the controls added to the CD Audio property page.

Table 32.24. Controls added to the CD Audio property page, listed in tab order.

Control	Resource ID	Attributes
Open pushbutton	IDC_CD_OPEN	
Play group frame	IDC_GRP_PLAY	Disabled
All radio button	IDC_CD_PLAY_OPT	Group, Disabled

continues

Table 32.24. continued

Control	Resource ID	Attributes
Select Tracks radio button	IDC_CD_PLAY_SEL	Disabled
From static text	IDC_CD_FROM	Group, Disabled
To static text	IDC_CD_TO	Disabled
From edit control	IDC_EDIT_FROM	Disabled
To edit control	IDC_EDIT_TO	Disabled
Play pushbutton	IDC_CD_PLAY	Disabled
Stop pushbutton	IDC_CD_STOP	Disabled
Close pushbutton	IDC_CD_CLOSE	Disabled

As with the property pages in previous sections, use ClassWizard to create a class derived from CPropertyPage that manages the new property page. Use the values provided in Table 32.25 for the new property page class.

Table 32.25. Values used to add a CAudioPage class.

Control	Value
Name	CAudioPage
Base Class	CPropertyPage
File	AudioPage.cpp
Dialog ID	IDD_PROPPAGE_AUDIO
OLE Automation	None
Component Gallery	Cleared

The next step is to use ClassWizard to associate CAudioPage member variables with controls located on the property page. Click on the Member Variables tab, and add the member variables listed in Table 32.26 to the CAudioPage class.

Table 32.26. Control member variables added to the CAudioPage class.

Control ID	Category	Variable Type	Variable Name
IDC_CD_PLAY_OPT	Value	int	m_rbTrack
IDC_EDIT_FROM	Value	DWORD	m_dwFrom
IDC_EDIT_TO	Value	DWORD	m_dwTo

Use ClassWizard to add six message-handling functions to the `CAudioPage` class, using the values from Table 32.27.

Table 32.27. Message-handling events added to the `CVideoPage` class.

Object ID	Message	Function Name
IDC_CD_CLOSE	BN_CLICKED	OnCdClose
IDC_CD_OPEN	BN_CLICKED	OnCdOpen
IDC_CD_PLAY	BN_CLICKED	OnCdPlay
IDC_CD_STOP	BN_CLICKED	OnCdStop
IDC_CD_PLAY_OPT	BN_CLICKED	OnCdPlayOpt
IDC_CD_PLAY_SEL	BN_CLICKED	OnCdPlaySel

One variable and one member function must be added manually to the `CAudioPage` class:

- The `m_id` member variable tracks the currently selected device.
- The `EnableCtrl` member function enables or disables a control given its resource ID and a flag that indicates whether the control is enabled or disabled.

Listing 32.16 shows the `CAudioPage` class declaration, with the changed lines shown in bold. Most unchanged lines are omitted for clarity.

Listing 32.16. Modifications made to the `CAudioPage` class (shown in bold).

```
class CAudioPage : public CPropertyPage
{
 .
 .
 .
// Implementation
protected:
    MCIDEVICEID m_id;
    void        EnableCtrl( UINT uID, BOOL fEnable );
 .
 .
 .
};
```

Listing 32.17 contains the source code for the new member functions added to the `CAudioPage` class.

Listing 32.17. Functions added to the `CAudioPage` class.

```cpp
void CAudioPage::OnCdClose()
{
    MCI_GENERIC_PARMS  genericParam;
    memset( &genericParam, 0, sizeof(genericParam) );
    DWORD dwError = mciSendCommand(  m_id,
                                     MCI_CLOSE,
                                     MCI_WAIT,
                                     (DWORD)&genericParam );

    if( dwError == 0 )
    {
        EnableCtrl( IDC_GRP_PLAY, FALSE );
        EnableCtrl( IDC_CD_PLAY, FALSE );
        EnableCtrl( IDC_CD_STOP, FALSE );
        EnableCtrl( IDC_CD_CLOSE, FALSE );
        EnableCtrl( IDC_CD_PLAY_OPT, FALSE );
        EnableCtrl( IDC_CD_PLAY_SEL, FALSE );
        EnableCtrl( IDC_CD_TO, FALSE );
        EnableCtrl( IDC_CD_FROM, FALSE );
        EnableCtrl( IDC_EDIT_TO, FALSE );
        EnableCtrl( IDC_EDIT_FROM, FALSE );
        EnableCtrl( IDC_CD_OPEN, TRUE );
    }
    else
    {
        TCHAR   szError[129];
        mciGetErrorString( dwError, szError, sizeof(szError) );
        AfxMessageBox( szError, MB_ICONHAND );
    }
}

void CAudioPage::OnCdOpen()
{
    DWORD           dwError;
    MCI_OPEN_PARMS  param;
    memset( &param, 0, sizeof(param) );
    param.lpstrDeviceType = (LPCTSTR)MCI_DEVTYPE_CD_AUDIO;
    dwError = mciSendCommand( NULL,
                              MCI_OPEN,
                              MCI_OPEN_TYPE¦MCI_OPEN_TYPE_ID,
                              (DWORD)&param );
    if( dwError == 0 )
    {
        m_id = param.wDeviceID;
        EnableCtrl( IDC_GRP_PLAY, TRUE );
        EnableCtrl( IDC_CD_PLAY, TRUE );
        EnableCtrl( IDC_CD_STOP, TRUE );
        EnableCtrl( IDC_CD_CLOSE, TRUE );
        EnableCtrl( IDC_CD_PLAY_OPT, TRUE );
        EnableCtrl( IDC_CD_PLAY_SEL, TRUE );
        EnableCtrl( IDC_CD_OPEN, FALSE );
    }
    else
    {
        TCHAR   szError[129];
        mciGetErrorString( dwError, szError, sizeof(szError) );
        AfxMessageBox( szError, MB_ICONHAND );
    }
}
```

```
void CAudioPage::OnCdPlay()
{
    DWORD           dwError;
    MCI_PLAY_PARMS  playParam;
    memset( &playParam, 0, sizeof(playParam) );

    UpdateData();

    if( m_rbTrack == 0 )
    {
        dwError = mciSendCommand( m_id,
                                  MCI_PLAY,
                                  0,
                                  (DWORD)&playParam );
    }
    else
    {
        playParam.dwFrom = m_dwFrom;
        playParam.dwTo   = m_dwTo;
        dwError = mciSendCommand( m_id,
                                  MCI_PLAY,
                                  MCI_FROM|MCI_TO,
                                  (DWORD)&playParam );
    }

    if( dwError != 0 )
    {
        TCHAR   szError[129];
        mciGetErrorString( dwError, szError, sizeof(szError) );
        AfxMessageBox( szError, MB_ICONHAND );
    }

}

void CAudioPage::OnCdPlayOpt()
{
    EnableCtrl( IDC_CD_TO, FALSE );
    EnableCtrl( IDC_CD_FROM, FALSE );
    EnableCtrl( IDC_EDIT_TO, FALSE );
    EnableCtrl( IDC_EDIT_FROM, FALSE );
}

void CAudioPage::OnCdPlaySel()
{
    EnableCtrl( IDC_CD_TO, TRUE );
    EnableCtrl( IDC_CD_FROM, TRUE );
    EnableCtrl( IDC_EDIT_TO, TRUE );
    EnableCtrl( IDC_EDIT_FROM, TRUE );
}

void CAudioPage::OnCdStop()
{
    DWORD               dwError;
    MCI_GENERIC_PARMS   genericParam;
    memset( &genericParam, 0, sizeof(genericParam) );
```

continues

Listing 32.17. continued

```
        dwError = mciSendCommand( m_id,
                                  MCI_STOP,
                                  MCI_WAIT,
                                  (DWORD)&genericParam );
        if( dwError != 0 )
        {
            TCHAR   szError[129];
            mciGetErrorString( dwError, szError, sizeof(szError) );
            AfxMessageBox( szError, MB_ICONHAND );
        }
}

void CAudioPage::EnableCtrl( UINT uID, BOOL fEnable )
{
    CWnd* pWnd = GetDlgItem( uID );
    ASSERT( pWnd );
    pWnd->EnableWindow( fEnable );
}
```

The member functions provided in Listing 32.17 use the `mciSendCommand` function to send various commands to the computer's CD audio device.

Modifying the Main Application Class

The `CMMApp` class is derived from `CWinApp` and is responsible for creating the main application window, in this case, a dialog box. It also handles all of the application-level interaction with Windows NT and the MFC framework. There are two changes to the `CMMApp` class:

- The property sheet must be created, and property pages must be added to the property sheet.
- The existing code for the standard dialog box must be removed, and the property sheet must be substituted for it.

Listing 32.18 contains the modifications to the `CMMApp` class; you can find these changes in the MMApp.cpp source file. Lines that have changed are shown in bold type.

Listing 32.18. Modifications to the `CMMApp::InitInstance` member function (shown in bold).

```
// MM.cpp : Defines the class behaviors for the application.
//

#include "stdafx.h"
#include "MM.h"

#include "BeepPage.h"
#include "SoundPage.h"
```

```
#include "VideoPage.h"
#include "AudioPage.h"
.
.
.
BOOL CMMApp::InitInstance()
{

#ifdef _AFXDLL
    Enable3dControls();
#else
    Enable3dControlsStatic();
#endif

    CPropertySheet   dlg( "Multimedia Demo" );
    CBeepPage        pgBeep;
    CSoundPage       pgSound;
    CVideoPage       pgVideo;
    CAudioPage       pgAudio;

    dlg.AddPage( &pgBeep );
    dlg.AddPage( &pgSound );
    dlg.AddPage( &pgVideo );
    dlg.AddPage( &pgAudio );
    m_pMainWnd = &dlg;
    int nResponse = dlg.DoModal();
    if (nResponse == IDOK)
    {
        // TODO: Place code here to handle when the dialog is
        //  dismissed with OK
    }
    else if (nResponse == IDCANCEL)
    {
        // TODO: Place code here to handle when the dialog is
        //  dismissed with Cancel
    }
    return FALSE;
}
```

After making these changes, compile and run the MM project. Experiment by clicking on each tab and playing different multimedia source files.

Summary

This chapter discussed many of the multimedia functions available with Windows NT and how you can use them to add multimedia features to your applications. You also saw a sample multimedia application that controls the CD player, runs AVI clips, and plays waveform audio files.

The next chapter, "OpenGL Programming," discusses OpenGL, a cross-platform graphics library that allows you to create three-dimensional graphics. Included as an example is a three-dimensional animation program.

OpenGL Programming

by Mickey Williams

This chapter shows you how to use the OpenGL graphics library to create three-dimensional objects. You will learn about the basic elements of the OpenGL library and create an MFC application using OpenGL to create 3D animation.

Understanding OpenGL

OpenGL is a platform-independent library used to draw 3D graphics. OpenGL is a popular graphics library because it is available on a wide variety of platforms. As an open standard supported on many platforms, OpenGL helps software vendors create applications that can be made available on many types of workstations quickly and easily. Instead of spending time porting graphics code between incompatible libraries, software vendors can concentrate on bringing a single product to market quickly.

Initially, OpenGL was available only on high-end workstations such as those from Silicon Graphics. OpenGL was introduced for the Windows NT operating system beginning with version 3.5.

The OpenGL standard is controlled by the OpenGL *Architecture Review Board* (ARB). Members of the ARB include manufacturers of high-end workstations, such as Silicon Graphics and DEC as well as Microsoft. The ARB deals with issues that arise over the implementation of OpenGL, as well as extensions to the OpenGL architecture.

If you are interested in learning graphics programming, you can find large amounts of OpenGL source code and examples, both on the Internet and in books such as this one. Because OpenGL is platform neutral, much of this code easily can be run on a Windows NT workstation.

Using OpenGL

This chapter shows you how to use OpenGL under Windows NT in an MFC application. The OpenGL code has nothing to do with MFC, however, so most of the code will work with a straight SDK project also. First, you'll look at some OpenGL basics.

Examining OpenGL Naming Conventions

OpenGL uses a unique naming convention for its functions and data types. For portability reasons, OpenGL programs generally use special `typedefs` instead of using the native types used on a particular machine. Instead of declaring a variable to be a `double`, for example, an OpenGL program should use `GLdouble`. Table 33.1 lists the available OpenGL data types.

Table 33.1. OpenGL data types and their Win32 equivalents.

OpenGL Type	Win32 Type
GLbitfield	unsigned int
GLboolean	unsigned char
GLbyte	char
GLclampd	double
GLclampf	float
GLdouble	double
GLenum	unsigned int
GLfloat	float
GLint	int
GLshort	short
GLsizei	int
GLubyte	unsigned char
GLuint	unsigned int
GLushort	unsigned short
GLvoid	void

Using typedef names enables the true type of the variable to be "hidden" behind a typedef. This allows the source code to remain portable between platforms, with any implementation-specific issues handled in the gl.h header file.

You can call many OpenGL functions with multiple parameter lists. The function used to set the current color, glColor, has 32 variations, including these:

```
glColor3d(1.0, 1.0, 1.0);          // white, using doubles
GLdouble vRed[] = {1.0, 0.0, 0.0};
glColor3dv(vRed);                  // red using a vector of doubles
glColor4f(0.0f, 0.0f, 1.0f, 1.0f);// blue with an alpha value
```

A function name always begins with the main function name—in this case, glColor. Functions that have versions accepting different numbers of parameters list the number of parameters next—in this case, three or four. Next, a single letter indicates the type of parameters passed to the function; in this case, d indicates double parameters and f indicates float. A v appended to the function indicates that the function accepts an array (or vector) as a parameter. Using an array is the most efficient method for passing a parameter list. Table 33.2 lists the suffixes appended to OpenGL function names.

Table 33.2. Function-naming conventions in OpenGL.

Suffix	Description
0-9	Number of parameters
b	GLbyte parameters
d	GLdouble parameters
f	GLfloat parameters
i	GLint parameters
s	GLshort parameters
ub	GLubyte parameters
ui	GLuint parameters
us	GLushort parameters
v	Vector parameters

Most OpenGL functions exist in only one version. Those that exist in more than one signature usually accept only a few of the possible types listed in Table 33.2.

Using the OpenGL State Machine

The OpenGL library works like a state machine. A *state machine* is an object that has a known state. It retains this state until an event causes the machine to move to a new state. Many of the OpenGL functions used in this chapter change the current state of the OpenGL machine and remain in effect until they are changed. The glColor command often is used to set the current color, for example, like this:

```
glColor3d( 1.0, 0.0, 0.0 );
```

After the color is defined using glColor, all objects created with the OpenGL library use this color. Similarly, any functions that describe the rotation or position information remain current until they are changed.

Using OpenGL with Windows NT

OpenGL is a cross-platform graphics library, so applications written using OpenGL can be expected to be portable between implementations. Every operating system that hosts an OpenGL implementation requires specific initialization steps before the OpenGL code can run, however. In addition, every operating system requires different steps to be taken when closing an OpenGL program, such as releasing system resources.

Listing 33.1 shows the format that many books use to implement an OpenGL program.

Listing 33.1. The generic format used to implement an OpenGL program.

```
int main()
{
    OpenWindow();
    DrawScene();
    KeepWindowOpen();
    CloseWindow();
    return 0;
}
```

In this code, `OpenWindow`, `KeepWindowOpen`, and `CloseWindow` are all system-specific routines that are different on every platform. In most cases, OpenGL functions are found only in the `DrawScene` function.

The next few sections describe how to create the Windows NT specific parts of an OpenGL program. After that, you'll create an OpenGL program.

Initializing

You must be aware of three issues when initializing your OpenGL application:

- Setting the window style for the OpenGL window
- Setting the pixel format
- Creating a rendering context

Each of these topics is covered in this section.

Setting the Window Style for an OpenGL Window

In order to use OpenGL, the output window must have several characteristics:

- The window class must not have the `CS_PARENTDC` style.
- For performance reasons, the window often has its own device context, which is specified by setting the window class's `CS_OWNDC` style bit.
- For performance reasons, the window class can use a null brush for erasing the background. The OpenGL library handles erasing the background.
- The window must have the `WS_CLIPSIBLINGS` and `WS_CLIPCHILDREN` style bits turned off.

When using MFC, this work is done with three functions: `Create`, `OnCreate`, and `PreCreateWindow`. If you are using OpenGL to display images in a view, your `Create` member function must look like Listing 33.2.

Listing 33.2. A typical `Create` member function for an MFC-based OpenGL window.

```
BOOL CMyView::Create(LPCTSTR lpszClassName,
                     LPCTSTR lpszWindowName,
                     DWORD   dwStyle,
                     const   RECT& rect,
                     CWnd*   pParentWnd,
                     UINT    nID,
                     CCreateContext* pContext)
{
    LPCTSTR pszClass;
    pszClass = AfxRegisterWndClass( CS_OWNDC,
                                    NULL,
                                    (HBRUSH)(COLORWINDOW+1));
    return CWnd::Create( pszClass,
                         lpszWindowName,
                         dwStyle,
                         rect,
                         pParentWnd,
                         nID,
                         pContext);
}
```

In addition, in most cases, you should use a null brush handle that is used for the window background. Later in this chapter, the MFC OpenGL example demonstrates using a null brush.

A typical `PreCreateWindow` function sets the `WS_CLIPCHILDREN` and `WS_CLIPSIBLINGS` flags:

```
BOOL CMyView::PreCreateWindow(CREATESTRUCT& cs)
{
    cs.style |= WS_CLIPCHILDREN | WS_CLIPSIBLINGS;
    return CView::PreCreateWindow(cs);
}
```

Setting the Pixel Format and Rendering Context

During the initialization of your Windows NT OpenGL code, you must create an OpenGL rendering context. OpenGL uses a rendering context in much the same way that the GDI uses device contexts.

Before creating a rendering context and associating it with a device context, you must set the pixel format for the DC using the `ChoosePixelFormat` function:

```
CDC* pdc = GetDC();
int nPixelFormat = ChoosePixelFormat( pdc->m_hDC, &pd );
```

`ChoosePixelFormat` is a Windows NT function that was added to support OpenGL. You pass a pointer to a `PIXELFORMATDESCRIPTOR` to the `ChoosePixelFormat` function after filling the structure with information about the ideal rendering surface for your OpenGL application. Windows NT returns an index that represents the pixel format that most closely matches your requirements.

NOTE

With ChoosePixelFormat, there is no guarantee that you will get everything you ask for. You may ask for 32-bit color, but Windows NT may return an index representing an 8-bit pixel format. You can determine the characteristics of the pixel format index returned to you by calling the DescribePixelFormat function.

Table 33.3 lists the members of the PIXELFORMATDESCRIPTOR structure.

Table 33.3. PIXELFORMATDESCRIPTOR structure members.

Parameter	Function
bReserved	Must be set to 0.
cAccumAlphaBits	Specifies the number of alpha bitplanes in the accumulation buffer.
cAccumBits	Specifies the total number of bitplanes in the accumulation buffer.
cAccumBlueBits	Specifies the number of blue bitplanes in the accumulation buffer.
cAccumGreenBits	Specifies the number of green bitplanes in the accumulation buffer.
cAccumRedBits	Specifies the number of red bitplanes in the accumulation buffer.
cAlphaBits	Currently unused.
cAlphaShift	Currently unused.
cAuxBuffers	Currently unused.
cBlueBits	Specifies the number of blue bitplanes in each RGBA color buffer.
cBlueShift	Specifies the shift count for blue bitplanes in each RGBA color buffer.
cColorBits	Specifies the number of color bitplanes in each color buffer.
cDepthBits	Specifies the depth of the depth (z-axis) buffer.
cGreenBits	Specifies the number of green bitplanes in each RGBA color buffer.
cGreenShift	Specifies the shift count for green bitplanes in each RGBA color buffer.
cRedBits	Specifies the number of red bitplanes in each RGBA color buffer.

continues

Table 33.3. continued

Parameter	Function
cRedShift	Specifies the shift count for red bitplanes in each RGBA color buffer.
cStencilBits	Specifies the depth of the stencil buffer.
dwDamageMask	Specifies whether more than one pixel format shares the same frame buffer. This member usually is set to 0.
dwFlags	Specifies properties of the pixel buffer. Possible values for this member are discussed later in this section.
dwLayerMask	Resolves overlays. This value normally is set to 0.
dwVisibleMask	Specifies the visible mask, which is used with the dwLayerMask member to determine whether one layer overlays another. This value normally is set to 0.
iLayerType	Always set to PFD_MAIN_PLANE.
iPixelType	Specifies the type of pixel data. This member can have two values: PFD_TYPE_RGBA for pixels that have four components (red, green, blue, and alpha) or PFD_TYPE_COLOR_INDEX for pixels that use a color index.
nSize	Specifies the size of this data structure and must be set to sizeof(PIXELFORMATDESCRIPTOR).
nVersion	Specifies the version of this data structure and must be set to 1.

You can use one or more of the flags listed in Table 33.4 to set the value for the dwFlags member.

Table 33.4. Flags used for the dwFlags variable inside PIXELFORMATDESCRIPTOR.

Parameter	Function
PFD_DOUBLEBUFFER	Indicates that the buffer is double-buffered. This flag cannot be used with the PFD_SUPPORT_GDI flag.
PFD_DOUBLE_BUFFER_DONTCARE	Indicates that the requested pixel format can be single- or double-buffered.
PFD_DRAW_TO_BITMAP	Specifies a frame buffer that can draw to a memory bitmap.
PFD_DRAW_TO_WINDOW	Specifies a frame buffer that is able to draw to a window or device surface.

Parameter	Function
PFD_GENERIC_FORMAT	Specifies that the pixel format is supported by the Windows NT GDI software implementation, as opposed to special hardware driver support.
PFD_NEED_PALETTE	Indicates that the buffer uses RGBA pixels on a palette-managed device.
PFD_NEED_SYSTEM_PALETTE	Used with systems with OpenGL hardware that supports one hardware palette only.
PFD_SUPPORT_GDI	Indicates that the buffer supports GDI drawing. This flag cannot be used with the PFD_DOUBLEBUFFER flag.
PFD_SUPPORT_OPENGL	Specifies a frame buffer that supports OpenGL drawing.

After choosing a pixel format, you must set the pixel format for the device context by calling the SetPixelFormat function:

```
SetPixelFormat( pdc->m_hDC, nPixelFormat, &pd );
```

The SetPixelFormat function has three parameters:

- A handle to the target device context
- The index returned from ChoosePixelFormat
- A pointer to the PIXELFORMATDESCRIPTOR used in the call to ChoosePixelFormat

The next step is to create an OpenGL rendering context. This is the rendering context created by calling the wglCreateContext function, which returns a handle to an OpenGL rendering context or HGLRC:

```
HGLRC hglrc = wglCreateContext( pdc->m_hDC );
```

After creating a rendering context, it must be "made current" before it can be used. Use the wglMakeCurrent function:

```
wglMakeCurrent( pdc->m_hDC, hglrc );
```

Any time the device context is changed or replaced, the rendering context must be brought up to date with wglMakeCurrent. Creating and updating the OpenGL rendering context is quite expensive in terms of CPU cycles. For this reason, I always use windows that have their own device context, which can be held for the life of the window. This enables me to create and update the rendering context once, without updating the rendering context for every drawing operation.

Setting the Viewport and Perspective Information

Before your application's scene can be described properly to the OpenGL library, you must define a viewport and other information. You do not need to reset this information every time the scene is drawn. The best place to locate these function calls is in your handler for WM_SIZE. A typical OnSize handler from an MFC application looks like Listing 33.3.

Listing 33.3. Handling the WM_SIZE message for an OpenGL application using MFC.

```
void CMyView::OnSize(UINT nType, int cx, int cy)
{
    CView::OnSize(nType, cx, cy);

    GLsizei glnWidth = cx;
    GLsizei glnHeight = cy;
    GLdouble gldAspect = (GLdouble)glnWidth/(GLdouble)glnHeight;

    glMatrixMode( GL_PROJECTION );
    glLoadIdentity();
    gluPerspective( 30.0, gldAspect, 1.0, 15.0 );
    glViewport( 0, 0, glnWidth, glnHeight );
}
```

The first function called by CMyView::OnSize is glMatrixMode. Passing GL_PROJECTION as a parameter specifies that operations involving a matrix must be applied to the projection matrix. Other values for this parameter follow:

- GL_MODELVIEW: Specifies the matrix used for the current model
- GL_TEXTURE: Specifies the texture matrix

Next, glIdentity loads the identity matrix, which is similar to clearing the matrix of any current operations that have been applied to it.

The gluPerspective function is a utility function that sets the current perspective for the viewport. The gluPerspective function has four parameters:

- The view angle in the y (up-down) direction
- The aspect ratio in the x (left-right) direction
- The distance from the viewer to the front of the image area or clipping rectangle
- The distance from the viewer to the back of the image area or clipping rectangle

Figure 33.1 shows how these parameters interact with each other to define the image-viewing area.

FIGURE 33.1.

Perspective parameter relationships.

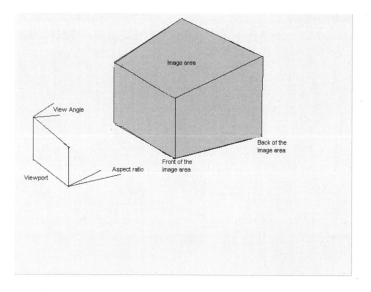

Finally, the actual viewport is set by calling the glViewport function. In this case, the parameters passed to glViewport specify that the entire window will be used as the viewport.

After calling these functions, you are ready to describe an image using OpenGL, which is covered in the next section.

Describing an Image with OpenGL

You can describe images using OpenGL at several different levels, each offering a different amount of performance and flexibility:

■ The OpenGL auxiliary library, or aux functions, enables you to specify an entire object with a single function call. These routines are easy to use but are not as flexible as other OpenGL functions.

■ The OpenGL utility, or glu functions, is a mid-level API that offers an even trade-off between performance and flexibility.

■ The most flexibility is obtained by using OpenGL glVertex functions to describe objects as a series of polygons, each made up of a number of vertices.

Using the Auxiliary Library

Using the auxiliary library, you can describe an object with just one function call. To draw a wire sphere, for example, you use the auxWireSphere function:

```
auxWireSphere( 1.0 );
```

Figure 33.2 is an example of a sphere rendered using auxWireSphere.

FIGURE 33.2.

A wire sphere drawn with `auxWireSphere`.

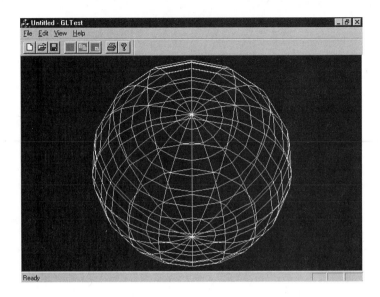

The auxiliary library includes functions that can be used to draw simple cones, cubes, cylinders, and other objects. When using the auxiliary library, you must include the glaux.h header file:

```
#include <gl/glaux.h>
```

You also must remember to link your program with glaux.lib.

Using the Utility Functions

At a somewhat lower level than the auxiliary library functions, OpenGL offers the utility library, or `glu` functions. These functions give you slightly more control over the objects that you describe. Before using any of the `glu` functions to create objects, a `GLUquadricObj` must be allocated. This object describes the OpenGL object and must be passed to the function used to display the object. It must be destroyed when the object no longer is used.

To create an open wire frame cylinder, for example, you use the `gluCylinder` function, as shown in Listing 33.4.

Listing 33.4. Creating, drawing, and destroying a cylinder using `glu` functions.

```
GLUquadricObj*  pCylinder;
.
.
.
// Initialization
pCylinder = gluNewQuadric();
ASSERT( m_pCylinder );
gluQuadricDrawStyle( m_pCylinder, GLU_LINE );
```

.
.
.
```
// Drawing
gluCylinder( m_pCylinder, 1.0, 1.0, 1.8, 15, 5 );
```
.
.
.
```
// Cleanup
gluDeleteQuadric( m_pCylinder );
```

FIGURE 33.3.

A wire frame cylinder drawn using gluCylinder.

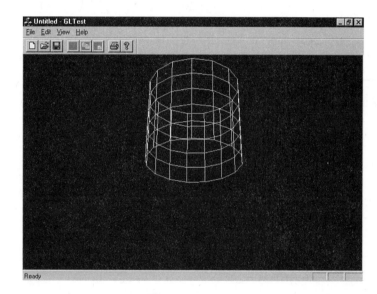

Figure 33.3 is an example of a cylinder rendered using gluCylinder.

In addition to gluCylinder, the utility library includes functions used to draw spheres, cones, cubes, and other objects.

Using glVertex

By far, the most flexible method for drawing objects using OpenGL is to break down the object into a series of polygons and to describe each polygon as a series of vertices. Although this approach can be a little tedious and results in large amounts of source code, you will have much more control over the image created by your application.

Drawing a cube using the OpenGL vertex functions, for example, requires you to describe all six sides of the cube. These six sides share eight vertices. It doesn't matter in which order they are described, but you must be sure to describe all sides, and you must match up the vertices correctly. Figure 33.4 shows the process required to describe a cube.

FIGURE 33.4.

The steps required to draw a cube.

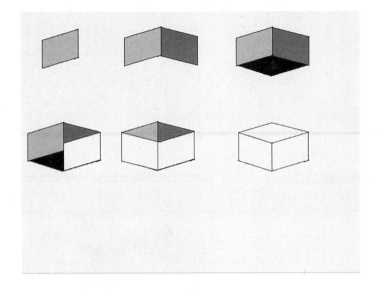

Listing 33.5 contains the OpenGL source code used to describe a small cube, with each side rendered in a different color. This source code is completely portable between different OpenGL implementations.

Listing 33.5. Drawing a cube using OpenGL.

```
void CMyView::DrawCube()
{
    // Draw a cube, describing all six sides as polygons:
    // Use red, blue, green, yellow, white, and gray sides.
    GLdouble vdRed[]    = { 1.0, 0.0, 0.0 };
    GLdouble vdBlue[]   = { 0.0, 0.0, 1.0 };
    GLdouble vdGreen[]  = { 0.0, 1.0, 0.0 };
    GLdouble vdYellow[] = { 1.0, 1.0, 0.0 };
    GLdouble vdWhite[]  = { 1.0, 1.0, 1.0 };
    GLdouble vdGray[]   = { 0.66, 0.66, 0.66 };

    // Vectors that describe vertices of the cube,
    // "looking down" at the center of the cube.
    GLdouble vdTopNW[] = { -0.5, 0.5, 0.5 };
    GLdouble vdTopNE[] = {  0.5, 0.5, 0.5 };
    GLdouble vdTopSW[] = { -0.5, 0.5, -0.5 };
    GLdouble vdTopSE[] = {  0.5, 0.5, -0.5 };
    GLdouble vdBotNW[] = { -0.5, -0.5, 0.5 };
    GLdouble vdBotNE[] = {  0.5, -0.5, 0.5 };
    GLdouble vdBotSW[] = { -0.5, -0.5, -0.5 };
    GLdouble vdBotSE[] = {  0.5, -0.5, -0.5 };
```

```
    glColor3dv( vdRed );
    glBegin( GL_POLYGON );
        glVertex3dv( vdTopNE );
        glVertex3dv( vdTopNW );
        glVertex3dv( vdBotNW );
        glVertex3dv( vdBotNE );
    glEnd();

    glColor3dv( vdBlue );
    glBegin( GL_POLYGON );
        glVertex3dv( vdTopSE );
        glVertex3dv( vdTopSW );
        glVertex3dv( vdBotSW );
        glVertex3dv( vdBotSE );
    glEnd();

    glColor3dv( vdGreen );
    glBegin( GL_POLYGON );
        glVertex3dv( vdTopNW );
        glVertex3dv( vdTopSW );
        glVertex3dv( vdBotSW );
        glVertex3dv( vdBotNW );
    glEnd();

    glColor3dv( vdYellow );
    glBegin( GL_POLYGON );
        glVertex3dv( vdTopNE );
        glVertex3dv( vdTopSE );
        glVertex3dv( vdBotSE );
        glVertex3dv( vdBotNE );
    glEnd();

    glColor3dv( vdWhite );
    glBegin( GL_POLYGON );
        glVertex3dv( vdTopNE );
        glVertex3dv( vdTopSE );
        glVertex3dv( vdTopSW );
        glVertex3dv( vdTopNW );
    glEnd();

    glColor3dv( vdGray );
    glBegin( GL_POLYGON );
        glVertex3dv( vdBotNE );
        glVertex3dv( vdBotSE );
        glVertex3dv( vdBotSW );
        glVertex3dv( vdBotNW );
    glEnd();
}
```

Figure 33.5 shows a sample program displaying the cube created using the source code from Listing 33.5.

FIGURE 33.5.

The cube created using the code from Listing 33.5.

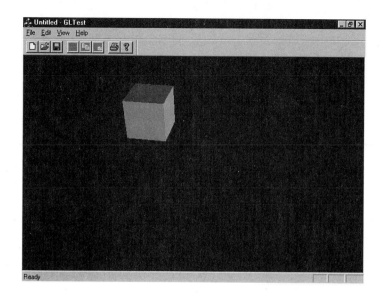

Cleaning Up OpenGL Objects

As your Windows NT application closes, you must perform several steps to clean up properly. The primary thing that you must do is destroy the OpenGL rendering context, using the wglDeleteContext function:

```
wglDeleteContext( m_hglrc );
```

In addition, you should destroy any GLUquadricObj objects you have created. The best place for this code is in your WM_DESTROY handler. In an MFC application, this function usually is named OnDestroy.

Looking at an OpenGL Animation Example

As an example of using OpenGL to display 3D animation in a Windows NT application, I have created an application named Ogl that is located on the accompanying CD-ROM. Ogl is an MFC-based SDI application that displays two animated objects in its main window: a cube and a pyramid, as shown in Figure 33.6.

You can compile and run the project "as is" from the CD, or you can follow along as I create the project in the following chapters. To get started, use AppWizard to create an SDI application named Ogl.

FIGURE 33.6.

The main window of the Ogl application.

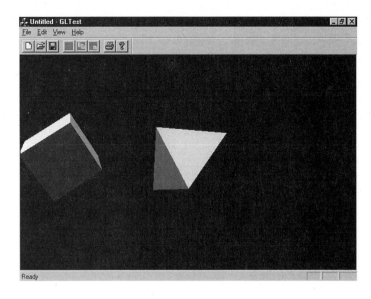

Modifying the View Class

Use ClassWizard to add four message-handling functions to the COglView class, using the values from Table 33.5.

Table 33.5. New message-handling functions for the COglView class.

Object ID	Message	Function Name
COglView	Create	Create
COglView	WM_CREATE	OnCreate
COglView	WM_DESTROY	OnDestroy
COglView	WM_SIZE	OnSize
COglView	WM_TIMER	OnTimer

In addition to the message-handling functions listed in Table 33.5, three additional member functions must be added to the COglView class. Listing 33.6 shows the modifications required for the COglView class, including two new member variables. The changed lines are shown in bold type, and most of the unchanged lines have been removed for clarity.

Listing 33.6. Modifications to the `COglView` class declaration, shown in bold.

```
class CGLTestView : public CView
{
.
.
.

// Implementation
protected:
    HGLRC   m_hglrc;
    CBrush  m_brNull;

    void Wobble( const GLdouble& gldRadius,
                 const GLdouble& gldLatitude,
                 const GLdouble& gldLongitude );
    void DrawCube();
    void DrawPyramid();
.
.
.

};
```

Listing 33.7 provides the source code for the new and changed `COglView` functions.

Listing 33.7. Modifications to the `COglView` member functions.

```
BOOL COglView::PreCreateWindow(CREATESTRUCT& cs)
{
    cs.style |= WS_CLIPCHILDREN | WS_CLIPSIBLINGS;
    return CView::PreCreateWindow(cs);
}

void COglView::OnDraw(CDC* pDC)
{
    static GLdouble gldRadius = -8.0;
    static GLdouble gldLatitude = 0.0;
    static GLdouble gldLongitude = 0.0;
    static GLdouble gldDelta = 0.0;

    gldLatitude += 4.0;
    gldLongitude += 2.5;
    gldDelta += 3.0;

    glEnable( GL_DEPTH_TEST );
    glClear( GL_COLOR_BUFFER_BIT | GL_DEPTH_BUFFER_BIT );
    glMatrixMode( GL_MODELVIEW );
    glLoadIdentity();
    Wobble( gldRadius, gldLatitude, gldLongitude );
    glPushMatrix();
    glRotated( gldDelta, 0.0, gldLatitude, gldLongitude );
    glTranslated( 2.0, 1.5, 0.0 );
    DrawCube();
    glPopMatrix();
    DrawPyramid();
    glFlush();
    SwapBuffers( wglGetCurrentDC() );
```

```
}

BOOL COglView::Create(LPCTSTR lpszClassName, LPCTSTR lpszWindowName, DWORD dwStyle,
const RECT& rect, CWnd* pParentWnd, UINT nID, CCreateContext* pContext)
{
    LOGBRUSH logBr;
    memset( &logBr, 0, sizeof(logBr) );
    logBr.lbStyle = BS_NULL;
    m_brNull.CreateBrushIndirect( &logBr );

    LPCTSTR     pszOglClass;
    pszOglClass = AfxRegisterWndClass( CS_OWNDC,
                                       NULL,
                                       m_brNull );
    return CWnd::Create( pszOglClass,
                         lpszWindowName,
                         dwStyle,
                         rect,
                         pParentWnd,
                         nID,
                         pContext);
}

int COglView::OnCreate(LPCREATESTRUCT lpCreateStruct)
{
    if (CView::OnCreate(lpCreateStruct) == -1)
        return -1;

    PIXELFORMATDESCRIPTOR pd;
    memset( &pd, 0, sizeof(pd) );
    pd.nSize = sizeof(pd);

    pd.nVersion = 1;
    pd.dwFlags = PFD_DRAW_TO_WINDOW¦
                 PFD_SUPPORT_OPENGL¦
                 PFD_DOUBLEBUFFER;
    pd.iPixelType = PFD_TYPE_RGBA;
    pd.iLayerType = PFD_MAIN_PLANE;
    pd.cDepthBits = 32;
    pd.cColorBits = 16;

    CDC* pdc = GetDC();
    int nPixelFormat = ChoosePixelFormat( pdc->m_hDC, &pd );
    SetPixelFormat( pdc->m_hDC, nPixelFormat, &pd );

    m_hglrc = wglCreateContext( pdc->m_hDC );
    wglMakeCurrent( pdc->m_hDC, m_hglrc );
    ReleaseDC( pdc );

    SetTimer( 0, 100, NULL );
    return 0;
}

void COglView::OnSize(UINT nType, int cx, int cy)
{
    CView::OnSize(nType, cx, cy);
    GLsizei glnWidth = cx;
    GLsizei glnHeight = cy;
```

continues

Listing 33.7. continued

```
    GLdouble gldAspect = (GLdouble)glnWidth/(GLdouble) glnHeight;

    glMatrixMode( GL_PROJECTION );
    glLoadIdentity();
    gluPerspective( 30.0,
                    gldAspect,
                    1.0,
                    15.0 );
    glViewport( 0, 0, glnWidth, glnHeight );
}

void COglView::Wobble( const GLdouble& gldRadius,
                       const GLdouble& gldLatitude,
                       const GLdouble& gldLongitude )
{
    glTranslated( 0.0, 0.0, gldRadius );
    glRotated( 0.0, 0.0, 0.0, 1.0 );
    glRotated( -gldLatitude, 1.0, 0.0, 0.0 );
    glRotated( gldLongitude, 0.0, 0.0, 1.0 );
}

void COglView::OnTimer(UINT nIDEvent)
{
    Invalidate(FALSE);
}

void COglView::DrawCube()
{
    // Draw a cube, describing all six sides as polygons:
    // Use red, blue, green, yellow, white, and gray sides.
    GLdouble vdRed[]    = { 1.0, 0.0, 0.0 };
    GLdouble vdBlue[]   = { 0.0, 0.0, 1.0 };
    GLdouble vdGreen[]  = { 0.0, 1.0, 0.0 };
    GLdouble vdYellow[] = { 1.0, 1.0, 0.0 };
    GLdouble vdWhite[]  = { 1.0, 1.0, 1.0 };
    GLdouble vdGray[]   = { 0.66, 0.66, 0.66 };

    // Vectors that describe vertices of the cube,
    // "looking down" at the center of the cube.
    GLdouble vdTopNW[] = { -0.5, 0.5, 0.5 };
    GLdouble vdTopNE[] = {  0.5, 0.5, 0.5 };
    GLdouble vdTopSW[] = { -0.5, 0.5, -0.5 };
    GLdouble vdTopSE[] = {  0.5, 0.5, -0.5 };
    GLdouble vdBotNW[] = { -0.5, -0.5, 0.5 };
    GLdouble vdBotNE[] = {  0.5, -0.5, 0.5 };
    GLdouble vdBotSW[] = { -0.5, -0.5, -0.5 };
    GLdouble vdBotSE[] = {  0.5, -0.5, -0.5 };

    glColor3dv( vdRed );
    glBegin( GL_POLYGON );
        glVertex3dv( vdTopNE );
        glVertex3dv( vdTopNW );
        glVertex3dv( vdBotNW );
        glVertex3dv( vdBotNE );
    glEnd();
```

```
    glColor3dv( vdBlue );
    glBegin( GL_POLYGON );
        glVertex3dv( vdTopSE );
        glVertex3dv( vdTopSW );
        glVertex3dv( vdBotSW );
        glVertex3dv( vdBotSE );
    glEnd();

    glColor3dv( vdGreen );
    glBegin( GL_POLYGON );
        glVertex3dv( vdTopNW );
        glVertex3dv( vdTopSW );
        glVertex3dv( vdBotSW );
        glVertex3dv( vdBotNW );
    glEnd();

    glColor3dv( vdYellow );
    glBegin( GL_POLYGON );
        glVertex3dv( vdTopNE );
        glVertex3dv( vdTopSE );
        glVertex3dv( vdBotSE );
        glVertex3dv( vdBotNE );
    glEnd();

    glColor3dv( vdWhite );
    glBegin( GL_POLYGON );
        glVertex3dv( vdTopNE );
        glVertex3dv( vdTopSE );
        glVertex3dv( vdTopSW );
        glVertex3dv( vdTopNW );
    glEnd();

    glColor3dv( vdGray );
    glBegin( GL_POLYGON );
        glVertex3dv( vdBotNE );
        glVertex3dv( vdBotSE );
        glVertex3dv( vdBotSW );
        glVertex3dv( vdBotNW );
    glEnd();
}

//
// DrawPyramid -
// Draws a four-sided pyramid (and a base) using
// five colors, with each face drawn as a separate
// polygon.
void COglView::DrawPyramid()
{
    glColor3f( 1.0f, 1.0f, 0.0f );
    glBegin( GL_POLYGON );
        glVertex3d( -1.0, 0.0, 0.0 );
        glVertex3d( 0.0, 0.0, -1.0 );
        glVertex3d( 0.0, 1.0, 0.0 );
    glEnd();

    glColor3f( 1.0f, 0.0f, 1.0f );
    glBegin( GL_POLYGON );
```

continues

Listing 33.7. continued

```
        glVertex3d( 0.0, 0.0, -1.0 );
        glVertex3d( 1.0, 0.0, 0.0 );
        glVertex3d( 0.0, 1.0, 0.0 );
    glEnd();

    glColor3f( 1.0f, 0.0f, 0.0f );
    glBegin( GL_POLYGON );
        glVertex3d( 1.0, 0.0, 0.0 );
        glVertex3d( 0.0, 0.0, 1.0 );
        glVertex3d( 0.0, 1.0, 0.0 );
    glEnd();

    glColor3f( 0.0f, 1.0f, 0.0f );
    glBegin( GL_POLYGON );
        glVertex3d( -1.0, 0.0, 0.0 );
        glVertex3d( 0.0, 0.0, 1.0 );
        glVertex3d( 0.0, 1.0, 0.0 );
    glEnd();

    glColor3f( 0.0f, 0.0f, 1.0f );
    glBegin( GL_POLYGON );
        glVertex3d( -1.0, 0.0, 0.0 );
        glVertex3d( 0.0, 0.0, 1.0 );
        glVertex3d( 1.0, 0.0, 0.0 );
        glVertex3d( 0.0, 0.0, -1.0 );
    glEnd();
}
```

Finally, Listing 33.8. shows the changes you need to make to the stdafx.h header file. The two changed lines are shown in bold type.

Listing 33.8. Modifications to the stdafx.h header file, shown in bold type.

```
#define VC_EXTRALEAN

#include <afxwin.h>         // MFC core and standard components
#include <afxext.h>         // MFC extensions
#ifndef _AFX_NO_AFXCMN_SUPPORT
#include <afxcmn.h>
#endif // _AFX_NO_AFXCMN_SUPPORT

#include <gl/gl.h>
#include <gl/glu.h>
```

The Ogl project must be linked with two OpenGL libraries: opengl32.lib and glu32.lib. Open the Project Settings dialog box by selecting Settings from the Build menu. Select the Link tab, and add these two libraries to the project using the Object/library modules edit control.

Compile and run the Ogl project. The main window of the SDI application displays a cube and pyramid, which rotate around the center of the window.

Summary

This chapter focused on the OpenGL library. You learned about the various functions used to create 3D objects using OpenGL. You also learned the steps used to integrate OpenGL functions into your MFC applications.

Cross-Platform Development

IN THIS CHAPTER

Introduction

Developers have dreamed of having one code base which could be deployed on many platforms, creating a larger market for their software. Customers have different platforms in their offices, all of which need access to the same data and in a similar fashion. They want applications that work the same way on the various platforms.

Unfortunately, in the past cross-platform based software just has not been available to the small developer. While it is true that the Windows GUI environment is dominant, it's not the only one. It is, however, the platform on which small developers release first because Windows has such a dominant position.

Nearly all the recent development technologies have focused on moving information between environments. The desire to share information is the basis for OLE, ODBC, MAPI, and now Visual C++.

There are several cross development tools on the market today. Most of these are proprietary APIs under which you develop the entire application, then build on the target platform. These tools assume you are starting a new cross-platform project. The latest tools use your existing Visual C++ and MFC-based code and enable true Windows cross development. In the UNIX Motif world there is Bristol Technologies Wind/U, which ports MFC applications. On the Macintosh, Microsoft supplies a cross-development tool which integrates into Visual C++.

While this chapter addresses Macintosh cross development, the process of using Wind/U to move to a UNIX Motif platform is very similar. These two tools enable the porting of existing products and also perform parallel cross development. Versions of Visual C++ and MFC are available for Windows NT on PowerPC, DEC Alpha, and MIPS platforms, which are included on the distribution CD with the Intel platform. On each of these machines, the Windows source code is recompiled under NT and Visual C++ to give a true native application.

Visual C++ is the standard development environment for Windows NT, regardless of what level developer you are. Using Visual C++ and MFC enables you to focus on writing 32-bit Windows NT software while enabling you to move to other platforms. By doing parallel development, you build and test code on all target platforms throughout the writing process.

This chapter focuses on cross-development for the Macintosh. Macintosh users want applications written that have the look and feel of Macintosh applications. Visual C++ does most of this, but there are several user interface issues that must be brought into the design and coding of the application. Sometimes functionality is not available on both platforms. This chapter presents a checklist of topics that need to be addressed in your cross-development project. By using this checklist to design your application for cross development, you can save steps and time.

Most of the work gets done for you by AppWizard and the MFC libraries. Compare Figure 34.1 and Figure 34.2. Both show the common dialog for printing and were generated by the same AppWizard-generated code. Notice the screen similarities and differences.

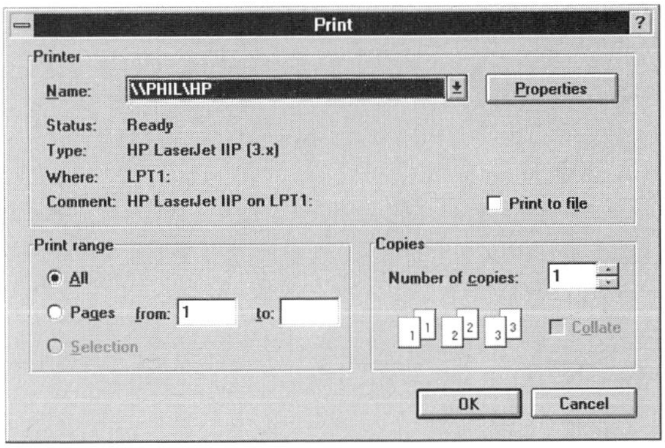

FIGURE 34.1.

AppWizard Windows application common dialog menu.

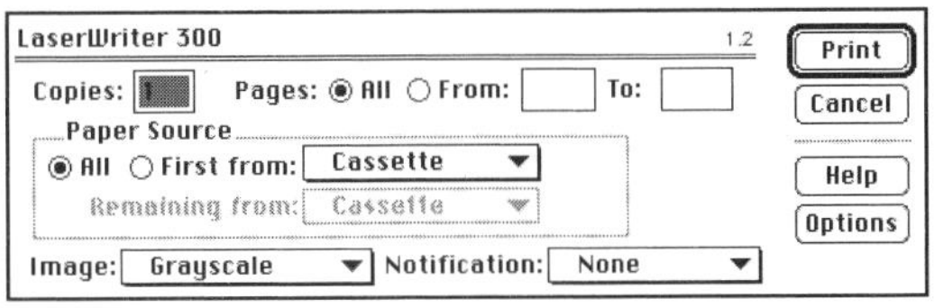

FIGURE 34.2.

AppWizard Macintosh application common dialog menu.

NT Macintosh Services

Macintosh clients on an NT network communicate with AppleTalk protocols built into every Macintosh computer. The network adapters can be LocalTalk, Ethernet, Token Ring, or FDDI. Windows NT server emulates an AppleShare server. The client software is downloaded when the Macintosh first logs into the NT server as a Guest user. This provides file sharing, printer sharing, administration, and routing support.

NT Services for Macintosh gives the Macintosh user access to printers in the NT server's domain. The PostScript-compatible printing engine enables any printer on the NT network to act as if it were a LaserWriter to the Macintosh. The Macintosh user gets print spooling from the NT server. The NT user can print to the Macintosh printer as another network laser printer.

To the Macintosh user, the NT file server looks like an AppleShare server. The server manages filenames, icons, and access permissions. NT server provides multistream file access, both resource and data forks, and 31 character long filenames. Macintosh users have access to PC-compatible CD-ROM drives attached to the NT server. However, Macintosh-compatible CDs cannot be read by NT Windows users because they are in a different format.

AppleTalk

AppleTalk is implemented as part of the Macintosh operating system. Macintosh users have a familiar graphical user interface to access network services. The usual physical connection is via LocalTalk connectors and RS-449/RS-422 connectors using telephone-type wiring (STP wiring). LocalTalk can operate up to 230Kbps and up to 300 meters distant, much slower than the 10 or 100Mbps Ethernet connections common in the NT environment. On an NT Server network, you will probably be using Ethernet cards, and you will need to add one to the Macintosh.

Data Link Layer

AppleTalk Address Resolution Protocol (AARP) is modeled after TCP/IP's ARP protocol with binding between OSI's upper layer network addresses and the data link layer addresses. AARP uses a simple address, 1 to 254, much easier to handle than the common 123.123.123.123 IP address. AARP makes it possible to use different data link technologies which Apple calls EtherTalk, TokenTalk, FDDITalk, as well as the Macintosh standard AppleTalk. A data link address is required to send a frame over the physical link. In the usual mode AARP knows the data link layer address of the destination. All nodes on the network receive the broadcast, but only the machine with the same address responds. These addresses are kept in an Address Mapping Table (AMT).

Dynamic address selection is also available. When a Macintosh boots, AARP sends a broadcast. If it receives a reply it knows that address is taken. It picks another address until no reply is received. This is the LocalTalk default stepping from 1 to 127 for user requests and from 128 to 254 for server requests.

The packet is defined as

> 2 bytes for hardware type
>
> 2 bytes for protocol type
>
> 1 byte for hardware address length
>
> 1 byte for protocol address length
>
> 2 bytes for function code, where 1 = AARP request, 2 = reply, 3 = probe for dynamic address selection

This information is followed by a source hardware address, source protocol address, destination hardware address, and destination protocol address.

AppleTalk Network Layer

The network layer uses sockets similar to IPX and TCP/IP sockets. AppleTalk calls these Datagram Delivery Protocol or (DDP). A DDP socket is a simple packet structure:

> 6 bits of 000000
>
> 10 bits length
>
> 8 bits destination socket
>
> 8 bits source socket
>
> 8 bits of type (which is the upper layer process the data is being sent to)
>
> 586 bytes of data

The network layer also defines Name Binding Protocol (NBP), which is similar to the DNS name on TCP/IP networks. This is a binding between the address and the more easy-to-use symbolic name called the Network Visible Entries (NVE).

AppleTalk sets up zones as a collection of nodes. This process is similar to NT Server's workgroups but without the associated security issues. When the Macintosh boots, it polls its Zone Information Table (ZIT) to determine what zone it belongs in. The ZIT is maintained on the router.

AppleTalk Transport Layer

The transport layer is broken into a transaction protocol (ATP) and a data stream protocol (ADSP). An ATP transaction is a request and response between the client and the server machine. In ATP each transaction is numbered, which enables the client to determine that it gets the correct response to its request.

The ADSP protocol is full duplex flow between two sockets, similar to TCP, with a maximum stream size of 64K. ADSP uses two types of packets, control and data.

AppleTalk Session Layer Protocol

This layer provides session protocols and printer access protocols. The AppleTalk Session protocol (ASP) uses the concept of transactions—a series of commands are sent from the client to the server and executed.

The Printer Access Protocol (PAP) creates, maintains, and disconnects connections to remote printers. PAP polls the Name Binding Protocol (NBP) from the network layer to map addresses from the server to printer settings on the client.

AppleTalk Application Layer

AppleTalk does not have the OSI presentation layer. The AppleTalk Filing Protocol (AFP) is defined in the application layer to locate files across the network or locally on the client. AFP defines the write, read, and search access controls as well as usernames, passwords, and directory access controls. AppleTalk Print Services (APS) communicates with the PAP layer to give the application printer access.

Installing the AppleTalk Network Protocol

Prior to NT 4.0, Macintosh services were only available on NT Advanced Server. You still need NT Advanced Server to set up a volume on which to store Macintosh files and to share printers. However, NT 4.0 Workstation allows you to connect to the Macintosh via AppleTalk or TCP/IP as well as serial.

1. Log on the NT server as Administrator.
2. In the Control Panel, select the network applet, go to the Protocols tab and select Add.
3. Select AppleTalk and enter the path to your distribution files. Continue copies the necessary files and sets up the Registry entries. It then rebinds the network and asks you to restart your computer.
4. Return to the network applet and the AppleTalk protocol and choose Configure as in Figure 34.3. NT detects the network connection and zones you have available from the Macintosh and displays a list. Zones are the Macintosh equivalent of workgroups.

FIGURE 34.3.

Setup of AppleTalk on NT Workstation.

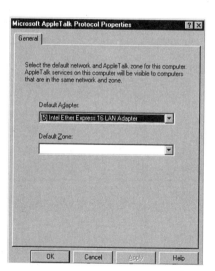

Visual C++ for Mac68K and PowerPC

Visual C++ for the Macintosh was released with Visual C++ 2.0 in 1994. Microsoft is a major supplier of Macintosh software, and many of its applications are nearly identical on PC and Macintosh platforms. Conspiracy Theory people have long believed that Microsoft, like the military, may have cool new toys that they haven't told us about yet. The first major revision of the Macintosh environment was in Visual C++ 4.0, which takes this cross-development extension from a little known add-on to a major component of Visual C++. Microsoft claims 90% of your MFC application will port with no changes.

Nearly all the features of Visual C++ 4.0 are available to the Macintosh developer. The total Win32 API is replaced with WLM.LIB. Macintosh-specific functionality is provided by a Macintosh extensions API. Although applications written using the Win32 API need moderate modification, 32-bit applications written with MFC should, in most cases, build on the Macintosh with only a few changes. Approximately 90 percent of the Win32 APIs have a Macintosh WLM equivalent. This chapter focuses on the MFC wrappers to those functions.

In general, MFC applications run faster than Win32 API applications when ported, but are almost twice as large. In general, Macintosh executables are five to seven times larger than their PC counterparts due to static linking of the Windows Portability Library. If you are targeting 680x0 Macintosh, MFC is available only as a static library. Power Macintosh projects use MFC in a shared DLL, MFC40.DLL.

The setup requires a Windows NT or Windows 95 machine running VC++ 4.x and a Macintosh running System 7+ with at least 5MB of RAM. The connection is either via serial cable, AppleTalk, or TCP/IP. VC++ 4.x cross development for the Macintosh supports 68K, PowerPC, and "Fat Mac" applications. Fat Mac applications are a merger of 68K and PowerPC applications that can be run on either machine. Code can be optimized for 68020, 68030, 68040, and the PowerPC Macintosh.

Although you can connect via serial cable, the process of copying data to the Macintosh and debugging the application by this method is so slow that this is not recommended. If you do go this route, use a null modem cable, which in the Mac world is called a printer cable.

In Visual C++ 4.x the target platform is switched from Intel Debug or Retail to the desired Macintosh platform and a complete rebuild is performed. If you are building an AppWizard MFC application, Visual C++ provides a Macintosh resource file ending in .R. If this is an existing application, you need to add a resource file to the project with a name slightly different than the Intel .RC file. I reuse a file called Mac.R built from a "do nothing" AppWizard application. In the initial builds of your Macintosh application this will suffice. Later, as the application is performance tuned, certain settings in this resource file, such as the minimum and preferred memory sizes, will be changed.

When you install Visual C++ on the Macintosh, you will notice that it copies Visual C++ Debug Monitor into your Control Panel folder and copies both the Debug Output and File Utilities applications into the Macintosh Startup Folder. Rebooting the Macintosh runs the software and lets you set the communication parameters for the PC and Macintosh.

Figure 34.4 and Figure 34.5 show the steps in setting up the communications.

FIGURE 34.4.

*Communications settings in
Visual C++ on NT.*

FIGURE 34.5.

*Communication setting on
the Macintosh.*

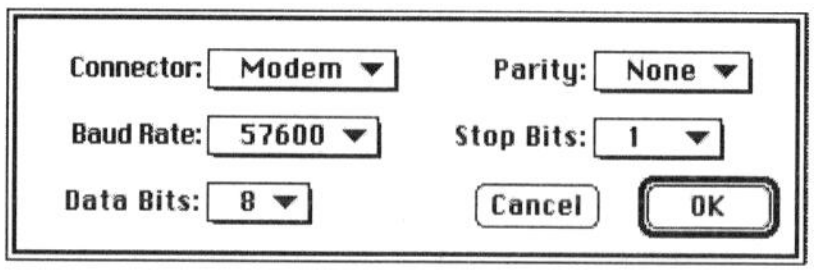

If you need to make changes, the following is what gets installed:

        Power Macintosh Install:
          extension folder:
          Visual C++ Power Mac File Utility
          Visual C++ Power Mac Serial Transport
          Visual C++ Power Mac TCP/IP Transport
          Visual C++ Power Mac ADSP Transport
         Startup
          (alias or application)
          Power Mac DebugServices
          VC++ Power Mac Debug Monitor
        68K Macintosh Install:
          Control Panel Folder:
          VC++ Debug Monitor
         Startup Folder
          (alias or application)
          VC++ File Utility

After the build, Visual C++'s MFILE asks you for the destination computer, folder, and file-name. (This is in the format of the Macintosh HD:folder:file.) The executable file is copied to the Macintosh.

All Visual C++ debugging is available. The PC can launch the Macintosh application. As you exercise the application on the Macintosh, watch windows are available even to the extent that Visual C++ now knows the differences in processor registers.

This cross-development environment has great potential for expanding your software's marketability. An existing 32-bit MFC application can be ported in less than an afternoon, expanding your offerings to a new class of users.

Macintosh versus Windows NT and Windows 95

If you're reading this, you're not a casual computer user or even a beginning C++ programmer. It's a fact—papers like this get buried deep in the documentation where the "faint-of-heart" dare not go. You might even think that experienced developers don't read documentation either. However, most likely you are devoted to one platform and disdain the other. Without delving into religious issues, some basic differences that you need be aware of in cross-platform development are outlined in this section. Simply stated, Macintosh people hate Windows-looking applications running on their Macintosh, period.

The Macintosh was designed with a large ROM, to which most system calls are made. In Windows, system DLLs are dynamically linked in at runtime as needed. The Macintosh traps system calls and supplies the corresponding ROM functionality. In Windows the same functionality is supplied by three dynamically linked libraries on the hard disk. The Windows KERNEL32.DLL corresponds to the Macintosh Operating System, the Windows GDI32.DLL to Macintosh QuickDraw, and Windows USER32.DLL to the Macintosh User Interface Toolbox.

Visually, Macintosh applications do not look like Windows applications. VC++ 4.0's cross-development environment does a good job of smoothing out the differences. VC++ will handle adjusting menus, adding the Macintosh Finder Apple on the left and changing the look of dialog boxes to be dialog windows on the Macintosh. Some things visually work better than others. Many Windows programs use the MDI interface with a frame containing a cascade of document windows. On the Macintosh the frame is gone, usually leaving the collage (shown in Figure 34.6) of seemingly unrelated document windows. Fortunately, this is the exception. In most cases, the MFC cross builds Macintosh-looking Macintosh applications.

Both the PC and the Macintosh are 32-bit machines. While the Macintosh uses cooperative type multitasking, the PC uses preemptive multitasking. Both Windows 95 and Windows NT are multithreaded. Because the Macintosh is not, this is the first area where you may need to modify your PC-based source code. NT also supports SMP (multiprocessors) and if you are the one developer on the planet who has force implemented this in your application, you will be the only one who needs to refine your code. Most programmers assume that the process object manager can handle SMP when and if they ever get a chance at a multiprocessor computer. On the Macintosh only one instance of a program can be running. DLLs (dynamically linked libraries) are commonplace in the PC world and now on the PowerPC, but you will build statically linked Macintosh 680x0 apps. This issue is readdressed at the end of this chapter.

FIGURE 34.6.

Document window cascade on the Macintosh.

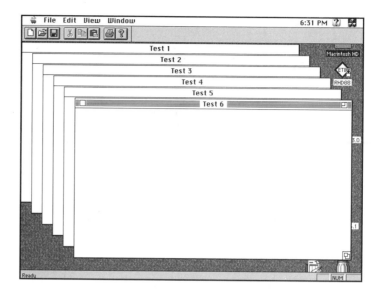

Lastly, there are file I/O and network component issues based on byte ordering and word size issues. The PC uses little-Endian encoding (least significant byte first) while the Macintosh is big-Endian (most significant byte first). This issue may require a good deal of platform-specific code if you've done extensive bit flipping. In fact, you should make few assumptions about data type sizes. All programmers just went through the 16- to 32-bit conversions, and now we will have to face the DEC Alpha with 64 bits (although NT for Alpha runs in 32-bit mode at this time). The big differences will be in the CDC classes (drawing, printing, and painting). If you look through the documentation you will notice that of the 86 MFC functions which don't port, 49 are CDC class functions. These unsupported MFC functions are listed in the Books-on-Line.

Other significant areas where you may need to write platform-specific code include communications, synchronization objects, exception handling, asynchronous I/O, metafiles, named pipes, and multimedia services. OpenGl, WinSockets, RPC, mailslots, and Unicode simply don't exist in the Macintosh world and these features would require considerable rewriting. If you have used the Clipboard extensively, and DDE, this area will probably need some hard coding because the Macintosh Clipboard uses only 4-character resource names. If you just use copy and paste, the application cross compiles fine, because Visual C++ handles these. It should be obvious that inline assembler stuff won't port. It should be more obvious that direct calls to DOS, like int24 calls, won't port. Windows uses 256 Binary Raster Ops, compared to the Macintosh's 16. The Macintosh supports exactly one printer per machine, and there is no concept of Landscape/Portrait printing.

On the plus side, both ODBC and OLE have been implemented on the Macintosh and these features should port without significant code changes. The exception is that OLE in-place activation is still in an early stage of development due to significant differences between DDE (PC Dynamic Data Exchange) and PPC (Macintosh Program-to-Program Communications).

As sample code snippets are developed in this chapter, differences are pointed out. Compiler directives that enable you to maintain one code base are demonstrated as well. This will usually be in the form of an `#ifdef _MAC`. You should always strive to keep one source code base for both platforms.

Windows

Most aspects of a window are similar on both systems. Both have vertical and horizontal scroll bars, which act similarly. On the Macintosh these belong to the content area (client area), not to the window frame as on the PC. The Macintosh has one zoom button in the upper-right corner which functions like the Windows maximize and minimize buttons. On the Macintosh, the size box in the lower-right corner (as shown in Figure 34.7) sizes the window in both dimensions, giving it a constant aspect ratio, while in Windows the sizing borders can make the window have a highly variable aspect ratio. If your Windows application has used the lower-right corner for a control, this may need to be moved. The size box is added by the Visual C++ cross compiler to windows with either `WS_HSCROLL` or `WS_VSCROLL` and the `WS_THICKFRAME` style bit set.

FIGURE 34.7.

Some common MFC controls on the Macintosh.

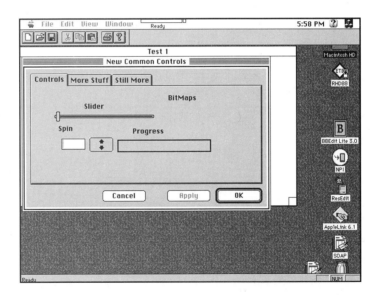

A Macintosh window doesn't have its own menu, just a title bar and close box. Any child window with the `WS_CAPTION` bit set is a separate window, separate from the parent.

An MDI frame window on the Macintosh is maximized at all times. If your application starts with several windows open, this will be a problem. You need to force the ordering with `SW_HIDE` (on the background windows) and `WS_EX_NOAUTOHIDE` (on the one you choose as top most). If you must open multiple MDI Child Windows on startup, here's a way to work around it.

In the derived `CMDIFrameWnd` class, `CMainFrame`, which the AppWizard creates, implement `MDIGetActive()` by copying the base class' version and making the following modifications:

```
CMyChild* CMainFrame::MDIGetActive(BOOL* pbMaximized) const
{
...
  HWND hWnd = (HWND)::SendMessage(m_hWndMDIClient, WM_MDIGETACTIVE, 0,
    (LPARAM)pbMaximized);
  if (pbMaximized) *pbMaximized = ::IsZoomed(hWnd); // Added this
...
  return (CMyChild*)pWnd;          // changed this line
```

Then derive a class from `CMDIChildWnd` called `CMyChild`. Override `ActivateFrame()` by copying the base class' version and making the following modifications:

```
void CMyChild::ActivateFrame(int nCmdShow)
{
...
  BOOL bMaximized;
  ((CMainFrame*)pFrameWnd)->MDIGetActive(&bMaximized); // changed this
...
}
```

Note that because `MDIGetActive()` is not virtual, the call to this function must be modified to explicitly call the derived class' version. In MFC, only `CMDIChildWnd::ActiveFrame()` calls this function with the `pbMaximized` flag so other calls to `MDIGetActive()` do not have to be modified.

Lastly, the Macintosh doesn't support minimize windows (iconization). Icons are shortcuts and are not running applications. Where you have used `SW_MINIMIZE`, you get a NO-OP call.

Character Sets

While the Macintosh has always used one standard character set, both NT and Win95 use Unicode, ANSI, and the extended IBM set (IBM OEM set). If you have used Unicode symbols that are 16 bits wide, you need to remap to the Macintosh 8-bit characters. Fonts under Windows are more complex than on the Macintosh. The cross-development environment maps fonts from Windows NT to the Macintosh. This mapping is set by Microsoft as shown in Table 34.1, but you may need to edit this file for your own use.

Table 34.1. Font mappings in FTAB.R.

Windows	*Macintosh*
ARIAL NARROW	N HELVETICA NARROW
AVANTGARDE	AVANT GARDE
ARIAL	HELVETICA
BOOK ANTIQUA	PALATINO

Windows	Macintosh
BOOKMAN OLD STYLE	BOOKMAN
CENTURY GOTHIC	AVANT GARDE
CENTURY SCHOOLBOOK	NEW CENTURY SCHLBK
COURIER NEW	COURIER
DUTCH PS	TIMES
DUTCH SWA	TIMES
HELV	HELVETICA
HELVETICA-NARROW	N HELVETICA NARROW
ITC ZAPF DINGBATS SWA	ZAPF DINGBATS
ITCZAPFDNGBATSWA	ZAPF DINGBATS
MS SANS SERIF	HELVETICA
MS SERIF	TIMES
MT SYMBOL	SYMBOL
MT SYMBOL ITALIC	SYMBOL
MODERN	MONOCO
MONOTYPE CORSIVA	ZAPF CHANCERY
MONOTYPE SORTS	ZAPF DINGBATS
NEWCENTURYSCHLBK	NEW CENTURY SCHLBK
ROMAN	TIMES
SWA DUTCH	TIMES
SWA DUTCH 801	TIMES
SWA ITC ZAPF DINGBATS	ZAPF DINGBATS
SWA SWISS	HELVETICA
SWA SWISS 721	HELVETICA
SWAITCZAPFDINGBAT	ZAPF DINGBATS
SCRIPT	ZAPF CHANCERY
SWISS PS	HELVETICA
SWISS SWA	HELVETICA
TERMINAL	COURIER
TIMES NEW ROMAN	TIMES
TIMES-ROMAN	TIMES
TMS RMN	TIMES

continues

Table 34.1. continued

Windows	Macintosh
ZAPFCHANCERY	ZAPF CHANCERY
ZAPFDINGBATS	ZAPF DINGBATS

FTAB.R also defines the Macintosh to Windows conversions when using existing Macintosh resource code.

Menus

The Macintosh uses an event model that doesn't translate literally to the Windows message loops. Each window on the PC can have its own menu bar, but the Macintosh has only one global menu bar at the top of the screen. The Macintosh does not support MF_OWNERDRAW or MF_BITMAP styles on the menu bar, so the cute little icon menus are out. The Macintosh menu bar is a separate resource from its submenus, but on the PC a Windows menu bar and the submenus are just one resource. A Macintosh menu bar simply lists submenu titles (every top-level menu must be MF_POPUP), whereas a Windows menu bar can have commands and submenus intermixed. Macintosh menus do not wrap, so keep them short. Windows has the system menu in the upper-left corner, but the Macintosh has the Apple with the desk accessories and frequently used item lists, as shown in Figure 34.8. Most importantly, when a Macintosh user clicks on a menu item, they must hold the mouse button and drag onto the submenu. When a Windows user clicks on a menu item, the submenu stays on the screen until an item is selected or until a second mouse click is made outside the submenu. In Windows, pushing the Alt key puts the keyboard into "Menu mode" where the arrow keys can be used to navigate the menu structure. In spite of the above, the cross compiler does a good job of making the application look Macintosh, even replacing EXIT with QUIT!

Keyboard

In general, Windows applications use keyboard mnemonics that are defined so that Alt plus a key moves rapidly to a menu choice. It is expected that a Windows application can be navigated without a mouse. The mouse takes precedence on the Macintosh. Macintosh menus generally do not use separator bars to group menu choices. In Windows, accelerators are also defined for commonly used commands, i.e. Ctrl+C for Copy and Ctrl+X for Cut. The Macintosh uses the Command key (the clover looking thing) for the Control key. For the Copy key you need to designate this yourself in your submenu by substituting Copy\t\021C for Ctrl+C.

FIGURE 34.8.

*The Apple Menu with our
About at the top.*

Figure 34.9 shows the default Edit menu on the Macintosh, with these changes made by AppWizard. While the Macintosh has defined several standard accelerators or Command key options, they generally are not defined in the Menu resource. Keyboard commands on the Macintosh are global to the entire program, while in Windows, keyboard commands are directed specifically to the window with the input focus. The Macintosh keyboard does not autorepeat. Windows users expect F1 to be mapped to "help," while on the Macintosh the default behavior of F1 is Undo. In fact, many Macintosh keyboards do not have a row of functions keys, so mapping them to integral functions in your application is not desired. Also, you cannot rely on standard Windows key sequences like Alt+Esc and Alt+Tab to switch applications.

FIGURE 34.9.

*Macintosh Edit options
with Command
Accelerator.*

Macintosh software does not have a system menu. It does have the Apple menu. When you build your Visual C++ Macintosh application through AppWizard, you see About has moved to the Apple menu. This is accomplished by changing the command ID to SC_DESKACCESSORY. Visual C++ provides an API, GetSystemMenu, for modifying the Apple Menu.

Mouse

All Macintosh users have a single button mouse. Windows users many not even have a mouse, or the mouse may have one, two, or three buttons. The Windows standard use of the right mouse button is to bring up a pop-up menu of the most common actions. If the Windows application has made extensive use of right button clicks, they have to be remapped on the

Macintosh. The default behavior is Shift+Click. The Macintosh cursor is always 16 × 16 pixels wide, and the Macintosh does not support colored cursors. The Windows cursor can vary in size and may even be an animation.

Files

File system differences between the Macintosh and Windows environments cause cross development issues for every application. Creator types, file types, and directory IDs do not exist in Windows. Each file on the Macintosh includes them, as seen in Figure 34.10, the Apple Get Info box. Windows pathnames do not translate to the Macintosh. Visual C++ handles some differences in the common dialogs, but you need to handle the others within your code.

FIGURE 34.10.

*Get Info Box on Macintosh
with file Kind, Size,
Creator, and Version.*

Users of cross-development applications expect that the data created on one platform can be read by the other. But, as stated earlier, the Macintosh assumes big-endian ordering and NT assumes little-endian. The PowerPC and MIPS CPUs allow byte ordering to be specified by the operating system. You just can't assume. You can let MFC do most of the work, however, by passing a CArchive object as the argument to serialize in a class derived from a CObject. Most classes derived from CObject are able to handle the cross-platform issues of byte ordering. You normally use a CFile object to read and write to a disk file. Your AppWizard-generated code did this as shown in the following example:

```
void CTestDoc::Serialize(CArchive& ar)
{
if (ar.IsStoring())
{
ar << m_Doc;
}
else
{
ar >> m_Doc;
}
}
```

An object should know how to write out its current state and read that state back in. This is the concept of serialization. In MFC, by adding the macros DECLARE_SERIAL and IMPLEMENT_SERIAL to your CObject class, it becomes serializable. You also need to implement the serialize member function as

```
virtual void Serialize(CArchive& ar);
```

CArchive objects use the insertion operator (<<) and extraction operator (>>) to move the object's state to and from the file. If you have memory allocated for an object, you would call the Serialize member function instead, as

```
void CMyDoc::Serialize(Carchive& ar)
{
m_myList.Serialize(ar);
}
```

The byte ordering is handled in the cross-development file ARCCORE.CPP. In ARCCORE.CPP, CArchive handles the simple value types as well as CPoint, CRect, CSize, CString, CByteArray, CObArray, CStringArray, CObList, CStringList, CTime, and CTimeSpan. A good idea is to examine the ARCCORE.CPP code. It demonstrates how operator << and operator >> are overloaded for each data type and shows you the actual code that swaps the bytes.

The other issue to address is pathnames. The Windows DOS pathname of C:\directory\ subdirectory\file.txt becomes Macintosh HD:folder:subfolder:file. The easiest way to address this difference is to let MFC handle the translation, saving you parsing or examining it as in this code snippet from the Scribble tutorial.

```
CString strPageTitle = GetDocument()->GetTitle();
...
pDc->TextOut(pInfo->m_rectDraw.right/s,-100,strPageTitle);
```

MFC translates the path in the GetTitle member function. If you need to do more, use MFC GetOpenFileName() and GetSaveFileName along with the Cross Development File API's function GetFullPathName.

Apple has a function FXMakeFSSpec documented in their *Inside Macintosh* series. This uses LMSetCurDirStore to set the Macintosh global CurDirStore to parID. If the file exists, it returns noErr, and if not, it returns fnfErr.

```
#include "macname1.h"
#include "files.h"
#include "lowmem.h"
#include "error.h"
#include "macname2.h"
{
  FSSpec spec;
  OSErr err;
  err = FSMakeFSSpec(0,0,"\pMacintosh HD:Folder:filename",&psec);
  if(err == noErr || err == fnfErr)
    LMSetCurDirStore(spec.parID);
  if (GetOpenFileNmae(&OpenFileName))
  //do your stuff
}
```

Bitmaps and DIBs

The first issue to address in graphic applications is the Macintosh's ability to change screen depth while an application is running.

When you copy a DIB to the screen on a Macintosh, the color table must be converted and the DIB reoriented. If you do this repeatedly, it slows your application. To speed this process, copy the DIB to a memory DC and then copy the DC to the screen instead of the DIB.

Before a Windows DIB file can be read or saved on the Macintosh, it must be in big-endian format. Microsoft supplies a good sample program, DIBLOOK, with the cross-development software which illustrates the differences. It handles the DIB format as

```
//source code from Microsoft DIBLOOK sample

#ifdef _MAC
#define SWAPWORD(x) MAKEWORD(HIBYTE(x), LOBYTE(x))
#define SWAPLONG(x) MAKELONG(SWAPWORD(HIWORD(x)),SWAPWORD(LOWORD(x)))
void ByteSwapHeader(BITMAPFILEHEADER* bmiHeader);
void ByteSwapInfo(LPSTR lpHeader, BOOL fWin30Header);
#endif

#ifdef _MAC
void ByteSwapHeader(BITMAPFILEHEADER* bmfHeader)
{
  bmfHeader->bfType = SWAPWORD(bmfHeader->bfType);
  bmfHeader->bfSize = SWAPLONG(bmfHeader->bfSize);
  bmfHeader->bfOffBits = SWAPLONG(bmfHeader->bfOffBits);
}


void ByteSwapInfo(LPSTR lpHeader, BOOL fWin30Header)
{
if (fWin30Header)
{
  LPBITMAPINFOHEADER lpBMIH = &(LPBITMAPINFO(lpHeader)->bmiHeader);

  //lpBMIH->biSize = SWAPLONG(lpBMIH->biSize);
  lpBMIH->biWidth = SWAPLONG(lpBMIH->biWidth);
  lpBMIH->biHeight = SWAPLONG(lpBMIH->biHeight);
  lpBMIH->biPlanes = SWAPWORD(lpBMIH->biPlanes);
  lpBMIH->biBitCount = SWAPWORD(lpBMIH->biBitCount);
  lpBMIH->biCompression = SWAPLONG(lpBMIH->biCompression);
  lpBMIH->biSizeImage = SWAPLONG(lpBMIH->biSizeImage);
  lpBMIH->biXPelsPerMeter = SWAPLONG(lpBMIH->biXPelsPerMeter);
  lpBMIH->biYPelsPerMeter = SWAPLONG(lpBMIH->biYPelsPerMeter);
  lpBMIH->biClrUsed = SWAPLONG(lpBMIH->biClrUsed);
  lpBMIH->biClrImportant = SWAPLONG(lpBMIH->biClrImportant);
}
else
{
  LPBITMAPCOREHEADER lpBMCH = &(LPBITMAPCOREINFO(lpHeader)->bmciHeader);

  lpBMCH->bcWidth = SWAPWORD(lpBMCH->bcWidth);
  lpBMCH->bcHeight = SWAPWORD(lpBMCH->bcHeight);
```

```
  lpBMCH->bcPlanes = SWAPWORD(lpBMCH->bcPlanes);
  lpBMCH->bcBitCount = SWAPWORD(lpBMCH->bcBitCount);
}
}

#endif
```

Dialogs

Visual C++ is a big help with dialogs because most of the user interface differences have to do with how dialog boxes present their controls. In Windows NT development you need to ensure that every control can be accessed via the keyboard. No mouse is assumed. The tab order (WM_NEXTDLGCTL) proceeds through the edit controls to the button controls. This is not the default behavior on the Macintosh.

Macintosh users expect the tab order to jump between edit boxes only, never to a button control. Visual C++ makes this change for you. Macintosh users expect one button to be the default (hit Enter) action, and that button is surrounded by a thick border. Visual C++ automatically makes the OK button the default and draws the border. Macintosh users expect list boxes to get a thick border when they are selected, as Figure 34.11 shows. Visual C++ gives you this as well. Macintosh users expect combo boxes to be blank before they have focus, and Windows C++ automatically adds the ES_HIDESEL style for you. On the Macintosh, combo boxes are a white rectangle with a down-pointing arrow and shadow. All of the above can be accomplished without creating a second Macintosh dialog resource.

FIGURE 34.11.

Macintosh dialog box with thick borders for control with focus and default button.

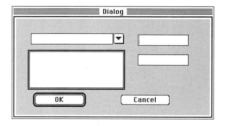

When you have certain features you want in the Macintosh resource, the process of making a Macintosh-specific resource is simple. Open the .RC file, make a copy of the PC resource, and rename it IDD_MYDIALOG$(_MAC). A shortcut is available: Use the right mouse button, choose Properties, and add _MAC to the Condition field. The $(_MAC) automatically does the same action as adding the code

```
#ifdef _MAC
do this
#else
do this
#endif
```

In fact, using `#ifdef _MAC` in the .RC file is discouraged. The resource compiler accepts the directives, but Visual C++ strips them out when you edit. Notice that when you build the application using AppWizard, Visual C++ actually creates double sets of Menu resources in this fashion. AppWizard did this when it created the Macintosh menu in Figure 34.12. You can also force the Macintosh application to have the behavior of the PC dialog box by adding the `DS_WINDOWSUI` style to the STYLE section of your .RC file. Although it may be desirable to have a consistent user interface across platforms, Macintosh users expect their applications not to act like Windows applications, and this may not be a wise bit of code to add.

FIGURE 34.12.

Both Windows and Macintosh Menu resources.

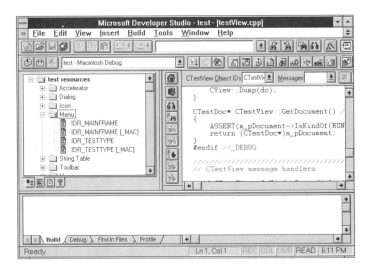

The Clipboard

The Macintosh clipboard is geared to the frontmost application. When your application is in the background, changes to the clipboard by other applications do not show up in your clipboard viewer until you move your application to the foreground. You may have done some automated processing, and this may need to be changed.

Macintosh clipboard format names are only four characters long. PICT format includes, bitmap, DIB, and palette as well as Metafilepict. The others are TEXT and RTF. You need to make these changes as

```
#ifdef _MAC
  cb = RegisterClipBoardFormat("RTF "); \\note spacing
#else
  cb = RegisterClipBoardFormat("RichTextFormat");
#endif
```

What's on the VC++ 4.0 for Macintosh CD?

The C/C++ LINKER and Resource Compiler in their Macintosh versions all have switch settings to generate COFF format object files, link in Macintosh-specific APIs, and build Macintosh-specific executable code. MRC is a PC implementation of the Macintosh REZ resource compiler.

On the PC, other utilities include MPROF, a source code profiler used to optimize the Macintosh code. MFILE is the file transfer utility to move the application to the Macintosh, and C++ File Utility is the Macintosh counterpart that talks to the PC. The C++ Debug Monitor handles the messaging between the Macintosh and Debug running within the PC's VC++ 4.0. Swapper is the Macintosh code swapping library. MacHelp is a Macintosh version of Microsoft help. Other software provided on the PC side include MPW2LIB, to covert OBJ files to COFF format, HC35, the Mac help file compiler, and VCPort_, a very handy profiler for identifying portions of your source code which may need to be touch specific or are platform specific.

These utilities are so important to your success that they need closer examination.

VCPORT

As long as you do *not* read the file VCPORT.WRI, installation and use of VCPORT is straight-forward.

NOTE

VCPORT is in an unusual location on the Visual C++ 4.0 CD-ROM, in the directory MSDEV\SAMPLES\MAC\UTILITY\VCPORT\. Finding it is the hardest part of its use. Copy the files from this directory to your MSDEV\BIN directory.

In VC++ 4.0, go to Tools, Customize, Add, and fill in the Property Page by putting VCPORT in Menu, c:\msdev\bin\VCPort.exe in Command, $(FilePath) /g in Arguments, and c:\nsdev\bin in Initial Directory. If you choose instead to use Microsoft's instructions, you are on your own, lost. The file VCPWIN.KWD lists the functions and their portability level. It's a good resource file.

From this point on the process is straightforward. After you choose a source file in the VC++ 4.0 IDE, choose VCPORT from the tools, and you will get

```
P:\SOAP95\Splash.cpp(58) : GetSystemMetrics: Modified Implementation

P:\SOAP95\Splash.cpp(91) : UpdateWindow: Portable Implementation

P:\SOAP95\Splash.cpp(87) : WS_VISIBLE: Portable Implementation
```

```
P:\SOAP95\Splash.cpp(266) : Catch: Not Implemented

P:\SOAP95\Splash.cpp(300) : Catch: Not Implemented

P:\SOAP95\Splash.cpp(367) : EnableWindow: Portable Implementation
```

The Modified Implementation messages need your attention. These are usually ported but function in a slightly different fashion on the Macintosh. Not Implemented means not implemented. For example, the macro "Catch" is part of an exception handling routine, and the Macintosh doesn't have structured exception handling.

There is one more important piece of information about VCPORT: In real life you will use it from the command line as VCPORT *.cpp > prn.

MRC

From the IDE you don't even see the Mac Resource Compiler do its work. When you installed the Macintosh VC++ 4.0 software, it installed a different version of RC, which takes the switch /M and outputs .RSC files instead of the .RES you're used to. In this process, the Windows resources are converted to Macintosh resources. This .RSC file is the input for MRC.

MRC implements all the functions of the Apple's Macintosh Programmer's Workshop (MPW) REZ resource compiler, except for the $$Packedsize function. This includes the preprocessor functions like #include, #define, #undef, #if, #else, and #endif. It also includes resource - specific statements declaring resources as data, changing resource IDs, and defining resource types.

The REZ language is documented in the Apple MPW documentation. The only step that the MFC programmer will usually come into contact with is setting the Macintosh memory requirements minimum and preferred sizes. If you take an existing MFC application and cross compile to the Macintosh, you will notice that you have the PC resource (.RC) file but do not have the Macintosh (.R) file. The application takes forever and a day to load on the Macintosh and runs very slowly. As a temporary fix you can edit the memory requirements on the Macintosh using the Get Info under File, as shown in Figure 34.13.

FIGURE 34.13.

Changing Size resources after the build.

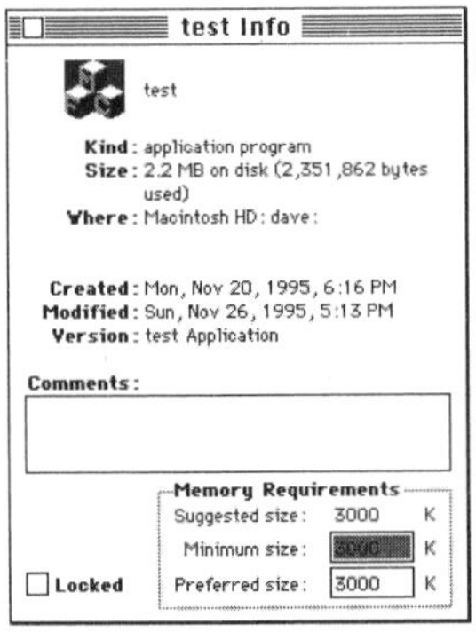

The permanent fix involves copying a Macintosh resource file into your project. You can build an AppWizard project and use this .R file as a template for projects. The file is quite small. Where you see the word "TEST," insert your app name.

```
//Mac.r: Macintosh-specific resources

#include "types.r"
#include "ftab.r"
#include "CodeFrag.r"

resource 'SIZE' (-1)
{
    reserved,
    acceptSuspendResumeEvents,
    reserved,
    canBackground,
    doesActivateOnFGSwitch,
    backgroundAndForeground,
    dontGetFrontClicks,
    ignoreAppDiedEvents,
    is32BitCompatible,
    isHighLevelEventAware,
    localAndRemoteHLEvents,
    isStationeryAware,
    useTextEditServices,
    reserved,
    reserved,
    reserved,

// Set different memory requirment sizes depending on whether we're compiling for
//   PowerMacintosh or 68K

#ifdef _MPPC_

    2500 * 1024,      //rule of thumb is size of executable plus 1 meg for data ..
this is preferred size
2500 * 1024      // this is required size

#else //!_MPPC_

#ifdef _DEBUG
3000 * 1024,  //large sizes if debug build
3000 * 1024
#else
2000 * 1024,
2000 * 1024
#endif //DEBUG

#endif //_MPPC

};

resource 'BNDL' (128, purgeable)  // test bundle resource ID
{
  'TEST',    // test signature
  0,  // resource ID of signature resource: // should be 0
  {
```

```
    'ICN#', // mapping local IDs in 'FREF's to 'ICN#' IDs
      {
      0, 128,
      1, 129
      },
    'FREF',  // local resource IDs for 'FREF's
      {
      0, 128,
      1, 129
      }
    }
};

resource 'FREF' (128, purgeable)  // test application
{
  'APPL', 0,
  ""
};

resource 'FREF' (129, purgeable)  // test document
{
'TEST', 1,
""
};

type "TEST' as 'STR ';

resource 'TEST' (0, purgeable)
{
  "TEST Application"
};

#ifdef _MPPC_

resource 'cfrg' (0)
{
  {
  kPowerPC,
  kFullLib,
  kNoVersionNum,
  kNoVersionNum,
  kDefaultStackSize,
  kNoAppSubFolder,
  kIsApp,
  kOnDiskFlat,
  kZeroOffset,
  kWholeFork,
  "TEST"
  }
};

#endif //_MPPC_
```

The includes are standard Apple REZ files for resource type mapping and font mapping. The BNDL resource defines the bundle of the icon and signature. A helpful note is to make sure the .RC file and the .R file have different first names. If not, the output files get overwritten, and you will have a tough time finding the reason.

MPROF

MPROF is the Macintosh application profiler used to optimize the Macintosh code and identify bottlenecks. To be more exact, MPROF is a report writer that formats the data from your profile builds. Remember Macintosh Word 6.0? It gave the cross compiler a bad rap. Microsoft found out that where they thought bottlenecks would develop was not where they did develop. The profiler is the only way to optimize your app on the Macintosh. Although in your regular development use, you would profile only small parts of the application at one time, this section documents profiling an entire application. This example code profiles an OnDialog function call. The process is the same regardless of which function you use, you simply have to adjust the procedure to your function.

The profile run can be up to 90 minutes long on a 680x0 Macintosh and 60 minutes on the PowerMac. The reason for this is the granularity of the profiler and the chip on the computer it uses as a timebase. On the Macintosh 68040, each tick is 1.2766 microseconds, in which 6 to 7 instructions are executed. On the Power Macintosh each tick is 128 nanoseconds. Each record is 10 bytes on the Macintosh and 14 bytes on the Power Macintosh, so you may also assume that it takes considerable disk space to store this number of measurements and adjust your runtime accordingly.

The MPROF has three parts, a header file, a library file, and the report writer, MPROF.EXE. Also included is the library, SWAPD.LIB, used for swappable applications. The process entails adding calls to your application, compiling and linking the profile ready app, and finally generating a report with MPROF.EXE.

Steps

To profile your application running on the Macintosh, you need to do a little extra work as outlined in the following steps:

1. Include the MPROF.H file in the .CPP file you are going to profile.
2. Declare the name of your output file in the source code to be profiled as

   ```
   char *meafile = "myapp.mea"
   ```
3. Just after your initial variable declarations in the source file, enable profiling with

   ```
   _FEnableMeas(meafile, opTimingSwap);
   ```
4. Just before the source file's return statement, disable profiling with

   ```
   _FDisableMeas();
   ```
5. Save the edited file.
6. To compile, first insert the /Gh compiler option and include /MAP myapp as a linker option. Also include MPROF.LIB as an object to be linked. If you have a swappable application, include SWAPD.LIB and also specify /NODEFAULTLIB linker option.

7. Compile, link, and exercise your application.

8. When you close the application you will find your myapp.mea file on the Macintosh. Use MFILE.EXE to transfer this file back to the NT machine.

9. Generate the report with the line

```
MPROF /ra /m myapp.map myapp.mea > myapp.mpf
```

The profile can be further tuned to your needs by the use of User Measurement macros, _StartUMeas, _StopUMeas, _PauseMeas, and _ResumeMeas. When profiling a section of code with these macros, you need to remove the /Gh compiler switch as _StartUMeas will start the timer.

This example had a dialog which took an extraordinary amount of time to show on the Macintosh. The first question was whether the time was spent in the class construction or the DoModal function. It is profiled as

```
void CTestView::OnWindowSeemydialog()
{
  char *meafile = "test.mea";
  _FEnableMeas(meafile, opTimingSwap);

  _StartUMeas(1);
  CMy mydialog;
  _StopUMeas(1);

  _StartUMeas(2);
  mydialog.DoModal();
  StopUMeas(2);
  _FDisableMeas();
}
```

The results were the following:

```
Microsoft (R) MPROF Version 1.00.5270 for 680x0
Copyright (C) Microsoft Corp 1994-95. All rights reserved.
options: /ra /m
MProf profiling started at Sun Nov 26 08:58:17 1995
Elapsed Time: 42.730120 sec
```

Call	Count Min	Avg	Max	Total	Pct
UserMeasurement(2)1	42695666	42695666	42695666	42695666	99.9
UserMeasurement(1)1	34454	34454	34454	34454	0.1

Clearly the DoModal() was where it was spending the time. The Pct column is significant when profiling the entire application, because it clearly shows the functions where time is being spent. The Segment information gives further clues.

Table 34.2. Segment information.

Segment Name	Seg Size	Hit Pct	SizeExe Pct	LCnt	UCnt
My (0001)	532	16.67	26.69	1	0
WlmClipboard(0031)	8604	3.23	2.93	1	0
WlmResListBox(0048)	37084	2.13	16.27	1	0
WlmNRListBox(0049)	10400	3.57	3.81	1	0
WlmCtlRare(004a)	2716	10.00	20.62	1	0
WlmBtnRare(004b)	1844	11.11	6.07	1	0
WlmBtn (004c)	11560	2.78	12.73	1	0
WlmCombo (004d)	23308	1.69	18.95	1	0
WlmEdit (0050)	37564	1.27	9.72	1	0
WlmDrag (0051)	7324	6.25	3.82	1	0
CRTCONVERT(0063)	458	16.67	13.10	1	0

MPW2LIB

This utility is provided with the VC++ 4.0 cross-development environment to convert a Macintosh object file from MPW format to the required COFF format. This enables existing libraries and object code from the Macintosh development environment to be linked into your application. Macintosh libraries may provide functionality you need that cannot be gotten through MFC or the Win32 API. The process is straightforward. Using MFILE, transfer the object file from the Macintosh to your working directory. The command is

```
MPW2LIB file.obj
```

This command creates the file.lib. The only 2 optional parameters are /f, to force far rather than near data segments, and /n, to read a names.txt file listing of object files to convert.

MFILE and the C++ File Utility

This is a pair of utilities that provide bidirectional transfer of files between Windows NT and the Macintosh. MFILE on the NT machine is called by Visual C++ after the linking step and establishes the transfer with C++ File Utility on the Macintosh. There are actually two versions of MFILE, one for talking to PowerMac and the other for the 680x0 Mac. To ensure that your configuration calls the correct version, run the batch file VCVARS32.BAT. You can use several connections: AppleTalk, Serial, or TCP/IP. The 680x0 Macintosh has a major disadvantage in that you don't get to use incremental file copy, which saves a good deal of time. Another note is that the Macintosh needs to be running C++ File Utility when MFILE is called.

You should probably use this mostly from the command line in the form

```
MFILE copy c:\test\program.txt":Macintosh:HD:temp:program"
```

The leading colon on the Macintosh pathname is required by MFILE and designates the direction of the control by the following silly rule: If the last file listed begins with a colon, the transfer is to the Macintosh in direction. Some MFILE examples follow:

MFILE COPY ..\MYFILE ":::FOLDER:MYFILE" copies the DOS file, MYFILE, to the Folder two levels up from where the FILE UTILITY resides on the Macintosh.

MFILE COPY "Macintosh HD:MYFOLDER:MYFILE" "::MYFILE" copies MYFILE from MYFOLDER to one level up from FILE UTILITY on the Macintosh.

MFILE DELETE "Macintosh HD:MYFOLDER:MYFILE" removes the MYFILE from the Macintosh.

Debugging the Macintosh Application

Visual C++'s integrated debugging environment continues to operate in its usual fashion. The application running on the Macintosh is sending debug messages to Visual C++ with the AppleTalk or Serial connection. You will also notice the Macintosh sending MacsBug messages to its own screen. The integrated debug environment also correctly displays the Macintosh register values and watch values, and matches the disassembly screen.

When Function Names Conflict

When writing functions using the API functions, which call the Macintosh Toolbox or the Macintosh Operating system, you'll find some functions that have the same name in Windows header files as they have in the MACOS header files. The libraries provide a method to avoid the conflict with two header files, MACNAMES1.h and MACNAMES2.h. Each provides a list of the conflicting functions. MACNAMES1.H renames the function with the prefix Mac, while MACNAMES2.h replaces it with Afx. This is used as

```
#include <windows.h>
#ifdef _Macintosh
#include <macname1.h>
#include <Menus.h>   //MacintoshOS Lib header file

MenuHandle hm;
hm = MacGetMenu(test);   //notice same GetMenu function with Afx added
SetItem(hm,0,"\pAdded just on Mac"_;

#endif
```

or, if with MacintoshNAME2.h,

```
#include <windows.h>
#ifdef _Macintosh
#include <macname2.h>
#include <Menus.h>   //MacintoshOS Lib header file
```

```
MenuHandle hm;
hm = AfxGetMenu(test);  //notice same GetMenu function with Afx added
SetItem(hm,0,"\pAdded just on Mac"_;

#endif
```

Table 34.3. Function name conflicts.

Each of the listed functions is renamed to "Macfunction" in MACNAME1.H and "AFXfunction" in MACNAME2.H

FlushInstructionCache	SetCursor
GetCurrentProcess	GetCursor
ReplaceText	ShowWindow
AnimatePalette	MoveWindow
LineTo	GetMenu
SetRect	DeleteMenu
EqualRect	AppendMenu
OffsetRect	InsertMenu
InsertRect	DrawMenuBar
UnionRect	InsertMenuItem
PtInRect	CloseWindow
InvertRect	FindWindow
FrameRect	GetNextWindow
FillRect	LoadResource
SetRectRgn	DrawText
CopyRgn	OpenDriver
UnionRgn	CloseDrive
XorRgn	StartSound
EqualRgn	StopSound
FillRgn	GetCurrentThread
FrameRgn	GetClassInfo
InvertRgn	SendMessage
PaintRgn	GetParent
OffsetRgn	CompareString
GetPixel	GetFileSize
Polygon	GetDoubleClickTime
ShowCursor	IsWindowVisible

If you are porting existing code with many conflicting API function calls, a second method may work better in which you define the macro _MACNAMES.

```
#ifdef _Macintosh
#define _MACNAMES
#include <windows.h>
#include <Menus.h>
#else
```

```
#include <windows.h>
#endif

#ifdef _MAC
  AfxDrawMenuBar(hwnd);
  hm = AfxGetMenu(hwnd);
#else
  DrawMenuBar(hwnd);
  hm = GetMenu(hwnd);
#endif
```

Macintosh Help Compiler

On the Macintosh, a call to the help function runs Microsoft's MacHelp, a Macintosh version of WinHelp. They function and look similar, as Figure 34.14 shows. Visual C++ 4.0 still ships with HC35.EXE, a help compiler which requires RTF files from Word version 2.0. HC31.505, a newer version for Word 6 and 7, can be obtained from Microsoft's WWW site.

FIGURE 34.14.

MacHelp.

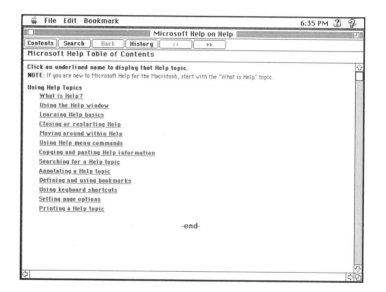

The main advantage of using the Visual C++ cross-development environment is that all the help files are the same. You need to open the help project file and change the first line to PLATFORM = MAC. MacHelp can display PICT files (not used in WinHelp), BMP files, and DIB files, but not Windows metafiles (WMF files). By using the #ifdef _MAC macro in your help switch statement, the user can go to the Macintosh version of the text where there are differences.

MacHelp does not, however, support all of the features of WinHelp. These nonsupported features include secondary windows, customizable menus, DLLs, and many of the macro commands. Your graphics will be scaled differently on the Macintosh. If you restrict your graphics to DIB files or BMP files, they display well on both.

Table 34.4. Support MacHelp macros.

```
About()
Back()
BrowseButtons()
CopyDialog()
CreateButton()
DestoyButton()
Exit()
History()
JumpId()
PopupId()
PositionWindow()
Print()
Search()
```

Using HC31.505 was recently discussed in detail on the Internet. Part of that discussion is excerpted in the following section.

> **NOTE**
>
> The problem with using HC31.505 is that all the bitmaps display too small. To get around this, process all the bitmaps with MRBC (Multi-Resolution Bitmap Compiler) and save them with Macintosh resolution. MRBC can be found in the \msdev\bin directory. The easiest way to do this is to copy/rename all of your bitmaps so that they have an extension *.MAC.
>
> Then you must run MRBC on each file with a /s switch. This generates an *.MRB file with the same name as the original file. You cannot specify a wildcard on the command line for MRBC. If you do, it compiles all of the bitmaps into a single MRB file. The easiest way to do this is to use a for statement in a batch file:
>
> ```
> for %%f in (*.mac) do mrbc /s %%f
> ```
>
> Once you have all of your *.MRB files, you can do one of two things:
>
> 1. Rename the files so that they are the same as the old name. The advantage to this method is that you don't have to modify the source files at all. Just make sure the BMROOT points to the directory with the MAC bitmaps.
>
> 2. Keep the MRB name and modify the sources to reference the new name. This takes more work, but you won't accidentally use a Windows bitmap instead of a Mac bitmap.
>
> Once you compile the help file, you must modify the Mac header for the file. You will have to do this after copying the file to the Mac. The Creator should be set to MSH2, and the Type should be set to HELP.

ODBC and Macintosh

The Cross Development tools for Macintosh supply ODBC SDK version 2.1, while Visual C++ 4.0 under NT uses the 2.5 SDK. If you have relied on some 2.5 functionality, you will need to rework this code. All the platform differences in the MFC libraries are handled by the cross compiler.

On the 680x0 Macintosh Apple Shared Library Manager (ASLM), libraries are placed in the extension folder, which means that you need to call the ASLM. On the Power Macintosh Code Fragment Manager (CFM), libraries are used. If you are targeting both platforms, you need to initialize the ASLM (register as an ASLM client) and then clean up before you quit. In `InitInstance` before any ODBC calls are made, initialize ASLM as the following:

```
#ifdef _68K_
InitLibraryManager(0, kCurrentZone, KNormalMemory);
#endif
```

Before exiting, clean up with

```
#ifdef _68K_
CleanupLibaryManager();
#endif
```

Only one other coding change is needed. When calling an ODBC function that takes a `HWND` as a parameter, you need to get the `HWND` provided by `GetWindowWrapper` as:

```
#ifndef _MAC    //notice the use of #ifndef
  nResult = SQLDriverConnect(hdbc, hWnd "",0,
      szBuffer, MAXBUFLEN, &swStrLen,
      SQL_DRIVER_COMPLETE_REQUIRED);
#else
  nResult = SQLDriverConnect(hdbc, GetWrapperWindow(hWnd) "",0,
      szBuffer, MAXBUFLEN, &swStrLen,
      SQL_DRIVER_COMPLETE_REQUIRED);
#endif
```

All other changes are done internally to MFC, and you only need to recompile. There are no other source code changes for Macintosh in the ODBC MFC files.

OLE and Macintosh

OLE for Macintosh is functionally identical to OLE for Windows NT. OLE was designed to be cross platform. Its only unsupported features are for inproc servers and OLE controls. In place server support is provided by calling Macintosh OLE directly. The differences in file pathnaming (monikers) and clipboard 4 character formats are the same as listed earlier. In Windows NT OLE is provided as a system DLL, and on the Macintosh OLE is provided as an extension folder item. To start the OLE extension on the Macintosh, it must be initialized with a call to `InitOleManager` and cleaned up with a call to `UninitOleManager`. Just as with ODBC in the prior section, the application must register as an ASLM client and clean up when it's done.

OLE Drag and Drop can get a little strange due to the definition of a window and a child window. In Windows NT, any window can be a drop target, whether it's a top-level window or a child. On the Macintosh, each top-level window maps to a Macintosh window, and each child maps to the same Macintosh window. Dropping an OLE object on a child causes ambiguity. The interface design needs to be aware of this inexact definition in the drop target.

If you have developed your cross-platform application through the AppWizard, most of the changes have been done for you. Your Macintosh OLE application will support OLE on the Macintosh. If you are porting an existing application with OLE common dialogs, you must include OLE2UI.H instead of OLEDLG.H and define two preprocessor symbols, INC_OLE2 (OLE declarations) and _WIN32REG (registry functions).

If you are a native Macintosh developer moving to OLE, Microsoft has documented a large collection of Macintosh-specific API functions in the Visual C++ Books-on-Line document entitled: "OLE for Macintosh: How it Differs from OLE for Windows."

Macintosh Shared Libraries

A big issue in making a cross-platform product for the Macintosh is providing the functionality of Windows DLLs. Visual C++ for Macintosh provides this in three ways.

1. **Apple Code Fragment Manager (CFM) shared libraries for the Power Macintosh.** These are similar to DLLs, but you create the main entry point as the default `WlmDllMain` function and provide a `DllMain` function if you wish to receive process attach/detach notifications. The library uses the CFM defined routine `WlmConnectionInitEx` to initialize, and the application uses `LoadLibraryEx` with the flag `LOAD_BY_FRAGMENT_NAME`. A cfrg resource needs to be added to the project, which provides the Macintosh with the name and options of the DLL. A default resource is defined for this as

   ```
   #include "CodeFrag.r"
   resource 'CFRG' (0)
   {
     {
       kPowerPc,
       kFullLib,
       kNoVersionNum,
       kNoVersionNum,
       kDefaultStackSize,
       kNoAppSubFolder,
       kIsLib,
       kOnDiskFlat,
       kZeroOffset,
       kWholeFork,
       "NameOfMyDLL"
     }
   };
   ```

2. **Stand-alone code.** Apple defines several stand-alone code resources: CDEF (control definition procedures for custom controls); cdev (control devices); INIT(initialization code); LDEF (list definitions); MDEF(menu definitions); WDEF (window custom defini-

tions); and XCMD (external hypercard commands). You can also define resource types yourself. Stand-alone code cannot use standard global variables, cannot make intersegment calls or jumps, and cannot be linked to library functions which use standard global variables. The Apple defined resources must be built with a small memory model.

3. **Apple Shared Library Manager (ASLM) for the 680x0 Macintosh**. These are copied to the Macintosh extensions folder. ASLMs must be built in the large memory module. You create the module definition DEF file as a listing of exported functions. This file needs definitions of LIBRARY, VERSION, FLAGS, LOADHEAP, and CLIENTDATA, followed by the EXPORTS listing of functions. Compile the Visual C++ library in the usual fashion using LIB and LINK. If you add Macintosh-specific resources, you need to use Apple REZ to build a Macintosh resource script file. Lastly, MRC combines the image file with the resources into the ASLM format.

The Visual C++ Books-on-Line chapter "Macintosh Shared Libraries" steps through creation of each of the three methods as well as documenting the process to move a Macintosh existing CFM library.

A Check List of Topics

I have included a check list of the items in your application that may need special handling during cross-platform development or features that may not be supported.

1. Run VCPort to flag areas which need to be touched.

2. Multithreaded applications, multiple instances, assembler routines, DOS calls, OpenGL, Winsockets, RPC, Mailslots, and Unicode don't exist in the Macintosh world.

3. Communication code, exception handling, metafiles, named pipes, and multimedia code need to use the Macintosh extensions and to be rewritten.

4. Look at the windows to see if there is a control in the lower-right corner where the sizing button overlaps. If this is an MDI application, all the child windows will open maximized. If you have multiple child windows, this gets messy. Child windows or dialog boxes with their own menus are not supported.

5. Review FTAB.R and the mapping for character sets to ensure strings fit their positions on the screen. Check dropped letters in long screen strings.

6. Menus are only MF-POPUP—a menu choice cannot run a command. Menus don't wrap. The About box moves to the Apple menu. Check that all the Control accelerators are changed to Command accelerators. Most Macintoshes don't have Function keys.

7. Macintosh users all have a one-button mouse, so you must rework the right mouse button choices to Shift+Click.

8. Try to open the same file you created on the Macintosh on the Windows NT PC. Make file formats cross-platform, too.

9. Check each dialog so that it has a default action when the user presses Enter. Redesign the tab order for the Macintosh so that the Tab key never takes you to a button control. If combo boxes come up empty, check to see if you have a default setting you depend upon. Be careful of your placement of the Combo Box choice list so that it doesn't obscure another control.

10. Cut and Copy to the clipboard and then paste to ensure functionality.

11. Carefully review the MacHelp file so that your jumps hit the correct places.

12. Profile functions that are slow and rework them.

Summary

Microsoft has developed an impressive tool with the Macintosh Cross Development version of Visual C++ 4.0. MFC applications can be ported in a very short period of time, expanding the market for your software. Visual C++ does most of the work in converting a Windows NT application to a Macintosh application.

Many sections of this book have addressed why Windows NT and Visual C++ are the standard development environment. Visual C++ for Macintosh adds to that standard, making NT a stable environment to develop both for Macintosh and UNIX Motif platforms. A true Macintosh application can be written while developing for Windows NT and can look and behave like a Macintosh application should. In fact, MacUser Magazine recently nominated an MFC application for its Eddy Software Award.

Online Help

by Mickey
Williams

35

In this chapter, you'll learn how to use the online help system provided with most Windows NT applications, as well as the steps required to add online help to your project. You will examine the various components that make up the Windows NT help system, as well as the support provided by AppWizard for creating context-sensitive help.

Creating Online Help in Windows NT

Applications written for Windows NT are expected to provide online help to users. Although a very simple application may be able to exist without online help, no serious programs are delivered without help systems. In fact, online help is so common that many programs, such as the Visual C++ Developer Studio, eliminate hard copy documentation altogether.

Unlike early versions of the Windows help system, the help system included with Windows NT 4.0 can be used to provide high-quality, hypertext-based help. Many Windows NT help systems include bitmaps and external routines in their online help systems.

Creating Hypertext Help Systems

A Windows help system is not arranged sequentially like printed documentation; instead, Windows help is a hypertext system that enables you to link topics together dynamically. A user navigates easily through a hypertext system because topics are linked together according to logical relationships between topics, as shown in Figure 35.1.

FIGURE 35.1.

Navigating hypertext.

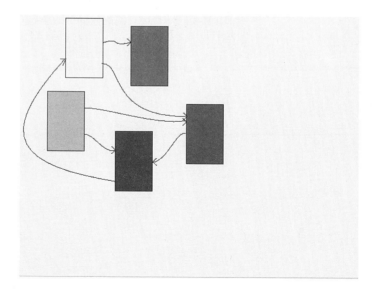

It is very easy for a user to navigate through a hypertext-based help system. Because there are no artificial boundaries created for topics, users easily can refer to information stored in various parts of the help system and return to their starting point. As shown in Figure 35.1, each page may be referenced by many other pages; many of these pages are not adjacent to each other.

Invoking Help

You can invoke online help in two ways in a Windows NT application:

- By explicit command, such as selecting a Help menu item or clicking a button.
- By pressing F1 or Shift+F1 to get context-sensitive help.

Many Windows NT 4.0 applications also include a "what is this," or question mark icon. This icon works just like using Shift+F1—the cursor is changed to a question mark, and help is provided for the item clicked.

A well-implemented Windows NT application enables the online help system to be started using both these methods. AppWizard and the MFC class library provide much of the code and framework required for these functions, as discussed later in this chapter, beginning with the section *Adding Help Features to a Windows NT Application*.

Looking at the Basic Help System Structure

Several components provide online help in a Windows NT application. Figure 35.2 shows how these components interact with each other.

FIGURE 35.2.

WinHelp is launched through Windows NT by the application.

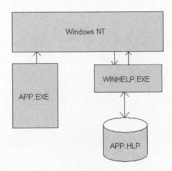

The primary component of the help system is the Windows Help Engine, which is invoked by a Windows NT application. Windows NT sends messages to applications after users select help topics from the menu or click help buttons. Windows NT also sends messages after users press the F1 key to request context-sensitive help.

Creating a Windows NT Help File

To create a help file to be used with Windows NT, you need to use tools outside of your compiler environment. In many ways, creating the help file used in your online help system is just like creating a new project.

Examining the Tools Used to Create a Help File

To create a Windows NT online help system, you need four things:

- An editor or other tool that creates RTF text used as the help file source
- The Win32 help compiler
- Optionally, a help project tool, such as the Microsoft Help Workshop supplied with the Win32 SDK and Visual C++
- Other content included in the help file, such as bitmaps

Figure 35.3 shows how these tools are related.

FIGURE 35.3.

Tools used to create Windows NT help files.

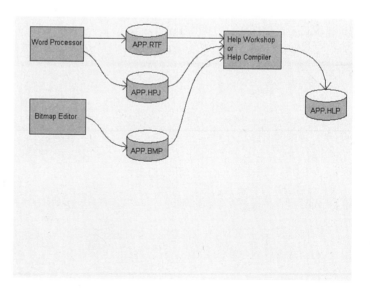

After creating the help file source using a text editor, characteristics about the help file are entered into a help project file. The help compiler reads the project file and compiles the RTF source, bitmaps, and other input into a help file. It then gives the file an .HLP extension.

Working with RTF Files

The source files used to create a Windows help file must be stored in the Rich Text Format (RTF). The RTF format includes information about the document's formatting, along with the actual document text. Most word processors, including Word for Windows, are capable of saving a document as an RTF file.

The examples and screen shots in this chapter assume that you're using Microsoft Word for Windows. You can use any tool that saves text as an RTF file to create these examples, however. Both WordPerfect and FrameMaker can create RTF files, for example.

Most of the help formatting is done in the form of special footnote tags. These special tags mark the topic titles, keywords, and context strings. Table 35.1 lists the most common footnote tags.

Table 35.1. Common footnote tags.

Tag	Usage	Used For
#	#HID_FOO	A help ID context string for a topic
$	$Foo	Topic title string
+	+Foo	Browse sequence
K	Kfoo;bar	A list of keywords separated by semicolons

Most of the help file sources you create will look just like a document with very short pages. In fact, I usually create my help file as a simple RTF document and then add the special help formatting after I'm happy with the contents.

Creating Topics

The basic unit of information provided to the end user is the help topic. As the author, you get to determine the size and content of every topic. Physically, a *help topic* is a section of your help source that is between two hard-coded page breaks. The page must have a help ID context string, and it usually has a topic title and keywords associated with it.

Figure 35.4 shows an example of a simple topic. The screen is split into two sections: The upper half shows the topic, and the bottom half displays the footnotes assigned for the document.

FIGURE 35.4.

Using Word to edit a help topic.

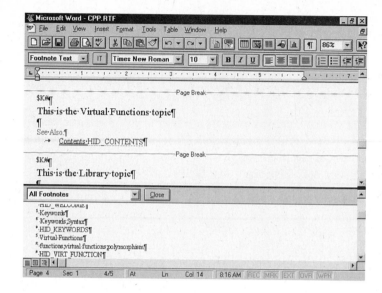

This topic has three footnotes:

- A help ID context string—in this case, HID_VIRT_FUNCTION
- A topic title—in this case, Virtual Functions
- A keyword list—in this case, functions;virtual functions;polymorphism

Each of these footnotes is marked by one of the special characters provided in Table 35.1. The topic title footnote, for example, is marked with a dollar sign ($).

To create a footnote using Word, choose Footnote from the Insert menu. A dialog box similar to the one in Figure 35.5 appears. Click the Custom Mark radio button. Add the appropriate tag in the edit control and click OK. The footnote is created, and the cursor is positioned automatically in the footnote area in the proper location.

When editing footnotes, take care not to disturb footnotes for adjacent topics. Sometimes it can be difficult to determine which footnotes are associated with a particular help topic. Take your time: Some footnote errors can be difficult to find.

Creating Jump Links

A *jump* is a link to a new topic. When the cursor moves over a jump *hot spot*, the cursor shape changes to a hand to indicate that clicking in this area displays a new topic. It is common to create a jump link to related topics when they appear in a help topic. It's also a common practice to have a list of related topics at the bottom of the page.

#### Chapter 35

FIGURE 35.5.

Adding a footnote using Word for Windows.

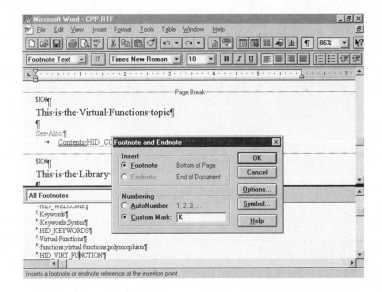

To create a jump in your help file, the hot spot must be double-underlined. Immediately following the hot spot, the help ID context string must appear in hidden text. This help ID must refer to the context string of the *jump target*—the new topic presented when this hot spot is selected. Figure 35.6 shows a jump created in a help topic.

FIGURE 35.6.

The source used to create a jump to another topic.

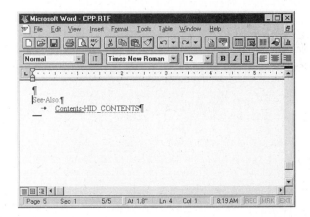

If you are using Word, you can set the underline and hidden text attributes for a block of text by choosing Font from the Format menu. Other word processors have similar features that enable you to change these settings for a block of text.

Creating Pop-Up Links

A *pop-up* is a link to a new topic. It is similar to a jump, except that a pop-up topic is displayed in a small window that overlaps the current help topic. When the cursor moves over a pop-up hot spot, the cursor shape changes to a hand, just as it does for a jump hot spot. Figure 35.7 shows a pop-up help topic displayed over an existing help topic.

FIGURE 35.7.

Displaying a pop-up help topic in WinHelp.

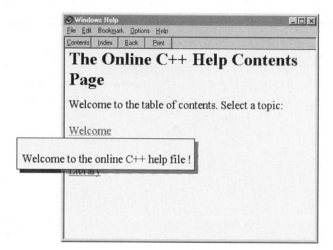

To create a pop-up link, the hot spot must be single-underlined. Immediately following the hot spot, the help ID context string must appear in hidden text. As with jump links, this help ID must refer to the context string of the new topic. Figure 35.8 shows an example of a pop-up created in a help topic.

FIGURE 35.8.

The source used to create a pop-up help topic.

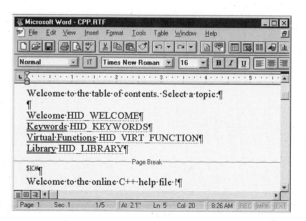

When creating a pop-up topic, remember that the pop-up is displayed only temporarily. Pop-up topics should not contain title text or links to other topics.

Designing a Help System Hierarchy

An important part of creating an online help system is designing the actual structure of its content. Although a number of tools are available to help you create online help directly from the files used to create user guides, this is not a good idea for several reasons:

- Online help enables you to take advantage of hypertext links, unlike printed documents, which tend to repeat information.

- Online documentation should consist of screen-size chunks of information rather than page-size chunks. Trying to use a help system that consists of large topics is frustrating.

- Online help topics generally are more direct and more topical. Context-sensitive topics can directly describe every dialog box, for example.

Figure 35.9 shows the hierarchy used by a typical help system.

FIGURE 35.9.

A typical help system hierarchy.

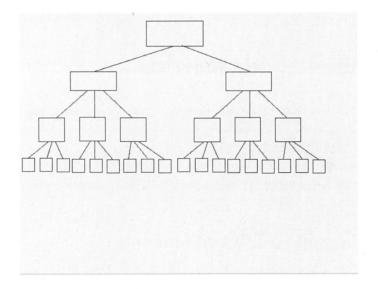

Two main trees exist in a help system:

- **Domain information:** Information about using the Windows application, including topics on manipulating the toolbars, using the printer, opening files, and similar topics. If you select the Online Help option, this information is provided for you in the default help files generated by AppWizard.

- **Problem domain information:** This is the information that deals specifically with your application.

Designing a help system structure is an iterative process. After laying out topics in a hierarchy, look for topics that contain similar or complementary information. Take advantage of hypertext links or pop-ups to refer to these topics.

Editing the Standard Help Source Files

If you create a skeleton project using AppWizard and select the Context-Sensitive Help option, one or more help source files are generated and placed in the `hlp` subdirectory. Each file represents one set of help topics. The `afxcore.rtf` file contains the help source that covers a basic MFC application, for example.

Each of these source files requires a small amount of customization. Areas that must be customized by you are designated between << and >> tags. When the name of your application is referenced, for example, you must specify its name in the help file.

The generic help source provided by AppWizard is an excellent starting point for your application's help system. After customizing the basic topics included in the help files, you can add topics that relate to your specific application.

Using the Help Workshop

Included with the Visual C++ Developer Studio is the *Microsoft Help Workshop*—an easy-to-use tool that manages your help project. AppWizard creates a help project compatible with the Help Workshop. This file is located in the project's hlp subdirectory; it has the same name as the project and an extension of .HPJ.

You can use the Help Workshop to change the help project settings, such as compression and files included in the project. Figure 35.10 shows Help Workshop after opening a help project created in AppWizard.

Creating a Table of Contents

Most help systems include a table of contents. Think of your table of contents as the "top" of the help system. It isn't necessary to have an entry for every available topic—just the high-level starting points. If you are creating a new help system for a Windows NT project, you should include a newer style table of contents that displays the contents in the Finder, as shown in Figure 35.11.

To add this type of table of contents, you must create a contents file with a .CNT file extension. Each line in the contents file describes a topic and its nesting level, as Listing 35.1 shows.

FIGURE 35.10.

Using Help Workshop to manage a help project created by AppWizard.

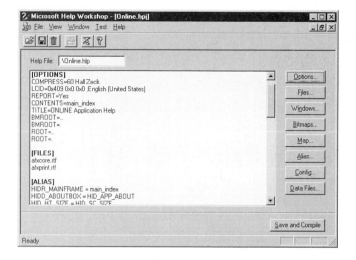

FIGURE 35.11.

The Windows NT Finder displaying a hierarchical contents listing.

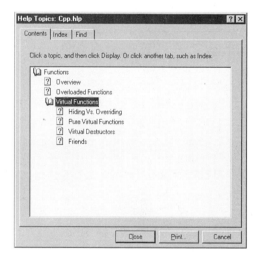

Listing 35.1. An example of a contents file.

```
:Base cpp.hlp
:C++ Help
1 Functions
2 Overview=HID_FUNC_OVERVIEW
2 Overloaded Functions=HID_FUNC_OVERLOAD
2 Virtual Functions
3 Hiding Vs. Overriding=HID_FUNC_VIRT_HIDING
3 Pure Virtual Functions=HID_FUNC_PURE
3 Virtual Destructors=HID_FUNC_VDTOR
2 Friends=HID_FUNC_FRIENDS
1 Pointers and Dynamic Memory
```

The first line of the file is a comment, which always begins with a colon. All other lines start with a nesting level: 1 indicates an item at the root level, 2 indicates an item nested below level 1, and so on. Every item associated with a help topic follows this format:

```
2 Overview=HID_FUNC_OVERVIEW
```

This line associates a second-level item named Overview with a help topic that has the context string HID_FUNC_OVERVIEW.

Adding Help Features to a Windows NT Application

When creating an MFC-based application using AppWizard, you can ask AppWizard to create a skeleton online help system for your application. You can select this option by enabling the Context-Sensitive Help checkbox in AppWizard, as shown in Figure 35.12.

FIGURE 35.12.

Requesting context-sensitive help for a new AppWizard project.

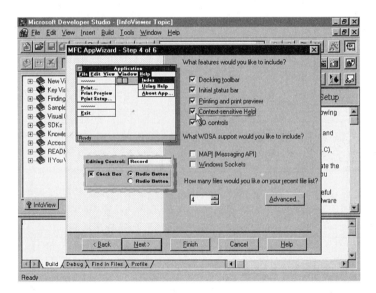

This wizard page is presented as step 4 when creating SDI or MDI applications. A similar wizard page is displayed as step 2 when creating dialog-based applications.

After you request AppWizard to add context-sensitive help, it does the following:

- Creates one or more help source files and stores them in the project's hlp subdirectory.
- Adds an F1 accelerator key.
- Adds a Help Topics item to the Help menu.
- Adds member function mapping for the F1 and Help menu items.

The number of RTF source files created by AppWizard depends on the optional features included in your project. If your project includes printing and database support, for example, help files for these topics automatically are added to your project.

The mapping of help commands is provided in your application's `MainFrame` window class. Listing 35.2 shows the `CMainFrame` message map for an SDI application generated with AppWizard.

Listing 35.2. Message maps used to route help commands in an SDI application.

```
BEGIN_MESSAGE_MAP(CMainFrame, CFrameWnd)
 //{{AFX_MSG_MAP(CMainFrame)
 // NOTE - the ClassWizard will add and remove mapping macros here.
 //    DO NOT EDIT what you see in these blocks of generated code !
     ON_WM_CREATE()
 //}}AFX_MSG_MAP
 // Global help commands
 ON_COMMAND(ID_HELP_FINDER, CFrameWnd::OnHelpFinder)
 ON_COMMAND(ID_HELP, CFrameWnd::OnHelp)
 ON_COMMAND(ID_CONTEXT_HELP, CFrameWnd::OnContextHelp)
 ON_COMMAND(ID_DEFAULT_HELP, CFrameWnd::OnHelpFinder)
END_MESSAGE_MAP()
```

The `ID_HELP` and `ID_HELP_FINDER` messages are generated from menu selections. The `ID_CONTEXT_HELP` message is generated by the Shift+F1 accelerator, and the `ID_DEFAULT_HELP` message is generated by the F1 accelerator.

Mapping Help Topics

As discussed earlier, every help topic has a context string associated with it. This context string identifies each topic. If you look up the `WinHelp` function, however, you will see that it accepts a `DWORD` parameter rather than a context string for the topic. In order to call a particular help topic, that help topic's context string ID must be mapped to a `DWORD` value that is passed in a call to `WinHelp`.

The help project file includes a mapping table used to coordinate the help topic's context string and the numeric value passed to `WinHelp`. The mapping table starts with a `[MAP]` entry and lists context strings on the left and numeric values on the right, like this:

```
[MAP]
HIDR_MAINFRAME                 0x20080
HIDR_ONLINETYPE                0x20081
HIDD_ABOUTBOX                  0x20064
```

Developer Studio and AppWizard handle this mapping process for you by using the `MAKEHM` utility to create a mapping table for all resource IDs found in the resource.h header file. `MAKEHM` actually is called by the MAKEHELP.BAT batch file when your program is compiled. This batch file uses MAKEHM to create a help ID based on the name of each resource. For example, a dialog box resource defined like this:

```
#define IDD_MACKENZIE   101
```

has a help ID named HIDD_MACKENZIE associated with it, as if it were defined like this:

```
#define HIDD_MACKENZIE   0x20065
```

If you call WinHelp directly from your application and have it display the topic using the context string HIDD_MACKENZIE, you must add an offset to the resource ID, like this:

```
CWinApp* pApp = AfxGetApp();
ASSERT( pApp );
pApp->WinHelp( HID_BASE_RESOURCE + IDD_MACKENZIE );
```

This enables you to use numeric symbols in all calls to WinHelp. Table 35.2 shows the mapping provided for resources that use the standard naming conventions.

Table 35.2. Resource-ID-to-help-topic-ID mapping performed by MAKEHELP.BAT and used by MFC.

Resource Type	Prefix	Help Prefix	Offset	
Menu	ID_, IDM_	HID_, HIDM_	HID_BASE_COMMAND	0x10000
Dialog, Frame	IDD_, IDR_	HIDD_, HIDR_	HID_BASE_RESOURCE	0x20000
Prompts	IDP_	HIDP_	HID_BASE_PROMPT	0x30000
Non-client	N/A	H_	HID_BASE_NCAREAS	0x40000
Frame Controls	IDW_	HIDW_	HID_BASE_CONTROL	0x50000
OLE Dispatch	N/A	HID	HID_BASE_DISPATCH	0x60000

In order to use the symbolic names for the offsets listed in Table 35.2, you must include the afxpriv.h header file.

Starting Help

As discussed earlier, the WinHelp function is used to start the Windows NT help system. CWinApp includes a WinHelp member function, which typically is called like this:

```
CWinApp* pApp = AfxGetApp();
ASSERT( pApp );
pApp->WinHelp( HID_BASE_RESOURCE + IDD_SETNAME );
```

In this code fragment, a DWORD value that corresponds to a help context string is passed as the only parameter. However, CWinApp::WinHelp actually accepts two parameters; the second parameter has a default value of HELP_CONTEXT. Table 35.3 lists some other commonly used values for the second parameter.

Table 35.3. Values for the second parameter.

Parameter	Function
HELP_COMMAND	Executes a help macro or macro string. The first parameter passed to WinHelp is the address of a string that specifies the name of the help macro. If the macro uses a long name, the short form of the name must be used.
HELP_CONTENTS	Displays an old-style contents page, which is the topic specified by the Contents option in the [OPTIONS] section of the help project file. If you are creating a new help file, you should provide a CNT file and use the HELP_FINDER command. The first parameter value is ignored.
HELP_CONTEXTPOPUP	Displays a help topic in a pop-up window. The first parameter must contain the help ID value that maps to a particular topic.
HELP_FINDER	Launches the new-style table of contents that uses the CNT file to display topics in a hierarchy. The value of the first parameter is ignored.
HELP_HELPONHELP	Displays help on how to use Windows help if the WINHELP.HLP file is available. The value of the first parameter is ignored.
HELP_INDEX	Displays the index in the Help Topics dialog box. If you are creating a new help file, you should use the HELP_FINDER command to display the index. The value of the first parameter is ignored.
HELP_KEY	Displays the topic in the keyword table that matches the specified keyword. If there is more than one match, the index is displayed. The first parameter must contain the address of the keyword string.
HELP_PARTIALKEY	Displays the topic in the keyword table that matches the specified keyword. If there is more than one match, the Finder index tab is displayed. The first parameter must contain the address of the keyword string. To open the index tab every time, pass an empty string.
HELP_QUIT	Closes Windows help. The value of the first parameter is ignored.

Handling F1 Help

Two types of F1 help exist. After a user presses F1, the MFC framework attempts to determine the proper menu item, dialog box, or other resource on which the user is requesting help. The

MFC framework then calls `WinHelp`, passing the appropriate value for the help topic associated with that resource.

The other type of F1 help occurs after the user presses Shift+F1. The cursor changes to a question mark, and the user can click the item for which help is requested. This type of help requires a hit test to be performed. A hit test involves determining which window is under the cursor when a mouse button is clicked. Again, the MFC framework handles this for MFC resources.

If you must provide context-sensitive help via a button, such as a Help button in a dialog box, you can just pass the call to `CWinApp::WinHelp`, as shown in Listing 35.3.

Listing 35.3. A message-handling function for a dialog box help button.

```
#include <afxpriv.h>
.
.
.
void CNameDlg::OnHelp()
{
    CWinApp* pApp = AfxGetApp();
    ASSERT( pApp );
    pApp->WinHelp( IDD_NAME + HID_BASE_RESOURCE );
}
```

This code calls the same help topic as if the user had pressed F1. This is an easy way to provide consistent help information to users, no matter which method they use to request help.

Summary

This chapter discussed the components used to provide context-sensitive help for Windows NT applications. You also learned about the tools you can use to create online help, and you examined the support provided by AppWizard and the MFC framework.

The next chapter, "Smart Install and Uninstall Programming," discusses how to create smart installation programs using the tools provided with Visual C++ and the Win32 SDK.

Smart Install and Uninstall Programming

36

by Mickey Williams

IN THIS CHAPTER

This chapter discusses creating smart install and uninstall packages for your Windows NT applications. Traditionally, Windows applications have included setup programs to assist the user in installation. For Windows 95 and Windows NT 4.0, programs are expected to include an uninstall option, which enables users to safely remove all traces of an application from their computer.

This chapter covers the steps required to create an installation program for Windows NT using the InstallShield SDK, the setup toolkit included with Visual C++, and the Win32 SDK. You also will create a sample setup program, which is located on the accompanying CD-ROM.

Looking at the Setup Program

Several different packages are available to help you create setup programs for your Windows NT application. If you have access to the Win32 SDK, you already have two such programs:

- The setup toolkit includes common dialog boxes and routines that enable you to write a setup program in C. This approach is fairly primitive.

- The InstallShield SDK from Stirling Software is a "light" version of the full-featured InstallShield 3 package. InstallShield SDK includes features that enable you to create an uninstall package for users of your application.

In addition, a large number of other third-party tools are available for creating installation programs, ranging from inexpensive shareware tools to very expensive, full-featured packages.

> **TIP**
>
> Don't make the mistake of trying to create your own setup and uninstall package. Many issues are involved in writing a good installation utility, and it's unlikely that you could write a new one in a short period of time.

The Basic Setup Process

The general purpose of a setup program is to install your application in a directory of the user's choice, to create an entry in the Start menu, and to initialize the application.

Most installation packages perform these basic steps:

- Copy the installation program to a temporary directory on the user's hard drive.
- Collect information from the user or from a configuration file.
- Copy the application from the setup disks and perform any required initialization.

During the setup process, the setup program often displays *billboards*—information bitmaps—to the user. These billboards usually advise users to register their software and advertise new or enhanced functionality in the product.

Microsoft's Help Guidelines

Microsoft has created a set of guidelines that should be used by application developers when developing installation programs. Some of these items are necessary in order to be certified as a BackOffice or Windows 95 application, whereas others are just common sense. The guidelines that have the most impact on a typical installation program follow:

■ Previous versions of Windows NT used DDE conversations with the Program Manager to create program groups. This interface still is supported, but the preferred method is to create a single entry in the Program menu for your application.

■ Offer several different installation options to users. These options often include Typical, Compact, and Custom installation options.

■ Offer a silent installation option. A silent installation does not require interaction with a user during the setup process. This enables a user to install your application from a batch file or a central location over the network.

■ Do not overwrite shared files unless the existing files have older version numbers than the files you are installing, and never overwrite without notifying the user.

■ Supply a common response to every option in your setup program that the user can choose just by confirming the default values.

■ Support installation from any location, not just from an MS-DOS drive.

■ Provide an uninstall option, preferably through the Control Panel Add/Remove Programs interface. Uninstallation is discussed in the next section.

The Basic Uninstall Process

Uninstallation is easier to manage in Windows NT than in Windows 95 because you actually can delete the uninstall program while it is being used. In Windows 95, this takes a bit of extra work.

As part of the uninstall process, your application should perform the following tasks:

■ Remove all its application files and directories from the user's hard drive, including the uninstall program.

■ Decrement the usage count on shared DLLs and other files and remove any files with a usage count of zero, after prompting users and enabling them to veto the operation.

■ Remove all traces of your application from the Registry.

■ Remove information from the Program menu bar.

Do not remove any of the user's data files or documents that may have been created using your application. If these files are located in your directory tree, give the user options for dealing with them, such as these:

- Delete the files.
- Move the files to a new location.
- Leave the files and directory path intact.

If you use InstallShield, the uninstallation program can be created with your installation program. As your program is installed, InstallShield can create a log file that removes your application when it is uninstalled.

Using the InstallShield SDK

When using the InstallShield SDK, your installation scripts are written using the InstallShield Script Language. This scripting language is very similar to the C language; in fact, any C programmer will be able to write installation scripts fairly easily.

Language Basics

InstallShield scripts look a lot like C programs, except for a few small differences:

- The equality and assignment operators both use a single equal (=) sign.
- Functions always return a 32-bit value.
- Function bodies are marked by `begin` and `end` statements rather than by the curly braces used in C.
- `If` statements are terminated with an `endif` statement.
- `Switch` statements are terminated with an `endswitch` statement.

Other differences exist that will become apparent as you examine an InstallShield installation script. The InstallShield SDK package includes a sample installation script and an online reference, and I have created an installation script on the accompanying CD-ROM. After working through a sample installation, you can modify an existing script or create a new one from scratch.

Control Flow

You can change the flow of an InstallShield script by using the following statements:

- `for`
- `goto`
- `if`

- repeat until
- switch
- while

The if statement used in an InstallShield script is very much like the C if statement. An if statement always is terminated by an endif statement and can include one or more else or elseif statements, as shown in Listing 36.1.

Listing 36.1. Using the if, else, and endif statements.

```
if( nType = BACK ) then
    goto GetTargetDirectory;
else
    goto GetName;
endif;
```

The switch statement is very much like the C switch statement, except that each case is not separated with break. Instead, a break is assumed between case statements. A switch always is terminated by an endswitch statement, as shown in Listing 36.2.

Listing 36.2. Using the case and switch statements.

```
switch (nType)
    case FOO:
        bIncludeReadme  = TRUE;
    case BAR:
        bIncludeProgram = TRUE;
    case BAZ:
        bIncludeNothing = TRUE;
endswitch;
```

The while statement is similar to the C while statement, except that it always is terminated with an endwhile statement, as Listing 36.3 shows.

Listing 36.3. Using the while and endwhile statements.

```
while( nFoo = TRUE )
    MessageBox( "Still Waiting", INFORMATION );
    nFoo = CalcFoo();
endwhile;
```

The for statement is not at all like the C for loop. It's actually much closer to the Pascal for loop. A for loop always is terminated with endfor, as Listing 36.4 shows.

Listing 36.4. Using the `for` and `endfor` statements.

```
for nFoo = 1 to 5
    WriteFoo();
endfor;
```

The `repeat until` statement is similar to the `do-while` loop used in C and C++ programs, as Listing 36.5 shows.

Listing 36.5. An example of using the `repeat until` loop.

```
repeat
    MessageBox( "Still Waiting...", INFORMATION );
    nFoo = GetFoo();
until( nFoo > 3 );
```

The `goto` statement is used to jump to a particular label—usually, to a previous dialog box label, as in this example:

```
goto GetTargetDirectory;
```

Using Dialog Boxes

The InstallShield SDK includes several dialog boxes that enable you to interact with the user. Each of the dialog boxes presented in the following sections is part of the basic InstallShield SDK package. You don't need to design any of these dialog boxes using a resource editor, and you don't need to include any special DLLs; they are part of the basic setup program.

You invoke all dialog boxes by using a simple function call, such as this:

```
nResult = AskDestPath( "", szMsg, svMainDirectory, 0 );
```

Navigating Using the Next and Back Buttons

Most of the dialog boxes are Wizard-type pages. The user can move forward and backward during the setup process by clicking the Next and Back buttons on each page. If a user clicks the Back button, the function used to display the dialog box returns BACK; you must use a `goto` statement to return to the preceding dialog box, as Listing 36.6 shows.

Listing 36.6. Handling the Back button.

```
WelcomeDlg:
    // Display welcome information
GetTargetDirectory:
    // Collect destination information
    if( AskDestPath( "", szMsg, svMainDirectory, 0 ) = BACK) then
```

```
    goto WelcomeDlg;
  endif;
DetermineUserSelection:
  // Ask for an installation option
  nType = SetupType( "", "", svMainDirectory, nType, 0 );
  if( nType = BACK ) then
    goto GetTargetDirectory;
  endif;
```

The actual code used in a real setup program has more steps, but Listing 36.6 shows the basic process used to handle navigating through the setup dialog boxes. Almost every dialog box has a label associated with it. After a user clicks the Next label, a goto statement returns the user to the preceding dialog box.

Customizing Dialog Box Titles

In most cases, the titles displayed by the InstallShield dialog boxes are reasonable defaults that will suit your needs. At times, however, you will need to customize the dialog box title. You can use the SetDialogTitle function to set a custom title for the setup dialog boxes, as in this example:

```
SetDialogTitle( DLG_ASK_TEXT, "User Name" );
```

The SetDialogTitle function has two parameters:

- The dialog box title to be changed
- A new title string for the dialog box

The first parameter must be one of the values provided in Table 36.1.

Table 36.1. Dialog ID values used for SetDialogTitle.

Dialog ID	Changes Title For
DLG_ASK_OPTIONS	Ask Options dialog box
DLG_ASK_PATH	Ask Path dialog box
DLG_ASK_TEXT	Ask Text dialog box
DLG_ASK_YESNO	Ask Yes No dialog box
DLG_MSG_INFORMATION	Information message dialog box
DLG_MSG_SEVERE	Severe message dialog box
DLG_MSG_WARNING	Warning message dialog box

Each of the dialog boxes listed in Table 36.1 is discussed in this section.

Welcome

Figure 36.1 shows the Welcome dialog box. This is the first dialog box displayed after the setup environment is initialized.

FIGURE 36.1.

The InstallShield Welcome dialog box.

You create the Welcome dialog box by calling the Welcome function:

```
Welcome( "Generic MFC Setup", 0 );
```

The first parameter passed to Welcome is used as the dialog box title. The second parameter always is set to zero.

The contents of the Welcome dialog box are customized by InstallShield based on information provided in the InstallationInfo function, as Listing 36.7 shows.

Listing 36.7. Calling the InstallationInfo function.

```
InstallationInfo( "Sams",
                  "Generic",
                  "1.0",
                  "Generic.exe" );
```

The first two parameters—the company name and product name—are used in the Welcome dialog box.

Choose Destination Location

You can get the destination path from the user by displaying the Choose Destination Location dialog box, which is shown in Figure 36.2. The user is presented with a default location and can accept this location or click the Browse button to search for a new destination.

#### Chapter 36

FIGURE 36.2.

The InstallShield Choose Destination Location dialog box.

You create the Choose Destination Location dialog box by calling the `AskDestPath` function, as Listing 36.8 shows.

Listing 36.8. Calling the `AskDestPath` function.

```
#define APPBASE_PATH            "Sams\\ProgWindowsNTUnleashed\\"
#define APPBASE_DIR             "Program Files"
.
.
.
svMainDirectory = TARGETDISK ^ APPBASE_DIR ^ APPBASE_PATH;
szMsg = "";
AskDestPath( "", szMsg, svMainDirectory, 0 );
```

Four parameters are passed to `AskDestPath`:

- The title of the dialog box or an empty string to use the default title
- A message string to be displayed to the user or an empty string to display the standard message
- The default path displayed to the user
- A zero for the last parameter, which is reserved

In Listing 36.8, `TARGETDISK` is an InstallShield system parameter that contains the current drive letter.

The return value from `AskDestPath` is one of these values:

- `BACK` indicates that the user has clicked the Back button.
- `NEXT` indicates that the user has clicked the Next button.
- A value of less than zero indicates that the user has clicked the Close button or that some other error has occurred.

After the user clicks Next, the buffer passed as the third parameter to `AskDestPath` contains the path selected by the user.

General Options

When installing an application, you might need to ask the user to make a selection from several options. InstallShield provides two dialog boxes for presenting general-purpose options:

- An exclusive options dialog box that displays the options with radio buttons
- A non-exclusive options dialog box that displays the options using checkboxes

Figure 36.3 shows an example of an options dialog box that uses checkboxes. You can display up to nine options in a single dialog box.

FIGURE 36.3.

Using checkboxes with the options dialog box to select several options.

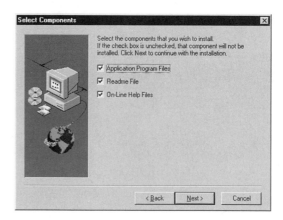

You create the options dialog box by calling the `AskOptions` function, as shown in Listing 36.9.

Listing 36.9. Calling the `AskOptions` function.

```
szMsg = "Select the components that you want to install.\n"+
        "If the checkbox is unchecked, that component will "+
        "not be installed. Click Next to continue with the "+
        "installation.";
nResult = AskOptions( NONEXCLUSIVE,
                      szMsg,
                      "Application Program Files",
                      bIncludeProgram,
                      "Readme File",
                      bIncludeReadme,
                      "On-Line Help Files",
                      bIncludeHelp );
```

The `AskOptions` function has between four and 20 parameters:

- A variable that indicates whether the dialog box will contain exclusive or non-exclusive options. In this case, NONEXCLUSIVE indicates that the dialog box will contain non-exclusive items. A value of EXCLUSIVE creates a dialog box that contains exclusive options.

- A message displayed in the dialog box.

- A title for the first option item.

- A BOOL variable that contains the initial state of the item. After the dialog box is closed, this variable contains the user's selection.

- Additional pairs of option item text and variables—up to nine.

Ask Text

An installation program often needs to collect text from the user, such as the user name, address, or product serial number. To gather general text responses, InstallShield provides an Ask Text dialog box, as shown in Figure 36.4.

FIGURE 36.4.

The InstallShield User Name dialog box.

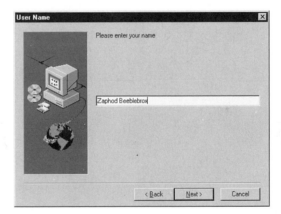

You can create an Ask Text dialog box by calling the AskText function, as Listing 36.10 shows.

Listing 36.10. Calling the AskText function.

```
nResult = AskText( "Please enter your name",
                   "Jennifer Smith",
                   svUser );
```

Three parameters are passed to the AskText function:

- A prompt displayed to the user just above the edit control
- A default value for the edit control
- A buffer that stores the result after the user clicks Next

The title of the Ask Text dialog box is set to Enter Information by default. To change this to a more suitable name, use the SetDialogTitle function, as discussed earlier in this chapter in *Customizing Dialog Box Titles.*

Question

At times, you may need to ask a user a yes or no question. InstallShield provides a Question dialog box for this purpose, as shown in Figure 36.5.

FIGURE 36.5.

The InstallShield Question dialog box.

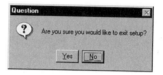

You create the Question dialog box by calling the AskYesNo function, as Listing 36.11 shows.

Listing 36.11. Asking a question using the AskYesNo function.

```
szMsg = "Are you sure you would like to exit setup?";
if( AskYesNo( szMsg, NO ) = YES) then
    abort;
endif;
```

The AskYesNo function has two parameters:

- The message displayed to the user, which normally is phrased as a question
- The default button—in this case, NO

The return value from AskYesNo is the button clicked by the user: YES or NO.

General Message

A general-purpose message dialog box also is provided by InstallShield in order to display messages to the user. Figure 36.6 shows a sample message dialog box—in this case, an Information dialog box.

FIGURE 36.6.

The InstallShield Information dialog box.

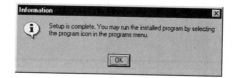

Three types of message dialog boxes are supplied by InstallShield:

- **WARNING**: Displays messages indicating that a minor problem has occurred that does not affect the installation.
- **SEVERE**: Displays messages indicating that a major error that affects the installation has occurred.
- **INFORMATION**: Displays general-purpose messages that do not imply that an error has occurred.

You create a message dialog box by calling the `MessageBox` function, as Listing 36.12 shows.

Listing 36.12. Displaying a message using the `MessageBox` function.

```
szMsg = "Setup is complete. You may run the installed"+
        " program by selecting the program icon in " +
        "the programs menu.\n\n";
MessageBox( szMsg, INFORMATION );
```

The `MessageBox` function has two parameters:

- The message displayed to the user
- The type of message box: WARNING, SEVERE, or INFORMATION

Selecting a Setup Type

Part of the setup guidelines provided by Microsoft indicates that you should provide several installation options for your application. In general, these follow:

- **Typical:** Sets up the application using common defaults.
- **Compact:** Installs the minimum version of your application.
- **Custom:** Enables an expert user to select the components to be installed.

The InstallShield SDK includes a Setup Type dialog box that enables a user to select these setup options, as shown in Figure 36.7.

You create the Setup Type dialog box by calling the `SetupType` function, as shown in Listing 36.13.

Listing 36.13. Determining the setup option using the `SetupType` function.

```
nType = SetupType( "", "", "", TYPICAL, 0 );
switch( nType )
    case TYPICAL:
                // Set typical options
    case COMPACT:
                // Set compact options
    case CUSTOM:
                // Create dialog and allow user to select options
endswitch
```

FIGURE 36.7.

The InstallShield Setup Type dialog box.

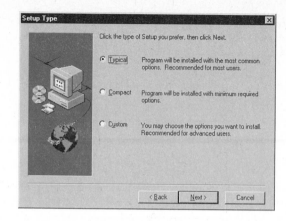

Five parameters are passed to SetupType, in the order shown here:

1. The title displayed for the dialog box or the empty string to display the default title
2. The message displayed to the user or the empty string to display the default message
3. Reserved: Must always be the empty string
4. The initially selected setup option: TYPICAL, COMPACT, or CUSTOM
5. Reserved: Must always be set to zero

The return value from SetupType is one of these values:

■ **BACK:** Indicates that the user has clicked the Back button.

■ **TYPICAL:** Indicates that the user has selected the Typical option.

■ **COMPACT:** Indicates that the user has selected the Minimal option.

■ **CUSTOM:** Indicates that the user has selected the Custom option.

Looking at an Installation Example Using InstallShield

As an example of using the InstallShield SDK to create a real installation on Windows NT 4.0, I have created a sample installation and uninstallation program. Like all these examples, these programs can be found on the accompanying CD-ROM.

The installation program copies a generic MFC application, a README file, the MFC40.DLL library, and a help file to the directory of your choice. It supports multiple installation options and the uninstall program.

Using the Generic Application

The generic application is exactly what it sounds like—a default MFC application created by AppWizard. Although the application itself is very simple, the installation program required to install it is very much a real Windows NT installation program.

Begin by arranging a directory hierarchy, as shown in Figure 36.8.

FIGURE 36.8.

The setup program directory and file hierarchy.

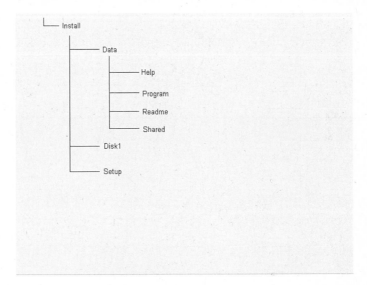

The root directory—in this case, Install—can have any name you want to give it. It must contain the following files:

- **build.bat**: A batch file (which is presented later in this section)
- **icomp.exe**: A program used to compress your application files
- **split.exe**: A program used to split files and programs too large to fit on a single distribution disk

The Data subdirectory contains all the files that will be installed by the setup program. In general, it's a good idea to create a separate subdirectory for each type of file used by your application. The generic setup program uses these subdirectories:

- **Help:** Contains the application's help files: generic.hlp and generic.cnt.
- **Program:** Contains the actual application: Generic.exe.
- **Readme:** Contains the readme.txt file.
- **Shared:** Contains the shared system files used by the application—in this case, MFC40.DLL.

The Setup subdirectory contains the script and packing list files, as well as the following programs used to compile these files:

- **compile.exe**: Compiles the Setup.rul script into a Setup.ins file
- **packlist.exe**: Compiles the Setup.lst file into a Setup.pkg file
- **Setup.lst**: The list of files installed as part of the installation process
- **Setup.rul**: The setup script file

The Disk1 subdirectory is used to store the contents of the first setup disk. If your setup program spans several disks, you must create separate directories for each disk.

Using the Build Batch File

To compile the setup program, just go to the Install directory and execute the `Build.bat` batch file. This batch file compresses the contents of the data subdirectory and creates the setup program, storing the results in the Disk1 subdirectory.

Listing 36.14 provides the source code for `Build.bat`.

Listing 36.14. The `Build.bat` batch file.

```
rem ....Build components...
del data.z
cd setup
compile setup.rul
copy setup.ins ..\disk1
packlist setup.lst
copy setup.pkg ..\disk1
cd ..
icomp -i data\*.* data.z
split -f1420 -d1@770 data.z
copy data.1 disk1
copy disk1.id disk1
```

After the compressed setup files are copied to the Disk1 subdirectory, you must manually add the InstallShield setup program and libraries to the subdirectory. These files follow:

- _inst32i.ex_
- _isdel.exe
- _setup.dll
- _setup.lib
- setup.exe
- uninst.exe

Running the Setup Program

To run the setup program, copy the contents of the Disk1 subdirectory to a floppy disk, or execute the setup.exe program found in the Disk1 subdirectory directly. The generic program then is installed on your computer using the options you select.

To uninstall the generic application, open the Control Panel and click the Add/Remove Programs icon. Select the Generic MFC item from the listbox, as shown in Figure 36.9. Click the Add/Remove button, and the application is removed.

FIGURE 36.9.

Removing the generic MFC application.

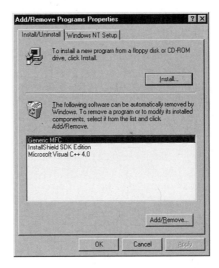

You can find the actual setup script used to create this setup program on the accompanying CD-ROM. It runs about 500 lines of source code and is too long to reproduce here, but it contains all the steps required to create a real setup program used for installing a Windows NT application.

Summary

This chapter discussed the steps required to create installation programs for Windows NT 4.0. Installation programs are expected not only to install an application properly, but they are also expected to leave an uninstallation program in place so that the application can be safely removed.

The easiest way to properly install a Windows NT application is to use a tool to create your setup program, such as InstallShield SDK, which is included with Visual C++ and the Win32 SDK. This chapter covered the steps involved with creating a setup program using InstallShield SDK.

INDEX

SYMBOLS

A V I A C O M   S E R V I C E-E

The Information SuperLibrary™

Bookstore	**Search**	**What's New**	**Reference**	**Software**	**Newsletter**	**Company Overviews**
Yellow Pages	**Internet Starter Kit**	**HTML Workshop**	**Win a Free T-Shirt!**	**Macmillan Computer Publishing**	**Site Map**	**Talk to Us**

CHECK OUT THE BOOKS IN THIS LIBRARY.

You'll find thousands of shareware files and over 1600 computer books designed for both technowizards and technophobes. You can browse through 700 sample chapters, get the latest news on the Net, and find just about anything using our

We're open 24-hours a day, 365 days a year.

You don't need a card.

We don't charge fines.

And you can be as **LOUD** as you want.

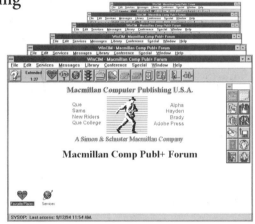

Building an Intranet with Windows NT 4

— *Scott Zimmerman & Tim Evans*

This hands-on guide teaches readers how to set up and maintain an efficient Intranet with Windows NT. It comes complete with a selection of the best software for setting up a server, creating content, and developing Intranet applications.

CD-ROM includes a complete Windows NT Intranet toolkit with a full-featured Web server, Web content development tools, and ready-to-use Intranet applications

Includes complete specifications for several of the most popular Intranet applications—group scheduling, discussions, database access, and more

Covers Windows NT 4.0

Price: $49.99 USA/$70.95 CDN   User Level: Casual-Accomplished
ISBN: 1-57521-137-8   600 pages   Trim Size: 7 $\frac{3}{8}$×9 $\frac{1}{8}$
Release Date: 07/01/96   Internet—Intranets

Client/Server Unleashed

— *Neil Jenkins, et al.*

This book leads the reader through the often confusing client/server world. It defines every aspect of the client/server architecture and gives an overview of all the products and tools. Readers will be conceptually led through all the major steps in planning and implementing their C/S architecture.

CD-ROM contains demonstrations of various products and a multimedia client/server product encyclopedia

Guides the reader through planning projects and evaluating business considerations

Covers migration from standard systems to C/S systems

Covers client/server

Price: $59.99 USA/$84.95 CDN   User Level: Accomplished-Expert
ISBN: 0-672-30726-x   1,200 pages   Trim Size: 7 $\frac{3}{8}$×9 $\frac{1}{8}$
Release Date: 08/01/96   Client/Server

Microsoft SQL Server Unleashed, Second Edition

— *David Solomon & Daniel Woodbeck, et al.*

This comprehensive reference details the steps needed to plan, design, install, administer, and tune large and small databases. In many cases, the reader will use the techniques in this tome to create and manage his or her own complex environment.

CD-ROM includes source code, libraries, and administration tools

Covers programming topics, including SQL, data structures, programming constructs, stored procedures, referential integrity, large table strategies, and more

Includes updates to cover all new features of SQL Server 6.5 including the new transaction processing monitor and Internet/database connectivity through SQL Server's new Web Wizard

Price: $59.99 USA/$84.95 CDN   User Level: Accomplished-Expert
ISBN: 0-672-30956-4   1,200 pages   Trim Size: 7 $\frac{3}{8}$×9 $\frac{1}{8}$
Release Date: 08/01/96   Databases

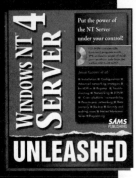

Windows NT 4 Server Unleashed

— Jason Garms

The Windows NT server has been gaining tremendous market share over Novell, and the new upgrade—which includes a Windows 95 interface—is sure to add momentum to its market drive. To that end, *Windows NT 4 Server Unleashed* is written to meet that growing market. It provides information on disk and file management, integrated networking, BackOffice integration, and TCP/IP protocols.

CD-ROM includes source code from the book and valuable utilities

Focuses on using Windows NT as an Internet server

Covers security issues and Macintosh support

Price: $49.99 USA/$70.95 CDN   User Level: Accomplished-Expert
ISBN: 0-672-30933-5   1,100 pages   Trim Size: 7³/₈×9¹/₈
Release Date: 08/01/96   Networking

Microsoft BackOffice Administrator's Survival Guide

— Arthur Knowles

This all-in-one reference focuses on what Microsoft BackOffice is and how it is used in the real world. It includes all the fundamental concepts required for daily maintenance and troubleshooting, and it explains the more arcane aspects of managing the BackOffice.

CD-ROM includes product demos, commercial and shareware utilities, and technical notes

Uses step-by-step written procedures interspersed with figures captured from the actual tools

Introduces Microsoft's new System Management Server

Covers Windows 95

Price: $59.99 USA/ $84.95 CDN   User Level: Accomplished-Expert
ISBN: 0-672-30849-5   1,008 pages   Trim Size: 7³/₈×9¹/₈
Release Date: 04/01/96   Networking

Paul McFedries Windows 95 Unleashed, Premier Edition

— Paul McFedries

Completely updated and revised. Best-selling author Paul McFedries has created a Windows 95 user's masterpiece. And in the traditional style of the Unleashed series, every new feature is discussed in detail, leaving the reader fully informed and completely functional within the new operating system. It also includes coverage of soon-to-be-released Microsoft Internet products, such as VBScript, Internet Studio, and Microsoft Exchange coverage not found anywhere else.

CD-ROM contains an easy-to-search online chapter on troubleshooting for Windows 95

Covers Internet topics, including the Microsoft Network

Discusses multimedia topics, internetworking, and communication issues

Price: $59.99 USA/$84.95 CDN   User Level: Accomplished-Expert
ISBN: 0-672-30932-7   1,400 pages   Trim Size: 7³/₈×9¹/₈
Release Date: 07/01/96   Programming

Add to Your Sams Library Today with the Best Books for Programming, Operating Systems, and New Technologies

The easiest way to order is to pick up the phone and call
1-800-428-5331
between 9:00 a.m. and 5:00 p.m. EST.
For faster service please have your credit card available.

ISBN	Quantity	Description of Item	Unit Cost	Total Cost
1-57521-137-8		Building an Intranet with Windows NT 4 (Book/CD-ROM)	$49.99	
0-672-30726-x		Client/Server Unleashed (Book/CD-ROM)	$59.99	
0-672-30956-4		Microsoft SQL Server Unleashed, Second Edition (Book/CD-ROM)	$59.99	
0-672-30933-5		Windows NT 4 Server Unleashed (Book/CD-ROM)	$49.99	
0-672-30849-5		Microsoft BackOffice Administrator's Survival Guide (Book/CD-ROM)	$59.99	
0-672-30932-7		Paul McFedries' Windows 95 Unleashed, Premier Edition (Book/2 CD-ROMs)	$59.99	
0-672-30901-7		Peter Norton's Complete Guide to Windows NT 4 Workstation (Book/CD-ROM)	$39.99	
1-57521-089-4		Windows NT 4 Web Development (Book/CD-ROM)	$59.99	

❏ 3 ½" Disk

❏ 5 ¼" Disk

	Shipping and Handling: See information below.	
	TOTAL	

Shipping and Handling: $4.00 for the first book, and $1.75 for each additional book. Floppy disk: Add $1.75 for shipping and handling. If you need to have it NOW, we can ship product to you in 24 hours for an additional charge of approximately $18.00, and you will receive your item overnight or in two days. Overseas shipping and handling adds $2.00 per book and $8.00 for up to three disks. Prices subject to change. Call for availability and pricing information on latest editions.

201 W. 103rd Street, Indianapolis, Indiana 46290

1-800-428-5331 — Orders   1-800-835-3202 — Fax   1-800-858-7674 — Customer Service

Book ISBN 0-672-30905-x